T0180161

Lecture Notes in Artificial Intelligence   11672

Subseries of Lecture Notes in Computer Science

Series Editors

Randy Goebel
University of Alberta, Edmonton, Canada
Yuzuru Tanaka
Hokkaido University, Sapporo, Japan
Wolfgang Wahlster
DFKI and Saarland University, Saarbrücken, Germany

Founding Editor

Jörg Siekmann
DFKI and Saarland University, Saarbrücken, Germany

More information about this series at http://www.springer.com/series/1244

Abhaya C. Nayak · Alok Sharma (Eds.)

PRICAI 2019: Trends in Artificial Intelligence

16th Pacific Rim
International Conference on Artificial Intelligence
Cuvu, Yanuca Island, Fiji, August 26–30, 2019
Proceedings, Part III

 Springer

Editors
Abhaya C. Nayak (iD)
Department of Computing
Macquarie University
Sydney, NSW, Australia

Alok Sharma (iD)
RIKEN Center for Integrative
Medical Sciences
Yokohama, Japan

ISSN 0302-9743   ISSN 1611-3349 (electronic)
Lecture Notes in Artificial Intelligence
ISBN 978-3-030-29893-7   ISBN 978-3-030-29894-4 (eBook)
https://doi.org/10.1007/978-3-030-29894-4

LNCS Sublibrary: SL7 – Artificial Intelligence

This Springer imprint is published by the registered company Springer Nature Switzerland AG
The registered company address is: Gewerbestrasse 11, 6330 Cham, Switzerland

Preface

These proceedings in three volumes contain the papers presented at the 16th Pacific Rim International Conference on Artificial Intelligence (PRICAI 2019) held during August 26–30, 2019, in Yanuca Island, Fiji. PRICAI started as a biennial conference inaugurated in Tokyo in 1990. It provides a common forum for researchers and practitioners in various branches of artificial intelligence (AI) to exchange new ideas and share experience and expertise. Over the past years the conference has grown, both in participation and scope, to be a premier international AI event for all major Pacific Rim nations as well as countries from further afield. Indeed, the growth has merited holding PRICAI on an annual basis starting this year.

Submissions to PRICAI 2019 were received through two different routes: (1) some papers were directly submitted to PRICAI as in earlier years, and (2) in a special arrangement with IJCAI 2019, authors of submissions that narrowly missed out being accepted were encouraged to resubmit to PRICAI, along with the reviews and meta-reviews they received. The submissions of the first category underwent a double-blind review process, and were reviewed by the PRICAI Program Committee (PC) members and external reviewers against criteria such as significance, technical soundness, and clarity of presentation. Every paper received at least two, and in most cases three, reviews. Submissions of the second category were not subjected to further review, keeping in mind the workload of the reviewers in the community.

Altogether we received 311 high-quality submissions (with 265 submissions being of the first category) from 34 countries, which was impressive considering that for the first time PRICAI was being held in consecutive years. The program co-chairs read the reviews, the original papers, and called for additional reviews if necessary to make final decisions. The entire review team (PC members, external reviewers, and co-chairs) expended tremendous effort to ensure fairness and consistency in the paper selection process. Of the 265 submissions under the first category, 105 (39.6%) were accepted as full papers for the main-track, and 6 as full papers for the industry-track. A small number of papers were also accepted as short papers for the main-track (6), short papers for the industry-track (7), and as posters (6) – with the understanding that papers in the last category will not be included in these proceedings. The papers are organized in three volumes, under three broad (and naturally overlapping) themes, "Cognition", "Investigation", and "Application."

The technical program consisted of two workshops, five tutorials, and the main conference program. The workshops and tutorials covered important and thriving topics in AI. The workshops included the Pacific Rim Knowledge Acquisition Workshop (PKAW 2019) and the Knowledge Representation Conventicle (2019). The former was co-chaired by Prof. Kouzou Ohara and Dr. Quan Bai, while the latter was organized by Dr. Jake Chandler. The tutorials focused on hot topics including Big Data in bioinformatics, Data Science, Cognitive Logics, and Identity Management. All papers at the main conference were orally presented over the three days in parallel, and in thematically organized sessions. The authors of the posters were also offered the opportunity to give short talks to introduce their work.

It was our great honor to have four outstanding keynote/invited speakers, whose contributions have pushed boundaries of AI across various aspects: Prof. Hiroaki Kitano (Sony Computer Science Laboratories Inc. and The System Biology Institute, Japan), Prof. Grigoris Antoniou (University of Huddersfield, UK), Prof. Mary-Anne Williams (University of Technology Sydney, Australia), and Prof. Byoung-Tak Zhang (Seoul National University, South Korea). We are grateful to them for sharing their insights on their latest research with us.

The success of PRICAI 2019 would not have been possible without the effort and support of numerous people from all over the world. First of all, we would like to thank the PC members and external reviewers for their engagements in providing rigorous and timely reviews. It was because of them that the quality of the papers in this volume is maintained at a high level. We wish to thank the general co-chairs, Professors Abdul Sattar and MGM Khan for their continued support and guidance, and Dr. Sankalp Khanna for his tireless effort toward the overall coordination of PRICAI 2019. We are also thankful to various chairs and co-chairs, namely the industry co-chairs, workshop co-chairs, the tutorial co-chairs, the web and publicity co-chairs, the sponsorship chair, and the local organization chair, without whose support and hard work PRICAI 2019 could not have been successful. We also acknowledge the willing help of Kinzang Chhogyal, Jandson S. Ribeiro, and Hijab Alavi toward the preparation of these proceedings.

We gratefully acknowledge the financial and/or organizational support of a number of institutions including the University of the South Pacific (Fiji), Griffith University (Australia), Macquarie University (Australia), Fiji National University (Fiji), RIKEN Center for Integrative Medical Sciences (Japan), University of Western Australia (Australia), Australian Computer Society (ACS), and Springer Nature. Special thanks to EasyChair, whose paper submission platform we used to organize reviews and collate the files for these proceedings. We are also grateful to Alfred Hofmann and Anna Kramer from Springer for their assistance in publishing the PRICAI 2019 proceedings in the *Lecture Notes in Artificial Intelligence* series, as well as sponsoring the best paper awards.

We thank the Program Chair and the Conference Chair of IJCAI 2019, Professors Sarit Kraus and Thomas Eiter, for encouraging the resubmission of many IJCAI submissions to PRICAI 2019. Last but not least, we thank all authors and all conference participants for their contribution and support. We hope all the participants took this valuable opportunity to share and exchange their ideas and thoughts with one another and enjoyed their time at PRICAI 2019.

August 2019   Abhaya C. Nayak
                                                                     Alok Sharma

Organization

Steering Committee

Tru Hoang Cao	Ho Chi Minh City University of Technology, Vietnam
Xin Geng	Southeast University, China
Guido Governatori	Data61, Australia
Takayuki Ito	Nagoya Institute of Technology, Japan
Byeong-Ho Kang	University of Tasmania, Australia
Sankalp Khanna	CSIRO, Australia
Dickson Lukose	GCS Agile Pty Ltd., Australia
Hideyuki Nakashima	Sapporo City University, Japan
Seong-Bae Park	Kyung Hee University, South Korea
Abdul Sattar	Griffith University, Australia
Zhi-Hua Zhou	Nanjing University, China

Honorary Members

Randy Goebel	University of Alberta, Canada
Tu-Bao Ho	JAIST, Japan
Mitsuru Ishizuka	University of Tokyo, Japan
Hiroshi Motoda	Osaka University, Japan
Geoff Webb	Monash University, Australia
Wai K. Yeap	Auckland University of Technology, New Zealand
Byoung-Tak Zhang	Seoul National University, South Korea
Chengqi Zhang	University of Technology Sydney, Australia

Organizing Committee

General Co-chairs

Abdul Sattar	Griffith University, Australia
M. G. M. Khan	University of the South Pacific, Fiji

Program Co-chairs

Abhaya C. Nayak	Macquarie University, Australia
Alok Sharma	RIKEN Center for Integrative Medical Sciences, Japan

Local Co-chairs

Salsabil Nusair	University of the South Pacific, Fiji
A. B. M. Shawkat Ali	Fiji National University, Fiji

Workshop Co-chairs

Nasser Sabar	La Trobe University, Australia
Anurag Sharma	University of the South Pacific, Fiji

Tutorial Co-chairs

Min-Ling Zhang	Southeast University, China
Yi Mei	Victoria University of Wellington, New Zealand

Industry Co-chairs

Duc Nghia Pham	MIMOS Berhad, Malaysia
Sankalp Khanna	CSIRO, Australia

Sponsorship Co-chairs

Andy Song	Royal Melbourne Institute of Technology, Australia
Sabiha Khan	Fiji National University, Fiji

Web and Publicity Co-chairs

Mahmood Rashid	Victoria University, Australia
Benjamin Cowley	Griffith University, Australia

Local Arrangements

Priynka Sharma	University of the South Pacific, Fiji
Gavin Khan	University of the South Pacific, Fiji
Wafaa Wardha	University of the South Pacific, Fiji
Goel Aman Lal	University of the South Pacific, Fiji

Program Committee

Eriko Aiba	University of Electro-Communications, Japan
Patricia Anthony	Lincoln University, New Zealand
Quan Bai	Auckland University of Technology, New Zealand
Yun Bai	University of Western Sydney, Australia
Blai Bonet	Universidad Simón Bolívar, Venezuela
Richard Booth	Cardiff University, UK
Zied Bouraoui	CRIL – CNRS, Université d'Artois, France
Arina Britz	CAIR, Stellenbosch University, South Africa
Rafael Cabredo	De La Salle University, Philippines
Longbing Cao	University of Technology Sydney, Australia
Lawrence Cavedon	RMIT University, Australia
Siqi Chen	Tianjin University, China
Songcan Chen	Nanjing University of Aeronautics and Astronautics, China
Wu Chen	Southwest University, China
Yingke Chen	Sichuan University, China
Wai Khuen Cheng	Universiti Tunku Abdul Rahman, Malaysia

Krisana Chinnasarn	Burapha University, Thailand
Phatthanaphong Chomphuwiset	Mahasarakham University, Thailand
Dan Corbett	Optimodal Technologies, USA
Célia da Costa Pereira	Université Côte d'Azur, France
Jirapun Daengdej	Assumption University, Thailand
Xuan-Hong Dang	IBM T.J. Watson, USA
Abdollah Dehzangi	Morgan State University, USA
Clare Dixon	University of Liverpool, UK
Shyamala Doraisamy	Universiti Putra Malaysia, Malaysia
Atilla Elci	Aksaray University, Turkey
Vlad Estivill-Castro	Griffith University, Australia
Eduardo Fermé	Universidade da Madeira, Portugal
Christian Freksa	University of Bremen, Germany
Katsuhide Fujita	Tokyo University of Agriculture and Technology, Japan
Naoki Fukuta	Shizuoka University, Japan
Marcus Gallagher	University of Queensland, Australia
Dragan Gamberger	Ruđer Bošković Institute, Croatia
Wei Gao	Nanjing University, China
Xiaoying Gao	Victoria University of Wellington, New Zealand
Yang Gao	Nanjing University, China
Xin Geng	Southeast University, China
Manolis Gergatsoulis	Ionian University, Greece
Guido Governatori	CSIRO, Australia
Alban Grastien	Data61, Australia
Fikret Gürgen	Boğaziçi University, Turkey
Peter Haddawy	Mahidol University, Thailand
Bing Han	Xidian University, China
Choochart Haruechaiyasak	NECTEC, Thailand
Kiyota Hashimoto	Prince of Songkla University, Thailand
Tessai Hayama	Nagaoka University of Technology, Japan
Jose Hernandez-Orallo	Universitat Politècnica de València, Spain
Juhua Hu	University of Washington, USA
Sheng-Jun Huang	Nanjing University of Aeronautics and Astronautics, China
Xiaodi Huang	Charles Sturt University, Australia
Van Nam Huynh	JAIST, Japan
Masashi Inoue	Tohoku Institute of Technology, Japan
Sanjay Jain	National University of Singapore, Singapore
Jianmin Ji	University of Science and Technology of China, China
Liangxiao Jiang	China University of Geosciences, China
Yichuan Jiang	Southeast University, China
Hideaki Kanai	JAIST, Japan
Ryo Kanamori	Nagoya University, Japan
Byeong-Ho Kang	University of Tasmania, Australia

C. Maria Keet   University of Cape Town, South Africa
Gabriele Kern-Isberner   Technische Universität Dortmund, Germany
Sankalp Khanna   CSIRO, Australia
Frank Klawonn   Ostfalia University of Applied Sciences, Germany
Sébastien Konieczny   CRIL - CNRS, France
Alfred Krzywicki   University of New South Wales, Australia
Young-Bin Kwon   Chung-Ang University, South Korea
Ho-Pun Lam   CSIRO, Australia
Jérôme Lang   CNRS, LAMSADE, University Paris-Dauphine,
                                 France
Roberto Legaspi   RIKEN Center for Brain Science, Japan
Gang Li   Deakin University, Australia
Guangliang Li   University of Amsterdam, The Netherlands
Li Li   Southwest University, China
Ming Li   Nanjing University, China
Tianrui Li   Southwest Jiaotong University, China
Yu-Feng Li   Nanjing University, China
Beishui Liao   Zhejiang University, China
Jiamou Liu   University of Auckland, New Zealand
Qing Liu   CSIRO, Australia
Michael Maher   Reasoning Research Institute, Australia
Xinjun Mao   National University of Defense Technology, China
Eric Martin   University of New South Wales, Australia
Maria Vanina Martinez   Universidad de Buenos Aires, Argentina
Sanparith Marukatat   NECTEC, Thailand
Michael Mayo   University of Waikato, New Zealand
Brendan Mccane   University of Otago, New Zealand
Thomas Meyer   University of Cape Town and CAIR, South Africa
James Montgomery   University of Tasmania, Australia
Abhaya Nayak   Macquarie University, Australia
Richi Nayak   QUT, Australia
Kourosh Neshatian   University of Canterbury, New Zealand
M. A. Hakim Newton   Griffith University, Australia
Shahrul Azman Noah   Universiti Kebangsaan Malaysia, Malaysia
Masayuki Numao   Osaka University, Japan
Kouzou Ohara   Aoyama Gakuin University, Japan
Hayato Ohwada   Tokyo University of Science, Japan
Mehmet Orgun   Macquarie University, Australia
Noriko Otani   Tokyo City University, Japan
Lionel Ott   University of Sydney, Australia
Maurice Pagnucco   University of New South Wales, Australia
Hye-Young Paik   University of New South Wales, Australia
Laurent Perrussel   IRIT, Université de Toulouse, France
Bernhard Pfahringer   University of Waikato, New Zealand
Duc Nghia Pham   MIMOS Berhad, Malaysia
Jantima Polpinij   Mahasarakham University, Thailand

Mikhail Prokopenko	University of Sydney, Australia
Chao Qian	University of Science and Technology of China, China
Yuhua Qian	Shanxi University, China
Joël Quinqueton	LIRMM, France
Fenghui Ren	University of Wollongong, Australia
Mark Reynolds	University of Western Australia, Australia
Ji Ruan	Auckland University of Technology, New Zealand
Kazumi Saito	University of Shizuoka, Japan
Chiaki Sakama	Wakayama University, Japan
Ken Satoh	National Institute of Informatics and Sokendai, Japan
Abdul Sattar	Griffith University, Australia
Torsten Schaub	University of Potsdam, Germany
Nicolas Schwind	National Institute of Advanced Industrial Science and Technology, Japan
Nazha Selmaoui-Folcher	University of New Caledonia, New Caledonia
Lin Shang	Nanjing University, China
Alok Sharma	RIKEN Center for Integrative Medical Sciences, Japan
Chuan Shi	Beijing University of Posts and Telecommunications, China
Zhenwei Shi	Beihang University, China
Daichi Shigemizu	NCGG, Japan
Yanfeng Shu	CSIRO, Australia
Guillermo R. Simari	Universidad del Sur in Bahia Blanca, Argentina
Tony Smith	University of Waikato, New Zealand
Chattrakul Sombattheera	Mahasarakham University, Thailand
Andy Song	RMIT University, Australia
Markus Stumptner	University of South Australia, Australia
Xing Su	Beijing University of Technology, China
Merlin Teodosia Suarez	De La Salle University, Philippines
Thepchai Supnithi	NECTEC, Thailand
Michael Thielscher	University of New South Wales, Australia
Shikui Tu	Shanghai Jiao Tong University, China
Miroslav Velev	Aries Design Automation, USA
Serena Villata	CNRS, France
Toby Walsh	University of New South Wales, Australia
Kewen Wang	Griffith University, Australia
Qi Wang	Northwestern Polytechnical University, China
Wei Wang	NJU, China
Paul Weng	UM-SJTU Joint Institute, China
Peter Whigham	University of Otago, New Zealand
Wayne Wobcke	University of New South Wales, Australia
Brendon J. Woodford	University of Otago, New Zealand
Chang Xu	University of Sydney, Australia
Guandong Xu	University of Technology Sydney, Australia
Ming Xu	Xi'an Jiaotong-Liverpool University, China
Shuxiang Xu	University of Tasmania, Australia

Xin-Shun Xu	Shandong University, China
Bing Xue	Victoria University of Wellington, New Zealand
Hui Xue	Southeast University, China
Bo Yang	Jilin University, China
Ming Yang	Nanjing Normal University, China
Roland Yap	National University of Singapore, Singapore
Kenichi Yoshida	University of Tsukuba, Japan
Chao Yu	University of Wollongong, Australia
Yang Yu	Nanjing University, China
Takaya Yuizono	JAIST, Japan
Yifeng Zeng	Teesside University, UK
Chengqi Zhang	University of Technology Sydney, Australia
Dongmo Zhang	Western Sydney University, Australia
Du Zhang	Macau University of Science and Technology, China
Min-Ling Zhang	Southeast University, China
Minjie Zhang	University of Wollongong, Australia
Qieshi Zhang	Chinese Academy of Sciences, Australia
Rui Zhang	University of Melbourne, Australia
Shichao Zhang	Guangxi Normal University, China
Wen Zhang	Beijing University of Technology, China
Yu Zhang	Hong Kong University of Science and Technology, SAR China
Zhao Zhang	Hefei University of Technology, China
Zili Zhang	Deakin University, Australia
Zongzhang Zhang	Soochow University, China
Li Zhao	MSRA, China
Yanchang Zhao	CSIRO, Australia
Shuigeng Zhou	Fudan University, China
Zhi-Hua Zhou	Nanjing University, China
Xiaofeng Zhu	Guangxi Normal University, China
Xingquan Zhu	Florida Atlantic University, USA
Fuzhen Zhuang	Chinese Academy of Sciences, China

Additional Reviewers

Shintaro Akiyama	Bayu Distiawan
Yuya Asanomi	Shaokang Dong
Mansour Assaf	Steve Edwards
Weiling Cai	Suhendry Effendy
Rohitash Chandra	Jorge Fandinno
Jairui Chen	Zaiwen Feng
Armin Chitizadeh	Chuanxin Geng
Laurenz A. Cornelissen	Sayuri Higaki
Emon Dey	Jin B. Hong
Duy Tai Dinh	Yuxuan Hu

Paul Salvador Inventado
Abdul Karim
Karamjit Kaur
Sunil Lal
Ang Li
Haopeng Li
Weikai Li
Yun Li
Yuyu Li
Shenglan Liao
Shaowu Liu
Yuxin Liu
Wolfgang Mayer
Kingshuk Mazumdar
Nguyen Le Minh
Risa Mitsumori
Taiki Mori
Majid Namaazi
Courtney Ngo
Aaron Nicolson
Lifan Pan
Asanga Ranasinghe
Vahid Riahi
Maria AF Rodriguez
Manou Rosenberg
Matt Selway
Cong Shang

Swakkhar Shatabda
Manisha Sirsat
Fengyi Song
Yixin Su
Adam Svahn
Trung Huynh Thanh
Yanlling Tian
Qing Tian
Jannai Tokotoko
Nhi N. Y. Vo
Guodong Wang
Jing Wang
Xiaojie Wang
Yi Wang
Yuchen Wang
Yunyun Wang
Shiqing Wu
Peng Xiao
Yi Xu
Wanqi Yang
Heng Yao
Dayong Ye
Jun Yin
Zhao Zhang
Zhu Zhirui
Zili Zhou
Yunkai Zhuang

Contents – Part III

Robotics, IOT and Traffic Automation

Biometrics and Bioinformatics

Other Applications

Detection and Classification

Attacking Object Detectors Without Changing the Target Object

Yi Huang[✉], Adams Wai-Kin Kong, and Kwok-Yan Lam

Nanyang Technological University, Singapore, Singapore
{S160042,adamskong,kwokyan.lam}@ntu.edu.sg

Abstract. Object detectors, such as Faster R-CNN and YOLO, have numerous applications, including in some critical systems, e.g., self-driving cars and unmanned aerial vehicles. Their vulnerabilities have to be studied thoroughly before deploying them in critical systems to avoid irrecoverable loss caused by intentional attacks. Researchers have proposed some methods to craft adversarial examples for studying security risk in object detectors. All these methods require modifying pixels inside target objects. Some modifications are substantial and target objects are significantly distorted. In this paper, an algorithm which derives an adversarial signal placing around the border of target objects to fool objector detectors is proposed. Computationally, the algorithm seeks a border around target objects to mislead Faster R-CNN to produce a very large bounding box and finally decease its confidence to target objects. Using stop sign as a target object, adversarial borders with four different sizes are generated and evaluated on 77 videos, including five in-car videos for digital attacks and 72 videos for physical attacks. The experimental results show that adversarial border can effectively fool Faster R-CNN and YOLOv3 digitally and physically. In addition, the experimental results on YOLOv3 indicate that adversarial border is transferable, which is vital for black-box attack.

Keywords: Adversarial examples · Attack · Object detection

1 Introduction

Computer vision methods have significant progress in recent years because of the advancement of deep neural networks (DNNs) and computational hardware, as well as the availability of large image and video datasets. Some of these methods have been deployed in real-world applications, e.g., face recognition methods in surveillance systems. However, the existence of adversarial examples in DNNs, which was first discussed by [23], raises great concerns on their deployment, especially in privacy and security-critical industries. Szgedy *et al.* demonstrated that DNN image classifiers can be easily fooled by images with deliberately designed perturbations. The perturbed images and the original ones are almost the same to the naked eye but DNNs classify them differently. Even worse, the adversarial examples are transferable [18], meaning that an adversarial example trained to mislead a DNN can likely mislead other DNNs with different parameters or even different architectures. In other words, attackers can carry out black-box attacks by exploiting this transferability.

© Springer Nature Switzerland AG 2019
A. C. Nayak and A. Sharma (Eds.): PRICAI 2019, LNAI 11672, pp. 3–15, 2019.
https://doi.org/10.1007/978-3-030-29894-4_1

In order to identify potential risks and to eventually improve the safety of DNN-based systems, researchers put great efforts on investigating adversarial examples. It can be summarized into three research directions: (1) designing new attack strategies [11,23][?][4,17,19,21] and countermeasures against adversarial examples [3,7,26], (2) estimating boundaries of DNNs against zero-day (new) attacks [2,10,12] and (3) explaining the existence of adversarial examples and their transferability [9,14,24]. From the application perspective, designing adversarial examples is arguably the most important because it reduces the number of possible zero-day attacks and provides critical information to develop countermeasures. Following Szgedy *et al.*'s research in 2014, researchers proposed different methods to generate adversarial example. Most of them targeted on DNN image classifiers and succeeded in misleading the classifiers with high misclassification rates digitally or physically. A question then arises: is it possible to attack more complex computer vision systems, such as those for object detection digitally and physically? Object detection has various applications, for instance, face detection, people counting, self-driving cars, etc. If an object detector is vulnerable to adversarial examples, it may not be wise to use it in a fully automatic environment before corresponding countermeasures are developed. Therefore, it is important and necessary to study the impact of adversarial examples on object detectors.

Object detection is different from image classification. Image classifier outputs a class label for an input image, while object detector localizes multiple objects in an image and predicts their class labels. Generally, object detector produces multiple bounding boxes internally for each object and uses non-maximum suppression or other techniques to select one bounding box for each object. Attacking object detectors is more difficult than attacking image classifiers because adversarial examples have to cause significant errors on all the internal bounding boxes [16]. Some researchers successfully attacked object detectors by changing every pixel in entire images [25], which generally cannot be implemented as physical attacks. Some researchers changed target objects extensively to achieve effective digital and physical attacks. Their adversarial examples are hard to be classified even for human beings. Is it possible to design adversarial examples, which are effective for digital and physical attacks, against object detectors without modifying target objects? According to the best knowledge of the authors, no existing adversarial examples can effectively fool object detectors digitally and physically without changing target objects. In this paper, an algorithm is proposed to craft adversarial examples, named adversarial borders to answer this question.

The rest of this paper is organized as follows. Section 2 reviews the existing adversarial examples against image classifiers and object detectors. Section 3 describes the proposed algorithm based on Faster R-CNN to craft adversarial border. Section 4 evaluates adversarial borders with different sizes on 77 videos for digitally and physically attacking Faster R-CNN and YOLOv3. Section 5 offers some conclusive remarks.

2   Related Work

2.1   Adversarial Examples Against Image Classifier

Szgedy *et al.* [23] introduced a method named L-BFGS to generate adversarial examples which are able to mislead DNN image classifiers into making wrong classifica-

Fig. 1. The 1st–3rd columns are adversarial stop signs generated by the methods in [Lu *et al.*, 2017a; Chen *et al.*, 2018; Eykholt *et al.*, 2017b], respectively.

tion. Their work revealed the potential risks of deep learning systems. Following their work, Goodfellow *et al.* [11] proposed a new method called Fast Gradient Sign Method (FGSM) for generating adversarial examples which is much faster than L-BFGS. Then, Rozsa *et al.* [21] proposed Fast Gradient method (FGM) based on FGSM, where they replaced the sign of the gradient with the original gradient to achieve more precise optimization direction. Papernot *et al.* [19] designed a new attack named Jacobian-based Saliency Map Attack (JSMA), which achieved higher adversarial success rate by modifying a small amount of pixels with higher computational cost. In addition to the above mentioned attacks, there are more attack methods such as Deepfool [17], C&W attack [4], Zeroth Order Optimization (ZOO) attack [5], etc. These attacks have a common assumption that attacker has access to the input of targeted DNN to perform the digital attacks. Comparing with the digital attacks, a more realistic scenario is that attacker can manipulate only adversarial examples in the physical world and these examples are fed into targeted DNN by an input device such as a camera. To evaluate the effectiveness of adversarial examples in the physical world, Kurakin *et al.* [13] extended FGSM by using a finer optimization scheme. Taking distance between camera and object, viewpoint variations and other noise in the physical world into account. Athalye *et al.* [1] used a function to model image transformation including scaling, rotation and translation, and then injected noise into the training process to increase robustness of their adversarial examples. Eykholt *et al.* [8] handled physical variations by selecting images with target object under diverse imaging conditions such as different viewpoints, distances and lighting conditions for training. They also used a synthetic transformation function to further increase the robustness of their adversarial examples. Those works proved that image classifiers are not safe in physical world.

2.2 Adversarial Examples Against Object Detector

After the success of adversarial examples against DNN image classifier, some researchers studied adversarial examples against object detector. Currently the attacks against object detector can also be classified into digital attacks and physical attacks. Lu [?] [16] set a target vector with all elements close to zero and employed the attack method in image classification to generate adversarial examples against YOLO detector. The experimental results showed that their method can successfully mislead YOLO digitally, but is ineffective in physical attack. Xie *et al.* [25] derived an attack named Dense Adversary Generation (DAG) to fool Faster R-CNN. They assigned an adversarial label to each object in an image and attacked the classification layer in Faster R-CNN by decreasing its output confidence to the original class label and increasing its confidence to the adversarial class label. Their method can mislead Faster R-CNN into outputting wrong object labels. Lu *et al.* [15] designed a method to construct an adversarial stop sign against Faster R-CNN. To make adversarial pattern robust, they selected a set of diverse frames which contain stop signs from a video to train their method. They minimized the mean score of the stop signs detected by Faster R-CNN in all the training frames. Their method relies on a shape matching function to map an adversarial stop sign in a root coordinate system to the stop signs in the training frames. It cannot be generalized to other objects, in particular those without well-defined shapes, e.g., chairs. Although their adversarial stop sign can attack Faster R-CNN successfully in the physical world, it is difficult even for humans to recognize it. Chen *et al.* [6] adapted the technique of expectation over transformation [1] and successfully produced an adversarial stop sign, which can physically fool Faster R-CNN. The perturbation in their attack is applied to the entire stop sign. However, it is also difficult for humans to recognize it. Song *et al.* [22] proposed a sticker attack which can successfully mislead both YOLO and Faster R-CNN when attaching their adversarial sticker to a stop sign. However their attack is not applicable when attackers have no access to the object in the physical world. All the previous methods require changing target objects. Figure 1 shows some adversarial stop signs generated by [6,15,22]. The proposed algorithm in the next section is to generate adversarial examples named adversarial border to attack object detectors digitally and physically without changing the objects.

3 The Algorithm Generating Adversarial Board

The proposed algorithm utilizes Faster R-CNN to derive adversarial board and therefore a brief summary of Faster R-CNN is first given. Faster R-CNN illustrated in the blue box in Fig. 2 adopts a two-stage detection strategy. In the first stage, a CNN takes an image as an input and produces feature maps. Then, a region proposal network (RPN) is used to generate bounding boxes called region proposals that may contain objects. The region proposals and the feature maps are taken into the second stage for classifying the objects and determining their locations and sizes, which are respectively performed by a classification layer and a regression layer. Finally, Faster R-CNN outputs classification results and refines bounding box coordinates of each region proposal. Currently, all adversarial examples against Faster R-CNN make use of the classification layer in the second stage only and require modifying pixels inside target objects. According to the best knowledge of the authors, no one attempted to use the regression layer to mislead Faster R-CNN and no one successfully misled Faster R-CNN without modifying pixels inside target objects.

The regression layer is used to compute bounding box coordinates of objects. For each region proposal, the regression layer outputs four values d_x, d_y, d_w, and d_h to refine the region proposal's coordinates (p_x, p_y, p_w, p_h), where (p_x, p_y) is the top left hand corner of the region proposal and p_w and p_h are its width and height, respectively. The bounding box coordinates are calculated by the following equations:

$$g_x = p_w \times d_x + p_x \tag{1}$$

$$g_y = p_h \times d_y + p_y \tag{2}$$

$$g_w = p_w \times e^{d_w} \tag{3}$$

$$g_h = p_h \times e^{d_h} \tag{4}$$

The equations imply that if d_w and d_h are slightly distorted, the bounding box coordinates will change a lot due to the exponential function. Adversarial border is designed to mislead regression layer such that it outputs very large bounding boxes for target object, e.g., stop sign and finally decreases the output confidence to it. The size of the bounding box, i.e., $g_w \times g_h$ and the size of the corresponding region proposal, i.e., $p_h \times p_w$ are always similar. Faster R-CNN is designed in such a way so that the parameters d_w and d_h can be learned more effectively. Mathematically, when $g_w \approx p_w$ and $g_h \approx p_h$, it implies that $d_w \approx 0$ and $d_h \approx 0$. If the regression layer is misled to output $d_w = v$ and $d_h = v$, where $v > 0$, the size of the output bounding box will be roughly $e^v \times e^v$ times larger than the size of the target object. In the experiments, v is set to 1, which corresponds roughly to 738% enlargement.

To handle the scale, distance and lighting variations in the physical world, n images are sampled from a video collection V which contains a target object T as a training set. Let the adversarial border be a patch Λ with a fixed size of $s \times s$ pixels and the bounding box predicated by Faster R-CNN for the target object T in a training image I_i be b_{ti} with a size of $h_{ti} \times w_{ti}$ pixels. The patch Λ is first enlarged to $\alpha h_{ti} \times \beta w_{ti}$ pixels, where $\alpha > 1$ and $\beta > 1$. Then, the enlarged patch is inserted to I_i at the location b_{ti}. Note that the image pixels inside b_{ti} are retained and only the pixels outside b_{ti} are replaced with the pixels in the enlarged Λ. These operations are represented by $Z_{\alpha\beta}$ and $I_{ip} = Z_{\alpha\beta}(\Lambda, b_{ti}, I_i)$ represents the perturbed image. Figure 5(a) shows some perturbed images in training. Note that in training, the adversarial border is inserted at the location of b_{ti}, which is determined by Faster R-CNN and therefore, it may overlap with the target object (Fig. 5(a)). However, in testing and attacking, it is assumed that b_{ti} is not available, which is important for black-box attacks, and the ground truth bounding box of the target object is used to insert the trained adversarial border. Figure 5(b) shows some testing images with a trained adversarial border. In fact, in preliminary experiments, the enlarged Λ was inserted in the ground truth location of the target object. However, its performance is not as good as the one inserted at the location of b_{ti}. Let $f_h(\cdot)$ and $f_w(\cdot)$ be two functions representing the operations in Faster R-CNN to compute the scaling values of d_w and d_h. Since the box-regression layer in Faster R-CNN outputs one boundary box for each region proposal and the number

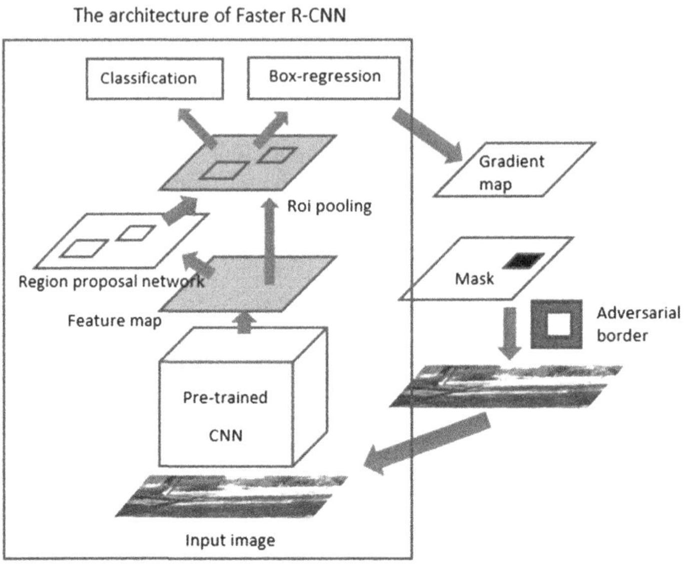

The architecture of Faster R-CNN

Fig. 2. A schematic diagram of Faster R-CNN and the construction of adversarial border. The blue box highlights the operations of Faster R-CNN and the outside is the construction of adversarial border. (Color figure online)

of region proposals is fixed for each image, f_h and f_w produce two fixed-length vectors, D_w and D_h, whose elements are respectively d_w and d_h of one bounding box and whose dimensions are same as the number of bounding boxes. Faster R-CNN uses non-maximum suppression and confidence values to determine final object bounding boxes. Mathematically, given an input image with an adversarial example i.e., $Z_{\alpha\beta}(\Lambda, b_{ti}, I_i)$, $D_w = f_w(Z_{\alpha\beta}(\Lambda, b_{ti}, I_i))$ and $D_h = f_h(Z_{\alpha\beta}(\Lambda, b_{ti}, I_i))$. To train an adversarial border, the minimization is performed through the equation:

$$\min_{\Lambda} \sum_{i=1}^{n} ||\mathbf{I} - f_w(Z_{\alpha\beta}(\Lambda, b_{ti}, I_i))||^2 + ||\mathbf{I} - f_h(Z_{\alpha\beta}(\Lambda, b_{ti}, I_i))||^2 \qquad (5)$$

where $\mathbf{I}$ represents a vector all whose elements are one and its dimension is same as D_h and D_w.

4   Experimental Results

To evaluate the risk caused by adversarial border, stop sign is selected as a target object because it was used in the previous adversarial example studies [6, 15, 16, 25] and is an important object for self-driving car. In this evaluation, both white-box attacks and black-box attacks are studied. For white-box attacks, adversarial border is trained and evaluated on Faster R-CNN with VGG-16 as a backbone network, while for black-box attacks, it is also trained on Faster R-CNN with VGG-16 but examined on YOLOv3 [20]. Both Faster

R-CNN and YOLOv3 were trained on the COCO dataset to detect multiple objects, including stop sign. In addition to white-box and black-box attacks, the performance of adversarial border for digital attacks and physical attacks is also investigated.

Fig. 3. Sample frames from the five videos for evaluating digital attack.

4.1   Digital Attack Evaluation

For evaluating adversarial border in digital attacks, five in-car videos with stop signs were downloaded from the Internet. Figure 3 shows sample frames from the videos. In each of the videos, a car was approaching to a stop sign. Since adjacent frames in the videos are similar, each alternative frame in the videos is sampled and five clips named Clip 1 to Clip 5 are constructed for evaluating adversarial border in digital attacks. All the images in these five clips have a stop sign facing to the camera. Table 2 summarizes the total number of images in each clip and the corresponding detection rates obtained by Faster R-CNN and YOLOv3. Clip 1 is used to train adversarial border and the other four clips are used to test its impact to Faster R-CNN and YOLOv3. The size of adversarial border is controlled by β and α. In the experiment, $\alpha = \beta$ is set and four values of α computed by the equation,

$$\alpha_i = 2 \times \left(\frac{i}{6}\right) + 1 \tag{6}$$

where $i \in \{1, 2, 3, 4\}$, are used to generate adversarial borders with four different sizes. Size 1 to Size 4 are used to denote the sizes of the adversarial borders computed from α_1 to α_4, respectively. Since the loss decreases slowly between the 200th iteration and the 300th iteration, the optimization is terminated at the 300th iteration. The adversarial borders generated at the 100th, 200th and 300th iterations are used in this experiment. The adversarial borders with different sizes and generated by different iterations are shown in Fig. 4. The number of detected stop signs with and without adversarial borders in each clip are denoted as Det_{adv} and Det_{org} respectively. The successful attack rate for digital attacks is defined as:

$$AR = 1 - Det_{adv}/Det_{org} \tag{7}$$

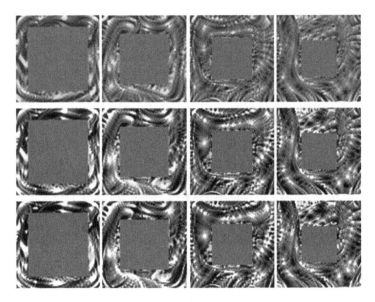

Fig. 4. The 12 adversarial borders used in the experiments. The adversarial borders in the 1st–4th columns are respectively computed from α_1 to α_4 and the adversarial borders in the 1st–3rd are respectively obtained at the 100th, 200th and 300th iterations.

Table 3 lists the average successful attack rates of Clip 2 to Clip 4 against Faster R-CNN and YOLOv3. It shows that the adversarial borders can successfully mislead Faster R-CNN and can also be transferred to YOLOv3 with high successful attack rates. In other words, adversarial border can be used in white-box and black-box attacks. Figure 7(a) shows the detection results with and without the adversarial examples.

4.2 Physical Attack Evaluation

For evaluating adversarial border in physical attacks, one original stop sign and the 12 adversarial borders (Fig. 3) with the original stop sign were printed on A3 paper using HP Colour LaserJet Enterprise flow MFP M880. The stop signs in these printouts were from the same image downloaded from Google image, not from the training video, Clip 1. The stop signs with the 12 different adversarial borders have the same size in the printouts but the sizes of the adversarial borders are different (Fig. 6). Each of them was placed in two different outdoor locations and three videos from the left hand side, the front view and the right hand side were taken from it using Samsung Galaxy 7. Totally, $72 (12 \times 3 \times 2)$ videos were taken from the 12 stop signs with the adversarial borders and $6 (1 \times 3 \times 2)$ videos were taken from the original stop sign without adversarial border. The resolution of the videos is 1080 by 1920 pixels. As with the previous experiment, images are extracted from every alternative frame from these videos for evaluation. Table 1 lists the detection rates of the six videos collected from the original stop sign. It shows that Faster R-CNN and YOLOv3 can detect around 80% and 60% of the frames, respectively. The successful attack rate for digital attacks defined Eq. (7) can-

(a)

(b)

Fig. 5. Examples for perturbed training images (left) and perturbed testing images (right).

Table 1. Detection rates of Faster R-CNN and YOLOv3 for the videos collected in location 1 and location 2 with adversarial borders.

Video	Location 1			Location 2		
	Total frames	Faster R-CNN	YOLOv3	Total frames	Faster R-CNN	YOLOv3
Left hand side view	181	0.796	0.751	107	0.813	0.542
Front view	194	0.743	0.557	106	0.887	0.774
Right hand side view	149	0.832	0.497	95	0.863	0.611
Mean	175	0.79	0.602	103	0.854	0.642

not be employed to evaluate physical attacks because the videos with and without the adversarial borders are different, e.g., viewpoints and the number of frames. Instead, the Faster R-CNN and YOLOv3 detection rates for the stop signs with the adversarial borders are computed and their means are given in Table 4. Each value in Table 4 is the mean detection rate computed from three different videos collected at the same location. Comparing with the detection rates with and without adversarial borders respectively in Tables 1 and 4, it shows that adversarial border can effectively mislead Faster R-CNN and YOLOv3 in the physical world. Figure 7(b) shows the detection results with and without the adversarial examples in the physical world.

Fig. 6. An adversarial border and the original stop sign on printouts.

Table 2. A summary of Clip 1–Clip 5 for digital attacks

	Resolution	Number of stop signs	Faster R-CNN	YOLOv3
Clip 1	1280 × 720	94	1.000	1.000
Clip 2	1280 × 720	100	0.800	0.790
Clip 3	1280 × 720	74	1.000	1.000
Clip 4	1280 × 720	157	0.981	0.987
Clip 5	406 × 720	298	0.997	0.876

Table 3. Average successful attack rates of digital attacks

Iteration	Faster R-CNN			YOLOv3		
	100	200	300	100	200	300
Size 1	0.626	0.790	0.826	0.626	0.847	0.885
Size 2	0.854	0.912	0.908	0.753	0.909	0.941
Size 3	0.882	0.857	0.819	0.884	0.871	0.904
Size 4	0.789	0.816	0.833	0.686	0.763	0.788

Table 4. Detection rates of Faster R-CNN and YOLOv3 for the videos collected in location 1 and location 2 with adversarial borders.

Iteration	Location 1						Location 2					
	Faster R-CNN			YOLOv3			Faster R-CNN			YOLOv3		
	100	200	300	100	200	300	100	200	300	100	200	300
Size 1	0.644	0.674	0.589	0.533	0.549	0.516	0.354	0.358	0.354	0.118	0.150	0.121
Size 2	0.421	0.532	0.675	0.393	0.385	0.506	0.035	0.118	0.248	0.108	0.107	0.145
Size 3	0.337	0.356	0.349	0.287	0.270	0.215	0.058	0.135	0.152	0.121	0.094	0.069
Size 4	0.441	0.413	0.488	0.296	0.301	0.282	0.300	0.301	0.266	0.144	0.115	0.093

(a)

(b)

Fig. 7. Detection results on images with and without adversarial borders. (a) Results from the digital attacks and (b) results from the physical attacks.

5   Conclusion and Discussion

Researchers demonstrated that deep image classifiers are vulnerable to adversarial examples with deliberately designed perturbations. Some researchers extended these adversarial examples to study vulnerability of deep object detectors. Comparing with the adversarial example studies for image classification, the studies for object detection are relatively limited. The previous studies for object detection require changing target objects significantly. In this paper, a new type of adversarial examples named adversarial border, which does not change any pixel in target object, is designed. The algorithm proposed to generate adversarial border sets the target values of the parameters d_w and d_h in Faster R-CNN to a large value such that the regression layer outputs very large bounding boxes and finally decreases the output confidence to the target object. The adversarial borders with four different sizes are evaluated on five in-car videos for digital attacks and 72 videos for physical attacks. The experimental results show that adversarial border can effectively fool Faster R-CNN and YOLOv3 digitally and physically. They also demonstrate that adversarial border can be used to perform white-box and black-box attacks.

Acknowledgement. This work is partially supported by the Ministry of Education, Singapore through Academic Research Fund Tier 1, RG30/17.

References

1. Athalye, A., Engstrom, L., Ilyas, A., Kwok, K.: Synthesizing robust adversarial examples. In: ICML (2018)
2. Bastani, O., Ioannou, Y., Lampropoulos, L., Vytiniotis, D., Nori, A.V., Criminisi, A.: Measuring neural net robustness with constraints. In: NIPS (2016)
3. Bhagoji, A.N., Cullina, D., Sitawarin, C., Mittal, P.: Enhancing robustness of machine learning systems via data transformations. In: 2018 52nd Annual Conference on Information Sciences and Systems (CISS), pp. 1–5 (2018)
4. Carlini, N., Wagner, D.A.: Towards evaluating the robustness of neural networks. In: 2017 IEEE Symposium on Security and Privacy (SP), pp. 39–57 (2017)
5. Chen, P.Y., Zhang, H., Sharma, Y., Yi, J., Hsieh, C.J.: ZOO: zeroth order optimization based black-box attacks to deep neural networks without training substitute models. In: AISec@CCS (2017)
6. Chen, S.-T., Cornelius, C., Martin, J., Chau, D.H.P.: ShapeShifter: robust physical adversarial attack on faster R-CNN object detector. In: Berlingerio, M., Bonchi, F., Gärtner, T., Hurley, N., Ifrim, G. (eds.) ECML PKDD 2018. LNCS (LNAI), vol. 11051, pp. 52–68. Springer, Cham (2019). https://doi.org/10.1007/978-3-030-10925-7_4
7. Das, N., et al.: Keeping the bad guys out: protecting and vaccinating deep learning with jpeg compression. CoRR abs/1705.02900 (2017)
8. Eykholt, K., et al.: Robust physical-world attacks on deep learning visual classification. In: 2018 IEEE/CVF Conference on Computer Vision and Pattern Recognition, pp. 1625–1634 (2018)
9. Fawzi, A., Fawzi, O., Frossard, P.: Fundamental limits on adversarial robustness. In: ICML 2015 (2015)
10. Fawzi, A., Fawzi, O., Frossard, P.: Analysis of classifiers' robustness to adversarial perturbations. Mach. Learn. **107**, 481–508 (2017)

11. Goodfellow, I., Shlens, J., Szegedy, C.: Explaining and harnessing adversarial examples. In: International Conference on Learning Representations (2015). http://arxiv.org/abs/1412.6572

12. Huang, X., Kwiatkowska, M., Wang, S., Wu, M.: Safety verification of deep neural networks. In: Majumdar, R., Kunčak, V. (eds.) CAV 2017. LNCS, vol. 10426, pp. 3–29. Springer, Cham (2017). https://doi.org/10.1007/978-3-319-63387-9_1

13. Kurakin, A., Goodfellow, I., Bengio, S.: Adversarial examples in the physical world. In: ICLR Workshop (2017). https://arxiv.org/abs/1607.02533

14. Liu, Y., Chang Liu, X.C., Song, D.: Delving into transferable adversarial examples and black-box attacks. In: Proceedings of 5th International Conference on Learning Representations (2017)

15. Lu, J., Sibai, H., Fabry, E.: Adversarial examples that fool detectors. CoRR abs/1712.02494 (2017)

16. Lu, J., Sibai, H., Fabry, E., Forsyth, D.A.: No need to worry about adversarial examples in object detection in autonomous vehicles. CoRR abs/1707.03501 (2017)

17. Moosavi-Dezfooli, S.M., Fawzi, A., Frossard, P.: DeepFool: a simple and accurate method to fool deep neural networks. In: 2016 IEEE Conference on Computer Vision and Pattern Recognition (CVPR), pp. 2574–2582 (2016)

18. Papernot, N., McDaniel, P.D., Goodfellow, I.J.: Transferability in machine learning: from phenomena to black-box attacks using adversarial samples CoRR abs/1605.07277 (2016)

19. Papernot, N., McDaniel, P.D., Jha, S., Fredrikson, M., Celik, Z.B., Swami, A.: The limitations of deep learning in adversarial settings. In: 2016 IEEE European Symposium on Security and Privacy (EuroS&P), pp. 372–387 (2016)

20. Redmon, J., Farhadi, A.: YOLOv3: an incremental improvement. CoRR abs/1804.02767 (2018)

21. Rozsa, A., Rudd, E.M., Boult, T.E.: Adversarial diversity and hard positive generation. In: 2016 IEEE Conference on Computer Vision and Pattern Recognition Workshops (CVPRW), pp. 410–417 (2016)

22. Song, D., et al.: Physical adversarial examples for object detectors. In: 12th USENIX Workshop on Offensive Technologies (WOOT 2018) (2018)

23. Szegedy, C., et al.: Intriguing properties of neural networks. In: International Conference on Learning Representations (2014). http://arxiv.org/abs/1312.6199

24. Tabacof, P., Valle, E.: Exploring the space of adversarial images. In: 2016 International Joint Conference on Neural Networks (IJCNN), pp. 426–433 (2016)

25. Xie, C., Wang, J., Zhang, Z., Zhou, Y., Xie, L., Yuille, A.L.: Adversarial examples for semantic segmentation and object detection. In: 2017 IEEE International Conference on Computer Vision (ICCV), pp. 1378–1387 (2017)

26. Zheng, S., Song, Y., Leung, T., Goodfellow, I.J.: Improving the robustness of deep neural networks via stability training. In: 2016 IEEE Conference on Computer Vision and Pattern Recognition (CVPR), pp. 4480–4488 (2016)

D_dNet-65 R-CNN: Object Detection Model Fusing Deep Dilated Convolutions and Light-Weight Networks

Yu Quan, Zhixin Li$^{(\boxtimes)}$, Fengqi Zhang, and Canlong Zhang

Guangxi Key Lab of Multi-source Information Mining and Security,
Guangxi Normal University, Guilin 541004, China
`lizx@gxnu.edu.cn`

Abstract. In recent years, object detection has become a popular direction of computer vision and digital image processing. All the research work in this paper is a two-stage object detection algorithm based on deep learning. First, this paper proposes the Deep_Dilated Convolution Network (D_dNet). That is, by adding the operation of dilated convolution into the backbone network, in this way, not only the number of training parameters can be further reduced, but also the resolution of feature map and the size of receptive field can be improved. Second, the Fully Convolutional Layer (FC) is usually involved in the re-identification process of region proposal in the traditional object detection. This too "thick" network structure will easily lead to reduced detection speed and excessive computation. Therefore, the feature map before training is compressed in this paper to establish a light-weight network. Then, transfer learning method is introduced in training network to optimize the model. The whole experiment is evaluated based on MSCOCO dataset. Experiments show that the accuracy of the proposed model is improved by 1.3 to 2.2% points.

Keywords: Object detection · Deep dilated convolution network · Light-weight network · Transfer learning · Convolutional neural network

1 Introduction

With the research of unstructured visual data, object detection algorithm has become a classic subject in the field of image processing and computer vision. The research on this topic is mainly based on two methods: one is based on traditional image processing and machine learning algorithm, the other is based on deep learning [4]. The two methods have their own characteristics in feature extraction, but the latter's region selection strategy is better than the former's SIFT, HOG and SURF methods in terms of pertinence, time complexity and window redundancy. In addition, the latter gradually realizes the end-to-end

© Springer Nature Switzerland AG 2019
A. C. Nayak and A. Sharma (Eds.): PRICAI 2019, LNAI 11672, pp. 16–28, 2019.
https://doi.org/10.1007/978-3-030-29894-4_2

target recognition and detection network from the initial R-CNN [6], Fast R-CNN [5] to the later Faster R-CNN [16], R-FCN [3], Mask R-CNN [12]. They can deal with the diversity change well, and the training and testing efficiency of the network has been greatly improved. This makes the computer vision have much room for improvement in object detection, instance segmentation [20] and object tracking.

First, RBG [6] proposed the R-CNN network framework, which provides a new way of thinking for object detection. From then on, the deep learning method has been brought into the field of object detection. Then, Girshick [5] introduced Fast R-CNN network structure, which improved the problems of long training time, large memory consumption and high complexity of R-CNN. The performance of object detection is further improved by improving image convolution operation and Region of Interest pooling (ROI pooling) input. Recently, He et al. [12] proposed Mask R-CNN network structure, and realized the instance segmentation [13] and key point detection [19]. In short, the implementation of Mask R-CNN algorithm is to add FCN to Faster R-CNN to generate corresponding object mask [12].

Inspired by the above related papers, this paper improves the network framework from two parts: the process of generating feature maps in the backbone network part and the process of identifying candidate areas in the head network [9] part. So, this paper proposes a deep dilated convolution network and a light-weight network model. Firstly, our basic network abandons AlexNet and VGG network, but integrates residual network (ResNet) [7] layer and dilated convolution network, which can not only avoid the problem of deep network degradation, but also reduce the number of parameters. Secondly, in order to improve the speed of classification and regression, we compress the feature map by mapping, and reduce the number of fully connected layers and the number of operations in the process of classification and regression operation. In this paper, we obtain better results within acceptable error range.

Structural improvement of backbone network: Firstly, from the point of view of reducing the number of parameters of deep network, this paper adds the structure of the dilated convolution network [1] while retaining the partial residual network (ResNet) layer. In this way, the stability of network performance is guaranteed, and the number of network parameters is reduced by 17 times. In addition, in order to obtain better semantic features, this paper adds an improved spatial feature pyramid network (FPN) [11] after convolution operation to further improve the performance of object detection and instance segmentation.

Head Network Structure Processing: In order to change the time-consuming and computational normality of the fully convolutional layer (FC layer), this paper compresses the classification of feature map into 10 categories (MSCOCO [2,8] datasets have 80 classifications), and changes the FC layer for classification and regression operation into single layer operation

In this paper, a series of comparative experiments on MSCOCO datasets are carried out. The experimental results of backbone network structure improvement are improved by 1.9% and head network improvement by 1.4%. To further

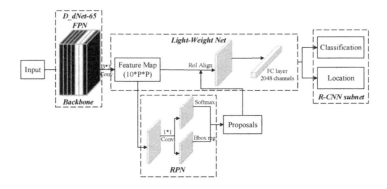

Fig. 1. D_dNet R-CNN network structure diagram

optimize the network model, this paper adds the transfer learning method, which improves the accuracy of the whole network model by up to 2.5%. The overall network framework of this article is shown as Fig. 1.

2   Models Description

2.1   Overview

In recent years, the research of object detection algorithm has turned to the detection technology based on a deep neural network. In the design of backbone network, AlexNet and VGG network are gradually replaced by ResNet network, because ResNet network structure has strong feature representation ability and can solve the problem of deep network degradation in the past. In the pre-training process, the deeper the feature map is, the vaguer the definition of the object's edge is, and the corresponding regression is weaker, so it is difficult to see smaller objects in the feature map with small resolution. In general, the step size of ResNet or VGG is equal to 32 (that is, the ratio of the input image to the final feature size). According to the decreasing rule of feature map size, trunk network usually has five stages (p1–p5). In addition, it is known that the FPN network contains p6, while RetinaNet contains p6 and p7 (p6 and p7 have no pretraining) [17]. So, against a background of 1/32 or smaller, small objects become invisible on them (that 32 × 32 objects are a point on them). Even if we add the shallow to the deeper semantics, most of the semantic information will be lost. To address this issue, two additional phases (p6 participation is in pretraining) have been added to the trunk network, as detailed in Sect. 2.2.

Although the two-stage object detection has higher accuracy than the one-stage object detection, the speed is slower. The main reason is that in order to achieve higher accuracy, the head design is usually "thick", which increases the calculation of the whole network and reduces the detection speed. This paper maps and performs compression operations on the feature diagrams output in the pretraining (the MSCOCO dataset's sample is always $81 \times P \times P$ that is compressed to $10 \times P \times P$ or $5 \times P \times P$). See Sect. 2.3 for details.

In addition, everyone knows that it is difficult to obtain high quality and large amount of data for deep neural network training in practical research. Transfer learning can solve the data embarrassment problem well. In addition, convolution neural network has good hierarchy. With the increase of network layer and the detection of image features, the more common the features detected by deep convolutional neural network are, the better the effect of transfer learning is. So we add the transfer learning method to the pretraining of the network. See Sect. 2.4 for details.

2.2   Deep Dilated Convolutional Neural Network

Firstly, considering the excellent performance of ResNet-50 network itself, it is often used as the backbone network of object detection. Therefore, the first four stages of Resnet-50 (1, 2, 3, 4) are still retained in the design of backbone network in this paper. The first stage passes $7 \times 7 \times 64$ convolution operation, batch normalization (BN), activation function (Rectified Linear Unit, ReLU) and maximum pooling layer (Max pooling layer). This ensures that the input image is only $1/4$ of the original image after passing through stage 1, thus ensuring a sufficiently large receptive field. However, considering that the feature map obtained in the first stage is large, the corresponding time is also large. Therefore, this paper still follows the practice of the Mask R-CNN: in the first stage, we only participated in the pretraining stage. In addition, each large layer in stages 2–4 is superimposed by the same repeat convolutional layer of remaining modules 1×1, 3×3 and 1×1.

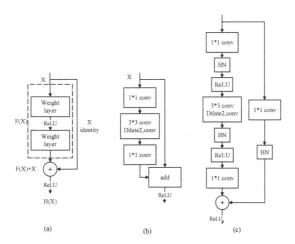

Fig. 2. Core module comparison diagram. (a) ResNet residual module, (b) DetNet core module, (c) D_dNet core module.

In stage 5–6, this paper absorbs the idea of DetNet network [10] design, changes the traditional residual convolutional module operation, and increases the bottleneck network structure of dilated convolution network [18]. In Fig. 2a, b, and c give the ResNet residual module, the DetNet core module, and the own network structure D_dNet core module respectively. First of all, the size of the feature map of these two stages is consistent, which is 1/16 of the original feature map and better than the resolution and receptive field effect of the original ResNet-50 network. Second, the first layer of stage 5–6 consists of two branches: main path and bypass. On the main road, the three convolution layers of 1×1, 3×3, and 1×1 are used as basic modules. Then, a processing operation of a batch normalization and activation function is respectively added between the convolution layers. Since the input first passes through the 1×1 convolution kernel, the feature map size is not changed, then the batch normalization and activation function processing operations are performed, and then the 3×3 convolution layer is entered. Since padding $= 1$ is set here, it does not change. Enter the size of the feature map so that the size of the feature map remains the same on the main road. On the bypass, in order to ensure that the input feature map can be added to the feature map output on the main road, a $1 \times 1 \times 256$ convolution operation is set on the bypass. The second and third layers in the two stages of stage 5–6 continue to use the residual module. In addition, it is found through analysis that directly outputting a 256-dimensional layer first passes through a $1 \times 1 \times 64$ convolution layer, then passes through a $3 \times 3 \times 64$ convolution layer, and finally passes through a $1 \times 1 \times 256$ convolution layer. The output is 256 dimensions, and the parameter quantity is reduced by 1/9. Therefore, increasing the depth expansion convolution network module reduces the pressure on the amount of computation and memory requirements to a certain extent. The complete pretraining model is shown as Fig. 3.

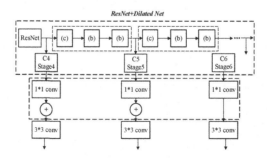

Fig. 3. D_dNet backbone network structure.

2.3   Light-Weight Head Network

At present, it is very difficult to improve the accuracy and computational speed of two-stage object detection. This paper assumes that in the network framework, if the computational load of the second stage is negligible compared with that of the first stage, the second stage has little effect on the computational speed of the whole network structure.

This paper analyses two decisive factors affecting the complexity of head network. One is that the feature map after pooling treatment is thicker and the other is that the fully connected layer is too thick. We try to compress the output feature map of pooling operation from $81 \times P \times P$ to $10 \times P \times P$ (based on MSCOCO dataset) in the framework of Mask R-CNN object detection, which is equivalent to compress more than 3900 channels to 490 channels. Then, this paper adds an 81-class fully connected layer before the classification and regression operations, and make the classification and regression operations all pass through a fully connected layer. Although the accuracy may be somewhat compromised, the design of head network structure within acceptable range is shown in Fig. 4.

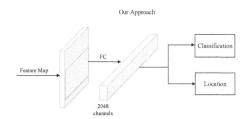

Fig. 4. Light-weight network structure diagram.

2.4   Training Model Based on Transfer Learning

This paper attempts to further optimize the first two models by adding a transfer learning method. This paper finds that the knowledge learned by convolutional neural network is actually the weight parameters obtained through pretraining, so the essence of transfer learning in this paper is the weight transfer. For example, in literature [14] and [15], classification and behavior recognition are realized based on the transfer learning task. In addition, studies in literature [14] have proved that knowledge movement among convolutional neural networks does not need to have strong semantic correlation.

In this paper, this paper modifies the number of output layer neurons according to the object task, and randomly initialize the weights of all connected layer neurons. At the same time, this paper initializes the parameters of other network layers using the weights that are obtained from the pre-training of MSCOCO datasets. Finally, this paper trains the whole network with the target task training set and get the final model. The whole process is shown in Fig. 5.

The model based on transfer learning can not only improve the accuracy of the classification part in object detection, but also refine the convolution layer

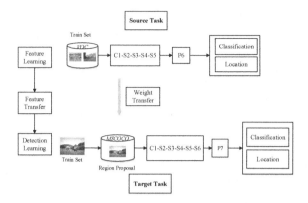

Fig. 5. Schematic diagram of the transfer learning process

parameters in the training target task network model to further improve the training accuracy and overall improve the performance of the model.

3   Experimental Results

3.1   Datasets and Evaluation Indicators

Dataset Description: This article chooses to use the extensive MSCOCO dataset, which has 80 categories in the direction of object detection. There are 80k images in the training set, 40k images in the test set and 40k images in the verification set. In addition, we combine the 80k training set with the 35k verification set and divide them into the 115k training set and the 5K small verification set. Here this paper uses the standard MSCOCO dataset indicators to evaluate the experiment. It mainly includes average precision (AP), average recall (AR) and variant criteria of different indicators.

Partial Parameter Settings: The GPU1080 configuration is selected in this paper. Due to the limitation of the processor, each GPU can only process one image at a time, and each image will set 2000 training regions of interest and 1000 test regions of interest. The learning rate is set to 0.01. The image input is still 1024×1024 size, but in a spatial pyramid operation the input size is 256×256 size feature map. The size of the pooling layer is set to 7.

Experimental evaluation criteria: This paper aims to obtain more persuasive evidence. Firstly, this paper validates and compares the proposed model and method. Then, this paper does a global comparative experiment, that is, this paper adds the transfer learning method to the two improved network models. The experimental analysis and results are as follows:

3.2   Deep Dilated Convolutional Neural Network Experiment

Experiment 1: In order to further verify the effectiveness of the proposed D_dNet-65 network in the feature space pyramid structure, the D_dNet-65 network is compared with the ResNet-50, ResNet-101, Mask R-CNN-50, Mask R-CNN-101 and DetNet networks. The specific results are shown in Table 1. The error rate of D_dNet-65 network is 23.8%, and the corresponding complexity reaches 5.2G. First of all, compared with ResNet-50 and Mask R-CNN-50, we found that the accuracy of the D_dNet-65 is better for the same basic network (up to 1.7% in mAP). Secondly, this paper also wants to further verify the effectiveness of the structure of the D_dnet-65 network with the increase of parameters. It can be seen from Table 1 that compared with resnet-101 and Mask R-CNN-101, D_dnet-65 has lower bit error rate and higher accuracy.

Table 1. Effects of various backbone networks on FPN in MSCOCO (%).

Backbone	Classification		FPN results					
	Toperr	FLops	mAP	AP_{50}	AP_{75}	AP_s	AP_m	AP_l
ResNet-50	24.1	3.8G	37.9	60.0	41.2	22.9	40.6	49.2
ResNet-101	23.0	7.6G	39.8	62.0	43.5	24.1	43.4	51.7
Mask R-CNN-50	**23.9**	**4.3G**	**37.8**	**60.2**	**41.5**	**20.1**	**41.1**	**50.4**
Mask R-CNN-101	23.6	4.6G	38.7	61.1	42.8	22.4	42.5	51.6
DetNet-59	23.5	4.8G	40.2	61.7	43.7	23.9	43.2	52.0
D_dNet-65	**23.8**	**5.2G**	**39.5**	**61.2**	**43.2**	**22.6**	**42.7**	51.9

Experiment 2: In this paper, in order to further verify the effectiveness of D_dNet-65 network, this paper takes Mask R-CNN network structure as the basic model, and only change its backbone network structure. Then, this paper compares their effects on border regression to prove the performance of the D_dNet-65. From Table 2, there is a slight gap between D_dNet-65 and the latest DetNet networking approach. However, the proposed the D_dNet-65 network structure can improve the performance of Mask R-CNN, even by 1.3 to 2.2% points.

Table 2. Effect of various backbone networks on border regression on MSCOCO (%).

Models	Backbone	Bounding box AP					
		mAP	AP_{50}	AP_{75}	AP_s	AP_m	AP_l
Mask R-CNN-50	ResNet-50-FPN	**39.1**	**61.7**	**42.9**	**21.3**	**42.3**	**50.7**
Mask R-CNN-101	ResNet-101-FPN	38.2	60.3	41.7	20.1	41.1	50.2
Mask R-CNN	DetNet-59-FPN	40.7	62.5	44.1	24.6	43.9	52.2
Mask R-CNN	D_dNet-65-FPN	**40.4**	**62.1**	**43.5**	**22.7**	**42.8**	**52.0**

Experiment 3: On backbone network, we consider the difference between the D_dNet-65 network and the Mask R-CNN network. Table 3 shows the comparison experiments of four kinds of backbone network from zero training FPN. We find that the D_dNet-65 network model proposed in this paper has good accuracy. Next, this paper wants to experiment further with the effectiveness of the D_dNet-65 network for different size objects.

Table 3. Results of zero-training of FPN network on MSCOCO (%).

Backbone	mAP	AP_{50}	AP_{75}	AP_s	AP_m	AP_l
ResNet-50	34.5	55.2	37.7	20.4	36.7	44.5
Mask R-CNN-50	**34.9**	**56.1**	**38.4**	**21.3**	**37.4**	**45.1**
DetNet-59	36.3	56.5	39.3	22.0	38.4	46.9
D_dNet-65	**35.6**	**56.3**	**38.9**	**21.7**	**38.1**	**46.4**

3.3 Light-Weight Head Network Experiment

Experiment 4: In order to verify the validity of the light-weight network model, we will do a series of comparative experiments on MSCOCO's small dataset. In this paper, it embeds the improved light-weight network into R-FCN, Mask R-CNN-50, D_dNet-65 and so on. In Table 4, the experimental effect of Mask R-CNN-50 was 1.8% lower than our own model. Although our results are slightly worse than those of Light-Head R-CNN, the computational speed is improved with the accuracy guaranteed. In addition, the regression loss of this paper is obviously smaller than the classified loss.

Table 4. Results of various models based on Light-weight network on MSCOCO (%).

Models	mAP	AP_s	AP_m	AP_l
R-FCN	33.1	18.8	36.9	48.1
Mask R-CNN-50	**37.9**	**21.1**	**40.5**	**51.2**
Light-Head R-CNN	41.5	25.2	45.3	53.1
D_dNet-65 R-CNN	**39.7**	**22.3**	**42.7**	**52.6**

3.4 Experiment Based on Transfer Learning Method

Experiment 5: In order to further optimize the network model, this paper adds transfer learning method in the training stage. In order to verify the effectiveness of the transfer learning method, we add the transfer learning method to the

ResNet (50, 100) and the Mask R-CNN (50, 100) networks and the D_dNet-65 R-CNN networks respectively, and verify the trained model with verification set (the verification set is 5k small verification sets separated from MSCOCO dataset).

In Table 5, this paper finds that the training accuracy and object detection performance of the network with the transfer learning method are very good. The improved Mask R-CNN-50 was increased by 1% point compared with the original experimental results in [12], and our D_dNet-65 R-CNN experimental results were 1.2% higher than the Mask R-CNN-50. In addition, this paper can fine-tune the parameters of convolution layer in the training process, so as to better improve the performance of the model.

Table 5. Multiple model training results based on transfer learning (%).

Models	Training accuracy	Performance test
ResNet-50	94.9	-
ResNet-101	94.7	-
Mask R-CNN-50	**95.1**	**39.3**
Mask R-CNN-101	95.3	39.1
D_dNet-65 R-CNN	**96.3**	**39.7**

4   Analysis of Results

Here this paper will analyze the comparison experiment of the D_dNet-65 R-CNN network model in detail. Our experiment is divided into four stages.

In the first stage, this paper validates the influence of network structure on FPN and border regression respectively. In order to further validate the performance of the D_dNet-65 network structure, we do experiments on the Mask R-CNN (50, 101). The results show that adding the D_dNet-65 network can effectively improve the instance segmentation performance of the Mask R-CNN (50, 101). In the second phase, in order to verify the effectiveness of light-weight network, comparative experiments were carried out on ResNet (50, 100), Mask R-CNN, D_dNet-65 and so on. In the third stage, this paper adds the proposed transfer learning method into the pretraining of several models for experimental analysis. In the fourth phase, as shown in Fig. 6, we do a comparative experiment on the whole network structure. In this paper, two models and transfer learning methods are embedded in the network of the graph and validated on MSCOCO dataset. Compared with the polygonal line of the inverted triangle, the polygonal line of the positive triangle tends to approach gradually with the increase of training time. Although inverted triangles do not work as well as regular triangles, the accuracy is much improved. Generally speaking, the method proposed in this paper has achieved good results in performance and speed.

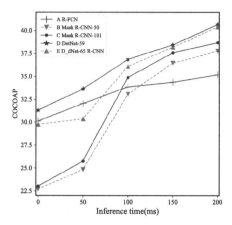

Fig. 6. Comparison of various models on MSCOCO

Finally, in order to further optimize the model, transfer learning method is used to train the model. Through the comparative analysis of several experiments, both single training and comprehensive experiments, have achieved good results.As shown in Fig. 7, Detection_activations look for trouble signs by checking the activation of different layers. Detection_anchors generate many anchors without location information through detection. Then, according to the size of the input image, the location information of each detection object can be accurately obtained. In this paper, better detection results are obtained.

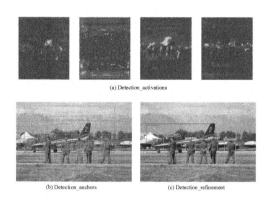

(a) Detection_activations

(b) Detection_anchors   (c) Detection_refinement

Fig. 7. D_dNet-65 R-CNN results on the MSCOCO test (a) Detection_activations, (b) Detection_anchors, (c) Detection_refinement

5   Conclusions

This paper presents a D_dNet-65 R-CNN model based on a two-stage object detection method. The model is based on MSCOCO dataset and consists of backbone network, head network and new transfer learning method. Firstly, based on the backbone network, a deep dilated convolution network is proposed. On the one hand, it can ensure the resolution of the feature map and the size of the receptive field, on the other hand, it can further reduce the number of parameters in the network. In addition, the "thickness" of the head network is reduced by compressing the feature map according to the characteristics of one-stage object detection, so that the training speed of the head network can be improved on the premise of guaranteeing the accuracy. Finally, to further optimize the model, transfer learning method is used to train the model. Through the comparative analysis of several experiments, both single training and comprehensive experiments, have achieved good results.

In addition, in addition to the proposed improved method and experimental verification, this paper also considers the next step of work. First, from the experimental direction, in addition to the possibility of adding multiple datasets for comparative experiments, it can also further study the effect of multi-scale images. Secondly, from the research direction, it can transfer the proposed object detection framework to the direction of instance segmentation and key point detection. Because transfer learning can solve the problem of data defects, it can consider adding unsupervised learning to further improve the performance of object detection.

Acknowledgments. This work is supported by the National Natural Science Foundation of China (Nos. 61663004, 61762078, 61866004), the Guangxi Natural Science Foundation (Nos. 2016GXNSFAA380146, 2017GXNSFAA198365, 2018GXNSFDA281009), the Research Fund of Guangxi Key Lab of Multi-source Information Mining and Security (16-A-03-02, MIMS18-08), the Guangxi Special Project of Science and Technology Base and Talents (AD16380008), Innovation Project of Guangxi Graduate Education (XYCSZ2019068), the Guangxi "Bagui Scholar" Teams for Innovation and Research Project, Guangxi Collaborative Innovation Center of Multi-source Information Integration and Intelligent Processing.

References

1. Anderson, P., et al.: Bottom-up and top-down attention for image captioning and visual question answering. In: Proceedings of the IEEE Conference on Computer Vision and Pattern Recognition, pp. 6077–6086 (2018)
2. Chen, X., et al.: Microsoft COCO captions: data collection and evaluation server (2015)
3. Dai, J., Li, Y., He, K., Sun, J.: R-FCN: object detection via region-based fully convolutional networks, pp. 379–387 (2016)
4. Erhan, D., Szegedy, C., Toshev, A., Anguelov, D.: Scalable object detection using deep neural networks. In: Proceedings of the IEEE Conference on Computer Vision and Pattern Recognition, pp. 2147–2154 (2014)

5. Girshick, R.: Fast R-CNN. In: Proceedings of the IEEE International Conference on Computer Vision, pp. 1440–1448 (2015)
6. Girshick, R., Donahue, J., Darrell, T., Malik, J.: Rich feature hierarchies for accurate object detection and semantic segmentation. In: Proceedings of the IEEE Conference on Computer Vision and Pattern Recognition, pp. 580–587 (2014)
7. He, K., Zhang, X., Ren, S., Sun, J.: Deep residual learning for image recognition. In: Proceedings of the IEEE Conference on Computer Vision and Pattern Recognition, pp. 770–778 (2016)
8. Jiang, W., Ma, L., Chen, X., Zhang, H., Liu, W.: Learning to guide decoding for image captioning (2018)
9. Li, Z., Peng, C., Yu, G., Zhang, X., Deng, Y., Sun, J.: Light-head R-CNN: in defense of two-stage object detector (2017)
10. Li, Z., Peng, C., Yu, G., Zhang, X., Deng, Y., Sun, J.: DetNet: design backbone for object detection. In: Ferrari, V., Hebert, M., Sminchisescu, C., Weiss, Y. (eds.) ECCV 2018. LNCS, vol. 11213, pp. 339–354. Springer, Cham (2018). https://doi.org/10.1007/978-3-030-01240-3_21
11. Lin, T.Y., Dollár, P., Girshick, R., He, K., Hariharan, B., Belongie, S.: Feature pyramid networks for object detection. In: Proceedings of the IEEE Conference on Computer Vision and Pattern Recognition, pp. 2117–2125 (2017)
12. Lin, T.Y., Goyal, P., Girshick, R., He, K., Dollár, P.: Focal loss for dense object detection. In: Proceedings of the IEEE International Conference on Computer Vision, pp. 2980–2988 (2017)
13. Long, J., Shelhamer, E., Darrell, T.: Fully convolutional networks for semantic segmentation, pp. 3431–3440 (2015)
14. Oquab, M., Bottou, L., Laptev, I., Sivic, J.: Learning and transferring mid-level image representations using convolutional neural networks, pp. 1717–1724 (2014)
15. Pan, S., Yang, Q.: A survey on transfer learning. IEEE Trans. Knowl. Discov. Data Eng. **22**(10), 1345–1359 (2010)
16. Ren, S., He, K., Girshick, R., Sun, J.: Faster R-CNN: towards real-time object detection with region proposal networks, pp. 91–99 (2015)
17. Ross, T.Y.L.P.G., Dollár, G.K.H.P.: Focal loss for dense object detection. In: Proceedings of the IEEE Conference on Computer Vision and Pattern Recognition (2017)
18. Shrivastava, A., Sukthankar, R., Malik, J., Gupta, A.: Beyond skip connections: top-down modulation for object detection (2016)
19. Steder, B., Rusu, R.B., Konolige, K., Burgard, W.: Point feature extraction on 3D range scans taking into account object boundaries. In: 2011 IEEE International Conference on Robotics and Automation, pp. 2601–2608. IEEE (2011)
20. Zheng, Y., Li, Z., Zhang, C.: A hybrid architecture based on CNN for cross-modal semantic instance annotation. Multimed. Tools Appl. **77**(7), 8695–8710 (2018)

Bi-directional Features Reuse Network for Salient Object Detection

Fengwei Jia[1], Xuan Wang[1(✉)], Jian Guan[2], Shuhan Qi[1], Qing Liao[1], and Huale Li[1]

[1] Computer Application Research Center, Harbin Institute of Technology, Shenzhen, Shenzhen 518055, China
`jfw129@gmail.com`,`{wangxuan,shuhanqi,hualeli}@cs.hitsz.edu.cn`, `liaoqing@hit.edu.cn`

[2] College of Computer Science and Technology, Harbin Engineering University, Harbin 150001, China
`j.guan@hrbeu.edu.cn`

Abstract. Recently, unidirectional convolutional neural networks have been widely used for salient object detection. However, most methods cannot solve common problems (i.e., the loss of valid information, tiny predicted feature, and isolated features in one block), which lead to inefficient feature reuse and blurred salient object edges. To address these problems, we propose a novel bi-directional features reuse network (BDFRN) for salient object detection, which consists of two subnets: forward-skip subnet and reverse-connect subnet. The forward-skip subnet employs an encoder-decoder structure to remedy the loss of salient details, and progressively refine the size of the predicted feature; meanwhile, the reverse-connect subnet can transmit the location features from top blocks to bottom blocks, such that these features can be reused and communicated between different blocks. Extensive experiments are conducted to demonstrate the performance of the proposed method, as compared with baseline methods.

Keywords: Salient object detection · Skip connection · Convolutional neural network

1 Introduction

As a pixel-wise image analysis task, salient object detection (SOD) aims to accurately pinpoint all the pixels of the most attractive objects in images, which has received broad attention, owing to its wide applications in the fields of object segmentation [2,14], fixation prediction [4] and object importance [18], etc.

The performance of SOD in these fields highly depends on the robustness of feature clues from images. Initially, only a single salient clue, such as objectivity, local or global color contrast, is exploited in SOD [8]. Then, the combinations of these single salient clues are applied, which can overcome shortcomings of using single clue [16]. Recently, convolutional neural networks (CNN) based

A. C. Nayak and A. Sharma (Eds.): PRICAI 2019, LNAI 11672, pp. 29–41, 2019.
https://doi.org/10.1007/978-3-030-29894-4_3

supervising methods have shown promising performance in the applications with artificially labeled data [3, 7, 12, 20, 22].

However, these CNN based networks still have limitations due to some inappropriate operations. Firstly, in spite of widely being used to extract high-level feature, multiple stages of spatial pooling and dropout operation are still the reasons that part features of valid and noise information are discarded simultaneously. In [6], a residual structure is applied to solve such problem, which can avoid the loss of valid information, however, because of small resolution of the output, it cannot be applied for SOD problem. Secondly, general unidirectional architecture can be beneficial for image classification, but the size of the final predicted map is too small to clearly distinguish object boundary. In [12], the authors employ a multi-level upsample and multiple masks strategy to enlarge the predicted map. However, to reshape feature, extra calculated fake data rather than true features are added into the network during frequent upsampling operations, which deteriorates predicted results. Thirdly, since the position and edge features of a salient object are learned respectively from the top and the bottom blocks, which are isolated across blocks in unidirectional network [7], hence the predicted outputs from top layers are often in an accurate position but blurred contour. In [3, 22], bidirectional networks are introduced to remedy this problem. Nevertheless, these works resort to merging all layers indiscriminately, which is hard to observe the status of different layers. In addition, the output of these networks comes only from the first or the last layer, and the features of each layer cannot be fully utilized.

From the discussions above, the unidirectional network cannot solve these three problems at the same time. Meanwhile, existing bidirectional networks equipped with simple structures and poor integration also have the same limitations, which becomes the bottleneck to further improve performance for the task of SOD.

To resolve these limitations, we present a bi-directional features reuse network, which can be decomposed into a forward-skip subnet and a reverse-connect subnet. By employing the encoder-decoder structure, the forward-skip subnet provides two ways to address the problem of the loss of valid information. The first is intra-block skip connection, where each layer is connected directly to its anterior layer to achieve the features reusing and decrease the features dropping; and the second is inter-block skip connection, where the outputs of the encoder are directly used and fed into the decoder. Regarding the problem of the small size of the output image, we gradually increase the width and length of predicted features by using multiple deconvolution layers, where the extra spatial features of encoder blocks add to decoder blocks. In the reverse-connect subnet, a reversing attention operation is carried out to solve the isolated features problem.

Thus, our contributions can be summarized as follows:

– We present a novel bi-directional features reuse network to solve problems of the loss of valid information, the tiny predicted feature, and the isolated features in a block.

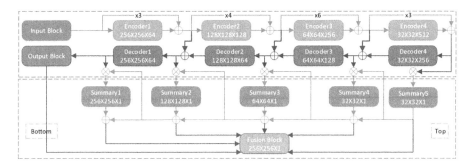

Fig. 1. The structure of the proposed bi-directional feature reuse network (BDFRN), where the top and bottom labels are given for the directional information. The sizes of the feature maps and channel numbers are shown within blocks as [height × width × channel]. (Color figure online)

- We weight all blocks' contribution and adaptively fuse multi-resolution features to balance the object position and edges at the same time.
- We improve the baseline methods and outperform current state-of-the-art results on five benchmarks.

2   The Proposed Method

As can be seen from Fig. 1, the structure of BDFRN includes two subnets. The blue dotted box denotes the forward-skip subnet, which mainly consists of encoder blocks and decoder blocks. The red dotted box represents the reverse-connect subnet, which is composed of several summary blocks and a fusion block. To avoid the directional confusion, the directions of the bottom and the top are given in the figure.

2.1   Forward-Skip Subnet

Existing networks [3,7,12,20,22] have a shortage structure that predicted outputs from the pipeline are small size images. Here, a forward connection subnet with encoder-decoder structure [2] is employed to solve the problem. This subnet contains four blocks: input block, output block, encoder block, and decoder block. The input block and the output block are a series of layers, which are used to initially process and finally integrate the image respectively. The configuration of the subnet is given in Table 1, where Conv denotes convolution operation, and Full-Conv is full-convolution [14]. The encoder block and decoder block are used to implement two connections: intra and inter block skip connection.

Intra-block Skip Connection. Inside a block, an encoder is applied to decrease the loss of valid information. The structure of the encoder block is

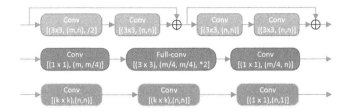

Fig. 2. Illustration of block structure. From top to bottom are the encoder block, decoder block and summary block respectively.

Table 1. The configuration of input block and output block

	Layer	In channel	Out channel	Filter size	Stride	Padding
Input block	Conv	3	64	7	2	3
	BatchNorm	64	64	-	-	-
	ReLU	-	-	-	-	-
	MaxPool	64	64	3	2	1
Output Block	Full-Conv	64	32	3	2	-
	ReLU	-	-	-	-	-
	Conv	32	32	3	1	-
	ReLU	-	-	-	-	-
	Full-Conv	32	1	2	1	1

given in Fig. 2. Here, $\mathtt{conv}(k \times k)(i, o)$ denotes convolution operation, where $(k \times k)$ is the kernel size, i and o represent the input channel and output channel, respectively. /2 means the step size of the convolution layer is set as 2, so that the width and length of features are reduced by half. To enhance the generalization and non-linear capability of the network, each convolutional layer is attached with a batch normalization layer and a ReLU layer. Given the input image I_{input}, the output features En_b of the encoder block b is

$$En_b = \begin{cases} Input(I_{input}), & b = 0 \\ Encoder_b(En_{b-1}), & b = 1, 2, 3, 4 \end{cases} \tag{1}$$

where the $Input(\dots)$ and $Encoder_b(\dots)$ denote the function of input block and encoder block b respectively.

Thus, each feature in a block can be fully utilized. Moreover, the intra-block skip structure can relieve the problem of vanishing gradient [6].

Inter-block Skip Connection. Among the blocks in the forward-skip subnet, we apply a jump connection strategy to connect each encoder block and its corresponding decoder block, as illustrated in Fig. 1.

Table 2. The configurations of encoder block, decoder block and summary block, where n, m, k denote the same means in Fig. 2.

Block	Encoder		Decoder		Summary	
	m	n	m	n	n	k
Block1	64	64	64	64	64	3
Block2	64	128	128	64	64	5
Block3	128	256	256	128	128	5
Block4	256	512	512	256	256	5
Block5	-	-	-	-	512	7

Mathematically, the output features De_b of the decoder block b can be expressed as

$$De_b = \begin{cases} Output(De_1), & b = 0 \\ Decoder_b(De_{b+1} + En_b), & b = 1, 2, 3 \\ En_4, & b = 4 \end{cases} \tag{2}$$

where $Output(\dots)$ and $Decoder_b(\dots)$ denote the function of output block and decoder block b respectively.

The structure of the decoder block is also given in Fig. 2. Here, $*2$ represents the transposed convolution operation with the stride set as 2, so that we can double the width and length of the features. Same as the encoder block, the convolutional layer is attached with a batch normalization layer and a ReLU Layer to enhance the generalization and non-linear ability of the network.

Since the inter-block skip connection is convenient for features reusing, the decoder block needs less weight and bias to resize the predicted map to the same as the input image.

Finally, the output features of the forward-skip subnet are from the output block, i.e. De_0 in Eq. 2. Table 2 details the configuration of every encoder block and decoder block in the forward-skip subnet.

2.2   Reverse-Connect Subnet

The reverse-connect subnet includes summary blocks, an operation of reversing effective region, and a fusion block.

Summary Block. Intuitively, in order to be able to simultaneously use the features of the encoder and decoder, the simple method is to directly merge the extracted features. The designed structure of summary block is shown in Fig. 2, and the configuration is given in Table 2. We use a convolutional layer followed by ReLU non-linearity. The outputs of summary block b is

$$S_b = Summary(En_{b-1} + De_b), \tag{3}$$

where $Summary(\dots)$ denotes the function of summary block.

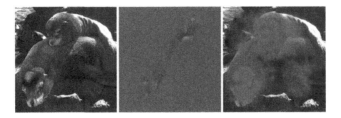

Fig. 3. From left to right: the input image, smallest sufficient region (SSR) and smallest destroying region (SDR). (The images are introduced from [4]).

The summary block is helpful in summarizing each feature by element addition between encoder block and decoder block. However, the performance was not perfect during the actual test. Therefore, it is necessary to introduce a new mechanism.

Reverse Effective Region. In the task of image classification, as the layers of the network gradually deepen, the network can learn the higher-level semantic information, and the top layer can provide the category label for the entire image. From a visualization point of view, the bottom layer of the network can see the texture and the edge. Whereas the features of the top layer are helpful for classification, due to the larger of the receptive field. To put it another way, the network will gradually increase the confidence of object classification in the image, which can determine the category. It is the existing special region that is identified by the top layer, which can contribute to the classification. This special region is called an effective region. For this interesting phenomenon, we introduce two concepts: **SSR** and **SDR** [4].

SSR, the smallest sufficient region, is the smallest region of the image that allows a confident classification. For example, the SSR is the middle image in Fig. 3, in which only parts of the seal can be seen. Even if humans see this region, it is difficult to identify what the preserved image is. However, this region contains all the features that the network can recognize and distinguish from other categories, such as the part of the face with whiskers.

The opposite concept is **SDR**, the smallest destroying region. SDR refers to the serious impact of classification when the region is removed from the image. This region and the counter-classification method have been discovered, i.e., generating adversarial artifacts. Because of the tiny and imperceivable region for human eyes, the SDR impedes right prediction from a classifier.

The top layer of the network would obtain an effective region between SSR and SDR to help the network to classify more accurately.

Reverse Effective Region. To get the clear edges of predicted salient objects, the operation of reversing effective region [3] is introduced into reverse-connect subnet, as illustrated in Fig. 4.

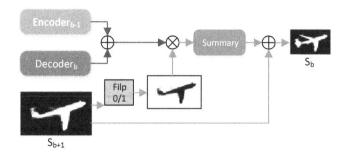

Fig. 4. The operation of reverse attention region

The region of an image can be divided into three parts: the effective object region, the object edges' region, and the background region. Initially, we flip the zero and one in the predicted map S_b of the summary block, hence the effective region is filled with zeros. Then, both of the flipped predicted map and the input of the next summary block are subjected to element-wise multiplication $\otimes$ to exclude the effective region of the object. The output features remain the edge region and the background region, except the effective region. At last, the summary blocks are connected with the predicted map S_{b+1}, which extract the features of salient object edges. The features of edges and the previous predict map are combined to perform element addition $\oplus$ operation. Therefore, regions of effective objects learned in the top layer can be accumulated back. Mathematically, for each input of the summary block $En_{b-1} + De_b$, the predicted map S_b by the previous predicted map S_{b+1} is

$$S_b = Summary\{(En_{b-1} + De_b) \otimes (1 - S_{b+1})\} \oplus S_{b+1}. \tag{4}$$

We calculate the extract predicted map from top to bottom by opposite direction along with the forward-skip subnet.

The advantage of reversing effective region is that the summary block can learn from the least amount of features, which avoids relearning from redundant effective regions used for object location. In addition, the effective region can propagate without losing object position.

Fusion Block. The information on the object position and edge are very important to the SOD performance, therefore, we focus on each summary block and the output of the forward-skip subnet, and apply adaptively self-learning to fuse five different sizes of predicted maps. The fusion block F_{fuse} is constructed by the combination of all summary blocks S_b with the output block F_{output}, expressed as

$$F_{fuse} = Fuse(S_b^{up}, F_{output} | \theta), \tag{5}$$

where $Fuse(\cdot)$ is a function of cumulative sum, S_b^{up} denotes enlarge S_b by transposed convolution operation. Fusion block adaptively learn multi-resolution features to boost predicted map performance of clear edges and right location.

2.3 Loss

Instead of binary cross entropy, the focal loss can solve the problem of the extreme foreground-background class imbalance [11]. Thus, we compare the predicted map Pr with its corresponding ground truth map GT by focal loss, as follows

$$\sigma(GT, Pr) = -(1 - p_t)^{\gamma} log(p_t), \tag{6}$$

where p_t represents the probability of pixel, and γ is the tunable focusing parameter, which is set to be 2, as suggested in [11].

The loss of the entire network should have the ability to adjust all the parameters contained in the two subnets. Therefore, we apply the loss consists of three parts: subnet loss, summary loss, and fusion loss. The whole loss for end-to-end training can be calculated as follows:

$$\begin{aligned} Loss &= \lambda\sigma(GT, F_{output}) \\ &+ \rho(\sum\nolimits_1^b \sigma(GT, S^{up}{}_b) + \sigma(GT, F_{fuse})), \end{aligned} \tag{7}$$

where F_{output} is the output feature from forward-skip subnet, λ and ρ are the trade-off control factors, which are set empirically as $\lambda = 2$ and $\rho = 1$ in our work.

2.4 Different from Existing Methods

Due to forward-skip subnet is built on encoder-decoder structure [2] and similar to the well-known U-Net [17], there is some improved design for better performance. One is that we simplify the downsampling layers from five to four, but add extra encoder blocks and skip connect between them. The input image is transformed into four features with different size. The advantage is to train deeper network and extract high-level semantic features without tiny feature size for the task of SOD. The other is that we obtain each scale of block features after decoder blocks instead of only the last layers for the balance of object position and edges. [7] show that bottom layers extract texture details and top layers achieve accurate location information. In order to predict salient object with clear contour and the right location of the salient object, each encoder block is bypassed to the output of its corresponding decoder and waiting for further operations in the reverse-connect subnet. The BDFRN$^-$ in Table 3 show the result of the single forward-skip subnet.

In the reverse-connect subnet, we introduce the concepts of SSR and SDR from RAS [3]. The way of adopting summary block helps to reduce the number of operational features in the operation of reverse effective region. Meanwhile, we choose a fusion method that can learn parameters, and adaptively obtain the parameters of the best performance. Table 3 show the proposed BDFRN is better than the RAS [3].

3   Experiments

Table 3. Quantitative comparison. Each cell from up to down composed of max and mean F-measure (higher better) and MAE (lower better).

	ECSSD	PASCAL-S	DUT-OMRON	HKU-IS	SOD
LEGS [19]	0.827	0.762	0.669	0.766	0.734
	0.785	0.704	0.592	0.723	0.683
	0.118	0.155	0.133	0.119	0.196
MCDL [23]	0.837	0.743	0.701	0.808	0.731
	0.796	0.691	0.625	0.757	0.677
	0.101	0.145	0.089	0.092	0.181
RFCN [20]	0.890	0.837	0.742	0.892	0.799
	0.834	0.751	0.627	0.835	0.751
	0.107	0.118	0.111	0.079	0.170
DHS [12]	0.907	0.829	0.881	0.890	0.827
	0.872	0.779	0.835	0.855	0.774
	0.059	0.094	0.077	0.053	0.128
Amulet [22]	0.915	0.837	0.742	0.895	0.806
	0.869	0.768	0.647	0.839	0.755
	0.059	0.098	0.098	0.052	0.141
DSS [7]	0.908	0.836	0.771	0.910	0.844
	0.873	0.804	0.729	0.895	0.795
	0.062	0.096	0.066	0.041	0.121
LinkNet [2]	0.901	0.829	0.766	0.905	0.812
	0.871	0.801	0.718	0.885	0.775
	0.068	0.099	0.070	0.048	0.131
RAS [3]	0.921	0.837	0.786	**0.913**	0.850
	0.889	0.785	0.713	0.871	**0.799**
	0.056	0.104	0.062	0.045	0.124
BDFRN⁻	0.909	0.832	0.775	0.905	0.821
	0.878	0.803	0.719	0.889	0.779
	0.066	0.092	0.070	0.045	0.128
BDFRN	**0.929**	**0.845**	**0.793**	0.909	**0.851**
	0.897	**0.818**	**0.741**	**0.890**	0.794
	0.051	**0.089**	**0.051**	**0.041**	**0.117**

3.1   Datasets and Evaluation Metrics

Here, the datasets and evaluation metrics applied in the next experiments are introduced simply.

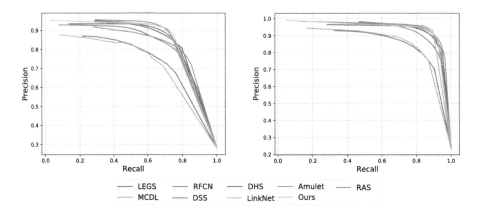

Fig. 5. PR curves on ECCSSD (left) and SOD (right).

Datasets. To demonstrate the effectiveness and robustness of the proposed network in salient object detection, we conduct evaluations on six widely used saliency detection datasets, including DUT-OMRON [5], ECSSD [21], HKU-IS [9], MSRA-B [13], PASCAL-S [10] and SOD [15].

Evaluation Metrics. Several evaluation metrics are used to evaluate the performance of BDFRN, including precision-recall (PR) curve, F-measure score, mean absolute error (MAE) score.

F-measure is defined as the harmonic mean of the average precision and the average recall, which is calculated as

$$F_\beta = (1 + \beta^2)\frac{\text{Precision} \times \text{Recall}}{\beta^2 \text{Precision} + \text{Recall}}, \tag{8}$$

where β is set to 0.3 as suggested in [1] to emphsize the precision. The max value and mean value of F-measure express the best detection and average characteristics in entire test images.

The MAE between predicted map S and groundtruth G can be computed as

$$\text{MAE} = \frac{1}{H \times W}\sum_{x=1}^{H}\sum_{y=1}^{W}|S(x, y) - G(x, y)|, \tag{9}$$

where W and H are width and height of the saliency map respectively.

3.2   Implementation Details

For the network initialization, the trained model of ResNet34 is used to initiate the encoder blocks of the forward-skip subnet. The random initialization is adopted for the rest of the layers. 5000 training images of MSRA-B are divided into two parts: 4500 images for training and 500 for validation. Network hyperparameters are set as follows: Adam optimizer is set $\beta = [0.9, 0.999]$, $\epsilon = 10^{-8}$, learning rate is set to $1e^{-4}$ and batch size is 32.

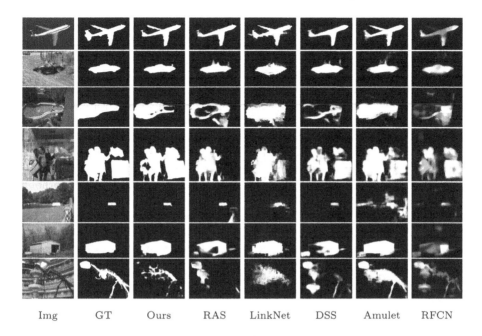

Img   GT   Ours   RAS   LinkNet   DSS   Amulet   RFCN

Fig. 6. Visual comparisons with other methods.

3.3   Performance Comparison

For comparison purpose, 9 state-of-the-art methods are tested as baseline methods, including LEGS [19], MCDL [23], RFCN [20], DHS [12], Amulet [22], DSS [7], LinkNet [2] and RAS [3].

Quantitative Evaluation. From the PR curves shown in Fig. 5, we can clearly find that BDFRN outperforms the state-of-the-art when recall ≤ 0.9. From Table 3, we can see that the proposed BDFRN outperforms all baseline methods in terms of max F-measure, mean F-measure and MAE score. Moreover, thanks to the design of the encoder-decoder structure, BDFRN$^-$, which only test forward-skip subnet, achieved competitive scores as the motivated method LinkNet [2]. However, BDFRN combined the forward-skip subnet and the reverse-connect subnet can completely defeat others, as shown from the table. BDFRN improves the max and mean F-measure over the LinkNet by 2.2% and 2.7% respectively, and reduce the MAE score by 25%. BDFRN also can achieve comparable performance as compared with RAS [3] on difficult datasets (i.e. HKU-IS and SOD), and better results on other datasets. The results show that the performance benefit from three kinds of connections (reverse connection, intra and inter block skip connection), gradually resizing the features and the adapted fusion can alleviate the loss of valid information and adds details to the object contour. BDFRN can solve three problems (the loss of valid information, tiny predicted feature, and isolated features in one block) at the same time.

Qualitative Evaluation. Figure 6 shows a visual comparison of saliency maps produced by state-of-the-art methods and the proposed BDFRN. It can be observed from the figure that BDFRN not only can detect the salient regions correctly with the less false location but also produce clear contour and coherent details. When compared to baseline methods, we can observe some characters as follows. In the first row, object overlapping semitransparent water, BDFRN can detect more torso part than RAS and less needless edge than LinkNet. In the second row, a salient object connects with some trees in the background, which shows BDFRN is good at distinguishing them. In the fourth row, we pick multiple objects in an image, which BDFRN can detect all the salient object. In the fifth row, the small salient object is detected clearly by BDFRN without any redundant object, especially for RAS and Amulet. Especially for the last row which is most difficult, it has the characteristic of large objects, rich edges, and complex background. Although all methods do not perfectly identify all the details, BDFRN recognizes more object boundary details than other methods without adding extra body torso.

4   Conclusion

In this paper, we propose an end-to-end method bi-directional features reuse network for salient object detection, which includes a forward-skip subnet and a reverse-connect subnet. The forward-skip subnet is able to effectively reuse features from inter and intra blocks, and gradually increase the size that can contribute to pixel-wise detection. The reverse side connection can enhance the salient object edge detail. By applying adaptive fusion, the whole network can gain a balance between the object position from the top layers and object edges from the bottom layers. Experimental results demonstrated the validity and performance of the proposed method.

Acknowledgment. This research is supported by Key Technology Program of Shenzhen, China (No. JSGG20170823152809704).

References

1. Achanta, R., Hemami, S., Estrada, F., Susstrunk, S.: Frequency-tuned salient region detection. In: CVPR, pp. 1597–1604 (2009)
2. Chaurasia, A., Culurciello, E.: LinkNet: exploiting encoder representations for efficient semantic segmentation. In: VCIP, pp. 1–4 (2017)
3. Chen, S., Tan, X., Wang, B., Hu, X.: Reverse attention for salient object detection. In: Ferrari, V., Hebert, M., Sminchisescu, C., Weiss, Y. (eds.) ECCV 2018. LNCS, vol. 11213, pp. 236–252. Springer, Cham (2018). https://doi.org/10.1007/978-3-030-01240-3_15
4. Dabkowski, P., Gal, Y.: Real time image saliency for black box classifiers. In: ANIPS, pp. 6967–6976 (2017)
5. Einhäuser, W., König, P.: Does luminance-contrast contribute to a saliency map for overt visual attention? Eur. J. Neurosci. **17**(5), 1089–1097 (2003)

6. He, K., Zhang, X., Ren, S., Sun, J.: Deep residual learning for image recognition. In: CVPR, pp. 770–778 (2016)
7. Hou, Q., Cheng, M.M., Hu, X., Borji, A., Tu, Z., Torr, P.: Deeply supervised salient object detection with short connections. In: CVPR, pp. 5300–5309 (2017)
8. Itti, L., Koch, C., Niebur, E.: A model of saliency-based visual attention for rapid scene analysis. IEEE Trans. Pattern Anal. Mach. Intell. **20**(11), 1254–1259 (1998)
9. Li, G., Yu, Y.: Visual saliency based on multiscale deep features. In: CVPR, pp. 5455–5463 (2015)
10. Li, Y., Hou, X., Koch, C., Rehg, J.M., Yuille, A.L.: The secrets of salient object segmentation. In: CVPR, pp. 280–287 (2014)
11. Lin, T.Y., Goyal, P., Girshick, R., He, K., Dollár, P.: Focal loss for dense object detection. In: ICCV, pp. 2980–2988 (2017)
12. Liu, N., Han, J.: DHSNet: deep hierarchical saliency network for salient object detection. In: CVPR, pp. 678–686 (2016)
13. Liu, T., et al.: Learning to detect a salient object. PAMI **33**(2), 353–367 (2011)
14. Long, J., Shelhamer, E., Darrell, T.: Fully convolutional networks for semantic segmentation. In: CVPR, pp. 3431–3440 (2015)
15. Martin, D., Fowlkes, C., Tal, D., Malik, J.: A database of human segmented natural images and its application to evaluating segmentation algorithms and measuring ecological statistics. In: ICCV, vol. 2, pp. 416–423 (2001)
16. Parkhurst, D., Law, K., Niebur, E.: Modeling the role of salience in the allocation of overt visual attention. Vis. Res. **42**(1), 107–123 (2002)
17. Ronneberger, O., Fischer, P., Brox, T.: U-Net: convolutional networks for biomedical image segmentation. In: Navab, N., Hornegger, J., Wells, W.M., Frangi, A.F. (eds.) MICCAI 2015. LNCS, vol. 9351, pp. 234–241. Springer, Cham (2015). https://doi.org/10.1007/978-3-319-24574-4_28
18. Spain, M., Perona, P.: Measuring and predicting object importance. Int. J. Comput. Vis. **91**(1), 59–76 (2011)
19. Wang, L., Lu, H., Ruan, X., Yang, M.H.: Deep networks for saliency detection via local estimation and global search. In: CVPR, pp. 3183–3192 (2015)
20. Wang, L., Wang, L., Lu, H., Zhang, P., Ruan, X.: Saliency detection with recurrent fully convolutional networks. In: Leibe, B., Matas, J., Sebe, N., Welling, M. (eds.) ECCV 2016. LNCS, vol. 9908, pp. 825–841. Springer, Cham (2016). https://doi.org/10.1007/978-3-319-46493-0_50
21. Yan, Q., Xu, L., Shi, J., Jia, J.: Hierarchical saliency detection. In: CVPR, pp. 1155–1162 (2013)
22. Zhang, P., Wang, D., Lu, H., Wang, H., Ruan, X.: Amulet: aggregating multi-level convolutional features for salient object detection. In: ICCV, pp. 202–211 (2017)
23. Zhao, R., Ouyang, W., Li, H., Wang, X.: Saliency detection by multi-context deep learning. In: CVPR, pp. 1265–1274 (2015)

Image Retrieval with Similar Object Detection and Local Similarity to Detected Objects

Sidra Hanif[1(✉)], Chao Li[1,2], Anis Alazzawe[1], and Longin Jan Latecki[1]

[1] Temple University, Philadelphia, PA 19122, USA
{sidra.hanif,aalazzawe,latecki}@temple.edu
[2] Huazhong University of Science and Technology, Wuhan 1037, China
chaol@hust.edu.cn

Abstract. Commercial image search applications like eBay and Pinterest allow users to select the focused area as bounding box over the query images, which improves the retrieval accuracy. The focused area image retrieval strategy motivated our research, but our system has three main advantages over the existing works. (1) Given a query focus area, our approach localizes the most similar region in the database image and only this region is used for computing image similarity. This is done in a unified network whose weights are adjusted both for localization and similarity learning in an end-to-end manner. (2) This is achieved using fewer than five proposals extracted from a saliency map, which speedups the pairwise similarity computation. Usually hundreds or even thousands of proposals are used for localization. (3) For users, our system explains the relevance of the retrieved results by locating the regions in the database images that are the most similar to the query object. Our method achieves significantly better retrieval performance than the off-the-shelf object localization-based retrieval methods and end-to-end trained triplet method with a region proposal network. Our experimental results demonstrate 86% retrieval rate as compared to 73% achieved by the existing methods on PASCAL VOC07 and VOC12 datasets. Extensive experiments are also conducted on the instance retrieval databases Oxford5k and INSTRE, where we exhibit competitive performance. Finally, we provide both quantitative and qualitative results of our retrieval method demonstrating its superiority over commercial image search systems.

Keywords: Object detection · Similarity measure · Image retrieval · Saliency map · Region proposals

1 Introduction

Today, on average 52 billion images are uploaded on image sharing applications each day [9]. Due to this proliferation of visual content, image-to-image search have gained substantial attention and now almost every commercial image search system has incorporated an image-to-image search engine in their framework. But the retrieval accuracy

We are grateful for the Amazon Research Award (ARA). This work was also supported in part by NSF grants IIS-1302164 and IIS-1814745.

© Springer Nature Switzerland AG 2019
A. C. Nayak and A. Sharma (Eds.): PRICAI 2019, LNAI 11672, pp. 42–55, 2019.
https://doi.org/10.1007/978-3-030-29894-4_4

of these systems particularly for small objects with background clutter and/or occlusion is still lacking in performance. For instance, Google's reverse image search facilitates the retrieval of similar images from vast online resources. But it only focuses on global image perspective, and often misses the relevant objects in images. To demonstrate this, let us consider the query focused area shown magnified in Fig. 1. The focused area, which usually contains a single object, is helpful to improve object search, as the query images may contain multiple objects and the user might be interested in one particular object for online search. Only this area is used as query. AS shown in Fig. 1, Google reverse search does not retrieve any image containing objects similar to those in the query focused area (*bottles*). The performance of triplet net is nearly as bad too. However, Pinterest [11] allows the selection of the focused area in query images. But, it still only considers global descriptors for database images. Therefore for small query objects, like *bottles*, it is unable to retrieve correct results. In contrast, all results of the proposed method are correct.

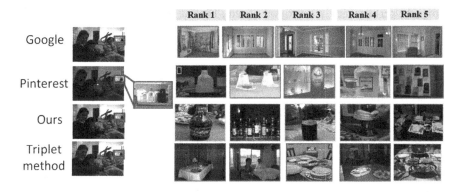

Fig. 1. Top-5 best matches for Google reverse search, Pinterest focused area search, the proposed method, and triplet net similarity (red shows wrong retrieval and   shows correct retrieval). (Color figure online)

The state-of-the-art approaches [21–23] to image retrieval discard the noisy background and keep the useful convolutional features to localize the main object. That is, they exclude the background in forming the final object descriptor [21]. The approach in [23] proposes parts detector consisting of convolutional filters to generate the probabilistic proposals, which highlight certain discriminative parts of the objects and suppress the noise of the background. These techniques show good results for fine-grained category retrieval [21] which only has a single category present in each image. However, these methods are ineffective for images with multiple objects as observed in [5, 14]. To cope with the presence of multiple objects in the image, [14] pool the feature representations from object detector. Their image search framework is based on faster R-CNN for object detection followed by a spatial re-ranking based on class scores. Faster R-CNN utilizes Region Proposal Network (RPN) [18] for object proposal generation. RPN generates region proposals combining both exhaustive search using sliding window, merging segmentation at varying threshold and group multiscale regions into object proposals. [5] train a separate triplet network and RPN, and combine both at test time. In this sequential setting, triplet network is trained for global image representation and RPN is trained for object localization using bounding box annotation. In another approach to image retrieval, [24] pick two neural activations from the convolutional networks, one for localization, and the other for object's feature description. In the last few years, image retrieval frameworks started adding object location as a part of retrieval problem, but these methods [5,14,23] either use two separate localization and feature embedding networks or rely on off-the-shelf object detection methods for object localization. Moreover, they utilize RPN which provide thousands of proposals but typically few indicate the actual object's locations. In our method, we generate region proposals from saliency maps at different threshold values. Even though we restrict the number of proposal to a maximum of five, we obtain better retrieval rate compared to these current methods [2,5].

1.1 Contributions

As mentioned above, we believe that localizing the query object in the target image can improve the performance of a retrieval system. The five main contributions of this paper can be summarized as follows:

(1) Localization−similarity module: A unified module for simultaneous localization and similarity learning is introduced.
(2) Saliency driven proposal set: We construct a saliency driven proposal set to localize objects in the target images.
(3) The localization in target images of the most similar region to the focus area in the query image not only makes the retrieval results better but also provides an explanation why the retrieved images are similar to the query.
(4) Proposed framework localizes the region most the similar to the query in the database images irrespective of the object class. Thus, it is applicable to visually diverse datasets without computing class scores.
(5) We demonstrate a better performance for the natural images as compared to commercially available image search applications.

To the best of our knowledge, this is a first attempt to combine localization and learning localized similarity embedding in a unified network for a class agnostic case in an end-to-end manner.

For our experimental evaluation, we consider the challenging PASCAL VOC07 [3], PASCAL VOC12 [3] datasets and the instance retrieval datasets namely Oxford5k [10] and INSTance-level object REtrieval and REcognition (INSTRE) [20]. We deliberately selected these datasets to evaluate our method, because they enable us to evaluate the performance on two visually different dataset types; with PASCAL set being the object detection dataset with cluttered or even overlapping objects in natural images, and Oxford5k [10] and INSTRE [20] being the instance retrieval datasets having small inter-class variability close to product search problem.

2   Method

A key motivation for our work is the fact that image retrieval can be addressed by combining object localization in target images with local similarity learning. In this section, we describe each component of our localization driven retrieval network. In Sect. 2.1 we explain the proposal generation by a recurrent convolutional neural network. Sect. 2.2 details the object localization. Sect. 2.3 describes the similarity learning in a unified network, and Sect. 2.4 defines the loss functions. The overall pipeline of our architecture is given in Fig. 2.

2.1 Saliency Driven Region Proposal Generation

In this work, we propose to simultaneously learn two functions $\Delta = f(y, z)$ and $\varphi = f(\Delta)$ for localization and local similarity respectively. We compare query image y with database image z predicting the area of interest Δ in the database image that is most similar to the focused area in query image. Similarity metric (φ) is close to 1 if y and z contain similar objects or 0 otherwise. The predicted variable Δ is simultaneously utilized by similarity learning module in the unified network. So Δ is the intermediate output of the unified network. To estimate the location of similar object in the database image, we start with the salient regions extracted from recurrent convolutional architecture. We term these salient regions as "Salient Proposal Boxes" (SPB). Lately, [19] uses saliency maps to indicate approximate position of objects. However, it utilizes the saliency information to filter the proposals extracted by selective search [18]. In contrast, we generate proposals based on saliency maps without any additional proposal generation module.

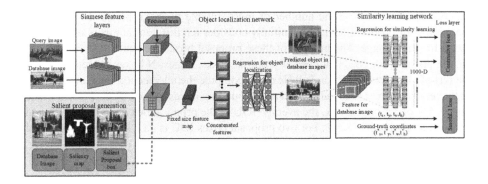

Fig. 2. The overall architecture of image retrieval with local similarity of the detected objects.

In the proposed work, saliency maps are extracted from recurrent convolutional architecture. Recurrent architecture refines the saliency prediction at each pass using the error from the previous iteration, details of the recurrent architecture can be found in [19]. We extract the saliency map at a third time step because it contains the refined saliency regions. The salient regions indicate probable presence of objects in the image. To convert them into proposal boxes, we apply multiple thresholds to the saliency map to obtain binary images followed by the connected component labeling. We use four threshold intervals $K = \{[0, 1], [1, 50], [50, 100], [100, 255]\}$ for partitioning saliency maps at multiple scales. Each of the intervals has the lower and the upper limit, denoted as k_l and k_u to capture the objects corresponding to particular scale. For instance, the threshold range [1, 50], $k_l = 1$ and $k_u = 50$, captures less salient objects, whereas the range [100, 255] captures highly salient objects. We use these thresholds to convert saliency map S to binary map B:

$$B_r = \begin{cases} 1 & \text{if} \quad k_l < S_r < k_u \\ 0 & \text{otherwise,} \end{cases} \tag{1}$$

where B_r is the binary map value and S_r is the saliency intensity levels at point r. To extract SPB from binary map B, we locally fit bounding boxes to connected components of B. The set of all SPB at the threshold interval $[k_l, k_u]$ is denoted as $\mathcal{B}(k_l, k_u)$. Connected components of the binary map may generate multiple proposal boxes depending on the quality of saliency map, but we retain only five proposal boxes with the largest area. Hence, $\mathcal{B}(k_l, k_u)$ denotes the set of at most five SPB for a given threshold interval. In the case when the set of SPB is empty for a given threshold interval, $\mathcal{B}(k_l, k_u)$ will contain the whole image frame as the only proposal box. A set of proposals extracted from the saliency map obtained by the recurrent fully convolution network at the four threshold intervals is illustrated in Fig. 3. As it can be seen, for small objects a low threshold of saliency map suggests better proposals (row 1). However, for large objects, as shown in rows 3 and 4, the proposal extracted at a higher thresholds give better prediction of object's location. If none of the proposal boxes is extracted at a given threshold, then the bounding box of the whole image is considered as a proposal box as shown in row 1 (columns 3 and 4). We actually performed experiments to determine the number of most suitable proposal boxes. To determine the number of proposal boxes, we initially consider ten different numbers of proposal boxes for each image. The number of these proposal boxes are set to 1, 2, 3, 4, 5, 10, 20, 30, 50 and 100. For N number of proposal boxes, largest N boxes are retained, and the rest of the boxes are discarded. Next, we compute the intersection over union (IOU) of the retained boxes with the ground truth bounding boxes of the objects present in the image. For one proposal box, the average IOU of the proposal box and objects' ground truth is reported to be 18.6%. For two proposal boxes IOU is 43.2%, for three proposal

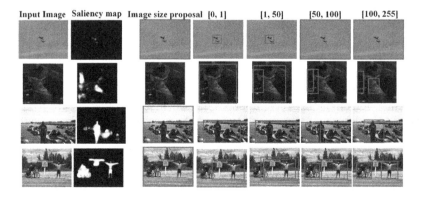

Fig. 3. The salient regions and SPB at four different threshold intervals.

boxes IOU is 46.0%, and for four and five proposal boxes IOU is 46.05%. For proposal boxes greater than 5 (that is, 10, 20, 30, 50 and 100), we observe the same IOU equal to 46.07%, which is very close to the IOU reported by 5 proposal boxes. Therefore, we used five proposal boxes for the rest of the analysis in this work. The salient regions provide a good starting guess for the location of the objects in the image. But these initial guesses may not fit the objects well, i.e., they may contain parts of the other objects or background around the object of interest, which may negatively effect the retrieval performance. Therefore, our next step is to find the object's exact location initialized from these proposal boxes. For this purpose, we train a unified localization-similarity network to find the exact location of objects of interest in the database images.

2.2 Object Localization

In the learning function $\Delta = f(y, z)$ of our convolutional neural network, Δ is the prediction offset for the proposal boxes that locate the similar object in database images. Δ is an intermediate network variable, which is implicitly learned in the network to localize the objects and simultaneously utilized by the network to generate feature embedding for the regions of the database images most similar to the query image's focused area.

Object localization in database images is useful for image retrieval as it helps to exclude the background in feature learning, consequently increasing the retrieval accuracy. Unlike our work, previous method applied the localization idea to retrieval problem by separately training localization and feature embedding [5]. Another work [14] on instance retrieval makes use of CNN features extracted from an established object detector i.e., faster-RCNN [13]. It provides a simple baseline that uses off-the-shelf faster R-CNN features to detect the object before retrieving similar images. In the proposed work, we used a different strategy as we train the complete network in an end-to-end manner without utilizing pre-trained networks [13, 14]. Hence, we propose a unified network in which one part is localization and the other part is the similarity learning fused together.

Since in our framework, the parameter regression works for SPB as well as other proposals. We also performed experiments with the complete image as a proposal box keeping the rest of the setting same. We construct a Siamese branches for feature learning using VGG layers cropped at pool5 layer [17]. These layers act as a backbone to learn high level features for object's location prediction and feature embedding of both the focused area in the query image and the most similar region in target image with shared network parameters. The location of similar objects in the database images is learned by regression layers initialized by SPB, which regress them to the exact location of the objects.

In regression layers, for positive pairs (query and database image both have a common objects), the proposal boxes regress to the location of the common object in the database image. For negative samples (both from different classes), proposal box remain unchanged. In other words, the network forces the proposal to stay where it is, so that they do not regress to any random location. The bounding box regression equations are taken from [13]. Moreover, the regression layer for localization is also able to perform object location regression initialized from the bounding box of the whole image (i.e., image size proposal box without using SPB).

The location of the object in the target image is then predicted from fully convolutional regression layer. The goal of this regression layer is to find the region in the target image that is the most similar to the focused area in the query image.

2.3 Similarity Learning

Concurrently, with object localization estimation, we learn a suitable feature embedding of the query focused area and the predicted location in the target image. Our goal is learning the local features embedding of the predicted location of the target image rather than considering the global image level features. The objective of this part is to minimize the error given by the localized similarity:

$$\phi(y, z) = \frac{1}{n}[f(y) - f(z')]^2, \tag{2}$$

where $f(y)$ is the feature vector of the focused area in the query image y, $f(z')$ is the feature vector of a regressed proposal box in database image z, and n is the dimension of the feature vectors. Small number of proposal boxes used in this research prevent us from an exhaustive search of query object over different scale ranges [5, 8, 14]. An alternate approach would be to utilize the off-the-shelf object detection methods (e.g., [14, 18]) to generate proposals. But these methods give large number of candidate proposals that increase the overhead of computation for the calculation of pairwise similarity values, making it unfeasible for real time computation. We compare our method to off-the-shelf object localization methods [13] combined with image re-ranking [14], and our method exhibits superior performance (Sect. 3). Our localization-similarity method integrates the object discovery and similarity scoring in a single unified convolutional neural network without any auxiliary network. In this way, we simultaneously estimate the location of objects in the target images as well as their similarities with focused area in query image.

2.4 Loss Function and Network Update

To train our network, we use a combination of two loss functions, regression $\mathcal{L}_{reg}(\Delta)$ and contrastive $\mathcal{L}_{cont}(\phi)$ loss, where Δ is the predicted location in database image and ϕ is a pairwise similarity defined in Eq. (2). The unified network is updated to minimize both the losses in a single pass. In our work, we evaluated the performance of the system with equal contribution from both loss functions:

$$\mathcal{L} = \mathcal{L}_{reg}(\Delta) + \mathcal{L}_{cont}(\phi). \tag{3}$$

The formula for regression loss is given as

$$\mathcal{L}_{reg}(\Delta) = \sum_{i=0}^{N}(g(x - x^*)) \tag{4}$$

Table 1. Comparison of Accuracy (%) for the localization−similarity network on PASCAL VOC07 and PASCAL VOC12.

Method	aero	bicy	bird	boat	bott	bus	car	cat	cha	cow	dtab	dog	hors	mbik	pers	plnt	shep	sofa	trai	tv	Avg
PASCAL VOC07																					
Our- Salient proposal [0, 1]	95	85.5	100	93	92.5	95	98	95.5	62.5	59	88	94	89	81.5	100	55.5	66	88.5	91.5	87	85.85
Our- Salient proposal [1, 50]	94	83.5	96	88	94.5	90.5	99.5	96	71.5	65.5	83	93.5	86.5	82	98.5	68	64.57	88.5	98	84	86.3
Our- Salient proposal [50,100]	94.5	84.5	96.5	91	86	89.5	100	98	69.5	60.5	83.5	92	80	83.5	94.5	61	77.5	87.5	98	79	85.3
Our- Salient proposal [100,255]	91	90.5	97.5	92	90.5	94	98.5	96.5	62	48.5	82.5	91	82	86.5	99.5	49	58	78.5	97.5	88.5	83.7
Our-Image size proposal	100	82.7	93.6	82.7	80	91.8	96.3	90	50.9	74.5	77.2	90.9	90	63.6	100	70	47.2	53.6	87.2	92.7	80.7
Triplet network (focused area) [16]	75	71.5	9.5	75.5	45.5	79.5	86	91.5	42.5	57.5	57.5	79	84	83.5	72	51	55	84	86	92.5	73.0
Deep retrieval [6]	94	61	5	60	26	77	69	65	35	55	46	56	67	70	83	62	44	52	55	64	59.6
Fast-RCNN based retrieval[15]	86	82	72	58	44	69	82	81	61	72	61	60	73	69	100	61	61	49	73	76	69.5
Activation map [22]	84	69	71	86.5	64	75	81	72	49.5	69.5	66.5	77.5	80	83	77	30.5	76.5	59.5	92	58	71.1
Cho [2]	51.1	45.3	12.7	12.1	11.4	21.2	61.9	11.6	19.2	9.7	3.9	17.2	29.6	34	43.7	10.2	8.1	9.9	24	27.3	23.2 -
PASCAL VOC12																					
Our- Salient proposal [0,1]	91.5	80	75.5	87.5	73	93	84	90.5	58	44	80.5	85.5	65.5	74	92	61.5	67	64	85	92.5	77.2
Our- Salient proposal [1,50]	90	67.5	78.5	88	79	91.5	82	90	58.5	43.5	74.5	85	76	76	93.5	66	77	59.5	79	96	77.5
Our- Salient proposal [50,100]	93.5	78.5	76.5	87	81	95	80.5	92.5	61	50.5	82	84	72	81.5	85.5	58.5	71.5	61.5	82	93.5	78.4
Our- Salient proposal [100, 255]	92	75	78	83	80	90.5	86	91	47.5	43.5	78	91	62	81	90	60	69	51.5	83.5	95	76.4
Our-Image size proposal	95.5	65.5	76	81	73.5	83.5	74.5	89	47.5	47.5	66.5	92	56.5	51	79.5	63.5	47.5	32.5	84	95.5	70.1
Triplet network (focused area) [16]	87.5	59.5	82	59.5	36	95.5	63	89	42	66.5	64	72.5	55	73	82	45.5	65.5	63.5	78.5	90.5	68.5
Deep retrieval [6]	93	62	48	43	25.5	84	57.5	70	32	50	51.5	42	48.5	72.5	80.5	28	60.5	51.5	64.5	76	57
Fast-RCNN based retrieval [15]	92	67	60.5	55	64	89	73	81	51	63.5	62.5	68	60.5	68	80.5	53	68.5	50.5	66.5	81	67.7
Activation map[22]	88.5	51	53	76.5	25.5	62	34.5	63	31.5	44.5	32	32.5	42.5	58.5	41	21	66	40.5	71.5	63	49.9

Here, x is the predicted coordinates and x^* is the ground-truth coordinates of the object. N is number of images in each batch. Function g is same as in Eq. (3) in [4]. The contrastive loss is given as,

$$\mathcal{L}_{cont}(\phi) = \delta(f(y) - f(z'))^2 + (1 - \delta)max(0, \text{m} - (f(y) - f(z'))^2) \quad (5)$$

Definitions of $f(y)$ and $f(z')$ are given in Sect. 2.3. For a pair of similar images $\delta = 1$ and otherwise $\delta = 0$. The margin value m is set to 3.

The gradient in the regression layers for localization (Δ) and similarity feature learning (ϕ) is updated as,

$$\frac{\partial \mathcal{L}_{reg}(\Delta)}{\partial X_p} = \frac{\partial \mathcal{L}_{reg}(\Delta)}{\partial \Delta} \cdot \frac{\partial \Delta}{\partial X_p}, \quad \frac{\partial \mathcal{L}_{cont}(\phi)}{\partial X_p} = \frac{\partial \mathcal{L}_{cont}(\phi)}{\partial \phi} \cdot \frac{\partial \phi}{\partial X_p} \quad (6)$$

where, X_p is the output at the feature extraction stage (features are extracted at pool5 layer of the VGG architecture. This backbone of Siamese feature extraction layers, used by both localization (Δ) and similarity embedding learning (ϕ), are updated simultaneously by adding the gradient from two regression layers:

$$\frac{\partial \mathcal{L}}{\partial y} = \frac{\partial \mathcal{L}_{reg}(\Delta)}{\partial X_p} \cdot \frac{\partial X_p}{\partial y} + \frac{\partial \mathcal{L}_{cont}(\phi)}{\partial X_p} \cdot \frac{\partial X_p}{\partial y} \quad (7)$$

where y is the input image (Eq. 7 is the same for z as well), substituting values from Eq. (6) to Eq. (7) gives the gradient for the overall loss function $\mathcal{L}$:

$$\frac{\partial \mathcal{L}}{\partial y} = \frac{\partial \mathcal{L}_{reg}(\Delta)}{\partial \Delta} \cdot \frac{\partial \Delta}{\partial X_p} \cdot \frac{\partial X_p}{\partial y} + \frac{\partial \mathcal{L}_{cont}(\phi)}{\partial \phi} \cdot \frac{\partial \phi}{\partial X_p} \cdot \frac{\partial X_p}{\partial y} \quad (8)$$

The weights of the unified network are adjusted in the way to optimize the performance of localization prediction and similarity feature embedding learning simultaneously. This makes sure that the unified networks is coherently optimized. In this way, the weights of the Siamese feature extraction layers as well as the regression layers for localization and similarity learning are adjusted simultaneously.

3 Experimental Evaluation

For the evaluation, we use PASCAL VOC07 [3], PASCAL VOC12 [3], Oxford5k [10] and INSTRE [20] datasets. We compare our results with previous methods [2, 5, 14, 15]. We use three performance metrics, namely, Accuracy (%), precision-recall curve and mean Average Precision (mAP).

3.1 PASCAL VOC07/PASCAL VOC12

In the first set of experiments, we use PASCAL VOC07 and PASCAL VOC12 datasets to find the retrieval accuracy. Accuracy is defined as the percentage of correct retrievals in the top-t retrieved images. In order to keep the value of t same as in [2], we use t = 10. We select the PASCAL VOC07 as benchmark dataset for object localization, because in this dataset 4,952 test images contain 12,032 objects, providing approximately 2.5 objects per image [3] and making this dataset favorable for testing the proposed localization−similarity network. For training, the ground-truth annotation of the objects is used to train the regression layer for localization, but for testing the object's location is predicted from regression network without ground truth annotation.

The retrieval accuracy for PASCAL VOC07 and PASCAL VOC12 are listed in Table 1, On both datasets, our method outperforms by a significant margin the triplet network based method [15], Faster-RCNN based instance retrieval [14], deep retrieval (triplet network+RPN) [5] and pretrained activation maps [21]. This is due to a better discriminatory ability of the proposed localization based retrieval for local perspective as opposed to global image similarity.

In Table 1, bold numbers show the maximum retrieval accuracy for each category. Our results are significantly better in the case of classes with multiple objects like *bicycles*, *motorbikes*, *sofa* and small occluded objects like *bottles*, *chairs* and *dining tables*. Overall, using SPB improves the Accuracy (%) from 69% to 86% in comparison with the baseline network [14]. Varying the threshold for SPB does not effect the performance much, but the optimal threshold is [1, 50] for both datasets.

We also evaluate our localization-similarity network with only one proposal being the bounding box of the whole image. It also yields results better than previous methods and validate the effectiveness of unified localization-similarity network for retrieval tasks. The reason of this improvement is the mutual benefit of the two sub networks (regression layers for localization and similarity embedding) in a unified network. The precision-recall (PR) curves for PASCAL VOC07 and PASCAL VOC12 are shown in Fig. 4. The PR curves give the holistic view of the effectiveness of our method. It can be seen that the performance of baseline method [14] is very poor, deep retrieval (triplet network+RPN) also have much lower precision compared to our method for all recall values. Thus, our method outperforms previous localization based methods for object search.

One of the challenges of evaluating object retrieval on PASCAL datasets is due to the overlapping objects in query image. Note that, all of our analysis is based on strict criteria for retrieval. For example, if the image has both *person* and *sofa* class and the query object *sofa* is overlapping with *person*, then retrieved images without *sofa* but

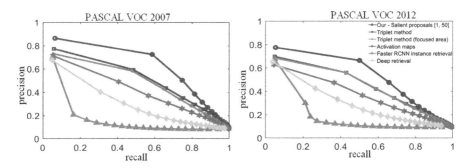

Fig. 4. PR curves for PASCAL VOC07 and PASCAL VOC12.

Table 2. Accuracy (%) of our method compared to Google reverse image search and Pinterest.

Method	Our-Image size proposal	Google reverse search	Pinterest
Accuracy (%)	**76.5**	63.5	68.7

with *person* are considered incorrect, irrespective of the fact that *person* class is over-lapping with *sofa* class in the focused area of the query image. The qualitative results of our method are shown in Fig. 5. In column 3–12, the localization of database object with respect to the query focused area is plotted with yellow boxes. For calculating the similarity of database image with query image's focused area, the feature descriptor from the localized yellow boxes are only extracted. This excludes the object's surrounding while ranking the images similar to query object. Our localization based retrieval method also explains retrieval results to the user. In Fig. 5 we present some example retrieval results of our localization-similarity network. In rows 1–5, we show the correct retrieval results with the correct localization. In row 6, one of the retrieved images does not belong to query class because the network localizes a similar object a *horse* instead of a query object which is *cow*, this is due to visual similarity of *horse* and *cow* class. The explanation of results to the user is more important when the network can inform user where it is actually looking in the target images. In row 7, the network can explain to the user that it is looking for *birds* in the target images, while the actual object in query focused area is a *boat*. However, after a closer look we discovered that there are *birds* above the *boat* in the query focused area.

In Table 2, we also provide a quantitative comparison to Google reverse search and Pinterest focused area search on 100 images sampled from PASCAL VOC07. Both quantitative (Table 2) and qualitative (Fig. 1) results of our retrieval method demonstrate its superiority over commercial image search systems.

3.2 Ensemble Model

We tried the ensemble of models which are trained at different thresholds. We used the threshold values of [0, 1], [1, 50] and [50, 100]. When we evaluate the model at these thresholds separately, we get the average accuracy of 85.85%, 86.3% and 85.3%

respectively. Whereas, when we apply the ensemble of the average of these models, we get the accuracy equal to 87.27%. Another way to construct the ensemble model is to max-pool individual model, that produces 86.6% accuracy, which is almost the same as the best performing model. These results for the average of models are better than the individual models but do not show noticeable improvement, so we did not include this aspect in the presented comparison.

3.3   Oxford5k and INSTRE-S1

We also compare the results for landmarks instance retrieval datasets Oxford5k [10] with existing localization based methods. This dataset has a lot of unlabeled ~4000/5008 images. The results are produced using image size proposal (the best performing for this application), to justify the effectiveness of localization-similarity network for instance retrieval. For Oxford5k dataset (which includes 4000 unlabeled images) we are able to get comparative results to the previous methods as shown in Table. 3, even though we used only 55 query images to finetune the network without any data augmentation. We believe that if we can increase the number of training images for Oxford5k dataset then the results would be a lot better.

For INSTRE dataset [20], which is an instance retrieval dataset with 100 classes, we perform better than the previous methods. The INSTRE dataset has more than 100 images per class for training, which validates our claim that our performance becomes better if we can increase the number of training images.

The mAP for INSTRE dataset is listed in Table 3. We are able to outperform previous region matching [12] and diffusion [7] based methods with our baseline method which uses only the image size proposal.

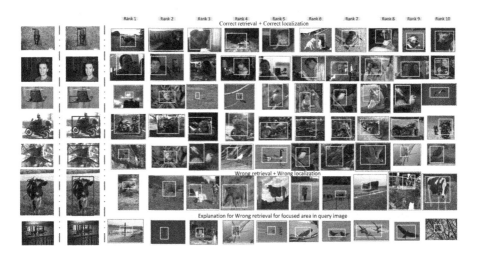

Fig. 5. Some example retrieval results of our localization-similarity network. Column 1: the query image, Column 2: the query image with the focused area marked. Columns 3–12: top-10 most similar images (frames mark correct retrieval, red frames wrong retrieval, and the bounding boxes localized by our method are shown in). Best viewed in colors. (Color figure online)

Table 3. Comparison of mAP on Oxford5k and INSTRE-S1.

Oxford5k	
Razavian et al. [16]	0.556
Babenko and Lempit [1]	0.657
Salvador et al. [14]	0.588
Our- Image size proposal (with unlabelled images)	0.536
Our- Image size proposal (without unlabelled images)	**0.681**

INSTRE	
R-MAC [6]	0.626
R-match [12]	0.71
Regional diffusion [7]	0.896
Our- Image size proposal	**0.92**

Table 4. Time required to perform image search in our unified network, Faster-RCNN based retrieval method [14] and image re-ranking [2]

Method	Our-Image size proposal	[2]	[14]
Time (seconds)	**54**	153	117

Our method not only yields good results but also takes less time to compute as compared to the baseline re-ranking methods for retrieval [14] as shown in Table 4.

The results are listed for PASCAL VOC07 dataset for 2000 database images, the set of query and database is consistent for all methods. The test time comparison of the proposed saliency-based object detection methods as compared to state-of-the-art object detection methods such as Fast RCNN, YOLO, Spatial Pyramid Pooling network (SPPnet) is as follows (in seconds/image): SPPnet = 28.65; Fast RCNN = 3.99; Our = 1.4829 (VGG = 1.052+regression layer = 0.4309); YOLO = 0.51 The test runtime for FastRCNN is 3.99, our method is computationally less costly than FastRCNN and far better than SPPnet. We computed these test times on NVIDIA GeForce GTX1080 GPU to ensure that it is a fair comparison.

3.4 Unknown Target Classes

To demonstrate the ability of our framework to handles unknown targets, we set up an additional experiment in which we included an unknown "zebra" class from MSCOCO datasets and tested its retrieval accuracy against the already trained system. The system has not seen the examples from this class before. For the unknown "zebras" class, we get 64% for top-5 and 80% for top-1 correct retrieval results. The important thing to note here is the visual closeness between "horse", "cow", "zebra" classes but still our system can perform well. For the unknown object retrieval case, we also tested our system for INSTRE, an instance retrieval dataset. This small object instance retrieval dataset is comprehensive with more than 11,000 database images. We trained the network for the subset of the INSTRE datasets and tested it on five randomly selected unknown classes. For these five classes, without image labels and bounding box information in the target images, we get 61.6% accuracy for top-5 correct retrieval and 76.0% accuracy for top-1 correct retrieval. These results show the effectiveness of our method for small object retrieval with unknown class information.

4 Conclusion

We present a unified method based on similar object localization for image retrieval. Our results demonstrate that the retrieval performance significantly improves by combining object localization and image similarity learning into a single network rather than perform object detection as a separate step before computing similarity. Our system also exhibits competitive performance with the previous instance search methods on Oxford 5k and INSTRE datasets. We also demonstrate the generalization ability of the proposed network to unseen queries without any retraining.

References

1. Babenko, A., Lempitsky, V.: Aggregating local deep features for image retrieval. In: Proceedings of the IEEE International Conference on Computer Vision, pp. 1269–1277 (2015)
2. Cho, M., Kwak, S., Schmid, C., Ponce, J.: Unsupervised object discovery and localization in the wild: part-based matching with bottom-up region proposals. In: Proceedings of the IEEE Conference on Computer Vision and Pattern Recognition, pp. 1201–1210 (2015)
3. Everingham, M., Van Gool, L., Williams, C.K., Winn, J., Zisserman, A.: The PASCAL visual object classes (VOC) challenge. Int. J. Comput. Vis. **88**(2), 303–338 (2010)
4. Girshick, R.: Fast R-CNN. In: Proceedings of the IEEE ICCV, pp. 1440–1448 (2015)
5. Gordo, A., Almazán, J., Revaud, J., Larlus, D.: Deep image retrieval: learning global representations for image search. In: Leibe, B., Matas, J., Sebe, N., Welling, M. (eds.) ECCV 2016. LNCS, vol. 9910, pp. 241–257. Springer, Cham (2016). https://doi.org/10.1007/978-3-319-46466-4_15
6. Gordo, A., Almazan, J., Revaud, J., Larlus, D.: End-to-end learning of deep visual representations for image retrieval. Int. J. Comput. Vis. **124**(2), 237–254 (2017)
7. Iscen, A., Tolias, G., Avrithis, Y.S., Furon, T., Chum, O.: Efficient diffusion on region manifolds: recovering small objects with compact CNN representations. In: CVPR, vol. 1, p. 3 (2017)
8. Li, Y., Liu, L., Shen, C., van den Hengel, A.: Image co-localization by mimicking a good detector's confidence score distribution. In: Leibe, B., Matas, J., Sebe, N., Welling, M. (eds.) ECCV 2016. LNCS, vol. 9906, pp. 19–34. Springer, Cham (2016). https://doi.org/10.1007/978-3-319-46475-6_2
9. Perret, E.: Here's How Many Digital Photos Will Be Taken in 2017 (2017). https://mylio.com/true-stories/tech-today/how-many-digital-photos-will-be-taken-2017-repost/
10. Philbin, J., Chum, O., Isard, M., Sivic, J., Zisserman, A.: Object retrieval with large vocabularies and fast spatial matching. In: 2007 IEEE Conference on Computer Vision and Pattern Recognition, CVPR 2007, pp. 1–8. IEEE (2007)
11. Pinterest: Pinterest (2018). https://www.pinterest.com/
12. Razavian, A.S., Sullivan, J., Carlsson, S., Maki, A.: Visual instance retrieval with deep convolutional networks. ITE Trans. Media Technol. Appl. **4**(3), 251–258 (2016)
13. Ren, S., He, K., Girshick, R., Sun, J.: Faster R-CNN: towards real-time object detection with region proposal networks. In: Advances in Neural Information Processing Systems, pp. 91–99 (2015)
14. Salvador, A., Giró-i Nieto, X., Marqués, F., Satoh, S.: Faster R-CNN features for instance search. In: Proceedings of the IEEE Conference on Computer Vision and Pattern Recognition Workshops, pp. 9–16 (2016)

15. Schroff, F., Kalenichenko, D., Philbin, J.: FaceNet: a unified embedding for face recognition and clustering. In: Proceedings of the IEEE Conference on Computer Vision and Pattern Recognition, pp. 815–823 (2015)
16. Sharif Razavian, A., Azizpour, H., Sullivan, J., Carlsson, S.: CNN features off-the-shelf: an astounding baseline for recognition. In: Proceedings of the IEEE Conference on Computer Vision and Pattern Recognition Workshops, pp. 806–813 (2014)
17. Simonyan, K., Zisserman, A.: Very deep convolutional networks for large-scale image recognition. arXiv preprint arXiv:1409.1556 (2014)
18. Uijlings, J.R., Van De Sande, K.E., Gevers, T., Smeulders, A.W.: Selective search for object recognition. Int. J. Comput. Vis. **104**(2), 154–171 (2013)
19. Wang, L., Wang, L., Lu, H., Zhang, P., Ruan, X.: Salient object detection with recurrent fully convolutional networks. IEEE Trans. Pattern Anal. Mach. Intell. **41**, 1734–1746 (2018)
20. Wang, S., Jiang, S.: INSTRE: a new benchmark for instance-level object retrieval and recognition. ACM Trans. Multimed. Comput. Commun. Appl. (TOMM) **11**(3), 37 (2015)
21. Wei, X.S., Luo, J.H., Wu, J., Zhou, Z.H.: Selective convolutional descriptor aggregation for fine-grained image retrieval. IEEE Trans. Image Process. **26**(6), 2868–2881 (2017)
22. Wei, X.S., Xie, C.W., Wu, J.: Mask-CNN: localizing parts and selecting descriptors for fine-grained image recognition. arXiv preprint arXiv:1605.06878 (2016)
23. Xu, J., Shi, C., Qi, C., Wang, C., Xiao, B.: Unsupervised part-based weighting aggregation of deep convolutional features for image retrieval. arXiv preprint arXiv:1705.01247 (2017)
24. Zhang, X., Xiong, H., Zhou, W., Lin, W., Tian, Q.: Picking neural activations for fine-grained recognition. IEEE Trans. Multimedia **19**(12), 2736–2750 (2017)

Audio-Based Music Classification
with DenseNet and Data Augmentation

Wenhao Bian[1,2], Jie Wang[2(✉)], Bojin Zhuang[2], Jiankui Yang[1],
Shaojun Wang[2], and Jing Xiao[2]

[1] Beijing University of Posts and Telecommnications, Beijing, China
[2] Ping An Technology (Shenzhen) Co., Ltd., Shenzhen, China
photonicsjay@163.com

Abstract. In recent years, deep learning technique has received intense attention owing to its great success in image recognition. A tendency of adaption of
deep learning in various information processing fields has formed, including
music information retrieval (MIR). In this paper, we conduct a comprehensive
study on music audio classification with improved convolutional neural networks (CNNs). To the best of our knowledge, this the first work to apply
Densely Connected Convolutional Networks (DenseNet) to music audio tagging, which has been demonstrated to perform better than Residual neural
network (ResNet). Additionally, two specific data augmentation approaches of
time overlapping and pitch shifting have been proposed to address the defi-
ciency of labelled data in the MIR. Moreover, an ensemble learning of stacking
is employed based on SVM. We believe that the proposed combination of strong
representation of DenseNet and data augmentation can be adapted to other audio
processing tasks.

Keywords: Music classification · Spectrogram · CNN · ResNet · DenseNet ·
Deep learning

1 Introduction

With the rapid development of digital technology, the amount of online music accu-
mulates so dramatically that structuring large-scale music is becoming a fundamental
problem. Since 2000s, music information retrieval (MIR) has been widely studied for
important applications including recommendation systems of music. As one of the
main top-level descriptors (Chathuranga 2013), music genre is a kind of label generally
created by human experts and used for categorizing. However, it is impossible to label
the gigabyte music manually. Thus, automatic music genre classification has been
considered as a great challenge and valuable for MIR systems.

Most of music classification problems mainly consist of two modules. One is the
preprocessing of raw audio data, the other is the design of classifier model. As a crucial
part of the system, preprocessed data is the key to the final classification accuracy.
Generally, there are three main ways to preprocess raw audio: (1) acoustic features
extraction (Auguin 2013); (2) spectrograms transformation (Costa 2011) (3) using raw
audio (Dielman 2011). Before the blossoming of deep learning, a common way is to

© Springer Nature Switzerland AG 2019
A. C. Nayak and A. Sharma (Eds.): PRICAI 2019, LNAI 11672, pp. 56–65, 2019.
https://doi.org/10.1007/978-3-030-29894-4_5

extract specific acoustic features and aggregate them as input using various machine-learning algorithms (Ogihara 2003). However, this method requires intense engineering effort and professional knowledge. With the fast development of deep learning, convolutional neural network (CNN) has received much success in image recognition and been tried in the MIR field (Nakashika 2012). On the other hand, labelled music audio is really deficient in this area due to high cost professional tagging of experts.

In this paper, we exploit the advanced DenseNet as the building block of CNN architectures to boost performance of music audio classification, achieving higher accuracy than ResNet and baseline. In the part of data processing, grayscale spectrograms transformed from music raw audio are used for feature engineering (Dieleman 2014). To address the shortage of labelled audio data, music-specific data augmentation is realized with the time overlapping and pitch shifting of spectrograms. All of the results verify that the methods we proposed achieve improvements over the state-of-the-art models on both of the FMA-small dataset (Defferrard 2017) and GTZAN (Sturm 2012).

This paper is structured as follows. In Sect. 2, a brief overview on related work is provided. We then describe the feature extraction in detail in Sect. 3. Section 4 discusses our methodologies, followed by the experimental results and some discussion. Finally, Sect. 6 provides conclusions and describes potential future work.

2 Related Work

As one of the high-level descriptors, music genre is always associated with harmonic, rhythm, pitch and other acoustic features (Aguiar 2018). In this sense, physical properties of audio signal have been studied for music analysis. For instance, Mel Frequency Cepstral Coefficients (MFCCs) have been proven effective in the analysis of structures of music signals (Mubarak 2006). Similar to other hand-crafted features, MFCCs is still a lossy representation. In order to fully utilize the information from the audio signal, raw audio has been directly used (Dielman 2011). However, results show the use of raw data did not exhibit better performance than spectrograms in classification tasks. Spectrogram retains more information than MFCCs but with lower dimension than raw audio, which is more suitable for classification tasks (Wyse 2017).

As a typical neural network of deep learning, CNN has been extensively applied in various image recognition tasks. Recently, CNN has been adapted for audio recognition tasks (Gwardys 2014). In this kind of tasks, audio data was first converted to 2D spectrograms and then classified with CNN. For instance, Lee et al. (2009) applied CNN to promote the classification accuracy of music genre and artist. And in (Choi 2016), the usual CNN network with 2D convolutional layers obtained state-of-the-art performance at that time, which demonstrated the effectiveness of feature extraction of CNN for diverse music classification tasks. Contrary to visual images, however, 2D convolution of spectrograms along the frequency axis is not musically plausible to some extent. Lately, Dieleman et al. (Dieleman 2014) introduced the network structure with '1D-CNN' to process spectrograms in music classification.

Recently, a number of sophisticated CNN models have emerged to improve the performance of image recognition drastically. For example, He et al. introduced ResNet (He 2016) with skip connections enabling a very deep CNN to be effectively trained. And Huang et al. (Huang 2017) proposed DenseNet which exploited feature reuse through dense connections instead of skip connection. Owing to the rapid advance of CNN in computer vision (CV), the ResNet architecture (Kim 2018) was successfully applied for music auto tagging by processing raw audio directly. In this paper, we explore a more advanced CNN architecture, i.e. DenseNet, to process spectrogram instead of raw audio for music classification. To avoid over fit of network training, data augmentation is effectively realized with the time overlapping and pitch shifting of original spectrograms.

3   Data Processing

3.1   Input Length

Spectrogram represents spectra sequences varied along with the time axis. Spectrogram preparation is key to successfully applying CNN on music genres classification. In this way, the music audio tagging is reformulated as an image classification task (Schluter 2013).

To generate grayscale spectrograms of music, Sound eXchange (SoX) package has been used. The spectrogram is with a fixed height of 128 pixels representing frequency per frame and varied widths dependent on 50 pixels per second of audio.

Additionally, the size of the spectrogram is also a hyper-parameter. If the full-scale spectrogram of an entire song is used, network size of CNN could be enlarged significantly. Following prior experiments in (Tokozume 2017), time slice $T = 1.0 - 2.5$ s is applied in this work. Thus, each slice takes approximately 2.56 s long segments. Finally, grayscale spectrograms with 128×128 dimension is input for CNN training. In the phase of evaluation, classification outputs of each slice of one song can be ensemble as a single song-level prediction.

3.2   Data Augmentation

Data Augmentation is a technique to avoid overfit of model training by increasing the volume of data. Based on the unique characteristics of music, two methods to augment the data are proposed. One is the time overlapping which is an effective way in the field of image processing. To increase the valid data size, window moving of audio signals generates extra data by setting the overlap of 50%. And the other way is pitch shifting. With a small change of pitch of a song, its classification still works. Thus, shifting the pitch of songs by a half of the tone is done with SoX. To increase the diversity of the data, extra data generated from two methods was mixed together, resulting in 3 times more data than the original one

Figure 1(a) illustrates 50% overlap of spectrograms and (b) compares the difference between the origin and the pitch shifting spectrogram.

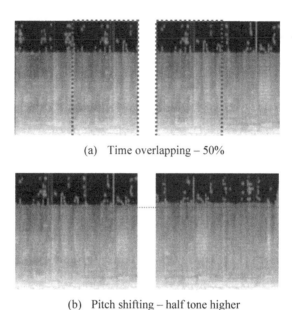

(a)   Time overlapping – 50%

(b)   Pitch shifting – half tone higher

Fig. 1.   Example of data augmentation techniques.

4   Methodology

Firstly, 1D CNN own less parameters and is computationally efficient (Nam 2019), which is more suitable for music tagging because of limited dataset in this area. Moreover, 2D convolution over frequency dimension is uninterpretable (Ulyanov 2016). Therefore, we choose 1D CNN as the basic block for spectrogram processing. Though time-consuming feature engineering can be alleviated by end-to-end training, the architecture of CNN network should be carefully designed for performance boost in specific tasks. In this paper, we firstly adapt DenseNet from CV to audio processing and compare its performance with ResNet and a regular CNN.

4.1   Basic Model

Our basic for music classification is shown in Fig. 2(a), which is inspired by (Park 2018). Gray-scale spectrograms with the size of 128×128 are prepared in the input layer. Instead of the popular 2D Conv, the convolution kernel of 1D Conv spans all the frequency of one time. As shown in Fig. 2, it mainly consists of 5 convolution layers with the kernel size of 4. After convolution layers, max-pooling layers with filter size of 4, 2 and 1 are applied in sequence. The last convolution layer with filter size of 1 is used instead of a fully connection layer (Lin 2014). Batch normalization and rectified linear unit (RELU) are applied behind each convolution layer. Before the softmax output layer, there are two dense layers with 1024 and 8 hidden units respectively. The dashed boxes in Fig. 2(a) are the regular CNN blocks.

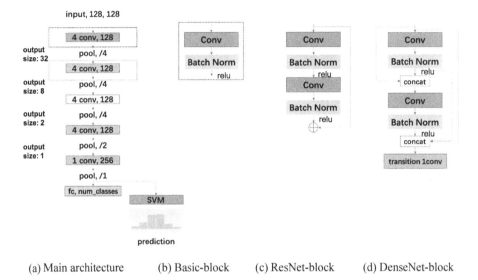

(a) Main architecture   (b) Basic-block   (c) ResNet-block   (d) DenseNet-block

Fig. 2. The proposed stacking model for music classification. (a) shows the main architecture with 5 convolution blocks and the SVM to predict the tags. (b) denotes the basic CNN block in the baseline model. (c)–(d) denotes the ResNet and DenseNet blocks to replace the basic one. (Color figure online)

4.2 Advanced Building Blocks

ResNet-Block Model. ResNet-block is inspired by residual learning (He 2016). The basic block idea is that $H(x)$ is considered as the desired underlying mapping when x is the input, then if one hypothesizes the net can approximate a residual function, i.e., $F(x) := H(x) - x$. The origin mapping becomes $F(x) + x$. Unlike (Kim 2018), we modified the ResNet-block to adapt the spectrogram input rather than the raw audio. As shown in Fig. 2(c), the ResNet-block contains two convolution layers. After the block, the max pooling layer is applied. A comparison experiment has been conducted by replacing the basic block of the black dotted box in Fig. 2(a).

DenseNet-Block Model The DenseNet-block is illustrated in Fig. 2(d). In some sense, DenseNet (Huang 2017) increases representational power of the basic CNN and capably improve performance over ResNet in classification tasks.

Contrary to the ResNet model, transition layers and connection methods are employed. Connectivity pattern in DenseNet is expressed $x_l = H_l([x_0, x_1, \ldots, x_{l-1}])$. the Lth layer receives the feature-maps of all former layers that is different from the $H_l(x) = F(x_{l-1}) + x_{l-1}$, which can alleviate the gradient vanishing problem, and feature reuse can present better performance with fewer parameters and lower computational cost than ResNet. One dense-block contains two convolution layers with filter size of 4 and the translation layer follows the dense block to prevent the channel growing exponentially. In the same way, the DenseNet-block is used to replace the basic block of the red dotted box in Fig. 2(a).

4.3 Ensemble of Audio Segments

During the data processing, a complete audio signal was clipped into small segments. Each segment is then predicted by the CNN classification model. Since these sliced segments belong to the same original audio clip, ensemble learning actually should be used. A common approach is to vote by selecting the most predicted labels among all segments as the final label. Inspired by (Gwardys 2014), however, we propose to use SVM as the stacking classifier. Feature vectors can be obtained by averaging each feature vector of each segment extracted from the trained CNN model, and handled by SVM for final genre prediction.

5 Experiments and Results

5.1 Dataset

Our proposed architectures are experimented on two different datasets: FMA-small and GTZAN. FMA-small dataset is a new influential music dataset to help alleviate data scarcity problem of MIR (Defferrard 2017), which contains 8000 tracks (.mp3 format) of 30 s per piece. There are 8 main genres with 1000 sub-classes per genre, such as Electronic, Experimental, Folk, Hip-hop, Instrumental, International, Pop, Rock. And most of them are with sampling rate of 44,100 Hz, bit rate 320 kb/s, and in stereo. The GTZAN dataset consists of 1000 audio tracks of 30 s long, which contains 10 genres with 100 tracks per genre. All tracks are 22,050 Hz, Mono 16-bit audio files in . wav format (Sturm 2012).

As described in Sect. 3, sound tracks are firstly processed into grayscale spectrograms and then is sliced into 10 segments with 2.56 s per one. As a result, images of 128×128 are input the model with 128 frequency bins as the channel. Data augmentation described in Sect. 3 is also employed.

5.2 Training Details

In all experiments, model training is implemented with SGD and the learning rate of $1e^{-2}$ and the decay of $1e^{-6}$. Dropout of 0.5 is applied to the output of the full connection layer. Zero padding is applied to each convolution layer to maintain its size. In addition, mini batch of 128 samples and regularization of L2 are used to prevent the model from overfitting.

5.3   Results

Table 1 summarizes the performance of baseline models with different parameters on FMA-small dataset. The kernel size of CNN cell is firstly optimized, where the model with kernel size of 4 outperform that of 3. In terms of ensemble methods, SVM offers higher accuracy than the voting method. When data augmentation is applied, significant improvement is achieved. Moreover, an interesting finding in Table 1 shows that the ResNet-block in the red box performs better than that in the black box. In our opinion, 1D-CNN in the black box connect the entire frequency range at once, which is different from other convolution layers to some extent.

Table 1. Summarization of test accuracies of the Baseline and ResNet models on FMA-small dataset. Note that k4 denotes the kernel size of 4 while k3 is of 3, data-aug represents the data augmentation, ResNet–black denotes that the ResNet block is in the black box in Fig. 2(a), and ResNet-red means in the red box.

Model+method	Accuracy (%)
Basic (k4+voting)	59.4
Basic (k3+SVM)	61.3
Basic (k4+SVM)	63.0
Basic (k4+SVM+data-aug)	64.7
ResNet-black (k4+SVM+data-aug)	63.7
ResNet-red (k4+SVM+data-aug)	66.3

Table 2. Comparison with previous state-of-the-art models on FMA-small and GTZAN. Note that ' ∼ ' denotes a round number because the accuracy is plot on the line chart but not provided.

Model	FMA-small	GTZAN
Transfer learning CNN (Gwardys 2014)	–	78.0
MRMR (Baniya 2014)	–	87.9
Transfer learning CNN (Choi 2017)	–	89.9
SVM (Arabi 2009)	–	90.8
Sparse representation-based classifier (Panagakis 2010)	–	93.7
SVM (Defferrard 2017)	54.8	–
Transfer learning CNN (Park 2018)	56.8	–
Transfer learning CNN (Lee 2019)	51.2 (∼)	92.2 (∼)
Our basic model	64.7	84.0
Our ResNet model	66.7	89.5
Our DenseNet model	68.9	90.2

Table 2 summarizes the results of our proposed DenseNet model compared to other state-of-the-art methods. On the FMA-small dataset, our models outperform all the previous results. Moreover, our proposed DenseNet model performs better than ResNet one owing to its strong feature extraction capability and cost less time to get a better result.

Since the FMA-small dataset is published in 2017 and related experiments are not many, we adapted our method to another dataset, i.e. GTZAN to compare with more approaches. Obviously, that also shows the better performance.

As can be seen, even without extra dataset, our DenseNet model performs close to the state-of-the-art deep learning method by using transfer learning CNN (Lee 2019). Note that our models which introducing the shortcut connections outperform (Park 2018) which using the same basic model by enhancing the representation of a layer.

6 Conclusion and Future Work

In this paper, a comprehensive study on music classification using a DenseNet deep learning method is conducted. To overcome the shortage of labelled music audio data, a music-specific data augmentation method is proposed with time overlapping and pitch shifting on spectrograms. Owing to the strong feature extraction capability of DenseNet, our stacking method achieves a state-of-the-art result on FMA-small dataset. We believe our presented approach can be adapted to other audio processing tasks.

In the future, we will investigate our DenseNet Model more thoroughly. We plan to investigate every layer expression and then try diverse connections. Then, we will adapt more advanced architectures which are designed for the image and language challenges in audio tasks.

Acknowledgement. This work was supported by Ping An Technology (Shenzhen) Co., Ltd, China.

References

He, K., Zhang, X., Ren, S., Sun, J.: Deep residual learning for image recognition. In: IEEE Conference on Computer Vision and Pattern Recognition (CVPR), Las Vegas, Nevada, pp. 770–778 (2016)

Huang, G., Liu, Z., van der Maaten, L.: Densely connected convolutional networks. In: IEEE Conference on Computer Vision and Pattern Recognition (CVPR), Honolulu, Hawaii, pp. 4700–4708 (2017)

Chathuranga, Y.M.D., Jayaratne, K.L.: Automatic music genre classification of audio signals with machine learning approaches. GSTF Int. J. Comput. (JoC) 3(2), 13 (2013)

Auguin, N., Huang, S., Fung, P.: Identification of live or studio versions of a song via supervised learning. In: Signal and Information Processing Association Annual Summit and Conference (APSIPA), pp. 1–4 (2013)

Costa, Y.M.G., Oliveira, L.S., Koericb, A.L., Gouyon, F.: Music genre recognition using spectrograms. In: 18th International Conference on Systems, Signals and Image Processing, pp. 1–4 (2011)

Dielman, S., Schrauwen, B.: End to end deep learning for music audio. In: IEEE International Conference on Music Information Retrieval (ISMIR) (2011)

Li, T., Ogihara, M., Li, Q.: A comparative study on content-based music genre classification. In: The 26th Annual International ACM SIGIR Conference on Research and Development in information Retrieval, pp. 282–289. ACM (2003)

Nakashika, T., Garcia, C., Takiguchi, T.: Local-feature-map integration using convolutional neural networks for music genre classification. In: 13th Annual Conference of the International Speech Communication Association (2012)

Dieleman, S., Schrauwen, B.: End-to-end learning for music audio. In: IEEE Acoustics, Speech and Signal Processing (ICASSP), pp. 6964– 6968 (2014)

Defferrard, M., Benzi, K., Vandergheynst, P., Bresson, X.: FMA: a dataset for music analysis. In: International Society for Music Information Retrieval Conference (ISMIR), pp. 316–323 (2017)

Sturm, B.L.: An analysis of the GTZAN music genre dataset. In: Proceedings of the Second International ACM Workshop on Music Information Retrieval with User-Centered and Multimodal Strategies, pp. 7–12. ACM (2012)

Aguiar, R.L., Costa, M.G.Y., Silla Jr, N.C.: Exploring data augmentation to improve music genre classification with convNets. In: International Joint Conference on Neural Networks (IJCNN) (2018)

Mubarak, O.M., Ambikai Rajah, E., Epps, J.: Novel features for effective speech and music discrimination. IEEE Engineering on Intelligent Systems, pp. 342–346 (2006)

Wyse, L.: Audio spectrogram representations for processing with Convolutional neural networks. In: Proceeding of the First International Workshop on Deep Learning for Music (2017)

Gwardys, G., Grzywczak, D.: Deep image features in music information retrieval. Int. J. Electron. Telecommun. 4(60), 321–326 (2014)

Lee, H., Pham, P., Largman, Y., Ng, A.Y.: Unsupervised feature learning for audio classification using convolutional deep belief networks. In: Neural Information Processing Systems, pp. 1096–1104 (2009)

Choi, K., Fazekas, G., Sandler, M.: Automatic tagging using deep convolutional neural networks. In: Society for Music Information Retrieval Conference, New York, NY, pp. 805–811 (2016)

Kim, T., Lee, J., Nam, J.: Sample-level CNN architectures for music auto- tagging using raw waveforms. In: IEEE International Conference on Acoustics, Speech, and Signal Processing, Aalborg, Denmark, pp. 366–370 (2018)

Schluter, J., Bock, S.: Musical onset detection with convolutional neural networks. In: 6th International Workshop on Machine Learning and Music (MML), Prague, Czech Republic (2013)

Tokozume, Y., Harada, T.: Learning environmental sounds with end-to-end convolutional neural network. In: IEEE International Conference on Acoustics, Speech and Signal Processing (ICASSP) (2017)

Nam, J., Choi, K., Lee, J.: Deep learning for audio-Based music classification and tagging. IEEE Signal Process. Mag. 36(1), 41–51 (2019)

Ulyanov, D., Lebedev, V.: Audio texture synthesis and style transfer (2016)

Park, J., Lee, J., Park, J., Ha, J., Nam, J.: Representation learning of music using artist labels. In: 19th International Society for Music Information Retrieval Conference (2018)

Lin, M., Chen, Q., Yan, S.: Network in network. In: Proceedings of ICLR (2014)

Choi, K., et al.: Transfer learning for music classification and regression tasks. In: 18th International Society of Music Information Retrieval (ISMIR) Conference, Suzhou, China (2017)

Arabi, A.F., Lu, G.: Enhanced polyphonic music genre classification using high level features. In: 2009 IEEE International Conference on Signal and Image Processing Applications (ICSIPA), pp. 101–106. IEEE (2009)

Panagakis, Y., Kotropoulos, C.: Music genre classification via topology preserving non-negative tensor factorization and sparse representations. In: 2010 IEEE International Conference on Acoustics Speech and Signal Processing (ICASSP), pp. 249–252. IEEE (2010)

Donmoon, L., Lee, J., Park, J., Lee, K.: Enhancing music features by knowledge transfer from user-item log data. In: Accepted paper at the International Conference on Acoustics, Speech, and Signal Processing (ICASSP) (2019)

Baniya, B.K., Ghimire, D., Lee, J.: A novel approach of automatic music genre classification based on timbrai texture and rhythmic content features. In: International Conference on IEEE Advanced Communication Technology (ICACT), pp. 96-102 (2014)

Bayesian Classifier Modeling for Dirty Data

Hongya Wang[1]([✉]), Weidong Cheng[1], Kaiyan Guo[1], Yingyuan Xiao[2], and Zhenyu Liu[3]

[1] School of Computer Science and Technology, Donghua University, Shanghai, China
hywang@dhu.edu.cn
[2] School of CSE, Tianjin University of Technology, Tianjin, China
yyxiao@tjut.edu.cn
[3] Shanghai Key Laboratory of Computer Software Testing and Evaluation, Shanghai, China

Abstract. Bayesian classifiers have been proven effective in many practical applications. To train a Bayesian classifier, important parameters such as prior and class conditional probabilities need to be learned from datasets. In practice, datasets are prone to errors due to dirty (missing, erroneous or duplicated) values, which will severely affect the model accuracy if no data cleaning task is enforced. However, cleaning the whole dataset is prohibitively laborious and thus infeasible for even medium-sized datasets. To this end, we propose to induce Bayes models by cleaning only small samples of the dataset. We derive confidence intervals as a function of sample size after data cleaning. In this way, the posterior probability is guaranteed to fall into the estimated confidence intervals with constant probability. Then, we design two strategies to compare the posterior probability intervals if overlap exists. Extension to semi-naive Bayes method is also addressed. Experimental results suggest that cleaning only a small number of samples can train satisfactory Bayesian models, offering significant improvement in cost over cleaning all of the data and significant improvement on precision, recall and F-Measure over cleaning none of the data.

Keywords: Bayesian classifiers · Data cleaning · Probability intervals

1 Introduction

Bayesian classifiers are statistical classifiers. They can predict class membership probabilities, that is, the probability that a given sample belongs to a particular class [4]. Naive Bayesian classifiers assume that attributes are independent with each other, which simplifies the computation involved and, in this sense, is considered naive [8]. Semi-naive Bayesian classifiers consider the dependencies among attributes. In order to avoid massive calculation, semi-naive Bayesian classifiers assume one attribute depends on only another one [10].

© Springer Nature Switzerland AG 2019
A. C. Nayak and A. Sharma (Eds.): PRICAI 2019, LNAI 11672, pp. 66–79, 2019.
https://doi.org/10.1007/978-3-030-29894-4_6

An industry survey shows that more than 25% of the critical data in top companies contained significant data errors [11]. Real-world data are commonly integrated from multiple sources, and the integration process may lead to a variety of data errors, such as incorrect values and duplicate representations of the same real-world entity [5]. While some domain-specific softwares have been developed for data cleaning, it is widely recognized that, in order to obtain reliable results, many cleaning techniques need humans to get involved. Thus, the procedure of data cleaning is often costly and time-consuming [1].

As will be shown shortly in Sect. 3.1, training a Bayesian classifier with dirty data may jeopardize classification accuracy dramatically. In order to deal with dirty data in Bayesian modeling, we usually have the following options: (1) Cleaning the whole dirty data, which leads to huge cost and, (2) Applying point estimation, namely, drawing a sample set and then cleaning the samples to train a Bayesian model. While in this case we decrease the cleaning cost, no theoretical guarantee is provided over the consistency between the models trained by point estimation and induced with the whole clean training set.

To this end, we propose IBCM, a probability-Interval-based Bayesian Classifier Modeling framework. With IBCM, we derive confidence intervals as a function of sample size for class conditional and prior probabilities after data cleaning. In this way, the posterior probability is guaranteed to fall into the estimated confidence intervals with constant probability. Two strategies are introduced to compare the overlapped posterior probability intervals. Both naive and seminaive Bayes methods are supported in our IBCM framework. To verify the effectiveness of IBCM, we conduct extensive experiments on four real datasets. The results suggest that cleaning only a small number of samples can train satisfactory Bayesian models, offering significant improvement in cost over cleaning all of the data and significant improvement on precision, recall and F-Measure over cleaning none of the data. It is worth nothing that we focus on Bayesian classifier modeling on dirty data from the efficiency point of view. How to build a more accurate and effective Bayesian classifier is beyond the scope of this paper.

The paper is organized as follows. Section 2 introduces the preliminaries and related work. We discuss IBCM in Sect. 3 and the two interval comparison strategies are presented in Sect. 4. We give the experimental results and discussions in Sect. 5. Section 6 concludes the paper.

2 Preliminary and Related Work

2.1 Naive Bayesian Classifier

The naive Bayesian classifier works as follows. Let T be a training set of samples, each with their class labels. There are k classes, $C_1, C_2, \ldots, C_k$. Each sample is represented by a n-dimensional vector, $X = \{x_1, x_2, \ldots, x_n\}$, depicting n measured values of the n attributes, $A_1, A_2, \ldots, A_n$, respectively. Given a sample X, the classifier will label X as the class with the highest posterior probability, i.e., the class that maximizes $P(C_i|X)$. By Bayes' theorem, $P(C_i|X) = \frac{P(X|C_i)P(C_i)}{P(X)}$.

As $P(X)$ is the same for all classes, the goal is reduced to compute $P(X|C_i)P(C_i)$ for each C_i.

In order to reduce computation overhead in evaluating $P(X|C_i)P(C_i)$, the assumption of class conditional independence is made, i.e., $P(X|C_i) = \prod_{k=1}^{n} P(x_k|C_i)$. The class conditional probability $P(x_1|C_i)$, $P(x_2|C_i)$, ..., $P(x_n|C_i)$ can easily be estimated from the training set. Naive Bayesian classifier treats discrete and continuous attribute somewhat differently. If A_k is discrete attribute, then $P(x_k|C_i)$ is modeled by a single real number between 0 and 1 which represents the probability that the attribute A_k will take on the particular value x_k in the case of C_i. If A_k is a continuous attribute, then for each class C_i μ_{C_i} follows a normal distribution with mean μ.

2.2 Semi-naive Bayesian Classifier

The posterior probability is calculated as $P(C_i|x_1, x_2) = P(C_i|x_2) \times \frac{P(x_1|C_i, x_2)}{P(x_1|x_2)}$ for semi-naive Bayesian classifier. The semi-naive Bayesian classifier uses the same method as the naive Bayesian classifier to compute parameters for discrete attributes. For two continuous attributes, semi-naive Bayesian classifier assumes that the two continuous attributes obey a two-dimensional normal distribution. The distribution of random variables X and Y that satisfy the following probability density distribution is called a two-dimensional normal distribution. (1) $f(x, y) = \theta \times exp(\eta \times \varepsilon)$. (2) $\theta = \frac{1}{2\pi\sigma_1\sigma_2\sqrt{1-\rho^2}}$. (3) $\eta = -\frac{1}{2(1-\rho^2)}$. (4) $\varepsilon = \frac{(x-\mu_1)^2}{\sigma_1^2} - \frac{2\rho(x-\mu_1)(y-\mu_2)}{\sigma_1\sigma_2} + \frac{(y-\mu_2)^2}{\sigma_2^2}$. ρ is correlation coefficient, and different ρ corresponds to different two-dimensional normal distribution.

2.3 Data Cleaning

It is becoming easier for enterprises to store and acquire large amounts of data. These datasets can facilitate decision making, richer analytics, and increasingly, provide training data for Machine Learning. However, data quality remains to be a major concern, and dirty data can lead to incorrect decisions and unreliable analysis. Examples of common errors include missing values, typos, mixed formats, replicated entries of the same real-world entity [?], and violations of rules [16]. Analysts must consider the effects of dirty data before making any decisions, and as a result, data cleaning is a key area of database research [14]. In this paper, we focus on two types of data errors: value errors and duplication errors.

Data cleaning is a broad area that encompasses extraction, deduplication, schema matching, and many other problems in relational data. While significant progress has been made in data cleaning, cleaning the entire data is still time consuming [13,17], and often requires user confirmation or crowdsourcing [3,15] to achieve satisfactory data quality. Thus, data cleaning is generally laborious and costly for large datasets.

3   IBCM Framework

3.1   Motivation

The following example shows that training Bayesian classifiers with dirty data may jeopardize classification accuracy.

Table 1. Toy example for Bayesian classifier modeling

Weight	Color	Shape	Good Apple	#dup
111(**106**)	green	irregular	No	2(**1**)
152	red	irregular	Yes	1
148	green(**red**)	circle	Yes	1
145	red(**green**)	circle	Yes(**No**)	1
147	green	irregular	No	2(**1**)
118	red	circle	Yes	1
135	green	circle(**irregular**)	No	1
121	red	circle(**irregular**)	No	3(**1**)
109	green	circle	No	1
138	red	irregular(**circle**)	Yes	1

In Table 1, the values in bold font indicate the correct values after data cleaning. *Good Apple* is the class attribute, and *Weight, Color, Shape* are observable attributes. Among these attributes, *Weight* is continuous, and *Color, Shape* and *Good Apple* are discrete. *#dup* represents the number of tuples duplicated.

Consider the dirty data in Table 1 and choose the naive Bayesian classifier for classification. We use the correct and dirty versions in Table 1 to train two Bayesian models, and then compare the classification accuracy of the two models. Assume that we have one test data {126, *red, circle*}. We can calculate the posterior probability $P(No|Weight = 126, red, circle) = 0.0012$ and $P(Yes|Weight = 126, red, circle) = 0.0042$ with the correct values. The test data {126, *red, circle*} belongs to the class "*Yes*". In contrast, we can calculate the posterior probability $P(No|Weight = 126, red, circle) = 0.0040$ and $P(Yes|Weight = 126, red, circle) = 0.0019$ with the dirty data. The test data {126, *red, circle*} belongs to the class "*No*". We can see that dirty data lead to the change of posterior probability and affect the result of classification.

In order to deal with the dirty data in Bayesian modeling, we usually have the following two options: (1) Cleaning the whole dirty data, which leads to huge cost and, (2) Applying point estimation, namely, drawing a sample set and then cleaning the samples to train a Bayesian model. While in this case we decrease the cleaning cost significantly, no theoretical guarantee is provided over the consistency between the models trained by point estimation and with the whole clean training set. To this end, we propose IBCM, a novel approach utilizing the Central Limit Theorem (CLT) and interval estimation to ensure that the posterior probability falls into the estimated confidence interval with constant probability.

3.2   Parameter Estimates Without Data Errors

We first introduce the parameter estimation using sampled data without data errors. We start with the dataset D of N tuples. From D, we draw a subset S of i.i.d samples with size K. Consider the discrete attribute in D. Suppose the proportions of a certain attribute value in D and S is denoted by m and m', respectively. According to the CLT, m' approximately follows the normal distribution $N(m, \frac{m(1-m)}{K})$. Thus, we can define a confidence interval of m parameterized by α (e.g., 95% indicates $Z_{\alpha/2} = 1.96$): $m' \pm Z_{\alpha/2}\sqrt{\frac{m'(1-m')}{K}}$.

Suppose we want to estimate the mean of a continuous attribute in D. We can calculate the mean of the continuous attribute in S and the CLT states that the estimate follows a normal distribution $N(mean(D), \frac{var(D)}{K})$. Thus, we can define a confidence interval of $mean(D)$ parameterized by α (e.g., 95% indicates $Z_{\alpha/2} = 1.96$): $mean(S) \pm Z_{\alpha/2}\sqrt{\frac{var(S)}{K}}$.

3.3   Estimation with Data Errors

Suppose D_{clean} is the correct version of the dirty data population D. We are interested in estimating the distribution of attributes in D_{clean}. However, since we do not have the cleaned data in the first place, we cannot directly sample from D_{clean}. We must draw our sample from the dirty data D and then clean the sample. We consider two types of errors: value error and duplication error. Reference [7] provides methods for dealing with value errors and duplication errors.

Value errors are caused by incorrect attribute values. These errors do not affect the size of the population, i.e., $|D| = |D_{clean}|$. Furthermore, correcting a value error only affects an individual tuple. Consequently, if we correct a tuple, we still preserve the uniform sampling properties of the sample, S. In other words, the probability that a given tuple is sampled does not change due to data cleaning.

Since duplication errors affect multiple tuples and the size of D_{clean} is different from the size of D, they do affect the uniformity of sampling. The duplicated data is more likely to be sampled and thus be over-represented in the estimate. Therefore, modification in estimates is needed. For each tuple $t_i \in S$, let m_i denote its number of duplicates in D. (1) For discrete attribute, The cleaned value of t_i is equal to the number of dirty value of t_i divided by m_i. (2) For continuous attribute, the result has to be scaled by the duplication rate $d = \frac{K}{K'}$, where $K' = \sum_{i=1}^{n} \frac{1}{m_i}$. The cleaned value is equal to the dirty value times d, and then divided by m_i. [7] proves that the above treatment of these two types of errors is unbiased.

Getting back to the example in Table 1 and assuming the test data is {126, *green*, *irregular*}, we will show how the confidence intervals for prior and class conditional probabilities are calculated in the presence of dirty data. For continuous attribute, assume we want to calculate the class conditional probability $P(Weight = 126|No)$. It is easy to see that the duplication rate is $d = \frac{10}{\frac{1}{2}+\frac{1}{1}+\cdots+\frac{1}{1}} = 1.2$. The values of cleaned column Weight under the condition of category No is equal to $\{\frac{1.2 \times 106}{2}, \frac{1.2 \times 145}{1}, \ldots, \frac{1.2 \times 109}{1}\}$. We calculate $mean(S)$ and $var(S)$ for cleaned column *Weight* under the condition of category *No* and return $mean(S) \pm Z_{\alpha/2}\sqrt{\frac{var(S)}{K}}$ as the estimated confidence interval, where $Z_{\alpha/2}$ is a constant derived from the user-specified confidence level. For discrete attribute, assume we want to calculate the class conditional probability $P(Color = green|No)$. Since we needn't to calculate the duplication rate for discrete attribute, we can easily obtain the number of *green* value for the clean column *Color* under the condition of category *No*, namely $\{\frac{1}{2}, \frac{1}{1}, \ldots, \frac{1}{1}\}$. We calculate m' for the value of *green* in clean column *Color* under the condition of category *No* and return $m' \pm Z_{\alpha/2}\sqrt{\frac{m'(1-m')}{K}}$ as the estimated population proportion interval, where $Z_{\alpha/2}$ is a constant derived from the user-specified confidence level.

3.4   Calculation of Posterior Probability Intervals

The posterior probability is equal to the product of the class conditional probability and the prior probability. In order to get the two endpoints of each posterior probability interval, we have to obtain the two endpoints of each class conditional and prior probability interval first. Since the confidence interval of the discrete attribute is just the probability interval, we can directly use the value of the two endpoints of the interval for multiplication.

For continuous attributes, identifying the two endpoints is more complicated since we assume that attributes are normally distributed, and the mean value is an interval. Thus, we actually obtain a family of density functions. For the sake of convenience, we let $u = mean(S)$, $t = Z_{\alpha/2}\sqrt{\frac{var(S)}{K}}$. The confidence interval of $mean(D)$ is $[u - t, u + t]$. We will show how we calculate the probability interval for continuous attribute for the naive and semi-naive Bayesian classifier respectively.

In the naive Bayesian classifier, given an x (x is determined by test data, namely a certain value of continuous attribute in the test data), we calculate the maximum value and minimum value of the density function according to the following two cases. (1) If x falls within $[u - t, u + t]$, the maximum value is taken at the midpoint of the interval, namely u, and the minimum value must be taken at either the left endpoint $u - t$ or the right endpoint $u + t$ of the interval. (2) If x does not fall within $[u - t, u + t]$, then the density function will be either monotonically increasing or monotonically decreasing on $[u - t, u + t]$. If the density function is monotonically increasing on $[u - t, u + t]$, the maximum value is taken at $u + t$, and the minimum value is taken at $u - t$. If the density

---

ALGORITHM 1. Computing probability intervals with IBCM

Given a sample S and columns $A_1, A_2, \ldots, A_k$;
Clean the sample for value errors and duplication errors;
for $i = 1; i \leq k; i + +$ do
    if A_i *is continuous attribute* **then**
        Get the confidence interval of $mean(D)$;
        return $mean(S) \pm Z_{\alpha/2} \sqrt{\frac{var(S)}{K}}$;
        Convert the confidence interval into the probability interval;
    end
    else
        Get the confidence interval of m;
        return $m' \pm Z_{\alpha/2} \sqrt{\frac{m'(1-m')}{K}}$;
        The confidence interval $m' \pm Z_{\alpha/2} \sqrt{\frac{m'(1-m')}{K}}$ is the probability interval;
    end
end
Calculate posterior probability intervals;

---

function is monotonically decreasing on $[u-t, u+t]$, the maximum value is taken at $u - t$, and the minimum value is taken at $u + t$.

In the semi-naive Bayesian classifier, given an x and a y (x and y are determined by test data, namely two values of two different continuous attributes in the test data), we will first rewrite $f(x, y)$ as a function of $f(\mu_1, \mu_2)$ by symmetry. We let $[u_1 - t_1, u_1 + t_1]$ and $[u_2 - t_2, u_2 + t_2]$ be the confidence interval of two mean values. We calculate the first order partial derivative with respect to μ_1 and μ_2 and set $\frac{\partial f}{\partial \mu_1} = 0$, $\frac{\partial f}{\partial \mu_2} = 0$. Thus, we can easily solve for μ_1 and μ_2. If μ_1 falls within $[u_1 - t_1, u_1 + t_1]$ and μ_2 falls within $[u_2 - t_2, u_2 + t_2]$, we should compare (μ_1, μ_2), $(u_1 - t_1, u_2 - t_2)$, $(u_1 - t_1, u_2 + t_2)$, $(u_1 + t_1, u_2 - t_2)$ and $(u_1 + t_1, u_2 + t_2)$. By comparing the values of the above five points in the density function, we can get the maximum value and minimum value of the density function. If μ_1 does not fall within $[u_1 - t_1, u_1 + t_1]$ or μ_2 does not fall within $[u_2 - t_2, u_2 + t_2]$, we should compare $(u_1 - t_1, u_2 - t_2)$, $(u_1 - t_1, u_2 + t_2)$, $(u_1 + t_1, u_2 - t_2)$ and $(u_1 + t_1, u_2 + t_2)$. By comparing the values of the above four points in the density function, we can get the maximum value and minimum value of the density function.

Once the probability intervals for class conditional and prior probabilities are obtained, calculating the posterior probability intervals is trivial. To sum up, we present the procedure of IBCM in Algorithm 1. As shown in Algorithm 1, for continuous attribute, we need to convert the confidence interval of $mean(D)$ into a probability interval following the aforementioned discussion. For discrete attribute, the confidence interval can be directly used as the class conditional or prior probability intervals, because the confidence interval of discrete attribute is the probability interval. Therefore, the posterior probability interval can be obtained by multiplying the class conditional probability intervals with the prior probability intervals (the product of two intervals is equal to multiply the left endpoints and the right endpoints of these two intervals respectively).

3.5   Theoretical Guarantee

As discussed earlier, for discrete and continuous attributes, the class conditional probability or prior probability fall into the estimated interval with confidence level α.

Theorem 1. *The probability that the true posterior probability falls into the posterior probability interval is greater than or equal to α^n (n is the number of attributes involved, typically $\alpha = 0.95$).*

Proof. Since we only care about the classification problem, the posterior probability is equal to the class conditional probability times the prior probability. Let B be the posterior probability, and let $A_1 \ldots A_n$ be the class conditional probability. According to Bayes' theorem, we have the equation $P(B) = P(A_1)P(A_2) \ldots P(A_n)$ (we ignore the prior probability since they are same for all cases). We know $P(B)$ and $P(A_1)P(A_2) \ldots P(A_n)$ are probability intervals. We also know $A_1 \ldots A_n$ have a *alpha* probability of falling within their respective probability interval. Thus, the worst probability that B falls into $P(B)$ is equal to α^n.

4   Interval Comparison

In this section the problem of comparing the probability intervals with overlaps is considered.

4.1   BoL Strategy

Suppose the two probability intervals are $a = [a^L, a^U]$ and $b = [b^L, b^U]$. In addition, we define the lengths of the two intervals as $L(a) = a^U - a^L$ and $L(b) = b^U - b^L$. Let $P(a \geq b)$ the possibility of $a \geq b$. As discussed in [2], $P(a \geq b)$ is defined as $P(a \geq b) = \frac{max[0, L(a) + L(b) - max(0, b^U - a^L)]}{L(a) + L(b)}$, which has the following properties: (1) If $P(a \geq b) = P(b \geq a)$, then $P(a \geq b) = P(b \geq a) = \frac{1}{2}$. (2) $P(a \geq b) + P(b \geq a) = 1$. (3) If $a \geq b$, then $P(a \geq b) \geq \frac{1}{2}$. If $P(a \geq b) \geq \frac{1}{2}$, then $a \geq b$. Property (3) can be used as the criteria for comparing two probability intervals.

Theorem 2. *If $a \geq b$, then the midpoint of a is greater than or equal to the midpoint of b.*

Proof. For the two intervals $a = [a^L, a^U]$ and $b = [b^L, b^U]$, $P(a \geq b) = max[0, a^U - a^L + b^U - b^L - max(0, b^U - a^L)]/(a^U - a^L + b^U - b^L)$ by definition. If $a \geq b$, then $P(a \geq b) \geq \frac{1}{2}$, which means $max[0, a^U - a^L + b^U - b^L - max(0, b^U - a^L)]/(a^U - a^L + b^U - b^L) \geq \frac{1}{2}$. Due to $a^U - a^L + b^U - b^L - max(0, b^U - a^L) \geq 0$, we can simplify the inequality as $a^U - a^L + b^U - b^L - max(0, b^U - a^L)/(a^U - a^L + b^U - b^L) \geq \frac{1}{2}$. Through the transposition, we obtain $\frac{a^U - a^L + b^U - b^L}{2} \geq max(0, b^U - a^L)$. If $b^U - a^L \leq 0$, then the above inequality is permanent establishment, which means the interval a is constantly greater than or equal to the interval b. If $b^U - a^L > 0$, then we can obtain the following inequality $\frac{a^U - a^L + b^U - b^L}{2} \geq b^U - a^L$. Through the transposition, we can finally get the inequality $\frac{a^L + a^U}{2} - \frac{b^L + b^U}{2} \geq 0$. It states clearly that the midpoint of the interval a is greater than or equal to the midpoint of the interval b.

Theorem 2 indicates that interval comparison is closely related with the comparison of the corresponding midpoints under the BoL strategy. In practice, using the BoL strategy makes interval comparison easier. As long as we know the two endpoints and the length of each interval, we can do interval comparison for overlapped posterior probability intervals.

4.2 BoAR Strategy

In BoAR strategy, we assume the true probabilities obey uniform distribution in a and b respectively, which are independent with each other. Therefore, the possible relationship between a and b can be transformed into the following problem: Find the value u and v randomly drawn from interval a and interval b, and then calculate the probability of u greater than or equal to v, that is, $P(a \geq b)$. The joint probability density function $h(u, v)$ of the two-dimensional random variable (u, v) is $h(u, v) = \frac{1}{(a^U - a^L)(b^U - b^L)}$.

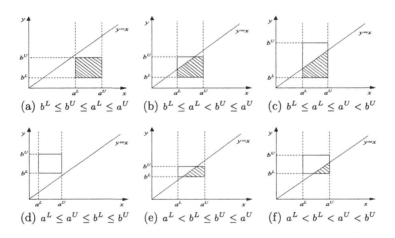

Fig. 1. Six cases for the probability density functions of u and v

In Fig. 1, x-coordinate indicates the data range of u, and y-coordinate indicates the data range of v. By the relationship between the boundary points of u and v, and the position relation between the boundary region and the line $y = x$, the probability density functions of u and v can be classified into six cases [6]. The probability $P(a \geq b)$ is the ratio of the shaded area to the rectangular area in Fig. 1.

According to the six cases for the probability density of u and v, we can figure out the formula of the possibility for each case. (1) $b^L \leq a^L$: (a) $b^U \leq a^L$, the distribution of $h(u, v)$ is shown in Fig. 1(a). We can get $P(a \geq b) = 1$. (b) $a^L < b^U \leq a^U$, the distribution of $h(u, v)$ is shown in Fig. 1(b). We can get $P(a \geq b) = 1 - \frac{1}{2} \frac{(b^U - a^L)^2}{L(a)L(b)}$. (c) $b^U > a^U$, the distribution of $h(u, v)$ is shown in Fig. 1(c). We can get $P(a \geq b) = \frac{1}{2} \frac{(a^L + a^U - 2b^L)}{L(b)}$. (2) $b^L > a^L$: (a) $a^U \leq b^L$, the distribution of $h(u, v)$ is shown in Fig. 1(d). We can get $P(a \geq b) = 0$. (b) $b^U \leq a^U$, the distribution of $h(u, v)$ is shown in Fig. 1(e). We can get $P(a \geq b) = \frac{1}{2} \frac{(2a^U - b^U - b^L)}{L(a)}$. (c) $b^U > a^U > b^L$, the distribution of $h(u, v)$ is shown in Fig. 1(f). We can get $P(a \geq b) = \frac{1}{2} \frac{(a^U - b^L)^2}{L(a)L(b)}$. As in BoL strategy, $a \geq b$ if $P(a \geq b) \geq \frac{1}{2}$.

5 Experiments

5.1 Experimental Settings and Datasets

In our experiments, we adopt three performance measures commonly used in machine learning, i.e., Precision, Recall and F-Measure. We evaluate the efficacy of our approach by controlling the following parameters: (1) Error%: The number of tuples affected by the error, ranging from 0% (all of the tuples clean) to 100% (all of the tuples dirty) for value and duplication errors. (2) Sampling Ratio%: The proportion of tuples that are sampled from the entire dataset.

We compare IBCM with either cleaning none of the data (AllDirty) or cleaning all of the data (AllClean) for naive and semi-naive Bayesian classifier. We used the following four datasets in the experiments.

(1) The SUSY dataset is from the UCI Machine Learning Repository. The data in SUSY dataset has been produced by using Monte Carlo simulations. The SUSY dataset contains about 5,000,000 rows with 17 feature columns and 1 categorical column.
(2) The Adult dataset is from the UCI Machine Learning Repository, which has census information. The Adult dataset contains about 48,842 rows with 14 feature columns and 1 categorical column. In the 14 feature columns of the Adult dataset, 6 feature columns are continuous, and the others are discrete.
(3) The Letter dataset is from the UCI Machine Learning Repository. The Letter dataset contains about 20,000 rows with 16 feature columns and 1 categorical column. All of the columns in the Letter dataset are discrete.
(4) The Bank dataset is related with direct marketing campaigns of a Portuguese banking institution. The Bank dataset contains about 45,224 rows with 16 feature columns and 1 categorical column. In the 16 feature columns of the Bank dataset, 3 feature columns are continuous, and the others are discrete.

Due to space limitation, we only report the results for SUSY dataset since it is of the largest size. The similar trends are observed for all the other datasets. The Naive Bayesian classifier is used as the default unless stated otherwise.

5.2   BoL vs. BoAR

We compare two interval comparison strategies in fixed error rate (30%) and sampling ratio (10%).

Table 2. BoL vs. BoAR for the SUSY dataset

	Precision	Recall	F-Measure
BoL	0.7341	0.9066	0.7843
BoAR	0.7289	0.9235	0.7919

In Table 2, we can see that the recall and F-Measure of BoAR strategy are better than those of BoL strategy, respectively. The precision of BoAR strategy is slightly lower than that of BoL strategy. Since BoL strategy do not utilize the distribution within the probability interval, the effect of BoL strategy is less accurate than that of BoAR. In the remaining experiments, BoAR is used as the default since it is superior to the BoL strategy.

5.3   IBCM with Different Error Ratios

We evaluated IBCM for a fixed sample size, and for each type of error, we varied the error percentage. For our experiments, we cleaned 10% of the training set, and evaluated the precision, recall and F-Measure.

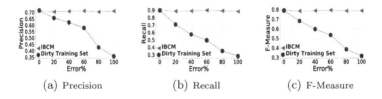

(a) Precision   (b) Recall   (c) F-Measure

Fig. 2. Results with different error ratios for the SUSY dataset

In Fig. 2(a), one can observe that the precision for dirty training set drops dramatically as the error rate increases. We repeated the same experiment for recall and F-Measure in Figs. 2(b) and (c), and then observed similar trends. Thus, using dirty data in Bayesian classifier modeling will get inaccurate results. However, with IBCM, we can see the precision, recall and F-Measure improve significantly compared with AllDirty. Therefore, IBCM appears to be more stable, that is, its performance is not dependent on the rate of errors. To sum up, IBCM is robust and returns more accurate results, regardless of the proportion of errors in the data set.

5.4   IBCM with Different Sample Sizes

We evaluated IBCM for a fixed proportion of errors and varied the sampling ratio. In addition, we uniformly sampled from the dataset and compared IBCM with AllClean and All Dirty. For the following experiments, we set a fixed error rate (30%), and evaluated the precision, recall and F-Measure.

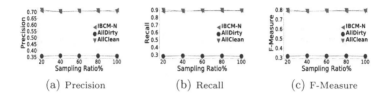

(a) Precision   (b) Recall   (c) F-Measure

Fig. 3. Performance of IBCM-N with different sampling ratios for the SUSY dataset

In Fig. 3, IBCM-N stands for applying naive Bayes method in the IBCM framework. We can see that as the sample size increases, the precision, recall and F-Measure for IBCM-N, AllDirty and AllClean almost have no change. The most likely reason is that when the number of samples reaches a certain threshold, the statistical probability tends to be stable. Results in Fig. 3 suggest that IBCM can quickly converge to the optimum and outperform AllDirty even though only a small number of sampled are cleaned. Particularly, we find that after cleaning only 6000 tuples (0.15% of all tuples), we are able to estimate more accurately than AllDirty. In addition, we observe that the effect of cleaning 0.15% for AllDirty is close to the effect of AllClean. As we all know, data cleaning is laborious and costly because many data cleaning techniques need humans to get involved in order to obtain reliable results. Therefore, IBCM achieves better results by cleaning only a small number of samples, which greatly improves the classification performance of Bayesian classifier and reduces the cleaning cost significantly.

5.5   Semi-naive Bayes Method

We also evaluated the semi-naive Bayes method in our IBCM framework with a fixed error rate (30%). When using semi-naive Bayes method, we choose two attributes that are actually related. It is worth noting that our purpose is not to compare the classification accuracy of the naive and semi-naive Bayes methods, but to illustrate that IBCM supports both methods well.

In Fig. 4, IBCM-S stands for applying the semi-naive Bayes method in the IBCM framework. We can see that using the semi-naive Bayes method to calculate internal parameters for two attributes which are actually correlated, the precision, recall and F-Measure improves significantly compared with the naive Bayes method. As expected, IBCM performs as well as AllClean, which means the proposed method supports both the naive and semi-naive Bayes methods.

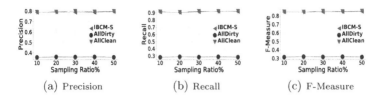

(a) Precision   (b) Recall   (c) F-Measure

Fig. 4. Performance of IBCM-S with different sampling ratios for the SUSY dataset

6   Conclusion

In this paper, we present IBCM, a novel approach that cleans only small samples of the dataset to train a Bayesian model. Our analysis and experimental results suggest that a few cleaned samples can train a good Bayesian model, offering significant improvement in cost over cleaning all of the data and significant improvement on precision, recall and F-Measure over cleaning none of the data.

Acknowledgment. The work reported in this paper is partially supported by NSFC under grant number 61370205 and NSF of Xinjiang Key Laboratory under grant number 2019D04024.

References

1. Fan, W., Li, J., Ma, S., Tang, N., Yu, W.: Towards certain fixes with editing rules and master data. PVLDB **3**(1), 173–184 (2010)
2. Nakahara, Y.: User oriented ranking criteria and its application to fuzzy mathematical programming problems. Fuzzy Sets Syst. **94**(3), 275–286 (1998)
3. Franklin, M.J., Kossmann, D., Kraska, T., et al.: CrowdDB: answering queries with crowdsourcing. In: SIGMOD Conference, pp. 61–72 (2011)
4. Bounhas, M., Mellouli, K., Prade, H., Serrurier, M.: From Bayesian classifiers to possibilistic classifiers for numerical data. In: Deshpande, A., Hunter, A. (eds.) SUM 2010. LNCS (LNAI), vol. 6379, pp. 112–125. Springer, Heidelberg (2010). https://doi.org/10.1007/978-3-642-15951-0_15
5. Lee, M.L., Ling, T.W., Low, W.L.: IntelliClean: a knowledge-based intelligent data cleaner. In: SIGKDD Conference, pp. 290–294 (2000)
6. Sengupta, A., Pal, T.K.: On comparing interval numbers. Eur. J. Oper. Res. **127**(1), 28–43 (2000)
7. Wang, J., Krishnan, S., Franklin, M.J., Goldberg, K., Kraska, T., Milo, T.: A sample-and-clean framework for fast and accurate query processing on dirty data. In: SIGMOD Conference, pp. 469–480 (2014)
8. Kazmierska, J., Malicki, J.: Application of the Naive Bayesian Classifier to optimize treatment decisions. Radiother. Oncol. **86**(2), 211–216 (2008)
9. Li, J., Yang, D., Ji, C.: Mine weighted network motifs via Bayes' theorem. In: ICSAI, pp. 448–452 (2017)
10. Zheng, Z., Webb, G.I.: Lazy learning of Bayesian rules. Mach. Learn. **41**(1), 53–84 (2000)
11. Swartz, N.: Gartner warns firms of 'dirty data'. Inf. Manage. J. **41**(3) (2007)

12. Gokhale, C., et al.: Corleone: hands-off crowdsourcing for entity matching. In: SIGMOD Conference, pp. 601–612 (2014)
13. Kolb, L., Thor, A., Rahm, E.: Dedoop: efficient deduplication with hadoop. PVLDB **5**(12), 1878–1881 (2012)
14. Rahm, E., Do, H.H.: Data cleaning: problems and current approaches. IEEE Data Eng. Bull. **23**(4), 3–13 (2000)
15. Kittur, A., Chi, E.H., Suh, B.: Crowdsourcing user studies with Mechanical Turk. In: SIGCHI Conference, pp. 453–456 (2008)
16. Beskales, G., Ilyas, I.F., Golab, L.: Sampling the repairs of functional dependency violations under hard constraints. PVLDB **3**(1–2), 197–207 (2010)
17. Khayyat, Z., Ilyas, I.F., Jindal, A., et al.: BigDansing: a system for big data cleansing. In: SIGMOD Conference, pp. 1215–1230 (2015)

Adversarial Feature Distillation for Facial Expression Recognition

Mengchao Bai[1,2], Xi Jia[1,2], Weicheng Xie[1,2], and Linlin Shen[1,2(✉)]

[1] School of Computer Science and Software Engineering, Shenzhen University,
Shenzhen, People's Republic of China
{baimengchao2017,jiaxi}@email.szu.edu.cn, {wcxie,llshen}@szu.edu.cn
[2] Guangdong Key Laboratory of Intelligent Information Processing,
Shenzhen University, Shenzhen, People's Republic of China

Abstract. Human face image contains abundant information including expression, age and gender, etc. Therefore, extracting discriminative feature for certain attribute while expelling others is critical for single facial attribute analysis. In this paper, we propose an adversarial facial expression recognition system, named expression distilling and dispelling learning (ED^2L), to extract discriminative expression feature from a given face image. The proposed ED^2L framework composed of two branches, i.e. expression distilling branch ED^2L-t and expression dispelling branch ED^2L-p. The ED^2L-t branch aims to extract the expression-related feature, while the ED^2L-p branch extracts the non-related feature. The disentangled features jointly serve as a complete representation of the face. Extensive experiments on several benchmark databases, i.e. the CK+, MMI, BU-3DFE and Oulu-CASIA, demonstrate the effectiveness of the proposed ED^2L framework.

Keywords: Facial expression recognition · Feature distilling ·
Feature dispelling · Adversarial learning

1 Introduction

Facial expression is one of the most important characteristics for people to express emotion and interact with others. In the field of computer vision and machine learning, numerous studies have been conducted on the facial expression recognition (FER) due to its practical importance in sociable robotics, medical treatment, driver fatigue surveillance, and many other human-computer interaction systems [1]. In [2], Ekman and Friesen firstly defined six basic emotions, including anger, disgust, fear, happiness, sadness and surprise. Contempt was subsequently added as one of the basic emotions [3].

The work is supported by National Natural Science Foundation of China (Grant No. 61672357, U1713214 and 61602315), the Science and Technology Project of Guangdong Province (Grant No. 2018A050501014) and the Science and Technology Innovation Commission of Shenzhen (Grant No. JCYJ20170302153827712).

A. C. Nayak and A. Sharma (Eds.): PRICAI 2019, LNAI 11672, pp. 80–92, 2019.
https://doi.org/10.1007/978-3-030-29894-4_7

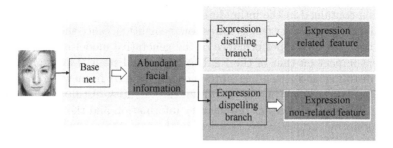

Fig. 1. Overview of our approach. A facial image contains abundant information. Our approach consists of two branches, which separate expression-related and non-related features for facial expression recognition by adversarial learning.

Current FER systems in the literature can be classified into two categories according to their feature extraction methods: hand-crafted features based methods and deep learning based methods. Majority of hand-crafted features based methods employed features such as LBP-TOP [4] and Gabor [5] to represent a given image. The extracted features are then used to classify facial expressions by Support Vector Machine (SVM) [6] or Nearest Neighbor classifier. Zhao and Pietikainen [4] proposed the LBP-TOP operator for expression recognition, which extracts co-occurrence features by computing concatenated LBP histograms from three orthogonal planes. Xie et al. [5] employed the Gabor surface feature (GSF) to represent the facial expression and SVM for classification. Since the extraction of hand-crafted features is separated from the training of classifier, these methods may lose useful facial information and achieve limited performance.

To extract sufficient and representative features, the deep learning based methods (e.g. IACNN [7] and DTAGN [8]) were adopted to facial expression analysis. Meng et al. [7] proposed an identity-aware CNN network to capture both expression-related and identity-related information, which achieved 95.37% accuracy on the CK+. Jung et al. [8] proposed the DTAGN composed of two different deep networks to extract temporal appearance feature from image sequences and temporal geometry feature from temporal facial landmark points, respectively. Although the performance of these methods are better than the hand-crafted features based methods, their capacities are still limited. Because a human face contains various attributes, e.g. age, skin color and gender, these expression features may be confused with other facial attributes related features.

With consideration to the aforementioned issues, some scholars tried to extract facial expression feature by comparing the differences between query face image and neutral face image. Yang et al. [9] proposed a De-expression Residue Learning (DeRL) method to extract expressive component (the difference between neutral expression and other expressions). The DeRL composed of two stages: First, a generator is trained using cGAN [10] to regenerate the neutral face image for a facial expression image. Then, the expression information contained in the intimidate layers of the generative model was captured and concatenated for facial expression recognition. Since the DeRL method contains two stages, the performance of the generative model in the first stage has a great impact on that of the FER in the second stage. Liu et al. [11] proposed a distilling and dispelling auto-encoder (D^{2}AE) framework to perform face editing. Its encoder contains two branches: identity-distilling and identity-dispelling branches, to extract the identity information and the complementary facial information, respectively. Features in the two streams represent different information of a face, which were then used by the decoder to manipulate facial attributes.

In this paper, inspired by the success of the DeRL [9] and D^{2}AE [11], we propose an end-to-end adversarial expression distilling and dispelling learning (ED^{2}L) framework for facial expression recognition, as depicted in Fig. 1. Similar to Liu et al. [11], the proposed ED^{2}L have two branches, i.e. the expression distilling and dispelling branches. Since the facial expression database is much smaller than those databases for face identification, the facial expression database is not large enough to train complex face identification network. We use SpherefaceNet-20 [12] instead of Inception-ResNet [13] as the backbone of our framework, which makes our network structure much lighter than D^{2}AE. The model parameter size of D^{2}AE is about 20 times larger than that of our approach, which saves computational resources and brings about a faster convergence during training our framework. In addition, Additive Margin Softmax [14] is used in our expression distilling branch as the loss function. Also, as shown with the purple dotted arrow in Fig. 2, the optimization of l_e^p in the expression dispelling branch updates Base net, $B_{\theta p}$ and dispeller simultaneously. The proposed ED^{2}L framework aims to separate discriminative expression feature from other face information. Our main contribution can be summarized as follows:

- A adversarial ED^{2}L framework is proposed to disentangle expression-related feature from a given face.
- The adversarial learning of the proposed ED^{2}L framework ensures the effective extraction of the expression-related and non-related features.
- The automatically learned expression-related feature achieves competitive performance in several benchmark databases.

2   Methods

In this section, we introduce the proposed ED^{2}L framework. As visualized in Fig. 2, the entire framework consists of three parts, the base net S_θ and two parallel branches: expression distilling branch ED^{2}L-t and expression dispelling branch ED^{2}L-p. Given a face image x, a variety of face attribute information $S_\theta(x)$ is extracted by the base net S_θ. Then, $S_\theta(x)$ is fed into expression distilling branch $B_{\theta t}$ and expression dispelling branch $B_{\theta p}$ to further extract expression-related and non-related features, respectively. The expression-related feature $\boldsymbol{f}_t \in R^{N_t}$ and non-related feature $\boldsymbol{f}_p \in R^{N_p}$ jointly serve as a complete representation of the face.

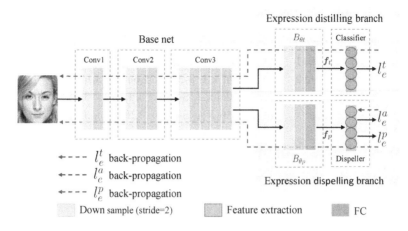

Fig. 2. The expression distilling and dispelling framework. (Color figure online)

2.1 Base Net

Adapted from SpherefaceNet-20 [12], the architecture of our framework is demonstrated in Table 1. Conv1, Conv2 and Conv3 denote convolutional blocks that contain multiple convolutional layers and residual units. $[3 \times 3, 64] \times 2$ denotes two cascaded convolution layers with 64 filters of size 3×3, and S-2 denotes stride 2 in the down sample layer. Each convolutional layer is followed by a batch normalization layer and a PReLU [15] layer. FC-256 denotes a fully connected layer with 256 neurons.

2.2 Expression Distilling Branch

We propose the expression distilling branch ED²L-t to extract discriminative expression-related information $\boldsymbol{f}_t$. As revealed in Fig. 2, $\boldsymbol{f}_t$ is extracted using the subnet $B_{\theta t}$ after the base net.

$$\boldsymbol{f}_t = B_{\theta t}(S_\theta(x)) \tag{1}$$

Then, $\boldsymbol{f}_t$ is mapped by a non-linear function *Additive Margin Softmax* [14], defined in Eq. (2),

$$\boldsymbol{y}_t = \frac{e^{s(W_{y_t}^T \boldsymbol{f}_t - m)}}{e^{s(W_{y_t^i}^T \boldsymbol{f}_t - m)} + \sum_{j=1, j \neq y_t^i}^{c} e^{s W_j^T \boldsymbol{f}_t}} \tag{2}$$

where $\boldsymbol{y}_t \in R^{N_t}$ is an N_t-dimensional vector, which represents the probabilities of belonging to the corresponding class, m and s are two hyper-parameters of the additive margin softmax which denote the margin among categories and scaling

Table 1. Architectures of the proposed ED^{2}L framework.

Components	Layers	Configurations
Base net	Conv1	$[3 \times 3, 32] \times 1$, S-2 $[3 \times 3, 32; 3 \times 3, 32] \times 1$
	Conv2	$[3 \times 3, 64] \times 1$, S-2 $[3 \times 3, 64; 3 \times 3, 64] \times 2$
	Conv3	$[3 \times 3, 128] \times 1$, S-2 $[3 \times 3, 128; 3 \times 3, 128] \times 4$
Expression distilling branch	$B_{\theta t}$	$[3 \times 3, 256] \times 1$, S-2 $[3 \times 3, 256; 3 \times 3, 256] \times 1$ FC-256
	Classifier	#Expression Category
Expression dispelling branch	$B_{\theta p}$	$[3 \times 3, 256] \times 1$, S-2 $[3 \times 3, 256; 3 \times 3, 256] \times 1$ FC-256
	Dispeller	#Expression Category

factor, respectively. The classification loss l_e^t is computed by the probability vector $\boldsymbol{y}_t \in R^{N_t}$, where i denotes the ground truth index.

$$l_e^t = -\log \boldsymbol{y}_t^i \tag{3}$$

The back-propagation route of l_e^t optimization including the expression distilling branch $B_{\theta t}$ and base net S_θ is indicated with the red dotted arrow in Fig. 2.

2.3   Expression Dispelling Branch

Similar to the ED^{2}L-t, the structure of expression dispelling branch ED^{2}L-p composed of a subnet $B_{\theta p}$ and an expression dispeller. The ED^{2}L-p inhibits expression-related feature and extracts the non-related feature $\boldsymbol{f}_p$ by the subnet $B_{\theta p}$ following the base net.

$$\boldsymbol{f}_p = B_{\theta p}(S_\theta(x)) \tag{4}$$

In order to ensure that the ED^{2}L-p can extract expression non-related feature, an adversarial supervised training method composed of two different loss functions l_e^a and l_e^p is employed.

The cross entropy loss $l_e^a = -\log \boldsymbol{y}_p^i$ is leveraged to supervise the training of the expression dispeller based on $\boldsymbol{y}_p$, which is computed by $\boldsymbol{y}_p = softmax(W_p\boldsymbol{f}_p+b_p)$. Note that the gradient of l_e^a is only back-propagated to the expression dispeller and does not update the previous layers, which is different from l_e^t.

l_e^p is proposed to fool the training of expression dispeller $\boldsymbol{y}_p$. In other words, l_e^p is required to be constant over all expressions and equal to $\frac{1}{N}$. Thus, the optimization goal is equivalent to minimize the negative entropy of the predicted expression distributions, where N denotes the number of expression categories.

$$l_e^p = -\frac{1}{N} \sum_j^N \log \boldsymbol{y}_p^j \tag{5}$$

The optimization of l_e^p updates the expression dispelling branch $B_{\theta p}$ and the base net S_θ.

The sum of l_e^a and l_e^p constitutes the total loss function of the expression dispelling branch. Note that y_p of the feature dispelling branch is not used to predict the expression category.

2.4 Objective Function

The ED^{2}L framework is jointly optimized by three loss functions l_e^t, l_e^a and l_e^p. The total loss function L is the weighted sum of l_e^t, l_e^a and l_e^p, as formulated in Eq. (6).

$$L = \lambda_t l_e^t + \lambda_p (l_e^a + l_e^p) \tag{6}$$

3 Experiments and Results

In this section, we evaluate the performance of the proposed approach on four benchmark databases, including CK+ [16], MMI [17], BU-3DFE [18] and Oulu-CASIA [19], and compare the results with the state-of-the-art methods.

3.1 Implementation Details

Data Preprocessing. For each database, the faces are first detected by the MTCNN [20] and aligned to the resolution of 128×110 according to their corresponding landmarks. Then, ten gray patches with the size of 112×96 are generated by cropping from four corners and center of each aligned image and the horizontal flipping mirror.

Hyperparameters. The proposed ED^{2}L framework is optimized using Adam optimizer [21] with betas of 0.9 and 0.999, ϵ of $1e-8$ and weight decay of 0.0005. The optimization is performed about 100 epochs with a batch size of 64 and an initial learning rate of $1e-4$. For objective function, we set $m = 0.35$, $s = 30$, $\lambda_t = 1$ and $\lambda_p = 10$.

3.2 Databases

The Extended Cohn-Kanade database (CK+) [16] is a representative laboratory-controlled database for facial expression recognition. It contains 593 video sequences from 123 subjects. Among these videos, only 327 sequences from 118 subjects are labeled with seven expressions (anger, contempt, disgust, fear, happiness, sadness and surprise). In order to compare with other methods, the 10-fold cross validation protocol in [9] is followed. The last three frames of each labeled sequence are selected and all subjects are divided into ten groups based their ID in an ascending order. Every subgroup is further selected as testing set to evaluate the model performance, and the remaining subgroups are used for training in the 10-fold cross validation.

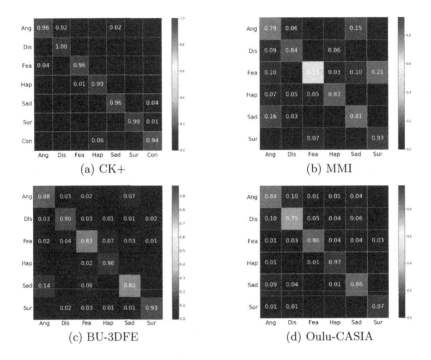

Fig. 3. Confusion matrix of the ED^{2}L framework with fine-tuning for the CK+, MMI, BU-3DFE and Oulu-CASIA databases. The labels on the vertical and horizontal axis represent ground truth and predicted expressions, respectively.

The MMI database [17] consists of 236 sequences from 32 subjects with six basic expressions. We select 209 sequences captured in front view. Since the sequences of this database begin with the neutral expression and show a peak expression near the middle of the sequences. We select three frames in the middle of each sequence and employ a 10-fold cross validation similar to that of the CK+ database.

The BU-3DFE database [18] consists of 2500 pairs of 3D face models and texture images of 100 subjects (56 female and 44 male subjects). Each subject displayed six basic facial expressions (anger, disgust, fear, happiness, sadness and surprise) with four intensity levels and a neutral expression. Following the test protocol in [9], only the texture images with high-intensity expressions (i.e. the last two levels) were selected. The selected pictures were further divided into 10 subject-independent groups.

The Oulu-CASIA database [19] contains two subsets, i.e. the Oulu-CASIA NIR database and the Oulu-CASIA VIS database, which were captured under three different illumination conditions (dark, weak and strong) using a NIR camera and a VIS camera, respectively. In our experiments, only the Oulu-CASIA VIS database under strong illumination condition is used. The Oulu-

Table 2. Overall accuracy on the CK+ database. Remark that $w.$ and $w.o.$ denote the use of fine-tuning, or not, respectively.

Method	Accuracy (%)
LBP-TOP [4]	88.99
3DCNN [23]	85.90
STM-Explet [24]	94.19
IACNN [7]	95.37
DTAGN-Joint [8]	97.25
DeRL [9]	97.30
Baseline($w.o.$)	94.19
Baseline($w.$)	94.50
Ours($w.o.$)	96.33
Ours($w.$)	**97.86**

CASIA VIS database includes 480 image sequences from 80 subjects labeled with six basic expressions (anger, disgust, fear, happiness, sadness and surprise). Similar to the CK+ database, the last three frames of each sequence are selected and a 10-fold cross validation is applied.

3.3 Experiments

Baseline. In order to prove the effectiveness of the proposed ED^{2}L framework, we employed a baseline network for comparison which has the same structure as the ED^{2}L framework without ED^{2}L-p branch.

Transfer Learning. Training of the CNN is prone to over-fitting because the number of images in the CK+, MMI, BU-3DFE and Oulu-CASIA databases are insufficient. Therefore, firstly, we trained the ED^{2}L framework on the FER2013 [22] database with the same parameter settings described in Sect. 3.1 and used the pretrained model as the base model. Then, the base model was further fine tuned using the CK+, MMI, BU-3DFE and Oulu-CASIA databases. When training the baseline model, the same procedure was adopted.

3.4 Results

CK+. The overall accuracy of 10-fold cross validation is displayed in Table 2. The proposed ED^{2}L framework outperforms the baseline with a 3.36% gap, which suggest the effectiveness of the adversarial learning between two branches. Compared to other methods, our approach achieves the best performance, i.e. 97.86% and beats all hand-crafted features based methods (LBP-TOP [4]) and CNN-based methods (3DCNN [23], STM-Explet [24], IACNN [7], DTAGN-Joint [8] and DeRL [9]). Figure 3(a) shows the confusion matrix of ED^{2}L framework for the CK+ database. Diagonal of this matrix, suggests that our method performed remarkably well in recognizing the expressions of disgust, happiness and surprise.

Table 3. Overall accuracy on the MMI database.

Method	Accuracy (%)
LBP-TOP [4]	59.51
STM-Explet [24]	75.12
DTAGN-Joint [8]	70.24
IACNN [7]	71.55
DeRL [9]	73.23
Baseline($w.o.$)	62.68
Baseline($w.$)	76.56
Ours($w.o.$)	72.73
Ours($w.$)	**80.38**

Table 4. Overall accuracy on the BU-3DFE database.

Method	Accuracy (%)
Wang et al. [25]	61.79
Berretti et al. [26]	77.54
Yang et al. [27]	84.80
Li et al. [28]	86.32
Lopes [29]	72.89
DeRL [9]	84.17
Baseline($w.o.$)	86.00
Baseline($w.$)	87.17
Ours($w.o.$)	87.83
Ours($w.$)	**88.67**

MMI. Table 3 lists the results of the proposed ED^2L framework, together with that of baseline and other approaches in literature. The accuracy of our approach with fine tuning, 80.38%, is significantly higher than that of baseline (76.56%), and the best results in literature (75.12%). As shown from the confusion matrix of MMI database in Fig. 3(b), the ED^2L framework has a remarkable recognition performance for the expression of surprise.

BU-3DFE. As it can be seen in Table 4, the accuracy of our approach, 87.83% show a better performance than that of the baseline (86.00%) and the best result in literature (86.32%). As illustrated in Fig. 3(c), our approach performed well in recognizing the expression of happiness.

Table 5. Overall accuracy on the Oulu-CASIA database.

Method	Accuracy (%)
LBP-TOP [4]	68.13
STM-Explet [24]	74.59
Atlases [30]	75.52
DTAGN-Joint [8]	81.46
PPDN [31]	84.59
DeRL [9]	**88.0**
Baseline($w.o.$)	83.96
Baseline($w.$)	84.58
Ours($w.o.$)	85.21
Ours($w.$)	**87.71**

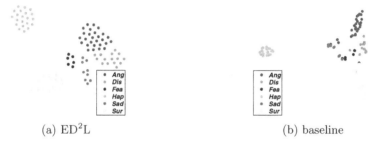

(a) ED^{2}L   (b) baseline

Fig. 4. Visualization of the features extracted by the adversarial ED^{2}L framework and baseline network, using t-SNE [32]. (Color figure online)

Oulu-CASIA. The overall accuracy of 10-fold cross validation is illustrated in Table 5. Fine-tuning has also been shown to improve the accuracy of our framework from 85.21% to 87.71%, which is again higher than that of baseline, 84.58%. When the performance of our framework is better than most of the approaches in literature, our accuracy is a little bit lower than that of DeRL, 88.0%. However, the number of training images (60,600) used for pretrained model in DeRL is much bigger than that of our approach (28,709). The amount of augmented training images in the second stage of DeRL is also about 10 times larger than that of our approach.

3.5   Visualization

In order to further illustrate the effectiveness of the proposed ED^{2}L framework, we extract the image features of the CK+ database from the FC-256 layer of the ED^{2}L-t branch and baseline, respectively. We use the first validation set of the 10-fold cross validation protocol to extract these features. Note that as subject independent division is used, the subjects in the first fold only present six expressions,

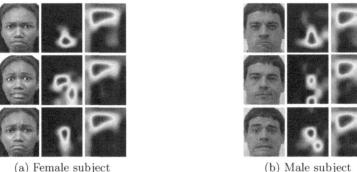

(a) Female subject   (b) Male subject

Fig. 5. Visualization of the feature heat-maps extracted from the down sample layers of ED^2L-t and ED^2L-p. The left column is the input image, the middle and right columns are the feature heat-maps extracted from ED^2L-t and ED^2L-p, respectively.

i.e. anger, disgust, fear, happiness, sadness and surprise. As depicted in Fig. 4, the features extracted by the ED^2L framework are densely clustered for each expression category and easy to distinguish. There are distinct boundaries between features of different expressions. While the features extracted by the baseline network are non-discriminative and have ambiguous boundaries, e.g. the points of fear expression (blue points) are mixed with others. The results qualitatively suggests that the proposed approach has an extraordinary ability to extract discriminative expression-related information, mainly due to the adversarial supervised learning of the expression distilling and dispelling branches.

In addition, we extract the feature maps of the CK+ database from the down sample layer of ED^2L-t and ED^2L-p, respectively. The 10th validation set of the 10-fold cross validation protocol is used to extract these feature maps composed of 256 channels. Then the sum of these feature maps is normalized to $[0, 1]$ to calculate the heat-maps. The feature heat-maps are resized to 112×96 to match the size of input image. In Fig. 5, we extract and visualize the feature maps for different expressions of two different subjects. For different expressions of the female subject shown in Fig. 5(a), the heat-maps extracted from ED^2L-t differ significantly with each other, while the ED^2L-p heat-maps are almost the same. The same conclusion can be drawn for the male subject shown in Fig. 5(b). The examples clearly suggest that ED^2L-t tries to look at regions sensitive to expressions like eyes, nose and mouth, while ED^2L-p focus on expression invariant regions like forehead.

4   Conclusions

In this paper, we present an adversarial expression distilling and dispelling learning (ED^2L) framework for facial expression recognition. The framework uses expression distilling (ED^2L-t) and dispelling (ED^2L-p) branches to extract expression-related and non-related features, respectively. The features learned by two branches jointly serve as a complete representation of the face. As evaluated on several facial expression benchmark databases, the ED^2L framework showed its superiority over both traditional hand-crafted features based methods and CNN-based methods.

References

1. Li, S., Deng, W.: Deep facial expression recognition: a survey. arXiv preprint arXiv:1804.08348 (2018)
2. Ekman, P., Friesen, W.V.: Constants across cultures in the face and emotion. J. Pers. Soc. Psychol. **17**(2), 124 (1971)
3. Matsumoto, D.: More evidence for the universality of a contempt expression. Motiv. Emot. **16**(4), 363–368 (1992)
4. Zhao, G., Pietikainen, M.: Dynamic texture recognition using local binary patterns with an application to facial expressions. IEEE Trans. Pattern Anal. Mach. Intell. **29**(6), 915–928 (2007)
5. Xie, W., Shen, L., Yang, M., Lai, Z.: Active AU based patch weighting for facial expression recognition. Sensors **17**(2), 275 (2017)
6. Chang, C.C., Lin, C.J.: LIBSVM: a library for support vector machines (2001). Software: http://www.csie.ntu.edu.tw/~cjlin/libsvm (2012)
7. Meng, Z., Liu, P., Cai, J., Han, S., Tong, Y.: Identity-aware convolutional neural network for facial expression recognition. In: 2017 12th IEEE International Conference on Automatic Face & Gesture Recognition (FG 2017), pp. 558–565 (2017)
8. Jung, H., Lee, S., Yim, J., Park, S., Kim, J.: Joint fine-tuning in deep neural networks for facial expression recognition. In: Proceedings of the IEEE International Conference on Computer Vision, pp. 2983–2991 (2015)
9. Yang, H., Ciftci, U., Yin, L.: Facial expression recognition by de-expression residue learning. In: Proceedings of the IEEE Conference on Computer Vision and Pattern Recognition, pp. 2168–2177 (2018)
10. Mirza, M., Osindero, S.: Conditional generative adversarial nets. arXiv preprint arXiv:1411.1784 (2014)
11. Liu, Y., Wei, F., Shao, J., Sheng, L., Yan, J., Wang, X.: Exploring disentangled feature representation beyond face identification. In: Proceedings of the IEEE Conference on Computer Vision and Pattern Recognition, pp. 2080–2089 (2018)
12. Liu, W., Wen, Y., Yu, Z., Li, M., Raj, B., Song, L.: Sphereface: deep hypersphere embedding for face recognition. In: Proceedings of the IEEE Conference on Computer Vision and Pattern Recognition, vol. 1, p. 1 (2017)
13. Szegedy, C., Ioffe, S., Vanhoucke, V., Alemi, A.A.: Inception-v4, inception-ResNet and the impact of residual connections on learning. In: Thirty-First AAAI Conference on Artificial Intelligence (2017)
14. Wang, F., Cheng, J., Liu, W., Liu, H.: Additive margin softmax for face verification. IEEE Signal Process. Lett. **25**(7), 926–930 (2018)
15. He, K., Zhang, X., Ren, S., Sun, J.: Delving deep into rectifiers: surpassing human-level performance on ImageNet classification. In: Proceedings of the IEEE International Conference on Computer Vision, pp. 1026–1034 (2015)
16. Lucey, P., Cohn, J.F., Kanade, T., Saragih, J., Ambadar, Z., Matthews, I.: The extended Cohn-Kanade dataset (CK+): a complete dataset for action unit and emotion-specified expression. In: 2010 IEEE Computer Society Conference on Computer Vision and Pattern Recognition Workshops (CVPRW), pp. 94–101 (2010)

17. Pantic, M., Valstar, M., Rademaker, R., Maat, L.: Web-based database for facial expression analysis. In: 2005 IEEE International Conference on Multimedia and Expo, p. 5 (2005)
18. Yin, L., Wei, X., Sun, Y., Wang, J., Rosato, M.J.: A 3D facial expression database for facial behavior research. In: 7th International Conference on Automatic Face and Gesture Recognition (FGR 2006), pp. 211–216. IEEE (2006)
19. Zhao, G., Huang, X., Taini, M., Li, S.Z., Pietikälnen, M.: Facial expression recognition from near-infrared videos. Image Vis. Comput. **29**(9), 607–619 (2011)
20. Zhang, K., Zhang, Z., Li, Z., Qiao, Y.: Joint face detection and alignment using multitask cascaded convolutional networks. IEEE Signal Process. Lett. **23**(10), 1499–1503 (2016)
21. Kingma, D.P., Ba, J.: Adam: a method for stochastic optimization. arXiv preprint arXiv:1412.6980 (2014)
22. Goodfellow, I.J., et al.: Challenges in representation learning: a report on three machine learning contests. In: Lee, M., Hirose, A., Hou, Z.-G., Kil, R.M. (eds.) ICONIP 2013. LNCS, vol. 8228, pp. 117–124. Springer, Heidelberg (2013). https://doi.org/10.1007/978-3-642-42051-1_16
23. Liu, M., Li, S., Shan, S., Wang, R., Chen, X.: Deeply learning deformable facial action parts model for dynamic expression analysis. In: Cremers, D., Reid, I., Saito, H., Yang, M.-H. (eds.) ACCV 2014. LNCS, vol. 9006, pp. 143–157. Springer, Cham (2015). https://doi.org/10.1007/978-3-319-16817-3_10
24. Liu, M., Shan, S., Wang, R., Chen, X.: Learning expressionlets on spatio-temporal manifold for dynamic facial expression recognition. In: Proceedings of the IEEE Conference on Computer Vision and Pattern Recognition, pp. 1749–1756 (2014)
25. Wang, J., Yin, L., Wei, X., Sun, Y.: 3D facial expression recognition based on primitive surface feature distribution. In: 2006 IEEE Computer Society Conference on Computer Vision and Pattern Recognition (CVPR 2006), vol. 2, pp. 1399–1406. IEEE (2006)
26. Berretti, S., Del Bimbo, A., Pala, P., Amor, B.B., Daoudi, M.: A set of selected SIFT features for 3D facial expression recognition. In: 2010 20th International Conference on Pattern Recognition, pp. 4125–4128. IEEE (2010)
27. Yang, X., Huang, D., Wang, Y., Chen, L.: Automatic 3D facial expression recognition using geometric scattering representation. In: 2015 11th IEEE International Conference and Workshops on Automatic Face and Gesture Recognition (FG), vol. 1, pp. 1–6. IEEE (2015)
28. Li, H., et al.: An efficient multimodal 2D + 3D feature-based approach to automatic facial expression recognition. Comput. Vis. Image Underst. **140**, 83–92 (2015)
29. Lopes, A.T., de Aguiar, E., De Souza, A.F., Oliveira-Santos, T.: Facial expression recognition with convolutional neural networks: coping with few data and the training sample order. Pattern Recogn. **61**, 610–628 (2017)
30. Guo, Y., Zhao, G., Pietikäinen, M.: Dynamic facial expression recognition using longitudinal facial expression atlases. In: Fitzgibbon, A., Lazebnik, S., Perona, P., Sato, Y., Schmid, C. (eds.) ECCV 2012. LNCS, pp. 631–644. Springer, Heidelberg (2012). https://doi.org/10.1007/978-3-642-33709-3_45
31. Zhao, X., et al.: Peak-piloted deep network for facial expression recognition. In: Leibe, B., Matas, J., Sebe, N., Welling, M. (eds.) ECCV 2016. LNCS, vol. 9906, pp. 425–442. Springer, Cham (2016). https://doi.org/10.1007/978-3-319-46475-6_27
32. Maaten, L.v.d., Hinton, G.: Visualizing data using t-SNE. J. Mach. Learn. Res. **9**, 2579–2605 (2008)

General Interaction-Aware Neural Network for Action Recognition

Jialin Gao[1(✉)], Jiani Li[2], Guanshuo Wang[1], Yufeng Yuan[2], and Xi Zhou[1,2]

[1] Cooperative Medianet Innovation Center, Shanghai Jiao Tong University,
Shanghai, China
{jialin_gao,guanshuo.wang}@sjtu.edu.cn
[2] CloudWalk Technology Co., Ltd., Shanghai, China
{lijiani,yuanyufeng,zhouxi}@cloudwalk.cn

Abstract. Second order representation, like non-local operation and bilinear pooling, has significantly outperformed the plain counterpart on a wide variety of visual tasks. However, these previous works focus on feature interactions either in spatiotemporal dimension or in channels, both of which have been ignored the joint effect of feature interactions along with different axes. We thus propose a general interaction-aware neural network that captures higher order feature interactions both in spatiotemporal and channel dimensions. In this paper, we illustrate how to implement the second and third order exemplar CNNs in a compacted way and evaluate their performance on action recognition benchmarks. Comprehensive experiments demonstrate that our method can achieve competitive or better performance than recent start-of-the-art approaches and visualization results illustrate that our scheme can generate more discriminative representations, focusing on target regions more properly.

Keywords: Interaction-aware neural network ·
High-order representations · Action recognition

1 Introduction

Human action recognition is a fundamental and important research field in computer vision, which can be widely applied in different areas such as public security and human-computer interaction. Inspired by the success of convolutional neural network (CNNs) for visual tasks in image domain [4,9,13], many recently works introduce deep models to recognize actions in videos [7,15,18,19], which outperform traditional approaches using hand-crafted representations [3,12,16] by a good margin. Despite of these progress, there are two crucial difficulties impeding on representation learning in action recognition: how to capture *longe-range* dependencies and how to depict spatio-temporal *interaction*.

This work was performed when Jialin Gao was an intern in CloudWalk Technology Co., Ltd.

© Springer Nature Switzerland AG 2019
A. C. Nayak and A. Sharma (Eds.): PRICAI 2019, LNAI 11672, pp. 93–106, 2019.
https://doi.org/10.1007/978-3-030-29894-4_8

To interpret actions in videos, it usually requires coping with three-dimensional spatio-temporal signals from video to construct appearance feature in each frame and model dynamics across frames. There are several genres of architectures for learning video representations: (1) two-stream CNNs [15], (2) 3D CNNs [11], (3) 2D CNNs inserted with temporal models, like LSTM [5], attention modelling [8], etc.

Two-stream CNNs model static appearance and motion information via two parallel branches. The spatial stream operates on individual video frames to characterize appearance descriptors and the temporal stream takes advantage of optical flow to capture local motion pattern, as well as exploiting long range interdependencies by stacking multiple frames. Nevertheless, high computational cost of generating optical flow and multi-stage training make it time-consuming and inefficient. In contrast, 3D convolutional operators dedicate to learn local features and relations directly from staked RGB volumes. Due to limited receptive field, it is required to stack multiple of these operations to process correlation within spatial, temporal or spatio-temporal regions in the long-range. Yet, this pipeline repeats the same operation again and again, hampering with optimization during the training. Even though carefully addressed, it causes inefficient computation and makes multi-hop feature interaction difficult. Similarly, temporal models encounter the same dilemma. CNNs with LSTM increase the optimization difficulties and attention models often merely sever as feature selectors.

Motivated by the non-local means algorithm [1], non-local neural network [20] explicitly models feature interactions between any two positions and captures long-range dependencies simultaneously, which boosts the performances on many video classification benchmarks. However, the original non-local module ignores correlation between channels, which is important for discriminating actions as suggested by a recent work [10]. Therefore, in this work, we aim to extend the non-local module to a general interaction-aware block aiming to exploiting correlations among the entire feature space. The core idea is to first compute long-range interaction between distant pixels in the whole spatio-temporal space and then add cross-channel correlations as complementary information.

Our general interaction-aware module is related to several recent works, including the Squeeze-and-Excitation Networks [10], compact generalized non-local network [22], and convolutional block attention module [21]. Nevertheless, our proposal has a number of unique merits: it captures dense interaction across channels while SENet [10] only computes correlations between statistical means obtained by the global average pooling. Our novel block employs two different branches to learn the interaction in spatio-temporal space and in channel space respectively, which eases the optimization compared with the joint modeling style in CGNL [22]. Although CBAM [21] sequentially infers attention maps for feature refinement, similar in some ways to us, it overlooks the feature interactions for discriminative representations, while we take both into consideration. Extensive experiments are conducted to evaluate our proposed method on the task of action recognition and to demonstrate the above advantages.

2   General Interaction-Aware Module

In this section, we first briefly review the original non-local module and kernel pooling in CNNs, then we propose our general interaction-aware block for action recognition based on these works.

2.1   Formulation

Suppose that the input feature map of a 3D convolutional layer is $\mathbf{X} \in \mathbb{R}^{t \times h \times w \times c}$, where t, h, w, c denote the time-span, height, width and the number of channels respectively. In [20], the non-local operation is defined as the weighted sum of features over all positions:

$$y_i = \frac{1}{Z(x)} \sum_{\forall j} f(\theta(x_i), \phi(x_j)) \tau(x_j) \tag{1}$$

where i is the index of an output position, $\theta(\cdot), \phi(\cdot), \tau(\cdot)$ represent the transformation or projection functions on the input signal $\mathbf{X}$ and f is a pairwise function to model the affinity, namely relationship, between i and all j. $Z(x)$ is a partition function, which satisfies $Z(x) = \Sigma_{\forall j} f(\theta(x_i), \phi(x_j))$. Equation 1 can be written into matrix form, $\mathbf{Y} = f(\theta(\mathbf{X}), \phi(\mathbf{X})) \tau(\mathbf{X})$

Specifically, the feature projection functions $\theta(\cdot)$, $\phi(\cdot)$, $\tau(\cdot)$ can be easily implemented via $1 \times 1 \times 1$ convolution with parameterized matrices $\mathbf{W}_\theta, \mathbf{W}_\phi, \mathbf{W}_\tau \in \mathbb{R}^{C_{in} \times C_{out}}$. The pairwise function $f(\cdot)$ has several instantiations, such as Gaussian, Embedded Gaussian, dot product. Apparently, the original module ignore channel-wise correlation due to its operation to aggregate all channel information together in Eq. 1.

However, a recent work [2] illustrates that learning higher-order interactions across channels can yield impressive performance gains on a number of visual tasks, including fine-grained classification, person re-id and visual question answering. The principle behind is that high-order pooling can provide more discriminative information than max or average pooling in classification tasks. Therefore, we integrate the powerful high-order pooling into the original non-local block to formulate general interaction-aware module, for enhancing the ability in modelling the relationships both in spatio-temporal and channel dimensions.

In order to learn the channel-wise correlations in neural network, we denote the input signal as a c dimensional feature vector, $\mathbf{X} = [x_1, x_2, ..., x_c]^T \in \mathbb{R}^c$, where $x_i \in \mathbb{R}^{thw}$ for 3D signals. A kernel function $\mathcal{K}(\cdot, \cdot)$ can usually be decomposed as the inner-product of two explicit feature transformation on the input signals $\mathcal{P}(\mathbf{X})$ and $\mathcal{P}(\mathbf{X})$ as:

$$\mathcal{K}(\mathbf{X}, \mathbf{Y}) = \langle \mathcal{P}(\mathbf{X}), \mathcal{P}(\mathbf{Y}) \rangle. \tag{2}$$

Various kernel functions can be applied here, such as polynomial kernels $(\mathbf{x}^T \mathbf{y})^p$, Gaussian RBF kernel $exp(-\gamma \|\mathbf{x} - \mathbf{y}\|^2)$, χ^2 kernel $\Sigma_{i=1}^c \frac{2x_i y_i}{x_i + y_i}$, etc. We introduce

Taylor series kernel in [2] to explore the interactions across channels, which could be implemented by tensor product.

For example, a 2nd order cross-channel interactions can be reformulated as outer product as:

$$g^2(\mathbf{X}, \mathbf{X}) = \mathbf{X} \otimes \mathbf{X} = \begin{bmatrix} x_1x_1 & x_1x_2 & \cdots & x_1x_c \\ x_2x_1 & x_2x_2 & \cdots & x_2x_c \\ \vdots & \vdots & \ddots & \vdots \\ x_cx_1 & x_cx_2 & \cdots & x_cx_c \end{bmatrix} \tag{3}$$

where $\otimes$ denotes the outer product operation and the results $g^2(\mathbf{X}, \mathbf{X}) \in \mathbb{R}^{c^2}$. From another perspective, bilinear pooling is a special case of second-order kernel pooling, which employs identity map as transformation functions, that is $\mathcal{K}(\mathbf{X}, \mathbf{Y}) = \mathbf{X}\mathbf{Y}^T \in \mathbb{R}^{c^2}$.

It is easy to deduce the cross-channel interactions formula based on the original non-local module and above kernel pooing method as:

$$\begin{aligned} \mathbf{Y} &= f(\theta(\mathbf{X}), \phi(\mathbf{X}))\tau(\mathbf{X})\mathcal{K}(\mathbf{X}, \mathbf{X}) \\ &= f(\theta(\mathbf{X}), \phi(\mathbf{X}))\tau(\mathbf{X})g^2(\alpha(\mathbf{X}), \beta(\mathbf{X})) \end{aligned} \tag{4}$$

where $\theta(\cdot)$, $\phi(\cdot)$, $\alpha(\cdot)$, $\beta(\cdot)$ and $\tau(\cdot)$ are projection functions, while $f(\cdot)$ and $g(\cdot)$ denote the spatio-temporal interactions and channel-wise correlations, respectively. Similarly, this operation can be generalized to model feature interactions of arbitrary order, when $n \geq 2$, via defining:

$$\begin{aligned} f^n(\theta(\mathbf{X}), \phi(\mathbf{X})) &= (\theta(\mathbf{X})^T\phi(\mathbf{X}))^{n-1} \\ g^n(\mathbf{X}) &= \mathbf{X} \underbrace{\otimes \cdots \otimes}_{n-1 \text{ times}} \mathbf{X} \in \mathbb{R}^{c^n}. \end{aligned} \tag{5}$$

where $f(\cdot), g(\cdot)$ represents spatial or spatio-temporal correlation and channel-wise interdependency respectively. To summarize, we have the general interaction-aware module as:

$$\mathbf{Y} = f^n(\theta(\mathbf{X}), \phi(\mathbf{X}))\tau(\mathbf{X})g^n(\Omega_1(\mathbf{X}), \cdots, \Omega_n(\mathbf{X})) \tag{6}$$

where $\theta, \phi, \tau, \Omega_i$ are projection functions. Equation 6 can model the n-order channel-wise and spatio-temporal correlations of video signals for discriminative representations. However, some kernels may refer to an infinite dimensional projection (e.g., Gaussian RBF), which is computationally infeasible. For example, a fourth order ($n = 4$) cross-channel interactions with $c = 256$ will lead to a 2^{32} dimensional feature space of $f^n(\cdot, \cdot)$. Thus, a compact approximation is crucial to implement our scheme.

2.2   Compact Approximation

The formulation of our proposed module has high time and space complexity due to the multiplication operations, thus, we employ Taylor series and kernel approximation with random feature projections to save time and space cost.

According to [2], a kernel can be approximated up to a certain order p with *Taylor series*:

$$\mathcal{K}(\mathbf{X}, \mathbf{Y}) \approx \sum_{i=0}^{p} \alpha_i^2 (\mathbf{X}^T \mathbf{Y})^i \tag{7}$$

where $(\mathbf{X}^T \mathbf{Y})^0 = 1, (\mathbf{X}^T \mathbf{Y})^1 = \mathbf{X}^T \mathbf{Y}$ and it has been proved in [14] that any i^{th} order tensor product is equivalent to the feature projection of the ith polynomial kernel, i.e. $(\mathbf{X}^T \mathbf{Y})^i = (\mathbf{X}^i)^T (\mathbf{Y}^i)$. Taking Gaussian RBF kernel as an example, the Taylor expansion can be formulated as $\mathcal{K}(\mathbf{X}, \mathbf{Y}) = exp(-\gamma \|\mathbf{X} - \mathbf{Y}\|^2) = \sum_{i=0}^{p} \alpha_i^2 (\mathbf{X}^T \mathbf{Y})^i$, where $\alpha_i^2 = exp(-\gamma(\|\mathbf{X}\|^2 + \|\mathbf{Y}\|^2)) \frac{(2\gamma)^p}{i!}$ and γ is a hyperparameter.

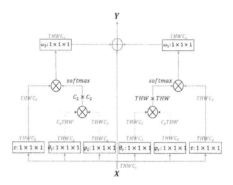

Fig. 1. A second-order exemplar of general interaction-aware module. $THWC$ denotes the shape of feature maps. "$\otimes$" represents matrix multiplication and "$\oplus$" denotes element-wise sum. Compared with the original non-local block, this exemplar increases a symmetric part for modelling interaction across channels.

According to Eq. 7, we have $n + 2$ parameter sets for optimization, given below:

$$\begin{aligned}
Param\{\theta\} &= [\alpha_0(\theta(\mathbf{X})^0), \cdots, \alpha_p(\theta(\mathbf{X})^p)] \\
Param\{\phi\} &= [\alpha_0(\phi(\mathbf{X})^0), \cdots, \alpha_p(\phi(\mathbf{X})^p)] \\
Param\{\Omega_i\} &= [\alpha_0 \Omega_i(\mathbf{X})^0, \cdots, \alpha_p \Omega_i(\mathbf{X})^p]
\end{aligned} \tag{8}$$

where $\theta(\mathbf{X})^0 = 1, \phi(\mathbf{Y})^0 = 1$ and they can be learned via back-propagation. We will show how to achieve simplified version via conducting related experiments and the results are shown in Table 5.

Second-Order Exemplar: For the second order terms, namely $f^2(\cdot), g^2(\cdot)$ in Eq. 6, as an exemplar for comparison with non-local and other methods. Thus, in Fig. 1, we have:

$$\mathbf{Y} = f^2(\theta_r(\mathbf{X}), \phi_r(\mathbf{X}))\tau(\mathbf{X}) + \varepsilon(\mathbf{X})\theta_l(\mathbf{X})^T \phi_l(\mathbf{X}) \tag{9}$$

where $\varepsilon(\mathbf{X}) = \alpha_1^2 f^2(\theta_r(\mathbf{X}), \phi_r(\mathbf{X}))\tau(\mathbf{X})$. We employ (θ_r, ϕ_r) and (θ_l, ϕ_l) to learn spatio-temporal correlation and cross-channel interdependency respectively via inner product of embedded input signal. It can also be regarded as an extension of the original non-local module, which adds channel-wise interaction as supplementary information. According to Eq. 9, (θ_r, ϕ_r) is used to model the relations across positions in spatio-temporal space and (θ_l, ϕ_l) is applied to obtain the cross-channel correlations.

3 Experiments

In this section, we evaluate our general interaction-aware neural network on several action recognition benchmarks and validate the complementarity between channel-wise feature interactions and spatio-temporal correlations. For consistency, we employ our second order instantiation comparing with the original non-local module and conduct several experiments for determining kernel functions and exploring weight-shared mode.

Table 1. Our backbone ResNet-50 3D model follows the $k = 3$ and for the 2D counterpart, $k = 1$. The input with $8 \times 224 \times 224$ dimensions was performed down-sampling in the temporal size only at layer $maxpool_2$. $T \times H \times W$ represents the dimensions on time, height, weight of filter kernel size and output feature maps.

Layer name	Net Architecture	Output size
$conv_1$	$1 \times 7 \times 7$, 64, s(1, 2, 2)	$8 \times 112 \times 112$
$maxpool_1$	$1 \times 3 \times 3$, s(1, 2, 2)	$8 \times 56 \times 56$
res_2	$\begin{matrix} 1 \times 1 \times 1\ 64 \\ 1 \times 3 \times 3\ 64\ \times 3 \\ 1 \times 1 \times 1\ 256 \end{matrix}$	$8 \times 56 \times 56$
$maxpool_2$	$2 \times 1 \times 1$, s(2, 1, 1)	$4 \times 56 \times 56$
res_3	$\begin{matrix} 1 \times 1 \times 1\ 128 \\ 1 \times 3 \times 3\ 128 \times 4 \\ 1 \times 1 \times 1\ 512 \end{matrix}$	$4 \times 28 \times 28$
res_4	$\begin{matrix} k \times 1 \times 1\ 256 \\ 1 \times 3 \times 3\ 256\ \times 6 \\ 1 \times 1 \times 1\ 1024 \end{matrix}$	$4 \times 14 \times 14$
res_5	$\begin{matrix} k \times 1 \times 1\ 512 \\ 1 \times 3 \times 3\ 512\ \times 3 \\ 1 \times 1 \times 1\ 2048 \end{matrix}$	$4 \times 7 \times 7$
$pool_3$	Global average pool	$1 \times 1 \times 1$

3.1   Implementation

In this part, we introduce datasets and the general configurations, including both training and test procedure. Some specific settings will be mentioned when it is used.

Dataset: Kinetics, Charades and UCF101 are used to conduct experiments for comparison with previous methods and ablation study. Due to the copyrights and unavailable download links of the original kinetics datasets, a large number of videos cannot be collected for training and testing. Thus we mainly analyze the results on mini-kinetics dataset, which test data is completed and it contains 200 action categories, 5000 videos for validation and 80000 videos for training. UCF101 collects 13,320 labeled videos from 101 action categories, which has three splits for train/test.

Configuration: Following [6], we adopt ResNet-50 in the slow pathway as the baseline, which is implemented as Table 1 and only the last two residual block inflated to 3D convolutions with $3 \times 3 \times 3$ kernels. In order to compare with the non-local module in [20], we also insert our GIAM into the network and construct our general interaction-aware neural network. Similarly, we also adopt the configuration of adding 1 and 5 blocks into baseline network, as [20]. Three kernel functions are explored in ablation studies: dot production, embedded Gaussian and Gaussian RBF using configurations following [20].

Table 2. Classification accuracy of 1 block with different kernel functions added into 2D ResNet-50 on **mini-Kinetics**, reported in percentage

Net(R50+)	Top-1	Top-5
C2D baseline	76.09	93.05
Gaussian RBF	77.15	93.13
Gaussian, embed	77.19	**93.57**
Dot production	**77.48**	93.48

Table 3. NL *vs.* **Ours** comparison on **Kinetics** via added 5 blocks into 3D ResNet-50. Accuracies are reported in percentage

Net(R50+)	Top-1	Top-5
C2D baseline	70.92	86.37
C3D baseline	71.33	87.76
5-block NL	72.48	90.37
5-block Ours	**72.97**	**90.77**

Table 4. 2D *vs.* 3D comparison between NL modules and ours on **mini-Kinetics** via added 5 blocks into 2D/3D ResNet-50 respectively

Net(R50+)	Top-1	Top-5
C2D NL	77.86	93.57
C2D Ours	**78.35**	**93.65**
C3D NL	78.01	94.02
C3D Ours	**78.64**	**94.13**

Training/Test Procedure: Our model are pretrained on ImageNet and fine-tuned on 8-frame input clips based ResNet-50 model with 0.005 learning rate, a momentum of 0.9 and a weight decay of $1e^{-4}$. We first resize the shorter side of each frame to 256 pixels and randomly crop a 224×224 region for training, while only one center crop for testing. The 8-frame clip is randomly sampled from 64 consecutive frames. We also set the BatchNorm (BN) layer learnable, which scale parameter in our module was initialized as zero for identity mapping and 64 clips are allocated on 8 GPUs evenly. Dropout is adopted after the global pooling with the ratio of 0.5 to avoid over-fitting. Stochastic gradient descent

(SGD) and multi-step learning strategy were employed in the training procedure, the learning rate decreases with a factor of 10 at 30, 50 epochs within 60 epochs.

3.2   Ablation Study

All of our experiments are based on ResNet-50, which is inflated to 3D CNNs following [6] for C3D configuration. The detailed architecture is shown in Table 1. First, we illustrate how to implement a second-order exemplar of our general interaction-aware network and compare different instantiations of kernel functions. Then we explore the influence of tied-weights and untied-weights on classification accuracy for compacted representation. We also demonstrate our second-order exemplar outperforms the original non-local module on action recognition benchmarks. Finally, we build a third-order instantiation of general interaction-aware network and conduct comparative experiments with our second-order one.

Kernel Functions: Three popular kernel functions are used in our experiments: Gaussian RBF, Embedded Gaussian and dot production. All the settings are consistent with [20]. We conduct experiments on mini-kinetics dataset and the results are shown in Table 2. All three kernel function achieve improvements compared with the ResNet-50 baseline and dot production obtained the best performance of top-1 accuracy, while embedded gaussian got the highest top-5 scores. In addition, the dot production is efficient and easy to implementation, thus we make it the main configuration for all later experiments.

Weight-Shared Mode: Our second-order exemplar in Fig. 1 was implemented without weight sharing, which could make the optimization difficult. It is naturally to consider exploring the weight-shared mode. In general, we have 4 combination of shared weight schemes for $\theta(\cdot)$, $\phi(\cdot)$, $\tau(\cdot)$, $\varepsilon(\cdot)$. As shown in Table 5, we conduct experiments for comparison in tied and untied τ, ε combined with tied and untied θ, ϕ. For C2D configuration, the tied τ, ε with tied θ, ϕ obtained the best results of top-1 accuracy, which is 78.35%, while the untied τ, ε with tied θ, ϕ achieved the highest top-5 accuracy, 93.82%. In C3D experiments, the untied τ, ε with tied θ, ϕ configuration achieved the best classifying performance in both, which was up to 78.64% in top-1 and 94.13% in top-5. It is worth

Table 5. Results on mini-Kinetics w/o tied weight

	Net	top-1	top-5
	Baseline	76.09	93.05
Tied τ, ε	Tied weight(θ, ϕ)	**78.35**	93.65
	Untied weight(θ, ϕ)	78.11	93.53
Untied τ, ε	Tied weight(θ, ϕ)	78.23	**93.82**
	Untied weight(θ, ϕ)	78.02	93.79

	Net	top-1	top-5
	Baseline	77.51	93.57
Tied τ, ε	Tied weight(θ, ϕ)	78.46	93.73
	Untied weight(θ, ϕ)	78.37	93.84
Untied τ, ε	Tied weight(θ, ϕ)	**78.64**	**94.13**
	Untied weight(θ, ϕ)	78.24	93.96

(a) Classification accuracy of ResNet-50 C2D configuration, reported in percentage

(b) Classification accuracy of ResNet-50 C3D configuration, reported in percentage

noting that the unshared weight style, namely untied τ, ε with untied θ, ϕ, got the least improvement on performance, not only in C2D configuration but also in C3D. This verified the initial conjecture that shared weight could ease the optimization processing for better performance. In addition, whether (τ, ε) is bound or, the classification accuracy of weight-shared model is higher than that of unshared mode. This indicates tied weight (θ, ϕ) models the spatio-temporal relations and channel-wise correlations on the same projection space, while the untied mode models them in different projection space. In other word, the modeling is not synchronized via using (θ_l, ϕ_l) and (θ_r, ϕ_r), that might cause (θ_l, ϕ_l) extracts relations in one space but (θ_r, ϕ_r) models correlations in another space. Therefore, we refine the architecture of our second-order exemplar in Fig. 1 via employing the same θ, ϕ to learn both spatio-temporal interactions and channel-wise correlations.

Compared with Non-Local (NL) Module: Due to the copyright of download link in Kinetics, comparative experiments were conducted on mini-kinetics and 5 blocks of NL or our exemplar were inserted into ResNet-50 backbone like Table 1. The results of Table 4 demonstrate our second-order exemplar outperforms the original NL module in both 2D and 3D configuration. For C2D experiments, our scheme achieved 78.35% top1-accuracy, which was round 0.5% higher than NL. Similar amount improvement could also be seen in C3D when we got 78.64% top-1 accuracy and NL achieved 78.01%. We also show the results of original non-local module and our second-order exemplar on incomplete Kinetics. In Table 3, our module got 72.97% top-1 accuracy while NL counterpart obtained 72.48%, 0.5% less than ours, which indicates the effect of supplementary information from channel-wise interaction.

Comparison to Other Competitive Methods: We compare the classification performance of our second-order exemplar with the state-of-the-art approaches on the validation set of Kinetics. The results are summarized in Table 6. We first compare with the three popular methods: CNN+LSTM [5],

Table 6. Comparison with competitive methods on the validation set of Kinetics via averaging Top-1 and Top-5 accuracy. For fairness, methods with only RGB input are considered

Method	Val set
ConvNet+LSTM	68.0%
Two-stream Spatial Net	66.6%
C3D Resnet-34	77.0%
C3D Baseline	79.5%
TSN Spatial Net	78.2%
ARTNet with TSN	80.0%
I3D NL	81.4%
I3D Ours	**81.9%**

Table 7. Classification mAP in Charades, NL and our scheme are based on ResNet-50 with 5 blocks, which was a litter lower than the published results of NL

Model	Modality	*train/val*
2-stream	RGB+flow	18.6%
2-stream+LSTM	RGB+flow	17.8%
Asyn-TF	RGB	22.4%
I3D	RGB	32.9%
NL I3D (5 blocks)	RGB	36.2%
I3D (5 blocks) [ours]	RGB	36.8%

Spatial Stream [15] and C3D (ResNet-34) [11]. Our proposed second-order exemplar significantly outperform these methods by a good margin, especially around 10% higher than the first two approaches. Then we evaluate our scheme with recent state-of-the-art methods, namely temporal segment network (TSN) [19] and Inflated 3D CNN (C3D baseline) [6], ARTNet with TSN [17] and non-local NN [20]. Our proposed achieved more than 3.7%, 2.4%, 1.9% and 0.5% accuracy higher than them, respectively. It is worth noting that the current published performance is 86.3% achieved by Resnet-101 with non-local module in slow-fast style. We reproduced I3D NL method based on our limited data and computing resource and got 81.4% classification accuracy. It is reasonable to infer that if the same experimental configuration achieved, including the data, computing resource and training epochs, our scheme still can outperform it.

Experiments on Charades: Charades contains round 8k training, 1.8k validation and 2k testing videos, which provides a multi-label classification task with 157 categories in actions. We initialize our model pre-trained on Kinetics and fine-tune it for 200 epochs, according the same setting in [20]. The detailed comparisons are shown in Table 7, the result of I3D is the 2017 competition winner in Charades and NL I3D was current highest mAP. Our proposed achieved better performance, which is 0.6% higher than that of NL I3D and round 4% above I3D.

Table 8. Comparison with state-of-the-art methods in UCF101. We report the average accuracy over three splits. For fair comparison, we only compare approaches with only RGB input and group the results according to its pre-train datasets

Net	Pre-train	Acc
LTC	Sport-1M	82.4%
MiCT	Sport-1M	**88.6%**
Two-stream Spatial Net	ImageNet	73.0%
ST-ResNet	ImageNet	82.3%
TSN Spatial Net	ImageNet	86.4%
C3D baseline	ImageNet	84.5%
Ours	ImageNet	**89.9%**
TSN-Inception V3	Kinetics	93.2%
C3D Baseline	Kinetics	92.5%
ARTNet	Kinetics	94.3%
Ours	Kinetics	**96.7%**

Experiments on UCF101: In this experiment we study the generalization of learned feature interactions on the Kinetics dataset via our second-order exemplar. The results are summarized in Table 8. Sport-1M, ImageNet and Kinetics are three popular dataset usually used for pre-trained model and we conduct our

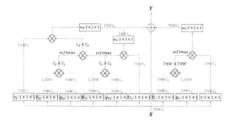 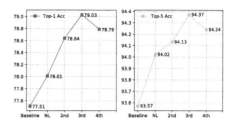

Fig. 2. Third-order exemplar of our general interaction-aware neural network. $THWC_i$ denotes the shape of feature maps. "$\otimes$" represents matrix multiplication and "$\oplus$" denotes element-wise sum.

Fig. 3. Results of different order exemplars on mini-kinetics

proposed scheme on the last two. First, we compare with competitive methods pre-trained on ImageNet. Our result is higher than two-stream spatial net more than 15% and outperform TSN spatial net by 3.5%, which demonstrates that the feature interactions learned in our proposed is more discriminative than them for generalization. In addition, our result is better than the MiCT pre-trained on Sport-1M by 1.3%, which demonstrated that high order information can extract better spatio-temporal representations. Then, we investigate the exemplar with approaches pre-trained on Kinetics and our proposed could still yield a slightly higher classification accuracy than others. It got 96.7%, higher than ARTNet and TSN, which are 94.3% and 93.2% respectively and improved the performance of C3D baseline by 4.2%.

Higher-Order vs Second-Order: According to Eq. 6, we can easily extend our second-order exemplar to any arbitrary order by repeating the left branch in Fig. 1. Taking the third-order one for example, as shown in Fig. 2, the output **Y** consists of four parts, which are the input signals, spatio-temporal relations, second-order channel-wise correlations and the third-order feature interactions in channel dimension. Based on these construction, we conduct the first four order NNs of our proposed module, due to [2] showing $p = 4$ enough for approximating. Figure 3 shows the trend of accuracy.

3.3 Visualization Results

In this section, we employ class activation mapping [23] method to show what models learned for qualitative analysis. Figures 4, 5, 6 and 7 show the heatmap of NL and ours via the same number of blocks (5) into ResNet-50. It can be observed that our model enhances the feature and help the baseline net focus more properly on the target object regions related to a certain human action. In Fig. 4, our model pays more attention to "cello" when recognizing "playing cello" activity in videos, the same observation can be seen from other samples. In Figs. 5 and 6, our model learns relations between scene and people, while NL focus on less related regions, which indicates that the joint feature interactions

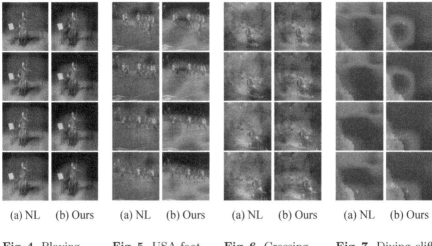

(a) NL   (b) Ours   (a) NL   (b) Ours   (a) NL   (b) Ours   (a) NL   (b) Ours

Fig. 4. Playing cello   **Fig. 5.** USA football   **Fig. 6.** Crossing river   **Fig. 7.** Diving cliff

from spatio-temporal and channel can help refine the feature map from baseline net and generate more discriminative representations for action recognition. In Fig. 7, NL fails to model the relationships among people, water and cliff, on the contrary, our scheme successfully capture the diving cliff action. These observations illustrate that the complementary effect of interactions between channels on spatio-temporal relationships.

4   Conclusion

In this paper, we present the general interaction-aware neural network for action recognition via learning high order feature interactions in both spatio-temporal and channel dimension. Our module can be easily combined with existing architectures and extensive experiments demonstrate significant improvement on classification performance due to modeling more discriminative representations.

References

1. Buades, A., Coll, B., Morel, J.M.: A non-local algorithm for image denoising. In: IEEE Computer Society Conference on Computer Vision and Pattern Recognition, CVPR 2005, vol. 2, pp. 60–65. IEEE (2005)
2. Cui, Y., Zhou, F., Wang, J., Liu, X., Lin, Y., Belongie, S.: Kernel pooling for convolutional neural networks. In: CVPR, vol. 1, p. 7 (2017)
3. Dalal, N., Triggs, B., Schmid, C.: Human detection using oriented histograms of flow and appearance. In: Leonardis, A., Bischof, H., Pinz, A. (eds.) ECCV 2006. LNCS, vol. 3952, pp. 428–441. Springer, Heidelberg (2006). https://doi.org/10.1007/11744047_33

4. Deng, J., Dong, W., Socher, R., Li, L.J., Li, K., Fei-Fei, L.: ImageNet: a large-scale hierarchical image database. In: IEEE Conference on Computer Vision and Pattern Recognition, CVPR 2009, pp. 248–255. IEEE (2009)
5. Donahue, J., et al.: Long-term recurrent convolutional networks for visual recognition and description. In: Proceedings of the IEEE Conference on Computer Vision and Pattern Recognition, pp. 2625–2634 (2015)
6. Feichtenhofer, C., Fan, H., Malik, J., He, K.: Slowfast networks for video recognition. arXiv preprint arXiv:1812.03982 (2018)
7. Feichtenhofer, C., Pinz, A., Wildes, R.: Spatiotemporal residual networks for video action recognition. In: Advances in Neural Information Processing Systems, pp. 3468–3476 (2016)
8. Gan, C., Wang, N., Yang, Y., Yeung, D.Y., Hauptmann, A.G.: DevNet: a deep event network for multimedia event detection and evidence recounting. In: Proceedings of the IEEE Conference on Computer Vision and Pattern Recognition, pp. 2568–2577 (2015)
9. Girshick, R., Donahue, J., Darrell, T., Malik, J.: Rich feature hierarchies for accurate object detection and semantic segmentation. In: Proceedings of the IEEE Conference on Computer Vision and Pattern Recognition, pp. 580–587 (2014)
10. Hu, J., Shen, L., Sun, G.: Squeeze-and-excitation networks. In: Proceedings of the IEEE Conference on Computer Vision and Pattern Recognition, pp. 7132–7141 (2018)
11. Ji, S., Xu, W., Yang, M., Yu, K.: 3D convolutional neural networks for human action recognition. IEEE Trans. Pattern Anal. Mach. Intell. **35**(1), 221–231 (2013)
12. Klaser, A., Marszałek, M., Schmid, C.: A spatio-temporal descriptor based on 3D-gradients. In: BMVC 2008-19th British Machine Vision Conference, pp. 275:1–275:10. British Machine Vision Association (2008)
13. Long, J., Shelhamer, E., Darrell, T.: Fully convolutional networks for semantic segmentation. In: Proceedings of the IEEE Conference on Computer Vision and Pattern Recognition, pp. 3431–3440 (2015)
14. Schölkopf, B., Smola, A.J., Bach, F., et al.: Learning with Kernels: Support Vector Machines, Regularization, Optimization, and Beyond. MIT Press, Cambridge (2002)
15. Simonyan, K., Zisserman, A.: Two-stream convolutional networks for action recognition in videos. In: Advances in Neural Information Processing Systems, pp. 568–576 (2014)
16. Wang, H., Schmid, C.: Action recognition with improved trajectories. In: Proceedings of the IEEE International Conference on Computer Vision, pp. 3551–3558 (2013)
17. Wang, L., Li, W., Li, W., Van Gool, L.: Appearance-and-relation networks for video classification. In: Proceedings of the IEEE Conference on Computer Vision and Pattern Recognition, pp. 1430–1439 (2018)
18. Wang, L., Qiao, Y., Tang, X.: Action recognition with trajectory-pooled deep-convolutional descriptors. In: Proceedings of the IEEE Conference on Computer Vision and Pattern Recognition, pp. 4305–4314 (2015)
19. Wang, L., et al.: Temporal segment networks: towards good practices for deep action recognition. In: Leibe, B., Matas, J., Sebe, N., Welling, M. (eds.) ECCV 2016. LNCS, vol. 9912, pp. 20–36. Springer, Cham (2016). https://doi.org/10.1007/978-3-319-46484-8_2
20. Wang, X., Girshick, R., Gupta, A., He, K.: Non-local neural networks. In: Proceedings of the IEEE Conference on Computer Vision and Pattern Recognition, pp. 7794–7803 (2018)

21. Woo, S., Park, J., Lee, J.-Y., Kweon, I.S.: CBAM: convolutional block attention module. In: Ferrari, V., Hebert, M., Sminchisescu, C., Weiss, Y. (eds.) ECCV 2018. LNCS, vol. 11211, pp. 3–19. Springer, Cham (2018). https://doi.org/10.1007/978-3-030-01234-2_1
22. Yue, K., Sun, M., Yuan, Y., Zhou, F., Ding, E., Xu, F.: Compact generalized non-local network. In: Advances in Neural Information Processing Systems, pp. 6511–6520 (2018)
23. Zhou, B., Khosla, A., Lapedriza, A., Oliva, A., Torralba, A.: Learning deep features for discriminative localization. In: Proceedings of the IEEE Conference on Computer Vision and Pattern Recognition, pp. 2921–2929 (2016)

Differential Privacy with Variant-Noise for Gaussian Processes Classification

Zhili Xiong[1,2(✉)], Longyuan Li[1,2], Junchi Yan[2], Haiyang Wang[1,2], Hao He[1,2], and Yaohui Jin[1,2]

[1] State Key Lab of Advanced Optical Communication System and Network, Shanghai Jiao Tong University, Shanghai, China
[2] Artificial Intelligence Institute, Shanghai Jiao Tong University, Shanghai, China
{zlx_9608,jeffli,yanjunchi,0103050180,hehao,jinyh}@sjtu.edu.cn

Abstract. Incredible capacity of machine learning models to mine the underlying information has led to concerns of privacy disclosure. This makes privacy-preserving learning algorithms become a hot spot. In this paper, we focus on Gaussian processes classification (GPC) with a provable secure and feasible privacy model, differential privacy (DP). First we apply a functional mechanism to design a basic privacy-preserving GP classifier. This involves finding the sensitivity of the outputs, and adding a Gaussian process noise proportional to the sensitivity to the trained classifier. Then we propose a variant-noise mechanism to perturb the classifier with different scaled noise based on the density of dataset. We show that this method can significantly reduce the added noise, whilst sufficiently maintaining the accuracy of the classifier both in theory and experiments.

Keywords: Machine learning · Gaussian processes · Differential privacy

1 Introduction

Massive data collected from our daily lives enables machine learning algorithms to find our habits and preferences, however, some information which we should have kept secret, such as financial records and health condition, may also be discovered. For this reason, privacy-preserving learning is becoming a burning issue. At the first glance, we just need "anonymise" the dataset – namely, removing or blurring all the identifiers about individuals (e.g. names, PIN codes, etc.) to keep the dataset private. However, such treatment and traditional $k-$anonymity or $l-$diversity based methods have been proved to be not sufficient due to the existence of "background" or auxiliary information related to the dataset [9,17]. Instead, differential privacy [7], as a standard of privacy with strict mathematical foundation, gives a more reliable and practical privacy-preserving framework with no assumption about auxiliary information, making the statistical characteristics of the dataset be remained, whilst any individual record will not be leaked.

© Springer Nature Switzerland AG 2019
A. C. Nayak and A. Sharma (Eds.): PRICAI 2019, LNAI 11672, pp. 107–119, 2019.
https://doi.org/10.1007/978-3-030-29894-4_9

In this paper our goal is to build a differentially private Gaussian processes (GP) classifier by perturbing GP's fit with specifically distributed noise. In our view, for a sample data point of the training dataset, the label of the sample, $\mathbf{y}$, is considered as the output, whilst the rest of features, $\mathbf{X}$, being the input, and we try to exploit the input to make the output private. This point of view is reasonable in that usually in actual structured dataset, only a portion of features need to be kept private (in our case, only one), and the rest can be directly exposed. With this treatment, the majority of information in the dataset can be still learned by classifier, whilst the private feature is perturbed. This will be a significative attempt to help dataset managers to share their data without fear of privacy disclosure.

To address this issue, we apply differential privacy to GP classifier by calculating the *sensitivity* of the classifier, which measures the maximum variation of classifier's predicted expectation when only one sample in the training dataset is changed. It's not necessary to calculate the sensitivity of the predicted variance in that we find the variance is not relevant to private features. Different from the case in GP regression (GPR), the sensitivity in GPC model is hard to obtain an accurate solution with analytical methods, but need approximation techniques to estimate. Here we use Laplacian approximation and find an upper bound of the sensitivity. Then we adopt a functional mechanism proposed by [10] to add Gaussian process noise to the predicted expectation. However, this is not the most efficient way. In real-world datasets, distribution of data points is not always uniform. If we take the "density"[1] of dataset into consideration, we can expect a privacy mechanism to add larger noise to sparse parts, and add smaller noise to dense parts. That means we need an approach to more accurately describe the similarity of data points. To achieve this, we introduce Mahalanobis distance to capture the density information of the dataset. In this condition, noise added to the outputs should be a multivariate Gaussian variable, instead of a Gaussian process. Experiments on both synthetic dataset and real-world dataset show that this variant-noise mechanism can sufficiently preserve the performance of the GP classifier.

In summary, this paper makes contributions as follows:

(a) To the best of our knowledge, our work is the first research on the design of a Gaussian processes classification model with differential privacy.
(b) We use Laplacian approximation method to present a simple GP classifier by bounding the changes in the predictive expectation caused by modification of a single record in the dataset. Then we take the density distribution of the dataset into consideration and redefine the sensitivity with Mahalanobis distance to propose a variant-noise privacy mechanism to reduce the scale of added noise.

---

[1] When we say a datapoint is of high density, that means in its neighbourhood of a given radius, there are a relatively larger amount of data points than that of a datapoint with low density.

(c) Experiments on synthetic datasets and real-world datasets verify that, our presented variant-noise privacy mechanism can sufficiently maintain the performance of a standard GP classifier.

2 Related Work

Gaussian processes based methods have been widely used in classical machine learning tasks, such as regression [3], classification [12], and dimensionality reduction [11]. Combination of GP and deep neural networks is a new attractive area. A typical instance is deep Gaussian processes (DGP), which is essentially a deep belief network (DBN) based on GP mappings [6]. Under the frame of DGP, data is modeled as the output of a multivariate Gaussian processes. Correspondingly, inputs are governed by another GP. Then GPLVM can be seen as a single layer of a DGP model. More generally, a fully-connected neural network of single layer with an i.i.d. prior over its parameters is equivalent to a GP [13].

A machine learning model with differential privacy [7] allows algorithms (or *queries*) to be sufficiently accurate without disclosing individual private information. Many basic machine learning algorithms, including logistic regression, expectation maximization and deep neural networks can become differentially private by adding noise to parameters of models [1,4,14]. A more universal approach is introducing a noise term to the empirical risk function of models then obtaining perturbed parameters by optimising this noised risk function [5]. But for functional data, where the functions are assumed to be lying in a reproducing kernel Hilbert space (RKHS) generated by a GP kernel, the noise should be a random process (e.g. Gaussian process) with a sensitivity measured in terms of the RKHS norm [10].

3 Preliminaries

3.1 Differential Privacy

For a dataset $\mathcal{D}$ and all potential *neighbouring* dataset $\mathcal{D}'$ (i.e. $\mathcal{D}'$ and $\mathcal{D}$ can only differ in one sample), a randomised query algorithm R is $(\varepsilon, \delta)-$differentially private if

$$\Pr\{R(\mathcal{D}) \in m\} \leqslant e^{\varepsilon} \cdot \Pr\{R(\mathcal{D}') \in m\} + \delta, \tag{1}$$

where m is any possible subset of query outputs, and ε and δ are two usually small positive numbers called privacy parameters. A smaller ε or δ provides a higher degree of privacy, and if we set δ to 0, a stronger definition named $\varepsilon-$differential privacy can be readily obtained. A differentially private algorithm guarantees that the output of the algorithm will not change significantly if a single record in dataset has been modified. In cryptography terms, differential privacy can be used to avoid *differential attack*. That means, an attacker can not get any new information about a specific user through comparing outputs generated from a pair of neighbouring datasets. Common methods to achieve differential privacy include perturbation and sampling [8].

3.2 Gaussian Processes Classification

Gaussian processes classification (GPC) can be considered as a natural generalisation of Gaussian processes regression (GPR). Concretely, if the output of a GP regressor is mapped onto the interval $[0, 1]$ through a *squash* function, then this output value represents the probability of a sample belonging to one of the two classes. In practical implementation [15], a GP is "interposed" between the data point and squash function. Then for a new data point $\boldsymbol{x}_*$, the GP classification involves a two-step procedure:

1. Place a GP prior over the *latent function* $f(\boldsymbol{x})$, which depicts the likelihood of one class versus the other with respect to $\boldsymbol{x}$.
2. Map the value $f(\boldsymbol{x}_*)$ onto $[0, 1]$ through a sigmoidal function: $\pi(f) = \mathrm{Pr}(y = 1|f)$.

The Gaussian cumulative distribution function, or *probit* function usually denoted as $\Phi(x)$ is the most frequently used squash function. Under this frame, the expected value of the probability $\pi_* = \pi(f_*) = \Phi(f_*)$ is

$$\bar{\pi}_* = \Phi\left(\frac{\bar{f}_*}{\sqrt{1 + \mathrm{var}(f_*)}}\right), \tag{2}$$

where the expectation and variance of the predictive distribution are as follows:

$$\bar{f}_* = \boldsymbol{k}_* K^{-1}\hat{\mathbf{f}}, \tag{3}$$

$$\mathrm{var}(f_*) = \boldsymbol{k}_{**} - \boldsymbol{k}_*(K')^{-1}\boldsymbol{k}_*^{\mathrm{T}}. \tag{4}$$

Here $k_{**} = k(\boldsymbol{x}_*, \boldsymbol{x}_*)$ is the prior variance of the new data point, k_* is the covariance vector between the new data point and the training dataset, and K' can be considered as the covariance of the training dataset (but not exactly the same). Due to the lack of space we omit a detailed explanation of these symbols, which can be found in [15]. The value of $\hat{\mathbf{f}}$ can not be calculated directly through analytical methods, but need some approximate techniques, such as Laplace approximation and expectation propagation [2].

4 Applying Differential Privacy to Gaussian Processes Classifier

One straightforward way to design a differentially private GP classifier is directly applying classical Laplacian mechanism to the predictive expectation $\bar{\pi}_*$ in Eq. (2). The sensitivity of $\bar{\pi}_*$ is also obvious: the range of probit function $\Phi(x)$ (or any other squash function) is $[0, 1]$, therefore $\Delta\bar{\pi}_* = 1$. But after being added noise based on this sensitivity, the new $\bar{\pi}_*$ may become an invalid value. We can adopt a "cut-off" Laplace mechanism to restrict the perturbed value of $\bar{\pi}_*$:

$$\tilde{\pi}_* = \begin{cases} 0, & \bar{\pi}_* + \mathrm{Lap}(\frac{\Delta\bar{\pi}_*}{\varepsilon}) < 0 \\ \bar{\pi}_* + \mathrm{Lap}(\frac{\Delta\bar{\pi}_*}{\varepsilon}), & 0 \leqslant \bar{\pi}_* + \mathrm{Lap}(\frac{\Delta\bar{\pi}_*}{\varepsilon}) \leqslant 1 \\ 1, & \bar{\pi}_* + \mathrm{Lap}(\frac{\Delta\bar{\pi}_*}{\varepsilon}) > 1 \end{cases} \tag{5}$$

where $\text{Lap}(\cdot)$ denotes the Laplacian distribution and $\Delta\bar{\pi}_*$ is taken as 1. However, many values of $\tilde{\pi}_*$ will be set to 0 or 1 if we handle it in this manner. This means that GP classification, as a probabilistic *soft* classification method, is approximately simplified to a *hard* classification method. Such a privacy mechanism remarkably reducing the practicality of algorithms is obviously not expected. Alternatively, we can privatise $\bar{\pi}_*$ by adding noise to $\dfrac{\bar{f}_*}{\sqrt{1+\text{var}(f_*)}}$.

It is worth noting that the variance $\text{var}(f_*)$ does not depend on the output $\boldsymbol{y}$ (or $\mathbf{f}$) of the training dataset, so we only need to make the expectation function $\bar{f}_*$ private. The proposed mechanism in [10] applies DP to functional data. Consider a continuous function f which we try to release with privacy. In RKHS space $\mathcal{H}$, f can be seen as a point. Now we use f' to denote the query function applying to the same dataset as the counterpart of f, except that one sample in the dataset has been modified. That means, the values of f and f' are generated using two neighbouring datasets, respectively. The sensitivity of f is defined as the supremum of the RKHS distance of f and f', $\|f - f'\|_{\mathcal{H}}$:

$$\sup_{D, D'} \|f - f'\|_{\mathcal{H}} \leqslant \Delta. \tag{6}$$

The seminal work [10] further proved that, a perturbed version of f formalised as

$$\tilde{f} = f + \frac{c(\delta) \cdot \Delta}{\varepsilon} G \tag{7}$$

is $(\varepsilon, \delta)-$ differentially private if $c(\delta)$ satisfies

$$c(\delta) \geqslant \sqrt{2 \log \frac{2}{\delta}} \tag{8}$$

and G is a sample function from a Gaussian process prior which has the same kernel as f. Notice that $c(\delta)$ should be set as a constant, instead of a function of δ.

Now our target is to find the concrete form of $\Delta(\bar{f}_*)$, which measures the variation of $\bar{f}_*$ if one record in dataset has been perturbed. Notice that $\boldsymbol{k}_*$ and K in Eq. (3) can be seen as constant in neighbouring datasets, then the sensitivity of $\bar{f}_*$ becomes

$$\Delta = \|\bar{f}_*(D) - \bar{f}_*(D')\| = \|\boldsymbol{k}_* K^{-1}\| \cdot \|\hat{\mathbf{f}}(D) - \hat{\mathbf{f}}(D')\|. \tag{9}$$

If we adopt Laplace method to approximate $\hat{\mathbf{f}}$, then its value is determined by

$$\hat{\mathbf{f}} = K \nabla \log p(\mathbf{y}|\hat{\mathbf{f}}). \tag{10}$$

This equation is difficult to solve with analytical method, but we only need to estimate an upper bound of $\|\hat{\mathbf{f}}(D) - \hat{\mathbf{f}}(D')\|$. We expand $p(\mathbf{y}|\hat{\mathbf{f}})$ to

$$p(\mathbf{y}|\hat{\mathbf{f}}) = \prod_{i=1}^{n} p(y_i|\hat{f}_i). \tag{11}$$

The logarithmic form is more convenient for further calculations, so take the logarithms of both sides in Eq. (11) and we have

$$\log p(\mathbf{y}|\hat{\mathbf{f}}) = \sum_{i=1}^{n} \log p(y_i|\hat{f}_i). \tag{12}$$

Therefore, $\hat{\mathbf{f}}(D) - \hat{\mathbf{f}}(D')$ can be written as:

$$
\begin{aligned}
&K\nabla \log p(\mathbf{y}|\hat{\mathbf{f}}(D)) - K\nabla \log p(\mathbf{y}|\hat{\mathbf{f}}(D')) \\
&= K\nabla[\log p(\mathbf{y}|\hat{\mathbf{f}}(D)) - \log p(\mathbf{y}|\hat{\mathbf{f}}(D'))] \\
&= K\nabla \sum_{i=1}^{n}[\log p(y_i|\hat{f}_i(D)) - \log p(y_i|\hat{f}_i(D'))].
\end{aligned}
\tag{13}
$$

Now we make an assumption similar to the kernel density estimation example in [10], that in D and D', variation happens at only one position, e.g. $\hat{f}_n$. This indicates $\hat{f}_i(D) = \hat{f}_i(D')$ for $1 \leqslant i \leqslant n-1$, then $p(y_i|\hat{f}_i(D)) = p(y_i|\hat{f}_i(D'))$ for $1 \leqslant i \leqslant n-1$. All but the last term in Eq. (13) thereby cancel, and Eq. (13) can be simplified to

$$\hat{\mathbf{f}}(D) - \hat{\mathbf{f}}(D') = K\nabla[\log p(y_n|\hat{f}_n(D)) - \log p(y_n|\hat{f}_n(D'))]. \tag{14}$$

As already mentioned, the form of $p(y_i|\hat{f}_i)$ is probit function $\Phi(\cdot)$, which yields

$$\frac{\partial}{\partial \hat{f}_n} \log p(y_n|\hat{f}_n) = \frac{y_n \mathcal{N}(\hat{f}_n)}{\Phi(y_n \hat{f}_n)}. \tag{15}$$

Put this result substitute into Eq. (14), we obtain

$$
\begin{aligned}
\|\hat{\mathbf{f}}(D) - \hat{\mathbf{f}}(D')\| &= \|\hat{f}_n(D) - \hat{f}_n(D')\| \\
&= |K| \left\| \frac{y_n \mathcal{N}(\hat{f}_n(D))}{\Phi(y_n \hat{f}_n(D))} - \frac{y_n \mathcal{N}(\hat{f}_n(D'))}{\Phi(y_n \hat{f}_n(D'))} \right\| \\
&= |K|y_n \left\| \frac{\mathcal{N}(\hat{f}_n(D))}{\Phi(y_n \hat{f}_n(D))} - \frac{\mathcal{N}(\hat{f}_n(D'))}{\Phi(y_n \hat{f}_n(D'))} \right\|.
\end{aligned}
\tag{16}
$$

Again, this equation is not analytically soluble since $\hat{f}_n(D)$ and $\hat{f}_n(D')$ appear on both sides. To obtain an upper bound, we might as well assume maximum of $\|\hat{f}_n(D) - \hat{f}_n(D')\|$ has been fund and let d be this maximum. Now consider the maximum of

$$|K|y_n \left\| \frac{\mathcal{N}(\hat{f}_n(D))}{\Phi(y_n \hat{f}_n(D))} - \frac{\mathcal{N}(\hat{f}_n(D'))}{\Phi(y_n \hat{f}_n(D'))} \right\|. \tag{17}$$

Because $\Phi(\cdot)$ is a continuous function with range $[0, 1]$, $\Phi(y_n \hat{f}_n(D))$ can be considered almost equal to $\Phi(y_n \hat{f}_n(D'))$. Consequently all that left to do is calculating the maximum value of $\|\mathcal{N}(\hat{f}_n(D)) - \mathcal{N}(\hat{f}_n(D'))\|$ given $\|\hat{f}_n(D) - \hat{f}_n(D')\| = d$.

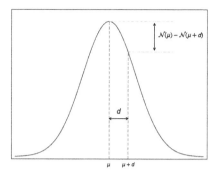

Fig. 1. If $\hat{f}_n(D)$ or $\hat{f}_n(D')$ equals the normal distribution's mean value, μ, $\|\mathcal{N}(\hat{f}_n(D)) - \mathcal{N}(\hat{f}_n(D'))\|$ is maximised.

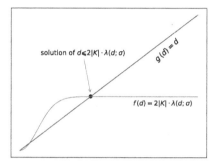

Fig. 2. An illustration of the function $\lambda(d;\sigma)$ and how its three features of this function determine the upper bound of d through Eq. (18): the solution of inequality $d \leqslant 2|K| \cdot \lambda(d;\sigma)$ must be in the form of $d \leqslant M$.

The bell shape of the normal distribution curve clearly demonstrates that $\|\mathcal{N}(\hat{f}_n(D)) - \mathcal{N}(\hat{f}_n(D'))\|$ reaches the maximum when $\hat{f}_n(D)$ or $\hat{f}_n(D')$ just lies in the expectation of the normal distribution, as shown in Fig. 1.

Therefore, for a specific normal distribution $\mathcal{N}(x;\mu,\sigma)$, we can use $\lambda(d;\mu,\sigma)$ to denote

$$\max_{\hat{f}_n(D),\hat{f}_n(D')} \|\mathcal{N}(\hat{f}_n(D)) - \mathcal{N}(\hat{f}_n(D'))\|,$$

when $\|\hat{f}_n(D) - \hat{f}_n(D')\| = d$. We can further notice that $\lambda(d;\mu,\sigma)$ is independent to μ, hence $\lambda(d;\sigma)$ is also an acceptable notation. Another obvious conclusion is that when $\|\hat{f}_n(D) - \hat{f}_n(D')\|$ reaches its maximum, y_n in Eq. (17) equals 1. Recall that both $\hat{f}_n(D)$ and $\hat{f}_n(D')$ lie in the expectation value of normal curve, then $\Phi(y_n\hat{f}_n(D)) \approx \Phi(y_n\hat{f}_n(D')) \approx \frac{1}{2}$. Now substitute these results into Eq. (16), we obtain

$$d \leqslant 2|K| \cdot \lambda(d;\sigma). \tag{18}$$

We only need to show this inequality did determine an upper bound of d without solving it and finding the concrete value. This can be guaranteed by three features of the function $\lambda(d;\sigma)$: (a) $\lambda(0;\sigma) = 0$; (b) $\frac{\partial}{\partial d}\lambda(d;\sigma) \geqslant 0$; (c) $|\lambda(d;\sigma)| \leqslant \mathcal{N}(\mu)$.

Figure 2 gives a brief illustration of how Eq. (18) determines a upper bound of d.

Now that the maximum of d is known, substitute it into Eq. (9) and Δ can be expressed as

$$\Delta = \|\boldsymbol{k}_* K^{-1}\|d, \tag{19}$$

where d is controlled by Eq. (18). If we assume further that values of kernel function is bounded, e.g. $0 \leqslant k(x_i, x_j) \leqslant 1$ (not unreasonable, as many kernels, such as the Gaussian kernel, satisfies this constraint), we get a more concise form of the sensitivity:

$$\Delta = d|K^{-1}|. \tag{20}$$

This is the sensitivity we need to make $\bar{f}_*$, or $\bar{\pi}_*$ private. However, privacy mechanism based on this sensitivity is not the most efficient approach to use our privacy budget. In a real-world dataset, distribution of data points can be uneven, which suggests that we can exploit a new mechanism to add larger noise to sparse area, whilst add smaller noise to dense area, instead of perturbing all the outputs with the same scaled noise. In the following section we show how to significantly reduce the added noise by introducing Mahalanobis distance to reflect the density distribution of dataset.

5   Differential Privacy with Variant-Noise for Gaussian Processes Classification

A theorem in [10] can help us to find a way to add variant noise according to the density of dataset: for a positive definite symmetric matrix (covariance matrix) $M \in \mathbb{R}^{d \times d}$, if vectors of query results denoted as $v_D \in \mathbb{R}^d$ satisfy

$$\sup_{D,D'} \|M^{-\frac{1}{2}}(v_D - v_{D'})\|_2 \leqslant \Delta, \tag{21}$$

then a released version of v_D defined as

$$\tilde{v}_D = v_D + \frac{c(\delta) \cdot \Delta}{\varepsilon}Z \tag{22}$$

achieves (ε, δ)−differential privacy. Here Z is a d−dimensional vector randomly sampled from a multivariate Gaussian distribution $\mathcal{N}_d(0, M)$ and $c(\delta)$ meets the same condition as in Eq. (8). In our case, v_D means the expectation values of the predictive distribution, $\bar{f}_*$. Compare Eq. (22) with Eq. (7), the main change is $\tilde{v}_D$ is *discretised*, i.e. functional data f_D becomes vectorised data v_D, and Gaussian process noise G becomes Gaussian distributed noise Z. This change can be interpreted as placing a priori upon test data points.

As in Eq. (21), now we introduce Mahalanobis distance matrix M, instead of simply using norm to define the sensitivity. In this way we can establish a linkage between the density of dataset and the sensitivity therein. In order to obtain a noise with smaller scale, we expect M to have larger covariance in sparser area, i.e. in those directions more stronger affected by changes in single training data point [16].

Let $\bar{\boldsymbol{f}}_*$ be the vector constructed by values of $\bar{f}_* = \boldsymbol{k}_* K^{-1} \hat{\mathbf{f}}$ for all test data points, and corresponding $\boldsymbol{k}_* K^{-1}$ can build a matrix $C = \mathbf{K}_* K^{-1}$. Then

$$\bar{\boldsymbol{f}}_*(D) - \bar{\boldsymbol{f}}_*(D') = C\big(\hat{\mathbf{f}}(D) - \hat{\mathbf{f}}(D')\big). \tag{23}$$

Here $\bar{\boldsymbol{f}}_*$ contains the predicted values for new test data points, and $\hat{\mathbf{f}}$ only depends on training data, therefore C entirely reflects how outputs on new data points will change after training dataset is modified. Substitute $\bar{\boldsymbol{f}}_*$ into Eq. (21), we have

$$\|M^{-\frac{1}{2}}(\bar{\boldsymbol{f}}_*(D) - \bar{\boldsymbol{f}}_*(D'))\|_2 = \|M^{-\frac{1}{2}}C(\hat{\mathbf{f}}(D) - \hat{\mathbf{f}}(D'))\|_2. \tag{24}$$

We have used the symmetry of M. Similar to the treatment described earlier in this article, now we still assume that $\hat{f}_n$ is the only position where change happens when D becomes D', and the difference between $\hat{f}_n(D)$ and $\hat{f}_n(D')$ is at most d. Note that d has been determined in Eq. (18). Let $\mathbf{c}_n$ be the n−th column of C, then

$$\begin{aligned}\|M^{-\frac{1}{2}}C(\hat{\mathbf{f}}(D) - \hat{\mathbf{f}}(D'))\|_2 &= \|M^{-\frac{1}{2}}d\mathbf{c}_n\|_2 \\ &= (dM^{-\frac{1}{2}}\mathbf{c}_n)^{\mathrm{T}}(dM^{-\frac{1}{2}}\mathbf{c}_n) \\ &= d^2(\mathbf{c}_n^{\mathrm{T}}M^{-1}\mathbf{c}_n).\end{aligned} \tag{25}$$

In this equation, for a given training dataset, d is a constant, and $\mathbf{c}_n$ reflects the distance or similarity of data points. For a new test point, $\mathbf{c}_n$ is also a definite vector. To reduce the scale of noise in Eq. (22), we just need to minimise Eq. (25) with respect to M, which can be solved by universal multivariate optimisation algorithms. Let M_* denote the optimal solution of M, then the sensitivity of $\hat{\boldsymbol{f}}_*$ is bounded by the inequality

$$\varDelta \leqslant d^2 \min_i(\mathbf{c}_i^{\mathrm{T}}M_{*i}^{-1}\mathbf{c}_i). \tag{26}$$

We have taken the random selection of $\mathbf{c}_n$ into consideration and use M_{*i} to denote the solution when $\mathbf{c}_i$ is chosen, i.e. when $\hat{f}_i$ is the only position where change happens. Obviously, the upper bound of $\varDelta$ in Eq. (26) is variant for different test points, which can help us to add variant noise to outputs based on the density distribution of dataset.

6   Experiments

In this section, we test our proposed method both on a synthetic dataset and an actual dataset. We use the standard non-private GP classification and the cut-off Laplacian mechanism for comparison.

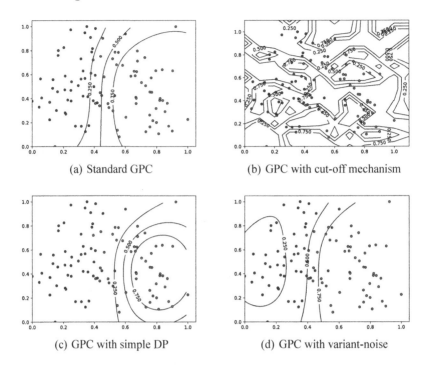

Fig. 3. Decision boundaries generated by a standard GP classifier and GP classifiers with three different noise mechanisms. We have set $\varepsilon = 1$ and $\delta = 0.01$ for all three differentially private GP classifiers. We can see that classification boundaries generated by cut-off mechanism are of many discontinuities, compared to smooth boundaries generated by another two privacy mechanisms. This is because continuity of $\Phi(\cdot)$ is seriously destroyed by cut-off treatment, but if indirect perturbation strategy is applied, squashed feature of $\Phi(\cdot)$ can overcome this limitation.

6.1   Results on Synthetic Data

First we experiment with a synthetic dataset to demonstrate how the accuracy of classifiers will degrade when our presented mechanisms are applied, compared to that of the standard non-private GP classification method. There are 100 sample data points in both training and test dataset.

In Fig. 3 we show an overview of decision boundaries generated by a standard GP classifier and three differentially private GP classifiers with different privacy mechanisms. We can easily see that, the cut-off strategy (Fig. 3(b)), i.e. directly adding noise to $\bar{\pi}_*$ in Eq. (2) then restricting the new values, generates "fragmented" decision boundaries, whilst indirect perturbation (Fig. 3(c) and (d)) by noising $\frac{\bar{f}_*}{\sqrt{1+\mathrm{var}(f_*)}}$ can well maintain the smoothness of classification boundaries. This is a natural result in that the cut-off treatment as in Eq. (5) gravely destroys the continuity of the function $\Phi(\cdot)$, but indirect perturbation can reduce such destruction through squashed feature of $\Phi(\cdot)$. Figure 4 describes the reduction of

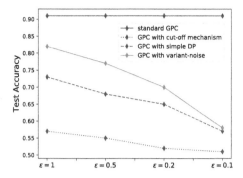

Fig. 4. The degradation of differentially private classifiers' accuracies when ε varies (We have set δ to 0.01 for all cases). Reduction of accuracies with the decrease of ε reflects the tradeoff between privacy and performance of models. Accuracy of the classifier with cut-off Laplacian mechanism is close to 50% throughout, i.e. a random classifier. Meanwhile, compared to the counterpart with simple DP, the classifier with variant-noise mechanism can better preserve the performance of the standard GP classifier.

the accuracy when we vary the value of ε in a more intuitive way. Noting that a smaller ε yields a noise with a larger scale, then accuracies of classifiers (with differential privacy) degrade with the decrease of ε. On the other hand, reducing ε corresponds to the strengthening guarantee of privacy. This reflects a tradeoff between privacy and usability of learning algorithms. From Fig. 4 we can find the cut-off mechanism achieve privacy at the expense of almost all the practicability of models: the accuracy is close to that of random classification. Results in this experiment also verify that our proposed variant-noise mechanism can better preserve the performance of the standard GP classifier than the simple DP functional mechanism (as an evenly noise adding strategy).

6.2   Results on Real-World Data

We also perform a simple test of our proposed method on an actual oil dataset provided by NCRG of Aston University[2]. This dataset is used to model measurements on a pipe-line transporting a mixture of oil, gas and water, including 2000 records. It contains 12 (real-valued) features to describe the mixture flow in the pipe with a category label. The flow of mixture belongs to one of three possible configurations: horizontally stratified, nested annular or homogeneous mixture.

We adopt the "one vs. rest" (OvR) strategy to train three GP binary classifiers for this multi-classification task. In Table 1 we give the results of our experiments. On this dataset, classifier with cut-off Laplacian mechanism become unstable, but two indirect perturbing strategies can still generate classifiers perform better than random classification even with large noise. Further more, our proposed variant-noise mechanism can best maintain the performance of the non-private model.

---

[2] http://www.aston.ac.uk/eas/research/groups/ncrg.

Table 1. Experimental results of test on NCRG oil dataset. ($\delta = 0.01$ for all ε)

Models	Test accuracy			
	$\varepsilon = 1$	$\varepsilon = 0.5$	$\varepsilon = 0.2$	$\varepsilon = 0.1$
Standard GPC	0.85	0.85	0.85	0.85
Cut-off mechanism	0.51	0.50	0.45	0.44
Simple DP	0.66	0.64	0.60	0.53
Variant-noise mechanism	0.75	0.72	0.66	0.56

Optimisation of Hyper-Parameters. So far we have not mentioned how we optimise hyper-parameters in a standard GP classification model, including $\hat{\mathbf{f}}$, K' in Eqs. (3) and (4), and the scale parameter l of the kernel function. This is because concrete optimisation of these hyper-parameters is not relevant to our privacy protection strategy. Note that we add noise to a *trained* classifier, instead of a *training* classifier, which guarantees that we can ignore the impact of the selection of optimisation methods. As a contrast, some models achieve differential privacy by being perturbed parameters during the training process (e.g. in gradient descent), including convolutional neural networks [1].

7   Conclusion

We have designed a differentially private Gaussian processes classifier. Through the analysis of the Laplacian approximation method, we find the sensitivity of a GP classifier. Then we make an improvement by introducing the density distribution of dataset into the calculation of sensitivity and present a variant-noise mechanism. Using this approach, we are able to add different scaled noise to outputs generated from different areas of the dataset. In this way, the total noise can be reduced compared with an evenly noise adding strategy, and the performance of GP classifier can be preserved to a great extent. As future work, we plan to apply differential privacy to online learning cases, and GP classification with other approximation techniques, e.g. expectation propagation.

Acknowledgements. This work is supported by National Key Research and Development Program of China (No. 2018YFC0830400) and Shanghai Electric Vehicle Public Data Center.

References

1. Abadi, M., et al.: Deep learning with differential privacy. In: ACM Conference on Computer and Communications Security (CCS) (2016)
2. Bishop, C.M.: Pattern Recognition and Machine Learning. Springer, New York (2006)
3. Quiñonero Candela, J., Rasmussen, C.E.: A unifying view of sparse approximate Gaussian process regression. J. Mach. Learn. Res. **6**, 1939–1959 (2005)

4. Chaudhuri, K., Monteleoni, C.: Privacy-preserving logistic regression. In: Advances in Neural Information Processing Systems (NIPS) (2008)
5. Chaudhuri, K., Monteleoni, C., Sarwate, A.D.: Differentially private empirical risk minimization. J. Mach. Learn. Res. **12**, 1069–1109 (2011)
6. Damianou, A., Lawrence, N.: Deep Gaussian processes. In: International Conference on Artificial Intelligence and Statistics (AISTATS) (2013)
7. Dwork, C.: Differential privacy. In: Bugliesi, M., Preneel, B., Sassone, V., Wegener, I. (eds.) ICALP 2006. LNCS, vol. 4052, pp. 1–12. Springer, Heidelberg (2006). https://doi.org/10.1007/11787006_1
8. Dwork, C., Roth, A.: The algorithmic foundations of differential privacy. Found. Trends Theor. Comput. Sci. **9**(3–4), 211–407 (2014)
9. Ganta, S.R., Kasiviswanathan, S.P., Smith, A.: Composition attacks and auxiliary information in data privacy. In: ACM Conference on Knowledge Discovery and Data Mining (SIGKDD) (2008)
10. Hall, R., Rinaldo, A., Wasserman, L.A.: Differential privacy for functions and functional data. J. Mach. Learn. Res. **14**(1), 703–727 (2013)
11. Lawrence, N.D.: Gaussian process latent variable models for visualisation of high dimensional data. In: Advances in Neural Information Processing Systems (NIPS) (2004)
12. Lawrence, N.D., Seeger, M., Herbrich, R.: Fast sparse Gaussian process methods: the informative vector machine. In: Advances in Neural Information Processing Systems (NIPS) (2002)
13. Lee, J., Sohl-dickstein, J., Pennington, J., Novak, R., Schoenholz, S., Bahri, Y.: Deep neural networks as Gaussian processes. In: International Conference on Learning Representations (ICLR) (2018)
14. Park, M., Foulds, J.R., Chaudhuri, K., Welling, M.: DP-EM: differentially private expectation maximization. In: International Conference on Artificial Intelligence and Statistics (AISTATS) (2017)
15. Rasmussen, C.E., Williams, C.K.I.: Gaussian Processes for Machine Learning. MIT Press, Cambridge (2005)
16. Smith, M.T., Álvarez, M., Zwiessele, M., Lawrence, N.D.: Differentially private regression with Gaussian processes. In: International Conference on Artificial Intelligence and Statistics (AISTATS) (2018)
17. Steffan, J., Schumacher, M.: Collaborative attack modeling. In: ACM Symposium on Applied Computing (SAC) (2002)

Language Technology

Zero-Shot Slot Filling via Latent Question Representation and Reading Comprehension

Tongtong Wu, Meng Wang, Huan Gao, Guilin Qi$^{(\boxtimes)}$, and Weizhuo Li

School of Computer Science and Engineering, Southeast University, Nanjing, China
{wutong8023,meng.wang,gh,gqi}@seu.edu.cn, liweizhuo@amss.ac.cn

Abstract. Slot filling is a demanding task of knowledge base population, which aims to extract facts about particular entities from unstructured text automatically. Most of the existing approaches rely on pretrained extraction models which may suffer from robustness caused by unseen slots, or the so-called zero-shot slot filling problem. Recent studies try to reduce the slot filling to a machine reading comprehension task and achieve certain improvements on unseen slots, but they still face challenges to generate appropriate questions for models and find the right answers. In this paper, we propose a novel end-to-end approach to address the zero-shot slot filling by unifying the natural language question generation and machine reading comprehension. Especially, we explore how to learn a well-organized latent question representation by incorporating external knowledge. We conduct extensive experiments to validate the effectiveness of our model. Experimental results show that the proposed approach outperforms the state-of-the-art baseline methods in zero-shot scenarios.

Keywords: Slot filling · Zero-shot learning · Reading comprehension

1 Introduction

Slot filling (SF) aims at extracting facts about particular entities from unstructured text automatically, and it has gradually become an important task for knowledge base population and completion. A slot is a named attribute, e.g., *spouse*, and fill the specified value of a slot for a given entity, e.g., for the entity *Mark Zuckerberg*, the fill for *spouse* is *Priscilla Chen*. Traditional approaches [6,18] usually treat slot filling as a typical relation extraction task. Given an entity and the slot, they first utilize natural language processing techniques (e.g., named entity recognition and disambiguation) to get several candidate fills from the unstructured text, and then determine the final fill by classifying relationships between the given entity and the candidate fills. Nevertheless, these approaches rely on pre-trained extraction models and fail on unseen slots, or the so-called zero-shot slot filling problem.

© Springer Nature Switzerland AG 2019
A. C. Nayak and A. Sharma (Eds.): PRICAI 2019, LNAI 11672, pp. 123–136, 2019.
https://doi.org/10.1007/978-3-030-29894-4_10

Recently, the template-based approach [8] and the question generation-based approach [11] are proposed to treat slot filling as a machine reading comprehension process and provide a pathway to zero-shot slot filling. Given an entity and the slot, these methods first formulate a natural language question. Then, they get the target fill by a question answering system over the unstructured text. During this process, the input questions for unseen slots could be generated from new manually annotated templates [8] or natural language question generation models [5,11,17]. Additionally, the generated questions of unseen slots can be directly fed into the pre-trained machine reading comprehension model [14] to extract the final answer from the relevant text.

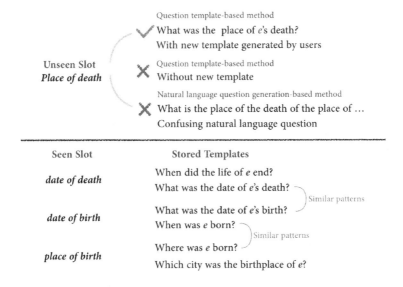

Fig. 1. Zero-shot cases in slot filling

However, existing reading comprehension-based approaches [8,11] still have limitations to generate appropriate questions for models to find the right answers. For instance, Fig. 1 illustrates the scenario of an unseen slot *place_of_death* comparing to several seen slot cases. The template-based model [8] requires skilled annotators to generate new templates for unseen slots in the testing phase and feeds the questions to the pre-trained question answering model. For the question generation-based approach [11], it may generate confusing and useless natural language questions because of lacking-related information in historical training instances. Moreover, since the gradients cannot be passed in natural language, the question generator and the reading comprehension extractor have to be trained individually. Such a pipeline framework combined by a question generator and extractor tends to result in cumulative errors. Therefore, the core issue of zero-shot slot filling is how to produce an appropriate potential question representation to unseen slots with limited manual annotations.

As shown in Fig. 1, we can observe that slots *date_of_birth* and *date_of_death* are both related to a *date* of an entity *e*, so the question could be formulated as "What was the date of *e*'s death (or birth)." It indicates that slots describing the same type of fills may share similar question patterns. We can also observe that *date_of_birth* and *place_of_birth* share the similar question pattern "When (or Where) was *e* born," because these two slots share the same topic word "birth." Therefore, given an unseen slot, although it is difficult to find the specific question template or generate the exact question for the slot, we can infer the target question by leveraging the related seen slots with the same fill type or topic word in training corpus, e.g., the unseen slot *place_of_death* can be asked by "What was the date of *e*'s death (inspired by *date_of_death*) or Where was *e* dead (inspired by *place_of_birth*)." However, directly adopting word embedding-based approaches [9, 12] to compute the similarity between unseen slots and seen slots will not achieve accurate results because of the limited information contained in the single entity and slot embeddings.

To improve the quality of the latent representation of questions and achieve better performance for zero-shot slot filling, we propose a knowledge-enhanced end-to-end framework, which consists of an encoder and an extractor. The encoder is used to capture semantic information of seen slots in a latent variable. This latent variable indicates the universal question distribution of both seen and unseen slots. Benefited from it, the extractor is designed to take the latent variable and the conditions as the question representation and determine the final fill. Especially, we incorporate external knowledge (i.e., Wikipedia abstracts) in both encoder and extractor to enhance the accuracy of questions sampling and fills extracting. We conduct experiments on the dataset proposed by [8], and the experimental results illustrate that the proposed method consistently and significantly outperformed state-of-the-art baselines concerning seen and unseen slots.

The contributions of our study are summarized as follows:

- We propose a knowledge-enhanced end-to-end framework to address slot filling by unifying the natural language question generation and machine reading comprehension. We learn the universal question distribution for sampling instead of generating concrete questions, which is simple but effective for handling the zero-shot slot filling problem.
- We incorporate external knowledge to improve questions sampling in the encoder and fills discovering in the extractor. This also frees the proposed model from human intervention in zero-shot slot filling scenarios.
- We conduct extensive experiments to validate the effectiveness of the proposed framework.

2   Method

To find the accurate fills for a given slot from relevant unstructured texts, we design a unified model with question representation learning and machine reading comprehension. Figure 2 illustrates the overview of the proposed slot filling framework.

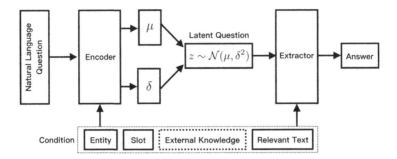

Fig. 2. Overview of the framework. A normal distribution $z \sim \mathcal{N}(\mu, \delta^2)$ of questions is learned into a latent vector space based on the existing slots and external knowledge. Then, the unseen slots can be further filled by the learned distribution and the reading comprehension process.

2.1   Encoder

As above mentioned in Sect. 1, the similar slots share similar questions, and the questions of unseen slots could be inferred from existing questions in the training data. To capture this similarity appropriately and accurately, the proposed framework starts from a variant of Variational Autoencoder (VAE) [7,15] to learn the distribution of latent variable z from question templates x of the seen slots. As questions obey a universal distribution, we can sample the question representation from the distribution for an unseen slot.

In the conventional VAE model, the log-likelihood $\log p(x^{(i)})$ could be written as a sum of the lower bound $\mathcal{L}(\theta; \phi; x^{(i)})$ and the KL divergence between the real posterior $p(z|x^{(i)})$ and the approximation $q_\phi(z|x^{(i)})$:

$$\log p(x^{(i)}) = D_{KL}(q_\phi(z|x^{(i)})||p(z|x^{(i)})) + \mathcal{L}(\theta; \phi; x^{(i)}), \tag{1}$$

where θ is the parameter of the model. Since the KL divergence is non-negative, $\mathcal{L}(\theta; \phi; x^{(i)})$ can be formulated as:

$$\mathcal{L}(\theta; \phi; x^{(i)}) = -D_{KL}(q_\phi(z|x^{(i)})||p(z|x^{(i)})) + \mathbb{E}_{q_\phi(z|x^{(i)})}[\log p_\theta(x^{(i)}|z)], \tag{2}$$

where $-D_{KL}(q_\phi(z|x^{(i)})||p(z|x^{(i)}))$ makes approximate posterior distribution close to prior, and $\mathbb{E}_{q_\phi(z|x^{(i)})}[\log p_\theta(x^{(i)}|z)]$ reconstructs the input data. In the proposed model, we do not need to reconstruct a concrete question $x^{(i)}$ and further modify $\mathbb{E}_{q_\phi(z|x^{(i)})}[\log p_\theta(x^{(i)}|z)]$ to $\mathcal{L}_{ext}(\theta; z)$ (i.e., Extractor in Sect. 2.2).

Following the definition of VAE, we utilize the standard normal distribution $\mathcal{N}(0, I)$ as the specified distribution of $p(z|x)$. Eventually, given an entity e and the slot s, to sample the latent question representation z from $\mathcal{N}(0, I)$ approximately, we take e and s as the condition c and define the approximate distribution as:

$$p(z|x^{(i)}; c^{(i)}) \sim \mathcal{N}(\mu(x^{(i)}; c^{(i)}), \delta^2(x^{(i)}; c^{(i)})), \tag{3}$$

where $\mu(x^{(i)}; c^{(i)})$ and $\delta(x^{(i)}; c^{(i)})$ are arbitrary deterministic functions with parameters ϕ that can be learned from data. To simplify the equation, we use $\mu^{(i)}$ and $\delta^{(i)}$ to represent them respectively:

$$\mathcal{L}(\theta; \phi; x^{(i)}; c^{(i)}) \simeq \frac{1}{2} \sum_{n=1}^{N} (1 + \log((\delta_n^{(i)})^2) - (\mu_n^{(i)})^2 - (\delta_n^{(i)})^2) + \mathcal{L}_{ext}(\theta; z; c^{(i)}). \tag{4}$$

Note that literal information of an unseen slot is limited. For instance, it is difficult to map the unseen slot *spouse* to *wife* or *husband* which are the usual expressions of the slot. Therefore, we incorporate external knowledge k (i.e., Wikipedia description of the slot) into the condition c.

For the structure of the encoder, we utilize Bidirectional Gated Recurrent Units (BiGRU) [4] to model the sequence data from questions and external knowledge. The encoder contains a stack of recurrent connections so that the hidden state h_{t+1} could be calculated based on the previous state and the input data x_t in current time step. The distribution over the latent variable z is obtained from the last state h_{end} of the BiGRU, defined as:

$$\begin{aligned}
\mu_{zx} &= \mathbf{W}_{\mu x}^{\top} h_{endx} + b_{\mu x}; & \log(\delta_{zx}) &= \mathbf{W}_{\delta x}^{\top} h_{endx} + b_{\delta x}, \\
\mu_{zc} &= \mathbf{W}_{\mu c}^{\top} h_{endc} + b_{\mu c}; & \log(\delta_{zc}) &= \mathbf{W}_{\delta c}^{\top} h_{endc} + b_{\delta c}, \\
\mu_z &= [\mu_{zx}, \mu_{zc}]; & \log(\delta_z) &= [\log(\delta_{zx}), \log(\delta_{zc})],
\end{aligned} \tag{5}$$

where μ_{zx} and $\log(\delta_{zx})$ are learned from h_{endx} which is the last state generated from questions. Analogously, the μ_{zc} and $\log(\delta_{zc})$ are learned from h_{endc} which is obtained from c. Finally, the intermediate variable μ_z and $\log(\delta_z)$ could be computed by concatenating both pair of parameters.

Further, the condition c is constituted by three parts, i.e., the given entity e, the specified slot s and the external knowledge k. Usually, e and s are short terms with no more than 5 words. Therefore, we only utilize a two-layer neural network to calculate the μ and $\log(\delta)$ of them. To capture the most related information from external knowledge, we employ the pre-trained word embedding and perform a simplified attention layer:

$$w_t' = [a_{et} w_t, a_{st} w_t], \tag{6}$$

where a_{et} is the attention value calculated by cosine similarity between entity embedding of e and the input w_t in current time step, and the a_{st} is the slot attention value. Each word in external knowledge would be modified as w_t' by this attention layer and generates the μ_k and $\log(\delta_k)$. Additionally, the condition variable μ_{zc} and $\log(\delta_{zc})$ could be expressed as:

$$\begin{aligned}
\mu_{zc} &= [\mu_{ze}, \mu_{zs}, \mu_{zk}], \\
\log(\delta_{zc}) &= [\log(\delta_{ze}), \log(\delta_{zs}), \log(\delta_{zk})].
\end{aligned} \tag{7}$$

Since it is difficult to optimize all parameters with a general normal distribution, we inspired by the work in [7] and obtain the latent variable $z = \mu + \delta\epsilon$, where $\epsilon \sim \mathcal{N}(0, I)$ could be seen as a constant which splits from the optimization.

Based on the above encoding process, the distribution of questions is learned, and the questions of unseen slots could be inferred from the distribution. In the next section, we will introduce how to extract the accurate fill for the slot of a given entity.

2.2 Extractor

Inspired by machine reading comprehension, we reduce the slot filling to a simplified question answering task. For instance, we could regard the given entity *Mark Zuckerberg* and slot *spouse* as a question, and try to extract the accurate answer *Priscilla Chen* as the fill from the relevant text.

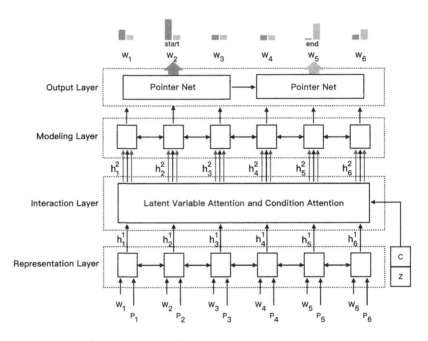

Fig. 3. Structure of the extractor. The extractor is a four-layer network to locate the expected slot value in text $t \supseteq \{w_1, w_2, w_3, \cdots, w_n\}$. Moreover, each word w_i is mapped to a part of speech (POS) tag p_i respectively. Each layer of the extractor is introduced respectively: (1) Representation layer refines the word embeddings and the POS tag embedding with contextual cues from surrounding words. (2) Interaction layer couples the representation of text t with z and c, aligning essential information between them. (3) Modeling layer employs an RNN to scan the context and refine the representation of each word. (4) Output layer returns the answer for the query which depends on the given entity e and the slot s.

In the encoder, we obtain the latent question representation z from $\mathcal{N}(0, I)$. Relatively, in the extractor, the latent variable z and the representation of conditions c (i.e., the given entity e, the slot s, and the external knowledge k) form the input question to the question answering model. As shown in Fig. 3, the extractor is a four-layer network to locate the expected slot value in the text.

Precisely, we utilize BiGRUs in the representation layer to model the temporal interactions between the contextual words of the relevant text t. Then, the hidden state h_i^1 of each time step of representation layer is inputted into the interaction layer which is responsible for aligning and fusing information between the text t and question q (i.e., the condition c and the latent variable z). As shown in Fig. 3, we define a latent variable attention to measure the correlation between each hidden state h_i and the latent variable z:

$$f_z(h_i^1) = \alpha(h_i^1, z)h_i^1, \tag{8}$$

where $\alpha_j \propto h_i^\top z$. Analogously, the condition attention value on each hidden state h_i is computed by:

$$f_c(h_i^1) = \alpha(h_i^1, c)h_i^1. \tag{9}$$

Note that there are three semantic parts, i.e., e, s and k contained in the condition representation. The attention values of these three parts will be computed respectively. Therefore, the modified hidden state h_i^2 (i.e., the combination of h_i^1, $f_z(h_i^1)$ and $f_c(h_i^1)$) is inputted into the modeling layer (or the so-called fusion layer) to combine the different information obtained from the previous layers. We also utilize BiGRUs to modeling this layer. Furthermore, the pointer networks are adapted to indicating the boundary of the expected answer. We mark the start index and end index of the answer as *start* and *end* respectively, and we obtain the probability distribution of the start index by:

$$p_{start} = \text{softmax}(\mathbf{W}_{start}^\top \mathbf{H}), \tag{10}$$

where $\mathbf{W}_{start}^\top$ is a trainable transformation matrix for start index detection, and $\mathbf{H}$ is the concatenated hidden state of the modeling layer. Moreover, we utilize the same strategy to obtain the p_{end}. Further, the objective function of the extractor is to maximize the log probabilities of the true start and end index by the predicted distributions which are averaged over all examples:

$$\mathcal{L}_{ext}(\theta; z; c) = \frac{1}{N} \sum_i^N \log p_{i_{start}} p_{i_{end}} \leq 0, \tag{11}$$

where N is the training sample capacity. Particularly, we modify the model in a way that allows it to decide whether an answer exists by marking the end-of-sentence (EOS) tag as the answer in negative examples. Finally, the total objective could be defined as to minimize the follow function:

$$\mathcal{L}(\theta; \phi; x; c) \simeq - \sum_{n=1}^{N/M} \sum_{i=1}^{M} \{ \frac{1}{2}(1 + \log((\delta_n^{(i)})^2) - (\mu_n^{(i)})^2 - (\delta_n^{(i)})^2) \\ + \log p_\theta(start|z_n^{(i)}, c_n^{(i)}) + \log p_\theta(end|z_n^{(i)}, c_n^{(i)}) \}, \tag{12}$$

where M is the batch size.

Based on the above-extracting process, the boundary of the expected fill is detected, and the span of the expected fill could be inferred from the boundary.

3 Experiments

To verify the performance of the proposed model, we conducted two types of experiments. First, we compare the proposed model to several baseline methods on typical slot filling, in which all slots appeared in the training data. Then, we evaluate the performance of the proposed model in zero-shot scenarios.

3.1 Dataset Construction

We mainly conduct experiments on the dataset in [8], which includes 1,192 high-quality question templates spanning 120 slots and 30,000,000 instances. Each instance is made up of a slot s, a question q, a relevant text t, and a set of answers a. We partitioned the dataset along with slots and randomly clustered each slot into one of three groups: train, dev, or test. Then, we sampled 1,000,000 examples for train, 1,000 for dev, and 10,000 for test. Moreover, we construct the slot descriptions from Wikipedia by extracting the abstract of the most related Wikipedia items automatically.

3.2 Comparison Systems

We take the models proposed in [8] and several variants of the proposed model as baselines. They are named after the preprocessing of the input of machine reading comprehension systems:

1. *KB Slot* only takes an indicator (e.g., R_7) as a question, that means it cannot be generalized to unseen slots.
2. *NL Slot* uses the slot name as the question, but the information of the question is still limited to extract answers from the relevant text.
3. *Single Template* leverages the crowed-source labeled question templates to generate natural language questions. There is only one template per slot could be observed in this model during training.
4. *MultipleTemplates* is a modified version based on *Single Template* and is trained on a diverse set of question templates.
5. *Question Ensemble* is the full vision of baseline, and leverages three questions per test instance and predict answers for each to improve the performance.

Compared with the above models, we consider a more rigorous experiment setting of zero-shot scenarios where there are no manually labeled question templates for unseen slots. Concretely, we leverage auto-aligned slot description as external knowledge and employ a unified model to handle the zero-shot issue. To evaluate the performance of each part, the baseline models are implemented incrementally:

1. $ES - ZES(Att)$ takes *slot* $(entity, ?)$ as the question directly without constraints of external knowledge and question templates, and the latent variable z serves as the only attention key in the extractor.

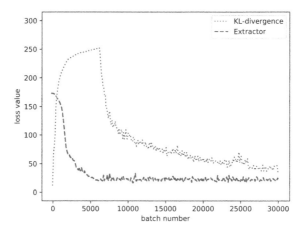

Fig. 4. Loss values in the training procedure

2. $ES - ZES(Cont)$ also takes the *slot* $(entity, ?)$ as the input, but the latent variable z will serve as the context in RNN labeler.
3. $QES(Att)$ takes question template with the entity e and slot s into consideration, such as "who is the wife of x" and *spouse* $(Zuckerberg, ?)$, the question could be formulated as "who is the wife of Zuckerberg" eventually. Such questions serve as the input of VAE, and the original query *slot* $(entity, ?)$ serves as the condition factor.
4. $QES(Wiki)(Att)$ is modified based on $QER(Att)$. External knowledge will be integrated into the model, i.e., slot description (gained from Wikipedia abstracts).
5. $QES(Wiki/POS)(Att)$ leverages the POS tag of each token (gained from the result of spaCy[1]) as the additional knowledge to Wikipedia abstracts.

3.3 Evaluation Metrics and Settings

Following the setting in typical reading comprehension, each instance is evaluated by comparing the predicted span with the tokens in the labeled answer set. Therefore, we employ Precision and Recall to evaluate the performance of the proposed model in the seen slot filling scenario and the zero-shot slot filling scenario at the test time. Precision is the true positive count divided by the number of times the system returned a non-null answer. The recall is the true positive count divided by the number of instances that have an answer.

We first initialized word embeddings with GloVe [12] trained on Wikipedia dataset. Additionally, we created ten folds of train/dev/test slot filling instances partitioned along with entities and slots respectively. We used a grid search strategy to determined the optimal parameters. The search ranges for each parameter follow: the learning rate λ for the Adam algorithm {0.1, 0.01, 0.001}, the

---

[1] https://spacy.io.

Table 1. Performance on seen slot filling

	Precision	Recall	F1
KB Slot	89.08%	91.54%	90.29%
NL Slot	88.23%	91.02%	89.60%
Single Template	77.92%	73.88%	75.84%
Multiple Templates	87.66%	91.32%	89.44%
Question Ensemble	88.08%	91.60%	89.80%
ES-ZES(Cont)	55.70%	57.32%	56.50%
ES-ZES(Att)	61.32%	63.46%	62.37%
QES(Att)	88.94%	91.34%	90.12%
QESK(Wiki)(Att)	90.93%	91.17%	91.05%
QESK(Wiki/POS)(Att)	**91.25%**	**91.63%**	**91.44%**

dimension of word embedding d_w {100, 300, 500}, the dimension of latent variable d_z {100, 300, 500, 1000}. The best configurations for the joint model were: $\lambda = 0.001$, $d_z = 300$, $d_w = 300$. Three epochs were enough for convergence, and each epoch contains 10,000 mini-batches. As shown in Fig. 4, the KL-divergence part converged rapidly in the training procedure, and this made it quite hard to distinguish the semantic information from the input question. To address this problem, we set a flag to control the convergence rate of each part in the loss function by not optimizing KL-divergence part until the extractor is trained to convergence.

3.4   Evaluation on Seen Slot Filling

In this section, we report the performance of the proposed model in a typical slot filling scenario, in which all slots appeared in the training data. As shown in Table 1, *QESK(Wiki/POS) (Att)* achieved the best performance compared with other models in [8]. Note that we obtained the highest F1 to 91.44% without manually annotated templates in testing.

In the listed results of the proposed models, *ES-ZES(Cont)* and *ES-ZES(Att)* performed differently because of the diverse utilization of latent variable generated from entity e and slot s. Specifically, *ES-ZES(Att)* incorporated latent variable z with the attention mechanism, whereas *ES-ZES(Cont)* treated z as the context of RNN in extractor. As a result, the F1 of the model with the attention mechanism is higher than the other one with 5.87%. With the help of natural language questions, the performance of *QES(Att)* (without external knowledge) improved significantly comparing with *ES-ZES(Cont)* and *ES-ZES(Att)*. The different results of *QES(Att)* and *QESK(Wiki)(Att)* show the benefit of incorporating external knowledge (i.e., Wikipedia abstracts) in the training phase. Moreover, with the help of POS tag of each token in the training corpus, *QESK(Wiki/POS)(Att)* achieved the best performance.

Table 2. Performance on unseen slot filling

	Precision	Recall	F1
KB Slot	19.32%	2.54%	4.32%
NL Slot	40.50%	28.56%	33.40%
Single Template	37.18%	31.24%	33.90%
Multiple Templates	43.61%	36.45%	39.61%
Question Ensemble	45.85%	37.44%	41.11%
ES-ZES(Cont)	20.20%	13.52%	16.19%
ES-ZES(Att)	21.36%	20.42%	20.84%
QES(Att)	30.24%	33.34%	31.71%
QESK(Wiki)(Att)	47.35%	40.36%	43.57%
QESK(Wiki/POS)(Att)	**48.52** %	**40.73**%	**44.28**%

3.5   Evaluation on Unseen Slot Filling

In this section, we present the performance of the proposed model in the zero-shot scenario. As shown in Table 2, our model *QESK(Wiki/POS)(Att)* performed better than the best model *Question Ensemble* in [8]. We analyze that there are mainly two reasons for the improvement. On the one hand, we sampled the latent question representation from the learned universal question distribution for an unseen slot, whereas *Question Ensemble* relied on the annotated templates to generate the corresponding question. On the other hand, incorporating external knowledge in both encoder and extractor enhanced the accuracy of question sampling and fills extracting.

Regarding the listed results of the proposed models, *ES-ZES(Cont)* and *ES-ZES(Att)* which only utilize the entity e and slot s are not competitive with the others. The performance of *QES(Att)* improved significantly with 10.87% F1 value comparing with the previous two variants owing to the help of natural language questions. However, *QES(Att)* still could not achieve the performance as well as the baseline *Question Ensemble*, which indicates simply utilizing entities, slots and natural language questions cannot learn and sample appropriate question representations very well. To address this issue, we utilized the Wikipedia abstract as the external knowledge in the training and testing phases. As a result, the performance of *QESK(Wiki)(Att)* shows that external knowledge can contribute to the unseen slot scenario with 11.86% F1 improvement than *QES(Att)*. Note that, *QESK(Wiki)(Att)* did not need a diverse set of question expressions while got a higher F1 score than *Question Ensemble*. Moreover, by adding more syntactic information, i.e., POS tags, in *QESK(Wiki/POS)(Att)*, we achieved the state-of-art performance.

4   Related Work

Slot filling is a significant issue in knowledge base population and completion. Traditional rule-based or pattern-based approaches [2,3,16] directly use rules or patterns to extract instances and usually suffer from the poor generalization and low recall. As mentioned in Sect. 1, many approaches are proposed to reduce the slot filling problem to a typical relation extraction task in recent years. Yu and Ji [18] proposed a graph-based model to fill the slot while they also needed to obtain all entity pairs and classify the relation between them. Adel et al. [1] proposed a conventional neural networks-based slot filling model with the presupposition of detected entities pairs as well. Huang et al. [6] used a pipeline framework to extract all candidate mentions in the source corpus. They proposed attention-based CNN for searching subgraph and detecting the slot type. As relation extraction-based approaches need to obtain all entity pairs by named entity recognition, they suffer from potential error accumulation between pipeline components and are disabled to extract open-type slot values. For instance, the fill is a short description of the appearance or the dead reason for someone.

To address the problem in conventional relation extraction, it is also possible to reduce slot filling to the task of answering simple reading comprehension questions. A typical machine reading task [10,13] could be formulated as utilizing the natural language question q to extract an answer a from the relevant text t, which is quite similar to slot filling tasks. In comparison, machine reading tasks focus on the open-domain natural language understanding, while slot filling focus the knowledge population under a schema and the information of question is limited. Nishida et al. [11] incorporated the information extraction and reading comprehension tasks by supervised multi-task learning, in which the extraction component can be trained by considering answer spans. Levy et al. [8] proposed a new method to utilize the reading comprehension models by modifying slots into natural language questions directly. Nevertheless, they did not solve the zero-shot problem in slot filling because manual annotation was still indispensable to obtain the question templates in testing.

5   Conclusion and Future Work

In this paper, we proposed a unified, end-to-end model with natural language question generation and machine reading comprehension to address the zero-shot slot filling problem. We first utilized a variant VAE to learn a latent variable to represent questions in the encoder. Then, we reduced the slot filling to a simplified question answering process from unstructured text in the extractor. Different from existing approaches, the proposed model learned the universal question distribution for unseen slot sampling instead of generating concrete questions, and we did not require human intervention for unseen slots owing to the external knowledge. Experimental results demonstrated that our model outperformed the state-of-the-art baseline methods in zero-shot scenarios with high precision and recall.

For the future work, we will explore a more general slot filling method based on transfer learning so that lots of labeled data related to machine reading comprehension or other areas can be utilized in the proposed framework. In addition, as introducing knowledge may introduce noise information, we will try to merge some manners (e.g., attention mechanism) to alleviate this issue.

Acknowledgment. This work was supported by National Key Research and Development Program of China (2018YFC0830200), National Natural Science Foundation of China Key Project (U1736204) and the Fundamental Research Funds for the Central Universities (3209009601).

References

1. Adel, H., Roth, B., Schütze, H.: Comparing convolutional neural networks to traditional models for slot filling. In: Proceedings of NAACL-HLT, pp. 828–838 (2016)
2. Bikel, D.M., Castelli, V., Florian, R., Han, D.J.: Entity linking and slot filling through statistical processing and inference rules. Theory Appl. Categ. (2009)
3. Chiticariu, L., Li, Y., Reiss, F.R.: Rule-based information extraction is dead! long live rule-based information extraction systems! In: Proceedings of EMNLP, pp. 827–832 (2013)
4. Cho, K., et al.: Learning phrase representations using RNN encoder-decoder for statistical machine translation. In: Proceedings of EMNLP, pp. 1724–1734 (2014)
5. Duan, N., Tang, D., Chen, P., Zhou, M.: Question generation for question answering. In: Proceedings of EMNLP, pp. 866–874 (2017)
6. Huang, L., Sil, A., Ji, H., Florian, R.: Improving slot filling performance with attentive neural networks on dependency structures. In: Proceedings of EMNLP, pp. 2588–2597 (2017)
7. Kingma, D.P., Welling, M.: Auto-encoding variational Bayes. In: Proceedings of ICLR, pp. 866–874 (2014)
8. Levy, O., Seo, M., Choi, E., Zettlemoyer, L.: Zero-shot relation extraction via reading comprehension. In: Proceedings of CoNLL, pp. 333–342 (2017)
9. Mikolov, T., Sutskever, I., Chen, K., Corrado, G.S., Dean, J.: Distributed representations of words and phrases and their compositionality. In: Proceedings of NeurIPS, pp. 3111–3119 (2013)
10. Nguyen, T., et al.: MS MARCO: a human-generated machine reading comprehension dataset. In: Proceedings of NeurIPS, pp. 2383–2392 (2017)
11. Nishida, K., Saito, I., Otsuka, A., Asano, H., Tomita, J.: Retrieve-and-read: multitask learning of information retrieval and reading comprehension. CoRR (2018)
12. Pennington, J., Socher, R., Manning, C.D.: GloVe: global vectors for word representation. In: Proceedings of EMNLP, pp. 1532–1543 (2014)
13. Rajpurkar, P., Zhang, J., Lopyrev, K., Liang, P.: Squad: $100,000+$ questions for machine comprehension of text. In: Proceedings of EMNLP, pp. 2383–2392 (2016)
14. Seo, M.J., Kembhavi, A., Farhadi, A., Hajishirzi, H.: Bidirectional attention flow for machine comprehension. In: Proceedings of ICLR, pp. 891–904 (2017)

15. Sohn, K., Yan, X., Lee, H.: Learning structured output representation using deep conditional generative models. In: Proceedings of NeurIPS, pp. 3483–3491 (2015)
16. Sun, A., Grishman, R., Xu, W., Min, B.: NY University 2011 system for KBP slot filling. In: Proceedings of TAC, pp. 328–338 (2011)
17. Wang, T., Yuan, X., Trischler, A.: A joint model for question answering and question generation. arXiv preprint arXiv:1706.01450 (2017)
18. Yu, D., Ji, H.: Unsupervised person slot filling based on graph mining. In: Proceedings of ACL, vol. 1, pp. 44–53 (2016)

Constrained Relation Network
for Character Detection in Scene Images

Yudi Chen[1,2], Yu Zhou[1(✉)], Dongbao Yang[1], and Weiping Wang[1]

[1] Institute of Information Engineering, Chinese Academy of Sciences, Beijing, China
{chenyudi,zhouyu,yangdongbao,wangweiping}@iie.ac.cn
[2] School of Cyber Security, University of Chinese Academy of Sciences,
Beijing, China

Abstract. Characters are the basic components of text. Accurate character detection plays an important role in text detection and recognition. Previous character detectors tackle characters as independent objects, without considering the meaningful context information among them. In this paper, we propose a new module named constrained relation module which utilizes both the geometric and contextual information to exploit the strong relationship between characters. With this module, we build a new network named constrained relation network for character detection and recognition. To the best of our knowledge it is the first work to utilize contextual information among texts for character detection in scene images. The module can improve the detection results by suppressing the confusing text-like regions and recalling the hard examples. Experiments on SynthText, ICDAR2013 and SCUT-FORU demonstrate the effectiveness of our method on both detection and recognition tasks.

Keywords: Character detection · Neural network · Context attention

1 Introduction

Detecting text in scene images has become a hot research topic for its broad applications in content based image retrieval, scene understanding, multilingual translation and industrial automation. Although great progress have been made, dilemmas such as vast variations of text scales, orientations, illumination, and fonts are still remained to be remedied.

According to the basic elements, text detection can be categorized into character based, word based and text line based methods. Though the mainstream text detection methods aim to detect words and text lines, character detection is indispensable in some cases, e.g. detecting characters for mathematical formula recognition and Chinese character extraction in equally row space and column space situation (Fig. 1). Moreover, the extremely large aspect ratio of text region is one of the most challenging problems unsolved in state-of-the-art text detection approaches because of the limited receptive fields of CNN. On the contrary, for most languages the character has limited aspect ratio. For region proposal

A. C. Nayak and A. Sharma (Eds.): PRICAI 2019, LNAI 11672, pp. 137–149, 2019.
https://doi.org/10.1007/978-3-030-29894-4_11

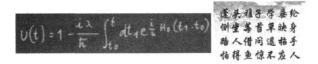

Fig. 1. Difficult patterns for text detection.

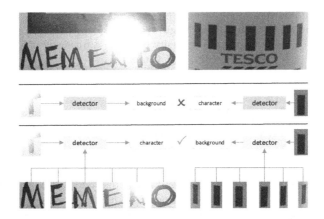

Fig. 2. Illustration of structure of conventional character detector and our detector. The first row shows the raw image. The second row shows the structure of conventional detectors. The third row shows the structure of our constrained relation module.

based methods, limited aspect ratio means fewer anchor boxes, which leads to less computation.

Conventional character detectors such as SWT [3] and MSER [16] try to make use of edge and region features of characters. Recently many works [10,20,26] based on deep learning use high-level visual features for character detection. However, all character detectors mentioned above consider characters as independent objects, and only use the corresponding deep features of themselves for classification. Many empirical studies have demonstrated that the contextual information can significantly improve the object detection and classification performance. Among them, the SIN [14] and the relation network [9] design simple structures to integrate geometrical and contextual information to the detection process. Inspired by these two contextual object detection methods, we find that even more strong relationships exist in scene characters as illustrated in Fig. 2. The left image in the top row has a hard example 'T', and the right image has some confusing text-like regions. The context-free detection methods may suffer from false negative and false positive errors. If we use the contextual detection method, the character 'T' can be recalled correctly and the text-like regions can be eliminated.

In this paper we propose the constrained relation network (CRN) for character detection. The CRN can take full use of context information to deal with most of the challenges mentioned above. The proposed architecture is based on Faster R-CNN [18], and the backbone is VGG-16. A constrained relation module is added after the FC layer. The constrained relation module utilizes both the geometric features and the appearance features to construct the relation network, and use a constrained mask to further select the appropriate context information.

Our contributions are as follows: (1) To the best of our knowledge it is the first character detection work which utilizes contextual information among texts in scene images. (2) We introduce the relation network to character detection and verify its effectiveness. (3) A constrained module is further proposed to precisely model the character context, and experimental results show that the proposed method is superior to the conventional relation network.

2   Related Works

Previous work for text detection and recognition can be roughly categorized into character-based [1–3,10,16,20,27] and word-based [6–8,12,13,15,25,29,31] methods. The character detection based methods usually first detect multiple character candidates coarsely. After that candidates are filtered by a text/non-text classifier to remove false positives. Finally, the identified characters are grouped into words or text lines by either heuristic rules or clustering models. Early works such as SWT [3] and MSER [16] use well-designed features to represent characters. They work well on focused text tasks, but will be vulnerable to complex background in scene images. With the development of deep learning, CNN based methods [10,20,27] play an important role in recent works.

The methods in the second category detect words directly. In [31] a neural network model is trained to directly predict the existence of text instances and their geometries from full images. [13] extracts features in different feature maps to jointly achieve text detection and bounding-box regression at multiple image scales. [12] designs a segmentation-based detector with multiple predictions for each text instance to deal with multi-oriented texts. Though the word detection approach is simpler, it does not work well with long aspect ratio texts and it is not robust enough to data patterns. In addition, visually defining a word boundary may not be feasible for texts in many non-Latin languages such as Chinese and Korean. Comprehensive surveys for scene text detection and recognition can be referred to [28].

Context has been demonstrated to be effective for object detection and recognition [9,14]. Recently, some approaches based on deep ConvNet have made some attempts to incorporate object context information to text detection [17,32]. In [23], RNN is used to explore meaningful context information of text line. However, it only considers the information of the sliding windows in the horizontal line. We find that even more strong relationships exist in all characters which in the same scene image, thus we propose a constrained relation module to exploit relations for characters in a self-adaptive mask.

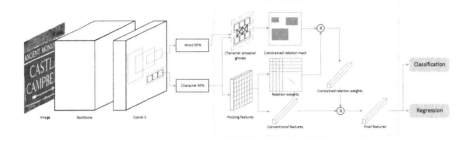

Fig. 3. Illustration of the architecture of the constrained relation network.

3   Methodology

In this section, the architecture of CRN is detailedly described, and the corresponding loss function is presented. The overall architecture of CRN is shown in Fig. 3.

We select Faster R-CNN as the character detection framework, and the network backbone is VGG-16. There are two RPNs to extract character proposals and word proposals respectively. The relation network is connected after the character RPN to generate relation weights for all character proposals. The character proposals are grouped according to the bounding boxes of the word RPN. Accordingly, the constrained mask is generated. After that, the constrained mask and the relation weights are fused to generate the constrained relation weights. The final feature are the combination of the conventional feature and the constrained relation weights. Classification and regression are implemented using the final feature.

In Sect. 3.1, we first review the conventional relation network. The constrained relation module and the loss function are described in the next two subsections respectively.

3.1   Relation Network

In Faster R-CNN, the classification and regression of a specific RoI only rely on its own feature. To take the context information into consideration, the relation network proposed an adapted attention module for object detection. The final feature f_R^n of the adapted attention module is calculated as:

$$f_R^n = \sum_m w^{mn}(W_V \cdot f_A^m)$$

(1)

where m, n is the index of RoI, W_V represent the weight parameters in the network, the appearance feature f_A is the output of RoI-Pooling layer, w^{mn} is the final weights formed by context information, it is computed as follow:

$$w^{mn} = softmax(\frac{W_K f_A^m \cdot W_Q f_A^n}{\sqrt{d_k}} + \log w_G^{mn})$$

(2)

where W_K, W_Q represent the weight parameters in the network, w_G^{mn} is the weight of geometry features of m_{th} RoI and n_{th} RoI, which is encoded by the embedding method in [24]. The feature dimension after projection is d_k. For more detailed information about the relation network, please refer to [9].

3.2 Constrained Relation Module

For character detection, we take the characters as the target objects. However, the relation network takes the relations of the character RoIs of the whole image into consideration, which is not the case sometimes. As shown in Fig. 4, the characters in the same word are more correlated while the characters in different words are not. It is straightforward that the closer characters are more helpful to the detection of the target character than those distant ones.

Algorithm 1. Constrained Relation Algorithm

Input: RoIs: R_w, R_c, Scores: S_w
Output: Constrained relation mask: M
1: **function** CRM(R_w, R_c, S_w)
2:     $r_t \leftarrow []$
3:     $R_w, S_w \leftarrow$ NMS(R_w, S_w)
4:     $R_w, S_w \leftarrow$ TopK(R_w, S_w, K)
5:     $p \leftarrow size(R_w, 0), q \leftarrow size(R_c, 0)$
6:     $P \leftarrow zeros(p, q), M \leftarrow zeros(q, q)$
7:     $P \leftarrow$ Cover(R_w, R_c)
8:     **for** $j = 0 \rightarrow size(R_c, 0)$ **do**
9:         $r_t \leftarrow find(P[:, j] == True)$
10:        **for** each $r \in r_t$ **do**
11:            $M[j, :] \leftarrow$ Logical_OR($M[j, :], P[r, :]$)
12:        **end for**
13:    **end for**
14:    **return** M, P;
15: **end function**

We propose the constrained relation module to implement the local attention strategy. The module takes the labels of word bounding boxes as the supervised information. An extra RPN process with different anchor sizes and aspect ratios is introduced to propose word RoIs. Next, an efficient algorithm is designed to group character RoIs. The details of the algorithm are summarized in Algorithm 1. R_w represents the RoIs of words and R_c represents the RoIs of characters. S_w is the text/non-text confidence scores of word RoIs. NMS represents a Non-Maximal Suppression algorithm [19] and TopK returns the first K results based on the input scores. M is the output of constrained relation module. r_t is the intermediate result. P is the matrix returned by the function Cover, $P[i, j]$ is True when the i_{th} word bounding box contains the j_{th} character bounding

Fig. 4. The relationship of the characters. Characters marked in the same color are closely related, while characters marked in different colors are uncorrelated with each other.

box. LOGICAL_OR(c, d) calculates the element-wise logical OR results of vectors c and d.

Once the constrained relation matrix M of character RoIs is calculated, it is sorted by the character groupings which is represented by P, and then fed into Conv(3,3) layer to get w_l. Then, an element-wise product is executed between w_l and w^{mn} (in Sect. 3.1). The result of the element-wise product is fed into FC layer to get the same shape of the feature after RoI-Pooling, then we get the constrained relation weights of the CRN. Another element-wise product is executed between the features and the constrained relation weights to get the final features, which is used for classification and regression in the second stage.

3.3 Loss Function

For learning the network, the loss function can be formulated as:

$$L = L_c + \alpha L_w \tag{3}$$

where L_c, L_w represent character loss and word loss respectively, α is a weight balancing these two losses. L_c is the same as in [18] and [4].

$$L_c = L_{rpn} + L_{rcnn} \tag{4}$$

L_{rpn} and L_{rcnn} are the RPN loss and the R-CNN loss respectively. Some characters in the scene images may be too small, even a 1-pixel error will change the prediction result. The loss function should be suitable for precise localization. Because the 2-stage strategy of Faster R-CNN is very suitable for precise localization, the loss function is inherited for character detection. For the word

RPN part, only the classification result is needed to help to group the character RoIs. Therefore only the cross entropy loss for classification is used. Moreover, the convolution parameters that are used to fuse the constrained relation mask (discussed in Sect. 3.2) should be learned during training. The word loss includes two loss functions L_{ws} and L_{lp} which are listed as follows:

$$L_w = L_{ws} + \beta L_{lp} \tag{5}$$

$$L_{ws} = -\frac{1}{N} \sum_{n}^{N} [y_n \log(x_n) + (1 - y_n) \log(1 - x_n)] \tag{6}$$

$$L_{lp} = 1 - \frac{2 \sum_{m,n} w_l^{m,n} * l^{m,n}}{\sum_{m,n}(w_l^{m,n})^2 + \sum_{m,n}(l^{m,n})^2} \tag{7}$$

where x_n is the pixel value in RPN scores map, y_n is the pixel label. In L_{lp}, the prediction is w_l, and the ground truth label is $l^{m,n} \in R^{N*N}$ which is generated by the matching of the ground truth character and word bounding boxes, N is the number of character RoIs. A dice loss is used here to deal with the class-imbalanced problem. In this work α, β are set to 1 and 0.5.

3.4   Implementation Details

The backbone network is VGG-16 pre-trained on the ImageNet dataset. The aspect ratios are set to $[1, \frac{1}{2}]$ for the character RPN and $[1, 2, 5]$ for the word RPN. The anchor sizes are set to $[2, 4, 8, 16, 32]$ for character RPN and $[8, 16, 32]$ for the word RPN. The CRN is trained on 100k images from the SynthText dataset for 240k iterations as the pre-trained model, then fine-tune is implemented on the ICDAR13 training dataset. The learning rate is set to 10^{-3} for the first 120K iterations and then is reduced by 10 times for the other 120K iterations. In the training stage, all the short edge of the input images are resized to 600 pixels while keeping the aspect ratio of the images.

All the experiments are conducted on an Intel Xeon E5-2630 CPU workstation with 32 GB RAM, NVIDIA M40 24 GB and Ubuntu 16.04 OS, and with the framework Tensorflow 1.8.0.

4   Experimental Results

Following the standard evaluation protocols, we evaluate our method on the SynthText, ICDAR13 and SCUT-FORU datasets. These three datasets have character-level annotations.

SynthText. The SynthText dataset [5] consists of 800,000 images, generated by a synthetic engine proposed in [5]. We randomly select 105k images, 100k of which are used for training and others for test. In fact, 20k images are already enough for character detection. Considering the character recognition process we choose 100k images here for the purpose of learning the semantic information.

We resize the short sides of all input images to 600 pixels and the aspect ratios are retained when evaluation. For multi-scale evaluation the short sides of the input images are randomly resized to four scales (300, 600, 1200, 2400). We use the same multi-scale resizing strategy for ICDAR13 and SCUT-FORU.

ICDAR13. The ICDAR13 datasets [11] are from the ICDAR 2013 Robust Reading Competition, containing 229 images for training, and 233 for test. We use 50k SynthText data for pre-training, and then fine-tune on 229 training images for 8 epochs. We resize the short sides of all input images to 1500 pixels and the aspect ratios are retained when evaluation.

SCUT-FORU. The samples of SCUT-FORU dataset [30] consist of 813 training images and 349 test images. The background and illumination vary in large scales in the dataset, so we use it to test the generalization performance of CRN. We do not train on any SCUT-FORU image, instead we use the model trained on ICDAR13 for evaluation.

Table 1. Character detection results on SynthText, P, R and F mean precision, recall and F1-measure respectively, MS means multi-scale

Method	Character detection			Character recognition		
	P	R	F	P	R	F
Hu *et al.* [10]	0.830	0.770	0.799	*	*	*
Hu *et al.* [9]	0.878	0.867	0.872	0.752	0.795	0.773
Base	0.793	0.853	0.822	0.649	0.763	0.701
CRN	0.930	0.874	0.901	0.824	0.812	0.818
CRN+MS	0.928	0.908	**0.918**	0.903	0.827	**0.863**

Three methods are compared to show the effectiveness of CRN. The first one is Faster R-CNN, in which some hyper parameters are changed for detecting characters, and it is marked as **Base**. The second one is an implementation of the relation network [9], in which embedding and multi-head attention are used. The third one is the proposed CRN, and it is marked as **CRN**.

Tables 1, 2 and 3 show the results on SynthText, ICDAR13 and SCUT-FORU datasets respectively. Since there is not much work related to character detection on these three datasets, we only choose the latest work for comparison. In addition to character detection, we also implement character recognition by simply replacing the classification of text and background with the classification of 36 characters and background in RCNN module.

The results shown in Table 1 demonstrate the effectiveness of CRN in large scale synthetic dataset. The detection f-measure of Faster R-CNN is 82.2%. By using relation network, the f-measure is increased by 5.0% compared to that of Faster R-CNN. Moreover CRN have increments of 7.9% and 2.9% f-measure

Table 2. Character detection results on ICDAR13, P, R and F mean precision, recall and F1-measure respectively, MS means multi-scale

Method	Character detection			Character recognition		
	P	R	F	P	R	F
Sung *et al.* [21]	0.864	0.743	0.799	*	*	*
Tian *et al.* [22]	0.718	0.854	0.780	*	*	*
Hu *et al.* [9]	0.919	0.826	0.870	0.856	0.769	0.810
Base	0.868	0.842	0.855	0.798	0.774	0.786
CRN	0.923	0.862	0.891	0.861	0.804	0.831
CRN+MS	0.917	0.898	**0.907**	0.821	0.856	**0.838**

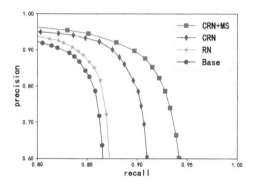

Fig. 5. P-R curves for character detection on ICDAR13

compared to Faster R-CNN and the relation network. CRN obtains another increment of 1.7% f-measure and finally achieves the f-measure of 91.8% for multi-scale evaluation. For recognition, the relation network, CRN and multi-scale CRN have increments of 7.2%, 11.7% and 16.2% separately. It can be seen that CRN has a greater improvement in multi-label classification task than two-class classification task. This fully demonstrates that semantic information between categories is important for classification tasks.

On the real scene text dataset ICDAR13, the consistent improvements are obtained. As shown in Table 2, the increments that from 85.5% to 89.1% and 78.6% to 83.1% are achieved respectively. Our method outperforms the method in [9] significantly by 3.7% F-score (90.7% vs 87.0%). The overall superior performance of CRN over Faster R-CNN and conventional relation network can be proved with the more detailed precision-recall curves of ICDAR13 dataset shown in Fig. 5.

As shown in Table 3, three key components in our pipeline are evaluated On SCUT-FORU dataset. With "relation network" branch, the f-measure is improved by about 1% with similar recall. If we further add "constrained mask",

Table 3. Character detection results on SCUT-FORU, P, R and F mean precision, recall and F1-measure respectively, MS means multi-scale

Relation network	Constrained mask	MS	P	R	F
✗	✗	✗	0.877	0.887	0.882
✔	✗	✗	0.913	0.873	0.893
✔	✔	✗	0.926	0.901	0.913
✔	✔	✔	0.921	0.951	0.936

the performance in recall increases by 3%. In accordance to our previous analysis in Sect. 3.2, information from other objects contributes differently to the detection of the current object. The detection process can benefit from a local attention strategy. All the models are only fine-tuned on ICDAR13 training set

(a)   (b)

(c)   (d)

Fig. 6. The Comparison between the Faster R-CNN based method and the Constrained Relation Network based method. (a) and (c) are the results with Faster R-CNN method, (b) and (d) are results with Constrained Relation Network method. The first row shows the promotion of recall, the second row shows the promotion of precision.

without using any training sample of SCUT-FORU dataset, and are directly used for evaluation in the SCUT-FORU test set, which demonstrate the generalization ability of CRN.

Two qualitative examples are shown in Fig. 6. (a) and (c) are the detection results with Faster R-CNN method, (b) and (d) are those with CRN. The character 'R' in the word 'COOKERY' in (a) is missed, but in (b) it is detected correctly and precisely, and many other tiny characters are additionally recalled by CRN. In (c) a whole line of false positive regions are detected as characters, but with the constrained relation module these false positive regions are eliminated, and at the same time all the true positive regions are correctly kept.

The above results indicate that a properly adjusted Faster R-CNN is suitable for character detection tasks. The relation network can improve test results to some extent by utilizing contextual information. But the global information fusion strategy will lead to the distraction of attention. By reasonably restricting the perceptual area, the CRN can achieve further improvements in detection task, especially for multi-category situations. All these quantitative and qualitative experimental results show the effectiveness of relation network and the constrained module for detection and recognition of characters.

5   Conclusions

In this paper we propose the constrained relation network (CRN) for character detection. The constrained relation module utilizes both the geometric features and the appearance features, and use a constrained mask to further select the appropriate context information. The F-Measure increments of 3.6% and 3.1% on ICDAR and FORU show the effectiveness of CRN for character detection. For future work, we will investigate whether the constrained mask can be trained to figure out the exactly grouping results.

Acknowledgments. This work is supported by the National Key R&D Program of China (2017YFB1002400) and the Strategic Priority Research Program of Chinese Academy of Sciences (XDC02000000).

References

1. Bai, F., Cheng, Z., Niu, Y., Pu, S., Zhou, S.: Edit probability for scene text recognition. In: CVPR, pp. 1508–1516 (2018)
2. Cheng, Z., Bai, F., Xu, Y., Zheng, G., Pu, S., Zhou, S.: Focusing attention: towards accurate text recognition in natural images. In: ICCV. pp. 5076–5084 (2017)
3. Epshtein, B., Ofek, E., Wexler, Y.: Detecting text in natural scenes with stroke width transform. In: CVPR, pp. 2963–2970 (2010)
4. Girshick, R.: Fast R-CNN. In: ICCV, pp. 1440–1448 (2015)
5. Gupta, A., Vedaldi, A., Zisserman, A.: Synthetic data for text localisation in natural images. In: CVPR, pp. 2315–2324 (2016)
6. He, P., Huang, W., He, T., Zhu, Q., Qiao, Y., Li, X.: Single shot text detector with regional attention. In: ICCV, pp. 3047–3055 (2017)

7. He, T., Tian, Z., Huang, W., Shen, C., Qiao, Y., Sun, C.: An end-to-end textspotter with explicit alignment and attention. In: CVPR, pp. 5020–5029 (2018)
8. He, W., Zhang, X.Y., Yin, F., Liu, C.L.: Deep direct regression for multi-oriented scene text detection. In: ICCV, pp. 745–753 (2017)
9. Hu, H., Gu, J., Zhang, Z., Dai, J., Wei, Y.: Relation networks for object detection. In: CVPR, pp. 3588–3597 (2018)
10. Hu, H., Zhang, C., Luo, Y., Wang, Y., Han, J., Ding, E.: WordSup: exploiting word annotations for character based text detection. In: ICCV, pp. 4940–4949 (2017)
11. Karatzas, D., et al.: ICDAR 2013 robust reading competition. In: ICDAR, pp. 1484–1493 (2013)
12. Li, X., Wang, W., Hou, W., Liu, R.Z., Lu, T., Yang, J.: Shape robust text detection with progressive scale expansion network. arXiv:1806.02559 (2018)
13. Liao, M., Shi, B., Bai, X.: TextBoxes++: a single-shot oriented scene text detector. TIP **27**(8), 3676–3690 (2018)
14. Liu, Y., Wang, R., Shan, S., Chen, X.: Structure inference net: object detection using scene-level context and instance-level relationships. In: CVPR, pp. 6985–6994 (2018)
15. Liu, Y., Jin, L.: Deep matching prior network: Toward tighter multi-oriented text detection. In: CVPR, pp. 1962–1969 (2017)
16. Nistér, D., Stewénius, H.: Linear time maximally stable extremal regions. In: Forsyth, D., Torr, P., Zisserman, A. (eds.) ECCV 2008. LNCS, vol. 5303, pp. 183–196. Springer, Heidelberg (2008). https://doi.org/10.1007/978-3-540-88688-4_14
17. Prasad, S., Wai Kin Kong, A.: Using object information for spotting text. In: ECCV, pp. 540–557 (2018)
18. Ren, S., He, K., Girshick, R., Sun, J.: Faster R-CNN: towards real-time object detection with region proposal networks. In: NIPS, pp. 91–99 (2015)
19. Rosenfeld, A., Thurston, M.: Edge and curve detection for visual scene analysis. IEEE Trans. Comput. **20**(5), 562–569 (1971)
20. Shi, B., Bai, X., Belongie, S.: Detecting oriented text in natural images by linking segments. In: CVPR, pp. 2550–2558 (2017)
21. Sung, M.C., Jun, B., Cho, H., Kim, D.: Scene text detection with robust character candidate extraction method. In: ICDAR, pp. 426–430. IEEE (2015)
22. Tian, S., Lu, S., Li, C.: WeText: scene text detection under weak supervision. In: ICCV, pp. 1492–1500 (2017)
23. Tian, Z., Huang, W., He, T., He, P., Qiao, Y.: Detecting text in natural image with connectionist text proposal network. In: Leibe, B., Matas, J., Sebe, N., Welling, M. (eds.) ECCV 2016. LNCS, vol. 9912, pp. 56–72. Springer, Cham (2016). https://doi.org/10.1007/978-3-319-46484-8_4
24. Vaswani, A., et al.: Attention is all you need. In: NIPS, pp. 5998–6008 (2017)
25. Xie, E., Zang, Y., Shao, S., Yu, G., Yao, C., Li, G.: Scene text detection with supervised pyramid context network. arXiv preprint arXiv:1811.08605 (2018)
26. Yao, C., Bai, X., Sang, N., Zhou, X., Zhou, S., Cao, Z.: Scene text detection via holistic, multi-channel prediction. arXiv:1606.09002 (2016)
27. Yao, C., Wu, W.: Mask TextSpotter: an end-to-end trainable neural network for spotting text with arbitrary shapes. In: ECCV, pp. 67–83 (2018)
28. Ye, Q., Doermann, D.: Text detection and recognition in imagery: a survey. TPAMI **37**(7), 1480–1500 (2014)
29. Yin, X.C., Yin, X., Huang, K., Hao, H.W.: Robust text detection in natural scene images. TPAMI **36**(5), 970–983 (2014)

30. Zhang, S., Lin, M., Chen, T., Jin, L., Lin, L.: Character proposal network for robust text extraction. In: ICASSP, pp. 2633–2637 (2016)
31. Zhou, X., Yao, C., Wen, H., Wang, Y., Zhou, S., He, W., Liang, J.: East: an efficient and accurate scene text detector. In: CVPR, pp. 5551–5560 (2017)
32. Zhu, A., Gao, R., Uchida, S.: Could scene context be beneficial for scene text detection? PR **58**, 204–215 (2016)

Effective Optical Braille Recognition Based on Two-Stage Learning for Double-Sided Braille Image

Renqiang Li, Hong Liu$^{(\boxtimes)}$, Xiangdong Wang, and Yueliang Qian

Beijing Key Laboratory of Mobile Computing and Pervasive Device,
Institute of Computing Technology, Chinese Academy of Sciences,
Beijing 100190, China
hliu@ict.ac.cn

Abstract. This paper proposes a novel two-stage learning framework TS-OBR for double-sided Braille images recognition. In the first stage, a Haar cascaded classifier with the sliding window strategy is adopted to quickly detect Braille recto dots with high confidence. Then a coarse-to-fine de-skewing method is proposed to correct original skewed Braille images, which maximizes the variance of horizontal and vertical projection at different angles. And an adaptive Braille cells grid construction method based on statistical analysis is proposed, which can dynamically generate the Braille cells grid for each Braille image. In the second stage, a decision-level SVM classifier with four classifiers recognition results is used to get recto dots detection results only on intersections of the Braille cells grid. Experimental results on the public double-sided Braille dataset and our Braille exam answer paper dataset show the proposed framework TS-OBR is effective, robust and fast for Braille dots detection and Braille characters recognition.

Keywords: Optical Braille Recognition · De-skewing ·
Braille dots detection · Braille cell location · Double-sided Braille

1 Introduction

There are about 1.3 billion visual impaired and 36 million blind in the world according to the WHO [13]. Braille is a tactile writing system for the visually impaired to learn knowledge and obtain information, which is designed by Frenchman Louis Braille. Automatic recognizing Braille document images into Braille characters can be called Optical Braille Recognition (OBR) [8]. OBR system is meaningful and important for republication of numerous early and valuable Braille books, translation of Braille exam papers in the special education field, and communication with others.

The Braille document consists of Braille characters based on rectangular cells, which contain six dots arranged in three rows and two columns. Many Braille books are double-sided to save papers, which may contain recto dots and verso

© Springer Nature Switzerland AG 2019
A. C. Nayak and A. Sharma (Eds.): PRICAI 2019, LNAI 11672, pp. 150–163, 2019.
https://doi.org/10.1007/978-3-030-29894-4_12

dots in one Braille document. Double-sided OBR is a challenging task for the diversity of Braille papers, disturbance of complex arrangement of recto and verso dots, deformation and skewness of Braille images by acquisition noise.

Generally, the OBR system contains several steps including Braille image acquisition, image de-skewing, Braille dots recognition and Braille cells location and recognition [8]. Image segmentation based OBR methods are widely used, which segment the Braille dots from the background and design some rules to identify them.

Antonacopoulos et al. [5] segmented the Braille image into shadow, highlight and background regions, and then identified them as recto dots or verso dots according to different combinations of highlight and shadow regions. Al-Shamma et al. [4] used canny method to detect dot edges and used holes filling and image filtering to detect Braille dots. They tested on several scanned single-sided Braille documents with the average time of 32.6 s for one document. Above segmentation based methods are simple and affected by designed rules and segmentation threshold values, and not robust for complex Braille images.

Some work used statistical learning methods to detect Braille dots and recognize Braille cells. Namba et al. [12] applied the neural network based on associative memory to classify Braille cell images into ten classes and obtained 87.9% recognition rate on Braille cell images. This method cannot deal the whole Braille image which is not suitable in real applications. Li et al. [9] used SVM with the sliding window strategy to recognize Braille characters, which needed 20 min to process one Braille image with the classification error of 5%. This method is time-consuming with low performance.

Recently, Li et al. [10] released the first public Braille images dataset DSBI [1]. They also proposed a Haar+Adaboost with the sliding window strategy to detect recto dots. Their strategy got 0.970 F1 value for recto dots detection on the DSBI dataset. However, they only evaluated on de-skewing images for recto dots detection. And the performance is not good enough, since even little error rate may lead dozens of Braille dots recognized wrong for a Braille page with over one thousand dots averagely.

Besides Braille dots detection, in real applications, one OBR system also should process the original Braille images with certain degree of skewness and deformation from acquisition noise or human errors. Most of existing OBR methods didn't mention this issue, some de-skewing methods are mentioned lightly and time-consuming in practice.

Braille cells locating is also a crucial stage of OBR systems. Most of existing methods are based on the standard arrangement of Braille dots, which are not robust for some complex situations with sparse Braille characters, incomplete Braille row or column groups and image deformation.

This paper focuses on the effective and quick double-sided Braille image recognition task for original images. The main contributions are as followings.

We propose a novel Two-Stage learning framework for double-sided Braille image recognition called TS-OBR. There are several advantages of our proposed framework TS-OBR, which contains the whole processing including image

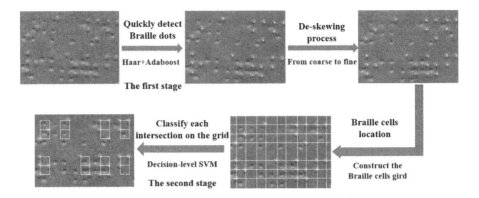

Fig. 1. Our proposed framework TS-OBR.

de-skewing, location of Braille cells and Braille dots detection and Braille characters recognition. We can directly process the original Braille images with skewness and deformation. Our system can recognize recto and verso Braille characters together so that we can only scan and process one side of the double-sided Braille image in real applications. Experimental results on the DSBI dataset and our Braille exam answer paper dataset show the effectiveness of our proposed method. The average F1 value is over 0.997 for both recto and verso dots detection and over 0.994 for Braille characters recognition on the DSBI. We also achieve an excellent performance with the average F1 value 0.992 for recto dots detection on our Braille exam answer paper dataset BEP directly using the model only trained on the DSBI. Unlike the DSBI, which is from printed Braille books, our dataset BEP comes from manually stabbed paper by blind student. The whole system TS-OBR only costs about 1.5 s for recto and verso dots detection respectively with high recognition rate on the two datasets.

2 The Proposed Framework

The proposed framework TS-OBR is shown in Fig. 1. The DSBI dataset provides the original color images and de-skewing color images. We just use original images to process. Firstly, we convert the original color image to the gray image. In our first stage, different from other methods, we use Haar+Adaboost with the sliding window strategy to quickly detect Braille dots rather than performing the de-skewing process. Then, the position of detected Braille dots will be used by a coarse-to-fine method to find an appropriate angle to correct the skewed image. A flexible Braille cells grid is then constructed to locate the Braille cells based on detected Braille dots and the statistical information of Braille cells arrangement. In our second stage, we further classify each intersection of the Braille cells grid using a decision-level SVM classifier to improve the performance of OBR.

3   Our Main Work

3.1   The First Stage for Braille Dots Initial Detection

Braille dots detection is the most crucial task in OBR systems. The existing segmentation based methods are not robust for complex double-sided Braille images. This paper regards Braille dots detection as general object detection in nature images. So we also adopt the classical object detection method, which uses Haar feature and Adaboost classifier [10,14] to detect Braille dots.

Different from [10], our first stage is only used for the initial Braille dots detection. Figure 2 shows one local region of recto dots detection with Haar+Adaboost and most of recto dots are detected successfully and reliably. Although some recto dots are missing, this problem can be resolved in our second stage with a higher performance classifier. Experimental results show that our first stage only takes average 0.29 s for each image with 200 dpi in the DSBI dataset.

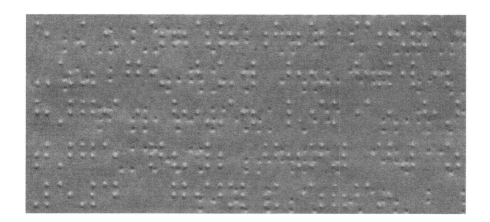

Fig. 2. Braille recto dots detection results with Haar+Adaboost.

3.2   De-skewing by a Coarse-to-Fine Strategy

The standard arrangement of Braille dots and cells should be regular in both horizontal and vertical directions, while the acquired Braille images have much noise. So de-skewing process is necessary and important. Most of original Braille images have a slight skewness in the DSBI dataset and our dataset, which will make the Braille cells location and Braille characters recognition more difficult.

Many existing de-skewing methods, including Linear regression [6] and Hough Transform [5], are not robust and fast for complex double-sided Braille images. Mennens et al. [11] used the deviation over the sum of the rows to calculate the image rotation angle. The image was slanted one pixel in vertical direction each time.

Algorithm 1. De-skewing by coarse-to-fine strategy

1. Create a white binary image $b(x, y)$ with the same size of the original image $oi(x, y)$.
2. Replace each detected dot $d(x, y)$ at the same position (x, y) in $b(x, y)$ with a black square with size of $s \times s$.
3. In the coarse de-skewing stage, rotate the image $b(x, y)$ from $-angle_1^\circ$ to $+angle_1^\circ$ with a large step ls.
4. For each angle $angle^\circ$, project the rotated binary image $b_a(x, y)$ in horizontal and vertical directions, and obtain the horizontal frequencies h and vertical frequencies v.
5. Calculate the projection variance var for $angle^\circ$:

$$\overline{h} = \frac{1}{n} \sum_i^n h_i, \overline{v} = \frac{1}{n} \sum_i^n v_i \qquad (1)$$

$$var_h = \frac{1}{n} \sum_i^n (h_i - \overline{h})^2, var_v = \frac{1}{n} \sum_i^n (v_i - \overline{v})^2 \qquad (2)$$

$$var = var_h + var_v \qquad (3)$$

6. Select the rotated angle with the maximum var as $a1^\circ$.
7. In the fine stage, rotate the binary image $b(x, y)$ from $(a1 - angle_2)^\circ$ to $(a1 + angle_2)^\circ$ with a small step ss to find a more accurate rotated angle.
8. Select the rotated angle with the maximum var as $a2^\circ$.
9. Rotate the original image $oi(x, y)$ with angle $-a2^\circ$, get the de-skewing image $dsi(x, y)$ and de-skewing dots DSD.

This paper proposes a coarse-to-fine de-skewing method with two levels angel interval by maximizing the variance of horizontal and vertical projection. And the angle with the maximum variance is the skewed angle. The details are described in Algorithm 1.

In our experiments, the parameters are set $s = 5$, $angle_1 = 5$, $angle_2 = 0.5$, $ls = 1^\circ$, $ss = 0.02^\circ$.

We use the coarse-to-fine projection strategy to quickly get the skewed angle with average 0.57 s for each image.

3.3   Dynamic Braille Cells Grid Location

Each Braille document consists of hundreds of Braille characters and each Braille character has a rectangular block called a Braille cell, which contains six Braille dots arranged in three rows and two columns. These six dots can be tiny bump called recto dots or flat to represent a certain Braille character. In ideal situations, the Braille cells grid is a regular grid, and the distances among horizontal and vertical lines are regular and easy to estimate at a specific resolution of scanned Braille images.

Most of Braille cells grid location methods are based on arrangement rules of Braille characters. Some methods used a preset fixed grid and selected a Braille dot as the starting point to construct a regular grid [3,9]. To enhance the robustness, Antonacopoulos et al. [5] used an adaptive method to form the Braille cells gird rather than the preset grid by calculating the distances of Braille rows and columns for each Braille document.

While in real applications, this grid is usually deformed due to acquired noise, thus the distances between lines are usually not fixed even in the same document. Besides these noise and deformation, Braille cells grid location is also difficult in some complex situations.

We introduce a robust and flexible method to construct the Braille cells grid by statistical information. The Braille cells grid can be dynamically generated by distribution of Braille dots. Our method contains four steps: detect Braille lines, group Braille lines, add missing Braille lines and construct the cells grid, which we will describe as followings.

Detect Braille Lines. With the de-skewing image and Braille dots, we firstly sort all the detected dots in ascending order by y coordinates and generate the first horizontal line according to the first dot. Then the distance of subsequent dots to the line is calculated. If the distance is below the threshold TH_1, it will be added to this line and the position of this line is updated by the average of y coordinates on this line dynamically. Otherwise, a new horizontal line will be generated. In this way, some candidate horizontal lines are extracted. Then we remove some very close lines and only remain those with many dots to reduce the influence of wrong detected dots.

Group Braille Lines. Based on the detected Braille lines, we select some reliable groups of three continuous horizontal lines from top to down, according to the arrangement rules of Braille cells. Set $\{hl_1, hl_2, hl_3\}$ is one group of lines, d_{12} and d_{23} are the distances of hl_1 and hl_2, hl_2 and hl_3 respectively, which should satisfies the following constraint:

$$d_{12}, d_{23} \leq TH_2 + \alpha \quad \&\& \quad d_{12}, d_{23} \geq TH_2 - \alpha \tag{4}$$

where TH_2 is the distances of lines in one Braille cell, and α is a penalty factor. We will update the value of TH_2 according to the d_{12} and d_{23} in each line group dynamically. Some overlapped line groups will be removed by statistical analysis.

Add Missing Braille Lines. The above steps can form some reliable groups with three lines. Other line groups will be inserted according to the remaining lines and the regular distance to make sure that line groups are placed in the regular interval by y coordinates.

Construct Cell Grid. The above steps construct the whole horizontal lines and line groups of current Braille image. Then the similar process is applied for detecting and grouping vertical lines according to x coordinates while each group only contains two vertical lines.

The threshold values in our method change dynamically to adapt the complex situations and could be tolerate some errors. Braille images in the DSBI dataset are scanned with 200 dpi, the initial parameters are: $TH_1 = 5$, $TH_2 = 21$, $\alpha = 3$ in our experiments. Experimental results show the effectiveness of our proposed Braille cells grid location method for complex double-sided Braille images.

3.4   The Second Stage for High-Precision OBR

With above accurate Braille cells grid information, we can further adopt a relatively complex and high performance machine learning method for Braille dots detection and Braille characters recognition. This stage can only process on the vertexes of Braille cells, also the intersections of Braille cells grid, instead of the whole image. This strategy is not mentioned in existing methods for OBR.

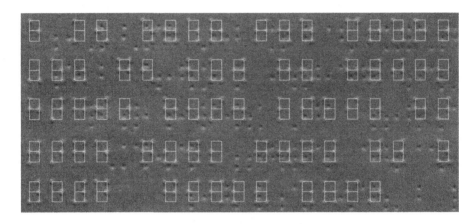

Fig. 3. Results of the second stage. The green dot is the detected recto dots and the white rectangle is the located Braille cells. (Color figure online)

This paper selects the feature of Histogram of Oriented Gradient (HOG) [7], Local Binary Pattern (LBP) [2] and fused HOG_LBP to train three SVM classifiers. We classify each intersection of the grid using them.

For better performance of Braille image recognition, the initial detection result will also be converted to the result based on the grid by assigning each detected dot to the nearest intersection. And then, we use a decision-level SVM to fuse the converted result and the classified results by three SVMs. We take these results as a 4-dimension feature to train the decision-level SVM for fusion so that we don't have to be stuck on how to balance the weight of each result.

The processing time has been reduced greatly in this strategy compared with general sliding window strategy. Our method can also help avoid the wrong dots detection beyond the grid intersections and then improve the precision and recall rate. One region of the recto dots detection and cells location result by the second stage is shown in Fig. 3.

4   Experiments and Analysis

4.1   Dataset

Unlike most existing methods which are tested on their small datasets, we use two Braille datasets to evaluate our method. Firstly, we choose the double-sided dataset DSBI [10]. DSBI is the first public and only Braille image dataset available, which contains 114 double-sided Braille images from several Braille books. These Braille images are acquired by the flatbed scanner with 200 dpi and the resolution is about 1700×2338 pixels. Some of Braille images have defects such as oil stains, distortion, cracks and abrasion Braille dots, which are complex and difficult for OBR.

The training set of DSBI contains 26 Braille images from 4 books and the test set contains remained 88 Braille images from all the books. This dataset also provides both the original Braille images and de-skewing images with detailed position annotation information of recto and verso dots, which can be used to evaluate the performance of dots and characters recognition.

In order to further verify the effectiveness of our proposed framework TS-OBR, we also constructed a Braille exam answer paper dataset called BEP. We have collected a total of 95 Braille exam answer papers from 28 blind students. Unlike Braille books, Braille papers are stabbed by blind students themselves using the special Braille writing tablet. Braille exam answer papers are usually one-sided, and the size of Braille dots stabbed varies greatly because of the difference of stab habits and strength.

What's more, many wrong-stabbed Braille dots are usually erased directly. But these erased dots are very difficult to distinguish from ordinary Braille dots visually, which are usually inferred by Braille teachers combined with context semantics. One local region of the Braille exam paper with some erased dots in our BEP is shown as Fig. 4. Therefore it's more challenging than the recognition of printed Braille books for these cases. We use all the pages in dataset BEP to evaluate the performance and generalization ability of our framework. And the models are the same as DSBI and only trained on the training set of DSBI.

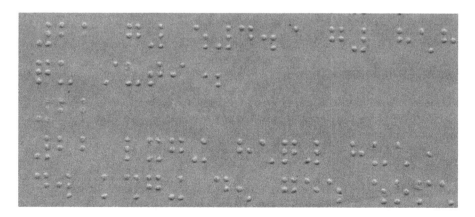

Fig. 4. One local region of the Braille exam paper with some erased and various appearance dots.

Unlike other datasets, each image contains only one or few objects, one Braille image contains averagely over 1,000 very small recto dots and hundreds of Braille characters. Table 1 gives us the statistical information of recto dots and Braille characters in both datasets. There are averagely over 1000 recto dots and around 400 Braille characters each Braille image no matter in the DSBI and BEP. The total number is very huge about over 100 thousands dots and around 40 thousands characters in each dataset. And we use 88 pages in DSBI and all 95 pages in BEP for evaluation.

Table 1. Statistical information of Braille recto dots and Braille characters.

Dataset	Recto dots	Braille characters	Total pages	Evaluated pages
DSBI	Average: 1071 ALL: 122117	Average: 401 ALL: 45725	114	88
BEP	Average: 1147 ALL: 109034	Average: 406 ALL: 38659	95	95

4.2 Metrics

We adopt precision, recall and F1 value to evaluate our method, which is used in [10]. Besides Braille dots detection, we also evaluate the performance of Braille characters recognition for double-sided Braille images. These metrics can be defined as follows:

$$Pre = \frac{TP}{TP + FP} \tag{5}$$

$$Rec = \frac{TP}{TP + FN} \tag{6}$$

$$F1 = \frac{2 \times Pre \times Rec}{Pre + Rec} \tag{7}$$

4.3 Experiment Details

All the experiments in this paper are carried out by the ordinary computer with Intel i7-6700@3.40 GHz and 16G RAM without GPU. We also evaluate our framework on several laptops. It's very fast and easy to run without extra setup so that Braille teachers and others can easily make use of our work to save their valuable time.

Haar+Adaboost Training. For recto dots training, we collect 9690 recto dots regions as positive samples and 28212 negative samples from the background and verso dots regions. The sample size is 20×20. We train a 7 cascaded classifier of Haar+Adaboost for recto dots using OpenCV. For verso dots training, we collect 10206 positive samples and 15016 negative samples to get a 9 cascaded classifier.

SVMs Training. For recto dots training, we collect 26908 positive and 33853 negative samples with the size of 24 × 24 to train three SVMs. For verso dots training, we collect 26590 positive and 33806 negative samples. For HOG feature, we adopt the block size of 16 × 16, the cell size of 4 × 4, bin number of 9 and get 1296 dimension feature. For LBP feature, we take the Uniform Pattern LBP with the cell size of 8 × 8 and get the 522 dimension feature. Then the fused HOG_LBP feature has 1818 dimension. Then the final decision-level SVM is trained by the 4 dimension feature vector from the detection results of Haar+Adaboost and three SVMs.

4.4 Results and Analysis

To objectively evaluate the performance of our proposed framework TS-OBR, we compare our method with the Braille dots detection in [10] which gave the results of segmentation based method and Haar+Adaboost method for only recto dots. Our paper gives the results of dots detection and Braille characters recognition including recto and verso. In order to evaluate the performance and generalization ability of our proposed framework TS-OBR, we also evaluate on our constructed Braille exam answer paper dataset BEP. To analysis the proposed method in detail, we also summary processing time and other statistical information.

4.4.1 Results on the Public Dataset DSBI

Braille Recto Dots Detection. Table 2 gives the recto dots detection results. The first two lines are from [10], which are on the de-skewing Braille images. Our first stage of the Haar+Adaboost with sliding windows method got the same F1 value 0.970, and a higher precision rate 98.38% compared with 97.65% of Haar in [10]. Since we want to ensure the detected dots are more reliable, we remain a high precision rate in our first stage. We also test the method of the HOG_LBP with SVM called HOG_LBP_SVM using the sliding window strategy on the entire de-skewing Braille image. And it got the 0.958 F1 value, which is 0.01 higher than the image segmentation based method but 0.012 lower than the Haar method. The initial recto dots detection by our Haar only took average 0.89 s (including the image de-skewing time) for a Braille image. But the HOG_LBP_SVM took average 15.02 s, which is time-consuming and about 17 times that of our Haar method.

The method SVM_Grid means that we only apply a SVM classifier with HOG_LBP on the cells grid, which got the 0.996 F1 value just using 1.22 s. This F1 value is higher than above four methods and is 0.038 higher than HOG_LBP_SVM with the sliding window strategy method. But our SVM_Grid used much less time, which can reduce much wrong detection on the background and also greatly reduce the number of windows to extract features and recognize.

This last method in Table 2 is our proposed framework TS-OBR, which uses two-stage dots detection. It got the highest F1 value 0.998 for recto dots detection, which is 0.028 higher than Haar in [10] and 0.002 than SVM_Grid.

Table 2. Results of Braille recto dots detection.

Method	Images	Pre	Rec	F1	Time
Segment [10]	De-skewing	91.72%	98.11%	0.948	/
Haar [10]	De-skewing	97.65%	96.38%	0.970	/
Haar(ours)	Original	98.38%	95.75%	0.970	0.89 s
HOG_LBP_SVM	De-skewing	93.14%	98.69%	0.958	15.02 s
SVM_Grid	Original	99.31%	99.97%	0.996	1.22 s
TS-OBR	**Original**	**99.65%**	**99.97%**	**0.998**	**1.45 s**

Our framework TS-OBR just took average 1.45 s to process one Braille image in the DSBI dataset. There are mainly three time-consuming steps in our framework, and the average time of them are 0.29 s for Haar+Adaboost, 0.57 s for de-skewing process and 0.52 s for decision-level SVM.

Statistical Analysis of Recto Dots Detection. In order to more intuitively illustrate the effectiveness of our TS-OBR framework, the average correctly detected dots number TP, wrong detected dots number FP, and missing dots number FN for recto dots detection of our methods are given in Table 3. There are averagely about 1085 recto dots on one double-sided Braille image in the DSBI dataset, which is much more than the general number of objects in natural image. As Table 3 shows, although in first stage, the Haar method had a high F1 value of 0.970, the average wrong detected dots number is 17.13 and the average missing dots number is 46.15.

Braille Verso Dots Detection. The experimental result shows the F1 value of Haar method in our first stage has dropped sharply from 0.970 to 0.895, which is influenced by the lower recall rate of 81.37%. But in our framework, the first stage is just used to quickly get some reliable Braille verso dots for next accurate Braille cells grid construction. So we remain the high precision rate of 99.53% with a lower recall rate. Finally, our TS-OBR method still obtains high performance with the F1 value 0.997 for verso dots detection, which is similar as recto dots. The processing time is average 1.58 s for verso dots detection with our TS-OBR framework (Table 4).

Table 3. Statistical information of Braille recto dots detection.

Method	Images	TP	FP	FN
Haar (ours)	Original	1039.38	17.13	46.15
TS-OBR	**Original**	**1085.16**	**4.03**	**0.34**

While our proposed framework TS-OBR with F1 value of 0.998, these can be reduced sharply to average 4.03 wrong detected dots and 0.34 missing dots for one Braille image. This statistical analysis results show the effectiveness of our framework for real applications.

Table 4. Results of Braille verso dots detection.

Method	Images	Pre	Rec	F1	Time
Haar (ours)	Original	99.53%	81.37%	0.895	0.86 s
TS-OBR	**Original**	**99.77%**	**99.74%**	**0.997**	**1.58** s

Braille Characters Recognition. Based on the detection of Braille dots and cells grid, we can easily get the results of Braille characters recognition as Table 5 shows. The F1 values are 0.995 and 0.994 for recto Braille characters and verso Braille characters respectively on the DSBI dataset. The results are little lower than F1 value of Braille dots detection, which lies in the evaluation of six-doted Braille character is stricter than a single Braille dot.

Table 5. Results of Braille characters recognition.

Method	Dots type	Pre	Rec	F1
TS-OBR	recto	99.06%	99.99%	0.995
TS-OBR	verso	99.10%	99.71%	0.994

4.4.2   Results on Our Dataset BEP

We use the models trained on the DSBI to directly evaluate all the Braille exam papers of BEP including recto dots detection and the Braille characters recognition. The detailed result is shown as Table 6.

For recto dots detection in the first stage, the method based on Haar+ Adaboost achieves a very high precision rate 99.25% on the BEP. Although the recall rate drops significantly from 95.75% to 90.50%, which means many dots are missing. However, the recall rate can be increased to 99.90% in the second stage. Compared with the results on DSBI, the precision rate on the BEP has a slight reduce from 99.65% to 98.46%. Braille exam papers are more complex than printed Braille books, for the size and appearance of Braille dots stabbed vary greatly because of the difference of stab habits and strength. And some detected errors are from those erased dots on BEP dataset, which are also difficult for manual detection. Finally, the F1 value on the BEP is 0.992, which demonstrates the good generalization ability of our proposed method and framework.

For Braille character recognition, the precision on the BEP reduced from 99.06% to 96.18% compared with the results on DSBI, which means there are average 12 wrong recognized characters in one Braille exam paper. Compared with Braille dots detection, Braille character recognition is more rigorous.

As long as one of the six points in the Braille cell is wrong, the whole Braille character recognition is wrong. Though our framework has gained an excellent performance on Braille dot detection, it still needs more efforts and study for manually stabbed Braille exam answer papers.

Table 6 also shows the whole system TS-OBR only costs about 1.5 s for recto dots detection with high recognition rate on the two datasets.

Table 6. Comparison of results on both datasets.

Dataset	Method	Type	Pre	Rec	F1	Time
DSBI	Haar	Recto dot	98.38%	95.75%	0.970	0.89 s
BEP	Haar	Recto dot	99.25%	90.50%	0.947	0.95 s
DSBI	TS-OBR	Recto dot	99.65%	99.97%	0.998	1.45 s
BEP	TS-OBR	Recto dot	98.46%	99.90%	0.992	1.54 s
DSBI	TS-OBR	Recto character	99.06%	99.99%	0.995	1.59 s
BEP	TS-OBR	Recto character	96.18%	99.93%	0.980	1.53 s

5   Conclusion

Double-sided Braille image recognition is challenging for various Braille papers, interference of recto and verso dots, deformation and skewness of Braille images. This paper proposes a novel two-stage learning framework for double-sided Braille image recognition. The experimental results on the public dataset DSBI and our Braille exam answer paper dataset BEP show the effectiveness, good generalization and fast ability for Braille dots detection and Braille characters recognition. Our future work is to further optimize our framework and apply it in real Braille images recognition applications.

Acknowledgement. This work is supported in part by Beijing Haidian Original Innovation Joint Foundation (L182054).

References

1. https://github.com/yeluo1994/DSBI
2. Ahonen, T., Hadid, A., Pietikäinen, M.: Face description with local binary patterns: application to face recognition. IEEE Trans. Pattern Anal. Mach. Intell. **28**, 2037–2041 (2006)
3. Al-Salman, A., AlOhali, Y., Alkanhal, M.I., AlRajih, A.: An Arabic optical Braille recognition system (2007)
4. Al-Shamma, S.D., Fathi, S.: Arabic Braille recognition and transcription into text and voice. In: 5th Cairo International Biomedical Engineering Conference, pp. 227–231 (2010)

5. Antonacopoulos, A., Bridson, D.: A robust Braille recognition system. In: Marinai, S., Dengel, A.R. (eds.) DAS 2004. LNCS, vol. 3163, pp. 533–545. Springer, Heidelberg (2004). https://doi.org/10.1007/978-3-540-28640-0_50

6. Babadi, M.Y., Jafari, S.: Novel grid-based optical Braille conversion: from scanning to wording (2011)

7. Dalal, N., Triggs, B.: Histograms of oriented gradients for human detection. In: IEEE Computer Society Conference on Computer Vision and Pattern Recognition (CVPR 2005), vol. 1, pp. 886–893 (2005)

8. Isayed, S., Tahboub, R.: A review of optical Braille recognition. In: 2nd World Symposium on Web Applications and Networking (WSWAN), pp. 1–6 (2015)

9. Li, J., Yan, X.: Optical Braille character recognition with support-vector machine classifier. In: International Conference on Computer Application and System Modeling (ICCASM 2010), vol. 12, pp. V12-219–V12-222 (2010)

10. Li, R., Liu, H., Wan, X., Qiang, Y.Z.: DSBI: double-sided Braille image dataset and algorithm evaluation for Braille dots detection. In: International Conference on Video and Image Processing (ICVIP) (2018)

11. Mennens, J., Tichelen, L.V., Francois, G., Engelen, J.J.: Optical recognition of Braille writing. In: ICDAR (1993)

12. Namba, M., Zhang, Z.: Cellular neural network for associative memory and its application to Braille image recognition. In: The 2006 IEEE International Joint Conference on Neural Network Proceedings, pp. 2409–2414 (2006)

13. World Health Organization: Visual impairment and blindness. http://www.who.int/en/news-room/fact-sheets/detail/blindness-and-visual-impairment. Accessed 2018

14. Viola, P.A., Jones, M.J.: Rapid object detection using a boosted cascade of simple features. In: CVPR (2001)

Document-Level Named Entity Recognition with Q-Network

Tingming Lu[1,2], Yaocheng Gui[1,2], and Zhiqiang Gao[1,2(✉)]

[1] Key Lab of Computer Network and Information Integration,
(Southeast University), Ministry of Education, Nanjing, China
`lutingming@163.com`, {`yaochgui,zqgao`}`@seu.edu.cn`
[2] School of Computer Science and Engineering, Southeast University, Nanjing, China

Abstract. Named entity recognition (NER) is typically viewed as a sequence labeling problem, where the solution is optimized in sentence level. In this paper, we explore utilizing document-level label consistency to improve NER performance by reinforcement learning. The process entails searching similar mentions and reconciling the labels, which are repeated until sufficient evidence is collected. We employ a Q-network, trained to maximize the total reward that reflects labeling accuracy while penalizing extra effort. On three publicly available datasets, our approach achieves an F_1 of 90.75%, outperforming the ensemble method (89.80%) by 0.95% and the best base tagger (88.16%) by 2.59% (The source code is available at https://github.com/KrisWentaoWong/dqnner/).

Keywords: Document-level named entity recognition · Q-network · Reinforcement learning

1 Introduction

Named entity recognition (NER) is a natural language processing task that aims to find mentions of named entities (NEs) in text and classify them into predefined categories, such as person, location, and organization [10]. Most previous studies formulate NER as a sequence labeling task and optimize the solution in sentence level with various learning models [6,7,16,17,24,27]. However, there are still some instances whose sentence-level context is ambiguous or lacks sufficient evidence [26].

The intuition for utilizing document-level label consistency is that within a particular document, similar mentions are likely to have the same label [3,5]. Taken from the AKSW-News dataset [18], Fig. 1 shows a document in which several mentions co-refer to a company "Nintendo". By looking only at local evidence it is unclear whether `NINTENDO` (mention 1) should be identified as a NE mention, but `Nintendo Co.` (mention 3) and `Nintendo` (mention 4) provide ample evidence that `NINTENDO` refers to a company.

In previous studies [3,5,20,26], document-level label consistency is incorporated into sequence models as constraints for boosting NER performance, while

© Springer Nature Switzerland AG 2019
A. C. Nayak and A. Sharma (Eds.): PRICAI 2019, LNAI 11672, pp. 164–178, 2019.
https://doi.org/10.1007/978-3-030-29894-4_13

```
BC-MICROSOFT-[NINTENDO]-INTERNET-BLOOM [NINTENDO], MICROSOFT,
                       1                          2
NOMURA ANNOUNCE INTERNET TIE-UP

...
[Nintendo Co.], Nomura Research Institute Ltd., and
              3
Microsoft Corp. will team up to offer entertainment,

sports, shopping and other information services through

home personal computers in Japan.

...
[Nintendo] will put up 40 percent of the initial
          4
investment, while Microsoft and Nomura will put up 30

percent each.

...
```

Fig. 1. A document from the AKSW-News dataset. NINTENDO (mention 1 and 2), Nintendo Co. (mention 3) and Nintendo (mention 4) are coreferential mentions.

in this paper, we explore utilizing it by reinforcement learning. Specially, for each mention m_{src} in an input document D, our strategy is to find other mentions in D which are similar to m_{src} but with clearer context, so as to collect additional evidence for labeling m_{src}.

The challenge of the strategy lies in propagating label information among these mentions, because label consistency does not hold so strictly. As an example, one document contains references to both The China Daily, a newspaper, and China, the country [3]. In order to label an ambiguous mention m_{src} in the document D correctly, one solution would be to select a similar mention m_{evi} in D, and to decide whether the label of m_{src} should be kept consistent with m_{evi}. However, if the evidence are still not enough, then we might wish to select the next similar mention. Thus, this is inherently a sequential decision problem.

We address the challenge using a reinforcement learning (RL) approach which combines similar mention selection and label reconciliation. For each mention m_{src} in D, a new episode is created. In each step, the state representation encodes information about the current and new labels along with the context of m_{src} and the selected similar mention m_{evi}. The RL agent takes an action for both similar mention selection and label reconciliation. The reward function reflects label accuracy and includes penalties for extra effort. We train the RL agent using a Deep Q-Network (DQN) [8] which predicts both selection and reconciliation choices simultaneously.

Our approach is evaluated on three publicly available datasets. Several base taggers are utilized to produce candidate NE mentions, including state-of-the-art Stanford NER [3] and an implementation of BiLSTM-CNN-CRF model [7, 17]. The experiments demonstrate that our approach outperforms the ensemble method as well as the best base tagger on all datasets, in terms of F_1.

The remaining part of this paper is organized as follows: In Sect. 2, we introduce related work. Section 3 introduces our RL approach. Section 4 describes the experiments, followed by results and analysis in Sect. 5. Finally, we conclude in Sect. 6.

2   Related Work

In this section, we introduce related work for document-level NER and reinforcement learning-based NER. Then we compare previous work with ours.

2.1   Document-Level NER

While sentence-level NER have been extensively studied [16,27], including recent work incorporating deep learning models [6,7,17,24], the studies on document-level NER are relatively rare. Finkel et al. [3] propose some penalties for inconsistency in labels based on the training data and then maximize an objective function with the penalties with Gibbs Sampling inference. Krishnan and Manning [5] propose a two-stage model with non-local features to make label consistency in both document-level and cross-document level. Radford et al. [15] exploit document-level tags to create document-level gazetteers at inference time to improve NER. Wang et al. [20] propose a document-level optimization approach to NER and apply it in a domain-specific NER task. Zhang et al. [26] propose a model that learns to incorporate document-level and corpus-level contextual information alongside local contextual information via global attentions, which dynamically weight their respective contextual information.

2.2   Reinforcement Learning-Based NER

Wang et al. [21] propose a deep RL based augmented general sequence tagging system, which contains two parts: a deep neural network based sequence tagging model and a deep RL based augmented tagger. The augmented tagger helps improve system performance by modeling the data with minority tags. Fang et al. [2] reframe the active learning as a RL problem to explicitly learn a data selection policy. The policy takes the role of the active learning heuristic. Yang et al. [25] design an instance selector based on RL to distinguish positive sentences from auto-generated annotations. Najafi et al. [11] frame the prediction of the output sequence as a sequential decision-making process, where the network is trained with an adjusted actor-critic algorithm.

2.3   Comparison with Previous Work

Thanks to the decades research on NER, many NE taggers are publicly available now. Our approach utilizes multiple existing NE taggers to produce candidate NE mentions, and then on the basis of ensemble method, we model the similar mention selection and label reconciliation process using a multi-step RL framework. Based on RL, our study is unique in the sense of the capability of integrating any existing NE tagger.

Our work is inspired by Narasimhan et al. [13]. They use a RL framework to acquire and incorporate external evidence to improve event extraction accuracy. However, our task–NER–is different from theirs–event extraction. NER finds multiple NE mentions in a document and classifies each mention into predefined categories, while event extraction task extracts predefined slots of special kind of events from a document.

3 Framework

An overview of our approach is illustrated in Fig. 2. For an input document, multiple existing NE taggers are used as base taggers to generate candidate mentions, then ensemble model assigns the most probable label and a confidence score to each mention, and finally the RL agent reconciles the label for each mention.

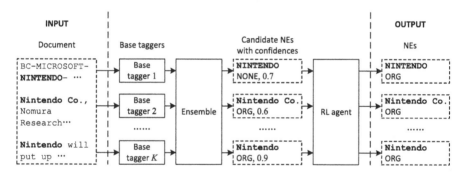

Fig. 2. Overview of our approach. The ensemble model incorrectly labels NINTENDO as NONE (red). Then the RL agent utilizes document-level label consistency and re-labels it as ORG (blue). (Color figure online)

3.1 Base Taggers

A base tagger takes a document D as input, and outputs a set of named entities. Suppose there are K base taggers. The kth base tagger outputs $E_k = \{e\}$, where $e = \langle m, l \rangle$, m is a mention and l is a label. The set of mentions produced by the kth base tagger is denoted by M_k. Then the set of mentions by K base taggers can be obtained by

$$M = \bigcup_{k=1}^{K} M_k. \tag{1}$$

3.2 Ensemble Model

For each $m \in M$ (Eq. (1)), the ensemble model takes multiple base taggers'
output as input, and then predicts the most probable label l and a confidence
score c based on a classifier, which are essential to our RL model. Features used
by ensemble model's classifier include base tagger features and context features.
Base tagger feature $f_{base}(m, k)$ represents label of m predicted by the kth base
tagger, defined as

$$f_{base}(m, k) = \begin{cases} l & \text{if } \exists \langle m, l \rangle, \langle m, l \rangle \in E_k, \\ \text{NONE} & \text{otherwise,} \end{cases} \tag{2}$$

$k \in \{1, 2, ..., K\}$. Context features are simply part-of-speech tags (postags).
$f_{postag}(m, i)$ represents postag of the token at position i within or around m,
$i \in \{\text{START}, \text{END}, \text{PREV}, \text{SUCC}\}$.

3.3 RL Framework

We model the multi-step process of similar mention selection and label reconciliation as a markov decision process (MDP). The MDP framework allows us to
sequentially perform label reconciliation, and in the same time, to choose different kinds of similar mentions for additional evidence. In each episode, the RL
agent handles one mention m_{src}. At each step, the agent has to reconcile a label
l_{evi} of a similar mention m_{evi} with the current label l_{curr} of m_{src}, and decide on
the next query for retrieving more similar mentions.

We represent the MDP as a tuple $\langle S, A, T, R \rangle$, where $S = \{s\}$ is the state
space, $A = \{a = (d, q)\}$ is the set of all actions, $R(s, a)$ is the reward function,
and $T(s', r | s, a)$ is the transition function. We describe these in detail below.

States. The state s in our MDP consists of the ensemble model's confidence
in predicted labels, and the context of mentions. We represent the state as a
continuous real valued vector incorporating information listed in Table 1. Values of nominal features (l_{curr}, l_{evi} and postag features) are encoded as one-hot
vectors. For feature $f_{postag}(m, i)$, $i \in \{\text{START}, \text{END}, \text{PREV}, \text{SUCC}\}$. For features
$f_{contain}(m, l)$, $f_{in}(m, l)$ and $f_{overlap}(m, l)$, $l \in \{\text{PER}, \text{LOC}, \text{ORG}\}$.

$X_{equal}(m_{src})$, $X_{super}(m_{src})$ and $X_{sub}(m_{src})$ are the list of *equal*, *super* and
sub mentions of m_{src}, respectively, each of which is sorted in descending order
of confidence. While deciding if two mentions are *equal* or hold a *super* mention
or *sub* mention relation, we ignore case, which will performs better than being
sensitive to case according to [5]. This is because our dataset contains many
mentions in all Caps especially in news headlines, and ignoring case enables us
to model dependences with other occurrences with a different case. For example, Nintendo Co. is a *super* mention of NINTENDO, and Nintendo is an *equal*
mention of NINTENDO.

Table 1. State feature of our RL framework.

Feature	Description
l_{curr}	current label of m_{src}
l_{evi}	label of m_{evi}
$\mathbb{1}_{l_{curr}=l_{evi}}$	match of l_{curr} and l_{evi}
c_{curr}	confidence score of m_{src} being labeled as l_{curr}
c_{evi}	confidence score of m_{evi} being labeled as l_{evi}
$c_{curr} - c_{evi}$	difference between c_{curr} and c_{evi}
$f_{postag}(m_{src}, i)$	postag of token at position i within or around m_{src}
$f_{postag}(m_{evi}, i)$	postag of token at position i within or around m_{evi}
$f_{equal}(m_{src}, m_{evi})$	m_{evi} exactly matches m_{src}
$f_{super}(m_{src}, m_{evi})$	m_{evi} is a super mention of m_{src}
$f_{sub}(m_{src}, m_{evi})$	m_{evi} is a sub mention of m_{src}
$|X_{equal}(m_{src})| > 0$	exists available $equal$ mentions of m_{src}
$|X_{super}(m_{src})| > 0$	exists available $super$ mentions of m_{src}
$|X_{sub}(m_{src})| > 0$	exists available sub mentions of m_{src}
$f_{contain}(m_{src}, l)$	m_{src} contains another mention with label l
$f_{in}(m_{src}, l)$	m_{src} lies in another mention with label l
$f_{overlap}(m_{src}, l)$	m_{src} overlaps with another mention with label l
$f_{contain}(m_{evi}, l)$	m_{evi} contains another mention with label l
$f_{in}(m_{evi}, l)$	m_{evi} lies in another mention with label l
$f_{overlap}(m_{evi}, l)$	m_{evi} overlaps with another mention with label l

Actions. At each step, the agent is required to take two actions–a reconciliation decision d and a query choice q. The decision d on the new label can be one of the following types: (1) *accept* the label, (2) *ignore* the label, or (3) *stop*. In cases (1) and (2), the agent continues to find more mentions, while the episode ends if a *stop* action (3) is chosen. The current label l_{curr} and confidence score c_{curr} are simply updated with the accepted label l_{evi} and the corresponding confidence c_{evi}.

The choice q is used to choose the next query in order to retrieve the next similar mention. Possible values of q are (1) *equal*, (2) *super* and (3) *sub*, indicating that the agent requests the environment to find an *equal* mention, a *super* mention, or a *sub* mention.

Rewards. The most obvious reward is to wait for the end of an episode, then measure whether the label for m_{src} is correct. However, this kind of reward is delayed, and is difficult to related to individual actions after a long episode. To compensate for this, we use reward shaping, whereby intermediate rewards are assigned which speed up the learning process. At each step, the intermediate reward is defined as below to maximize the final accuracy while minimizing the number of queries:

$$R(s, a) = \mathbf{1}_{l_{curr}=l^*} - \mathbf{1}_{l_{prev}=l^*} - \zeta \tag{3}$$

where l_{prev} is the label of m_{src} before taking action a, l_{curr} is the one after taking a, l^* is the gold standard label of m_{src}, and ζ is a penalty.

Transitions. Each episode starts off with a single mention m_{src} in a document D. The subsequent steps in the episode involve *equal*, *super* or *sub* mentions of m_{src} in D. A single transition in the episode consists of the agent being given the state s containing information about m_{src} and m_{evi}. The transition function $T(s', r|s, a)$ incorporates the reconciliation decision d from the agent in state s along with the information from the next similar mention retrieved using query q, and produces the next state s' as well as the reward r. The episode stops whenever d is a *stop* decision.

3.4 Q-Network

The MDP described in the previous subsection can be viewed as a sequence of transitions (s, a, r, s'). In order to learn a policy maximizing the accumulative rewards in episodes, we adopt a value-based RL algorithm Q-learning [22], which updates its Q-function estimate according to

$$Q_{i+1}(s, a) \leftarrow Q_i(s, a) + \alpha \left[r + \gamma \max_{a'} Q_i(s', a') - Q_i(s, a) \right], \tag{4}$$

where $\alpha \in (0, 1]$ is a learning rate.

We use Deep Q-Network (DQN) [8] as the function approximator $Q(s, a) \approx Q(s, a; \theta)$, in which the Q-function is approximated using a neural network, to capture non-linear interactions between the different pieces of information in state [4, 12]. DQN uses experience replay that randomizes over the data, thereby removes correlations in the observation sequence and smoothing over changes in the data distribution. In addition, it uses an iterative update which adjusts the action-values towards target values that are only periodically updated, thereby reduces correlations with the target.

3.5 Algorithm

Algorithm 1 details the entire MDP framework for document-level NER in the training phase, in which transitions are sent to DQN to learn the Q-function. During the test phase, each mention is handled only once in a single episode, where actions are selected under a greedy policy with respect to the learned Q-function.

Algorithm 1. MDP framework for document-level NER

---

1 Initialize set of training documents $\mathcal{D}$
2 **for** *epoch = 1,N* **do**
3   **for** $D \in \mathcal{D}$ **do**
4   Obtain candidate mentions M by tagging D using base taggers
5   Obtain the most probable label and a confidence score for each mention in M
6   **for** $m_{src} \in M$ **do**
7   Construct $X_{equal}(m_{src})$, $X_{super}(m_{src})$ and $X_{sub}(m_{src})$
8           $l_{curr} \leftarrow$ label of m_{src}
9           $c_{curr} \leftarrow$ confidence of labeling m_{src} with l_{curr}
10          $d \leftarrow ignore$, $q \leftarrow random()$, $r \leftarrow 0$
11   **while** $d \neq stop$ **do**
12   Pop next mention m_{evi} from $X_q(m_{src})$
13   Form state s
14   Send (s, r) to agent
15   Get decision d, query q from agent
16             $l_{prev} \leftarrow l_{curr}$
17   **if** $d = accept$ and $m_{evi} \neq null$ **then**
18                $l_{curr} \leftarrow l_{evi}$
19                $c_{curr} \leftarrow c_{evi}$
20             $r \leftarrow \mathbf{1}_{l_{curr}=l^*} - \mathbf{1}_{l_{prev}=l^*} - \zeta$

---

4 Experimental Setup

In this section, we first introduce evaluation metric. Then we detail datasets, base taggers and classifiers for ensemble model used in our experiments. Finally, parameters of our RL model are described.

Evaluation. Performance on NER is evaluated by measuring the precision and recall of tagged mentions (and not tokens), combined into F_1 score. There is no partial credit for labeling part of a mention correctly; an incorrect mention boundary is penalized as both a false positive and as a false negative.

Datasets. All the datasets in our experiments are publicly available. Each dataset is divided equally into three parts: (1) *train-e* for training the ensemble model, (2) *train-q* for training the Q-network, and (3) *test* for evaluation.

The AKSW-News dataset consists of 325 newspaper articles [18], most of which are reports in aerospace domain. The CoNLL-2003 shared task [19] data is widely used in NER task. Since one of our base taggers (Stanford NER) is trained on the training part of CoNLL-2003, we only use the testing part. The OntoNotes 5.0 [14] dataset contains 3,145 annotated documents. These documents come from a wide range of sources which include newswire, bible, transcripts, magazines, and web blogs. 719 documents are sampled randomly from the dataset and are used in our experiments.

Base Taggers. Seven existing NE taggers are used as base taggers. For outputs of the base taggers, only three classes are considered in our experiments, namely person, location, and organization. Their performance[1] is listed in Table 2 for comparison with the ensemble method and the RL model.

Table 2. Precision (P), Recall (R) and F_1-score of the base taggers. The best base tagger (Stanford) achieves an F_1 score of 88.16% averaged on three datasets.

Tagger	AKSWNews			CoNLL'03			Ontonotes 5.0		
	P	R	F_1	P	R	F_1	P	R	F_1
Stanford	**93.61**	**88.52**	**90.99**	**91.85**	87.22	**89.48**	**85.80**	**82.30**	**84.01**
BLCC	81.97	81.12	81.54	88.97	**88.74**	88.85	72.75	75.68	74.18
Illinois	78.18	67.30	72.33	89.83	80.70	85.02	67.80	61.36	64.42
GATE	83.84	74.80	79.06	68.82	56.46	62.03	61.00	53.41	56.95
OpenNLP	59.63	54.21	56.79	81.32	75.79	78.46	54.17	54.37	54.27
Balie	66.86	61.03	63.81	56.09	47.32	51.33	55.11	44.95	49.51
LinePipe	52.34	56.16	54.18	51.48	42.08	46.31	52.80	56.81	54.73

The Stanford Named Entity Recognizer (Stanford) is a CRF-based tagger [3]. BiLSTM-CNN-CRF (BLCC) [7, 17] is a neural network architecture that benefits from both word- and character-level representations automatically, by using combination of bidirectional LSTM, CNN and CRF. Base taggers also include Illinois Named Entity Tagger (Illinois) [16], General Architecture for Text Engineering (GATE) [1], Apache OpenNLP Name Finder (OpenNLP), Ottawa Baseline Information Extraction (Balie) [9] and LingPipe[2]. Although their performance is lower compared to Stanford and BLCC, we believe more base taggers are beneficial because they produce more candidate NE mentions and hence increase the potential of our approach.

Classifiers for Ensemble Model. Four classifiers are used for building different ensemble models in our experiments, including Bagging, Decision Tree,

---

[1] For performance of BiLSTM-CNN-CRF (BLCC), there is a difference between the results reported by its authors (https://github.com/UKPLab/emnlp2017-bilstm-cnn-crf/blob/master/docs/Pretrained_Models.md) and the results by us listed in Table 2, although its authors and us use the same implementation. This is because its authors use CoNLL format (in which texts have been tokenized) as input, while we use raw text of documents so as to make our approach "end-to-end".

[2] http://alias-i.com/lingpipe/ (version 4.1.0).

Random Forest and Support Vector Machine (SVM). We use the implementations of these classifiers in the Waikato Environment for Knowledge Analysis (Weka) [23] with default parameters.

Parameters of RL Model. We train the RL model for 30 epochs ($N = 30$) and evaluate on the test set every epoch. The final performance scores reported are averaged over 10 epochs after 20 epochs of training. The penalty per step is set to 0.1. Following [13], the Q-network consists of two linear layers (20 hidden units each) followed by rectified linear units (ReLU), along with two separate output layers. We also use a learning rate of $2.5E^{-5}$, a discount (γ) of 0.8, and a replay memory of size 500k. The target-Q network is updated every 5k steps.

5   Results and Analysis

5.1   Results

Figure 3 shows the learning curve of the RL agent by measuring F_1 score on the test set after each training epoch. The F_1 scores increase gradually and converge after about 20 training epochs.

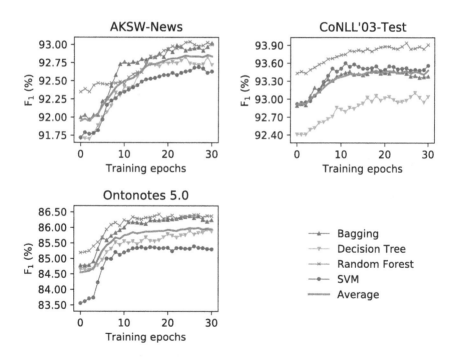

Fig. 3. Evolution of F_1 scores on the three datasets using different classifiers for ensemble, averaged on 2 independent runs.

Performance of the ensemble method and our approach (ensemble+RL) is listed in Table 3, averaged on the four classifiers (Bagging, Decision Tree, Random Forest and SVM) for ensemble. Performance of the best base tagger (Stanford) is also listed for comparison. In term of F_1, our approach outperforms the best base tagger and the ensemble method on all the datasets. With the RL agent which utilizes document-level label consistency and learns to reconcile labels among similar mentions, our approach achieves an F_1 of 90.75%, outperforming the ensemble method (89.80%) by 0.95% and the best base tagger (88.16%) by 2.59%.

Table 3. Precision (P), recall (R) and F_1 score of ensemble and ensemble+RL methods averaged on the four ensemble classifiers and 2 independent runs. Performance of the best base tagger (Stanford) is also listed for comparison.

Dataset	Tagger	P	R	F_1
AKSW-News	best base tagger	**93.61**	88.52	90.99
	ensemble	93.39	90.56	91.95
	ensemble+RL	93.51	**92.18**	**92.84**
CoNLL'03-Test	best base tagger	91.85	87.22	89.48
	ensemble	**94.86**	91.05	92.91
	ensemble+RL	94.51	**92.42**	**93.45**
Ontonotes 5.0	best base tagger	85.80	**82.30**	84.01
	ensemble	**91.56**	78.54	84.55
	ensemble+RL	91.03	81.41	**85.95**
Avg.	best base tagger	90.42	86.01	88.16
	ensemble	**93.27**	86.72	89.80
	ensemble+RL	93.02	**88.67**	**90.75**

5.2   Analysis

Compared to the ensemble method, ensemble+RL improves recall by 1.62%, 1.37% and 2.87% on the three datasets separately, with precision slightly increased by 0.12% or decreased by 0.35% and 0.53% (see Table 3). In average, RL boosts the recall by 1.95% over ensemble. We explain the reason below.

There are some NE mentions (such as mention 1 and mention 2 in Fig. 1) whose local context is ambiguous, and hence they are hard to be identified by base taggers which usually look only at context in current sentence. They are also hard to be assigned with correct labels by the ensemble method, since ensemble classifier takes only the base taggers' outputs and local context as input. However, the RL agent learns to find similar mentions which are not so ambiguous in the scope of the current document, and then propagates labels.

Table 4. Statistics of label propagations by the RL agent. It makes more correct propagations than incorrect ones, on the basis of the ensemble method.

Propagation	AKSW-News		CoNLL'03-Test		Ontonotes 5.0	
	Correct	Incorrect	Correct	Incorrect	Correct	Incorrect
NONE→PER	15.3	5.0	16.5	4.6	5.0	4.8
NONE→LOC	12.1	4.0	9.6	5.1	11.8	10.6
NONE→ORG	41.6	4.0	14.8	8.9	121.9	39.3
PER→LOC	0.4	0.0	1.9	0.3	0.0	0.0
PER→ORG	0.3	0.3	2.3	0.0	21.8	1.6
LOC→PER	6.3	0.5	0.9	0.6	0.0	0.0
LOC→ORG	0.0	0.0	4.4	0.6	0.5	0.9
ORG→PER	11.5	2.6	1.4	2.3	0.0	0.6
ORG→LOC	0.9	0.6	0.6	0.5	0.1	1.3
Total	88.3	17.0	52.3	22.9	161.0	59.0

Taking AKSW-News as an example, the RL agent correctly propagates labels for 88.3 mentions which are incorrectly classified by the ensemble method, although the RL agent also introduces 17.0 errors (see Table 4). Especially, about 80% of the propagations are made for mentions which are assigned with NONE labels by the ensemble method. This demonstrates that the RL agent is

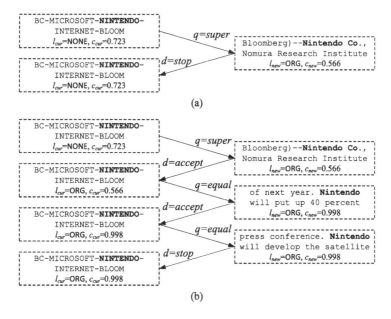

Fig. 4. The learned policies after 5 (a) and 10 (b) training epochs.

capable of propagating labels for mentions which are with ambiguous local context and hence are hard to be identified by the base taggers as well as the ensemble method.

5.3 Case Study

Going back to the example in Fig. 1, five of the base taggers fail to identify NINTENDO (mention 1), while only Balie and LingPipe identify it as an organization. As a result, the ensemble method assigns it with a NONE label.

Figure 4 illustrates two episodes under the policies learned after different number of training epochs. After 5 epochs training (a), the RL agent fails to accept the correct label ORG. It stops very early, to avoid penalties on further steps. But after 10 epochs training (b), the RL agent has learned a better policy. It accepts the label ORG from two similar mentions–Nintendo Co. (mention 3) and Nintendo (mention 4), despite the penalty on each step. Finally it stops after the confidence is high enough.

6 Conclusion

In this paper, we utilize document-level label consistency to improve NER performance by reinforcement learning. Multiple existing NE taggers are used as base taggers to generate candidate NE mentions, and then on the basis of the ensemble method, the RL agent trained using a Q-network chooses similar mentions and reconciles the labels. We evaluate our approach on three publicly available datasets, and four classification models are employed to build different ensemble models. With the RL agent searching evidence in the scope of a document, our approach boosts the recall by 1.95% over the ensemble method, with a slight decrease of precision by 0.25%, and finally achieves an F_1 of 90.75%, outperforming the ensemble method (89.80%) by 0.95% and the best base tagger (88.16%) by 2.59%. Our approach is flexible, as it can incorporate any existing NE tagger.

Acknowledgement. This work is partially funded by the National Science Foundation of China under Grant 61602260, 61702279, 61502095. We would like to thank all the anonymous reviewers for their helpful comments.

References

1. Cunningham, H., Wilks, Y., Gaizauskas, R.J.: Gate: a general architecture for text engineering. In: Proceedings of the 16th conference on Computational linguistics-Volume 2, pp. 1057–1060. Association for Computational Linguistics (1996)
2. Fang, M., Li, Y., Cohn, T.: Learning how to active learn: a deep reinforcement learning approach. In: Proceedings of the 2017 Conference on Empirical Methods in Natural Language Processing, pp. 595–605 (2017)
3. Finkel, J.R., Grenager, T., Manning, C.: Incorporating non-local information into information extraction systems by Gibbs sampling. In: Proceedings of the 43rd Annual Meeting on Association for Computational Linguistics, pp. 363–370. Association for Computational Linguistics (2005)

4. He, J., et al.: Deep reinforcement learning with an action space defined by natural language. In: Proceedings of ICLR (2016)
5. Krishnan, V., Manning, C.D.: An effective two-stage model for exploiting non-local dependencies in named entity recognition. In: Proceedings of the 21st International Conference on Computational Linguistics and the 44th Annual Meeting of the Association for Computational Linguistics, pp. 1121–1128. Association for Computational Linguistics (2006)
6. Lample, G., Ballesteros, M., Subramanian, S., Kawakami, K., Dyer, C.: Neural architectures for named entity recognition. In: Proceedings of NAACL-HLT, pp. 260–270 (2016)
7. Ma, X., Hovy, E.: End-to-end sequence labeling via bi-directional LSTM-CNNs-CRF. In: Proceedings of the 54th Annual Meeting of the Association for Computational Linguistics (Volume 1: Long Papers), vol. 1, pp. 1064–1074 (2016)
8. Mnih, V., et al.: Human-level control through deep reinforcement learning. Nature **518**(7540), 529 (2015)
9. Nadeau, D.: Balie-baseline information extraction: multilingual information extraction from text with machine learning and natural language techniques. Technical report, University of Ottawa (2005)
10. Nadeau, D., Sekine, S.: A survey of named entity recognition and classification. Lingvisticae Investigationes **30**(1), 3–26 (2007)
11. Najafi, S., Cherry, C., Kondrak, G.: Efficient sequence labeling with actor-critic training. arXiv preprint arXiv:1810.00428 (2018)
12. Narasimhan, K., Kulkarni, T., Barzilay, R.: Language understanding for text-based games using deep reinforcement learning. In: Proceedings of the 2015 Conference on Empirical Methods in Natural Language Processing, pp. 1–11 (2015)
13. Narasimhan, K., Yala, A., Barzilay, R.: Improving information extraction by acquiring external evidence with reinforcement learning. In: Proceedings of the 2016 Conference on Empirical Methods in Natural Language Processing, pp. 2355–2365 (2016)
14. Pradhan, S., Moschitti, A., Xue, N., Uryupina, O., Zhang, Y.: CoNLL-2012 shared task: modeling multilingual unrestricted coreference in OntoNotes. In: Joint Conference on EMNLP and CoNLL-Shared Task, pp. 1–40. Association for Computational Linguistics (2012)
15. Radford, W., Carreras, X., Henderson, J.: Named entity recognition with document-specific KB tag gazetteers. In: Proceedings of the 2015 Conference on Empirical Methods in Natural Language Processing, pp. 512–517 (2015)
16. Ratinov, L., Roth, D.: Design challenges and misconceptions in named entity recognition. In: Proceedings of the Thirteenth Conference on Computational Natural Language Learning, pp. 147–155. Association for Computational Linguistics (2009)
17. Reimers, N., Gurevych, I.: Reporting score distributions makes a difference: Performance study of LSTM-networks for sequence tagging. In: Proceedings of the 2017 Conference on Empirical Methods in Natural Language Processing, pp. 338–348 (2017)
18. Speck, R., Ngonga Ngomo, A.-C.: Ensemble learning for named entity recognition. In: Mika, P., et al. (eds.) ISWC 2014. LNCS, vol. 8796, pp. 519–534. Springer, Cham (2014). https://doi.org/10.1007/978-3-319-11964-9_33
19. Tjong Kim Sang, E.F., De Meulder, F.: Introduction to the CoNLL-2003 shared task: language-independent named entity recognition. In: Proceedings of the Seventh Conference on Natural Language Learning at HLT-NAACL 2003-Volume 4, pp. 142–147. Association for Computational Linguistics (2003)

20. Wang, L., Li, S., Yan, Q., Zhou, G.: Domain-specific named entity recognition with document-level optimization. ACM Trans. Asian Low-Resource Lang. Inf. Process. (TALLIP) **17**(4), 33 (2018)
21. Wang, Y., Patel, A., Jin, H.: A new concept of deep reinforcement learning based augmented general sequence tagging system. In: Proceedings of the 27th International Conference on Computational Linguistics, pp. 1683–1693 (2018)
22. Watkins, C.J., Dayan, P.: Q-learning. Mach. Learn. **8**(3-4), 279–292 (1992)
23. Witten, I.H., Frank, E., Trigg, L.E., Hall, M.A., Holmes, G., Cunningham, S.J.: Weka: practical machine learning tools and techniques with Java implementations (1999)
24. Yadav, V., Bethard, S.: A survey on recent advances in named entity recognition from deep learning models. In: Proceedings of the 27th International Conference on Computational Linguistics, pp. 2145–2158 (2018)
25. Yang, Y., Chen, W., Li, Z., He, Z., Zhang, M.: Distantly supervised NER with partial annotation learning and reinforcement learning. In: Proceedings of the 27th International Conference on Computational Linguistics, pp. 2159–2169 (2018)
26. Zhang, B., Whitehead, S., Huang, L., Ji, H.: Global attention for name tagging. In: Proceedings of the 22nd Conference on Computational Natural Language Learning, pp. 86–96 (2018)
27. Zhou, G., Su, J.: Named entity recognition using an HMM-based chunk tagger. In: Proceedings of the 40th Annual Meeting on Association for Computational Linguistics, pp. 473–480. Association for Computational Linguistics (2002)

Deep Learning Method with Attention for Extreme Multi-label Text Classification

Si Chen[1], Liangguo Wang[2(✉)], Wan Li[1], and Kun Zhang[2]

[1] Beijing University of Posts and Telecommunications, Beijing, China
chens_bupt@163.com, liwan@bupt.edu.cn
[2] Information Science Academy of China Electronics Technology Group Corporation, Beijing, China
chenwangliangguo@163.com, acneedforspeed@126.com

Abstract. Extreme multi-label text classification (XMTC), the problem of finding the most relevant label subset of each document from hundreds or even millions labels, has been a practical and important problem since the boom of big data. Significant progress has been made in recent years by the development of machine learning methods. However, although deep learning method has beaten traditional method in other related areas, it has no clear advantage in XMTC when we consider the performance of prediction. In order to improve the performance of deep learning method for Extreme multi-label text classification, we propose a novel feature extraction method to better explore the text space. Specifically, we build the model consisting of attention mechanism, convolutional neural network and recurrent neural network to extract multiview features. Extensive experiments on four public available datasets show that our method achieves better performance than several strong baselines, including traditional methods and deep learning methods.

Keywords: Extreme multi-label classification · Deep learning · Feature extraction

1 Introduction

Multi-label text classification task is an important problem and has been applied in many areas such as relational classification [18] and document classification [19]. When the number of labels grows larger, such as hundreds, thousands and even millions, multi-label classification is called extreme multi-label text classification (XMTC for short). For example, Amazon products datasets can easily have millions of labels due to the wide variety of products and each product may be associated with a large number of labels.

Traditional methods for XMTC have made significant progress in recent years such as target-embedding methods [10], tree-based ensemble methods [11] and linear methods [13]. This kind of methods represents text by bag-of-words with no semantic considered. Deep learning models, solving this problem by distributed word embedding, have gained a great success in many areas, such as

© Springer Nature Switzerland AG 2019
A. C. Nayak and A. Sharma (Eds.): PRICAI 2019, LNAI 11672, pp. 179–190, 2019.
https://doi.org/10.1007/978-3-030-29894-4_14

text summarization [14,16], automatic question answering [1] and multi-label text classification [5,18,19]. For XMTC, deep learning models have also been explored more and more. Zhang et al. [17] propose a deep embedding method to explore the label space, Liu et al. [8] employ convolutional neural network (CNN) to encode the source sequence and then predict the labels by the extracted features. However, these deep learning methods simply use CNN to encode text by extracting the local information and treat them equally. We believe convolutional results in different position have different importance [15]. Meanwhile, CNN mostly focuses on the local features of the text while global features play an important role in classification task. Inspired by the above, we explore the improvement of feature extraction method in the XMTC field. We employ self-attention [12] to allocate different weights for different convolution results in different position and add a long short-term memory (LSTM) neural network into our model to obtain the global features.

To investigate the advantage of our model on XMTC, we conduct experiments on four benchmark datasets. Experimental results demonstrate that our model significantly and consistently outperforms the traditional methods as well as some other deep learning methods on all datasets and evaluation metrics.

Specifically, we accomplish this paper with the following contributions:

- To the best of our knowledge, this is the first work to focus on the convolutional results in different position and introduce attention mechanism into the extreme multi-label text classification.
- We propose a deep learning model with novel feature extraction module by combining the advantages of existing CNN, LSTM and self-attention. mechanism [12] to extract more effective text features for XMTC.
- Extensive experiments on various public benchmark datasets show that our method can perform competitively against or even outperform state-of-the-art methods including traditional models and deep learning models.

The remainder of this paper is organized as follows: after reviewing the related work in Sect. 2, we present the framework of our method in Sect. 3. Experimental results are presented in Sect. 4 and we conclude this paper in Sect. 5.

2   Related Work

XMTC has drawn lots of attention recently and several methods have been proposed to solve it. Similar with many other tasks, these methods could be divided into traditional methods where text is represented by bag of words and deep learning methods where distributed word vector is used to encode text.

In traditional methods, there are three kinds of representative work: target-embedding methods [10], tree-based ensemble methods [8] and linear methods [13]. For target-embedding method, since the size of labels is huge, the idea is to learn a mapping $F1$ from the true label vector L to an auxiliary label vector $\hat{L}$ with a much smaller size, then another mapping $F2$ from the feature vector to the label vector $\hat{L}$ and $F3$ from the label vector $\hat{L}$ back to label vector L

should be learned. Much work focus on finding the best mapping $F1$ and $F3$ [4], such as Bloom filters [3], Landmark labels [2], SLEEC [10] and so on. For tree-based ensemble, it is motivated by the decision tree classification model. This method induces a tree structure which recursively partitions the instance space or sub-spaces at each non-leaf node, so that the classifier of each leaf only focuses on a part of the labels [11]. Most tree-based ensemble methods use decision tree as the selector, and the representative method is FastXML [11], which has better performance in the multi-label field. Linear methods differ from the above two. It is a standard training method by using linear relation, and imposes some penalty limit. For example, the well-known model PD-Sparse [13] uses elastic net regularization with multi-class hinge loss and exploits primal and dual sparsity.

Deep learning models, on the other hand, have achieved great successes recently in other related domains by automatically extracting context-sensitive features from raw text. Deep learning method uses distributed vector (word embedding) to represent words, so similar words have high similarity. One simple neural network model called FastText [5] is to average the word embedding directly and then sends the averaged embedding to the final layer for prediction. Other deep learning models include the CNN [6], the RNN [7] and so on. These models are widely used but not optimized for XMTC. Recently, some researchers have begun to study how to solve XMTC problems with deep learning methods. For example, Zhang et al. [17] propose a deep embedding method to explore the label space, and Liu et al. [8] employ convolutional neural network (CNN) to encode the source sequence and then predict the labels by the extracted features. However, their researches are only a small step forward and far from enough.

3 Method

In this section, we introduce the problem definition of XMTC first and then describe the proposed model in detail. The overall architecture of our model (DSANN for short) is shown in Fig. 1.

3.1 Problem Definition

Our problem setup is the same as [8]. Given an input text sequence, we denote it by $x = \{w_1, w_2, .., w_n\}$, where $w_i \in V$. V is the vocabulary collected in a large training data and n is the length of text sequence.

We assume that we have a set of training sequences and their corresponding labels, denoted as $D = (x_j, y_j)_{j=1}^{N}$, where N is the size of training set, y_j is the label set owned by x_j. Our goal is to learn a classifier model from D and predict labels for any unseen sequence x.

3.2 The Structure of DSANN

In this part, we first introduce our novel feature extraction module in which multi-view features are extracted. Then, we describe the k-max pooling which

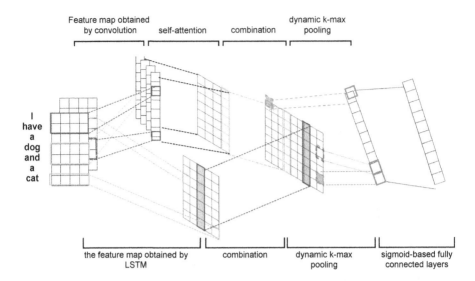

Fig. 1. Architecture of our proposed model. Our feature extraction module consists of CNN, LSTM and self-attention. With combining the features selected from CNN with self-attention and LSTM respectively, we extract features from multi-view.

is inspired by XML-CNN [8]. Finally, we show the output layer and the loss function of our model.

Feature Extraction: We input the text into two modules at the same time. One module is composed of TextCNN and self-attention, and the other module is LSTM. These two modules combined together to form final feature of the text.

For input sequence, let us use $x = \{w_1, w_2, ..., w_n\}$ to denote the sequence of word embedding vectors, where $w_i \in R^d$, d is the dimensional size. Next, we input the x into our proposed model.

We use convolution kernels of different sizes to obtain different receptive field features. In addition, in order to combine the features obtained by convolution kernels of different sizes together, a padding operation is adopted, which can ensure the length of all feature vectors are equal to the length of the text. The convolutional result obtained by one convolution kernel is defined as a vector $c = \{c_1, c_2, ..., c_n\}^T$. For each c_i:

$$c_i = g_c(v \cdot w_{i:i+m+1}) \tag{1}$$

where g_c represents the nonlinear activation function of the convolutional layer, m refers to the filter size and v is the convolutional filter. Then all the feature vectors obtained by different convolution kernel are combined together.

Convolutional results in different position have different importance. Therefore, on top of convolutional results, we use self-attention [12] to solve this problem. Formally, after the convolutional part, we use the following equation to calculate the attention:

$$A\left(Q, K, V\right) = softmax\left(\frac{QK^T}{\sqrt{d_k}}\right) V \tag{2}$$

$$head_i = A\left(QW_i^Q, KW_i^K, VW_i^V\right) \tag{3}$$

$$MultiHead\left(Q, K, V\right) = Concat(head_1, ..., head_h)W^O \tag{4}$$

where W_i^Q, W_i^K, W_i^V, W^O are the trainable parameters, n is the sequence length and d_f is the number of convolution kernel. $W_i^Q \in R^{d_f \times d_k}$, $W_i^K \in R^{d_f \times d_k}$, $W_i^V \in R^{d_f \times d_v}$, and $W^O \in R^{hd_v \times d_f}$. We employ h parallel attention layers, or heads. For each of these we use $d_k = d_v = d_f/h$. In our work, Q, K, V are the convolutional result C, where $C \in R^{n \times d_f}$.

After the self-attention, important convolution result has a larger weight and vice versa. But this kind of features extracted are locally defined because of the limitation of CNN. Therefore, we employ a LSTM neural network to capture the global features. All hidden state is obtained as follows:

$$H_{1...n} = LSTM(w_1, ..., w_n) \tag{5}$$

where $H_{1...n} \in R^{n \times d_h}$ and d_h is the hidden vector size.

Thus, H and MultiHead (M for short) have obtained different views on the text sequence and then we concatenate them together as our final features:

$$X_{1...n} = H \oplus M \tag{6}$$

K-Max Pooling: After feature extraction, the matrix X is sent to the Dynamic k-max pooling layer as the same with XML-CNN [8] model. We use maxk($\cdot$) function to select the top k max features of $X^{(i)}$ which defined as each column of X.

$$P\left(O\right) = [maxk\left(X^{(1)}\right), ..., maxk\left(X^{(d_t)}\right)] \tag{7}$$

where $d_t = d_f + d_h$.

Output Layer: Finally, the pooling results are sent into a fully connected layer to predict the optimal labels.

$$\hat{O} = W_h P(O) \tag{8}$$

where W_h are parameters to be learned.

Loss Function: On XMTC, the most common used loss function is the cross-entropy loss, we follow this setting in our experiments and use the following formula [9] to calculate it:

$$min_\Theta \; -\frac{1}{n}\sum_{i=1}^{n}\sum_{j=1}^{L} y_{ij}log\left(\sigma\left(\hat{O}_{ij}\right)\right) + (1 - y_{ij})log\left(1 - \sigma\left(\hat{O}_{ij}\right)\right) \tag{9}$$

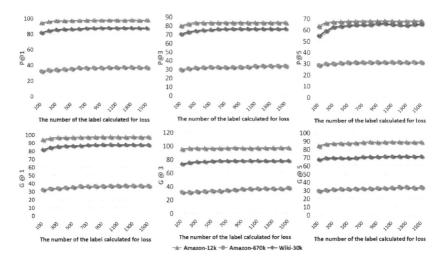

Fig. 2. Results of P@K with loss calculated by top k labels. The x-axis represents the label size modeled, y-axis represents the performance in terms of different evaluations metrics.

Table 1. Datasets Information. F is the total number of features, L is the total number of class labels, N is the number of training instances, M is the number of test instances, $\hat{L}$ is the average number of documents per label, $\hat{N}$ is the average number of label per document.

Datasets	F	L	N	M	$\hat{L}$	$\hat{N}$
RCV1-2K	48,367	103	23,149	5674	745.56	3.79
Amazon-12K	135,895	12,277	490,310	152,981	214.45	5.37
Wiki-30K	100,623	29,875	12,456	5,543	8.15	18.42
Amazon-670K	135,895	670,091	490,449	153,025	3.99	5.45

where σ is sigmoid function defined as $\sigma(x) = \frac{1}{1+e^{-x}}$.

During the experiments, we found that each instance is only related to few labels. The rest labels are completely unrelated to this instance. After a few steps of training, these unrelated labels can be easily predicted correctly. But calculating their loss is time consuming and slowing down the convergence rate. So after a few steps of normal training, we only calculate the loss function on top k predicted labels where k is manually defined. For example, on one of the dataset, we calculate the loss function on the whole labels in the first 100 training step and then we only calculate the loss on top 800 predicted labels. In this manner, the model convergence from 3000 to 2500 steps.

Since the number of label sets of RCV1 dataset is too small, we have not experimented with them. The results of other datasets are shown in the Fig. 2. It can be seen that for different datasets, we always have a k to achieve the best result.

4   Experiments

In this part, we first introduce the datasets and experiment settings which include baseline methods we compared with, metrics for performance evaluation and hyper-parameters setting for our and compared methods. Then we present the experiment result and our analysis. After that, we finish this part with the ablation test where components of our method are test step by step.

4.1   Datasets and Experiment Settings

Datasets. We evaluate our model with the following four datasets:

1. RCV1: This is an English news text and the corresponding news categories data which is widely used in text classification and many other natural language processing task. The data we use consists of about thirty thousand samples and more than one hundred labels.
2. Amazon-12K: This data is collected from Amazon products and their corresponding product categories. There are more than six hundred thousand samples and more than one hundred thousand labels.
3. Wiki-30K: This data contains about eighteen thousand samples and thirty thousand labels, which is collected from Wikipedia.
4. Amazon-670K: This is another data collected from Amazon products and their categories. It is much larger than **Amazon-12K**, which has six hundred thousand labels and six hundred thousand samples.

The detail information about these four datasets[1] are listed in Table 1.

Baselines. We adopt the following seven representative methods of text classification as baselines to compare with our model, including traditional learning methods and deep learning methods. Each of these methods has its own advantages and characteristics, which are described in detail below:

– FastXML [11]: This is a tree-based approach in XMTC. It uses tree ensemble to learn hierarchy of the target labels.
– SLEEC [10]: This is a representative method of target-embedding methods in XMTC. It clusters the labels first and then uses KNN to classify new samples.
– PD-Sparse [13]: This is one of the most representative linear methods which has a max-margin designed for Extreme multi-label classification.
– FastText [5]: This is a simple and effective deep learning method for classification. It encodes the source sequence by averaging the embedding of words.
– TextCNN [6]: This is a widely used text classification model. The model uses CNN to encode text sequence and makes prediction based on the features extracted by CNN.

---

[1] Available at http://manikvarma.org/downloads/XC/XMLRepository.html.

- TextRNN [7]: Different from TextCNN, this model replaces CNN with RNN for text sequence encoding and prediction.
- XML-CNN [8]: This is an advanced deep learning CNN model designed for XMTC. It designed the model by considering multi-label co-occurrence patterns in the CNN architecture.

Evaluation Metrics. Same with [8], we evaluate the performance by Precision at top k (P@K) and the Normalized Discounted Cumulative Gains (NDCG@K) [11], with $k = 1, 3, 5$. Let us use $\hat{y} = \{\hat{y_1}, \hat{y_2}, ..., \hat{y_L}\}$ and $y = \{y_1, y_2, ..., y_L\}$ represent the predicted score vector and the ground truth respectively, where L is the number of labels. Then the metrics are defined as follows:

$$P@k = \frac{1}{k} \sum_{l \in r_k(\hat{y})} y_l$$

$$DCG@k = \sum_{l \in r_k(\hat{y})} \frac{y_l}{log(l+1)}$$

$$NDCG@k = \frac{DCG@k}{\sum \sum_{l=1}^{min(k, \|y\|_0)} \frac{1}{log(l+1)}}$$

where $r_k(\hat{y})$ is the set of rank indices of the truly relevant labels among the top-k portion of the system-predicted ranked list for a document, and $\|y\|_0$ counts the number of relevant labels in the ground truth label vector y. P@k and NDCG@k are calculated for each test document and then averaged over all the documents.

Hyper-parameter Setting. In the experiments, we experiment with each dataset several times and get the average performance of the experimental results as the final experimental results.

In our proposed model, the window sizes of one-dimensional convolutional filters is [3, 5, 7]. The number of feature maps for each filter was 128 for all datasets. Dropout rate was $p = 0.5$. The hidden vector size of RNN is set to 128 and we use bidirectional LSTM specifically. These hyper-parameters were fixed across all datasets. For SLEEC, the number of learners was set to 15, and embedding dimension was set to 100. For FastXML, the number of trees was set to 50 and hyper-parameter $C_\delta = C_r = 1.0$. For PD-Sparse, the tuning parameter C was set to 1.0. All other hyper-parameters of these methods were chosen on the validation set. For word embeddings in deep learning models, we used pre-trained 300-dimensional Glove vectors. The model is trained by Adam and the learning rate is set to 10^{-3}. Batch size is set to 128.

4.2   Result Analysis

The result of the experiments are showed in Tables 2 and 3. From the result, we can see that traditional methods, unexpectedly have a relatively good performance on XMTC. By contrast, without adjusting to the problem, deep learning methods such as TextCNN and TextRNN are difficult to beat traditional methods. Therefore, XMTC is different from traditional classification task where deep learning models can easily beat traditional methods. XML-CNN, which takes multi-label co-occurrence patterns into account in a CNN architecture and is specially designed for XMTC, achieves better performance on most metrics compared with other methods (excluding our model). It could be inferred that correlation of labels in XMTC is actually helpful for building models. Different from XML-CNN, our deep learning model focus on feature extraction and combines local and global text features for prediction, the experiments result demonstrates its effectiveness. Even compared with the second place, our model can increase the evaluation metrics by 1.01–3.91%, we outperform all the baselines and achieve a new state-of-the-art.

4.3   Ablation Test

Our method is characterized by a novel feature extraction module which could be divided into three components: CNN, RNN and self-attention. We conduct ablation test to investigate the effectiveness of each component for XMTC.

Based on CNN model, we evaluate the performance by adding these components step by step and record the performance on three datasets: **RCV1, Wiki-30k** and **Amazon-12k**. The models are defined as follows:

- **CN**: This is the model [8] which uses CNN with k-max pooling to encode the source text sequence.
- **CN+SA**: In this model, we employ the self-attention on top of convolution to calculate the weight of each convolutional result.

Table 2. P@K performance. '-' means the result is unavailable, and bold fonts represent the best performance on the dataset.

Datasets	Metrics	FastXML	SLEEC	PD-Sparse	FastText	TextCNN	TextRNN	XML-CNN	DSANN
RCV1-2K	P@1	94.73	95.32	95.43	95.40	93.43	92.53	96.86	**98.06**
	P@3	78.52	79.64	79.46	80.12	76.15	75.43	81.23	**82.98**
	P@5	54.35	54.67	55.61	55.75	53.47	53.63	56.03	**57.56**
Amazon-12K	P@1	94.62	93.84	88.96	82.23	90.39	89.75	95.23	**97.35**
	P@3	78.95	79.25	71.35	71.94	74.36	77.86	81.02	**83.62**
	P@5	63.72	64.27	56.28	58.99	59.40	59.42	64.98	**67.99**
Wiki-30K	P@1	83.72	86.03	82.69	66.86	80.24	79.45	85.34	**87.54**
	P@3	68.79	74.23	67.03	55.83	55.98	55.21	74.98	**76.26**
	P@5	59.03	63.82	55.83	48.74	36.73	37.42	64.11	**65.45**
Amazon-670K	P@1	36.26	35.37	–	9.08	17.47	13.57	35.68	**36.98**
	P@3	31.87	30.89	–	9.07	15.78	12.35	32.34	**33.76**
	P@5	28.84	28.93	–	9.02	14.73	11.32	29.56	**31.15**

Table 3. NDCG@K performance. '-' means the result is unavailable, and bold fonts represent the best performance on the dataset.

Datasets	Metrics	FastXML	SLEEC	PD-Sparse	FastText	TextCNN	TextRNN	XML-CNN	DSANN
RCV1-2K	G@1	94.73	95.32	95.43	95.40	93.43	92.53	96.86	**98.06**
	G@3	89.21	91.37	90.72	91.02	88.26	87.83	92.34	**94.65**
	G@5	88.64	89.36	89.93	89.78	87.96	87.37	91.63	**93.26**
Amazon-12K	G@1	94.62	93.84	88.96	82.23	90.39	89.75	95.23	**97.35**
	G@3	88.83	89.56	81.56	80.86	84.80	84.56	89.98	**91.86**
	G@5	85.37	87.04	78.57	80.78	82.19	81.47	87.21	**88.96**
Wiki-30K	G@1	83.72	86.03	82.69	66.86	80.24	79.45	85.34	**87.54**
	G@3	72.78	76.45	70.98	58.23	60.88	60.36	76.94	**78.04**
	G@5	65.43	68.98	61,86	52.45	53.84	53.02	69.32	**71.23**
Amazon-670K	G@1	36.26	35.37	–	9.08	17.47	13.57	35.68	**36.98**
	G@3	33.62	33.27	–	9.51	16.60	13.65	33.89	**35.12**
	G@5	32.32	31.54	–	9.74	15.38	12.48	32.98	**33.99**

- **CN+SA+RN**: We employ the feature extraction module with self-attention on top of convolution and then concatenate it with the LSTM hidden vectors. The combination of the features are sent to the k-max pooling and then used to predict the labels (i.e. DSANN).

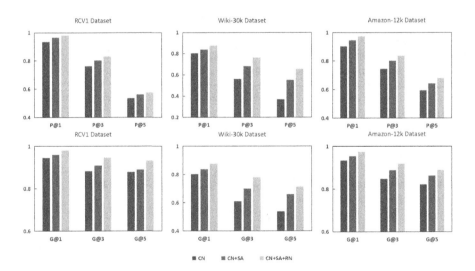

Fig. 3. Performance by adding components. The meanings of CN, CN+SA and CN+SA+RN are explained in the ablation test section.

The experiment results are shown in the Fig. 3. The results prove the effectiveness of attention mechanism and LSTM. For attention mechanism, due to self-attention, the model pays more attention to important information by giving greater weights to convolution result in important position. The perform value could be increased by 2%–18% after adding self-attention. For LSTM, It extracts global features and thus improve the performance of the model on XMTC tasks. In our experiment, after using LSTM, the evaluation score could be increased by 1%–8%.

5   Conclusion

Different from traditional text classification, the number of predicted labels for XMTC could be very large, reach hundreds of thousands or million. Therefore, existing deep learning models can not apply to XMTC directly. In this paper, we analyze the shortcomings of existing deep learning model for XMTC, and propose a new method to solve this problem. Specifically, we focus on the convolutional results in different position and introduce self-attention mechanism on top of CNN. Instead of using CNN to encode the text sequence only, we input the text into two modules at the same time. One module is composed of TextCNN and self-attention, and the other module is LSTM. Features extracted by these two modules are combined to predict the result. We conduct experiments on four real-world datasets, the experiment results show that our approach outperforms baseline methods and achieves new state-of-the-art under different evaluation metrics.

Acknowledgment. This work is supported by Information Science Academy of China Electronics Technology Group Corporation. The work was conducted during the first author's internship in the Information Science Academy of China Electronics Technology Group Corporation.

References

1. Allaouzi, I., Ahmed, M.B.: Deep neural networks and decision tree classifier for visual question answering in the medical domain. In: Working Notes of CLEF 2018 - Conference and Labs of the Evaluation Forum, Avignon, 10–14 September 2018 (2018)
2. Balasubramanian, K., Lebanon, G.: The landmark selection method for multiple output prediction. In: Proceedings of the 29th International Conference on Machine Learning, ICML 2012, Edinburgh, 26 June–1 July 2012 (2012)
3. Cissé, M., Usunier, N., Artières, T., Gallinari, P.: Robust bloom filters for large multilabel classification tasks. In: Advances in Neural Information Processing Systems 26: 27th Annual Conference on Neural Information Processing Systems 2013. Proceedings of a Meeting Held 5–8 December 2013, Lake Tahoe, pp. 1851–1859 (2013)
4. Hsu, D.J., Kakade, S., Langford, J., Zhang, T.: Multi-label prediction via compressed sensing. In: Advances in Neural Information Processing Systems 22: 23rd Annual Conference on Neural Information Processing Systems 2009. Proceedings of a Meeting Held 7–10 December 2009, Vancouver, pp. 772–780 (2009)
5. Joulin, A., Grave, E., Bojanowski, P., Mikolov, T.: Bag of tricks for efficient text classification, pp. 427–431 (2016)

6. Kim, Y.: Convolutional neural networks for sentence classification. CoRR abs/1408.5882 (2014)
7. Lai, S., Xu, L., Liu, K., Zhao, J.: Recurrent convolutional neural networks for text classification (2015)
8. Liu, J., Chang, W., Wu, Y., Yang, Y.: Deep learning for extreme multi-label text classification. In: Proceedings of the 40th International ACM SIGIR Conference on Research and Development in Information Retrieval, Shinjuku, 7–11 August 2017, pp. 115–124 (2017)
9. Nam, J., Kim, J., Loza Mencía, E., Gurevych, I., Fürnkranz, J.: Large-scale multi-label text classification — revisiting neural networks. In: Calders, T., Esposito, F., Hüllermeier, E., Meo, R. (eds.) ECML PKDD 2014, Part II. LNCS (LNAI), vol. 8725, pp. 437–452. Springer, Heidelberg (2014). https://doi.org/10.1007/978-3-662-44851-9_28
10. Nonweiler, T.R.F.: SLEEC: a space station ambulance. Philos. Trans. Math. Phys. Eng. Sci. **357**(1759), 2157–2176 (1999). http://www.jstor.org/stable/55137
11. Prabhu, Y., Varma, M.: FastXML: a fast, accurate and stable tree-classifier for extreme multi-label learning, August 2014
12. Vaswani, A., et al.: Attention is all you need. CoRR abs/1706.03762 (2017)
13. Yen, I.E.H., Huang, X., Ravikumar, P., Zhong, K., Dhillon, I.S.: PD-Sparse: a primal and dual sparse approach to extreme multiclass and multilabel classification. In: Balcan, M.F., Weinberger, K.Q. (eds.) ICML. JMLR Workshop and Conference Proceedings, vol. 48, pp. 3069–3077. JMLR.org (2016)
14. Yousefi-Azar, M., Hamey, L.: Text summarization using unsupervised deep learning. Expert Syst. Appl. **68**, 93–105 (2017)
15. Yu, A.W., et al.: QANet: combining local convolution with global self-attention for reading comprehension. CoRR abs/1804.09541 (2018)
16. Zhang, C., et al.: Semantic sentence embeddings for paraphrasing and text summarization. CoRR abs/1809.10267 (2018)
17. Zhang, W., Wang, L., Yan, J., Wang, X., Zha, H.: Deep extreme multi-label learning. CoRR abs/1704.03718 (2017)
18. Zhang, Z., Wang, H., Liu, L., Li, J.: Multi-label relational classification via node and label correlation. Neurocomputing **292**, 72–81 (2018)
19. Zou, Y., OuYang, J., Li, X.: Supervised topic models with weighted words: multi-label document classification. Front. IT EE **19**(4), 513–523 (2018)

Rule-Based HierarchicalRank:
An Unsupervised Approach to Visible Tag
Extraction from Semi-structured Chinese Text

Jicheng Lei[1], Jiali Yu[2], Chunhui He[3(✉)] [iD], Chong Zhang[3], Bin Ge[3],
and Yiping Bao[4]

[1] CETC Big Data Research Institute Co., Ltd., Chengdu, China
[2] Tus-Holdings Co., Ltd., Beijing, China
[3] Science and Technology on Information Systems Engineering Laboratory,
National University of Defense Technology,
Changsha, Hunan, People's Republic of China
xtuhch@163.com
[4] Guizhou Wingscloud Co. Ltd., Guiyang, China

Abstract. The large and growing amounts of semi-structured Chinese text present both challenges and opportunities to enhance text mining and knowledge discovery. One such challenge is to automatically extract a small set of visible tag from a document that can accurately reveal the document's topic and can facilitate fast information processing. Unfortunately, at this stage, there is still a certain gap between the existing methods and truly engineering application.

In order to narrow this gap, we propose Rule-Based HierarchicalRank (RBH), an unsupervised method for visible tag extraction from semi-structured Chinese text via a documents' title and non-title two levels. In different level, we use inconsistent methods to extract the candidate visible tags. The experiment results show that the performance of the RBH method is far better than all the baseline methods on visible tag extraction task on two distinct experiment datasets. Specifically, On Paper-Dataset, the rule-based HierarchicalRank methods' precision and F1-score achieves 18.6% and 14.1%, while TOP K = 5. In addition, on Event-Dataset, the best precision of our method is higher 7% than the state-of-the-art method PositionRank with TOP K = 1. Furthermore, the best Recall of RBH achieves 37.7% when TOP K = 5.

Keywords: Tag extraction · RBH · Text mining · Knowledge discovery · PageRank

1 Introduction

With the development of the internet and information technology, and using text to store data or information is very common in the modern life. These texts are usually divided into three forms: structured, semi-structured and unstructured. Such as a basic table information, academic papers and Weibo content. Among these three forms, semi-structured text is the most commonly used. Because on the one hand, it can store not only structured data, but also unstructured information. Semi-structured text usually

© Springer Nature Switzerland AG 2019
A. C. Nayak and A. Sharma (Eds.): PRICAI 2019, LNAI 11672, pp. 191–205, 2019.
https://doi.org/10.1007/978-3-030-29894-4_15

contains a lot of text information. Because it is not fully structured, most of the unstructured information can't be directly used. It needs to exploit multiple advanced analysis techniques to further complete the structure task to mining the data potential value. Extracting useful tag information from these rapidly-growing semi-structured text has become very challenging.

Text tag it is a general concept in current academe. In order to describe it more details, we divided it into visible tag and hidden tag two categories, which are described as follows:

Visible tag: it is a visible topic-word for the original text, such as an entity name or a keyphrase.
Hidden tag: it is an invisible topic-word for the original text, such as a meta-physical category.

Refining research tasks by classification is a common way. For different classification, we can use different method to extract tags. In this paper, we mainly study visible tag extraction instead of hidden tag extraction.

According to the definition of visible tag, we can know that keyword or keyphrase extraction at most of the time will be very similar to the visible tag extraction task. Via extracting tag can well summarize the topic of a document and can as the basis support for efficient information processing and application task. Such as scientific article summarization [1] or text classification [2], and information retrieval [3] or recommendation [4]. In the field of tag extraction, many methods have been proposed in recently. Related works are mainly divided into two categories: supervised [5] and unsupervised [6].

Kim [7] has pointed out that the supervision method in the field of visible tag extraction is better than the unsupervised method. However, the shortcoming of the supervision method is that it requires a large amount of annotation data to complete the training of the model. This labeling cost is too high to support the automatic extraction of tag for the open-domain task. For unsupervised method, Florescu [8] proposed using the global positional information that appears in the text to improve the extraction of key-phrases and achieve better experimental results on scholarly documents. Huang [9] point out selecting special POS (for example, noun, verb, adj) feature and length of the word can improve keyphrase extraction quality. In addition, via deeply analysis of semi-structured text, it is found that the title of the document is much shorter than the abstract or content, but the part of title often included some tags. Figure 1 shows a semi-structured text (Chinese/English) sample [10], and it contains title, abstract, and keywords of the document.

SLA 感知的事务型组合服务容错方法

摘　要：　针对组合服务容错逻辑与执行逻辑不分离,以及容错过程易出现 SLA(service level agreement)违反的现状,提出一种 SLA 感知的事务型组合服务容错方法.该方法首先采用有限状态机建模组合服务执行过程,对其状态进行监控;其次,采用监控自动机监控执行过程中的 SLA 属性,确保不出现 SLA 违反;然后,对于补偿过程,采用改进的差分进化算法快速寻找最优恢复规划;最后,该方法与组合服务执行逻辑相分离,所以易于开发、维护和更新.基于真实数据集的实验结果验证了所提方法在故障处理时间与组合最优度方面优于其他方法,并且对不同故障规模适应良好.

关键词：　组合服务;容错;服务级别协议(SLA);差分进化算法;有限状态机

SLA-Aware Fault-Tolerant Approach for Transactional Composite Service

Abstract: Addressing the status quo that fault-tolerant logic of composite service is not separated from execution logic and service level agreement (SLA) violation appears frequently, this article proposes a SLA-based fault-tolerant approach for transactional composite services. Firstly, finite-state machine is adopted to model the execution process of the composite service and monitor the execution status. Secondly, monitoring automata is employed to monitor the SLA attributes during its execution to avoid SLA violation. Thirdly, an improved differential evolution algorithm is used to quickly determine the optimal recovery plan for the compensation process. Finally, a process is given to illustrate that as the approach is isolated from the execution logic of the composite service, it is easy to develop, maintain and update. The experimental results based on the real data sets show that the proposed approach is superior to other approaches in both the fault handling time and composition optimization. Meanwhile, the approach can deal with different fault scales.

Key words: composite service; fault tolerance; service level agreement (SLA); differential evolution algorithm; finite-state machine

Fig. 1. The sample of a semi-structured (Chinese/English) text

Nguyen [11] has finished a preliminary study for the type of sample with Fig. 1, by selecting some features such as the distribution of candidate phrases in different sections of a research paper, and the acronym status of a phrase to improve extraction quality.

For the visible tag extraction task, although the advantages are obvious and some research progress has been made. However, the state-of-the-art method still can't support engineering application of the Chinese text visible tag extraction task. In order to improve this situation, via using hierarchical strategies, we propose rule-based HierarchicalRank method to achieve visible tag extraction task from semi-structured Chinese text. In this paper, our contributions are as follows:

(a) Based on our knowledge, for the first time, we propose to segment the text tag as visible tag and hidden tag two categories, and it via the dynamic extension method to automatic extract the visible tags between the title and non-title part in a document.
(b) We propose an unsupervised rule-based and hierarchical extraction model, called HierarchicalRank, that using different extraction strategies at different field, and combine a words' occurrences into a biased PageRank [12] to extract visible tag from semi-structured Chinese text.
(c) We summarize some effective general rules in Chinese tag extraction task, which can assist in the extraction of keyphrase or keyword.
(d) we improved the PositionRank method, and via introduce words' length to compute the weight of the word.

The rest of the paper is organized as follows. The related work is summarized in the next section. rule-based HierarchicalRank method is described in Sect. 3. And then, give the experimental results and analysis in Sect. 4. In Sect. 5, we did a simple discussion. Finally, we conclude the paper and future work in Sect. 6.

2 Related Work

For visible tag extraction task, many approaches have been proposed [13, 14]. Using supervised method to complete the extraction of key-phrases, mainly KEA [15], GenEx [16], BDT [17]. In 2012, Chuang [18] proposed a model that incorporates a set of statistical and linguistic features for identifying descriptive terms in a text. In addition, some researches to map the corresponding tag and non-tag in the document into a binary classification problem by labeling the data, and train the relevant classifier according to the labeled data to realize automatic extraction of tags. a method was proposed for visible tag extraction based on the Naive Bayes [15]. Using SVM classifier and combined N-gram language model to extract tags from meeting transcripts has been proven to improve performance [19]. Recently, proposed a neural network architecture based on a Bi-LSTM or RNN that is able to detect the main topic on the well-known INSPEC datasets [20].

In addition, utilizing unsupervised method to extract keyword or keyphrase is also very popular. For this case, tag extraction task is seen as a statistical and ranking problem [21]. A typical approach in the early date was to use TF-IDF to implement visible tag extraction [22, 23]. At present, it is more common to use co-occurrence and graph theory to construct a graph-based ranking algorithm to automatically extract tags. TextRank [24] is a classic method, based on which a series of methods have been derived and have achieved well performances in visible tag extraction in different fields. For example, ExpandRank [25] and PositionRank [8]. In addition, PTR [26] and WAM [27] are also belong to efficient methods on some special tasks.

Usually, different extraction methods are also used for different type of the text. Hu [28] through combined Skip-gram model to propose PKEA algorithm to extract patent keywords. Naidu [29] proposed an algorithm that automatically extract keywords for text summarization in Telugu e-newspaper dataset. In order to improve the accuracy of keyword extraction, Yuan [30] put forward a framework of keyword extraction based on meta-learning. Biswas [31] proposed an unsupervised graph-based visible tag extraction method from Tweets content, called KWG which uses Node-Edge rank centrality measure to calculate the importance of nodes closeness centrality measure to break the ties among the nodes.

In contrast to the above approaches, we propose HierarchicalRank, aimed at capturing both word's POS information and highly frequent weights in a document via hierarchical extraction strategies. The strong contribution of this paper is the design of hierarchical extraction strategies, which is different from existing methods that use the same level to extract visible tags. Our method assigns priority extraction strategy to the title in a document instead of using a uniform distribution over all content.

3 Rule-Based HierarchicalRank Method

In this section, we describe a fully unsupervised method HierarchicalRank. Considering that visible tags contain not only keyword or keyphrase, but also some representative entity names. So, in the hierarchical segmentation phase, we segment the title and non-title content as two parts in a contains title's semi-structured text. Particularly, if the semi-structured text being processed is missing a title, the algorithm will be automatically set the title to Null-value. After segmentation as described above, the length of the title will be shorter, while the content of non-title will be longer. For this case, for the title of text, we prefer to use a rule-based approach for automatic extraction of visible tags. For the non-title part, an unsupervised method will be used for the extraction of visible tags. Finally, the extracted results of the two parts are combined according to the visible tag selecting strategies to merge the TOP-K topic words as the visible tags of the semi-structured text. Figure 2 shows the flow chart of the rule-based HierarchicalRank method.

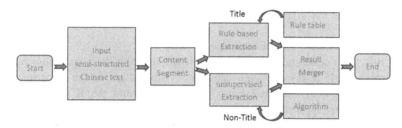

Fig. 2. The flow chart of the rule-based HierarchicalRank method

3.1   Rule Setting

In order to extract higher quality visible tags from the title of semi-structured text. Based on two semi-structured Chinese text experiment datasets, we made in-depth statistics and analysis for the title with all of the documents, and found that more than 84% of the title contained one or two visible tags. According to the analysis results from the Chinese text part-of-speech (POS) information, it is found that the visible tag in the title include the following eight categories: (1) Person Name; (2) Institution Name; (3) English Proper Noun; (4) Chinese Proper Noun; (5) Subject Proper Noun; (6) Geographic Location Noun; (7) Biological Proper Noun; (8) Compound word of Nouns, Verbs and Adjectives. Based on these statistics results, we set an eight-level rules table for the extraction of visible tags in the title. The detailed level as shown in Table 1:

Table 1. Rule table level divide status

Rule-Level	Rule-Content (POS)	Rule-Level	Rule-Content (POS)
I	Person Name (nr)	V	Geographic Location Noun (ns)
II	Institution Name (nt|nz|ni)	VI	Subject Proper Noun (g)
III	English Proper Noun (nx)	VII	Biological Proper Noun ([nb|nf|nh])
IV	Chinese Proper Noun (nn)	VIII	Compound word ([n+v]|[adj+n]|[n+n]|[v+n])

In Table 1, we list all the general rules for the tag extraction from the title. Specially, the priority is decremented from **I** to **VIII**. The end of each rule represents part of speech, for example, 'nr' in rule **I** represent the word belong to a person name, and (nt|nz|ni) in Table 1 indicates OR relationship.

3.2   Candidate Tags Hierarchical Extraction

According to Fig. 2, we can know that candidate tags are derived from both the title and non-title two parts. Because the title length is very shorter and the length of the non-title is longer, a hierarchical ranking approach is applied to the different content. For the title, we using a rule-based extraction approach, and the unsupervised approach will be used in the non-title part.

3.2.1   Title Candidate Tags Extraction

For the title, by combining the rules have listed in Table 1, it can efficiently and easily extract TOP K no duplicate candidate visible tags. In the experiment, we select TOP K (K = 2) candidate tags from the title, and the K-value should be adjusted in different application scenarios. Here, using the title in Fig. 1 as the visible tags extraction sample. The original title is 'SLA 感知的事务型组合服务容错方法 (SLA-Aware Fault-Tolerant Approach for Transactional Composite Service)'. The result after the word segmentation is '[SLA/nx, 感知/v, 的/ude1, 事务型/b, 组合/v, 服务/n, 容错/b, 方法/n]' . Finally, Matching the rules **III (nx)** and **VIII (v+n)** in Table 1, we easily get two tags ['SLA' ,'组合服务(composite service)'] as the titles' candidate visible tags.

3.2.2   Non-titles Candidate Tags Extraction

Considering that the non-title content is relatively longer than the title, it is not appropriate to use a rule-based method to extract the tag. Therefore, we propose to use an unsupervised method to complete the extraction of the tag. Based on the current state-of-the-art method PositionRank [8], we have made some fine-tuning and improvements to make it better adapt to the hierarchical extraction architecture.

The part of fine tuning: PositionRank method is to extract the keyphrase by using both the title and non-title content as input of the algorithm, but now we only use the non-title part as the input of the improved PositionRank algorithm to extract the visible tag. Improvements: (1) the original PositionRank not well support Chinese text processing, and we introduced the Chinese words segmentation module jieba[1] tokenizer to support Chinese text processing; (2) the PositionRank using the regular expression [(adjective)*(noun)+] to match phrase, for Chinese, we expand it to [(noun)*(verb)+| (adjective)*(noun)+|(noun)*(noun)+|(verb)*(noun)+]; (3) the PositionRank using all position information of the word to calculate the words' weight, we add length of the word to compute the weight. The improved PositionRank method detail described as followed.

---

[1] https://pypi.org/project/jieba/.

Suppose D is a target document for tags extraction. For non-title of D, via using jieba to finish words segment, and combine both POS filter and words' co-occurrence to build an undirected graph $G = (V, E)$ for D. Two nodes v_i and v_j are connected by an edge $(v_i, v_j) \in E$ if the word corresponding to these nodes co-occur within a window of w contiguous tokens in the content of D. The weight of an edge $(v_i, v_j) \in E$ is computed based on the co-occurrence count on the two words within a window of w successive tokens in D. Let M as its adjacency matrix. An element $m_{ij} \in M$ is set to the weight of edge (v_i, v_j) if there exist an edge between nodes v_i and v_j, and is set to zero otherwise. M is the normalized form of matrix with $m_{ij} \in M$ defined as:

$$m_{ij} = \begin{cases} m_{ij} / \sum_{j=1}^{|V|} m_{ij}, & if \ \sum_{j=1}^{|V|} m_{ij} \neq 0 \\ 0, & otherwise \end{cases} \tag{1}$$

Where $|V|$ is the number of nodes. The rank score of a node v_i is recursively computed by summing the normalized scores of node v_j, which are linked to v_i. Let S denote the vector of rank scores, for all $v_i \in E$. The initial values of S are set to $1/|V|$. The rank score of each node at step T+1, can than be computed recursively using:

$$S(T+1) = M \cdot S(T) \tag{2}$$

To ensure that the PageRank does not get stuck into cycles of the graph, a damping factor α is added to allow the 'teleport' operation to another node in the graph. Hence, the computation of S as followed:

$$S = \alpha \cdot M \cdot S + (1 - \alpha) \cdot P \tag{3}$$

Where S is the principal eigenvector and P is a vector of length $|V|$ with all elements $1/|V|$.

The idea of improved PositionRank is to assign big weights with the word that both appeared early and have a big length of the word in a document. Specifically, we want to assign a higher weight to a word appeared in third position as compared to a word found on the tenth position with the same length of word. If the same word appears multiple times in the target document, then we sum all its position weights and product with the length of the word as the word total weight. For example, if the length of the word = 2, and it appears in the 5th and 8th, its weight is:

$$W = 2 * \left(\frac{1}{5} + \frac{1}{8} \right) = 0.65$$

Then, the vector P is set to the normalized weight for each candidate word as follows:

$$P = \left[\frac{P_1}{P_1 + P_2 + \ldots + P_{|V|}}, \frac{P_2}{P_1 + P_2 + \ldots + P_{|V|}}, \ldots, \frac{P_{|V|}}{P_1 + P_2 + \ldots + P_{|V|}} \right] \quad (4)$$

The rank score of a vertex v_i, i.e., $S(v_i)$, can be obtained in an algebraic way recursively computing the following equation:

$$S(v_i) = (1 - \alpha) \cdot P_i + \alpha \cdot \sum_{v_j \in Adj(v_i)} \frac{w_{ji}}{O(v_j)} S(v_j) \quad (5)$$

Where P_i is the weight found in the vector P for vertex v_i, and $O(v_j) = \sum_{(v_k) \in Adj(v_j)} w_{jk}$.

When all candidate words have finished the computation of rank score, we according to appearing contiguous positions in the original document to concatenated the words into a phrase. Then, using the expand regular expression to match all phrases with the phrases' length more than L (L is the least length of a phrase). Finally, via ranking the value of sum (scores) of individual words that include the phrase to extract the TOP K candidate tags.

In our experiments, we setting $\alpha = 0.85$, co-occur window size = 6, candidate tag number $K = 6, L = 3$, and the words' rank scores are recursively computed until the difference between two consecutive iteration is less than 0.001 or a number of 200 iterations is reached.

3.3 Candidate Tags Merger

According to Sect. 3.2, for a semi-structured Chinese document, by using Hierarchi-calRank method, we can get title_Tags (TOP 2) and non-title_Tags (TOP 6) two candidate tag lists. Follow the extraction rule, we can know that title_tags contains no more than two non-repeating tags, and non-title_tags contains no more than six non-repeating tags. Considering that they use an independent extraction method, there may exist duplicate or similar tags within two tags' lists.

In order to merge the candidate tags, we use the Longest Common Sequence (LCS) [32] value of the strings to filter similar tags. The detail merge algorithm is as followed.

```
Algorithm Input (two lists): title_Tags, non-title_Tags.
Initialize a Null list called Tags;
if title_Tags is Null:
    if non-title_Tags is Null:
        Return Tags #(Tags=Null)
    else:
        Tags=non-title_Tags
        Return Tags #(Tags=non-title_Tags)
else:
    if non-title_Tags is Null:
        Tags=title_Tags
        Return Tags #(Tags=title_Tags)
    else:
        Tags=title_Tags;
        for non-title_tag in non-title_Tags:
            flag=false
            for title-tag in title_Tags:
                if LCS[non-title_tag, title-tag].length<C:
                    flag=true
                else:
                    flag=false
                    break
            if flag==true:
                Tags.append(non-title_tag)
        Return Tags # Tags merged title_tag and non-title_tag
```

Using this algorithm, we can easily to get all the visible tags, and for Chinese, we suggest C = 2.

4 Experimental Results and Analysis

4.1 Datasets and Evaluation Metrics

Datasets Introduction. In order to evaluate the performance of HierarchicalRank, we carried out experiments based on two Chinese datasets. The first dataset consists of all the Chinese research papers published by the Journal of Software[2] in 2018. The second dataset consists of the mainly China hot social events published by zhiweidata[3] from January 1st to January 15th, 2019. For the first dataset, we use the title and abstract of

---

[2] http://www.jos.org.cn/jos/ch/index.aspx.

[3] http://ef.zhiweidata.com/#!/down.

each paper to extract visible tags. The author-input keywords are used as gold-standard for evaluation. For the second dataset, we use the title and description content of each event to extract visible tag. The original visible events' tags are used as gold-standard for evaluation. All two datasets are summarized in Table 2, which show the number of documents in each dataset, the total number of visible tags (Vt), and the average number of visible tags per document (AvgVt).

Table 2. A summary of the datasets

Dataset	#Docs	Vt	AvgVt
Paper dataset (Journal of Software 2018)	56	267	4.8
Event dataset (zhiweidata)	50	71	1.4

Evaluation Metrics. We use the mean reciprocal rank (MRR) curve to illustrate our experimental results. MRR value revealed the averaged ranking of the first correct prediction and is defined as:

$$MRR = \frac{1}{|D|} \sum_{d \in D} \frac{1}{rd} \tag{6}$$

where D is the collection of documents and rd is the rank at which the first correct keyphrase of document d was found. In addition, we also summarize the results in terms of Precision, Recall, and F1-score in a table to contrast HierarchicalRank with previous methods since these metrics are widely used in previous works.

4.2   Core Parameter Setting and Analysis

For the rule-based HierarchicalRank extraction methods, the number of best candidate tags in the title is an important parameter. Considering that the length of the title is very short, and the number of best candidate tags in the title is recommended between 1 and 3. An effective method of processing is to sample and statistic the extracted text and calculate the AvgVt value of this type. For example, the first dataset AvgVt is 4.8, and the second dataset AvgVt is 1.4. Then, set the number of best candidate tags to 1, if the AvgVt <= 2, and the number of best candidate tags set 2, if the AvgVt > 2 and the AvgVt <= 6, in addition, if the AvgVt > 6, we can set 3 as the number of best candidate tags. For the choice of the number of non-title best candidate tags and words co-occur window size, we can refer to PositionRank [8] method to set it.

Figure 3 shows the MRR curve of rule-based HierarchicalRank and TextRank for different values of the number of best candidate tags in the title, on all two datasets.

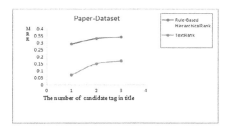 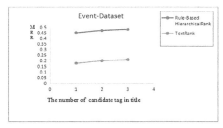

Fig. 3. MRR curves with different values for the number of best candidate tags in title

According to Fig. 3, the MRR curve shows that the performance of our method is better than TextRank algorithm for title-tag extraction on all two experiment datasets.

In addition, for improved PositionRank, we add the words' length to compute word weights. In order to evaluate the performance of improved PositionRank algorithm. We combining the original PositionRank and the improved PositionRank algorithm to do comparative experiment in all two datasets. Figure 4 shows the MRR curve for the experiment.

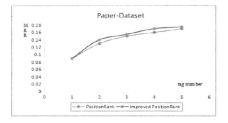 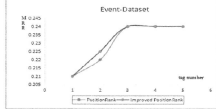

Fig. 4. MRR curves of the PositionRank and improved PositionRank algorithm

From Fig. 4, through the MRR curve, we can know that the performance of the improved PositionRank algorithm is slightly better than the original PositionRank algorithm in complete tags extraction task for all two experimental datasets.

Another core parameter of the HierarchicalRank is the total number of extracted visible tags (title_tags + non-title_tags) in a document, and this parameter is usually sensitive to the average length of the document. In our experiments, we set the total number of tag in a document between 1 and 5. Figure 5 shows the MRR curve of rule-based HierarchicalRank and another four unsupervised baselines method, PositionRank, Improved PositionRank, TextRank, and TF-IDF for different total number of the tags within all two datasets.

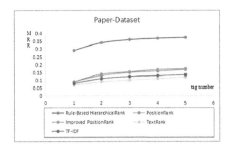 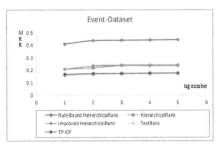

Fig. 5. MRR curves of the rule-based HierarchicalRank and baselines algorithm

Via Fig. 5, shows the MRR curve, we can know that the performance of the rule-based HierarchicalRank algorithm is far better than all the baselines method on visible tags extraction task for all two experiment datasets.

4.3   Overall Performance

In order to consistent with these prior works on visible tag extraction report results also in terms of precision (P), Recall (R), F1-score (F1). We also calculate the P, R and F1 in our experiment. In Table 3, we show the results of the comparison of rule-based HierarchicalRank with all baselines, in terms of P, R and F1 for TOP K = 1, 3, 5 predicted number of total tags, on all two datasets.

Table 3. rule-based HierarchicalRank against baselines in terms of P, R and F1

Dataset	Unsupervised methods	TOP #1 (%)			TOP #3 (%)			TOP #5 (%)		
		P	R	F1	P	R	F1	P	R	F1
Paper-Dataset	rule-based HierarchicalRank	**18.6**	**6.0**	**9.1**	**15.5**	**9.7**	**12.0**	**14.3**	**13.9**	**14.1**
	Improved PositionRank	9.0	2.1	3.4	9.0	5.8	7.1	7.3	6.9	7.1
	PositionRank	8.9	1.9	3.1	8.9	5.6	6.9	7.0	6.7	6.9
	TextRank	7.1	1.5	2.5	4.8	3.0	3.7	4.0	3.7	3.9
	TF-IDF	7.8	1.7	2.8	5.2	3.3	4.0	4.5	3.9	4.2
Event-Dataset	rule-based HierarchicalRank	**36.0**	**23.7**	**28.6**	**21.0**	**37.7**	**27.0**	**20.6**	**37.7**	**26.6**
	Improved PositionRank	29.7	16.6	21.3	17.1	16.7	16.9	16.5	16.7	16.6
	PositionRank	29.0	16.0	20.6	16.4	16.0	16.2	16.0	16.0	16.0
	TextRank	16.0	8.3	10.9	11.4	11.1	11.3	11.1	11.1	11.1
	TF-IDF	17.2	8.6	11.5	12.1	11.6	11.8	11.2	11.6	11.4

As show from Table 3, the rule-based HierarchicalRank method outperforms all baselines, on all two datasets. The performance of the improved PositionRank algorithm is slightly better than the PositionRank, but it is not obviously on the Paper-Dataset. The rule-based HierarchicalRank method in Paper-Dataset achieves 18.6% Precision and

14.1% F1-score, when TOP K = 5, it is double the PositionRank method on Precision and F1-score. On Event-Dataset, the best Precision of our method higher 7% than PositionRank with TOP K = 1, and the best Recall achieves 37.7% when TOP K = 5.

5 Discussion

The main purpose of the rule-based HierarchicalRank method proposed in this paper is to solve the visible tag extraction task of semi-structured text, but it can also adapt the keyphrase or keyword extraction task by adjusting the corresponding parameters. In addition, the method also can be used to processed have title and content unstructured text, such as Chinese Weibo text.

Considering the setting of the rules, one of the shortcomings of this method is that only the visible tag extraction task of Chinese text is currently supported. If reader use this method to process non-Chinese text, it is a new task to redesign the rules according to interrelated text corpus.

In the processing of Chinese text, the accuracy of word segmentation and part-of-speech (POS) annotation often have a greater impact on the performance of the algorithm. In order to improve the performance of the rule-based HierarchicalRank method, when dealing with Chinese text, we suggest that increase the accuracy of word segmentation by introducing the domain dictionary to improve the quality of tag extraction.

For the setting of the core parameters of the method, the relevant solutions are given for the papers of our experimental datasets. If the algorithm is used in other application scenarios, it is recommended that to adjust and test the parameters according to the specific data feature, it will give fuller play to the performance of the algorithm.

This paper only studies the visible tags extraction task. For the hidden tags extracting task, and it may be solved in the future by using supervised learning method or deep learning method.

6 Conclusion and Future Work

We proposed a novel hierarchical unsupervised method, called HierarchicalRank, which segment both the title and non-title content of the semi-structured Chinese text to extract the visible tags. In addition, we improved the PositionRank algorithm via introduce words' length to compute the weights. To our knowledge, we are the first to propose using hierarchical method in unsupervised visible tag extraction. Specifically, in title level, the experimental results show that the quality of the extraction of the visible tag can be effectively improved via combining some general rules.

In a addition, the experimental results on two datasets show that rule-based Hierarchical Rank method achieves better performance than the currently state-of-the-art method. In the future, it would be interesting to explore the performance of Hierarchical Rank on other types of unstructured text, e.g., web news. Finally, combined HierarchicalRank to extract hidden tag belong to another very important direction in text mining.

Acknowledgment. This paper was supported by the National Natural Science Foundation of China (NSFC) via grant No. 61872446 and Natural Science Foundation of Hunan Province, China via grant No. 2018JJ2475 and No. 2018JJ2476.

References

1. Abujbara, A., Arbor, A.: Coherent Citation-Based Summarization of Scientific Papers. Meeting of the Association for Computational Linguistics: Human Language Technologies. DBLP (2011)
2. Yang, Y., Pedersen, J.O.: A comparative study on feature selection in text categorization. In: Proceedings of the International Conference on Machine Learning (1997)
3. Liu, T.Y.: Learning to rank for information retrieval. ACM SIGIR Forum **41**(2), 904 (2010)
4. Li, Y., Nie, J., Yi, Z., Wang, B., Yan, B., Weng, F.: Contextual recommendation based on text mining. In: International Conference on Computational Linguistics: Posters (2010)
5. Caragea, C., Bulgarov, F.A., Godea, A., Gollapalli, S.D.: Citation-enhanced keyphrase extraction from research papers: a supervised approach (2014)
6. Wang, M., Zhao, B., Huang, Y.: PTR: phrase-based topical ranking for automatic keyphrase extraction in scientific publications. In: Hirose, A., Ozawa, S., Doya, K., Ikeda, K., Lee, M., Liu, D. (eds.) ICONIP 2016. LNCS, vol. 9950, pp. 120–128. Springer, Cham (2016). https://doi.org/10.1007/978-3-319-46681-1_15
7. Kim, S.N.: Automatic keyphrase extraction from scientific articles. Lang. Resour. Eval. **47**(3), 723–742 (2013)
8. Florescu, C., Caragea, C.: PositionRank: an unsupervised approach to keyphrase extraction from scholarly documents. In: Proceedings of the 55th Annual Meeting of the Association for Computational Linguistics (Volume 1: Long Papers), vol. 1, pp. 1105–1115 (2017)
9. Huang, C.M., Wu, C.Y.: Effects of word assignment in LDA for news topic discovery. In: IEEE International Congress on Big Data (BigData Congress), pp. 374–380. IEEE (2015)
10. Zhang, J.N., Wang, S.G., Sun, Q.B., Yang, F.C.: SLA-Aware fault-tolerant approach for transactional composite service. J. Softw. **29**(12), 3614–3634 (2018). http://www.jos.org.cn/1000-9825/5313.htm. (in Chinese)
11. Nguyen, T.D., Kan, M.-Y.: Keyphrase extraction in scientific publications. In: Goh, D.H.-L., Cao, T.H., Sølvberg, I.T., Rasmussen, E. (eds.) ICADL 2007. LNCS, vol. 4822, pp. 317–326. Springer, Heidelberg (2007). https://doi.org/10.1007/978-3-540-77094-7_41
12. Page, L., Brin, S., Motwani, R., Winograd, T.: The PageRank citation ranking: bringing order to the web. Stanford InfoLab (1999)
13. Hasan, K.S., Ng, V.: Automatic keyphrase extraction: a survey of the state of the art. In: Proceedings of the 52nd Annual Meeting of the Association for Computational Linguistics (Volume 1: Long Papers), vol. 1, pp. 1262–1273 (2014)
14. Merrouni, Z.A., Frikh, B., Ouhbi, B.: Automatic keyphrase extraction: an overview of the state of the art. In: 4th IEEE International Colloquium on Information Science and Technology (CiSt), pp. 306–313. IEEE (2016)
15. Frank, E., Paynter, G.W., Witten, I.H., et al.: Domain-specific keyphrase extraction. In: International Joint Conference on Artificial Intelligence (1999)
16. Turney, P.D.: Learning algorithms for keyphrase extraction. Inf. Retrieval **2**(4), 303–336 (2002)

17. Lopez, P., Romary, L.: HUMB: automatic key term extraction from scientific articles in GROBID. In: Proceedings of International Workshop on Semantic Evaluation, pp. 248–251 (2010)
18. Chuang, J., Manning, C.D., Heer, J.: "Without the clutter of unimportant words": ldescriptive keyphrases for text visualization. ACM Trans. Comput. Hum. Interact. **19**(3), 1–29 (2012)
19. Sheeba, J.I., Vivekanandan, K.: Improved keyword and keyphrase extraction from meeting transcripts. Int. J. Comput. Appl. **52**(13), 11–15 (2013)
20. Basaldella, M., Antolli, E., Serra, G., Tasso, C.: Bidirectional LSTM recurrent neural network for keyphrase extraction. In: Serra, G., Tasso, C. (eds.) IRCDL 2018. CCIS, vol. 806, pp. 180–187. Springer, Cham (2018). https://doi.org/10.1007/978-3-319-73165-0_18
21. Alqaryouti, O., Khwileh, H., Farouk, T., Nabhan, A., Shaalan, K.: Graph-based keyword extraction. In: Shaalan, K., Hassanien, A.E., Tolba, F. (eds.) Intelligent Natural Language Processing: Trends and Applications. SCI, vol. 740, pp. 159–172. Springer, Cham (2018). https://doi.org/10.1007/978-3-319-67056-0_9
22. Zhang, Y., Zincirheywood, N., Milios, E.: Narrative text classification for automatic key phrase extraction in web document corpora (2005)
23. Li, J., Zhang, K.: Keyword extraction based on tf/idf for Chinese news document. Wuhan Univ. J. Nat. Sci. **12**(5), 917–921 (2007)
24. Mihalcea, R., Tarau, P.: TextRank: bringing order into texts. In: EMNLP, pp. 404–411 (2004)
25. Wan, X., Xiao, J.: Single document keyphrase extraction using neighborhood knowledge. In: National Conference on Artificial Intelligence. AAAI Press (2008)
26. Liu, Z., Huang, W., Zheng, Y., Sun, M.: Automatic keyphrase extraction via topic decomposition. In: Proceedings of the 2010 Conference on Empirical Methods in Natural Language Processing, EMNLP 2010, 9–11 October 2010, MIT Stata Center, Massachusetts, A meeting of SIGDAT, a Special Interest Group of the ACL. Association for Computational Linguistics (2010)
27. Liu, Z., Chen, X., Zheng, Y., Sun, M.: Automatic keyphrase extraction by bridging vocabulary gap. In: Fifteenth Conference on Computational Natural Language Learning. Association for Computational Linguistics (2011)
28. Hu, J., Li, S., Yao, Y., Yu, L., Yang, G., Hu, J.: Patent keyword extraction algorithm based on distributed representation for patent classification. Entropy **20**(2), 104 (2018)
29. Naidu, R., Bharti, S.K., Babu, K.S., Mohapatra, R.K.: Text summarization with automatic *Keyword* extraction in Telugu e-Newspapers. In: Satapathy, S.C., Bhateja, V., Das, S. (eds.) Smart Computing and Informatics. SIST, vol. 77, pp. 555–564. Springer, Singapore (2018). https://doi.org/10.1007/978-981-10-5544-7_54
30. Yuan, M., Zou, C.: Text keyword extraction based on meta-learning strategy. In: International Conference on Big Data and Artificial Intelligence (BDAI), pp. 78–81. IEEE (2018)
31. Biswas, S.K.: Keyword extraction from tweets using weighted graph. In: Mallick, P.K., Balas, V.E., Bhoi, A.K., Zobaa, A.F. (eds.) Cognitive Informatics and Soft Computing. AISC, vol. 768, pp. 475–483. Springer, Singapore (2019). https://doi.org/10.1007/978-981-13-0617-4_47
32. Ge, B., He, C.H., Hu, S.Z., Guo, C.: Chinese news hot subtopic discovery and recommendation method based on key phrase and the LDA model. DEStech Transactions on Engineering and Technology Research, ECAR (2018)

A POS Tagging Model for Vietnamese Social Media Text Using BiLSTM-CRF with Rich Features

Ngo Xuan Bach[✉], Trieu Khuong Duy, and Tu Minh Phuong

Department of Computer Science,
Posts and Telecommunications Institute of Technology, Hanoi, Vietnam
{bachnx,duytk,phuongtm}@ptit.edu.vn

Abstract. This paper deals with the task of part-of-speech (POS) tagging for Vietnamese social media text, which poses several challenges compared with tagging for conventional text. We introduce a POS tagging model that takes advantages of deep learning and manually engineered features to overcome the challenges of the task. The main part of the model consists of several bidirectional long short-term memory (BiLSTM) layers that are used to learn intermediate representations of sentences from features extracted at both the character and the word levels. Conditional random field (CRF) is then used on top of those BiLSTM layers, at the inference layer, to predict the most suitable POS tags. We leverage various types of manually engineered features in addition to automatically learned features to capture the characteristics of Vietnamese social media data and therefore improve the performance of the model. Experimental results on a public POS tagging corpus for Vietnamese social media text show that our model outperforms previous work [4] by a large margin, reaching 91.9% accuracy with 27% error rate reduction. The results also reveal the effectiveness of using both automatically learned and manually designed features in a deep learning framework when only a limited amount of training data is available.

Keywords: Part-of-speech tagging · Social media text · Bidirectional long short-term memory · Conditional random field

1 Introduction

Part-of-speech (POS) tagging is the task of determining a proper POS tag for each word in an input sentence according to its context. For example, a good English POS tagger is expected to be able to differentiate the proper POS tag of the word "play" in the following two sentences: (1) *I saw that play yesterday*; and (2) *He can play piano*. While the word "play" in the first sentence is a noun, it is a verb in the second sentence. The outputs of POS taggers provide useful information for most natural language processing (NLP) tasks as well as applications, including syntactic parsing, semantic role labeling, question answering, information extraction, and machine translation.

© Springer Nature Switzerland AG 2019
A. C. Nayak and A. Sharma (Eds.): PRICAI 2019, LNAI 11672, pp. 206–219, 2019.
https://doi.org/10.1007/978-3-030-29894-4_16

POS tagging for social media text has received a great attraction in NLP research community in recent years [1,2,4,7,10,23,28,31]. The task for noisy text generated by social users exposes several challenges compared with tagging for conventional text. The first challenge comes from the characteristics of social media text, which is not always written conforming to the formal grammar and correct spelling. Social users often use abbreviations, wrong capital letters, jargons, typos, and emoticons. There are other problems specific to Vietnamese social media text such as frequent use of foreign language words like English words, or use of words without tone marks. Another challenge is the lack of large-scale annotated POS tagged corpora for social data. Developing a robust and accurate POS tagger for social media text is therefore difficult, especially in low resource languages like Vietnamese.

Previous studies on POS tagging usually train statistical classifiers or sequence labeling models using annotated corpora. The most popular learning algorithms include maximum entropy models (MEMs) [30,35], support vector machines (SVMs) [9], hidden Markov models (HMMs) [5], and conditional random fields (CRFs) [4,10]. To achieve good tagging performances, such algorithms need to be trained with a set of manually engineered features. "The current word", "the previous word", "the next word", "the POS tag of the previous word", "whether the first letter of the current word is capitalized", and "whether the current word contains digits" [30] are among the most effective manually designed features.

The last few years have seen much success of deep learning in various fields of computer science, especially in computer vision [13,21] and natural language processing [11,39]. Convolutional neural networks (CNNs) [20] and recurrent neural networks (RNNs) [8] are among the most popular and successful deep learning architectures. A number of research works have applied CNNs and RNNs for POS tagging and achieved impressive results [14,16,17,22,26,29,32,37]. The advantage of deep learning models is the ability to automatically learn effective features from raw inputs. Deep models, however, are data hungry, which performances usually degrade when only a small amount of training data is available.

The aim of this work is to develop an accurate and robust POS tagging model for Vietnamese social media text, in which we tackle two problems: (1) characteristics of Vietnamese social media text; and (2) the lack of large-scale available annotated datasets. To this end, we employ advanced learning techniques, i.e. deep learning models. We leverage various types of manually engineered features in addition to automatically learned features, which are the advantage of deep architectures. Such manually designed features can capture characteristics of social media data and makes the model accurate when training on a relatively small size corpus, which is the drawback of deep learning models. We present a BiLSTM-CRF model in which BiLSTM is used for learning word and sentence representations and CRF is employed at the inference layer to capture the relations between POS tags of adjacent words. Experimental results on a public POS tagging dataset for Vietnamese social media text show that our model outperforms the best previous work by a large margin.

The rest of this paper is structured as follows. Section 2 presents related work. Section 3 introduces our proposed POS tagging model for Vietnamese social media text. Experimental results and analyses are described in Sect. 4. Finally, Sect. 5 concludes the paper and discusses future work.

2   Related Work

This section gives a brief review of related work, including POS tagging for social media text, neural network based POS taggers, and POS tagging for Vietnamese language.

POS Tagging for Social Media Text. Gimpel et al. [10] present a study on POS tagging for Twitter in English. They employ CRFs as the learning method and got 89.4% tagging accuracy on a corpus consisting of 1,827 tweets. Owoputi et al. [28] propose to utilize word cluster features to improve POS tagging for English tweets, and report an accuracy improvement of more than 3% over a baseline. Derczynski et al. [7] investigate existing English POS taggers for tweet data and introduce a method to combine the outputs of taggers, which use different tagsets. In addition to English, several studies have been conducted on POS tagging for social media text in other languages. Nooralahzadeh et al. [27] address the task for French. Their model with CRFs achieves 91.9% and 51.1% token and sentence accuracy on a dataset consisting of 1,700 French sentences extracted from social media services like Twitter, Facebook and forums. Albogamy and Ramsay [1,2] conduct empirical studies on POS tagging for Arabic tweets. They provide a detailed error analysis of state-of-the-art POS taggers when applied to Arabic tweets and introduce a fast and robust POS tagger for Arabic tweets using agreement-based bootstrapping. Rehbein [31] uses CRFs on a collection of 1,426 German tweets and reports the tagging accuracy of 88.8%. Neunerdt et al. [23] investigate the task for German social media text. They evaluate state-of-the-art German POS taggers on multiple types of data sources, including chat messages, blog comments, Merkur and YouTube comments.

Neural Network Based POS Taggers. Several neural network based models have been developed for POS tagging. RNNs are among the most popular choice due to their power in modeling sequence data. Efficient POS taggers usually combine RNNs or their variants such as bidirectional RNNs, LSTM, bidirectional LSTM with other types of networks, including CNNs and CRFs. Plank et al. [29] with bidirectional LSTM, Wang et al. [37] with bidirectional LSTM-RNN, Labeau et al. [17] with CNN-Bidirectional RNN, Shao et al. [32] with bidirectional RNN-CRF, Huang et al. [16] with LSTM-CRF and bidirectional LSTM-CRF, and Ma and Hovy [22] with bidirectional LSTM-CNN-CRF are examples of successful neural network architectures for POS tagging. Our model also exploits bidirectional LSTM for feature representation learning and CRF for inference, but focuses on Vietnamese social media text. Moreover, we use a rich feature set consisting of both automatically learned and manually designed features to tackle the lack of annotated social media data.

POS Tagging for Vietnamese Language. Most previous work on Vietnamese POS tagging focuses on general text, which usually formulates the task as a sequence labeling problem. Various kinds of learning algorithms have been investigated, including MEMs [19,36], SVMs [24], CRFs [25,36], guided online learning [25], dual decomposition [3], and neural networks [26]. The most closely related previous work is that of Bach et al. [4]. They introduce a POS tagged corpus for Vietnamese social media text consisting of 4,150 Vietnamese sentences extracted from Facebook. A series of experiments have been conducted on the corpus using CRFs. Our work also focuses on Vietnamese social media text, but introducing a model with advanced learning techniques, i.e. deep neural networks. As shown in experiments, our model achieves impressive results on the same corpus of Bach et al. [4].

3   Tagging Model

This section describes our POS tagging model for Vietnamese social media text. Given an input sentence in Vietnamese language represented by a sequence of words $s = (w_1, w_2, \ldots, w_m)$, the goal of the model is to determine the most proper POS tag $l_i \in L$ for each word w_i, where m denotes the length of sentence s, and L is the set of POS tags.

3.1   Model Overview

As shown in Fig. 1, our model consists of three main stages: word representation, sentence representation, and inference.

- **Word representation**: The goal of this stage is to produce a representation vector for each word in the input sentence. To utilize various types of information, our model combines both automatically learned features and manually engineered features extracted at the character and word levels. While the former ones use words directly, the later ones are carefully extracted in a preprocessing step with human knowledge.
- **Sentence representation**: At this stage, BiLSTM is used to capture left-to-right and right-to-left information of the word sequence to generate the intermediate representation for the input sentence. We stack two BiLSTM layers to build deeper representations[1].
- **Inference**: At the inference layer, CRF takes the sentence representation as the input and output the most suitable POS tag sequence.

In the next sections, we describe how to build word representations and how BiLSTM and CRF are used in our model. For notation, we denote vectors with bold lower-case (e.g., $\mathbf{x}$, $\mathbf{y}_t$), matrices with bold upper-case (e.g., $\mathbf{W}$, $\mathbf{H}_i$), and scalars with italic lower-case (e.g., c, α).

---

[1] Goldberg [11] shows that by stacking several BiLSTM layers we can produce better representations for sentences.

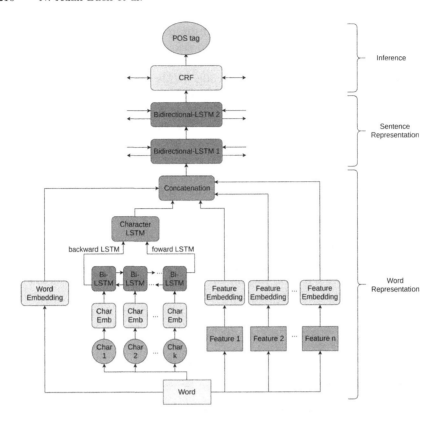

Fig. 1. Model architecture.

3.2 Word Representation

The representation vector $\mathbf{x}_t$ of word w_t is made by concatenating both auto-matically learned features and manually engineered features. We consider two types of manually engineered features, including features extracted from words (call handcrafted features) and features extracted from word clusters trained by using a corpus of plain text (call word cluster features).

- **Automatically learned features**: Automatically learned features consists of word-level features and character-level features. For word-level features, we use word embeddings directly. For character-level features, character embed-dings are employed as the input to a BiLSTM to capture left-to-right and right-to-left information of the character sequence. Both word and character embeddings are initialized randomly and learned in the training process.
- **Handcrafted features**: Like the work of Bach et al. [4], we use the following handcrafted features:
  - A feature that checks whether the word is a special character (hyphen, punctuation, mathematical operation, dash, and so on)

- A feature that checks whether the word is an icon or emoticon
- A feature that detects whether the word contains digits
- Features looking at capitalization patterns (the first letter and all the letters) in the word
- Features that detect hashtags and URLs
- A feature generated by applying Metaphone[2] algorithm to create a coarse phonetic normalization of the word to simpler keys
- The predicted POS tag of vnTagger [19], a widely-used Vietnamese POS tagger trained on general text.

- **Word cluster features**: Word cluster features have been shown to be an important information source for POS tagging, both conventional and social media text [4,25,27,28,34]. We extract word cluster features using Brown word clustering [6] and CCA word clustering [33] in a similar way of Bach et al. [4]. Both Brown and CCA are hard hierarchical agglomerative word clustering algorithms, which produce a word-cluster hierarchy in a binary tree style from a plain text corpus. While the Brown algorithm performs clustering directly on words, the CCA algorithm derives a low-dimensional representation of words and builds word clusters on the obtained representations.

We also use feature embeddings for both handcrafted features and word cluster features, which are initialized randomly and learned in the training process.

3.3 BiLSTM

Long short-term memory (LSTM) networks [15] are a variant of recurrent neural networks (RNNs) [8], a class of neural network architectures specially designed for modeling sequence data. LSTM networks deal with the long-range dependency problem in RNNs by introducing some gates at each position to control the passing of information along the sequence.

Let $\mathbf{X} = (\mathbf{x}_1, \mathbf{x}_2, \ldots, \mathbf{x}_m)$ denote an input sentence consisting of the feature representations of m words. At each position t, the RNN outputs an intermediate representation based on a hidden state $\mathbf{h}$:

$$\mathbf{y}_t = \sigma(\mathbf{W}_y \mathbf{h}_t + \mathbf{b}_y),$$

where σ denotes the element-wise Softmax, $\mathbf{W}_y$ and $\mathbf{b}_y$ are parameter matrix and vector which are learned in the training process. The hidden state $\mathbf{h}_t$ is updated using a non-linear activation function on the previous hidden state $\mathbf{h}_{t-1}$ and the current input $\mathbf{x}_t$ as follows:

$$\mathbf{h}_t = f(\mathbf{h}_{t-1}, \mathbf{x}_t).$$

Each type of RNNs has different ways to implement the function f. LSTM cells use a few gates, including an input gate $\mathbf{i}_t$, a forget gate $\mathbf{f}_t$, an output gate $\mathbf{o}_t$ and a memory cell $\mathbf{c}_t$ to update the hidden state $\mathbf{h}_t$ as follows:

$$\mathbf{i}_t = \sigma(\mathbf{W}_i \mathbf{x}_t + \mathbf{V}_i \mathbf{h}_{t-1} + \mathbf{b}_i),$$

---

[2] http://commons.apache.org/codec/.

$$\mathbf{f}_t = \sigma(\mathbf{W}_f \mathbf{x}_t + \mathbf{V}_f \mathbf{h}_{t-1} + \mathbf{b}_f),$$

$$\mathbf{o}_t = \sigma(\mathbf{W}_o \mathbf{x}_t + \mathbf{V}_o \mathbf{h}_{t-1} + \mathbf{b}_o),$$

$$\mathbf{c}_t = \mathbf{f}_t \odot \mathbf{c}_{t-1} + \mathbf{i}_t \odot \tanh(\mathbf{W}_c \mathbf{x}_t + \mathbf{V}_c \mathbf{h}_{t-1} + \mathbf{b}_c),$$

$$\mathbf{h}_t = \mathbf{o}_t \odot \tanh(\mathbf{c}_t),$$

where $\odot$ denotes the multiplication operator function, and $\mathbf{W}_*$, $\mathbf{V}_*$, and $\mathbf{b}_*$ (* denotes i,f,o,c) are weight matrices and vectors to be learned.

To capture both left and right information, we employ bidirectional long short-term memory (BiLSTM) networks [12], which combine an LSTM that moves forward from the start of the sentence with another LSTM that moves backward from the end of the sentence. The hidden state $\mathbf{h}_t$ of the BiLSTM is the concatenation of the forward $\overrightarrow{\mathbf{h}_t}$ and backward $\overleftarrow{\mathbf{h}_t}$ hidden states, $\mathbf{h}_t = [\overrightarrow{\mathbf{h}_t}, \overleftarrow{\mathbf{h}_t}]$, where $\overrightarrow{\mathbf{h}_t} = \text{LSTM}(\overrightarrow{\mathbf{h}_{t-1}}, \mathbf{x}_t)$ and $\overleftarrow{\mathbf{h}_t} = \text{LSTM}(\overleftarrow{\mathbf{h}_{t+1}}, \mathbf{x}_t)$.

Here, we present the BiLSTM layer for learning sentence representations from sequences of words. The BILSTM layer for learning word representations from sequences of characters is exactly the same.

3.4   CRFs

The inference layer takes the sentence representation $\mathbf{Y} = (\mathbf{y}_1, \mathbf{y}_2, \ldots, \mathbf{y}_m)$ as the input and outputs a POS tag l_t, at each position t $(t = 1, 2, \ldots, m)$. It is beneficial to consider the correlations between the current POS tag and neighboring tags since there are syntactical constrains in natural language sentences. For example, in Vietnamese, nouns (tag N) usually precede adjectives (tag A) and verbs (tag V) usually come after proper nouns (tag Np). If we simply feed the tth element y_t to a Softmax layer to predict the POS tag, such constraints are more likely to be violated. Our tagging model, therefore, employs Conditional random fields (CRFs) [18], a powerful framework to deal with structure prediction problems. CRFs have been shown to be an effective model for building POS taggers for social media text [4,10,27].

CRFs define the probability of a tag sequence $\mathbf{l} = (l_1, l_2, \ldots, l_m)$ given the sentence representation $\mathbf{Y}$ as follows:

$$p(\mathbf{l}|\mathbf{Y}, \boldsymbol{\lambda}, \boldsymbol{\mu}) = \frac{1}{Z(\mathbf{Y})} exp(\sum_j \lambda_j f_j(l_{t-1}, l_t, \mathbf{Y}, t) + \sum_k \mu_k g_k(l_t, \mathbf{Y}, t))$$

where $f_j(l_{t-1}, l_t, \mathbf{Y}, t)$ is a transition feature function, which is defined on the entire input sentence $\mathbf{Y}$ and the POS tags at positions t and $t - 1$ in the tag sequence $\mathbf{l}$; $g_k(l_t, \mathbf{Y}, t)$ is a state feature function, which is defined on the entire input sentence $\mathbf{Y}$ and the tag at position t in the tag sequence $\mathbf{l}$; λ_j and μ_k are model parameters, which are estimated in the training process; and $Z(\mathbf{Y})$ is a normalization factor. CRFs are commonly trained by maximizing the likelihood function using convex optimization techniques. Searching the most likely output label sequence, i.e. inference step, can be done by using the Viterbi algorithm.

Table 1. Statistical information about the tagset

Tag	Description	%	Tag	Description	%
Np	Proper noun	3.54	CC	Coordinating conjunction	0.49
Nc	Classifier	1.15	I	Interjection	1.55
Nu	Unit noun	0.32	T	Auxiliary, modal words	3.52
N	Common noun	18.46	X	Unknown	1.75
V	Verb	19.20	AB	Abbreviation	5.23
A	Adjective	6.68	FL	Foreign language	1.31
P	Pronoun	5.89	AR	Angry (emoticon)	0.05
R	Adverb	8.04	CF	Confused (emoticon)	0.79
L	Determiner	0.93	HP	Happy (emoticon)	2.36
M	Numeral	2.41	IL	Inlove (emoticon)	0.21
E	Preposition	3.80	SD	Sad (emoticon)	0.30
C	Subordinating conjunction	3.17	PUN	Punctuation	8.86

4 Experiments

4.1 Dataset

We conducted experiments on the Vietnamese POS tagging corpus introduced by Bach et al. [4]. The corpus consists of a tagset for Vietnamese social media text with 24 POS tags and 4,150 annotated Vietnamese sentences extracted from Facebook. The list of POS tags and their percentages are shown in Table 1. V (verbs, 19.20%), N (common nouns, 18.46%), PUN (punctuations, 8.86%), R (adverbs, 8.04%), A (adjectives, 6.68%), P(pronouns, 5.89%), and AB (abbreviations, 5.23%) are the most frequent POS tags.

4.2 Models to Compare

We conducted experiments to compare the performances of the following POS tagging models:

- **CRF**: This model is presented by Bach et al. [4]. We include two variants of the model using different feature sets as follows:
  1. using handcrafted features only, and
  2. using word cluster features in addition to handcrafted ones.
- **BiLSTM-CRF**: This is our proposed model with bidirectional LSTM and CRF. We conducted experiments with three variants of the model using different feature sets as follows:
  1. using automatically learned features (word and character embeddings),
  2. using both automatically learned and handcrafted features, and
  3. using word cluster features in addition to automatically learned and handcrafted features.

– **BiLSTM-Soft**: This model was similar to BiLSTM-CRF, but using the Softmax function at the inference layer instead of using CRF. We also conducted experiments with three variants of the model using different feature sets like BiLSTM-CRF.

The performances of tagging models were measured using accuracy, precision, recall, and the F_1 score. While accuracy was computed over all kinds of POS tags, precision, recall, and the F_1 score were computed for each kind of POS tag. We performed 10-fold cross-validation in all experiments[3].

4.3 Network Training

We trained the networks using NCRF++, an open-source neural sequence labeling toolkit[4] developed by Yang and Zhang [38]. The dimensions of word embeddings, character embeddings, and feature embeddings (for manually engineered features) were set to 100, 50, and 20, respectively. All models were trained using standard stochastic gradient descent (SGD) with batches of size 128. We chose the initial learning rate $\eta_0 = 0.003$, and the learning rate η_i was updated on each epoch of training as $\eta_i = \frac{\eta_0}{1+\rho i}$, with decay rate $\rho = 0.05$ and i denotes the number of epochs completed. To mitigate overfitting, dropout was applied to the outputs of both word representation and sentence representation stages with dropout rate of 0.5.

4.4 Experimental Results

In the first experiment we compared the effectiveness of different tagging models. Table 2 summarizes the accuracies for each model. As can be seen, LSTM models that do not use handcrafted features achieved the lowest accuracy. BiLSTM-Soft and BiLSTM-CRF models that take only word and character embeddings as input assigned correct tags only to 87.4% and 87.3% tokens respectively, which is almost 1% worse than CRF with handcrafted features. The bad performance of pure deep learning models compared to CRFs may be attributed to the small size of training data and/or the informativeness of features that were chosen manually. There is no clear winner between BiLSTM-Soft (87.4%) and BiLSTM-CRF (87.3%) when no additional features are used, which is somewhat surprising. The next observation is that handcrafted features are very useful in improving the accuracy of BiLSTM models. Both BiLSTM models augmented with such features achieved substantial improvements of 3% or more over the original models (90.3% vs 87.4% for BiLSTM-Soft and 90.7% vs 87.3% for BiLSTM-CRF). These results confirm the importance of manually engineered features in some NLP tasks, which are complement to features learned by deep learning models. The results also show the usefulness of word cluster features when used with both traditional CRF and BiLSTM. Adding these features to CRF improved the accuracy from 88.3% to 88.9%. Even more significant improvements were observed

---

[3] The division into training and test sets is the same as the work of Bach et al. [4].
[4] Software available at https://github.com/jiesutd/NCRFpp.

when adding word cluster features to BiLSTM. BiLSTM-Soft achieved 0.8% improvement whereas BiLSTM-CRF achieved 1.2% improvement in accuracy when using cluster features in addition to others. Among the models, BiLSTM-CRF achieved the highest accuracy of 91.9%, which is substantially higher than that of the second best BiLSTM-Soft. The superiority of BiLSTM-CRF over BiLSTM-Soft is consistent with previous work on the effectiveness of using CRF as the final inference layer for BiLSTM models. Overall, the best proposed model achieved 3% accuracy improvement (or 27% error rate reduction) over the best model of Bach et al. [4].

Table 2. Accuracies of POS tagging models

Model	Features	Accuracy(%)
CRF (Bach et al. [4])	Handcrafted features	88.3
	+ Word cluster features	**88.9**
BiLSTM-Soft	Word & Character embeddings	87.4
	+ Handcrafted features	90.3
	+ Word cluster features	91.1
BiLSTM-CRF	Word & Character embeddings	87.3
	+ Handcrafted features	90.7
	+ Word cluster features	**91.9**

Next, we look more closely on how well the proposed models work with each type of POS tags. Table 3 shows the F_1 scores for different types of POS tags. Note that the model of Bach et al. [4] employs a post processing step, in which the model utilizes a dictionary of emoticons to correct the output. Their model, therefore, achieved perfect scores for all emoticon tags (AR, CF, HP, IL, SD). We argue that their method is corpus-dependent and may limit its use in practice. Thus, we did not perform a similar post processing step. Even without post-processing, our models still got very good results for emoticon tags. Specifically, BiLSTM-CRF achieved 100%, 100%, 99.8%, 98.8%, and 92.7% F_1 values for HP, SD, CF, IL, and AR, respectively. Given the prevalence of emoticons in social media texts, this result demonstrates the appropriateness of the proposed tagger for the problem at hand. Among 19 types of POS tags other than emoticons, both BiLSTM-Soft and BiLSTM-CRF improved CRF on 17 types and got comparative results on the two other ones. Moreover, we achieved a big improvement on many word types, including foreign language words (FL, 30.4%), unknown words (X, 14.2%), abbreviation words (AB, 8.3%), interjections (I, 6.6%), proper nouns (Np, 6.2%), auxiliary and modal words (T, 4.6%), common nouns (N, 4.4%), verbs (V, 4.1%), adjectives (A, 2.9%), and adverbs (R, 2.9%). The superior performance of BiLSTM-CRF over BiLSTM-Soft on almost all tags showed the effectiveness of using CRF at the inference layer.

Table 3. F_1 scores (%) on each type of POS tags

Tag	Models			Tag	Models		
	CRF	BiLSTM-Soft	BiLSTM-CRF		CRF	BiLSTM-Soft	BiLSTM-CRF
Np	76.9	**81.3 (+4.4)**	**83.1 (+6.2)**	CC	98.4	**99.2 (+0.8)**	**99.2 (+0.8)**
Nc	84.7	**86.6 (+1.9)**	**87.4 (+2.7)**	I	70.9	**76.1 (+5.2)**	**77.5 (+6.6)**
Nu	82.7	82.5	82.1	T	77.7	**80.8 (+3.1)**	**82.3 (+4.6)**
N	86.5	**90.4 (+3.9)**	**90.9 (+4.4)**	X	46.9	**53.4 (+6.5)**	**61.1 (+14.2)**
V	89.0	**92.3 (+3.3)**	**93.1 (+4.1)**	AB	86.8	**94.2 (+7.4)**	**95.1 (+8.3)**
A	82.6	**84.9 (+2.3)**	**85.5 (+2.9)**	FL	52.5	**78.9 (+26.4)**	**82.9 (+30.4)**
P	92.4	**94.1 (+1.7)**	**94.6 (+2.2)**	AR	100	60.0	92.7
R	91.1	**93.5 (+2.4)**	**94.0 (+2.9)**	CF	100	**99.7**	**99.8**
L	93.1	**94.0 (+0.9)**	**94.3 (+1.2)**	HP	100	**100**	**100**
M	96.0	**97.6 (+1.6)**	**97.7 (+1.7)**	IL	100	93.6	98.8
E	96.1	**97.0 (+0.9)**	**97.3 (+1.2)**	SD	100	**100**	**100**
C	90.2	**91.5 (+1.3)**	**91.7 (+1.5)**	PUN	99.7	**99.7**	**99.7**

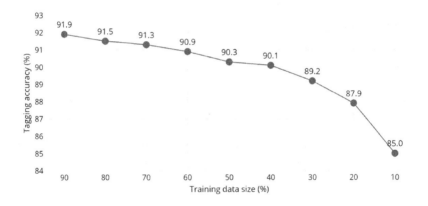

Fig. 2. Tagging performances with different training data sizes.

In the previous experiments, we conducted 10-fold cross-validation, i.e. 90% data were used for training and 10% data were used for testing. The results were then averaged over 10 folds. The next experiment was designed to investigate the POS tagging performance of the proposed model when smaller datasets were used to train the model. Figure 2 shows tagging accuracies when reducing the amount of training data, from 90% to 80%, 70%, 60%, 50%, 40%, 30%, 20%, and 10%. Our model achieved relatively good results when using a very small a mount of training data, 85.0% and 87.9% accuracies when using only 10% and 20% data for training, respectively. The model need only 30% (three times less) data for training to get better result compared with the best model of Bach et al. [4]. The performance stably improved when we increased the size of training data, reaching 91.9% accuracy when using 90% of data for training. This stability can be attributed to the appropriate combination of different types of features which we use in the proposed method, which alleviate the dependence of deep learning models on the availability of large training datasets.

5 Conclusion

We have presented in this paper a neural network based POS tagger for Vietnamese social media text. By utilizing a rich feature set consisting of both automatically learned and manually engineered features in a BiLSTM-CRF framework, our model achieved impressive results compared with the best previous work even when the amount of training data is small. We plan to investigate other types of neural network architectures for reducing the dependence on manually designed features. Studying neural network based models for other Vietnamese NLP tasks is also an interesting direction for future research.

References

1. Albogamy, F., Ramsay A.: POS tagging for Arabic tweets. In: Proceedings of RANLP, pp. 1–8 (2015)
2. Albogamy, F., Ramsay, A.: Fast and robust POS tagger for Arabic tweets using agreement-based bootstrapping. In: Proceedings of LREC, pp. 1500–1506 (2016)
3. Bach, N.X., Hiraishi, K., Minh, N.L., Shimazu, A.: Dual decomposition for Vietnamese part-of-speech tagging. In: Proceedings of KES, pp. 123–131 (2013)
4. Bach, N.X., Linh, N.D., Phuong, T.M.: An empirical study on POS tagging for Vietnamese social media text. Comput. Speech Lang. **50**, 1–15 (2018)
5. Brants, T.: TnT: a statistical part-of-speech tagger. In: Proceedings of the Sixth Conference on Applied Natural Language Processing, pp. 224–231 (2000)
6. Brown, P.F., Desouza, P.V., Mercer, R.L., Pietra, V.D., Lai, J.: Class-based n-gram models of natural language. Comput. Linguist. **18**(4), 467–479 (1992)
7. Derczynski, L., Ritter, A., Clark, S., Bontcheva, K.: Twitter part-of-speech tagging for all: overcoming sparse and noisy data. In: Proceedings of the RANLP, pp. 198–206 (2013)
8. Elman, J.L.: Finding structure in time. Cogn. Sci. **14**(2), 179–211 (1990)
9. Gimenez, J., Marquez, L.: SVM-tool: a general POS tagger generator based on support vector machines. In: Proceedings of LREC, pp. 43–46 (2004)
10. Gimpel, K. et al.: Part-of-speech tagging for twitter: annotation, features, and experiments. In: Proceedings of ACL, pp. 42–47 (2011)
11. Goldberg, Y.: Neural Network Methods for Natural Language Processing. Morgan & Claypool, San Rafael (2017)
12. Graves, A., Schmidhuber, J.: Framewise phoneme classification with bidirectional LSTM and other neural network architectures. Neural Netw. **18**(5–6), 602–610 (2005)
13. He, K., Zhang, X., Ren, S., Sun, J.: Deep residual learning for image recognition. arXiv:1512.03385 (2015). https://arxiv.org/abs/1512.03385
14. Heigold, G., Neumann, G., Genabith, J.V.: An extensive empirical evaluation of character-based morphological tagging for 14 languages. In: Proceedings of EACL, pp. 505–513 (2017)

15. Hochreiter, S., Schmidhuber, J.: Long short-term memory. Neural Comput. **9**(8), 1735–1780 (1997)
16. Huang, Z., Xu, W., Yu, K.: Bidirectional LSTM-CRF models for sequence tagging. arXiv:1508.01991. https://arxiv.org/abs/1508.01991 (2015)
17. Labeau, M., Loser, K., Allauzen, A.: Non-lexical neural architecture for fine-grained POS tagging. In: Proceedings of EMNLP, pp. 232–237 (2015)
18. Lafferty, J., McCallum, A., Pereira, F.: Conditional random fields: probabilistic models for segmenting and labeling sequence data. In: Proceedings of ICML, pp. 282–289 (2001)
19. Le, H.P., Roussanaly, A., Nguyen, T.M.H., Rossignol, M.: An empirical study of maximum entropy approach for part-of-speech tagging of Vietnamese texts. In: Proceedings of the TALN (2010)
20. LeCun, Y., Bottou, L., Bengio, Y., Haffner, P.: Gradient-based learning applied to document recognition. Proc. IEEE **86**(110), 2278–2324 (1998)
21. LeCun, Y., Bengio, Y., Hinton, G.: Deep Learning. Nature **521**, 436–444 (2015)
22. Ma, X., Hovy, E.: End-to-end sequence labeling via bi-directional LSTM-CNNs-CRF. In: Proceedings of ACL, pp. 1064–1074 (2016)
23. Neunerdt, M., Trevisan, B., Reyer, M., Mathar, R.: Part-of-speech tagging for social media texts. In: Gurevych, I., Biemann, C., Zesch, T. (eds.) GSCL 2013. LNCS (LNAI), vol. 8105, pp. 139–150. Springer, Heidelberg (2013). https://doi.org/10.1007/978-3-642-40722-2_15
24. Nghiem, M., Dinh, D., Nguyen, M.: Improving Vietnamese POS tagging by integrating a rich feature set and support vector machines. In: Proceedings of RIVF, pp. 128–133 (2008)
25. Nguyen, L.M., Ngo, X.B., Nguyen, V.C., Pham, Q.N.M., Shimazu, A.: A semi-supervised learning method for Vietnamese part-of-speech tagging. In: Proceedings of KSE, pp. 141–146 (2010)
26. Nguyen, D.Q., Vu, T., Nguyen, D.Q., Dras, M., Johnson, M.: From word segmentation to POS tagging for Vietnamese. In: Proceedings of ALTA, pp. 108–113 (2017)
27. Nooralahzadeh, F., Brun, C., Roux, C.: Part of speech tagging for French social media data. In: Proceedings of COLING, pp. 1764–1772 (2014)
28. Owoputi, O., O'Connor, B., Dyer, C., Gimpel, K., Schneider, N., Smith, N.A.: Improved part-of-speech tagging for online conversational text with word clusters. In: Proceedings of NAACL, pp. 380–390 (2013)
29. Plank, B., Sogaard, A., Goldberg, Y.: Multilingual part-of-speech tagging with bidirectional long short-term memory models and auxiliary loss. In: Proceedings of ACL, pp. 412–418 (2016)
30. Ratnaparkhi, A.: A maximum entropy model for part-of-speech tagging. In: Proceedings of EMNLP, pp. 133–142 (1996)
31. Rehbein, I.: Fine-grained POS tagging of German tweets. In: Gurevych, I., Biemann, C., Zesch, T. (eds.) GSCL 2013. LNCS (LNAI), vol. 8105, pp. 162–175. Springer, Heidelberg (2013). https://doi.org/10.1007/978-3-642-40722-2_17
32. Shao, Y., Hardmeier, C., Tiedemann, J., Nivre, J.: Character-based joint segmentation and POS tagging for Chinese using bidirectional RNN-CRF. In: Proceedings of IJCNLP, pp. 173–183 (2017)
33. Stratos, K., Kim, D., Collins, M., Hsu, D.: A spectral algorithm for learning class-based n-gram models of natural language. In: Proceedings of UAI, pp. 762–771 (2014)
34. Stratos, K., Collins, M.: Simple semi-supervised POS tagging. In: Proceedings of NAACL-HLT, pp. 79–87 (2015)

35. Toutanova, K., Manning, C.: Enriching the knowledge sources used in a maximum entropy part-of-speech tagger. In: Proceedings of EMNLP, pp. 63–70 (2000)
36. Tran, T.O., Le, A.C., Ha, Q.T., Le, H.Q.: An experimental study on Vietnamese POS tagging. In: Proceedings of IALP, pp. 23–27 (2009)
37. Wang, P., Qian, Y., Soong, F.K., He, L., Zhao, H.: Part-of-speech tagging with bidirectional long short-term memory recurrent neural network. arXiv:1510.06168 (2015). https://arxiv.org/abs/1510.06168
38. Yang, J., Zhang, Y.: NCRF++: an open-source neural sequence labeling toolkit. In: Proceedings of ACL-System Demonstrations, pp. 74–79 (2018)
39. Young, T., Hazarika, D., Poria, S., Cambria, E.: Recent trends in deep learning based natural language processing. arXiv:1708.02709v8 (2018). https://arxiv.org/abs/1708.02709

AutoEncoder Guided Bootstrapping of Semantic Lexicon

Chenlong Hu[1(✉)], Mikio Nakano[2], and Manabu Okumura[1]

[1] Tokyo Institute of Technology, Tokyo, Japan
huchenlong@lr.pi.titech.ac.jp, oku@pi.titech.ac.jp
[2] Honda Research Institute Japan Co., Ltd., Wako, Japan
nakano@jp.honda-ri.com

Abstract. Mutual bootstrapping is a commonly used technique for many natural language processing tasks, including semantic lexicon induction. Among many bootstrapping methods, the *Basilisk* algorithm achieved successful applications through two key iterative steps: scoring context patterns and candidate instances. In this work, we improve Basilisk by modifying its two scoring functions. By incorporating AutoEncoder to the scoring functions of patterns and candidates, we can reduce the bias problems and obtain more balanced results. The experimental results demonstrate that our proposed methods for guiding bootstrapping of a semantic lexicon with AutoEncoder can boost overall performance.

Keywords: Bootstrapping · AutoEncoder · Semantic lexicon

1 Introduction

Acquiring large amounts of knowledge for natural language processing tasks can be costly when performed manually. Therefore, there is an increasing need to acquire knowledge, such as semantic relations, from raw text corpora. Such semantic knowledge is beneficial for the other numerous application scenarios (e.g., domain-specific dialogue systems). Hearst started the early work with manually-constructed lexico-syntactic patterns to infer hyponyms (Hearst 1992). Given a set of expert-designed patterns, high-precision results could be achieved. However, this method cannot be easily applied directly to other corpora or tasks (Jurafsky and Martin 2009) because each task requires specific expert-designed patterns. A supervised algorithm trained on human-labeled samples is another straightforward and effective approach (Santos et al. 2015). However, it is time-consuming to obtain annotated data for a sizable language corpus. Due to the above reasons, weakly supervised or semi-supervised approaches have attracted more attention for obtaining semantic resources from a large-scale corpus. The weakly supervised method, also known as distant supervision, attempts to build an alignment between a raw corpus and a knowledge database (Mintz et al. 2009). By using a database like *Freebase* (Bollacker et al. 2008), a large

© Springer Nature Switzerland AG 2019
A. C. Nayak and A. Sharma (Eds.): PRICAI 2019, LNAI 11672, pp. 220–233, 2019.
https://doi.org/10.1007/978-3-030-29894-4_17

number of samples with noisy labels and features can be created and used for training a normal supervised mechanism. However, the use of distant supervision is limited only to existing available knowledge databases.

Compared with the approaches described above, mutual *bootstrapping* can be considered a more effective and adaptable algorithm as it is not required to construct complex patterns and knowledge bases. This technique has been frequently used in a variety of tasks, including relation extraction (Hearst 1992; Brin 1998; Agichtein and Gravano 2000), semantic lexicon induction (Lin et al. 2003; Thelen and Riloff 2002), and word sense disambiguation (Yarowsky 1995). Given raw text and a limited number of initial seed instances (an initial seed list), bootstrapping methods can learn context patterns and expand the seed list with newly obtained candidate instances. As a minimal supervision algorithm, iterative bootstrapping does not need extensive annotation and knowledge base alignment, unlike the supervised methods.

Basilisk (Thelen and Riloff 2002) is an effective and commonly used bootstrapping approach for constructing a semantic lexicon from a corpus. Its performance depends on its two fundamental steps: evaluating patterns and candidate instances alternately. On the basis of our experimental observation and analysis, which we describe later, the results of Basilisk are easily biased due to poor scoring functions for patterns and candidates.

In this paper, we propose methods that can improve the global performance of the bootstrapping approach based on Basilisk. The key idea is to modify the two scoring functions: *candidate scoring* and *pattern scoring*. To better score *candidate* instances, AutoEncoder is used to score and identify the better candidates. Our motivation is that while we have only a small amount of seed (positive) instances, we can train AutoEncoder only on the positive samples, extracted by previous iterations. In this setting, we do not rely on any negative samples, unlike other related bootstrapping approaches (Curran et al. 2007; Lin et al. 2003). To better score *patterns*, we attempt to use a more balanced scoring mechanism by also using AutoEncoder. This new metric of *pattern scoring* could benefit downstream steps, resulting in boosting the results of the bootstrapping approach based on Basilisk.

Our methods can be summarized as follows:

- We improve candidate evaluation by incorporating AutoEncoder, which does not rely on any additional training data.
- We also present a new function to boost the scoring of patterns such that better candidates will be pooled in subsequent steps. The performance of candidate scoring can be improved by including our new pattern scoring function.

The rest of the paper is as follows: Sect. 2 introduces Basilisk and some related work for our improved methods. Section 3 describes our motivation and proposed methods. The experimental setup and results are presented in Sect. 4. Finally, we conclude this paper.

2 Basilisk

Basilisk, proposed in (Thelen and Riloff 2002), acquires a high-quality semantic lexicon in a bootstrapping manner. To alleviate the semantic drift phenomenon, Basilisk's direct predecessor (Riloff et al. 1999) rated candidate instances, on the basis of collective evidence from a large set of patterns. The process of Basilisk is illustrated in Algorithm 1.

Algorithm 1: Process of Basilisk

Input: Seed list, patterns, and their extractions in the corpus
Output: Seed list (Updated)
Parameter : k, N
1 Score all patterns
2 Select top-(k+i) patterns to *pattern_pool*
3 Select all extractions of patterns in *pattern_pool* to *candidate_instance_pool*
4 Score all candidate words in *candidate_instance_pool*
5 Add top-N candidates to seed list
6 $i = i + 1$,
7 Repeat *Steps 1 to 6*

Prior to the actual iterative process, a list of seed instances with a limited number is inputted to the system. The seed instances are considered to be members of a specific semantic category. Basilisk first generates and stores all context patterns where the inputted seed instances appear in the corpus and then starts with *pattern scoring* as shown below:

1. **Pattern Scoring**: Basilisk uses *RlogF* to score and rank patterns:

$$RlogF(p_i) = F_i/N_i * log(F_i), \tag{1}$$

   where F_i represents the number of seed instances extracted by pattern p_i, and N_i is the total number of extracted instances related to the pattern.
2. Pattern Selection: on the basis of the score, the top-(k+i) patterns are selected and placed in the *pattern_pool*.
3. Candidate Pool: all the instances newly extracted by the patterns in the *pattern_pool* are put into the *candidate_instance_pool*, except for those already in the seed list.
4. **Candidate Scoring**: to evaluate candidates in the *candidate_instance_pool*, *AvglogF* is used as the scoring metric, as defined below:

$$AvglogF(c_i) = \sum_{j=1}^{P_i} log_2(F_j + 1)/P_i, \tag{2}$$

   where c_i is the candidate to be evaluated, P_i is the number of patterns that extract c_i, and F_j is the number of correct instances corresponding to pattern

p_j. This function calculates the mean value of productivity for patterns. The most important step is step 4, where candidate instances are scored. Note that the candidates are evaluated on the basis of all the patterns.

5. Top-N words are added to the seed list for the semantic lexicon.

Figure 1 shows the process in Basilisk.

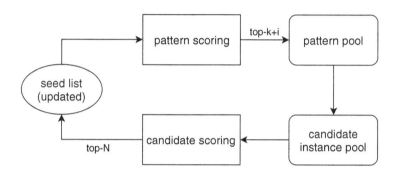

Fig. 1. Basilisk's process

In the paper of Basilisk (Thelen and Riloff 2002), rather than using $AvglogF$ (Eq. 2), the authors first investigated the effect of another candidate scoring function $AvgF$:

$$AvgF(c_i) = \sum_{j=1}^{P_i} F_j / P_i. \tag{3}$$

However, the simple *average* strategy is prone to be biased by one pattern with a large number of extractions F_j (the ability to extract candidates). To minimize this problem, *logarithm* is added to constrain the effect of any single pattern. The improved version, $AvglogF$, as shown in Eq. 2, was adopted for the final version of Basilisk.

However, our preliminary experiments showed that this bias still occurred during candidate estimation. If one candidate c_i is extracted by a low number of high-score patterns (larger $logF$), it is still prone to be overrated.

An intuitive method for alleviating the problem is to set a threshold for the number of patterns, i.e., to discard candidate words recalled by fewer than M patterns. Although several values were used for the threshold in our preliminary experiments, there was no significant improvement when compared with $AvglogF$. Furthermore, setting a good threshold value is also a problem. All in all, we can say that this intuitive method "treats the symptoms rather than curing the disease."

The reason for the bias problem is that lexicon induction does not effectively rely on collective evidence over all patterns. Therefore, we can improve candidate scoring by considering confidences from more patterns. We thus turn our attention to the related bootstrapping work. *NoisyOR* is an effective technique used in *Snowball* (Agichtein and Gravano 2000) and *NOMEN* (Lin et al. 2003). *NoisyOR* assesses each instance, on the basis of the contribution of wider range of patterns. In contrast to *AvglogF*, which prefers clues from a small number of high-quality patterns, *NoisyOR* considers the evidence on the quantity of patterns. We can attempt to use *NoisyOR* for candidate scoring.

$$NoisyOR(c_i) = 1 - \prod_{j=1}^{P_i}(1 - conf(p_j)), \tag{4}$$

where i is the index of a candidate and p_j is one pattern. P_i is calculated from the number of patterns candidate c_i is extracted. The confidence of each pattern can be described as $conf(p_j) = F_j/N_j$, as shown in Eq. 1. Given *NoisyOR*, the acceptance of candidate c_i is based on the backing of as many patterns as possible. This metric prevents the ranking and selection from being easily biased to the lexicon selected by high-confidence patterns, as in the cases with *AvglogF*. Now, we utilized both *AvglogF* and *NoisyOR* as the two baseline scoring functions to evaluate candidates in Step 4 of Algorithm 1.

3   Proposed Methods

3.1   Candidate Scoring with AutoEncoder

The above-mentioned baseline candidate scoring methods, *NoisyOR* and *AvglogF*, along with other bootstrapping systems, like *WMEB* (McIntosh and Curran 2008) and *Espresso* (Pantel and Pennacchiotti 2006), evaluate instances by using the information from pattern confidence or co-occurrence between patterns and instances. Another type of knowledge, a set of instances acquired in previous iterations of bootstrapping, can also be directly used to evaluate candidates. The characteristics of the acquired lexicon in the updating seed list are as follows:

1. Both the initial set of instances and the acquired instances in the seed list can be seen as *positive* samples belonging to the target semantic category.
2. The vocabulary in the seed list is expanded over time.
3. The seed list from the different initial seed list will be updated and acquired independently with each other.

To utilize this resource in the bootstrapping, one option would be to train a supervised classifier or regression model on the acquired lexicon. However, it needs "appropriate" *negative* labeled samples, which are hard to obtain in different bootstrapping iterations with a varying initial seed list. One trick is to input a *negative* list as well as a *positive* list (Agichtein and Gravano 2000). While general negative instances (e.g., "the" and "a") cannot cover and reflect differences among patterns, too specific instances are only adaptive to a few patterns.

Therefore, our motivation is to evaluate candidate instances only with positive seed instances. On the basis of the above motivation, we utilize a neural model called AutoEncoder (Japkowicz et al. 1995), which can be trained in an unsupervised manner. AutoEncoder is an unsupervised neural network that learns the data description of positive instances. With the *bottleneck* structure between input and reconstruction output layers, the identity in the small set of examples is in fact learnable (Bengio et al. 2015). This can avoid issues with saturation in learning only from positive instances, and enable AutoEncoder to take into account the first characteristic of a seed list in which its instances are all positive.

Another characteristic of a seed list is that its size is enlarged by iterations. AutoEncoder can not only boost training in an incremental mode but also acquire adaptability to different iterations. Therefore, we can also train independent models for a different initial seed list, such that the learned model can fit its own initial seed list. Thus, AutoEncoder can match our objectives and the three characteristics of the seed list.

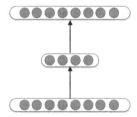

Fig. 2. Architecture of AutoEncoder

The architecture of AutoEncoder is shown in Fig. 2. We first use feature vectors (learned from word embeddings) of instances as the input at the bottom. Then, the input is compressed into a smaller number of hidden states. Finally, the output layer tries to rebuild the input signals with the reconstruction loss function. After being trained with only positive instances, AutoEncoder can output positive instances with smaller reconstruction loss, which enables distinct features to be acquired from positive instances such that it is hard to reconstruct negative instances. The scoring function with AutoEncoder can be defined as follows:

$$AE(c_i) = 1 - softmax(reconstruct(c_i, c_i')), \tag{5}$$

where output c_i' represents the reconstruction output for input c_i, and reconstruction loss is measured by $reconstruct()$. We use $softmax = exp(x_i)/\sum exp(x_j)$ to output a probability value $AE(c_i)$, in which we can rank and select the better candidates with larger $AE(c_i)$ values using Eq. 5. This value can also be used for the pattern scoring step introduced in Subsect. 3.2 below.

3.2   Pattern Scoring with AutoEncoder

As shown in Fig. 1, all candidates come from the candidate pool acquired on the basis of the pattern pool, which is determined during the pattern scoring step. Therefore, if low-quality patterns are selected, credible results are hard to be obtained even when there is a better candidate assessment metric. We hypothesize the following:

Hypothesis 1 (H1): *Better pattern evaluation results in better candidate selection, and so the pattern scoring function contributes to the performance improvement in candidate selection.*

Therefore, our motivation is to modify the pattern scoring function for better pattern evaluation. Reviewing the first step of the Basilisk loop (see Algorithm 1), the score for each pattern p_i is computed by Eq. 1. Here, we rewrite it as follows:

$$RlogF(p_i) = F_i/N_i * log(F_i) = R_i * logF \quad (Rewriting), \qquad (6)$$

where $R_i = F_i/N_i$ denotes "reliability" that computes the correct probability of extracting pattern p_i, while $logF = log(F_i)$ measures the potential "productivity." The characteristics of $RlogF$ are as follows:

1. "Reliability": $R = F/N$ assumes all extracted instances other than previous seed instances as *False Positive*.
2. "Productivity": $logF = log(F)$ is not a probability.
3. "Combination": $RlogF$ combines R_i and $logF$ by a "multiplication."

First, we attempt to incorporate AutoEncoder into the calculation of $R_i = F_i/N_i$. Since N_i consists of correctly extracted seed instances F_i and other instances whose correctness is unknown, it is ill-advised to regard all the unidentified ones as negative when calculating R_i. For each unknown candidate x_i in Unk (unknown instances extracted by a pattern), $1 - AE(x_i)$ is incorporated to score the probability of the instance being a "*False Positive.*" The formula of R_i could be replaced by the following:

$$autoR_i = F_i/(F_i + \sum_{x_i \in Unk} (1 - AE(x_i))). \qquad (7)$$

Second, we replace $log(F_i)$ with a new measure $L_i = F_i/L$, where L is the size of the updated seed list. Now, the "productivity" is represented as L_i, which is a probability that agrees with "reliability."

Finally, we combine the previous two metrics, $autoR_i$ and L_i. Rather than "multiply" the two metrics, as $RlogF$, a more balanced combination operation named *harmonic mean* can be used:

$$autoRL(p_i) = 2 * autoR_i * L_i/(autoR_i + L_i), \qquad (8)$$

where $autoR_i$ and L_i are defined as above. Similar to the F1 measure, the *harmonic mean* is a metric for averaging two measures.

3.3   Summarizing Proposed Methods

We summarize our proposed methods in accordance with the motivations presented above. We utilize the basic framework of Basilisk and modify two key steps.

Candidate Scoring. To evaluate candidate seed instances, we modify $AvglogF$ (Eq. 2) or another baseline $NoisyOR$, adapted in the other bootstrapping systems, to AutoEncoder (AE) for the candidate scoring step:

$$AE(c_i) = 1 - softmax(reconstruct(c_i, c_i')).$$

Pattern Scoring. As described in Subsect. 3.2, we substitute $RlogF$ with $autoRL$, combining two new probability metrics of $autoR_i$ and L_i that represent "reliability" and "productivity," respectively:

$$autoRL(p_i) = 2 * autoR_i * L_i/(autoR_i + L_i).$$

The above formula is used as the new pattern scoring function in Step 1 of Basilisk.

4   Experiments

In this section, we first introduce the data for the experiments and the evaluation metrics, and then show the experimental results and their analysis. We also perform ablation studies to understand the behavior of each component in our methods.

4.1   Data

The objective of this research is to acquire a lexicon from a general corpus for a specific semantic domain (specifically, the *food* domain). We used the Wikipedia dataset as the corpus. The dataset was preprocessed by a Spacy2 pipeline, including a tokenizer and a noun phrase chunker (Honnibal and Montani 2017). With minimal syntactic structure information, we used only a *conjunction* pattern with the form of multiple conjunctive items (t_{i-1}, t_i, t_{i+1}) (a trigram of noun phrases or nouns). Here, candidates are selected irrespective of order and can be at any position in (t_{i-1}, t_i, t_{i+1}). Once an instance t is chosen, the pattern including the instance will be extracted as a candidate pattern.

4.2   Evaluation Metrics

We evaluated the results in terms of Precision, Recall, and F1-measure (F1). Precision is defined as the ratio of correct instances in all the extracted instances.

Each result instance was manually evaluated by inspecting whether it was correct. For Recall, we calculated two different values with a small and large list of correct instances. The small list with 68 instances consists of more single-token instances. The large list with 457 instances consists of more noun phrases. Recall values were the ratio of the number of instances in the lists that can be acquired in the bootstrapping. Therefore, two recall metrics are recorded: Recall (small) and Recall (large). As F1 considers both the precision and the recall, we have two corresponding F1s: F1 (small) and F1 (large).

4.3   Experimental Setting

All experiments were performed using ten initial seed instances. In each iteration, $top-(20+i)$ patterns were added to the pattern pool. The top-5 best candidate instances were then added to the expanded seed list for the next iteration. For the inputs of the AutoEncoder model, Glove embeddings (300 dimensions) trained on Common Crawl were used (Pennington et al. 2014)[1]. We transformed each instance to one input vector by averaging the embedding vectors of its words. Each input to AutoEncoder was compressed by a hidden layer with 100 dimensions. Sigmoid was selected as the decoder activation to reconstruct input. Mean Squared Error (MSE) loss is optimized by the Adam algorithm. For each training phase, AutoEncoder was trained with the early stopping strategy by the maximum number of epochs (128). Because bootstrapping approaches can be easily influenced by different input seed instances (McIntosh and Curran 2008; Riloff and Jones 2018), we evaluated the results with five different initial seed lists for all compared bootstrapping systems for 20 iterations. There were no overlaps among the five seed lists to ensure reliable experiments. For fair comparisons, all the results for the methods were the average of the metrics over the five disjoint seed lists.

4.4   Experimental Results and Analysis

Candidate Scoring. First, we compared our AutoEncoder-guided scoring function with the two baseline methods: $AvglogF$ and $NoisyOR$.

Table 1. Results for candidate scoring. All metrics are averaged over five independent initial seed lists. The best scores are in bold.

Method	F1(small)	F1(large)	Precision	Recall(small)	Recall(large)
$AvglogF$	0.119	0.147	0.840	0.065	0.082
$NoisyOR$	0.202	0.165	0.870	0.115	0.091
AE	**0.254**	**0.280**	**0.878**	**0.150**	**0.172**

---

[1]   https://nlp.stanford.edu/projects/glove/.

As shown in Table 1, $NoisyOR$ outperforms $AvglogF$ in all five metrics. AE, with AutoEncoder, outperforms both the previous baseline systems. As for F1, $AvglogF$ and AE obtain higher scores for F1 (large) than for F1 (small). In contrast, $NoisyOR$ achieves higher scores for F1 (small) than for F1 (large). This may be due to its preference for single-token instances of which the small list consists. $NoisyOR$ evaluates candidates by collecting evidence from a larger range of patterns, and so extracts more general single-token instances. In summary, our AutoEncoder-based candidate scoring function improved overall performance compared with the two baseline methods.

Pattern Scoring. This subsection investigates the performance of our new pattern scoring function $autoRL$, to validate **Hypothesis** 1 and our motivation in Subsect. 3.2.

In the experimental setting, we used the same baseline candidate scoring functions ($AvglogF$ and $NoisyOR$) and modified the pattern evaluation function.

As shown in Table 2, $autoRL$ improved performance, especially in F1 (small), which increased to 0.232. The same scale of improvement (from 0.165 to 0.253) was also achieved in F1 (large) for the method with $NoisyOR$, at the cost of a slight precision drop. Precision is affected, especially for the $AvglogF$ method. One possible reason is that the candidate instances extracted by few patterns can be also derived by using $autoRL$. Table 2 shows that the overall performance of both the baseline methods in candidate scoring could be enhanced by using $autoRL$ in pattern scoring.

Table 2. Results for pattern scoring. $autoRL + AvglogF$ denotes that $autoRL$ is used for pattern evaluation, and candidate scoring still uses $AvglogF$. $autoRL + NoisyOR$ represents $autoRL$ plus $NoisyOR$. The best scores are in bold.

Method	F1(small)	F1(large)	Precision	Recall(small)	Recall(large)
$AvglogF$	0.119	0.147	**0.840**	0.065	0.082
$autoRL + AvglogF$	**0.232**	**0.213**	0.774	**0.138**	**0.124**
$NoisyOR$	0.202	0.165	**0.870**	0.115	0.091
$autoRL + NoisyOR$	**0.259**	**0.253**	0.838	**0.153**	**0.149**

Ablation Study 1: Impact of Each Part in the Pattern Scoring Function. To assess the contribution of each part in our new pattern scoring method, we performed an ablation study. Table 3 summarizes the results in F1 scores. In Basilisk's original formula $RlogF(p_i) = R_i * logF$, R_i represents "reliability" and $logF$ measures "productivity." They are combined by the "multiply" operation. Therefore, our $autoRL$ (Eq. 8) modifies three parts of $RlogF$. More specifically, we can replace R_i with $autoR$ for "reliability" and F/L for "productivity."

Finally, harmonic mean, instead of "multiply", can be used to combine "reliability" and "productivity." In this ablation study, we kept the basic *Basilisk* framework and investigated the contribution of the changes in "productivity," "reliability," and their combination. Because $logF$ is not a probability, we do not show its score in the *Harmonic* cell.

Index 0 shows the results of the original Basilisk as the baseline. The first adjustment is $autoR$, which is a new reliability metric based on AutoEncoder. It significantly outperformed R, multiplied by $logF$ (index 0). Specifically, F1 (small) increased from 0.119 to 0.176 and F1 (large) increased from 0.147 to 0.192. By changing "productivity" to F/L, $R * F/L$ also achieved a better F1 (small) score than $RlogF$, as shown in the third row (index 2). However, it could not boost $logF$ in F1 (large), which remained at 0.147. As for index 3, where both parts were modified, $autoR$ multiplying F/L obtained a comparable F1 (small) result (0.151) to R multiplying F/L (0.149) and a significantly higher F1 (large) result (0.199). The last four columns for F1 show that replacing "multiply" with "harmonic mean" also improved performance. The results for "Harmonic" were around 0.056–0.08 in F1 (small) and 0.014–0.035 in F1 (large) higher than those for "Multiply." Therefore, in the combination operation, harmonic mean is a better choice than multiplying "reliability" and "productivity." In the comparison of the two adjustment methods, the improvement of $autoR$ over R demonstrates the benefit of AutoEncoder to improve the representation of "reliability." Overall, our proposed method enhanced the performance on the basis of the contribution of the multiple different parts.

Table 3. Impact of each part in pattern scoring function. The index 0 row denotes the initial pattern scoring function $RlogF$, while indexes 1–3 denote three ablation studies. The numbers in the last two columns denote F1-scores for the small and large lists for different combination operations including "Multiply" and "Harmonic Mean," respectively. "nan" indicates that we did not receive any result. Bold numbers indicate the best F1 scores.

Index	Reliability	Productivity	F1(small)		F1(large)	
			Multiply	Harmonic	Multiply	Harmonic
0	R	$logF$	0.119	nan	0.147	nan
1	$autoR$	$logF$	0.176	nan	0.192	nan
2	R	F/L	0.149	0.205	0.147	0.182
3	$autoR$	F/L	0.151	**0.232**	0.199	**0.213**

Ablation Study 2: Impact of the Size of the Training Data for AutoEncoder. We performed another ablation study to investigate the effect of the training data size for AutoEncoder. The results are reported in Table 4. Here, 100 additional human-crafted positive instances were added to the training set with each initial seed list. We report the influences on F1 (small) and F1 (large) on the basis of the two training data: the original data (10 seed instances) and the augmented seed list with extra examples (110 seed instances). The first column, "Step," denotes in which step the augmented training data is used among the two steps in Basilisk: pattern scoring and candidate scoring. In "Pattern Scoring," we tested two baseline methods for candidate scoring: $AvglogF$ and $NoisyOR$. The performance was improved with the augmented data for $AvglogF$. Table 4 shows that F1 (small) increased from 0.232 to 0.252 and F1 (large) increased from 0.213 to 0.235 when the augmented data was used. In contrast to $AvglogF$, it is more beneficial to train AutoEncoder only with Data (Base) than with Data (Augm). The performances for $NoisyOR + AE$ degraded when more training instances were used, as shown in the second row from bottom. One possible interpretation is that random selection of augmented data caused a biased set of training instances, that resulted in a performance degradation. The augmented data may also break the characteristics of a seed list, as illustrated in Subsect. 3.1. For example, it violates the adaptiveness of AutoEncoder to each independent initial seed list.

Table 4. Impact of the training data size. "Step" indicates in which step we used augmented training data. "Data(Augm)" denotes the augmented data. "Data(Base)" denotes the base seed set. Bold numbers denote the **better** scores in each row comparison ("Data(Base)" vs "Data(Augm)").

Step	Method	Data(Base)		Data(Augm)	
		F1(small)	F1(large)	F1(small)	F1(large)
Pattern scoring	$AvglogF$	0.232	0.213	**0.252**	**0.235**
	$NoisyOR$	**0.259**	**0.253**	0.224	0.221
Candidate scoring	AE	**0.254**	**0.280**	0.226	0.259

5 Conclusion

In this paper, we presented methods for improving bootstrapping of a semantic lexicon that uses AutoEncoder to better evaluate candidate instances. The experimental results, including ablation studies, validated the effectiveness of the proposed methods. By training AutoEncoder on the updated seed lists, we could provide a better candidate scoring function. Additionally, our more balanced pattern evaluation function, guided by AutoEncoder, also improved the overall performances. In future work, we plan to incorporate more knowledge into our methods for bootstrapping.

Acknowledgments. We would like to thank the anonymous reviewers for their helpful comments and suggestions. Chenlong Hu gratefully acknowledges the support from China Scholarship Council (CSC).

References

Agichtein, E., Gravano, L.: Snowball: extracting relations from large plain-text collections. In: Proceedings of the Fifth ACM Conference on Digital Libraries, pp. 85–94. ACM (2000)

Bengio, Y., Goodfellow, I.J., Courville, A.: Deep learning. Nature **521**(7553), 436–444 (2015)

Bollacker, K., Evans, C., Paritosh, P., Sturge, T., Taylor, J.: Freebase: a collaboratively created graph database for structuring human knowledge. In: Proceedings of the 2008 ACM SIGMOD International Conference on Management of Data, pp. 1247–1250. ACM (2008)

Brin, S.: Extracting patterns and relations from the world wide web. In: Atzeni, P., Mendelzon, A., Mecca, G. (eds.) WebDB 1998. LNCS, vol. 1590, pp. 172–183. Springer, Heidelberg (1999). https://doi.org/10.1007/10704656_11

Curran, J.R., Murphy, T., Scholz, B.: Minimising semantic drift with mutual exclusion bootstrapping. In: Proceedings of the 10th Conference of the Pacific Association for Computational Linguistics, vol. 6, pp. 172–180. Pacific Association for Computation Linguistics, Australia (2007)

Hearst, M.A.: Automatic acquisition of hyponyms from large text corpora. In: Proceedings of the 14th Conference on Computational Linguistics, vol. 2, pp. 539–545. Association for Computational Linguistics (1992)

Honnibal, M., Montani, I.: Spacy 2: natural language understanding with bloom embeddings, convolutional neural networks and incremental parsing (2017, to appear)

Japkowicz, N., Myers, C., Gluck, M., et al.: A novelty detection approach to classification. In: IJCAI, vol. 1, pp. 518–523 (1995)

Jurafsky, D., Martin, J.H.: Speech and language processing: an introduction to natural language processing, computational linguistics, and speech recognition, 2nd edn. Prentice Hall series in artificial intelligence. Prentice Hall, Pearson Education International (2009)

Lin, W., Yangarber, R., Grishman, R.: Bootstrapped learning of semantic classes from positive and negative examples. In: Proceedings of ICML-2003 Workshop on the Continuum from Labeled to Unlabeled Data, vol. 1, p. 21 (2003)

McIntosh, T., Curran, J.R.: Weighted mutual exclusion bootstrapping for domain independent Lexicon and template acquisition. In: Proceedings of the Australasian Language Technology Association Workshop 2008, pp. 97–105 (2008)

Mintz, M., Bills, S., Snow, R., Jurafsky, D.: Distant supervision for relation extraction without labeled data. In: Proceedings of the Joint Conference of the 47th Annual Meeting of the ACL and the 4th International Joint Conference on Natural Language Processing of the AFNLP: Volume 2-Volume 2, pp. 1003–1011. Association for Computational Linguistics (2009)

Pantel, P., Pennacchiotti, M.: Espresso: leveraging generic patterns for automatically harvesting semantic relations. In: Proceedings of the 21st International Conference on Computational Linguistics and the 44th annual meeting of the Association for Computational Linguistics, pp. 113–120. Association for Computational Linguistics (2006)

Pennington, J., Socher, R., Manning, C.: GloVe: global vectors for word representation. In: Proceedings of the 2014 Conference on Empirical Methods in Natural Language Processing (EMNLP), pp. 1532–1543 (2014)

Riloff, E., Jones, R.: A retrospective on mutual bootstrapping. AI Mag. **39**(1), 51–61 (2018)

Riloff, E., Jones, R., et al.: Learning dictionaries for information extraction by multi-level bootstrapping. In: AAAI/IAAI, pp. 474–479 (1999)

Santos, C.N.d., Xiang, B., Zhou, B.: Classifying relations by ranking with convolutional neural networks. arXiv preprint arXiv:1504.06580 (2015)

Thelen, M., Riloff, E.: A bootstrapping method for learning semantic lexicons using extraction pattern contexts. In: Proceedings of the ACL-02 Conference on Empirical Methods in Natural Language Processing, vol. 10, pp. 214–221. Association for Computational Linguistics (2002)

Yarowsky, D.: Unsupervised word sense disambiguation rivaling supervised methods. In: Proceedings of the 33rd Annual Meeting on Association for Computational Linguistics, ACL 1995, pp. 189–196. Association for Computational Linguistics (1995)

Hierarchical Convolutional Attention Networks Using Joint Chinese Word Embedding for Text Classification

Kaiqiang Zhang[1,2], Shupeng Wang[1], Binbin Li[1], Feng Mei[3(✉)],
and Jianyu Zhang[3]

[1] Institute of Information Engineering, Chinese Academy of Sciences, Beijing, China
{zhangkaiqiang,wangshupeng,libinbin}@iie.ac.cn
[2] School of Cyber Security, University of Chinese Academy of Sciences,
Beijing, China
[3] Changan Communication Technology Co., LTD., Beijing, China
{meifeng,zhangjianyu}@chanct.com

Abstract. We propose a hierarchical convolutional attention network using joint Chinese word embedding for text classification. Compared with previous methods, our model has three notable improvements: (i) it considers not only words but also their characters and fine-grained sub-character components; (ii) it employs self-attention mechanisms with the benefits of convolution feature extraction, enable it to attend differentially to more and less important content; (iii) it has a hierarchical structure that can get the document vector. We demonstrate the effectiveness of our architecture by surpassing the accuracy of the current state-of-the-art on four classification datasets. Visualization of our hierarchical structure illustrates that our model is able to select informative sentences and words in a document.

Keywords: Joint Chinese word embedding · Self-attention · Hierarchical structure

1 Introduction

Text classification is one of the fundamental tasks in natural language processing (NLP). It has broad applications including topic labeling (Wang and Manning 2012), sentiment classification (Maas et al. 2011; Pang and Lee 2008), and spam detection (Sahami et al. 1998). Traditional approaches of text classification utilize features generated from vector space models such as bag-of words or term frequency-inverse document frequency (TF-IDF) (Sebastiani 2005), and then use a linear model or kernel methods on these features (Wang and Manning 2012; Joachims 1998).

More recently, deep learning approaches typically rely on architectures based on convolutional neural networks (CNN) (Blunsom et al. 2014) or recurrent

© Springer Nature Switzerland AG 2019
A. C. Nayak and A. Sharma (Eds.): PRICAI 2019, LNAI 11672, pp. 234–246, 2019.
https://doi.org/10.1007/978-3-030-29894-4_18

neural networks (RNN) (Young et al. 2017) to learn text representations. These newer approaches have been shown to outperform traditional approaches.

Among the two, RNN has attained remarkable achievement in handling serialization tasks. As RNN is equipped with recurrent network structure which can be used to maintain information, it can better integrate information in certain contexts. For the purpose of avoiding the problem of gradient exploding or vanishing in a standard RNN, long short-term memory (LSTM) (Hochreiter and Schmidhuber 1997) and other variants (Cho et al. 2014) have been designed for the improvement of remembering and memory accesses. Living up to expectations, LSTM does show a remarkable ability in the processing of natural language. Moreover, the other popular neural network, CNN, has also displayed a remarkable performance in computer vision (Krizhevsky and Hinton 2012), speech recognition, and natural language processing (Kalchbrenner et al. 2014) because of its remarkable capability in capturing local correlations of spatial or temporal structures. In terms of natural language processing, CNN is able to extract n-gram features from different positions of a sentence through convolutional filters and then it learns both short- and long-range relations through the operations of pooling.

Although neural-network-based approaches to text classification have been quite effective (Kim 2014; Zhang et al. 2015; Johnson and Zhang 2014; Tang et al. 2015), we still find the following two shortcomings.

Firstly, when it comes to document representation, most of the above methods use word-level distributed word representation. Among these embedding methods (Bengio et al. 2003; Mnih and Hinton 2009), CBOW and Skip-Gram models can learn good embeddings of words from large scale training corpora (Mikolov et al. 2013a, 2013b). However, when use these methods which treat each word as the minimum unit, it is easy to ignore the morphological information of words. There are also related works that used character-level features for text classification (Zhang et al. 2015)(charCNN). They first applied CNN only on characters and obtained the advantage that abnormal character combinations such as misspellings and emoticons may be naturally learnt.

In Chinese, the characters themselves are usually composed of sub-character components, which have semantic information. The components of a character can be roughly divided into two types: semantic component and phonetic component[1]. The semantic component represents the meaning of the character, while the phonetic component represents the sound of the character. For example (see Figs. 1 and 2), we intercepted a sentence from the Fudan text classification dataset C36-Medical007 and extracted the keyword "症" (symptom).

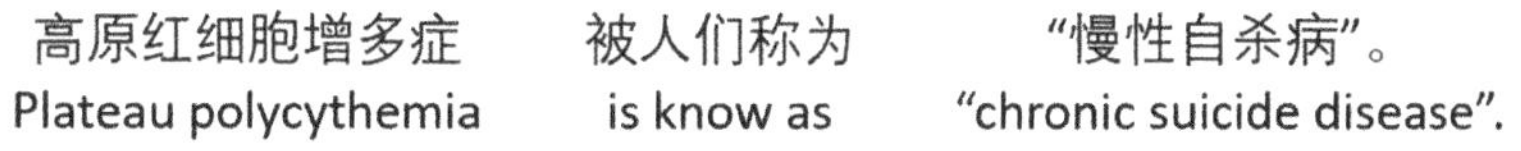

高原红细胞增多症   被人们称为   "慢性自杀病"。
Plateau polycythemia   is know as   "chronic suicide disease".

Fig. 1. Component example.

---

[1] https://en.wikipedia.org/wiki/Written_Chinese.

Fig. 2. Semantic and phonetic component. (Color figure online)

As mentioned above, "症" consists of "疒" (green part in the figure) and "正" (blue part in the figure). "疒" (sick) is the semantic component, while "正 (positive)" is the phonetic component. If methods pay more attention to the character "症" and the component "疒", it is easy to correctly classify this document into the Medical class.

Secondly, not all parts of a document are equally relevant for a query. In the above example, "高原红细胞增多症" (Plateau polycythemia) plays a more important role than "被人们称为" (is known as) in the final classification result.

The current state-of-the-art in text classification are Hierarchical Attention Networks (HAN), developed by Yang et al. (2016). HAN use a hierarchical structure in which each hierarchy uses the same architecture - a bidirectional RNN with gated recurrent units (GRU) (Chung et al. 2014), followed by an attention mechanism that creates a weighted sum of the RNN outputs at each timestep. The HAN processes documents by first breaking a long document into its sentence components, then processing each sentence individually before processing the entire document. By breaking a document into smaller, more manageable chunks, the HAN can better locate and extract critical information useful for classification. This approach surpassed the performance of all previous approaches across several text classification tasks.

Our work focuses mainly on Chinese text classification, which is known as a completely different language from English. We propose Hierarchical Convolutional Attention Network using Joint Chinese Word Embedding(HCAje), an architecture based off joint Chinese word embedding that can generate document representations from words as well as their characters and fine-grained sub-character components. Meanwhile, we use the convolution feature extraction to improve the self-attention architecture (Vaswani 2017) and adapt it into an effective approach for text classification. To evaluate the performance of our model in comparison to other common classification architectures, we look at 4 Chinese data sets. HCAje can achieve accuracy that surpasses the current state-of-the-art on several classification tasks.

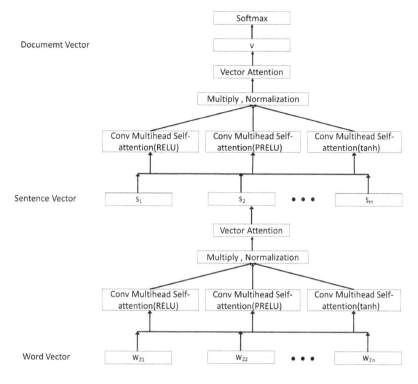

Fig. 3. Architecture for HCAje.

2 Hierarchical Convolutional Attention Network Using Joint Chinese Word Embedding

The overall architecture of our HCAje is shown in Fig. 3. It consists of several parts: joint Chinese word embedding, hierarchical structure, convolution feature extraction, parallel convolutional multihead self-attention and vector attention. We describe the details of different components in the following sections.

2.1 Joint Chinese Word Embedding

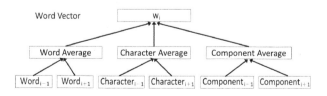

Fig. 4. Illustration of joint Chinese word embedding.

Our joint Chinese word embedding model is based on CBOW model (Mikolov et al. 2013a) and combines words, characters and components information. In the Sect. 3.5, we verified the effects of different combinations, and the following combinations worked best. It uses the average of context word vector, the average of context character vector and the average of context component vector to predict the target word, and use the sum of these three prediction losses as the objective function. We denote D as the training corpus, $W = (w_1, w_2, ..., w_n)$ as the vocabulary of words, $C = (c_1, c_2, ..., c_m)$ as the vocabulary of characters, $O = (o_1, o_2, ..., o_k)$ as the vocabulary of component, and T as the context window size respectively. As illustrated in Fig. 4, our model aims to maximize the sum of log-likelihoods of three predictive conditional probabilities for target w_i:

$$L(w_i) = \sum_{k=1}^{3} \log P(w_i \mid h_{i_k}) \tag{1}$$

where h_{i_1}, h_{i_2}, h_{i_3} are the composition of context words, context characters, context components respectively. Let v_{w_i}, v_{c_i}, v_{o_i} be the "input" vectors of word w_i, character c_i, and component o_i respectively, $\hat{v}_{w_i}$ be the "output" vectors of word w_i. The conditional probability is defined by the softmax function as follows:

$$p(w_i \mid h_{i_k}) = \frac{\exp\left(h_{i_k}^T \hat{v}_{w_i}\right)}{\sum_{j=1}^{N} \exp\left(h_{i_k}^T \hat{v}_{w_j}\right)}, \quad k = 1,2,3 \tag{2}$$

where h_{i_1} is the average of the "input" vectors of words in the context:

$$h_{i_1} = \frac{1}{2T} \sum_{-T \leq j \leq T, j \neq 0} v_{w_{i+j}} \tag{3}$$

Similarly, h_{i_2} is the average of character "input" vectors in the context, h_{i_3} is the average of component "input" vectors in the context. Given a corpus D, our model maximizes the overall log likelihood:

$$L(D) = \sum_{w_i \in D} L(w_i) \tag{4}$$

where the optimization follows the implementation of negative sampling used in CBOW model (Mikolov et al. 2013a).

2.2   Convolution Feature Extraction

As mentioned in the Introduction, our model refers to Scaled Dot Product Attention which is a type of self-attention and multihead attention developed by Vaswani et al. Rather than use the same input for Q, K, and V, we used a convolution to extract different features from input for each of the Q, K, and V embeddings. This allows for more expressive comparison between entries in a sequence; for example, certain features may be useful when comparing Q and

K but may not be necessary when creating the output sequence from V. For our feature extractor function, we use a 1D convolution with d filter maps and a window size of three words, which provides more context for each center word when extracting important features.

$$Q = GELU(Conv1D(E, W^q) + b^q)$$
$$K = GELU(Conv1D(E, W^k) + b^k) \tag{5}$$
$$V = GELU(Conv1D(E, W^v) + b^v)$$

In the equation above, $Conv1D(A, B)$ is a 1D convolution operation with A as the input as B as the filter. We found gaussian error linear units (GELU) (Hendrycks and Gimpel 2016) to perform better than rectified linear units (ReLUs) and other activation functions. The GELU nonlinearity is the expected transformation of a stochastic regularizer which randomly applies the identity or zero map to a neuron's input. The GELU nonlinearity weights inputs by their magnitude, rather than gates inputs by their sign as in ReLUs.

2.3   Parallel Multihead Convolutional Self-attention

As we know, attention mechanisms are designed to produce a weighted average of an input sequence. However, a weighted average is not sufficient when capture the overall content within a linguistic sequence. To better capture the linguistic information, we use two multihead convolutional self-attentions (Eq. 6) in parallel followed by elementwise multiplication. Compared to simple weighted average, our approach can capture more complex interactions between elements in the sequence. After many attempts, we found that the combination of these two activation functions obtains the best performance. Among them, tanh outputs a value between -1 and 1, and prevents the final output from becoming too small or large after elementwise multiplication. GELU' s convergence rate is rapid.

$$Parallel(E) = Multihead(Q^a, K^a, V^a)$$
$$\odot Multihead(Q^b, K^b, V^b)$$
$$where\ Multihead(Q, K, V) = [head_1, ..., head_h]$$
$$head_i = Attention(Q, K, V)$$
$$Q^a = GELU(Conv1D(E, W^{qa}) + b^{qa})$$
$$K^a = GELU(Conv1D(E, W^{ka}) + b^{ka}) \tag{6}$$
$$V^a = GELU(Conv1D(E, W^{va}) + b^{va})$$
$$Q^b = tanh(Conv1D(E, W^{qb}) + b^{qb})$$
$$K^b = tanh(Conv1D(E, W^{kb}) + b^{kb})$$
$$V^b = tanh(Conv1D(E, W^{vb}) + b^{vb})$$

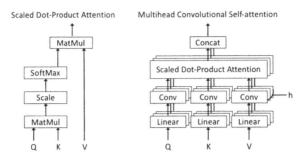

Fig. 5. Scaled dot-product attention and multihead convolutional self-attention.

2.4 Vector Attention

The output of parallel multihead convolutional self-attention is a sequence $E^{output} \in R^{l \times d}$ in which l is the length of the input sequence, and d is the embedding dimension. To obtain a single fixed-length vector which represents each sequence, we introduce vector attention which is same as the traditional attention mechanism that is used on RNN. For word level,

$$u_{it} = \tanh\left(W_w z_{it} + b_w\right) \tag{7}$$

$$\alpha_{it} = \frac{\exp\left(u_{it}^\top u_w\right)}{\sum_t \exp\left(u_{it}^\top u_w\right)} \tag{8}$$

$$s_i = \sum_t \alpha_{it} z_{it} \tag{9}$$

Firstly, we feed the word vector z_{it} (obtained by w_{it} through parallel multihead convolutional self-attention and elementwise multiplication) through a one-layer MLP to get u_{it} as a hidden representation of z_{it}. Then we measure the importance of the word as the similarity of u_{it} with a word level context vector u_w and get a normalized importance weight α_{it} by softmax. After that, we compute the sentence vector s_i as a weighted sum of the word annotations based on the weights. The context vector u_w is randomly initialized and learned in training process.

For sentence level,

$$u_i = \tanh\left(W_s z_i + b_s\right) \tag{10}$$

$$\alpha_i = \frac{\exp\left(u_i^\top u_s\right)}{\sum_i \exp\left(u_i^\top u_s\right)} \tag{11}$$

$$v = \sum_i \alpha_i z_i \tag{12}$$

where v is the document vector that summarizes all the information of sentences in this document, z_i is obtained by s_i through parallel multihead convolutional self-attention and elementwise multiplication, u_s is a sentence level context vector.

2.5   Hierarchical Structure

We utilize a hierarchical structure that breaks up documents into sentences and attained state-of-the-art performance. This structure consists of two levels: the word level and the sentence level. The word level reads in word vectors from a given sentence and outputs a sentence vector representing the content within that sentence, and the sentence level reads in the sentence vectors and outputs a document vector representing the content of the entire document. Each hierarchical consists of two parallel multihead convolutional self-attentions followed by a normalization layer and an vector attention layer (see Fig. 3).

2.6   Document Classification

The document vector v is our final representation of the document and can be fed into a softmax and used for classification purposes:

$$p = \text{softmax}\left(W_d v + b_d\right) \tag{13}$$

We use the negative log likelihood of the correct labels as training loss:

$$L = -\sum_d j_d \log p_d \tag{14}$$

where j is the label of document d.

3   Experiments

3.1   Datasets

We evaluate the effectiveness of our model on three document classification datasets. The statistics of the datasets are summarized in Table 1. We use 80% of the data for training and the rest are used as testing set to evaluate the performance.

Table 1. Datasets.

Dataset	Categories	Documents	Train Samples	Test Samples
Fudan-large	5	6,121	4,894	1,227
Fudan-small	5	294	233	61
THUCNews	14	21,000	16,800	4,200
SogouNews	11	50,000	40,000	10,000

Fudan corpus[2] contains 20 categories of documents, including economy, politics, sports and etc. The number of documents in each category ranges from 27

---

[2] http://www.nlpir.org/download/tc-corpus-answer.rar.

to 1061. In this paper, we refer to the processing method by Zhang et al. (2015). To avoid imbalance, we select 10 categories and organize them into 2 groups. One group is named Fudan-large and each category in this group contains more than 1000 documents. The other is named Fudan-small and each category contains less than 100 documents. The publish information for each document is also removed because it contains strong indication of the categories, which will bias the classifier with unfair benefits.

THUCNews is obtained from (Guo et al. 2016). It consists of 740,000 news spanning 2005 to 2011. For our evaluation, we selected 14 popular categories and extracted 1,500 randomly selected news from each: economy, lottery, real estate, stock, home, education, technology, society, fashion, politics, sports, constellation, entertainment and game.

Sogou news is a combination of the SogouCA and SogouCS news corpora (Wang et al. 2008), containing in total 2,909,551 news articles in various topic channels. We then labeled each piece of news using its URL, by manually classifying their domain names. This gives us a large corpus of news articles labeled with their categories. We choose 14 categories and extracted 50,000 randomly selected news from each: sports, finance, entertainment, automobile, house, education, travel, female, culture, health and technology.

3.2 Baselines and Hyperparameters

To offer fair comparisons to competitive models, we conducted a series of experiments with both traditional methods such as **Naïve Bayes (NB)** and **logistic regression (LR)**. For logistic regression, we use L1 regularization with a penalty strength of 1.0. We also compare HCAje with five deep learning methods.

Word-based CNN like that of (Kim 2014) are used. We use three parallel convolution layers with 3-, 4-, and 5-word windows, all with 100 feature maps and apply 50% dropout on the concatenated vector. We use the pretrained word2vec embedding.

Character-based CNN are reported in (Zhang et al. 2015). To ensure fair comparison, the models for each case are of the same size as Word-based CNN, in terms of both the number of layers and each layer' s output size.

Bi-directional GRU We also offer a comparison with a recurrent neural network model, namely Bi-directional Gated Recurrent Unit. The Bi-directional GRU model used in our case is word-based, using pretrained word2vec embedding as in previous models.

Hierarchical Attention Networks (HAN) are the current state-of-the-art. For our experiments, we use the same optimized hyperparameters as those used by Yang - each hierarchy is composed of a bi-directional GRU with 50 units and an attention mechanism with a hidden layer of 200 neurons.

BERT or Bidirectional Encoder Representations from Transformers, is a new method of pre-training language representations which obtains state-of-the-art results on a wide array of Natural Language Processing (NLP) tasks. We fine-tuned Google's pre-trained Chinese Bert model on the data set mentioned above.

For our HCAje, we tuned the hyperparameters on the remaining text of the Sogou news. We use 8 heads for our final implementation. As for joint Chinese word embedding, we adopt the Chinese Wikipedia Dump[3] as our training corpus and removed pure digits and non-Chinese characters. After Chinese word segmentation and POS tagging, we obtained a 1 GB training corpus with 153,071,899 tokens and 3,158,225 unique words. The components information of Chinese character is crawled from HTTPCN[4]. For fair comparison, we used the same parameter settings with the pretrained word2vec embedding. We fixed the word vector dimension to be 100, the window size to be 5, the training iteration to be 100, the initial learning rate to be 0.025, and the subsampling parameter to be. Words with frequency less than 5 were ignored during training. We used 10-word negative sampling for optimization.

3.3   Model Configuration and Training

For training, we use a mini-batch size of 64 and documents of similar length (in terms of the number of sentences in the documents) are organized to be a batch. All models are trained using the Adam optimizer (Kingma and Ba 2015) with learning rate 2E–5, beta1 0.9, and beta2 0.99. We save the model parameters with the highest validation accuracy and use those parameters to evaluate on the test set.

3.4   Results and Analysis

The experimental results on all datasets are shown in Table 2. For each model, we record the final test accuracy. Results show that HCAje gives the best performance across all datasets.

The improvement is regardless of data sizes. For small datasets such as Fudan-small and Fudan-large, our model outperforms the previous baseline methods by 1.7% and 1.4% respectively. This finding is consistent across other larger datasets. Our model outperforms previous best models by 2.2% and 2.5% on THUCNews and Sogou news.

Within the HCAje, using joint Chinese word embedding achieves better accuracy than using word2vec, using two parallel multihead convolutional self-attentions achieves better accuracy than using one or three, and using vector attention outperforms using maxpool. Here PCMS stands for parallel convolutional multihead self-attention.

---

[3] http://download.wikipedia.com/zhwiki.
[4] http://tool.httpcn.com/zi/.

Table 2. Test set accuracy.

Methods	Fudan-small	Fudan-large	THUCNews	Sogou news
Naïve Bayes	65.28	74.95	84.36	80.97
Logistic Regression	68.30	76.57	84.91	82.65
Word-based CNN	70.05	78.58	85.81	83.61
Character-based CNN	70.34	78.88	85.73	84.23
Bi-directional GRU	70.70	78.84	85.53	84.07
HAN	70.92	79.75	86.76	85.67
HCAje(word2vec, 2 PCMS, maxpool)	70.81	79.43	86.38	85.13
HCAje(word2vec, 2 PCMS, vector attention)	71.29	80.15	87.07	85.89
HCAje(joint word embedding, 2 PCMS, maxpool)	70.89	79.51	86.58	85.27
HCAje(joint word embedding, 1 PCMS, vector attention)	70.44	79.62	86.12	85.49
HCAje(joint word embedding, 3 PCMS, vector attention)	71.07	79.70	86.74	85.66
HCAje(joint word embedding, 2 PCMS, vector attention)	**72.12**	**80.87**	**88.67**	**87.81**

3.5 Different Combinations of Embedding

As mentioned above, Chinese words can be divided into words, characters and components. We try different combinations to represent Chinese words, and test the classification effect on four datasets. The results are shown Table 3. By comparing the experimental results, the combination of words, words and components has the best classification results, while the combination of words and components has the worst classification results.

Table 3. Test set accuracy.

Methods	Fudan-small	Fudan-large	THUCNews	Sogou news
HCAje(word, character)	71.01	78.43	83.18	84.06
HCAje(word, component)	71.21	79.5	84.19	84.21
HCAje(character, component)	70.75	80.20	83.14	82.31
HCAje(word, character, component)	**72.12**	**80.87**	**88.67**	**87.81**

3.6 Visualization of Attention

In order to validate that our model is able to select informative sentences and words in a document, we visualize the hierarchical structure in Fig. 3 for one document from the sports classification of Fudan corpus. Every line is a sentence (the upper lines are the original Chinese texts, and the lower lines are the translated English texts). Red denotes the importance of sentences and blue denotes the importance of words (The darker the color, the more important it is). Figure 6 shows that our model can select the words carrying strong information like "国际足联 (the FIFA)", "世界杯 (World Cup)" and their corresponding sentences.

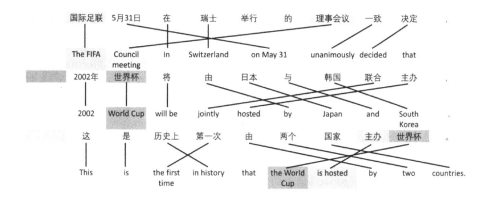

Fig. 6. Visualization of attention.

4   Conclusion

In this paper, we introduced a new self-attention based Chinese text classification architecture, HCAje, and compared its performance with the traditional approaches and deep learning approaches, in four classification datasets. In all four tasks HCAjes achieved slightly better performance than previous methods. Visualization of these attention layers illustrates that our model is effective in picking out important words and sentences. Although our model is introduced to classified Chinese text, the idea can also be applied to other languages that share a similar writing system. In the future, we would like to further explore learning representations for traditional Chinese words and Japanese Kanji.

References

Wang, S., Manning, C.D.: Baselines and bigrams: simple, good sentiment and topic classification. In: Proceedings of the 50th Annual Meeting of the Association for Computational Linguistics: Short Papers, vol. 2, pp. 90–94. Association for Computational Linguistics (2012)

Guo, Z., Zhao, Y., Zheng, Y., Si, X., Liu, Z., Sun, M.: THUCTC: An Efficient Chinese Text Classifier (2016)

Wang, C., Zhang, M., Ma, S., Ru, L.: Automatic online news issue construction in web environment. In: Proceedings of the 17th International Conference on World Wide Web, WWW 2008, New York, NY, USA, pp. 457–466 (2008)

Pang, B., Lee, L.: Opinion mining and sentiment analysis. Found. Trends Inf. Retrieval **2**(1–2), 1–135 (2008)

Hochreiter, S., Schmidhuber, J.: Long short-term memory. Neural Comput. **9**(8), 1735–1780 (1997)

Cho, K., et al.: Learning phrase representations using RNN encoder-decoder for statistical machine translation. arXiv 2014. arXiv:1406.1078 (2014)

Krizhevsky, A.I.S.A., Hinton, G.E.: ImageNet classification with deep convolutional neural networks. In: Proceedings of the Advances in Neural Information Processing Systems, Lake Tahoe, NV, USA, 3–6 December 2012, pp. 1097–1105 (2012)

Kalchbrenner, N., Grefenstette, E., Blunsom, P.: A convolutional neural network for modelling sentences. arXiv 2014. arXiv:1404.2188 (2014)

Maas, A.L., Daly, R.E., Pham, P.T., Huang, D., Ng, A.Y., Potts, C.: Learning word vectors for sentiment analysis. In: Proceedings of the 49th Annual Meeting of the Association for Computational Linguistics: Human Language Technologies, vol. 1, pp. 142–150. Association for Computational Linguistics (2011)

Sahami, M., Dumais, S., Heckerman, D., Horvitz, E.: A Bayesian approach to filtering junk e-mail. In: Learning for Text Categorization: Papers from the 1998 workshop, vol. 62, pp. 98–105 (1998)

Sebastiani, F.: Text Categorization [OL]. Encyclopedia of Database Technologies and Applications (2005)

Joachims, T.: Text categorization with Support Vector Machines: learning with many relevant features. In: Nédellec, C., Rouveirol, C. (eds.) ECML 1998. LNCS, vol. 1398, pp. 137–142. Springer, Heidelberg (1998). https://doi.org/10.1007/BFb0026683

Blunsom, P., Grefenstette, E., Kalchbrenner, N., et al.: A convolutional neural network for modelling sentences. In: Proceedings of the 52nd Annual Meeting of the Association for Computational Linguistics (2014)

Young, T., Hazarika, D., Poria, S., Cambria, E.: Recent trends in deep learning based natural language processing. arXiv preprint arXiv:1708.02709 (2017)

Hendrycks, D., Gimpel, K.: Gaussian Error Linear Units (GELUs). arXiv:1606.08415 (2016)

Kim, Y.: Convolutional neural networks for sentence classification. In: EMNLP, pp. 1746–1751 (2014)

Zhang, X., Zhao, J., LeCun, Y.: Character-level convolutional networks for text classification. In: NIPS, pp. 649–657 (2015)

Tang, D., Qin, B., Liu, T.: Document modeling with gated recurrent neural network for sentiment classification. In: Proceedings of the 2015 Conference on Empirical Methods in Natural Language Processing, pp. 1422–1432 (2015)

Bengio, Y., Ducharme, R., Vincent, P., Jauvin, C.: A neural probabilistic language model. J. Mach. Learn. Res. **3**(Feb), 1137–1155 (2003)

Mnih, A., Hinton, G.E.: A scalable hierarchical distributed language model. In: Proceedings of NIPS, pp. 1081–1088 (2009)

Mikolov, T., Chen, K., Corrado, G., Dean, J.: Efficient estimation of word representations in vector space. arXiv preprint arXiv:1301.3781 (2013)

Mikolov, T., Sutskever, I., Chen, K., Corrado, G.S., Dean, J.: Distributed representations of words and phrases and their compositionality. In: Proceedings of NIPS, pp. 3111–3119 (2013)

Vaswani, A., et al.: Attention is all you need. In: NIPS (2017)

Lin, Z., et al.: A structured self-attentive sentence embedding. In: ICLR (2017)

Cheng, J., Dong, L., Lapata, M.: Long Short-term Memory-networks for Machine Reading, pp. 551–561 (2016)

Paulus, R., Xiong, C., Socher, R.: A deep reinforced model for abstractive summarization. arXiv preprint arXiv:1705.04304 (2017)

Kingma, D.P., Ba, J.L.: Adam: a method for stochastic optimization. In: ICLR (2015)

Machine Learning Based Cross-border E-Commerce Commodity Customs Product Name Recognition Algorithm

Jing Ma[1][(✉)], Xiaofeng Li[1][(✉)], Chi Li[2], Bo He[1], and Xiaoyu Guo[1]

[1] College of Economics and Management, Nanjing University of Aeronautics and Astronautics, Nanjing 211106, China
majing5525@126.com, 13820650@QQ.com
[2] Alibaba Zhejiang Rookie Supply Chain Management Co., Ltd., Hangzhou 310000, China

Abstract. This paper aims to solve the problem of identifying commodity names in the field of cross-border e-commerce by using some machine learning algorithms. As far as we know, this is the first attempt to use machine learning algorithms to solve this kind of problems in this field. A model of commodity name recognition algorithm based on the SVM and TF-IDF models is proposed. For 115,521 commodity description texts containing 2,128 different commodities, experiments show that the recognition accuracy of the algorithm is 91% and the recall rate is 93%. At the same time, compared with the traditional manual method, the algorithm can improve the efficiency of commodity export declaration by about 20% during the "Double Eleven" period. It is proved by experiment and practice that this algorithm is reasonable, effective and practical.

Keywords: Cross-border e-commerce · Commodity description · Commodity name · Commodity name recognition · SVM · Feature extraction

1 Introduction

1.1 Background

With the advent of the "Internet plus" era, cross-border e-commerce has been on top of the market. Alibaba is a well-known e-commerce enterprise in China. In addition to having the Taobao and Tmall e-commerce platforms, it also provides a good cross-border e-commerce platforms Ali Express and Ali to Global (AE and ATG) for global e-commerce users.

Currently, Alibaba's cross-border e-commerce platforms use the customs declaration mode by entrusting the generated order of goods to a third party customs declaration agency to complete the customs declaration by filling in the customs declaration form manually. This mode of manual declaration through a third-party agency company is inefficient, costly and inaccurate, and there is also a risk of business data leakage. In order to achieve intelligent automatic declaration, it first need to accurately identify the cross-border goods' name. This paper firstly describes the use of machine

© Springer Nature Switzerland AG 2019
A. C. Nayak and A. Sharma (Eds.): PRICAI 2019, LNAI 11672, pp. 247–256, 2019.
https://doi.org/10.1007/978-3-030-29894-4_19

learning algorithms to process the commodity description text information for product name recognition.

1.2 Problem Definition

The cross-border e-commerce commodity description name recognition is a new problem, which is aimed at accurately identify the correct name of the goods in the short text of commodity description and that this short text is usually no more than 50 Chinese characters.

As shown in the Fig. 1, the title, written by merchants, usually contain a lot of information in order to maximize the likelihood of a product getting search engine hits. Such descriptive title is characterized by strong randomness of words, poor correlation between words, non-strict grammatical structure, colloquial semantic expression and repeated synonyms.

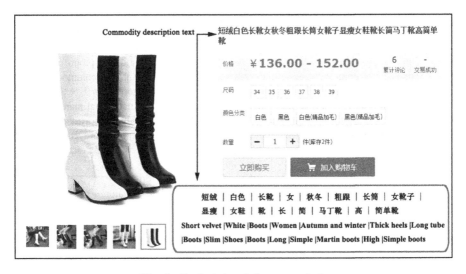

Fig. 1. Product description example 1

This problem can be defined as a "special" problem of "weak correlation short text multi-classification". Compared with the traditional short text classification, the particularities are mainly manifested in the classification rules. Traditional short text classification rules usually include whether the short text contains a given topic, whether the semantics are related to a given topic, whether the similarity of the text meets a given classification threshold, and so on. However, the precondition of commodity name recognition is that the commodity name must be recognized in the given commodity description text, that is, the identified commodity name vocabulary must be included in the commodity description text; while in the traditional short text classification problem, the category words are not necessarily included in the original short text. For example, the short text commentary text "China J-20 (Chinese new stealth fighter), so cool!" There is no word "military" in this article, but the classification result should classify this short text into "military" category. While, for the commodity description in the Fig. 2, It is likely to be classified into the category of "film and television works" because it contains words such as "The mummy", "Mission: Impossible" and "Tom Cruise".

Fig. 2. Product description example 2

Through the above analysis, the conclusions are as follows: the problem of commodity name recognition in cross-border e-commerce is a new kind of short text multi-classification problem, which is different from the traditional short text classification problem. So, how to accurately identify the commodity name in the short text of commodity description with the above characteristics has become a very interesting issue and it is also worth to explore and research.

1.3   Contribution

The main contributions of this paper are as follows:

(1) For the first time, this paper explores and presents a cross-border e-commerce commodity name recognition algorithm based on the machine learning model. The recognition accuracy of over 2,000 commodities is more than 90%.

(2) In collaboration with Alibaba Group, the first cross-border e-commerce product description text dataset at home and abroad was constructed with about 120,000 commodity description texts. All the texts in the dataset are standardized and labeled manually, which can provide high quality dataset for follow-up research in this field.

(3) For this problem, the text feature extraction effects of Word2vec model and TF-IDF model are compared. The reasons for the difference in effect are analyzed in principle. Furthermore, the text feature extraction model which is most suitable for this problem is given.

(4) The product name optimization algorithm proposed in this paper has achieved good practical results in the practical application process of "Double Eleven" (November 11 is the Chinese e-commerce festival, named "Double Eleven") in 2017, and the clearance speed of cross-border goods has increased by more than 20%.

2 Related Work

As far as we know, there are few algorithms for recognition commodity names by using commodity description texts in cross-border e-commerce at home and abroad. The most relevant research is the short text classification.

The research of short text classification began in the 1990s. Sriram et al. [1] proposed a new short text classification method based on the combination of Twitter users' personal information and the internal characteristics of message organization, and the effect was improved significantly. However, the feature selection in this method needs to be done manually, which leads to poor generality, so it has not been popularized. Phan et al. [2] used Wikipedia data as classified data set, and used Latent Dirichlet Allocation (LDA) [3] to train to get the theme model of the document. After a series of processing and calculation, the theme feature vectors of the short text were obtained and used to represent the short text. This method combined text vectors and topics at the same time, so it achieved good classification results.

With the emergence and development of machine learning algorithms, many classical machine learning algorithms, such as Naïve Bayes, CART and Random Forest, have also been applied to short text classification. With the popularity of deep learning algorithms, neural network models such as RNN and LSTM also show good results on short text classification [4]. However, depth learning models also have some shortcomings, such as large amount of calculation, long training time, poor interpretability, difficulty in adjusting parameters and over-fitting. For comparison of effects, the paper also selected the RNN model as a comparative experimental model.

Literature review shows that the above algorithms have strong pertinence and good performance in solving problems in their fields. However, for the problem of commodity name recognition studied in this paper, the results are not satisfactory. The short texts of this problem have the characteristics of weak correlation between words, disorder, irregular grammatical structure and repetition of synonyms. This leads to the coexistence of similar features, the ambiguity of feature differences and the high dimensionality of features in text classification. So, the selection of classification model has become a difficult problem.

3 Data Collection and Preprocessing

The raw data is obtained directly from the commodity trading information database in Alibaba's cross-border e-commerce platforms.

Three-month trading records of October, November and December in the "Double Eleven" period of 2016 were selected. The top 30% of the trading records was extracted as the sample dataset. The sample dataset contains different 2,597 commodities, which represent the most popular commodities during the "Double Eleven" e-commerce festival and are also the most frequently declared commodities for export declaration.

Total about 149,672 short texts have been filtered and labeled. After filtering and cleaning, the dataset contains 2,128 different commodities and 115,521 commodity description texts.

4 Model Introduction

Word2vec and TF-IDF are the two most commonly used models for extracting text features. In this paper, the two feature extraction models are used to extract text features, respectively.

Support Vector Machine (SVM) model has high classification accuracy. This paper chooses the support vector machine model as the kernel algorithm to solve this problem.

4.1 Word2vec

Word2vec is a neural network probabilistic language model proposed by Mikolov et al. [5] Word2vec model contains two training models: CBOW and Skip-gram. The CBOW model can predict a given word by context. This paper used the CBOW training model in the experiment.

4.2 TF-IDF

TF-IDF model is often used to measure how important a word in a text dataset. TF-IDF is the product of the TF value and the IDF value of a word [6]. The characteristic extraction formula of TF-IDF is as follows:

$$f(w) = TF(w) \cdot IDF(w) = TF(w) \cdot \log \frac{N}{n(w) + 1} \tag{1}$$

Where N is the total number of texts, n(W) is the number of texts, which contain the word w.

4.3 Support Vector Machine (SVM) Model

The Support Vector Machine (SVM) model was proposed by Vapnic et al. in 1995 [7].
Linear SVM finds the hyperplane with the largest edge, so it is also called the maximal
edge classifier. The smaller the decision boundary, the worse the generalization ability
is. Therefore, it is necessary to design a linear classifier that maximizes the decision
boundary to ensure that the generalization error is minimized at the worst.

A binary classification problem involving N training samples is considered. Each
sample can be represented as a two-tuples $(X_i, Y_i)(i = 1, 2, \ldots N)$, where, x_i represents
the attribute set of the i sample. Let $y_i \in \{-1, 1\}$ represent its class label. Then the
decision boundary of a linear classifier can be expressed as follows:

$$w * x + b = 0 \tag{2}$$

Where w and b are the parameters of the model. The optimized separation
hyperplane can be expressed in the following form:

$$y = \text{sign}\left[w^T \varphi(x_i) + b\right] \tag{3}$$

It is obtained by solving the following Quadratic Optimization problem:

$$\min Q(w) = \frac{\|w\|^2}{2} + C\left(\sum_{i=1}^{N} \xi_i\right) \tag{4}$$

Where C is a user-specified parameter indicating a penalty for misclassified training
instances, $\xi \geq 0$ is a slack variable. The SVM Support vector is only a small part of the
training set, which greatly reduces the model's dependence on the data and improves its
generalization ability.

5 Experiment

5.1 Experimental Design

First, short-form texts for cross-border e-commerce products were pre-processed,
including data cleaning, filtering and manual labeling. Then, a user dictionary composed of labels was established. It was added to the jieba word segmentation system.
Then, the jieba system was used to segment the corpus. After that, the stop word list
was expanded to remove the stop words.

Next, the two models of word2vec and TF-IDF were used to extract the features of
the pre-processed corpus. The word vector matrix and the TF-IDF matrix were got.
Then, the 10-fold cross-validation method was used and the dataset was divided into
the training set and the test set according to 9:1.

Lastly, many machine learning models, such as Linear SVC, SVM (RBF), Naïve
Bayes, Logistic Regression, XGBoost, RNN, etc., were used to train the commodity
description corpus for commodity name recognition. Then, all experimental results
were compared and evaluated.

5.2   Evaluation

In this paper, three metrics: accuracy, recall and F1_score value, which are widely used in supervised machine learning, are used to evaluate the quality of the results.

$$Precison = \frac{TP}{TP + FP} \tag{5}$$

$$Recall = \frac{TP}{TP + FN} \tag{6}$$

$$F1\_score = \frac{2 \cdot Pr \cdot Re}{Pr + Re} \tag{7}$$

Where TP: True Positive; FP: False Positive; FN: False Negative.

5.3   Contrastive Experiment

First, Word2vec was used to extract features. According to the Table 1, the SVM model with linear kernel function performs best by using Word2vec model to extract features. However, the difference between the experimental results of various machine learning models is not very significant (Table 2).

Table 1. Word2vec comparative experiment

Feature Extract Model / ML Model	word2vec		
	Precision	Recall	F1_SCORE
Naïve Bayes	0.75	0.66	0.69
Logistic Regression	0.72	0.79	0.74
Random Forest	0.73	0.75	0.73
XGBoost	0.75	0.77	0.75
RNN	0.72	0.68	0.70
SVM(RBF)	0.76	0.79	0.76
SVM(linear)	*0.79*	*0.83*	*0.80*

Table 2. Word2vec parameter setting table (others use default value setting)

name	values	Parameter description
sentence	/	The corpus to be trained is a list of lists
size	300	Dimensions of training feature vectors
window	10	The maximum distance is between the current word and the prediction word in a sentence
sg	0	sg=0, use CBOW model sg=1, use skip-gram model
Min_count	2	Words whose frequencies are less than Min_count times will be discarded

Next, the TF-IDF model was used to extract features. The experimental results are shown in the Table 3. By using the TF-IDF model to extract features, the experimental results of various machine learning models were significantly different. The SVM model that uses linear kernel functions still performs the best.

Table 3. TF-IDF comparison experiment

Feature Extract Model ML Model	TF-IDF		
	Precision	Recall	F1_SCORE
Naïve Bayes	0.44	0.53	0.42
Logistic Regression	0.77	0.85	0.80
Random Forest	0.85	0.87	0.86
XGBoost	0.83	0.84	0.83
RNN	/	/	/
SVM(RBF)	0.06	0.24	0.09
SVM(linear)	*0.91*	*0.93*	*0.92*

In the two comparative experiments using different feature extraction models, the SVM using linear kernel functions always performs well.

6 Discussion

The experimental results of SVM+TF-IDF composite model by using linear kernel function are not only better than those of SVM+Word2vector composite model, but also better than those of other machine learning algorithm models. Comparing the two schemes, the Precision values differ by 0.12, the Recall values differ by 0.10, and the F1_score values differ by 0.12.

7 Conclusion and Summary

Through the experiment results, we found that the TF-IDF model is better than Word2vec model in representing the commodity description short texts. For such an interesting result, this paper provides the following analysis:

(1) The characteristics of cross-border e-commerce commodity description corpus are the primary reason for the impact of results.

(2) The principle of Word2vec based on the CBOW training model is precisely to predict the current word according to the previous N words and the subsequent N words. The advantage of the model is that it can extract the relationship between words well. However, the special features of the corpus have some deviations from the principle of the Word2vec model, so the performance of the powerful Word2vec model is not good enough.

(3) The principle of the TF-IDF model is to express every word in the text using the product of word frequency and inverse word frequency. However, this model often ignores the relevance between words. That is why TF-IDF model performs better in this kind of short-text corpus.

(4) Through experiments, we also found that the performance of the deep learning model RNN is too general. The principle of RNN is that you can use the previous information to help infer the current information. So, it is easy to explain why, for such independent distribution, low correlation corpus, the effect is not good enough.

(5) The SVM model with linear kernel function in traditional machine learning model stands out, which shows its strong multi-classification ability, good robustness and generalization ability. But the principle of the model determines that it is sensitive to outliers or noise, so it is very important to preprocess the dataset used for training.

Recognition of commodity names from short descriptive texts in cross-border e-commerce is the basis for automatic declaration of commodities. Up until the present, this is the first time to study this problem in the field where the algorithm scheme of TF-IDF with linear SVM is used. For more than 2000 different commodities, the precision and recall rate of the algorithm reach 0.91 and 0.93 respectively.

In 2017, during the Alibaba "Double Eleven" period, the algorithm improved the efficiency of commodity export declaration by about 20%. The experimental and practical tests prove that the algorithm is reasonable, effective and has practical application value.

In our future work, we will explore how to use deep learning composite neural networks to research the case of commodity name recognition. I sincerely hope to share this work with the vast number of scholars who are working in this field.

Acknowledgements. This work is sponsored by the National Natural Science Foundation of China (No. 71373123), the Fundamental Research Funds for the Central Universities (NO. NW2018004).

References

1. Sriram, B., Fuhry, D., Demir, E., et al.: Short text classification in twitter to improve information filtering. In: Proceedings of the 33rd International ACM SIGIR Conference on Research and Development in Information Retrieval, pp. 841–842. ACM (2010)
2. Phan, H.X., Nguyen, L.M., Horiguchi, S.: Learning to classify short and sparse text & web with hidden topics from large-scale data collections. In: Proceedings of the 17th International Conference on World Wide Web, pp. 91–100. ACM (2008)
3. Chaozhen, L.V., Donghong, J.I., Feifei, W.U.: Short text classification based on expanding feature of LDA. Comput. Eng. Appl. **51**(4), 123–127 (2015)
4. Zhou, Y., Xu, J., Cao, J., et al.: Hybrid attention networks for chinese short text classification. Computacion Y Sistemas **21**(4), 759–769 (2017)
5. Lin, J., Dongbo, W.: Automatic extraction of domain terms using continuous bag-of-words model. New Technol. Libr. Inf. Serv. **32**(2), 9–15 (2016)
6. Salton, G., Clement, T.Y.: On the construction of effective vocabularies for information retrieval. In: Proceedings of the 1973 Meeting on Programming Languages and Information Retrieval. ACM, New York, November 1973
7. Liu, B., Xiao, Y., Cao, L.: SVM-based multi-state-mapping approach for multi-class classification. Knowl.-Based Syst. **129**(1), 79–96 (2017)

A Syllable-Structured, Contextually-Based Conditionally Generation of Chinese Lyrics

Xu Lu[1,2], Jie Wang[2(✉)], Bojin Zhuang[2], Shaojun Wang[2], and Jing Xiao[2]

[1] Beijing University of Posts and Telecommunications, Beijing, China
[2] Ping An Technology (Shenzhen) Co., Ltd., Shenzhen, China
photonicsjay@163.com

Abstract. This paper presents a novel, syllable-structured Chinese lyrics generation model given a piece of original melody. Most previously reported lyrics generation models fail to include the relationship between lyrics and melody. In this work, we propose to interpret lyrics-melody alignments as syllable structural information and use a multi-channel sequence-to-sequence model with considering both phrasal structures and semantics. Two different RNN encoders are applied, one of which is for encoding syllable structures while the other for semantic encoding with contextual sentences or input keywords. Moreover, a large Chinese lyrics corpus for model training is leveraged. With automatic and human evaluations, results demonstrate the effectiveness of our proposed lyrics generation model. To the best of our knowledge, there is few previous reports on lyrics generation considering both music and linguistic perspectives.

Keywords: Natural Language Processing · Natural Language Generation · Seq2Seq · Lyrics generation

1 Introduction

Natural language generation (NLG) plays an important role in machine translation, dialogue generation and other fields. In the recent years, owing to the fast rise of deep learning, RNN and other alternate neural networks are often used in NLG applications. In particular, an encoder-decoder based sequence-to-sequence (Seq2Seq) generation framework has been widely applied in various NLG problems including poetry and short essays generation. The main idea behind the Seq2Seq model is to encode input sequences into a fixed-length dense vector, and then decode corresponding sequences from this contextual vector. Moreover, attention mechanism has also been incorporated into this architecture to learn to soft alignments between contextual semantics.

Given a piece of melody, automatic lyrics generation is a challenging task. Completely different from prose text, lyrics generation should include both knowledge and consideration of music-specific properties including melody structure, rhythms, etc. For instance, word boundaries in lyrics and the rests in a melody should be consistent. As depicted in Fig. 1, it sounds unnatural if a single syllable spans beyond a long melody rest. During the procedure of lyrics writing, such constraints in content and lexical selection could impose extra cognitive loads.

© Springer Nature Switzerland AG 2019
A. C. Nayak and A. Sharma (Eds.): PRICAI 2019, LNAI 11672, pp. 257–265, 2019.
https://doi.org/10.1007/978-3-030-29894-4_20

Because of Chinese language specificity, one Chinese character represents one syllable. Therefore, beat patterns of melody can be interpreted as character number of lyrics and its fine sections. Different from regular poems, the form of lyrics is more free. To address this issue, this paper proposes a novel two-channel Seq2Seq for lyrics generation, which combines both syllable-pattern and contextual semantic information. With attention mechanism, singable lyrics can be generated and perfectly matched with the original melody.

(You ask me how deep I love you, how much I love you.)

Fig. 1. Structural alignment between lyrics and melody of a Chinese popular song.

The remainder of this paper is organized as follows. In Sect. 2, background about NLG is introduced. In Sect. 3, our lyrics generation model is described at detail. Section 4 discusses the model structure and experimental results. Section 5 concludes the work. Main contributions of our work are also listed:

- We propose a syllable-structured lyrics generation model, considering both music specialty and language attribute simultaneously with a two-channel encoder.
- To improve the singability of generated lyrics, the beat pattern of melody has been approximately interpreted as syllable structural information.
- To enhance the coherence and entirety of generated lyrics, the contextually-based conditional generation model can take in previous sentences or keywords.
- We leverage a large Chinese lyrics corpus of 300,000 pop songs to pre-train this model.

2 Background

2.1 Prior Work

Automatic text generation has been always a popular but challenging research topic. Recent work (Oliveira 2012) has been conducted to address this problem with grammatical and semantic templates. Statistical machine translation methods (He 2012) have also been exploited, in which each new line is considered as a "translation" of the previous line. Deep learning has also been proposed for language generation. For instance, an attention-based bidirectional RNN model (Yi 2016) was proposed for generating 4-line Chinese poems. Except for Chinese regular poems, Chinese iambic poems with free forms has also been demonstrated (Wang 2016). Moreover, the language model of LSTM (Potash 2015) was used to generate rap lyrics with a desired style, but failed to control the structure flexibly. In order to consider music properties, a melody-conditioned language model (Watanabe 2018) was proposed to generate Japanese lyrics. However, lyric-melody aligned data was really rare and highly cost if labelled by experts. Moreover, a RNN based language model is really difficult to capture long-term contextual information and hard to generate coherent multi-paragraph lyrics. To address this issue, we propose a two-channel Seq2Seq model which can contextually generate texts by taking in previous sentences or keywords.

2.2 RNN Encoder-Decoder

The RNN encoder-decoder framework (Sutskever 2014) is firstly introduced, of which the encoder and decoder are two separate RNN modules. The encoder converts a sequence of input $(x_1, \ldots, x_t)$ to a contextual dense vector c. Vector c encodes information of the whole source sequence, and is incorporated into decoder to generate the target output sequence. Thus, the probability distribution of prediction is defined as:

$$P(Y) = \prod_{t=1}^{T} P(y_t|y_{t-1}, c) \tag{1}$$

where y_{t-1} represents the generated output sequence prior to time step t. Different from an RNN based language model, the encoder-decoder model is capable of mapping sequence to sequence even from different domains. To apply explicit alignment between source and target sequences, attention mechanism is incorporated into this model.

3 Proposed Methods

In this section, a baseline model of lyric generation with an attention based encoder-decoder architecture is described. Following that, we describe the proposed method to control the generation of syllable structure and content with a multi-channel Seq2Seq model.

3.1 Baseline Model

In the encoder of the baseline model, a bidirectional RNN is used, which has been successfully applied in text generation and spoken language understanding. In addition, LSTM is used as the basic RNN unit because of its better long-term dependencies than vanilla RNN.

During the lyrics generation, context-aware generation is realized by inputting $(x_1, \ldots, x_t)$. The bidirectional LSTM reads the source word sequence forward and backward. The forward RNN reads the word sequence in its original order and generates a hidden state h_{fi} at each time step. Similarly, the backward RNN reads the word sequence in the reverse order and generate a sequence of hidden states $(h_{bT}, \ldots, h_{b1})$. The final encoder hidden state h_i at each time step i is a concatenation of the forward state h_{fi} and backward state h_{bi} i.e. $h_i = [h_{fi}, h_{bi}]$.

Therefore, last state of the forward and backward RNN carries information of the entire source sequence. We use the last state of the backward encoder as the initial decoder hidden state following the approach (Bahdanau 2014). The decoder is a uni-directional LSTM. At each decoding step i, the decoder state s_i is calculated as a function of the previous decoder state s_{i-1}, the previous predicted token y_{i-1}, the encoder hidden state h_i and the context vector c_i:

$$s_i = f(s_{i-1}, y_{i-1}, h_i, c_i) \tag{2}$$

where the context vector c_i is computed as a weighted sum of the encoder states $h = (h_1, \ldots, h_T)$ (Liu and Lane 2016):

$$c_i = \sum\nolimits_{j-1}^{T} \alpha_{i,j} h_j \tag{3}$$

And

$$\alpha_{i,j} = \frac{\exp(e_{i,j})}{\sum_{k=1}^{T} \exp(e_{i,k})}, \qquad e_{i,k} = g(s_{i-1}, h_k) \tag{4}$$

where g is a feed-forward neural network. At each decoding step, the explicit aligned input is the encoder state h_i. The context vector c_i provides extra information to the decoder and can be seen as a continuous bag of weighted features $(h_1, \ldots, h_T)$.

3.2   Multi-channel Seq2Seq with Attention

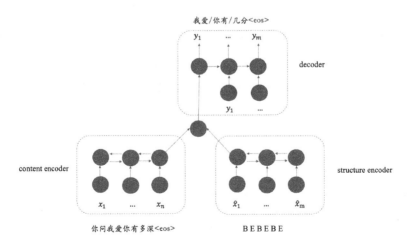

Fig. 2. Scheme of the multi-channel Seq2Seq generation model with structure and content encoders. Tokens of 'S', 'B', 'M', 'E' represent the syllable structure of lyrics, meaning the start of a sentence, the beginning, middle and end of a music segmentation of a melody.

As shown in Fig. 1, there is a finer structural alignment between lyrics and melody, except for sentence length. To be consistent with the beat pattern of melody, finer control of lyrics structures is required. Due to specialty of Chinese, phrase groups with certain character numbers retain both semantic and beat pattern information. To fuse both music and language into sentence decoding, we propose a multi-channel Seq2Seq model as shown in Fig. 2. Two different Bi-LSTMs read the structural token sequence and previous sentences, while text generation is only modeled with one forward LSTM.

When the attention mechanism is enabled, the context vector c_i provides partial information from input sequences that is used together with the aligned hidden state h_i for generating Chinese characters. Different from the contextual vector in Sect. 3.1, c_i in this model is calculated based on the concatenation of the two encoders' hidden states. But the initial state of the decoder is still same with the last state of content encoder.

Other than syllable structural encoding, two approaches of content encoding have been conducted to determine new sentence generation. In one case, two neighboring sentences extracted from lyrics are processed as previous and next sequence pairs. Similar to a kind of monolingual translation, next sentence can be generated by taking the previous one as input. In the other case, one keyword was retrieved from one lyric sentence to form training corpus of keyword-sentence pair. For keyword retrieval, a text-rank algorithm was used.

4 Experiments

4.1 Data

A large corpus of Chinese lyrics of 160,000 songs has been prepared to pre-train our lyrics generation language model. From this corpus, corresponding music notations of 50,000 songs have been manually interpreted with crowdsourcing. Among them, 4.15 million previous-next sentence/keyword-sentence pairs have been accumulated for model training. 10,000 lyric sentences are used for evaluation of model.

4.2 Training Procedure

LSTM cell is used as the basic RNN unit in all models, of which the dimension size of hidden state is 128. And then 4 layers of LSTM networks are used in the proposed models. Embedding size of 128 of Chinese characters are randomly initialized and then fine-tuned by training with mini-batch size of 16. Dropout rate of 0.3 is used to the non-recurrent connections for model regularization. Maximum norm for gradient clipping is set to 1. Adam method is used for model optimization and Bahdanau attention is applied. Schedule sampling with probability of 0.1 instead of teaching force is used for preparing ground truth. For inference, beam search decoding with beam width size of 35 is used.

4.3   Evaluation Metric

Automatic Evaluation

To evaluate our proposed model, a test lyric corpus has been selected as ground truth reference. For the melody structure control, the melody-alignment accuracy between prediction and ground truth will be calculated. In the case of semantic prediction, BLEU scores of generations will be computed. Even if BLEU is not a suitable metric for this NLG task, we believe that it can still reflect the semantic coherence and relevance of generation. Note that Bi-gram is the max length of n-gram. And BLEU can reflect the degree of control of the content which is very important.

Human Evaluation

Since lyrics generation belongs to literature creation, human evaluation might be a better way for performance evaluation. Following the reference (Yi 2016), three criteria has been designed: Fluency (fluency of generated sentences), Meaningfulness (do generated lyrics convey some certain messages and the contextual relevance?), Diversity (do generated sentences often show similar phrases or word?), and Entirety (general impression on sentences). Five thousand of generated lyrics samples were cross-scored by five Chinese language experts with score range of 0 to 5.

4.4   Results and Analysis

Automatic Evaluation Result

Compared to previous work, main contribution of this paper is to fuse syllable-structural control into text generation. As seen in Table 1 and Fig. 3, the multi-channel generation model can completely control the output sentence length, and melody-matching accuracy is also very high. With a beam-search decoder, the baseline model tends to generate sentences with shorter length and results in lower BLEU scores. However, BLEU of the keyword-aware generation model (KG) is higher than others including the sentence-aware generation model (SG), because the encoded keyword provides more context information, which offers a promising approach for structure and semantic control in NLG.

Table 1. Accuracy of automatic evaluation

Models	Length control	Melody matching	BLEU
Baseline	8.20%	2.00%	2.83%
SG	**100.00%**	**87.60%**	4.61%
KG	99.93%	83.85	**16.22%**

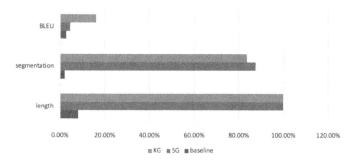

Fig. 3. Overall comparison of automatic evaluation.

4.5   Human Evaluation Result

As seen from Table 2 and Fig. 4, our model performs much better than the baseline. One main reason is that the generic Seq2Seq baseline model tends to generate short sentences, often less than five words, which decreases the meaningfulness and increases repeatability of generated sentences. While with our generation model, two encoders of structure and content will mutually promote the effect of decoding referred to (Ghazvininejad 2016).

Table 2. Score of human evaluation

Models	Fluency	Meaningful	Diversity	Entirety
Baseline	3.01	2.11	1.2	2.11
SG	4.21	3.74	3.92	4
KG	**4.25**	**4.54**	**4.43**	**4.4**

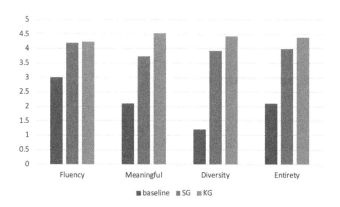

Fig. 4. Human evaluation of three models.

Moreover, the KG model owns higher scores than SG, because the encoded keyword represents global context of next generation, resulting in the increase of meaningfulness and diversity scores. Overall, both the KG and SG models have achieved satisfactory results. Furthermore, during the generation of an entire lyrics, it is too cumbersome to give one keyword for each sentence. Therefore, in the real lyrics generation, SG and KG models fuse together to compose a full-paper lyrics samples. Figure 5 shows a typical example.

Fig. 5. Generated lyrics with tune of Chinese song "Water for Forgotten Love" (忘情水).

5 Conclusion and Future Work

In this paper, we consider lyrics generation as a sequence-to-sequence learning problem, and propose a two-channel Seq2Seq generation model conditioned on input melody. Better than the baseline, our model jointly learns contextual information and syllable structures, verified by both automatic and human evaluation. Moreover, our proposed approach can be extended to other kinds of language structure control, including poetry rhythm and specific language templates.

To generate perfect lyrics, there are still further works for model polishing. The topic and emotion of the entire lyrics is difficult to handle only through encoding keywords and contextual sentences. Therefore, encoding channels can be scaled to fuse more controlling information, including global theme, sentiment or other literature styles.

Acknowledgement. This work was supported by Ping An Technology (Shenzhen) Co., Ltd., China.

References

Oliveira, H.: PoeTryMe: a versatile platform for poetry generation. Computational Creativity (2012)

He, J., Zhou, M., Jiang, L.: Generating Chinese classical poems with statistical machine translation models. In: Proceedings AAAI (2012)

Yi, X., Li, R., Sun, M.: Generating Chinese classical poems with RNN encoder-decoder. arXiv: 1604.01537 (2016)

Wang, Q., Luo, T., Wang, D., Xing, C.: Chinese song iambics generation with neural attention-based model. arXiv:1604.06274 (2016)

Potash, P., Romanov, A., Rumshisky, A.: Ghostwriter: using an LSTM for automatic rap lyric generation. In: EMNLP, pp. 1919–1924 (2015)

Sutskever, I., Vinyals, O., Le, Q.V.: Sequence to sequence learning with neural networks. In: Advances in Neural Information Processing Systems, pp. 3104–3112 (2014)

Mikolov, T., Kombrink, S., Burget, L., Černocký, J.H., Khudanpur, S.: Extensions of recurrent neural network language model. In: 2011 IEEE International Conference on Acoustics, Speech and Signal Processing (ICASSP), pp. 5528–5531. IEEE (2011)

Bahdanau, D., Cho, K., Bengio, Y.: Neural machine translation by jointly learning to align and translate. arXiv preprint arXiv:1409.0473 (2014)

Ghazvininejad, M., Shi, X., Choi, Y.: Generating topical poetry. In: Proceedings of the 2016 Conference on Empirical Methods in Natural Language Processing (2016)

Liu, B., Lane, I.: Attention-Based Recurrent Neural Network Models for Joint Intent Detection and Slot Filling (2016)

Watanabe, K., Matsubayashi, Y., Fukayama, S., Goto, M., Inui1, K., Nakano, T.: A melody-conditioned lyrics language model. In: Proceedings of NAACL-HLT, pp. 163–172 (2018)

An End-to-End Preprocessor Based on Adversiarial Learning for Mongolian Historical Document OCR

Xiangdong Su[✉], Huali Xu[✉], Yue Zhang[✉], Yanke Kang, Guanglai Gao,
and Batusiren

College of Computer Science, Inner Mongolia University, Hohhot, China
sxddxs5747@sina.com, xuhuali.purple@gmail.com, 31709030@mail.imu.edu.cn

Abstract. In Mongolian historical document recognition, preprocessing mainly involves image binarization and denoising. This is a challenging task and greatly effects the accuracy of the recognition result. Concerning the fact that image binarization and denoising are both image-to-image tasks, this paper proposes an end-to-end preprocessor for Mongolian historical document OCR. The preprocessor is trained in an adversarial learning fashion and deal with binarization and denoising simultaneously. The input of the preprocessor is the color image of Mongolian document images, and the output is the clean binary images which can be used for word recognition. The preprocessor was trained on a limited dataset and performed better than the combination of binarization and denoising methods used in earlier Mongolian historical document OCR systems.

Keywords: Adversiarial learning · Preprocessing · Binarization · Denoising · OCR

1 Introduction

Recently, a trend of digitizing historical documents has emerged to facilitate access and preservation. Inner Mongolia, an autonomous region of northern China, is home to a substantial number of ancient Mongolian books. The Mongolian Kanjur is well known among these books and is considered to be an encyclopedia. It consists of 108 volumes altogether. Each volume contains 800 pages. The total number of words is about 20,000,000. It encompasses history, literature, religion, sociology, and many other subjects. To protect this native literature and facilitate its retrieval, a more efficient way involves converting these images into text using optical character recognition (OCR).

Document OCR is usually divided into three stages, including preprocessing, word recognition and post-processing. The first stage involves image binarization and denoising. It has a great influence on the accuracy of the recognition result. In fact, there are two challenges in the preprocessing step of Mongolian

© Springer Nature Switzerland AG 2019
A. C. Nayak and A. Sharma (Eds.): PRICAI 2019, LNAI 11672, pp. 266–272, 2019.
https://doi.org/10.1007/978-3-030-29894-4_21

historical document OCR. The first one is finding the best threshold for binarization. The second is denoising these document images which contain severe and various noises. The noise is mainly caused by several reasons. At first, since the Mongolian Kanjur was produced using woodblock printing during the Qing Dynasty, ink spreading caused the spur noise in the documents. Meanwhile, pigment shedding introduced much noise during the preservation of this ancient book. Besides, the scanning process results in some noise since the protective film is worn during scanning. Therefore, a more sophisticate preprocessor is necessary for the OCR system.

From the perspective of image processing, document image binarization and denoising are both image-to-image tasks. The former is converting the color image to a binary image, and the latter is converting the binary images with noise to clean ones. A more efficient way is integrating the binarization and denoising into a unified framework. In this paper, the preprocessor tackles binarization and denoising in one step with conditional GAN, which was proved to be suitable for the image-to-image task. Denton et al. in [8] introduce a generative model capable of producing high-quality samples of natural images. Gauthier in [9] applies a conditional GAN to generate faces with specifc attributes. Inspired by the pix2pix work [1], we take conditional GAN [2] as a solution to preprocessing of Mongolian historical document OCR and learned an end-to-end preprocessor for this task. The input of the preprocessor is the color image of Mongolian Kanjur, and the output is the clean binary images which can be used for word recognition.

As a deep learning model, GAN was first proposed by Goodfellow in 2014 [3]. It cast generative modeling as a game between two networks: a generator network produces synthetic data given some noise source and a discriminator network discriminates between the generator's output and true data. After training, the generator can produce fairly good output. When adding a condition to the generator in GAN, we can control the output of the generator more closer to our expectations. This allows the condition GAN is quite suitable for image-to-image problems.

There are three main advantages of the proposed approach. First, we formulate the document image preprocessing as a pix2pix problem and take condition GAN to solve this problem. The whole process requires no threshold computing, filter design and mapping function formulation. Second, our approach performs better than the combination of binarization and denoising methods used in earlier Mongolian historical document OCR systems. Third, our approach runs faster than multi-stage preprocessor. This paper also set an example of document preprocessing for other OCR systems.

2 Proposed Preprocessor

2.1 Module Architecture

This paper takes conditional GAN [2] as a solution to preprocessing of Mongolian historical document OCR and learned an end-to-end preprocessor for this task. As shown in Fig. 1, the conditional GAN consists of two components. The discriminator network D maps from an output image to a probability that the image is from the real data distribution: $D(x) \rightarrow (0, 1)$. In contrast, the generator network G maps from random noise vector z and observed condition x (Mongolian historical document image) to target clean image y: $G(z, x) \rightarrow y$. These two networks are trained iteratively. For a fixed generator G, the discriminator D is trained to classify the output image as either being from the training data (close to 1) or a fixed generator (close to 0). When the discriminator is optimal, it can be frozen, and the generator G can continue to be trained to lower the accuracy of the discriminator. The generator possesses an encoder-decoder structure. The input (including the noise z and the color image y) is first compressed into a higher level representation through a series of encoders (convolution + activation function). Then, the compressed representation is converted into the target image through a series of decoders (deconvolution + activation function).

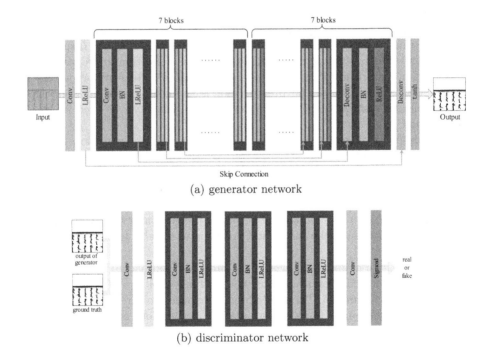

(a) generator network

(b) discriminator network

Fig. 1. The generator network and discriminator network

Batch normalization is used in each convolutional layer to ensure network performance and stability [10,11]. Both of the modules here take the form convolution-BatchNorm-ReLu [10]. The discriminator also uses an encoder-like structure, in which the inputs are the preprocessed images from the generator and the ground truth. They are concatenated together and passed through the processing modules in sequence.

The objective of the conditional GAN can be expressed as Eq. (3):

$$\mathcal{L}_{conditionalGAN}(G, D) = \mathbb{E}_{x,y}[logD(x, y)] + \mathbb{E}_{x,z}[log(1 - D(x, G(x, z)))] \quad (1)$$

Where G tries to minimize this objective against an adversarial D that tries to maximize it.

The previous study has proved that it is beneficial to mix the GAN objective with a $L1$ loss function [1]. The discriminator's job remains unchanged, but the generator is tasked with not only fooling the discriminator but also being near the ground truth output from a $L1$ perspective. The $L1$ loss function can be written as Eq. (2):

$$\mathcal{L}_{L1}(G) = \mathbb{E}_{x,y,z}[y - G(x, z)] \quad (2)$$

Thus, the final objective is Eq. (3):

$$G^* = \arg\min_{G}\max_{D}(\mathcal{L}_{conditionalGAN}(G, D) + \lambda\mathcal{L}_{L_1}(G)) \quad (3)$$

2.2 Optimization

We follow the literature [12] to design the generator in conditional GAN. We directly give an output of each ith convolution layer to the $(n-i)$th deconvolution layer by adding a skip connection between them, where n is the total number of layers. Previous work [13] has proved the fact that $L1$ loss can excellently capture the low frequencies of the images and Patch-GAN can sufficiently model high-frequency structure of those images. Therefore, the PatchGAN used in image-to-image tasks also adopted in our approach. This discriminator D tries to classify if each $N \times N$ patch in an output image is real or fake, averaging all responses to provide the ultimate output of discriminator D.

3 Experiments

3.1 Data Set and Evaluation Metric

In this section, we evaluate the proposed preprocessor on Mongolian historical documents images with complex noise. The dataset consists of the scanned images of Mongolian Kanjur, whose width and height are 17196 pixels and 5621 pixels individually. Since the preprocessor is trained with several paired color images and their corresponding clean binary images, we created the clean binary image in a semiautomatic way. At first, we automatically binarize the color image with OTSU [4], and then manually remove the noise in the binary image. The repaired binary image is used as the ground truth.

To train the model more efficiently, images need to be cut into 2048×2048 blocks. In the segmentation process, we start with the upper left corner of the image. For the image edge part whose width and height are less than 2048 pixels, we recalculate 2048 pixels from the right and the bottom, and segment them.

There are 405 samples in the training dataset (2048×2048 pixel), 135 samples in validation dataset, and 135 samples in the test dataset.

In our experiment, we use three metrics to evaluate the proposed preprocessor, including peak signal-to-noise ratio (PSNR), structural similarity measure (SSIM) and mean opinion score (MOS).

3.2 Related Methods for Comparison

To systematically evaluate the proposed system, we compare the proposed preprocessor with four methods. The first one is the combination of OTSU algorithm [4] (image binarization) and Gaussian Filter (image denoising), belonging to the traditional method. Three other methods are recently proposed deep learning methods, including Grid LSTM [5], SAE [6], and FCN [7].

3.3 Result and Discussion

The experimental results are summarized in Table 1. Our model achieves a PSNR 43.89, an SSIM 0.9942, and a MOS 4.6. It performs best among the listed models, indicating that it does a very good job at binarization and denoising for Mongolian historical document. This is owing to the well-defined network architecture. Compared to the deep learning based models, the combination of OTSU and Gaussian Filter is the worst.

Table 1. Performance comparison in terms of PSNR, SSIM and MOS

Model	PSNR	SSIM	MOS
OTSU+Gaussian Filter	14.82	0.8665	3.2
Grid LSTM [5]	26.81	0.9273	3.2
SAE [6]	38.52	0.9812	3.9
FCN [7]	41.78	0.9881	4.4
Ours	**43.89**	**0.9942**	**4.6**

Figure 2 shows the results coming from the proposed preprocessor and related methods for comparison. Due to each image of the Mongolian historical document (Mongolian Kanjur) is very large, we only show a clip of them. From the figure, we can see that the proposed preprocessor obtains the best performance.

From the point of denoising, the proposed preprocessor can distinguish between noise and text in images, so that the noise can be well removed while the text part does not be interfered in the preprocessing. This is because the model is trained in an adversarial way with a few of paired images (color images with noise and clean binary images). The proposed approach can automatically fill the incomplete parts of text resulting from pigment shedding. Filling actions are learned from hand-restored images, and the repaired results are is consistent with our expectations. Figure 3 shows a word in the Mongolian Kanjur, in which Fig. 3(a) is the word in the color document image, Fig. 3(b) is its appearance

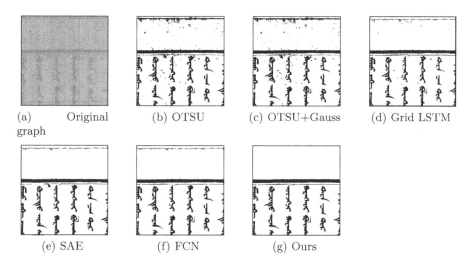

(a)   Original   (b) OTSU   (c) OTSU+Gauss   (d) Grid LSTM
graph

(e) SAE   (f) FCN   (g) Ours

Fig. 2. Illutstration of the processing results with different methods

after binarization with OTSU method, and Fig. 3(c) is its appearance proposed by our approach. It demonstrates that our approach can handle noise resulting from pigment shedding in document reservation.

(a) a Mongo-
lain word

(b) word pro-
cessed with
OTSU

(c) word pro-
cessed with our
approach

Fig. 3. Single word comparison

4   Conclusion

To deal with image binarization and denoising in Mongolian historical document OCR, this paper proposes an end-to-end preprocessor based on adversarial learning. The preprocessor is trained in an adversarial learning fashion and deal with binarization and denoising simultaneously. The input of the preprocessor is the color image of Mongolian historical document images, and the output is the clean binary images which can be used for word recognition. Compared with the combination models of a binarization method (OTSU) and several deep learning methods, the proposed preprocessor obtains the best performance in processing effect. It can removed the noise well and fill the incomplete parts of text resulting from pigment shedding. This also set an example of document preprocessing for other OCR systems.

Acknowledgment. This work was funded by National Natural Science Foundation of China (Grant No. 61762069), Natural Science Foundation of Inner Mongolia Autonomous Region (Grant No. 2017BS0601, Grant No. 2018MS06025) and program of higher-level talents of Inner Mongolia University (Grant No. 21500-5165161).

References

1. Isola, P., Zhu, J.-Y., Zhou, T., Efros, A.A.: Image-to-image translation with conditional adversarial networks. CoRR, vol. abs/1611.07004 (2016)
2. Mirza, M., Osindero, S.: Conditional generative adversarial nets. CoRR, vol. abs/1411.1784 (2014)
3. Goodfellow, I., et al.: Generative adversarial nets. In: Advances in Neural Information Processing Systems, pp. 2672–2680 (2014)
4. Otsu, N.: A threshold selection method from gray-level histograms. IEEE Trans. Syst. Man Cybern. **9**(1), 62–66 (1979)
5. Florian, W.: Efficient document image binarization using heterogeneous computing and interactive machine learning, Licentiate Dissertation (2018)
6. Calvo-Zaragoza, J., Gallego, A.: A selectional auto-encoder approach for document image binarization (2017)
7. Tensmeyer, C., Martinez, T.: Document Image Binarization with Fully Convolutional Neural Networks (2017)
8. Szlam, A., Denton, E., Chintala, S., Fergus, R.: Deep generative image models using a laplacian pyramid of adversarial networks. In: Computer Vision and Pattern Recognition (2015)
9. Gauthier, J.: Conditional generative adversarial nets for convolutional face generation. In: Convolutional Neural Networks for Visual Recognition (2014)
10. Ioffe, S., Szegedy, C.: Batch normalization: accelerating deep network training by reducing internal covariate shift (2015)
11. Collis, J.: Glossary of deep learning: batch normalisation (2017)
12. Fischer, P., Ronneberger, O., Brox, T.: U-net: convolutional networks for biomedical image segmentation (2015)
13. Tamura, S., Waibel, A.: Noise reduction using connectionist models. In: International Conference on Acoustics, Speech, and Signal Processing, pp. 553–556 (1988)

UFANS: U-Shaped Fully-Parallel Acoustic Neural Structure for Statistical Parametric Speech Synthesis

Dabiao Ma[1], Zhiba Su[1], Wenxuan Wang[2], Yuhao Lu[1], and Zhen Li[2($\boxtimes$)]

[1] Turing Robot Ltd. Multi-modal Group, Beijing, China
{madabiao,suzhiba,luyuhao}@uzoo.cn
[2] School of Science and Engineering, Chinese University of Hong Kong, Shenzhen,
Shenzhen, Guangdong, China
wangwenxuan1@link.cuhk.edu.cn, lizhen@cuhk.edu.cn

Abstract. Neural networks with auto-regressive structures, such as Recurrent Neural Network (RNN), have become the most appealing structures for acoustic model in parametric text-to-speech synthesis (TTS). Despite the prominent ability to generate high quality results, high inference cost of RNN model prevents its usage in industry TTS applications and services. In this paper, we propose a fully-parallel convolutional neural network based acoustic model, U-shaped Fully-parallel Acoustic Neural Structure (UFANS). Experiments show our model achieves 20 times speed up in inference and is 300 times faster than real time with comparable speech quality, which is suitable for industrial level TTS services.

Keywords: Text-to-speech · Acoustic model · UFANS · U-Net · Fully-parallel

1 Introduction

Text-to-speech (TTS) systems aim to convert texts to human-like speeches. Acoustic model is a model in TTS system that maps linguistic features to acoustic features. RNNs [1,15] and auto-regressive CNNs [2,8] based acoustic models have achieved great success due to its capacity to capture long-term information. However, those types of models usually result in high time latency in computations, since the computation of current step relies on the results of previous steps.

U-Net [11], a fully-parallel convolutional neural network, is first proposed for image segmentation tasks. Down-sampling and up-sampling operation make the receptive field of U-Net increase exponentially. Skip connection structure in U-Net enable the information flow across different layers. The combination of these prominent characteristics make U-Net successful in image segmentation. Inspired by the success, U-shaped models are applied in various acoustic applications, e.g. denoise [5], audio source separation [13].

D. Ma, Z. Su and W. Wang—Equal contribution.

A. C. Nayak and A. Sharma (Eds.): PRICAI 2019, LNAI 11672, pp. 273–278, 2019.
https://doi.org/10.1007/978-3-030-29894-4_22

In this paper, we propose a fully-parallel acoustic neural structure (UFANS), motivated by U-Net, aiming to reduce industrial cost. Our model is a fully-parallel gated convolutional structure with skip connections. The characteristic of parallel ensures our system highly concurrent. The skip connection structure and the gate in convolution block control the information flows. And large receptive field helps our model capture long-term information. The experimental results show 2 things: (1) Our model is 300 times faster than real time in inference with comparable speech quality. (2) Large receptive field, the gate structure, and the skip connection structure improve speech quality. Low time latency and high speech quality are essential for industrial TTS services.

2   U-Shaped Fully-Parallel Acoustic Neural Structure (UFANS)

2.1   Overall Structure

We apply a modified U-shaped structure to speech synthesis tasks which used RNN based [1,15] acoustic model in the past. The main difference between UFANS and U-Net are listed here:

- **Different convolution structure.** We use gated convolutions [7] instead of regular convolutions. The gate structure is able to control the information flows within layers. The experiments also show that UFANS benefits from gated convolutions.
- **Different pooling method.** Image segmentation is a classification task, U-Net uses maximal pooling [3] to extract the most important spatial features. TTS is a regression task, we replace maximal pooling by average pooling to utilize all information along time dimension. The experiments also show that average pooling performs better.
- **Different input dimension.** The inputs of U-Net are 2-Dimension data, pixel values of images. Pooling and up-sampling are performed along height and width dimensions of images. The inputs of UFANS are 1-Dimension data, frames of linguistic features. Pooling and up-sampling are performed along time dimensions.

2.2   Convolution Blocks

Gated convolution is used in the two phases in UFANS; Fig. 1 is convolution block in contraction phase. 'Conv' doubles the channel dimension, after which the output of 'Conv' is split from middle along the channel dimension.

Figure 2 is the convolution block in expansive phase. The input of this block consists of two parts, 'Input1' and 'Input2'. 'Input1' is the output of the previous layer; 'Input2' is the output of the corresponding layer in contraction phase. We use dropout [12] to do generalization.

2.3   Down-Sampling and Up-Sampling

The average pooling operation plays a role of a down-sampling layer. The time dimension is reduced to half after average pooling. The deconvolution layer plays a role of up-sampling. The time dimension is doubled after the deconvolution layer. The combination of down-sampling and up-sampling makes receptive field increase exponentially.

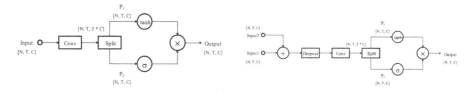

Fig. 1. Contraction phase   **Fig. 2.** Expansive phase.

Suppose the depth of UFANS is N, which means there are N down-sampling and up-sampling operations. The number of adjacent frames S_N that offer information to one specific acoustic frame is determined by the following iteration.

$$S_i = 2 * (S_{i-1} + 2), S_0 = 0, i = 1, ..., N \tag{1}$$

3   Experiments and Results

3.1   Dataset

We use two female Mandarin datasets to do experiments. Each dataset has about 10500 utterances, each utterance lasts from 3 s to 7 s and sample rate is 24 kHz. We extracted 60-dimensional mel-cepstral coefficients, 5-dimensional band-aperiodicity parameters, 1-dimensional logarithmic fundamental frequency and their delta, delta-delta dynamic features [14], and one additional voiced/unvoiced dimension. The inputs are frame based linguistic features with dimension 165, up-sampled and aligned with manually annotated ground truth duration tagging. WORLD [6] deterministic vocoder is used to synthesize audios. Both the linguistic and acoustic features are normalized before training.

3.2   Model Hyper-Parameters

As far as we know, no fully-parallel convolutional structure has been applied as a acoustic system in speech synthesis. So we compare our model with several RNN based baseline systems.

The Bi-LSTM baseline system consists of four dense layers with 1024 channels, followed by one Bi-LSTM layer with 384 channels for each direction, as is used in [15]. We also train a larger one that consists of one dense layer with 2048 channels and three Bi-LSTM layers with 1024 channels for each direction, which is used as baseline model in [1]. The Bi-SRU system consists of three dense layers with 1024 channels and four Bi-SRU layers with 512 channels in each direction. The DNN system consists of three dense layers with 1024 channels [10]. UFANS uses nine down-samplings and up-samplings, $3 * 3$ kernel gated convolutions with 256 channels in all blocks except in the final block where a regular convolution with 512 channels is used.

Table 1. Comparison of objective results.

Model	MSE	Parameter size (MB)	Parallel	Inference time (ms)	Training time (s)
Bi-LSTM [1]	192.8	292	No	243	184917
Bi-LSTM [15]	195.3	30	No	69	49260
Bi-SRU	194.9	74	No	44	35491
DNN [10]	209.2	9.5	Yes	0.84	5214
UFANS	194.6	42	Yes	3.2	6724

The frame level based mean squared error (MSE) is taken as the training criteria. We train all models by Adam [4] method with batch size 16, initial learning rate 0.0004 and β_1, β_2 to be $0.9, 0.999$. The model is implemented with MXNET. We trained all models to achieve best validation records. Training is finished in 5 h on a single GTX Titan X GPU.

3.3   Performance Comparison

Two methods are used to evaluate the performance of our generated speeches, i.e., quantitative results and user study.

Quantitative Results. The quantitative results of our experiments are presented in Table 1, where MSE is averaged between the two speaker cases. The inference speed is evaluated as the time latency to synthesize one-second speech, which includes data transfer from main memory to GPU global memory, GPU calculations and data transfer back to main memory. The larger Bi-LSTM system got the lowest MSE while at the cost of a much larger parameter size and a much lower inference speed. Actually, as we will see in the following section, the speeches synthesized from UFANS even have comparable quality with the speeches synthesized from the larger Bi-LSTM system. Bi-SRU got slightly better MSE than Bi-LSTM system used in [15], while Bi-SRU is faster. UFANS got better MSE than Bi-LSTM system in [15] with a speed-up factor of 23, and a speed-up of 76 compared with the larger Bi-LSTM system. We did all experiments on GeForce GTX TITAN X devices.

User Study. We did a user study to compare the quality of synthesized speeches with above systems. We randomly selected 20 Mandarin reviewers (10 female and 10 male) who are qualified to judge qualities of speeches. The score ranges from 1 (bad) to 5 (excellent). We also computed 95% confidence interval for each score using crowdMOS method [9]. The results show that UFANS is able to generate comparable or better speeches than RNN based baseline systems.

4   Conclusion

In this paper, we propose an U-shaped Fast Acoustic Neural Structure (UFANS). Our structure greatly reduces the time cost in training and inference with comparable speech quality. We show the possibility and promising prospect of applying fully-parallel CNN structure to industrial TTS applications and services. We also show that large receptive field (long-time information dependency), the gate structure (information flows) and the skip connection structure(combination of different level features) in UFANS ensure high speech quality.

References

1. Bi, M., Lu, H., Zhang, S., Lei, M., Yan, Z.: Deep feed-forward sequential memory networks for speech synthesis. In: ICASSP (2018). http://arxiv.org/abs/1802.09194
2. Blaauw, M., Bonada, J.: A neural parametric singing synthesizer. arXiv preprint arXiv:1704.03809 (2017)
3. Ciresan, D.C., Meier, U., Schmidhuber, J.: Multi-column deep neural networks for image classification. In: CVPR, pp. 3642–3649 (2012). http://arxiv.org/abs/1202.2745
4. Kingma, D.P., Ba, J.: Adam: a method for stochastic optimization. In: 3rd International Conference for Learning Representations (2014). http://arxiv.org/abs/1412.6980
5. Liu, B., Nie, S., Zhang, Y., Ke, D., Liang, S., Liu, W.: Boosting noise robustness of acoustic model via deep adversarial training. arXiv preprint arXiv:1805.01357 (2018)
6. Morise, M., Yokomori, F., Ozawa, K.: World: a vocoder-based high-quality speech synthesis system for real-time applications. IEICE Trans. Inf. Syst. **99**(7), 1877–1884 (2016)
7. van den Oord, A., Kalchbrenner, N., Vinyals, O., Espeholt, L., Graves, A., Kavukcuoglu, K.: Conditional image generation with PixelCNN decoders. In: Neural Information Processing Systems (2016). http://arxiv.org/abs/1606.05328
8. Ping, W., et al.: Deep Voice 3: Scaling Text-to-Speech with Convolutional Sequence Learning (2018)
9. Protasio Ribeiro, F., Florencio, D., Zhang, C., Seltzer, M.: CROWDMOS: an approach for crowdsourcing mean opinion score studies. In: ICASSP. IEEE, May 2011. https://www.microsoft.com/en-us/research/publication/crowdmos-an-approach-for-crowdsourcing-mean-opinion-score-studies/

10. Qian, Y., Fan, Y., Hu, W., Soong, F.K.: On the training aspects of deep neural network (DNN) for parametric TTS synthesis. In: 2014 IEEE International Conference on Acoustics, Speech and Signal Processing (ICASSP), pp. 3829–3833. IEEE (2014)

11. Ronneberger, O., Fischer, P., Brox, T.: U-net: Convolutional networks for biomedical image segmentation. In: Medical Image Computing and Computer Assisted Intervention, pp. 234–241 (2015). http://arxiv.org/abs/1505.04597

12. Srivastava, N., Hinton, G.E., Krizhevsky, A., Sutskever, I., Salakhutdinov, R.: Dropout: a simple way to prevent neural networks from overfitting. J. Mach. Learn. Res. **15**(1), 1929–1958 (2014). http://www.cs.toronto.edu/ rsalakhu/papers/srivastava14a.pdf

13. Stoller, D., Ewert, S., Dixon, S.: Wave-u-net: a multi-scale neural network for end-to-end audio source separation. arXiv preprint arXiv:1806.03185 (2018)

14. Tokuda, K., Yoshimura, T., Masuko, T., Kobayashi, T., Kitamura, T.: Speech parameter generation algorithms for HMM-based speech synthesis. In: ICASSP (2000)

15. Wu, Z., Watts, O., King, S.: Merlin: an open source neural network speech synthesis system. In: 9th ISCA Speech Synthesis Workshop 2016, pp. 202–207, September 2016. https://doi.org/10.21437/SSW.2016-33

A Hierarchical Attention Based Seq2Seq Model for Chinese Lyrics Generation

Haoshen Fan[1,2(✉)], Jie Wang[2(✉)], Bojin Zhuang[2], Shaojun Wang[2], and Jing Xiao[2]

[1] University of Science and Technology of China, Hefei, China
[2] Ping An Technology (Shenzhen) Co., Ltd., Shenzhen, China
photonicsjay@163.com

Abstract. In this paper, we comprehensively study on context-aware generation of Chinese song lyrics. Conventional text generative models generate a sequence or sentence word by word, failing to consider the contextual relationship between sentences. Taking account into the characteristics of lyrics, a hierarchical attention based Seq2Seq (Sequence-to-Sequence) model is proposed for Chinese lyrics generation. With encoding of word-level and sentence-level contextual information, this model promotes the topic relevance and consistency of generation. A large Chinese lyrics corpus is also leveraged for model training. Eventually, results of automatic and human evaluations demonstrate that our model is able to compose complete Chinese lyrics with one united topic constraint.

Keywords: Natural language generation · Seq2Seq · Gate recurrent unit · Attention

1 Introduction

Natural language generation (NLG) (Mann 1982), also known as text generation, is one of most important tasks in the field of natural language processing (Chowdhury 2003). NLG has been extensively studied in many applications, such as dialogue system (Chen et al. 2017), machine translation (Cho et al. 2014), text summarization (Nallapati et al. 2016) and so on. In this paper, however, we concentrate on Chinese lyric text generation. Different from prose texts, lyrics exhibits its own significant characteristics, including rhyme, rhetoric and repeated structures. In the perspective of narrative, a lyrics paragraph always concentrates on one main topic due to its limited length, which is totally different from long documents often covering several topics. Moreover, sentence length of lyrics is always short, in a range of 8 to 15 words, which results in close contextual relationship between adjacent sentences.

In general, most of text generation models can be extended for lyrics generation. In the area of text generation, there exist two main approaches, one of which is probabilistic language model (LM) and the other is Sequence-to-Sequence (Seq2Seq). LM has been successfully used in various NLG applications, which is capable of predicting next words on the premise of prior contexts. For instance, Bengio used n-gram model of three layers to construct a language model (Bengio et al. 2003). Then, Mikolov

© Springer Nature Switzerland AG 2019
A. C. Nayak and A. Sharma (Eds.): PRICAI 2019, LNAI 11672, pp. 279–288, 2019.
https://doi.org/10.1007/978-3-030-29894-4_23

promoted LM with recurrent neural network (RNN) (Mikolov 2010). However, LM even with long-short term memory (LSTM) network would suffer from semantic shift along with the accumulation of sequence length (Hochreither and Schmidhuber 1997). To address sequence transduction between heterogeneous data, a sequence-to-sequence model was proposed (Sutskever et al. 2014). Taking a sequence as input, Seq2Seq can encode it into a fixed dense vector and then decode to another sequence. Moreover, Bahdanau applied the attention mechanism to the Seq2Seq in order to diffuse decoding weights into different parts of input (Bahdanau et al. 2015). Based on Seq2Seq, text generation can be defined as next sentence prediction on the premise of prior sentences. In most of Seq2Seq applications, however, input contexts are formed based on sequential concatenation of previous sentences directly. Consequently, the semantic effect of sub-sequences far from the decoder could become weaker on prediction.

To generate long-paragraph Chinese lyrics with high contextual relevance and consistence, in this paper, we propose a hierarchical recurrent encoder (HRE) incorporated into the seq2seq framework. HRE can extract both sentence-level and word-level semantics from prior sentences, providing more contextual information for decoding. Moreover, the attention mechanism covering the most adjacent sentence is applied, considering the closest connection with next prediction. The rest of the article will be structured as follows: Sect. 4.1 describes the data preprocess of Chinese lyrics corpus, Sect. 3 describes the details of our model, Sect. 4 describes the experiments on several models, Sect. 2 briefly introduces the related work and we make some conclusion in Sect. 5.

2 Related Work

NLG is an essential part of natural language processing (NLP). According to the modality of input, there exist text-to-text generation, meaning-to-text generation, data-to-text generation, image-to-text generation etc. In this paper, lyrics generation is modeled as a specific text-to-text generation with previous sentences as input. Similar tasks including Chinese poetry generation (Wang et al. 2016), essay generation (Feng et al. 2018) and comment generation (Tang et al. 2016) have been extensively studied. Chinese poetry generation generate a kind of hierarchical text with strict format which often has a fixed number of sentences and each sentence has a fixed number of words. For instance, to generate context-aware comments, Tang proposed to encode the context as a continuous semantic representation into a basic RNN model. Moreover, essay generation covering several topic words has also been demonstrated by similar methods.

Various hierarchical models have been used for generating coherent long texts. For example, Li proposed a hierarchical neural auto-encoder to build an embedding for a paragraph (Li et al. 2015). Lin presented a novel hierarchical recurrent neural network language model (HRNNLM) to maintain overall coherence in a document (Lin et al. 2015). Following the HRED proposed by Sordoni (2015), Serban extended the hierarchical model to promote dialogue generation with long-term contexts (Serban and Bengio et al. 2016). Later, he enhanced the HRED model with a latent variable at the decoder (Serban and Sordoni et al. 2016). Furthermore, a hierarchical seq2seq with attention is proposed by us for Chinese lyrics generation to address the long-term coherence.

3 Model

In this section, a hierarchical attention based Seq2Seq model for lyrics generation is described. Original lyrics has been preprocessed into the paragraph format for model training in advance. Here, a lyrics paragraph comprises a sequence of M sentences, i.e. $P = \{S_1, S_2, \ldots, S_M\}$. Each sentence S_m consists of a sequence of N_m words $S_m = \{\omega_{m,1}, \omega_{m,2}, \ldots \omega_{m,N_m}\}$, where $\omega_{m,n}$ represents the word at position n in sentence m.

3.1 Recurrent Neural Network

A recurrent neural network (RNN) model recurrently calculates a vector named recurrent state or hidden state h_n by taking a sequence of words $\{\omega_1, \omega_2, \ldots, \omega_N\}$:

$$h_n = f(h_{n-1}, \omega_n), n \in (1, N), h_0 = 0 \tag{1}$$

Particularly, the h_0 denote the initial state and always is set as zero at the time of training. Usually, h_n depends on the current word ω_n and previous ones before the current time step. In Eq. 1, f denotes a parametrized non-linear function, such as sigmoid, hyperbolic tangent, long-short term memory (LSTM) and gate recurrent unit (GRU). The hidden state will lose long contextual information when a vanilla RNN such as sigmoid or hyperbolic tangent is used. Through bringing in a memory cell, LSTM or GRU can handle longer-term contexts. Moreover, GRU requires less computational cost compared with LSTM. Thus, GRU is used as the RNN cell unit. The equations of GRU are summarized as follows:

$$z_t = \sigma(W_z \omega_t + U_z h_{t-1}) \tag{2}$$

$$r_t = \sigma(W_r \omega_t + U_r h_{t-1}) \tag{3}$$

$$\widetilde{h}_t = \tanh(W \omega_t + U(r_t * h_{t-1})) \tag{4}$$

$$h_t = (1 - z_t) * h_{t-1} + z_t * \widetilde{h}_t \tag{5}$$

In the Equation above, the σ is the non-linear function i.e. logistic sigmoid, which limits output to range [0, 1]. z_t is the update gate deciding the weight of input information past, and r_t is the reset gate determining the weight of last state. The candidate update $\widetilde{h}_t$ controls the percentage of information obtained from h_{t-1} with reset gate. The final update h_t depends on the update gate and candidate update. The subscript letter t represents the time step.

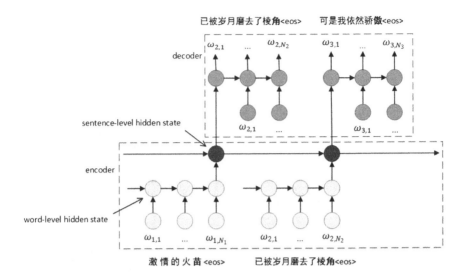

Fig. 1. The graph of HRED model constructing a Chinese lyrics paragraph with three sentences. The word-level encoder the sentences into a fix dense vector and the sentence-level encoder map the vectors into the representation of paragraph, which is the input of decoder. We bold the last rhyming word.

3.2 Hierarchical Recurrent Encoder

Sordoni proposed a hierarchical recurrent encoder-decoder (HRED) to predict a next web query conditioned on previous queries submitted by users (Sordoni et al. 2015). The hierarchical encoder consists of query-level and session-level encoders, which has been demonstrated very successful for web query prediction. Following this HRED work, a lyrics paragraph is considered with hierarchical structure of word-level and sentence-level as shown in Fig. 1. At the bottom of the network, the sentence-level RNN encodes each sentence into a fix dense vector. This higher-level semantic vector is used to predict the next sentence S_{m+1}.

Different from web queries, however, a lyrics paragraph always contains more than ten sentences. Thus, we adapt this HRE to handle a certain number of sentences before decoding as shown in Fig. 2. The number of sub-group sentences is denoted as *Num*, which is a hyper-parameter. After some trial and error, the *Num* is optimized as 5. Note that GRU is used as the basic RNN cell unit. Moreover, the word-level encoder and the decoder share same parameters.

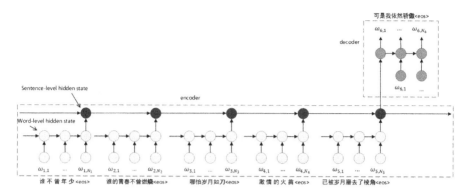

Fig. 2. Hierarchical Seq2Seq extending HRED.

3.3   Decoder

In the decoder, the last state of the sentence-level RNN is used as the initial state. The probability distribution in the time t. represented:

$$p(\omega_t|s, \omega_1, \ldots, \omega_{t-1}) = g\big(h_{t,dec}, \omega_{t-1}, s\big) \tag{6}$$

In the Eq. 6, the s is the last state of the sentence-level encoder. The state $h_{t,dec}$ can be denoted as:

$$h_{t,dec} = f\big(h_{t-1,dec}, \omega_{t-1}, s\big) \tag{7}$$

S2Seq with attention was first proposed by Dzmitry and has achieved a great success in various NLG applications. Here, the attention mechanism is incorporated into the hierarchical model and applied to the word-level encoder. The difference between seq 2seq with attention and conventional seq2seq is that the decoder uses different context vector s_t in each step as:

$$h_{t,dec} = f\big(h_{t-1,dec}, \omega_{t-1}, s_t\big) \tag{8}$$

The context vector s_t is a weighted sum of the encoder hidden states $\big\{h_{1,dec}, h_{2,dec}, \ldots, h_{N_m,dec}\big\}$:

$$s_t = \sum\nolimits_{j=1}^{N_m} a_{tj} h_{j,enc} \tag{9}$$

where the a_{tj} is computed by decoder hidden state $h_{t-1,dec}$ and each encoder hidden state $\big\{h_{1,dec}, h_{2,dec}, \ldots, h_{N_m,dec}\big\}$. As shown in Fig. 3, we only use the sequence of hidden states of last sentence S_{m-1} as the input of attention while predicting the next sentence S_m because of the strongest semantic relationship between adjacent sentences. Finally, beam search is used in the inference stage.

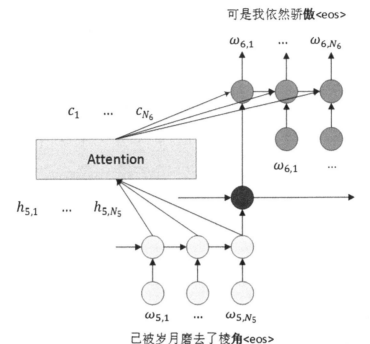

Fig. 3. Hierarchical Seq2Seq with attention.

4   Experiments and Results

In this section, settings of experimental parameters are described at detail. A generic Seq2Seq model is applied as a baseline. Tensorflow framework is used to implement the hierarchical attention based Seq2Seq model because of its flexibility and accumulated development experiences shared in community (Tang 2016).

4.1   Data Processing

Lyrics in monolingual Chinese was collected to guarantee the same data structure. 100,000 pop song lyrics has been prepared, which is familiar with most Chinese Netizens. Based on this corpus, a prior vocabulary of 7030 words was achieved. Filtering out 1985 low frequency words which occur less than 10 times in the paragraphs, our vocabulary size is eventually 5045. Additionally, the following three symbols have been added into this vocabulary, including 'unk' representing unknown words, 'go' and 'eos' donating the start and end of sentences. Besides, the maximum length of all sentences is limited to 20. Those sentences longer than 20 have been filtered out. Finally, the prepared corpus was divided into two parts, 90% as training data while 10% as test data.

4.2   Parameters Setting

We use the word embedding with dimension 300 to represent the words. Specifically, the word embedding is defined as the trainable parameters, which will be fine-tuned as the training progress. The word-level encoder has 1000 hidden unit. To keep the sentences talking the same topic and memorizing complex topics and emotion, we set the dimensionality of sentence-level encoder and decoder to 1500. Moreover, the word-level encoder has 3 layers to ensure the model can encode the complex lyrics sentences while the sentence-level encoder and decoder has 1 layer. Finally, the beam width k is set to 5. All of the parameters are randomly initialized within the range [−0.5, 0.5]. They are trained to minimize the cross-entropy loss function with the Adam optimizer (Kingma and Ba 2015). We set the mini-batch to 256. We train the model until the loss function has a minimum value and is no less than that in the next three epochs.

4.3   Evaluation Metrics

Human Evaluation
Nine Chinese experts are asked to evaluate the performance of our model. They are asked to mark generated lyrics samples from three different aspects: Topic Relevance, Fluency and Semantic Coherence. The score is range from 1 to 5. 5000 lyrics paragraphs are randomly generated for graduate students majored in Music to score.

BLEU
Additionally, we use Bilingual Evaluation Understudy (BLEU) as our automatic evaluation (Papineni et al. 2002). BLEU is an evaluation method widely used for machine translation. In this paper, the test dataset is used as the reference ground truth for automatic evaluation.

Table 1. Averaged score of different model for lyrics text generation.

Model	Topic relevance	Fluency	Semantic coherence	Average score
Seq2Seq	2.34	2.99	2.38	2.57
Hierarchical Seq2Seq	2.99	2.79	2.76	2.85
Hierarchical Seq2Seq with attention	**3.11**	**3.17**	**3.46**	**3.24**

4.4   Experimental Results

Table 1 shows the final results of human evaluation of different models. The basic Seq2Seq model exhibits the worst performance since it only considers the adjacent sentences, which can't maintain the long-term semantic coherence. In comparison, the hierarchical Seq2Seq model boosts the performance in terms of "Topic Relevance" and "Semantic Coherence". The main reason is that the hierarchical model is able to remember higher-level semantics due to the sentence-level encoding. However, the poor performance of the hierarchical model in "Fluency" is attributed to the omission of word-level encoding. Thus, the hierarchical Seq2Seq with attention performs best in all three perspectives. The attention mechanism helps the model directly connect the semantic relationship between adjacent sentences while retaining higher-level contextual information.

Table 2. BLEU scores of different models.

Model	BLEU score
Seq2Seq	0.189
Hierarchical Seq2Seq	0.274
Hierarchical Seq2Seq with attention	0.288

Table 3. Example of generated lyrics. The blue text is the lyrics generated by the hierarchical Seq 2Seq model with attention. Note that the first line "Homeland" is the title of the lyrics.

故乡
Homeland

看那田地看那原野,
Look-at-the-farmland-and-look-at-the-field,

一片美丽好风光,
It's-a-beautiful-scenery.

俄罗斯的大自然啊,
Nature-in-Russia,

这是我的故乡。
Is-my-hometown.

看那高山看那平地,
Look-at-the-mountain-and-the-at-land,

无边草原和牧场。
Borderless-grasslands-and-pastures.

俄罗斯的辽阔地方,
Russia's-vast-territory,

是我梦中的故乡。
Is-my-dream-home.

看那远方的山,
Look-at-the-mountains-in-the-distance,

看那辽阔的草原,
Look-at-the-vast-grassland,

是那遥远的天堂,
It's-a-distant-paradise,

那遥远的故乡。
The-remote-homeland.

In order to make the evaluation result more objective, we also show the BLEU result in Table 2. Obviously, the results of BLEU show the same trend as those of human evaluation. The hierarchical Seq2Seq preforms better than Seq2Seq model and the hierarchical Seq2Seq with attention performs better than the hierarchical Seq2Seq. Compared with other area of text generation such as machine translation, the BLEU results are very small. The reason is that the generated lyrics use different word combinations to express the same meaning while each word of the text to be translated often has a unique correct answer. Finally, a sample of generated lyrics is given in Table 3. Those underlined and bold Chinese characters at the ending of sentences are rhyming.

5 Conclusions

In this paper, we propose a novel hierarchical Seq2Seq model with attention for Chinese lyrics generation. A large-scale Chinese lyrics corpus has been leveraged for model training. Results of human and BLEU evaluation demonstrate the effectiveness of this model owing to its sentence-level semantic encoding and attended to adjacent sentences. Moreover, this hierarchical encoder method offers a promising approach of context fusing for other NLG applications.

Acknowledgement. This work was supported by Ping An Technology (Shenzhen) Co., Ltd, China.

References

Mann, W.: Text generation. Comput. Linguist. **8**, 62–69 (1982)

Chowdhury, G.G.: Natural language processing. Annu. Rev. Inf. Sci. Technol. **37**, 51–89 (2003)

Chen, H., Liu, X., Yin, D., Tang, J.: A survey on dialogue systems: recent advances and new frontiers. ACM SIGKDD Explor. Newslett. **19**, 25–35 (2017)

Cho, K., et al.: Learning phrase representations using RNN encoder-decoder for statistical machine translation. Computer Science (2014)

Nallapati, R., Zhou, B., dos santos, C.N., Gulcehre, C., Xiang, B.: Abstractive text summarization using sequence-to-sequence RNNs and beyond. In: Conference on Computational Natural Language Learning (2016)

Bengio, Y., Ducharme, R., Vincent, P., Janvin, C.: A neural probabilistic language model. J. Mach. Learn. Res. **3**, 1137–1155 (2003)

Mikolov, T.: Recurrent neural network based language model. Interspeech **2**, 3 (2010)

Hochreither, S., Schmidhuber, J.: Long short-term memory. Neural Comput. **9**, 1735–1780 (1997)

Sutskever, I., Vinyals, O., Le, Q.V.: Sequence to sequence learning with neural networks. In: Advances in Neural Information Processing Systems, pp. 3104–3112 (2014)

Bahdanau, D., Cho, K., Bengio, Y.: Neural machine translation by jointly learning to align and translate. In: International Conference on Learning Representations (2015)

Wang, Z., He, W., Wu, H., Li, W., Wang, H., Chen, E.: Chinese poetry generation with planning based neural network. In: International Conference on Computational Linguistics, pp. 1051–1060 (2016)

Feng, X., Liu, M., Liu, J., Qin, B., Sun, Y., Liu, T.: Topic-to-essay generation with neural networks. In: International Joint Conferences on Artificial Intelligence, pp. 4078–4084 (2018)

Tang, J., Yang, Y., Carton, S., Zhang, M., Mei, Q.: Context-aware natural language generation with recurrent neural networks. Computing Research Repository (2016)

Li, J., Luong, M.T., Dan, J.: A hierarchical neural autoencoder for paragraphs and documents. Computing Research Repository (2015)

Lin, R., Liu, S., Yang, M., Li, M., Zhou, M., Li, S.: Hierarchical recurrent neural network for document modeling. In: Conference on Empirical Methods in Natural Language Processing, pp. 899–907 (2015)

Sordoni, A., Bengio, Y., Vahabi, H., Lioma, C., Simonsen J.G., Nie, J.Y.: A hierarchical recurrent encoder-decoder for generative context-aware query suggestion. Computing Research Repository, pp. 553–562 (2015)

Serban, I.V., Sordoni, A., Bengio, Y., Courville, A., Pineau, J.: Building end-to-end dialogue systems using generative hierarchical neural network models. In: Association for the Advance of Artificial Intelligence, pp. 3776–3784 (2016)

Serban, I.V., et al.: A hierarchical latent variable encoder-decoder model for generating dialogues. In: Association for the Advance of Artificial Intelligence, pp. 3295–3301 (2016)

Tang, Y.: TF.Learn: tensorflow's high-level module for distributed machine learning (2016)

Kingma, D., Ba, J.: Adam: a method for stochastic optimization. In: International Conference on Learning Representations, San Diego (2015)

Papineni, K., Roukos, S., Ward T., Zhu, W.J.: BLEU: a method for automatic evaluation of machine translation. Association for Computational Linguistics (2002)

Benchmarking NLP Toolkits
for Enterprise Application

Kok Weiying$^{(\boxtimes)}$, Duc Nghia Pham, Yasaman Eftekharypour,
and Ang Jia Pheng

MIMOS Berhad, Kuala Lumpur, Malaysia
{kok.weiying, nghia.pham,
yasaman.eftekhary, jp.ang}@mimos.my

Abstract. Natural Language Processing (NLP) is an important technology that motivates the form of AI applications today. Many NLP libraries are available for researchers and developers to perform standard NLP tasks (such as segmentation, tokenization, lemmatization, POS tagging, and NER) without the need to develop from scratch. However, there are some challenges in selecting the most suitable library such as data type, performance, and the compatibility. In this paper, we assessed five popular NLP libraries for performing the standard processing tasks on datasets crawled from different online news sources in Malaysia. The obtained results are analysed and differences of those libraries are listed. The goal of this study is to provide a clear view for users to select the suitable NLP library for their text analysis task.

Keywords: Natural language processing · Sentence segmentation ·
Tokenization · Lemmatization · POS tagging · Named entity recognition

1 Introduction

Natural Language Processing (NLP) plays an important role in current AI applications that require an understanding of human language such as contextual extraction, machine translation, content categorization, and so on. Some of the most common and practical examples of NLP-related applications are Google translate, Bing translate, spam email filtering, customer services, and voice assistants (e.g. Alexa, Cortana, Siri or Google Assistant).

Different libraries are available for researchers and developers to perform standard processing of widely-spoken languages, such as sentence segmentation, tokenization, part-of-speech tagging (POS), lemmatization and named entity recognition (NER). Factors such as update frequency, cost integration, language support, and accuracy performance need to be considered for implementing a robust application [1].

In this paper, we will focus on the comparison between five popular NLP libraries that are publicly available (i.e. CoreNLP, NLTK, OpenNLP, SparkNLP, and spaCy) to help in sentence segmentation, tokenization, lemmatization, POS tagging, and NER tasks. In summary, the selected libraries are reviewed and evaluated based on the choice of programming language, license type, supported NLP tasks, and the algorithms used. The results found using the pre-trained models of these NLP libraries are compare in detailed.

A. C. Nayak and A. Sharma (Eds.): PRICAI 2019, LNAI 11672, pp. 289–294, 2019.
https://doi.org/10.1007/978-3-030-29894-4_24

2   Common NLP Tasks

Table 1 lists the common NLP tasks and their dependencies/difficulties in processing.

Table 1. List of common NLP tasks.

NLP Task	Description	Difficulties/Dependencies
Sentence segmentation	Divide a bunch of text into sentences	- Language dependency: each written language has its own sentence structure or rules such as the full stop punctuation used to end a sentence for Chinese (。) and English (.) is in a different form and has a different meaning in a context [2] - Application dependency: there is no absolute definition on what constitutes a sentence and is relatively arbitrary distinction across different written languages [2] - Corpus dependency: a robust NLP approach is needed with the increasing number of text corpora that contain irregular features, punctuation or misspelling that are unable to be processed by algorithm that is trained to process well-formed sentences [2]
Tokenization	Break a sentence into tokens (words, numbers or punctuation)	Difficulties in tokenization: - Space-delimited languages (Latin alphabet): Tokenization ambiguity exists with the uses of punctuation such as apostrophes, hyphen, commas, etc. - Unsegmented languages (Chinese, Japanese or Thai) do not contain word boundaries or whitespace between each word where additional lexical and morphological information is needed while tokenizing these languages [2]
Lemmatization	Remove the inflectional ending of a word to lemma	Lemmatization provides a better precision are usually used to improve the performance of text similarity metrics [3]
POS tagging	Classify words in a sentence to the proper morphosyntactic tags	The most common POS tagger for English is the Penn Treebank tag set which contains 36 POS tags and 12 other tags [4]
Named entity recognition	Identify unique entities and classify them into predefined categories (e.g. person, location, organization, etc.)	Linguistic grammar-based techniques show a higher precision but lower recall and time consuming for expert linguist to craft the rules whereas statistical machine learning models required large amount of annotated training data [5]. Both methods suffer from shortcomings on the maintenance and development of large scale NER system [5]

Table 2. List of five popular NLP libraries. They all provide pre-trained models for the 5 common NLP tasks in Table 1, except that OpenNLP doesn't support lemmatization.

Library	Description	Licence	Language
Stanford CoreNLP	Highly flexible and extensible. Can be used as an integrated toolkit with a wide range of grammatical analysis tools and provides a number of wrappers that can be used in various major modern programming languages [6]	GPL v3	Java
NLTK	Provides ready-to-use computational linguistics courseware. Contains over 50 corpora and lexical sources such as Penn Treebank Corpus, Open Multilingual Wordnet and a suite of text processing libraries for almost all NLP [7]	Apache v2.0	Python
OpenNLP	Contains various components that enable user to build a full NLP pipeline to execute respective NLP tasks, or train and evaluate a model via its API [8]	Apache v2.0	Java
SparkNLP	A natural language processing library built on top of Apache Spark ML. SparkNLP provides simple, performance & accurate NLP annotations for machine learning pipelines that can be scale easily in a distributed environment [9]	Apache v2.0	Python
spaCy	Designed specifically for production use which helps to build applications that process a large volume of text [10]. spaCy can be used to build information extraction or natural language understanding system or pre-processing text for deep learning [10]	MIT	Python

3 NLP Libraries

In this study, five NLP libraries (as shown in Table 2) are selected based on (i) the availability of pre-trained model, (ii) the ability to perform the five common NLP tasks mentioned above, (iii) the ability to process English language text, and (iv) the support of Java or Python programming language.

Table 3. The accuracy of 5 NLP libraries for sentence segmentation, tokenization, lemmatization & POS tagging based on the annotated data.

Library	#Sentences	#Tokens	Segmentation (%)	Token. (%)	Lemma. (%)	POS (%)	NER (%)
CoreNLP	117	881	**96.85**	**99.89**	**97.26**	97.17	**97.67**
NLTK	111	871	**96.85**	96.69	82.67	92.45	94.43
OpenNLP	116	870	90.55	99.09	N/A	96.89	96.72
SparkNLP	150	881	74.16	98.97	96.01	93.56	93.08
spaCy	150	906	75.59	98.86	90.08	**97.20**	93.92

Table 4. Detailed comparison of results processed by 5 NLP libraries and human. Results that different to human annotation are bold.

Task	Human	CoreNLP	NLTK	OpenNLP	SparkNLP	spaCy
Tokenization	"anti-graft"	"anti-graft"	"anti-graft"	"anti-graft"	"anti-graft"	**"anti", "-", "graft"**
	"KG-DWN-98/2"	"KG-DWN-98/2"	"KG-DWN-98/2"	"KG-DWN-98/2"	"KG-DWN-98/2"	**"KG", "-", "DWN-98/2"**
	"US$8.5mil"	**"US$", "8.5", "mil"**	**"US", "$", "8.5mil"**	**"US$", "8.5mil"**	"US$8.5mil"	**"US$", "8.5mil"**
Lemmatization	"was"	"was"	**"wa"**	"was"	"was"	"was"
	"as"	"as"	**"a"**	"as"	"as"	"as"
	"MyEG Services Bhd"	"MyEG Services Bhd"	"MyEG Services Bhd"	"MyEG Services Bhd"	"MyEG Services Bhd"	**"myeg services bhd"**
POS tagging	"co" (NN), "-" (HYPH), "founder" (NN)	**"co-founder" (NN)**	"co" (NN), "-" (HYPH), "founder" (NN)	"co" (NN), "-" (HYPH), "founder" (NN)	"co" (NN), "-" (HYPH), "founder" (NN)	"co" (NN), "-" (HYPH), "founder" (NN)
NER	"AirAsia" (ORG)	**"AirAsia" (LOC)**	**"AirAsia" (PER)**	**"AirAsia" (PER)**	**"AirAsia" (PER)**	**"AirAsia" (LOC)**

4   Results and Discussion

We collected 171 news articles from Malaysian news sites from July to August 2018. Images and unwanted symbols were removed. We then ranked these articles based on the number of words, named entities, different sentence structure and punctuation used. Finally, ten highest ranking articles were manually annotated and processed with sentence segmentation, tokenization, lemmatization, POS tagging and NER.

Table 3 shows the results of these 5 NLP libraries on the 10 highest ranking news articles. The results show that CoreNLP has the highest accuracy in four of NLP tasks (segmentation, tokenization, lemmatization, and NER) and slightly (0.03%) worse than spaCy on POS tagging. Table 4 highlights the differences between human annotated results and these 5 libraries on processing the 5 common NLP tasks.

The available pre-trained models are unable to detect Malaysian named entities: they were either left untagged or incorrectly tagged. Hence, we selected CoreNLP, OpenNLP and, spaCy – the three best libraries on the other four NLP tasks – and retrained their NER models using our local news dataset of 171 articles (80% training and 20% testing). Table 5 shows the results of these three libraries on NER tagging. CoreNLP and spaCy both reached an F-score of 0.78 whilst OpenNLP only scored 0.62.

Table 5. Precision, Recall, F-score results for NER of CoreNLP, OpenNLP, and spaCy.

Library	Algorithm	Tagging format	Precision	Recall	F-score
CoreNLP	Conditional Random Field [11]	where labeles are separated by a tab "\t" e.g. "word \tLABEL"	0.83	0.73	0.78
OpenNLP	Maximum Entropy [8]	each sentence has a mark with entity e.g. "<START: person> Entity <END>"	0.87	0.48	0.62
spaCy	Word embedding strategy using sub-word features and "Bloom" embedding, CNN with residual connections, transition-based approach to named entity parsing [10]	Wikipedia scheme IOB Scheme BILUO Scheme	0.79	0.77	0.78

5   Conclusion

Selection of the right NLP library is critical in developing an NLP-based application as it affects the accuracy of analysis tasks. Our results showed that both CoreNLP and spaCy produced higher accuracy than others. Between the two libraries, spaCy is significantly faster than CoreNLP, up to 10 times faster on certain tasks. We hope that our findings can help developers or researchers in selecting the right NLP library for their tasks, saving them the time and effort to retrain and compare different libraries for common NLP tasks.

References

1. Al Omran, F.N.A., Treude, C.: Choosing an NLP library for analyzing software documentation: a systematic literature review and a series of experiments, pp. 187–197. IEEE Press, Piscataway (2017)
2. Palmar, D.D.: Text preprocessing. In: Indurkhya, N., Damerau, F.J. (eds.) Handbook of natural language processing, vol. 2, pp. 9–30. CRC Press, Boca Raton (2010)
3. Aker, A., Petrak, J., Sabbah, F.: An extensible multilingual open source lemmatizer. In: Proceedings of the International Conference Recent Advances in Natural Language Processing, RANLP, pp. 40– 45. ACL (2017)
4. Marcus, M., Beatrice, S., Mary, A.: Building a large annotated corpus of. English: The Penn Treebank (1993)
5. Epaminondas, K., Tatar, D., Sacarea, C.: Named entity recognition. In: Natural Language Processing: Semantic Aspects, pp. 297–309. CRC Press, Boca Raton (2013)
6. Pinto, A., Gonçalo Oliveira, H., Oliveira Alves, A.: Comparing the performance of different NLP toolkits in formal and social media Text. In: 5th Symposium on Languages, Applications and Technologies (SLATE2016). Schloss Dagstuhl-Leibniz-Zentrum fuer Informatik (2016)

7. Loper, E., Bird, S.: NLTK: the natural language. arXiv preprint cs/0205028 (2002)
8. Foundation, T.A.: Apache OpenNLP Developer Documentation. (The Apache Software Foundation) (2011). https://opennlp.apache.org/docs/1.9.1/manual/opennlp.html, Accessed 01 Mar 2019
9. John Snow Labs: SparkNLP - Documentation and Reference (2019). https://nlp.johnsnow-labs.com/components.html, Accessed 11 Mar 2019
10. Honnibal, M.: Introducing spaCy (2016). https://explosion.ai/blog/introducing-spacy, Accessed 01 Mar 2019
11. Manning, C., Surdeanu, M., Bauer, J., Finkel, J., Bethard, S., McClosky, D.: The Stanford CoreNLP natural language processing toolkit. In: Proceedings of 52nd Annual Meeting of the Association for Computational Linguistics: System Demonstrations, pp. 55–60 (2014)

Robotics, IOT and Traffic Automation

Unsupervised Data Augmentation for Improving Traffic Sign Recognition

Sisi Cao[1], Wenbo Zheng[1(✉)], and Shaocong Mo[2(✉)]

[1] School of Software Engineering, Xi'an Jiaotong University, Xi'an, China
zwb2017@stu.xjtu.edu.cn
[2] College of Computer Science and Technology, Zhejiang University,
Hangzhou, China
mosc@zju.edu.cn

Abstract. Traffic sign recognition is a key function in driver assistant systems and autonomous vehicles. Several benchmark datasets had been proposed to test the performance of various recognition models. However, two related problems remained unsolved. First, whether the data samples are enough to evaluate the performance of the proposed recognition models? Second, whether data augmentation could be introduced to build better benchmark datasets? To solve these two problems, we show in this paper that some famous benchmark datasets can be further improved via appropriate data augmentation. Specially, we propose a feature-space data augmentation algorithm that first determines an appropriate feature space for the available data, then generates potentially useful new samples in the feature space and finally maps these new samples into original spaces to get new data samples. Numerical tests show that this algorithm helps to increase the accuracies of recognition models.

Keywords: Traffic signs recognition · Benchmark datasets · Data generation

1 Introduction

Traffic sign recognition is a basic function of advanced driver assistant systems (ADAS) and autonomous vehicles [23,26]. Prompt and accurate traffic sign recognition enable drivers or autonomous vehicles to notify the change of road conditions in time, so as to avoid making traffic accidents or violating traffic laws.

Various methods had been proposed to detect and recognize traffic signs. For example, Adaboost method was applied in [3,5]; sparse coding models were studied in [25]; supporting vector machines were used in [5,10]; extreme learning models were examined in [15]; and convolutional neural networks (CNN) were tested in [24,29,33].

Several benchmark datasets had also been proposed to test the performance of these methods [13]. Testing results on these benchmark datasets indicate that

---

S. Cao and W. Zheng—Contribute equally to this study.

© Springer Nature Switzerland AG 2019
A. C. Nayak and A. Sharma (Eds.): PRICAI 2019, LNAI 11672, pp. 297–306, 2019.
https://doi.org/10.1007/978-3-030-29894-4_25

some methods could recognize the given traffic sign data with an impressively high accuracy. For example, it was shown in that [13] several recognition models yielded more than 99% accuracy on testing datasets.

However, most existing approaches in this direction focused on model selection for traffic sign recognition and paid less attention to the data used for training and testing. Particularly, few studies in this field thoroughly answer the following question: *Whether these data samples are enough to evaluate the performance of the proposed recognition models?*

That is, we are interested in whether the obtained recognition model had been well trained to deal with various instances of traffic signs, based on these limited data samples [14,22]. Notice that all existing recognition models are data-driven, we may get insufficient models, if training data do not cover the whole space of the traffic sign of interests.

If we found any existing benchmark dataset is not abundant for a thorough test, another corresponding question can be naturally raised as: *How to generate more useful training and testing data from a limited number of sample data?*

Such a question attracted great interests and received many efficient answers [9,16,19]. Generally, we can categorized the approaches into two kinds: data-space based data augmentation methods and feature space based data augmentation methods. The first kinds of approaches directly change the data; while the second kinds of approaches first retrieve the common features of the existing data points, then change the corresponding points in the feature space, and finally map the changed points back into the data space.

In other words, feature space based approaches generate new data points that share the same common features. For example, the recently popular Variational Autoencoder (VAE)[19], Generative Adversarial Networks (GAN)[9], autoregressive model [4], and Glow [18]. However, as we know, the deep generative model based on deep neural networks is a black-box method [35], and it is not easy to explain the process of a deep generative model of generating samples. According to the Geometric view [21], we can regard these deep generative models as the two process: one is the process of feature selection, the other is the process of optimal transportation based on selected feature. This views can be good to explain the process of generative model and need less demand of the hardware. So why not we use the feature selection and optimal transportation to simulate the process of generating samples?

However, for traffic sign testing problem, we aim to generate more critical data points that are often rare event to sample but are crucial to build recognition models. Existing approaches are not designed for this purpose and are thus ineffective.

To solve these problems, we propose a feature-space data augmentation algorithm using optimal mass transport that first determines an appropriate feature space for the available data, then generates potentially useful new samples in the feature space and finally maps these new samples into original spaces to get new data samples. Numerical tests show that this algorithm helps to increase the accuracies of recognition models. The rest of this short paper is arranged as follows. Section 2 explains the details of the algorithm. Section 3 gives some numerical testing results based on the famous benchmark GTSRB datasets and Sect. 4 concludes the paper.

2 Data Augmentation Methods

2.1 Data-Space Data Augmentation

Data augmentation usually refers to applying deformations to the labeled data and meanwhile keep the semantic meaning of the labels unchanged [7,32].

In this paper, we had considered the following four widely used data-space data augmentation:

1. Flip. The upper part and the lower part of the image are transformed with the image horizontal central axis as the center axis.
2. Rotation. We rotate the image 30° clockwise according to the center point to form a new image.
3. Scale. We used the closest interpolation algorithm to zoom up to twice the size of the original image.
4. Crop. We only keep a quarter image of the center of the image center.

2.2 Feature-Space Data Augmentation

Notations. For presentation simplicity, in the rest of this paper, we define $F := \{1, 2, 3, \ldots, D\}$ as the feature set for $D \in \mathbb{N}$. For a matrix $L \in \mathbb{R}^{D \times D}$, L_{ij} is its (i, j)-th component.

Given two discrete probability distributions over vector $\boldsymbol{x}$, $p(\boldsymbol{x})$ of sizes N and $q(\boldsymbol{x})$ of sizes M, $\forall i \in \{1, 2, 3, \ldots, N\}, \forall j \in \{1, 2, 3, \ldots, M\}$, we define $p(x_i)$ and $q(x_j)$ are the i-th competent of $p(\boldsymbol{x})$ and the j-th competent of $q(\boldsymbol{x})$ respectively.

We suppose get i.i.d. samples from these two probability distributions of sizes N and M, respectively. We define P and Q are two histograms from samples of $p(\boldsymbol{x})$ and $q(\boldsymbol{x})$ respectively, their discrete joint distribution is f_{ij} and $\bigcup f_{i*} = P, \bigcup f_{*j} = Q$ [11].

Suppose the key features S_p from the discrete probability distributions $p(\boldsymbol{x})$ and the key features S_q from the discrete probability distributions $q(\boldsymbol{x})$, the space where S_p and S_q are located is Ω. The dimension of S_p is recorded as d_{S_p}, the dimension of S_q is recorded as d_{S_q}, and the number of S_p and S_q is recorded as α. In Ω, T is a self-mapping, the map T maps the key features S_p into a key features S_q, is recorded as $T \otimes S_p = S_q$. To compute fast, we could introduce the Frobenius dot product $< \cdot, \cdot >_F$, for matrix A and B, $< A, B >_F = Tr(A^T B)$, where $Tr(\cdot)$ the function of the trace of the matrix.

Feature-Space Data Augmentation Using Optimal Mass Transport.
According to the Geometric view [21], we can regard the deep generative model
as the two process: the first process is feature selection, the second process is
optimal transportation based on selected feature. Therefore, we can use the
feature selection method using Wasserstein distance to get the key features of
the input data and use optimal mass transport based on selected feature to
generate specific samples.

In the first process, we use feature selection method using Wasserstein distance to find a subset S of feature set $F = \{1, 2, \ldots, D\}$ in which these two kinds
of distributions do not match.

We can define a distance/divergence matrix $L \in \mathbb{R}^{D \times D}$ that estimates the
difference between $p(\boldsymbol{x})$ and $q(\boldsymbol{x})$ based on the available sampling data. Then,
we can formulate our problem as an optimization problem that seeks a sparse
approximation of matrix L [11]

$$\min_{S \subseteq F} \sum_{i,j \in S} L_{i,j} - \|L\|_1, \quad \text{s.t.} |S| = \alpha \tag{1}$$

where α is the pre-selected number of features, $\|L\|_1$ denotes the entrywise
1-norm of matrix L, $|S|$ is the cardinality of S.

We can introduce the Wasserstein distance to estimate the difference between
$p(\boldsymbol{x})$ and $q(\boldsymbol{x})$. Specifically, we denote flow f_{ji} and define another all-zero histogram R to be the sum that is moved from the bin j in R to the bin i in P
[2]. Wasserstein distance between P and Q can then be defined as the minimum
total flow that is needed to make R to be equivalent to Q, can be written as

$$L^{WD} = WD(p(\boldsymbol{x}), q(\boldsymbol{x})) =$$
$$\min_{\{f_{i,j}, i=1,2,3,\ldots,n, j=1,2,3,\ldots,m\}} \sum_{j=1}^{m} \sum_{i=1}^{n} f_{ij} d_{ij} \tag{2}$$

where $f_i = p_i, f_j = q_j$. $i = 1, 2, 3, \ldots, n; j = 1, 2, 3, \ldots, m$. d_{ij} is the distance
between the bins i and j. In this paper, we simply use the $L1$ distance, i.e.,
$d_{ij} = |i - j|$.

According [31], once we design matrix L, the problem (1) is seen as the
sparsest k-subgraph problem and we can find a suboptimal solution in polynomial time.

By this process, we can get the selected feature to provide the input and
foundations for the next process.

In second process, we use optimal mass transport to transforms selected feature using previous process to specific samples. Specifically, the optimal mass
transport problem is to find a map that minimizes the inter-domain transportation cost [27]. On the basis of the statistical view of machine learning, we can
transform one space for all possible input data to another space. For $\Omega \subset \mathbb{R}^n$, let
us take the process of transforming the features S_p from $p(\boldsymbol{x})$ to the features S_q
from $q(\boldsymbol{x})$ to be an example to illustrate this process of optimal mass transport.

Assume Ω have an equal total measure as

$$\int_{\Omega} dS_p = \int_{\Omega} dS_q \tag{3}$$

We aim to find a region to its own foem mapping (diffeomorphism), T : $(\Omega, S_p) \rightarrow (\Omega, S_q)$. According to the theory of Gu et al. [20,21], $T : (\Omega, S_p) \rightarrow (\Omega, S_q)$ is a unique optimal transport mapping. We transform initial probability distribution S_p into target probability distribution S_q, $T \otimes S_p = S_q$. At the same time, minimizing the transport cost,

$$Cost(T) := \min_{T \otimes S_p = S_q} \int_{\Omega} |x - T(x)|^2 dS_p \tag{4}$$

Otherwise, we can use the fast computer optimal transport method by Perrot et al. [28] proposed to estimate the mapping of Eq.(4), it can be written as:

$$f(\gamma, T) = \frac{1}{\alpha \times d_{S_q}} ||T(S_p) - \alpha \times \gamma \times S_q||_2^2$$
$$+ \frac{\lambda_\gamma}{\max(C)} < \gamma, C >_F \tag{5}$$
$$+ \frac{\lambda_T}{d_{S_p} \times d_{S_q}} R(T)$$

where $f(\gamma, T)$ is the estimation function by Perrot et al. proposed, $T(S_p)$ is a short-hand for the application of T on each example in S_p, the parameter γ to control the closeness between S_p and S_q, C is the cost matrix related to the function $Cost(T)$, $R(\cdot)$ is a regularization term, λ_γ and λ_T are two hyper-parameters controlling the trade-off between the three terms in (5).

We choose the $\ell_1\ell_2$ regularization [6] as $R(\cdot)$. According to the Perrot's advices [28], we define the value of λ_T, λ_γ are 10^{-2}, 10^{-7} respectively.

By this process and previous process, we can get the specific samples by controlling the parameter γ.

To sum up, our method contains three steps. Firstly, we use the feature selection method to get the key features of the input data. Then, we use the optimal transportation model [28] to simulate the process of generating samples based on the key features of samples. Finally, we use the fast computer optimal transport method (5) [8] to get final results. See Algorithm 1 below, where the Feature-Select-Solution function is mentioned in Algorithm 2, the Solve-Optimal-Transport function is mentioned in POT library [8] and Perrot's method [28].

3   Numerical Tests

We randomly select 2000 images from the traffic sign dataset [13] as original dataset.

Algorithm 1. Feature-Space Data Augmentation Algorithm Using Optimal Mass Transport

---

Input: Parameter γ
Output: Generated Samples $Sample_{Part}$
1: $[Sub_P, Sub_Q] = $FEATURE-SELECT-SOLUTION$(P, Q)$
2: $Sample_{Part} =$
       SOLVE-OPTIMAL-TRANSPORT(Sub_P, Sub_Q, γ)
3: **return** Generated Samples $Sample_{Part}$

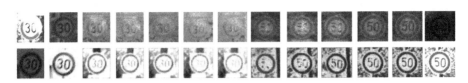

Fig. 1. The results of transforming speed limit 30 to speed limit 50 of the selected features. From left to right, in turn, the original image of speed limit 30, the transport result when the parameter γ is $\{10^{-5}, 10^{-4}, \cdots, 10^4, 10^5\}$, and the original image of speed limit 50.

Table 1. Contrast the results of the first experiment

Data Augmentation Method	Recognition Method	HOG+SVM	NMF+KNN	NMF+SVM	PCA+KNN	PCA+SVM
Data-Space Data Augmentation	Flip	45%	49%	56%	63%	64%
	Rotation	45%	52%	60%	62%	70%
	Scale	46%	56%	62%	64%	68%
	Crop	47%	53%	57%	58%	60%
Our Methods		65%	67%	74%	84%	84%

Table 2. Contrast the results of the second experiment

Data Augmentation Method	Recognition Method	HOG+SVM	NMF+KNN	NMF+SVM	PCA+KNN	PCA+SVM
Data-Space Data Augmentation	Flip	50%	53%	57%	58%	63%
	Rotation	48%	48%	56%	59%	59%
	Scale	47%	55%	58%	61%	64%
	Crop	50%	51%	55%	64%	72%
Our Methods		79%	82%	91%	95%	93%

We set the parameter γ in $\{10^{-5}, 10^{-4}, \cdots, 10^4, 10^5\}$, and use the fast computer optimal transport algorithm [8, 28] to get the generated samples. For example, the portion of generated samples is shown in Fig. 1. We choose clear generated samples and mark them as the newly generated data.

To test whether the newly generated data bring benefit of traffic sign recognition problems, we design the following test.

First, HOG+SVM [34], NMF+KNN [17], NMF+SVM [12], PCA+KNN [1] and PCA+SVM [30] are trained merely based on the original dataset provided in GTSRB [13]. The obtained HOG+SVM [34], NMF+KNN [17], NMF+SVM [12], PCA+KNN [1] and PCA+SVM [30] are then tested on the newly generated data.

Second, another HOG+SVM [34], another NMF+KNN [17], another NMF+S–VM [12], another PCA+KNN [1] and another PCA+SVM [30] are trained based on a mixture of the original dataset provided in GTSRB and the newly generated data. The obtained HOG+SVM [34], NMF+KNN [17], NMF+SVM [12], PCA+KNN [1] and PCA+SVM [30] are then tested on the rest of data.

Finally, we compare their performance in Tables 1 and 2. For Tables 1 and 2, it is obvious that the recognition rate of the five models using our method is better than others. It means our method is robust and effective for increasing the recognition rate of traffic sign recognition.

4   Conclusion

Based on optimal mass transport theory, we have proposed a novel data augmentation for traffic sign recognition. In our method, we have first got the key features of the input data using the feature selection method and then transformed the key features of input data using optimal mass transport theory. Our method can generate any Wasserstein distance of generated samples that you desire. We design the experiment of traffic sign recognition problem to prove the effectiveness of the way to improve the performance of exacting methods using generated samples. Our experimental results show that many simple methods can improve their the recognition rate of special traffic sign recognition problem.

The above findings indicate that optimal mass transport theory might be used as an effective alternative and explanation of intelligence test [22] in many applications. We expect more attention could be drawn in this direction in the near future.

A   A Feature-Select Solution Based Wasserstein Distance

The Feature-Select-Solution function is shown in Algorithm 2.

Algorithm 2. Feature-Select-Solution

1: **function** $DP(i)$
2:     **for** $L^{WD}[i] \leq 0$ **do**
3:         **if** $\sim isempty(Sub[i])$ **then**
4:             $Sub_{temp} = Sub[i];$
5:             $i = i + 1;$
6:             $Sub[i] = DP(i)$
7:         **end if**
8:         **if** $Sub_{temp} \neq$ Continue **then**
9:             $Sub \leftarrow Sub \cup Sub_{temp}$

10:             **return** Sub
11:         **end if**
12:     **end for**
13:     **return** Continue
14: **end function**
15: **function** RELEVANCE ANALYSIS(f_{ij})
16:     **for** $i = 1 : 1 : N$ **do**
17:         **for** $j = 1 : 1 : M$ **do**
18:             $L^{WD}(i,j) = f_{ij} * |i - j|$
19:         **end for**
20:     **end for**
21: **end function**
22: **function** SOLVE-K-SUBGRAPH-PROBLEM
23:     $Sub \leftarrow \emptyset, [N, M] = size(L^{WD})$
24:     **for** $i = 1 \rightarrow max(N, M)$ **do**
25:         $Sub[i] \leftarrow \text{DP}(i)$
26:     **end for**
27:     **return** Score vector Sub
28: **end function**
29: $f_{ij} =$ SOLVE-JOINT-DISTRIBUTION(P, Q)
30: $L^{WD} =$ RELEVANCE ANALYSIS(f_{ij})
31: $Sub =$ SOLVE-K-SUBGRAPH-PROBLEM(L^{WD})
32: **return** Score vector Sub

References

1. Abukhait, J., Zyout, I., Mansour, A.M.: Speed sign recognition using shape-based features. Int. J. Comput. Appl. **84**, 31–37 (2013)
2. Anderson, D.T., Zare, A., Price, S.: Comparing fuzzy, probabilistic, and possibilistic partitions using the earth mover 's distance. IEEE Trans. Fuzzy Syst. **21**(4), 766–775 (2013)
3. Baro, X., Escalera, S., Vitria, J., Pujol, O., Radeva, P.: Traffic sign recognition using evolutionary adaboost detection and forest-ecoc classification. IEEE Trans. Intell. Transp. Syst. **10**(1), 113–126 (2009)
4. Bos, R., de Waele, S., Broersen, P.M.T.: Autoregressive spectral estimation by application of the burg algorithm to irregularly sampled data. IEEE Trans. Instrum. Meas. **51**(6), 1289–1294 (2002)
5. Chen, T., Lu, S.: Accurate and efficient traffic sign detection using discriminative adaboost and support vector regression. IEEE Trans. Veh. Technol. **65**(6), 4006–4015 (2016)
6. Courty, N., Flamary, R., Tuia, D.: Domain adaptation with regularized optimal transport. In: Calders, T., Esposito, F., Hüllermeier, E., Meo, R. (eds.) ECML PKDD 2014. LNCS (LNAI), vol. 8724, pp. 274–289. Springer, Heidelberg (2014). https://doi.org/10.1007/978-3-662-44848-9_18
7. DeVries, T., Taylor, G.W.: Dataset Augmentation in Feature Space. arXiv e-prints, February 2017
8. Flamary, R., Courty, N.: Pot python optimal transport library (2017)

9. Goodfellow, I.J., et al.: Generative Adversarial Networks. arXiv e-prints, June 2014
10. Greenhalgh, J., Mirmehdi, M.: Real-time detection and recognition of road traffic signs. IEEE Trans. Intell. Transp. Syst. **13**(4), 1498–1506 (2012)
11. Hara, S., Katsuki, T., Yanagisawa, H., Ono, T., Okamoto, R., Takeuchi, S.: Consistent and efficient nonparametric different-feature selection. In: Artificial Intelligence and Statistics, pp. 130–138 (2017)
12. Hillebrand, M., Kreßel, U., Wöhler, C., Kummert, F.: Traffic sign classifier adaption by semi-supervised co-training. In: Mana, N., Schwenker, F., Trentin, E. (eds.) ANNPR 2012. LNCS (LNAI), vol. 7477, pp. 193–200. Springer, Heidelberg (2012). https://doi.org/10.1007/978-3-642-33212-8_18
13. Houben, S., Stallkamp, J., Salmen, J., Schlipsing, M., Igel, C.: Detection of traffic signs in real-world images: the german traffic sign detection benchmark. In: The 2013 International Joint Conference on Neural Networks (IJCNN), pp. 1–8, August 2013
14. Huang, W., Wen, D., Geng, J., Zheng, N.: Task-specific performance evaluation of UGVs: case studies at the IVFC. IEEE Trans. Intell. Transp. Syst. **15**(5), 1969–1979 (2014)
15. Huang, Z., Yu, Y., Gu, J., Liu, H.: An efficient method for traffic sign recognition based on extreme learning machine. IEEE Trans. Cybern. **47**(4), 920–933 (2017)
16. Rezende, D.J., Mohamed, S., Wierstra, D.: Stochastic backpropagation and approximate inference in deep generative models. arXiv e-prints, January 2014
17. Kalayeh, M.M., Idrees, H., Shah, M.: NMF-KNN: image annotation using weighted multi-view non-negative matrix factorization. In: 2014 IEEE Conference on Computer Vision and Pattern Recognition, pp. 184–191, June 2014
18. Kingma, D.P., Dhariwal, P.: Glow: Generative Flow with Invertible 1x1 Convolutions. arXiv e-prints, July 2018
19. Kingma, D.P., Welling, M.: Auto-Encoding Variational Bayes. arXiv e-prints, December 2013
20. Lei, N., Luo, Z., Yau, S.-T., Gu, D.X.: Geometric Understanding of Deep Learning. arXiv e-prints, May 2018
21. Lei, N., Su, K., Cui, L., Yau, S.-T., Gu, D.X.: A Geometric View of Optimal Transportation and Generative Model. arXiv e-prints, October 2017
22. Li, L., Huang, W., Liu, Y., Zheng, N., Wang, F.: Intelligence testing for autonomous vehicles: a new approach. IEEE Trans. Intell. Veh. **1**(2), 158–166 (2016)
23. Li, L., Wang, F.Y.: Advanced motion control and sensing for intelligent vehicles (2007)
24. Li, Y., Møgelmose, A., Trivedi, M.M.: Pushing the "speed limit": high-accuracy us traffic sign recognition with convolutional neural networks. IEEE Trans. Intell. Veh. **1**(2), 167–176 (2016)
25. Lu, K., Ding, Z., Ge, S.: Sparse-representation-based graph embedding for traffic sign recognition. IEEE Trans. Intell. Transp. Syst. **13**(4), 1515–1524 (2012)
26. Mogelmose, A., Trivedi, M.M., Moeslund, T.B.: Vision-based traffic sign detection and analysis for intelligent driver assistance systems: perspectives and survey. IEEE Trans. Intell. Transp. Syst. **13**(4), 1484–1497 (2012)
27. Ning, L., Georgiou, T.T., Tannenbaum, A.: Matrix-valued monge-kantorovich optimal mass transport. In: 52nd IEEE Conference on Decision and Control, pp. 3906–3911, December 2013
28. Perrot, M., Courty, N., Flamary, R., Habrard, A.: Mapping estimation for discrete optimal transport. In: Lee, D.D., Sugiyama, M., Luxburg, U.V., Guyon, I., Garnett, R. (eds.) Advances in Neural Information Processing Systems, vol. 29, pp. 4197–4205. Curran Associates Inc., New York (2016)

29. Sermanet, P., LeCun, Y.: Traffic sign recognition with multi-scale convolutional networks. In: The 2011 International Joint Conference on Neural Networks, pp. 2809–2813, July 2011
30. Shi, M., Wu, H., Fleyeh, H.: Support vector machines for traffic signs recognition. In: 2008 IEEE International Joint Conference on Neural Networks (IEEE World Congress on Computational Intelligence), pp. 3820–3827, June 2008
31. Watrigant, R., Bougeret, M., Giroudeau, R.: Approximating the sparsest k-subgraph in chordal graphs. Theory Comput. Syst. **58**(1), 111–132 (2016)
32. Wong, S.C., Gatt, A., Stamatescu, V., McDonnell, M.D.: Understanding data augmentation for classification: when to warp? In: 2016 International Conference on Digital Image Computing: Techniques and Applications (DICTA), pp. 1–6, November 2016
33. Yang, Y., Luo, H., Xu, H., Wu, F.: Towards real-time traffic sign detection and classification. IEEE Trans. Intell. Transp. Syst. **17**(7), 2022–2031 (2016)
34. Yao, C., Wu, F., Chen, H., Hao, X., Shen, Y.: Traffic sign recognition using hog-SVM and grid search. In: 2014 12th International Conference on Signal Processing (ICSP), pp. 962–965, October 2014
35. Yao, C., Cai, D., Jiajun, B., Chen, G.: Pre-training the deep generative models with adaptive hyperparameter optimization. Neurocomputing **247**, 144–155 (2017)

Detection of Anomalous Traffic Patterns and Insight Analysis from Bus Trajectory Data

Xiaocai Zhang[1] (ORCID), Xuan Zhang[1], Sunny Verma[1], Yuansheng Liu[1],
Michael Blumenstein[2], and Jinyan Li[1(✉)] (ORCID)

[1] Advanced Analytics Institute, FEIT, University of Technology Sydney,
Sydney, Australia
`Xiaocai.Zhang@student.uts.edu.au`, `Jinyan.Li@uts.edu.au`
[2] Centre for Artificial Intelligence, School of Computer Science, FEIT,
University of Technology Sydney, Sydney, Australia
`Michael.Blumenstein@uts.edu.au`

Abstract. Detection of anomalous patterns from traffic data is closely related to analysis of traffic accidents, fault detection, flow management, and new infrastructure planning. Existing methods on traffic anomaly detection are modelled on taxi trajectory data and have shortcoming that the data may lose much information about actual road traffic situation, as taxi drivers can select optimal route for themselves to avoid traffic anomalies. We employ bus trajectory data as it reflects real traffic conditions on the road to detect city-wide anomalous traffic patterns and to provide broader range of insights into these anomalies. Taking these considerations, we first propose a feature visualization method by mapping extracted 3-dimensional hidden features to red-green-blue (RGB) color space with a deep sparse autoencoder (DSAE). A color trajectory (CT) is produced by encoding a trajectory with RGB colors. Then, a novel algorithm is devised to detect spatio-temporal outliers with spatial and temporal properties extracted from the CT. We also integrate the CT with the geographic information system (GIS) map to obtain insights for understanding the traffic anomaly locations, and more importantly the road influence affected by the corresponding anomalies. Our proposed method was tested on three real-world bus trajectory data sets to demonstrate the excellent performance of high detection rates and low false alarm rates.

Keywords: Traffic · Anomalous pattern · Bus trajectory ·
Deep sparse autoencoder

1 Introduction

Detection of anomalous traffic patterns is to find out the traffic patterns which are not expected but which are helpful for traffic management [10]. Anomalous patterns in moving transportation carriers' trajectories can reflect abnormal traffic

© Springer Nature Switzerland AG 2019
A. C. Nayak and A. Sharma (Eds.): PRICAI 2019, LNAI 11672, pp. 307–321, 2019.
https://doi.org/10.1007/978-3-030-29894-4_26

streams on the transportation networks [13]. These patterns can be caused by various factors such as traffic accidents, traffic controls, parades, sports events, disasters or other events. To our knowledge, existing trajectory-based traffic anomalies/outliers detection methods are based on taxi trajectory data [3,7,13,16,19]. However, many accessible trajectory data sources of the bus have not been investigated for traffic anomalies probing. Bus service operates along almost all main roads in metropolitan cities everyday, which facilitates commuters substantially. Moreover, GPS has equipped bus with high-resolution positioning information, which probes the city-wide traffic situations factually.

Models based on bus trajectory data have the following advantages: (i) As public transportation carrier, there is not much risk of privacy leaking; (ii) Easy to get access to the real-time bus data for many cities via API; and (iii) Each bus service has its own regular route, bus trajectory is more independent of the drivers' preference, which can probe the real road traffic conditions. On the contrary, taxi trajectory data may lose much information about traffic situation, since taxi drivers can choose paths for themselves [6,20]. If a taxi driver gets the traffic information ahead, the driver very likely chooses the optimal route to avoid a foreseeable congestion, which may not get useful information regarding anomalous traffic pattern discovery.

Our **contributions** in this research are summarized as follows:

1. We present a deep neural network architecture to extract deep hidden features and devise a novel algorithm for anomalous traffic patterns detection.
2. We visualize features by mapping them into red-green-blue (RGB) color space and conduct GIS map fusion for getting insights into anomalies regarding of uncovering anomaly locations as well as impacts to road traffic.
3. We perform comprehensive experiments on three real-world data sets to confirm the effectiveness and superiority of the deep neural network architecture on feature extraction, our proposed anomaly detection algorithm and insight of anomaly.

2   Related Work

Anomalous pattern detection from spatio-temporal data is a popular topic in the domain of data mining and knowledge discovery [13]. For anomaly/outlier detection, principal component analysis (PCA) based methods [8], random projection [5], clustering based method [14] and one-class SVM [9] have been widely adopted.

The study of road traffic anomaly detection has also been investigated in many studies, most of which are based on city-wide taxi trajectories. Pang et al. [16] have applied likelihood ratio tests which have been commonly used in epidemiological studies to represent traffic patterns. Experiments on real taxi GPS data show the accurate and rapid detection of traffic anomalies. Liu et al. [13] constructed anomaly detection model by building a region graph from taxi GPS data, where a node represents a region and the link between every two nodes denotes the traffic flow, and the extreme outliers can be detected from graph links. Chawla *et al.* [3] used PCA to identify traffic anomaly form GPS trajectory data based on their deviation from their respective historical traffic profile. Zhang *et al.* [19] proposed an isolation based anomalous taxi trajectory detection method and get high detection rate. Kuang *et al.* [7] employed wavelet transform and PCA to uncover anomalous traffic events in urban areas using taxi GPS data.

Apart from using taxi trajectory data, there are also a few papers utilizing other kinds of data sources. Nguyen *et al.* [15] developed a real-time system using social media (Twitter) data for traffic incident detection. Li *et al.* [11] introduced a traffic anomaly detection algorithm based on the massive traffic video. Riveiro *et al.* [17] constructed a visual analytics framework that employs large amounts of multidimensional and heterogeneous road traffic data for traffic anomaly detection.

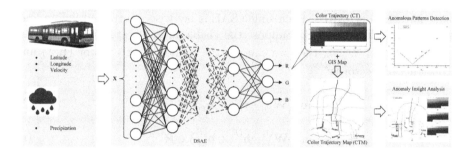

Fig. 1. The workflow of anomalous traffic pattern detection and insight analysis.

3 Proposed Method

Figure 1 illustrates the overall workflow of our proposed method. First, feature extraction is conducted by a deep learning method; and a color trajectory (CT) is established and visualized for traffic anomalous insight analysis. Then, anomalous patterns are uncovered by extracting spatial and temporal properties and devised anomaly detection algorithm.

3.1 Feature Extraction and Visualization Using Deep Learning

We employ deep sparse autoencoder (DSAE) to extract hidden features, which can also be used for bus trajectory visualization. A GPS trajectory trip $\mathbf{T}$ is defined as

$$\mathbf{T} = \left((\varphi_1, \lambda_1, v_1)^T, \cdots, (\varphi_N, \lambda_N, v_N)^T \right) \in \mathbb{R}^{D \times N} \qquad (1)$$

where φ, λ and v denote latitude and longitude and velocity (unit: km/h), N denotes the number of time series and D denotes the dimensionality. In this study, we have $D = 3$.

We also consider the impact of rainfall on traffic conditions, as the consensus that heavy rainfall can significantly affect traffic flow characteristics and lead to traffic congestion or even accidents. Therefore, we integrate trajectory data with precipitation data r_i (unit: mm/h) to get

$$\mathbf{Z} = \left((\varphi_1, \lambda_1, v_1, r_1)^T, \cdots, (\varphi_N, \lambda_N, v_N, r_N)^T \right) \in \mathbb{R}^{(D+1) \times N} \tag{2}$$

Before feeding the data to DSAE, data normalization and windowing operation are conducted. We set a time window size ω to move z_i by one step along the time axis, therefore, we have the windowed data as the network input $\mathbf{X}$

$$x_i = (\varphi_i, \lambda_i, v_i, r_i, \cdots, \varphi_{i+\omega-1}, \lambda_{i+\omega-1}, v_{i+\omega-1}, r_{i+\omega-1})^T \in \mathbb{R}^{4*\omega} \tag{3}$$

$$\mathbf{X} = (x_1, x_2, \cdots, x_{N_X-1}, x_{N_X}) \in \mathbb{R}^{(4*\omega) \times N_X} \tag{4}$$

where $N_X = N - \omega + 1$, ω is an integer and $0 < \omega < N$.

We feed $\mathbf{X}$ into the DSAE, which is a deep neural network stacked by many sparse autoencoder (SAE). Each single SAE is lay-wise pre-trained before fine-tuning of the whole network. Suppose the visible layer's vector in the lth SAE denotes $\mathbf{v}^{(l)} \in \mathbb{R}^{D_V \times N_X}$, then we can get the hidden layer's vector ($\mathbf{h}^{(l)}$) and reconstruction vector ($\mathbf{r}^{(l)}$).

$$\mathbf{h}^{(l)} = \tanh(\mathbf{W}_{en}^{(l)} \cdot \mathbf{v}^{(l)} + \mathbf{b}_{en}^{(l)}) \in \mathbb{R}^{D_H^{(l)} \times N_X} \tag{5}$$

$$\mathbf{r}^{(l)} = \tanh(\mathbf{W}_{de}^{(l)} \cdot \mathbf{h}^{(l)} + \mathbf{b}_{de}^{(l)}) \in \mathbb{R}^{D_R^{(l)} \times N_X} \tag{6}$$

where $\mathbf{W}_{en}^{(l)}$ and $\mathbf{W}_{de}^{(l)}$ are the weights of lth layer of encoder and decoder. $\mathbf{b}_{en}^{(l)}$ and $\mathbf{b}_{de}^{(l)}$ are the biases of lth layer of encoder and decoder. The reconstruction error is

$$\min L^{(l)} = \frac{1}{2} \left\| \mathbf{h}^{(l)} - \mathbf{r}^{(l)} \right\|_2^2 + \alpha \left(\left\| \mathbf{W}_{en}^{(l)} \right\|_2^2 + \left\| \mathbf{W}_{de}^{(l)} \right\|_2^2 \right) + \beta \sum_{j=1}^{D_H^{(l)}} \mathrm{KL} \left(\rho || \rho_j^{(i)} \right) \tag{7}$$

$$\mathrm{KL} \left(\rho || h^{(i)} \right) = \rho \log \frac{\rho}{\rho_j^{(i)}} + (1 - \rho) \log \frac{1 - \rho}{1 - \rho_j^{(i)}} \tag{8}$$

where α, β and ρ are the preset parameters. $\rho_j^{(i)}$ is the average activation of units in the lth hidden layer.

We embed a 3-neuron layer as the output layer of DSAE to get 3-dimensional hidden features, corresponding to red, green and blue channel in RGB color space.

$$\mathbf{Y} = (o_r, o_g, o_b)^T \in \mathbb{R}^{3 \times N_Y} \tag{9}$$

where $N_Y = N - \omega + 1$. Then we normalize the red channel o_r into range $[0, 255]$.

$$R = \mathrm{Round} \left(\frac{o_r - \min(o_r)}{\max(o_r) - \min(o_r)} \times 255 \right) \tag{10}$$

In a similar way, we can also get the green channel (G) and blue channel (B).

$$\mathbf{CT} = (R, G, B)^T \in \mathbb{R}^{3 \times N_{CT}} \tag{11}$$

where $N_{CT} = N - \omega + 1$, and we call $\mathbf{CT}$ the *color trajectory* (CT) forementioned.

3.2 Anomalous Patterns Detection

For the ith complete trajectory, we have τ_i called *trajectory representation*.

$$\tau_i = \left(N_{CT_i}, \mathbf{CT}_i\right) = \left(N_{CT_i}, (R_i, G_i, B_i)^T\right) \tag{12}$$

where N_{CT_i} is a temporal feature that reflects the trajectory duration. A longer duration indicates a higher confidence that traffic anomaly might have occurred. However, if a trajectory duration is located in a normal zone, there also might be traffic anomaly happened.

We choose a trajectory representation τ_k as *exemplar*, which we recommend to choose with small N_{CT}, as it is more impossible to be anomaly. We define $s(\tau_i, \tau_k)$ as the similarity between $\mathbf{CT}_i$ and $\mathbf{CT}_k$ of exemplar. To calculate the similarity, there is precondition that $N_{CT_i} = N_{CT_k}$. If $N_{CT_k} < N_{CT_i}$, we append $N_{CT_i} - N_{CT_k}$ points of white color (rgb(255, 255, 255)) to $\mathbf{CT}_k$. In that way, we construct a new trajectory representation τ_j to make $N_{CT_i} = N_{CT_j}$, while the temporal feature N_{CT_k} keeps the same.

$$\tau_j = \left(N_{CT_k}, \mathbf{CT}_j\right) = \left(N_{CT_k}, (R_j, G_j, B_j)^T\right) \tag{13}$$

Similarly, if $N_{CT_k} > N_{CT_i}$, we do the same processing on $\mathbf{CT}_i$. Then, the similarity between $\mathbf{CT}_i$ and $\mathbf{CT}_k$ can be derived by Eq. (14).

$$s(\tau_i, \tau_k) = \begin{cases} \sum_{n=1}^{N_{CT_i}} \left(\frac{(R_i^n - R_k^n)^2 + (G_i^n - G_k^n)^2 + (B_i^n - B_k^n)^2}{255^2 + 255^2 + 255^2} \right) & \text{if } N_{CT_i} = N_{CT_k} \\ \sum_{n=1}^{N_{CT_i}} \left(\frac{(R_i^n - R_j^n)^2 + (G_i^n - G_j^n)^2 + (B_i^n - B_j^n)^2}{255^2 + 255^2 + 255^2} \right) & \text{if } N_{CT_i} > N_{CT_k} \\ \sum_{n=1}^{N_{CT_k}} \left(\frac{(R_k^n - R_m^n)^2 + (G_k^n - G_m^n)^2 + (B_k^n - B_m^n)^2}{255^2 + 255^2 + 255^2} \right) & \text{if } N_{CT_i} < N_{CT_k} \end{cases} \tag{14}$$

Suppose $d_{ab}^n = \frac{(R_a^n - R_b^n)^2 + (G_a^n - G_b^n)^2 + (B_a^n - B_b^n)^2}{255^2 + 255^2 + 255^2}$, we introduce a small positive threshold ε, if the similarity between two color points is smaller than ε, we regard that they are the same and the similarity equals 0. Therefore, we have Eq. (15) in Eq. (14).

$$d_{ab}^n = \begin{cases} d_{ab}^n & \text{if } d_{ab}^n \geq \varepsilon \\ 0 & \text{if } d_{ab}^n < \varepsilon \end{cases} \tag{15}$$

For the ith complete trajectory, we have

$$\epsilon_i = \left(N_{CT_i}, s(\tau_i, \tau_k)\right) \tag{16}$$

where $s(\tau_i, \tau_k)$ is a spatial property which reflects the spatial distribution of the moving object. By mapping all ϵ to a two-dimensional space which we refer to as *spatio-temporal plane* here, we could categorize anomalous trajectories into two categories: *class 1 anomaly* and *class 2 anomaly*. They are defined as follows:

Class 1 anomaly: An anomalous trajectory whose associated spatial and temporal feature values are both different from both spatial and temporal feature values of its spatio-temporal neighbors.

Class 2 anomaly: An anomalous trajectory whose associated spatial feature value is very different from the spatial feature values of its temporal neighbors.

Spatio-temporal outliers points can be detected with devised anomalous traffic patterns detection (**ATPD**) algorithm (Algorithm 1), where steps 4 to 13 divide the whole observations into different candidature sets for different detection tasks (class 1 and class 2 anomaly detection) by adopting a threshold N_C. For class 2 anomaly detection, we employ Boxplot rule with a threshold

---

Algorithm 1. ATPD algorithm

---

1 **Parameters**: N_C, δ, r, K;
2 **Input**: ϵ;
3 **Output**: C;
4 $m \leftarrow 0, n \leftarrow 0$;
5 **for** $\epsilon_i \in \epsilon$ **do**
6   **if** $N_{CT_i} \geq N_C$ **then**
7         $m \leftarrow m + 1$;
8         $\epsilon_{C1}(m) \leftarrow N_{CT_i}$;
9   **else**
10         $n \leftarrow n + 1$;
11         $\epsilon_{C2}(n) \leftarrow N_{CT_i}$;
12   **end if**
13 **end for**
14 **for** $\epsilon_{C2}(n) \in \epsilon_{C2}$ **do**
15     $TN \leftarrow$ Temporal K neighbors selection (N_{CT_n}, K);
16     $S \leftarrow$ Get corresponding similarity set (TN, ϵ);
17     $Q_1, Q_3 \leftarrow$ Compute the first and third quartile (S);
18     $IQR \leftarrow Q_3 - Q_1$;
19     $U \leftarrow Q_3 + \delta * IQR$;
20     $L \leftarrow Q_1 - \delta * IQR$;
21   **if** $s_{C2}(\tau_n, \tau_k) > U$ **or** $s_{C2}(\tau_n, \tau_k) < L$ **then**
22         $C_{C2}(n) \leftarrow$ True;
23   **else**
24         $C_{C2}(n) \leftarrow$ False;
25   **end if**
26 **end for**
27 **for** $\epsilon_{C1}(m) \in \epsilon_{C1}$ **do**
28     $D \leftarrow$ Compute distance to the nearest spatio-temporal neighbor $(\epsilon_{C1}(m))$;
29   **if** $D > r$ **then**
30         $C_{C1}(m) \leftarrow$ True;
31   **else**
32         $C_{C1}(m) \leftarrow$ False;
33   **end if**
34 **end for**
35 $C \leftarrow$ Combine (C_{C1}, C_{C2});

δ to uncover anomalous observations (steps 14 to 26). Simultaneously, class 1 anomaly could be detected by computing Euclidean distance from the nearest neighbor and employing a threshold r (steps 27 to 34).

3.3   Anomaly Insight Analysis

We combine Eqs. (1) and (11) together to construct *color trajectory map* (CTM) by integrating $\mathbf{CT}$ with GIS map. Note that $N_{CT} < N$ as the windowing processing introduced. We construct *location vector* l_i and *location matrix* $\mathbf{L}$.

$$l_i = (\varphi_i, \lambda_i)^T \in \mathbb{R}^2 \tag{17}$$

$$\mathbf{L} = \left(l_{\left|\frac{w-1}{2}\right|+1}, l_{\left|\frac{w-1}{2}\right|+2}, \cdots, l_{\left|\frac{w-1}{2}\right|+N-w}, l_{\left|\frac{w-1}{2}\right|+N-w+1} \right) \in \mathbb{R}^{2 \times N_L} \tag{18}$$

where $N_L = N_{CT} = N - \omega + 1$.

We combine the location matrix $\mathbf{L}$ and $\mathbf{CT}$ together to get

$$\mathbf{L}' = (\mathbf{L}, \mathbf{CT}) \tag{19}$$

For each L_i', map color with value of $(R_i, G_i, B_i)^T$ to coordinate $(\varphi_i, \lambda_i)^T$ on the GIS map. So that the CTM of a whole trajectory has been generated.

$$L_i' = \left((\varphi_i, \lambda_i)^T, (R_i, G_i, B_i)^T \right) \tag{20}$$

Color trajectory ($\mathbf{CT}$) and CTM are linked together via rgb value $((R_i, G_i, B_i)^T)$. By comparing the $\mathbf{CT}$ of an anomalous trajectory and non-anomalous trajectories, the anomalous color with significant difference could be found intuitively. Then, the anomaly happened location (road section) could also be discovered on CTM intuitively.

4   Experiments and Analysis

In this section, we conduct extensive experiments for answering the following questions:

Q1: Is **ATPD** effective while detecting all anomalies i.e. high detection rate?

Q2: Does our developed feature visualization method useful for capturing anomaly locations and traffic impacts with detected anomalies using **ATPD**?

Q3: How does our proposed **ATPD** for feature extraction and anomaly detection performs in comparison to the state-of-the-art anomaly detection methods?

4.1 Experimental Settings

Data Sets: We use the GPS trajectory data of bus Route 66, Route 50 and Route 18 in Guiyang, China. All the data (including the local hourly precipitation data) is available at Guiyang Open Government Data Platform [1]. All the data are divided into training and test set: three months for training, and the following one month for testing. Table 1 gives detail description of data sets.

Table 1. Data sets description

Route no	Day type	Whole sample	Training sample	Test sample	Training set period	Test set period	Input dimension
66	Weekend	486	324	162	1 Aug.~ 31 Oct	1 Nov.~ 30 Nov	118041 × 40
50	Weekend	1304	950	354	1 Aug.~ 31 Oct	1 Nov.~ 30 Nov	406030 × 40
18	Weekday Off-peak	1117	824	293	1 Sept.~ 30 Nov	1 Dec.~ 31 Dec	238555 × 40

Parameters: The parameters are set as: $(\omega, \alpha, \beta, \rho, \varepsilon) = (10, 10^{-5}, 10^{-4}, 0.05, 0.01)$ for all the data sets, as suggested by the literature work [12]. The algorithm's parameters are set as: $(N_C, \delta, r, K) = (450, 2.2, 50, 2)$ for Route 66, $(N_C, \delta, r, K) = (500, 1.7, 50, 2)$ for Route 50 and $(N_C, \delta, r, K) = (350, 0.9, 40, 2)$ for Route 18, with the understanding and trials from training set. Besides, we employ a DSAE with four encoding layers with the dimensions of $40 \rightarrow 20 \rightarrow 10 \rightarrow 3$ to get the three-dimensional hidden features.

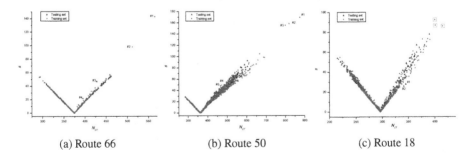

(a) Route 66	(b) Route 50	(c) Route 18

Fig. 2. Spatio-temporal planes of Route 66, 50 and 18. Objects inside   are not with high confidence to be regarded as anomalies, as their spatial and temporal features are not far away from their spatio-temporal neighbors.

4.2 Result from Anomalous Patterns Detection (Answering Q1)

To evaluate this criteria we utilize the detection rate (precision) calculated as $TP/(TP + FN)$ and false alarm rate calculated as $FP/(FP + TN)$ [18]. The performance comparisons of our proposed **ATPD** versus popular baselines are shown in Table 3, note that we transfer the anomalous observations in training set to test set in order to enlarge the anomalous sample size for performance testing. The proposed **ATPD** detects all anomalies with low false alarm rate. Visualizations of spatio-temporal planes for Route 66, 50 and 18 are shown in Fig. 2, where points are distributed along the tick ($\checkmark$) with the pattern that similarity s increases with N_{CT} when $N_{CT} > N_{CT_k}$, while it decreases with N_{CT} when $N_{CT} < N_{CT_k}$. Moreover, at first glance, we can discern those anomalous objects that are not located in the expected zones from the spatio-temporal planes shown in Fig. 2. Also, in Fig. 2(a), anomalies #1 and #2 are referred as *class 1 anomaly* as their spatial and temporal features are both far away from their spatio-temporal neighbors, and so does anomalies #1, #2, and #3 in Fig. 2(b). However, we regard anomaly #3, #4 in Fig. 2(a), #4, #5 in Fig. 2(b) and #1, #2 in Fig. 2(c) as *class 2 anomaly*, as only their spatial features are far away from their temporal neighbors. In general, class 1 anomaly has more serious impact on traffic than class 2 anomaly, while class 2 anomaly is more difficult to uncover.

The detected outliers by using our model are all coincide with the known traffic anomalous events (Table 2). They are listed in the following:

Known event 1: A sedan bumped another car at the Shachong East Road in the late afternoon of 14 August 2016, the driver of the sedan ran away after accident resulting in severe traffic congestion. Note that it was raining during this time period and the event only affected services for Route 50.

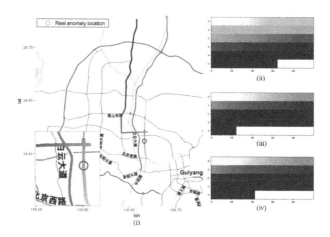

Fig. 3. Insight analysis example of anomaly #1 in Route 66. (i) CTM of anomaly #1. (ii) CT of anomaly #1. (iii) CT of an non-anomaly. (iv) CT of another non-anomaly. (Color figure online)

Known event 2: A severe car crash (a SUV and a truck) happened in the West No.2 Ring Road in the morning of 18 September 2016. Two men died and one got injured. This event imposed impacts on Route 66 and Route 50 bus services.

Known event 3: Two cars crashed at a bus station near the Guizhou Cancer Hospital (West Beijing Road) around the noon on 26 November 2016. A pedestrian died. This event only affected Route 66 service.

Known event 4: A SUV crashed an electric motorcycle in North Wenchang Avenue in the morning of 14 December 2016. Two riders on the electric motorcycle got injured while trapping under the vehicle. Only Route 18 service was influenced by this event.

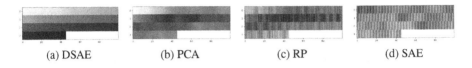

(a) DSAE   (b) PCA   (c) RP   (d) SAE

Fig. 4. A color trajectory in Route 66 generated by methods of DSAE, PCA, RP and SAE. The CT generated by our DSAE based method is the most smooth and distinct. (Color figure online)

4.3 Result from Visualization and Anomaly Insight Analysis (Answering Q2)

Figure 4(a) gives an example of the CT from a real-world bus trajectory. For Fig. 4(a), the bus trajectory starts at color of yellow   , with the bus proceeding to the destination, the color changes gradually and finally terminates at blue ■. The horizontal axis indicates the trajectory duration (N_{CT}, 1 unit equals 10 seconds, each row contains 100 units).

Table 2. Detected anomalies

Route	Anomaly	Date	Running Time	Event	Category
66	#1	18 Sept. 2016	07:29-09:00	Event 2	Class 1 anomaly
	#2	18 Sept. 2016	07:00-08:23	Event 2	Class 1 anomaly
	#3	26 Nov. 2016	12:43-13:55	Event 3	Class 2 anomaly
	#4	26 Nov. 2016	12:07-13:09	Event 3	Class 2 anomaly
50	#1	18 Sept. 2016	06:58-09:25	Event 2	Class 1 anomaly
	#2	18 Sept. 2016	07:22-09:40	Event 2	Class 1 anomaly
	#3	18 Sept. 2016	07:34-09:48	Event 2	Class 1 anomaly
	#4	14 Aug. 2016	19:41-21:01	Event 1	Class 2 anomaly
	#5	14 Aug. 2016	17:32-18:51	Event 1	Class 2 anomaly
18	#1	14 Dec. 2016	09:31-10:28	Event 4	Class 2 anomaly
	#2	14 Dec. 2016	09:50-10:48	Event 4	Class 2 anomaly

After detecting anomalous trajectory we can get the CTM of these trajectories by fusion of the GIS map (Eq. 20). We illustrate an anomalous trajectory by taking the CTM of anomaly #1 for Route 66 as example as displayed in Fig. 3, where ○ in (i) denotes the actual event site. In contrast the CT of anomaly #1 (Fig. 3 (ii)) and non-anomalies (Fig. 3 (iii) and (iv)) we could have an intuitive perspective that the anomaly might have occurred around light yellow ▨ color. Since, the trajectory part with such color is quite different from those of non-anomalies. However, when it proceeds to color of grey ■, the rest partial colors turn to be similar to those of non-anomalies. Therefore, we could infer that the anomaly indeed happened at the locations highlighted between locations ▨ and ■ in Fig. 3, which is in line with the real location (○) of event 2. Apart from location detection, we also provide influential insights to this car crash by highlighting road between ▨ and ■ (left bottom of Fig. 3).

4.4   Baseline and Comparison (Answering Q3)

Feature Extraction and Visualization: We compare our model with other popular baselines in dimensionality reduction: PCA, random projection (RP) and sparse autoencoder (SAE). In contrast the CTs generated by DSAE (Fig. 4(a)) and baselines ((Fig. 4)(b) (c) (d)), we can find that DSAE gets a more smooth and distinct color distribution. In Fig. 5, by comparing the spatio-temporal planes derived by above baselines, we can find that none of these baselines can get favorable detection performance than the DSAE-based model on all data sets. Some anomalies (especially for class 2 anomaly) are mixed together with non-anomalies (#3, #4 in Route 66 with PCA and SAE, #4, #5 in Route 50 with RP and SAE, #1, #2 in Route 18 with PCA, RP and SAE), which is quite difficult to detect. Moreover, many non-anomalies can be mis-detected as outliers with high confidence (labeled ○ in Fig. 5).

We define an evaluation index named averaged moving standard deviation (AMSD) to evaluate the concentration of tick shape ($\checkmark$) distributed data. We employ a window size (κ) for windowing operation along N_{CT} (horizontal axis), compute the sample standard deviation of all normalized $s\left(\tau_{ij}, \tau_k\right)$ (denoted as $\hat{s}\left(\tau_{ij}, \tau_k\right)$) within each κ-sized N_{CT}. Following this, we get the mean standard deviation of all κ-sized N_{CT} for AMSD. We remove those anomalous trajectories from training sets, and calculate the AMSD value of all the non-anomalies derived from DSAE-based model and other baselines. In Fig. 6, our model performs best in data sets of Route 66 and Route 18. RP can get fairly good performance in Route 50, however, its performance in anomaly detection is poorly as it mis-detected quite a number of points in Route 50.

$$AMSD = \frac{1}{m} \sum_{i=1}^{m} \sqrt{\frac{1}{n_i - 1} \sum_{j=1}^{n_i} \left(\hat{s}\left(\tau_{ij}, \tau_k\right) - \bar{s}_i\right)} \tag{21}$$

Anomaly Detection: We also compare our model (**ATPD**) with other baselines that employed in outlier/anomaly detection: classification based (one-class SVM, long short-term memory (LSTM) networks), clustering based (affinity

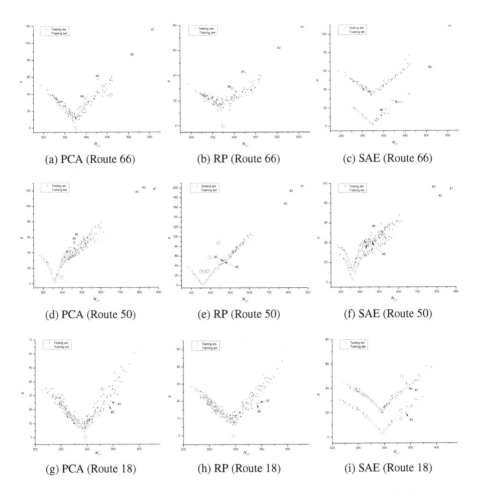

Fig. 5. Spatio-temporal planes from baselines of PCA, RP and SAE.

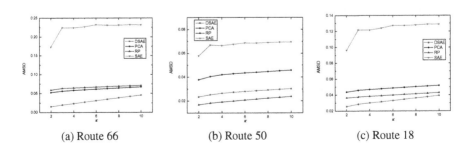

Fig. 6. Concentration performance evaluation in training sets.

propagation (AP) clustering) and nearest-neighbor based (kNN) [2]. We also feed the extracted features via DSAE into those baselines. The performances are given in Table 3. Since there is no anomalous trajectory in Rout 18 training set, supervised learning of SVM, LSTM and kNN cannot be conducted. Overall, **ATPD** can get superior performance, SVM performs poorly since it might have exploited inadequacies of the soft-margin maximization paradigm when handling extremely imbalanced data [4].

Table 3. Comparison of performance in test set with baselines

Route	Detection Rate					False Alarm Rate				
	ATPD	SVM	LSTM	AP	kNN	**ATPD**	SVM	LSTM	AP	kNN
66	100%	0	25.00%	50.00%	50.00%	0.63%	38.12%	0	12.50%	0
50	100%	0	20.00%	60.00%	60.00%	1.69%	51.98%	0	0	0
18	100%	—	—	0	—	3.09%	—	—	0.34%	—

5   Conclusion and Future Work

In this paper, we proposed an anomalous traffic patterns detection method for bus trajectory data analysis. We extracted spatial and temporal properties from the color trajectory derived from deep learning method, and then devised an algorithm based on Boxplot rule and nearest neighbor for anomalous patterns detection. We integrated the visualized color trajectory with GIS map to generate color trajectory map, from which we can get intuitive insights into the locations of these anomalies and also the traffic influences to road by the corresponding anomalies. Experiments on three real-world bus route data sets confirmed the effectiveness and superiority of our proposed method compared with baselines of PCA, RP, SAE, SVM, LSTM, AP and kNN. Some cities have adopted 'Bus Lane' strategy for some metropolitan roads in certain periods to improve the reliability and efficiency of bus services. In that case, our approach may not be efficient to detect some city-wide incident-based anomalies, as the situation that some incidents that affect other vehicles on the road might not affect buses. However, from the perspective of bus service operation or management, such situation does not make much sense, since those anomalies that impose little impact on bus service will not be taken into account for decision making. In the future, we plan to study the online approach based on the developed methodology for real-time traffic anomaly detection, which is essential as buses run on almost all major roads of the city area.

References

1. Guiyang open government data platform. http://www.gyopendata.gov.cn/city/index.htm. Accessed 1 Feb 2018
2. Chandola, V., Banerjee, A., Kumar, V.: Anomaly detection: a survey. ACM Comput. Surv. (CSUR) **41**(3), 15 (2009)
3. Chawla, S., Zheng, Y., Hu, J.: Inferring the root cause in road traffic anomalies. In: Proceedings of 2012 IEEE 12th International Conference on Data Mining, pp. 141–150 (2012)
4. He, H., Garcia, E.A.: Learning from imbalanced data. IEEE Trans. Knowl. Data Eng. **9**, 1263–1284 (2008)
5. Juvonen, A., Hamalainen, T.: An efficient network log anomaly detection system using random projection dimensionality reduction. In: Proceedings of 2014 6th International Conference on New Technologies, Mobility and Security (NTMS), pp. 1–5. IEEE (2014)
6. Kong, X., Song, X., Xia, F., Guo, H., Wang, J., Tolba, A.: LoTAD: long-term traffic anomaly detection based on crowdsourced bus trajectory data. World Wide Web **21**(3), 825–847 (2018)
7. Kuang, W., An, S., Jiang, H.: Detecting traffic anomalies in urban areas using taxi GPS data. Math. Probl. Eng. **2015**, 1–14 (2015)
8. Lakhina, A., Crovella, M., Diot, C.: Diagnosing network-wide traffic anomalies. In: ACM SIGCOMM Computer Communication Review, vol. 34, pp. 219–230. ACM (2004)
9. Li, K.L., Huang, H.K., Tian, S.F., Xu, W.: Improving one-class SVM for anomaly detection. In: Proceedings of 2003 International Conference on Machine Learning Cybernetics, vol. 5, pp. 3077–3081. IEEE (2003)
10. Li, Y., Guo, T., Xia, R., Xie, W.: Road traffic anomaly detection based on fuzzy theory. IEEE Access **6**, 40281–40288 (2018)
11. Li, Y., Liu, W., Huang, Q.: Traffic anomaly detection based on image descriptor in videos. Multimedia Tools Appl. **75**(5), 2487–2505 (2016)
12. Liu, H., Taniguchi, T., Tanaka, Y., Takenaka, K., Bando, T.: Visualization of driving behavior based on hidden feature extraction by using deep learning. IEEE Trans. Intell. Transp. Syst. **18**(9), 2477–2489 (2017)
13. Liu, W., Zheng, Y., Chawla, S., Yuan, J., Xing, X.: Discovering spatio-temporal causal interactions in traffic data streams. In: Proc. 17th ACM SIGKDD International Conference on Knowledge Discovery and Data Mining, pp. 1010–1018. ACM (2011)
14. Münz, G., Li, S., Carle, G.: Traffic anomaly detection using k-means clustering. In: GI/ITG Workshop MMBnet, pp. 13–14 (2007)
15. Nguyen, H., Liu, W., Rivera, P., Chen, F.: TrafficWatch: real-time traffic incident detection and monitoring using social media. In: Bailey, J., Khan, L., Washio, T., Dobbie, G., Huang, J.Z., Wang, R. (eds.) PAKDD 2016. LNCS (LNAI), vol. 9651, pp. 540–551. Springer, Cham (2016). https://doi.org/10.1007/978-3-319-31753-3_43
16. Pang, L., Chawla, S., Liu, W., Zheng, Y.: On detection of emerging anomalous traffic patterns using GPS data. Data Knowl. Eng. **87**, 357–373 (2013)
17. Riveiro, M., Lebram, M., Elmer, M.: Anomaly detection for road traffic: a visual analytics framework. IEEE Trans. Intell. Transp. Syst. **18**(8), 2260–2270 (2017)
18. Tsai, C.F., Lin, C.Y.: A triangle area based nearest neighbors approach to intrusion detection. Pattern Recogn. **43**(1), 222–229 (2010)

19. Zhang, D., Li, N., Zhou, Z.H., Chen, C., Sun, L., Li, S.: iBAT: detecting anomalous taxi trajectories from GPS traces. In: Proceedings of 13th International Conference on Ubiquitous Computing, pp. 99–108. ACM (2011)
20. Zhang, X., Zhao, Z., Zheng, Y., Li, J.: Prediction of taxi destinations using a novel data embedding method and ensemble learning. IEEE Trans. Intell. Transp. Syst 1–11 (2019). https://doi.org/10.1109/TITS.2018.2888587

Knowledge-Based Robotic Agent
as a Game Player

Misbah Javaid$^{(\boxtimes)}$ ⓘ, Vladimir Estivill-Castro ⓘ, and Rene Hexel ⓘ

School of Information and Communication Technology, Griffith University,
Nathan, QLD 4111, Australia
misbah.javaid@griffithuni.edu.au

Abstract. To investigate, how a *Robot*'s communication ability in terms
of *explanations* can cultivate better trust relationships between a *Robot*
and it's human teammates. We opted a partial information game-
playing environment, to immerse interaction between humans and a
Robotic Agent. We designed our *Robotic Agent* as a *Knowledge-Based
(KB) Robotic Agent* that does not play perfectly, but plays with significant expertise and approximates well enough by updating it's *belief*
all the time in a partially observable environment. We developed the
explanation-generation mechanism on top of the game that generates
meaningful *explanations* for the strategy of a game at a level that the
human teammates appreciate and understand. The generated *explanations* adapt according to the game situation that can increase human's
overall understanding of the task domain. We evaluated the individual
effectiveness of our *KB Robotic Agent*, by developing a *Case Study* with
the partial information game *Domino*. In a computational experiment,
our *KB Robotic Agent* played 10,000 game matches with other agents
and exhibited a reasonable winning rate. With this victory proportion,
we can conclude that our *KB Robotic Agent* captured and analysed all
available information intelligently and forecast the possible moves of the
opponents correctly.

Keywords: Trust · Explanations · Human-robot interaction

1 Introduction

The diverse and growing number of robotic application has created a significant
effect on human society [10], and a human's interaction with a robot has evolved
from operator interaction to peer interaction. Yet, it has also generated different
challenges that require to be overcome before a human-robot team could work
successfully [5]. One of the primary challenges is to ensure appropriate levels
of human's trust in a robot [1,6]. Trust is a challenging aspect for humans and
robots to perform together as a team [3]. Trends in the literature have shown that
if humans do not trust autonomous systems, the interaction between human and
system may suffer that ultimately leads to abortion of future interaction [4,7]. We

© Springer Nature Switzerland AG 2019
A. C. Nayak and A. Sharma (Eds.): PRICAI 2019, LNAI 11672, pp. 322–336, 2019.
https://doi.org/10.1007/978-3-030-29894-4_27

argue that by augmenting a robot with the capability of providing *explanations* can tailor human-robot interaction and make it possible for a human to trust a robot. In human-human interaction, *explanations* serve to make something clear and understandable and are given to change, clarify or impart knowledge. Similarly, in human-robot interaction (HRI), *explanations*, by virtue of making the performance of a *Robot* transparent to its human teammates, solve the challenging problem of human's trust in robots. In this manner, hand-craft explanations have also shown to be promising in providing enough transparency to humans [2]. Therefore, the research at hand rendering more human like approach by augmenting a robot with the *explanations* capability to establish a trust relationship between human and a robot. We developed an HRI scenario in which a *Robotic Agent* plays a partial information game with humans in teams (four players are divided in two teams). The *Robotic Agent* plays a dual role, i.e., as an adversary with two humans and as a team partner with a human. We selected a team-based scenario, in which humans and a *Robot* interact and play together. We expect, by supplementing the *Robotic Agent* with the *explanation* ability also help in improving human-robot team performance.

1.1 Main Contributions of this Study

This study addresses four main contributions:

1. The development and implementation of a *Knowledge-Based(KB) Robotic Agent* that can deal with the hidden information of a game.
2. Autonomous decision-making of the *KB Robotic Agent* to play a multi-player strategy game with humans with significantly expertise by playing a dual role, i.e. an adversary and a team partner.
3. The implementation details of the *Explanation-Generation* mechanism of the *KB Robotic Agent*.
4. The evaluation of the individual effectiveness of the *KB Robotic Agent*, by developing a *Case Study* with the partial information game *Domino*, which has not been studied before in Artificial Intelligence (AI).

We chose *Domino* for our study because (1) environment in the game of *Domino* is partially observable. (2) There is no explicit verbal communication during the game in the environment. (3) It is also a multi-player team-based game that requires teammates to develop trust in each other. (4) It is also played in teams (in pairs) that adds an element of cooperation and competition among teammates. We divided the paper into different sections. Section 2 shows complete system architecture of our HRI scenario, by highlighting the main components of our *Knowledge Base Robotic Agent* that generates autonomous behaviour within the HRI scenario. Section 3 presents a *Case Study* with the help of a partial information game *Domino*, to describe the performance evaluation of our *Knowledge Base Robotic Agent*. Section 4 describes how our *Knowledge Base Robotic Agent* generates different types of *explanations*.

2   Complete System Architecture for HRI

Figure 1, shows the complete integration framework that organises all the main modules involved in the HRI scenario.

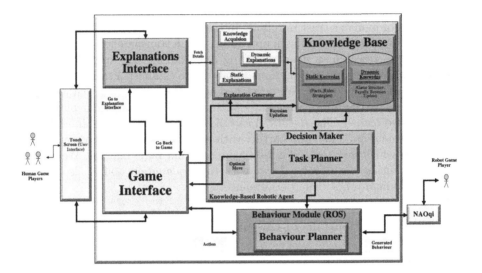

Fig. 1. Complete architectural overview of our HRI scenario.

2.1   Detailed Overview of Our Knowledge-Based Robotic Agent

We created our *Robotic Agent*, as an intelligent *"Knowledge-Based (KB) Agent"* which has three main modules.

1. **The Knowledge-Based Module:** On the implementation facet, the central component of our *KB Robotic Agent* is the *Knowledge-Base* module that incorporates an up-to-date repository of well organised data for the accurate and quick response to other modules (i.e. *Decision Maker module, Explanation Generator module*) for further computations. Its primary responsibility is to store two types of knowledge. (1) *Static Knowledge* that includes rules, facts and mechanics regarding the task[1]. (2) *Dynamic Knowledge*: Direct knowledge of the task environment is inaccessible because of the partial observability. Therefore, the *KB Robotic Agent* uses *Bayesian Inference* to capture the information regarding the task environment in terms of observations and return those observations as *belief* states to the *Knowledge-Base*. Also, the *KB Robotic Agent* updates its *belief space* after every new information is revealed (*Bayesian Updation*).

---

[1] Here task means game.

2. **The Decision-Maker Module:** that gleans insight from the information housed in the *Knowledge Base* and uses that information for doing all the reasoning (decision-making) for the game-play according to some strategy. To do so, the *Decision-Maker* module uses *MinMax* algorithm with *Alpha-beta pruning* in it's reasoning process to approximate well enough and make inferences to provide a solution for a given problem based on the current state of the game.
3. **The Explanation-Generator Module:** we adopt a human-in-the-loop approach by augmenting the *KB Robotic Agent* with the capability of providing different types of *explanations* to make complex behaviour of the *KB Robotic Agent* more understandable and intuitive for a human that will lead to build the trust of the human on it's *KB Robotic Agent* (see Sect. 4 for details).

2.2 Behaviour Module

The *Behaviour Module* stabilises the decisions made by the *Decision Maker* module by taking the *final decided move* from the *Decision-Maker* module and produces an appropriate sequence of behaviour. The *Behavioural Module* uses *ROS* (Robotic Operating System) that is predominantly used to interface with the *KB Robotic Agent* itself, through the *NAOqi* framework[2], is mainly responsible for *KB Robotic Agent's* physical behaviour according to *game-play* events i.e., *click and play*.

3 Case Study

The remainder of this paper highlight the performance evaluation of our *KB Robotic Agent* by developing a *Case Study* scenario with the help of partial information game *Domino*. Before moving forward, first, we discuss the mechanics of the partial information game *Domino*.

3.1 Mechanics of the Game Domino

The version of the *Domino* game is four players P_i (for $i = 0,1,2,3$), with some partnering, where P_i is in the same team as P_j if $i \cong j$ mod 2. We have our focus on the *"Block Type Game of Domino"* in which a player can have only two choices (1) to make a legal move by putting a tile with an endpoint matching one of the open ends (either left or right) of the current board (2) *Pass* if the player has no legal move, and turn will be forwarded to next player. Let S represents a double-six set of 28 unique *Domino* tiles of the form: $S_{uv} = \{u,v\}$, $0 \leq u, v \leq 6$ and u can be equal to v. The total number of dots d of a *Domino* tile is defined as $d(S_{uv}) = u + v$. The game starts by setting a constant permutation ($P_{uv} = \pi(S_{uv})$) and at the start of each game, each player i gets seven random

---

[2] *NAOqi* is the main programming framework, that runs on the robot and controls it.

Domino tiles from the permutation $\{P_{8(i-1)+1}, P_{8(i-1+2)}, \ldots, P_{8i}\}$. Players take their turn clockwise. The first move of the first round must be made by the player with the highest pips, i.e., (6,6). The 28 *Domino tiles* can also be labeled as the edges E of the complete graph K_v on $V = \{0,1,2,3,4,5,6\}$ including loops (i.e., (v,v) is an edge in E for all $v \in V$). *Domino* is a non-deterministic game, because of the random shuffling and dealting of tiles among four players at the beginning of every game. However, the element of non-determinism is resolved, after all players receive their *HAND*.[3]

3.2   Dynamic Knowledge Acquision

In the game, our *KB Robotic Agent* continuously updates it's *belief* using *Bayesian Inference*. (1) When it receives it's *HAND*, before the start of every game and (2) when any player makes a move or fails to make a move because this changes the environment and reveals information about someone's *HAND* and strategy to play the game.

Bayesian Inference: *Bayesian Inference* derives a *posterior* probability as a consequence of two antecedents, a *prior* probability and a *likelihood function* derived from a statistical model for the observed data. *Bayesian Inference* computes the *posterior* probability according to Bayes' theorem:

$$Prob(H|E) = \frac{Prob(E|H)\ Prob(H)}{Prob(E)} \qquad (1)$$

where:

- Conditional probability has been denoted by (i.e., *given* with |)
- H stands for the *belief* whose probability may be affected by new data.
- the evidence E is an observation that is captured through a sensor
- Prob(H), *the prior probability*, is the probability of H before E is observed
- Prob($H \mid E$), *the posterior probability* is the probability of H given E (after E is observed)
- Prob($E \mid H$), is the probability of observing E given H[4]
- Prob(E) is sometimes termed the marginal likelihood or *model evidence*.

Before the game begins, our *KB Robotic Agent* has some initial *belief* ahead of time for certain regarding the position of 28 tiles among four players. The initial *belief* is some previous estimation known as *prior* probability before gaining the current evidence E. For each player P_i the initial *belief* is as: $Prob(H_{p_i,(u,v)}) = 1/4$ (or 7/28) regarding the position of the 28 tiles among four players (discrete probability mass function).

---

[3] A *HAND* represents a set of seven tiles of a player.

[4] In some literature, it is considered as sensor model, that is the probability of observing E given that H is true.

Belief Updation After Every Player Received it's HAND: After the tiles are dealt among four players, our *KB Robotic Agent* P_i collects it's seven tiles and makes the fundamental *belief* for making a move as:

$$H_{P_i,(u,v)} = \text{Player } P_i \text{ is supplied } (u,v) \text{ initially} \tag{2}$$

for all $i \in \{0,1,2,3\}$ and all edges (u,v) in E.

The *KB Robotic Agent* P_i learns by collecting it's HAND and updates it's *prior belief* based on the tiles it received using Bayes' theorem. The updation of *belief* is after seeing the evidence E as: if P_i is given a tile (u,v), then $Prob(H_{P_i,(u,v)}) = 1$, while $Prob(H_{p_j,(u,v)}) = 0$, for all $j \neq i$. Similarly, if the *KB Robotic Agent* P_i is not given a tile (u,v), then: $Prob(H_{P_i,(u,v)}) = 0$, while $Prob(H_{P_j,(u,v)}) = 7/21$ (or $1/3$), for all $j \neq i$.

Belief Space: Figure 2, shows a glimpse of *belief space* before and after every player received it's *HAND*. Our *KB Robotic Agent* is sure[5] only about those tiles which are in it's *HAND*. As the game proceeds, the *KB Robotic Agent* gets more information about the true state of the environment[6] and updates it's *belief space*.

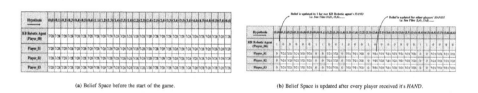

(a) Belief Space before the start of the game.   (b) Belief Space is updated after every player received it's *HAND*.

Fig. 2. Change in belief space before and after every player received it's HAND.

Belief Updation When a Player Put a Tile on the Board: Let's take a simple example of the fundamental *belief* updation when a player j put a tile (u,v) on the board. Now the *KB Robotic Agent* P_i has seen the evidence E as: *The player j holds the tile (u,v)*. The *KB Robotic Agent* P_i has already some previous estimate in the form of *prior* probability $1/3$ (less than one) for the hypothesis $(H_j = (H_{P_j,(u,v)})$, for other players holding (u,v). Moreover, our *KB Robotic Agent* P_i also knows that he does not hold the tile (u,v) because it has already *updated* it's *belief* for all those tiles, it did not get as $Prob(H_{P_i,(u,v)}) = 0$ for all $j \neq i$. Therefore, further evidence that the *KB Robotic Agent* P_i does not hold the tile (u,v) will not change it's *belief*

---

[5] Sure means the *belief* computed after seeing the evidence, which is basically *posterior* probability because it reflects the level of *belief* computed in the light of the new evidence.

[6] By keeping track of the moves played by each player including *passes* and the number of *tiles* in other players' *HAND*.

and $Prob(H_i = (H_{P_i,(u,v)})$ will remain 0. Actually, Bayes' theorem explains it that our *KB Robotic Agent* already knows it doesn't hold a tile *(u,v)* so any further evidence that our *KB Robotic Agent* doesn't hold it will not change it's *belief* and $Prob(H_i \mid E) = 0$ will remain same.[7] Now, interestingly, our *KB Robotic Agent* P_i will learn through the evidence E that when some other player j holds the tile (u,v) then any other player k can not hold it. Bayes' theorem explains it in this way that if a player j holds the tile (u,v), then the player k could not have revealed it. That is, the *KB Robotic Agent* will never observe that a player k holding a tile (u, v). Therefore, the *KB Robotic Agent* updates it's *belief* for any other player k as $Prob(E \mid H_k) = 0$, and for player j who has revealed a tile (u,v) as:

$$Prob(H_j \mid E) = \frac{Prob(E \mid H_j)\ Prob(H_j)}{\sum_{t=0,1,2,3} Prob(E \mid H_t)Prob(H_t)} \tag{3}$$

$$Prob(H_j \mid E) = \frac{Prob(E \mid H_j)\ Prob(H_j)}{Prob(E \mid H_j)Prob(H_j)} = 1 \tag{4}$$

This is because when $t \neq j$, the *KB Robotic Agent* knows $Prob(E \mid H_t) = 0$. It is impossible to see the evidence E, when some other player holds it.[8]

Belief Updation When a Player Passed it's Turn for Making a Move. Let's take an example, when a player j *passes* it's turn for a tile *(u,v)*. Now, our *KB Robotic Agent* P_i knows for sure that a player P_j is lack of having any tile with a value matching to any of the open ends on the board (means having 0 probability). Therefore, it *updates* it's *belief* for the player j as 0 for all those tiles containing the number matching to any of the open ends on the board and renormalises the probabilities pertaining to the other players for all those tiles containing that particular number(s). However, the player who has more unplayed tiles, has more chances of having a tile with that specific numbers as compared to the player who has less unplayed tiles. Figure 3(b), shows an example of Player_ 02 *passed* it's turn for making a move, when there is number 6 on the both open ends of the board. The Player_ 03 has more unplayed tiles, therefore, it has more chances of having a tile with the numbers 6 as compared to the Player_ 01, who has less unplayed tiles. As the game proceeds and more actual knowledge gets disclosed, the estimated *belief space* becomes true *belief space*. Based on the player's set of moves, *Bayesian Inference* not only allows an implicit deduction of what a player's tiles are but it also makes explicit expectations over the tiles and gives observed information more accurately. The *KB Robotic Agent* not only *updates* it's *belief* space regarding the probabilities of all other tiles pertaining to each player, but it can also estimate the location of a tile by making prediction ie. how likely are the remaining unknown tiles among other players (*Bayesian Prediction*).

---

[7] Because it is the probability of the hypothesis given the observed evidence.

[8] When $Prob(E \mid H)$ is considered as likelihood, it is seen as a function of H with E fixed. It indicates the compatibility of the evidence with the given hypothesis.

Belief Space After the First Move and When a Player Passed it's Turn for Making a Move: Figure 3(a), shows the whole *belief space* is *updated* after the first move and the probability of all other tiles have also been slightly increased. Figure 3(b), shows when a player fails to make a move, the whole *belief space* gets *updated* because it changes the environment and reveals information about the *HAND* of the player who *passed* it's turn. The probability also gets bigger of any tile belonging to a player at the expense of more unplayed tiles than one with fewer.

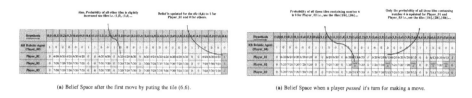

(a) Belief Space after the first move by puting the tile (6,6).   (a) Belief Space when a player *passed* it's turn for making a move.

Fig. 3. Updation in belief space.

3.3   Decision-Making

The *KB Robotic Agent* uses *MinMax* algorithm with *Alpha-beta pruning* to calculate the best possible moves. The *KB Robotic Agent* and his teammate represent *max* players and the opponents two players are *min* players. We used standard *MinMax* algorithm and allowed each possible move's score to be disconnected from their current probabilities by rounding them off to 1 and assign 0 to rest of the moves. This approach provided not only provided a simple heuristic to estimate the position of few *Domino* tiles play but also permitted the use of *alpha-beta pruning* algorithm, which optimises the *MinMax* technique by adjusting the parameters towards the value of a more in-depth search and culling the search paths that could not contribute to the final result. In this way, the *KB Robotic Agent* estimates the order of some given *Domino* tiles by using the approach for *perfect information* game. Rounding off to the nearest 0's and 1's is an approximation-space that leaves out a few states based upon the observations while keeping track of all possible sets of *Domino* tiles that have been observed before. Given the current state of the game[9], the *KB Robotic Agent* determines what *HANDS* the other players could possibly have and returns the best possible move[10].

3.4   Evaluation of Our Knowledge-Based Robotic Agent

We present the performance comparison between our *KB Robotic Agent* with other players based on how many rounds it wins/loses or draw against a team of

---

[9] Open ends on the board, the sizes of all other players' *HANDS*, moves played by every player including *passes* and current *belief space*.

[10] Choose an adequate tile to play.

(1) *Random* players, who prefers to play random moves (2) *Perfect Information* players, who are skilled enough and know everyone's *HAND* during the game through *cheating*. We played total 10,000 team-based games. Please note, for the sake of simplicity, we call the *Perfect Information* players as the "*Perfect*" player and our *Knowledge-Base Robotic Agent* as "*KB*" player.

First Simulation of Games: Team of KB Players vs. Team of Random Players: In the first simulation of *games*, we partnered our *KB* player with another *KB* player and played 5000 games against two *Random* players.

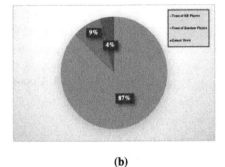

No. of Games Played	No. of games team of KB players Won	No. of games team of KB players Loss	Games Draw
5000	4350	450	200

(a)

(b)

Fig. 4. (a) Game statistics. (b) Overall performance comparison of both teams.

Overall, the performance of our team of *KB* players maintained their highest victory proportion in this short experiment of 5000 games, as shown in the Fig. 4.

Second Simulation Experiment: Team of KB Players vs. Team of Perfect Players. In the second experiment, our team of *KB* players played a total of 5000 *games* against a team of *Perfect* players. The overall performance of our team *KB* Players does not seem to be on the same par with the team of *Perfect* players, who maintained their highest victory proportion. We not only account for wins and loses between two teams, but we also investigated that the team of *Perfect* players always turn out with positive score, even in the games the team of *Perfect* players lost. The difference between our team of *KB* players and the team of *Perfect* players is quite straightforward in the sense that the team of *Perfect* players know every other player's *HANDS* including the *HANDS* of their team partner's (Fig. 5).

Therefore, the team of *Perfect* Players have more chances of winning because they compute all possible paths of the game from an initial configuration that leads to success. Therefore, the only way for the team of *Perfect* Players to lose is if one or both *Perfect* Players are dealt with a very bad *HAND* at the beginning of the game(s).

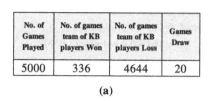

No. of Games Played	No. of games team of KB players Won	No. of games team of KB players Loss	Games Draw
5000	336	4644	20

(a)

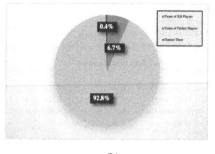

(b)

Fig. 5. (a) Game statistics. (b) Overall performance comparison of both teams.

Third Simulation of Game: Team of KB Players vs. Team of Random Players - (Two Sets of Tiles Randomly Selected and Fixed:). In the third simulation, we shuffled the tiles and randomly selected two sets of tiles. The set of the selected tiles remained fixed throughout the game. However, the position of the players exchanged. We gave both the teams an opportunity to play with the same set of tiles. Basically, this simulation constitutes a *HAND*, and we want to analyse the difference of the lost margin of both teams in terms of the difference of the tiles *left* in each player's *HAND* (Fig. 6).

Player_00 (*KB Player*)	(3,6),(4,6),(2,2),(0,4),(0,2),(2,5),(2,4)
Player_01 (*Random Player*)	(2,3),(0,6),(3,4),(2,6),(0,5),(3,5),(0,1)
Player_02 (*KB Player*)	(6,6),(1,6),(0,0),(1,3),(1,2),(5,6),(0,3)
Player_03 (*Random Player*)	(1,4),(1,1),(4,4),(5,5),(1,5),(4,5),(3,3)

(a) Tiles of the players'

Player_00 (*KB Player*)	(2,5),(2,4)
Player_01 (*Random Player*)	(3,5),(0,1)
Player_02 (*KB Player*)	(0,3)
Player_03 (*Random Player*)	(4,4),(5,5),(1,5),(4,5),(3,3)

(b) Tiles' left in each player's HAND

Player_00 (*Random Player*)	(3,6),(4,6),(2,2),(0,4),(0,2),(2,5),(2,4)
Player_01 (*KB Player*)	(2,3),(0,6),(3,4),(2,6),(0,5),(3,5),(0,1)
Player_02 (*Random Player*)	(6,6),(1,6),(0,0),(1,3),(1,2),(5,6),(0,3)
Player_03 (*KB Player*)	(1,4),(1,1),(4,4),(5,5),(1,5),(4,5),(3,3)

(c) Tiles of the players' after position of the players' is swapped

Player_00 (*Random Player*)	(2,2),(2,4)
Player_01 (*KB Player*)	
Player_02 (*Random Player*)	(1,2)
Player_03 (*KB Player*)	(1,4),(5,5)

(d) Tiles' left in each player's HAND after position of the players' is swapped

Fig. 6. First set of tiles.

We observed that with the same tile-set, our team of *KB* players analysed the open ends of the board more intelligently as compared to team of *Random* players, and won both the games. We interpreted this to mean that, in the early phase of the game where most *Domino* tiles are uncertain. Our team of *KB* players had a potentially better deduction of what a player's tiles are based on their current set of moves (Fig. 7).

Player_00 (*KB* Player)	(6,6),(0,2),(1,1),(0,3),(2,5),(1,4),(0,6)
Player_01 (*Random* Player)	(3,6),(2,3),(1,6),(4,5),(5,5),(4,4),(3,4)
Player_02 (*KB* Player)	(3,5),(1,3),(5,6),(3,3),(1,5),(1,2),(0,1)
Player_03 (*Random* Player)	(0,5),(4,6),(0,4),(2,4),(0,0),(2,6),(2,2)

(a) Tiles of the players'

Player_00 (*KB* Player)	
Player_01 (*Random* Player)	(4,5),(5,5),(4,4),(3,4)
Player_02 (*KB* Player)	(3,5)
Player_03 (*Random* Player)	(0,0),(2,4),(4,6),(2,2)

(b) Tiles' left in each player's HAND

Player_00 (*Random Player*)	(6,6),(0,2),(1,1),(0,3),(2,5),(1,4),(0,6)
Player_01 (*KB Player*)	(3,6),(2,3),(1,6),(4,5),(5,5),(4,4),(3,4)
Player_02 (*Random Player*)	(3,5),(1,3),(5,6),(3,3),(1,5),(1,2),(0,1)
Player_03 (*KB Player*)	(0,5),(4,6),(0,4),(2,4),(0,0),(2,6),(2,2)

(c) Tiles of the players' after position of the
players' is swapped

Player_00 (*Random Player*)	(0,6)
Player_01 (*KB Player*)	
Player_02 (*Random Player*)	(1,2),(0,1)
Player_03 (*KB Player*)	(2,6),(0,0),(2,2)

(d) Tiles' left in each player's HAND after
position of the players' is swapped

Fig. 7. Second set of tiles.

4   Explanation Generator

There are five different *goals* of *explanations* i.e. *Conceptualisation, Justification, Learning, Transparency* and *Relevance* [4,8,9] that provide with the fertile ground of understanding why an *explanation* is required. For current work, we mainly concentrate on *Learning, Transparency* and *Justification* goals of *explanations*. Our *Explanation-Generation mechanism* provides support for generating two possible types of *explanations* keeping in view different goals of *explanations*:

1. **Static Explanations**
2. **Dynamic Explanations**

Static Explanations (Goal of Learning): *Static Explanations* have a predefined explicit goal of enhancing a human's *Learning* by offering *explanations* that differ between *Declarative* knowledge, i.e., *what is the main purpose of the game* and *Procedural* knowledge, i.e., *how to play the game. Static Explanations* which are central ones in our study are (1) Rules of the game (2) History and facts about the game (3) Game-play Tips. Figure 8, shows *Static Explanations* generation mechanism.

Dynamic Explanations (Goal of Transparency, Justification, Learning): Our method of generating *Dynamic Explanations* is meaningful for the strategy of a game and is more like a goal-driven[11], *constrastive* approach that explains the *cause* of an event relative to some other event that did not occur. The perspective of *constrastive* approach can motivate human that among all *available choices*, the *final decision made* is best according to the current game situation.

---

[11] Which means based on the goal state, our *KB Robotic Agent* tracks back to find the game state in which the decision was made. To do so, the *KB Robotic Agent* basically leaves a reasoning trace behind a goal tree, which makes it possible to answer questions about it's behaviour (decision-made).

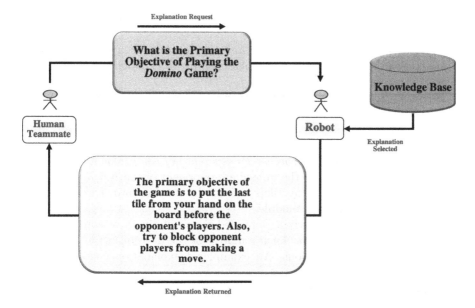

Fig. 8. Static explanation-generation mechanism.

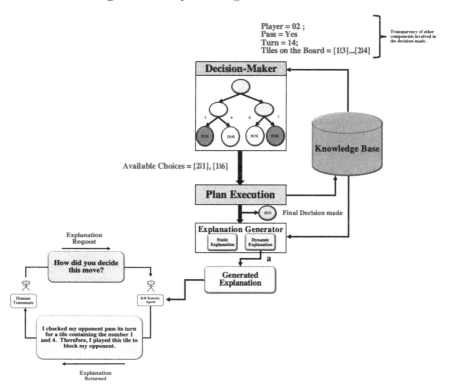

Fig. 9. Dynamic explanation-generation mechanism.

Dynamic Explanations provide a human with the:

1. *Transparency* of how did the *KB Robotic Agent* make a decision and are more towards *how*-type questions. An example of explanation contains goal of *Transparency* is below:
   Human: *How did you decide this move?*
   KB Robotic Agent: *"I played this tile to block my opponent for making a move, because my opponent is lack of having a tile matching open ends of the board"*.
   The human teammates' can access *Transparency of Knowledge Acquision* sub-module to verify whether the immediate opponent of the *KB Robotic Agent* has *passed* his turn for any tile(s) or not by looking into *Transparency of Knowledge Acquision* sub-module.

2. *Justification* for the underlying intended cause offering a reason in terms of explaining the *KB Robotic Agent*'s motive of the decision made and mainly focus on *why*-type questions. An example of explanation contains goal of *Justification* is:
   Human: *why did we lose the game?*
   KB Robotic Agent: *"I did not have an excellent HAND to play the game, I have to pass my turn more then once, so we lost the game. Better next time"*.
   The human teammates' can access *Transparency of Knowledge Acquision* to verify whether the *KB Robotic Agent passed* his turn or not.
   Figure 9, shows *Dynamic Explanations* generation mechanism.

3. *Dynamic Explanations* also hold the capacity to improve a human's learning[12]. An example of explanation contains goal of *Learning* is:
   if it is *Game_01* and the *KB Robotic Agent* plays the tile (6,6), then if the human asks: **Human**: *How did you decide to play this move?*
   KB Robotic Agent: *"it is a basic rule to play the first tile with the highest pips on the board. Therefore, I put this tile on the board"*.
   Human teammates learn a fundamental rule of playing the game.

4. *Transparency of Knowledge Acquision:* that provides a human with the concrete and individual segments of stored knowledge from the *Knowledge Base*. The main segments are (1) raw sensor *belief space* (observations) of the *KB Robotic Agent* that consists of objective facts about the environment. (2) The known *HANDS* of the players in terms of complete and accurate record of what moves have been played by players. (3) All other known public information.[13] (4) Information with all the *HANDS* of the players whose owner is unknown[14] and each time any player plays a move, it is removes from the set of all *HANDS*.

---

[12] We did not make strategies of playing the *game*, as a part of *Static Explanations* because we want that the human teammates should learn different strategies by observing the *KB Robotic Agent's* way of playing (decisions).

[13] For example, in the game *Domino, pass* information of a player (which player *passes* it's turn and on which tile number).

[14] A complete set of 28 *Domino* tiles in terms of the "number" of tiles that left in each player's *HAND*.

5   Discussion

In this paper, we discussed the design and implementation of an HRI scenario in which a *KB Robotic Agent* plays a partial observable strategy game with humans in teams and provides different *explanations* to its human teammates. We mainly described the implementation details of our *KB Robotic Agent* and it's *Explanation-Generation* mechanism. We implemented the *Robotic Agent* as a "Knowledge-Based" *Agent* that keeps a rapid update of knowledge to play a partial information game with humans in teams. We developed *Explanation-Generation* mechanism on top of the game that generates multiple *Static* and *Dynamic Explanations* along with the *Transparency* of different components of the *Knowledge-Base* mainly involved in the decision-making of the *Robot*. *Static Explanations* are based upon rules and tips of playing the *game*. While *Dynamic Explanations* provide insight into the *KB Robotic Agent's* decisions, so that the human teammates are better equipped to understand and therefore trust on the *KB Robotic Agent* teammate. We evaluated the performance efficacy of our *KB Robotic Agent* with a partial information game "Domino" against a team of *Perfect Information* players and *Random* players. Overall, our team of *KB Robotic Agent game* players won a remarkable number of games. We are hopeful that our *KB Robotic Agent* will work better with a human as a teammate and will also win a significant number of *games* against a team of human players. We also included different game elements, i.e., number of games win/loss and game score that not only reflect a teammate's individual performance but also encourage them to engage (cooperate and compete) and improve joint-team performance. Our immediate next step is to evaluate this interactive scenario in a lab experiment to gather data on how much a *Robot's* *explanations* influence a human's level of trust. We are hopeful that with the physical presence of a *Robot* in the same human environment and the *Robot's* enhanced capability of communicating via *explanations* can upraise human's stakes of trusting the *Robot*.

References

1. Yagoda, R.E., Gillan, D.J.: You want me to trust a ROBOT? The development of a human-robot interaction trust scale. Int. J. Soc. Robot. **4**(3), 235–248 (2012)
2. Dzindolet, M.T., Peterson, S.A., Pomranky, R.A., Pierce, L.G., Beck, H.P.: The role of trust in automation reliance. Int. J. Hum. Comput. Stud. **58**(6), 697–718 (2003)
3. Lee, J.D., See, K.A.: Trust in automation: designing for appropriate reliance. Hum. Factors **46**(1), 50–80 (2004)
4. Nothdurft, F., Minker, W.: Justification and transparency explanations in dialogue systems to maintain human-computer trust. In: Rudnicky, A., Raux, A., Lane, I., Misu, T. (eds.) Situated Dialog in Speech-Based Human-Computer Interaction. SCT, pp. 41–50. Springer, Cham (2016). https://doi.org/10.1007/978-3-319-21834-2_4
5. Adams, B.D., Bruyn, L.E., Houde, S., Angelopoulos, P.A.: Trust in Automated Systems: Literature Review, 1st edn. Humansystems Incorporated, Canada (2003)

6. Billings, D.R., Schaefer, K.E., Chen, J.Y., Hancock, P.A.: Human-robot interaction: developing trust in robots. In: Proceedings of the Seventh Annual ACM/IEEE International Conference on Human-Robot Interaction, pp. 109–110. ACM, Boston (2012)
7. Nothdurft, F., Richter, F., Minker, W.: Probabilistic human-computer trust handling. In: Proceedings of the 15th Annual Meeting of the Special Interest Group on Discourse and Dialogue (SIGDIAL), Philadelphia, U.S.A, pp. 51–59 (2014)
8. Nothdurft, F., Ultes, S., Minker, W.: Finding appropriate interaction strategies for proactive dialogue systems—an open quest. In: Proceedings of the 2nd European and the 5th Nordic Symposium on Multimodal Communication, pp. 73–80. Linköping University Electronic Press, Tartu (2015)
9. Sørmo, F., Cassens, J.: Explanation goals in case-based reasoning. In: Proceedings of the ECCBR 2004 Workshops, Number 142–04, pp. 165–174 (2004)
10. Xin, M., Sharlin, E.: Playing games with robots-a method for evaluating human-robot interaction. In: Human Robot Interaction, p. 522. Itech Education and Publishing, Vienna (2007)

Urban Traffic Control
Using Distributed Multi-agent Deep
Reinforcement Learning

Shunya Kitagawa[✉], Ahmed Moustafa, and Takayuki Ito

Department of Computer Science, Nagoya Institute of Technology, Nagoya, Japan
kitagawa.shunya@itolab.nitech.ac.jp,
{ahmed,ito.takayuki}@nitech.ac.jp

Abstract. There are many economic losses due to the crowded and poorly managed traffic conditions in urban areas. In this regard, reinforcement learning (RL) has emerged as a promising approach for optimizing urban traffic control (UTC) based on the real-time traffic conditions. One of the RL-based algorithms is Distributed W-Learning (DWL) in which each agent has multiple policies and then this agent learns to optimize the traffic light control (green, red and so on) based on these policies. In this context, there are situations in which it is only necessary for the control agent to achieve its own policy, and other situations where the priority must be given to the performance of other control agents. As a result, DWL is able to learn how to optimize the entire UTC. In addition, DWL has a mediator that informs the control agents the traffic volume of each road, and these agents learn based on that information. However, the limitation of DWL is that it is based on Q-learning, therefore, it is difficult to optimize multiple policies when the control area expands. In addition, because the action values are represented by tables, these tables grow exponentially when applied to large-scale action spaces. Likewise, the ability to adapt to new environments becomes poor. Therefore, in this paper, we propose an approach to address this problem. The proposed approach uses Deep Q Network (DQN) algorithm in order to optimize the traffic conditions more flexibly. The proposed approach utilizes deep learning for value function approximation. Therefore, the proposed approach has the advantage of being highly extensible and capable of predicting an action in large-scale action spaces even in unknown environments. The experimental results show the proposed approach is capable of optimizing multiple policies of the UTC, efficiently.

Keywords: Reinforcement learning · Urban traffic control · Deep learning

1 Introduction

The population of the world as of 2019 is set to become 7.6 billion people. In addition, this population is estimated to be around 10 billion people by 2050. Therefore, it is suggested that the number of people who utilize cars will increase exponentially from now on. In order to solve this challenge, a rule based UTC system called Split Cycle Offset Optimisation Technique (SCOOT) was proposed [3–5].

© Springer Nature Switzerland AG 2019
A. C. Nayak and A. Sharma (Eds.): PRICAI 2019, LNAI 11672, pp. 337–349, 2019.
https://doi.org/10.1007/978-3-030-29894-4_28

However, there is still a limit to the volume of traffic that can be optimized in SCOOT, due to its reliance on a set of predefined rules, and due to the centralized nature of this system. On the other hand, multi-agent RL has proven flexible and suitable to solve a wide spectrum of problems, especially those that require cooperation among the control agents. Therefore, in recent years, UTC systems based on multi-agent RL has attracted attention [15,16,18]. Because multi-agent RL is very effective as an approach to optimize changes in complex and dynamic environments such as real-world urban traffic control. In this regard, many optimization approaches based on multi-agent reinforcement learning for urban traffic control have been proposed [1,2,6,7,17]. One of these RL-based algorithms is Distributed W-Learning. However, this algorithm has the problem of lack of scalability, i.e., it does not scale well in the face of large-scale environments. Because this algorithm is based on Q-learning so each control agent learns the action value in a tabular format. Therefore, in order to overcome this challenge, we propose a novel approach for UTC that fits large-scale environments using DQN. In this context, DQN expresses the action value function by an approximate function rather than a table. In specific, the proposed approach deploys six agents and each agent has ten learning models to improve the traffic conditions. Therefore, the proposed approach learns how to optimize the traffic conditions by learning models whose total number is sixty. We evaluate the proposed approach using the multi-modal traffic flow simulation software (VISSIM). Towards this end, a detailed map of the road network around Nagoya Institute of Technology in Japan is used. In addition, we use a set of records that shows the traffic volume in 2015 at Nagoya City, Japan [19] for input. The experimental evaluation assesses the performance of the proposed approach against the existing state-of-the-art approaches. In specific, those experiments consider UTC optimization with three policies, which are improving the traffic conditions of the entire cars, minimizing the stop time of the official vehicles, and minimizing the stop time of the emergency vehicles.

The rest of this paper is organized as follows. Section 2 presents the preliminaries and the challenges of modern UTC systems. In Sect. 3, we introduce the proposed approach that is able to optimize UTC in large-scale environments with multiple policies. Extensive experimental results are presented in Sect. 4. Discussions of the proposed approach are presented in Sect. 5. Finally, the paper is concluded in Sect. 6.

2   Preliminary

2.1   SCOOT

At the beginning, a system called SCOOT was proposed in order to control the traffic in urban areas. This system, i.e., SCOOT, is a rule based system that aims to optimize the flow of the traffic in urban areas using a set of predefined rules. Towards this end, SCOOT changes the color of the of traffic lights (green and red) when the traffic volume in each direction of a certain junction exceeds a preset threshold. Since it depends on a predefined set of specific rules, SCOOT is a system that lacks flexibility. In addition, SCOOT adopts a centralized system perspective which proved challenging in large-scale environments. Therefore, in order to optimally control the large traffic volumes in urban environments, there exists a pressing need for learning-based systems. These learning-based systems are envisioned to learn rather than optimize, and hence, become flexible in the face of dynamic traffic environments. In addition, these learning-based systems are envisioned to show a form of cooperative behavior by distributing the control among multiple nodes.

2.2 DWL

There are many endeavours for developing learning based UTC systems where various data input formats are used. Among these endeavours, there is a UTC system that aims to improve the traffic conditions based on the data input from satellite images using convolutional neural networks (CNN) [11]. In addition, there are many other proposed systems to control real-time traffic volumes, using several techniques including image processing, and remote sensing [12–14]. One notable implementation of the learning-based systems that is able to control traffic in dynamic urban environments is DWL [8–10,20]. DWL is based on the action value learning strategy of RL, i.e., Q-learning. In this regard, DWL is an algorithm that learns and utilizes the dependencies among the learning agents, and the dependencies among the control policies in order to improve the entire system performance. Towards this end, each control agent proposes a certain action, that is selected by Q-learning, to its surrounding agents in order to determine the group action, while placing a greater weight on the action of the agent with the highest importance. This way, each control agent learns how to cooperate and how to improve the entire system performance. Comparing DWL to SCOOT, the traffic conditions have improved, as the traffic volume per time unit is reduced, and it is demonstrated that the traffic conditions have improved by 5% even when the traffic volume is high [9]. However, DWL has many limitations. In specific, DWL takes time to learn the optimal control policy because the reward given to the control agent is a constant value. In addition, DWL does not take into account the change of the learning rate especially when selecting an action. Moreover, given the fact that DWL is based on Q-learning, the learning speed becomes slow once the control area has increased. Furthermore, with the increase in the number of learning policies, the state/action space explodes exponentially and it becomes difficult to learn correctly. Besides, there is another serious drawback, DWL can not estimate the best action in those situations that have not been experienced during the learning phase. Since DWL is learning discretely with a table, it fails to predict the optimal action under continuous traffic conditions. However, this problem can be solved by defining action value as a function by using DQN. It can be assumed that there is a linear relationship between agent action and traffic conditions. Therefore, we think that it is possible to estimate even if the traffic condition of the road becomes unlearned situation.

3   Distributed W-Learning with Deep Q-Networks

In order to overcome the limitations of DWL, this paper proposes a learning-based approach that is able to optimize traffic control in large-scale environments. Towards this end, the proposed approach employs DQN in order to estimate the value function of the control agents, and therefore, it enables theses control agents to adapt efficiently in continuous traffic control scenarios with multiple optimization policies. The proposed approach is called Distributed W-learning with Deep Q-Networks (DWDQN). This proposed approach, i.e., DWDQN, works as follows.

3.1   Overview

In this approach, we aim to improve the traffic control by optimizing the traffic volume of each road. In specific, each agent in this approach has four choices (30, 40, 50, 60) as candidate actions. This action value represents the duration that the traffic signal lasts. For example, if the action with the value 30 is selected to control the green signal, the action of sustaining the green signal for 30 s is performed. In this approach, each control agent presumably has three policies and needs learning in order to optimize these policies. Figure 1 shows a description of the action selection of each DWDQN agent. It is important to note that the number of learning models depends on the number of policies each agent needs to learn. For example, the proposed approach assumes three models per policy to learn, and each of these learning models is used to select an action. Therefore the total number of learning models can be represented by the number of control policies multiplied by three and then added to the base learning model. For the purpose of urban traffic control, the three control policies are set as in Table 1.

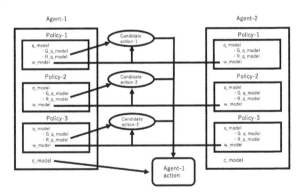

Fig. 1. Action selection of DWDQN

Table 1. Control policies of agents

Policy	Feature
1	Optimize the entire traffic volume
2	Optimize the traffic volume of official vehicles (e.g., bus, taxi and so on)
3	Optimize the traffic volume of emergency vehicles (e.g., ambulance)

As a result, the proposed approach, i.e., DWDQN, has ten models each of which independently learns. These learning models can be divided into nine models that learn control policies and a baseline model that learns choosing the group action that coordinates among these policies. All of these models, i.e., ten models, learn using Deep Q-Network (DQN). Therefore, these models learn the approximate function of the action value. This means that even if the area of traffic control is large, it is possible to scale the learning up. In addition, the proposed approach assumes that the criteria for selecting a certain action in UTC is linearly related to the traffic volume per time unit in a certain place. In addition, learning the action value by approximate function improves the learning efficiency. For example, when expressing the traffic volume at a crossroad intersection as (a, b), where a and b represent the traffic volume in each direction. In the case of $(10, 100)$, the priority is given to the traffic on the right side, i.e., 100. This also applies to the case of $(10, 50)$. The consideration here is how much time it takes to control the right side traffic. In other words, it is enough to learn what to control while the duration of the green signal. On the other hand, in the case of DWL, since learning is performed independently for the action value between $(10, 100)$ and $(10, 50)$, the learning time becomes exponential as the control area increases.

3.2 Learning Models

As mentioned above, DWDQN employs ten models for learning. The basic structure of these learning models is demonstrated in Table 2. In addition, each control agent learns the optimal group action by linking these ten models. The types of these learning models are listed in Table 3. In this context, each control agent employs one G_q_model, one R_q_model, one w_model in order to learn each control policy, and only one baseline c_model in order to learn the group action.

Table 2. Basic structure of learning models

Layer (type)	Output Shape	Param #
dense_1 (Dense)	(None, 2, 128)	512
activation_1 (Activation)	(None, 2, 128)	0
flatten_1 (Flatten)	(None, 256)	0
dense_2 (Dense)	(None, 128)	32896
activation_2 (Activation)	(None, 128)	0
dropout_1 (Dropout)	(None, 128)	0
dense_3 (Dense)	(None, 128)	16512
activation_3 (Activation)	(None, 128)	0
dropout_2 (Dropout)	(None, 128)	0
dense_4 (Dense)	(None, 1)	129
activation_4 (Activation)	(None, 1)	0

Total params: 50,049
Trainable params: 50,049
Non-trainable params: 0

Table 3. Learning models for each agent

Model	Feature
G_q_model	This model is used to learn each control policy and is used when the traffic light is Green. The state of this model is expressed by the tuple (a, b) which represents the traffic volume of each junction. This model is employed by each agent
R_q_model	This model is used to learn each control policy and is used when the traffic light is Red. The other settings are the same as G_q_model
w_model	This model is used to learn the weights among neighbor agents in each policy. In specific, each agent is able to observe its neighbor agent selections (the traffic light of junction). Therefore, this learning model increases the weight of the action which improves the entire traffic performance. The state of this model depends on the number of neighbor agents. For example, Crossroads (+) is expressed by the tuple (a, b, c, d), T-junction is expressed by the tuple (a, b, c) which represents the traffic volume of neighbor agents. This model focuses on multiple agents
c_model	This baseline model is used to learn the relative weights of each policy. In other words, this model is used to learn the concession degree of those candidate actions. In this case, since the number of policies is three, the candidate actions based on each policy are initialized with equal weights $(0.33, 0.33, 0.33)$. The concession degree is described by (Lines 6 to 14) in Algorithm 3. In specific, DWDQN subtracts all the actions with the minimum values among the candidate actions in order to define the inclination among the respective policies as their importance degree. The reason for adding base reward is to avoid setting the minimum value to 0. Besides, if we know beforehand that a certain policy is important, we can optimize more quickly by increasing the base weight value of this certain policy. This makes it possible to make significant concessions like $(0.8, 0.1, 0.1)$ among the control policies. For example, action 30 is selected for Policy 1, action 50 is selected for Policy 2, action 60 is selected for Policy 3 and the weights of these policies are set as $(0.7, 0.1, 0.2)$. In this case, the group action is calculated as $30 \times 0.7 + 50 \times 0.1 + 60 \times 0.2 = 38$, this result is rounded to 40 because the action space is defined as $(30, 40, 50, 60)$

3.3   Algorithm

The reason why the control agents use different learning models to control the traffic lights in both the green and red modes is that we consider the following situation. At the crossroads, where the action space that the control agent can take is $(30, 40, 50, 60)$, when the traffic volume in one direction is large, UTC can be optimized with assuming the green light time is set to 30 s, and the red light is set to 60 s. In other words, it is best to just take the reverse action selected at the green signal. Therefore one learning model becomes sufficient. However, if the traffic volume in the area to which the control belongs is low, optimizing the entire system can be achieved by setting both the green signal and the red signal to 30 s. In order to cope with such situations, it is necessary to learn each model separately from both the green signal and the red signal. The proposed DWDQN approach works, in details, as follows. The initial step is to initialize each agent state and its reward value. This step is described in Algorithm 1.

Algorithm 1. DWDQN Initialization of each agent

1: **while** Agents **do**
2:     $InitializeAgent.state_q(P_i\ states,\ A_i\ actions)$
3:     $InitializeAgent.state_w(Neighbor\ agents\ states)$
4:     $InitializeAgent.state_c(P_i\ states,\ W_i\ states)$
5:     $InitializeAgent.reward$
6:     $Agent.Green\_switch \leftarrow 0$ ▷ 0 means signal is red
7: **end while**

Firstly, each agent learns q_model, w_model, and c_model, independently. Then, each agent selects the candidate actions based on each policy. At this time, each agent can learn the best action for each policy based on the q_model and w_model. The detailed procedure for action selection is described by Algorithm 2. In addition, Algorithm 2 shows the detailed procedure for calculating the reward value. In the proposed approach, cooperation is promoted among the control agents. But, at the time of initial selection of candidate actions based on the relative policy, local reward is multiplied by 10 in order to make a choice that maximizes the utility of each control agent. In addition, the reason for adding a base reward is that the learning agent can select actions with negative reward values. In this context, it is important to note that the ReLU function is used to perform normalization, but since this function may take a lot of negative values, learning does not proceed if all the values are treated as 0. On the other hand, adding a base reward reduces the part that was truncated as 0. In addition, the reason to divide by max_reward is to perform normalization so that DWDQN can scale up especially in these scenarios where the size of the state/action space is large.

Algorithm 2. DWDQN agent get_action and get_reward on each policy

1: **function** GET_ACTION($current\_state$)
2:     $Initialize(max\_index\_list)$
3:     **while** policies **do**
4:         $weight \leftarrow Agent.w\_model(current\_state)$
5:         $q\_value \leftarrow Agent.q\_model(current\_state)$
6:         $value \leftarrow weight \times q\_value$
7:         $max\_index\_list.append(max(value))$
8:     **end while**
9:     **return** $random.choice(max\_index\_list)$
10: **end function**
11:
12: **function** GET_REWARD($previous\_state,\ current\_state$)
13:     $reward \leftarrow ReLU(local\_reward \times 10 + global\_reward + base\_reward)/max\_reward$
14:     **return** reward   /* Reward function used for each models.*/
15: **end function**

Finally, DWDQN learning algorithm works as follows. Each agent selects its candidate actions based on each control policy. In the proposed approach, the number of control policies is set to three so the learning agents receive three candidate actions. Those candidate actions are weighed by the c_model, and the final action is decided. In this regard, each control agent proceeds through the steps that are presented in Algorithm 3.

Algorithm 3. DWDQN agent select_action_step and learn_step

1: /* While simulation in progress*/
2: **while** Agents **do**
3:     **while** policies **do**
4:         $Agent.reward \leftarrow GET\_REWARD(previous\_state, \ current\_state)$
5:         $Agent.Green\_switch \leftarrow convert(0, 1)$
6:         $Agent.action\_p \leftarrow GET\_ACTION(current\_state)$
7:                                       ▷ The action is candidate action on policy
8:         $Agent.memory\_append(previous\_state, \ Agent.action\_p,$
9:                                     $Agent.reward, \ current\_state)$
10:        $Agent.p\_weight \leftarrow Agent.c\_model(p\_state) - min\_p\_weight + base\_weight$
11:     **end while**
12:     $Agent.action \leftarrow Agent.action\_p1 \times Agent.p\_weight(p1\_state)$
13:                     $+Agent.action\_p2 \times Agent.p\_weight(p2\_state)$
14:                     $+Agent.action\_p3 \times Agent.p\_weight(p3\_state)$
15: **end while**
16: /* Learning by DQN*/
17: **while** Agents **do**
18:     $replay\_experience(Agent.memory)$
19: **end while**

---

4 Experimentation

We created and implemented a map that represents the area around Nagoya Institute of Technology in VISSIM. In addition, we set the number of vehicles based on the "27th National road/street traffic situation survey that was conducted" by the Japanese government [19]. Besides, we implemented SCOOT, DWL, and DWDQN in the road network in order to compare those algorithms. The destination of each vehicle is determined by the simulator. The actually implemented road network is represented in Fig. 2. As shown in Fig. 2, the number of signal/control agents is set to six and each agent can observe the conditions of other neighbor agents. Therefore, Agent 1 in Fig. 2 can observe Agent 2, Agent 3 and Agent 6. Those conditions of neighbour agents are used when learning w_model. In this experiment, the traffic volume for 12 h is simulated by VISSIM, and the traffic volume every 5 s in the simulator is recorded and compared. In addition, we change the traffic volume in a scale from 0.5 to 1.5 in order to confirm the robustness of UTC. In this context, the number 1.0 in Figs. 4, 5 and 6 means the simulated traffic volume is based on the actual traffic volume. For the sake of evaluation, the average value of running the simulation 50 times by

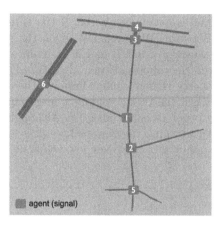

Fig. 2. Region to which the UTC is applied in this paper

each algorithm (SCOOT, DWL, DWDQN) is recorded and compared. In order
to avoid overfitting, we randomly increase or decrease the number of vehicles
deployed to each road by 20% each round we run the simulations. However, at
the initial step, the total number of vehicles, i.e., vehicle volume, is set as the
same. On the other hand, we set the required number of training epochs according to each algorithm. However, given the fact that SCOOT is not a learning
based algorithm, so there is no training phase. In specific, in DWL, the number
of training epochs is set to 400 because the quality of the control/learning policy could not be improved beyond 400 training epochs. On the other hand, in
DWDQN, the number of training epochs is set to 200. It is important to note
that, at the initial stage, it was planned to set the number of training epochs to
400 for all learning algorithms, i.e., DWL and DWDQN. However, in DWDQN,
the obtained results seemed to overfit, therefore, we set the number of training epochs to 200 instead. Figures 4, 5 and 6 show the results using the actually
learned UTC policies. On the other side, Fig. 3 signifies the accumulated rewards
during the learning step. In this regard, we define the reward function using the
following equations.

$$p1\_reward = total\_traffic\_volume \tag{1}$$

$$p2\_reward = official\_vehicle\_volume \tag{2}$$

$$p3\_reward = emergency\_vehicle\_volume \tag{3}$$

$$reward = -(p1\_reward + 2 \times p2\_reward + 5 \times p3\_reward) \tag{4}$$

The reason for using multiplication when calculating the reward value is to
express the relative importance of each policy through multiplying by its weight
value. As shown in Fig. 3, after running around 120 training epochs, DWDQN
receives higher rewards than DWL, and it can be confirmed that DWDQN
achieves higher rewards also in the final learning results. On the other hand,
Fig. 4 compares the total traffic volume of each algorithm (Policy 1). As shown

in Fig. 4, DWDQN achieves better results in all the three traffic volume situations (0.5, 1.0, 1.5). Between DWL and DWDQN, the result of conducting p test, returns a p-value where $p < 0.001$, and it is significant. In addition, Fig. 5 compares the official vehicle volume of each algorithm (Policy 2). Please note that DWL has the property that it cannot improve the official vehicle volume compared to SCOOT when the traffic volume is large (1.5). This property has also been confirmed in other recent studies [9]. Although it has a significance test value with $p > 0.05$, we think the obtained result is acceptable, because we set the priority of this policy to a relatively low value, i.e., 2.

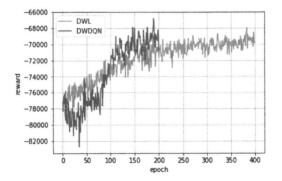

Fig. 3. Accumulated rewards in learning step

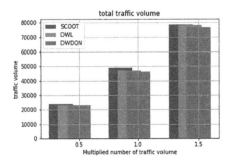

Fig. 4. Total traffic volume per hour in the UTC area

Fig. 5. Official-vehicle traffic volume per hour in the UTC area

times	Algorithm	SCOOT	DWL	DWDQN
	0.5	23881	23100	**23055**
	1.0	48809	47020	**46127**
	1.5	78612	78037	**76587**

times .eps	Algorithm	SCOOT	DWL	DWDQN
	0.5	1513	1497	**1475**
	1.0	3123	3109	**3011**
	1.5	5120	5137	**4989**

Furthermore, Fig. 6 compares the emergency vehicle volume of each algorithm (Policy 3). Between DWL and DWDQN, the result of conducting p-test, returns a p-value where $p = 0.01$, and it is significant. The reason we obtain better results than Policy 2 is that we set Policy 3 with a higher weight, i.e., 5. Finally, Fig. 7 compares the total stop vehicle volume of each algorithm. In specific, the traffic of the entire UTC is recorded every 5 s, the number of stopped (velocity is 0 km/h) vehicles is counted, and the results are shown in Fig. 7. This is an indicator that measures how people actually perceive the improvement in traffic conditions. In other words, this indicator can be regarded as an individual satisfaction metric that is calculated when applying a certain control algorithm in order to control large-scale traffic volumes. In this experiment, as well, it is clear that DWDQN is able to obtain the best results. In specific, the p-test result is confirmed to be very small and significant with $p = 6.2\text{e-}12$.

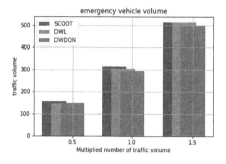

Fig. 6. Emergency-vehicle volume per hour in the UTC area

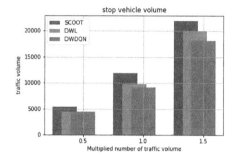

Fig. 7. Stop-vehicle volume per hour in the UTC area

	Algorithm	SCOOT	DWL	DWDQN
	0.5	156	**147**	149
times	1.0	314	304	**296**
	1.5	514	513	**499**

	Algorithm	SCOOT	DWL	DWDQN
	0.5	5434	**4404**	4416
times	1.0	11933	9844	**9195**
	1.5	21859	19836	**18096**

5 Discussion

We run the simulations 50 times in order to obtain the average of the experimental results for each algorithm. In this regard, it is observed that DWDQN has less dispersion than DWL, and therefore, good performance can be achieved with high accuracy. Towards this end, the max, median, min and variance of the obtained values from the experimental results are shown in Table 4. In addition, the obtained p value when comparing the total traffic volume of DWL and DWDQN based on the actual traffic volume is $p < 0.001$. Moreover, as shown in Table 4, it is clear that DWL has larger variance than DWDQN. This can be attributed to the fact that DWL employs Q-learning as a baseline algorithm. As a characteristic of the Q-learning algorithm, the agent can only learn the situation it has experienced once, so the control agent cannot optimize the traffic well if it gets into a state of traffic that did not exist at all during the learning phase. Therefore, the learning agent has the possibility to select extreme actions with negative reward values. Furthermore, if we increase the learning time during the experimentation, it may reduce the variance of the results, but this would also increase the possibility of overfitting. Therefore, we believe that it is difficult to stabilize the learning results any more beyond the settings in the current experiments. In contrast, DWDQN is also based on RL, however, it can be observed that its variance is small. In other words, DWDQN can adapt for variable traffic conditions swiftly compared to DWL. On the other hand, in the conducted experiments, in order to make it easy to compare DWDQN and DWL, the agent's action space is set to 4 choices (30, 40, 50, 60). However, this action space is only a measure to ensure the learning efficiency by the Q-learning agent used for DWL. Contrarily, in the proposed DWDQN approach, since the action value is expressed by an approximate function, even if the action space is made finer like (30, 31, 32, ..., 58, 59, 60), the learning efficiency is not lowered. This means, DWDQN can further improve the traffic volume. Finally, regarding the scalability, we run the conducted experiments while increasing the number of control agents/signals to 2, 4, 6, respectively. In the future, we plan to experiment the proposed approach with larger number of control agents. In terms of the learning time, DWL suffered an increase in its learning time exponentially. On the other hand, this exponential increase did not happen in the case of DWDQN.

Table 4. 50 times experimental results

Algorithm	SCOOT	DWL	DWDQN
Max	49659	48357	46697
Median	48960	46811	46130
Min	48076	46406	45803
Variance	563	556	261

6   Conclusion and Future Work

This paper proposes a novel approach for urban traffic control using multi-agent deep reinforcement learning. The proposed approach employs DQN in order to estimate the value function of the traffic control agents, and therefore, it enables those control agents to adapt efficiently in lare-scale traffic control scenarios. The experimental results has shown the efficiency of the proposed approach in urban traffic control, especially with multiple optimization policies. Future work is set to investigate the extension of the action space and the increase of the number of control policies.

References

1. Chu, T., Wang, J.: Traffic signal control by distributed reinforcement learning with min-sum communication. In: 2017 American Control Conference (ACC), pp. 5095–5100 (2017)

2. Tahifa, M., Boumhidi, J., Yahyaouy, A.: Swarm reinforcement learning for traffic signal control based on cooperative multi-agent framework. In: Intelligent Systems and Computer Vision (ISCV), pp. 1–6 (2015)
3. Robertson, D.I., Bretherton, R.D.: Optimizing networks of traffic signals in real time - the SCOOT method. IEEE Trans. Veh. Technol. **40**, 11–15 (1991)
4. Zhaomeng, C.: Intelligent traffic control central system of Beijing-SCOOT. IEEE, June 2010
5. Zhang, B., Wang, Q., Liu, F., Kang, L.: Bus signal priority based on SCOOT. IEEE, September 2017
6. Tahifa, M., Boumhidi, J., Yahyaouy, A.: Swarm reinforcement learning for traffic signal control based on cooperative multi-agent framework. In: ISCV (2015)
7. Rezzai, M., Dachry, W., Mouataouakkil, F., Medromi, H.: Reinforcement learning for traffic control system: study of exploration methods using Q-learning. In: IRJET, October 2017
8. Dusparic, I., Cahill, V.: Distributed w-learning: multi-policy optimization in self-organizing systems. IEEE, Septemeber 2009
9. Dusparic, I., Cahill, V.: Autonomic multi-policy optimization in pervasive systems: overview and evaluation. ACM **7** (2012). Article no. 11
10. Dusparic, I., Monteil, J., Cahill, V.: Towards autonomic urban traffic control with collaborative multi-policy reinforcement learning. IEEE, November 2016
11. Kanzaki, Y., Ohno, K., Takaya, E., Kurihara, S.: Multi-agent traffic signal control system using deep Q-Network. In: The 32nd Annual Conference of the Japanese Society for Artificial Intelligence (2018)
12. Akoum, A.H.: Automatic traffic using image processing. J. Softw. Eng. Appl. 765–776 (2017)
13. Sochor, J., Juránek, R., Herout, A.: Traffic surveillance camera calibration by 3D model bounding box alignment for accurate vehicle speed measurement. J. Comput. Vis. Image Underst. **167**, 87–98 (2017)
14. Liu, H., Ma, J., Yan, W., Liu, W., Zhang, X., Li, C.: Traffic flow detection using distributed fiber optic acoustic sensing. IEEE Access **6**, 68968–68980 (2018)
15. Zhang, K., Yang, Z., Liu, H., Zhang, T., Basar, T.: Fully decentralized multi-agent reinforcement learning with networked agents. PMLR (2018)
16. Omidshafiei, S., Pazis, J., Amato, C., How, J.P., Vian, J.: Deep decentralized multi-task multi-agent reinforcement learning under partial observability. In: PMLR (2017)
17. Ma, C., Hao, W., Wang, A., Zhao, H.: Developing a coordinated signal control system for urban ring road under the vehicle-infrastructure connected environment. IEEE, September 2018
18. Calvo, J.A., Dusparic, I.: Heterogeneous multi-agent deep reinforcement learning for traffic lights control. In: AICS (2018)
19. MLIT homepage. http://www.mlit.go.jp/road/census/h27/. Accessed 16 Feb 2019
20. Dusparic, I., Monteil, J., Cahill, V.: Towards autonomic urban traffic control with collaborative multi-policy reinforcement learning. In: ITSC, pp. 1–4, Decemeber 2016

Limited Receptive Field Network
for Real-Time Driving Scene Semantic
Segmentation

Dehui Li[1], Zhiguo Cao[1], Ke Xian[1(✉)], Jiaqi Yang[1], Xinyuan Qi[1], and Wei Li[2]

[1] School of Artificial Intelligence and Automation,
Huazhong University of Science and Technology, Wuhan 430074, China
{ldh,zgcao,kexian,jqyang,silliam_qi}@hust.edu.cn
[2] Queen Mary University of London, London, UK
w.li@qmul.ac.uk

Abstract. Most existing real time semantic segmentation models focus on leveraging global context information and large receptive field. However, these undoubtedly introduce more computational cost and limit the inference speed. Inspired by the mechanism of human eyes, we propose a novel Limited Receptive Field Network (LRFNet) which achieves a good balance between the segmentation speed and accuracy. Specifically, we design two sub-encoders: the fine encoder which encodes sufficient context information, and the coarse encoder which supplements spatial information. In order to recover high-resolution accurate outputs, we fuse the features from the two sub-encoders followed by a lightweight decoder. Extensive comparative evaluations demonstrate the advantages of our LRFNet model for real-time driving scene semantic segmentation task over many state-of-the-art methods on two standard benchmarks (Cityscapes, CamVid).

Keywords: Neural network · Semantic segmentation · Real-time

1 Introduction

Semantic segmentation is about labeling all pixels of the whole image. It is widely applied in applications that highly demand real-time inference speed for fast interaction and response, such as autonomous driving, indoor navigation, and virtual reality devices. Existing studies typically focus on learning global context information via introducing heavy network structure [1–3] or achieving comprehensive information aggregation using the large receptive field. As we all know, the driving scene semantic segmentation task is inherently computationally intensive due to the notorious high resolution of input images, especially when heavy network structures were widely chosen for better performance. Also, large receptive field embedded in network blocks for useful information aggregation would definitely bring the difficulty of having high inference speed. There is

A. C. Nayak and A. Sharma (Eds.): PRICAI 2019, LNAI 11672, pp. 350–362, 2019.
https://doi.org/10.1007/978-3-030-29894-4_29

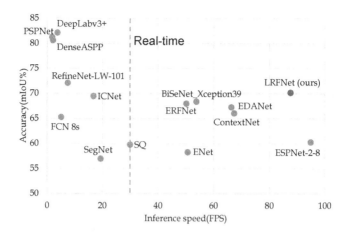

Fig. 1. Comparison of inference speed and mIoU on Cityscapes test set [5].

consequently an inevitable need for a better designed model for achieving good balance of inference accuracy and speed for real-time driving scene semantic segmentation.

In this work, we argue that it is unnecessary to incorporate global context information and large receptive field for real-time semantic segmentation. As mentioned in [4], humans cannot distinguish all the objects within the field of view but can only distinguish a very limited area projected on the macula lutea which is a small sensitive region on the center of retina. The structure of human eyes indicates that the global information or large receptive field may be unnecessary in driving scene semantic segmentation. Inspired by this insight, we propose the Limited Receptive Field Network (LRFNet). LRFNet can save a lot of calculation by discarding the additional structure to acquire global information or large receptive field. To figure out the influence of limited receptive field, we visualize the empirical receptive field of LRFNet and LRFNet with additional global structure. Our experiments demonstrate that they have the similar empirical receptive field which is limited in a small region around the classified pixel (Table 6), even though very large theoretic receptive field is adopted in the latter network. These results are coincide with the human visual system. LRFNet is very effective and efficient. Significantly, LRFNet achieves 70.2% mean IoU on the Cityscapes [5] test dataset with speed of 91.0 FPS on a NVIDIA TITAN Xp card, which gives the highest accuracy and one of the fastest speed among real-time semantic segmentation networks. The accuracy and speed compared with the exiting state-of-the-art methods are shown in Fig. 1.

Our main contributions are summarized as follows:

- We rethink the global information of semantic segmentation and point out the global information or too large receptive field is unnecessary especially in broad view scene such as driving scene, since it brings a mass of redundant information which will be suppressed by the network eventually.
- We design a novel semantic segmentation network using no global information nor too large receptive field, i.e. the Limited Receptive Field Network (LRFNet). Without the effort to acquire global information and the effort to suppress the plenty of redundant information, LRFNet is of great effectiveness and efficiency.
- We achieve state-of-the-art results on Cityscapes and CamVid dataset. More specifically, we obtain 70.2% mean IOU on the Cityscapes test dataset with the speed of 91.0 FPS.

The remainder of this paper is structured as follows. Section 2 discusses about some related works on the task of semantic segmentation. Section 3 discusses the model design of our work, including the motivation and the description of LRFNet. Section 4 compares our work with state-of-the-arts, and then performs a comprehensive set of experiments to figure out the influence of global information and each element in LRFNet. Section 5 summarizes this work.

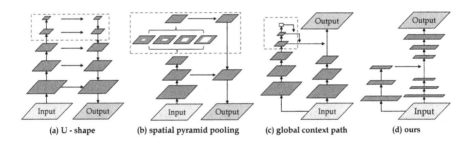

(a) U - shape   (b) spatial pyramid pooling   (c) global context path   (d) ours

Fig. 2. Illustration of different network structure. (a) displays the U-shape structure. This kind of networks downsample feature maps to very small size to acquire large receptive field. Networks presented in (b) use spatial pyramid pooling to obtain multi-scale information and large receptive field. (c) exhibits the multi-path networks among which Context Path adopt global information. (d) demonstrates our proposed LRFNet. All the first three kinds of networks use additional structure to gain global information or large receptive field (emphasized with red boxes). By contrast, LRFNet uses no additional structure to obtain global information or large receptive field and saves a lot of calculation. Without too much redundant information, LRFNet can achieve high performance with lightweight structure. (Color figure online)

2   Related Work

In this section, we introduce the related work in semantic segmentation, including global information and real-time semantic segmentation.

2.1   Global Information in Semantic Segmentation

Larger receptive field means more context information. Based on such hypothesis, many networks use different kinds of structure to obtain global information or large receptive field. U-shape like methods [3] used very deep networks to downsample the feature maps to very low resolution to acquire large receptive field. [6–8] used spatial pyramid pooling to obtain multi-scale information and large receptive field. [1,2] used very deep Context Path to gain large receptive field. [9,10] used global pooling or large kernel to get more context information. However, these methods paid a lot of efforts to enlarge theoretic receptive field superficially while taking no consideration of empirical receptive field. Our experiments show that the empirical receptive field is much smaller than the theoretic one. The empirical receptive field will be limited in a small region around the classified pixel even though very large theoretic receptive field is adopted (Table 6). In other words, too large receptive field is unnecessary in broad view scene such as driving scene, since a lot of redundant information will be brought in by over large receptive field and the redundant information will be suppressed by the network eventually.

2.2   Real-Time Semantic Segmentation

Semantic segmentation has achieved great progress in the recent works [6–8,11]. These networks achieved pretty high accuracy but paid little attention on efficiency. [12] adopted ResNet [13] structure but used bottleneck to reduce computation, which is one of the first networks aiming at semantic segmentation in real-time. [14] designed an efficient spatial pyramid (ESP) module that uses point-wise convolution in front of the spatial pyramids to reduce computational cost. These two networks improved efficiency greatly but significantly sacrificed accuracy. [15] employed a subset of ResNet [13] at three resolution levels which were later combined to provide semantic segmentation results, but its complicate structure brought quite a few computation. [1] used different branches to get context and spatial information, respectively. In context path, they used pre-trained backbone to downsample the feature maps to $\frac{1}{32}$ and then used global pooling to get global information. These operations bring a lot of redundant information and consuming calculation, which eliminate the opportunity of higher accuracy and faster speed.

3   Model Design

3.1   Motivation

Proper size of the receptive field is very important for real-time semantic segmentation. Unlike existing networks taking global information or large receptive field immoderately [1,6–10], we argue that over large receptive field is unnecessary for semantic segmentation especially in broad view scene. For example, when to classify a pixel of a car (the yellow dot) from the surrounding region of the car (region within red box) in Fig. 3(a), it is unnecessary to compare the information like the sky and trees in a large distance. This is similar to the mechanism of macula lutea (a sensitive region on the center of the retina) found in the human eye system [4], which allows human can efficiently achieve this task without taking the whole field of information.

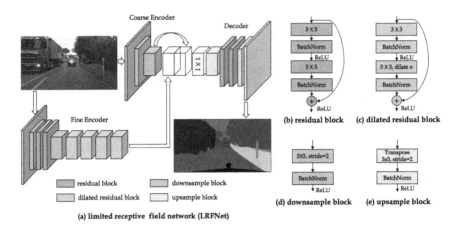

Fig. 3. An overview of the Limited Receptive Field Network (LRFNet). (Color figure online)

3.2   Limited Receptive Field Network

Armed by the insights above, we now propose the Limited Receptive Field Network (LRFNet) that aims to discover and capture representative information effectively and efficiently for the input driving scene image by incorporating small receptive model units. This contrasts to most existing semantic segmentation models typically using large receptive units or learning global information with high-level semantics. The overall design of the proposed LRFNet is demonstrated in Fig. 3(a). In general, we follow the standard encoder-decoder [3] model design. Our model consists of three parts: (i) one *coarse encoder*, with a shallow network design, to capture widespread spatial information, (ii) another *fine encoder*, with deeper stacked blocks, to capture rich contextual semantics, and (iii) a carefully designed *decoder* responsible for recovering segmentation details and producing the accurate prediction after fusing the features of the two encoders. Since no additional structure to acquire global information or lager receptive field is introduced, LRFNet can save a lot of calculations. Also, without redundant information, LRFNet is able to learn expressive representations with a lighter weight model structure.

Fine Encoder. We design a fine encoder (FE) to encode sufficient context information. Specifically, FE has three downsampling stages as shown in Fig. 3(a), which consists of three downsample layers, two residual blocks and four dilated residual blocks. Different from other networks [1,6–10], FE uses no additional structure to encode global information or lager receptive field, which saves a lot of calculation and makes itself very efficient.

Downsample Rate: Most exiting semantic segmentation networks attach great importance to large receptive field or global information [1,3,6,8–10]. In these networks, feature maps are downsampled to pretty low resolution, $\frac{1}{32}$ of the input size for example, and more convolution layers are employed which brings heavy calculations. However, based on our motivation, instead of using large downsample rate to encode too much context information, the encoder of LRFNet only downsample the feature maps to $\frac{1}{8}$ of the input size which is much shallower and much more lightweight than most exiting methods. Besides, more details are reserved with small downsample rate.

Residual Learning: Traditional convolution layers only receive the information from the previous one. Residual learning network add skip-connection between nonadjacent layers to reuse features and improve gradient back-propagation during training. This operation has been proven to be useful in many networks [13,16]. Therefore, we adopt residual learning in LRFNet and name related layers as residual block (RB) which is shown in Fig. 3(b).

Dilated Convolution: Dilated convolution is another powerful tool used to encode context information while retaining resolution of feature maps. Since we use finite downsample rate, we adopt dilated convolution in the fine encoder to adjust networks ability to obtain context information. It should be noted that these dilated convolutions could be adjusted according to specific scenarios and tasks. In this paper, we use dilated convolution in the last four convolution blocks of the fine encoder which dilated rates are 2, 4, 8, 16, respectively. We call these blocks as dilated residual block (DRB) which is shown in Fig. 3(c).

Coarse Encoder. On the other hand, coarse encoder (CE) is designed to provide accurate spatial information, and its objective is to refine the results of the fine encoder. As shown in Fig. 3(a), coarse encoder has only three downsample blocks and the feature maps will be downsample to 1/8 size quickly. Without too much convolution processing to destroy the original spatial structure of image, CE reserves spatial location information effectively.

Fusion. The outputs of fine encoder and coarse encoder complement each other. We concatenate the outputs and then reduce them to fewer channels by an 1×1 convolution for subsequent processing.

Decoder. To get sufficient semantic information, the feature maps are downsampled to 1/8 of input size and lots of details are lost. Some methods used bilinear interpolation to upsample the feature maps to the input size directly [1,15] which cannot recover the details. On the other hand, other methods used heavy decoder in their models [3,17], which make their network inefficient. To recover object segmentation details without reducing the efficiency of the whole network, we propose a lightweight decoder which has only three upsample blocks and two RBs as illustrated in Fig. 3(a).

Loss Function. The loss function is the sum of cross-entropy terms for each spatial position in the output score map as shown in Eq. 1, where N is the pixel number of feature map, i is the true class the pixel belongs to, p_i is the prediction on the true class position, and c is the number of classes.

$$loss = \frac{1}{N} \sum_i -log \frac{e^{p_i}}{\sum_{j=1}^c e^{p_j}} .$$ (1)

4   Experiments

Datasets and Evaluation Protocol. For evaluation, we used two standard driving scene benchmarks Cityscapes [5] and CamVid [18]. We adopted the standard semantic segmentation setting including the training/validation/test image split (Table 1). Following previous works use the standard Intersection-over-Union (IoU) metric for model evaluations.

Table 1. Evaluation protocol.

Dataset	Image resolution	# Train	# Validation	# Test	# Classes
Cityscapes	2048×1024	2,975	500	1,525	19
CamVid	960×720	367	101	233	11

Implementation. We implemented our LRFNet in the PyTorch framework. For optimization, we use Adam [19] with batch size 20, betas $= (0.9, 0.999)$, and weight decay 0.0001 during training. We employ the "poly" learning rate policy, in which we set base learning rate to 0.0005 and power to 0.9. The epoch is set to 300 in ablation studies and 600 in final results reported in Sect. 4.1. Noted that, we trained our model from scratch in all experiments. The unlabeled pixels are ignored. For a fair comparison, the speed test reported in this paper is evaluated on PyTorch and performed on a workstation with NVIDIA TITAN Xp cards.

4.1   Comparison to State-of-the-Arts

Evaluation on Cityscapes. Table 2 shows the comparisons of LRFNet against 13 existing models on Cityscapes. On this dataset, the best mean IoU is 82.1%

with extremely slow speed (3.7 FPS) achieved by DeepLabv3+ [8], which benefits a lot from heavy ImageNet pre-trained backbone and additional coarse label supervision. Our LRFNet can provide around 24 times (91.0/3.7) speed gain while getting considerable performance (70.2–82.1). Also, it is evident that LRFNet outperforms the fastest model ESPNet [14] in terms of mean IoU by 9.9% (70.2–60.3) with only 3.9 FPS (94.9–91.0) drop. These validate the clear superiority of our LRFNet in balancing the inference speed and performance for real-time driving scene semantic segmentation.

Table 2. Evaluation results on Cityscapes test set. "Sub": the downsampling factor of the input images. "ImN": ImageNet dataset (Deng et al. 2009). "coa.": the coarse annotation set of Cityscapes dataset. "PaC.": the Pascal Context dataset. Since all the mean IoUs are reported at full resolution (2048 × 1024), the time of upsampling the outputs to full resolution is counted if the input images are downsampled.

Method	Publication	Extra data	Sub	Pre-trained model	mIoU (%)	FPS
FCN8s [20]	CVPR'15	ImN+PaC	No	VGG16	65.3	5.1
SegNet [17]	T-PAMI'17	ImN	4	From scratch	57.0	19.4
PSPNet [6]	CVPR'17	ImN+coa.	No	ResNet50	78.4	1.8
ICNet [15]	ECCV'18	ImN	No	PSPNet50	69.5	16.8
denseASPP [7]	CVPR'18	No	No	DenseNet161	80.6	2.1
DeepLabv3+ [8]	ECCV'18	ImN+coa.	No	Xception71	82.1	3.7
ENet [12]	CVPR'17	No	2	From scratch	58.3	50.8
SQ [21]	NIPSW'16	ImN	No	SqueezeNet	59.8	30.0
ERFNet [22]	T-ITS'17	No	2	From scratch	68.0	50.2
BiSeNet [1]	ECCV'18	ImN	$\frac{4}{3}$	Xception39	68.4	53.8
ESPNet [14]	ECCV'18	No	2	From scratch	60.3	94.9
EDANet [23]	arXiv'18	No	2	From scratch	67.3	66.4
ContextNet [2]	BMVC'18	No	No	From scratch	66.1	67.4
LRFNet (ours)	-	No	2	From scratch	70.2	91.0

Evaluation on CamVid. We evaluated the performance of LRFNet against 7 competitors on CamVid, a more challenging dataset with much fewer training images (CamVid: 367 vs. Cityscapes: 2,975). This generally carries out an unavoidable challenge to the deep model training, especially when no auxiliary data pre-training is available. Table 3 shows that LRFNet still achieves the best performance under the setting of real-time inference, surpassing the 2nd best ICNet [15] by 1.2% (68.3–67.1) in terms of mean IoU with significant 34.4 (80.4–46.0) higher FPS. Also, LRFNet can gain 11.7% (68.3–56.6) higher mean IoU compared with the fastest ESPNet [14]. Importantly, it is worth pointing out that the performance advantage of our model is achieved by the proposed model design rather than knowledge transferring. For example, the best model PSPNet50 [6] relies on the heavy ResNet50 backbone [13] (pre-trained on ImageNet), whilst LRFNet is only 0.8% (69.1–68.3) lower in terms of mean IoU and about 15 times (80.4/5.3) faster in terms of FPS.

4.2   Further Analysis and Discussions

We further studied three components that affect the performance on the Cityscapes dataset: global information, fine and coarse encoders, and decoder. More specifically, we used the Fine Encoder (shown in Fig. 3) as our baseline. All of the following experiments are evaluated on Cityscapes validation set.

Influence of Global Information. We studied the influence of global information by incorporating an extra global structure shown in Fig. 2(c) with our LRFNet. Table 4 shows that global information can bring slight gain in terms of mean IoU by 0.58% (71.23–70.65) while resulting in significant speed drop (54.7–91.0). This indicates that global information or large receptive field is not so important in high-resolution image segmentation such as driving scene. We also visualized the empirical receptive field using the method proposed by [24]. As shown in Table 6, the empirical receptive field of global network is similar

Table 3. Evaluation results on CamVid test set.

Method	Publication	mIoU (%)	FPS
SegNet [17]	T-PAMI'17	52.4	14.8
SQ [21]	NIPSW'16	60.2	24.3
PSPNet50 [6]	CVPR'17	69.1	5.3
ENet [12]	CVPR'17	60.0	51.0
ICNet [15]	ECCV'18	67.1	46.0
ERFNet [22]	T-ITS'17	64.4	43.9
ESPNet [14]	ECCV'18	56.6	96.9
LRFNet (ours)	-	68.3	80.4

Table 4. Evaluation of global information.

Downsample rate	mIoU (%)	FPS
4	48.53	147.3
8 (LRFNet)	70.65	91.0
16	71.43	69.8
32	71.29	56.2
32 with global pooling	71.23	54.7

Table 5. Performance comparison of each component in LRFNet. FE: Fine Encoder; CE: Coarse Encoder.

Method	mIoU (%)
FE (A)	62.53
FE+CE (B)	63.35
CE+Decoder (C)	45.10
FE+Decoder (D)	69.70
FE+CE+Decoder (E)	70.65

to the network without global information, and it is limited in a small region around the classified pixel even though the theoretic receptive field is across all the picture. This means that the global network learns to focus on the crucial region while suppressing the irrelevant region, which coincides with the physiological structure of human eye. In other words, the additional structure to get global information in network is in vain since a lot of information the additional structure brings in is redundant and will be suppressed eventually.

Influence of Different Downsample Rates. We compared the mean IoU and FPS on Cityscapes dataset under different downsample rates. The compared results in Table 4 show that the downsample rate of 16 achieves the best performance, surpassing LRFNet by 0.77% (71.42–70.65) in terms of mean IoU with significant 22.1 (91.0–68.9) lower FPS. To achieve a balance between mean IoU and speed, the downsample rate of 8 is adopted in LRFNet.

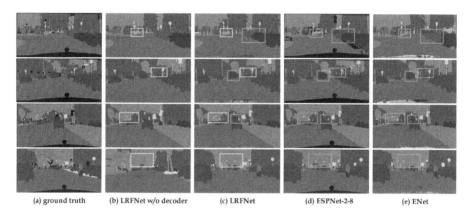

Fig. 4. Examples of predictions. Yellow boxes indicate the differences between LRFNet and LRFNet without decoder. Green boxes show the differences compared with other real-time semantic segmentation networks. (Color figure online)

Table 6. The empirical receptive field of car, sky and pole.

Table 7. Examples of error maps.

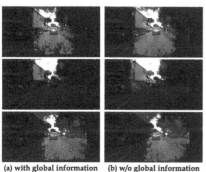

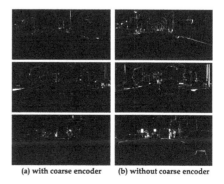

Complementary of Fine and Coarse Encoders. We evaluated the complementary effects of our jointly learned fine and coarse encoders by comparing their independent performance against that of the dependent. Table 5 shows that a performance gain is obtained from the joint feature representation of both encoders. To further investigate how does the CE can bring the benefit of enriching information learned from inputs, we compared some prediction error maps of Model D (without CE) and E (with CE), as illustrated in Table 7. These examples indicate that the model with CE makes less error near the objects edge since CE can capture more accurate spatial information.

Importance of Decoder. Since a lot of details are lost in downsampled feature maps, we use a decoder in LRFNet to recover more details from the coarse prediction. To investigate the effectiveness of the decoder, we evaluate its performance and compare the results in Table 5. Apparently, decoder gains higher accuracy of network. Also, we exhibit some comparative predictions in Fig. 4. From the qualitative results, we observe that the predictions of network without decoder are much coarser and lost a lot of details as indicated with yellow boxes.

5 Conclusion

In this paper, we rethought global information and too large receptive field for semantic segmentation. Inspired by human eye systems, we proposed a novel architecture named Limited Receptive Field Network (LRFNet). LRFNet is lightweight by discarding the additional structure to acquire global information or very large receptive filed. We lucubrated with experiments to figure out the influence of limited receptive field in driving scene semantic segmentation. We found that global information or very large theoretical receptive field is unnecessary, since the empirical receptive field is limited in a small region around the classified pixel even when the theoretical receptive field is across all the image. In other words, LRFNet is still effective in driving scene semantic segmentation with limited receptive field. We achieved state-of-the-art performance on two standard benchmarks (Cityscapes and CamVid). Specifically, we achieved 70.2% mean IoU on the Cityscapes test dataset with speed of 91.0 FPS on a NVIDIA TITAN Xp card, which is the highest accuracy and one of the fastest speed among real-time semantic segmentation networks.

References

1. Yu, C., Wang, J., Peng, C., Gao, C., Yu, G., Sang, N.: BiSeNet: bilateral segmentation network for real-time semantic segmentation. In: Ferrari, V., Hebert, M., Sminchisescu, C., Weiss, Y. (eds.) ECCV 2018. LNCS, vol. 11217, pp. 334–349. Springer, Cham (2018). https://doi.org/10.1007/978-3-030-01261-8_20
2. Poudel, R.P.K., Bonde, U., Liwicki, S., Zach, C.: ContextNet: exploring context and detail for semantic segmentation in real-time. In: The British Machine Vision Conference (BMVC) (2018)

3. Ronneberger, O., Fischer, P., Brox, T.: U-Net: convolutional networks for biomedical image segmentation. In: Navab, N., Hornegger, J., Wells, W.M., Frangi, A.F. (eds.) MICCAI 2015. LNCS, vol. 9351, pp. 234–241. Springer, Cham (2015). https://doi.org/10.1007/978-3-319-24574-4_28
4. Gross, H., Blechinger, F., Achtner, B.: Handbook of Optical Systems, Volume 4, Survey of Optical Instruments (2008)
5. Cordts, M., et al.: The cityscapes dataset for semantic urban scene understanding. In: IEEE Conference on Computer Vision and Pattern Recognition (CVPR) (2016)
6. Zhao, H., Shi, J., Qi, X., Wang, X., Jia, J.: Pyramid scene parsing network. In: IEEE Conference on Computer Vision and Pattern Recognition (CVPR) (2017)
7. Yang, M., Yu, K., Zhang, C., Li, Z., Yang, K.: DenseASPP for semantic segmentation in street scenes. In: IEEE Conference on Computer Vision and Pattern Recognition (CVPR) (2018)
8. Chen, L.-C., Zhu, Y., Papandreou, G., Schroff, F., Adam, H.: Encoder-decoder with atrous separable convolution for semantic image segmentation. In: Ferrari, V., Hebert, M., Sminchisescu, C., Weiss, Y. (eds.) ECCV 2018. LNCS, vol. 11211, pp. 833–851. Springer, Cham (2018). https://doi.org/10.1007/978-3-030-01234-2_49
9. Liu, W., Rabinovich, A., Berg, A.: ParseNet: looking wider to see better. In: International Conference on Learning Representations (ICLR) (2016)
10. Peng, C., Zhang, X., Yu, G., Luo, G., Sun, J.: Large kernel matters-improve semantic segmentation by global convolutional network. In: IEEE Conference on Computer Vision and Pattern Recognition (CVPR) (2017)
11. Lin, G., Milan, A., Shen, C., Reid, I.F.: RefineNet: multi-path refinement networks for high-resolution semantic segmentation. In: IEEE Conference on Computer Vision and Pattern Recognition (CVPR) (2017)
12. Paszke, A., Chaurasia, A., Kim, S., Culurciello, E.: ENet: a deep neural network architecture for real-time semantic segmentation. arXiv preprint arXiv:1606.02147 (2016)
13. He, K., Zhang, S., Ren, S., Sun, J.: Deep residual learning for image recognition. In: IEEE Conference on Computer Vision and Pattern Recognition (CVPR) (2016)
14. Mehta, S., Rastegari, M., Caspi, A., Shapiro, L., Hajishirzi, H.: ESPNet: efficient spatial pyramid of dilated convolutions for semantic segmentation. In: Ferrari, V., Hebert, M., Sminchisescu, C., Weiss, Y. (eds.) ECCV 2018. LNCS, vol. 11214, pp. 561–580. Springer, Cham (2018). https://doi.org/10.1007/978-3-030-01249-6_34
15. Zhao, H., Qi, X., Shen, X., Shi, J., Jia, J.: ICNet for real-time semantic segmentation on high-resolution images. In: Ferrari, V., Hebert, M., Sminchisescu, C., Weiss, Y. (eds.) ECCV 2018. LNCS, vol. 11207, pp. 418–434. Springer, Cham (2018). https://doi.org/10.1007/978-3-030-01219-9_25
16. Huang, G., Liu, Z., Van Der Maaten, L., Weinberger, K.Q.: Densely connected convolutional networks. In: IEEE Conference on Computer Vision and Pattern Recognition (CVPR) (2017)
17. Kendall, A., Badrinarayanan, V., Cipolla, R.: SegNet: a deep convolutional encoder-decoder architecture for scene segmentation. IEEE Trans. Pattern Anal. Mach. Intell. **39**(12), 2481–2495 (2017)
18. Brostow, G.J., Fauqueur, J., Cipolla, R.: Semantic object classes in video: a high-definition ground truth database. Pattern Recogn. Lett. **30**(2), 88–97 (2009)
19. Kingma, D.P., Ba, J.L.: Adam: a method for stochastic optimization. In: International Conference on Learning Representations (ICLR) (2015)
20. Long, J., Shelhamer, E., Darrell, T.: Fully convolutional networks for semantic segmentation. In: IEEE Conference on Computer Vision and Pattern Recognition (CVPR) (2015)

21. Treml, M., et al.: Speeding up semantic segmentation for autonomous driving. In: Conference on Neural Information Processing Systems (NIPS), Workshop (2016)
22. Romera, E., Alvarez, J.M., Bergasa, L.M., Arroyo, R.: ERFNet: efficient residual factorized convnet for real-time semantic segmentation. IEEE Trans. Intell. Transp. Syst. **19**(1), 263–272 (2018)
23. Lo, S.-Y., Hang, H.-M., Chan, S.-W., Lin, J.-J.: Efficient dense modules of asymmetric convolution for real-time semantic segmentation. arXiv preprint arXiv:1809.06323 (2018)
24. Zhou, B., Khosla, A., Lapedriza, A., Oliva, A., Torralba, A.: Object detectors emerge in deep scene CNNs. In: International Conference on Learning Representations (ICLR) (2015)

A Truthful Online Mechanism for Resource Allocation in Fog Computing

Fan Bi[1]([⊠]), Sebastian Stein[1], Enrico Gerding[1], Nick Jennings[2],
and Thomas La Porta[3]

[1] University of Southampton, Southampton, UK
{fb1n15,ss2,eg}@ecs.soton.ac.uk
[2] Imperial College London, London, UK
[3] Penn State University, State College, USA

Abstract. Fog computing is a promising Internet of Things (IoT) paradigm in which data is processed near its source. Here, efficient resource allocation mechanisms are needed to assign limited fog resources to competing IoT tasks. To this end, we consider two challenges: (1) near-optimal resource allocation in a fog computing system; (2) incentivising self-interested fog users to report their tasks truthfully. To address these challenges, we develop a truthful online resource allocation mechanism called flexible online greedy. The key idea is that the mechanism only commits a certain amount of computational resources to a task when it arrives. However, when and where to allocate resources stays flexible until the completion of the task. We compare our mechanism to four benchmarks and show that it outperforms all of them in terms of social welfare by up to 10% and achieves a social welfare of about 90% of the offline optimal upper bound.

Keywords: Mechanism design · Fog computing · IoT · Resource allocation

1 Introduction

The Internet of Things (IoT) is developing rapidly, and it is estimated that by 2025, 22 billion active devices will be in the IoT (Lueth 2018). Since it is impossible to let the often low-powered IoT devices perform all computing tasks, some of which are highly computationally demanding, a common solution is to combine IoT and cloud computing (Doukas and Maglogiannis 2012; Sajid et al. 2016). However, cloud computing alone cannot satisfy all the computing requirements from the IoT (Bonomi et al. 2012). The main reason is that transferring all the data from the IoT to the cloud to analyse requires a huge amount of bandwidth, and many IoT applications, such as autonomous vehicles, augmented reality and virtual reality, need very low latency, which cloud computing cannot guarantee. Consequently, fog computing has been proposed to make up for these shortcomings (Bonomi et al. 2012). In simple terms, the key difference is that the fog is

© Springer Nature Switzerland AG 2019
A. C. Nayak and A. Sharma (Eds.): PRICAI 2019, LNAI 11672, pp. 363–376, 2019.
https://doi.org/10.1007/978-3-030-29894-4_30

closer to the IoT devices than the cloud (CIS 2015). To make the most of the fog resources and maximise the efficiency, good resource allocation mechanisms for fog computing are needed. However, unlike cloud computing, fog computing cannot ignore bandwidth constraints because it is common to send large volumes of traffic between IoT devices and fog nodes (FNs). Another difference is that many tasks in the fog are time-oriented, which means that they need a certain amount of computational time to achieve their maximum value, but they can still achieve part of the value if they are allocated less time. For example, suppose a user wants to run a video surveillance application with facial recognition to surveil their shops for 24 h. In this case, the large volume of video streams from the cameras in their shops will be sent to a nearby FN instead of a remote data centre to do the compute-intensive analysis. Furthermore, it is still of value to them if the surveillance lasts less than 24 h, say, 18 h.

To address these challenges, researchers have proposed many resource allocation mechanisms for fog computing (or similar computing paradigms such as cloud computing, edge computing or geo-distributed clouds) in order to save energy, reduce cost or improve quality of service (Aazam and Huh 2015; Cardellini et al. 2015; Gu et al. 2018). However, most of these mechanisms were not specifically designed for settings where users act strategically to maximise their utility (e.g., users may misreport higher value for their tasks to increase their chances of acceptance). To address this problem, some researchers have proposed truthful mechanisms that incentivise users to truthfully reveal their private information. However, these approaches cannot be applied directly to our model due to subtle but important differences. For example, several truthful mechanisms are designed to schedule tasks in the cloud (Wang et al. 2012; Lucier et al. 2013; Wang et al. 2015; Chawla et al. 2017; Zhu et al. 2018). However, they all assume single-minded agents (i.e., agents who do not get any value for a partially executed task). In addition, the model by Lucier et al. (2013) assumes that each task requires a certain amount of resource to complete rather than a certain running time, which is very different from the time-oriented tasks in the fog. Furthermore, Zhang et al. (2015) and Shi et al. (2017) also propose truthful mechanisms for single-minded users in a geo-distributed cloud, and they assume users can specify all the details about the placement of resources among data centres for their tasks, which is not very practical mainly because users rarely have the knowledge of the system structure. Finally, Hayakawa et al. (2018) introduce the price-based mechanisms for homogeneous resource allocation, whereas there are several heterogeneous resources in the fog. So their resource allocation framework needs to be adapted in this case. In addition, we choose online greedy (OG) and Social Welfare Maximisation Online Auction 2 (SWMOA2), which are adapted from mechanisms in (Wang et al. 2012; Shi et al. 2017) respectively, as the state-of-the-art benchmarks that we will evaluate our mechanism against.

In this paper, we are the first to address these shortcomings. Specifically, we design *dominant-strategy incentive compatible* (DSIC) and *individually rational* (IR) mechanisms for realistic fog settings to maximise social welfare[1]. DSIC mechanisms guarantee that regardless of others' behaviours, users always maximise their utility by reporting truthfully. Furthermore, under an IR mechanism, no user will get a negative utility by participation. Such mechanisms provide two major benefits. First, they can elicit the true information about the tasks. Second, fog users do not need to invest their resources into optimally manipulating their bids to increase their utility. In addition, we focus on improving social welfare in this paper and leave the objective of maximising the fog provider's revenue to future work.

To design a truthful mechanism which addresses these problems, we significantly extend the framework proposed by Hayakawa et al. (2018) to our problem model. This is because their resource allocation model is similar to ours, and they show that a well-defined price-based mechanism can achieve high efficiency. In brief, we extend the state of the art as follows:

- We are the first to formulate the resource allocation in fog computing (RAFC) problem as a constraint optimisation problem that considers the bandwidth constraints and allows flexible allocation of virtual machines (VMs) (i.e., emulations of real computers that contain all the necessary elements to run fog tasks) and of the bandwidth. We also show that it can be modelled as an online mechanism design problem where a fog user requests an amount of usage time with a given resource configuration.
- We design a DSIC and IR online mechanism called flexible online greedy (FlexOG) for RAFC and show by extensive simulations, that it achieves a social welfare better than that achieved by the state-of-the-art benchmarks (up to 10%) and is close to the offline optimal value (around 90%).

The remainder of the paper is organised as follows: In Sect. 2, we propose a formal model of the RAFC problem. In Sect. 3, we present our proposed resource allocation mechanism as well as other benchmark mechanisms. In Sect. 4, we show the results of simulations and evaluate the performance of our mechanism. Finally, in Sect. 5, we conclude the paper.

2   The Fog Resource Model

We briefly describe our model of RAFC. The fog computing system is owned by a fog provider. It contains a set P of geo-distributed FNs and a set L of locations, which are interconnected through a set $\mathbb{E}$ of data links, as shown in Fig. 1. Furthermore, there is a set E_l of IoT devices in each location l. An IoT device (e.g., a smart TV, surveillance camera, smart speaker or smartphone) is denoted as $e \in E_l$. Every FN $p \in P$ has a set R of limited computational

---

[1] We define social welfare as the difference between the value of all fog tasks and the operational costs of all fog tasks.

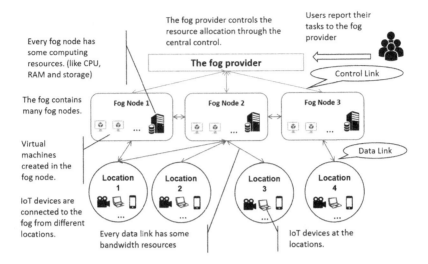

Fig. 1. General view of a fog computing system.

resources (e.g., CPU, RAM and disk storage). Moreover, there are $A_{p,r}$ units of type $r \in R$ resources in FN p, and the unit operational cost of resource r in FN p is $o_{p,r}$. In addition, the bandwidth capacity and the unit operational cost of link $(j,k) \in E$ are $b_{j,k}$ and $o_{j,k}$ respectively. For simplicity, we assume that the bandwidth capacity and unit bandwidth costs are symmetrical for all links (i.e., $b_{j,k} = b_{k,j}$, $o_{j,k} = o_{k,j}$, $\forall (j,k) \in E$). FNs and data links together offer their resources to satisfy the needs of fog users. In particular, we assume that VMs can be created in an FN to run fog tasks as long as there are enough computational resources in that FN, and the total resource requirements of several virtual machines are just the sum of their resource requirements. Furthermore, the fog provider controls the resource allocation of the fog through a central control system, which is a server that receives reports of tasks from fog users, makes decisions of how to allocate resources and executes them through control links.

Fog users with tasks arrive over time and I denotes the set of all tasks. Note that we adopt a continuous time system, but the tasks can only start execution at discrete time steps, denoted by the set $T = \{1, 2, \ldots, |T|\}$. Each task $i \in I$ is owned by a user, which is also denoted as i for simplicity. In addition, the arrival time of task i is $T_i^a \in [0, |T|]$, which is the time when user i becomes aware of its task i, and the time interval that the task can run is from its start time T_i^s to its finish time T_i^f. Here, we assume that no tasks arrive at the exact same time. User i reports its task's type $\hat{\theta}_i$ (as defined in the following) at time $\hat{T}_i^a$ to run a certain application (e.g., a video surveillance application or a picture processing application). We assume that user i wants to know the number of time steps $\tilde{t}_i$ it will get and the payment $\tilde{p}_i$ for its task also by time $\hat{T}_i^a$ because users want to run the tasks locally or elsewhere if their tasks get rejected. The operational cost of task i is denoted as o_i, which is the sum of costs of all resources allocated to task i, including the cost of bandwidth. Furthermore, we also assume that every task only requires one VM to run but may require connections to several IoT devices $e \in E$ (in the same location or in different locations) because this is common in an IoT system. Users are also assumed to be stationary, which means that the IoT devices of users do not change locations over time. Furthermore, we also assume VMs can migrate between FNs and the migration costs are negligible, and all tasks are preemptible, which means that they can always be paused and resumed. Finally, we focus on one type of task called time-oriented tasks (e.g., video surveillance and video processing tasks), which are common in fog computing. Such a task i needs a certain capacity of resources for a time length t_i to get its full value, but can still get part of the value if the processing time is less than t_i. Formally, the type of task i: θ_i is a tuple $(T_i^a, T_i^s, T_i^f, v_i, \{a_{i,r}\}_{r \in R}, \{\Gamma_l^i\}_{l \in L})$, where $a_{i,r}$ denotes the amount of resource $r \in R$ required, and Γ_l^i denotes the bandwidth demand between its VM and location $l \in L$. For simplicity, bandwidth demands are symmetrical. That is, Γ_l^i denotes both the bandwidth demands to and from location $l \in L$. In this paper, the valuation function $v_i = \{v_{i,0}, v_{i,1}, \ldots, v_{i,t_i}\}$, where $v_{i,t}$ is the value when task i gets usage time of t time steps and t_i denotes the usage time needed to get the full value of the task. We make a mild assumption that the value monotonically increases with usage time (i.e., $v_{i,t'} \geq v_{i,t''}, \forall t' \geq t''$). We choose this type of valuation function because it corresponds to many applications in the fog, which achieve better results as processing time increases. Moreover, the reported type of task i: $\hat{\theta}_i$ is a tuple $(\hat{T}_i^a, \hat{T}_i^s, \hat{T}_i^f, \hat{v}_i, \{\hat{a}_{i,r}\}_{r \in R}, \{\hat{\Gamma}_l^i\}_{l \in L})$, and $\hat{\theta}^{\langle t \rangle}$ denotes the set of all reported types until and including time t.

Now, a key assumption in our work is that users are strategic, so $\hat{\theta}_i$ may not be equal to θ_i. Moreover, we assume limited misreports (Nisan et al. 2007) based on the nature of our problem (i.e. $\hat{T}_i^a \geq T_i^a, \hat{T}_i^s \geq T_i^s, \hat{T}_i^f \leq T_i^f, \hat{a}_{i,r} \geq a_{i,r}, \hat{\Gamma}_l^i \geq \Gamma_l^i$). This is reasonable because a user cannot bid for a task before it becomes aware of it, and cannot bid a looser time constraint ($\hat{T}_i^s < T_i^s$ or $\hat{T}_i^f > T_i^f$) because the provider can check whether i is ready to run at $\hat{T}_i^s$ and withhold the results for i until $\hat{T}_i^f$. So bidding $\hat{T}_i^s < T_i^s$ will be detected and penalised by cancelling the task and bidding $\hat{T}_i^f > T_i^f$ will get no value. Finally, user i will not misreport a lower resource requirement because its task cannot run in that case.

Next, when receiving the bid $\hat{\theta}_i$ for task i, the fog provider will decide the resource allocation scheme λ_i to this task, how much usage time $\tilde{t}_i$ will be allocated, and the payment $\tilde{p}_i$ right away because of the assumption we made earlier. Formally, the fog provider solves a constraint optimisation problem, and the decision variables are: (1) $\{z_{p,t}^i \in \{0,1\}\}_{i \in I, p \in P, t \in T}$, indicating that the VM of task i is placed in FN p ($z_{p,t}^i = 1$), or not ($z_{p,t}^i = 0$) at time step t. (2) $\{f_{l,p,j,k,t}^i \in \mathbb{R}^+\}_{i \in I, l \in L, p \in P, (j,k) \in E, t \in T}$, indicating allocation of the bandwidth on each link for task i at time step t. (3) $\tilde{p}_i(\lambda_i, \hat{\theta}^{\langle \hat{T}_i^a \rangle}) \in \mathbb{R}^+$, denoting the payment of task i, which is a function of the allocation: λ_i and all information received by $\hat{T}_i^a$: $\hat{\theta}^{\langle \hat{T}_i^a \rangle}$. So, for task i, its usage time $\tilde{t}_i = \sum\limits_{p \in P, t \in T} z_{p,t}^i$, resource allocation scheme $\lambda_i = \{z_{p,t}^i\}_{i \in I, p \in P, t \in T} \cup \{f_{l,p,j,k,t}^i\}_{i \in I, l \in L, p \in P, (j,k) \in E, t \in T}$ and its utility is $u_i = v_i(\tilde{t}_i) - \tilde{p}_i(\lambda_i, \hat{\theta}^{\langle \hat{T}_i^a \rangle})$. The objective function of this optimisation problem maximises the social welfare:

$$\underset{\lambda_i}{\text{maximise}} \sum_{i \in I} \boldsymbol{v}_i \Big(\sum_{p \in P, t \in T} z_{p,t}^i \Big) - o \tag{1}$$

where $o = \sum_{i \in I, r \in R, p \in P, t \in T} a_{i,r} z_{p,t}^i o_{p,r} + \sum_{i \in I, l \in L, p \in P, (j,k) \in \mathbb{E}, t \in T} 2 o_{j,k} f_{l,p,j,k,t}^i$

The constraints of the optimisation problem include resource constraints in the fog system and time constraints for fog tasks. Please refer to Bi et al. (2019) for details on these constraints. This is a mixed integer linear programming problem, and we use the IBM ILOG CPLEX optimiser to solve it in our simulations.

3   Allocation Mechanisms

In this section, we present the details of the mechanisms used in this paper.

3.1   Price-Based Mechanisms

First, we introduce a class of online resource allocation mechanisms called price-based mechanisms that guarantee DSIC and IR for our resource allocation problem. Specifically, the properties that this class of mechanisms should have are:

Definition 1. *A monotonic payment function is (weakly) monotonically increasing over $\hat{T}_i^a$, $\hat{T}_i^s$, $\hat{t}_i$, $\hat{a}_{i,r}, r \in R$ and $\hat{\Gamma}_l^i, l \in L$, and (weakly) monotonically decreasing over $\hat{T}_i^f$.*

Definition 2. *An online mechanism belongs to the price-based mechanisms class if it has the following properties:*

1. *The mechanism computes the payment $\tilde{p}_i$ for any possible allocation λ_i to task i by using a payment function $\tilde{p}_i(\lambda_i, \hat{\theta}^{\langle \hat{T}_i^a \rangle})$ that is independent of $\hat{v}_i$ and monotonic.*
2. *The payment for tasks with no resource allocated is zero.*
3. *The resource allocation scheme λ_i for task i maximises $\hat{v}_i - \tilde{p}_i$ (over all λ_i that can be made to task i for any $\hat{v}_i$).*

Then, the following theorem guarantees that any mechanism in the class of price-based mechanisms is DSIC and IR.

Theorem 1. *Any online mechanism that satisfies Definition 2 is DSIC and IR.*

This theorem can be proved in a similar way to Theorem 1 in (Hayakawa et al. 2018), and the proof is omitted for space reasons.

3.2   Benchmark Mechanisms

We describe the benchmark mechanisms used in this paper in detail below.

Offline Optimal Mechanism. Under this mechanism, we assume that we know all the information about future tasks and allocate resources to optimise the social welfare with no need to incentivise fog users to bid truthfully. This theoretical and idealised case can be achieved by solving the optimisation problem 1.

Online Optimal Mechanism. This mechanism is similar to the offline optimal except that the optimisation problem is solved at each time step with knowledge only of the tasks that have arrived so far (and not of future tasks). Note that this mechanism is non-truthful, but we use this to determine the social welfare that could be achieved in an online setting if all users report truthfully. In Sect. 4, we also evaluate this mechanism in settings where some users misreport.

Online Greedy Mechanism (OG). This mechanism is an extension of the greedy algorithm from (Wang et al. 2012), and greedily allocates resources to maximise the utility of a task when it arrives and commits to this allocation. Furthermore, it computes the payment as this task's corresponding operational costs ($\tilde{p}_i = o_i = \sum_{r \in R, p \in P, t \in T}(a_{i,r} z^i_{p,t} o_{p,r}) + \sum_{l \in L, p \in P, (j,k) \in \mathbb{E}, t \in T}(2o_{j,k} f^i_{l,p,j,k,t}))$. Note that OG belongs to the price-based mechanisms and thus is DSIC and IR.

SWMOA2. Although the Social Welfare Maximisation Online Auction (SWMOA) mechanism from (Shi et al. 2017) cannot be directly applied to our model, we develop a variant of it called SWMOA2 as a suitable benchmark. The main difference between this mechanism (given in Algorithm 1) and OG is that it keeps a virtual cost instead of an operational cost for every

---

Algorithm 1. The SWMOA2 mechanism

$\theta_{all} \leftarrow \emptyset$ ▷ The set of arrived tasks
$\Lambda \leftarrow \emptyset$ ▷ The set of committed allocation decisions
$\kappa_{m,t} \leftarrow 0, \forall m, t$ ▷ The load factors of resources
$c_{m,t} \leftarrow 0, \forall m, t$ ▷ The virtual costs of resources
for t **in** T **do**
  while *new tasks arrive within t* **do**
    When a new task i arrives   ▷ Tasks arrive over time
    $\theta_{all} \leftarrow \theta_{all} \cup i$ ▷ Update the set of arrived tasks
    Solve the maximum virtual utility allocation for task i (i.e.,
    $\arg\max_{\lambda_i}(\hat{v}_i(\lambda_i) - c_i(\lambda_i)))$ ▷ Find the allocation that maximises task i's virtual
    utility
    $\Lambda \leftarrow \Lambda \cup \lambda_i$ ▷ Commit this allocation
    $\tilde{p}_i \leftarrow c_i(\lambda_i)$ ▷ Compute the payment for task i
    $\kappa_{m,t} \leftarrow \kappa_{m,t} + z^i_{p,t} a_{i,r}/A_{p,r}, \forall m \in P \times R, t \in T$ ▷ Update load factors of
    computational resources
    $\kappa_{m,t} \leftarrow \kappa_{m,t} + \sum_{l \in L, p \in P} f^i_{l,p,j,k,t}/b_{j,k}, \forall m \in \mathbb{E}, t \in T$ ▷ Update load factors of
    bandwidth resources
    $c_{m,t} = \mu^{\kappa_{m,t}} - 1, \forall t \in T, m \in M$ ▷ Update the virtual costs of resources
  end
  Allocate resources for next time step $(t + 1)$ according to Λ
end

resource. For convenience, we use M to denote the set of every computational resource at each FN and the bandwidth resource on each link, and m is one type of them. To compute the virtual costs, we define the load factor $\kappa_{m,t}$ to be the proportion of occupied resource m at time step t. Then, the virtual cost accordingly is: $c_{m,t} = \mu^{\kappa_{m,t}} - 1, \forall t \in T, m \in M$, where $\mu = 2|M|F + 2$, and F is the upper limit of the ratio between the highest and the lowest task valuation per time step. Then, the virtual cost of task i is $c_i = \sum_{r \in R, p \in P, t \in T}(a_{i,r}z_{p,t}^i c_{p,r,t}) + \sum_{l \in L, p \in P, (j,k) \in \mathbb{E}, t \in T}(2c_{j,k,t}f_{l,p,j,k,t}^i)$. SWMOA2 also belongs to the price-based mechanisms and is DSIC and IR.

3.3   Flexible Online Greedy Mechanism (FlexOG)

Our mechanism, FlexOG (Algorithm 2), builds upon OG by allocating newly arrived tasks greedily but keeps their specific allocation schemes flexible. This gives it the DSIC property of OG but adds more flexibility. This also results in higher social welfare because there is more space for optimisation when high-value tasks arrive in the future. After receiving a report of task i, FlexOG finds the allocation that maximises the social welfare of all flexible tasks given the constraints of their committed usage time. Then, FlexOG computes the usage time $\tilde{t}_i$ for task i from its corresponding allocation scheme, and commits it to task i, which means that task i is guaranteed to get $\tilde{t}_i$ usage time before its

---

Algorithm 2. The FlexOG mechanism

$\theta_{all} \leftarrow \emptyset$ ▷ The set of arrived tasks
$\theta_{flex} \leftarrow \emptyset$ ▷ The set of flexible tasks
$o \leftarrow 0$ ▷ The total operational costs
$\tilde{T} \leftarrow \emptyset$ ▷ The set of committed processing times
for t *in* T **do**
    while *new tasks arrive within* t **do**
        When a new task i arrives   ▷ Tasks arrive over time
        $\theta_{all} \leftarrow \theta_{all} \cup i$ ▷ Update the set of arrived tasks
        $\theta_{flex} \leftarrow \theta_{flex} \cup i$ ▷ Update the set of flexible tasks
        Solve the maximum utility allocation for tasks in θ_{flex} (i.e.,
        $\arg\max_{\lambda_j} \sum_{j \in \theta_{flex}} (\hat{v}_j(\lambda_j) - o_j(\lambda_j)))$ ▷ Find the allocation for tasks in θ_{flex} that
        maximise their social welfare, given their committed usage time
        $\tilde{T} \leftarrow \tilde{T} \cup \tilde{t}_i(\lambda_i)$ ▷ Commit the processing time to i
        $\tilde{p}_i \leftarrow \sum_{j \in \theta_{all}} o_j(\lambda_j) - o$ ▷ Compute the payment for i
        $o \leftarrow \sum_{j \in \theta_{all}} o_j(\lambda_j)$ ▷ Update the total operational costs
    end
    for i *in* θ_{flex} **do**
        Allocate resources for the next time step $(t+1)$ according to λ_i
        $\tilde{t}_i \leftarrow \tilde{t}_i - \sum_{p \in P} z_{p,t+1}^i$ ▷ Update the remaining processing time of task i
        if $\tilde{t}_i = 0$ **then**
            $\theta_{flex} \leftarrow \theta_{flex} \setminus i$ ▷ Delete task i from flexible tasks if it gets its
            comitted usage time
        end
    end
end

---

reported finish time $\hat{T}_i^f$. Afterwards, FlexOG requires payment for task i as the marginal total operational cost, and task i is put to the set of flexible tasks. In addition, at the end of each time step, FlexOG allocates resources for the next time step according to the latest allocation schemes. Finally, if a task will get all of its committed usage time in the next time step, it will be removed from the set of flexible tasks. In summary, the key idea of our mechanism is that we only commit the usage time $\tilde{t}_i$ to task i but keep its allocation scheme flexible.

Theorem 2. *The FlexOG mechanism is DSIC and IR.*

We only give a proof sketch here because of space reasons. Obviously, FlexOG satisfies condition 2 in Definition 2 by charging zero to a rejected task. The payment $\tilde{p}_i(\lambda_i, \hat{\theta}^{\langle \hat{T}_i^a \rangle})$ is independent of $\hat{v}$ because by maximising $\sum_{j \in \theta_{flex}} (\hat{v}_j(\lambda_j) - o_j(\lambda_j))$ FlexOG actually minimises the total operational cost, which is independent of $\hat{v}$. The payment function is also monotonic because increasing $\hat{T}_i^a, \hat{T}_i^s$, $\hat{t}_i$, $\{\hat{a}_{i,r}\}_{r \in R}$, $\{\hat{I}_l^i\}_{l \in L}$ or decreasing $\hat{T}_i^f$ can only increase the total operational cost $\sum_{j \in \theta_{flex}} o_j$. Hence, this mechanism satisfies condition 1. The mechanism also satisfies condition 3 because it maximises $\sum_{j \in \theta_{flex}} (\hat{v}_j(\lambda_j) - o_j(\lambda_j))$, which is equivalent to maximise $(\hat{v}_i - \tilde{p}_i)$ according to how the payment is computed by FlexOG. From the above, FlexOG is DSIC and IR by Theorem 1.

4   Simulations and Analysis

In this section, we describe the setup of our experiments and evaluate our proposed mechanism by simulations. The aim is to compare the social welfare achieved by FlexOG to benchmark mechanisms in different situations.

4.1   Experimental Setup

We generate the following synthetic data to use in simulations because there currently exists no comprehensive data set of real-world fog computing tasks. The basic parameters of the synthetic data are as follows. The time span of our discrete time period is $|T| = 12$. The fog provider has 6 FNs ($|P| = 6$) and 6 locations ($|L| = 6$). The topology of this setup is shown in Fig. 2. Additionally, there are $|R| = 3$ types of computational resources (CPU, RAM, and disk storage) at each FN. We choose this small setting so that we can run more trials in a reasonable time for all mechanisms, and we get similar results in other settings on a similar scale.

The number of tasks in this time period is $|I| = 40$. The arrival time T_i^a follows a continuous uniform distribution $U(0, 10)$, so that no tasks arrive at exactly the same time. Moreover, the number of IoT devices for each task E_i is generated uniformly from $\{1, 2, \ldots, 6\}$. The location of each IoT device $u_{e,l}^i$ is chosen uniformly at random from all locations L with replacement.

Furthermore, we choose a special valuation function v_i in our simulation for simplicity, which is a non-decreasing linear function of the usage time $\tilde{t}_i$.

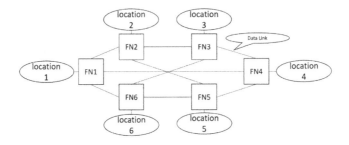

Fig. 2. The topology of the fog computing system.

$$v_i(\tilde{t}_i) = \begin{cases} g_i \times \tilde{t}_i & \text{if } \tilde{t}_i \leq t_i \\ g_i \times t_i & \text{if } \tilde{t}_i > t_i \end{cases}$$

where the coefficient g_i represents task i's obtained value per usage time.

To make the resource allocation more realistic, there are two types of tasks in this synthetic data: low-value tasks and high-value tasks, and the proportion of high-value tasks is denoted as $q \in [0,1]$. For task i of either type: $a_{i,r}, \forall r \in R$ and Γ_l^i are all generated from a Gaussian distribution $\mathcal{N}(1,1)$ with negative results discarded. The usage duration t_i is a positive integer uniformly chosen from $\{1,2,3,4\}$, and the start time T_i^s is an integer uniformly chosen within 2 time steps after the arrival time: $\{\lceil T_i^a \rceil, \lceil T_i^a \rceil + 1, \lceil T_i^a \rceil + 2\}$. Furthermore, the finish time T_i^f is an integer uniformly chosen between a and b time steps after the earliest finish time (not exceeding the last time step): $\{T_i^s + t_i - 1 + a, T_i^s + t_i + a, \ldots, min(T_i^s + t_i - 1 + b, |T|)\}$, and (a,b) defines the deadline slackness of the task, which is an important parameter because it reflects the task's flexibility. For low-value task i, g_i is uniformly chosen from a continuous interval: $[8,30]$. However, for high-value task i, g_i is uniformly chosen from a continuous interval: $[180,200]$. Thus, $F = 200/8 = 25$ in this case. Finally, users who misreport only misreport their valuation coefficient as one million.

Furthermore, the overall resource capacity of each computational resource r: $\sum_{p \in P} A_{p,r}$ is set to be a k fraction of the corresponding total resource demand: $\sum_{i \in I} a_{i,r}$, and the overall bandwidth capacity: $\sum_{(j,k) \in \mathbb{E}} b_{j,k}$ is set to be a $2k$ fraction of the total bandwidth demands: $\sum_{i \in I, l \in L} \Gamma_l^i$. Then, each FN receives the same fraction of resource r: $\frac{\sum_{p \in P} A_{p,r}}{|P|}$, and each data link receives the same fraction of the available total bandwidth: $\frac{\sum_{(j,k) \in \mathbb{E}} b_{j,k}}{|\mathbb{E}|}$. Finally, the unit operational costs at different FNs and links: $o_{p,r}, p \in P, r \in R, o_{j,k}, (j,k) \in \mathbb{E}$ are all generated uniformly from $[0.03, 0.1]$.

4.2   Simulation Results

We have tested the robustness of our mechanism by running simulations with different parameters, such as the number of tasks, the value distribution, the arrival time distribution, the operational costs of resources, deadline slackness, and resource scarcity in FNs and data links. We only show representative results below due to the space limitation. Across all of these settings, trends are similar. In particular, the FlexOG's performance in social welfare is typically around 90% of the offline optimal, and between 5–10% better than OG's.

First, we compare the total social welfare achieved by FlexOG with other benchmarks under different resource coefficients k indicating the scarcity of the resources in Fig. 3.[2] Note that we normalise the results to the performance of offline optimal so that it is easier to compare the performance of different mechanisms. The figure shows that FlexOG consistently achieves better social welfare than other truthful benchmark mechanisms. In particular, SWMOA2 always has the worst performance mainly because its virtual price function is exponential to the amount of occupied resource, and this hinders tasks from getting allocated even when there is enough resource for them. It is worth noting that, although the price function of SWMOA can guarantee that the allocation will not break the resource constraints for the problem model in (Shi et al. 2017), it no longer has this function in our model. The reason FlexOG performs better than OG is the way in which committed time steps are allocated to tasks is flexible, and so it can reschedule unfinished tasks to allocate more time steps for the newly arrived task. In addition, our mechanism also performs close to offline optimal, achieving around 90%, which indicates that our mechanism is efficient even though it is online. Although online optimal performs about 10% better than FlexOG, its performance drops below that of FlexOG when just 20% of users misreport. In addition, we have also tested whether users have the incentive to misreport by comparing utilities of truthful and non-truthful users, and the result shows on average non-truthful users get a higher utility. This means that, in a strategic setting where users can misreport, FlexOG can actually achieve significantly more social welfare than online optimal. The figure also shows that the performance difference between FlexOG and OG shrinks when the resource coefficient k is relatively low or high. Intuitively, this is because when there are few resources or there are abundant resources the performance of OG will be closer to the optimal, and there is less space for FlexOG to improve social welfare by rescheduling tasks.

Next, we compare the performance in social welfare under different levels of task slackness in Fig. 4. A task with more slackness has more time steps between its earliest and latest finish times. Such tasks are more flexible to allocate. As can be seen from the figure, the gap between FlexOG and OG increases as the tasks becomes more slack. This is because when tasks are more slack, FlexOG is more likely to reschedule low-value tasks to allocate more high-value tasks, while OG cannot benefit from this since its resource allocation schemes are fixed once they have been made.

---

[2] All figures are with 95% confidence intervals based on 200 trials, and the relative tolerance is set to 1% for offline optimal, and 5% for others. (A 1% tolerance means that the CPLEX optimiser stops when a solution is within 1% of optimality).

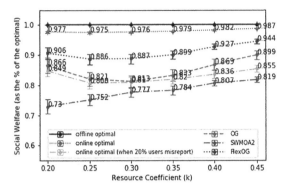

Fig. 3. Social welfare achieved by the mechanisms $((a, b) = (5, 10), F = 25, q = 0.1)$

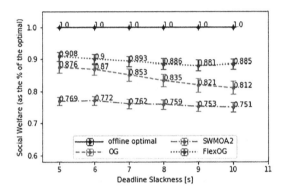

Fig. 4. Social welfare achieved by the mechanisms $((a, b) = \{(0, 5), (1, 6), (2, 7)(3, 8), (4, 9), (5, 10)\}, F = 25, q = 0.1, k = 0.3)$.

Finally, the evaluation of processing time is shown in Fig. 5. We plot the processing time of all mechanism only under resource coefficient 0.25, 0.35 and 0,45

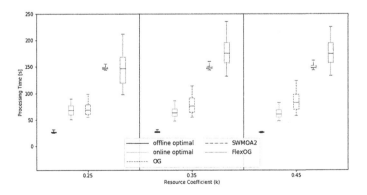

Fig. 5. Processing time of the mechanisms $((a, b) = (5, 10), F = 25, q = 0.1)$.

because the trend is similar under other coefficients. Note that the boxes show the lower to upper 25% values of the data with whiskers showing 5–95 percentile of the data, and the outliers are not shown in the figure. It can be seen from the figure that in general, offline optimal takes the least processing time, online optimal, OG, and SWMOA2 take more, and FlexOG uses the most time. This is mainly because offline optimal only needs to solve the optimisation problem once, while all other mechanisms need to solve the optimisation problem multiple times. FlexOG not only needs to solve the optimisation problem $|I| = 40$ times, but its optimisation problems also have more decision variables. Thus FlexOG is feasible for tasks where users can forecast their time constraints. Whereas for task requests that need immediate processing or task requests that come very frequently, the processing time of FlexOG would become an issue.

5 Conclusions

This paper formulates the RAFC problem as a constrained optimisation problem and proposes a novel truthful online mechanism for solving it. We made two key contributions. The first is that we extend price-based online mechanisms to our RAFC problem. The second is that we propose a truthful fog resource allocation mechanism called FlexOG, and we show its performance in terms of social welfare is significantly better than state-of-the-art mechanisms.

In the future, we plan to improve the scalability of FlexOG and to combine online mechanism design and machine learning to enhance social welfare further.

Acknowledgments. This research was sponsored by the U.S. Army Research Laboratory and the U.K. Ministry of Defence under Agreement Number W911NF-16-3-0001. The views and conclusions contained in this document are those of the authors and should not be interpreted as representing the official policies, either expressed or implied, of the U.S. Army Research Laboratory, the U.S. Government, the U.K. Ministry of Defence or the U.K. Government. The U.S. and U.K. Governments are authorized to reproduce and distribute reprints for Government purposes notwithstanding any copyright notation hereon.

References

White paper: Fog computing and the internet of things: Extend the cloud to where the things are (2015). https://www.cisco.com/c/dam/en_us/solutions/trends/iot/docs/computing-overview.pdf Accessed 20 May 2019

Aazam, M., Huh, E.N.: Fog computing micro datacenter based dynamic resource estimation and pricing model for IoT. In: Proceedings of 29th International Conference on AINA, pp. 687–694. IEEE (2015)

Bi, F., Stein, S., Gerding, E., Jennings, N., La Porta, T.: A truthful online mechanism for allocating fog computing resources. In: Proceedings of the 18th International Conference on AAMAS, pp. 1829–1831 (2019)

Bonomi, F., Milito, R., Zhu, J., Addepalli, S.: Fog computing and its role in the internet of things. In: Proceedings of the First MCC Workshop, pp. 13–16. ACM (2012)

Cardellini, V., Grassi, V., Presti, F.L., Nardelli, M.: On QoS-aware scheduling of data stream applications over fog computing infrastructures. In: ISCC, pp. 271–276. IEEE (2015)

Chawla, S., Devanur, N.R., Holroyd, A.E., Karlin, A.R., Martin, J.B., Sivan, B.: Stability of service under time-of-use pricing. In: Proceedings of the 49th Annual ACM SIGACT Symposium on Theory of Computing, pp. 184–197. ACM (2017)

Doukas, C., Maglogiannis, I.: Bringing IoT and cloud computing towards pervasive healthcare. In: Proceedings of Sixth International Conference on IMIS, pp. 922–926. IEEE (2012)

Gu, Y., Chang, Z., Pan, M., Song, L., Han, Z.: Joint radio and computational resource allocation in IoT fog computing. IEEE Trans. Veh. Technol. $67(8)$, 7475–7484 (2018)

Hayakawa, K., Gerding, E.H., Stein, S., Shiga, T.: Price-based online mechanisms for settings with uncertain future procurement costs and multi-unit demand. In: Proceedings of the 17th International Conference on AAMAS, pp. 309–317 (2018)

Lucier, B., Menache, I., Naor, J.S., Yaniv, J.: Efficient online scheduling for deadline-sensitive jobs. In: Proceedings of the Twenty-Fifth Annual ACM Symposium on Parallelism in Algorithms and Architectures, pp. 305–314. ACM (2013)

Lueth, K.L.: State of the IoT 2018: Number of IoT devices now at 7b – market accelerating, August 2018. https://iot-analytics.com/state-of-the-iot-update-q1-q2-2018-number-of-iot-devices-now-7b/. Accessed 14 Feb 2019

Nisan, N., Roughgarden, T., Tardos, E., Vazirani, V.V.: Algorithmic Game Theory. Cambridge University Press, New York (2007)

Sajid, A., Abbas, H., Saleem, K.: Cloud-assisted IoT-based scada systems security: a review of the state of the art and future challenges. IEEE Access 4, 1375–1384 (2016)

Shi, W., Wu, C., Li, Z.: An online auction mechanism for dynamic virtual cluster provisioning in geo-distributed clouds. IEEE Trans. Parallel Distrib. Syst. $28(3)$, 677–688 (2017)

Wang, C., Ma, W., Qin, T., Chen, X., Hu, X., Liu, T.Y.: Selling reserved instances in cloud computing. In: Proceedings of the 24th IJCAI, pp. 224–230 (2015)

Wang, Q., Ren, K., Meng, X.: When cloud meets ebay: towards effective pricing for cloud computing. In: Proceedings of INFOCOM, pp. 936–944. IEEE (2012)

Zhang, X., Wu, C., Li, Z., Lau, F.C.M.: A truthful $(1-\epsilon)$-optimal mechanism for on-demand cloud resource provisioning. In: Proceedings of INFOCOM, pp. 1053–1061. IEEE (2015)

Zhu, Y., Fu, S.D., Liu, J., Cui, Y.: Truthful online auction toward maximized instance utilization in the cloud. IEEE/ACM Trans. Netw. $26(5)$, 2132–2145 (2018)

Graph Representation of Road and Traffic for Autonomous Driving

Jianglin Qiao[1(✉)], Dongmo Zhang[1], and Dave de Jonge[1,2]

[1] University of Western Sydney, Sydney, Australia
19469397@student.westernsydney.edu.au,
{d.zhang,d.dejonge}@westernsydney.edu.au
[2] IIIA-CSIC, Barcelona, Spain
davedejonge@iiia.csic.es

Abstract. Autonomous driving has the potential to radically change the way vehicles interact each other. This paper aims to develop a formal method to model high level interaction between autonomous vehicles. We introduce a concept of road graph to represent complex road situations such as intersections, road merging, unmarked roads, and traffic hazards. We then extend the concept to further represent status of vehicles, dynamics of traffic and protocols of traffic control. Specifically, we formalise two categories of traffic control protocols, time-based protocols and priority-based protocols.

1 Introduction

Over the last decade, research on autonomous vehicles (AVs) has made revolutionary progress, which brings us hope of safer, more convenient and efficient means of transportation [2,9]. A great number of tech giants and research institutes alone with the major automakers are striving for the developments of new technologies for autonomous driving with the ultimate target that all vehicles eventually become fully autonomous without human intervention at their highest automation level [4,8].

An autonomous vehicle system is an integration of many technologies, including computer vision, graphical processing, navigation, sensor technologies and so on. Most significantly, the recent advance of machine learning technologies enables a self-driving car to learn to drive in any complex road situations with millions of accumulated driving hours, which are way higher than any experienced human driver can reach. However, driving is not a purely technical job but involves complicated social activities, which could be hard to learn from experience. For instance, if two cars meet in a narrow road or a long bridge on which only one car can go through, how do the cars decide which one should reverse to give way to the other? Many of such a situation requires direct interaction among vehicles, vehicles and infrastructures, or vehicles and authorities [3,5]. Such demands push the research on AVs to a different direction from machine learning with regards to communication, negotiation and cooperation among autonomous vehicles. Unfortunately the studies along, this direction is far from adequate.

Existing research on vehicle to vehicle (V2V) allows exchange of information collected from local sensors to achieve a form of 'collaborative awareness' [1,7]. However, the information exchanged between vehicles are normally signal data or messages. Such low level communication cannot achieve high-level interaction for the purpose

© Springer Nature Switzerland AG 2019
A. C. Nayak and A. Sharma (Eds.): PRICAI 2019, LNAI 11672, pp. 377–384, 2019.
https://doi.org/10.1007/978-3-030-29894-4_31

of automated negotiation, cooperative maneuvering, collaborative auto-piloting among autonomous vehicles [6].

The primary goal of our research is to establish a high-level communication protocol for autonomous vehicles, which can solve various traffic conditions through negotiation between vehicles. Herein, we propose the *road graph*; a novel concept for representing roads and traffic which includes fully autonomous vehicles, as the basis of our research. With this road graph model we describe various traffic-related elements, such as traffic flow, traffic-control protocols, vehicle information and vehicle management processes. It should be mentioned that at this point our work is only for theoretical research. Its purpose is to develop an abstract model that allows self-driving vehicles to understand roads and traffic, so as to pave the way for more advanced vehicle negotiation. We leave it as future work to develop models that are closer to real-world traffic.

The structure of this paper is as follows. In Sect. 2 we introduce the representation of roads, vehicle and traffic setting, and traffic state and traffic flow. In Sect. 3, we give traffic control protocols in detailed. In Sect. 4 we summarise the paper with conclusions and future research directions.

2 Traffic Representation

To allow autonomous vehicles to reason about complicated traffic situations, we introduce a formal method to represent roads, traffic flows and traffic control protocols. As a generic assumption of this work and a way of abstraction, time occurs at distinct, separate "points in time", throughout each non-zero region of time ("time period"), represented by natural numbers $T = \{1, 2, 3, \cdots\}$.

2.1 Road Graph

In order to specify any complicated road, we divide a road into a number of blocks or road segments. Each block of a road allows one car to travel at each time[1], represented as a vertex in a graph. Directed edges in a graph represent connections and travel directions between road blocks. If two vertices have no edge to link them, no vehicle can travel directly between these two blocks. In addition, we assume that each road contain a number of entries and a number of exits. For each entry, it must have at least one out-going edge, and for each exit, it must have at least one incoming edge. Formally we have the following definition.

Definition 1. *A* road graph *G is a tuple $(B, \mathcal{E}, B_n, B_x)$, where:*

- *B is a non-empty and finite set of blocks;*
- *$\mathcal{E} \subseteq B \times B$ is a set of arcs. An arc $(b, b') \in \mathcal{E}$ refers to a connection and travel direction from block b to block b' ;*
- *$B_n \subseteq B$ is a set of blocks to represent the road entries;*
- *$B_x \subseteq B$ is a set of blocks to represent the road exits.*

Figure 1 shows a simple road graph representing a typical two-way two-lane road. The vertices $b_1, \cdots, b_{20}$ represent the segments of the road while the arcs indicate the traffic flows that are allowed from segments to segments. For instance, b_1, b_2, b_3, b_4, b_5 are the blocks of the left most lane. The arc from b_2 to b_8 means a vehicle on block b_2 can change lane to block b_8 but is not allowed to shift to block b_7. Blocks b_1, b_6, b_{11} and b_{16} are entries of the road, and blocks b_5, b_{10}, b_{15} and b_{20} are exits of the road.

---

[1] We will use discrete time to represent traffic flows thus a time point represents a period of time.

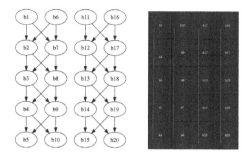

Fig. 1. A road graph representing a two-way two-lane road

As an abstraction of roads, a road graph can represent more complicated road situations and configurations, such as multi-way junctions, roundabout, no-through road and U-turns. The following example shows a representation of a typical four-way intersection.

Example 1. *Figure 2 shows an example of road graph for a four-way intersection which will be used as running example of the paper. Each direction has one lane. Note that the road graph indicates that a vehicle turning right is not allowed to travel in diagonal inside the intersection. For instance, a vehicle at b_2 turning to b_{19} must travel via b_3, b_4 and b_{10} rather than a sharp turn from b_3 to b_{10}. This is by no means a restriction of road graph representation but reflects an actual setting of the road.*

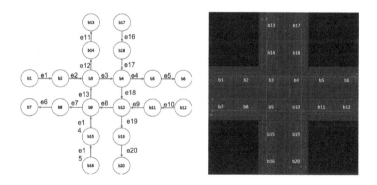

Fig. 2. A road graph for four-way intersection

Given a road graph, a road path can be easily defined as path in terms of the standard graph theory terminology. Formally we have the following definition:

Definition 2. *Given a road graph* $(B, \mathcal{E}, B_n, B_x)$*, a* path ρ *is a sequence* $b_0 \xrightarrow{e_1} b_1 \xrightarrow{e_2} b_2 \cdots \xrightarrow{e_m} b_m$*, where*

- $b_i \in B$ *for all* $0 \le i \le m$
- $e_i = (b_{i-1}, b_i) \in \mathcal{E}$ *for all* $0 < i \le m$
- $b_i \ne b_j$ *for any* $i \ne j$

ρ *is called a* complete path *if* $b_0 \in B_n$ *and* $b_m \in B_x$*. We use* $\hat{\rho}$ *to denote the start block of the path and* $\check{\rho}$ *the end block of the path, i.e.,* $\hat{\rho} = b_0$ *and* $\check{\rho} = b_m$*.*

2.2   Vehicles and Traffic Settings

Vehicles are road users. We assume that all vehicles are fully autonomous, which means that decision-making of each vehicle is not centralised but by the vehicle itself, no matter they driven by human or computers. We also assume that each vehicle has a designated complete path, which specified its entry block, exit block and intended travel path. In the context of automated negotiation between autonomous vehicles, these pieces of information are initial settings of a vehicle before it enters a road. They are negotiable when it travels on the road. In addition, we also assume each vehicle has a designated time point to enter the road. Formally, we specify the information of vehicles with the following concept:

Definition 3. *Given a road graph* $G = (B, \mathcal{E}, B_n, B_x)$ *and a set* $\mathcal{V}$ *of possible vehicles, the* vehicle information, $\mathcal{I}$, *on* G *is represented by a tuple* $(\mu, \sigma, \eta, \mathcal{P})$ *where*

- $\mu : \mathcal{V} \to B_n$ *is a function that maps each vehicle to a road entry;*
- $\sigma : \mathcal{V} \to B_x$ *is a function that maps each vehicle to a road exit;*
- $\eta : \mathcal{V} \to T$ *is a function that maps each vehicle to a time point indicating the time the vehicle is expected to enter the road;*
- $\mathcal{P} : \mathcal{V} \to P$ *is a function that maps each vehicle to a complete path such that for each vehicle* $v \in \mathcal{V}$, $\overset{\frown}{\mathcal{P}}(v) = \mu(v)$ *and* $\overset{\smile}{\mathcal{P}}(v) = \sigma(v)$.

In the rest of the paper, we call $(G, \mathcal{V}, \mathcal{I})$ *a traffic setting.*

2.3   Traffic States and Traffic Flows

Traffic means that vehicles move on a road. A snapshot of traffic on a road can be viewed as a set of vehicles that currently on the road and the positions they occupy. As we mentioned before, we assume that each block can only contain one vehicle at each time point. Therefore vehicles' location can be represented with an injective function from a vehicle to a block of the road. Formally we introduce the following concept:

Definition 4. *Given a traffic setting* $(G, \mathcal{V}, \mathcal{I})$, *a* traffic state *with respect to the traffic setting is a pair* (V, τ) *where*

- $V \subseteq \mathcal{V}$, *indicating the vehicles that are currently on the road;*
- $\tau : V \to B$ *is an injective function that maps each vehicle to a block of the road. In other words, for any* $v, v' \in V$, $\tau(v) = \tau(v')$ *implies* $v = v'$.

A traffic state represents a snapshot of a traffic flow, thus, is a static view of traffic. However, traffic is dynamic. In order to model a flow of traffic, we define traffic on a road as a set of traffic states in time sequence:

Definition 5. *Let* $(G, \mathcal{V}, \mathcal{I})$ *be a traffic setting. A* traffic flow $\mathcal{F} = \langle (V_t, \tau_t) \rangle_{t \in T}$ *is a temporal sequence of traffic states such that for each time point* $t \in T$,

1. $v \in V_{t+1} \setminus V_t$ *implies* $\tau_{t+1}(v) = \mu(v)$, *i.e., a vehicle must enter the road from its specified entry.*
2. *for each* $v \in V_t$, *exactly one of the following conditions holds*
   (a) $\tau_t(v) = \tau_{t+1}(v)$
   (b) $(\tau_t(v), \tau_{t+1}(v)) \in \mathcal{E}$
   (c) $\tau_t(v) = \sigma(v)$ *and* $v \notin V_{t+1}$
3. *for any* $v, v' \in V_t$ *such that* $v \neq v'$ *and* $\tau_t(v) = \tau_{t+1}(v')$, $\tau_{t+1}(v) \neq \tau_t(v')$.

3 Traffic Control Protocols

Traffic must be controlled to ensure road safety and efficiency. The way of traffic control is to instruct vehicles taking appropriate measures or actions in order to avoid collisions or delays. Complex operational procedures, rules and laws, and physical equipment (such as signs, markings, and lights) have been used in real-world traffic control systems. The most common traffic control devices and methods are traffic lights, stop signs, roundabouts and other facilities. Despite of the significant differences between different traffic control methods and systems, the mechanisms of all traffic control methods can be categorised into two fundamental traffic control protocols: *time-based traffic control* and *priority-based traffic control*.

3.1 Time-Based Traffic Control Protocols

The time-based traffic control utilises protocols that control traffic by restricting accessibility or impassability of roads in different time periods. With the road graph representation, we can simply define a time-based traffic protocol as a temporal sequence of arc groups, indicating which road segments are accessible at each time. A typical application of time-based traffic control protocols is traffic light systems.

Definition 6. *Given a road graph* $G = (B, \mathcal{E}, B_n, B_x)$. *A time-based traffic control protocol* $\alpha : T \to 2^{\mathcal{E}}$ *is a function from each time point to a subset of arcs. Furthermore, a traffic flow* $\mathcal{F} = \langle (V_t, \tau_t) \rangle_{t \in T}$ *is said to be* complied with *a time-based protocol* α *if for any time point* t *and any vehicle* v, *if* $v \in V_t$, $\tau_t(v) \neq \sigma(v)$ *and* $\tau_t(v) \neq \tau_{t+1}(v)$, *then* $(\tau_t(v), \tau_{t+1}(v)) \in \alpha(t)$.

Intuitively, a time-based traffic control protocol specifies which segment of road can go through at each time point. In other words, for each time point t, all the arcs in $\alpha(t)$ are passible (green light), while all the arcs in $\mathcal{E} \setminus \alpha(t)$ are impassible (red light). When a traffic control protocol is enforced on a road, traffic is shaped to form specific patterns of traffic flow. A traffic flow is complied with a time-based protocol means any vehicle must travel at green lights. The following example shows a representation of traffic in a four-way intersection when time-based protocol is enforced.

Example 2. *Consider a road graph for a four-way intersection in Example 1, and a time-based traffic control protocol* α *on the road graph as follows:*

$$
\alpha(t) = \begin{cases}
E_g \cup \{e_2, e_3, e_9, e_8\}, & \text{if } 0 \leq t \bmod l < 1_1 \\
E_g \cup \{e_2, e_3, e_{18}, e_{14}\}, & \text{if } l_1 \leq t \bmod l < l_2 \\
E_g \cup \{e_{14}, e_{13}, e_{17}, e_{18}\}, & \text{if } l_2 \leq t \bmod l < l_3 \\
E_g \cup \{e_9, e_8, e_{13}, e_{17}\}, & \text{if } l_3 \leq t \bmod l < l
\end{cases}
$$

where $0 < l_1 < l_2 < l_3 < l$ *and* $E_g = \{e_1, e_4, e_5, e_6, e_7, e_{10}, e_{11}, e_{12}, e_{15}, e_{16}, e_{19}, e_{20}\}$. $t \bmod l$ *means* "t *modulo* l".

The protocol specifies four time intervals in each period of length l : $[0, l_1)$, $[l_1, l_2)$, $[l_2, l_3)$ and $[l_3, l)$. The first time interval allows vehicles from east or west to travel straight or take a left turn. The second interval allows traffic from west to take right turn and traffic from south to take left turn. The other two intervals are similar for traffic from other directions.

3.2 Priority-Based Traffic Control Protocol

A priority-based protocol controls traffic based on preset priorities of roads at each road junction. For instance, in a left driving country, vehicles give way to the traffic on right whenever they are approaching an intersection, which means that the road on right has higher priority than the road a vehicle travels on. With the help of graph representation of roads, we can formalise a priority-based traffic control protocol as follows:

Definition 7. *Given a road graph* $G = (B, \mathcal{E}, B_n, B_x)$. *A priority-based protocol* $\beta : \mathcal{E} \to 2^{\mathcal{E}}$ *is a function from each arc of the road to a subset of the arcs* $\mathcal{E}$ *such that*

1. *for any* $(b_1, b_2) \in \mathcal{E}$, *if* $(b'_1, b'_2) \in \beta(b_1, b_2)$, *then* $b_2 = b'_2$;
2. *if* $e' \in \beta(e)$, $e \notin \beta(e')$.

To understand the conditions of the definition, the first condition means that an arc gives priority to another arc only if they meet at the same block. The second condition means that two vehicles on different roads do not give way to each other. Similar to time-based traffic control protocols, we can also define whether a traffic flow is complied with a priority-based traffic control protocol.

Definition 8. *Let* $(G, \mathcal{V}, \mathcal{I})$ *be a traffic setting. A traffic flow* $\mathcal{F} = \langle (V_t, \tau_t) \rangle_{t \in T}$ *is said to be complied with a priority-based protocol* β *if for any* $t \in T$ *and any* $v, v' \in V_t$, *such that* $v \neq v'$, $\tau_t(v) \neq \tau_{t+1}(v)$ *implies* $(\tau_t(v'), \tau_{t+1}(v)) \notin \beta(\tau_t(v), \tau_{t+1}(v))$ *unless* $(\tau_t(v'), \tau_{t+1}(v)) \notin \mathcal{P}(v)$.

It means that a vehicle does not have to give way to another vehicle only if the road that the other vehicle travels on does not have a higher priority or the other vehicle does not travel into the same block.

Example 3. *Figure 3 shows a road graph representing a T-junction. Imagine there is a stop sign in block* b_{15}. *Then all vehicles entering* b_9 *via* e_{14} *must stop at the stop sign and observe the coming vehicles towards* b_9 *from other roads. Assume that we enforce the following priority-based traffic control protocol* β *at this T-junction:*

- $\beta(e) = \emptyset$, *where* $e \in \{e_1, e_3, e_4, e_5, e_6, e_7, e_8, e_{10}, e_{11}, e_{13}, e_{14}, e_{15}, e_{16}\}$.
- $\beta(e_2) = \{e_{13}\}$; $\beta(e_{12}) = \{e_8\}$; $\beta(e_9) = \{e_{14}\}$;

Let $\mathcal{F}(t) = (V_t, \tau_t)$ *be a traffic state at time* t *where* $V_t = \{v_1, v_2\}$, $\tau_t(v_1) = b_{10}$ *and* $\tau_t(v_2) = b_{15}$. *Assume that both vehicles* v_1 *and* v_2 *are travelling towards block* b_9. *Since* e_8 *has a higher priority than* e_{14}, *only vehicle* v_1 *can go through but* v_2 *must stay in block* b_{15}. *If* $\mathcal{F}(t+1)) = (V_{t+1}, \tau_{t+1})$ *represents the next state, we then have* $\tau_{t+1}(v_1) = b_9$ *and* $\tau_{t+1}(v_2) = b_{15}$.

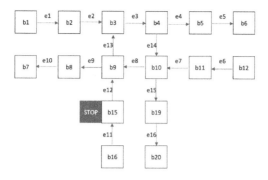

Fig. 3. An example of priority-based protocol on a T-junction

4   Conclusion and Future Work

In this paper, we proposed a way to represent traffic roads, traffic flow, and control protocol at first. And then we introduce a process to generate a traffic flow within traffic control protocols, which are time-based protocol and priority-based protocol. Autonomous vehicle will determine the future of road transportation systems. These technologies aim to improve mobility, safety, comfort, and fuel consumption while reducing emissions. However, the extent of this improvement is unknown. Although the impact on the driving environment has extensively analysed in the literature, more comprehensive studies are needed. Our research can not only describe a single type of traffic situation but also cover different traffic situations. However, this article is just the basis for our research. We will pave the way for future vehicle negotiations by indicating roads, traffic flow, and traffic control protocols.

References

1. Azimi, S., Bhatia, G., Rajkumar, R., Mudalige, P.: Reliable intersection protocols using vehicular networks. In: 2013 ACM/IEEE International Conference on Cyber-Physical Systems (ICCPS), pp. 1–10 (2013)
2. Banerjee, T., Bose, S., Chakraborty, A., Samadder, T., Kumar, B., Rana, T.K.: Self driving cars: a peep into the future. In: 2017 8th Annual Industrial Automation and Electromechanical Engineering Conference (IEMECON), pp. 33–38 (2017)
3. Cui, S., Seibold, B., Stern, R., Work, D.B.: Stabilizing traffic flow via a single autonomous vehicle: possibilities and limitations. In: 2017 IEEE Intelligent Vehicles Symposium (IV), pp. 1336–1341 (2017)
4. Dikmen, M., Burns, C.M.: Autonomous driving in the real world: experiences with tesla autopilot and summon. In: Proceedings of the 8th International Conference on Automotive User Interfaces and Interactive Vehicular Applications (AutomotiveUI), pp. 225–228 (2016)
5. Gruel, W., Stanford, J.M.: Assessing the long-term effects of autonomous vehicles: a speculative approach. Transp. Res. Procedia **13**, 18–29 (2016)
6. Hobert, L., Festag, A., Llatser, I., Altomare, L., Visintainer, F., Kovacs, A.: Enhancements of V2X communication in support of cooperative autonomous driving. IEEE Commun. Mag. **53**(12), 64–70 (2015)

7. Liu, C., Lin, C.W., Shiraishi, S., Tomizuka, M.: Improving efficiency of autonomous vehicles by V2V communication. In: 2018 Annual American Control Conference (ACC), pp. 4778–4783 (2018)
8. Ross, P.E.: Robot, you can drive my car. IEEE Spectrum **51**(6), 60–90 (2014)
9. Thorpe, C., Herbert, M., Kanade, T., Shafer, S.: Toward autonomous driving: the CMU Navlab. I. Perception. IEEE Expert **6**(4), 31–42 (1991)

Biometrics and Bioinformatics

Primate Face Identification in the Wild

Ankita Shukla[1]([⊠])(iD), Gullal Singh Cheema[1](iD), Saket Anand[1],
Qamar Qureshi[2], and Yadvendradev Jhala[2]

[1] Indraprastha Institute of Information Technology Delhi, New Delhi, India
{ankitas,gullal1408,anands}@iiitd.ac.in
[2] Wildlife Institute of India, Dehradun, India
{qnq,jhalay}@wii.gov.in

Abstract. Ecological imbalance owing to rapid urbanization and deforestation has adversely affected the population of several wild animals.
This loss of habitat has skewed the population of several non-human
primate species like chimpanzees and macaques and has constrained
them to co-exist in close proximity of human settlements, often leading to human-wildlife conflicts while competing for resources. For effective wildlife conservation and conflict management, regular monitoring
of population and of conflicted regions is necessary. However, existing
approaches like field visits for data collection and manual analysis by
experts is resource intensive, tedious and time consuming, thus necessi-
tating an automated, non-invasive, more efficient alternative like image
based facial recognition. The challenge in individual identification arises
due to unrelated factors like pose, lighting variations and occlusions due
to the uncontrolled environments, that is further exacerbated by limited
training data. Inspired by human perception, we propose to learn representations that are robust to such nuisance factors and capture the notion
of similarity over the individual identity sub-manifolds. The proposed
approach, Primate Face Identification (PFID), achieves this by training
the network to distinguish between positive and negative pairs of images.
The PFID loss augments the standard cross entropy loss with a pairwise
loss to learn more discriminative and generalizable features, thus making
it appropriate for other related identification tasks like open-set, closed
set and verification. We report state-of-the-art accuracy on facial recognition of two primate species, rhesus macaques and chimpanzees under
the four protocols of classification, verification, closed-set identification
and open-set recognition.

Keywords: Face recognition · Deep learning · Primates · Social good

1 Introduction

One of the key indicators of a healthy ecosystem is its constituent biodiversity.
Over the last several decades, technological progress has substantially improved

---

A. Shukla and G.S. Cheema—Equal Contribution.

© Springer Nature Switzerland AG 2019
A. C. Nayak and A. Sharma (Eds.): PRICAI 2019, LNAI 11672, pp. 387–401, 2019.
https://doi.org/10.1007/978-3-030-29894-4_32

human quality of life, albeit at a cost of rapid environmental degradation. Specifically, to meet the needs of the growing human population, various factors like urban and infrastructural development, agricultural land expansion and livestock ranching have resulted in soaring rates of deforestation. In addition to the risk of extinction for many species, shrinking natural habitats have led to increased interactions between humans and wildlife, often raising safety concerns for both (Fig. 1).

Conflicts with primarily forest-dwelling species like big cats (tigers, leopards, mountain lions, etc.), elephants, bears or wolves may cause severe injuries or even death to humans. On the other hand, there are species which have transitioned into a commensal relationship with humans, i.e., they rely on humans for food without causing direct harm. Due to their apparent harmlessness, several commensal (or semi-commensal) species like wild herbivores, wild boars, macaques and other non-human primates often dwell in close proximity of human settlements. This co-existence leads to indirect conflicts in the form of crop-raiding and property damage as well as occasional direct conflicts such as attacks or biting incidents. An example image of crop raiding and primates in close vicinity of humans is shown in Fig. 2. Certain species like the rhesus macaque (*Macaca mulatta*) have become a cause of serious concern due to their resilience and ability to co-exist with humans in rural, semi-urban and urban areas. Their prolific breeding and short gestation periods lead to high population densities, thereby increasing the chances and extent of conflicts with humans. As a consequence, organizations have resorted to lethal conflict management measures like culling [2], which become infeasible when the conflicted species have declining populations, e.g., the human-primate conflict crisis in Sri Lanka where two of the responsible primate species are endangered: Toque macaques (*Macaca sinica*) and the purple faced langur (*Trachypithecus vetulus*) [5]. Besides, the effectiveness of lethal measures is well debated and poorly designed initiatives could have unexpected consequences like increased aggression or even extinction of the conflicted species [16]. On the other hand, non-lethal approaches are easier to adopt across geographies as they avoid complex socio-religious issues [19]. Two recurring non-lethal themes in conflict management discussions are population monitoring and stakeholder engagement [16], both of which can be easily achieved with a combination of smartphone and AI technology. Pursuing a crowdsourcing approach to population monitoring and conflict reporting has two direct benefits: the cost and scalability of data collection for population monitoring can be improved drastically and active involvement of the affected community can help increase awareness, which in turn abates the human behavioral factors that often influence human-wildlife conflicts.

In this work, we focus on addressing the human-primate conflicts, largely because of the frequency and magnitude of encounters in urban, rural and agricultural regions across developing South Asian nations [1]. Inspired by the success and scalability of human face recognition, we propose a Primate Face Identification (PFID) system. Automatic identification capabilities could serve as a backbone for a crowdsourcing platform, where geo-referenced images submitted by users are automatically indexed by individuals, gender, age, etc. Such an indexed database could simplify downstream tasks like primate population monitoring and analysis of conflict reports, enabling better informed and effective strategies for conflict as well as conservation management.

Fig. 1. Example images showing primates in human shared space and crop raiding [source: google images].

We summarize the contributions of this paper as follows:

- We propose *Primate Face Identification* (PFID), a deep neural network based system for automated identification of individual primates using facial images.
- We introduce a guided pairwise loss using similar and dissimilar image pairs to learn robust and generalizable representations.
- Our fully automatic pipeline convincingly beats state-of-the-art methods on two datasets (macaques and chimpanzees) under *all* settings.

2 Existing Work on Face Recognition

There is a vast body of literature in human face recognition. Without attempting to present a comprehensive survey, we briefly discuss prior work relevant to facial identification of primates. We broadly categorize these approaches into two categories: Non Deep Learning Approaches and Deep Learning Approaches.

Non Deep Learning Approaches. Traditional face recognition pipelines comprised of face alignment, followed by low level feature extraction and classification. Early works in primate face recognition [13], adapted the Randomfaces [25] technique for identifying chimpanzees in the wild and follows the standard pipeline for face recognition. Later, LemurID was proposed in [6], which additionally used manual marking of the eyes for face alignment. Patch-wise multiscale Local Binary Pattern (LBP) features were extracted from aligned faces and used with LDA to construct a representation, which was then used with an appropriate similarity metric for identifying individuals.

Deep Learning Approaches. Freytag et al. [9] used Convolutional Neural Networks (CNNs) for learning a feature representation of chimpanzee faces. For increased discriminative power, the architecture uses a bilinear pooling layer after the fully connected layers (or a convolutional layer), followed by a matrix log operation. These features are then used to train an SVM classifier for classification of known identities. Later, [4] developed face recognition for gorilla images captured in the wild. This approach fine-tuned a YOLO detector [17] for gorilla faces. For classification, a similar approach was taken as [9], where pre-trained CNN features are used to train a linear SVM. More recently, [7] proposed PrimNet, a deep neural net based approach that uses the *Additive Margin Softmax* loss [22] and achieves state of the art performance for identifying individuals across different primate species including lemur, chimpanzee and golden monkey. However, it requires substantial manual effort to designing landmark templates for face alignment prior to identification process, which can adversely affect adoption rates in a crowdsourced mobile app setting. For human face recognition techniques, various approaches have improved performance by combining the standard cross entropy loss with other loss functions such as contrastive loss [21] and center loss [23] to learn more discriminative features.

3   Primate Face Identification (PFID) System

Pose Invariant Representation Learning. We would like to motivate the choice of our loss function with the following reasons

1. Our approach is inspired by the human perception system, which is robust to nuisance factors like illumination and pose and is able to identify individual faces captured in unconstrained environments and extreme poses. Geometrically, face images of an identity defines a sub-manifold [15] in image manifold of faces. This allows one to devise a metric such that sample pairs of the same identity have small distances regardless of pose and other nuisance factors, while those of different identities have larger distances. In PFID, we use a deep neural network to learn such a representation through a specially designed loss function over similar and dissimilar pairs of primate face images.
2. Learning invariant features has long been a challenging issue in computer vision. Owing to the high curvature of original image data manifold [14], simple metric like euclidean distance fails to capture the underlying data semantics. Consequently, linear methods also are inappropriate to learn decision boundaries for tasks like image recognition. In such scenarios, deep learning approaches have come in handy, with their ability to flatten the data manifold owing to the successive non linear operations applied though a series of layers [3]. However, deep models are often trained with a cross-entropy based classification loss, to drive the class probability distribution for a given image independently to one hot encoding vector. Given sufficient training data, this training protocol often generalizes well for classification task, however, its performance is often limited on other related tasks like verification and unseen class generalizabilty. The latter's performance crucially depends on the ability to learn a representation space that can model class-level similarities. By incorporating a pairwise similarity loss term operating on the class

probability (softmax) distributions, we drive the learned representations to be semantically more meaningful, and hence invariant to other factors.

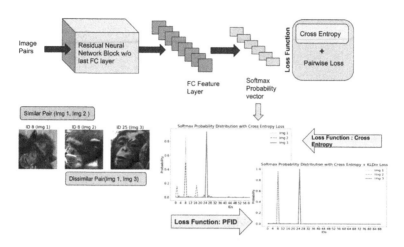

Fig. 2. Illustration of proposed PFID loss function vs. the standard cross entropy loss on the learned class probability distributions with ResNet model.

We now present our proposed PFID loss function for unique identification of primates using cropped facial images that can be obtained using state of the art deep learning based detectors. We note that images will be largely collected by the general public, professional monkey catchers and field biologists. Typically, we expect the images to be captured in uncontrolled outdoor scenarios, leading to significant variations in facial pose and lighting. These conditions are challenging for robust eye and nose detection, which need to be accurate in order to be useful for facial alignment. Consequently, we train our identification model to work without facial alignment and capture the semantic similarities of the underlying space.

The proposed loss formulation combines the standard cross entropy network with a guided pairwise KL divergence loss imposed on similar and dissimilar pairs. Using pairwise loss terms ensure that the underlying features are more discriminative and generalize better. Our analysis in Sect. 4.4 show empirical evidence that the learned features are more clusterable than when trained with the standard cross-entropy loss.

An illustration of the effect of loss function is shown in Fig. 2. A similar pair corresponds to images of same individual, while a dissimilar pair corresponds to images from two different identities. The learned class probability distribution for a similar pair and dissimilar pair using two different loss functions is shown. In case of network trained with PFID loss, the class probabilities are maximally similar for a similar pair as oppose to standard cross entropy loss.

Let, $\mathcal{X} = \{x_1, x_2, \ldots, x_n\}$ be the training dataset of n samples with $l_i \in \{1, 2, \ldots, K\}$ as the associated labels. We use the labeled training data to create sets of similar image pairs, $\mathcal{C}_s = \{(i,j) : x_i, x_j \in \mathcal{X}, l_i = l_j\}$, and that of dissimilar pair, $\mathcal{C}_d = \{(i,j) : x_i, x_j \in \mathcal{X}, l_i \neq l_j\}$ for $i, j \in \{1, 2, \cdots, n\}$. The KL divergence between two distribution p^i and q^j corresponding to points x_i and x_j is given by

$$KL(p^i||q^j) = \sum_{k=1}^{K} p_k^i \log \frac{p_k^i}{q_k^j} \tag{1}$$

For a similar pair $(i,j) \in \mathcal{C}_s$, we use the symmetric variant of (1) given by

$$\mathcal{L}_s^{ij} = KL(p^i||q^j) + KL(q^j||p^i) \tag{2}$$

and for a dissimilar pair $(i,j) \in \mathcal{C}_d$, we use its large-margin variant for improving discriminative power

$$\mathcal{L}_d^{ij} = \max(0, m - KL(p^i||q^j)) + \max(0, m - KL(q^j||p^i)) \tag{3}$$

where m is the desired margin width between dissimilar pairs. It is important to note that during training, when both x_i and x_j are misclassified by the model, minimizing (2) may lead to an increase in the bias.

Guided Pairwise Loss Function. Since we use class labels for the cross-entropy loss, we incorporate them in the pairwise loss terms to guide the training. Subsequently, we modify the terms in (2) and (3) to get the following guided KL divergence loss term

$$\mathcal{L}_s = \sum_{i,j \in \mathcal{C}_s} a\mathcal{L}_s^{ij}, \qquad \mathcal{L}_d = \sum_{i,j \in \mathcal{C}_d} a\mathcal{L}_d^{ij} \tag{4}$$

where, $a = 1$ if either $\arg\max p^i = l_i$ or $\arg\max q^j = l_j$ and $a = 0$ otherwise. The loss function for PFID is given by the sum of standard cross entropy $(\mathcal{L}_{CE})$ and the guided KL divergence loss

$$\mathcal{L}(\theta) = \mathcal{L}_{CE} + \frac{1}{|\mathcal{C}_s|} \sum_{j,k \in \mathcal{C}_s} a\mathcal{L}_s^{jk} + \frac{1}{|\mathcal{C}_d|} \sum_{j,k \in \mathcal{C}_d} a\mathcal{L}_d^{jk} \tag{5}$$

This loss function is used to train the network with a mini-batch gradient descent. Here $|\mathcal{C}_s|$ and $|\mathcal{C}_d|$ are the number of similar and dissimilar pairs respectively in a given batch. More details on the training are provided in Sect. 4.3.

4   Experimental Setup and Results

4.1   Dataset

We evaluate our model using three datasets, the details of which are given in Table 1. As is typical of wildlife data collected in uncontrolled environments, all the three datasets have a significant class imbalance as reported in the Table 1.

Rhesus Macaque Dataset. The dataset is collected using DSLRs in their natural dwelling in an urban region in the state of Uttarakhand in northern India. The dataset is cleaned manually to remove images with no or very little facial content (e.g., extreme poses with only one ear or only back of head visible). The filtered dataset has 59 identities with a total of 1399 images. An illustrative set of pose variations for the datasets are shown using the cropped images in Fig. 3. Due to the small size of this dataset, we combined our dataset with the publicly available dataset by Witham [24]. The combined dataset comprises 7679 images of 93 individuals. Note that we use the combined dataset only for the individual identification experiments, as the public data by Witham comprises of pre-cropped images. On the other hand, the detection and the complete PFID pipeline is evaluated on a test set comprising full images from our macaque dataset.

Fig. 3. Pose variations for one of the Rhesus Macaque (Top) and Chimpanzee (Below) from the dataset.

Chimpanzee Dataset. The C-Zoo and C-Tai dataset consists of 24 and 66 individuals with 2109 and 5057 images respectively [9]. The C-Zoo dataset contains good quality images of chimpanzees taken in a Zoo, while the C-Tai dataset contains more challenging images taken under uncontrolled settings of a national park. We combine these two datasets to get 90 identities with a total of 7166 images.

Table 1. Dataset Summary. The numbers in the brackets show the range of samples per individual ([min,max]), highlighting the imbalance in the datasets.

Dataset	Rhesus Macaques	C-Zoo	C-Tai
# Samples	7679	2109	5057
# Classes	93	24	66
# Samples/individual	[4,192]	[62,111]	[4,416]

4.2 Evaluation Protocol

We evaluate and compare the performance of our PFID system under four different experimental settings, namely: classification, closed-set identification, open-set identification and verification.

Classification: To evaluate the classification performance the dataset is divided into 80/20 train/test splits. We present the mean and standard deviation of classification accuracy over five stratified splits of the data. As opposed to other evaluation protocols discussed below, all the identities are seen during the training, with unseen samples of same identities in the test set.

Open and Closed-Set Identification: Both, closed-set and open-set performance is reported on *unseen* identities. We perform 80/20 split of data w.r.t. to identities, which leads to a test set with 18 identities in test for both chimpanzee and macaque datasets. We again use five stratified splits of the data. For each split, we further perform 100 random trials for generating the probe and gallery sets. However, the composition of the probe and gallery sets for the closed-set scenario is different from that of open set.

Closed-Set: In case of closed-set identification, all identities of images present in the probe set are also present in the gallery set. Each probe image is assigned the identity that yields the maximum similarity score over the entire gallery set. We report the fraction of correctly identified individuals at Rank-1 to evaluate the performance.

Open-Set: In case of open-set identification, some of the identities in the probe set may not be present in the gallery set. This allows to evaluate the recognition system to validate the presence or absence of an identity in the gallery. To validate the performance, from the test of 18 identities, we used all the images of odd numbered identities as probe images with no images in the gallery. The rest of the even numbered identities are partitioned in the same way as closed-set identification to create probe and gallery sets. We report Detection and Identification Rate (DIR) at 1% FAR to evaluate open-set performance.

Verification: We compute positive and negative scores for each sample in test set. The positive score is the maximum similarity score of the same class and negative scores are the maximum scores from each of the classes except the true class of the sample. In our case, where the test data has 18 identities, each sample is associated with a set of 18 scores, with one positive score from the same identity and 17 negative scores corresponding to remaining 17 identities. The verification accuracy is reported as mean and standard deviation at 1% False Acceptance Rates (FARs).

4.3 Network Details and Parameter Setting

We resize all the face images in macaque and chimpanzee dataset to 112×112. We add the following data augmentations: random horizontal flips and random rotations within $5°$ for both the datasets. We use the following base network architectures for PFID: ResNet-18 [10] and DenseNet-121 [11] and remove the first maxpool layer because of small image size. For CE setting, we fine-tuned the imagenet pre-trained networks with cross-entropy loss and a batch size of 16. For the PFID setting, for each image in a batch, a similar class image is sampled to make a batch size of 8 pairs (16 images in a batch). The dissimilar pairs are then exhaustively created from these pairs. We used SGD for optimization with an initial learning rate of 10^{-3} and weight decay of $5e-4$. We trained all the models for both datasets for 40 epochs with learning rate decay by 0.1 at 25th and 35th epoch. We observed better performance with batch size of 16 instead of 32 or higher especially in case of training with only cross-entropy loss. It is recommended to use a lower batch size given that the training data is less in both the datasets.

4.4   Results

We present the results corresponding to PFID and other state of the art approaches for face recognition.

Baseline Results. For the baseline results, we extracted the penultimate (FC) layer features from both ResNet-18 and DenseNet-121 models. For all the evaluation protocols, the features are $l2$-normalized and in addition for classification, they are used to train a SVM (Support Vector Machine) classifier by performing a grid-search over the regularization parameter. The results are given in the first 2 rows of the Tables 2 and 3. We directly used the features and did not perform PCA (Principal Component Analysis) to reduce the number of feature dimensions because it had no impact on the performance in each evaluation.

Comparison with State of the Art Approaches. We compare PFID with recent work PrimNet [7] that achieved state of the art performance on chimpanzee face dataset. While our approach outperforms PrimNet by a large margin, it is worth noting that our results are reported on non-aligned face images, that makes PFID better suited for the application of crowdsourced population monitoring by eliminating the need for manual annotations of fiducial landmarks. Since ResNet-18 and DenseNet-121 are pretrained on imagenet data, we additionally fined-tuned ArcFace [8] and SphereFace [12] models that are pre-trained on human face images, specifically on CASIA [26] dataset. We use ResNet-50 as the backbone for ArcFace and 20-layer network for SphereFace, and use the parameters given in the respective papers. We observed best performance with batch size 32 in all the three methods. We used a learning rate of 0.1, 0.01 and 0.001 for PrimNet (trained from scratch), SphereFace and ArcFace respectively and weight decay as $5e-4$. We trained all the models for 30 epochs to avoid over-fitting with learning rate decay by 0.1 at 15th and 25th epoch. The results are reported in Tables 2 and 3 for both the datasets. The results highlight that the imagenet pre-trained models generalize well in our case where the training data is not huge. Further, it should be noted that the results reported for the three models ArcFace, SphereFace and PrimNet are also reported without face alignment as oppose to the results reported in the respective papers. While we report results with non-aligned face images, we would also like to point out that the performance dropped in all the approaches with aligned face images in case of chimpanzee dataset owing to loss of features in aligned faces.

Table 2. Evaluation of Chimpanzee dataset for classification, closed-set, open-set and verification setting. Baseline results are reported by taking the penultimate layer features of the network and training a SVM for classification. For all the remaining settings the features are directly used for the evaluation protocol.

Method	Classification Rank-1	Closed-set Rank-1	Open-set Rank-1	Verification 1% FAR
Baseline (ResNet-18 FC + SVM)	55.38 ± 1.18	70.51 ± 2.98	12.80 ± 5.73	37.10 ± 4.63
Baseline (DenseNet-121 FC + SVM)	61.78 ± 1.4	75.34 ± 3.98	30.51 ± 6.61	54.80 ± 3.65
ArcFace (ResNet-50)	85.47 ± 0.86	78.47 ± 5.81	41.24 ± 7.82	63.91 ± 5.37
SphereFace-20	78.38 ± 1.23	72.72 ± 3.44	35.49 ± 8.34	57.74 ± 6.38
PrimNet	70.86 ± 1.19	72.22 ± 5.33	37.27 ± 5.48	62.83 ± 5.98
CE (ResNet-18)	85.29 ± 1.43	86.44 ± 5.42	48.62 ± 9.05	75.19 ± 8.16
CE (DenseNet-121)	86.74 ± 0.74	87.01± 5.39	53.60 ± 13.04	76.86 ± 9.55
PFID (ResNet-18)	88.98 ± 0.26	88.26 ± 5.01	59.36 ± 9.12	80.06 ± 6.62
PFID (DenseNet-121)	**90.78 ± 0.53**	**91.87 ± 2.92**	**66.24 ± 8.08**	**83.23 ± 6.07**

PFID Results. To show the efficiency of our approach, we fine-tuned ResNet-18 and DenseNet-121 models with standard cross entropy (CE) loss and report in the Tables 3 and 2 for macaque and chimpanzee datasets respectively and compared it with the PFID loss. We observe an increase in performance for the four evaluation protocols with PFID loss as opposed to traditional cross entropy fine-tuned network. Imposing a KL-divergence loss has improved the discriminativeness of features by skewing the probability distributions of similar and dissimilar pairs. For chimpanzee dataset an improvement of **4.04%, 4.86%, 12.64%** and **6.97 %** is achieved in case of classification, closed-set, open-set and

Table 3. Evaluation of Rhesus Macaque dataset for classification, closed-set, open-set and verification setting. Baseline results are reported by taking the penultimate layer features of the network and training a SVM for classification. For all the remaining settings the features are directly used for the evaluation protocol.

Method	Classification Rank-1	Closed-set Rank-1	Open-set Rank-1	Verification 1% FAR
Baseline (ResNet-18 FC + SVM)	85.28 ± 0.25	88.29 ± 2.95	50.09 ± 7.35	66.98 ± 9.21
Baseline (DenseNet-121 FC + SVM)	88.3 ± 0.57	89.24 ± 3.63	53.93 ± 10.27	71.34 ± 8.88
ArcFace (ResNet-50)	98.23 ± 0.47	93.98 ± 2.99	67.07 ± 13.91	95.16 ± 1.56
SphereFace-20	97.61 ± 0.74	93.41 ± 2.19	95.62 ± 12.21	93.18 ± 1.95
PrimNet	97.11 ± 0.65	90.94 ± 2.54	65.98 ± 15.23	92.14 ± 2.82
CE (ResNet-18)	97.91 ± 0.58	95.94 ± 2.94	79.69 ± 8.12	96.35 ± 2.06
CE (DenseNet-121)	97.99 ± 0.69	96.24 ± 0.85	71.36 ± 10.05	96.01 ± 3.01
PFID (ResNet-18)	98.71 ± 0.41	96.18 ± 1.58	83.02 ± 7.36	97.71 ± 0.91
PFID (DenseNet-121)	**98.91 ± 0.40**	**97.36 ± 1.73**	**84.00 ± 7.43**	**98.24 ± 0.94**

verification respectively using DenseNet-121. The corresponding CMC (Cumulative Matching Characteristic) and TAR (True Acceptance Rate) vs FAR plots for the datasets are shown in Fig. 4.

Feature Learning and Generalization. To further show the effectiveness of PFID loss function and robustness of features, we perform cross dataset experiments in Table 5. We used model trained on chimpanzee dataset and extracted features on macaque dataset to evaluate the performance for closed-set, open-set and verification task and vice versa. We compared the quality of the features learned with PFID with the features learned with cross entropy based fine-tuning. We also show the generalizability between two chimpanzee datasets captured in different environments i.e. CZoo and CTai. The results clearly highlight the advantage of PFID over cross entropy loss for across data generalization. Additionally, to highlight the discriminativeness and clusterability of the class specific features, we cluster the feature representations of unseen (identities) test data using K-means clustering algorithm. We report the clustering performance in Table 4 and compare with the standard cross entropy loss.

Comparison with Siamese Network Based Features. One might draw similarity of our approach with the popular siamese networks [20] that are trained on similar and dissimilar pairs to result in a similarity score at the output. We

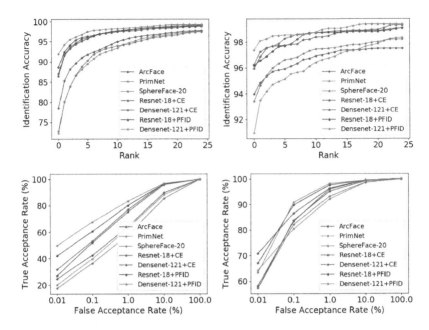

Fig. 4. CMC (Top) and TAR vs FAR (Bottom) plots for (Left) C-Zoo+CTai and (Right) Rhesus Macaques dataset.

Table 4. Comparison of K-means clustering performance on the learned representations with DenseNet-121. The results highlight that the PFID learns more clusterable space.

Model	Macaque	Chimpanzee
	NMI	NMI
CE	0.868 ± 0.008	0.686 ± 0.084
PFID	0.897 ± 0.030	0.715 ± 0.089

Table 5. Evaluation of learned model across datasets. Left of the arrow indicates the dataset on which the model was trained on, and right of the arrow indicates the evaluation dataset. All the results are reported for DenseNet-121 network.

	Macq. → Chimp.		Chimp. → Macq.		CZoo → CTai		CTai → CZoo	
	CE	PFID	CE	PFID	CE	PFID	CE	PFID
Closed Set	54.58	**63.48**	83.02	**88.38**	59.92	**70.35**	87.54	**91.96**
Open Set	13.56	**34.29**	32.04	**43.00**	17.21	**27.21**	43.25	**64.75**
Verification	43.02	**63.77**	67.51	**75.37**	48.68	**60.57**	66.71	**82.22**

train ResNet-18 on chimpanzee data in siamese setting with pairwise hinge-loss on features to show that the learned features in the classification setting are not discriminative as compared to our PFID. While training in siamese setting, we also observe that the network overfits on the training data and performs poorly on unseen classes. The results for different evaluation protocols are: Classification (83.97 ± 1.42), Closed-set (75.45 ± 5.51), Verification (57.28 ± 7.37) and Open-set (22.22 ± 8.07).

Identification on Detected Face Images. The above results evaluated the performance of PFID on cropped face images *i.e.* the true bounding box of the test samples. As the captured images with handheld devices like cameras would also have background, we evaluate the performance of PFID on the detected faces on test samples. Since, we had 1191 full images for the Macaque dataset, the detector is trained and tested with a split of 80/20. We fine-tune state-of-the-art Faster-RCNN [18] detector for detecting macaque faces and achieve highly accurate face detection performance. The identification results on the cropped faces obtained from the detector is shown in Table 6. For identification evaluation, we have 10 identities and 227 images for both closed-set and verification, whereas for open-set we extend the probe set by adding 8 identities and 1100 samples which are not part of the dataset.

4.5   Integration with Crowd Sourcing App

We have developed a simple app to work as a front-end for PFID, which permits a user to upload geo-tagged images of individuals and troops as well as report a conflict incident. Augmented with the PFID based back-end service, this app could help maintain an updated database of reported conflicts, along with a primate database indexed by individuals, troop and last-sighted locations, which can be used with techniques like Capture-Recapture to estimate population densities.

Table 6. Evaluation of detected macaque faces for closed set, open set and verification setting.

Method	Closed-set Rank-1	Open-set Rank-1	Verification 1% FAR
CE (ResNet-18)	95.00	70.78	89.22
PFID (ResNet-18)	97.20	78.80	91.11
CE (DenseNet-121)	95.30	80.67	91.56
PFID (DenseNet-121)	**97.80**	**89.67**	**95.11**

5   Conclusion

In this work, we discussed the problem of unique identification of non-human primates using face images captured in the wild. From existing literature, we found that population monitoring is an important step in the management strategies and largely rely only on field-based efforts. In this work, we identified this challenge and proposed an alternate solution that can simultaneously improve monitoring of commensal primates as well as actively involve the affected human community without any serious cost implications. We developed a novel face identification approach that is capable of learning pose invariant features, thus allowing to generalize well across poses without the requirement of a face alignment step. Additionally, the proposed approach leverages the pairwise constraints to capture underlying data semantics enabling it to perform effectively for unseen classes. With the effectiveness of our approach in different identification tasks on real world data, we foresee that the PFID system could become a part of widely used wildlife management tools like SMART[1].

Acknowledgement. This work is supported by Microsoft AI for Earth Grant 2017-18 and Infosys Center for AI at IIIT Delhi, India.

References

1. Anand, S., Radhakrishna, S.: Investigating trends in human-wildlife conflict: is conflict escalation real or imagined? J. Asia Pac. Biodivers. **10**(2), 154–161 (2017)
2. Anderson, C.J., Johnson, S.A., Hostetler, M.E., Summers, M.G.: History and status of introduced rhesus macaques (macaca mulatta) in silver springs state park, Florida (2016). http://edis.ifas.ufl.edu/uw412
3. Brahma, P.P., Wu, D., She, Y.: Why deep learning works: a manifold disentanglement perspective. IEEE Trans. Neural Netw. Learn. Syst. **27**, 1997–2008 (2016)
4. Brust, C.A., et al.: Towards automated visual monitoring of individual gorillas in the wild. In: CVPR, pp. 2820–2830 (2017)
5. Cabral, S.J., Prasad, T., Deeyagoda, T.P., Weerakkody, S.N., Nadarajah, A., Rudran, R.: Investigating Sri Lanka's human-monkey conflict and developing a strategy to mitigate the problem. J. Threatened Taxa **10**(3), 11391–11398 (2018)
6. Crouse, D., et al.: LemurFaceID: a face recognition system to facilitate individual identification of lemurs. BMC Zool. **2**(1), 2 (2017)
7. Deb, D., et al.: Face recognition: primates in the wild. arXiv preprint arXiv:1804.08790 (2018)
8. Deng, J., Guo, J., Xue, N., Zafeiriou, S.: ArcFace: additive angular margin loss for deep face recognition. arXiv preprint arXiv:1801.07698 (2018)
9. Freytag, A., Rodner, E., Simon, M., Loos, A., Kühl, H.S., Denzler, J.: Chimpanzee faces in the wild: log-Euclidean CNNs for predicting identities and attributes of primates. In: Rosenhahn, B., Andres, B. (eds.) GCPR 2016. LNCS, vol. 9796, pp. 51–63. Springer, Cham (2016). https://doi.org/10.1007/978-3-319-45886-1_5
10. He, K., Zhang, X., Ren, S., Sun, J.: Deep residual learning for image recognition. In: Proceedings of the IEEE Conference on Computer Vision and Pattern Recognition, pp. 770–778 (2016)

---

[1] http://smartconservationtools.org/.

11. Iandola, F., Moskewicz, M., Karayev, S., Girshick, R., Darrell, T., Keutzer, K.: DenseNet: implementing efficient convNet descriptor pyramids. arXiv preprint arXiv:1404.1869 (2014)
12. Liu, W., Wen, Y., Yu, Z., Li, M., Raj, B., Song, L.: SphereFace: deep hypersphere embedding for face recognition. In: Proceedings of the IEEE Conference on Computer Vision and Pattern Recognition, pp. 212–220 (2017)
13. Loos, A., Ernst, A.: Detection and identification of chimpanzee faces in the wild. In: 2012 IEEE International Symposium on Multimedia (ISM), pp. 116–119. IEEE (2012)
14. Lu, H.M., Fainman, Y., Hecht-Nielsen, R.: Image manifolds. In: Applications of Artificial Neural Networks in Image Processing III, vol. 3307, pp. 52–64. International Society for Optics and Photonics (1998)
15. Murphy-Chutorian, E., Trivedi, M.M.: Head pose estimation in computer vision: a survey. IEEE Trans. Pattern Anal. Mach. Intell. **31**(4), 607–626 (2008)
16. Nyhus, P.J.: Human-wildlife conflict and coexistence. Annu. Rev. Environ. Resour. **41**(1), 143–171 (2016)
17. Redmon, J., Divvala, S., Girshick, R., Farhadi, A.: You only look once: unified, real-time object detection. In: CVPR, pp. 779–788 (2016)
18. Ren, S., He, K., Girshick, R., Sun, J.: Faster R-CNN: towards real-time object detection with region proposal networks. In: NIPS, pp. 91–99 (2015)
19. Saraswat, R., Sinha, A., Radhakrishna, S.: A god becomes a pest? Human-rhesus macaque interactions in Himachal Pradesh, Northern India. Eur. J. Wildl. Res. **61**(3), 435–443 (2015)
20. Schroff, F., Kalenichenko, D., Philbin, J.: FaceNet: a unified embedding for face recognition and clustering. In: The IEEE Conference on Computer Vision and Pattern Recognition (CVPR), June 2015
21. Sun, Y., Chen, Y., Wang, X., Tang, X.: Deep learning face representation by joint identification-verification. In: Advances in Neural Information Processing Systems, pp. 1988–1996 (2014)
22. Wang, F., Cheng, J., Liu, W., Liu, H.: Additive margin softmax for face verification. IEEE Signal Process. Lett. **25**(7), 926–930 (2018)
23. Wen, Y., Zhang, K., Li, Z., Qiao, Y.: A discriminative feature learning approach for deep face recognition. In: Leibe, B., Matas, J., Sebe, N., Welling, M. (eds.) ECCV 2016. LNCS, vol. 9911, pp. 499–515. Springer, Cham (2016). https://doi.org/10.1007/978-3-319-46478-7_31
24. Witham, C.L.: Automated face recognition of rhesus macaques. J. Neurosci. Methods **300**, 157 (2017)
25. Wright, J., Yang, A.Y., Ganesh, A., Sastry, S.S., Ma, Y.: Robust face recognition via sparse representation. IEEE Trans. Pattern Anal. Mach. Intell. **31**(2), 210–227 (2009)
26. Yi, D., Lei, Z., Liao, S., Li, S.Z.: Learning face representation from scratch. arXiv preprint arXiv:1411.7923 (2014)

Evaluation of Human Body Detection Using Deep Neural Networks with Highly Compressed Videos for UAV Search and Rescue Missions

Piotr Rudol[1]([✉])(iD) and Patrick Doherty[1,2](iD)

[1] Department of Computer and Information Science, Linköping University,
58183 Linköping, Sweden
{piotr.rudol,patrick.doherty}@liu.se
[2] School of Intelligent Systems and Engineering, Jinan University (Zhuhai Campus),
Zhuhai, China
https://www.ida.liu.se/divisions/aiics/

Abstract. Dealing with compressed video streams in mobile robotics is an unavoidable fact of life. Transferring images between mobile robots or to the Cloud using wireless links can practically only be achieved using lossy video compression. This introduces artifacts that often make image processing challenging. Recent algorithms based on deep neural networks, as advanced as they are, are commonly trained and evaluated on datasets of high-fidelity images which are typically not captured from aerial views. In this work we evaluate a number of deep neural network based object detection algorithms in the context of aerial search and rescue scenarios where real-time and robust detection of human bodies is a priority. We provide an evaluation using a number of video sequences collected in-flight using Unmanned Aerial Vehicle (UAV) platforms in different environmental conditions. We also describe the detection performance degradation under limited bitrate compression using H.264, H.265 and VP9 video codecs, in addition to analyzing the timing effects of moving image processing tasks to off-board entities.

Keywords: CNN · Compression · UAV · Search & rescue · Cloud robotics

1 Introduction and Motivation

Industrial scale data and computing power used by companies such as Google or Facebook is revolutionizing applications of image processing and speech recognition in all walks of life. The basic driving force behind these advances is the use

Supported by the ELLIIT network organization for Information and Communication Technology, the Swedish Foundation for Strategic Research (SymbiKBot Project), and the Wallenberg AI, Autonomous Systems and Software Program (WASP) - Research Arena Public Safety (WARA-PS).

© Springer Nature Switzerland AG 2019
A. C. Nayak and A. Sharma (Eds.): PRICAI 2019, LNAI 11672, pp. 402–417, 2019.
https://doi.org/10.1007/978-3-030-29894-4_33

of deep learning which is based on many-layered neural networks. Embedding deep-learning based image processing functionality in autonomous systems such as Unmanned Aircraft Systems (UAS's) with the intent of operating in-the-field and in near real-time, introduces a number of additional issues that require much deeper analysis in terms of execution speed, memory requirements and accuracy tradeoffs.

For example, in the case of object detection for static stand alone systems, what meta-architectures for convolutional neural networks are most adequate for a particular application in terms of speed/memory/accuracy tradeoffs? What does the analysis show and how can such results be used in choosing the most efficient meta-architecture for a particular application? Several of these issues have been considered in Huang et al. [6] which presents results of an extensive study and serves as a good starting point for this kind of research. Although related, the main emphasis in this paper is to determine how such an analysis carries over to the use of autonomous or other systems in-the-field and what additional parameters and constraints specific to autonomous systems need to be studied in order to understand the tradeoffs in this context while taking full advantage of the new algorithms.

In this paper, the target application context is outdoor emergency search and rescue operations using collaborating teams of heterogenous systems that include smaller quadrotor helicopter platforms operating together with human rescue responders and other resources. Such teams collaborate to achieve complex goals such as aerial-based human body detection and delivery of medical and food supplies to the injured in a timely manner. In this application, it is assumed that each quadrotor system has embedded image processing capabilities or access to such external capabilities. Figure 1 (right) depicts three of several quadrotor platforms used in our experimentation.

The operational environments in which these combined human and aerial robotic teams operate are supported by a larger distributed system consisting of Ground Operation (GOP) centers, information sources for the querying and storage of mission data, maps, images and video streams. Cloud technology is also used for additional data storage and access to additional computational processing capabilities that can be leveraged during missions. Cloud Robotics is the terminology used for integrating Cloud technologies with robotic systems, where robotic sensing, computation and storage can be shared between the robotic system and the Cloud infrastructure. A comprehensive survey of research within the field of Cloud Robotics can be found in [13].

For a particular quadrotor platform, there are options for executing computationally intensive image processing algorithms on-board the system itself; leveraging resources in another UAV; outsourcing some or all of the computation to workstations in ground operation centers; using Cloud resources for computation, or using different combinations of the above.

Figure 1 depicts the basic experimental setup for this paper and also that used in actual in-the-field emergency rescue experimentation. The top-left part of the figure depicts several different computational sources for a specific UAV to

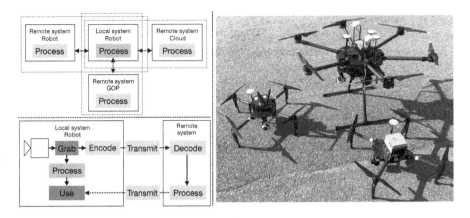

Fig. 1. Overview of the system components in focus in this work. Top-left: computational resources available to a UAS. Bottom-left: detailed view of the most relevant system components. Right: three quadrotor platforms used for experimentation. (Color figure online)

leverage. The bottom-left part of the figure provides the configuration that will be studied in this paper, where we assume one local robotic system interfacing with a remote system with computational resources that in our context could be the Cloud, another UAV, or a ground operation center.

The combination of autonomous UAVs, embedded computer vision algorithms, Cloud Robotics, and a highly distributed collaborative system of teams introduces additional complexities besides speed/memory/accuracy tradeoffs for deep-learning based image processing. In particular, the encoding, transmission and decoding phases in an image processing pipeline that may be distributed must be taken into account as is clearly visible in Fig. 1.

For many computer vision algorithms it is assumed that the input images are of high fidelity. However, this is not the case in application areas such as surveillance or robotics in general, due to the way acquisition, transmission and even storage of video signals is performed. This situation is further degraded in the case of aerial robots since generally the carrying capacity does not permit the use of high fidelity cameras and sufficient on-board computational power. Moreover, for very small size UAVs (e.g. below 1.0 kg), on-board image processing is severely limited as the latest developments and state-of-the-art algorithms using deep neural networks require computational power offered mainly by Graphics Processing Units (GPU) in order to deliver timely results.

Even though there exist mobile processing solutions that can achieve acceptable levels of performance, complementing the on-board computations with off-board processing can be very beneficial. In such cases, wireless transmission of video signals is inevitable in order to transport data to remote processing units. However, this comes at the price of increased delays as well as introducing compression artifacts, especially if the available bandwidth is limited as shown in Fig. 2.

Fig. 2. Example frames from the evaluation sequence showing degradation of image quality when using different video encoding techniques with the same bitrate of 50 kbps. From the right: H.265, VP9, H.264.

An example of taking advantage of off-board and in-the-cloud computation for image processing and UAVs is presented in [7]. The authors describe a system that first performs a local check of *objectness* to find potentials for detecting objects that is executed on a remote computer in the Cloud. Substantial speedup of computation is reported due to the use of powerful hardware. However, the authors do not investigate issues related to image compression and transmission.

The results presented in [3] show the influence of the blur, noise, contrast, JPEG and JPEG2000 compression on a number of deep neural networks in the classification task. The authors investigate how these quality distortions influence the performance in a per-frame setting. In this work we investigate the degradation of performance under limited bitrate video compression.

1.1 Contributions

In this paper, we investigate the use of deep neural networks for human body object detection in the context of emergency rescue using aerial robots. In particular, we evaluate the performance of a number of existing neural networks under various video compression techniques when the available video transmission bandwidth is limited. We quantify the degradation of object detection performance when dealing with video compression as well as investigate the timing properties of the components involved in leveraging remote processing such as computation in the Cloud.

The remainder of this paper is structured as follows. In Sect. 2, we review a number of deep network structures and provide basic information about three families of networks as well as specific information about the networks used in this work. Section 3 includes a description of the dataset used for the evaluation. Section 4 describes the video compression techniques investigated. Evaluation results are then presented in Sect. 5. Final remarks and conclusions are provided in Sect. 6.

2 Network Architectures and Configurations

There exists a plethora of techniques based on deep neural networks developed in recent years for dealing with the issue of object detection. Some of them are general [11], some are designed for a specific application, and some are adapted to specific circumstances through transfer learning. The objective of the evaluation performed in this research is to test the applicability of existing successful families of neural networks used in the task of object detection under limited bandwidth video compression. We believe that this approach offers more insight and can provide guidelines for choosing an appropriate class of methods given specific practical limitations when operating in-the-field (e.g. computational resources or communication links). An alternative approach would be to fine-tune a number of methods to the task at hand. However, this would provide a different type of insight and it also runs the risk of overfitting the model to the datasets used. Both approaches have their merits and the latter will be pursued in future research.

The aim of detecting objects in images (using deep neural networks or otherwise) is to find bounding boxes of objects belonging to specific classes including detection confidence measures for each box. Similarly to [6], we focus on three families of detection networks which encompass a number of specialized variations: Single Shot MultiBox Detectors (SSD) [9], Faster Region-based Convolutional Network (R-CNN) [12], and Region-based Fully Convolutional Network (R-FCN) [2]. For different network meta-architectures one of the following feature extractors were used: ResNet [5], Inception v2 [15], and Inception ResNet v2 [14]. In-depth description of the network architectures as well as feature extractors can be found in [6] and in the respective publications. A short description of these methods is given below.

2.1 Networks

The following neural network architectures will be considered in the evaluation:

- *SSD*: The Single Shot MultiBox Detector architecture uses a single feedforward convolutional network to directly predict classes and bounding boxes. By using a single stage, the need for a second stage where a number of proposals are classified is omitted. This is in contrast to networks which operate in two stages as described below. The approach discretizes the output space into a set of default boxes with different aspect ratios and scales per feature map location. Moreover, predictions from multiple feature maps with different resolutions are combined to account for different sizes of objects. During inference, the network computes scores for objects detected in each default box and adjusts its shape to better fit the object [9].
- *Faster R-CNN*: Region-based Convolutional Networks (R-CNN) operate in two stages. First, a Region Proposal Network (RPN) is used to generate detection region proposals. In the second stage, the generated proposals are evaluated using a classifier and the class-specific box is refined for each proposal as well [12]. Faster R-CNN uses a network architecture which overcomes shortcomings of its previous versions: R-CNN and Fast R-CNN. Due to the speed improvements, Faster R-CNN is suitable for real-time operation.

– *R-FCN*: The Region-based Fully Convolutional Network structure is similar to Faster R-CNN but the cropping of features happens in the last layer before the object class prediction takes place. This is unlike Faster R-CNN where the cropping is done from the same layer where region proposals are predicted. This allows for significant gain in speed as the amount of per-region computations is minimized [2].

2.2 Feature Extractors

In all network families mentioned above first a convolutional feature extractor transforms an input image to a set of high level features. We chose the following feature extractors in our evaluation:

– *ResNet* (50 and 101): The training of very deep networks becomes difficult and the vanishing gradient problem is one of the reasons that accuracy starts to saturate and can even degrade. To overcome this issue the authors [5] reformulated the layers as learning residual functions with reference to the inputs. Here, the residual can be understood as a subtraction of a feature learned from the input of the layer. The ResNet structure also uses shortcut connections between layers. Due to these changes, the learning of networks of this form is easier to do than with simple deep networks. The issue with degrading accuracy is also resolved. The introduction of Residual Networks is considered as one of the bigger breakthroughs in the area. The designation of 50 and 101 (also 152) refers to the number of layers in the network [5].
– *Inception v2*: The choice of kernel size depends on the locality of the salient information (object of a class) in an image. For local information, a small kernel is better, and for global information, a larger one is more suitable. Very deep networks are prone to overfitting. To solve this issue, the authors [15] decided to go *wider* instead of *deeper*. Filters with multiple sizes are placed on the same level (1×1, 3×3, 5×5 convolutions) creating an inception module. This basic idea with a few additional aspects omitted here is known as GoogLeNet (Inception v1). Inception v2 increased the speed and accuracy by factorizing 5×5 into two 3×3 convolutions and $n \times n$ to a combination of $1 \times n$ and $n \times 1$ to improve the speed [15].
– *Inception ResNet v2*: This is a hybrid of ResNet and Inception networks which introduces residual connections that add the output of the convolution operation of the inception module to the input [14].

2.3 Configurations

The table in Fig. 3 presents the network configurations evaluated in this paper. In addition to the network family, the type of feature extractor is also specified. For all networks the input image is first resized in one of two ways. Either it is scaled to a fixed size (300×300, or 600×600 pixels) or it is resized such that the shorter edge is 600 pixels and the longer is scaled to be no longer than

Network		Feature extractor	Input Resizer	Region Proposals
Faster R-CNN	-	Resnet-50	Keep aspect: 600, 1024	300
	LP	Resnet-50		20
	-	Resnet-101		100
	LP	Resnet-101		20
	-	Inception Resnet (v2)		300
	LP	Inception Resnet (v2)		20
	R-FCN	Resnet-101		100

Network	Feature extractor	Input Resizer
SSD	Inception (v2)	Fixed: 300, 300
SSD	Resnet-50	Fixed: 640, 640
SSD	MobileNet (v2)	Fixed: 300, 300

Fig. 3. Network configurations used for evaluation. LP refers to low-proposal versions.

1024 pixels. In the latter case the scaling is done in a manner that preserves the aspect ratio.

Finally, the number of produced region proposals is specified where applicable. A typical number of proposals evaluated by Faster R-CNN and R-FCN is 300. In order to speedup the detection process the number of proposals can be reduced with a small penalty on the recall performance, as reported in [6]. Since our interest is in close to real-time performance, we also investigated the effect of using a lower number of proposals on our dataset. For the evaluation, we used already pre-trained networks available within the TensorFlow [1] models zoo[1]. The networks were trained on the COCO (Common Objects in Context) dataset [8] which contains over 90 object classes. However, we report results only for the *person* class due to the chosen application area.

3   Evaluation Dataset

In order to evaluate the degradation of performance of the detectors due to image compression, a number of aerial sequences were selected from videos collected during a two year period. The selection was made to assure variations in weather conditions, times of year, locations, detection subjects' poses and appearance (clothing), and backgrounds (grass, gravel, wood, asphalt, dirt road, water). Over 69 min of source video footage was used.

The table in Fig. 4 presents descriptions of the sequences collected at four locations abbreviated as T, M, V, and K. Figure 4 (right) shows a number of sample images from these locations. The distance of the camera and objects to be detected is characterized by the percentage of objects belonging to groups defined in the COCO evaluation protocol: small (area $< 32^2$ pixels), medium (32^2 pixels $<$ area $< 96^2$ pixels), and large (area $> 96^2$ pixels).

The original sequences were recorded using DJI Zenmuse Z3 cameras on DJI Matrice 100 and Matrice 600 Pro platforms (see Fig. 1). The videos were recorded on the cameras' internal SD Cards with 1920 × 1080 resolution and a 60 Hz framerate using an H.264 codec with a bitrate of 60 Mbps.

---

[1] TensorFlow detection model zoo: https://github.com/tensorflow/models/blob/master/research/object_detection/g3doc/detection_model_zoo.md (2019).

Name	Weather	Month	Class: person				Length m:s
			Small %	Med. %	Large %	Total	
T1	Overcast	April	12	78	10	618	5:25
T2	Sunny	May	12	87	1	628	5:22
T3	Sunny	May	4	82	14	744	6:23
T4	Overcast	May	12	84	4	2799	6:19
M1	Sunny	June	3	97	0	30	0:29
M2	Sunny	June	22	69	8	131	1:21
M3	Sunny	June	34	60	7	173	2:25
M4	Sunny	June	26	69	5	170	3:15
M5	Sunny	June	1	98	1	318	2:35
M6	Sunny	May	6	81	14	426	3:01
M7	Sunny	May	0	93	7	290	2:38
M8	Sunny	May	4	88	8	729	6:23
M9	Overcast	October	18	80	2	907	8:32
M10	Sunny	April	5	90	4	568	4:36
V1	Sunny	Sep.	5	95	0	64	2:59
V2	Sunny	Sep.	20	80	0	219	4:23
V3	Overcast	June	78	22	0	497	0:43
K1	Sunny	May	23	75	2	1352	2:17

Fig. 4. Summary of video sequences and example images used for evaluation: four locations (T, M, V, K), different weather conditions and times of year, percentage size composition (small, medium, and large) and total number of objects of class person.

In producing the evaluation sequences, the originals were transcoded using the codecs described in Sect. 4, to a resolution of 1024×576 and a 30 Hz framerate. This resolution and framerate were chosen as they are more common for cameras typically used on UAV platforms for on-board processing, as well as to fit to the inputs of the evaluated networks. A wide range of bitrates were tested, spanning from 20 Mbps, down to the extremely low 50 kbps.

For SSD networks which use fixed size input images with aspect ratio of 1:1, no additional pre-processing has been applied. It has the disadvantage that the input images are deformed when scaled from the original 16:9 aspect ratio. To remedy this, it is common to crop the images or add padding in order to preserve the aspect ratio. This however will be investigated in future work.

Finally, images at the rate of 2 Hz were extracted from the transcoded sequences to produce more than 8200 images per all codec and bitrate combinations. Because we are dealing with video sequences, unlike the case of typical image datasets, the consecutive images are similar. For this reason, images at a lower rate are still representative of the full sequences. Finally, the evaluation images were annotated with the *person* class and used as ground truth during evaluation. In the research presented here, we focus on human body detection due to the targeted application area of search and rescue. However, the results should be applicable to objects of other classes (in fact, the evaluated networks can detect over 90 object classes).

4   Video Compression

Three common video compression techniques were investigated in the experimentation: H.264, H.265, and VP9. The H.264 (MPEG-4 AVS) coding format is currently one of the most commonly used techniques for a multitude of applications. Compared to its predecessor (MPEG-2 Part 2), it offers bitrate savings of up to 50% with comparable quality. The H.265 (High Efficiency Video Coding - HEVC) is a successor to H.264 and is quickly gaining market share. Again, it offers up to 50% of the required bitrate reduction as compared to H.264. The third codec under evaluation is an open, royalty-free media file format called VP9. It offers bitrate savings of up to 20–50% when compared to H.264. More details about the coding techniques can be found in [10], or [4].

The encoding configurations for the application considered in this paper have been chosen to minimize the encoding time, i.e. to allow to transfer, decode and process the data with minimum delay. The evaluation and results characterize the degradation and performance of object detection, where minimal time increase is paramount. For applications where timely delivery of results is not a priority (e.g. off-line and/or batch processing), different encoding configurations can be more suitable. This would result in either better image quality at the same bitrate or decreased required bitrate for the same quality. The results presented below correspond to the *worst case* i.e. lowest quality settings with minimal delays.

Video sequences described in the previous section were encoded using the FFMpeg[2] multimedia framework. The most important parameters were chosen as follows: *1-pass* encoding with a target bitrate and *ultrafast* preset. The latter parameter allows for achieving a very fast encoding time, but the resulting compression level is not optimal.

5   Evaluation

The evaluation of the degradation of object detection performance under limited bitrate compression has been performed using two parameters: *precision* and *recall*. In machine learning, *precision* answers the question: what proportion of positive identifications was actually correct? In other words, a model that produces no false positives has a precision of 1. Similarly, *recall* answers the question: what proportion of actual positives was identified correctly? A model that produces no false negatives has a recall of 1. The two parameters together describe the behavior of an algorithm. In many applications there exists an inverse relationship between precision and recall, so that it is possible to increase one at the cost of the other.

From the perspective of the application investigated in this paper, the second parameter is more important as its high value means a low number of *false negatives*. In the context of detecting human bodies in search and rescue missions, it is more important not to miss a potential victim than it is to deal with a larger

---

[2] FFmpeg multimedia framework: https://www.ffmpeg.org.

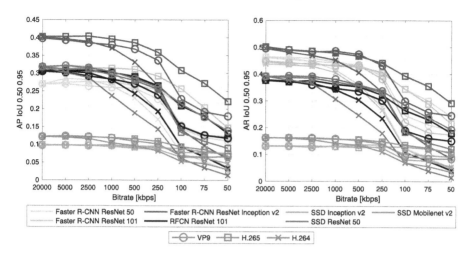

Fig. 5. Average Precision and Recall for different networks and bitrates.

number of false positives. But of course, a proper balance is also important to avoid accepting an overwhelming number of false positive detections.

The results presented below were obtained by performing evaluations using TensorFlow with COCO detection metrics. The parameter, Intersection over Union (IoU), measures how much overlap there is between areas of two regions. If the ground truth and prediction regions are identical, IoU is equal to 1. In other words IoU measures how good the prediction in the object detector is. For COCO, Average Precision is the average over multiple IoUs (e.g. a detection is considered positive if IoU > 0.5). The label, AP 0.50 0.95, in the vertical axis, corresponds to the Average AP for IoU from 0.5 to 0.95 with a step size of 0.05.

5.1   Accuracy

Figure 5 presents Average Precision and Average Recall values for different networks, codecs, and bitrates. In general, all networks show little degradation as the bitrate is reduced down to 2.5 Mbps. This applies for all encoding techniques. Below this value, the performance deteriorates rapidly for H.264 and more gracefully for VP9 and H.265, respectively. The relatively best performance is achieved using H.265 even when the bitrate is reduced to 500 kbps.

The performance of the SSD Inception v2 and Mobilenet v2 networks is consistently poor relative to other networks and stays constantly poor for almost all bitrates. If these networks are the only available option, there is no need to devote additional bitrate for video transmission. Additionally, these networks do not greatly benefit from using GPU computations instead of standard Central Processing Units (CPUs). This will be shown in the next subsection.

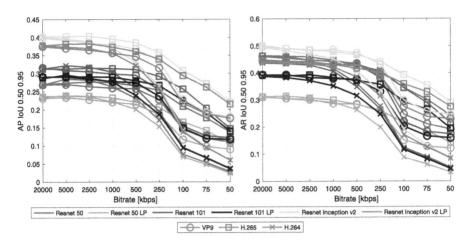

Fig. 6. The degradation of Average Precision and Recall of Faster R-CNN networks with lower number of proposals (LP).

Figure 6 presents the difference in Average Precision and Recall for Faster R-CNN networks depending on the number of proposals used. The configuration of networks is presented in Fig. 3. The decrease in number of proposals does not significantly lower the accuracy but gives big gains in computation times as described in Sect. 5.2. However, if the best object detection performance is required, a higher number of proposals is better. The general performance of codecs at specific bitrates follows the findings described above. Figure 7 presents the Precision and Recall for objects of different sizes as defined in the COCO evaluation protocol for different networks and bitrates.

The accuracy of the networks on large and medium size objects follows the above findings about codecs and bitrates. However, for small objects the overall performance is low and its degradation is very rapid for all codecs and bitrates. Therefore, if the application at hand requires detecting small objects, the highest available bitrate should be used. Alternatively, care should be taken to make sure the distance between an object and a camera is small. This can be achieved by performing search flights at a lower altitude.

5.2   Timing

When off-loading or complementing computationally intensive tasks such as object detection to a remote unit, introduction of delays is inevitable. Figure 1 (right) presents a schematic of steps involved in processing the image data locally (e.g. directly on a robotic system) as well as using a remote entity. Comparison between local processing (in green) with processing on a remote entity, a number of additional steps (in blue) introduce delays in the processing pipeline.

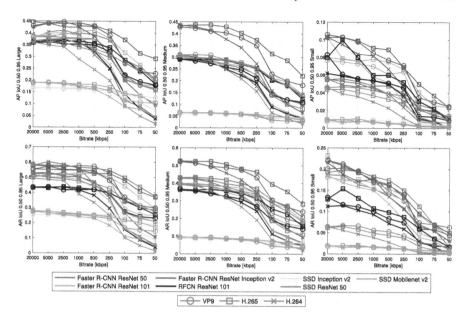

Fig. 7. Average Precision (top) and Recall (bottom) at IoU 0.5 0.95 for objects of different sizes: large (left), medium (middle), and small (right).

These delays are caused by encoding and decoding times as well as transmission to and from the remote unit. For off-board processing to make sense, one or both of the following has to be true: (a) the total time of remote processing has to be smaller than the total time of local processing (due to the availability of more powerful hardware) or (b) off-board processing has to provide a solution which is not achievable on the local system alone. In the evaluation, we omit the time taken to grab images, since it is the same for both cases.

It is important to note that both cases are hardware dependent and reproducibility of the results is not straight forward. The computation speed is highly dependent on the specific hardware configuration and even software versions used. Consequently, the results should be treated as indicators or relative measurements rather than absolute values. Furthermore, the inference setup can be tailored to specific hardware to achieve maximum performance. Here, we analyze the performance *as-is* without attempting to improve it through an optimized deployment. At this stage of investigation, we do not perform any comparative evaluation of specific technologies that can be used to transmit video data between systems. WiFi, 3G, 4G or even 5G have different properties and their use is dependent on availability. Instead, we provide the time gains of processing using different hardware components. Based on this data, an appropriate transmission technology can be chosen.

The table in Fig. 8, presents the hardware used for the timing evaluation of the models presented in previous sections. Four system configurations denoted as A, B, C and D were used, each with an increasing amount of discrete GPU

	A	B	C	D
CPU	Intel Core i7-7567U, 3.5GHz (max: 4.0GHz), 2+2 cores	Intel Core i7-6700T, 2.8GHz (max: 3.6GHz), 4+4 cores	Intel Xeon E5-1620 v4, 3.5GHz (max: 3.8GHz), 4+4 cores	Intel Core (Skylake) 3.2GHz, 4 cores
GPU	-	Nvidia GeForce GTX 1070, 8GB	Nvidia Titan Xp, 12GB	Nvidia Tesla V100-SXM2, 16GB
RAM	16GB	16GB	16GB	28GB
Location	Robot	Desktop	Desktop	Datacenter

Fig. 8. Hardware configurations of systems used for execution timing analysis.

power available. System A is a small form-factor computer from the Intel NUC family. Due to its size, it is suitable for usage on-board smaller UAV platforms (see Fig. 1 right), but it lacks a dedicated discrete GPU. System B is a typical desktop computer with a mid-range gaming class GPU and a corresponding CPU. System C has been configured for the purpose of machine learning. It is equipped with a GPU tailored for this purpose. System D is a machine in a datacenter. Its configuration is heavily tailored to machine learning tasks.

The table in Fig. 9 presents the average per-frame execution times of the networks listed when performing inference on the evaluation sequences described in Sect. 3. Additionally, time differences are listed to easily assess the performance gain in computations using different hardware components. The overall speedup of computations using GPUs compared to CPUs is also provided.

Figure 10 (left), compares the inference performance using GPUs. Average frame inference times as well as minimum and maximum values are provided (note the logarithmic time scale).

The gains in performance using the faster GPU systems were as follows. System C was on average 1.52 times faster than System B. System D was 1.72 and 1.09 times faster than Systems B and C, respectively. Unsurprisingly, the most

	Model / System	CPU [ms] A	B	C	D	GPU [ms] B	C	D	CPU-GPU time diff. [ms] B	C	D	CPU/GPU speedup B	C	D
Faster R-CNN	Inception Resnet v2	21030	15487	13299	12969	801	390	263	14686	12909	12706	19,3	34,1	49,3
	Inception Resnet v2 LP	8012	6412	5403	5270	395	207	149	6017	5196	5121	16,2	26,1	35,4
	Resnet 101	3493	2509	2130	2057	130	79	69	2379	2051	1988	19,3	27,0	29,8
	Resnet 101 LP	2259	1673	1418	1344	102	64	55	1571	1354	1289	16,4	22,2	24,4
	Resnet 50	2610	1860	1594	1567	104	66	61	1756	1528	1506	17,9	24,2	25,7
	Resnet 50 LP	1372	1025	882	860	64	51	48	961	831	812	16,0	17,3	17,9
RFCN Resnet 101		2956	2157	1813	1725	123	75	67	2034	1738	1658	17,5	24,2	25,7
SSD	Inception v2	118	88	81	86	27	29	34	61	52	52	3,3	2,8	2,5
	Mobilenet v2	68	61	53	65	25	26	35	36	27	30	2,4	2,0	1,9
	Resnet 50 v1	1990	1461	1192	1186	80	50	56	1381	1142	1130	18,3	23,8	21,2

Fig. 9. Execution times, gains of time and speedup of GPU over CPU processing.

computationally demanding (and most accurate) is the Faster R-CNN ResNet Inception v2. It executes 3.05 and 2.05 times faster using System D, as compared to systems B and C, respectively. In the case of the least computationally demanding models, SSD Inception v2 and SSD Mobilenet v2, a slight decrease in performance was observed using the more powerful GPU systems C and D. This can be explained by the fact that the more powerful GPUs are not required as these networks have very little demand and the potential gains disappear in the overhead before a GPU can actually process a frame. It is also important to note that these two network configurations scale input images to a lower resolution of 300 × 300 as specified in the table in Fig. 3.

The speedup of GPU frame inference due to using a lower number of proposals (as described in Sect. 2) is substantial. For the three variants of networks as ordered in Fig. 10 (left), the average speedup for the three GPUs was, 1.89, 1.25, and 1.40 times, respectively.

Figure 10 (right), presents the timing analysis results of performing inference using CPUs. The average, as well as minimum and maximum times are shown (note the logarithmic scale). The differences between performing inference using CPU computations using the four hardware configurations, is not as large as in the case of GPUs. This is expected, as performing inference using CPUs is known not to be optimal and the CPUs used are similar in computational power. SSD Inception v2 and SSD Mobilenet v2 models are the fastest to compute. These models are the most suitable for use when GPU power is not available, as is often the case with on-board computation on aerial vehicles.

However, as expected, the gain of using GPUs over CPUs is dramatic. For example, comparing the execution times for the most accurate network, the Faster R-CNN ResNet Inception v2, the gain of the slowest CPU execution (System A) versus the fastest GPU execution (System D) is 80 times (21030 ms vs 263 ms). This clearly demonstrates the gains of taking advantage of remote computational resources in the Cloud Robotics setting. The speedup gained

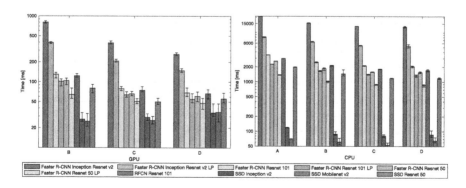

Fig. 10. Inference times (logarithmic scale) for a number of models using three GPU systems. Average, minimum and maximum times are shown.

makes up for any reasonable delays introduced by encoding and transmitting the data for off-board processing. The same applies to the other networks (excluding SSD Inception v2 and SSD Mobilenet v2) as the average speedup is 20 times.

The speedup of frame inference using CPUs is also substantial due to using a lower number of proposals (as described in Sect. 2). For the three variants of networks as ordered in Fig. 10, the average speedup for the four CPU systems was: 2.49, 1.52, and 1.84 times, respectively.

The time gains for using GPU over CPU processing (as shown in Fig. 9) allow us to assess if processing on a remote unit makes sense. For most networks, the time difference is larger than 1 s which should compensate for the time of encoding, transmitting, and decoding of the video stream. As mentioned earlier, for the most extreme case, the gain in processing time is larger than 20 seconds per frame.

6   Conclusion

We have evaluated a number of deep neural network-based object detection algorithms from the perspective of in-the-field usage where video transmission bandwidth is limited. We showed how the detection performance of human bodies degrades under a decreasing bitrate using three common video compression algorithms. For the evaluation, we used a novel dataset of video sequences collected during real flights in various environmental conditions which are representative for a wide variety of search and rescue missions. We also presented the performance of the algorithms in terms of per-frame calculation times on four hardware systems with varying performance of CPU and GPU components. The results presented can provide criteria for choosing an appropriate object detection algorithm given the available computational and communication hardware, or for assessing the tradeoffs in performing image processing tasks on-board or off-board with UAV platforms.

References

1. Abadi, M., et al.: TensorFlow: large-scale machine learning on heterogeneous systems (2015). https://www.tensorflow.org/. software available from tensorflow.org, 2019
2. Dai, J., Li, Y., He, K., Sun, J.: R-FCN: object detection via region-based fully convolutional networks. In: Proceedings of the 30th International Conference on Neural Information Processing Systems, NIPS 2016, pp. 379–387. Curran Associates Inc., USA (2016). http://dl.acm.org/citation.cfm?id=3157096.3157139
3. Dodge, S., Karam, L.: Understanding how image quality affects deep neural networks. In: 2016 Eighth International Conference on Quality of Multimedia Experience (QoMEX), pp. 1–6, June 2016
4. Guo, L., Cock, J.D., Aaron, A.: Compression performance comparison of x264, x265, libvpx and aomenc for on-demand adaptive streaming applications. In: 2018 Picture Coding Symposium, PCS 2018, San Francisco, CA, USA, 24–27 June 2018, pp. 26–30 (2018). https://doi.org/10.1109/PCS.2018.8456302

5. He, K., Zhang, X., Ren, S., Sun, J.: Deep residual learning for image recognition. In: 2016 IEEE Conference on Computer Vision and Pattern Recognition (CVPR), pp. 770–778 (2016)

6. Huang, J., et al.: Speed/accuracy trade-offs for modern convolutional object detectors. CoRR abs/1611.10012 (2016). http://arxiv.org/abs/1611.10012

7. Lee, J., Wang, J., Crandall, D., Šabanović, S., Fox, G.: Real-time, cloud-based object detection for unmanned aerial vehicles. In: 2017 First IEEE International Conference on Robotic Computing (IRC), pp. 36–43, April 2017

8. Lin, T.-Y., et al.: Microsoft COCO: common objects in context. In: Fleet, D., Pajdla, T., Schiele, B., Tuytelaars, T. (eds.) ECCV 2014. LNCS, vol. 8693, pp. 740–755. Springer, Cham (2014). https://doi.org/10.1007/978-3-319-10602-1_48

9. Liu, W., et al.: SSD: single shot multibox detector. In: Leibe, B., Matas, J., Sebe, N., Welling, M. (eds.) ECCV 2016. LNCS, vol. 9905, pp. 21–37. Springer, Cham (2016). https://doi.org/10.1007/978-3-319-46448-0_2

10. Ohm, J.R., Sullivan, G., Schwarz, H., Tan, T., Wiegand, T.: Comparison of the coding efficiency of video coding standards including high efficiency video coding (HEVC). IEEE Trans. Circ. Syst. Video Technol. **22**, 1669–1684 (2012). https://doi.org/10.1109/TCSVT.2012.2221192

11. Redmon, J., Divvala, S.K., Girshick, R.B., Farhadi, A.: You only look once: unified, real-time object detection. CoRR abs/1506.02640 (2015). http://arxiv.org/abs/1506.02640

12. Ren, S., He, K., Girshick, R., Sun, J.: Faster R-CNN: towards real-time object detection with region proposal networks. IEEE Trans. Pattern Anal. Mach. Intell. **39**(6), 1137–1149 (2017)

13. Saha, O., Dasgupta, P.: A comprehensive survey of recent trends in cloud robotics architectures and applications. Robotics **7**(3) (2018). https://doi.org/10.3390/robotics7030047

14. Szegedy, C., Ioffe, S., Vanhoucke, V.: Inception-v4, inception-ResNet and the impact of residual connections on learning. CoRR abs/1602.07261 (2016)

15. Szegedy, C., Vanhoucke, V., Ioffe, S., Shlens, J., Wojna, Z.: Rethinking the inception architecture for computer vision. In: 2016 IEEE Conference on Computer Vision and Pattern Recognition (CVPR), pp. 2818–2826 (2016)

A Deep Learning Approach for Dog Face Verification and Recognition

Guillaume Mougeot[(✉)], Dewei Li, and Shuai Jia

Department of Control Science and Engineering,
Shanghai Jiao Tong University, 800 Dongchuan Road, Shanghai, China
{gmougeot,dwli,liu2596615}@sjtu.edu.cn

Abstract. Recently, deep learning methods for biometrics identification have mainly focused on human face identification and have proven their efficiency. However, little research have been performed on animal biometrics identification. In this paper, a deep learning approach for dog face verification and recognition is proposed and evaluated. Due to the lack of available datasets and the complexity of dog face shapes this problem is harder than human identification. The first publicly available dataset is thus composed, and a deep convolutional neural network coupled with the triplet loss is trained on this dataset. The model is then evaluated on a verification problem, on a recognition problem and on clustering dog faces. For an open-set of 48 different dogs, it reaches an accuracy of 92% on a verification task and a rank-5 accuracy of 88% on a one-shot recognition task. The model can additionally cluster pictures of these unknown dogs. This work could push zoologists to further investigate these new kinds of techniques for animal identification or could help pet owners to find their lost animal. The code and the dataset of this project are publicly available (https://github.com/GuillaumeMougeot/DogFaceNet).

Keywords: Dog face recognition · Dog face identification · Pet animal identification

1 Introduction

Nowadays, the main techniques for dog identification are collars, tattoos and microchip implants [12]. As these methods can be unreliable or harmful for the animals, zoologists and computer scientists have started exploring new strategies through the use of machine learning. Machine learning techniques have now become reliable enough for human face identification [27]. They can thus potentially be used on the more complex problem of dog face identification.

This project is mainly inspired by the recent development of deep learning in face verification: does these two pictures represent the same individual?, in face recognition: who is this individual? and in face clustering: group these pictures by individuals [22, 26].

A. C. Nayak and A. Sharma (Eds.): PRICAI 2019, LNAI 11672, pp. 418–430, 2019.
https://doi.org/10.1007/978-3-030-29894-4_34

However, animal face identification needs improvement. There is no publicly available dataset and little development in used techniques. This work aims thus at developing the existing methods by using recent deep learning research in face verification and recognition on a novel dataset of dog faces.

A brief review of the last development in human and animal identification is presented in Sect. 2. In Sect. 3, we first build a dataset using pictures we took and images retrieved from the Internet. The face pictures are then aligned and grouped into triplets. In Sect. 4, a ResNet-like model [9] coupled with the triplet loss [22] is designed to be trained on this dataset. In Sect. 5, the trained model is evaluated on a verification, a recognition and a clustering task. The main applications of this work could be to find stray animals or track free-ranging animals in smart cities.

2   Related Work

So far, research on animal biometrics recognition has mainly focused on cattle identification [2,8,13,15,17,18] or endangered species identification [5,6]. Kumar et al. [19] present a complete review on the latest development in this field. Dog faces are mainly subject to studies in landmark detection [29] and breed classification [20,29]. A method for dog face identification was recently proposed in [16]. In this paper they classify the most recent development in animal biometrics identification into four categories: muzzle points, iris pattern, retina vascular and face images. As human fingerprints identification, muzzle points identification is a reliable way to identify individual animals but in order to extract features, pictures have to be in a high resolution and well exposed or muzzles prints should be retrieved using an appropriate scanner. In both cases, data collection on animals is difficult and time consuming. Iris pattern and retina vascular identification suffer from the same problems. On the other hand, a lot of high resolution dog faces can now be found on the Internet. The work of Kumar et al. [16] on dog faces is inspired by classical machine learning methods for face recognition like Fisherfaces. Their image dataset is composed of one face per individual animal and data augmentation is then used to create new representations of these individual animals. Their model reached a top-1 accuracy of 82% on a *closed-set* of test data.

A more realistic goal would be to consider several actual pictures per individual animal taken in the wild. A trained model could then to be tested on an *open-set* of test data. These changes increase the difficulty of the problem significantly. The same difficulty arises for human face identification. To deal with it, researchers have created deep learning methods. As human face recognition represents a key domain in computer vision, many related research results can be found [1,3,4,26,27]. The work of Schroff et al. in [22] illustrates the importance of this new types of methods: the previously published error rate on the Labeled Faces in the Wild (LFW) dataset [11] has been reduced by 30%.

The determinant part in face identification method based on deep learning is the loss definition for which a lot of important improvements have been developed during the past few years [7,21,22,28,30]. Among these different losses, the triplet loss generates better results on a small *open-set* of data. Even though CosFace [28] or ArcFace [7] should normally work better regarding their accuracy on standard human face datasets as LFW, they rapidly overfit when trained on small datasets with a low level of regularity such as dog faces.

In order to train a network with the triplet loss, triplets of pictures have to be defined. A triplet is composed of an anchor picture x_a, a positive picture x_p and a negative picture x_n. The anchor picture is a picture of a randomly chosen individual inside the dataset. The positive picture is a different picture of the same individual. The negative picture is a picture of another individual. For an image x the network f will generate an embedding vector $f(x)$. The goal of the model is to ensure that the Euclidean distance between the anchor embedding vector $f(x_a)$ and the positive image one $f(x_p)$ is lower than the Euclidean distance between the anchor embedding vector and the negative image one $f(x_n)$. In order to increase the margin between the different classes, a constant α is added in the previous inequality. This can be written as follows:

$$||f(x_a) - f(x_p)||^2 + \alpha < ||f(x_a) - f(x_n)||^2 \qquad (1)$$

The final objective of the network is then to minimize the following loss L defined as the triplet loss in [22] (N is the number of triplets per batch):

$$L = \sum_{i=0}^{N} max(||f(x_a^{(i)}) - f(x_p^{(i)})||^2 - ||f(x_a^{(i)}) - f(x_n^{(i)})||^2 + \alpha, 0) \qquad (2)$$

Regarding the model selection, a VGG network [23] was used in Schroff et al. [22] paper. This network is a standard for image classification. Nevertheless, it has been improved by He et al. in [9]. Their created structure, called ResNet, has five time less parameters and a better accuracy on the ImageNet classification task. More complex networks have lately been developed such as InceptionNet [25], SENet [10] or NASNet [31]. These methods are the current state-of-the-art regarding image classification.

3   Dataset Creation and Pre-processing

3.1   Data Collection

As no open source dog face datasets are available, a new one is created. This dataset is a collection of dog face pictures we took ourselves and pictures found on the Internet. The main contributions on this dataset can be found on non-profit pet adoption websites: Streunerhilfe[1], Tiko[2], Pfotenhilfe[3], La SPA[4], Tieronline[5] and Animal-happyend[6].

---

[1] https://www.streunerhilfe-bulgarien.de/.
[2] https://www.tiko.or.at/de/tiere/.
[3] https://www.pfotenhilfe.org/tiervermittlung/.
[4] https://www.la-spa.fr/.
[5] https://www.tieronline.ch/.
[6] https://www.animal-happyend.ch/.

Fig. 1. Data pre-processing. Left: a raw image with its corresponding labels, **Right:** a set of aligned images after similarity transform.

In order to increase the network accuracy, only dogs with more than 5 pictures are selected. The final dataset contains 3148 pictures of 485 dogs.

3.2 Data Pre-processing

As the dataset is small, feeding the model with only raw images would give a bad accuracy. Three labels are thus manually added on the images: the left eye, the right eye and the muzzle, as shown on the left part of Fig. 1.

Dog faces are then aligned using the position of the eyes. Face alignment creates regularities in images and facilitates dog face parts automatic detection. A similarity transformation, i.e. a translation, a rotation and a re-sizing, is used to align the raw images. The eyes are horizontally constrained in the upper third of the picture. It creates a strong similarity between pictures and leaves enough space in the bottom part for the dog muzzle. The right eye of the dog is placed in position $(0.7/2.4 \times$ *new height*, $0.7/2.4 \times$ *new width*$)$ and the left eye in position $(0.7/2.4 \times$ *new height*, $1.7/2.4 \times$ *new width*$)$. It is a good compromise between reducing the background regions and ensuring enough space for long dog noses to appear on the pictures. The pictures are finally re-sized to $($*new height*, *new width*, *depth*$) = (104 \times 104 \times 3)$ pixels. Figure 1 represents an example of different aligned dog faces.

To properly train the model, the dataset is split into a training set and a testing set. There are two main methods to define the testing set: either to create what is called a *closed-set* or to create an *open-set*. A closed-set is a set of unknown images of known dogs, which means that the network has already seen pictures of these dogs during the training stage. An open-set is a mixture of unknown dog pictures, the network sees these dogs for the first time during the testing stage. The open-set problem is a harder problem to solve and closer to a real life problem. The testing set is thus defined as an open-set. If an application has to be developed later, a network that manages to correctly identify dog faces from an open-set of images will be a necessity.

The training set is composed of 2850 pictures of 437 dogs, and the testing set contains 298 pictures of 48 dogs. As specified above, there is no intersection between these two sets of dogs.

In order to prevent overfitting, to increase the size of the dataset and to foster generalization, the training set is augmented by slightly zooming into the pictures (*zoom range* = 0.1), by rotating them (*rotation range* = 8°) and by shifting their channels (*channel shift range* = 0.1).

The images are finally grouped into triplets following the procedure defined in Sect. 2. The final dataset, ready for training, contains: 10000 triplets (30000 pictures) of augmented dog faces for the training set and 1000 triplets (3000 pictures) of non-augmented dog faces for the testing set.

4 Model Definition and Training

4.1 Model Definition

Because of the novelty of the problem a new model has to be designed to solve it. This model is a deep convolutional neural network inspired by the recent development on this type of structure. Many different VGG-like [23] and ResNet-like [9] models have been trained on the dataset. The final model has the best performance on both verification and recognition task. It is described on Fig. 2. It is mainly inspired from the ResNet [9] structure to which a lot of dropout layers [24] are added. The network takes an image x of size $(104 \times 104 \times 3)$ as input and outputs an embedding vector $f(x)$ of size 32. In order to scale the Euclidean distance in the loss defined in Eq. (2), the output vector has to rely on the unit hypersphere, hence $||f(x)||^2 = 1$.

To design this model the utmost attention is paid to prevent overfitting. In order to extract a sufficient number of features from pictures, the network has to be as deep as possible. The residual layers allow to design such a deep network: it prevents the gradient from vanishing during back-propagation. The final model contains 92 layers for a total of 5.8 million of parameters. However, a too deep model would rapidly overfit to the small training set and its accuracy on the testing set would decrease. The model also contains many dropout layers to create a sparse network during training. Each of these dropout layers will set three fourths of the previous output to zero. This technique thus strongly prevents the network to specialize too much.

4.2 Training

The model is trained using a GPU Tesla K80 with a margin $\alpha = 0.3$. However, the model rapidly overfits if it is only trained on the dataset defined in Sect. 3. In order to fix such a problem we could have re-generated augmented triplets. Although this solution can temporarily work, it rapidly overfits again. A better solution is described in [22]: to generate so-called *hard triplets*. It consists in taking a subset of dogs, and then for each picture x_a:

- among pictures of the same class, find the most different positive picture x_p from x_a, that is, compute $argmax_{x_p}||f(x_a) - f(x_p)||^2$

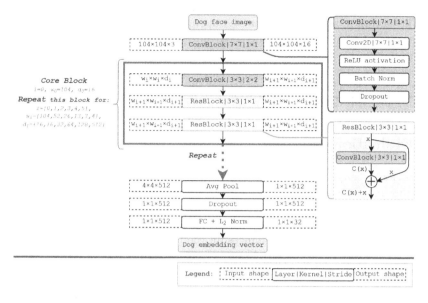

Fig. 2. Model definition. The model takes a dog face image as input and outputs its corresponding embedding vector. The core block (inside the blue box) is sequentially repeated 6 times. The *ConvBlock* and the *ResBlock* descriptions are presented on the right side of the figure. (Color figure online)

- among pictures of the other classes, find the most similar negative picture x_n from x_a, that is, compute $argmin_{x_n}||f(x_a) - f(x_n)||^2$

These hard triplets can be generated either online (during training) or offline (every n epochs). We choose to use offline training for computation power reasons: the online generation needs a minimal number of images per classes, which leads to a too big sized batch for our available computational power. Offline training consists in re-generating hard augmented triplets every $n = 3$ epochs, what will be called a *cycle*. The model is finally compiled using the Adam optimizer [14]. To improve the convergence, the learning rate is scheduled during training as shown in Table 1.

Table 1. Learning rate scheduling.

	Cycles	Epochs	Learning rates
	13	39	0.001
	4	12	0.0005
	4	12	0.0003
	2	6	0.0001
Total	23	69	-

The accuracy is monitored on the open test set defined in Sect. 3. In this set, a triplet is considered as correct if it respects the hard condition defined by inequality (1). As shown on Fig. 3, the model loss decreases during a cycle and increases after hard augmented triplets generation. If the model is trained more than 70 epochs, it starts overfitting: the validation loss will increase as the training loss will decrease.

5 Evaluation

As previously emphasized, the model is evaluated on an open-set of dogs. These dogs are unknown to the network during training. This set is composed of 298 pictures of 48 dogs. After feeding the network with these images, 298 embedding vectors are computed. These vectors will finally be used by a specific algorithm to evaluate the network performances on the three following tasks:

- **Verification:** given a pair of pictures, the algorithm has to say if it is the same dog or not. In term of embedding vectors, it means that the distance d between the vectors of a pair is compared with a threshold t. If $d < t$ then the algorithm considers that the pair represents the same dog. A random choice algorithm will obtain an accuracy of 50% here.
- **Recognition:** given one or several pictures per dog that are considered as *learned* by the algorithm, the algorithm has to determine for every *non-learned* picture which dog it represents. Given a newly computed vector the algorithm looks at its closest neighbors in the set of *learned* vectors and outputs the most frequent class in this set: it is the k-nearest neighbors (k-NN) algorithm. This task is harder than the previous one: a random choice algorithm will obtain an accuracy of one over the number of dogs, so 2.08% here.

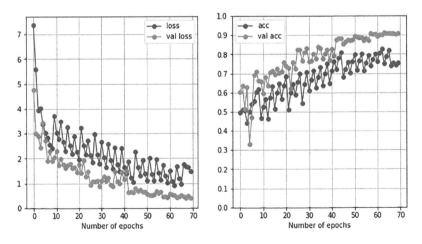

Fig. 3. Model convergence. Left: training and validation loss. **Right:** training and validation accuracy.

- **Clustering:** given all the images, the algorithm has to group them by dogs. After computing all the embedding vectors, the clustering algorithm creates groups of vectors that are close to each other. The algorithm applied here is the classic k-means algorithm.

In order to highlight the efficiency of ResNet-like structure, the results obtained with it will be compared to the one obtained with the best VGG-like structure designed to solve this problem. The latter network is composed of 14 million parameters and just like the ResNet-like structure, it contains many dropout layers.

5.1 Face Verification

For this first test, 2500 positive pairs and 2500 negative pairs are generated. A positive pair is a pair of pictures representing the same dog. A negative pair is a pair of pictures representing two different dogs. The Table 2 sums up the main results for this task. The first row shows the models' performances using their best thresholds. The second row shows the models' performances using the value of α used for training. Additionally Fig. 4 illustrates the ROC curve of these models for this binary classification task. The best accuracy reached with the ResNet-like model is 92%. Although it could be considered as low compared to human face identification models (FaceNet methods reaches 99.63% accuracy on LFW dataset), it is high regarding the size of our dataset and the high complexity of dog faces. Indeed human face models are normally trained on datasets of millions of human faces and thanks to the strong similarity between human faces, the model can extract key features more easily.

Finally some examples of false positive and false negative pairs are presented on Fig. 5. Mistakes are mainly due to a too big difference in light exposure between the two pictures and due to a too large angle between the two dog faces. Verification problems can also sometimes come from occlusions, for instance due to the dog tongue or to a muzzle protection.

Table 2. Verification results. First row: results obtained with the best distance threshold. **Second row:** results obtained with the α margin used for training.

ResNet-like		VGG-like	
Threshold	Accuracy	Threshold	Accuracy
$best = 0.63$	**92.0%** ± 0.3	$best = 0.99$	$91.3\% \pm 0.3$
$\alpha = 0.3$	$85.8\% \pm 0.3$	$\alpha = 0.3$	$68.3\% \pm 0.3$

5.2 Face Recognition

This is the main issue for an identification tool. As previously explained, after embedding vector computation by the model, this task is simply a k-NN problem.

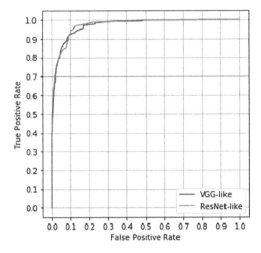

Fig. 4. Verification task. ROC curve comparing VGG with ResNet for a face verification task.

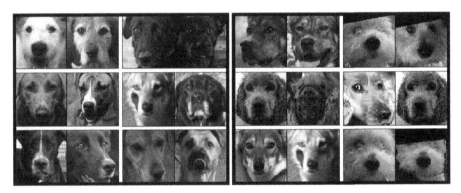

Fig. 5. Verification task. Left: some false positive pairs. **Right:** some false negative pairs.

The testing set is divided into a sub training set and a sub testing set. The sub training set is used to train the k-NN algorithm and the sub testing set to evaluate it. In order to create the sub training set, M embedding vectors per dog are selected. The rest of the embedding vectors composes the sub testing set. For instance, if $M = 1$ then it means that a single vector per dog is selected (48 vector in our case) and the rest of them (250 vectors) are used for testing: it is called a one-shot recognition problem. In this case $k = 1$, which means that the class of a vector in the sub testing set is given by the class of its closest neighbor in the sub training set. For $M > 1$, taking $k = M + 1$ gives the best accuracy for this task.

As the M vectors are randomly selected within a class, the output accuracy on the sub testing set is different depending on this selection. In order to be more accurate on this evaluation task, for each possible value of M, 1000 different sub training/sub testing sets are created and evaluated. The Table 3 represents the different rank-1 results obtained for different values of M. The *Mean*, *Minimum* and *Maximum* columns contain the average, the minimum and the maximum accuracy of the algorithm over these 1000 sub sets.

Table 3. Recognition results. This table presents the rank-1 accuracy on this task.

M	k	ResNet-like			VGG-like		
		Mean	Minimum	Maximum	Mean	Minimum	Maximum
1	1	**60.44%**	50.80%	69.60%	57.03%	44.00%	66.00%
2	3	67.49%	56.43%	79.21%	63.13%	51.98%	72.77%
3	4	73.25%	61.54%	83.33%	64.99%	54.49%	74.36%
4	5	73.92%	60.34%	86.21%	65.13%	54.72%	74.54%

The ResNet-like network reaches a rank-1 accuracy of 60.44% for the one-shot recognition task. This is lower than a normal human face recognition algorithm. However, as mentioned in the previous section, this is due to the very small amount of available data and the dog face complexity. It can also be noticed that the performances of the algorithms improve with the number of embedding vectors per class into the sub training set. Indeed the more information that are provided to the network the more accurate its predictions are.

As one of the potential applications of this project is to find a lost pet it could be interesting to look at the rank-5 accuracy. It means that the answer of the algorithm is considered as correct if the right dog is given within the 5 first suggestions. Indeed, the application could suggest to the user a list of possible dogs and the user could then select the correct animal. The obtained results are presented in Table 4. The model accuracy on this task reveals the potential of this project: for a one-shot recognition problem the model reaches 88% accuracy and given at least 3 pictures per dogs the model reaches a maximum accuracy of 100%.

Table 4. Recognition results. This table presents the rank-5 accuracy on this task.

M	k	ResNet-like			VGG-like		
		Mean	Minimum	Maximum	Mean	Minimum	Maximum
1	1	**88.41%**	80.00%	94.40%	85.92%	78.80%	91.60%
2	3	**92.83%**	87.13%	98.83%	89.68%	85.64%	95.05%
3	4	**95.97%**	86.54%	**100%**	92.22%	87.18%	96.15%
4	5	**96.10%**	88.79%	**100%**	93.44%	87.93%	97.41%

5.3   Face Clustering

We finally try to cluster the 48 dogs' pictures after embedding vector computation using the k-means clustering algorithm. Over the 48 clustered sets created, the algorithm manages to output 20 sets of correctly clustered dogs. These results are good regarding the complexity of this task: as shown on the left side of Fig. 6, the network can cluster pictures of a dog taken with very different angles and lighting. This figure also shows one of the mistakes made by the algorithm: two badly clustered dogs from the same breed that look very similar.

This kind of application could, for example, help zoologists to automatically sort their animal photos.

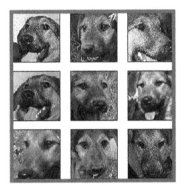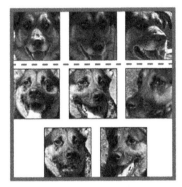

Fig. 6. Clustering task. Left: the algorithm correctly clustered 9 pictures of the same dog with different angles and lighting. **Right:** the algorithm wrongly clustered pictures of two different dogs (3 pictures for the first one and 5 for the other one).

6   Conclusion

Animal identification has until now relied on standard tagging tools and on classical computer vision and machine learning methods. Very little research on this problem has been conducted using deep learning techniques. Recent improvements in deep learning methods have created a breakthrough for human face identification and can now be employed to solve the more complex problem of animal face identification.

A novel method to identify dog faces using deep learning is presented here. Dog face identification is a more complicated task than for human faces due to the lack of available data and to the large range of texture variations in dog face pictures. A new dataset is built and a new model is designed to solve this problem. The trained network reaches a satisfying accuracy on both verification and recognition tasks. This project could thus allow researchers to pay more attention on these new kinds of techniques for their future work on animal identification.

However, there is still room for improvement. Our dataset is significantly small compared to the standard in deep learning domain and too few dogs per breed are represented. The images have to be labeled by hand which could be improved by automatic landmarks detection. Dog muzzle riddles or other dog features could also have been used to help the network with its task. The model is not accurate enough to solve a real identification problem but has its usefulness in other problems such as helping dog owners finding their lost pet. To showcase the potential of the developed method, a mobile app is currently under development to achieve the latter objective.

References

1. Amos, B., Ludwiczuk, B., Satyanarayanan, M.: OpenFace: a general-purpose face recognition library with mobile applications. Technical report, CMU-CS-16-118, CMU School of Computer Science (2016)
2. Awad, A.I.: From classical methods to animal biometrics: a review on cattle identification and tracking. Comput. Electron. Agric. **123**, 423–435 (2016). https://doi.org/10.1016/j.compag.2016.03.014. http://www.sciencedirect. com/science/article/pii/S0168169916300837
3. Cao, K., Rong, Y., Li, C., Tang, X., Loy, C.C.: Pose-robust face recognition via deep residual equivariant mapping. CoRR abs/1803.00839 (2018). http://arxiv. org/abs/1803.00839
4. Chen, S., Liu, Y., Gao, X., Han, Z.: MobileFaceNets: efficient CNNs for accurate real-time face verification on mobile devices. CoRR abs/1804.07573 (2018). http:// arxiv.org/abs/1804.07573
5. Crouse, D., et al.: LemurFaceID: a face recognition system to facilitate individual identification of lemurs. BMC Zool. **2**(1), 2 (2017). https://doi.org/10.1186/ s40850-016-0011-9
6. Deb, D., et al.: Face recognition: primates in the wild. CoRR abs/1804.08790 (2018). http://arxiv.org/abs/1804.08790
7. Deng, J., Guo, J., Zafeiriou, S.: ArcFace: additive angular margin loss for deep face recognition. CoRR abs/1801.07698 (2018). http://arxiv.org/abs/1801.07698
8. Hansen, M.F., et al.: Towards on-farm pig face recognition using convolutional neural networks. Comput. Ind. **98**, 145–152 (2018)
9. He, K., Zhang, X., Ren, S., Sun, J.: Deep residual learning for image recognition. CoRR abs/1512.03385 (2015). http://arxiv.org/abs/1512.03385
10. Hu, J., Shen, L., Sun, G.: Squeeze-and-excitation networks. CoRR abs/1709.01507 (2017). http://arxiv.org/abs/1709.01507
11. Huang, G.B., Ramesh, M., Berg, T., Learned-Miller, E.: Labeled faces in the wild: a database for studying face recognition in unconstrained environments. Technical report 07-49, University of Massachusetts, Amherst, October 2007
12. Blancou, J.: A history of the traceability of animals and animal products. Revue scientifique et technique (International Office of Epizootics) (2001). https://www. ncbi.nlm.nih.gov/pubmed/11548516
13. Jarraya, I., Ouarda, W., Alimi, A.M.: A preliminary investigation on horses recognition using facial texture features. In: 2015 IEEE International Conference on Systems, Man, and Cybernetics, pp. 2803–2808, October 2015. https://doi.org/10. 1109/SMC.2015.489
14. Kingma, D.P., Ba, J.: Adam: a method for stochastic optimization. CoRR abs/1412.6980 (2014). http://arxiv.org/abs/1412.6980

15. Kumar, S., et al.: Deep learning framework for recognition of cattle using muzzle point image pattern. Measurement **116**, 1–17 (2018). https://doi.org/10.1016/j.measurement.2017.10.064. http://www.sciencedirect.com/science/article/pii/S0263224117306991

16. Kumar, S., Singh, S.K.: Monitoring of pet animal in smart cities using animal biometrics. Future Gener. Comput. Syst. **83**, 553–563 (2018). https://doi.org/10.1016/j.future.2016.12.006. http://www.sciencedirect.com/science/article/pii/S0167739X16307385

17. Kumar, S., Singh, S.K., Abidi, A.I., Datta, D., Sangaiah, A.K.: Group sparse representation approach for recognition of cattle on muzzle point images. Int. J. Parallel Program. **46**, 812–837 (2017)

18. Kumar, S., Singh, S.K., Singh, R.S., Singh, A.K., Tiwari, S.: Real-time recognition of cattle using animal biometrics. J. Real-Time Image Process. **13**(3), 505–526 (2017). https://doi.org/10.1007/s11554-016-0645-4

19. Kumar, S., Singh, S.K., Singh, R., Singh, A.K.: Animal Biometrics: Techniques and Applications. Springer, Singapore (2017). https://doi.org/10.1007/978-981-10-7956-6. https://www.springer.com/us/book/9789811079559

20. Liu, J., Kanazawa, A., Jacobs, D., Belhumeur, P.: Dog breed classification using part localization 7572, 172–185, October 2012

21. Liu, W., Wen, Y., Yu, Z., Li, M., Raj, B., Song, L.: SphereFace: deep hypersphere embedding for face recognition. CoRR abs/1704.08063 (2017). http://arxiv.org/abs/1704.08063

22. Schroff, F., Kalenichenko, D., Philbin, J.: FaceNet: a unified embedding for face recognition and clustering. CoRR abs/1503.03832 (2015). http://arxiv.org/abs/1503.03832

23. Simonyan, K., Zisserman, A.: Very deep convolutional networks for large-scale image recognition. CoRR abs/1409.1556 (2014). http://arxiv.org/abs/1409.1556

24. Srivastava, N., Hinton, G., Krizhevsky, A., Sutskever, I., Salakhutdinov, R.: Dropout: a simple way to prevent neural networks from overfitting. J. Mach. Learn. Res. **15**, 1929–1958 (2014). http://jmlr.org/papers/v15/srivastava14a.html

25. Szegedy, C., Ioffe, S., Vanhoucke, V.: Inception-v4, Inception-ResNet and the impact of residual connections on learning. In: AAAI (2016)

26. Taigman, Y., Yang, M., Ranzato, M., Wolf, L.: DeepFace: closing the gap to human-level performance in face verification (2014). https://research.fb.com/publications/deepface-closing-the-gap-to-human-level-performance-in-face-verification/

27. Trigueros, D.S., Meng, L., Hartnett, M.: Face recognition: from traditional to deep learning methods (2018)

28. Wang, H., et al.: CosFace: large margin cosine loss for deep face recognition. CoRR abs/1801.09414 (2018). http://arxiv.org/abs/1801.09414

29. Wang, X., Ly, V., Sorensen, S., Kambhamettu, C.: Dog breed classification via landmarks, pp. 5237–5241, January 2015. https://doi.org/10.1109/ICIP.2014.7026060

30. Zheng, Y., Pal, D.K., Savvides, M.: Ring loss: convex feature normalization for face recognition. CoRR abs/1803.00130 (2018). http://arxiv.org/abs/1803.00130

31. Zoph, B., Vasudevan, V., Shlens, J., Le, Q.V.: Learning transferable architectures for scalable image recognition. CoRR abs/1707.07012 (2017). http://arxiv.org/abs/1707.07012

A Modern Approach for Sign Language Interpretation Using Convolutional Neural Network

Pias Paul[(⊠)], Moh. Anwar-Ul-Azim Bhuiya, Md. Ayat Ullah,
Molla Nazmus Saqib, Nabeel Mohammed, and Sifat Momen

Department of Electrical and Computer Engineering, North South University,
Plot-15, Block-B, Bashundhara, 1229 Dhaka, Bangladesh
{paul.pias,anwar.bhuiyan,ayat.ullah,nazmus.saqib,nabeel.mohammed,
sifat.momen}@northsouth.edu

Abstract. There are nearly 70 million deaf people in the world. A significant portion of them and their families use sign language as a medium for communicating with each other. As automation is being gradually introduced to many parts of everyday life, the ability for machines to understand the act on sign language will be critical to creating an inclusive society. This paper presents multiple convolutional neural network based approaches, suitable for fast classification of hand sign characters. We propose two custom convolutional neural network (CNN) based architectures which are able to generalize 24 static American Sign Language (ASL) signs using only convolutional and fully connected layers. We compare these networks with transfer learning based approaches, where multiple pre-trained models were utilized. Our models have remarkably outperformed all the preceding models by accomplishing 86.52% and 85.88% accuracy on RGB images of the ASL Finger Spelling dataset.

Keywords: Image processing · CNN · Transfer learning · ASLR · Finger Spelling dataset

1 Introduction

A language that needs manual communication and involvement of body language to convey meaning as opposed to conveyed sound patterns is known as sign language. This can involve a simultaneous combination of handshapes, orientation, and movement of the hands, arms or body, and different facial expressions to fluidly express a speaker's thoughts. In some cases, sign language is the only method that is used to communicate with a person with hearing impairment. Sign languages such as the American Sign Language (ASL), British Sign Language (BSL), Quebec Sign Language (LSQ), Spanish sign language (SSL) differ in the way an expression is made. They share many similarities with spoken languages, which is why linguists consider sign languages to be a part of natural languages.

A. C. Nayak and A. Sharma (Eds.): PRICAI 2019, LNAI 11672, pp. 431–444, 2019.
https://doi.org/10.1007/978-3-030-29894-4_35

Sign Language Recognition (SLR) system which is required to perceive gesture-based communications, has been widely studied for years. It provides a way to help deaf/mute individuals interact easily with technology. However, just like speech recognition, this is not an easy task. However, recent advances in computer vision, particularly the use of convolutional neural networks (CNN), has created opportunities to create effective solutions to problems previously thought to be almost unattainable. In this paper, we present multiple CNN-based models to classify 24 characters from the ASL Finger Spelling Dataset. We present models which were custom made for this problem, as well as models which leverage transfer learning. One of our custom models achieved a test accuracy of 86.52%, which is better than the current best published result.

2   Related Works

In 2013 Pugeault and Bowden [18] proposed an interactive keyboard-less graphical user interface that can detect hand shapes in real time. In that work, they used a Microsoft Kinect device for collecting both appearance and depth images, OpenNI+NITE framework for hand detection and tracking, features based on Gabor filters and a Random Forest classifier for classification. From the ASL dataset, which was also proposed in that paper, they have ignored and discarded images of letter j and z since both of these letters require motion and used leftover 48000 images; 50% for training and 50% for validation. Using both appearance and depth images together brought them better classification result compared to the usage of appearance and depth information separately.

Tripathi et al. have proposed a continuous hand gesture recognition system [29]. In their approach, keyframes were extracted using gradient-based methods and HoG features were used for actual feature extraction. For classification, several distance metrics were used including City Block, Mahalanobis, Chess Board, Cosine, etc. They created a dataset using 10 sentences signaled by 5 different people. They found that using a higher number of bins for HoG resulted in better performance and the best performance was found when Euclidean distance employed.

Masood et al. [15] proposed a method to bridge the gap for the people who do not know and want to communicate using sign languages through isolated sign language recognition using methods based on computer vision. They used an Argentinean dataset (LSA) with 2300 video samples and substantial gesture variation with 46 categories. Their model used the Inception-v3 pre-trained CNN, and combined with the use of Long Short Term Memory (LSTM) for sequence predictions. They tried 3 models such as a single layer of 256 LSTM units, a wider Recurrent neural network(RNN) network with 512 LSTM units, a deep RNN network consisting of 3 layers with each 64 LSTM units. Empirically, they found the model with 256 LSTM units gave the best performance. Two approaches were taken for training, one was a prediction approach in which predictions of frames made by CNN were fed as input to the LSTM. In the other approach, the output of the pooling layers was directly fed into the LSTM. The second approach gave a better result with an accuracy of 95.2%.

3 Experimental Setup

This section provides details of the setup used for the experiments performed. We initially present the dataset on which we will train and compare the different models. This is followed by a brief description of the data preprocessing and partitioning. The proposed models are discussed next, which includes descriptions of the custom models as well as the transfer learning techniques.

3.1 Dataset

The work is based on ASL Finger Spelling dataset that consists of images which were obtained from 5 different users. In the proposed dataset [18], images were obtained in 2 different ways, each user was asked to perform 24 ASL static signs which were captured in both color and depth format. There are a total of **131,670** number of images where **65,774** images have RGB channels and rest are depth images that contain the intensity values in the image which represent the distance of the object or simply depth from a viewpoint. The reason behind choosing American Sign Language (ASL) for this work was that ASL is widely learned as a second language and the dataset contains sign from only using one hand which reduces the task of over-complicated feature extraction. Here, the dataset comprises 24 static signs which have similar lighting and background excluding the letters j and z since these 2 letters require dictionary lookup and involve motion (Table 1).

Table 1. Types of images collected from each user

User	Image type	
	RGB	Depth+RGB
A	12,547	25,118
B	13,898	27,820
C	13,393	26,810
D	13,154	26,332
E	12,782	25,590

3.2 Data Preprocessing and Feature Extraction

From the total of **5** user samples, **4** were considered in such a way that the proposed dataset [18] was divided into two parts. First part is Dataset-A which contains only color images and the other one is Dataset-B which contains both

Table 2. Preparing the dataset

Image type	Training set	Validation set	Label
RGB	26,547	26,445	**DataSet-A**
Depth+RGB	53,142	52,938	**DataSet-B**

depth and color images. This is shown in Table 2. In both the DataSet-A and DataSet-B, images from users C and D were used as the training set and images from user A and B were used to make validation/test set. As the images were of different sizes, all of them were re-sized to 200×200 pixels. Pixel color values were re-scaled between 0 and 1 and then each image was normalized by subtracting the mean (Fig. 1).

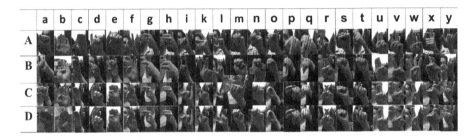

Fig. 1. Illustration on the variety of the dataset where each column represents images of individual letters that has been collected from 4 different users.

To increase the amount of training data, each training image was augmented using the transformations mentioned in Table 3. The augmentations were applied single (not compositionally) and were only applied to RGB images. The validation data were not augmented per say, but were modified.

Table 3. Augmentation techniques applied on Dataset-A and Dataset-B

Training data set		Validation data set	
Arguments	Parameters	Arguments	Parameters
Rescale	1./255	Rescale	1./255
Center-Cropped	True	Center-Cropped	True
Shear_Range	0.2 Degree		
Zoom_range	0.1		
Random_Rotation	20 Degree		
Horizontal_Flip	True		
Height_Shift_Range	0.1		
Width_Shift_Range	0.1		
Fill_Mode	Nearest		

3.3   The Proposed Architecture

Table 4 shows the details of the two custom models used for comparison. Both models were trained and tested on DataSet-A and DataSet-B. For Custom-Model-A, conv3-32 means respective field size 3 and number of channels 64. The images were resized to 128×128 dimension which will go through the convolutional layers. The model uses LeakyReLU as activation function. We found LeakyReLU to work better than RelU for this model after experimentation. Apart from using max pooling, Global Average Pooling (GAP) was also used to downsample the input dimension from each layer using a 2×2 window. After flattening the output of the last pooling layer was passed through four fully connected layers with the final layer having 24 neurons for the 24 classes. The last layer also uses the softmax activation function.

In custom-Model-B, 2×2 strided convolution [27] was used to reduce the size of the output feature maps instead of the more commonly used pooling techniques. Surprisingly, for this model, our tests showed better performance using the RelU activation function (an investigation looking into the discrepancy is currently under progress and will be reported in a later paper). Batch normalization was also used in this model. This model also flattens the output of the last convolutional layer and forwards the output to four fully connected layers, although the configurations are slightly different from Custom-Model-A.

3.4   Transfer Learning Using Pre-trained Models

Apart from our custom models, we have also experimented using Transfer Learning which leverages the weights or filters of a pre-trained model on a new problem as in the case of most real-world problems when there are insufficient data points to train complex models. The premise is if knowledge from an already trained machine learning model is applied to a different but related problem, it may facilitate the learning process as the model is already trained to identify some potentially useful features.

Figure 2 shows the overall strategy used for transfer learning. This method is one which has been used in many different tasks, where the softmax layer of the original pre-trained model is discarded and replaced by a new classification layer with random weights. All layers except this new one are frozen and then the newly crafted model is trained until the random weights change to be compatible with the rest of the model. Then the frozen layers are unfrozen and the entire model is trained.

For this work, we experimented with five different models all pre-trained on the ImageNet dataset. These are MobileNetV2, NASNetMobile, DenseNet21, VGG16 and VGG19.

3.5   Training Details

We arrived at a set of hyper parameters which worked well through experimentation. Table 5 summarizes this information.

Table 4. Configuration of the customized models

Configuration of the proposed architectures	
Custom-Model-A	**Custom-Model-B**
input (128 × 128image)	**input (200 × 200 image)**
conv3-32. LeakyReLU conv3-32. LeakyReLU conv3-32. LeakyReLU	conv3-64 Sequential (conv3-64.ReLU, BatchNorm conv3-64.Relu, BatchNorm)
MaxPool (stride=2)	**conv3-64 (stride = 2)**
Dropout(0.6) conv3-32. LeakyReLU conv3-32. LeakyReLU conv3-32. LeakyReLU	Sequential (conv3-64.ReLU, BatchNorm conv3-64.Relu, BatchNorm) Sequential (conv3-64.ReLU, BatchNorm)
MaxPool (stride=2)	**conv3-64 (stride = 2)**
DepthwiseConv3. LeakyReLU BatchNormalization conv3-32. LeakyReLU BatchNormalization	Sequential (conv3-64.ReLU, BatchNorm, conv3-64.Relu, BatchNorm) Sequential (conv3-64.ReLU, BatchNorm, conv3-64.Relu, BatchNorm) Dropout(0.6)
conv3-64. LeakyReLU conv3-64. LeakyReLU conv3-64. LeakyReLU conv3-64. LeakyReLU	**conv3-64 (stride = 2)** Sequential (conv3-64.ReLU, BatchNorm, conv3-64.Relu, BatchNorm) Sequential (conv3-64.ReLU, BatchNorm, conv3-64.Relu, BatchNorm)
MaxPool (stride=2)	**conv3-64 (stride = 2)** **conv3-64 (stride = 2)**
conv3-64. LeakyReLU conv3-64. LeakyReLU conv3-64. LeakyReLU conv3-64. LeakyReLU	Sequential (conv3-64.ReLU, BatchNorm, conv3-64.Relu, BatchNorm) Sequential (conv3-64.ReLU, BatchNorm, conv3-64.Relu, BatchNorm)
GlobalAveragePooling **MaxPool (stride=2)**	**conv3-64 (stride = 2)**
FC-1024 Dropout(0.4) ReLU	Dropout(0.6) FC-576 ReLU
FC-576 Dropout(0.4) ReLU	Dropout(0.6) FC-256 ReLU
FC-256 Dropout(0.4) ReLU	Dropout(0.6) FC-128 ReLU
FC-128 Dropout(0.4) ReLU	Dropout(0.6) FC-64 ReLU
FC-24, softmax	FC-24, softmax

The loss function of choice was categorical cross entropy as shown in Eq. 1, which measures the classification error as a cross entropy loss when multiple categories are in use. Here, the double sum is over the observations i, whose number is N, and the categories c, whose number is C and the term $1_{y_i \in C_c}$

Table 5. Training details

Training details	
Batch Size	64
Input size	200*200*3
Learning Rate	0.001
Optimizer	Adam
Loss Function	Categorical Crossentropy
Epoch	25

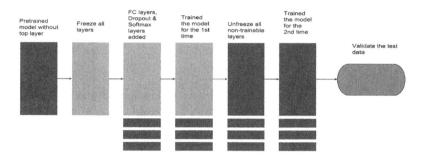

Fig. 2. The proposed transfer learning process

is the indicator function of the ith observation belonging to the cth category. Finally, the probability predicted by the model for the ith observation belongs to which of the cth category is determined by $P_{model}[y_i \in C_c]$.

$$-\frac{1}{N}\sum_{i=1}^{N}\sum_{c=1}^{C}1_{y_i \epsilon C_c}logP_{model}[y_i \epsilon C_c] \tag{1}$$

For this work the base **learning rate was set to 0.001** with which the network starts to train itself but as mentioned earlier the learning rate is being adapted step wise here by using Eq. 2. Here **last_epoch**, the value of **Step_Wise_LR** will be updated as if an epoch completes all its steps.

$$Step\_Wise\_LR = (base\_lr * gamma * (\frac{last\_epoch}{step\_size})) \tag{2}$$

4   Results

The task of finding a model which will detect the signs based on ASL was divided into two parts. In the first segment, two custom models were built from which accuracy of **86.52%** and in the second segment, an accuracy of **85.88%** was achieved using pre-trained models on Dataset-A.

4.1 Results from Custom Model

To evaluate the model several approaches were taken. At first, two custom models (custom-model-A) and (custom-model-B) were created using the corresponding configurations mentioned in Sect. 3.3. Using the custom-model-A mentioned in Table 6, **77.19% accuracy was achieved** while validating images from Dataset-A. Here to minimize overfitting **40% and 60% of dropout, L2 regularization and Global Average Pooling (GAP)** were used. After **25 epochs** a training accuracy of 96.33% and a validation accuracy of **77.19%** were achieved using 5,214,840 trainable parameters for RGB images.

Table 6. Results obtained using the custom models

Model name	No. of trainable parameters	DataSet-A		DataSet-B	
		Training accuracy (%)	Validation accuracy (%)	Training accuracy (%)	Validation accuracy (%)
Custom-Model-A	5,214,840	96.33	77.19	86.54	**66.79**
Custom-Model-B	**428,728**	**98.54**	**86.52**	**89.45**	62.16

The custom-model-B from Table 6 which architecture was discussed in Sect. 3.3, gave the best validation accuracy compared to the custom-model-A for Dataset-A.

Between two custom models, training and validation accuracy for each model in every epoch are recorded to find out the best model that gives comparatively better validation accuracy. From Fig. 3, we can see that after a certain epoch training accuracy highlighted with blue color remains almost the same where validation accuracy highlighted with orange color drops and doesn't increase

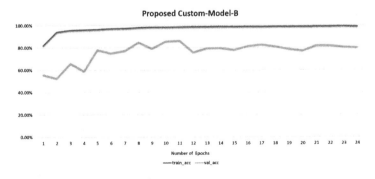

Fig. 3. Illustration of training and validation accuracy of the proposed Custom-Model-B (Color figure online)

prominently. This indicates that there was no need for running the model after that certain epochs. To overcome overfitting some regularization techniques such as **Dropout, L2 Regularization** were applied by tuning the hyperparameters which lead to the best performance on the validation set. For this work, 3 different instances of dropout value for custom model-B were considered where dropping 60% of neurons reduces the overall validation loss by an amount of **0.25** that helped to increase the validation accuracy.

4.2   Results from Transfer Learning

Table 7. Results from pre-trained models using DataSet-A

Pre-trained model	No. of total parameters	DataSet-A	
		Training accuracy (%)	Validation accuracy (%)
MobileNetV2	4,297,816	99.88	84.93
NASNetMobile	5,044,012	99.60	85.88
DenseNet121	7,467,480	96.18	76.92
VGG19	29,076,312	84.75	59.93
VGG16	20,024,384	86.50	55.57

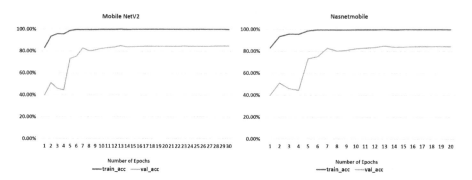

Fig. 4. Illustration of training and validation accuracy of the best two transfer learning models

To improve the validation accuracy, fine-tuning process was introduced where the model was initialized using the technique mentioned in Sect. 3.4. From this configuration, with trainable parameters-9,051,928 and non-trainable parameters-20,024,384 a validation accuracy of 55.57% was achieved using VGG16 model which weights were pre-trained on **imagenet** dataset and from VGG19 with Trainable parameters-9,051,928 & Non-trainable parameters-14,714,688, a validation accuracy of 59.93% was achieved where the training accuracy was 84.75%. In both the models, parameters except in fully connected layers were being frozen. As this result was not even close to our custom models, a different technique with other pre-trained models was implied. With this technique, the top layers or fully connected layers of the model was first trained for 10 epochs, then the weights of all the pre-trained layer and the top layer were unfrozen and the same model was trained for the second time. In the first scenario, when the model was only trained with top layers weighs the activation function "Softmax" that relied upon the last fully connected layers trained itself in a way that when in the second time model retrained itself for 25 epochs, it gives much better validation accuracy mentioned in Table 7. From this process using 'MobileNetV2' & 'NASNetMobile' model's pre-trained weights with 2072 and 1176 corresponding neurons, accuracy of **84.93% and 85.88%** were recorded. In the case of Densenet121, VGG16 and VGG19 same configuration could not be applied as there is a huge number of parameters or weights in terms of memory. In case of all the pre-trained models, "MobilenetV" and "NASNetMobile" gives linear growth in terms of validation accuracy. From Fig. 4 we can see that, after running for several epochs, validation accuracy has gone lower for the first 3–4 epochs, then it jumps to 75% and gradually increases to 84% and stabilizes for the remaining epochs. On the other hand, the training accuracy gains 98% accuracy in first 5–6 epoch and remain stable for the rest of the epochs.

4.3   Discussion on Results

The previous work that gave best validation accuracy based on **ASL fingerspelling** dataset was conducted by Pugeault and Bowden [18] where they recorded accuracy on three different instances. They obtained 73% accuracy for using only RGB images, 69% for using only depth information and 75% accuracy for using RGB+depth images. In our work, we have considered only two instances as we only used RGB("DataSet-A") and Depth+RGB("DataSet-B") to measure performances. Although our customized models could not perform better on "DataSet-B" compared to their [18] work but all the other models performed better than [18] on RGB images. A total of 240 unseen color images were used to measure f1 score of both the customized models. Both the models were asked to measure ground truth values of 10 images from each class. Based on the precision and recall values, f1 score was then generated for each class that is shown in Table 8.

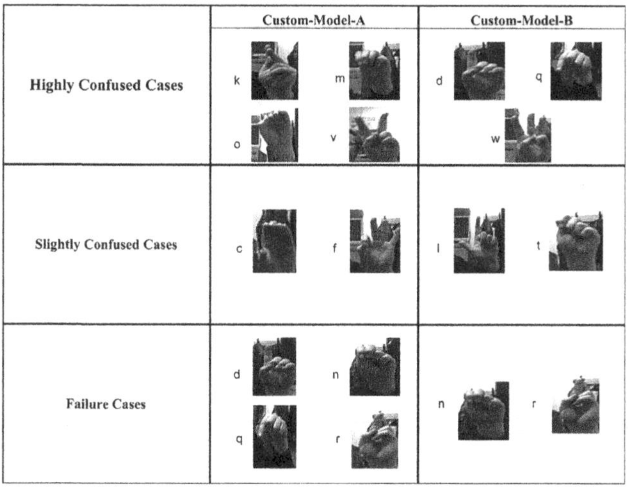

Fig. 5. Illustration of different scenarios of our custom models predictions

For "Custom-Model-A" recall values are significantly higher than the precision values for classes k, m, o, v where for "Custom-Model-B" those classes are d, q, w. The reason behind this might be because signs of c and o, w and f, d and l, m and n, k and r shown in Fig. 5 are quite similar which is why models may get confused while classifying for those particular classes. In case of both the models, the classifiers could not predict n, r out of given images. In case of letter c, f "Custom-Model-A" shows small confusion as the precision values are slightly lower than the recall values for those classes wherein for "Custom-Model-B" those classes are l, t. Although for some classes the custom models could not give accurate predictions overall performance of both the models was good as the macro-average value of "Custom-Model-A" is nearly 59% and for "Custom-Model-B" it is nearly 68%.

Table 8. F1 score obtained from customized models

Class	F1-score		Predicted accurately	
	Custom Model-A	Custom-Model-B	Custom-Model-A	Custom Model-B
a	0.89	1.00	8	10
b	0.89	0.17	8	1
c	0.83	1.00	10	10
d	**0.00**	0.46	**0**	4
e	0.46	0.75	3	9
f	0.91	0.89	10	10
g	0.95	1.00	9	10
h	1.00	0.9	10	8
i	0.84	0.68	8	7
k	0.33	0.95	8	10
l	1.00	0.79	10	7
m	0.62	0.93	10	10
n	**0.00**	**0.00**	**0**	**0**
o	0.12	0.36	1	3
p	0.3	1.00	3	10
q	**0.00**	0.57	**0**	7
r	**0.00**	**0.00**	**0**	**0**
s	1.00	1.00	10	10
t	0.53	0.67	4	5
u	0.95	0.89	9	8
v	0.27	0.74	4	6
w	0.75	0.24	6	2
x	**0.00**	0.71	**0**	7
y	0.83	0.35	10	9

5   Conclusion

In this paper, we present an image-based comparison wise approach to finding
models that can interpret sign languages in a much more efficient way from ASL
finger Spelling dataset. For that, we have developed two custom models and
several transfer learning models based on convolutional neural network. Then for
training and validating the network, two approaches were considered in which
one approach was to use only RGB images and the other one was to use both
RGB and depth information. Our classification results of RGB images exceeded
all the previous models. For further improvement, the letters j and z will be
included in the video dataset which will be utilized to recognize continuous
hand signs.

References

1. Anderson, R., Wiryana, F., Chandra, M., Putra, G.: Sign language recognition application systems for deaf-mute people: a review based on input-process-output. Procedia Comput. Sci. **116**, 441–448 (2017)
2. Arge, F.O.R.L., Mage in CI: Vdcnl-s i r, pp. 1–14 (2015)
3. 2014 IEEE International Conference on Advanced Communications, Control and Computing Technologies, pp. 1412–1415 (2014)
4. Núñez Fernández, D., Kwolek, B.: Hand posture recognition using convolutional neural network. In: Mendoza, M., Velastín, S. (eds.) CIARP 2017. LNCS, vol. 10657, pp. 441–449. Springer, Cham (2018). https://doi.org/10.1007/978-3-319-75193-1_53
5. Ghotkar, A., Kharate, G.K.: Study of vision based hand gesture recognition using Indian sign language (2017)
6. Chollet, F.: Xception: deep learning with depthwise separable convolutions (2014)
7. Hoque, T., Kabir, F.: Automated Bangla sign language translation system: prospects, limitations and applications, pp. 856–862 (2016)
8. Hosoe, H., Sako, S.: Recognition of JSL finger spelling using convolutional neural networks, pp. 85–88 (2017)
9. Huang, G., Weinberger, K.Q.: Densely connected convolutional networks (2016)
10. Karabasi, M., Bhatti, Z., Shah, A.: A model for Real-time recognition and textual representation of Malaysian sign language through image processing. In: 2013 International Conference on Advanced Computer Science Applications and Technologies (2013)
11. Karmokar, B.C., Alam, K.R., Siddiquee, K.: Bangladeshi sign language recognition employing neural network ensemble (2012)
12. Kishore, P.V.V., Kumar, P.R.: Segment, track, extract, recognize and convert sign language videos to voice/text. IJACSA **3**, 35–47 (2012)
13. Koller, O., Forster, J., Ney, H.: Continuous sign language recognition: towards large vocabulary statistical recognition systems handling multiple signers. Comput. Vis. Image Underst. **141**, 108–125 (2015)
14. Kumar, P.K., Prahlad, P., Loh, A.P.: Attention based detection and recognition of hand postures against complex backgrounds (2012)
15. Masood, S., Srivastava, A., Thuwal, H.C., Ahmad, M.: Real-time sign language gesture (word) recognition from video sequences using CNN and RNN. In: Bhateja, V., Coello Coello, C.A., Satapathy, S.C., Pattnaik, P.K. (eds.) Intelligent Engineering Informatics. AISC, vol. 695, pp. 623–632. Springer, Singapore (2018). https://doi.org/10.1007/978-981-10-7566-7_63
16. Mekala, P., Gao, Y., Fan, J., Davari, A.: Real-time sign language recognition based on neural network architecture, pp. 195–199 (2011)
17. Prajapati, R., Pandey, V., Jamindar, N., Yadav, N., Phadnis, P.N.: Hand gesture recognition and voice conversion for deaf and dumb. IRJET **5**, 1373–1376 (2018)
18. Pugeault, N., Bowden, R.: Spelling it out: real-time ASL fingerspelling recognition (2011)
19. Rahaman, M.A., Jasim, M., Ali, H.: Real-time computer vision-based Bengali sign language recognition, pp. 192–197 (2014)
20. Rajam, P.S., Balakrishnan, G.: Real time Indian sign language recognition system to aid deaf-dumb people, pp. 1–6 (2011)
21. Rao, G.A., Kishore, P.V.: Selfie video based continuous Indian sign language recognition system. Ain Shams Eng. J. **9**, 1929 (2017)

22. Sandler, M., Zhu, M., Zhmoginov, A., Howard, A., Chen, L.-C.: MobileNetV2: inverted residuals and linear bottlenecks (2018)
23. Savur, C.: Real-time American sign language recognition system by using surface EMG signal, pp. 497–502 (2015)
24. Sarawate, N., Leu, M.C., ÖZ, C.: A real-time American sign language word recognition system based on neural networks and a probabilistic model. Turk. J. Electr. Eng. Comput. Sci. **23**, 2107–2123 (2015)
25. Seth, D., Ghosh, A., Dasgupta, A., Nath, A.: Real time sign language processing system. In: Unal, A., Nayak, M., Mishra, D.K., Singh, D., Joshi, A. (eds.) Smart-Com 2016. CCIS, vol. 628, pp. 11–18. Springer, Singapore (2016). https://doi.org/10.1007/978-981-10-3433-6_2
26. Singha, J., Das, K.: Recognition of Indian sign language in live video. Int. J. Comput. Appl. **70**, 17–22 (2013)
27. Springenberg, J.T., Dosovitskiy, A., Brox, T., Riedmiller, M.: Striving for simplicity: the all convolutional net, pp. 1–14 (2015)
28. Szegedy, C., Vanhoucke, V., Shlens, J., Wojna, Z.: Rethinking the inception architecture for computer vision (2014)
29. Tripathi, K., Baranwal, N., Nandi, G.C.: Continuous Indian sign language gesture recognition and sentence formation. Procedia Comput. Sci. **54**, 523–531 (2015)
30. Uddin, S.J.: Bangla sign language interpretation using image processing (2017)
31. Wazalwar, S., Shrawankar, U.: Interpretation of sign language into English using NLP techniques. J. Inf. Optim. Sci. **38**, 895 (2017)
32. Zoph, B., Shlens, J.: Learning transferable architectures for scalable image recognition (2017)

Clustering of Small-Sample Single-Cell RNA-Seq Data via Feature Clustering and Selection

Edwin Vans[1,2(✉)], Alok Sharma[1,5,6,7], Ashwini Patil[8], Daichi Shigemizu[3,4,5,6], and Tatsuhiko Tsunoda[4,5,6]

[1] School of Engineering and Physics, University of the South Pacific, Suva, Fiji
vans.edw@gmail.com, alok.fj@gmail.com
[2] School of Electrical and Electronics Engineering, Fiji National University, Suva, Fiji
edwin.vans@fnu.ac.fj
[3] Medical Genome Center, National Center for Geriatrics and Gerontology, Obu, Aichi 474-8511, Japan
[4] Department of Medical Science Mathematics, Medical Research Institute, Tokyo Medical and Dental University (TMDU), Tokyo 113-8510, Japan
[5] RIKEN Center for Integrative Medical Sciences, Yokohama, Kanagawa 230-0045, Japan
[6] CREST, JST, Tokyo 113-8510, Japan
[7] Institute for Integrated and Intelligent Systems, Griffith University, Brisbane, QLD 4111, Australia
[8] Institute of Medical Science, University of Tokyo, 4-6-1, Shirokanedai, Minato-ku, Tokyo 108-8639, Japan

Abstract. We present FeatClust, a software tool for clustering small sample size single-cell RNA-Seq datasets. The FeatClust approach is based on feature selection. It divides features into several groups by performing agglomerative hierarchical clustering and then iteratively clustering the samples and removing features belonging to groups with the least variance across samples. The optimal number of feature groups is selected based on silhouette analysis on the clustered data, i.e., selecting the clustering with the highest average silhouette coefficient. FeatClust also allows one to visually choose the number of clusters if it is not known, by generating silhouette plot for a chosen number of groupings of the dataset. We cluster five small sample single-cell RNA-seq datasets and use the adjusted rand index metric to compare the results with other clustering packages. The results are promising and show the effectiveness of FeatClust on small sample size datasets.

Keywords: Single-cell RNA-Seq · Hierarchical clustering · Feature selection

1 Introduction

Single-cell RNA sequencing (RNA-Seq) is at the cutting edge of cell biology. It quantifies the gene expression profile of the whole transcriptome of individual cells. Analysis of single-cell RNA-seq data through unsupervised clustering

© Springer Nature Switzerland AG 2019
A. C. Nayak and A. Sharma (Eds.): PRICAI 2019, LNAI 11672, pp. 445–456, 2019.
https://doi.org/10.1007/978-3-030-29894-4_36

enables researchers to identify cell type and function and to discover heterogeneity within the cell populations. Heterogeneity within a cell population is common [11] and it occurs in a variety of different cell populations such as tumor cells [10,24], embryonic stem cells (ESCs) [21], hematopoietic stem cells (HSCs) [12] and T cells [5].

Recently, several clustering software packages were developed for analysis of single-cell datasets. One such software package is called SEURAT, developed by Satija Labs for analysis of single cell data-sets [6,18,20]. The original version of SEURAT used PCA on highly variable genes. It then selected statistically significant principal components and projected these to two-dimensional space using t-SNE. Density clustering (DBSCAN) algorithm was then used to identify clusters. The newer version of SEURAT uses PCA and graph-based clustering similar to [16,26].

Žurauskienė and Yau [28] developed a hierarchical clustering based method which they called pcaReduce. pcaReduce works by first reducing the dimensionality of the gene expression matrix to $k - 1$ using PCA, where k is the initial cluster size. It then uses k-means to divide the data into k clusters and obtains the mean and the covariance matrix for each cluster. pcaReduce does the following steps in a loop. A probability distribution based on multivariate Gaussian is used to find the probability of merging pairs of clusters for every possible pair of clusters. The pair with the highest probability is merged. The principal component in the reduced data that explains the least variance is removed iteratively. The mean and covariance are updated, and the algorithm repeats until only one principal component is left.

A recently developed software package for clustering of single cell data is called SC3 [15]. The SC3 package utilises three different metrics for calculation of the distance between cells. They use Euclidean, Pearson's and Spearman's distances. Also, the authors use PCA and graph Laplacian for transforming the data into a lower dimensional space. They then use k-means and select some clusterings corresponding to the reduced dimension for consensus. They choose a range of reduced dimensions and finally perform consensus using various results. While the consensus approach improves clustering accuracy and provides stable cluster assignments, the method is very complicated to use for small datasets.

The clustering packages described here use either centroid based k-means clustering, connectivity based hierarchical clustering or graph-based clustering. The k-means clustering algorithm also commonly referred to as Lloyd's algorithm [17] finds k centroids and assigns each of the samples to its closest centroid to minimise the sum of the squared distance between the centroids and each of its assigned sample point. While the k-means clustering algorithm does converge in finding k optimal centroids or means, it can get stuck in local minima. Another problem is that different initialisation can result in different cluster centroids, which makes the algorithm unstable. Hence, the k-means algorithm is usually run a few times using different initialisation. The k cluster means are the parameters of the algorithm, and it can be initialised by randomly choosing k

samples from the dataset. There are numerous initialisation methods. However, one favorite initialisation technique is kmeans++ [3].

Connectivity-based methods such as hierarchical clustering work by dividing the data points into a hierarchy of clusters. A standard version is agglomerative hierarchical clustering which is the bottoms up approach. Initially, each data point in the training set is its cluster. In other words, all the clusters initially are singletons. Subsequently, pairs of clusters are merged at each step of the algorithm by minimising the linkage criterion until only one cluster remains (containing all the data points). One useful measure is Ward's criterion [25]. Ward's criterion merges two clusters by minimising their within-cluster variance. Thus it is also known as minimum variance criterion. Hierarchical clustering, while giving very stable groupings is prone to noise which can lead to incorrect clusters of the data. Furthermore, computational requirements increase with increasing number of samples.

Graph-based clustering methods treat samples as nodes in a graph. Graph-based clustering methods identify groups of nodes that are highly connected, for example, by constructing a k-nearest neighbour graph. Two nodes can be combined if they share at least one nearest neighbour (shared nearest neighbour). The k in k-nearest neighbour graph affects how many clusters are detected. In the results section, we describe how we used SEURAT which uses graph-based clustering to obtain the desired number of groups. Graph-based methods are more suited to large datasets with a high number of samples.

One of the challenges in clustering single-cell RNA-Seq data is the high dimensionality of the genes in the dataset. For clustering purposes, genes which are expressed in all the cells (ubiquitous genes) do not contribute much to determining the groupings of the cells. On the other hand, genes which are only expressed in a few cells also do not assist to identifying the clusters of the cells. Many of the dimensions also contain noise which can prevent correct clustering of the sample cells. Removing these genes is one way of reducing the dimensionality of the dataset to some extent. This approach is called gene filtering, and many clustering packages such as SC3 and SEURAT use this approach for reducing data dimensionality.

Popular clustering packages discussed here perform feature extraction through PCA, t-SNE or graph Laplacian-based methods prior to clustering. Through such techniques, the features are projected to a lower dimensional space which contains essential information in the data and the dimensions that include noise are removed. Also, these methods do not require grouping information of the samples to be known *a priori*. On the other hand, selecting important features through feature selection for clustering of single cell data has not been explored much. Feature selection involves applying a statistical technique to select informative features or genes in the data. For example, genes with the highest variance across cells could be instructive in determining cell type. Through feature selection, features which do not give valuable information for clustering the samples, or noisy features may be removed.

In this paper, we explore the idea of feature selection for reducing the high dimensionality of gene expression data and for improving clustering accuracy. We propose the concept of first clustering similar features in the data into groups, finding the mean of the feature groups and then iteratively removing those groups of features from the dataset which contain low cluster mean variance across the samples. FeatClust selects the optimal number of feature groups by performing silhouette analysis; that is, computing silhouette score in each iteration after the clustering the samples. FeatClust can additionally generate silhouette plots that can be used to visually determine the number of clusters if it is not known. The method is simple to understand and easy to implement. Also, the clustering results on five small sample single-cell datasets show that this approach successfully removes less informative features and improves clustering accuracy. This paper is organized as follows. Section 2 describes the method in more details. Section 3 presents the clustering results of the technique on three small sample datasets and provides a discussion of the results. Section 4 draws the conclusions and recommendations for future work.

2 FeatClust Method

The proposed FeatClust method takes an iterative feature elimination approach where we first cluster features into some groups and then iteratively remove less important groups of features. The proposed algorithm is given in Algorithm 1. The input to the proposed approach is the gene expression matrix X which is a $d \times n$ matrix where d represents features (or genes), and n represents samples (or cells) and the number of clusters q, which is known a priori. The output y_{samples} is a n-dimensional vector which contains the cluster labels in the range $[1, 2, ..., q]$ of each cell in X.

2.1 Gene Filtering and Normalization

As a pre-processing step, we take the counts or the normalised counts matrix where rows represent genes and columns represent cells and apply log transformation after adding a pseudo-count of 1. Thus we get $X = \log_2(\text{counts} + 1)$. A gene filter is applied which rejects highly and lowly expressed genes. The gene filter removes genes expressed (expression value > 0) in less than $r\%$ of cells and genes expressed in greater than $(100 - r)\%$ of the cells. By default we choose $r = 10$ as ubiquitous and rare genes do not provide much information to improve clustering. This reduces the dimensionality of the cells, thus increasing the computational speed of the method. Finally, the features are normalised to the L2 unit norm. This is done by computing the L2 norm across all samples for each feature and then dividing the feature by the L2 norm.

2.2 Feature Clustering

The proposed approach starts by clustering the features of the input X into k groups, where k can be any integer in the range $[q + 1, q + 2, ..., d]$. If k is

---

Algorithm 1. Proposed FeatClust Algorithm

Input: X a $(d \times n)$ gene expression matrix, q and k
Output: $y_{\text{samples}} \in \{1, 2, ..., q\}$, an n-dimensional vector of cluster labels of the samples

1 Cluster the features of X into k groups using agglomerative clustering
2 For the k feature groups compute cluster centres to get μ_i, where $i = 1, 2, ..., k$ and μ_i is a n-dimensional vector
3 Compute the variance σ_i^2 of μ_i across samples
4 $X' \leftarrow X$
5 $i \leftarrow 0$
6 **for** $j = k$ *to* q **do**
7 $\quad$ Perform hierarchical clustering on samples of X',
   $\quad y_i \leftarrow$ hierarchical_clustering(X', q)
8 $\quad$ s_score$_i \leftarrow$ silhouette_score(X, y_i)
9 $\quad$ Remove all features from X' belonging to feature group having lowest cluster mean variance so that only $j - 1$ feature clusters remain
10 $\quad$ $i \leftarrow i + 1$
11 index $\leftarrow \underset{i}{\arg \max}$ s_score$_i$
12 $y_{\text{samples}} \leftarrow y_{\text{index}}$

---

d, then we have singleton clusters of the features. Setting a very large value of k can slow down the algorithm while on the other hand setting a very small value can result in the algorithm not being able to properly separate and remove low variance features. We suggest setting k to about 20% of n to create a balance between removing less informative features and computational speed of the algorithm. The features are then clustered using agglomerative hierarchical clustering employing Ward linkage criterion and Euclidean distance measure. Once the features are clustered into groups, the cluster centres of the k groups are computed resulting in μ_i which is a n-dimensional vector. The variance σ_i^2, where $i = 1, 2, ..., k$, across samples of each of the feature cluster means is also computed.

The proposed approach then iteratively clusters the samples, again using hierarchical clustering employing Ward's criterion, computes the silhouette score using the cluster labels obtained through hierarchical clustering and then removes the feature group which has the least variance of the cluster means. The iteration starts with all k groups of features and stops when q groups of features remain.

2.3   Optimal Feature Groups

The silhouette score is computed as the mean of individual silhouette coefficient of the samples. The silhouette coefficient for each sample is computed as follows

$$S = \frac{s_n - s_w}{\max(s_w, s_n)} \tag{1}$$

where s_w is the mean within cluster distance and s_n is the mean nearest cluster distance for the sample. Usually, silhouette analysis is done to determine the number of clusters in the dataset visually. We also use silhouette analysis to determine the optimal number of groups of features. To select the optimal number of feature groups, we take the clustering which gives the maximum silhouette score. In addition to clustering, the FeatClust method provides functions to visualise the clustering result as silhouette plots, and its corresponding 2D scatter plot. Figure 1 shows silhouette and its relevant PCA scatter plots in 2D generated by FeatClust for two different clustering results. It is seen that the average silhouette score of all the samples (depicted by the red dashed line) is greater in the plots corresponding to higher ARI score.

3   Results

We tested our clustering method five small sample single cell datasets containing very high dimension. Here we define small sample datasets as datasets having less than 200 samples. These datasets include Biase et al. [4], Yan et al. [27], Goolam et al. [8], Fan et al. [7] and Treutlein et al. [22]. The Biase et al., Goolam et al. and Fan et al. datasets contain single cells from various stages of mouse embryo development. The Yan et al. dataset contains single cells from human preimplantation embryos, and embryonic stem cells and the Treutlein et al. dataset contains single cells from various mouse tissues. A summary of the datasets is given in Table 1.

Table 1. Summary of single cell datasets used in experiments. The last column, clusters, refers to the number of different cell types in the dataset as reported by the original authors.

Dataset	Features (genes)	Samples (cells)	Clusters
Biase	25737	49	3
Yan	20214	90	7
Goolam	41480	124	5
Fan	26357	66	6
Treutlein	23271	80	5

The datasets were downloaded in R `SingleCellExperiment` object format from [1]. The counts/normalised counts and column/row meta-data (e.g., names of genes etc.) were extracted from SCE object and stored in comma-separated values (CSV) files to be accessed by our Python script. We compared our method with the various recent state of the art single cell clustering packages such as SEURAT, SC3, SIMLR [23], pcaReduce, SINCERA [9] and TSCAN [13]. We applied the same pre-processing and normalisation steps as we did in our method to the datasets before running the clustering functions of various methods.

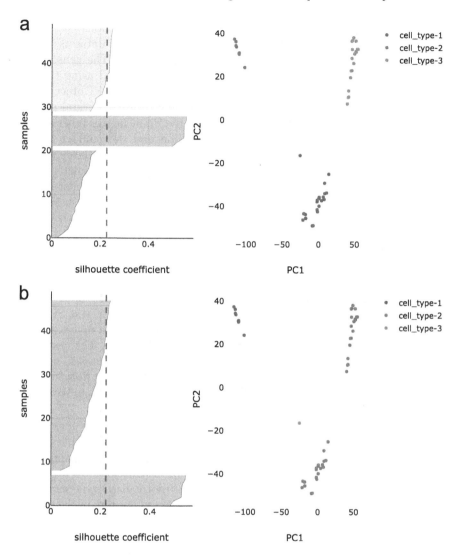

Fig. 1. Silhouette plot and the corresponding PCA 2D scatter plot for Biase et al. dataset for two different clustering results; (a) result with ARI of 0.95 and (b) result with ARI of 0.37. The cells are clustered and labelled by our clustering method, Feat-Clust. The red dotted lines show the average silhouette score for all the samples. The average silhouette score is slightly higher for (a) thus FeatClust selects clustering obtained in (a). One can see that (a) is a better clustering result than (b) because more samples in (a) have higher than average silhouette score and the 2D scatter plot differentiates between the three clusters in the dataset. (Color figure online)

The SEURAT R package was installed using the instructions on [2] on 5 December 2018. To run SEURAT's clustering algorithm on the datasets, we first imported the RDS datasets which were downloaded earlier. The gene expression matrix was extracted, and a SEURAT object was created using the gene expression matrix. PCA was performed separately on the SEURAT object before performing clustering. The SEURAT clustering algorithm had several parameters which we set as follows. All default values of the FindClusters function were used except for the three parameters; k, resolution and the number of principal components to use in the clustering algorithm. k defines the number of neighbours for the k-nearest neighbour algorithm. Resolution parameter can be used to adjust the number of clusters. The resolution and the number of principal components to use was set to 1 and 1:10 (this means use first 10 PC's) respectively. The k parameter was adjusted experimentally to obtain the desired number of clusterings.

The SC3 R package was downloaded and installed from Bioconductor on 19 September 2018. Since SC3 works on single cell experiment (SCE) objects, a `SingleCellExperiment` library and class are needed to create SCE objects and pass it to the SC3 function. The originally downloaded datasets were already SCE objects. Thus, we passed these objects to SC3 function to test SC3. The parameters of SC3 for various datasets were set as follows. The first parameter is ks where we can either give a range of values or a single value. This parameter sets the number of clusters in the SC3 algorithm. For each dataset, we knew the number of clusters. We set this parameter as a single value representing the number of clusters for each dataset. The second parameter is *biology*. We set this as FALSE since we only wanted to test the clustering part of SC3.

The SIMLR R package was downloaded and installed from Bioconductor on 3 March, 2019. An R script was written to test the SIMLR clustering method on the datasets that we have obtained. We followed the examples given in [19] to test SIMLR on our datasets. The parameters of SIMLR were set as follows. The X parameter was set to the preprocessed and normalized gene expression matrix. The c parameter was set to the actual number of clusters in the dataset. The k parameter which is the tuning parameter was set to default value of 10. The rest of the parameters were set to defaults.

The pcaReduce clustering package was downloaded from GitHub https:// github.com/JustinaZ/pcaReduce on 4 March 2019 and installed using the instructions in the readme file. An R script was developed to test the pcaReduce method. The pcaReduce algorithm had four arguments. The first is the D_t which is the dataset argument. We provided the filtered and normalised gene expression matrix. The second parameter is nbt which is the number of times to perform the pcaReduce algorithm. This parameter was set to 100. The next argument is q which refers to the number of reduced dimension to start pcaReduce. This parameter was set to the default 30. The last parameter of pcaReduce is the method parameter. We set it to the character value 'S' which means to perform sample-based merging of clusters.

The SINCERA package was installed on 4 March 2019 following the instructions on their GitHub page https://github.com/xu-lab/SINCERA. An R script was written to test the method on our selected datasets following a demonstration file on their GitHub page. To run SINCERA, an S4 object was created using the filtered and normalized data. Then, PCA was run on the S4 object and finally cluster assignment function was run on the S4 object to obtain the clustering of the datasets. For this method, PCA features were used. The clustering method was hierarchical clustering and the first 10 reduced dimensions were used. The default clustering method in SINCERA was used which is hierarchical clustering with Pearson's correlation distance and average linkage.

The TSCAN package in R was installed directly from Bioconductor on 3 March, 2019. The TSCAN reference manual [14] was followed and an R script was implemented to test the method on our selected datasets. The TSCAN method was relatively simple to test. There is one function `exprmclust` which runs TSCAN clustering on the datasets directly. We passed the filtered and normalized gene expression matrix, together with the target number of clusterings (`clusternum`) into this function. The rest of the parameters were defaults.

The results were compared using the adjusted rand index (ARI) metric which compares two different clusterings. The ARI is defined as follows. Given a set of n samples in the data and two clusterings of these samples, the overlap between the two groupings can be summarized in a contingency table, where each entry n_{ij} represents the number of samples in common between i-th group of the first clustering and the j-th group of the second clustering. The adjusted rand index is computed as follows

$$ARI = \frac{\sum_{ij} \binom{n_{ij}}{2} - \left[\sum_i \binom{a_i}{2} \sum_j \binom{b_j}{2} \right] / \binom{n}{2}}{\frac{1}{2} \left[\sum_i \binom{a_i}{2} + \sum_j \binom{b_j}{2} \right] - \left[\sum_i \binom{a_i}{2} \sum_j \binom{b_j}{2} \right] / \binom{n}{2}} \tag{2}$$

where a_i and b_j are the sums of rows and columns of the contingency table respectively. The ARI values are in the range $[-1, 1]$. A value of 1 indicates perfect grouping. A value of 0 indicates a random assignment of samples to groups, and negative values indicate wrong cluster assignments. For all the datasets we computed the ARI between the cluster assignments obtained by the methods and the original groupings of the samples into cell types. We performed 100 trials for each method on all the datasets as some methods included a random component. The results reflect the median of 100 trials. The ARI of our approach and various methods are shown as a bar plot in Fig. 2. Compared to the rest of the methods FeatClust performed better in four out of the five datasets.

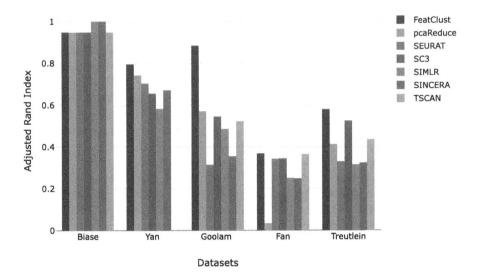

Fig. 2. Bar plot showing the ARI score for various methods on five datasets. FeatClust performs better in clustering in four out of five datasets compared to the rest of the methods. Note that no results for the method TSCAN on the Yan et al. dataset was obtained.

4   Conclusion

We have presented FeatClust, a software tool for clustering and visualisation of small sample size single-cell RNA-seq datasets containing high dimensionality. The method is based on feature selection by iteratively removing groups of features which give less information for performing clustering on the samples. The feature clustering and sample clustering is both performed using agglomerative hierarchical clustering employing Ward linkage criterion. The FeatClust method on each iteration removes the feature cluster group giving least variance, where the variance across samples of the cluster means is computed. The result in terms of ARI on five selected datasets shows the effectiveness of the proposed approach. The FeatClust method can also be applied to cluster larger sample datasets. However, the computation speed will reduce if the sample size increases as the method clusters features also. To take advantage of FeatClust's good clustering capability, we recommend using it in a hybrid approach where a smaller subset of cells can be sampled uniformly from large datasets and clustered using FeatClust. The remaining cells can be classified using supervised learning.

Software Availability. The FeatClust algorithm was implemented in Python programming language and is available on GitHub https://github.com/edwinv87/featclust. The installation and usage instructions are provided on the readme file on GitHub.

References

1. Single-cell RNA-seq datasets. https://hemberg-lab.github.io/scRNA.seq. datasets/. Accessed 08 Sep 2018
2. SEURAT: R toolkit for single cell genomics (2018). https://satijalab.org/seurat/. Accessed 5 Dec 2018
3. Arthur, D., Vassilvitskii, S.: k-means++: the advantages of careful seeding. In: Eighteenth Annual ACM-SIAM Symposium on Discrete Algorithms (2007)
4. Biase, F.H., Cao, X., Zhong, S.: Cell fate inclination within 2-cell and 4-cell mouse embryos revealed by single-cell RNA sequencing. Genome Res. **24**(11), 1787–1796 (2014). https://doi.org/10.1101/gr.177725.114
5. Buettner, F., et al.: Computational analysis of cell-to-cell heterogeneity in single-cell RNA-sequencing data reveals hidden subpopulations of cells. Nat. Biotechnol. **33**(2), 155–160 (2015). https://doi.org/10.1038/nbt.3102
6. Butler, A., Hoffman, P., Smibert, P., Papalexi, E., Satija, R.: Integrating single-cell transcriptomic data across different conditions, technologies, and species. Nat. Biotechnol. **36**(5), 411–420 (2018). https://doi.org/10.1038/nbt.4096
7. Fan, X., et al.: Single-cell RNA-seq transcriptome analysis of linear and circular RNAs in mouse preimplantation embryos. Genome Biol. **16**(1) (2015). https://doi.org/10.1186/s13059-015-0706-1
8. Goolam, M., et al.: Heterogeneity in Oct4 and Sox2 targets biases cell fate in 4-cell mouse embryos. Cell **165**(1), 61–74 (2016). https://doi.org/10.1016/j.cell.2016.01.047
9. Guo, M., Wang, H., Potter, S.S., Whitsett, J.A., Xu, Y.: SINCERA: a pipeline for single-cell RNA-seq profiling analysis. PLOS Comput. Biol. **11**(11), e1004575 (2015). https://doi.org/10.1371/journal.pcbi.1004575
10. Hebenstreit, D.: Methods, challenges and potentials of single cell RNA-seq. Biology **1**(3), 658–667 (2012). https://doi.org/10.3390/biology1030658
11. Islam, S., et al.: Characterization of the single-cell transcriptional landscape by highly multiplex RNA-seq. Genome Res. **21**(7), 1160–1167 (2011). https://doi.org/10.1101/gr.110882.110
12. Jaitin, D.A., et al.: Massively parallel single-cell RNA-seq for marker-free decomposition of tissues into cell types. Science **343**(6172), 776–779 (2014). https://doi.org/10.1126/science.1247651
13. Ji, Z., Ji, H.: TSCAN: pseudo-time reconstruction and evaluation in single-cell RNA-seq analysis. Nucleic Acids Res. **44**(13), e117–e117 (2016). https://doi.org/10.1093/nar/gkw430
14. Ji, Z., Ji, H.: TSCAN: Tools for Single-Cell ANalysis, October 2018. https://bioconductor.org/packages/release/bioc/html/TSCAN.html
15. Kiselev, V.Y., et al.: SC3: consensus clustering of single-cell RNA-seq data. Nat. Methods **14**(5), 483–486 (2017). https://doi.org/10.1038/nmeth.4236
16. Levine, J.H., et al.: Data-driven phenotypic dissection of AML reveals progenitor-like cells that correlate with prognosis. Cell **162**(1), 184–197 (2015). https://doi.org/10.1016/j.cell.2015.05.047
17. Lloyd, S.: Least squares quantization in PCM. IEEE Trans. Inf. Theory **28**(2), 129–137 (1982). https://doi.org/10.1109/tit.1982.1056489
18. Macosko, E.Z., et al.: Highly parallel genome-wide expression profiling of individual cells using nanoliter droplets. Cell **161**(5), 1202–1214 (2015). https://doi.org/10.1016/j.cell.2015.05.002

19. Ramazzotti, D., Wang, B., Sano, L.D., Batzoglou, S.: Single-cell Interpretation via Multi-kernel LeaRning (SIMLR), January 2019
20. Satija, R., Farrell, J.A., Gennert, D., Schier, A.F., Regev, A.: Spatial reconstruction of single-cell gene expression data. Nat. Biotechnol. **33**(5), 495–502 (2015). https://doi.org/10.1038/nbt.3192
21. Tang, F., et al.: mRNA-seq whole-transcriptome analysis of a single cell. Nat. Methods **6**(5), 377–382 (2009). https://doi.org/10.1038/nmeth.1315
22. Treutlein, B., et al.: Reconstructing lineage hierarchies of the distal lung epithelium using single-cell RNA-seq. Nature **509**(7500), 371–375 (2014). https://doi.org/10.1038/nature13173
23. Wang, B., Zhu, J., Pierson, E., Ramazzotti, D., Batzoglou, S.: Visualization and analysis of single-cell RNA-seq data by kernel-based similarity learning. Nat. Methods **14**(4), 414–416 (2017). https://doi.org/10.1038/nmeth.4207
24. Wang, D., Bodovitz, S.: Single cell analysis: the new frontier in 'omics'. Trends Biotechnol. **28**(6), 281–290 (2010). https://doi.org/10.1016/j.tibtech.2010.03.002
25. Ward, J.H.: Hierarchical grouping to optimize an objective function. J. Am. Stat. Assoc. **58**(301), 236–244 (1963). https://doi.org/10.1080/01621459.1963.10500845
26. Xu, C., Su, Z.: Identification of cell types from single-cell transcriptomes using a novel clustering method. Bioinformatics **31**(12), 1974–1980 (2015). https://doi.org/10.1093/bioinformatics/btv088
27. Yan, L., et al.: Single-cell RNA-seq profiling of human preimplantation embryos and embryonic stem cells. Nat. Struct. Mol. Biol. **20**(9), 1131–1139 (2013). https://doi.org/10.1038/nsmb.2660
28. Žurauskienė, J., Yau, C.: pcaReduce: hierarchical clustering of single cell transcriptional profiles. BMC Bioinform. **17**(1) (2016). https://doi.org/10.1186/s12859-016-0984-y

Stratifying Risk of Coronary Artery Disease Using Discriminative Knowledge-Guided Medical Concept Pairings from Clinical Notes

Mahdi Abdollahi[1(✉)], Xiaoying Gao[1], Yi Mei[1], Shameek Ghosh[2], and Jinyan Li[3]

[1] Victoria University of Wellington, Wellington, New Zealand
{mahdi.abdollahi,xiaoying.gao,yi.mei}@ecs.vuw.ac.nz
[2] Medius Health, Sydney, Australia
shameek.ghosh@mediushealth.org
[3] University of Technology Sydney, Sydney, Australia
Jinyan.Li@uts.edu.au

Abstract. Document classification (DC) is one of the broadly investigated natural language processing tasks. Medical document classification can support doctors in making decision and improve medical services. Since the data in document classification often appear in raw form such as medical discharge notes, extracting meaningful information to use as features is a challenging task. There are many specialized words and expressions in medical documents which make them more challenging to analyze. The classification accuracy of available methods in medical field is not good enough. This work aims to improve the quality of the input feature sets to increase the accuracy. A new three-stage approach is proposed. In the first stage, the Unified Medical Language System (UMLS) which is a medical-specific dictionary is used to extract the meaningful phrases by considering disease or symptom concepts. In the second stage, all the possible pairs of the extracted concepts are created as new features. In the third stage, Particle Swarm Optimisation (PSO) is employed to select features from the extracted and constructed features in the previous stages. The experimental results show that the proposed three-stage method achieved substantial improvement over the existing medical DC approaches.

Keywords: Medical text classification · Particle swarm optimization · Feature selection · Feature construction · Conceptualization · Ontology

1 Introduction

Document classification has many important applications such as filtering spam emails, labeling client queries and tagging patient reports. In general, text mining

© Springer Nature Switzerland AG 2019
A. C. Nayak and A. Sharma (Eds.): PRICAI 2019, LNAI 11672, pp. 457–473, 2019.
https://doi.org/10.1007/978-3-030-29894-4_37

includes preprocessing, representing text, weighting features, selecting features, training, testing and evaluating.

There is a principal difference between clinical text mining and standard text mining in terms of text terminology and their frequency. In clinical text mining, the text describes a set of clinical events within a narrative, with the goal of producing an explanation as precisely and comprehensively as possible when describing the health status of a patient. Generally, such text heavily uses domain-specific terminology and acronyms, making clinical text analysis very different from standard text mining. Moreover, various combinations of domain-specific medical events in a clinical report can describe patient's conditions totally differently. Hence, extracting meaningful information to analyze medical discharge notes is very important.

Information extraction (IE) task targets to extract structured information from the unstructured and semi-structured texts. The process involves transforming an unstructured text or a collection of texts into structured data that can be used in a database. As our society became more data oriented, many different communities of researchers bring in techniques from machine learning, databases, information retrieval, and computational linguistics for various aspects of the information extraction problem in different fields such as the medical domain.

In medical document classification, there are thousands of features and often there are redundant and irrelevant features which can make noise in the training step to create a model. Consequently, the obtained model may have poor classification accuracy. This issue can be addressed by utilizing feature engineering approaches such as feature selection (Bai et al. 2018) and feature construction to improve the quality of features by removing irrelevant and noisy features.

Most previous approaches for document classification are not effective enough for feature extraction due to a large number of redundant features (Bai et al. 2018). To solve this issue and improve the performance of document classification, this paper proposes a three-stage method by using discriminative knowledge-guided medical concept pairings from clinical notes for stratifying risk of coronary artery disease (CAD).

In this method, a tool is employed to extract concepts and detect most related features to the candidate classification problem. As medical domain is the main focus, a domain-specific ontology is used for feature extraction. After extracting features from the documents, all the possible pairs of the extracted features are constructed to create new features. Then, particle swarm optimization (PSO) is utilized for feature selection. This paper aims to investigate the following research questions:

1. Whether the concept pairs can construct meaningful features from the extracted information of document set;
2. Whether PSO can reduce the number of features and keep the meaningful features; and
3. Whether the suggested approach can increase the classification accuracy in the aimed clinical notes classification.

The rest of the paper is organized as follows: Sect. 2 gives the problem description and related works. The proposed method is described in Sect. 3. The experiment design and results are presented in Sects. 4 and 5. At the end, the conclusions and future works are showed in Sect. 6.

2   Background

2.1   Document Classification in Medical Domain

The first application of classifier models in predicting medical research results was presented in (Bellazzi and Zupan 2008). In this study, the authors tried to make use of data mining in the field of medicine. Yoo et al. investigated the advantages and disadvantages of using data mining algorithms in the biomedical field (Yoo et al. 2012), in which the proposed medical features include prediction health costs, prognosis and diagnosis, hidden knowledge from biomedicine data, relationship among diseases and among drugs are tested using data mining methods, and the extracted information is used in prediction. In (Wagholikar et al. 2012) more than ten methods have been used to identify more than ten types of diseases. Based on the results of this study, the efficacy of these methods is better for some diseases such as gastroenterology, oncology and cardiovascular.

2.2   Information Extraction in Medical Document Classification

There has been research on using statistical methods from the distribution of the features in document classification problems for ranking features (Shah and Patel 2016). Existing methods employed metrics associated with word frequency, information gain, mutual information, term frequency-inverse document frequency (tf-idf) for extracting textual features. However, they tend to treat each feature separately, and ignore the dependencies between features. Ontology-based classification methods is introduced in (Dollah and Aono 2011). They use ontologies such as Medical Subject Headings (MeSH), Systematized Nomenclature of Medicine (SNOMED) and Unified Medical Language System (UMLS) to improve classification.

Clinical documents has been used in tasks such as finding risk factors for diabetic patients, assessing Framingham risk score (FRF) for candidate population, distinguishing heart disease risk factors, and finding the risk of heart disease (Shivade et al. 2015). In this research, we use ontology as a feature extraction technique for document classification to identify Coronary Artery Disease (CAD).

2.3   Feature Selection in Medical Document Classification

In medical document classification, choosing a more efficient feature selection method that works with small sets of features from a high dimensional set of features is necessary. In some research, traditional feature selection methods, such as information gain, are generally employed (Gaizauskas et al. 2014).

And then, after selecting a small set of features, learning algorithms such as Support Vector Machine (SVM) are used to learn classifiers. One of the promising methods in feature selection is PSO.

PSO has been used to predict and analyze different diseases in medical field. For example, (Eberhart and Hu 1999) utilized PSO to check human tremor. PSO is used to improve a neural network that makes a distinction between normal people and those have tremor. Fong et al. (2014) employed PSO to find optimal feature subsets.

3   Our Three-Stage Method

In this section, the developed three-stage algorithm and the employed tools for extracting concepts of phrases and constructing new features are described in detail. Figure 1 presents the flowchart of the proposed three-stage method.

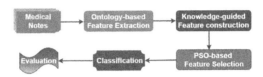

Fig. 1. The proposed three-stage method

The input of the proposed method is a set of medical discharge notes. Firstly, the method detects all of the meaningful phrases in the discharge notes by utilizing the MetaMap tool (Aronson and Lang 2010) to extract their concepts from the United Medical Language System (UMLS). After eliminating unrelated features in the first stage, all the possible pairs of extracted expressions are created as the constructed features. Then, Particle Swarm Optimisation (PSO) is applied to select a feature subset from all of the extracted features in the first stage and the constructed features in the second stage. The classifier is learned along with the PSO feature selection.

It is expected that the proposed algorithm extracts meaningful features and selects more informative subset of the constructed features and maintains or enhances the classification accuracy.

3.1   Feature Extraction Method

UMLS is a dictionary in the biomedical area. An ontology structure of clinical vocabulary concepts is provided by UMLS. In this work our medical documents are the inputs of UMLS, and the detected meaningful expressions are the outputs. In the first stage, the MetaMap tool is utilized to send all of the discharge documents to UMLS to extract the concepts of the detected meaningful expressions. Then, the classification task and the target label of the candidate problem is considered in the concept selection step. As the class label of the problem is the name of a disease and diseases have symptoms, all of the phrases whose concepts belong to "Disease or Syndrome" or "Sign or Symptom" are selected as a feature subset and the rest of the concepts are deleted. Figure 2 shows the outline of the feature extraction and feature construction method.

A paragraph is given below as an example to describe how MetaMap works on the input discharge notes and what output it provides in classification process. Below is an example of a raw clinical notes.

"Hyperlipidemia: The patient's Lipitor was increased to 80 mg q.d. A progress note in the patient's chart from her assisted living facility indicates that the patient has had shortness of breath for one day. The patient is a 63-year-old female with a three-year history of occasional weakness. Increasing large right-sided pulmonary edema."

Figure 3 presents the extracted concepts from MetaMap for the detected meaningful expressions from the notes. Table 1 shows the detected phrases based on their concepts. Some of the phrases such as "hyperlipidemia" and "shortest of breath" belong to more than one concept. As this research targets "[Disease or Syndrome]" and "[Sign or Symptom]" concepts, the scientific names of "hyperlipidaemia", "shortness of breath", "weakness" and "pulmonary oedema" are selected as a feature subset and the rest of the concepts are deleted. The scientific names of the expressions "Hyperlipidemia", "Dyspnea", "Weakness" and "Pulmonary Edema" are shown in lines 7, 19, 32 and 40 of Fig. 3, respectively.

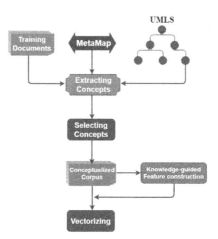

Fig. 2. Feature extraction method

```
1  Phrase: hyperlipidemia .
2  >>>>> Phrase
3  hyperlipidemia
4  <<<<< Phrase
5  >>>>> Mappings
6  Meta Mapping (1000):
7     1000   Hyperlipidaemia, NOS (Hyperlipidemia) [Disease or Syndrome]
8  Meta Mapping (1000):
9     1000   Hyperlipidemia (Serum lipids high (finding)) [Finding]
10 <<<<< Mappings
11 Processing 00000000.tx.7: MEDICATIONS ON ADMISSION : Lipitor , Flexeril ,
12 hydrochlorothiazide and Norvasc .
```
```
13 Phrase: shortness of breath
14 >>>>> Phrase
15 shortness of breath
16 <<<<< Phrase
17 >>>>> Mappings
18 Meta Mapping (1000):
19    1000   SHORTNESS OF BREATH (Dyspnea) [Sign or Symptom]
20 Meta Mapping (1000):
21    1000   shortness of breath (Shortness of breath:-:Point in time:^Patient:-) [Clinical Attribute]
22 Meta Mapping (1000):
23    1000   Shortness of breath (How Often Shortness of Breath) [Intellectual Product]
24 <<<<< Mappings
```
```
25 Phrase: occasional weakness
26 >>>>> Phrase
27 occasional weakness
28 <<<<< Phrase
29 >>>>> Mappings
30 Meta Mapping (644):
31    569   Occasional (Infrequent) [Temporal Concept]
32    569   WEAKNESS (weakness) [Sign or Symptom]
33<<<<< Mappings
```
```
34 Phrase: pulmonary edema
35 >>>>> Phrase
36 pulmonary edema
37 <<<<< Phrase
38 >>>>> Mappings
39 Meta Mapping (1000):
40    1000   PULMONARY OEDEMA (Pulmonary Edema) [Disease or Syndrome]
43 <<<<< Mappings
```

Fig. 3. A segment of returned results of extracted concepts using MetaMap

3.2   Feature Construction Method

After the feature extraction, the obtained features are used to construct new features. To consider the relationship between the extracted diseases and symptoms, all of the possible pairs of (disease, disease), (disease, symptom) and (symptom,

Table 1. The extracted concepts of the example notes using MetaMap.

Sentences	Detected phrases	Extracted concepts	Selected
First sentence	Hyperlipidaemia	**[Disease or Syndrome]**	✓
		[Finding]	✗
	Patient	[Patient or Disabled group]	✗
	Lipitor	[Organic Chemical, Pharmacologic Substance]	✗
	80%	[Quantitative Concept]	✗
	mg++ increased	[Finding]	✗
Second sentence	Progress note	[Clinical Attribute]	✗
		[Intellectual Product]	✗
	Patient chart	[Manufactured Object]	✗
	Assisted living facility	Healthcare Related Organization, Manufactured Object	✗
	Patient	[Patient or Disabled group]	✗
	Shortness of breath	**[Sign or Symptom]**	✓
		[Clinical Attribute]	✗
		[Intellectual Product]	✗
	One day	[Temporal Concept]	✗
Third sentence	Occasional	[Temporal Concept]	✗
	Weakness	**[Sign or Symptom]**	✓
Fourth sentence	Pulmonary oedema	**[Disease or Syndrome]**	✓

symptom) are constructed for each document and added to the extracted features. Table 2 shows the constructed features for the extracted features from the sample sentences.

Table 2. The constructed features for the extracted features from the sample sentences

Cases	Pairs	Constructed Features
Case 1	(Disease, Disease)	(Hyperlipidemia, Pulmonary Edema)
Case 2	(Disease, Symptom)	(Hyperlipidemia, Dyspnea), (Hyperlipidemia, Weakness), (Pulmonary Edema, Dyspnea), (Pulmonary Edema, Weakness)
Case 3	(Symptom, Symptom)	(Dyspnea, Weakness)
Case 4	Case 1 + Case 2	(Hyperlipidemia, Pulmonary Edema), (Hyperlipidemia, Dyspnea), (Hyperlipidemia, Weakness), (Pulmonary Edema, Dyspnea), (Pulmonary Edema, Weakness)
Case 5	Case 1 + Case 3	(Hyperlipidemia, Pulmonary Edema), (Dyspnea, Weakness)
Case 6	Case 2 + Case 3	(Hyperlipidemia, Dyspnea), (Hyperlipidemia, Weakness), (Pulmonary Edema, Dyspnea), (Pulmonary Edema, Weakness), (Dyspnea, Weakness)
Case 7	Case 1 + Case 2 + Case 3	(Hyperlipidemia, Pulmonary Edema), (Hyperlipidemia, Dyspnea), (Hyperlipidemia, Weakness), (Pulmonary Edema, Dyspnea), (Pulmonary Edema, Weakness), (Dyspnea, Weakness)

After the feature construction step, all of the created pairs are added to the obtained feature set in the concept selection step. In Table 2, the last column presents the total feature size for each case. The obtained output will be used instead of the original documents in the binary classification problem. The first stage keeps the informative features and the second stage enrich the feature set. For giving weights to the extracted phrases of the documents, TF-IDF is utilized in the vectorization phase and each document is represented as a vector of weights based on the TF-IDF function.

3.3   PSO-Based Algorithm for Feature Selection

In the second step, different pairs are made from disease and symptoms. As the pairs are constructed using all the extracted features, there might be redundant features among the obtained feature set. Hence, it is necessary to do feature selection. In this stage, PSO is applied to remove the irrelevant and unnecessary features from the extracted and constructed features in the first and second stage. The value for each particle is initialized randomly between $[-1, 1]$. Each particle in PSO indicates a feature subset and is represented as a vector. For instance, a negative value indicates the feature is not selected and a positive value means the feature is selected. The dimension of each vector is d and each vector includes real numbers. The dimension of the search space is represented by d which is equal to the size of the obtained features by the first and second steps.

Table 3. Possible Pairs and the number of features

Cases	Pairs	Number of original features (100%)	Number of UMLS features (10.33%)	Number of features (UMLS + Pairs)(%)
Case 1	(Disease, Disease)	7554	780	10107(133.80)
Case 2	(Disease, Symptom)	7554	780	11261(149.07)
Case 3	(Symptom, Symptom)	7554	780	4199(55.59)
Case 4	(Disease, Disease) + (Disease, Symptom)	7554	780	20578(272.41)
Case 5	(Disease, Disease) + (Symptom, Symptom)	7554	780	13518(178.95)
Case 6	(Disease, Symptom) + (Symptom, Symptom)	7554	780	14670(194.20)
Case 7	(Disease, Disease) + (Disease, Symptom) + (Symptom, Symptom)	7554	780	24074(318.69)

The position and velocity of each particle is initialized randomly. Then, particles moves by updating their *gbest* (the best position) and *pbest* (best position has found so far). At the end of the method, *gbest* is found using the fitness values of particles and also the obtained best particle is used to form the selected feature set. Algorithm 1 shows the pseudocode for PSO for feature selection in the third stage. The fitness value for each particle is calculated by the classification accuracy (see line 5).

The method used in this work is a wrapper approach. Hence, a classifier is utilized to run with PSO to calculate the value of fitness function.

Algorithm 1. Pseudo-code of PSO to select the best feature subset

```
Input  : Training instances
Output : The best feature subset (gbest)
1:  Keep only the features that are extracted in the first and second stages;
2:  Randomly initialize the position and velocity of particles;
3:  iter ← 0
4:  while iter < maxIter do
5:      Evaluation: Evaluate fitness of particles based on classification accuracy on the training set;
6:      for i = 1 to |Particle| do
7:          Update pbest and gbest for particle i;
8:      end
9:      for i = 1 to |Particle| do
10:         for d = 1 to dimension do
11:             Update the velocity of particle i
12:             Update the position of particle i
13:         end
14:     end
15:     iter ← iter + 1
16: end
17: return the position of gbest;
```

The process of calculating the fitness function value for each particle is presented in Fig. 4. All of the training documents are feeded as input to PSO for selecting features. Fitness value of a particle is computed by 10-fold cross validation. The training document set is separated into 10 subsets. One training subset is used for evaluating the particle's fitness value and the nine remained training subsets are utilized as input to PSO for training a classifier. The fitness value of a particle is the average of computed ten classification accuracies. In this stage, only the training set is considered to train the candidate classifier and the test set is only utilized after the training to evaluate the classification accuracy of the selected best feature subsets.

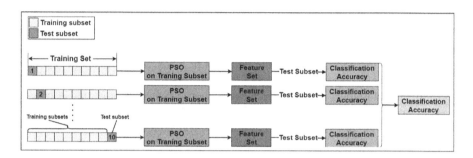

Fig. 4. PSO for feature selection using 10 fold cross validation

4   Experimental Design

4.1   Dataset and Preprocessing

The performance of the proposed three-stage method is evaluated on the 2010 Informatics for Integrating Biology and the Bedside (i2b2) data set. The labels of the 2010 i2b2 data set are CAD (Coronary Artery Disease) and non-CAD that form a binary classification problem. The data set includes 426 documents which 170 documents for training and 256 documents for testing. All of the features are extracted by considering two specific concepts ("Disease or Syndrome" and "Sign or Symptom") by employing the MetaMap tool and utilizing the UMLS. Then, all of the possible pairs of obtained features are constructed for the output of each document separately. Next, the following preprocessing steps are applied on the obtained results of the feature extraction step:

- Hold only words and delete punctuation, numbers, etc. Convert all words to lowercase.
- Delete words which are less than 3 letters long. For example, removing "am" but keeping "are".
- Remove the 524 SMART stopwords.
- Extract stems of the remained words.

4.2 Parameter Settings

The 2010 i2b2 data set includes 426 documents with 7554 various terms. Table 3 shows the total number of attributes for each case after applying the first and second stages (check the last column). Five different classifiers (Logistic Regression (LR), Linear Support Vector Machine (LSVM), Naive Bayes (NB), Decision Tree (DT) and K-Nearest Neighbor (KNN)) are employed for the experimental comparison. The classification accuracy is calculated on the testing documents to evaluate the performance of the classifiers. Table 4 presents the set parameters of PSO which are proposed in (Bai et al. 2018). The values for particles are initialised using numbers in $[-1, 1]$, and the threshold (θ) is set to zero, hence, about 50% of the features will be selected. Some documents will disappear if less than 50% of features are selected.

Some of the classifiers' parameters are tuned to get better results. The inverse of regularization strength ("C") is adjusted to 10 in the Logistic Regression. The number of the neighbors is set to the value 28 in KNN. The maximum depth of the tree and the random number generator are adjusted to values 14 and 11 in Decision Tree classifier, respectively. Furthermore, early stopping rule is chosen to avoid overfitting in training Linear SVM and Logistic Regression classifiers. The rest of the classifiers' parameters are kept the same as default values.

Table 4. PSO parameter setting

PSO Parameters	Value
Population size	30
Maximum number of iteration	100
Dimension of All+PSO (Abdollahi et al. 2019)	7554
Dimension of UMLS+PSO (Abdollahi et al. 2019)	780
Dimension of case 1	10107
Dimension of case 2	11261
Dimension of case 3	4199
Dimension of case 4	20578
Dimension of case 5	13518
Dimension of case 6	14670
Dimension of case 7	24074
Velocity	$[-3, 3]$
Threshold (θ)	0
Acceleration coefficients	2.0
Run times	40

5   Results and Further Analysis

5.1   Results

Five different classifiers are employed to assess the proposed approach, and the results are shown in Figs. 5, 6, 7, 8 and 9 for each classifier respectively. Our three-stage approach has seven cases (case1 to case7) and they use different pair combinations shown in Table 3. The seven methods are compared with four other methods: "All_Deter" which uses all unique term features; "UMLS_Deter" which uses UMLS concepts as features; "All+PSO" (Abdollahi et al. 2019) which uses PSO to select features from all terms; and "UMLS+PSO" (Abdollahi et al. 2019) which uses PSO to select from UMLS concepts. The efficiency of the classifiers are assessed based on classification accuracy. From Figs. 5, 6, 7, 8 and 9 it is obvious that the proposed technique with three stages (case 1 to case 7) is significantly better than the other compared methods.

5.2   Further Analysis

Number of Selected Features: Table 5 shows the average (and standard deviation values for stochastic methods) of the selected features by different approaches. "Original", "UMLS" and "UMLS+Pairs" methods are deterministic and use all of the features without any feature selection. "Original" is using all unique terms in the original documents. "UMLS" approach is using the extracted features from UMLS by applying MetaMap tool. "UMLS+Pairs" method is utilizing the detected features from UMLS and the constructed pairs of features. "All+PSO" (Abdollahi et al. 2019), "UMLS+PSO" (Abdollahi et al. 2019) and "UMLS+Pairs+PSO" are stochastic methods by applying PSO to select a feature subset. The smallest feature subset belongs to "UMLS+PSO" method which contains only 10.33% of the original features. The smallest number of features is allocated for case 3 in "UMLS+Pairs" and "UMLS+Pairs+PSO" with 55.59% and 27.02%, respectively. By comparing the number of the selected features for the deterministic and stochastic versions of the proposed approach, it can be concluded that case 3 has the smallest size of the features in both methods which is

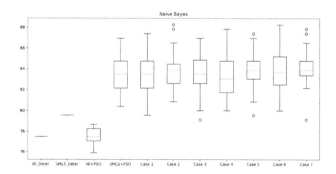

Fig. 5. Comparison of Naive Bayes classifier accuracy

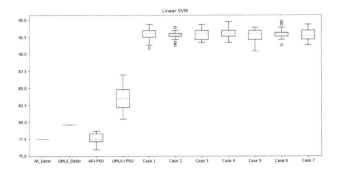

Fig. 6. Comparison of Linear SVM Classifier accuracy

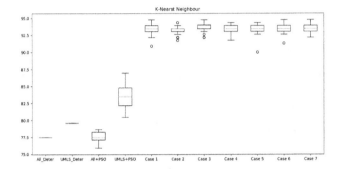

Fig. 7. Comparison of k-Nearest Neighbor classifiers accuracy

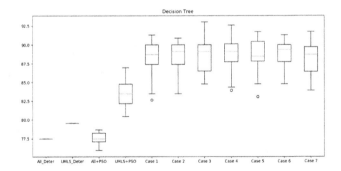

Fig. 8. Comparison of Decision Tree classifier accuracy

smaller than "Original" method's feature size and the feature size of stochastic method is approximately 50% smaller than the deterministic method.

With or Without PSO: Table 6 compares the statistical results of the deterministic and stochastic versions of the proposed approach with the pairs.

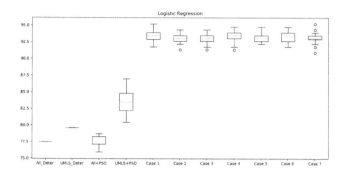

Fig. 9. Comparison of Logistic Regression classifier accuracy

Table 5. Number of selected features

#	Classifiers	NB	LSVM	KNN	DT	LR
	Cases	Ave±Std				
1	Original (100%) (Abdollahi et al. 2018)	7554	7554	7554	7554	7554
2	UMLS (Abdollahi et al. 2018)	780	780	780	780	780
3	All+PSO (Abdollahi et al. 2019)	3779.35 ± 38.01	3768.75 ± 48.22	3774.13 ± 39.36	3775.25 ± 43.04	3767.65 ± 32.77
4	UMLS+PSO (Abdollahi et al. 2019)	387.20 ± 14.61	386.08 ± 14.79	394.35 ± 10.68	388.60 ± 15.14	388.25 ± 12.31
5	UMLS+Pairs (Case 1)	10107	10107	10107	10107	10107
6	UMLS+Pairs (Case 2)	11261	11261	11261	11261	11261
7	UMLS+Pairs (Case 3)	4199	4199	4199	4199	4199
8	UMLS+Pairs (Case 4)	20578	20578	20578	20578	20578
9	UMLS+Pairs (Case 5)	13518	13518	13518	13518	13518
10	UMLS+Pairs (Case 6)	14670	14670	14670	14670	14670
11	UMLS+Pairs (Case 7)	24074	24074	24074	24074	24074
12	UMLS+Pairs+ PSO (Case 1)	5051.68 ± 56.22	5055.95 ± 51.53	5048.78 ± 52.02	5049.85 ± 55.25	5041.68 ± 53.57
13	UMLS+Pairs+ PSO (Case 2)	5630.18 ± 56.41	5625.6 ± 53.50	5616.0 ± 44.85	5625.1 ± 51.37	5630.55 ± 54.53
14	UMLS+Pairs+ PSO (Case 3)	2097.25 ± 34.79	2090.85 ± 34.84	2100.0 ± 35.59	2089.93 ± 33.19	2103.33 ± 29.34
15	UMLS+Pairs+ PSO (Case 4)	10276.4 ± 81.09	10292.38 ± 81.56	10275.6±83.59	10288.23 ± 67.09	10274.93 ± 80.68
16	UMLS+Pairs+ PSO (Case 5)	6756.98±71.62	6747.9 ± 59.01	6762.73 ± 47.58	6763.4 ± 63.10	6752.05 ± 56.78
17	UMLS+Pairs+ PSO (Case 6)	7310.73 ± 53.22	7329.95 ± 55.86	7343.43 ± 59.93	7343.9 ± 68.94	7329.78 ± 59.80
18	UMLS+Pairs+ PSO (Case 7)	12038.48 ± 75.39	12042.25 ± 79.63	12037.60 ± 62.95	12035.55 ± 77.71	12026.95 ± 69.64

Table 6. Accuracy of Classifiers for the Seven Cases without PSO and with PSO

Classifiers	NB		LSVM		KNN		DT		LR	
Cases	Accuracy (%) Ave±Std									
	Without PSO	With PSO	Without PSO	With PSO	Without PSO	With PSO	Without PSO	With PSO	Without PSO	With PSO
Case 1	81.05 ± 0.00	**83.47** ± 0.018	92.49 ± 0.00	**92.75** ± 0.007	92.09 ± 0.00	**93.32** ± 0.007	**91.30±0.00**	88.50 ± 0.022	92.89 ± 0.00	**93.32** ± 0.007
Case 2	81.42 ± 0.00	**83.85** ± 0.016	92.49 ± 0.00	**92.80** ± 0.006	**93.28 ± 0.00**	93.22 ± 0.006	**92.09 ± 0.00**	88.49 ± 0.019	92.09 ± 0.00	**93.03** ± 0.006
Case 3	79.45 ± 0.00	**83.66** ± 0.017	92.89 ± 0.00	**92.98** ± 0.007	92.89 ± 0.00	**92.98** ± 0.007	90.12 ± 0.00	**88.42 ± 0.020**	92.49 ± 0.00	**92.91** ± 0.007
Case 4	81.03 ± 0.00	**83.39** ± 0.019	92.89 ± 0.00	**92.97** ± 0.007	93.28 ± 0.00	**93.37** ± 0.006	**91.70 ± 0.00**	88.85 ± 0.021	91.70 ± 0.00	**93.35** ± 0.008
Case 5	81.03 ± 0.00	**83.84** ± 0.017	93.28 ± 0.00	92.77 ± 0.008	91.30 ± 0.00	**93.33** ± 0.007	88.14 ± 0.00	**88.60 ± 0.020**	91.70 ± 0.00	**92.97** ± 0.006
Case 6	81.42 ± 0.00	**83.79** ± 0.021	92.49 ± 0.00	**92.99** ± 0.007	92.49 ± 0.00	**93.52** ± 0.007	**90.91 ± 0.00**	88.92 ± 0.016	90.91 ± 0.00	**93.34** ± 0.008
Case 7	81.03 ± 0.00	**84.05** ± 0.016	92.49 ± 0.00	**92.90** ± 0.008	93.28 ± 0.00	**93.47** ± 0.005	86.56 ± 0.00	**88.10 ± 0.022**	91.30 ± 0.00	**93.15** ± 0.007

Table 7. Comparison of classification accuracy and standard deviation averages using 40 independent runs. The highlighted entries are significantly better (Wilcoxon Test, $\alpha = 0.05$)

Methods	Three-Stage (Stochastic)		All (Deterministic) (Abdollahi et al. 2018)		UMLS (Deterministic) (Abdollahi et al. 2018)		UMLS+Pairs (Deterministic)		All+PSO (Stochastic) (Abdollahi et al. 2019)			Two-Stage (Stochastic) (Abdollahi et al. 2019)		
Classifiers	Accuracy Ave±Std	Accuracy Best(Lowest)	Accuracy	T	Accuracy	T	Accuracy	T	Accuracy Ave±Std	Accuracy Best(Lowest)	T	Accuracy Ave±Std	Accuracy Best(Lowest)	T
NB	**83.79 ± 0.021**	**88.26(80.00)**	77.47	+	79.57	+	81.42	+	77.58 ± 0.007	78.66(75.89)	+	83.50 ± 0.018	86.96(80.43)	+
LSVM	**92.99 ± 0.007**	**94.78(91.30)**	87.35	+	92.61	+	92.49	+	87.22 ± 0.008	88.93(84.98)	+	92.87 ± 0.007	93.91(91.30)	+
KNN	93.52 ± 0.007	**94.78(91.30)**	84.98	+	94.78	+	93.28	+	86.80 ± 0.014	89.33(82.21)	+	93.61 ± 0.005	94.78(92.61)	=
DT	88.92 ± 0.016	91.30(84.78)	85.77	+	87.39	+	92.09	−	90.09 ± 0.011	**92.25(86.96)**	−	88.71 ± 0.021	91.30(82.61)	=
LR	**93.34 ± 0.008**	**94.78(91.74)**	86.96	+	92.61	+	92.09	+	87.62 ± 0.008	89.33(86.17)	+	93.27 ± 0.007	94.35(91.74)	+

The best results are highlighted and three-stage method (with PSO) shows better performance than two-stage method (without PSO) (Abdollahi et al. 2019) in Naive Bayes, Linear SVM, KNN and Logistic Regression classifiers.

Significance Test: The suggested three-stage approach is applied on the training set using 40 independent PSO runs. Next, the quality of the selected feature subsets is evaluated on the test set by using the gained best feature subsets from each run. The experimental results are computed by considering the classification accuracies of the 40 selected feature subsets. Table 7 compares the statistical results for six approaches. The standard deviation and average of accuracies are calculated for all of the classifiers and the Wilcoxon signed ranks test with significance level of 0.05 is used to test whether the suggested approach has made significant difference in classification accuracy. In Table 7, "T" column presents the significance test of the proposed approach against the other five approaches, where "+" means the suggested three-stage method is significantly more accurate, "=" means no significant difference, and "−" means significantly less accurate. The best results are highlighted in the table.

6 Conclusions and Future Work

This work introduces a three-stage method to utilise domain concepts and their relations to enrich the input data for a classification problem. The proposed approach is able to improve the quality of the input data set by constructing new features and increase the classification accuracy in the majority of the targeted classifiers. From the experimental and statistical examinations it can be seen that the suggested approach can achieve significantly better classification accuracy.

This work shows promise in using a third-stage feature extraction, construction and selection method in clinical document classification, however, it still needs more research to improve the classification performance. We will study other ways to construct features for the second stage by analyzing the distance of the detected features in the document to guide our feature construction method in making pairs. In the meantime, we will consider different fitness functions to enhance the PSO method.

References

Abdollahi, M., Gao, X., Mei, Y., Ghosh, S., Li, J.: Uncovering discriminative knowledge-guided medical concepts for classifying coronary artery disease notes. In: Mitrovic, T., Xue, B., Li, X. (eds.) AI 2018. LNCS (LNAI), vol. 11320, pp. 104–110. Springer, Cham (2018). https://doi.org/10.1007/978-3-030-03991-2_11

Abdollahi, M., Gao, X., Mei, X., Ghosh, S., Li, J.: An ontology-based two-stage approach to medical text classification with feature selection by particle swarm optimisation. In: 2019 IEEE Congress on Evolutionary Computation (CEC), pp. 1–8. IEEE (2019)

Aronson, A.R., Lang, F.-M.: An overview of metamap: historical perspective and recent advances. J. Am. Med. Inform. Assoc. **17**(3), 229–236 (2010)

Bai, X., Gao, X., Xue, B.: Particle swarm optimization based two-stage feature selection in text mining. In: 2018 IEEE Congress on Evolutionary Computation (CEC), pp. 1–8. IEEE (2018)

Bellazzi, R., Zupan, B.: Predictive data mining in clinical medicine: current issues and guidelines. Int. J. Med. Inform. **77**(2), 81–97 (2008)

Dollah, R.B., Aono, M.: Ontology based approach for classifying biomedical text abstracts. Int. J. Data Eng. **2**(1), 1–15 (2011)

Eberhart, R.C., Hu, X.: Human tremor analysis using particle swarm optimization. In: Proceedings of the 1999 Congress on Evolutionary Computation-CEC99, vol. 3, pp. 1927–1930. IEEE (1999)

Fong, S., Deb, S., Yang, X.-S., Li, J.: Feature selection in life science classification: metaheuristic swarm search. IT Prof. **16**(4), 24–29 (2014)

Gaizauskas, R., Barker, E., Paramita, M.L., Aker, A.: Assigning terms to domains by document classification. In: Proceedings of the 4th International Workshop on Computational Terminology (Computerm), pp. 11–21 (2014)

Shah, F.P., Patel, V.: A review on feature selection and feature extraction for text classification. In: 2016 International Conference on Wireless Communications, Signal Processing and Networking (WiSPNET), pp. 2264–2268. IEEE (2016)

Shivade, C., Malewadkar, P., Fosler-Lussier, E., Lai, A.M.: Comparison of umls terminologies to identify risk of heart disease using clinical notes. J. Biomed. Inform. **58**, S103–S110 (2015)

Wagholikar, K.B., Sundararajan, V., Deshpande, A.W.: Modeling paradigms for medical diagnostic decision support: a survey and future directions. J. Med. Syst. **36**(5), 3029–3049 (2012)

Yoo, I., et al.: Data mining in healthcare and biomedicine: a survey of the literature. J. Med. Syst. **36**(4), 2431–2448 (2012)

Improving the Results of *De novo* Peptide Identification via Tandem Mass Spectrometry Using a Genetic Programming-Based Scoring Function for Re-ranking Peptide-Spectrum Matches

Samaneh Azari[1]([⊠]), Bing Xue[1], Mengjie Zhang[1], and Lifeng Peng[2]

[1] School of Engineering and Computer Science, Victoria University of Wellington, PO Box 600, Wellington 6140, New Zealand
{samaneh.azari,bing.xue,mengjie.zhang}@ecs.vuw.ac.nz
[2] Centre for Biodiscovery and School of Biological Sciences, Victoria University of Wellington, PO Box 600, Wellington 6140, New Zealand
lifeng.peng@vuw.ac.nz

Abstract. *De novo* peptide sequencing algorithms have been widely used in proteomics to analyse tandem mass spectra (MS/MS) and assign them to peptides, but quality-control methods to evaluate the confidence of *de novo* peptide sequencing are lagging behind. A fundamental part of a quality-control method is the scoring function used to evaluate the quality of peptide-spectrum matches (PSMs). Here, we propose a genetic programming (GP) based method, called GP-PSM, to learn a PSM scoring function for improving the rate of confident peptide identification from MS/MS data. The GP method learns from thousands of MS/MS spectra. Important characteristics about goodness of the matches are extracted from the learning set and incorporated into the GP scoring functions. We compare GP-PSM with two methods including Support Vector Regression (SVR) and Random Forest (RF). The GP method along with RF and SVR, each is used for post-processing the results of peptide identification by PEAKS, a commonly used *de novo* sequencing method. The results show that GP-PSM outperforms RF and SVR and discriminates accurately between correct and incorrect PSMs. It correctly assigns peptides to 10% more spectra on an evaluation dataset containing 120 MS/MS spectra and decreases the false positive rate (FPR) of peptide identification.

Keywords: Genetic programming · Symbolic regression · Peptide-spectrum match · Tandem mass spectrometry

© Springer Nature Switzerland AG 2019
A. C. Nayak and A. Sharma (Eds.): PRICAI 2019, LNAI 11672, pp. 474–487, 2019.
https://doi.org/10.1007/978-3-030-29894-4_38

1   Introduction

Mass spectrometry (MS) is the most commonly used method for the accurate mass determination and characterisation of proteins in complex biological samples. The common method for MS-based protein identification and characterising their amino acid sequences involves digesting proteins into peptides, which are then separated, fragmented, ionised, and captured by mass spectrometers. One of the common methods for assigning MS/MS spectra to peptide sequences is *de novo* peptide sequencing which is particularly appropriate for discovering novel peptides which are not presented in any protein sequence database. Given a set of MS/MS spectra to a *de novo* peptide sequencing algorithm, the results of peptide sequencing for each spectrum is a set of candidate peptides each having a confidence score indicating the quality of match between the spectrum and the candidate peptide. Normally, the highest-scoring (first ranked) candidate in each set of candidate peptides is regarded as the correct match for each spectrum. However, even with the identification of highest scoring PSMs, the fraction of peptide sequences that are fully correctly predicted by existing *de novo* sequencing algorithms cannot achieve 70% [1]. The existence of noise, low quality of spectra, incomplete fragmentation and missing fragment ions could be possible reasons of incorrect full-length peptide sequencing. Therefore, the top-scored candidate does not necessary indicate a correct match and the correct match could be in the second or third rank in the candidate list.

As we do not want to assign a spectrum to a peptide which is not presented in the biological sample because incorrect peptide assignments result in incorrect protein identifications and the search scores in the current *de novo* peptide sequencing algorithms do not always guarantee to find the true(correct) matches from many false matches, therefore, it is essential to apply a post-processing step as a PSM validation phase on the results of *de novo* sequencing in order to improve peptide identification sensitivity and accuracy. Current *de novo* peptide sequencing algorithms suffer from the lack of suitable scoring functions. The existing PSM-scoring functions to measure the goodness of a match between a spectrum and a peptide have the following limitations. A number of them are based on the simple shared peak count (SPC) approach where the number of peaks matched between experimental and theoretical (simulated) spectrum are counted [2] and the weight of all peaks are considered equal although some peaks are more informative than other peaks. Cross correlation based scores or statistical measures like the expectation value also have been previously used, but each one on its own does not serve as a strong discriminatory scoring function [3]. In addition, some methods put a prior assumption and built a linear scoring function from combination of different similarity scores which measure the goodness of match between a spectrum and a peptide [4].

Building a new scoring function from the possible combinations of different (sub)scores can be considered as a regression problem, where the (sub)scores are treated as features. Symbolic regression is a type of regression analysis that attempts to find the model that best fits a given dataset by discovering both model structure and parameters at the same time. Being a function identification process, symbolic regression does not face the problem of unknown gap in domain knowledge or human bias [5,6]. Having symbolic nature of solutions and being independent of any prior knowledge, GP is a promising method for symbolic regression problems. Symbolic regression using GP has been successfully applied to many real-world applications such as finance [7], industrial processing [8], and software engineering [9]. Therefore, it is worth discovering how GP employs different database search (sub)scores as its features and builds a regression model to reveal the intrinsic relationship of the data. The regression model will be used as the PSM-scoring function. The new scoring function will be used to re-score a collection of candidate PSMs resulting from *de novo* peptide sequencing of MS/MS data. It is expected that the new GP-based function gives the highest score (first rank) to the correct match among other peptides belonging to the same candidate set, finding the correct peptide candidate for the given spectrum.

1.1   Research Goals

The main goal of this paper is developing an effective GP-based PSM scoring function to re-score and re-rank the PSMs which are the output of *de novo* sequencing algorithms, aiming at improving the rate of full-length correct peptide identification of the *de novo* algorithm. This problem will be formulated as a symbolic regression. The following objectives are specifically investigated:

1. Design appropriate terminal set, function set and a fitness function that help GP to explore the space of all possible combinations of similarity (sub)scores.
2. Compare the performance of GP with other benchmark algorithms.
3. Evaluate the effectiveness of the new GP-based scoring function on the results of *de novo* sequencing in terms of improvement in FDR.

2   Background

2.1   Assigning MS/MS Spectra to Peptide Sequences

Basically, proteins and peptides are fundamentally the same as, being comprised of chains of amino acids that are held together by peptide bonds. Peptide and protein identification is one of the significant challenges of proteomics. Mass spectrometry is the most commonly used techniques to overcome the challenge. A MS/MS spectrum is a mass to charge ratio plot which is the result of ionisation the biological sample by a mass spectrometer. The spectrum is used to identify the peptides in the sample and then from combining the peptides, proteins are identified. Mainly there are two main peptide identification strategy including database search and *de novo* sequencing. A database search method matches the input experimental MS/MS spectra against the theoretical spectra predicted for the peptides included in a protein sequence database search. However, when the protein database is not available or the biological sample contains unknown peptides and proteins *de novo* sequencing methods are used. Peptide sequences are extracted directly from the MS/MS spectrum by measuring the mass differences between two informative peaks (b-/y-ions) corresponding to the mass of an amino acid and then linking the amino acids together to build a peptide.

2.2   Genetic Programming and MS/MS Data Analysis

Genetic Programming (GP) is a technique whereby a population of computer programs is evolved using an evolutionary algorithm to perform well in a predefined task. Randomly generating a set of individual as an initial population, GP searched for the solutions during the evolutionary search process. A set of genetic operators is applied on the individuals to generate fitter offsprings for the next generation [10]. GP simulates evolution by employing fitness based selection where the fittest program is expected to be chosen. The process can be stopped based on the stopping criteria which can be finding an ideal individual with a specified fitness value or reaching a maximum number of generations.

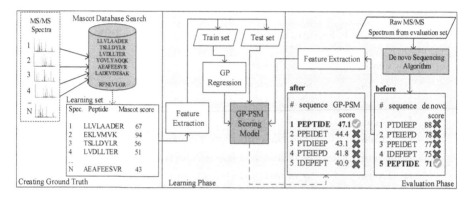

Fig. 1. The workflow of the proposed GP-PSM method consisting of three phases.

3   The Proposed Ranking GP Method

The proposed GP-PSM workflow designed for scoring the PSMs is presented in Fig. 1. The workflow proceeds in three phases: creating the ground truth, learning the GP-based PSM scoring function followed by an evaluation step to re-score the results of *de novo* sequencing using the new scoring function.

Our ground truth is a set of MS/MS spectra with known identifications. The spectra used in the learning set are composed of various qualities with different peptide lengths varied from 5 to 12. More details about the learning set and validation set is given in Table 2. It is important to mention that the correct identification for each spectrum in both sets is known. This is an essential requirement since the existence of false positive PSMs in the learning set would not allow GP to find discriminating scoring functions. Therefore, here we have used a set of high confident PSMs identified and validated by Mascot database search, a benchmark database search tool. The Mascot database search has already identified the correct peptide corresponding to each spectrum with a Mascot score indicating the confidence level of the identification.

For each instance in the learning set, a set of features explained in Table 1 is extracted. The features are the (sub)scores or similarity scores which measure the quality of match between the experimental spectrum s and the theoretical spectrum t, the simulated spectrum of peptide p, from different perspectives. After feature extraction, the instances from the learning set are divided into two sets train and test set (70% and 30%) to be used by GP to build the PSM scoring model. Therefore, the features are used as the independent variables and the Mascot score is the dependant variable in the GP regression model. GP uses train set to learn the model and applies the model on the test set. After generating the GP-PSM model, it is used to re-score the set of PSMs from the evaluation set. Each feature used in the model is relatively useful at determining if a PSM is correct or not, but the GP-PSM model incorporates them into a strong discriminatory scoring function for PSMs.

Table 1. Features used in GP-PSM to represent a PSM.

	Feature name	Description
f_1	$I_{matched}$	sum of intensities of matched peaks
f_2	$N_{matched}$	# of matched peaks
f_3	$N_{not-matched}$	# of un-matched peaks
f_4	Δmass	The mass difference between the s and p
f_5	Nterm	# of matched b-ions from N-terminus
f_6	Cterm	# of matched y-ions from C-terminus
f_7	Cos	Fixed length Normalised Dot product
f_8	Euc	Fixed length normalised Euclidean distance
f_9	Hamming	Hamming distance between two vectorised
f_{10}	SeqFix	Fixed length SEQUEST-like scoring function
f_{11}	SeqVar	Variable length SEQUEST-like scoring function

After building the GP-PSM model, the effectiveness of this model is evaluated on the evaluation set and using the current *de novo* sequencing algorithms. Given a raw MS/MS spectrum from the evaluation set to the *de novo* sequencing algorithm, the result is a set of PSMs each having a *de novo* score. The spectrum has been previously identified by Mascot database search and its corresponding peptide is known to us, but the *de novo* sequencing algorithm does not know that and needs to assign a peptide to the spectrum. As it can be seen in the example, for the input spectrum, five candidate peptides are listed as the results of identification by the *de novo* sequencing tool. The *de novo* sequencing algorithm normally reports the highest-scoring candidate peptide as the results of the identification. As it can be seen in the example, the correct candidate is sit at the lowest score in the list ('before'list). The scores of the PSMs in this list can be refined by using the GP-PSM model. So the first step is applying feature extraction and the second step is applying the GP model to re-score the PSMs. It is worth mentioning that the *de novo* scores in the 'before'list are not used when the GP model is applied. As the result it can be seen that in the new re-scored list ('after'list) the correct PSM got the highest score among the other candidates and this is what we would like to obtain.

3.1   Feature Extraction

For each PSM, a vector of 11 features summarised in Table 1 is computed. These features measure the quality of match between the spectrum s and the peptide p based on different criteria. In order to match the experimental spectrum s against the peptide p, a theoretical spectrum t is constructed from peptide p based on the CID fragmentation rules [11]. $I_{matched}$ as the first feature in Table 1, calculates the sum of intensities of peaks matched between the experimental spectrum s and the theoretical spectrum t. $N_{matched}$ and $N_{not-matched}$ equals to the number of peaks in the theoretical spectrum t, which are match and not matched against the spectrum s, respectively. Δmass is the mass difference between the spectrum s and the peptide p. The *Nterm* feature counts the number of consecutive b-ions matched from N-terminus (left to right) of t against s. Similarly, the *Cterm* feature counts the number of y-ions from t matched against s from C-terminus side (right to left). The first six features were previously used as the fitness function of a genetic algorithm based *de novo* sequencing [12] where all features were linearly combined with each feature having equal weights of 1. However, in this work we will not put the prior linear assumption on their combination and let GP to find the non-linear relationship between them.

Features $\{f_7, f_8, f_9, f_{10}, f_{11}\}$ vectorise the experimental spectrum s and the theoretical spectrum t into two binned vectors and then measure how well s fits t. Features $\{f_7, f_8, f_9, f_{10}\}$ have fix length of 4,000, whereas f_{11} has a variable length. The value in each bin in the vectorised experimental spectrum equals to the sum of the intensities of all peaks within the corresponding bin, whereas in the case of the vectorised theoretical spectrum the bin gets a value of one. The Cos feature, $\{f_7\}$, uses dot/scalar product between two vectors s and t to calculate and normalises the result of the dot product to be in the range of [0,1] by dividing it into multiplication of the magnitude of the two vectors. A value of 0 for f_7 indicates that the two spectrum vectors s and t have no peaks matched in between, whereas $f_7 = 1$ indicates a perfect match, and represents that all peaks in t are matched against those of s. The Euc and Hamming features, $\{f_8, f_9\}$, calculate the normalised Euclidean distance and hamming distance between s and t, respectively.

The features SeqFix and SeqVar, (f_{11}, f_{12}) are inspired from the scoring function used in SEQUEST, a benchmark database search engine [13]. Both features apply a preprocessing step on the experimental spectrum in order to remove the potential noise peaks and normalise the intensities and then vectorise the spectra. SeqVar has a variable length for each spectrum and is determined by dividing the mass of the experimental spectrum into the fragment ion tolerance which here is 0.5. Both features use normalised dot product to measure the goodness of the match between s and t.

3.2   GP Program Representation

A tree based GP structure is considered to represent each GP individual in GP-PSM. Each individual represents a scoring function that returns a real number as the match score. A terminal set consisting of 11 features and random constants and a function set of arithmetic operators including $\{+, -, \times, /(\text{protected})\}$ are considered for GP. A population size of 300 and maximum number of generations $G = 100$ are considered. The initial population is created based on ramped half-and half. The mutation and crossover rates are 0.1 and 0.9, respectively and the best individual is copied to the next generation. Tournament selection with size 5 selects the parental individuals. The algorithm is implemented in Python 3.6 and uses DEAP (Distributed Evolutionary Algorithms in Python) package [14].

Table 2. The MS/MS spectra used in this study.

Dataset		# of MS/MS	# of PSMs
Learning set	Train	7,000	7,000
	Test	3,000	3,000
Evaluation set		120	600

3.3   An Effective Fitness Function for PSMs Scoring

The GP method tries to generate a scoring function which combines different similarity (sub) scores as features and produces a real value score as the confidence score of the match between the experimental spectrum and the theoretical spectrum. The scoring function should be discriminating enough in order to distinguish a correct match from false matches in the evaluation phase (please see the flowchart in Fig. 1). As the GP problem is formulated as a symbolic regression task, we use relative sum of squared error (RSS) in Eq. (1) to compute the error of the prediction.

$$RSS = \frac{\sum_{i=1}^{N}(\hat{Y}_i - Y_i)^2}{\sum_{i=1}^{N}(\overline{Y} - Y_i)^2} \tag{1}$$

where $\hat{Y}_i$ is the output of the GP individual corresponding to the target value Y_i, $\overline{Y}$ is the mean of the target values, and N is the number of instances. A model with good performance has RSS < 1. Therefore, in this problem GP tries to minimise the RSS.

4   Experiment Design

4.1   MS/MS Datasets

To build the learning set and the evaluation set, the MS/MS spectra from the comprehensive full factorial LC-MS/MS benchmark dataset are used [15].

This dataset contains 50 protein samples extracted from *Escherichia coli* K12 designed for evaluating MS/MS analysis tools. The MS/MS spectra are acquired from the linear ion trap Fourier-transform with the collision-induced dissociation (CID) technique. The peptide identification has been already applied by Wessels et al. [15] using Mascot v2.2 [16] with maximum missed cleavage of 1, precursor mass tolerance of 10 ppm, and fragment error of 0.8 Da with a cutoff q-value of 0.01. Therefore, the so called ground truth data (the peptide corresponding to each spectrum) is included in the full factorial dataset.

Since the fragmentation pattern strongly relies on the peptide's charge and the precursor mass, this study only focuses on doubly charge peptides. The MS/MS spectra used in both learning and evaluation set have following characteristics: doubly charged, maximum precursor mass of 1150 Dalton, peptide length of 7 to 12 with no modifications. As it can be seen from Table 2, a set of 10,000 MS/MS spectra corresponding to 10,000 peptides are selected from the full factorial dataset to create the learning set. The learning set is split by 70% and 30% to create the train and test set, respectively. Also a set of 120 spectra as selected from the comprehensive dataset to create the evaluation set. These spectra later are given to a benchmark *de novo* sequencing algorithm, called PEAKS [17], for peptide identification. For each spectrum, PEAKS produces at least five candidate peptides as the results of identification. That is the reason that the number of PSMs in evaluation set is not equal to the number of MS/MS spectra. The evaluation set is used for evaluating the effectiveness of GP-PSM in terms of improving the false discovery rate of the *de novo* sequencing algorithm. More details is given in Experiments Section.

4.2 Benchmark Algorithm

As GP is used to learn a scoring function in a regression task, the proposed method is compared with Random Forest (RF) and Support Vector Regression (SVR). Also as mentioned previously, the effectiveness of the scoring functions generated by GP, RF, SVR is evaluated by applying the model on the results of PEAKS. The results are evaluated in terms of false positive rate (FPR) before and after applying the model. Given the ground truth, FPR is the ratio of the number of correct matches to the total number of MS/MS spectra.

$$FPR = \frac{FP}{N} \qquad (2)$$

Where FP is the number of false-positive PSMs and N indicates the number of MS/MS spectra. After applying the new GP-based scoring function on the results of PEAKS, in each group of five candidate peptides corresponding to the same spectrum, if the highest scoring peptide is not the correct match, the value of false positive increases by 1.

4.3   Experiments

Experiment I: Learning the PSM Scoring Functions. Based on the learning phase in the GP-PSM flowchart in Fig. 1, the three algorithms including GP, RF and SVR are used to learn the PSM scoring functions using the train set of the learning set from Table 2. The three algorithms are evaluated in terms of RSS measure in Eq. (1) on both train and test sets. As previously mentioned, the intention of the models is minimising the RSS value on both train and test sets. However, a method with low accuracy is sometimes superior to the one with high accuracy, therefore regardless of the performance of these three algorithms in learning phase, in evaluation phase each of them is applied on the evaluation set to investigate the effectiveness of each model as a post-processing method.

Experiment II: Evaluating the Effectiveness of GP-PSM, RF and SVR. This experiment measures the performance of the three algorithms in terms of FPR before and after applying the models on the evaluation set. One question that might arise here is that what is the difference between the test set in the learning set and evaluation set. To answer this question we should explain how each set is created. The PSMs in the test set are the results of peptide identification by Mascot database search from the full factorial dataset. However, the PSMs in evaluation set are produced by PEAKS which is a *de novo* sequencing algorithm.

Table 3. The RSS results of the three methods in learning phase using the PSMs in learning set.

Method	Train	Test
RF	0.13	0.53
SVR	0.69	0.67
GP-PSM	0.55 ± 0.04	0.55 ± 0.03
Best GP individual	0.49	0.50

Given an MS/MS spectrum to PEAKS, the output is a set of peptide sequences each having a confidence score between 0 and 100 [17]. As previously mentioned even the highest-scored PSM does not necessary indicate a correct match for the corresponding spectrum, therefore the output of PEAKS is given as the input to the scoring functions generated by GP, RF and SVR for rescoring. Then for each spectrum, the highest-scored PSM is reported as the final peptide identification. That is the reason that FPR before and after applying post-processing on the results of PEAKS for each algorithm is calculated. It is worth mentioning the already the correct peptide corresponding to the spectra in evaluation set is known, that is why FPR can be calculated.

Another important point about the difference between the PSMs in the learning set and in the evaluation set is that as PEAKS reports five candidate peptide for each spectrum, the candidate are highly similar to each other, therefore, the value of their features also very close to each other. So the scoring function generated by the regression-based method should be strongly discriminated in order to give the highest score to the correct candidate peptide.

5   Results and Discussions

5.1   Results of Experiment I

Table 3 presents the results of the experiment I when three methods including RF, SVR and GP were used to learn the PSM scoring function. The three methods are evaluated in terms of RSS on both train and test sets. For GP experiments, 30 individual runs using 30 different random seeds are considered.

As it can be seen from Table 3 that RF has the best result of train set and the second best is the Best individual of GP. On test set the best individual of GP has the best result. However, as it was previously mentioned from the results of learning set we might not be able to conclude which scoring function is the best, therefore, the three algorithm are applied on the evaluation set to check the effectiveness of the model. For GP the best individual in terms of RSS on train set is used at the PSM scoring function. More details are explained in the following section.

Table 4. The results of PEAKS using the MS/MS spectra from evaluation set.

Method	TP (Target PSMs)	FP		FPR
		# of MS/MS spectra that it's correct match		
		is not first-rank (Missed Target PSMs)	does not exist among the five candidates	
PEKAS	67	25	28	0.44

Table 5. The results of PEAKS peptide identification after post-processing by RF, SVR and GP using the PSMs from evaluation set.

Method	# of Target PSMs which are missed (out of 67)	# of identified Missed Target PSMs (out of 25)	TP	FP	FPR	FPR reduction after post-processing
RF	**6**	7	68	52	0.43	1%
SVR	**6**	11	72	48	0.40	4%
GP-PSM	8	**20**	**79**	**41**	**0.34**	**10%**

5.2   Results of Experiment II

This experiment is conducting in order to evaluate the performance of the new scoring functions generated by the three methods RF, SVR and GP on the evaluation set. PEAKS is used to perform *de novo* sequencing using 120 MS/MS spectra from the evolution set. For each spectrum, PEAKS reports 5 candidate peptides each having a confidence score indicating the reliability of the match. In each set of candidates, the top-scored candidate is selected as the corresponding match for the input spectrum. Having the ground truth (from full factorial dataset), we can calculate the peptide identification rate. The results of peptide identification by PEAKS is shown in Table 4. It can be seen that out of 120 total number of spectra, only 67 of them are correctly identified by PEAKS (labelled as TP or Target PSMs in this table). However, there are 25 spectra that their corresponding correct peptide did not get the highest-rank in the candidate list. We call these PSMs as Missed Target PSMs which means they are those target PSMs which wrongly got lower scores by PEAKS. Therefore, other PSMs which were not supposed to get the highest scores belong to FP. Moreover, there are 28 spectra that non of the peptides in their candidate lists were correct. It can be seen that the FPR of PEAKS using evaluation set before applying the post-processing is 0.44. In overall, we expect the post-processing method to increase the number of TPs or Target PSMs, reduce the number of Missed Target PSMs and decrease the FPR. Please notice that for the set of 28 spectra, the post-processing method cannot help as the correct match does not exist among the candidate list of each spectrum.

Table 5 presents the results of PEAKS *de novo* peptide sequencing after post-processing by RF, SVR and GP using the PSMs from evaluation set which are the output of PEAKS. The second column in this table, # of target PSMs which are missed, presents the number of target PSMs previously identified by PEAKS, but now are wrongly got low scores by the post-processing method. Also the third column in this table, number of identified missed target PSMs, indicates the number of missed target PSMs by PEAKS that are now identified by the post-processing method.

The results show that the PSM scoring function generated by GP is able to identify 80% (= $(\frac{20}{25} \times 100)$) of the missed target PSMs whereas SVM and RF only found 44% and 28%, respectively. However, it can be seen that the RF and SVR are relatively better than GP in terms of keeping the target PSMs which are already got the highest ranks by PEAKS.

Getting the lowest rate of FPR amongst the other methods, the GP method in overall outperforms other methods by 10% reduction in FPR. The reason of the overall good performance of GP is its good discriminating ability. More analysis on the results of RF reveals that in most of failure cases assigned the similar rank to two candidate peptides in the list. As a rule in our method, if two PSMs belonging to the same candidate list if get the similar rank score, the identification is rejected even if one of them is the correct match. In the case of SVR, quite often the target PSM did not have the change to get the highest score. This could be due to the low RSS results of SVR in the learning phase.

5.3   Analysis on the Best GP Evolved Program

Figure 2 shows the best GP-based scoring function among the 30 independent runs in terms of RSS on train set. The Tree contains 67 nodes. Having implicit feature selecting ability, GP automatically discarded irrelevant or redundant features such as $\{f_4\}$, $\Delta mass$, and $\{f_8\}$, Euclidean distance. These discards highly makes sense as for all the PSMs $\Delta mass$ is a small value and almost the same for all instances since the MS/MS spectra selected in this study do not have any post translation modifications so the mass difference between each spectrum and its corresponding peptide is very close to zero. As Cos feature and Euclidean features used here are both normalised and are mathematically equivalent and GP already has selected Cos feature, $\{f_7\}$, seven times so, $\{f_8\}$, Euc, is discarded by GP. As previously mentioned about finding the non-linear relationship between features $\{f_1\}$ to $\{f_6\}$, it can be seen that the left big sub-tree is mainly responsible for this task. It has 17 features and 13 of them are among features $\{f_1, f_2, f_3, f_4, f_5, f_6\}$, whereas the right big sub-tree is looking after the combination of the vectorised features including $\{f_7, f_8, f_9, f_{10}, f_{11}\}$.

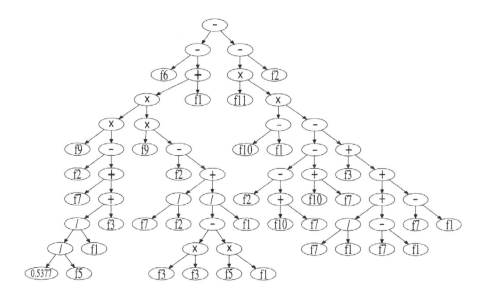

Fig. 2. The best GP evolved program (the PSM ranking function).

6   Conclusions and Future Work

This work developed a genetic programming (GP) based method to automatically generate a PSM scoring function aiming at reducing the rate of false discovery peptide identification from MS/MS data. The effective fitness function let GP to generate a strong discriminative scoring function which was able to improve the peptide identification. The GP method learns from thousands of

MS/MS spectra. Important characteristics about goodness of the matches are extracted from the learning set and incorporated into the GP scoring functions. We compare GP-PSM with two methods including Support Vector Regression (SVR) and Random Forest (RF). The GP method along with RF and SVR, each is used for post-processing the results of peptide identification by PEAKS, a commonly used *de novo* sequencing method. The results show that GP-PSM outperforms RF and SVR and discriminates accurately between correct and incorrect PSMs. It correctly assigns peptides to 10% more spectra on an evaluation dataset containing 120 MS/MS spectra and decreases the false positive rate (FPR) of identification. The results show that GP-PSM outperformed RF and SVR by 9% and 4% in terms of reduction the FPR, resulting in improving the PEAKS peptide identification. Not being a black box, GP with its interpretability characteristic gives the chance to identify the important features which proven to be more informative for discriminating the correct PSMs from incorrect ones. The non-linear combination of the selected features can be used as the fitness function for other *de novo* sequencing algorithms.

As for future work, we will investigate how to design a wrapper GP method by considering the learning phase as the feature selection and the evaluation phase as the classification part of the wrapper method. We will also investigate how the new scoring function generated in this study can be used as a new feature for PSM scoring.

References

1. Yang, H., et al.: pSite: amino acid confidence evaluation for quality control of De Novo peptide sequencing and modification site localization. J. Proteome Res. **17**(1), 119–128 (2017)
2. Colinge, J., Bennett, K.L.: Introduction to computational proteomics. PLoS Comput. Biol. **3**(7), e114 (2007)
3. Fenyö, D., Beavis, R.C.: A method for assessing the statistical significance of mass spectrometry-based protein identifications using general scoring schemes. Anal. Chem. **75**(4), 768–774 (2003)
4. Keller, A., Nesvizhskii, A.I., Kolker, E., Aebersold, R.: Empirical statistical model to estimate the accuracy of peptide identifications made by MS/MS and database search. Anal. Chem. **74**(20), 5383–5392 (2002)
5. Babovic, V., Keijzer, M.: Genetic programming as a model induction engine. J. Hydroinformatics **2**(1), 35–60 (2000)
6. Smits, G., Kotanchek, M.: Pareto-front exploitation in symbolic regression. In: O'Reilly, U.M., Yu, T., Riolo, R., Worzel, B. (eds.) Genetic Programming Theory and Practice II. Genetic Programming, vol. 8, pp. 283–299. Springer, Boston (2005). https://doi.org/10.1007/0-387-23254-0_17
7. Ong, C.-S., Huang, J.-J., Tzeng, G.-H.: Building credit scoring models using genetic programming. Expert Syst. Appl. **29**(1), 41–47 (2005)
8. Lee, Y.-S., Tong, L.-I.: Forecasting energy consumption using a grey model improved by incorporating genetic programming. Energy Convers. Manag. **52**(1), 147–152 (2011)

9. Harman, M., Jia, Y., Krinke, J., Langdon, W.B., Petke, J., Zhang, Y.: Search based software engineering for software product line engineering: a survey and directions for future work. In: Proceedings of the 18th International Software Product Line Conference, vol. 1, pp. 5–18. ACM (2014)
10. Langdon, W.B., Poli, R., McPhee, N.F., Koza, J.R.: Genetic programming: an introduction and tutorial, with a survey of techniques and applications. In: Fulcher, J., Jain, L.C. (eds.) Computational Intelligence: A Compendium. SCI, vol. 115, pp. 927–1028. Springer, Heidelberg (2008). https://doi.org/10.1007/978-3-540-78293-3_22
11. Beardsley, R.L., Herrmann, K.A., Hilderbrand, A.E.: Peptide fragmentation overview. In: Principles of Mass Spectrometry Applied to Biomolecules, vol. 10, p. 279 (2006)
12. Azari, S., Xue, B., Zhang, M., Peng, L.: GA-Novo: *De Novo* peptide sequencing via tandem mass spectrometry using genetic algorithm. In: Kaufmann, P., Castillo, P.A. (eds.) EvoApplications 2019. LNCS, vol. 11454, pp. 72–89. Springer, Cham (2019). https://doi.org/10.1007/978-3-030-16692-2_6
13. Eng, J.K., McCormack, A.L., Yates, J.R.: An approach to correlate tandem mass spectral data of peptides with amino acid sequences in a protein database. J. Am. Soc. Mass Spectrom. **5**(11), 976–989 (1994)
14. Fortin, F.-A., De Rainville, F.-M., Gardner, M.-A., Parizeau, M., Gagné, C.: DEAP: evolutionary algorithms made easy. J. Mach. Learn. Res. **13**, 2171–2175 (2012)
15. Wessels, H.J.C.T., et al.: A comprehensive full factorial LC-MS/MS proteomics benchmark data set. Proteomics **12**(14), 2276–2281 (2012)
16. Cottrell, J.S., Perkins, D.N., Pappin, D.J., Creasy, D.M.: Probability-based protein identification by searching sequence databases using mass spectrometry data. Electrophoresis **20**(18), 3551–3567 (1999)
17. Ma, B., et al.: Peaks: powerful software for peptide de novo sequencing by tandem mass spectrometry. Rapid Commun. Mass Spectrom. **17**(20), 2337–2342 (2003)

Computational Prediction of Lysine Pupylation Sites in Prokaryotic Proteins Using Position Specific Scoring Matrix into Bigram for Feature Extraction

Vineet Singh[1(✉)], Alok Sharma[2,3,4,5,6(✉)], Abel Chandra[5],
Abdollah Dehzangi[7], Daichi Shigemizu[3,4,6,8],
and Tatsuhiko Tsunoda[3,4,6]

[1] Faculty of Science Technology and Environment,
University of the South Pacific, Suva, Fiji
vineet.singh@usp.ac.fj
[2] Institute for Integrated and Intelligent Systems,
Grifth University, Brisbane, QLD 4111, Australia
alok.sharma@griffith.edu.au
[3] Department of Medical Science Mathematics, Medical Research Institute,
Tokyo Medical and Dental University, Tokyo 113-8510, Japan
[4] Laboratory for Medical Science Mathematics, RIKEN Center for Integrative
Medical Sciences, Yokohama 230-0045, Kanagawa, Japan
[5] School of Engineering and Physics, Faculty of Science Technology
and Environment, University of the South Pacific, Suva, Fiji
[6] CREST, JST, Tokyo 113-8510, Japan
[7] Department of Computer Science,
Morgan State University, Baltimore, MD, USA
[8] Division of Genomic Medicine, Medical Genome Center,
National Center for Geriatrics and Gerontology, Obu 474-8511, Japan

Abstract. Post-transcriptional modification (PTM) in a form of covalently attached proteins like ubiquitin (Ub) are considered an exclusive feature of eukaryotic organisms. Pupylation, a crucial type of PTM of prokaryotic proteins, is modification of lysine residues with a prokaryotic ubiquitin-like protein (Pup) tagging functionally to ubiquitination used by certain bacteria in order to target proteins for proteasomal degradation. Pupylation plays an important role in regulating many biological processes and accurate identification of pupylation sites contributes in understanding the molecular mechanism of pupylation. The experimental technique used in identification of pupylated lysine residues is still a costly and time-consuming process. Thus, several computational predictors have been developed based on protein sequence information to tackle this crucial issue. However, the performance of these predictors are still unsatisfactory. In this work, we propose a new predictor, PSSM-PUP that uses evolutionary information of amino acids to predict pupylated lysine residues. Each lysine residue is defined through its profile bigrams extracted from position specific scoring matrices (PSSM). PSSM-PUP has demonstrated improvement in performance compared to other existing predictors using the benchmark dataset from Pupdb Database. The proposed method achieves highest

© Springer Nature Switzerland AG 2019
A. C. Nayak and A. Sharma (Eds.): PRICAI 2019, LNAI 11672, pp. 488–500, 2019.
https://doi.org/10.1007/978-3-030-29894-4_39

performance in 10-fold PSSM-PUP with accuracy value of 0.8975, sensitivity value of 0.8731, specificity value of 0.9222, precision value of 0.9222 and Matthews correlation coefficient value of 0.801.

Keywords: Post-translational modification · Lysine pupylation prediction · Position specific scoring matrices (PSSM)

1   Introduction

The chemical alterations of proteins after being transformed in the ribosome creates a relevant biological reaction in the cell. Post-translational modification (PTM) is alteration of amino acids in the protein sequence, which contributes to diversify the proteome [1, 2]. There are many PTMs, listed from methylation [3] and ubiquitination [4] to acetylation [5], succinylation [6, 7] and phosphoglycerylation [8]. Recently, the scientific community are looking into another PTM called pupylation. A bacterial prokaryotic ubiquitin-like protein (Pup) is an intrinsically unstructured protein with 64 amino acids [9]. Pupylation is a process of Pup attaching substrate lysine via is opeptide bonds which plays important role in regulating various cellular processes such as protein degradation and signal transduction in prokaryotic cells [10]. Although pupylation and ubiquitylation are functionally the same, the enzymology involved in the two are different. Ubiquitylation requires three enzymes (activating enzyme, conjugating enzyme, and protein ligase), whereas pupylation requires only two enzymes; deamidase of Pup (DOP) and proteasome accessory factor A (PafA) [11–13]. Firstly, C-terminal glutamine of Pup is deamidated to glutamate via DOP and then deamidated Pup is attached to specific lysine of substrate proteins by PafA. The prokaryotic pupylation is still mostly unknown [14–16].

It is important to accurately identify pupylation sites to understand the fundamental mechanisms of pupylation. The traditional wet-lab experiment to identify pupylated site is expensive, inefficient and time-consuming and therefore computational tools for prediction are essential. Although there a number of computational methods developed for this, the prediction performance is still unsatisfactory. The first predictor to predict pupylation sites was proposed by Liu et al. called GPS-PUP which used a group-based prediction system (GPS) sequence encoding [17]. Zhao et al. employed the bi-profile Bayes feature extraction with support vector machine (SVM) classifier to develop EnsemblePup [18]. Zhao et al. also proposed another computational predictor PrePup which uses multiple feature encoding such as position-specific scoring matrix (PSSM) conservation scores, structural disorder score, amino acid index property (AAindex), secondary structure, solvent accessibility, and feature space with a SVM classifier [19]. Another computational predictor PUL-PUP, was established by Jiang and Cao using positive-unlabeled learning with a composition of k-spaced amino acid pairs feature (CKSAAP) and SVM algorithm [20]. Ju et al. proposed a predictor IMP-PUP by constructing features based on the composition of k-spaced amino acid pairs and on the basis of semi-supervised self-training SVM algorithm [21]. In SVM based predictor iPUP, Tung et al. also used the CKSAAP [22]. Chen et al. proposed PupPred, where the sequential, structural and evolutionary hallmarks around pupylation sites were investigated and employed some of the sequence-derived features [23]. The features included physicochemical properties, binary features, protein secondary structures, amino acid pairs and PSSM with a k-nearest neighbor algorithm in SVM-based classifier. Hasan et al. developed pbPUP predictor on the basis of profile-based composition of k-spaced amino acid pair (pbCKSAAP) encoding with SVM classifier [24]. In recent paper by Hasan et al. shows the progress and challenges faced in protein pupylation sites prediction [25]. Most recently, Xuanguo et al. proposed an enhanced positive-unlabeled learning algorithm (EPuL) which employs only positive and unlabeled samples. The EPuL algorithm is implemented to select the reliably negative initial dataset and then iteratively picking out the non-pupylation sites [26]. In very recent work, Bao et al. developed CIPPN which identifies pupylation sites using neural network [27]. Most of the predictors have used the benchmark datasets from the PupDB database [28].

Although there are several predictors available, performance of pupylated lysine residues prediction remains unsatisfactory. Therefore, better approaches are needed by using relevant characteristics of amino acids for perception information. From the existing predictors, PrePup [19] and PupPred [23] incorporated evolutionary information, but performance can be further improved. In this work, we propose a new predictor named as PSSM-PUP (position specific scoring matrix into bigram for pupylation prediction) which employs evolutionary features of amino acids where we computed PSSM for each protein for predicting pupylated lysines. We selected a segment comprising 21 amino acids, 10 upstream and 10 downstream corresponding to each lysine residue for feature extraction. Afterward, profile bigram [29] was computed on this segment which is used to define the features of lysine residue. Since there is not enough information available from the knowledge of primary sequences, PSSM-PUP is designed to obtain information by evaluating each protein sequence related to pupylation sites.

For this work, we used a benchmark dataset consisting of 153 proteins from PupDB database [28]. This dataset has a very high number of non-pupylated lysine residues (negative samples) over the pupylated lysine residues (positive samples). We employed k-nearest neighbors cleaning treatment [1] to reduce this imbalance. Finally, a LIBSVM (library for support vector machines) package was used to develop pupylation prediction. PSSM-PUP has shown improvement in performance compared to existing predictors [20, 21].

2   Materials and Methods

This paper discusses the predictor called PSSM-PUP, which uses PSSM of a protein with the profile bigram of amino acids around lysines to predict pupylated and non-pupylated lysine residues [29]. The following sections discusses the benchmark data used for this study, extraction of evolutionary feature via PSSM, computation of profile bigram from PSSM for a segment of amino acids around corresponding lysine reside and SVM classifier used for pupylation prediction.

2.1 Benchmark Dataset

The dataset used in this study was downloaded from PupDB database [28]. It comprises of 153 protein sequences with pupylated and non-pupylated lysine residues. All the protein sequences were used for computing the sequence identity of the dataset. We used the cd-hit program [30] to have less than 40% sequence alignment. We evaluated each protein sequence and retrieved its pupylated and non-pupylated lysine residues. We obtained 181 pupylation sites (positive samples) and 2290 non-pupylation sites (negative samples).

2.2 Evolutionary Feature via PSSM

For a given amino acid, PSSM gives its substitution probability with the 20 amino acids of the human genome, according to its location in the protein sequence. These probabilities are obtained using PSI-BLAST tool that aligns the protein sequence to similar sequences found in the protein data bank [31]. PSI-BLAST calculates the probabilities for all the protein sequences in our benchmark dataset. The output of this tool are two $L \times 20$ matrices in which L represents the protein sequence length and 20 the amino acids of the genetic code. One matrix is called log-odds, while the other one, the linear probabilities of amino acids. In this work, the latter is used, i.e., the linear probabilities of amino acids. PSSM extracts promising features relevant for evolutionary information [32–38].

2.3 Feature Extraction

In this work, PSSM feature is used to discriminate the pupylated and non-pupylated sites by considering 10 downstream and 10 upstream amino acids to the lysine residue. The lysine residue in the center, with downstream and upstream amino acids (see Fig. 1) and makes a total window size equal to 21. We computed predictor's performance with window sizes of 15, 21, 25, 27, 31, 37, 41 and 21 gave the best result. Four of the previous studies [19–21, 26] also used window size 21 for pupylation prediction. For the case where a lysine is located towards the N or C terminus of the protein sequence and there are not enough residues for either downstream or upstream, the mirroring effect [1, 6, 8, 39, 40] is used (see Fig. 2). Usage of the mirror technique to deal with the issue of insufficient residues may not be biologically correct procedure, but it has been the most effective solution by far. We can represent each lysine residue with 10 amino acids downstream and 10 amino acids upstream by

$$S = [L_{-10}, L_{-9}, \ldots, L_{-2}, L_{-1}, K, L_1, L_2, \ldots, L_9, L_{10}] \tag{1}$$

The residues L_{-i} $(1 \leq i \leq 10)$ are the upstream amino acids and L_i $(1 \leq i \leq 10)$ are the downstream amino acids. It can be observed from Eq. (1) that each lysine residue is represented by 21 amino acids, including the lysine itself in the center. The segment S describing each lysine residue belongs to one of the two classes (c = {0,1}), where a non-pupylated site falls in class 0 (c = 0) while a pupylated site is categorized as class 1 (c = 1). The vector that represents each segment S are extracted from the PSSM values obtained for the entire protein sequence. Furthermore, this vector was transformed into frequency vector with bigram [29]. The resulting 20 × 20 matrix obtained after the PSSM + bigram transformation was reordered into a 400-dimensional vector, which are the evolutionary features representing the segment S.

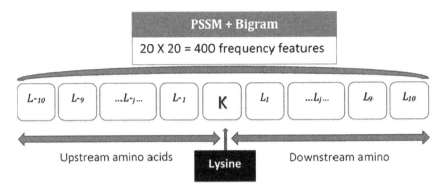

Fig. 1. Shows neighboring residues to the one lysine residues (K). Lysine site with enough upstream and downstream amino acids.

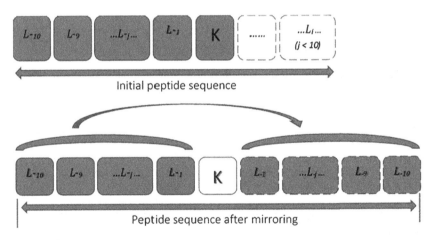

Fig. 2. Illustrates lysine with insufficient number of amino acids on either left or right of lysine residue (K). Left mirroring carried out to get adequate upstream and right mirroring is done to get missing downstream amino acids.

The PSSM + bigram procedure and how each segment S are represented is outlined below. PSSM obtained from PSI-BLAST for each protein sequence is a matrix of size $L \times 20$. Each element of the matrix, which can be labeled as m_{ij}, indicates the transitional probability of j-th amino acid at i-th location in the protein sequence concerned.

In this manner, PSSM results in the substitution probabilities of the 20 amino acids for the given protein sequence. The segment S, which is a small part of the entire protein sequence, is therefore a 21×20 feature vector after the extraction. The profile bigram [29] of segment size 21 was calculated by

$$B_{p,q} = \sum_{k=1}^{20} m_{k,p} m_{k+1,q} \text{ where } 1 \le p \le 20 \text{ and } 1 \le q \le 20 \qquad (2)$$

The Eq. (2) returns 400 frequencies that correspond to 400 bigram transitions. Profile bigram is known to give good performance in the different areas of protein analysis [29, 41, 42]. The matrix B (PSSM + bigram) was reordered into a 400 element feature vector F as shown in Eq. (3) below. The superscript T denotes transpose.

$$F = \begin{bmatrix} B_{1,1}, B_{1,2}, \ldots, B_{1,20}, B_{2,1}, B_{2,2}, \ldots, B_{2,20}, B_{20,1}, B_{20,2}, \ldots, B_{20,20} \end{bmatrix}^T \qquad (3)$$

The evolutionary information was computed for the 181 lysine residues in the positive set (c = 1), as well as for the 2471 in the negative set (c = 0). It is worth noting that this method provides a 400-dimensional feature vector in spite of the length of the segment size. This is an important property of profile bigram where the size of feature vector does not increase when larger segment sizes are used.

2.4   Support Vector Machine

SVM [43] is one type of supervised learning algorithm in the field of machine learning. SVM has been used for both regression and classification purposes but is mostly common for classification tasks and used in many existing pupylation predictors [19–22, 24, 26]. The way this algorithm works is by finding a hyperplane that best discriminates the two classes i.e. it finds a plane that has the maximum distance between data points of the two classes. Moreover, the number of features of these data points has the effect on the dimensionality of the hyperplane. For instance, feature size of 2 requires a hyperplane that is 1 dimensional (a line). Furthermore, not all classes are linearly separable. In these cases, non-linear kernels are used. Non-linear kernels map the nonlinear input space to a feature space of higher dimension in which the classes can be linearly separated. LIBSVM [44] predictor has been employed in this work on Matlab platform and the SVM type selected was radial basis function kernel and cost value of 2 and gamma value of 0.0250.

2.5   Statistical Measures

To evaluate the performance of the proposed predictor and compare with the existing predictors, few measures which are sensitivity (Sn), specificity (Sp), accuracy (Acc), precision (Pre) and Matthews correlation coefficient (MCC) are employed in this work.

One of the key measure is sensitivity, which evaluates the percentage of pupylated residues correctly classified by the model. The predictor achieving high sensitivity shows that it can accurately detect those positive instances (pupylated residues) in the dataset. Simply when sensitivity equals to 1 makes an accurate predictor and when it equals to 0 makes it an inaccurate one. The formula for sensitivity is defined as:

$$Sensitivity = \frac{PL_+}{PL_+ + PL_-} \tag{4}$$

where PL_+ is number of pupylated lysine predicted correctly and PL_- represents the number of pupylated lysine incorrectly classified by the predictor.

On the other hand, specificity assesses the proportion of correctly identified non-pupylated lysine residues. Specificity of 1 demonstrates an accurate predictor which is able to predict negative instance of the dataset (non-pupylated residues) and specificity equals to 0 shows predictor is unable to identify non-pupylated residues. The metric for specificity is defined as

$$Specificity = \frac{NPL_+}{NPL_+ + NPL_-} \tag{5}$$

where NPL_+ is the number of non-pupylated lysine predicted correctly and NPL_- represents the number of incorrectly classified non-pupylated lysine by the predictor.

For a predictor to correctly distinguish between positive samples and negative samples is evaluated by the accuracy of the predictor. Predictor with accuracy equals to 1 shows an accurate predictor whereas a zero accuracy means predictor is totally incorrect. Accuracy is calculated as

$$Accuracy = \frac{PL_+ + NPL_+}{PL + NPL} \tag{6}$$

where PL and NPL are the total numbers of pupylated and non-pupylated lysine residues, respectively.

Precision is another assessment measure of the predictor defined as the ratio of the number of correctly identify pupylated lysine over sum of correctly classified pupylated and non-pupylated lysine residues.

$$Precision = \frac{PL_+}{PL_+ + NPL_+} \tag{7}$$

Final statistical measure used in this paper is the Matthews correlation coefficient (MCC). It shows the value of correlation coefficient between predicted and observed instances. If a predictor has MCC equals to 1, it implies a perfect correlation between prediction and observation whereas, MCC equals to -1 does not show any agreement. MCC metric is calculated as

$$MCC = \frac{(NPL_+ \times PL_+) - (NPL_- \times PL_-)}{\sqrt{(PL_+ + PL_-)(PL_+ + NPL_-)(NPL_- + PL_-)(NPL_+ + NPL_-)}} \quad (8)$$

A best predictor is the one that achieves high performance in the five statistical measures discussed. However, it should perform better at least in some of the measures compared to the existing predictors. A predictor which is unable to predict pupylated lysine correctly (low sensitivity) cannot be used for pupylation prediction.

2.6 Validation Scheme

The effectiveness of a new predictor needs to be assessed with a validation method. There are several validation methods discussed in literature, however, two most used ones are the jackknife and n-fold validation scheme [45, 46]. In validation phase, an independent test set has to be used to assess the predictor. The Jackknife validation is less arbitrary than the n-fold cross-validation and provides unique results for a dataset [47]. From the literature, the same validation scheme [19–22, 26, 48] (n-fold cross-validation) technique is used in this study. The n-fold cross-validation technique is carried out in following steps listed in Table 1:

Table 1. Steps for cross-validation approach

---

1. Split the data samples complementary into n folds of roughly equal sample size with similar positive and negative sample size in each.
2. Use one fold as independent test set and the remaining $n - 1$ folds as training data.
3. Use the training data, adjust the parameters of the predictor
4. Compute all the statistical measures on independent test set
5. Repeat steps 1 to 4 for the remaining folds for assessment and calculated the average of each statistical measure.

In this study, we conducted 6-, 8- and 10-fold cross-validations for assessing the PSSM-PUP predictor and result were recorded.

3   Results and Discussion

Any proposed predictors need to be assessed in order to measure it performance. For this study, we used five statistical metrics: sensitivity, specificity, precision, accuracy and Matthews correlation coefficient [19, 20, 22, 24, 49] which are commonly used in the literature. The following sections discusses how the class imbalance were treated and also presents the results of support vector machine classification. The overall performance of PSSM-PUP and comparison with existing pupylation predictors with five metrics are also discussed.

3.1 Reducing the Imbalance Between Classes

After analyzing the protein sequence of our dataset, we found out the number of positive samples (pupylation sites) is much smaller than the negative samples (non-pupylation sites). This led to a high class imbalance samples that can cause biased classification results. Imbalance between samples of different classes is a common issue in machine learning and it is crucial to mitigate this problem. This proposed predictor removes redundant instances before the classification takes place. We used k-nearest neighbor technique in this study to deal imbalance of samples between classes. K-nearest neighbor technique is very popular in pattern recognition which was reintroduced for protein attribute prediction by Chou [50]. To balance both negative and positive classes, we removed redundant negative samples using k-nearest neighbors cleaning treatment [25]. We calculated Euclidean distance between all the samples in the dataset. We first set the cut-off by dividing the number of negative instance and positive instances (2,290/181) which came to a ratio of 12.65. Thus, K = 12 was initially set for reducing class imbalance. In other terms, we remove a negative sample if one of 12 nearest neighbor is a positive sample (calculation based on the Euclidean distance between the negative sample and all other samples in the entire dataset). After this first filtering, the imbalance classes still remained, therefore, we kept increasing the K value until the both the sets were almost similar in size. This method reduced the initial negative samples of 2,290 to 180 with a threshold value of 70, meaning a negative sample was removed if at least one positive sample is present within the 70 nearest neighbor. The negative instances were reduced to 180 samples. The positive instances remained 181 as it can affect the sensitivity. The final dataset after filtering (filtered negative samples and positive samples) was used to carry out 6-, 8-, 10- fold cross-validation and assess the predictor's performance.

3.2 Comparison with Existing Predictors

We compared our proposed PSSM-PUP predictor with two recently proposed predictors: PuL-PUP [19] by Jiang and Cao, and IMP-PUP [20] by Ju et al. Unfortunately, we could not compare with EPuL algorithm [25] since the given webserver was not working and the software package also did not work. The software package for testing were given for these two predictors PuL-PUP [19] and IMP-PUP [20]. Since all exiting predictors used the same dataset, it is worth noting that the trained model in existing predictors would have utilized some of the same protein sequences in their training which are in my test samples. Therefore, for comparison purposes, we used the feature extraction method to extract the features from the given software package and trained and tested using the LIBSVM classifier. The same train and test sets used in our proposed PSSM-PUP predictor was used to train and test for different folds when comparing with other predictors. We calculated the sensitivity, specificity, precision, accuracy, MCC for PSSM-PUP, PuL-PUP and IMP-PUP for 6-, 8- and 10-fold cross-validation trials (Table 2).

Table 2. Table shows performance assessment of two benchmark predictors and PSSM-PUP for 6-, 8-, 10- fold cross validation. The highest values in each metric are highlighted in bold.

Fold	Predictor	Sensitivity	Specificity	Precision	Accuracy	MCC
6	PSSM-PUP	85.645	92.222	91.920	88.916	0.782
	PUL-PUP	80.054	74.444	76.188	77.272	0.552
	IMP-PUP	82.276	72.222	74.856	77.272	0.549
8	PSSM-PUP	85.598	92.762	92.523	89.174	0.788
	PUL-PUP	79.891	77.841	78.552	78.873	0.583
	IMP-PUP	81.719	72.826	75.231	77.280	0.551
10	PSSM-PUP	**87.310**	**92.222**	**92.290**	**89.752**	**0.801**
	PUL-PUP	81.754	76.111	77.693	78.956	0.584
	IMP-PUP	82.310	70.556	74.145	76.441	0.537

The comparison of predictor PuL-Pup [19], IMP-PUP [20] with PSSM-PUP is shown Table 1. Improvement in performance for PSSM-PUP is seen over PuL-Pup [19] and IMP-PUP [20] on sensitivity, specificity, precision, accuracy and MCC. The performance improved slightly for sensitivity but significantly for specificity, precision, accuracy and MCC. It is worth noting that only the feature extraction methods were used to get the training and test sets. Same LIBSVM classifier with the same SVM parameters was used to train and test the predictors for comparison.

The promising results shows the ability of proposed PSSM-PUP predictor to correctly identify pupylated and non-pupylated lysine residues. This is possible since proposed predictor uses significant evolutionary information of protein sequences effectively. This information which is stored in the PSSM of each amino acid around lysine, when placed in one matrix of bigram shows important characteristic for detecting modified lysines. The SVM classifier and its effective use in PTM also improves the outcome. In short, the combination of PSSM + bigram extracts more information around lysine residues, which plays a vital role in predicting pupylated and non-pupylated lysine residues.

Our PSSM-PUP predictor's software package can be accessed from: https://github.com/vinzsingh09/PSSM-PUP.

4   Conclusion

This paper discussed a new predictor named PSSM-PUP, which has used the combination of *PSSM + Bigram* efficiently for pupylation prediction. The evolutionary information hidden in PSSMs that is converted to bigram occurrences shows to be a significant feature which can used for prediction. The k-nearest neighbors cleaning treatment also plays an important role to solve imbalance data issue and removing redundant samples to balance the dataset. A balanced dataset with support vector machine (LIBSVM) has shown PSSM-PUP to perform better than exiting existing predictors. For future study, we intend to use structural properties of amino acids for pupylation prediction and further explore the use of a 21-residue window for describing lysine residues.

References

1. Jia, J., Liu, Z., Xiao, X., Liu, B., Chou, K.-C.: iSuc-PseOpt: identifying lysine succinylation sites in proteins by incorporating sequence-coupling effects into pseudo components and optimizing imbalanced training dataset. Anal. Biochem. **497**, 48–56 (2016)
2. Walsh, C.T., Garneau-Tsodikova, S., Gatto Jr., G.J.: Protein posttranslational modifications: the chemistry of proteome diversifications. Angew. Chem. Int. Ed. **44**, 7342–7372 (2005)
3. Liu, Z., Xiao, X., Qiu, W.-R., Chou, K.-C.: iDNA-Methyl: identifying DNA methylation sites via pseudo trinucleotide composition. Anal. Biochem. **474**, 69–77 (2015)
4. Qiu, W.-R., Xiao, X., Lin, W.-Z., Chou, K.-C.: iUbiq-Lys: prediction of lysine ubiquitination sites in proteins by extracting sequence evolution information via a gray system model. J. Biomol. Struct. Dyn. **33**, 1731–1742 (2015)
5. Hou, T., et al.: LAceP: lysine acetylation site prediction using logistic regression classifiers. PLoS ONE **9**, e89575 (2014)
6. Dehzangi, A., et al.: PSSM-Suc: accurately predicting succinylation using position specific scoring matrix into bigram for feature extraction. J. Theor. Biol. **425**, 97–102 (2017)
7. López, Y., et al.: SucStruct: prediction of succinylated lysine residues by using structural properties of amino acids. Anal. Biochem. **527**, 24–32 (2017)
8. Chandra, A., et al.: PhoglyStruct: prediction of phosphoglycerylated lysine residues using structural properties of amino acids. Sci. Rep. **8**, 17923 (2018)
9. Burns, K.E., Liu, W.-T., Boshoff, H.I., Dorrestein, P.C., Barry, C.E.: Proteasomal protein degradation in Mycobacteria is dependent upon a prokaryotic ubiquitin-like protein. J. Biol. Chem. **284**, 3069–3075 (2009)
10. Chen, X., Solomon, W.C., Kang, Y., Cerda-Maira, F., Darwin, K.H., Walters, K.J.: Prokaryotic ubiquitin-like protein pup is intrinsically disordered. J. Mol. Biol. **392**, 208–217 (2009)
11. Burns, K.E., Cerda-Maira, F.A., Wang, T., Li, H., Bishai, W.R., Darwin, K.H.: "Depupylation" of prokaryotic ubiquitin-like protein from mycobacterial proteasome substrates. Mol. Cell **39**, 821–827 (2010)
12. Imkamp, F., et al.: Dop functions as a depupylase in the prokaryotic ubiquitin-like modification pathway. EMBO Rep. **11**, 791–797 (2010)
13. Striebel, F., Imkamp, F., Özcelik, D., Weber-Ban, E.: Pupylation as a signal for proteasomal degradation in bacteria. Biochim. Biophys. Acta (BBA)-Mol. Cell Res. **1843**, 103–113 (2014)
14. Striebel, F., Imkamp, F., Sutter, M., Steiner, M., Mamedov, A., Weber-Ban, E.: Bacterial ubiquitin-like modifier Pup is deamidated and conjugated to substrates by distinct but homologous enzymes. Nat. Struct. Mol. Biol. **16**, 647 (2009)
15. Georgiou, D., Karakasidis, T., Megaritis, A.: A short survey on genetic sequences, Chou's pseudo amino acid composition and its combination with fuzzy set theory. Open Bioinform. J. **7**, 41–48 (2013)
16. Poulsen, C., et al.: Proteome-wide identification of mycobacterial pupylation targets. Mol. Syst. Biol. **6**, 386 (2010)

17. Liu, Z., Ma, Q., Cao, J., Gao, X., Ren, J., Xue, Y.: GPS-PUP: computational prediction of pupylation sites in prokaryotic proteins. Mol. Biosyst. **7**, 2737–2740 (2011)
18. Zhao, X., Zhang, J., Ning, Q., Sun, P., Ma, Z., Yin, M.: Identification of protein pupylation sites using bi-profile Bayes feature extraction and ensemble learning. Math. Probl. Eng. **2013**, 7 (2013)
19. Zhao, X., Dai, J., Ning, Q., Ma, Z., Yin, M., Sun, P.: Position-specific analysis and prediction of protein pupylation sites based on multiple features. Biomed. Res. Int. **2013**, 109549 (2013)
20. Jiang, M., Cao, J.-Z.: Positive-unlabeled learning for pupylation sites prediction. Biomed. Res. Int. **2016**, 5 (2016)
21. Ju, Z., Gu, H.: Predicting pupylation sites in prokaryotic proteins using semi-supervised self-training support vector machine algorithm. Anal. Biochem. **507**, 1–6 (2016)
22. Tung, C.-W.: Prediction of pupylation sites using the composition of k-spaced amino acid pairs. J. Theor. Biol. **336**, 11–17 (2013)
23. Chen, X., Qiu, J.-D., Shi, S.-P., Suo, S.-B., Liang, R.-P.: Systematic analysis and prediction of pupylation sites in prokaryotic proteins. PLoS ONE **8**, e74002 (2013)
24. Hasan, M.M., Zhou, Y., Lu, X., Li, J., Song, J., Zhang, Z.: Computational identification of protein pupylation sites by using profile-based composition of k-spaced amino acid pairs. PLoS ONE **10**, e0129635 (2015)
25. Hasan, M.M., Khatun, M.S.: Recent progress and challenges for protein pupylation sites prediction. EC Proteomics Bioinform. **2**, 36–45 (2017)
26. Nan, X., et al.: EPuL: an enhanced positive-unlabeled learning algorithm for the prediction of pupylation sites. Molecules **22**, 1463 (2017)
27. Bao, W., You, Z.-H., Huang, D.-S.: CIPPN: computational identification of protein pupylation sites by using neural network. Oncotarget **8**, 108867 (2017)
28. Tung, C.-W.: PupDB: a database of pupylated proteins. BMC Bioinform. **13**, 40 (2012)
29. Sharma, A., Lyons, J., Dehzangi, A., Paliwal, K.K.: A feature extraction technique using bi-gram probabilities of position specific scoring matrix for protein fold recognition. J. Theor. Biol. **320**, 41–46 (2013)
30. Li, W., Godzik, A.: Cd-hit: a fast program for clustering and comparing large sets of protein or nucleotide sequences. Bioinformatics **22**, 1658–1659 (2006)
31. Berman, H., et al.: The protein data bank. Nucleic Acids Res. **28**, 235–242 (2000). http://www.rcsb.org/pdb/
32. Dehzangi, A., Paliwal, K., Lyons, J., Sharma, A., Sattar, A.: Proposing a highly accurate protein structural class predictor using segmentation-based features. BMC Genomics **15**, S2 (2014)
33. Faraggi, E., Zhang, T., Yang, Y., Kurgan, L., Zhou, Y.: SPINE X: improving protein secondary structure prediction by multistep learning coupled with prediction of solvent accessible surface area and backbone torsion angles. J. Comput. Chem. **33**, 259–267 (2012)
34. Heffernan, R., et al.: Improving prediction of secondary structure, local backbone angles, and solvent accessible surface area of proteins by iterative deep learning. Sci. Rep. **5**, 11476 (2015)
35. McGuffin, L.J., Bryson, K., Jones, D.T.: The PSIPRED protein structure prediction server. Bioinformatics **16**, 404–405 (2000)
36. Taherzadeh, G., Zhou, Y., Liew, A.W.-C., Yang, Y.: Sequence-based prediction of protein–carbohydrate binding sites using support vector machines. J. Chem. Inf. Model. **56**, 2115–2122 (2016)
37. Taherzadeh, G., Yang, Y., Zhang, T., Liew, A.W.C., Zhou, Y.: Sequence-based prediction of protein–peptide binding sites using support vector machine. J. Comput. Chem. **37**, 1223–1229 (2016)

38. Dehzangi, A., Paliwal, K., Lyons, J., Sharma, A., Sattar, A.: A segmentation-based method to extract structural and evolutionary features for protein fold recognition. IEEE/ACM Trans. Comput. Biol. Bioinform. (TCBB) **11**, 510–519 (2014)

39. Jia, J., Liu, Z., Xiao, X., Liu, B., Chou, K.-C.: pSuc-Lys: predict lysine succinylation sites in proteins with PseAAC and ensemble random forest approach. J. Theor. Biol. **394**, 223–230 (2016)

40. López, Y., et al.: Success: evolutionary and structural properties of amino acids prove effective for succinylation site prediction. BMC Genomics **19**, 923 (2018)

41. Dehzangi, A., Heffernan, R., Sharma, A., Lyons, J., Paliwal, K., Sattar, A.: Gram-positive and Gram-negative protein subcellular localization by incorporating evolutionary-based descriptors into Chou's general PseAAC. J. Theor. Biol. **364**, 284–294 (2015)

42. Dehzangi, A., et al.: Improving succinylation prediction accuracy by incorporating the secondary structure via helix, strand and coil, and evolutionary information from profile bigrams. PLoS ONE **13**, e0191900 (2018)

43. Meyer, D., Leisch, F., Hornik, K.: Benchmarking support vector machines (2002)

44. Chang, C.-C.: LIBSVM: a library for support vector machines. ACM Trans. Intell. Syst. Technol. **2**, 27:1–27:27 (2011). http://www.csie.ntu.edu.tw/~cjlin/libsvm

45. Chou, K.-C., Shen, H.-B.: Cell-PLoc: a package of Web servers for predicting subcellular localization of proteins in various organisms. Nat. Protoc. **3**, 153 (2008)

46. Alpaydin, E.: Introduction to Machine Learning. MIT Press, Cambridge (2014)

47. Hajisharifi, Z., Piryaiee, M., Beigi, M.M., Behbahani, M., Mohabatkar, H.: Predicting anticancer peptides with Chou's pseudo amino acid composition and investigating their mutagenicity via Ames test. J. Theor. Biol. **341**, 34–40 (2014)

48. Zhao, X., Ning, Q., Chai, H., Ma, Z.: Accurate in silico identification of protein succinylation sites using an iterative semi-supervised learning technique. J. Theor. Biol. **374**, 60–65 (2015)

49. Bao, W., Jiang, Z.: Prediction of lysine pupylation sites with machine learning methods. In: Huang, D.-S., Jo, K.-H., Figueroa-García, J.C. (eds.) ICIC 2017, Part II. LNCS, vol. 10362, pp. 408–417. Springer, Cham (2017). https://doi.org/10.1007/978-3-319-63312-1_36

50. Chou, K.-C.: Some remarks on protein attribute prediction and pseudo amino acid composition. J. Theor. Biol. **273**, 236–247 (2011)

A Light-Weight Context-Aware Self-Attention Model for Skin Lesion Segmentation

Dongliang Ma[1], Hao Wu[1], Jun Sun[1(✉)], Chunjing Yu[2], and Li Liu[2]

[1] JiangSu Provincial Engineering Laboratory of Pattern Recognition
and Computational Intelligence, JiangNan University, Wuxi, China
mdl.viper@gmail.com, wuhao940917@gmail.com, junsun@jiangnan.edu.cn
[2] Affiliated Hospital of JiangNan University, Wuxi, China
ycj_wxd1978@163.com, liuli_sytu@hotmail.com

Abstract. Dermoscopy imaging analysis is the basic operation for diagnosing and treating skin lesions. Recently, deep neural networks have been able to segment melanoma from surrounding skin accurately. However, because of the limitation of demanding a large amount of floating point operations and having long runtime on skin lesion segmentation network, it is difficult to deploy models to existing medical devices. In this paper, we design LCASA-Net, a novel light-weight neural network architecture, which applies Context-Aware Self-Attention block to effectively and efficiently capture informative features in dermoscopic images. Our model is created specifically for skin lesion segmentation task requiring low latency operation with higher precision. LCASA-Net is up to 2× faster, requires 5× less FLOPS, possesses 10× less parameters and achieves higher performance to existing state-of-the-art methods on ISBI 2017 dataset.

Keywords: Dermoscopy image · Skin lesion segmentation · Light-weight neural network · Context-Aware Self-Attention block

1 Introduction

As shown in Skin Cancer Foundation statistics [11], malignant melanoma is a kind of deadly cutaneous cancer, for the number of patients has increased dramatically in recent years. Early diagnosis and therapy can greatly reduce the risk of death. With the rapid development over the past decades, deep learning has achieved great success in segmentation of skin lesions [2,7,8,12], which assists dermatologists correctly segment and analyze melanomas. Most of them follow the design principles of pursuing remarkable accuracy, which makes them have poor efficiency of floating point operations and long runtime. Therefore, they are unsuitable for existing medical devices. To address the above issue, we introduced traditional small semantic segmentation model named ENet [9] into skin lesion segmentation tasks, which requires making a good trade-off on accuracy

© Springer Nature Switzerland AG 2019
A. C. Nayak and A. Sharma (Eds.): PRICAI 2019, LNAI 11672, pp. 501–505, 2019.
https://doi.org/10.1007/978-3-030-29894-4_40

and model parameters or memory footprint. As displayed in our experiments, although the above network achieved high running speed in the field of semantic segmentation, the requirements of low latency operation with high performance for skin lesion segmentation is difficult to be met.

In this paper, we employ context aware local features with attention modules as the basic unit to propose a fast light-weight model in dermoscopic images for skin lesion segmentation. In particular, our model achieved the Jaccard index of 80.9% on ISBI 2017 [4] Skin Lesion Segmentation dataset. Furthermore, our model has less than 0.5M parameters, and can process a dermoscopy image with 768 * 1024 resolution at a speed of 20 fps on only one NVIDIA TITAN X. To the best of our knowledge, it is the first time that a small semantic model has been used in the field of skin lesion segmentation.

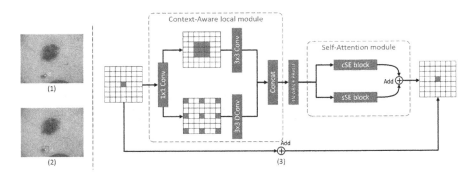

Fig. 1. It is difficult to distinguish whether a and b are benign point or lesion when we only pay attention to themselves. The red contour represents the lesion region which is annotated by doctors. (2) With the help of its surrounding context, it is easier to recognize that a is benign point and b is lesion. (3) The architectural design of Context-Aware Self-Attention block. (Color figure online)

2   Methodology

The challenge is presented in dermoscopic images that makes it difficult for computers to identify automatically the edge contour of lesion region from healthy skin with large variations (e.g., skin colors, different resolutions of images, presence of hair, variations of illumination or reflection, etc.). Specially, the information for border of lesion would be easily ignored in the final segmentation, resulting in poor performance for skin lesion analysis. Figure 1(1) shows the problem that some pixels in skin lesion segmentation tasks are difficult to be distinguished whether it is a lesion (red point) or not (yellow point).

It is known that context information could greatly improve performance for scene labeling [3,5]. Inspired by the success of the Context Contrasted Local (CCL) [5], which is proposed to reach a equilibrium between the informative context and the local information for semantic segmentation, we integrate coarse context and delicate local to extract multi-level context aware local features. The informative features are extracted by concatenating different branches. However, context of different positions tends to be dominated by consistency representation, which may result in lacking in discrimination. It is difficult to obtain apposite and effective high-quality features for lesions, which is more serious around the border. To address this issue, we introduce an attention module [10] after each Context-Aware local module to improve the discriminability of the representation. The architecture of the Context-Aware Self-Attention block is illustrated in Fig. 1(3). Table 1 shows our proposed network architecture in detail.

Table 1. LCASA-Net architecture. Input size is given for an image resolution of 3 * 768 * 1024. CASA means the Context-Aware Self-Attention block proposed by us.

Name	Type	Output size
Stem	3 * 3 conv with stride = 2	32 * 384 * 512
	3 * 3 conv with stride = 1	32 * 384 * 512
	3 * 3 conv with stride = 1	32 * 384 * 512
Pooling 1	Average pooling with stride = 2	3 * 384 * 512
Pooling 2	Average pooling with stride = 2, repeat 2 times	3 * 192 * 256
Concat 1	Concat stem and pooling 1	35 * 384 * 512
Down-sample 1	CASA with stride = 2	64 * 192 * 256
Stage 1	CASA with stride = 1, repeat 8 times	64 * 192 * 256
Concat 2	Concat stage 1, Down-sample 1 and Pooling 2	131 * 192 * 256
Down-sample 2	CASA with stride = 2	128 * 96 * 128
Stage 2	CASA with stride = 1, repeat 16 times	128 * 96 * 128
Concat 3	Concat stage 2, Down-sample 2	256 * 96 * 128
Classifier	1 * 1 conv	1 * 96 * 128
Up-sampling	Bilinear interpolation	1 * 768 * 1024

3 Experiments

Dataset. In our work, we employed ISBI 2017 [4] dataset of dermoscopy images to test the robustness of LCASA-Net. Images of the dataset were annotated by different doctors in various top medical centers. The dataset of ISBI 2017 [4] consists of training, validation, and test set, which contains 2000, 150 and 600 images, respectively.

Implementation Details. LCASA-Net was implemented on PyTorch, which is an open source deep learning library. The SGD optimization algorithm was employed with $momentum = 0.9$ and $weightdecay = 1 * 10^{-4}$ for adjusting learning rate. We used the learning rate of $5 * 10^{-2}$ with a power of 0.9. To prevent overfitting, we selected color distortion, flipped horizontally with 0.5 probability, randomly cropped and resized the cropped region into 768-by-1024 pixels for our model. During training, we set the batchsize to 8 and the epochs to 500. As for loss function, the *lovaâz* loss [1] and OHEM [6] were combined for watershed energy. We conducted the experiments on NVIDIA TITAN X with 12 GB memory.

Results. Quantitative results are displayed in Table 2. We compared LCASA-Net against 4 state-of-the-art methods on ISBI 2017 [4] test subset. The segmentation performance of our model reached an overall Jaccard index of more than 80.9%, which is the new state-of-the-art result. Specially, Table 2 provides a comparison of LCASA-Net with other state-of-the-art skin lesion segmentation networks to memory footprint, parameters and inference speed, and it is shown that LCASA-Net is 10 times smaller and 2 times faster than MtSinai [12], which makes use of color spaces to train a model and has achieved great success in the skin lesion segmentation challenge [4]. Compared with the current smallest semantic segmentation model, the number of parameters and the inference speed of LCASA-Net are close to ENet [6], and our method is about 6.8% higher than it in Jaccard index. With fewer parameters, less memory footprint, less inference time, and significantly higher accuracy, our method is shown to be very suitable to be deployed in existing medical devices for skin lesion segmentation.

Table 2. Performance, memory, parameters and inference speed analysis, evaluated on 768 * 1024 high resolution images on ISBI 2017 dataset. For fairness, we reimplemented these methods on NVIDIA TITAN X.

Methods	ACC	JAC	DIC	FLOPS (G)	Parameters (M)	Speed (fps)
RECOD [8]	0.931	0.754	0.839	275.95	44.78	<1
ResNet [2]	0.934	0.758	0.842	55.48	25.56	6.14
FCN [7]	0.930	0.752	0.837	24.21	134.27	3.60
MtSinai [12]	0.934	0.765	0.849	42.67	5.04	9.28
ENet [9]	0.929	0.741	0.827	5.27	0.36	22.80
Ours	0.947	0.809	0.879	8.08	0.49	19.56

4   Conclusion

In this work, we designed a novel light-weight network named LCASA-Net for skin lesion segmentation, including the proposed Context-Aware Self-Attention block which can capture informative features in dermoscopic images effectively and efficiently. The quantitative results showed that LCASA-Net is a robust segmentation technique as it achieved high performance, owned little parameters, and processed a dermoscopy image with fast speed. Future work aims to demonstrate the versatility of LCASA-Net for a variety of medical applications.

References

1. Berman, M., Triki, A.R., Blaschko, M.B.: The lovász-softmax loss: a tractable surrogate for the optimization of the intersection-over-union measure in neural networks. In: Proceedings of the IEEE Conference on Computer Vision and Pattern Recognition, pp. 4413–4421 (2018)
2. Bi, L., Kim, J., Ahn, E., Feng, D.: Automatic skin lesion analysis using large-scale dermoscopy images and deep residual networks. arXiv preprint arXiv:1703.04197 (2017)
3. Chen, L.-C., Zhu, Y., Papandreou, G., Schroff, F., Adam, H.: Encoder-decoder with atrous separable convolution for semantic image segmentation. In: Proceedings of the European Conference on Computer Vision (ECCV), pp. 801–818 (2018)
4. Codella, N.C.F., et al.: Skin lesion analysis toward melanoma detection: a challenge at the 2017 international symposium on biomedical imaging (ISBI), hosted by the international skin imaging collaboration (ISIC). In: IEEE 15th International Symposium on Biomedical Imaging (ISBI 2018), pp. 168–172. IEEE (2018)
5. Ding, H., Jiang, X., Shuai, B., Liu, A.Q., Wang, G.: Context contrasted feature and gated multi-scale aggregation for scene segmentation. In: Proceedings of the IEEE Conference on Computer Vision and Pattern Recognition, pp. 2393–2402 (2018)
6. Li, Q., Arnab, A., Torr, P.H.S.: Holistic, instance-level human parsing. arXiv preprint arXiv:1709.03612 (2017)
7. Long, J., Shelhamer, E., Darrell, T.: Fully convolutional networks for semantic segmentation. In: Proceedings of the IEEE Conference on Computer Vision and Pattern Recognition, pp. 3431–3440 (2015)
8. Menegola, A., Tavares, J., Fornaciali, M., Li, L.T., Avila, S., Valle, E.: RECOD Titans at ISIC challenge 2017. arXiv preprint arXiv:1703.04819 (2017)
9. Paszke, A., Chaurasia, A., Kim, S., Culurciello, E.: ENet: a deep neural network architecture for real-time semantic segmentation. arXiv preprint arXiv:1606.02147 (2016)
10. Roy, A.G., Navab, N., Wachinger, C.: Concurrent spatial and channel 'Squeeze & Excitation' in fully convolutional networks. In: Frangi, A., Schnabel, J., Davatzikos, C., Alberola-López, C., Fichtinger, G. (eds.) MICCAI 2018. LNCS, vol. 11070, pp. 421–429. Springer, Cham (2018). https://doi.org/10.1007/978-3-030-00928-1_48
11. Siegel, R.L., Miller, K.D., Jemal, A.: Cancer statistics, 2015. CA Cancer J. Clin. **65**(1), 5–29 (2015)
12. Yuan, Y., Lo, Y.-C.: Improving dermoscopic image segmentation with enhanced convolutional-deconvolutional networks. IEEE J. Biomed. Health Inform. **23**, 519–526 (2017)

Development of an Assistive Tongue Drive System for Disabled Individuals

Rahul Kumar[1] ⓘ, Krishneel Sharma[1], Mansour Assaf[1(✉)],
Bibhya Sharma[2], and Som Naidu[3]

[1] School of Engineering and Physics, The University of the South Pacific,
Suva, Fiji
assaf_m@usp.ac.fj
[2] School of Computing Science and Information Systems,
The University of the South Pacific, Suva, Fiji
[3] Centre for Flexible Learning, The University of the South Pacific, Suva, Fiji

Abstract. The authors propose a preliminary design and development of an assistive technology, which addresses the problem for people with disabilities to communicate with learning environments. An assistive Tongue Drive System (TDS) has been proposed which permits the end user to make use of their tongue for communication. In this paper, the hardware/software co-design of the proposed TDS system is presented and discussed in detail.

Keywords: Assistive technologies · Tongue-computer interface · Spinal cord injury · Brain computer interfaces · Magnetic field

1 Introduction

In this study, the authors propose a wearable device which enables the end users with disabilities to operate a laptop/computer without the need of keyboard or mouse. Not only the proposed system is capable to operate a laptop/computer, but also has the potential to enable people with disabilities to interact with the environment. This will help the disabled individuals to lead more independent lives.

With an ever-increasing technology, recent advancements have been made when it comes to wearable devices with assists in improving the lives of individuals, specifically those who live with complete paralysis [1, 2]. Through these types of assistive technologies and wireless communication systems, individuals with severe disabilities are able to communicate with other devices such as television set, radio, wheelchair, laptop, tablet etc.

The prime objectives of this study are; firstly, to model the problem mathematically in order to grasp the situation and simulate the underlying design solutions. Next is to acquire enough data from the sensors to learn the mechanical singularities in the proposed system and prepare countermeasures to refine the proposed design. Actually, this step is very important because it involves the adjustments been made to the proposed design so that outputs are recognized accurately which is then used to translate specific tongue gesture into computer commands. Final objective is to make

© Springer Nature Switzerland AG 2019
A. C. Nayak and A. Sharma (Eds.): PRICAI 2019, LNAI 11672, pp. 506–511, 2019.
https://doi.org/10.1007/978-3-030-29894-4_41

use of a wireless technology for communicating the information between the magnetic field sensing device and the peripherals. Next we present the design methodology.

2   Methodology

The proposed assistive TDS is equipped with multiple magnetic sensors together with a magnetic tracer which makes it capable to detect the position and movement in 3D space. Figure 1 describes the overall system setup for the TDS.

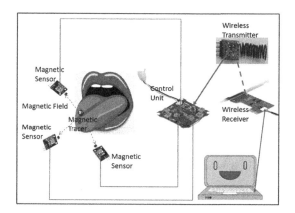

Fig. 1. Proposed TDS system representation

The TDS comprises of an array of magnetic sensors carefully positioned and worn by placing it around user's head via means of a headset like structure. By means of the magnetic tracer, the tongue movement is detected (magnetic tracer is a spherical permanent magnet of approximately 2.5 mm in diameter and placed as shown in Fig. 1) through measurement of differential changes in magnetic field around the mouth. These signals from the sensors are transmitted wirelessly to a laptop for further processing in order to decode/classify the tongue gesture, which is then translated into computer commands or actions.

The incoming data samples then undergoes segmentation and feature extraction procedure at the receiving workstation. Once the appropriate features are acquired, it is then subjected to a classifier which translates the sensor signals to one of the five tongue gestures. In this study, these five tongue gestures (which are basically the output commands) are: NO MOVEMENT, UP, DOWN, LEFT and RIGHT patterns. It must be noted that the classifier development plays a major role in this study and various different machine-learning algorithms have been tested and the best one turned out to be a shallow neural network classifier.

2.1 Data Pre-processing

The magnetic induction signals are continuous in nature (in both amplitude and in time). In order to analyze the data, a pre-requisite is to digitize the continuous signal. The time scale is made discrete sampling the continuous waveform at a given interval while the amplitude is made discrete by means of an analog-to-digital converter (ADC). After conversion of the signal samples, the data is stored as real numbers for further processing.

In this study, the statistical time features (STF) of the digitized version of the signal is studied in detail and have been used to extract significant attributes of the signal for the purpose of training the classifier. Table 1 below shows 15 statistical time features used for feature extraction prior to training.

Table 1. Feature list

STF (1–5)	STF (6–10)	STF (11–15)
Variance	Root mean square	Latitude factor
Mean	Square root mean	Crest factor
Max value	Normalized 5th central moment	Shape factor (with RMS)
Standard deviation	Normalized 6th central moment	Shape factor (with SRM)
Kurtosis	Skewness	Impulse factor

Since there are three magnetic sensors proposed for the system, the feature set will contain a total of 45 features at one instance. This number is of features is very high and would be cumbersome when it comes to hardware deployment stage. Thus, an additional step to reduce the number of features via principal component analysis was carried out. By preserving 95% of the variability, only first 22 set of linear combinations of the features was preserved and used for training the classifier.

2.2 Development of the Classifier

To this aim, various classification algorithms have been used to train the classifier. Using 1500 samples of data, following methods were used to train the classifier: these include, neural networks, support vector machines, k-nearest neighbor, family of trees as well as ensemble based classifiers.

After the feature extraction step, the feature set is normalized and trained by splitting the data randomly in partitions of: 50% for training, 25% for validation and 25% for the test set. The best performance after comparison among the aforementioned methods is demonstrated by a shallow neural network classifier which has an accuracy of 93.4% (Table 2). Using neural networks is advantageous because not only it has higher accuracy, but also due to its error function and output layer, we are able to analyze how confident the network is when it comes to the output class. The designed neural network is equipped with a cross entropy error function and has a softmax function in its output layer, which gives the class based on its probabilities.

Table 2. Comparison of the classifiers

Classification model	Accuracy (%)
1. Support vector machine (best configuration is with fine Gaussian kernel with box constraint of 1.0)	84.7
2. Medium kNN (best configuration is with k = 10)	86.9
3. Decision Trees (best configuration under complex tree with maximum no. splits = 100)	83.3
4. Ensemble Classifier (Boosted tree)	80.3
5. Ensemble Classifier (Bagged tree)	81.6
6. Artificial neural network (shallow network with only single hidden layer with 11 neurons)	93.4

In the next section, we present the hardware implementation details.

3   Hardware Arrangement of TDS

The process on how the proposed system works is given in Fig. 2. The major components are shown in red. The control module on the right of Fig. 2 detects tongue movement which then activates the data acquisition from the magnetic sensors using the inbuilt DSP module, the signal is filtered and digitized. Thereafter, the signal is transmitted to the receiving end, which is basically a laptop via a Bluetooth connection. Then, the oncoming signal is then classified on a real time basis by means of the developed neural network based classifier. The output is the tongue gesture as mentioned in the previous section. The tongue gesture is then displayed and conveyed via means of a speaker.

3.1   Wireless Data Transfer

The inbuilt Bluetooth module of Raspberry Pi Zero carries out the data transfer as described in Fig. 2. After the filtering and digitizing step, the signal is transmitted to the main processing module for classification (laptop) which classifies the signal in question on a real time basis. In order to quantify the time delay of the developed system, 300 samples were taken for each type for gesture (class) which underwent the testing phase. It is apparent from Fig. 3, that the developed system has an average time delay of less than approximately 0.25 s. This signifies that the proposed system response is fast and robust. Next we present the conclusion.

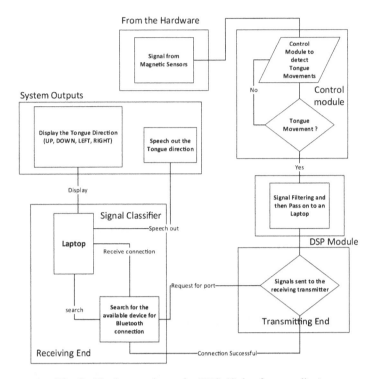

Fig. 2. Hardware scheme for TDS (Color figure online)

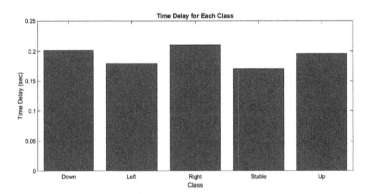

Fig. 3. Time-delay graph for all the classes

4 Conclusion

The proposed assistive TDS does not only provide a portable solution but also, due to its open architecture can be easily integrated with other peripherals. With an average time delay of less than 0.25 s and a system accuracy of 93.4%, the proposed system is very responsive and efficient when it comes to assess the performance of the TDS. It also has a power saving feature which governs the sensor and communication modules only when the tongue is in motion. The proposed solution will be able to assist many individuals with Spinal Cord Injuries (SCI) at much lower cost which would revolve around US$30.

Moreover, the system is versatile as it can work with any other type of laptop/computer device. It can also act as a control module for computer mouse, keyboard and as well as for wheelchairs. In this study, the TDS language is limited to only five classes. Future research will focus on extending the current TDS language to a more explanatory level and develop a curriculum such that end users can exploit the full potential of the developed TDS.

References

1. Christopher and Dana Reeve Foundation. One degree of separation: paralysis and spinal cord injury in the United States (2008). www.christopherreeve.org/site/c.ddJFKRNoFiG/b. 5091685/k.58BD/One_Degree_of_Separation.htm
2. National Institute of Neurological Disorders and Stroke (NINDS), NIH. Spinal cord injury: hope through research (2003). www.ninds.nih.gov/disorders/sci/detail_sci.htm

Other Applications

Deep Transfer Collaborative Filtering for Recommender Systems

Sibo Gai[1], Feng Zhao[1], Yachen Kang[1], Zhengyu Chen[1], Donglin Wang[1(✉)],
and Ao Tang[2]

[1] School of Engineering, Westlake University, Hangzhou 310024, China
{gaisibo,zhaofeng,kangyachen,chenzhengyu,wangdonglin}@westlake.edu.cn
[2] WeCar(Shenzhen) Technology Co., Ltd., Shenzhen, China
ao.tang@weicheche.cn

Abstract. Collaborative filtering (CF) is among the most effective techniques for recommendations. However, it suffers from data sparsity and cold-start issue. One solution is to incorporate the side information and the other is to learn knowledge from relevant domains. In this paper, we consider both aspects and propose a generic deep transfer collaborative filtering (DTCF) architecture, which integrates collective matrix factorization and deep transfer learning. We exhibit one instantiation of our architecture by employing non-negative matrix tri-factorization and stacked denoising autoencoder (SDAE) in both source and target domains. Deep learning copes with both the ratings' statistic characteristics and the side information to generate effective latent representations. Matrix tri-factorization produces private latent factors linked with per SDAE and common latent factors connected with different domains. Extensive experimental results on real datasets exhibit a superiority of our approach in comparison to state-of-the-art works.

Keywords: Collaborative filtering · Recommender system ·
Matrix tri-factorization · Side information · Knowledge transfer

1 Introduction

Recommendation becomes important and draws much attention in current information-overload era. Plenty of classical recommendation methods have been proposed during the last decade, which are largely categorized as content-based methods and collaborative filtering (CF) based methods [24]. Content-based methods consider user profile or item content information while CF-based methods utilize the user's past activities or preferences for recommendation. The CF-based methods are preferred owe to a better performance than content-based methods. Among various CF methods, matrix factorization acts out as a powerful tool for recommendations in large datasets [3].

Matrix factorization techniques are the main cornerstone of CF [12], which can produce effective latent factors for users and items from the rating matrix

© Springer Nature Switzerland AG 2019
A. C. Nayak and A. Sharma (Eds.): PRICAI 2019, LNAI 11672, pp. 515–528, 2019.
https://doi.org/10.1007/978-3-030-29894-4_42

[10,22]. However, there are two primary challenges for CF-based methods: data sparsity and cold start [4,6,8]. When the historical data is very sparse, CF-based methods degrade significantly [7]. On the other hand, the recommender systems are incapable of recommending users any new item that has not received rating information yet.

In order to overcome these problems, one solution is to integrate CF with the side information like users' profiles or items' properties to exploit prior features [25,26]. The side information has been either loosely utilized as regularizations [26] or tightly coupled with CF by using deep learning [13,28]. Another solution is to transfer the knowledge from relevant domains to a target domain and the cross-domain recommendation techniques address such problems [8]. In practice, we can track the same user's participation in a couple of recommendation systems to acquire various information in different domains. Deep transfer learning improves the recommendation performance in the target domain [9,14].

In this paper, we investigate the combination of CF and deep learning in both source and target domains to improve the recommendation performance. The generic architecture of deep transfer collaborative filtering (DTCF) is proposed by integrating cross-domain collective matrix factorization and deep learning. One DTCF instantiation is exhibited in detail, in which each stacked denoising autoencoder (SDAE) deals with both the ratings' statistic characteristics and the side information to achieve effective latent representations. Non-negative matrix tri-factorization [2] on the ratings engenders the private latent factors for both users and items in each domain, which are respectively connected with an individual SDAE. On the other hand, this factorization also generates the common latent factors, representing the association between users' latent factors and items' latent factors, which are treated as a bridge between source and target domains due to the across-domain stability [29]. DTCF jointly optimizes deep representation learning and CF for both source and target domains.

The main contribution of this paper lies in that we propose a generic architecture of deep transfer collaborative filtering and each deep structure SDAE in DTCF deals with both the ratings' statistic characteristics and the side information, where a feature extraction technique is used to deal with the rating's sparsity. DTCF addresses the knowledge transfer in a deep manner under the constraint of matrix factorization. We specifically study the simultaneous optimization of empirical likelihood and deep structure in source and target domains.

The remaining of this paper is organized as follows. Section 2 introduces the related work in general. Section 3 describes the preliminary and our proposed novel generic architecture. The proposed DTCF instantiation is presented in detail in Sect. 4, including the specific strategy, the loss function and the optimization. Performance evaluations on three real datasets are reported in Sect. 5, followed by Conclusion in Sect. 6.

2   Related Work

In general, our work is related to the following topics: matrix factorization based CF, deep learning based CF and matrix factorization based transfer learning.

2.1   Matrix Factorization Based CF

MF is the most popular technique to derive latent factors [11]. By adopting different loss function, a variety of matrix factorization models have been investigated, such as non-negative matrix factorization [12], probabilistic matrix factorization [22], Bayesian probabilistic matrix factorization [21], and max-margin matrix factorization [20]. By incorporating side information in sparse ratings, CF methods have shown an improved performance [18,19]. However, it is not sufficient because the side information is loosely coupled. Different from these methods, we further take the advantage of deep structure and transfer knowledge.

2.2   Deep Learning Based CF

Deep learning based CF is comparatively new, which could alleviate those intractable problems. Restricted Boltzmann machine is modified for CF tasks in [23] while ordinal Boltzmann machines are proposed for CF tasks in [27]. Recently, several deep learning models learn latent factors by tightly coupling with the side information [17]. Based on generalized Bayesian SDAE, a collaborative deep learning is proposed in [28] that only extracts deep features for items. Deep collaborative filtering based on marginalized denoising autoencoder is proposed for learn both items and users in a deep manner [13]. An alternative model of incorporating the side information is investigated in [3]. Deep heterogeneous autoencoder is proposed in [14] for dealing with heterogeneous data. Different from these methods, we further consider the transfer of knowledge from related domains in target domain.

2.3   Matrix Factorization Based Transfer Learning

Knowledge can be transferred across domains by using multiple decomposed matrices via collective matrix factorization (CMF) [26]. Its tri-factorization variants have been extensively studied for transfer learning [5]. CMF jointly factorizes multiple matrices with correspondences between rows and columns while sharing a set of common latent factors across different matrices [15]. CMF maximizes the empirical likelihood among multiple domains and the common latent factors are then used as a bridge for knowledge transfer [16,29]. Different from these methods, we further take the advantage of deep structure to integrate the side information and the ratings' statistic characteristics.

In addition, different from the traditional deep transfer structures that share cross-domain information via hidden connections [8] or learn a common network via domain separation network [1,9], we share the common latent factors.

3   Preliminary and Our Proposed Generic Architecture

Prior hybrid CF models combine deep structure and matrix factorization [3, 13,28], where deep structure deals with either the side information or both the

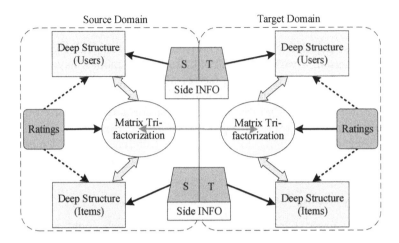

Fig. 1. Generic architecture of our proposed model.

ratings and side information, and matrix factorization on the ratings considers the production of users' latent matrix and items' latent matrix. However, this architecture cannot be used for cross-domain recommendations in the absence of a linkage between source and target domains.

In this paper, we attempt to propose a novel architecture to achieve cross-domain CF recommendations. Figure 1 shows the generic architecture, which utilizes non-negative matrix tri-factorization in each domain to generate an additional association matrix that could link different domains. For convenient description, define by $\mathcal{D}_s$ the source domain and $\mathcal{D}_t$ the target domain. *And the domain indices are denoted as $d \in \{s, t\}$.* In a recommendation setting, the user-item matrix can be decomposed as the production of three non-negative matrices $\mathbf{R}_d = \mathbf{U}_d \mathbf{H} \mathbf{V}_d^{\mathrm{T}}$ in domain $\mathcal{D}_d$, where $\mathbf{U}_d$ indicates the user latent factors, $\mathbf{V}_d$ indicates the item latent factors, and $\mathbf{H}$ indicates the association of $\mathbf{U}_d$ and $\mathbf{V}_d$. Non-negative matrix tri-factorization is integrated with deep structure by private latent factors $\mathbf{U}_d$, $\mathbf{V}_d$ and deep latent representations, where an individual deep structure deals with either only the side information or both the side information and the feature from ratings (dashed in Fig. 1). The source domain $\mathcal{D}_s$ is connected with the target domain $\mathcal{D}_t$ via common latent factors $\mathbf{H}$.

As in Fig. 1, we have an individual deep structure to learn effective latent representation of users or items in each domain, which possibly incorporates the side information and the ratings in various ways. Based on the generic cross-domain architecture, we will present one specific DTCF instantiation in the following, which takes the SDAE as deep structure to learn latent representation. For convenience, Table 1 summarizes the primary symbols used in our approach.

Table 1. Summary of primary notations.

Notation	Description
m_d	Number of users in $\mathcal{D}_d$
n_d	Number of items in $\mathcal{D}_d$
$\mathbf{R}_d = [r_{d,ij}]_{m_d \times n_d}$	Rating matrix in $\mathcal{D}_d$
$\mathbf{U}_d = [u_{d,ij}]_{m_d \times k_1}$	Users' latent factor matrix in $\mathcal{D}_d$
$\mathbf{u}_{d,i} \in \mathbb{R}^{1 \times k_1}$	Latent factor vector (user i) in $\mathcal{D}_d$
$\mathbf{V}_d = [v_{d,ij}]_{n_d \times k_2}$	Items' latent factor matrix in $\mathcal{D}_d$
$\mathbf{v}_{d,j} \in \mathbb{R}^{1 \times k_2}$	Latent factor vector (item j) in $\mathcal{D}_d$
$\mathbf{H} \in \mathbb{R}^{k_1 \times k_2}$	Common latent factors
$\mathbf{X}_d^{(u)}, \mathbf{X}_d^{(v)}$	Transformed rating matrix in $\mathcal{D}_d$
$\mathbf{x}_{d,i}^{(u)}, \mathbf{x}_{d,j}^{(v)}$	Transformed rating vectors
$\mathbf{p}_{d,i}^{(u)}, \mathbf{p}_{d,j}^{(v)}$	Side Information for $\mathbf{u}_{d,i}, \mathbf{v}_{d,j}$ in $\mathcal{D}_d$
$\mathbf{W}_d^{(u)} = [\mathbf{W}_{d,l}^{(u)}]_1^{L_d^{(u)}}$	Weights of users' SDAE in $\mathcal{D}_d$
$\mathbf{W}_d^{(v)} = [\mathbf{W}_{d,l}^{(v)}]_1^{L_d^{(v)}}$	Weighs of items' SDAE in $\mathcal{D}_d$
$\mathbf{z}_d^{(u)}, \mathbf{z}_d^{(v)}$	Weights for side Information in SDAE
$\mathbf{z}_{d,l}^{(u)}, \mathbf{z}_{d,l}^{(v)}$	Weights for side Information at layer l
$\mathbf{b}_d^{(u)}, \mathbf{b}_d^{(v)}$	Biases of users/items' SDAE
$\mathbf{b}_{d,l}^{(u)}, \mathbf{b}_{d,l}^{(v)}$	Biases of users/items' at layer l
$\mathbf{h}_{d,o}^{(u_i)}, \mathbf{h}_{d,o}^{(v_j)}$	Latent representation of $\mathbf{u}_{d,i}, \mathbf{v}_{d,j}$

4   Deep Transfer Collaborative Filtering

4.1   Structure of DTCF

Figure 2 shows the specific DTCF instantiation, where we have an individual SDAE for users or items in each domain to integrate the side information and learn effective latent representations. The TFE block in Fig. 2 denotes the transformation and feature extraction (TFE), where the transformation is similar to [3] and feature extraction considers statistical characteristics. Specifically, we have $\mathbf{X}_d^{(u)} = [\mathbf{R}_d]_F$ and $\mathbf{X}_d^{(v)} = [\mathbf{R}_d^{\mathrm{T}}]_F$, where the operator $[\cdot]_F$ considers each row of the matrix and sequentially concatenates one-hot coding of the maximum, the minimum, the median, the mode, the quartiles and the rounding mean. Moreover, $\mathbf{x}_{d,i}^{(u)}$ and $\mathbf{x}_{d,j}^{(v)}$, the vector of $\mathbf{X}_d^{(u)}$ and $\mathbf{X}_d^{(v)}$, are obtained to feed SDAEs. Please be noted that we also consider the case without feature extraction in our experiments, where $\mathbf{X}_d^{(u)} = \mathbf{R}_d$ and $\mathbf{X}_d^{(v)} = \mathbf{R}_d^{\mathrm{T}}$ instead.

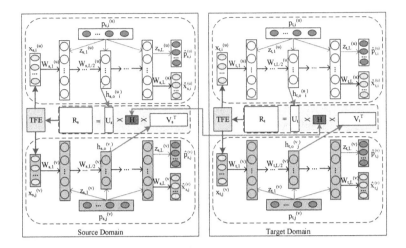

Fig. 2. The proposed DTCF instantiation.

Furthermore, the hidden representation at layer l and the output at layer $L_d^{(u)}$ can be obtained as

$$\mathbf{h}_{d,l}^{(u)} = g\left(\mathbf{W}_{d,l}^{(u)}\mathbf{h}_{d,l-1}^{(u)} + \mathbf{z}_{d,l}^{(u)}\tilde{\mathbf{p}}_{d,i}^{(u)} + \mathbf{b}_{d,l}^{(u)}\right)$$

$$\hat{\mathbf{x}}_{d,i}^{(u)} = f\left(\mathbf{W}_{d,L_d^{(u)}}^{(u)}\mathbf{h}_{d,L_d^{(u)}}^{(u)} + \mathbf{b}_{d,L_d^{(u)}}^{(u)}\right)$$

$$\hat{\mathbf{p}}_{d,i}^{(u)} = f\left(\mathbf{z}_{d,L_d^{(u)}}^{(u)}\mathbf{h}_{d,L_d^{(u)}}^{(u)} + \mathbf{b}_{d,n}^{(u)}\right) \tag{1}$$

where $l \in \{1, 2, \cdots, L_d^{(u)} - 1\}$; $\tilde{\mathbf{p}}_{d,i}^{(u)}$ is the corrupted *side information*; $g(\cdot)$ and $f(\cdot)$ are active functions for the hidden and output layers; $\mathbf{b}_{d,n}^{(u)}$ is the biases in the output layer for the side information. $\mathbf{x}_{d,i}^{(u)}$ is the input to the first layer, effective latent representation is obtained in the middle layer and $\hat{\mathbf{x}}_{d,i}^{(u)}$ denotes the output. Similar results can be obtained for the items' SDAE by replacing (u) with (v), i with j.

As in Fig. 2, non-negative matrix tri-factorization is integrated with deep structure by approximating private latent factors as deep representation. Specifically, for both source and target domains, the users' SDAE takes as input the side information of users to learn effective latent representation $\mathbf{h}_{d,o}^{(u_i)}$ that is used to compensate latent factor vector $\mathbf{u}_{d,i}$ in matrix tri-factorization. And the items' SDAE takes as input the side information of items to learn effective latent representation $\mathbf{h}_{d,o}^{(v_j)}$ that is used to compensate latent factor vector $\mathbf{v}_{d,j}$ in matrix tri-factorization. The source domain is linked with the target domain by common latent factors $\mathbf{H}$.

4.2   Loss Function

The overall loss of DTCF consists of three components: the matrix tri-factorization loss, the reconstruction cost of the side information, and the approximation error between deep representations and private latent factors.

Firstly, the loss of matrix tri-factorization in source and target domains can be expressed as

$$\min_{\boldsymbol{\theta}_m} \mathcal{L} = \sum_{d \in \{s,t\}} \left\| \mathbf{C}_d \odot \left(\mathbf{R}_d - \mathbf{U}_d \mathbf{H} \mathbf{V}_d^{\mathrm{T}} \right) \right\|^2, \tag{2}$$

where $\boldsymbol{\theta}_m = \{ \mathbf{U}_s, \mathbf{V}_s, \mathbf{H}, \mathbf{U}_t, \mathbf{V}_t \}$ the binary matrix $\mathbf{C}_d$ is an indicator of sparsity and $\odot$ is the element-wise operation. Here, $\mathbf{U}_d \mathbf{H} \mathbf{V}_d^{\mathrm{T}}$ can be further written as

$$\left[\mathbf{U}_d \mathbf{H} \mathbf{V}_d^{\mathrm{T}} \right]_{ij} = \left[\mathbf{u}_{d,i} \mathcal{H}_1^c, \mathbf{u}_{d,i}^c \mathcal{H}_2^c, \cdots, \mathbf{u}_{d,i} \mathcal{H}_{k_2}^c \right] \mathbf{v}_{d,j}^{\mathrm{T}}$$
$$= \mathbf{u}_{d,i} \left[\mathcal{H}_1^r \mathbf{v}_{d,j}^{\mathrm{T}}, \mathcal{H}_2^r \mathbf{v}_{d,j}^{\mathrm{T}}, \cdots, \mathcal{H}_{k_1}^r \mathbf{v}_{d,j}^{\mathrm{T}} \right], \tag{3}$$

where $\mathcal{H}_k^c$ with $k \in \{1, 2, \cdots, k_1\}$ denotes the column of $\mathbf{H}$; $\mathcal{H}_k^r$ with $k \in \{1, 2, \cdots, k_2\}$ denotes the row of $\mathbf{H}$. By defining $\bar{\mathbf{u}}_{d,i} \triangleq \left[\mathbf{u}_{d,i} \mathcal{H}_1^c, \mathbf{u}_{d,i}^c \mathcal{H}_2^c, \cdots, \mathbf{u}_{d,i} \mathcal{H}_{k_2}^c \right]$ and $\bar{\mathbf{v}}_{d,j}^{\mathrm{T}} \triangleq \left[\mathcal{H}_1^r \mathbf{v}_{d,j}^{\mathrm{T}}, \mathcal{H}_2^r \mathbf{v}_{d,j}^{\mathrm{T}}, \cdots, \mathcal{H}_{k_1}^r \mathbf{v}_{d,j}^{\mathrm{T}} \right]$, it can be rewritten as

$$\left[\mathbf{U}_d \mathbf{H} \mathbf{V}_d^{\mathrm{T}} \right]_{ij} = \bar{\mathbf{u}}_{d,i} \mathbf{v}_{d,j}^{\mathrm{T}} = \mathbf{u}_{d,i} \bar{\mathbf{v}}_{d,j}^{\mathrm{T}}. \tag{4}$$

Furthermore, the reconstruction cost at both source and target domains can be expressed as

$$\min_{\boldsymbol{\theta}_r} \mathcal{L}_r = \sum_d \alpha_d \sum_i \left(\mathbf{x}_{d,i}^{(u)} - \hat{\mathbf{x}}_{d,i}^{(u)} \right)^2 + \sum_d \beta_d \sum_j \left(\mathbf{x}_{d,j}^{(v)} - \hat{\mathbf{x}}_{d,j}^{(v)} \right)^2$$
$$+ \sum_d (1 - \alpha_d) \sum_i \left(\mathbf{p}_{d,i}^{(u)} - \hat{\mathbf{p}}_{d,i}^{(u)} \right)^2 + \sum_d (1 - \beta_d) \sum_j \left(\mathbf{p}_{d,j}^{(v)} - \hat{\mathbf{p}}_{d,j}^{(v)} \right)^2$$

where $\boldsymbol{\theta}_r = \left\{ \mathbf{W}_s^{(u)}, \mathbf{b}_s^{(u)}, \mathbf{W}_s^{(v)}, \mathbf{b}_s^{(v)}, \mathbf{W}_t^{(u)}, \mathbf{b}_t^{(u)}, \mathbf{W}_t^{(v)}, \mathbf{b}_t^{(v)} \right\}$. α_d and β_d are penalty parameters.

Thirdly, the approximation error between deep representations and latent factor vectors can be expressed as

$$\min_{\boldsymbol{\theta}_a} \mathcal{L}_a = \sum_d \rho_d \sum_i \left(\mathbf{u}_{d,i} - \mathbf{h}_{d,o}^{(u_i)} \right)^2 + \sum_d \gamma_d \sum_j \left(\mathbf{v}_{d,j} - \mathbf{h}_{d,o}^{(v_j)} \right)^2,$$

where $\boldsymbol{\theta}_a = \left\{ \mathbf{U}_s, \mathbf{V}_s, \mathbf{W}_s^{(u)}, \mathbf{b}_s^{(u)}, \mathbf{W}_s^{(v)}, \mathbf{b}_s^{(v)} \right\} \cup \left\{ \mathbf{U}_t, \mathbf{V}_t, \mathbf{W}_t^{(u)}, \mathbf{b}_t^{(u)}, \mathbf{W}_t^{(v)}, \mathbf{b}_t^{(v)} \right\}$; ρ_d and γ_d are penalty parameters.

Therefore, the overall loss function of the proposed DTCF is finally obtained as

$$\min_{\Theta} \mathcal{J} = \mathcal{L} + \mathcal{L}_r + \mathcal{L}_a + \lambda f_{reg}, \tag{5}$$

where $\boldsymbol{\Theta} = \boldsymbol{\theta}_m \cup \boldsymbol{\theta}_r \cup \boldsymbol{\theta}_a$, f_{reg} is the regularization that prevents overfitting,

$$
\begin{aligned}
f_{reg} = \sum_d &\left(\sum_i \| \mathbf{u}_{d,i} \|^2 + \sum_j \| \mathbf{v}_{d,j} \|^2 \right) \\
&+ \sum_d \left(\| \mathbf{W}_d^{(u)} \|^2 + \| \mathbf{W}_d^{(v)} \|^2 + \| \mathbf{b}_d^{(u)} \|^2 + \| \mathbf{b}_d^{(v)} \|^2 \right) \\
&+ \sum_d \left(\| \mathbf{z}_d^{(u)} \|^2 + \| \mathbf{z}_d^{(v)} \|^2 \right)
\end{aligned}
\tag{6}
$$

and λ is a penalty parameter.

4.3   Optimization

To solve this problem, the alternate optimization algorithm is considered by utilizing the following three-step procedure.

Step I: Given all weights $\mathbf{W}_d^{(u)}$, $\mathbf{W}_d^{(v)}$, and biases $\mathbf{b}_d^{(u)}$, $\mathbf{b}_d^{(v)}$ in source and target domains, the gradients of $\mathcal{J}$ in (5) with respect to $\mathbf{u}_{d,i}$ and $\mathbf{v}_{d,j}$, $d \in \{s,t\}$, can be obtained as

$$
\frac{\partial \mathcal{J}}{\partial \mathbf{u}_{d,i}} = - \sum_j c_{d,ij} \left(r_{d,ij} - \mathbf{u}_{d,i} \bar{\mathbf{v}}_{d,j}^{\mathrm{T}} \right) \bar{\mathbf{v}}_{d,j} + \rho_d \left(\mathbf{u}_{d,i} - \mathbf{h}_{d,o}^{(u_i)} \right) + \lambda \mathbf{u}_{d,i},
$$

$$
\frac{\partial \mathcal{J}}{\partial \mathbf{v}_{d,j}} = - \sum_i c_{d,ij} \left(r_{d,ij} - \bar{\mathbf{u}}_{d,i} \mathbf{v}_{d,j}^{\mathrm{T}} \right) \bar{\mathbf{u}}_{d,j} + \gamma_d \left(\mathbf{v}_{d,j} - \mathbf{h}_{d,o}^{(v_j)} \right) + \lambda \mathbf{v}_{d,j}, \tag{7}
$$

where the binary $c_{d,ij}$ indicates whether the corresponding rating $r_{d,ij}$ is observed $(=1)$ or not $(=0)$. By using coordinate ascent similar to [28], we have

$$
\mathbf{u}_{d,i} = \left(\bar{\mathbf{V}}_d \mathbf{C}_{d,i} \bar{\mathbf{V}}_d^T + (\rho_d + \lambda)\mathbf{I} \right)^{-1} \left(\bar{\mathbf{V}}_d \mathbf{C}_{d,i} \mathbf{R}_{d,i} + \rho_d \mathbf{h}_{d,o}^{(u_i)} \right) \tag{8}
$$

$$
\mathbf{v}_{d,j} = \left(\bar{\mathbf{U}}_d \mathbf{C}_{d,j} \bar{\mathbf{U}}_d^T + (\gamma_d + \lambda)\mathbf{I} \right)^{-1} \left(\bar{\mathbf{U}}_d \mathbf{C}_{d,j} \mathbf{R}_{d,j} + \gamma_d \mathbf{h}_{d,o}^{(v_j)} \right) \tag{9}
$$

with $\bar{\mathbf{U}}_d = [\bar{\mathbf{u}}_{d,i}]_1^{k_1}$ and $\bar{\mathbf{V}}_d = [\bar{\mathbf{v}}_{d,j}]_1^{k_2}$; $\mathbf{C}_{d,i} = \mathrm{diag}(c_{i1}, \cdots, c_{ik_2})$ and $\mathbf{C}_{d,j} = \mathrm{diag}(c_{1j}, \cdots, c_{k_1j})$; $\mathbf{R}_{d,i} = (\mathbf{R}_{d,i1}, \cdots, \mathbf{R}_{d,ik_2})^{\mathrm{T}}$ and $\mathbf{R}_{d,i} = (\mathbf{R}_{d,1j}, \cdots, \mathbf{R}_{d,k_1j})^{\mathrm{T}}$.

Step II: Fixed the users' latent factors $\mathbf{U}_d$ and the items' latent factors $\mathbf{V}_d$, $d \in \{s,t\}$, by referring to [2], the association between the users' latent factors and items' latent factors $\mathbf{H}$ can be updated by

$$
\mathbf{H} \leftarrow \mathbf{H} \odot \sqrt{ \frac{ \left\{ \sum_{d \in \{s,t\}} \mathbf{U}_d^{\mathrm{T}} (\mathbf{C}_d \odot \mathbf{R}_d) \mathbf{V}_d \right\} }{ \left\{ \sum_{d \in \{s,t\}} \mathbf{U}_d^{\mathrm{T}} \left(\mathbf{C}_d \odot (\mathbf{U}_d \mathbf{H} \mathbf{V}_d^{\mathrm{T}}) \right) \mathbf{V}_d \right\} } }, \tag{10}
$$

where $\odot$ is the element-wise operation defined as above and $\frac{\{\cdot\}}{\{\cdot\}}$ is the element-wise division.

Step III: Fixed the users' latent factors $\mathbf{U}_d$, the items' latent factors $\mathbf{V}_d$ and the common latent factors $\mathbf{H}$, $d \in \{s,t\}$, all weights $\mathbf{W}_d^{(u)}$, $\mathbf{W}_d^{(v)}$, and biases $\mathbf{b}_d^{(u)}$, $\mathbf{b}_d^{(v)}$, of SDAEs in both domains, can be learnt by backpropagation with stochastic gradient decent (SGD) method

$$\frac{\partial \mathcal{J}}{\partial \mathbf{W}_d^{(u)}} = -\rho_d \sum_i \left(\mathbf{u}_{d,i} - \mathbf{h}_{d,o}^{(u_i)}\right) \frac{\partial \mathbf{h}_{d,o}^{(u_i)}}{\partial \mathbf{W}_d^{(u)}} + \alpha_d \sum_i \left(\mathbf{x}_{d,i}^{(u)} - \hat{\mathbf{x}}_{d,i}^{(u)}\right) \frac{\partial \hat{\mathbf{x}}_{d,i}^{(u)}}{\partial \mathbf{W}_d^{(u)}} + \lambda \mathbf{W}_d^{(u)},$$

$$\frac{\partial \mathcal{J}}{\partial \mathbf{W}_d^{(v)}} = -\gamma_d \sum_j \left(\mathbf{v}_{d,j} - \mathbf{h}_{d,o}^{(v_j)}\right) \frac{\partial \mathbf{h}_{d,o}^{(v_j)}}{\partial \mathbf{W}_d^{(v)}} + \beta_d \sum_j \left(\mathbf{x}_{d,j}^{(v)} - \hat{\mathbf{x}}_{d,j}^{(v)}\right) \frac{\partial \hat{\mathbf{x}}_{d,j}^{(v)}}{\partial \mathbf{W}_d^{(v)}} + \lambda \mathbf{W}_d^{(v)}. \quad (11)$$

Furthermore, $\frac{\partial \mathcal{J}}{\partial \mathbf{b}_d^{(u)}}$ and $\frac{\partial \mathcal{J}}{\partial \mathbf{b}_d^{(v)}}$ can be easily obtained by replacing $\mathbf{W}$ with $\mathbf{b}$ in (11). $\frac{\partial \mathcal{J}}{\partial \mathbf{z}_d^{(u)}}$ and $\frac{\partial \mathcal{J}}{\partial \mathbf{z}_d^{(v)}}$ are obtained by

$$\frac{\partial \mathcal{J}}{\partial \mathbf{z}_d^{(u)}} = -\rho_d \sum_i \left(\mathbf{u}_{d,i} - \mathbf{h}_{d,o}^{(u_i)}\right) \frac{\partial \mathbf{h}_{d,o}^{(u_i)}}{\partial \mathbf{z}_d^{(u)}} + (1 - \alpha_d) \sum_i \left(\mathbf{p}_{d,i}^{(u)} - \hat{\mathbf{p}}_{d,i}^{(u)}\right) \frac{\partial \hat{\mathbf{p}}_{d,i}^{(u)}}{\partial \mathbf{z}_d^{(u)}} + \lambda \mathbf{z}_d^{(u)},$$

$$\frac{\partial \mathcal{J}}{\partial \mathbf{z}_d^{(v)}} = -\gamma_d \sum_j \left(\mathbf{v}_{d,j} - \mathbf{h}_{d,o}^{(v_j)}\right) \frac{\partial \mathbf{h}_{d,o}^{(v_j)}}{\partial \mathbf{z}_d^{(v)}} + (1 - \beta_d) \sum_j \left(\mathbf{p}_{d,j}^{(v)} - \hat{\mathbf{p}}_{d,j}^{(v)}\right) \frac{\partial \hat{\mathbf{p}}_{d,j}^{(v)}}{\partial \mathbf{z}_d^{(v)}} + \lambda \mathbf{z}_d^{(v)}. \quad (12)$$

Iterate all three steps until the convergence.

5 Experiments

We evaluate our DTCF instantiation on the challenging movie and book recommendations, where experiments are conducted on three popular datasets: MovieLens-100K (MLK)[1], MovieLens-1M (MLM) (see Footnote 1) and BookCrossing (BC)[2].

5.1 Dataset

MLK consists of 100 K ratings of 943 users and 1682 movies while MLM consists of 1 million ratings of 6040 users and 3706 movies. Each rating is an integer in the range of 1 to 5. The ratings are highly sparse, where no ratings occupy 93.7% in MLK and 95.8% in MLM. The side information for users contains the user's age, gender, occupation and zipcode while the side information for items contains the category of movie genre and release date. BC contains 1149780 books from 278858 users, where each rating is an integer from 0 to 10 and no ratings occupy 99.9%. Some attributes of books and users are also provided and being utilized as the side information.

---

[1] http://www.grouplens.org/datasets/movielens.
[2] http://www2.informatik.uni-freiburg.de/~cziegler/BX/.

Table 2. RMSE comparison of various methods on three pairs of datasets.

Algorithm	MLK(s) vs MLM(t)			MLM(s) vs MLK(t)			BC(s) vs MLK(t)		
	60%	80%	95%	60%	80%	95%	60%	80%	95%
NMF	1.0258	1.0127	1.0040	1.0381	1.0276	1.0195	1.0381	1.0276	1.0195
GCMF	1.023	1.0116	1.0107	1.0326	1.0215	1.0123	1.0337	1.0319	1.0205
CDL	1.0113	1.0027	0.9871	1.0207	1.0168	0.9984	1.0207	1.0168	0.9984
PMF	0.9204	0.9131	0.9100	0.9590	0.9380	0.9236	0.9590	0.9380	0.9236
RGCMF	0.9173	0.9123	0.9079	0.9585	0.9366	0.9213	0.9614	0.9371	0.9220
CMF	0.9090	0.8857	0.8746	0.9476	0.9232	0.9162	0.9476	0.9232	0.9162
DCF	0.8864	0.8632	0.8571	0.9348	0.9157	*0.8981*	0.9348	*0.9157*	*0.8981*
aSDAE	0.9964	0.9777	0.9701	0.9345	0.9278	0.9227	0.9964	0.9777	0.9701
DTCFr	*0.8716*	*0.8575*	*0.8490*	*0.9282*	*0.9100*	0.8993	*0.9290*	0.9242	0.9219
DTCF	**0.8582**	**0.8471**	**0.8420**	**0.9124**	**0.8957**	**0.8897**	**0.9157**	**0.8980**	**0.8902**

To incorporate the side information in movie recommendation, the side information for users and items are encoded into a binary valued vector of length 139 and 28 in both domains respectively. Similarly, for book recommendation, the side information for users and items is encoded into binary vectors of length 62 and 1003 respectively.

We organize MLK(s) vs MLM(t), MLM(s) vs MLK(t) and BC(s) vs MLK(t) as three pairs for evaluation, where the former acts as the *source* domain and the latter acts as the *target* domain. For all compared methods, we train each compared method with different percentages of the user-item ratings, where 60%, 80% and 95% of the whole rating data are randomly selected as the training data and the remaining data are taken as the test data. We repeat the evaluation five times with different randomly selected training data.

We employ the root mean squared error (RMSE) and the mean absolute error (MAE) as the evaluation metric, which are defined respectively as

(1) RMSE:

$$\text{RMSE} = \sqrt{\frac{1}{N_{\mathcal{T}}} \sum_{R_{ij}^t \in \mathcal{T}} \left(R_{ij}^t - \hat{R}_{ij}^t \right)^2}, \tag{13}$$

(2) MAE:

$$\text{MAE} = \frac{\sum_{R_{ij}^t \in \mathcal{T}} \left| R_{ij}^t - \hat{R}_{ij}^t \right|}{N_{\mathcal{T}}}, \tag{14}$$

where R_{ij}^t is the ground-truth rating of user i for item j, $\hat{R}_{ij}^t$ denotes the estimated rating of R_{ij}^t, $N_{\mathcal{T}}$ is the total number of ratings in the test dataset $\mathcal{T}$.

5.2   Baselines

In order to evaluate the performance of our proposed DTCF, we consider the following methods as baselines:

- **NMF** - Non-negative matrix factorization [12] is a single-domain recommendation model.
- **GCMF** - Graph-based collective matrix factorization [16] is a transfer model and attempts to combine factorization with graph co-regularization that does not work well for sparse datasets.
- **CDL** - Collaborative deep learning [28] is a hierarchical deep Bayesian model to achieve deep representation learning for the item information.
- **PFM** - Probabilistic matrix factorization [22] assumes that there exists Gaussian observation noise and Gaussian priors on the latent factors.
- **RGCMF** - Revised GCMF (RGCMF) is a revision and extension of the original GCMF [16]. We improve this method by considering the data sparsity and inducing a binary indicating matrix as in (2).
- **CMF** - Collective matrix factorization [26] is a model factorizing multiple sources, including the ratings and the additional side information.
- **DCF** - Deep collaborative filtering [13] is a single-domain recommendation model which combines PMF with marginalized SDAE.
- **aSDAE** - Additional denoising autoencoder [3] is a single-domain model which has autoencoders with both side information and raw rating.
- **DTCFr** - DTCFr is similar to DTCF, which considers the transformation of ratings but not feature extraction.

For our DTCF instantiation, we set the parameters α_d and β_d as 0.1, the parameters γ_d, ρ_d as 0.9, the regularization coefficient λ as 0.2, respectively. The learning rate η is set to 0.001. We use a masking noise with a noise level of 0.1 to get the corrupted inputs. In terms of the SDAE in both source and target domains, the number of layers for the encoder or decoder is set to 2 and the total number of layers for the encoder-decoder is equal to 7. Moreover, the dimensionality of learned latent factor vectors for users is set to 30 while the dimensionality of learned latent factor vectors for items is set to 100. The size of the hidden layers is 37 and 55 for users and items respectively in both MLK and MLM, and 58 and 86 in BC.

5.3   Experimental Results

Tables 2 and 3 shows respectively the average RMSE and MAE of all baselines and our proposed DTCFr and DTCF on three pairs of datasets, where the lowest and second lowest value of each dataset is highlighted in boldface and italic, respectively. As observed, DTCF performs the best for all cases and DTCFr performs the second best in most of cases.

From Tables 2 and 3, it is observed that DTCF, DTCFr, DCF and CMF achieve a better performance than NMF, PMF, GCMF and RGCMF, indicating the effectiveness of incorporating the side information. Moreover, DTCF,

Table 3. MAE comparison of various methods on three pairs of datasets.

Algorithm	MLK(s) vs MLM(t)			MLM(s) vs MLK(t)			BC(s) vs MLK(t)		
	60%	80%	95%	60%	80%	95%	60%	80%	95%
NMF	0.8241	0.8207	0.8169	0.8283	0.8249	0.8225	0.8283	0.8249	0.8225
GCMF	0.8214	0.8183	0.8172	0.8261	0.821	0.8196	0.8275	0.8254	0.8249
CDL	0.8173	0.8146	0.8061	0.8209	0.8187	0.8116	0.8209	0.8187	0.8116
PMF	0.7619	0.7553	0.7517	0.7903	0.7815	0.7694	0.7903	0.7815	0.7694
RGCMF	0.7232	0.7186	0.7124	0.7741	0.7702	0.7649	0.7843	0.7782	0.7680
CMF	0.7214	0.7066	0.6993	0.7876	0.7652	0.7447	0.7876	0.7652	0.7447
DCF	0.7122	0.6918	0.6852	0.7632	0.7407	0.7236	0.7632	0.7407	0.7236
aSDAE	0.8029	0.7850	0.7769	0.7475	0.7404	0.7355	0.8029	0.7850	0.7769
DTCFr	*0.6832*	*0.6711*	*0.6638*	*0.7276*	*0.7125*	*0.7034*	*0.7285*	*0.7258*	*0.7235*
DTCF	**0.6728**	**0.6640**	**0.6596**	**0.7151**	**0.7021**	**0.6960**	**0.7167**	**0.7021**	**0.6961**

DTCFr and DCF outperform CMF, NMF, PMF, GCMF and RGCMF, indicating that deep structures can exploit better feature quality of the side information. Furthermore, DTCF outperform DCF and CDL, validating the effectiveness of cross-domain learning in recommendations. DTCFr outperform DCF in general except a few cases in terms of RMSE because BC dataset is extremely sparse and learning from the ratings gets difficult.

DTCF outperforms DTCFr, validating the effectiveness of feature extraction for highly sparse ratings. Both aSDAE and DTCFr takes the extreme-sparse ratings into the SDAE so that it is very difficult to learn effective latent representation from the ratings. Therefore, on the one hand, we design the TFE block to improve the way of incorporating the sparse ratings in deep structure to learn effective latent representation. Using statistic characteristics to raising the encoding of raw ratings from different users is reasonable.

In addition, the cross-domain RGCMF is comparative to CMF that incorporates the side information, which implies the effectiveness of both transfer learning and the incorporation of the side information. To sum up, our proposed DTCF achieves a superiority in comparison to state-of-the-art methods, which demonstrates the effectiveness of the integration of deep learning and cross-domain non-negative matrix tri-factorization.

From Tables 2 and 3, it is observed that the performance of our proposed DTCF, DTCFr, GCMF and RGCMF on the pair of MLM vs MLK is better than that on the pair of BC vs MLK, in terms of both RMSE and MAE. That indicates that the source domain of MLM has more common characteristics with the target domain of MLK than it of BC. In other words, the dataset of MLK is more like MLM instead of BC, which is consistent with our intuition. On the other hand, the remaining techniques including NMF, CDL, PFM, CMF and DCF have an equal performance on both data pairs because they are not cross-domain recommendation techniques and the source domain thus becomes useless.

6   Conclusion

DTCF is proposed for cross-domain recommendation. In both source and target domains Non-negative matrix tri-factorization is integrated with deep structure, where common latent factors conduct a bridge between domains and private latent factors link with per deep structure. The feature extraction technique is used to improve the performance. Effective latent representations of users and items are learned by jointly optimizing matrix tri-factorization and SDAEs in both source and target domains. The proposed scheme has been demonstrated by extensive experiments.

References

1. Bousmalis, K., Trigeorgis, G., Silberman, N., Krishnan, D., Erhan, D.: Domain separation networks. In: Advances in Neural Information Processing Systems, pp. 343–351 (2016)
2. Ding, C.H.Q., Li, T., Peng, W., Park, H.: Orthogonal nonnegative matrix t-factorizations for clustering, pp. 126–135 (2006)
3. Dong, X., Yu, L., Wu, Z., Sun, Y., Yuan, L., Zhang, F.: A hybrid collaborative filtering model with deep structure for recommender systems. In: AAAI, pp. 1309–1315 (2017)
4. Dziugaite, G.K., Roy, D.M.: Neural network matrix factorization. arXiv:1511.06443 (2015)
5. Gupta, S.K., Phung, D.Q., Adams, B., Tran, T., Venkatesh, S.: Nonnegative shared subspace learning and its application to social media retrieval. In: KDD, pp. 650–658 (2010)
6. He, X., Liao, L., Zhang, H., Nie, L., Hu, X., Chua, T.S.: Neural collaborative filtering, pp. 173–182 (2017)
7. Hoyer, P.O.: Non-negative matrix factorization with sparseness constraints. J. Mach. Learn. Res. **5**, 1457–1469 (2004)
8. Hu, G., Zhang, Y., Yang, Q.: MTNeT: a neural approach for cross-domain recommendation with unstructured text. In: KDD Deep Learning Day, pp. 1–10 (2018)
9. Kanagawa, H., Kobayashi, H., Shimizu, N., Tagami, Y., Suzuki, T.: Cross-domain recommendation via deep domain adaptation. In: Azzopardi, L., Stein, B., Fuhr, N., Mayr, P., Hauff, C., Hiemstra, D. (eds.) ECIR 2019. LNCS, vol. 11438, pp. 20–29. Springer, Cham (2019). https://doi.org/10.1007/978-3-030-15719-7_3
10. Koren, Y., Bell, R., Volinsky, C.: Matrix factorization techniques for recommender systems. IEEE Comput. J. **8**, 30–37 (2009)
11. Lee, D.D., Seung, H.S.: Learning the parts of objects by non-negative matrix factorization. Nature **401**(6755), 788 (1999)
12. Lee, D.D., Seung, H.S.: Algorithms for non-negative matrix factorization. In: NIPS, pp. 556–562 (2001)
13. Li, S., Kawale, J., Fu, Y.: Deep collaborative filtering via marginalized denoising auto-encoder. In: ACM International on Conference on Information and Knowledge Management, pp. 811–820 (2015)
14. Li, T., Ma, Y., Xu, J., Stenger, B., Liu, C., Hirate, Y.: Deep heterogeneous autoencoders for collaborative filtering. In: ICDM, pp. 1164–1169 (2018)
15. Long, M., Cheng, W., Jin, X., Wang, J., Shen, D.: Transfer learning via cluster correspondence inference. In: ICDM, pp. 917–922 (2011)

16. Long, M., Wang, J., Ding, G., Shen, D., Yang, Q.: Transfer learning with graph co-regularization. IEEE Trans. Knowl. Data Eng. **26**(7), 1805–1818 (2014)
17. Ouyang, Y., Liu, W., Rong, W., Xiong, Z.: Autoencoder-based collaborative filtering. In: Loo, C.K., Yap, K.S., Wong, K.W., Beng Jin, A.T., Huang, K. (eds.) ICONIP 2014. LNCS, vol. 8836, pp. 284–291. Springer, Cham (2014). https://doi.org/10.1007/978-3-319-12643-2_35
18. Park, S., Kim, Y.D., Choi, S.: Hierarchical Bayesian matrix factorization with side information. In: IJCAI, pp. 1593–1599 (2013)
19. Porteous, I., Asuncion, A.U., Welling, M.: Bayesian matrix factorization with side information and Dirichlet process mixtures. In: AAAI, pp. 563–568 (2010)
20. Rennie, J.D.M., Srebro, N.: Fast maximum margin matrix factorization for collaborative prediction. In: ICML, pp. 713–719 (2005)
21. Salakhutdinov, R.: Bayesian probabilistic matrix factorization using Markov chain Monte Carlo. In: ICML, pp. 880–887 (2008)
22. Salakhutdinov, R., Mnih, A.: Probabilistic matrix factorization. In: NIPS, pp. 1257–1264 (2007)
23. Salakhutdinov, R., Mnih, A., Hinton, G.E.: Restricted Boltzmann machines for collaborative filtering. In: ICML, pp. 791–798 (2007)
24. Shi, Y., Larson, M., Hanjalic, A.: Collaborative filtering beyond the user-item matrix: a survey of the state of the art and future challenges. ACM Comput. Surv. **47**(1), 1–45 (2014)
25. Singh, A., Gordon, G.J.: A Bayesian matrix factorization model for relational data. In: UAI, pp. 556–563 (2010)
26. Singh, A.P., Gordon, G.J.: Relational learning via collective matrix factorization. In: KDD, pp. 650–658 (2008)
27. Truyen, T.T., Phung, D.Q., Venkatesh, S.: Ordinal Boltzmann machines for collaborative filtering. In: UAI, pp. 548–556 (2009)
28. Wang, H., Wang, N., Yeung, D.Y.: Collaborative deep learning for recommender systems. In: KDD, pp. 1235–1244 (2015)
29. Zhuang, F., et al.: Mining distinction and commonality across multiple domains using generative model for text classification. IEEE Trans. Knowl. Data Eng. **24**(11), 2025–2039 (2012)

Multiple Knowledge Transfer for Cross-Domain Recommendation

Quan Do, Sunny Verma$^{(\boxtimes)}$, Fang Chen, and Wei Liu

Advanced Analytics Institute, School of Computer Science,
University of Technology Sydney, Sydney, Australia
{DucMinhQuan.Do,Sunny.Verma}@student.uts.edu.au,
{Fang.Chen,Wei.Liu}@uts.edu.au

Abstract. Collaborative filtering based recommendation systems rely on underlying similarities among users and items across multiple dataset and hence requires sufficiently large amount of ratings data to achieve accurate and reliable results. However, newly established businesses do not have sufficient ratings data and hence this requirement is rarely met. In this research, we propose Multiple Latent Clusters (**MultLC**) transfer to exploit the correlations among multiple datasets that do not necessarily have an identical dimension of information. In particular, we transfer different aspects of knowledge across different data sources where while transferring each aspect from a source to the target, we only soft-transfer common latent clusters while preserving unique (domain-specific) latent clusters of the target. By soft-transfer, we mean that we minimize the difference among the shared clusters (while not making them identical). Comprehensive experiments on real-world datasets demonstrate the effectiveness of our proposed **MultLC** over other widely utilized cross-domain recommendation algorithms. The performance improvements demonstrate the benefits of transferring knowledge from multiple sources while preserving the unique information of the target-domain for cross-domain recommendations.

Keywords: Recommendation systems · Cross-domain ·
Coupled matrix factorization · Collaborative filtering ·
Transfer learning

1 Introduction

Recommendation systems have been widely deployed in many products and service providers. One of the most popular methods is matrix factorization (MF) which demonstrated its effectiveness notably in the Netflix Prize competition [13]. MF decomposes an incomplete rating matrix of n-user-by-m-movie into two lower rank matrices. Even though MF has shown its capability in many recommendation problems, it is based only on observed ratings to predict missing ones [12] and hence suffer cold start problems i.e., problem of users' with few ratings [5,20]. Thus, it fundamentally requires sufficient observations to provide

© Springer Nature Switzerland AG 2019
A. C. Nayak and A. Sharma (Eds.): PRICAI 2019, LNAI 11672, pp. 529–542, 2019.
https://doi.org/10.1007/978-3-030-29894-4_43

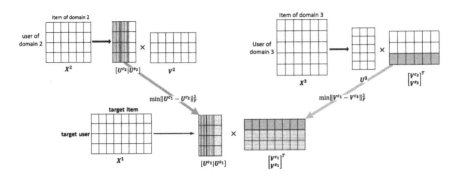

Fig. 1. An illustration of Multiple Latent Clusters Transfer Learning model for a target rating matrix $\mathbf{X}^1$. $\mathbf{X}^2$ is a source matrix having the same users as those in the target. $\mathbf{X}^3$ is another source matrix having the same items as those in the target.

accurate and reliable recommendations. In other words, only established businesses with a massive collection of their users' preferences can take advantages of these technique. Hence, new businesses with limited ratings are unable to utilize MF techniques to achieve reliable recommendations.

Given a wide variety of public datasets on the Internet, one can borrow some knowledge from related sources. It is the way human beings develop new fields. For example, data mining borrows many concepts, ideas, and methodologies from machine learning, statistics and database systems. Instead of developing all new theories, data mining re-uses knowledge from related fields in addition to its own domain's specialties. Inspired by this intuition, we propose a multiple knowledge transfer approach in which different aspects of a target are transferred from related aspects of various sources, each from a correlated one.

Formally, suppose target $\mathbf{X}^1$ contains ratings collected from n users for m items, $\mathbf{X}^2$ and $\mathbf{X}^3$ are rating matrices from other domains, where $\mathbf{X}^1$ and $\mathbf{X}^2$ have the same n users, and $\mathbf{X}^1$ and $\mathbf{X}^3$ have the same m items; in other words, the user dimension is the shared aspect between $\mathbf{X}^1$ and $\mathbf{X}^2$ whereas item dimension is the shared aspect between $\mathbf{X}^1$ and $\mathbf{X}^3$. Our research problem is how to utilize $\mathbf{X}^2$ and $\mathbf{X}^3$ to improve the prediction accuracy of missing ratings on $\mathbf{X}^1$. Although researchers have proposed several approaches [4,10,14,15,17] for transfer learning, there are still two gaps in the literature. Firstly, many researchers attempted to use the correlations from only one source. Secondly, and more importantly all of them assumed the source and the target share an identical dimension of information. Because the datasets come from different domains, *they have unique characteristics even in the shared aspects*. Thus, enforcing them to share an identical dimension of information may lead to a false knowledge transfer, reducing the recommendation accuracy.

In this paper, we propose a Multiple Latent Clusters (**MultLC**) transfer learning which is the first method to learn from cross-domain datasets that do not necessarily have identical dimensions of information. In particular, our approach firstly extracts latent clusters from matrix tri-factorization. When the source matrices are decomposed into user factors (the factors on user dimension) and item ones with rank r, where r latent clusters of users in $\mathbf{X}^2$ are captured in r columns of its user factor. Similarly, r latent clusters of items in $\mathbf{X}^3$ are captured in r columns of its item factor. Then, we only transfer latent clusters in the shared dimension between the source and the target, e.g., the user latent clusters between $\mathbf{X}^2$ and $\mathbf{X}^1$ and the item latent clusters between $\mathbf{X}^3$ and $\mathbf{X}^1$. Unlike traditional methods, our key hypothesis is that the source $\mathbf{X}^2$ and the target $\mathbf{X}^1$ share only some parts of their user latent clusters. Besides, they have parts of the user latent clusters which are unique for their domains. In a similar hypothesis, the source $\mathbf{X}^3$ and the target $\mathbf{X}^1$ share some parts of their item latent clusters. Our idea is to transfer the shared parts from the sources to the target as illustrated in Fig. 1 from $\mathbf{X}^2$ to $\mathbf{X}^1$ and from $\mathbf{X}^3$ to $\mathbf{X}^1$, where we minimize the difference between latent variables of shared dimensions (i.e. $min \ \|U^{c_1} - U^{c_2}\|_F^2$ and $min \ \|V^{c_1} - V^{c_3}\|_F^2$ in Fig. 1) instead of making them identical. In summary, our main contributions are:

1. **Multiple sides knowledge transfer**: We provide theories for utilizing both source dimensions of the matrix and validate its advantages with real-world data. Our model is generic that can be easily extended to high-dimensional matrices such as multi-mode tensors.
2. **Common latent clusters transfer with preservation of unique clusters**: We propose a novel model for transferring common latent clusters from a source to a target-domain while preserving their respective unique clusters. We show that this way of transfer learning can better capture the actual correlations of cross-domain datasets.
3. **Real-world cross-domain datasets validation**: Our algorithm is validated on real-world datasets in comparisons with other cross-domain methods including matrix factorization and deep neural network based algorithms. Empirical results suggest our proposed idea is the best choice for transferring knowledge from other domains to improve the performance of cross-domain recommendation systems.

2 Related Work

We briefly review three major approaches applied to leverage closely related datasets for cross-domain recommendation systems: (a) transfer learning [14,18]; (b) co-factorization [1,7,19]; and (c) related deep learning based approach [6].

Transfer Learning was proposed to transfer knowledge from a source matrix to a target matrix for improving prediction of the target. Li et al. [14] proposed Code Book Transfer (CBT) for transferring rating patterns, weighting low-rank factor $\mathbf{S}$ from the source to improve recommendation accuracy on the target.

Improving the method for transferring latent similarities of users or items, Weike et al. proposed Coordinate System Transfer (CST) to transfer identical latent clusters, called principal coordinates, between the source and the target-domain [18]. The principal coordinates from the source were used as a regularization term in the loss function of the target decomposition.

Joint Analysis. Collective Matrix Factorization (CMF) [19], jointly analyzes both $\mathbf{X}^1$ and $\mathbf{X}^2$ for utilizing the correlation between them. It assumed they share an identical low-rank subspace in their common dimension. Suppose $\mathbf{X}^1$ and $\mathbf{X}^2$ be correlated in their user dimension, their identical low-rank subspace is expressed by the same latent factor $\mathbf{U}$ in the following coupled loss function: $\mathcal{L} = \left\|\mathbf{X}^1 - \mathbf{U} \times \mathbf{V}^{1^{\mathrm{T}}}\right\|^2 + \left\|\mathbf{X}^2 - \mathbf{U} \times \mathbf{V}^{2^{\mathrm{T}}}\right\|^2$. This identical low-rank subspace basis connects both datasets to provide a deeper understanding of their underlying structure [1]. Thus, it helps improving recommendation for both $\mathbf{X}^1$ and $\mathbf{X}^2$.

A recent approach on CMF is proposed in [3] where the authors studied the problem of recommending items to user based on item-item (co-occurrence matrix) lists. The co-occurrence lists for items are generated using word embeddings based on correlation of items. However, this approach utilizes an additional source of data (a correlation matrix of items) for joint factorization; it is unclear how can this approach extended for cross-domain recommendation with multiple data sources that does not necessarily having similar information.

Deep Learning. Recent technique leverages deep learning to capture similarities and latent relationships between users and items. In this regard several deep networks have been introduced for collaborative filtering and recommendation systems. For collaborative filtering few recently frameworks are proposed in [8,11,16]. These deep networks are either generic neural network based frameworks or they combine content-based filtering and collaborative filtering in a unified framework as in [16]. However, in case of the cross-domain recommendation system, [6] proposed a multi-view deep learning approach (DSSM) in which users and items of each dataset inputted through two neural networks. These networks were then mapped into semantic vectors. In this approach, the relationships between users and items were defined as the cosine similarity of their corresponding semantic vectors. Besides, the common dimension among datasets shared the same network. For example, in case $\mathbf{X}^1$ and $\mathbf{X}^2$ have the same users, their users would be fed to the same network to learn the parameters.

3 Proposed Multiple Latent Clusters Transfer Learning

This section explains our algorithm to transfer common latent clusters from multiple sources to the target while preserving the target's specific clusters. To achieve this, the first step is to extract latent clusters from both the sources and the target. Since we utilize matrix tri-factorization to extract the latent clusters, we briefly introduce the matrix tri-factorization technique and how the latent clusters are captured in the low-rank factors.

3.1 Matrix Tri-Factorization as a Clustering Method

Matrix tri-factorization decomposes a matrix $\mathbf{X} \in \mathbb{R}^{n \times m}$ into three low-rank factors: user $\mathbf{U} \in \mathbb{R}^{n \times r}$, weight $\mathbf{S} \in \mathbb{R}^{r \times r}$ and item factor $\mathbf{V}^T \in \mathbb{R}^{r \times m}$, where r is the rank of the factorization.

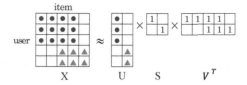

Fig. 2. A demonstration of matrix tri-factorization for clustering. $\mathbf{X}$ has two user clusters based on their similar preferences: users with blue circles and those with green triangle ones. When decomposing $\mathbf{X}$ into low-rank factors $\mathbf{U}$, $\mathbf{S}$ and $\mathbf{V}$ with $r = 2$, the first user cluster is captured in the first column of the user factor matrix $\mathbf{U}$. Whereas, the second user cluster is captured in the second column of the user factor matrix $\mathbf{U}$. (Color figure online)

$$\mathbf{X} \approx \mathbf{U} \times \mathbf{S} \times \mathbf{V}^{\mathrm{T}} \tag{1}$$

where $\mathbf{U}^{\mathrm{T}} \times \mathbf{U} = \mathbf{I}$ and $\mathbf{V}^{\mathrm{T}} \times \mathbf{V} = \mathbf{I}$ are enforced with the factorization. $\mathbf{U}$ and $\mathbf{V}$ contain clusters of users and items respectively [2], as illustrated in Fig. 2.

3.2   One Side Knowledge Transfer

We first explain the case a single source $\mathbf{X}^2$ (from another domain) and the target $\mathbf{X}^1$. The case of transferring from multiple sources is discussed later.

Suppose $\mathbf{X}^1$ and $\mathbf{X}^2$ are correlated in their user dimension, i.e., $\mathbf{X}^1$ is a rating matrix from n users for m items and $\mathbf{X}^2$ is another rating matrix from the same n users for different p items. Our proposed idea is to transfer common latent user clusters from the source to the target while preserving unique ones of the target. To this end, the first step is to extract user latent clusters from the source domain with matrix tri-factorization:

$$\mathbf{X}^2 \approx \mathbf{U}^2 \times \mathbf{S}^2 \times \mathbf{V}^{2^{\mathrm{T}}} \tag{2}$$

such that $\mathbf{U}^{2^{\mathrm{T}}} \times \mathbf{U}^2 = \mathbf{I}$; $\mathbf{V}^{2^{\mathrm{T}}} \times \mathbf{V}^2 = \mathbf{I}$, where $\mathbf{I}$ is the identity matrix.

As discussed in Sect. 3.1, each column of $\mathbf{U}^2$ is a cluster of users and that of $\mathbf{V}^2$ is a group of items. Because $\mathbf{X}^1$ and $\mathbf{X}^2$ are correlated in their user dimension, their latent user clusters are closely related. However, as they are from different domains, we propose that they share only a few user latent clusters and possess their domain's user latent clusters. In other words, among r clusters of users captured in columns of $\mathbf{U}^2$, only c_u of them have corresponding user clusters in the target and hence Eq. 2 can be rewritten as below:

$$\mathbf{X}^2 \approx [\mathbf{U}^{c_2} \mid \mathbf{U}^{s_2}] \times \mathbf{S}^2 \times \mathbf{V}^{2^{\mathrm{T}}} \tag{3}$$

where $\mathbf{U}^{c_2} \in \mathbb{R}^{n \times c_u}$ and $\mathbf{U}^{s_2} \in \mathbb{R}^{n \times (r-c_u)}$; $c_u \in [1, r]$ is the number of common user latent clusters shared between the source and the target.

We then transfer this $\mathbf{U}^{c_2}$ to the corresponding user clusters of the target: $\mathbf{U}^{c_1} = \mathbf{U}^{c_2}$. However, we relax this relationship so that the shared user clusters between the target and the source does not have to be identical. We use this constraint to regularize the target's corresponding user clusters to be as close to the source's as possible. As a result, our loss function for factorization becomes

$$\mathcal{L} = \| \mathbf{X}^1 - [\mathbf{U}^{c_1} | \mathbf{U}^{s_1}] \times \mathbf{S}^1 \times {\mathbf{V}^1}^T \|_F^2 + \rho_u \| \mathbf{U}^{c_1} - \mathbf{U}^{c_2} \|_F^2 + \lambda\theta \qquad (4)$$

where θ is the weighted λ-regularization [21], $[\mathbf{U}^{c_1} | \mathbf{U}^{s_1}]^T \times [\mathbf{U}^{c_1} | \mathbf{U}^{s_1}] = \mathbf{I}$, ${\mathbf{V}^1}^T \times \mathbf{V}^1 = \mathbf{I}$, $\mathbf{U}^{c_1} \in \mathbb{R}^{n \times c_u}$, and $\mathbf{U}^{s_1} \in \mathbb{R}^{n \times (r - c_u)}$.

Rows of $\mathbf{U}^{c_1}$, $\mathbf{U}^{s_1}$ and $\mathbf{V}^1$ are independent. Thus, this computation can be performed row-wise in parallel either by multi-threaded or distributed programming paradigms; Eq. 4 can now be rewritten for each row as below:

$$\mathcal{L} = \sum_{i,j}^{n,m} \| \mathbf{X}_{i,j}^1 - [\mathbf{u}_i^{c_1} | \mathbf{u}_i^{s_1}]^T \times \mathbf{S}^1 \times \mathbf{v}_j^1 \|_F^2 + \rho_u \| \mathbf{u}_i^{c_1} - \mathbf{u}_i^{c_2} \|_F^2 + \lambda\theta \qquad (5)$$

Equation 5 is a non-convex function but, it is convex with respect to each factor when the others are fixed. Therefore, we employ the alternating least square (ALS) [9] for optimization where each factor is updated by freezing others factors as constant. This process then alternates among all the factor which needs to be computed, whose derivations are presented in the following subsections.

Updating Rule for $\mathbf{U}^{c_1}$: Let $\begin{bmatrix} \mathbf{w}_j^{c_1} \\ \mathbf{w}_j^{s_1} \end{bmatrix} = \mathbf{S}^1 \times \mathbf{v}_j^1$, then Eq. 5 becomes

$$\mathcal{L} = \sum_{i,j}^{I,J} \| \mathbf{X}_{i,j}^1 - {\mathbf{u}_i^{c_1}}^T \mathbf{w}_j^{c_1} - {\mathbf{u}_i^{s_1}}^T \mathbf{w}_j^{s_1} \|_F^2 + \rho_u \sum_i^I \| \mathbf{u}_i^{c_1} - \mathbf{u}_i^{c_2} \|_F^2$$
$$+ \lambda (\sum_i^I \| \mathbf{u}_i^{c_1} \|_F^2 + \sum_i^I \| \mathbf{u}_i^{s_1} \|_F^2 + \| \mathbf{S}^1 \|_F^2 + \sum_j^J \| \mathbf{v}_j^1 \|_F^2) \qquad (6)$$

The optimal value of $\mathbf{u}_i^{c_1}$ is achieved when $\frac{\partial \mathcal{L}}{\partial \mathbf{u}_i^{c_1}}$ equals to zero.

$$\frac{\partial \mathcal{L}}{\partial \mathbf{u}_i^{c_1}} = -2 \sum_j^J (\mathbf{X}_{i,j}^1 - {\mathbf{u}_i^{c_1}}^T \mathbf{w}_j^{c_1} - {\mathbf{u}_i^{s_1}}^T \mathbf{w}_j^{s_1}) {\mathbf{w}_j^{c_1}}^T + 2\rho_u (\mathbf{u}_i^{c_1} - \mathbf{u}_i^{c_2}) + 2\lambda \mathbf{u}_i^{c_1}$$
$$= -2 {\mathbf{x}_{i,*}^1}^T \mathbf{W}^{c_1} + 2 {\mathbf{u}_i^{c_1}}^T {\mathbf{W}^{c_1}}^T \mathbf{W}^{c_1} + 2\rho_u \mathbf{u}_i^{c_1} + 2\lambda \mathbf{u}_i^{c_1} + \mathbf{b} \qquad (7)$$

where $\mathbf{b} = 2 {\mathbf{u}_i^{s_1}}^T {\mathbf{W}^{s_1}}^T \mathbf{W}^{c_1} - 2\rho_u \mathbf{u}_i^{c_2}$ and $\mathbf{x}_{i,*}^1$ is a vector of observed $\mathbf{X}_{i,j}^1, \forall j \in J$. Let $\frac{\partial \mathcal{L}}{\partial \mathbf{u}_i^{c_1}} = 0$, we can find the updating rule for $\mathbf{u}_i^{c_1}$:

$$\mathbf{u}_i^{c_1} = \left({\mathbf{W}^{c_1}}^T \mathbf{W}^{c_1} + (\lambda + \rho_u) \times \mathbf{I} \right)^{-1} \left({\mathbf{x}_{i,*}^1}^T \mathbf{W}^{c_1} - \mathbf{b} \right) \qquad (8)$$

Updating Rule for $\mathbf{U}^{s_1}$: Analogy to $\mathbf{U}^{c_1}$, Eq. 6 is a convex function with respect to $\mathbf{U}^{s_1}$ when all other factors are fixed.

Optimal $\mathbf{U}^{s_1}$ can be achieved the same way by setting $\frac{\partial \mathcal{L}}{\partial \mathbf{u}_i^{s_1}}$ equal to zero.

$$\mathbf{u}_i^{s_1} = \left({\mathbf{W}^{s_1}}^T \mathbf{W}^{s_1} + \lambda \times \mathbf{I} \right)^{-1} \left({\mathbf{x}_{i,*}^1}^T \mathbf{W}^{s_1} - \mathbf{b} \right) \qquad (9)$$

Updating Rule for $\mathbf{V}^1$: Let $\mathbf{w}_i^1 = [\mathbf{u}_i^{c_1} | \mathbf{u}_i^{s_1}]^T \times \mathbf{S}^1$, then Eq. 5 becomes:

$$\mathcal{L} = \sum_{i,j}^{I,J} \| \mathbf{X}_{i,j}^1 - \mathbf{w}_i^{1^T} \mathbf{v}_j^1 \|_F^2 + \lambda \, (\sum_j^J \|\mathbf{v}_j^1\|_F^2 + const \,) \tag{10}$$

where $const$ is the remaining of the regularization term.

Similar to solving $\mathbf{U}^{c_1}$ updating rule for $\mathbf{v}_j^1$ can be derived by setting $\frac{\partial \mathcal{L}}{\partial \mathbf{v}_j^1} = 0$.

$$\frac{\partial \mathcal{L}}{\partial \mathbf{v}_j^1} = -2\sum_i^I (\mathbf{X}_{i,j}^1 - \mathbf{w}_i^{1^T}\mathbf{v}_j^1)\mathbf{w}_i^{1^T} + 2\lambda\mathbf{v}_j^1 = -2\mathbf{W}^{1^T}\mathbf{x}_{*,j}^1 + 2\mathbf{W}^{1^T}\mathbf{W}^1\mathbf{v}_j^1 + 2\lambda\mathbf{v}_j^1 = 0 \tag{11}$$

$$\Leftrightarrow \mathbf{v}_j^1 = (\mathbf{W}^{1^T}\mathbf{W}^1 + \lambda\mathbf{I})^{-1}(\mathbf{W}^{1^T}\mathbf{x}_{*,j}^1)$$

where $\mathbf{x}_{*,j}^1$ is a column vector of all observed $\mathbf{X}_{i,j}^1$, $\forall i \in I$.

Updating Rule for $\mathbf{S}^1$: Let

$$\mathbf{s}^T = \begin{bmatrix} \mathbf{S}_{1,1}^1, \mathbf{S}_{2,1}^1, ..., \mathbf{S}_{R,1}^1 \\ \mathbf{S}_{1,2}^1, \mathbf{S}_{2,2}^1, ..., \mathbf{S}_{R,2}^1 \\ ....., ..., ..., ... \\ \mathbf{S}_{1,R}^1, \mathbf{S}_{2,R}^1, ..., \mathbf{S}_{R,R}^1 \end{bmatrix}, \quad \mathbf{a}^T = \begin{bmatrix} \mathbf{U}_{i,1}^1\mathbf{V}_{j,1}^1, \mathbf{U}_{i,2}^1\mathbf{V}_{j,1}^1, ..., \mathbf{U}_{i,R}^1\mathbf{V}_{j,1}^1 \\ \mathbf{U}_{i,1}^1\mathbf{V}_{j,2}^1, \mathbf{U}_{i,2}^1\mathbf{V}_{j,2}^1, ..., \mathbf{U}_{i,R}^1\mathbf{V}_{j,2}^1 \\ ...., ..., ..., ... \\ \mathbf{U}_{i,1}^1\mathbf{V}_{j,R}^1, \mathbf{U}_{i,2}^1\mathbf{V}_{j,R}^1, ..., \mathbf{U}_{i,R}^1\mathbf{V}_{j,R}^1 \end{bmatrix} \tag{12}$$

then Eq. 5 can be rewritten as below:

$$\mathcal{L} = \sum_{i,j}^{I,J} \| \mathbf{X}_{i,j}^1 - \mathbf{s}^T\mathbf{a} \|_F^2 + \lambda \, (\|\mathbf{s}\|_F^2 + const) \tag{13}$$

where $const$ is the remaining of the regularization term.

$$\frac{\partial \mathcal{L}}{\partial \mathbf{s}} = -2\sum_{i,j}^{I,J} (\mathbf{X}_{i,j}^1 - \mathbf{s}^T\mathbf{a})\mathbf{a}^T + 2\lambda\mathbf{s} = -2\mathbf{x}_{*,*}^{1\,T}\mathbf{A} + 2\,\mathbf{s}^T\mathbf{A}^T\mathbf{A} + 2\,\lambda\mathbf{s} = 0 \tag{14}$$

$$\Leftrightarrow \mathbf{s}^T = (\mathbf{A}^T\mathbf{A} + \lambda \times \mathbf{I})^{-1}(\mathbf{x}_{*,*}^{1\,T}\mathbf{A})$$

where $\mathbf{x}_{*,*}^{1\,T}$ contains observed entries of $\mathbf{X}_{i,j}^1$.

3.3 Both Sides Knowledge Transfer

There are situations when we can find from another domain an extra $\mathbf{X}^3$ which has the same items as $\mathbf{X}^1$ does. In this case, $\mathbf{X}^1$ and $\mathbf{X}^2$ are correlated in their user dimension and $\mathbf{X}^1$ and $\mathbf{X}^3$ are correlated in their item dimension as illustrated in Fig. 1. Now we propose how $\mathbf{X}^1$ use not only knowledge from $\mathbf{X}^2$ but also that from $\mathbf{X}^3$ to improve its recommendation performance.

As an analogy to the case where common user latent clusters from $\mathbf{X}^2$ are transferred to $\mathbf{X}^1$, we also transfer shared item latent clusters from $\mathbf{X}^3$ to $\mathbf{X}^1$. Thus, item factor of $\mathbf{X}^3$ is computed to group items in latent space.

$$\mathbf{X}^3 \approx \mathbf{U}^3 \times \mathbf{S}^3 \times \begin{bmatrix} \mathbf{V}^{c_3} \\ \mathbf{V}^{s_3} \end{bmatrix}^T \tag{15}$$

where $c_v \in [1, r]$ is the number of common latent clusters shared between $\mathbf{X}^3$ and $\mathbf{X}^1$; $\mathbf{U}^{3^T} \times \mathbf{U}^3 = \mathbf{I}$; $\begin{bmatrix} \mathbf{V}^{c_3} \\ \mathbf{V}^{s_3} \end{bmatrix}^T \times \begin{bmatrix} \mathbf{V}^{c_3} \\ \mathbf{V}^{s_3} \end{bmatrix} = \mathbf{I}$; $\mathbf{V}^{c_3} \in \mathbb{R}^{c_v \times m}$; $\mathbf{V}^{s_3} \in \mathbb{R}^{(r-c_v) \times m}$.

Algorithm 1. MultLC: Transferring multiple common latent clusters while preserving unique latent clusters of the target

---

1: **Input:** $\mathbf{X}^1$, $\mathbf{X}^2$, $\mathbf{X}^3$, c_u, c_v, $\mathcal{E}$
2: Extract user latent clusters in $\mathbf{X}^2$ by matrix tri-factorization
3: Extract item latent clusters in $\mathbf{X}^3$ by matrix tri-factorization
4: Randomly initialize all factors
5: Initialize $\mathcal{L}$ by a small number
6: **while** ($\frac{\mathrm{Pre}\mathcal{L}-\mathcal{L}}{\mathrm{Pre}\mathcal{L}} < \mathcal{E}$) **do**
7:     $\mathrm{Pre}\mathcal{L} = \mathcal{L}$
8:     **if** $c_u > 0$ **then**
9:         Solve common $\mathbf{U}^{c1}$ while fixing other factors following Eq. 8
10:         Solve target's specific $\mathbf{U}^{s1}$ while fixing other factors following Eq. 9
11:     **else**
12:         Solve $\mathbf{U}^1$ while fixing all other factors
13:     **if** $c_v > 0$ **then**
14:         Solve common $\mathbf{V}^{c1}$ while fixing other factors
15:         Solve target's specific $\mathbf{V}^{s1}$ while fixing other factors
16:     **else**
17:         Solve $\mathbf{V}^1$ while fixing the
18:         other factors following Eq. 11
19:     Solve $\mathbf{S}^1$ while fixing all other factors following Eq. 14
20:     Compute $\mathcal{L}$ following Eq. 16
21: **Output:** $\mathbf{U}^1, \mathbf{S}^1, \mathbf{V}^1$

Then, both the shared item latent clusters from $\mathbf{X}^3$ and the common user latent clusters from $\mathbf{X}^2$ are utilized in our new loss function:

$$\mathcal{L} = \left\| \mathbf{X}^1 - [\mathbf{U}^{c1}|\mathbf{U}^{s1}] \times \mathbf{S}^1 \times \begin{bmatrix} \mathbf{V}^{c1} \\ \mathbf{V}^{s1} \end{bmatrix}^T \right\|_F^2 + \rho_u \|\mathbf{U}^{c1} - \mathbf{U}^{c2}\|_F^2 + \rho_v \|\mathbf{V}^{c1\,T} - \mathbf{V}^{c3\,T}\|_F^2 + \lambda\theta \quad (16)$$

Our model, as defined in Eq. 16, allows the number of latent clusters c_u shared between $\mathbf{X}^1$ and $\mathbf{X}^2$ and c_v shared between $\mathbf{X}^1$ and $\mathbf{X}^3$ to be different depending on their correlations' nature. This idea guarantees their actual relationships are best utilized. Following the same procedures for finding all factors in Sect. 3.2, we can effectively find $\mathbf{U}^{c1}$, $\mathbf{U}^{s1}$, $\mathbf{S}^1$, $\mathbf{V}^{c1}$, and $\mathbf{V}^{s1}$.

A pseudo-code of our proposed multiple latent clusters for cross-domain transfer learning is shown in Algorithm 1. User latent clusters in $\mathbf{X}^2$ are extracted in line 1. Then, the item latent clusters in $\mathbf{X}^3$ are extracted in line 2. Only the shared latent clusters are transferred to $\mathbf{X}^1$. For this transfer learning process, we randomly generate all $\mathbf{U}^{c1}$, $\mathbf{U}^{s1}$, $\mathbf{S}^1$, $\mathbf{V}^{c1}$ and $\mathbf{V}^{s1}$ in line 3, and initialize a loss value in line 4. If there are shared common user latent clusters between $\mathbf{X}^1$ and $\mathbf{X}^2$, every row of $\mathbf{U}^{c1}$ and $\mathbf{U}^{s1}$ is computed in line 8 and 9, respectively. If not, full $\mathbf{U}^1$ is computed in line 11. Solving $\mathbf{V}^1$ is performed similarly in lines 12 to 16. Factor $\mathbf{S}^1$ is solved in line 17. These steps are repeated until the loss function converges (Table 1).

4   Experiments and Results

In this section we evaluate performance of our proposed **MultLC** with other existing models and present a comprehensive study of how well these models leverage the correlations from observed ratings from different source domains.

Table 1. Dimension and observation size of ABS census data of New South Wales ($\mathbf{X}^1$), Victoria states ($\mathbf{X}^2$), and crime data from BOCSAR ($\mathbf{X}^3$).

Characteristics	$\mathbf{X}^1$	$\mathbf{X}^2$	$\mathbf{X}^3$
Dimension	$154 \times 7{,}889$	$81 \times 7{,}889$	154×62
Training	91,069	47,900	661
Validation	4,793	2,521	34
Testing	23,965	12,605	173

4.1 Data for the Experiments

We use three pairs of data collected from different public sources.

Datasets 1: We extract this dataset from census data of New South Wales (NSW) state and that of Victoria state. Australian Bureau of Statistics[1] (ABS) has published their collected data about Australia states' demography profile. Population and family profiles for NSW are separated by 154 local government areas (LGA). We form this information into a matrix $\mathbf{X}^1$ of 154 LGAs by 7,889 demography categories. As for Victoria state, census data in 81 LGAs are provided; a matrix $\mathbf{X}^2$ of 81 LGAs by 7,889 demography categories is created. $\mathbf{X}^1$ and $\mathbf{X}^2$ have the second dimension (demography categories) in common.

Datasets 2: This dataset is constructed from the crime statistics in New South Wales state reported by Bureau of Crime Statistics and Research (BOSCAR). Crimes are grouped into 62 specific offenses within 154 LGAs in NSW. This data is used to create a matrix $\mathbf{X}^3$ of 154 LGAs by 62 crimes. $\mathbf{X}^3$ has the first dimension (LGA) identical with the first dimension of $\mathbf{X}^1$.

Datasets 3: $\mathbf{X}^1$ and $\mathbf{X}^2$ are of the same demography profiles whereas $\mathbf{X}^1$ and $\mathbf{X}^3$ are of the same LGAs. The correlations between $\mathbf{X}^1$'s and $\mathbf{X}^2$'s demography coordinates and between $\mathbf{X}^1$'s and $\mathbf{X}^3$'s LGA coordinates can be leveraged altogether for this dataset.

4.2 Empirical Results

Case #1. Transferring States Demographic Similarities from a Source to a Target-Domain. Table 2 shows recommendation performance of all algorithms when the source ($\mathbf{X}^2$) and the target ($\mathbf{X}^1$) have correlations on their demography latent factors. In general, models shared same factors (CST, CBT, CMF) achieve lower accuracy (higher RMSE) as they do not properly utilize the correlations between datasets. In particular, CMF which assumes both $\mathbf{X}^1$ and $\mathbf{X}^2$ have the same factor on demography dimension performs the worst. Their factors on demography dimension are highly correlated, but they are not the same. Thus, forcing them to be identical does not help. Similarly, CST transfers

---

[1] http://www.abs.gov.au/websitedbs/censushome.nsf/home/datapacks.

Table 2. Mean and standard deviation of test RMSE on X^1 with transfer across ABS VIC data (X^2) with different algorithms and decomposition ranks. A lower RMSE means a higher accuracy. Best results for each rank are in bold. The last row represent p-values of t-tests between each algorithm and our proposed **MultLC**.

Rank	CST [18]	CBT [14]	CMF [19]	our **MultLC**
5	0.0168 ±0.0003	0.0159 ±0.0008	0.0235 ±0.0035	**0.0127** ±0.0004
7	0.0180 ±0.0003	0.0143 ±0.0001	0.0213 ±0.0007	**0.0127** ±0.0001
9	0.0193 ±0.0004	0.0139 ±0.0001	0.0224 ±0.0013	**0.0127** ±0.0003
11	0.0205 ±0.0004	0.0137 ±0.0001	0.0222 ±0.0022	**0.0129** ±0.0003
13	0.0216 ±0.0002	0.0138 ±0.0001	0.0238 ±0.0020	**0.0127** ±0.0001
15	0.0227 ±0.0006	0.0141 ±0.0001	0.0242 ±0.0020	**0.0128** ±0.0002
t-tests	5.57×10^{-4}	6.10×10^{-3}	3.34×10^{-6}	–

all latent clusters on demography dimension from X^2 to X^1, losing the target's specific demography groups. This transfer leads to the second lowest accuracy. CBT produces the best RMSE among the three. One reason could be X^1 and X^2 are closely related, so their weighting factors are quite similar.

Table 2 clearly demonstrates that preserving the target's specific information while utilizing common knowledge improves recommendation performance significantly. Our method proposes to transfer common parts of demography latent clusters of X^2 while preserving the unique demography latent clusters of X^1, providing a more accurate understanding of the underlying structure of X^1. Thus, it achieves the highest accuracy (the lowest RMSE).

To confirm the statistical significance of our method, we perform t-tests to validate if the average RMSE of each baseline (CST, CBT, CMF) and that of **MultLC** differ significantly. As shown in Eq. 2, all p-values $< \alpha(0.05)$ validating that the observed improvements of our method are statistically significant.

Case #2. Transferring Local Area Similarities from a Source to a Target. Table 3 re-confirms the above reasoning with another pair of datasets. Although X^1 and X^3 are from the same LGAs, their LGAs latent factors do have their respective unique latent clusters in addition to their common ones. Transferring those common latent clusters while preserving the target's specific ones accurately leverages the correlations between these datasets. Thus, this produces the best accuracy. We perform the same t-tests as of the case #1.

Since all p-values $< \alpha(0.05)$, the observed difference between each algorithm and our proposed method is statistically significant.

Table 3. Mean and standard deviation of tested RMSE on $\mathbf{X}^1$ with correlations from BOCSAR NSW crime data ($\mathbf{X}^3$) with different algorithms and ranks. A lower RMSE means a higher accuracy. Best results for each rank are in bold. The last row represent p-values of t-tests between each algorithm and our proposed **MultLC**

Rank	CST [18]	CBT [14]	CMF [19]	our **MultLC**
5	0.0158 ±0.0001	0.0153 ±0.0012	0.0167 ±0.0020	**0.0128** ±0.0001
7	0.0162 ±0.0002	0.0142 ±0.0001	0.0171 ±0.0017	**0.0127** ±0.0002
9	0.0167 ±0.0002	0.0141 ±0.0001	0.0155 ±0.0010	**0.0127** ±0.0001
11	0.0176 ±0.0001	0.0139 ±0.0001	0.0158 ±0.0010	**0.0129** ±0.0001
13	0.0178 ±0.0001	0.0140 ±0.0001	0.0155 ±0.0011	**0.0130** ±0.0002
15	0.0185 ±0.0003	0.0143 ±0.0001	0.0154 ±0.0010	**0.0132** ±0.0002
t-tests	1.88×10^{-4}	7.09×10^{-4}	5.10×10^{-5}	–

Table 4. Mean and standard deviation of tested RMSE on $\mathbf{X}^1$ with transfer across ABS VIC data and BOCSAR NSW crime data. Only CST and our **MultLC** support this scenario. Best results for each rank are in bold.

Rank	CST [18]	our **MultLC**
5	0.0228 ±0.0002	**0.0127** ±0.0002
7	0.0235 ±0.0001	**0.0125** ±0.0001
9	0.0256 ±0.0001	**0.0125** ±0.0002
11	0.0244 ±0.0002	**0.0125** ±0.0002
13	0.0265 ±0.0002	**0.0128** ±0.0003
15	0.0251 ±0.0002	**0.0129** ±0.0001
t-tests	4.19×10^{-6}	-

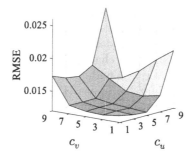

Fig. 3. Tested mean RMSEs under different numbers of common latent demography clusters c_v and different numbers of common latent LGA clusters c_u transferred to both dimensions of the target. Results are with rank 9. The lowest RMSE is not achieved when full latent clusters in both dimensions are transferred ($c_u = c_v = 9$) with no target's specific preservation, suggesting the disadvantages of existing methods.

Case #3. Transferring both Sides: Demography and Local Area Dimensions. Table 4 displays the results when common latent clusters on both dimensions of $\mathbf{X}^1$ are transferred from $\mathbf{X}^2$ and $\mathbf{X}^3$. In particular, common latent clusters on demography factor of $\mathbf{X}^2$ and those on LGA factor of $\mathbf{X}^3$ are utilized in corresponding factors of $\mathbf{X}^1$. Only CST and our proposed model support this case, thus, we compare their results with ours. There are two conclusions we can draw here. Firstly, recommendation performance of **MultLCSpace** is improved more than two times compared to CST, a significant difference confirmed by our t-tests. This improvement again clearly demonstrates the advantages of preserving unique latent clusters in the target-domain. Secondly, when information in both dimensions is utilized, the accuracy is even further improved in comparison with the case when knowledge in either dimension is transferred. This accuracy improvement is very encouraging as it suggests the potential to extend our multiple knowledge transfer approaches to high-dimensional matrices.

We also analyze how **MultLC** works with different numbers of common and unique latent clusters in both dimensions. Figure 3 illustrates the results of **MultLC** when decomposition rank equals 9. The best accuracy is achieved when $c_u = 5$ and $c_v = 1$. On the contrary, the worst case is produced when $c_u = c_v = r$ which is the case of the CST model. The results confirm the importance of the target's specific latent clusters on cross-domain transfer learning.

5   Conclusion and Future Work

In this paper, we proposed **MultLC** to transfer a single aspect of knowledge from multiple sources for improving target-domain recommendations. As the sources come from different domains, our model transfers only shared latent clusters without requiring the shared latent variables to be identical and preserves the unique ones of the target on both sides of the target matrix. This idea better leverages similarities of the first dimension or those of the second dimension or both. Validated on real-world datasets, our proposed approach significantly outperforms existing models. These results demonstrate the importance of transferring common latent clusters from a source while preserving the target's specific ones. Moreover, our findings show that the multiple knowledge transfers on both dimensions further improves the performance in cross-domain recommendations. Our experimental results suggest possibility of simultaneous transfer of multiple dimensions in high-dimensional matrices (tensors) providing us an interesting future work.

References

1. Acar, E., Kolda, T.G., Dunlavy, D.M.: All-at-once optimization for coupled matrix and tensor factorizations. arXiv preprint arXiv:1105.3422 (2011)
2. Bauckhage, C.: K-means clustering is matrix factorization. arXiv preprint arXiv:1512.07548 (2015)

3. Cao, D., Nie, L., He, X., Wei, X., Zhu, S., Chua, T.S.: Embedding factorization models for jointly recommending items and user generated lists. In: Proceedings of the 40th International ACM SIGIR Conference on Research and Development in Information Retrieval (2017)
4. Chen, W., Hsu, W., Lee, M.L.: Making recommendations from multiple domains. In: Proceedings of the 19th ACM SIGKDD International Conference on Knowledge Discovery and Data Mining (2013)
5. Cheng, Z., Ding, Y., He, X., Zhu, L., Song, X., Kankanhalli, M.S.: Aˆ3NCF: an adaptive aspect attention model for rating prediction. In: IJCAI (2018)
6. Elkahky, A.M., Song, Y., He, X.: A multi-view deep learning approach for cross domain user modeling in recommendation systems. In: Proceedings of the 24th International Conference on World Wide Web (2015)
7. Gao, S., Luo, H., Chen, D., Li, S., Gallinari, P., Guo, J.: Cross-domain recommendation via cluster-level latent factor model. In: Blockeel, H., Kersting, K., Nijssen, S., Železný, F. (eds.) ECML PKDD 2013. LNCS (LNAI), vol. 8189, pp. 161–176. Springer, Heidelberg (2013). https://doi.org/10.1007/978-3-642-40991-2_11
8. He, X., Liao, L., Zhang, H., Nie, L., Hu, X., Chua, T.S.: Neural collaborative filtering. In: Proceedings of the 26th International Conference on World Wide Web (2017)
9. Hu, Y., Koren, Y., Volinsky, C.: Collaborative filtering for implicit feedback datasets. In: Proceedings of the IEEE International Conference on Data Mining (2008)
10. Jiang, M., Cui, P., Chen, X., Wang, F., Zhu, W., Yang, S.: Social recommendation with cross-domain transferable knowledge. IEEE Trans. Knowl. Data Eng. **27**(11), 3084–3097 (2015)
11. Karatzoglou, A., Hidasi, B.: Deep learning for recommender systems. In: Proceedings of the Eleventh ACM Conference on Recommender Systems (2017)
12. Koren, Y., Bell, R.: Advances in collaborative filtering. In: Ricci, F., Rokach, L., Shapira, B., Kantor, P.B. (eds.) Recommender Systems Handbook, pp. 145–186. Springer, Boston (2011). https://doi.org/10.1007/978-0-387-85820-3_5
13. Koren, Y., Bell, R., Volinsky, C.: Matrix factorization techniques for recommender systems. Computer **42**(8), 30–37 (2009)
14. Li, B., Yang, Q., Xue, X.: Can movies and books collaborate?: cross-domain collaborative filtering for sparsity reduction. In: Proceedings of the 21st International Joint Conference on Artificial Intelligence (2009)
15. Li, C.Y., Lin, S.D.: Matching users and items across domains to improve the recommendation quality. In: Proceedings of the 20th ACM SIGKDD International Conference on Knowledge Discovery and Data Mining (2014)
16. Lian, J., Zhang, F., Xie, X., Sun, G.: CCCFNeT: a content-boosted collaborative filtering neural network for cross domain recommender systems. In: Proceedings of the 26th International Conference on World Wide Web Companion (2017)
17. Liu, Y.F., Hsu, C.Y., Wu, S.H.: Non-linear cross-domain collaborative filtering via hyper-structure transfer. In: Proceedings of the 32nd International Conference on Machine Learning (2015)
18. Pan, W., Xiang, E., Liu, N., Yang, Q.: Transfer learning in collaborative filtering for sparsity reduction. In: AAAI Conference on Artificial Intelligence (2010)
19. Singh, A.P., Gordon, G.J.: Relational learning via collective matrix factorization. In: ACM SIGKDD International Conference on Knowledge Discovery and Data Mining (2008)

20. Wang, X., He, X., Feng, F., Nie, L., Chua, T.S.: TEM: tree-enhanced embedding model for explainable recommendation. In: Proceedings of the 2018 World Wide Web Conference on World Wide Web (2018)
21. Zhou, Y., Wilkinson, D., Schreiber, R., Pan, R.: Large-scale parallel collaborative filtering for the Netflix prize. In: Fleischer, R., Xu, J. (eds.) AAIM 2008. LNCS, vol. 5034, pp. 337–348. Springer, Heidelberg (2008). https://doi.org/10.1007/978-3-540-68880-8_32

Joint Extraction of Opinion Targets and Opinion Expressions Based on Cascaded Model

Quanchao Liu[1,2(✉)] and Yue Hu[1,2]

[1] Institute of Information Engineering, Chinese Academy of Science,
Beijing 100093, China
liuquanchao@iie.ac.cn
[2] University of Chinese Academy of Science, Beijing 100049, China

Abstract. Fine-grained opinion analysis is a very important task, especially identifying opinion target and opinion expression. In this paper, a new neural architecture is proposed for the sentence-level joint extraction of opinion target and opinion expression. The neural architecture namely cascaded model includes pre-trained model BERT Base, linguistic features, bi-directional LSTM, soft attention network and CRF layer from bottom to top. The cascaded model provides the best joint extraction results in the SemEval-2014/2016 Task 4/5 data sets compared with the state-of-the-art. There are three main contributions in our work, (1) attention network is introduced into the task of sentence-level joint extraction of opinion target and opinion expression, which enhances the dependence between opinion target and opinion expression. (2) pre-trained model BERT-Base and linguistic features are introduced into our work, which greatly improve the convergence speed and the performance of the cascaded model. (3) opinion target and opinion expression are synchronously extracted, and achieved better results compared with the most of the existing pipelined methods.

Keywords: Opinion target · Opinion expression · Joint extraction · LSTM · Cascaded model

1 Introduction

Fine-grained opinion analysis aims to discover opinion expressions, subjective intensity, emotional orientation (such as "positive" or "negative") and opinion targets in sentence. For example, in the sentence *"Tom says, the cellphone runs very slowly."*, tom expresses a very negative opinion towards the target *"cellphone"* using the opinionated expression *"slowly"*. In this work, we focus on the joint extraction of opinion targets and opinion expressions based on cascaded model.

Opinion targets, *T*, which are the entities or topics that the opinion is about;

Opinion expressions, *O*, which are direct subjective expressions toward target, explicit mentions of private states or expressive subjective elements in the sentence are expressed entirely by the words in text [1].

© Springer Nature Switzerland AG 2019
A. C. Nayak and A. Sharma (Eds.): PRICAI 2019, LNAI 11672, pp. 543–554, 2019.
https://doi.org/10.1007/978-3-030-29894-4_44

Compared with the traditional serialization method, the serialization method usually first identifies the opinion expression, and then identifies the opinion targets according to the relationship clue between opinion expressions and opinion targets. In order to identify opinion targets, many researchers regard opinion words as obvious identification [2, 3], their work is based on the observation that opinion words are generally around the opinion targets, and there is a strong correlation between them. Therefore, most of the previous methods extract opinion targets mainly depending on the correlation, and the extraction of opinion word and opinion target is a mutually reinforcing process [3]. However, the correlation between opinion word and opinion target can not be obtained accurately and effectively, especially in the case of long-distance semantic association. So, how to discover the correlation is the key to solve this problem. Many researchers used dependency tree to solve the problem of long-distance semantic association [4, 5], the effect of this method depends on the results of parsing, and all kinds of user-generated content are often irregular texts, many errors occur in the process of parsing. At the same time, some researchers regard the extraction of opinion targets and opinion words as a problem of sequence labeling. For example, many variations of conditional random fields have been successfully applied to the joint extraction of opinion targets and opinion expressions [2, 6]. However, the method of conditional random fields need to design a large number of features manually, sometimes including dependency trees, opinion-bearing words and other pre-processed components. The process of feature extraction is very time-consuming, and it is unrealistic that manual feature design relies heavily on a large number of human prior knowledge and the experience of experts and linguists.

In recent years, feature-based deep learning has become a research hotspot and applied to various tasks of natural language processing. Especially RNN, CNN, LSTM and transformer model have been used in fine-grained opinion mining [7–10]. Considering the strong dependence and mutually reinforcing relationship between opinion target and opinion expressions, in the process of fine-tuning we combine pre-trained model with bi-directional LSTM recurrent neural network for joint extraction. The main contributions of this work are summarized as follows:

(1) attention network is introduced into the task of sentence-level joint extraction of opinion target and opinion expression, which enhances the dependence between opinion target and opinion expression.
(2) pre-trained model BERT-Base and linguistic features are introduced into our work, which greatly improve the convergence speed (than without BERT-Base) and the performance of the cascaded model.
(3) opinion target and opinion expression are synchronously extracted, and achieved better results compared with the most of the existing pipelined methods.

2 Related Work

For natural language processing tasks, deep neural network, which regards sentences as word sequences, has been successfully applied to language model, word segmentation and other tasks. The work of (Collobert et al. [24]) utilized convolutional neural network to tackle sequence labeling problem, their model consists of a convolutional neural network and a CRF layer on the output. The Conv-CRF model has generated promising results on sequence labeling tasks.

At the same time, several RNN-based neural network models have been proposed to solve sequence labeling tasks like POS tagging [11] and NER [12, 13], achieving competitive performance against traditional models, but the performance of these models drops rapidly when the models solely depend on neural embeddings. Some experts and researchers have tried Elman-RNN, Jordan-RNN and LSTM models in fine-grained opinion mining [7]. Yao et al. employed LSTM network for tagging [14], the work didn't make use of bi-directional LSTM and CRF layers and thus the tagging accuracy may be suffered. However, the work in (Huang et al.), they used the bi-directional LSTM CRF model and obtained better tagging accuracy than a single CRF model with identical feature sets [11]. Especially the work in (Lample et al.), they presented a LSTM-CRF architecture with a char-LSTM layer learning spelling features from supervised corpus and didn't use any additional resources or gazetteers except a massive unlabeled corpus for unsupervised learning of pre-trained word embeddings [15]. Meanwhile, the work in (Zheng et al.) investigated different kinds of LSTM-based end-to-end models to jointly extract the entities and relations, they found that the tagging-based methods are better than most of the existing pipelined and joint learning methods [16]. Further, both [17] and [18] used attention networks to extract fine-grained information from different text contents, and obtained better results.

In our work, we acquire pre-trained word embeddings from pre-trained model BERT-Base (Cased, 110M parameters) to give better initialization to our cascaded model [19]. The cascaded model then fine-tune the word vectors during training to learn task-specific embeddings. We present an architecture to incorporate other linguistic features into our cascaded model. The results on the task of joint extraction of opinion targets and opinion expressions show that BERT-Base, linguistic features and attention network improve the performance of state-of-the-art LSTM-CRF model. Meanwhile, our cascaded model also can be easily applied to a wide range of sequence labeling tasks on different languages and domains.

3   Method

3.1   System Architecture

Our cascaded model can be divided into three parts as shown in Fig. 1. The first is a feature rich word encoder which uses pre-trained model BERT-Base and other linguistic features to encode words into a vector with semantic and contextual information from raw sentences, this part uses three layers bi-directional LSTM recurrent neural network to encode words. The second is attention layer which uses attention network to generate word representation. And the last part of the cascaded model is CRF layer, it takes into account neighboring tags and yields the final predictions for every word.

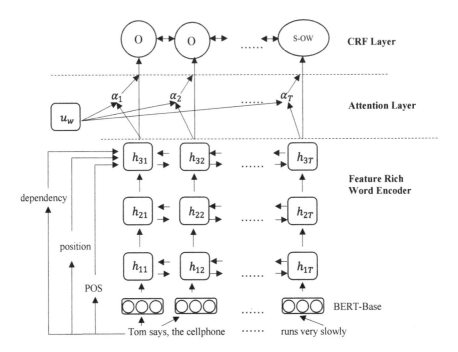

Fig. 1. System architecture.

3.2   Feature Rich Word Encoder with Pre-trained Model BERT-Base

The work of (Devlin et al.) is mainly divided into two parts [10]. One is the pre-train part of the language model. Another is the fine-tune part of the training task-specific. We know in a neural language model, the higher-level hidden state usually captures context information and the low-level hidden state usually captures syntax information. In our cascaded model, we take advantage of both of them and use pre-trained model BERT-Base and three layers bi-directional LSTM to fine-tune contextualized word w_i at position i:

$$w_i = \sum_{l=1}^{L} \delta_l h_{i,l} \tag{1}$$

where L is the number of layers, $\delta_l \in R$ is the weight of each layer learned by bi-directional LSTM, $h_{i,l} \in R^T$ is the hidden state of each layer, T is the hidden size, and the loss function is the cross entropy.

   In addition, we consider some other linguistic features, because POS information, position information and dependency relation between opinion target and opinion expression are also very important when identifying role of argument. Formally, given a source sentence (s, OT, OW) where $s = [w_1, w_2, \cdots, w_m]$, OT represents *opinion target*, OW represents *opinion expression*. For each word w_i in s, we generate a multi-type embedding: $\widetilde{v}_i = \left[v_i, p_i, d_i, \widetilde{d}_l, t_i \right]$ where v_i denotes a pre-trained word embedding, p_i denotes POS information when considering word embedding, and we give every

POS tag a unique id and note it as a one-hot vector for word at position i. d_i and $\widetilde{d}_l$ are position embeddings (Al-Badrashiny et al.) indicating the distance from w_i to OT and OW respectively [20]. t_i is a binary digit indicating whether the word is within the shortest dependency path between OT and OW [21]. Thus the sentence is a sequence of word representations $V = \{\widetilde{v}_1, \widetilde{v}_2, \cdots, \widetilde{v}_m\}$ where m is the length of the sentence.

Finally, our feature rich word encoder concatenates BERT-Base embeddings after fine-tuned and linguistic features embeddings together.

3.3 Attention Layer

In previous works [7–9, 11], CNN, RNN and bi-directional LSTM were directly used to extract features and then do prediction based on them. However, not all words contribute equally to the representation of opinion target in a sentence, or not all words contribute equally to the representation of opinion expression. Hence, we introduce attention mechanism to jointly extract opinion target and opinion expression, which is important while computing sentence representation.

In our cascaded model, we propose soft attention network to explicitly encode BERT-Base after fine-tuned and linguistic features into sentence representation. Specifically,

$$u_{lt} = \tanh(W_w h_{lt} + b_w) \tag{2}$$

$$\alpha_{lt} = \frac{\exp(u_{lt}^T u_w)}{\sum_t \exp(u_{lt}^T u_w)} \tag{3}$$

$$s_l = \sum_t \alpha_{lt} h_{lt} \tag{4}$$

where in our model $l = 3$. We first feed the word annotation h_{lt} through bi-directional LSTM to get u_{lt} as a hidden representation of h_{lt}, then we measure the importance of the word as the similarity of u_{lt} with a word-level context vector u_w and get a normalized importance weight α_{lt} through a softmax function. u_w is initialized by pretrained model BERT-Base and jointly learned during the training process. After that, we compute the sentence vector s_l as a weighted sum of the word annotations based on the weights. So s_l effectively includes a representation of a word in sentence, which is useful for numerous tagging applications.

3.4 CRF Layer

We model tagging decisions jointly using a conditional random field (CRF). For an input sentence $X = (x_1, x_2, \cdots, x_m)$, we consider P to be the matrix of scores output by soft attention network. P is of size $T \times K$, where K is the number of distinct tags, including *B-OT, I-OT, E-OT, S-OT, B-OW, I-OW, E-OW, S-OW, O*. The BIESO tagging scheme means (**Beginning, Inside, End, Single, O**ther), which is used to label every word. $P_{i,j}$ corresponds to the score of the jth tag of the ith word in a sentence. For a sequence of predictions $Y = (y_1, y_2, \cdots, y_m)$. The score is defined as follows:

$$s(X, Y) = \sum_{i=0}^{m} \left(A_{y_i, y_{i+1}} + P_{i, y_i} \right) \tag{5}$$

where A is a matrix of transition scores such that $A_{i,j}$ represents the score of a transition from the tag i to tag j.

A soft attention network over all possible tag sequences generates a probability for the sequence Y:

$$p(Y|X) = \frac{e^{s(X,Y)}}{\sum_{\widetilde{y} \in Y_X} e^{s(X, \widetilde{y})}} \tag{6}$$

where Y_X represents all possible tag sequences for a sentence X. During training, we maximize the $\log(p(Y|X))$ of the correct tag sequence. From the formulation (6), we know while decoding, we predict the output sequence that obtains the maximum score given by:

$$Y^* = arg \max_{\widetilde{y} \in Y_X} s(X, \widetilde{y}) \tag{7}$$

both the summation in (6) and the maximum a posteriori sequence Y^* in (7) can be computed using dynamic programming. More information can refer to the work of [15].

3.5 Training

We learn word-level features while training instead of hand-engineering prefix and suffix information about words. Our cascaded model uses a generic SGD forward and backward training procedure. We divide the whole training data to batches and process one batch at a time.

For each batch, we first run cascaded model (three layers bi-directional LSTM-soft attention network) forward pass which includes the forward pass for both forward state and backward state of LSTM. As a result, we get the output score for all words (tags) at all positions. We then run CRF layer forward and backward pass to compute gradients for network output and state transition edges. After that, we can back propagate the errors from the output to the input, which includes the backward pass for both forward state and backward state of LSTM. Finally, we update the cascaded model parameters.

4   Experiments

In this section, we present our experimental settings and results for the task of joint extraction of opinion targets and opinion expressions from customer reviews.

4.1 Data Sets and Evaluation Metric

Data Sets. In our experiments, data sets come from two sources. One is the *REST* and *LAPT* two review data sets provided by the SemEval-2016 Task 5: Aspect Based Sentiment Analysis (Pontiki et al.) which are annotated at the sentence-level [22]. The other is from the SemEval-2014 Task 4: Aspect Based Sentiment Analysis. Given an opinionated document about a target entity (e.g. a laptop or a restaurant), the goal is to identify all the opinion tuples with the type of {*Aspect Category Detection#Opinion Target Expression, Sentiment Polarity*}. Take "*I was very disappointed with this restaurant.*" for example, the expected output is {RESTAURANT#GENERAL, "*restaurant*", negative, from = "34" to = "44"}. According to the requirements of the experiments, we revise the data sets manually to meet the training data. The specific operation is to tag opinion expressions in sentences which have tags of "target" ("target" cannot be "NULL", or "term" from SemEval-2014) and "negative/positive". As to "*I was very disappointed with this restaurant.*", we additionally label opinion expression "*disappointed*" and change the expected output to {RESTAURANT#GENERAL, "*restaurant*", from = "34" to = "44", "*disappointed*", from = "11" to = "23"}. Certainly, some sentences have no opinion target entity (or opinion expression) and some have more than one opinion target entity (or opinion expression). We use the standard labelling and training to compare our results. For example, "*Service was slow, but the people were friendly.*" corresponds to {RESTAURANT#GENERAL, "*Service*", from = "0" to = "7", "*slow*", from = "12" to = "16"; "*people*", from = "26" to = "32", "*friendly*", from = "38" to = "46"} but "*The waiter is beautiful and generous.*" corresponds to {RESTAURANT#GENERAL, "*waiter*", from = "4" to = "10", "*beautiful and generous*", from = "14" to = "36"}. Finally, from two domains data sets we only retain 10120 sentences that contain both opinion targets and opinion expressions, Table 1 shows basic statistics about the data sets.

Table 1. Corpora statistics.

	REST		LAPT (Only 2014)	
	Train	Test	Train	Test
Total sentences from SemEval	5041	1476	3045	800
Retained sentences	4937	1403	3021	759
One opinion target and expression	1908	869	1803	439
Multiple opinion targets and expressions	3029	534	1218	320

Evaluation Metric. The evaluation metric measures the standard precision (P), recall (R) and F1 score based on exact matches. This means that a pair of opinion target and its opinion expression is considered to be correct only if it exactly matches with the pair of {opinion target, opinion expression} annotated by the human. In all our experiments when comparing two models, we use P, R, $F1$ scores to measure statistical significance and report the corresponding value.

4.2 Model Configuration

We use 100 dimensions for POS, position embeddings and dependency relation, 768 dimensions for deep contextualized word representation, 200 dimensions for the bi-directional LSTM hidden layers. The dropout is set to 0.5, and the cascaded model is trained using SGD for 30 epochs with a learning rate of 0.05, where a batch size of 100 sentences is used. The cross-entropy is used as the loss function.

The implementation of cascaded model is based on TensorFlow. We get POS and dependency of words through using standfordNLP. And use pre-trained model BERT Base representations to compute deep contextualized word representation. During training, both SGD and 10-fold cross-validation are used to update model parameters.

4.3 Results and Analysis

In this section, we will present the procedure of our experiments and make further comparative analysis with other state-of-the-art approaches.

First of all, we need determine the number of layers in neural network. Generally speaking, we can choose a shallow and wide neural network or a deep and narrow neural network to fit the same function. But the latter (deep network) expresses more rich semantic and contextual information. We test the performance of our cascaded model with different number of bi-directional LSTM layers. As a result, the performance obtains slight improvement, as shown in Table 2, bi-LSTM-1 means a bi-directional LSTM network with one layer, and bi-LSTM-2 means a bi-directional LSTM network with two layers, the others are the same. But adding layers becomes not so effective when the number of bi-directional LSTM layers exceeds three, and the convergence speed of training has been affected to a certain extent. So we set three layers in our cascaded model. From Table 2 we know that LSTM units become less effective in higher level layers and there is no need to build very deep neural network for extracting contextual information.

Table 2. Performance of cascaded model with different number of layers.

Number of layers	REST			LAPT		
	P(%)	R(%)	F1(%)	P(%)	R(%)	F1(%)
Bi-LSTM-1 layer	70.9	73.9	72.4	67.2	69.3	68.2
Bi-LSTM-2 layers	73.1	78.1	75.5	69.1	72.1	70.6
Bi-LSTM-3 layers	74.9	79.1	77.0	70.3	72.9	71.6
Bi-LSTM-4 layers	74.1	78.2	76.1	69.0	71.7	70.3
Bi-LSTM-5 layers	74.2	77.9	76.0	69.3	71.9	70.6

Secondly, we compare it with the works of [7, 11, 15, 17, 18]. Table 3 lists the performances from different models. Liu et al. [7] used LSTM RNN and different pre-trained word embeddings to validate fine-grained opinion mining, in our comparative experiments, google embeddings is used for their word embeddings. Huang et al. [11] proposed a variety of LSTM and finally utilized bi-directional LSTM-CRF for POS and

NER. Lample et al. [15] also used bi-directional LSTM-CRF to achieve NER, but their works generated a word embedding for a word from its characters. Gao et al. [17] built the architecture for hierarchical attention network as 2 hierarchies. The lower hierarchy processed one line at a time, fed in as word embeddings. These were processed by a bi-directional LSTM/GRU with an attention mechanism that determined which words are most important. The upper hierarchy processed an entire document at a time by taking in the line embeddings generated from the lower hierarchy. In our comparative experiments, the lower hierarchy is adopted and processes one sentence at a time. Ding et al. [18] built three parts for event extraction, including a feature rich word encoder, a multi-attention layer and a classifier. The input of classifier was obtained by con-catenating event vector and sentence representation. However, in our comparative experiments CRF is used as the output layer of our model for synchronously extracting opinion target and opinion expression.

Our cascaded model achieved competitive performance compared to their works. However, different from their works, advanced pre-trained model BERT, linguistic features, attention mechanism and CRF model are introduced, which makes the performance of our cascaded model significantly improved. In addition, opinion target and opinion expression from the same sentence are synchronously extracted compared with the most of the existing pipelined methods.

Table 3. The compare of the performances from different models.

Models	REST			LAPT		
	P(%)	R(%)	F1(%)	P(%)	R(%)	F1(%)
(Liu et al. 2015)	68.3	69.1	68.7	65.8	67.2	66.5
(Huang et al. 2015)	65.9	66.1	66.0	62.8	64.1	63.4
(Lample et al. 2016)	70.1	72.8	71.4	65.9	68.7	67.3
(Gao et al. 2018)	67.9	70.3	69.1	64.7	66.9	65.8
(Ding et al. 2018)	73.3	76.1	74.7	68.9	70.6	69.7
Ours	74.9	79.1	77.0	70.3	72.9	71.6

In order to show contributions of each item in cascaded model, finally we perform a cascaded model ablation experiment. The ablation experimental results are shown in Table 4. It should be noted that each experimental ablation is only one item, while the rest is retained in the cascaded model. From Table 4 we know that pre-trained model BERT Base contributes the most performance gains. The remaining items are position, attention network, dependency and POS in turn. So the pre-trained word representation based on massive data is the key for the identification of opinion target and opinion expression. In addition, both position and attention network also play an important role for the joint extraction, but dependency and POS are not so important to our cascaded model, mainly because they have a small ability to capture token sequence relations.

Table 4. The ablation experimental results.

Model ablation	REST			LAPT		
	P(%)	R(%)	F1(%)	P(%)	R(%)	F1(%)
Cascaded model	74.9	79.1	77.0	70.3	72.9	71.6
- BERT Base	59.9	63.2	61.5	55.8	59.1	57.4
- POS	72.1	75.9	74.0	69.1	72.3	70.7
- Dependency	72.9	75.1	74.0	68.0	71.9	69.9
- Position	65.6	68.3	66.9	61.9	64.7	63.3
- Attention	68.9	70.3	69.6	64.9	66.1	65.5

5 Discussions

Our work is close to the work of [18] as both of them utilized deep neural networks for sequence labeling problem. While their work used classifier to give a confidence score to each argument role, ours used CRF to predict the output sequence. Further, we also utilized pre-trained model BERT-Base and different linguistic features to improve the performance of cascade model.

Our work is also close to the work of [7] as both of them regarded the tasks in opinion mining as either a word-level sequence labeling problem or as a semantic compositional task. They emphasized the influence of different word embeddings on feature engineering, but we utilized advanced pre-trained model BERT-Base and soft attention network.

Finally, our work is also related to the work of [11, 15, 23] as all of them employed bi-directional LSTM and conditional random fields (CRF) to tackle sequence labeling problem. But we showed that with the pre-trained model BERT-Base, essential linguistic features and soft attention network, we consistently obtained better tagging accuracy than the simple combination of bi-directional LSTM and CRF.

In addition, we try to explore a new information extraction scenario, that is the joint extraction of opinion target and its maximized opinion expression, which provides more all-round opinion information for fine-grained opinion mining.

6 Conclusion and Future Direction

In this paper, we present a new neural architecture for the joint extraction of opinion target and opinion expression. The neural architecture namely cascaded model includes pre-trained model BERT, linguistic features, bi-directional LSTM, soft attention network and CRF model from bottom to top. The cascaded model provides the best joint extraction results in the SemEval-2016 Task 5 data sets compared with LSTM-CRF model. In general, there are three main key to success. One is to model output label dependencies via CRF model. The second is the attention mechanism, which enhances the word-level features between opinion target and opinion expression. Thirdly, the pre-trained model BERT is used for word representations, which captures deep semantic and contextual information.

In the future, we would like apply our models to other fine-grained opinion mining tasks including opinion expression detection and characterizing the intensity and sentiment of the opinion expressions. We would also like to explore to what extent these tasks can be jointly modeled in the BERT-BLSTM (Bi-directional LSTM)-ATTENTION based multi-task learning framework.

Acknowledgments. We are grateful to the anonymous reviewers for their insightful comments and suggestions to improve the paper. This research is financially supported by The National Key Research and Development Program of China (No. 2018YFC0704306, No. 2017YFB0803301, No. 2018YFC0704304).

References

1. Wiebe, J., Wilson, T., Cardie, C.: Annotating expressions of opinions and emotions in language. Lang. Resour. Eval. **39**(2–3), 165–210 (2005)
2. Qiu, G., Liu, B., Bu, J., et al.: Opinion word expansion and target extraction through double propagation. Comput. Linguist. **37**(1), 9–27 (2011)
3. Liu, K., Xu, L., Zhao, J.: Extracting opinion targets and opinion words from online reviews with graph co-ranking. In: Proceedings of the 52nd Annual Meeting of the Association for Computational Linguistics (Volume 1: Long Papers), vol. 1, pp. 314–324 (2014)
4. Culotta, A., Sorensen, J.: Dependency tree kernels for relation extraction. In: Proceedings of the 42nd Annual Meeting on Association for Computational Linguistics, p. 423. Association for Computational Linguistics (2004)
5. Stevenson, M., Greenwood, M.A.: Dependency pattern models for information extraction. Res. Lang. Comput. **7**(1), 13 (2009)
6. Yang, B., Cardie, C.: Joint inference for fine-grained opinion extraction. In: Proceedings of the 51st Annual Meeting of the Association for Computational Linguistics (Volume 1: Long Papers), vol. 1, pp. 1640–1649 (2013)
7. Liu, P., Joty, S., Meng, H.: Fine-grained opinion mining with recurrent neural networks and word embeddings. In: Proceedings of the 2015 Conference on Empirical Methods in Natural Language Processing, pp. 1433–1443 (2015)
8. Poria, S., Cambria, E., Gelbukh, A.: Aspect extraction for opinion mining with a deep convolutional neural network. Knowl.-Based Syst. **108**, 42–49 (2016)
9. Yao, Y., Huang, Z.: Bi-directional LSTM recurrent neural network for Chinese word segmentation. In: International Conference on Neural Information Processing, pp. 345–353. Springer, Cham (2016)
10. Devlin, J., Chang, M.W., Lee, K., et al.: Bert: pre-training of deep bidirectional transformers for language understanding. arXiv preprint arXiv:1810.04805 (2018)
11. Huang, Z., Xu, W., Yu, K.: Bidirectional LSTM-CRF models for sequence tagging. arXiv preprint arXiv:1508.01991 (2015)
12. Chiu, J.P.C., Nichols, E.: Named entity recognition with bidirectional LSTM-CNNs. Trans. Assoc. Comput. Linguist. **4**, 357–370 (2016)
13. Hu, Z., Ma, X., Liu, Z., et al.: Harnessing deep neural networks with logic rules. arXiv preprint arXiv:1603.06318 (2016)
14. Yao, K., Peng, B., Zhang, Y., et al.: Spoken language understanding using long short-term memory neural networks. In: 2014 IEEE Spoken Language Technology Workshop (SLT), pp. 189–194. IEEE (2014)

15. Lample, G., Ballesteros, M., Subramanian, S., et al.: Neural architectures for named entity recognition. arXiv preprint arXiv:1603.01360 (2016)
16. Zheng, S., Wang, F., Bao, H., et al.: Joint extraction of entities and relations based on a novel tagging scheme. arXiv preprint arXiv:1706.05075 (2017)
17. Gao, S., Young, M.T., Qiu, J.X., et al.: Hierarchical attention networks for information extraction from cancer pathology reports. J. Am. Med. Inform. Assoc. **25**(3), 321–330 (2018)
18. Ding, R., Li, Z.: Event extraction with deep contextualized word representation and multi-attention layer. In: Gan, G., Li, B., Li, X., Wang, S. (eds.) ADMA 2018. LNCS (LNAI), vol. 11323, pp. 189–201. Springer, Cham (2018). https://doi.org/10.1007/978-3-030-05090-0_17
19. GitHub. https://github.com/google-research/bert#pre-trained-models. Accessed 25 Dec 2018
20. Al-Badrashiny, M., Bolton, J., Chaganty, A.T., et al.: TinkerBell: cross-lingual cold-start knowledge base construction. In: TAC (2017)
21. Huang, L., Sil, A., Ji, H., et al.: Improving slot filling performance with attentive neural networks on dependency structures. arXiv preprint arXiv:1707.01075 (2017)
22. Pontiki, M., Galanis, D., Papageorgiou, H., et al.: SemEval-2016 task 5: aspect based sentiment analysis. In: Proceedings of the 10th International Workshop on Semantic Evaluation (SemEval-2016), pp. 19–30 (2016)
23. Ma, X., Hovy, E.: End-to-end sequence labeling via bi-directional LSTM-CNNs-CRF. arXiv preprint arXiv:1603.01354 (2016)
24. Collobert, R., Weston, J., Bottou. L., et al.: Natural language processing (almost) from scratch. J. Mach. Learn. Res. 12(Aug), 2493–2537 (2011)

Towards Effective Data Augmentations via Unbiased GAN Utilization

Sunny Verma[1,2(✉)], Chen Wang[2], Liming Zhu[2], and Wei Liu[1]

[1] Advanced Analytics Institute, School of Computer Science,
University of Technology Sydney, Sydney, Australia
Sunny.Verma@student.uts.edu.au, Wei.Liu@uts.edu.au
[2] CSIRO, Data61, Sydney, Australia
{Chen.Wang,Liming.Zhu}@data61.csiro.au

Abstract. The parameters of any machine learning (ML) model are obtained from the dataset on which the model is trained. However, existing research reveals that many datasets appear to have strong build-in biases. These biases are inherently learned by the learning mechanism of the ML model which adversely affects their generalization performance. In this research, we propose a new supervised data augmentation mechanism which we call as **Data Augmentation Pursuit (DAP)**. The **DAP** generates labelled synthetic data instances for augmenting the raw datasets. To demonstrate the effectiveness of utilizing **DAP** for reducing model bias, we perform comprehensive experiments on real world image dataset. CNN models trained on augmented dataset obtained using **DAP** achieves significantly better classification performance and exhibits reduction in the bias learned by their learning mechanism.

Keywords: Generative Adversarial Networks · Data Augmentation · Dataset bias

1 Introduction

In today's era of Artificial Intelligence (AI) the machine learning models are increasingly used in our daily lives, such as product recommendations and bank loan approvals. The complexity of decision rules for models trained with deep neural networks have grown exponentially resulting in high decision accuracy on many benchmark datasets. However, there exists evidences [8] which strongly recommend that the accuracy of such models must not be the sole criteria with their deployment for social purposes. Since the problems inherent within the datasets like dataset-bias [2] affects the decision made by these models. Sometimes the consequences of false decisions made by these models can be catastrophic, for example the Uber self driving car's accident[1] or the racial biases in Google searches[2].

---

[1] https://www.bbc.com/news/technology-44243118.
[2] http://www.bbc.com/news/technology-21322183.

© Springer Nature Switzerland AG 2019
A. C. Nayak and A. Sharma (Eds.): PRICAI 2019, LNAI 11672, pp. 555–567, 2019.
https://doi.org/10.1007/978-3-030-29894-4_45

Although the benchmark datasets are created with an attempt to capture unbiased real world representations, there are evidence in the literature that show that strong build-in biases exists in these datasets [22,23]. Various biases are induced while generating datasets, for example the "capture" bias which is related to the devise utilized while capturing the data instances; it is also related to collectors preferences of views for the real world. The category or label bias arises when the visual categories are poorly defined, like similar images may be annotated with different names. These biases cause poor generalization performance of machine learning models. An over-simplified solution to alleviate this phenomenon is to remove the culprit data instances. However, the identification of such data instances is a challenge and more importantly the performance of models trained on unbiased dataset might deteriorate [14]. This will lead to roll-back of the previous biased model which contradicts the objective of removing biases from the datasets.

Motivated by the aforementioned issues, in this paper we address the issue of bias management in the datasets by developing a data provisioning mechanism which we call as **Data Augmentation Pursuit (DAP)**. Contrary to previous works, where sophisticated machine learning models are devised to mitigate the dataset-biases while learning ML models [7,14], **we are interested in how we can use the available data to augment these datasets with synthetic instances, resulting in lesser bias learned by the ML models**.

To achieve this objective, we utilize generative adversarial networks (GANs) [5] to generate synthetic examples for augmenting the existing datasets. However, we argue that blindly augmenting the datasets with synthetic examples generated by GANs does not guarantee reduction in bias learned by the machine learning models [24]. Rather the bias in the augmented dataset might increase, therefore, a principled approach is required to augment these datasets. In this regard, we devise **DAP** an iterative filtering with an objective to ensure that the retained synthetic examples do not increase the biases while augmenting the datasets. The ML models thus trained performs better than the original model and exhibits decrease in the biases learned from the dataset.

Our contributions can be summarized as:

- *We propose **Data Augmentation Pursuit (DAP)** for augmenting dataset with synthetic examples. The **DAP** regulates the fraction of sample inputs to GAN and controls the synthetic examples selection for dataset augmentation. ML models trained with the obtained augmented using **DAP** exhibits least model and achieves significantly better classification performance.*
- *We propose a filtering strategy for sieving synthetic examples generated by GAN. Our filtering strategy ensures the reduction in semantic gap between real and synthetically generated data instances.*
- *We perform extensive experimentation on CIFAR-10 dataset by utilizing various GAN's frameworks for data augmentation and empirically demonstrate that proper attention is required while augmenting datasets.*

The rest of the paper is organized in the following sections: Literature review is presented in Sect. 2, followed by Sect. 3 on preliminaries of GANs.

Our proposed **DAP** is described in Sect. 4 and finally experiments, results, and conclusions are discussed in Sect. 5, Sect. 6, and Sect. 7 respectively.

2   Literature Review

Data augmentation has played a crucial role in object and image recognition tasks. In order to improve recognition accuracy using CNN, several state of the art models has applied extensive data augmentation to the training datasets [11,21]. Conventionally, for generating synthetic examples trivial image transformation techniques like random rotation, cropping, contrast normalization, etc., have been applied extensively. However, not all synthetic examples help in improving the classifier's learning algorithm and selecting good examples is critically important [15]. However, for large datasets, the number of possible data augmentations are exhaustive and the number of parameters in CNN is exponential. Hence selecting good synthetic examples is almost intractable. Therefore, we require a clever way to select synthetic examples which adds value to datasets and the classifiers inexpensively. Therefore, we focus our literature review on the work which augments the training data by adding "virtual samples" following a systematic procedure and not blindly applying basic image transformations.

Paulin et al. [15] proposed a novel approach for creating augmented data sets by greedily selecting set of image transformations. Their approach "Image Transformation Pursuit" (ITP) iteratively and greedily selects a set of optimal transformations which maximizes the classifier's performance. While testing, the transformations selected by ITP are first applied to the test instances and then those transformed instances are classified. Similarly, in [14], the authors proposed sophisticated data augmentations which exists in the real world scenarios but might not exists in the training data. Performance of classifier's trained with their proposed augmentations generalize better on cross-datasets.

Similarly Sato et al. [18] authors proposed an online data augmentation procedure called APAC (Augmented PAttern Classification), which applies random deformations to the data samples in an online fashion. Here the classifier is only trained with multiple deformed samples from the training instances. The expected loss from these deformed instances is then utilized to train the classifier. Similar to ITP, the testing data instance undergoes the same deformation process while performing classification. However, both ITP and APAC requires heavy computational resources, and hence extensive pursuit is not possible when deep networks with a huge number of parameters are trained.

Conversely, Khosla et al. [7] proposed a discriminative framework that explicitly defines bias associated with each dataset and, attempts to approximate weights for the generalization. Their model applies max margin principle to perform better on cross datasets by taking into account label of the originating datasets for the data instances. Their model can be considered as a sophisticated domain adaptation technique which simultaneously trains a classifier on multiple datasets.

Besides the above, some recent techniques have applied data augmentation by utilizing the images generated by GANs. However, each of the devised mechanism has to apply domain-specific knowledge in-order to increase the quality of generated images prior their utilization. In [20], the authors proposed refinement of synthetic images by processing them with a refiner trained on unlabeled real data called *SimGAN*. The refiner adds realism to the synthetic images such that the synthetic images looks similar to the real image but preserves the annotated information of the generator. Classifier's trained with these refined images improves the state of the art in gaze estimation. Similarly in [10], the authors proposed refinement of synthetic images by conditioning on the image quality and achieved improvement in presentation attacks in biometric applications.

Our work is similar to ITP, as both targets selection of synthetic examples for augment the datasets. But our work differs in two ways: (1) we focus on harnessing the gains from available synthetic images generated by GANs, whereas ITP first selects the transformations to augment the dataset and then generate synthetic examples accordingly. (2) In ITP, both training and testing data were augmented, while we only augment the training dataset and does not alter the testing dataset.

3   Generative Adversarial Networks

Generative Adversarial Networks (**GANs**) first introduced in [5] are composed of deep networks. The first network is called the discriminator (**D**), while the second network is called the generator (**G**). The generator network aims to generates realistic images starting from noise prior (z) resembling true images of the dataset. In other words, if p_x is the distribution over true data then $\mathbf{G}(z)$ learns the distribution $p_g \sim p_x$. On the other hand, **D** aims at learning the discrimination between the distributions p_x and p_g, where $\mathbf{D}(input)$ represents the probability $(p_x|input)$ and $\mathbf{G}(z)$ represents the output from **G** having noise (z) as its input. Formally, the learning algorithm of GANs is formulated as minimax two-player game with objective function $V(G, D)$ as in Eq. (1).

$$\min_{G} \max_{D} V(G, D) = \mathbb{E}_{x \sim p_{data}(x)}[log D(x)] + \mathbb{E}_{z \sim p_{data}(z)}[log(1 - D(G(z)))] \quad (1)$$

both the networks compete against each other in the GAN learning framework maximizing their gains by applying alternatively updates rules defined in Eq. (2) and Eq. (3) respectively, where m is the size of minibatch.

$$\Delta_{\theta_d} \frac{1}{m} \sum_{i=1}^{m} [log D(x^i) + log(1 - D(G(z^i)))] \quad (2)$$

$$\Delta_{\theta_g} \frac{1}{m} \sum_{i=1}^{m} [log(1 - D(G(z^i)))] \quad (3)$$

The gradient based updates on parameters of **G** (θ_g) in Eq. (3) are dependent on **D**, whose parameters (θ_d) are updated prior updating parameters of **G**.

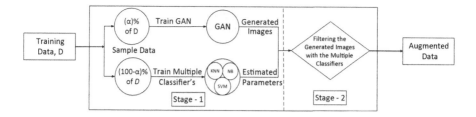

Fig. 1. Procedure of generating sieved synthetic data

Due to this update strategy, the bias leaned by the discriminator network eventually gets inherited by the learning mechanism of the generator network.

In other words, the discriminator which is itself a deep model that falls prey to inevitable dataset biases. Hence the same biases are eventually transferred to the learning mechanism of the generator network. Therefore, the resultant augmented dataset will eventually contain these biases inherently affecting any classifiers' learning mechanism. Also, currently the generator is not capable of adding real world flavors to the synthetic examples unless domain specific operations as in [10,20] are not applied on the synthetic images.

Recent novel advances in GANs include *CoGAN* (Coupled GAN) [13] which couples a pair of generative adversarial networks to learn joint distribution over multiple modalities; this is achieved by sharing weights among higher convolution layers. Similarly, *InfoGAN* [3] is an information-theoretic extension allowing learning meaningful representations of objects with the GAN framework. While, in *CycleGAN* [25] allows style and domain transfer by learning cross-domain relationships. Furthermore works, like ImprovedGAN [17] extended the GAN framework for semi-supervised classification.

Despite the recent advancements in GAN, synthetic images generated by them on datasets with high variability like CIFAR or ImageNet are of low quality [6,24]. Improving the quality of the images generated by GANs is currently an active research topic, but this paper does not focus on improving the learning framework of GANs. Rather, this work focuses on how one selects a subset of images to train GANs such that, the generated synthetic images can be utilized to augment the training dataset.

4   Data Augmentation Pursuit

As explained in Sect. 3, blindly augmenting datasets with synthetic examples can increase the bias in the augmented datasets. Therefore, we design a two stage filtering technique to control the training data instances utilized to train GANs and sieve unbiased synthetic examples generated by the generator. Our filtering technique is based on the ensemble classifier learning which outperforms a single classifier by creating diversity in the ensemble [12]. This leads to a reduction in bias on the final prediction from an ensemble classifier [2]. Hence, synthetic

---

Algorithm 1. *Data Augmentation Pursuit*

1: **Input:** Training Data D, Train labels $T_L \in \mathbb{Z}_2^M$, splitting percentage α
2: $GAN_\Theta \leftarrow$ Train GAN on $\alpha\%$ of D
3: $I \leftarrow$ generate synthetic examples by trained GAN conditioned on T_L
4: $E_\theta \leftarrow$ Train SVM, naive Bayes, and KNN classifiers on the remaining $(100 - \alpha)\%$ of D
5: $Pred_L \leftarrow \theta(I)$, predict the labels for synthetic examples using ensemble classifiers
6: $Index \leftarrow$ select the indices from $Pred_L$ where ensemble classifiers has consensus (majority vote) on the prediction and the synthetic example is correctly classified
7: $[D_{Aug}, D_{Lab}] \leftarrow I[Index]$, $T_L[Index]$ retain synthetic examples filtered from above
8: **Output:** Augmented Data $[D_{Aug}]$ and Augmented Label $[D_{Lab}]$

---

images selected using **DAP** does not adversely affect the learning system of classifier's when trained on them.

Moreover, due to filtering of synthetic images with an ensemble classifier; synthetic instances which closely resembles true data distribution receives consensus on prediction from classifiers' in the ensemble. As a result, the semantic gap between true data and synthetic data is reduced and, augmenting datasets with these filtered images results in reducing the variance learned by the alternating models which reduces the affects dataset biases in the learning mechanism of ml models. Our 2-stage filtering technique is shown in Fig. 1.

Stage-1. Randomly sample $\alpha\%$ of data instances from the true dataset (denoted as D) to train conditional GAN. A conditional GAN is simply a GAN framework conditioned with certain priors. This conditioning helps in generating synthetic examples by selecting the priors in the generator. Once the GAN is trained, we generate adequate number of synthetic examples denoted as I by conditioning the generator with data labels as priors. The utilization of conditional GAN generates synthetic examples with known ground truth. Simultaneously, we utilize $(100 - \alpha)\%$ of the remaining true dataset to train our ensemble classifier (naive Bayes, SVM, and KNN).

The motivation behind splitting the dataset D in '$\alpha\%$' and '$(100 - \alpha)\%$' while training GAN and ensemble classifier is to ensure that the biases learned by the two sub-processes are dissimilar. Later in **Stage-2** when filtering synthetic images generated by GANs utilizing ensemble classifier, the biases of the two sub-processes will work against each other resulting in removal of synthetic examples which are misclassified by the ensemble classifier.

Stage-2. Utilize the pre-trained ensemble classifier from **Stage-1** to classify the synthetic images generated by the GANs. The synthetic images which are correctly classified and achieving a consensus from the ensemble classifier are retained. Since the bias learned by the ensemble classifier and the GAN are complementary due to the random split of training data between them. The complementary biases act against each other while filtering synthetic images generated by GAN with ensemble classier. Hence, this strategy cancels the bias learned by the two mechanisms guaranteeing that augmenting dataset with these retained synthetic images will reduce the dataset bias and eventually the model

---

Algorithm 2. Calculation of Bias Variance and Accuracy

1: **Input:** Training Data D_{train}, Training Label L_{train}, Testing Data D_{test}, Testing Label L_{test}, Augmented Data D_{Aug}, Augmented Label L_{Aug}, Cross-folds = k, $\alpha \in [0, 10, 20, ..., 90, 100]$
2: $(D_1, L_1), (D_2, L_2), ..., (D_k, L_k) \leftarrow CV(D_{train}, L_{train})$ ▷ Create K cross folds of the training data and training labels
3: $(D_{A_1}, L_{A_1}), (D_{A_2}, L_{A_2}), ..., (D_{A_k}, L_{A_k}) \leftarrow CV(D_{train}, L_{train})$ ▷ Create K cross folds of the augmented data and augmented label
4: $[Pred_{Label}, Accuracy] \leftarrow [\ ], [\ ]$
5: **for** iter = 1 to k **do**
6:     **if** isequal$(\alpha, 0)$ **then**
7:         $[train, label] \leftarrow D_{iter}, L_{iter}$ ▷ Use true training data and labels
8:     **else**
9:         $train \leftarrow [D_{iter}, D_{A_{iter}}]$ ▷ add synthetic examples to training data
10:        $label \leftarrow [L_{iter}, L_{A_{iter}}]$ ▷ add synthetic labels to training labels
11:    $Model_\Theta \leftarrow$ **CNN**$(train, label)$ ▷ Train model parameters on the training data
12:    $[Pred_{Label}, Accuracy] \leftarrow$ **CNN**$(test, \Theta_{CNN})$ ▷ predict labels and accuracy of testing examples using CNN and append them to the List
13: $Accuracy \leftarrow mean(Accuracy)$ ▷ calculate mean of k-fold accuracies
14: $Bias \leftarrow bias^2(L_{test}, Pred_{Label})$ ▷ calculate bias using Equation (4)
15: $Variance \leftarrow variance(Pred_{Label})$ ▷ calculate bias using Equation (5)
16: **Output:** Bias, Variance, Accuracy

---

bias. The whole procedure of augmenting datasets with *Data Augmentation Pursuit* is described in Algorithm 1.

5   Experiments

We utilized publicly available implementation of DCGAN[3] [16] and IWGAN[4] [6] architectures on CIFAR-10 dataset [11]. The dataset consists of natural *RGB* images of size 32×32 distributed among 10 categories. Since we require labelled synthetic data generation the implementation for DCGAN was modified by conditioning both the discriminator and the generator on input labels.

However, the current state of GANs are not able to generate images which can span the whole manifold of the training data i.e. can be utilized for training ML models [19, 24]. We downscale our experiments to binary categories as this reduces the search space required by the generator drastically and recognizable synthetic images are generated. Furthermore, the bootstrap sampling parameter 'α' Algorithm 1 is initialized with a value equal to 10% of the true data and incremented with 10% on each iteration Algorithm 1.

5.1   Experimental Setup

In our experiments, we compare the performance of the CNN[5] classifier on four datasets (1) original CIFAR-10 dataset 'Org'; (2) dataset augmented blindly with synthetic examples generated using DCGAN [16] 'DCGAN'; (3) dataset augmented blindly with synthetic examples generated using IWGAN [6] 'IWGAN'; and (4) dataset augmented by applying two stage filtering strategy of **DAP**.

---

[3] https://github.com/kvfrans/generative-adversial.
[4] https://github.com/igul222/improved_wgan_training.
[5] https://github.com/soumith/DeepLearningFrameworks.

For evaluating the performance of the classifier's, we utilized three performance metrics: (a) classification accuracy, (b) bias, and (c) variance. We performed 3-$fold$ cross-validation on multiple binary categories and reported the mean accuracy, whereas the bias and the variance inherited by the learning mechanism of classifier's are obtained by bias-variance decomposition technique for zero-one loss functions [9] and are mathematically calculated as below:

$$bias_x^2 \equiv \frac{1}{2} \sum_{y \in Y} \left[P(Y_F = y|x) - P(Y_H = y|x) \right]^2 \tag{4}$$

$$variance_x \equiv \frac{1}{2} \left(1 - \sum_{y \in Y} [P(Y_H = y|x)^2 \right) \tag{5}$$

where, Y_F represents the ground truth of data instance x represented as a probability distribution (one hot vector), and Y_H represents the probability distribution for the predictions made by the classifier for the data instance x.

5.2   Feature Extraction for Ensemble Classifier

We utilized K-means triangle features [4] for training ensemble classifier in stage-1 Fig. 1 of **DAP**. The process begins with extracting random sub-patches from the input data neglecting its labels, denoted as $\mathbf{X} \in \mathbb{R}^{M \times N}$, where M is the total number of sub-patches and each sub-patch $x_i \in \mathbb{R}^N$ and $i \in [1, M]$. The vectors in $\mathbf{X}$ are then normalized by subtracting the mean and dividing them by the standard deviation of its elements, followed by whitening procedure. After preprocessing, K-means clustering technique is applied to learn 'k' centroids $c^{(k)}$. Finally for each $x_i \in X$, K-means triangle features are extracted [4]. Briefly, K-means triangle features are a form of non-linear mapping where each feature f_k is encoded with the following rule.

$$f_k(x) = max\{0, \mu(z) - z_k\} \tag{6}$$

where $z_k = \|x - c^{(k)}\|_2$ and $\mu(z)$ is the mean of the elements of z. This mapping assigns '0' for any feature f_k where the distance from $c^{(k)} > \mu(z)$.

6   Results and Discussions

In this section we study the performance of CNN and SVM classifiers with various degrees of dataset augmentation. We divide the discussion in two subsections, where in the first subsection we study the performance of the CNN classifier trained on the four datasets described in Sect. 5.1. Our hypothesis of measuring the model bias consists of three performance metrics namely the bias, variance, and the accuracy of the classifier. In the second subsection we study the effect of how does the classifier performs by regularizing the level of data augmentation i.e., by varying the hyper-parameter α in proposed **DAP**.

Table 1. Performance comparisons using CNN classifier on baselines datasets and augmented dataset obtained using **DAS**. The $p - values$ obtained using $t - tests$ on pairs 'Baseline vs **DAP**' are tabulated in the last column. Note that we follow the scientific notation[a] where we use $1Ex$ to present 1×10^x. Please note that, for bias and variance lower is better whereas for accuracy higher is better.

Categories	Accuracy				Bias				Variance			
	Org	DCGAN	IWGAN	**DAP**	Org	DCGAN	IWGAN	**DAP**	Org	DCGAN	IWGAN	**DAP**
Frog - Truck	.962	.965	.961	**.976**	.028	.026	.029	**.016**	.010	.009	.010	**.006**
Frog - Ship	.965	.973	.963	**.976**	.027	.020	.026	**.017**	.008	.006	.010	**.005**
Cat - Truck	.942	.946	.933	**.953**	.047	.042	.051	**.036**	.011	.012	.016	**.010**
Bird - Truck	.954	.960	.946	**.963**	.034	.030	.041	**.027**	.012	.010	.013	**.009**
Dog - Ship	.954	.962	.956	**.964**	.034	.030	.034	**.027**	.012	**.008**	.009	.009
Mobile - Cat	.953	.958	.952	**.960**	.038	.032	.035	**.031**	.009	.010	.013	**.007**
Dog - Truck	.958	.962	.945	**.965**	.031	.030	.041	**.026**	.011	.008	.014	**.007**
Frog - Horse	.951	.954	.951	**.961**	.034	.034	.036	**.028**	.015	.012	.014	**.011**
Mobile - Dog	.967	.971	.968	**.973**	.025	.023	.024	**.021**	.008	**.006**	.008	**.006**
Horse - Truck	.953	.952	.942	**.959**	.034	.036	.044	**.030**	.013	.012	.014	**.009**
Deer - Dog	.852	.870	.859	**.871**	.110	.099	.106	**.096**	.038	**.031**	.035	.032
Plane - Truck	.921	.925	.913	**.928**	.060	.056	.065	**.053**	.019	.019	.021	**.017**
Deer - Frog	.896	.905	.902	**.908**	.075	.069	.069	**.066**	.029	.027	.030	**.025**
Dog - Frog	.906	.913	.921	**.919**	.067	.065	.057	**.060**	.026	.022	.022	**.021**
Mobile - Bird	.964	.966	.957	**.968**	.026	.025	.029	**.023**	.011	.010	.014	**.009**
Mobile - Horse	.977	.982	.972	**.980**	.015	.013	.021	**.013**	.008	**.006**	.007	**.006**
Plane - Ship	.899	.908	.903	**.910**	.074	.069	.072	**.066**	.027	.023	.025	**.024**
Mobile - Frog	.971	.969	.960	**.973**	.022	.022	.029	**.019**	.008	.009	.011	**.007**
Mobile - Deer	.975	.974	.967	**.979**	.018	.018	.023	**.016**	.007	.007	.010	**.005**
Dog - Horse	.858	**.875**	.866	.874	.105	**.095**	.102	**.095**	.037	**.030**	.033	**.030**
p-values	1E−8	3E−5	1E−8	-	3E−8	2E−6	1E−7	-	6E−8	6E−5	7E−9	-

[a] https://en.wikipedia.org/wiki/Scientific_notation

6.1 How Does Data-Augmentation Affect the Performance of Classifier?

In order to evaluate the above research question, we study the performance of the CNN (and SVM) classifier when trained on dataset augmented with (1) original dataset i.e. without data augmentation; (2) blindly augmenting with synthetic DCGAN examples; (3) blindly augmenting with synthetic IWGAN examples; and (4) augmenting by applying our two stage filtering strategy of **DAP**.

Similarly, we evaluate bias, variance, and accuracy of SVM classifier on 20 randomly selected pairs from the dataset, and the results are shown in Table 2. Again, the values under the **DAP** column is chosen with the optimal value of α; i.e., the value of α where the reduction in the bias of the classifier is maximum.

Besides, to test the significance of the developed approach we use paired t-test to test the null hypothesis: the difference of the two distributions in the pair comes from the same normal distribution. Where each pair consists of the values obtained through the baselines one at a time against values obtained through **DAP** as shown in Table 1. The last row of Tables 1 and 2 reflects the $p-value$ of the t-statistics obtained at 5% level of significance. These low $p - values$ reject the null hypothesis, and the improvements achieved using proposed **DAP** are statistically significant.

Table 2. Performance comparison using SVM classifier on baselines datasets and augmented dataset obtained using **DAS**. The $p - values$ obtained using $t - tests$ on pairs 'Baseline vs **DAP**' are tabulated in the last column. Note that we follow the scientific notation[a] where we use $1Ex$ to present 1×10^x. Please note that, for bias and variance lower is better whereas for accuracy higher is better.

Categories	Accuracy				Bias				Variance			
	Org	DCGAN	IWGAN	DAP	Org	DCGAN	IWGAN	DAP	Org	DCGAN	IWGAN	DAP
Plane - Cat	.934	.936	.909	**.945**	.047	.042	.059	**.037**	.018	.021	.030	**.016**
Mobile - Frog	.975	.979	.966	**.980**	.018	.016	.021	**.014**	.006	.004	.011	**.004**
Frog - Ship	.979	.977	.962	**.983**	.015	.015	.024	**.012**	.005	.006	.012	**.004**
Mobile - Bird	.969	.972	.954	**.973**	.020	.019	.027	**.017**	.010	.009	.017	**.008**
Horse - Truck	.960	.960	.941	**.969**	.026	.027	.039	**.022**	.012	.012	.018	**.007**
Plane - Mobile	.941	.943	.933	**.950**	.041	.039	.042	**.035**	.017	.017	.023	**.015**
Mobile- Deer	.978	.980	.961	**.982**	.014	.012	.024	**.012**	.007	.007	.0144	**.005**
Mobile - Horse	.973	.974	.960	**.979**	.016	.017	.025	**.014**	.009	.008	.013	**.006**
Plane - Truck	.929	.931	.910	**.936**	.050	.046	.058	**.043**	.020	.021	.031	**.018**
Bird - Ship	.952	.949	.937	**.955**	.032	.034	.040	**.028**	.015	.016	.022	**.013**
Mobile - Ship	.941	.941	.934	**.945**	.040	.037	.044	**.035**	.017	.020	.021	**.017**
Plane - Horse	.951	.948	.934	**.957**	.033	.036	.041	**.030**	.014	.015	.024	**.010**
Ship - Truck	.937	.941	.926	**.945**	.043	.042	.051	**.039**	.018	.016	.022	**.013**
Cat - Truck	.953	.954	.941	**.958**	.032	.030	.037	**.028**	.014	.015	.020	**.011**
Dog - Truck	.963	**.969**	.952	.967	.025	**.021**	.030	.023	.011	.009	.017	**.008**
Plane - Bird	.895	.892	.879	**.904**	.070	.072	.079	**.064**	.034	.035	.040	**.029**
Plane - Frog	.969	.968	.944	**.972**	.022	.023	.035	**.020**	.008	.008	.020	**.006**
Bird - Deer	.856	.853	.847	**.864**	.099	.097	.102	**.091**	.044	.048	.050	**.042**
Frog - Horse	.958	.959	.950	**.961**	.028	.028	.033	**.026**	.013	.012	.015	**.009**
p-values	1E−7	9E−6	9E−12	-	1E−5	1E−4	1E−10	-	5E−8	2E−7	1E−12	-

[a]https://en.wikipedia.org/wiki/Scientific_notation

It is clearly visible that the improvement in classification performance is achieved via reduction in bias within the models trained on augmented datasets obtained using our proposed augmentation service. This clearly validates that one must not blindly augment datasets with available synthetic examples in order to achieve higher recognition performance. Instead, proper attention must be given to the bias of ML models which these synthetic examples affect.

6.2 How Does the Percentage of Input Data Affect the Quality of Data-Augmentation?

In order to evaluate how does the bias in training dataset reduces by varying the amount of examples shown to GAN. We plot the performance of classifiers by varying α (data split percentage in Stage-1 of **DAP**) between 10% to 90% of the training data. The accuracy and bias of the CNN and SVM classifier with various amount of data-split is shown in Fig. 2 and Fig. 3 respectively. Note that, the y-axis in the plots are scaled for visualization.

While the performance of the classifiers in these plots are fluctuating however their performance is mostly better than the baseline i.e. (a) no data-augmentation ($x - axis = 0$) and (b) augmenting blindly ($x - axis = 1$) in the plots. The reason for performance drop at certain α (for example Plane-Mobile accuracy plot in Fig. 3) can be due to the mode-collapsing in GAN [1].

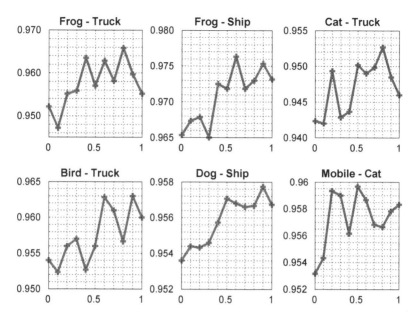

Fig. 2. Accuracy-plot of top 6 pairs from Table 1. The x−axis in subplots represents the values of α used in experiments, where $x = 0, 1$ corresponds to *Org, DCGAN*. The y−axis represents the mean accuracy obtained after 3-fold *crossvalidation*.

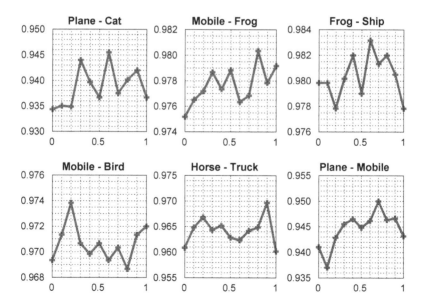

Fig. 3. Accuracy-plot of top 6 pairs from Table 2. The x−axis in subplots represents the values of α used in experiments, where $x = 0, 1$ corresponds to *Org, DCGAN*. The y−axis represents the mean accuracy obtained after 3-fold *crossvalidation*.

7   Conclusion and Future Works

We presented a formal analysis of bias and variance associated with the learning system of GANs and their affects on the bias of the learning systems of classifiers. The proposed data augmentation strategy **DAP** is empirically shown to alleviate the affects of dataset bias induced in the ML model. ML models trained on augmented datasets obtained with **DAP** shows reduction in their bias and achieves significantly better classification performance on multiple binary categories of CIFAR-10. Besides, the results measuring the bias and variance on classifier's learning system advocates the need for effective bias management while augmenting datasets with synthetic images generated using GANs.

Development of **DAP** in multi-class settings is planned as future work of this research. Besides, the formulation of an optimization procedure to estimate α in **DAP** can benefit real-world systems and is another interesting future work for this research.

References

1. Arjovsky, M., Chintala, S., Bottou, L.: Wasserstein generative adversarial networks. In: Precup, D., Teh, Y.W. (eds.) Proceedings of the 34th International Conference on Machine Learning. Proceedings of Machine Learning Research, 06–11 August 2017, vol. 70, pp. 214–223. PMLR, International Convention Centre, Sydney, Australia (2017)
2. Brain, D., Webb, G.I.: The need for low bias algorithms in classification learning from large data sets. In: Elomaa, T., Mannila, H., Toivonen, H. (eds.) PKDD 2002. LNCS, vol. 2431, pp. 62–73. Springer, Heidelberg (2002). https://doi.org/10.1007/3-540-45681-3_6
3. Chen, X., Duan, Y., Houthooft, R., Schulman, J., Sutskever, I., Abbeel, P.: Info-GAN: interpretable representation learning by information maximizing generative adversarial nets. In: Advances in Neural Information Processing Systems, pp. 2172–2180 (2016)
4. Coates, A., Ng, A., Lee, H.: An analysis of single-layer networks in unsupervised feature learning. In: Proceedings of the Fourteenth International Conference on Artificial Intelligence and Statistics, pp. 215–223 (2011)
5. Goodfellow, I., et al.: Generative adversarial nets. In: Advances in Neural Information Processing Systems, pp. 2672–2680 (2014)
6. Gulrajani, I., Ahmed, F., Arjovsky, M., Dumoulin, V., Courville, A.: Improved training of Wasserstein GANs. In: NIPS (2017)
7. Khosla, A., Zhou, T., Malisiewicz, T., Efros, A.A., Torralba, A.: Undoing the damage of dataset bias. In: Fitzgibbon, A., Lazebnik, S., Perona, P., Sato, Y., Schmid, C. (eds.) ECCV 2012. LNCS, vol. 7572, pp. 158–171. Springer, Heidelberg (2012). https://doi.org/10.1007/978-3-642-33718-5_12
8. Kleinberg, J., Mullainathan, S., Raghavan, M.: Inherent trade-offs in the fair determination of risk scores. In: ITCS (2017)
9. Kohavi, R., Wolpert, D.H., et al.: Bias plus variance decomposition for zero-one loss functions. In: Machine Learning, Proceedings of the Thirteenth International Conference (ICML), pp. 275–283 (1996)

10. Kohli, N., Yadav, D., Vatsa, M., Singh, R., Noore, A.: Synthetic iris presentation attack using iDCGAN. In: IJCB (2017)
11. Krizhevsky, A., Hinton, G.: Learning multiple layers of features from tiny images. Department of Computer Science, University of Toronto (2009)
12. Kuncheva, L.I., Whitaker, C.J.: Measures of diversity in classifier ensembles and their relationship with the ensemble accuracy. Mach. Learn. **51**(2), 181–207 (2003)
13. Liu, M.Y., Tuzel, O.: Coupled generative adversarial networks. In: Advances in Neural Information Processing Systems, pp. 469–477 (2016)
14. McLaughlin, N., Del Rincon, J.M., Miller, P.: Data-augmentation for reducing dataset bias in person re-identification. In: 2015 12th IEEE International Conference on Advanced Video and Signal Based Surveillance (AVSS). IEEE (2015)
15. Paulin, M., Revaud, J., Harchaoui, Z., Perronnin, F., Schmid, C.: Transformation pursuit for image classification. In: Proceedings of the IEEE Conference on Computer Vision and Pattern Recognition, pp. 3646–3653 (2014)
16. Radford, A., Metz, L., Chintala, S.: Unsupervised representation learning with deep convolutional generative adversarial networks. In: ICLR (2016)
17. Salimans, T., Goodfellow, I., Zaremba, W., Cheung, V., Radford, A., Chen, X.: Improved techniques for training GANs. In: Advances in Neural Information Processing Systems, pp. 2234–2242 (2016)
18. Sato, I., Nishimura, H., Yokoi, K.: APAC: augmented pattern classification with neural networks. arXiv preprint arXiv:1505.03229 (2015)
19. Shmelkov, K., Schmid, C., Alahari, K.: How good is my GAN? In: Ferrari, V., Hebert, M., Sminchisescu, C., Weiss, Y. (eds.) ECCV 2018. LNCS, vol. 11206, pp. 218–234. Springer, Cham (2018). https://doi.org/10.1007/978-3-030-01216-8_14
20. Shrivastava, A., Pfister, T., Tuzel, O., Susskind, J., Wang, W., Webb, R.: Learning from simulated and unsupervised images through adversarial training. In: Proceedings of the IEEE Conference on Computer Vision and Pattern Recognition, pp. 2242–2251 (2017)
21. Szegedy, C., et al.: Going deeper with convolutions. In: Proceedings of the IEEE Conference on Computer Vision and Pattern Recognition, pp. 1–9 (2015)
22. Tommasi, T., Patricia, N., Caputo, B., Tuytelaars, T.: A deeper look at dataset bias. In: Csurka, G. (ed.) Domain Adaptation in Computer Vision Applications. ACVPR, pp. 37–55. Springer, Cham (2017). https://doi.org/10.1007/978-3-319-58347-1_2
23. Torralba, A., Efros, A.A.: Unbiased look at dataset bias. In: 2011 IEEE Conference on Computer Vision and Pattern Recognition (CVPR). IEEE (2011)
24. Xian, Y., Lorenz, T., Schiele, B., Akata, Z.: Feature generating networks for zero-shot learning. In: CVPR (2018)
25. Zhu, J.Y., Park, T., Isola, P., Efros, A.A.: Unpaired image-to-image translation using cycle-consistent adversarial networks. In: ICCV (2017)

Weakly Supervised Joint Entity-Sentiment-Issue Model for Political Opinion Mining

Sandeepa Kannangara[✉] and Wayne Wobcke

School of Computer Science and Engineering, University of New South Wales, Sydney, NSW 2052, Australia
{s.kannangara,w.wobcke}@unsw.edu.au

Abstract. Microblogging has become an important source of opinion-rich data that can be used for understanding public opinion. In this paper, we propose a novel weakly supervised probabilistic topic model, Joint Entity-Sentiment-Issue (JESI), for political opinion mining from Twitter. The model automatically identifies the target entity of the expressed sentiment, the issues discussed and the sentiment towards the issues and entity simultaneously. Unlike other machine learning approaches to opinion mining which require labelled data for training classifiers, JESI requires only a small number of seed words for each entity and issue, and a sentiment lexicon. The model is evaluated on a dataset of tweets collected during the 2016 Australian Federal Election. Experimental results demonstrate that JESI outperforms baselines for sentiment, entity and issue classification, especially achieving higher recall and F1.

Keywords: Opinion mining · Sentiment analysis · Topic modelling

1 Introduction

The massive amount of opinion-rich data in microblogs such as Twitter provides worldwide access to understand public opinion on a wide range of issues. Thus exploiting such information to understand opinions is useful in many scenarios, for example by political analysts interested in determining public opinion towards policy decisions or legislative changes. To automatically analyse such data, research in opinion mining has attracted considerable attention in recent years.

Much early opinion mining research focused on business and e-commerce applications, such as product and movie reviews. There is less research on understanding opinions in a political context. Among them, the majority of methods are concerned with mining political sentiment to predict the outcome of elections. The approaches employed range from lexicon based methods [13] to supervised algorithms [1], and deep learning approaches [18]. Although the supervised and deep learning approaches are claimed to perform well [1], labelled data for such

© Springer Nature Switzerland AG 2019
A. C. Nayak and A. Sharma (Eds.): PRICAI 2019, LNAI 11672, pp. 568–581, 2019.
https://doi.org/10.1007/978-3-030-29894-4_46

approaches are not easily obtainable in practical applications. Further, most work on political sentiment focuses on sentiment classification, though Maynard and Funk [13] identified the opinion target and Vijayaraghavan et al. [18] classified topics along with the sentiment.

The work described in this paper concerns opinion mining in the political domain, developing a model to identify sentiment, sentiment target and aspects of the target using a weakly supervised approach. The weakly supervised approach is motivated by the difficulty of obtaining a sufficient amount of labelled data. Further, the identification of sentiment, target and aspects from each opinion is vital for proper opinion analysis in the political domain due to the nature of the posts. As an example, the tweet (underlining added):

Voting for the <u>Liberals/Nationals</u> & their "<u>Free market</u>" has killed the <u>dairy industry</u>. Don't vote for them!! #Auspol #Ausvotes #ozagchat

expresses a negative sentiment towards the Liberal Party on their economic management and dairy industry policies. The Liberal Party is the target, and economic management and dairy industry are the aspects. In general, it is common for people to write political tweets to express their sentiment towards targets such as a political party or person, possibly with aspects of the target. This argument can be further motivated by considering the definition of an *opinion* as a quintuple: sentiment target, aspect of the target, sentiment on the aspect of the target, opinion holder and time [10]. Mining these components of opinion is called *fine-grained opinion mining*.

Latent Dirichlet Allocation (LDA) [2] based sentiment-topic models are considered to perform well for fine-grained opinion mining [6,8,9,19]. The strength of such models is that all the dimensions can help to improve each other during the joint modelling process. Recent methods show that weakly supervised sentiment-topic models which utilise lexical information such as sentiment lexicons perform well compared to unsupervised models. However, many of the proposed sentiment-topic models focus only on identifying aspects and sentiment, ignoring the target entity of the opinion. Further, the majority of such models are evaluated on lengthy reviews. To the best of our knowledge, there is no existing LDA-based opinion mining model which jointly models sentiment, target and aspect from microblogging posts in the political domain.

In this paper, we propose a novel LDA-based weakly supervised fine-grained opinion mining model, Joint Entity-Sentiment-Issue (JESI), to jointly identify target **entity**, target aspect (**issue**) and **sentiment** from political tweets. Sentiment generation in JESI is conditioned on both the entity and issue distributions. JESI is weakly supervised, where the only supervision comes from seed words for entities and issues, and the SentiStrength classifier [17] to identify sentiment words.

The hypothesis underlying JESI is that the sentiment of an opinion depends on both entity and issue. To validate the hypothesis, JESI is evaluated on a dataset of tweets collected during the 2016 Australian Federal Election and compared to the performance of weakly supervised JST [9] as a baseline. We select JST as a baseline since the topic generation of JST depends on sentiment, which is the reverse order compared to JESI. JST is the basis of many LDA-based sentiment-topic models which detect sentiment and topic simultaneously [3,4].

Experimental results demonstrate JESI outperforms the baseline for sentiment, entity and issue classification. Further, the qualitative analysis of topic extraction demonstrates that JESI is capable of identifying more coherent topic words for each entity, issue and sentiment.

The remainder of this paper is organised as follows. In Sect. 2, we present the JESI model followed by the experimental setup in Sect. 3. The empirical analysis and discussion are in Sect. 4. In Sect. 5 we briefly review related work.

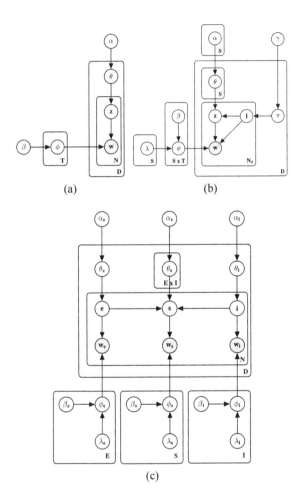

Fig. 1. (a) LDA model (b) JST model (c) JESI model

2 Joint Entity-Sentiment-Issue Model

In this section, we present the proposed model for fine-grained opinion mining which aims to extract target entities (e.g. candidates or political parties), issues discussed (e.g. tax, refugees, etc.) and sentiment (positive or negative) on the entity and issues from political tweets. The model is an LDA-based weakly supervised fine-grained political opinion mining model called Joint Entity-Issue-Sentiment (JESI), that jointly models entity, sentiment and issue. Figure 1 shows LDA, JST and JESI models.

The LDA model [2] is based on the assumption that documents are a mixture of topics, where a topic is a probability distribution over words. The model has three hierarchical layers, where topics are associated with documents, and words are associated with topics. In general, the procedure of generating a word in a document under LDA can be broken down into two steps: first to choose a distribution over a mixture of T topics, second to select a topic from the topic distribution randomly, and then draw a word from that topic according to the topic's word distribution.

Table 1. Parameter notations used in the JESI model

Notation	Description
D	Number of documents in the collection
N	Number of words in document d
E, I, S	Number of entities, issues and sentiments
e, i, s	An entity, an issue and a sentiment for the nth word in the dth document
w_e, w_i, w_s	Entity, issue and sentiment words for the nth word in the dth document
$\theta_e, \theta_i, \theta_s$	Entity, issue and sentiment distributions for document d
ϕ_e, ϕ_i, ϕ_s	Word distribution for entity e, issue i and sentiment s
$\alpha_e, \alpha_i, \alpha_s$	Symmetric Dirichlet priors for θ_e, θ_i and θ_s
$\beta_e, \beta_i, \beta_s$	Symmetric Dirichlet priors for ϕ_e, ϕ_i and ϕ_s
$\lambda_e, \lambda_i, \lambda_s$	Transformation matrices for encoding prior-information

To model entity, issue and sentiment jointly, we propose the JESI model with three variables instead of the topic variable in LDA. In JESI, entity and issue are associated with documents, the sentiment is associated with entity and issue, and entity, issue and sentiment words are associated with entity, issue and sentiment respectively.

Compared to LDA, which is an unsupervised model, JESI is a weakly supervised model. In JESI, we add additional dependency links of ϕ_e, ϕ_i and ϕ_s on the matrices λ_e, λ_i and λ_s respectively, which we use to encode word prior entity, issue and sentiment information into the model. This weakly supervised approach is inspired by the weakly supervised JST model [9]. JST incorporated only the sentiment prior knowledge using a sentiment lexicon. More details on incorporating prior information into the JESI model are given in Sect. 2.1. A graphical model JESI is shown in Fig. 1(c) and notations are described in Table 1.

Consider that we have a corpus with a collection of D documents denoted by $C = \{d_1, \cdots, d_D\}$; each document in the corpus is a sequence of N_d words denoted $d = (w_1, \cdots, w_{N_d})$, and each word in the document is an item from a vocabulary with V distinct terms. Also let E be the total number of entities, I be the total number of issues and S be the number of distinct sentiments. The procedure for generating words w_{e_n}, w_{i_n} and w_{s_n} in document d under JESI can be resolved into three steps. Firstly, an entity l is chosen from the document-entity distribution θ_{e_d} and an issue k is chosen from the document-issue distribution θ_{i_d}. Following that, a sentiment j is chosen from the sentiment distribution $\theta_{s_{d,l,k}}$ which is conditioned on the sampled entity l and issue k. Finally, an entity word w_{e_n}, an issue word w_{i_n} and a sentiment word w_{s_n} is drawn from the per-corpus word distribution conditioned on generated entity l, issue k and sentiment j separately. The generative process in JESI is:

- For each entity $l \in \{1, \cdots, E\}$, draw $\phi_{e_l} \sim \text{Dir}(\lambda_{e_l} \times \beta_{e_l}^E)$
- For each sentiment $j \in \{1, \cdots, S\}$, draw $\phi_{s_j} \sim \text{Dir}(\lambda_{s_j} \times \beta_{s_j}^S)$
- For each issue $k \in \{1, \cdots, I\}$, draw $\phi_{i_k} \sim \text{Dir}(\lambda_{i_k} \times \beta_{i_k}^I)$
- For each document d, choose distributions $\theta_{e_d} \sim \text{Dir}(\alpha_e)$ and $\theta_{i_d} \sim \text{Dir}(\alpha_i)$
- For each entity and issue under document d, choose a distribution $\theta_{s_{d,l,k}} \sim \text{Dir}(\alpha_s)$
- For each word w_i in document d
  - Choose an entity $l_n \sim \text{Mult}(\theta_{e_d})$, an issue $k_n \sim \text{Mult}(\theta_{i_d})$ and a sentiment $j_n \sim \text{Mult}(\theta_{s_{d,l_n,k_n}})$
  - Choose words $w_{e_n} \sim \text{Mult}(\phi_{e_{l_n}})$, $w_{i_n} \sim \text{Mult}(\phi_{i_{k_n}})$ and $w_{s_n} \sim \text{Mult}(\phi_{s_{j_n}})$

In our implementation, we use symmetric priors $\alpha_e, \alpha_i, \alpha_s, \beta_e, \beta_i,$ and β_s, which can be treated as the prior observation counts before having any actual words.

2.1   Incorporating Model Priors

Similar to JST, we add a dependency link of ϕ_s to matrix λ_s of size $S \times V$, which we use to encode word prior sentiment information into the JESI model. Additionally, we use a similar approach for ϕ_e and ϕ_i to encode word prior entity and issue information which is not available in the JST model. Further, for the initialisation of posterior distributions e, i and s, we utilise model prior information. If the word is not found in the prior information, we initialise e, i and s randomly.

For entity and issue prior information, we use manually constructed seed word lists. For example, the procedure of incorporating entity prior knowledge into the JESI model is: first, λ_e is initialised with all the elements taking a value of 1. Then for each term $w \in \{t_1, ..., t_V\}$ in the corpus vocabulary and for each entity $l \in \{l_1, ..., l_E\}$, if w is found in the entity seed word list of entity l_n, the element $\lambda_{e_{l_n,w}}$ is kept as 1 and other entities for word w updated to 0. For instance, assume that there are only 3 predefined entities and the word 'liberal' with index n in the vocabulary is relevant to the 'Liberal' entity. The corresponding row vector in λ_e is $[1, 0, 0]$ with elements representing Liberal (l_1), Labor (l_2) and Greens (l_3). Multiplying $\lambda_{e_{l_n}}$ with $\beta_{e_{l_n}}$, only the values of $\beta_{e_{l_{1_n}}}$ are retained, and $\beta_{e_{l_{2_n}}}$ and $\beta_{e_{l_{3_n}}}$ are set to 0. Thus, "liberal" can only be drawn from the Liberal entity word distributions generated from the Dirichlet distribution with parameter $\beta_{e_{l_1}}$.

2.2   Model Inference

In order to obtain the distributions of θ_e, θ_i, θ_s, ϕ_e, ϕ_i and ϕ_s, we first estimate the posterior distribution over e, i and s. The sampling distribution for a word given the remaining entity, issue and sentiment is $P(e_n = l, i_n = k, s_n = j | w_e, w_i, w_s, e^{\neg n}, i^{\neg n}, s^{\neg n}, \alpha_e, \alpha_i, \alpha_s, \beta_e, \beta_i, \beta_s)$ where $e^{\neg n}$, $i^{\neg n}$ and $s^{\neg n}$ are vectors of assignment of entities, issues and sentiments for all the words in the collection except for the word at the position n in document d. The joint probability of the words, entities, issues and sentiment is $P(w_e, w_i, w_s, e, s) = P(w_e|e)P(w_i|i)P(w_s|s)P(s|e,i)P(e)P(i)$.

For the first term, by integrating out ϕ_e yields

$$P(w_e|e) = \left(\frac{\Gamma(V\beta_e)}{\Gamma(\beta_e)^V}\right)^E \prod_l \frac{\prod_n \Gamma(N_{l,n} + \beta_e)}{\Gamma(N_l + V\beta_e)} \tag{1}$$

where $N_{l,n}$ is the number of times word n appears in entity l, N_l is the number of times words are assigned to entity l, and Γ is the gamma function.

Similarly, for the second and third terms, by integrating out ϕ_i and ϕ_s separately,

$$P(w_i|i) = \left(\frac{\Gamma(V\beta_i)}{\Gamma(\beta_i)^V}\right)^I \prod_k \frac{\prod_n \Gamma(N_{k,n} + \beta_i)}{\Gamma(N_k + V\beta_i)} \tag{2}$$

$$P(w_s|s) = \left(\frac{\Gamma(V\beta_s)}{\Gamma(\beta_s)^V}\right)^S \prod_j \frac{\prod_n \Gamma(N_{j,n} + \beta_s)}{\Gamma(N_j + V\beta_s)} \tag{3}$$

where $N_{k,n}$ is the number of times word n appears in issue k, N_k is the number of times words are assigned to issue k, $N_{j,n}$ is the number of times word n appears with sentiment j, and N_j is the number of times words are assigned to sentiment j.

For the fourth term, by integrating out θ_s yields

$$P(s|e,i) = \left(\frac{\Gamma(S\alpha_s)}{\Gamma(\alpha_s)^S}\right)^{D \times E \times I} \prod_d \prod_l \prod_k \frac{\prod_j \Gamma(N_{d,l,k,j} + \alpha_s)}{\Gamma(N_{d,l,k} + S\alpha_s)} \tag{4}$$

where D is the total number of documents in the collection, $N_{d,l,k,j}$ is the number of times a word from document d being associated with sentiment j, entity l and issue k, and $N_{d,l,k}$ is the number of times entity l and issue k is assigned document d.

For the fifth and sixth terms, by integrating out θ_e and θ_i respectively, we obtain

$$P(e) = \left(\frac{\Gamma(E\alpha_e)}{\Gamma(\alpha_e)^E}\right)^D \prod_d \frac{\prod_l \Gamma(N_{d,l} + \alpha_e)}{\Gamma(N_d + E\alpha_e)} \tag{5}$$

$$P(i) = \left(\frac{\Gamma(T\alpha_i)}{\Gamma(\alpha_i)^I}\right)^D \prod_d \frac{\prod_k \Gamma(N_{d,k} + \alpha_i)}{\Gamma(N_d + T\alpha_i)} \tag{6}$$

where $N_{d,l}$ is the number of times entity l being assigned to some word token in document d, and N_d is the total number of words in document d. Similarly, $N_{d,k}$ is the number of times issue k is assigned to some word token in document d.

Gibbs sampling is used to estimate the posterior distribution by sampling the variables of interest, e_n, i_n and s_n here, from the distribution over the variables given the current values of all the variables and data. The conditional posterior for e_n, i_n and s_n by marginalising out random variables θ_e, θ_i, θ_s, ϕ_e, ϕ_i and ϕ_s is

$$P(e_n = l, s_n = j, i_n = k | w_e, w_i, w_s, e^{\neg n}, i^{\neg n}, s^{\neg n}, \alpha_e, \alpha_i, \alpha_s, \beta_e, \beta_i, \beta_s) \propto$$

$$\underbrace{\frac{N_{l,w_n}^{\neg n} + \beta_e}{N_l + V\beta_e}}_{\theta_e} \cdot \underbrace{\frac{N_{j,w_n}^{\neg n} + \beta_s}{N_j + V\beta_s}}_{\theta_s} \cdot \underbrace{\frac{N_{k,w_n}^{\neg n} + \beta_i}{N_k + V\beta_i}}_{\theta_i} \cdot \underbrace{\frac{N_{d,l}^{\neg n} + \alpha_{e_l}}{N_d^{\neg n} + E\alpha_e}}_{\phi_e} \cdot \underbrace{\frac{N_{d,k}^{\neg n} + \alpha_{i_k}}{N_d^{\neg n} + T\alpha_i}}_{\phi_i} \cdot \underbrace{\frac{N_{d,l,k,j}^{\neg n} + \alpha_s}{N_{d,l,k}^{\neg n} + S\alpha_s}}_{\phi_s} \tag{7}$$

Samples obtained from the Gibbs sampling are then used to approximate the per-corpus entity (ϕ_e), issue (ϕ_i) and sentiment (ϕ_s) word distributions and the per-document entity (θ_e), issue (θ_i), and entity and issue specific sentiment (θ_s) distributions.

3   Experimental Setup

3.1   Dataset

As the evaluation dataset, we collected nearly 50,000 tweets with hashtags #auspol and #ausvotes posted during the 2016 Australian Federal Election (8 May – 2 July). We performed several standard preprocessing tasks on the tweets, including punctuation, number, URL and stop words removal, and stemming. Additionally, mention tags in tweets were replaced with the display name of the Twitter user using the available Twitter metadata. After completing the preprocessing, we removed duplicate tweets, which result in a dataset of 49,000 tweets as the training dataset.

Labelled data is not required to train the JESI model. However, to evaluate the resulted model's performance, it is required to have labelled data. Since

Table 2. Statistics of the datasets

	Training	Test
Number of tweets in corpus	49,000	1,407
Number of words in corpus	461,297	13,896
Vocabulary size	29,030	3,860
Average number of words/tweet	9	10

it is difficult to annotate the full dataset manually, we selected a portion of the training dataset randomly to annotate and prepare the labelled data for the evaluation. Before the annotation, we independently predefined 18 entities based on the analysis of frequently used mention tags in the dataset and 16 issues based on the major parties' policy analysis articles[1].

Then, from the training dataset, tweets were selected randomly for annotation by selecting 15% of tweets for each day between 8 May – 2 July. Three annotators independently annotated entity, sentiment, and issues for each tweet. Among them, we selected only the positive and negative tweets, which resulted in 1,407 tweets as the test data. From the test data, 89% tweets contain negative sentiment and only 11% contain positive sentiment. We test annotation reliability using Cohen's kappa statistics, and for all the cases, it is above 75%.

We use the labels only for evaluation and not for training and inference. To train the model, we use 49,000 tweets, and for evaluation, the labelled portion of tweets (1,407) is used. Table 2 shows some statistics of the datasets.

3.2 Hyperparameter Settings

In the JESI model implementation, we empirically set the symmetric priors $\beta_e = 1.5$, $\beta_i = 1$ and $\beta_s = 1$. For symmetric prior α values we adapted the approach proposed by JST [9]. We set $\alpha_e = (L \times 0.001)/E$, $\alpha_i = (L \times 0.001)/I$ and $\alpha_s = (L \times 0.05)/S$, where L is the average document length, E is the total number of entities, T is the total number of issues and S is the total number of sentiments. The value of 0.001 on average allocates 0.1% of probability mass for mixing entity and issue, and similarly, 5% for sentiment.

3.3 Model Priors

For the entity and issue prior information, we use manually constructed seed word lists. The seed word lists contain a maximum of 20 word tokens for each entity and issue.

To select sentiment prior information, we compared the MPQA lexicon[2], NRC Emotion Lexicon [14], SentiStrength [17] and Stanford CoreNLP Sentiment [16]. According to the type of output from each lexicon and classifier, we use different approaches to update $\lambda_{s_j,w}$.

The MPQA lexicon contains positive, negative and neutral words. If a word in the vocabulary is found under the positive or negative category j in the lexicon, $\lambda_{s_j,w}$ is updated to 1. A similar approach is used for the NRC Emotion Lexicon. However, in the NRC Lexicon, we consider trust, anticipation and joy as positive, and anger, fear, sadness and disgust as negative in addition to positive and negative words.

---

[1] https://www.abc.net.au/news/2016-05-13/election-2016-policy-big-issues/
7387588, https://electionwatch.unimelb.edu.au/australia-2016/categories/policies.
[2] https://mpqa.cs.pitt.edu/lexicons/.

SentiStrength and Stanford CoreNLP Sentiment return a sentiment score for a given word. Based on the returned value we use empirically found different weights on $\lambda_{s_j,w}$. SentiStrength returns a strength from 1 to 5 for positive (S_{pos}) and from -1 to -5 negative (S_{neg}) for each word. We update $\lambda_{s_j,w}$ as 1 if $|S_{pos} + S_{neg}|$ is 4, 0.8 if 3, 0.6 if 2, 0.4 if 1, or 0.2 if 1. Stanford CoreNLP Sentiment returns a score from 0 to 4 where 3 and 4 are for positive, 0 and 1 are for negative and 2 is for neutral words. We update $\lambda_{s_j,w}$ as 1 if the score is 4 or 0, or as 0.8 if the score is 3 or 1.

4   Experimental Results

We modified the JGibbLDA[3] package for implementation of JESI with Gibbs sampling. Gibbs sampling is used with 1000 iterations to produce a sample of results. We take 10 such samples of result sets, and for each sample, we calculate the macro-averaged results to measure effectiveness on small classes [12] such as the positive sentiment class in the evaluation dataset. Finally, we report the average for results of samples to compare the performance of document-level sentiment, issue and entity classification. We train JESI and baselines using the training dataset and evaluate the model on test dataset as discussed above.

4.1   Sentiment Classification

The document sentiment is classified based on $P(s|e, i)$, the probability of sentiment given entity and issue. From the output of the JESI model, we use the θ_s distribution to select the sentiment with maximum probability for each tweet.

Sentiment Prior Information Selection. We compare the performance on sentiment classification of JESI with different sentiment prior information, as discussed in Sect. 3.3. For entities and issues, we use seed words as prior information.

Table 3. JESI sentiment classification with different sentiment prior information

Prior information	Positive			Negative			Macro-averaged		
	Pre	Rec	F1	Pre	Rec	F1	Pre	Rec	F1
MPQA Lexicon	16.6	69.2	26.8	93.7	56.5	70.5	55.1	62.8	58.7
NRC Emotion Lexicon	16.1	**83.5**	26.9	**95.7**	45.6	61.8	55.9	64.5	59.9
Stanford CoreNLP	20.4	50.4	29.1	92.4	75.6	83.2	56.4	63.0	59.5
SentiStrength	**25.6**	55.3	**35.0**	93.5	**79.8**	**86.1**	**59.5**	**67.6**	**63.3**

The results in Table 3 demonstrate that the model performs better for sentiment classification on the evaluation dataset with SentiStrength as sentiment

---

[3] http://jgibblda.sourceforge.net/.

prior information. SentiStrength detects the highest percentage (9%) of negative words and the NRC Emotion Lexicon covers the highest percentage (10%) of positive words compared to other prior information which explains why SentiStregth gives the highest recall for the negative class and the NRC Emotion Lexicon gives the highest recall for the positive class. However, overall, JESI performs better with SentiStrength.

JESI vs SentiStrength. We evaluate the sentiment classification performance of JESI with SentiStregth as sentiment prior information, to the performance of the SentiStrength classifier on tweets.

The results in Table 4 show that JESI with SentiStength as sentiment prior information outperforms SentiStrength's sentiment classification. Notably, SentiStrength alone does not perform well for the negative class, which resulted in 70.8% F1 compared to 80.6% for JESI. Overall, it can be concluded that JESI is capable of learning more sentiment words during the learning process than the initial identification of sentiment words using SentiStrength as prior information, which helps to improve the overall sentiment classification performance of JESI.

JESI vs JST. We compare sentiment classification performance of JESI with JST [9]. We use SentiStrength and seed word lists as prior information for both models. However, in JST, words are generated conditioned on both sentiment and topic. Therefore, it is not possible to incorporate topic prior information to update Dirichlet priors β. However, to initialise posterior distributions l and z, we use sentiment and topic prior information, respectively.

In JST, we use the π distribution (Fig. 1(b)) to select the sentiment associated with the highest probability for each tweet as the predicted sentiment. However, in JST, there is only a topic latent variable in addition to sentiment variable. Therefore, here, we consider two JST models by considering JST topic are equivalent to entities and issues in two models. For JST, we use its original hyperparameter settings proposed in the paper [9].

The results in Table 5 show that JESI outperforms JST for sentiment classification. The main difference between JESI and JST is the sentiment generation order where, in JESI, the sentiment is generated condition on entity and issue and in JST entity/issue generation is conditioned on sentiment. Therefore, the results demonstrate the effectiveness of sentiment generation of JESI over JST.

Table 4. JESI sentiment classification vs SentiStrength sentiment classification

Model	Pre	Rec	F1
SentiStrength	55.5	64.0	59.4
JESI	**59.5**	**67.6**	**63.3**

Table 5. Sentiment classification performance comparison of JESI vs JST

Model	Pre	Rec	F1
JST (topic as entity)	56.4	65.2	60.5
JST (topic as issue)	56.6	65.5	60.7
JESI	**59.5**	**67.6**	**63.3**

Table 6. Entity classification performance comparison of JESI vs JST

Model	Pre	Rec	F1
JST (Topic as entity)	23.3	44.6	30.6
JESI	**77.9**	**52.4**	**62.6**

Table 7. Issue classification performance comparison of JESI vs JST

Model	Pre	Rec	F1
JST (Topic as issue)	37.6	36.3	36.9
JESI	**76.6**	**61.7**	**68.4**

Finally, we can conclude that the hypothesis of JESI is valid and in political opinions, the sentiment is generate conditioned on the target entity of the sentiment and issues of the target entity.

4.2   Entity Classification

Next, we evaluate the performance of JESI for entity classification. Entity classification is a multi-class classification task since there are 18 entity classes in the dataset. In JESI, the document-level entity is classified based on $P(e)$ which is the θ_e distribution. From the output of JESI model, we use θ_e distribution to select the entity for a given tweet by selecting the entity associated with the highest probability value for a given tweet.

We compare JESI entity classification with JST as a baseline. For JST, we use entity seed words as prior information for topics and SentiStrength for the sentiment. However, as discussed in the previous section for JST, we use topic (entity) prior information only to initialise the posterior distribution z. As hyperparameter values, for JST, we use the original values proposed in the paper [9]. In JST, we use the θ distribution to select the entity associated with the highest probability for each tweet as the predicted entity.

The results in Table 6 show that JESI outperforms JST for entity classification. In JST, the topic (entity) is conditioned on sentiment $P(t|s)$ while in JESI the entity generation is conditioned on the document $P(e)$. Therefore, we conclude that entity classification performs well when entity generation is not conditioned on sentiment.

4.3   Issue Classification

Issue classification is a multi-label multi-class classification task since there are 16 issue classes and each tweet can have multiple issues in the dataset. From the output of JESI, we use the θ_i distribution to select the issues for a given tweet by selecting the issues associated with the probabilities higher than a threshold value. For threshold selection, we use the PCut [7] method.

To compare performance, we use JST as a baseline. For JST, we use issue seed words as prior information for topics and SentiStrength for the sentiment. As discussed in the previous section for JST, we use topic (issue) prior information only to initialise the posterior distribution z. As hyperparameter values, for JST, we use the values proposed in [9]. In JST, we use the θ distribution to select the issues associated with probability values higher than the threshold for each tweet as the predicted issues.

Table 8. Examples of entity, issue and sentiment words generated by JESI

Entity	Liberal	*lnp, liberal, #lnp, vote, coalition, put, cut, #parakeelia, election, #lnpfail*
	Turnbull	*turnbull, malcolm, pm, news, cut, tax, vote, election, plan, #turnbull*
Issue	Refugees	*dutton, refugee, peter, labor, boat, asylum, bill, border, seeker, #refugees*
	Jobs	*turnbull, job, labor, pay, shorten, work, growth, union, leave, worker*
Sentiment	Positive	*shorten, labor, bill, abbott, news, policy, good, abc, support, vote*
	Negative	*turnbull, malcolm, lnp, liberal, vote, peter, lie, tax, cut, govt*

The results in Table 7 show that JESI outperforms JST for issue classification. In JST, the topic (issue) is conditioned on sentiment $P(t|s)$ while in JESI the issue generation is conditioned on the document $P(i)$. Therefore, we conclude that the issue classification performs well when issue generation is not conditioned on sentiment.

4.4 Topic Extraction

We perform a qualitative analysis of the generated entity, issues and sentiment words from the Twitter dataset to evaluate the effectiveness of topic words learnt by the JESI model. Some examples of entities, issues and sentiment along with the top words extracted by the model are shown in Table 8. In the model, the distributions of words given entity, issue and sentiment were estimated using ϕ_e, ϕ_i and ϕ_s respectively.

It can be seen from the table that the extracted topic words are informative and coherent. The majority of top entity words under the Liberal and Turnbull entities represent the different terms commonly used to represent them when writing tweets. Other than that it includes words such as 'tax' and 'cut', which are jointly used with the government party or leading candidates. Similarly, the issue words also contain the relevant entity's representative words, such as 'dutton' and 'peter' (the name of the Immigration Minister) under the Refugee issue. The extracted top sentiment words contain mixtures of entity words such as 'shorten' and 'turnbull', issue words such as 'tax' and 'cut' and sentiment words such as 'lie' and 'support'. In the annotated tweets, 40% of negative tweets are for the Liberal Party and, 30% are for Turnbull. We can expect the same distribution in the full dataset also. Therefore, the majority of top negative words are words relevant to Turnbull and the Liberal Party. Overall, the analysis of extracted words under the entity, issue and sentiment illustrate the effectiveness of JESI in extracting topics from a corpus of political tweets.

5 Related Work

Fine-grained opinion mining is an active research area of opinion mining, which consists of the identification of opinion target, aspects of the target and sentiment on the target and aspects. Previous methods have proposed different approaches to extract target, aspect and sentiment separately, and others have proposed models to identify components jointly.

Three approaches can be identified for aspect extraction: language dependency rules [11], sequential learning algorithms such as Conditional Random Fields (CRF) [5], and topic models such as LDA [15]. However, supervised methods such as CRF require substantial effort to label datasets word by word.

To jointly model sentiment and aspect, probabilistic topic models are utilised heavily due to their ability to identify and concisely represent latent topics in documents. The methods which used LDA as a basis to formulate joint topic-sentiment models achieved good performance. For example, the Joint Sentiment-Topic (JST) model [8], assumes that each sentiment has a multinomial distribution over topics and that each sentiment has a multinomial distribution over words. A hybrid model MaxEnt-LDA [19] was proposed to detect both aspects and aspect-specific opinion words concurrently.

Recent methods show that lexical information such as sentiment labels can be used to build weakly supervised topic models to improve sentiment analysis. The baseline of this paper, weakly supervised JST [9], which extended the previous JST model [8], is an example of such models. Later, most methods such as Hierarchical Aspect-Sentiment Model (HASM) [6] which uses sentiment seed words as supervised information, Multimodal Joint Sentiment-Topic (MJST) [4] which uses emoticons as supervised data, and WS-TSWE [3] which uses word embeddings for word co-occurrence statistics and sentiment lexicon, extended the weakly supervised JST model.

6   Conclusion and Future Work

In this paper, we presented the LDA-based weakly supervised Joint Entity-Sentiment-Issue (JESI) model for jointly identifying sentiment, sentiment target (entity) and aspect of the target (issue). Extensive experiments conducted on a Twitter dataset of political tweets show that the model outperforms JST, an existing sentiment-topic model, on sentiment, entity and topic classification, with higher precision, recall and F1. The results show that the hypothesis underlying JESI that the sentiment of an opinion depends on both entity and issue is valid. Further, JESI is capable of generating informative and coherent topic words for entities, issues and sentiment.

Future directions include (i) extending the JESI model to detect the political ideology of individuals, (ii) modifying JESI for stance detection by jointly modelling stance and target of the stance.

Acknowledgments. This work was supported by Data to Decisions Cooperative Research Centre. We would like to thank Caleb Morgan and Florim Binakaj for annotating the dataset. The first author would also like to thank Michael Bain and Alfred Krzywicki for their continuous mentoring and constant support.

References

1. Bakliwal, A., Foster, J., van der Puil, J., O'Brien, R., Tounsi, L., Hughes, M.: Sentiment analysis of political tweets: Towards an accurate classifier. In: Proceedings of the Workshop on Language Analysis in Social Media, pp. 49–58 (2013)

2. Blei, D.M., Ng, A.Y., Jordan, M.I.: Latent Dirichlet Allocation. J. Mach. Learn. Res. **3**, 993–1022 (2003)
3. Fu, X., Sun, X., Wu, H., Cui, L., Huang, J.Z.: Weakly supervised topic sentiment joint model with word embeddings. Knowl.-Based Syst. **147**, 43–54 (2018)
4. Huang, F., Zhang, S., Zhang, J., Yu, G.: Multimodal learning for topic sentiment analysis in microblogging. Neurocomputing **253**(C), 144–153 (2017)
5. Jakob, N., Gurevych, I.: Extracting opinion targets in a single-and cross-domain setting with conditional random fields. In: Proceedings of the 2010 Conference on Empirical Methods in Natural Language Processing, pp. 1035–1045 (2010)
6. Kim, S., Zhang, J., Chen, Z., Oh, A., Liu, S.: A hierarchical aspect-sentiment model for online reviews. In: Proceedings of the Twenty-Seventh AAAI Conference on Artificial Intelligence, pp. 526–533 (2013)
7. Lewis, D.D., Ringuette, M.: A comparison of two learning algorithms for text categorization. In: Proceedings of the Third Annual Symposium on Document Analysis and Information Retrieval, pp. 81–93 (1994)
8. Lin, C., He, Y.: Joint sentiment/topic model for sentiment analysis. In: Proceedings of the 18th ACM Conference on Information and Knowledge Management, pp. 375–384 (2009)
9. Lin, C., He, Y., Everson, R., Ruger, S.: Weakly supervised joint sentiment-topic detection from text. IEEE Trans. Knowl. Data Eng. **24**(6), 1134–1145 (2012)
10. Liu, B.: Sentiment Analysis and Opinion Mining. Morgan & Claypool Publishers, San Rafael (2012)
11. Liu, K., Xu, L., Zhao, J.: Opinion target extraction using word-based translation model. In: Proceedings of the 2012 Joint Conference on Empirical Methods in Natural Language Processing and Computational Natural Language Learning, pp. 1346–1356 (2012)
12. Manning, C.D., Raghavan, P., Schütze, H.: Introduction to Information Retrieval. Cambridge University Press, New York (2008)
13. Maynard, D., Funk, A.: Automatic detection of political opinions in tweets. In: García-Castro, R., Fensel, D., Antoniou, G. (eds.) ESWC 2011. LNCS, vol. 7117, pp. 88–99. Springer, Heidelberg (2012)
14. Mohammad, S.M., Turney, P.D.: Crowdsourcing a word-emotion association lexicon. Comput. Intell. **29**(3), 436–465 (2013)
15. Paul, M., Girju, R.: A two-dimensional topic-aspect model for discovering multi-faceted topics. In: Proceedings of the Twenty-Fourth AAAI Conference on Artificial Intelligence, pp. 545–550 (2010)
16. Socher, R., et al.: Recursive deep models for semantic compositionality over a sentiment treebank. In: Proceedings of the 2013 Conference on Empirical Methods in Natural Language Processing, pp. 1631–1642 (2013)
17. Thelwall, M., Buckley, K., Paltoglou, G.: Sentiment strength detection for the social web. J. Am. Soc. Inform. Sci. Technol. **63**(1), 163–173 (2012)
18. Vijayaraghavan, P., Vosoughi, S., Roy, D.: Automatic detection and categorization of election-related tweets. In: Proceedings of the Tenth International AAAI Conference on Web and Social Media, pp. 703–706 (2016)
19. Zhao, W.X., Jiang, J., Yan, H., Li, X.: Jointly modeling aspects and opinions with a MaxEnt-LDA hybrid. In: Proceedings of the 2010 Conference on Empirical Methods in Natural Language Processing, pp. 56–65 (2010)

A Case-Based Reasoning Approach for Facilitating Online Discussions

Wen Gu[1,2(✉)], Ahmed Moustafa[1], Takayuki Ito[1], Minjie Zhang[2], and Chunsheng Yang[3]

[1] Department of International Collaborative Informatics,
Nagoya Institute of Technology, Nagoya, Japan
{gu.wen,ahmed.moustafa}@itolab.nitech.ac.jp, ito.takayuki@nitech.ac.jp
[2] School of Computing and Information Technology, University of Wollongong,
Wollongong, Australia
minjie@uow.edu.au
[3] Digital Technology Research Center, National Research Council Canada,
Ottawa, Canada
chunsheng.yang@nrc.gc.ca

Abstract. In online discussion platforms, human facilitators are introduced in order to facilitate the discussions to proceed smoothly and build consensus efficiently. However, problems such as human bias and scalability are becoming critical with increasing sophistication of these online discussion platforms. In order to address these problems, online discussion facilitation support becomes more and more essential. Towards this end, in this paper, a novel case-based reasoning (CBR) based online discussion facilitation support approach, which consists of a case definition method and a case retrieval algorithm, is proposed to support online facilitation in large-scale discussion environments. The proposed approach models the online discussions using the issue based information system (IBIS) discussion style, where complex problems are modelled as a conversation amongst several stockholders. In the proposed approach, discussion cases are generated and retrieved based upon the structure features of their discussions. The experimental results show the proposed discussion case generation approach is able to reflect more precise discussion features than those approaches that are based only on the quantitative features, and the ability of the proposed case retrieval algorithm to retrieve the most similar case from the case base.

Keywords: Online discussion platforms · Facilitation support · Case-based reasoning · Issue based information system

1 Introduction

One effective approach to solve critical social problems is to collect the wisdom from a crowd of participant people. However, it grows difficult to organize a large number of people to discuss in one particular place during a particular time. With the development of the Internet, online discussion forums have attracted much attention as the platform of gathering a crowd of people together to solve

© Springer Nature Switzerland AG 2019
A. C. Nayak and A. Sharma (Eds.): PRICAI 2019, LNAI 11672, pp. 582–592, 2019.
https://doi.org/10.1007/978-3-030-29894-4_47

common problems. The core advantage of online discussion is that people can join the discussion via the Internet from different places whenever they are free. Therefore, platforms such as Climate CoLab [1], Deliberatorium [2] and Collagree [3] have been developed to encourage people to discuss in online environments. These platforms have been utilized to organize people to participant in online discussions about topics such as global climate change, law reform and city planning. In order to facilitate the discussion to proceed smoothly and achieve consensus efficiently, many platforms [2,3] introduce human facilitators into the discussions to conduct facilitation. Facilitators can promote the development of the discussion, integrate ideas and opinions, and help the group to build consensus [4]. However, as there is no general definition of online discussion facilitation, a human bias cannot be avoided. In addition, with the increase of the participants number in a certain discussion, scale issues and schedule issues also become critical problems for human facilitators.

As a result, it becomes more and more necessary to develop online discussion facilitation support techniques to help human facilitators relieve their burdens. The challenging part of facilitation in online discussion forums is that it is a very complicated problem, which changes significantly with the discussion development. It means that plenty of information need to be considered for facilitation and it is difficult to describe the method in a number of specific rules. Existing research [5] emphasizes the importance of experiences for human facilitators, since they reuse the successful experience they had in the past to solve new similar problems.

In this paper, we propose using CBR to support online discussion facilitation. CBR is one of the famous artificial intelligence techniques that have been successfully used in real-world applications [6,7]. In this regard, it provides an effective reasoning paradigm for solving new problems by adopting similar solutions that have been proposed for similar problems in the past [8]. This is very similar to the human facilitator thinking paradigm. Experienced human facilitators facilitate better than novice human facilitators because they have more experience that is derived from the past facilitation they have done. And experienced human facilitators are able to utilize these sorts of experience when they try to conduct facilitation in new discussion situations. Towards this end, in this paper, we propose a CBR based approach to support online discussion facilitation. When using CBR to solve a problem, the first and most important part is to find out the essential characteristics which can be used to express this problem in order to define the problem as a case. As a result, this proposed approach introduces a novel method of defining online discussion cases from their structures. In addition, a case retrieval algorithm is implemented to retrieve the most similar cases from the case base.

The rest of this paper is organized as follows. Section 2 introduces the related work of this research. In Sect. 3, the proposed CBR based online discussion facilitation support approach is introduced. Section 4 presents the experimental settings along with the experimental results.

2   Related Work

Many research efforts have been attempted in order to support group discussion facilitation. In this regard, Dickson et al. [9] explored three human-based facilitation modes in Group Decision Support System(GDSS) meeting and showed that group consensus improved in all the three modes. In addition, Anson et al. [10] showed human facilitators maintain high quality group interactions and improved group processes and greater cohesion. Also, an automated facilitation technique has been developed to support group discussion. Limayem et al. [11] showed both human-facilitated decision making groups and automated-facilitated decision making groups experienced significantly higher post-meeting consensus and perceived decision quality than non-facilitated groups in GDSS meeting. Aiken and Vanjani [12] showed that automated facilitator is better than human facilitator for simple idea generation and voting tasks. Wong and Aiken [13] showed both expert-human facilitated groups and automated facilitated groups perform significantly better than novice-human groups in electronic meetings when faced with relatively simple idea generating and ranking tasks. Derrick et al. [14] demonstrated that automated facilitation of system requirement generation is possible and showed that the agent-facilitated groups generate more complete requirements than non-facilitated groups. As shown in the above mentioned research works, just like human facilitators, automated facilitation techniques can also support group discussions.

However, there are still some problems in group-discussion facilitation. In specific, most of the group-discussion facilitation techniques can only support tasks such as agenda preparer, timekeeper, simple idea generation and voting. Therefore, it becomes difficult to use these techniques to support high level online discussion facilitation, since high level discussion facilitation, such as proper facilitation time detection and facilitation pattern decision, needs to be generated on the basis of the dynamically changing discussion situation. As a result, it is highly critical to develop novel discussion facilitation techniques to support high level facilitation in online discussion forums.

On the other hand, Gu et al. [15] proposed a CBR based online discussion facilitation support approach that is able to adapt to different discussion situations. Specifically, they proposed to use IBIS style to model the discussion structure and to define discussion cases from the quantitative perspective of the IBIS structure elements. IBIS style is based on the principle that the design process for complex problems is fundamentally a conversation amongst several stakeholders [16]. This has been used as a visual aid to help participants and facilitators to understand the discussion structure. However, in this IBIS based discussion process, a lot of inner characteristics cannot be reflected if we just consider the quantitative features. For example, we consider the similarity between $Case(a)$ and $Case(b)$ that are demonstrated in Fig. 1. In this situation, if we use the quantitative features to define a case base, the differences between $Case(a)$ and $Case(b)$ cannot be distinguished because their quantitative features are the same. Even though, they are constituted by different structures, these differences cannot be reflected because they have the same number of issues, ideas, and arguments. On the other hand, it is critical to consider the structure characteristics in the case definition because the discussion structure reflects the relationship among the discussion contents. For example, the connections among different vertexes need to be considered because they reflect the consistency in the discussion while those vertexes which are not connected cannot reflect the consistency in the discussion. As a result, it is critical to design new approaches to define the discussion case in order to reflect the structure characteristics of the discussion.

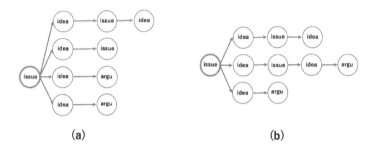

(a)   (b)

Fig. 1. Two IBIS style discussion cases

3   Proposed Approach

3.1   Problem Description

In this research, we aim to develop CBR based online discussion facilitation support approach that can be used to help human facilitators conduct facilitation in online discussion platforms.

In order to design a CBR based online discussion facilitation support approach, as the first step, we need to build a reasonable case base that represents the system's experience in online discussion facilitation. For each case, the definition consists of a problem description part and a problem solution part. In this paper, we propose a novel structure perspective method to describe the online discussion facilitation problem. The solution of the problem is a result that whether facilitation is necessary to be added or not. In addition, we propose a case retrieval algorithm in order to find the most similar case from the case base.

Specifically, we consider the discussion process that is represented in issue based information structure(IBIS) style [16]. We generate IBIS structures of the discussions by using three sorts of elements which are issue, idea, and argument. Issues are defined as the questions that need to be answered during the discussions. Ideas are defined as the possible answers to the issues. Arguments contains both pros and cons. Pros are defined as the support to an issue or an idea and cons are defined as the object to an issue or an idea. Each element in the IBIS style discussion structure is represented as a vertex. Facilitations are the posts that facilitators generated to promote the discussion. Each association between two elements is represented as a directed edge. For example, discussion in Fig. 2, (a) can be represented in IBIS style as demonstrated in Fig. 2, (b). FA represents facilitation posts and argu represents argument posts.

(a)   **(b)**

Fig. 2. IBIS style discussion expression

3.2 Discussion Case Definition

Discussion case definition has been proposed from the quantitative perspective which focuses on the numeric IBIS style discussion features such as issue number, idea number and argument number [15]. However, in order to reflect more precise features of the generated IBIS style discussion graphs, the characteristics of the structure in the graph also need to be considered. One of the examples is demonstrated in Fig. 3.

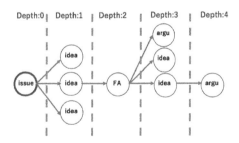

Fig. 3. IBIS style discussion expression

As shown in Fig. 3, one of the salient characteristics in the IBIS style discussion structure is the original vertex. The original issue vertex, which equals to the root topic of the discussion, can be considered as the parent vertex of all other vertexes. All other vertexes show the discussion details which are generated to solve the original discussion issue. Considering the discussion structure, it is obvious that the depth of the vertexes in the discussion structure can reflect status information in the discussion. For example, if two issues hold the same number of ideas, the issue which has more deep ideas can be considered as better discussed than the issue which has fewer deep ideas.

In this research, we define the original vertex's depth as 0. All other vertexes are in a depth which is more than 0. And we define the discussion case as a sort of labeled graph on the basis of the IBIS style discussion structure. Specifically, we define a labeled discussion graph as a directed graph in which each vertex and each edge is associated with one label. A labeled graph is defined by a triple $G = <V, r_V, r_E>$, where.

- V is a finite set of vertexes.
- $r_V \subseteq V \times L_V$ shows the relation between vertexes and labels. Each vertex has only one related label, which can be issue, idea or argument. The situation that v_i has label l_{v_i} is represented by a tuple (v_i, l_{v_i}). r_V is the set of tuples v_i.
- $r_E \subseteq V \times L_V \times V' \times L_{V'}$ shows the relation between edges and labels. One edge $(v_i, l_{v_i}, v_j, l_{v_j})$ is defined as the combination of two labeled vertexes (v_i, l_{v_i}) and (v_j, l_{v_j}). r_E is the set of quaternaries $(v_i, l_{v_i}, v_j, l_{v_j})$.

For example, one labeled IBIS style discussion case graph as demonstrated in Fig. 4(a) can be formulated by a labeled group as demonstrated in Fig. 4(b).

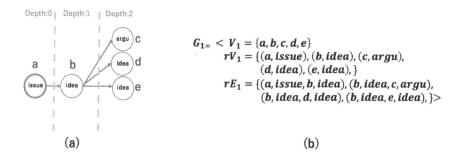

$$G_1 = < V_1 = \{a, b, c, d, e\}$$
$$rV_1 = \{(a, issue), (b, idea), (c, argu),$$
$$(d, idea), (e, idea),\}$$
$$rE_1 = \{(a, issue, b, idea), (b, idea, c, argu),$$
$$(b, idea, d, idea), (b, idea, e, idea),\}>$$

(a)   (b)

Fig. 4. IBIS style discussion expression

3.3   Discussion Case Retrieval

In this research, we calculate the similarity between two discussion cases on the basis of labeled graph similarity algorithm [18].

When we measure the similarity between two labeled IBIS style discussion graphs, we use the idea that comparing the number of features which are common to both objects, to the total number of the features [19]. In our situation, the total number of the features of a labeled IBIS style discussion graph can be represented as a triple G. When we compare the similarity of two graphs $G_1 = <V_1, r_{V_1}, r_{E_1}>$ and $G_2 = <V_2, r_{V_2}, r_{E_2}>$, such that $V_1 \cap V_2 = \emptyset$, one additional thing that we need to consider is the relation that connects the two graphs. In this research, we define the relation that connects two graphs as: if two vertexes hold same sort of label and are in the same structure depth, these two vertexes are consider to be similar. Similarity between two graphs G_1 and G_2 can be calculated by Eq. 1.

$$sim_S(G_1, G_2) = \frac{f(descr(G_1) \cap descr(G_2))}{f(descr(G_1) \cup descr(G_2))} \tag{1}$$

$descr(G_1)$ and $descr(G_2)$ are the descriptions of labeled graph G_1 and G_2, respectively. Each description is made up by all the labeled graph vertex features in addition to the edge features. The similarity between the two graphs, i.e., G_1 and G_2, is calculated by using the common features that the two graphs share divided by the set of all the two graph features.

There is a special state where new discussion case is the subgraph of more than two cases in the case base, and the number of common features of these two cases is the same. If these two cases are retrieved from the case base together, and then the algorithm retains the subbranch that includes the new discussion case and cut off other subbranches from the origin vertex. After that, the similarity is recalculated between these two cases in order to choose the most similar case.

4   Experiments

In this section, we introduce the experimental results of comparing the proposed structural perspective discussion case definition with the quantitative discussion case definition in case retrieval results.

In order to demonstrate the ability of the proposed CBR-based approach to retrieve similar discussion cases efficiently, we built a synthetic test case base that includes seven discussion cases. The quantitative information of the case base is shown in Table 1.

Table 1. Synthetic cases in test case base

Case ID	Case1	Case2	Case3	Case4	Case5	Case6	Case7
Number of issues	1	1	1	1	1	3	3
Number of ideas	1	3	3	1	5	5	5
Number of arguments	2	4	3	1	5	2	2
Idea depth	1	1	2	1	3	3	3
Facilitation	1	0	0	1	0	1	0

We choose four sorts of quantitative information as the parameters, number of issues, number of ideas, number of arguments and idea depth. The idea depth means the depth of the deepest idea in the discussion case. And the structural information of the case base is demonstrated in Fig. 5.

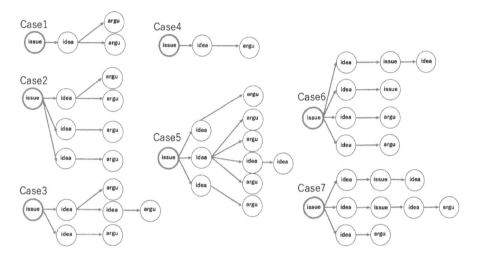

Fig. 5. Experiment case base

In addition, we built two synthetic test cases whose information is demonstrated in Table 2 and Fig. 6.

Table 2. Synthetic test cases

Case ID	Case_t1	Case_t2
Number of issues	1	1
Number of ideas	1	6
Number of arguments	2	6
Idea Depth	1	2

In this experiment, firstly, we retrieve the most similar case to our test cases from the case base by using the Nearest Neighbor (NN) algorithm [17]. In NN algorithm, similarity is calculated on the basis of the euclidean distance of each feature parameter. Two cases are more similar if the euclidean distance between them is smaller. If the euclidean distance between two cases is 0, it means that the two cases are identical, i.e., the two cases hold the same number of quantitative perspective features. Secondly, we retrieve the most similar case to our test case from the case base by using the proposed labeled graph similarity algorithm we

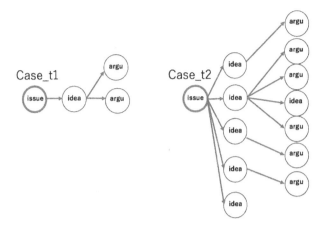

Fig. 6. Synthetic test cases

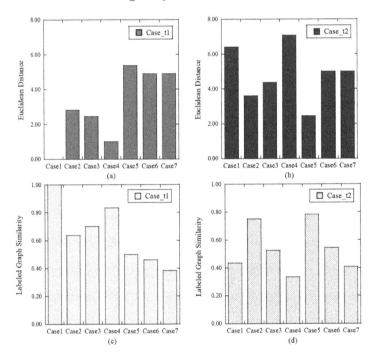

Fig. 7. Experiment results

introduced in Sect. 3. Two cases are more similar if the labeled graph similarity between them is higher.

Specifically, two test cases, $Case\_t1$ and $Case\_t2$ are designed to test our proposed approach. $Case\_t1$, which is identical to $Case1$ of the test case base, is designed to test whether identical cases can be calculated as identical by our proposed approach. $Case\_t2$, which is similar to $Case5$, $Case6$ and $Case7$ of the test case base, is designed to test whether structure details can be reflected by our proposed approach.

The results of the experiments are shown in Fig. 7. From these results, we can see that proposed approach can work as good as the quantitative perspective discussion case definition method. In specific, it finds the most similar case to $Case\_t1$ and $Case\_t2$ from the case base, which are $Case1$ and $Case5$, respectively. $Case\_t1$ is also identified to be identical with $Case1$ because the labeled graph similarity is 1. In addition, for the similarity results of $Case6$ and $Case7$, differences are not reflected when using the quantitative features, as shown in Fig. 7(a) and (b). However, this sort of difference can be reflected when using the structure perspective features and the proposed algorithm, as shown in Fig. 7(c) and (d). This reflects the situation that the quantitative features are the same, but the structures are different.

5   Conclusion

In this paper, we proposed a novel CBR based online discussion facilitation support approach to support online discussion facilitation. In the proposed approach, IBIS style discussion structure format is employed to define discussion cases on the basis of their discussion structure. Labeled graph similarity algorithm is utilized to retrieve the most similar discussion cases from the case base. Experimental results demonstrated the ability of the proposed case definition method to reflect structural discussion cases differences that the quantitative features cannot reflect and the ability of the proposed case retrieval algorithm to retrieve most similar cases from the case base. One of the directions for future work is to improve the efficiency of the proposed case retrieval algorithm when handling large-scale case base. The possible solution is to consider comparing the extracted features from each case instead of comparing two graphs. Another direction of future work is to introduce more information into the case definition in order to reflect more precise discussion situation. One possible solution is to consider the semantic information of each IBIS vertex. These additional information can be added as sub-vertexes that can ensure more precise case retrieval.

Acknowledgment. This work was supported by JST CREST Grant Number JPMJ-CR15E1, Japan.

References

1. Introne, J., Laubachar, R., Olson, G., Malone, T.: The climate Colab: large scale model-based collaborative planning. In: Proceedings of the International Conference on Collaboration Technologies and Systems (CTS 2011) (2011)
2. Klein, M.: How to harvest collective wisdom on complex problems: an introduction to the MIT deliberatorium. CCI working paper (2011)

3. Ito, T., Imi, Y., Ito, T.K., Hideshima, E.: COLLAGREE: a faciliator-mediated large-scale consensus support system. In: Collective Intelligence 2014, 10–12 June 2014. MIT, Cambridge (poster) (2014)

4. Ito, T.: Towards agent-based large-scale decision support system: the effect of facilitator. In: The 51st Hawaii International Conference on System Sciences, Hilton Waikoloa Village, USA, 3–6 January 2018 (2018)

5. McLean, M.: What can we learn from facilitator and student perceptions of facilitation skills and roles in the first year of a problem based learning curriculum. BMC Med. Educ. **3**, 1–10 (2003)

6. Yang, C., Orchard, R., Farley, B., Zaluski, M.: Authoring cases from free-text maintenance data. In: Perner, P., Rosenfeld, A. (eds.) MLDM 2003. LNCS, vol. 2734, pp. 131–140. Springer, Heidelberg (2003). https://doi.org/10.1007/3-540-45065-3_12

7. Lopes, E.C., Schiel, U.: Integrating context into a criminal case-based reasoning model. In: The Proceedings of 2nd International Conference on Information, Process, and Knowledge management (2010)

8. Schank, R.C.: Dynamic Memory: A Theory of Reminding and Learning in Computers and People. Cambridge University Press, New York (1983)

9. Dickson, G.W., Partridge, J.-E.L., Robinson, L.H.: Exploring modes of facilitative support for GDSS technology. MIS Q. **17**(2), 173–194 (1993)

10. Anson, R., Bostrom, R.P., Wynne, B.: An experiment assessing group support system and facilitator effects on meeting outcomes. Manage. Sci. **41**, 189–208 (1995)

11. Limayem, M., Lee-Partridge, J.E., Dickson, G.W., DeSanctis, G.: Enhancing GDSS effectiveness: automated versus human facilitation. In: Proceedings of the Twenty-Sixth Hawaii International Conference on System Sciences, vol. 4, pp. 95–101, January 1993

12. Aiken, M., Vanjani, M.: An automated GDSS facilitator. In: Proceedings of the 29th Annual Conference of the Southwest Decision Sciences Institute, Dallas, TX, 3–7 March 1998, pp. 87–89 (1998)

13. Wong, Z., Aiken, M.: Automated facilitation of electronic meetings. Inf. Manage. **41**(2), 125–134 (2003)

14. Derrick, D.C., Read, A., Nguyen, C., Callens, A., de Vreede, G.: Automated group facilitation for gathering wide audience end-user requirements. In: 2013 46th Hawaii International Conference on System Sciences, pp. 195–204, January 2013

15. Gu, W., Moustafa, A., Ito, T., Zhang, M., Yang, C.: A case-based reasoning approach for automated facilitation in online discussion systems. In: The Proceedings of The 2018 International Conference on Knowledge, Information and Creativity Support Systems (KICSS 2018), Thailand, November 2018

16. Kunz, W., Rittel, H.W.J.: Issues as elements of information systems. Center for Planning and Development Research, Institute of Urban and Regional Development, Working Paper No. 131, University of California, Berkeley (1970)

17. Dasarathy, B.V. (ed.): Nearest Neighbor Pattern Classification Techniques. IEEE Computer Society Press, Los Alamitos (1991)

18. Champin, P.-A., Solnon, C.: Measuring the similarity of labeled graphs. In: Ashley, K.D., Bridge, D.G. (eds.) ICCBR 2003. LNCS (LNAI), vol. 2689, pp. 80–95. Springer, Heidelberg (2003). https://doi.org/10.1007/3-540-45006-8_9

19. Lin, D.: An information-theoretic definition of similarity. In: Proceedings of ICML 1998, Fifteenth International Conference on Machine Learning, pp. 296–304. Morgan Kaufmann (1998)

Building Adversarial Defense
with Non-invertible Data Transformations

Wenbo Guo[1], Dongliang Mu[1,2(✉)], Ligeng Chen[2], and Jinxuan Gai[1]

[1] College of Information Sciences and Technology,
The Pennsylvania State University, State College, USA
{wzg13,dzm77,jug273}@ist.psu.edu
[2] National Key Laboratory for Novel Software Technology,
Nanjing University, Nanjing, China
dz1733001@smail.nju.edu.cn

Abstract. Deep neural networks (DNN) have been recently shown to be susceptible to a particular type of attack possible through the generation of particular synthetic examples referred to as adversarial samples. These samples are constructed by manipulating real examples from the training data distribution in order to *"fool"* the original neural model, resulting in misclassification of previously correctly classified samples. Addressing this weakness is of utmost importance if DNN is to be applied to critical applications, such as those in cybersecurity. In this paper, we present an analysis of this fundamental flaw lurking in all neural architectures to uncover limitations of previously proposed defense mechanisms. More importantly, we present a unifying framework for protecting deep neural models using a non-invertible data transformation–developing two adversary-resistant DNNs utilizing both linear and nonlinear dimensionality reduction techniques. Empirical results indicate that our framework provides better robustness compared to state-of-art solutions while having negligible degradation in generalization accuracy.

Keywords: Deep neural network · Adversarial sample defense · Non-invertible data transformation

1 Introduction

DNN has been applied to various critical fields such as medical imaging [2], self-driving cars [11] and malware detection [5,18,23]. However, recent work [15, 20] uncovered DNNs are vulnerable to *adversarial sample* – a synthetic sample generated by modifying a real example with imperceptible perturbations but causing a target DNN model to believe it belongs to the wrong class with high confidence.

To mitigate the aforementioned kind of attack, previous defenses [3,12,14] generally follow the basic idea of *adversarial training* in which a DNN is trained with both samples from the original data distribution as well as artificially synthesized adversarial ones. A recent unification of previous approaches [16]

© Springer Nature Switzerland AG 2019
A. C. Nayak and A. Sharma (Eds.): PRICAI 2019, LNAI 11672, pp. 593–606, 2019.
https://doi.org/10.1007/978-3-030-29894-4_48

showed that they were all special cases of a general, regularized objective function *DataGrad*. However, because the adversarial samples space is unbounded, this framework is still vulnerable to a certain type of adversarial sample. To be specific, as we will show later in Sect. 5, these defense can be easily bypassed if an attacker generate adversarial samples from the network trained with *DataGrad* (*i.e.*, post-defense model).

In this paper, we present a new defense framework that increases the difficulty for attackers to craft adversarial samples from both the original DNN and the post-defense model. At a high level, we integrate an data transform layer in front of a DNN model, which transform an input sample into an latent representation before being inputted into the DNN. Technically speaking, this data transformation layer employs a non-invertible dimensionality reduction approach which increases the computational cost of mapping an adversarial sample generated from the latent space back to the input space. Evaluation results on MNIST data set demonstrate an non-invertible data transformation layer improves the robustness of a DNN and preserves the classification performance on clean testing samples. In summary, we make the following contributions:

- We propose a comprehensive framework that makes a DNN model resistant to adversarial samples by integrating an input transformation into the model.
- We develop two new defense mechanisms by injecting different dimensional reduction methods into the proposed framework.
- We theoretically and empirically evaluate the DNN models, showing that our new defense framework is resistant to adversarial samples.

2   Existing Defences

The existing defense mainly falls in to the following categories: (1) augmenting the training set and (2) enhancing model complexity. As is mentioned in Sect. 1, most of the defenses augment the training set with a group of adversarial samples [1,4,16,22] and retrain the model with the augmented data (*i.e.*, adversarial training). These defenses can be viewed as adding a regularization term to a DNN's loss function [16], which penalizes the subspace where adversarial samples lies in. Another line of works building defences by increasing the complexity of a DNN and improve the tolerance of complex DNN models with respect to adversarial samples generated from simple DNN models. For example, [17] develops a defensive distillation mechanism, which trains a DNN from data samples that are distilled by another DNN. By using the knowledge transferred from the other DNN, the learned DNN classifiers become less sensitive to adversarial samples. Similar to [17], [9] proposed stacking an auto-encoder together with a normal DNN.

Though the above approaches, both from data augmentation and model complexity perspectives, have proven effective in handling samples generated from normal adversarial DNN models, they do not handle all adversarial samples. In light of this, we propose a framework that blocks the gradient flow from the output to input variables, a solution that prove effective even when the architecture and parameters of a given a DNN are publicly disclosed.

3   Data Transformation Enhanced DNN Framework

In this section, we introduce our framework's design goals and choose a particular type of data transformation that will fulfill these goals.

3.1   Design Goals

As is mentioned in Sect. 1, we build a novel DNN framework by integrating a data transformation layer before an ordinary DNN. And we want our framework to achieving the following goals:

- It has minimal impact on the performance of a DNN model when legitimate samples are seen.
- It increases the computational cost of finding a group of adversarial samples that can bypass the post-defense model.
- it is independent from the subsequent DNN model.

3.2   Framework Overview

As is mentioned before, to generate an adversarial samples from our framework, an attack need to map an adversarial sample generated from the latent space back to the input space. This indicates that if a selected data transformation is Non-invertible, an attacker is not able to generate adversarial samples. To be specific, non-invertible data transformation stands for the following properties: (1) inverting the data transformation is computationally too complex to be tractable; or (2) inverting the data transformation will cause significant reconstruction error. Besides non-invertible, the data transformation layer should preserve the semantic meanings for an original input, which will ensure the classification of our framework. Last but not least, the transformation should also be computationally efficient and more importantly, incremental. The latter requirement is essential given that any data transformation method must be capable of handling unseen samples as they are presented. Otherwise, the data transformation will need to be retrained, and subsequently, the DNN on top of the newly retrained transform layer.

Dimensionality reduction is one particular data transformation mechanism that satisfies these design objectives. First, dimensionality reduction methods are often designed to preserve at least the most important aspects of the original data. Second, dimensionality reduction can serve as a filter for adversarial perturbations when a DNN is confronted with adversarial samples generated from the post-defence models. Third, dimensionality reduction helps reduce the dimensionality of the input distribution that is fed into the DNN. Finally, it is easier to develop non-invertible data transformation methods, since recovering higher dimensional data from lower dimensional data is difficult. The following sections introduce details of two developed defence mechanisms using different non-invertible dimensional reduction methods.

4   Data Transformation Enhanced DNNs

4.1   Designed Linear Mapping (DLM) DNN

We first propose a novel linear dimensional reduction method, which stems from principal component analysis (PCA). And we provide a theorem that places the lower bound on the reconstruction error.

PCA is computationally efficient and easy to implement [13]. Additionally, it preserves critical information by finding a low-dimensional subspace with maximal variance. In another word, it is convenient for an attacker to generate adversarial examples by mapping the low dimensional data back to the high one.

PCA preserves meaningful features of the original data when mapping them to a lower dimension. Given a data matrix $X \in \mathbb{R}^{n \times p}$, the transformation matrix W can be obtained by solving the optimization function as:

$$\arg \min_{Y,W} \frac{1}{2} \left\| X - YW^T \right\|_F \tag{1}$$

where $W \in \mathbb{R}^{p \times q}$, $W^T W = I_q$ and $Y \in \mathbb{R}^{n \times q}$. According to the Eckart-Young Theorem [7], the optimal solution is obtained when W consists of the q largest eigenvalues of $X^T X$. Therefore, the low dimensional mappings can be computed as follows:

$$Y = XW \tag{2}$$

Accordingly, we can approximately reconstruct the high dimensional X from the transformed data Y by:

$$\hat{X} = YW^T \tag{3}$$

which represents the process of reconstructing high dimensional approximation using only low dimensional mappings and a transform matrix. Therefore, using PCA alone for a data transformation doesn't satisfy the non-invertible criteria we introduced in Sect. 3.

To deal with this problem and yet preserve computational efficiency, we equip PCA with our first non-invertible characteristic. To do this, we propose a novel dimension reduction method we call a designed linear mapping (DLM). This design ensures that the PCA operation continues to preserve the critical information while the column-wise highly correlated transformation matrix guarantees that inverting the DLM will generate significant reconstruction error. To explain the consequence of this, we now introduce DLM in detail and examine its properties.

Much as in (2), we shall formally define DLM as:

$$Y = XC^T + \omega, \tag{4}$$

where $X \in \mathbb{R}^{n \times p}$, $Y \in \mathbb{R}^{n \times p_c}$. $\omega \in \mathbb{R}^{n \times p_c}$ denotes a normally distributed noise matrix, where each entry of ω generated from a normal distribution $N(0, \sigma^2)$. $C \in \mathbb{R}^{p_c \times p}$ is the transformation matrix obtained by following equation:

$$C = [B; A], \tag{5}$$

where C is constructed by combining a loading matrix $B \in \mathbb{R}^{p_b \times p}$ obtained via PCA with a designed matrix $A \in \mathbb{R}^{(p_c - p_b) \times p}$, of which all columns are highly correlated. This combination integrates PCA's information-preserving effects into our DLM. As such, the lower dimensional projection Y can provide a better representation of the original X.

Since the DLM described by (4) has a simple linear form, we estimate reconstruction $\hat{X}$ for X using high-dimensional linear regression [19] (we omit calculation details due to space constraints). According to Theorem 1 in [19], we can obtain a lower bound of the reconstruction error, which is the L_2 norm of the difference between X and $\hat{X}$ as shown in (6):

$$\left(L_2(X, \hat{X})\right)^2 \geq \kappa_0 \; \sigma^2 \frac{s \; log(p/s)}{p_c}, \tag{6}$$

where s denotes the sparsity of X. κ_0 is a constant whose value depends closely on the data set. Therefore, given a certain set of data, any linear transformation method is restricted by a constant lower bound calculated according to (6). In addition, according to Theorem 2 in [19], there also exists an upper bound of the reconstruction error as follows:

$$\left(L_2(X, \hat{X})\right)^2 \leq f(C) \frac{s \; log(p)}{p_c}, \tag{7}$$

where $f(C)$ is a function of C. According to [19], the upper bound of the reconstruction error depends on both the data transformation matrix C and noise ω. When C is a an independent correlation matrix, as in PCA, then the upper bound will approach the aforementioned lower bound. However, since we specifically design C to be highly correlated, the upper bound will be significantly larger than the lower bound [6,8], and thus result in a larger range for the reconstruction error.

4.2 Dimensionality Reduction by Learning an Invariant Mapping (DrLIM) DNN

When adversarial samples are processed by normal DNN models, the decisions made in a lower dimensional space are completely different from those made for legitimate samples, even though adversarial samples are highly similar to legitimate ones. Therefore, we intend to employ a dimensionality reduction method that preserves the similarity of high dimensional samples in their lower dimensional mappings. Furthermore, our method needs to be capable of extracting critical information contained in the original data. Since the training of a DNN is already computationally intensive, our approach needs to be incremental in order to avoid the need for retraining the DNN.

Because of these considerations, we employ the dimensionality reduction method *DrLIM* proposed in [10]. DrLIM is specifically designed for preserving similarity between pairs of high dimensional samples when they are mapped to a lower dimensional space. As a result, there is a significantly lower chance that an adversarial sample acts as an outlier in the lower dimensional space, since its mapped location is bounded by the mapped locations of similar, legitimate samples. DrLIM can also be used in an online setting.

More importantly, we theoretically prove that inverting DrLIM is an NP-hard problem. Therefore, DrLIM is suitable for our framework in that it satisfies the second characteristic of non-invertibility defined in Sect. 3. But first, we briefly review DrLIM.

DrLIM consists of a convolutional neural network (CNN) model designed for optimizing the cost function:

$$\sum_{i=1}^{P} L\left(W, (Y, X_{i_1}, X_{i_2})^i\right), \tag{8}$$

where W denotes the coefficients. X_{i_1} and X_{i_2} denote the ith pair of input sample vectors with $i = 1 \ldots P$. Y is a binary label assigned to each pair of samples, with $Y = 0$ denoting a similar pair of X_{i_1} and X_{i_2}, and $Y = 1$ for dissimilar pairs. Any prior knowledge can be applied to representing dissimilarity. Let the loss function for measuring the cost for each pair be defined as:

$$L\left(W, Y, X_1, X_2\right) = (1 - Y)\frac{1}{2}\left(D(X_1, X_2)\right)^2 + \frac{Y}{2}\{max\left(0, m - D(X_1, X_2)\right)\}^2, \tag{9}$$

where $D(X_1, X_2) = \|G(X_1) - G(X_2)\|_2$ is the Euclidean distance measured between the output lower dimension mapping $G(X_1)$ and $G(X_1)$ for the sample pair X_1 and X_2. Let m be a predefined constant which indicates whether all dissimilar pairs are pushed or pulled towards to maintain a constant distance m.

Since G represents a mapping by the CNN to enable the recovery of high dimensional data from the low dimensional data $G(X)$, we need to first get $G^{-1}(X)$. For the forward pass of a conventional neural network, it is not guaranteed that the weight matrices are invertible [24], implying that information lost during pooling cannot be recovered. Thus, it is very difficult to compute $G^{-1}(X)$ and recover the original data from a low dimensional representation. Since inverting the CNN is nearly impossible, one option is to reconstruct original X according to (9) given W and Y. In the following, we demonstrate that even this approach can be mapped to a NP-hard problem.

As discussed before, the most important property of DrLIM that allows it to fit into our framework is that it is provably non-invertible. Assuming $G(X)$ takes a simple linear form of $G(X) = WX$, then we have $D(X_1, X_2)^2 = (X_1 - X_2)^T W^T W(X_1 - X_2)$. Here we denote $\delta X = (X_1 - X_2)$. Following this assumption, we can reformulate (9) as follows:

$$\min_{\delta X, z} \sum (1 - Y)\delta X^T W^T W \delta X + Y z^2, \tag{10}$$

$$\text{s.t. } z \geq 0, z \geq m - \sqrt{\delta X^T W^T W \delta X},$$

where $z = max\left(0, m - D(X_1, X_2)\right)$. Here we reformulate the second constraint as $\sqrt{\delta X^T W^T W \delta X} \geq m - z$. Since $m - z \geq 0$, we have following:

$$\delta X^T W^T W \delta X \geq (m - z)^2. \tag{11}$$

Therefore, W is positive semi-definite. When both sides of (11) are multiplied by -1 and substituted into (10), we find that:

$$\min_{\delta X, z} \sum (1 - Y)\delta X^T W^T W \delta X + Y z^2,$$
$$\text{s.t. } z \geq 0, -\delta X^T W^T W \delta X \leq -(m - z)^2. \tag{12}$$

From earlier work [21], the formulation (12) implies a quadratic problem with a non-positive semi-definite constraint, which is an NP-hard problem.

Note that solving (12) can yield the distance δX. There are multiple pairs of X_1 and X_2 that satisfy that $\delta X = (X_1 - X_2)$. This makes the problem even harder to solve. Additionally, since the linear relaxation (12) is already NP-hard, the original problem (9) is also NP-hard given that $G(X)$ is commonly regarded as a nonlinear function approximated by a neural network.

5   Evaluation

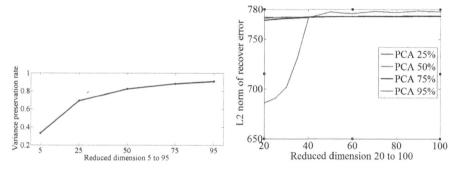

Fig. 1. Variance preservation rates with different reduced dimensions of PCA.

Fig. 2. Reconstruction errors with varying parameters for inverting DLM.

Going beyond theoretical analysis the non-invertible ability of the proposed defenses, we empirically demonstrate these defenses achieve the goals mentioned in Sect. 3. To be specific, We evaluate our framework using the widely-used MNIST data set [18]. MNIST contains a training split with 60000 greyscale images of handwritten digits and a test set containing 10000 images. Each image has a dimensionality of $28 \times 28 = 784$ pixels (Fig. 1).

In the following experiments, we evaluate the proposed approaches under two types of adversarial samples. In order to first demonstrate that our mechanisms do indeed preserve the classification performance of the DNN, we test them with the original test set. We then test our methods with adversarial samples generated from the post-defence models to show that we achieve our secondary design goal.

5.1   Limitations of Adversarial Training

In this section, We demonstrate the limitations of widely adopted defense mechanism: adversarial training. We build two different DNNs (model A and B) that share the same purpose–image recognition. Furthermore, we utilize adversarial training in learning both models A and B, which we denote as models A_{ADT} and B_{ADT}. Note that all following experiment results are the result of evaluating model A_{ADT} using different samples.

The results appear in Table 1. The second row '*Legitimate*' presents the classification error rates achieved by model A_{ADT} when testing with normal samples. In the next third and fourth row, we show classification error rates using adversarial samples generated from model A and model B respectively. The error rate obtained when testing with adversarial samples generated from model A itself is higher than the error rate found when testing with adversarial sample generated from a different model B. This is because adversarial samples generated from a specific model are more powerful for attacking that specific model. The result showed below demonstrates that adversarial samples generated from enhanced DNN models maintain their cross-model efficacy.

Table 1. Classification performance of testing an adversarial training enhanced model with various adversarial samples

Different testing sets	Classification error rates of model A_{ADT}
Legitimate	0.0213
Adversarial samples from A	0.2506
Adversarial samples from B	0.1633
Adversarial samples from A_{ADT}	0.7810
Adversarial samples from B_{ADT}	0.5715

5.2   Classification Performance

Classification Performance of DLM-DNN. In this experiment, we fix the reduced dimensionality to 100. These mappings are found by DLM and PCA. In order to better explore the effect of combining DLM with PCA, we vary the percentage P_{pca} of PCA mappings used in the fixed 100 dimension. Meanwhile, the percentage of DLM mappings used varies according to $100 - P_{pca}$. In addition, we also change the level of noise added to study its influence on classification performance.

We first show the classification performance when testing with legitimate samples in the column named as '*Legitimate*' in Table 2. The noise coefficient is set to be either 0.1 or 0.3, while P_{pca} varies from 5% to 95%. This performance degradation is due to the increase of noise injected into the lower dimensional mappings. Therefore, we conclude that if properly set, DLM-DNN can result in performance comparable to adversarial training.

Table 2. Classification performance of DLM-DNN and DrLIM-DNN

Trained model			Classification error rates with different testing sets	
			Legitimate	Adversarial
Normal DNN			0.0198	0.8981
Adversarial training enhanced DNN			0.0213	0.2506
DLM-DNN	Noise coefficient of 0.1	PCA(95%)	0.0226	0.3591
		PCA(75%)	0.0247	0.3211
		PCA(50%)	0.0258	0.2893
		PCA(25%)	0.0268	0.2735
		PCA(5%)	0.3101	0.5212
	Noise coefficient of 0.3	PCA(95%)	0.0386	0.2869
		PCA(75%)	0.0403	0.2685
		PCA(50%)	0.0427	0.2609
		PCA(25%)	0.0452	0.2699
		PCA(5%)	0.3710	0.5529
DrLIM-DNN			0.0384	0.1380

Fig. 3. 2D mapping generated by DrLIM (legitimate samples on the left and adversarial sample on the right)

We further examine the influence of varying P_{pca} on classification performance. As shown in Table 2, the classification performance slightly improves with the increase of PCA dimensionality. When P_{pca} is 95%, most of critical information about original samples are preserved. However, as P_{pca} reaches 25%, enough information is preserved resulting in only a slight decrease in classification error. Meanwhile, when P_{pca} varies from 25% to 95%, the benefit of preserving any further information diminishes as with only a negligible decrease in the error rate.

We next evaluate the classification performance of DLM-DNN when confronted with adversarial samples. We list the classification error rates in the column noted as '*Adversarial*'. According to Table 2, the error rates obtained by the DLM-DNN are considerably lower than that of a standard DNN, 0.8981. Again, when P_{pca} is properly set, the DLM-DNN achieves results comparable to adversarial training. Interesting enough, as P_{pca} ranges from 25% to 95%, classification error goes up. This observation might imply that the impact of adversarial samples is mitigated to a larger degree when more random disturbances are added.

DrLIM-DNN Classification Performance. In this experiment we demonstrate the classification performance of DrLIM-DNN. The training set used for evaluation includes 5 classes from the MNIST data, and each class contains 2000 samples. For testing, each of the 5 classes contains 1000 testing samples.

For training the DrLIM, we label a pair of image samples as similar when they have the same label. This simplifies the training of DrLIM utilizing strong prior knowledge. We further set the reduced dimension to 30 during the experiments. Classification performance is shown in Table 2. According to these results, using DrLIM-DNN results in a slightly higher error rate (0.0384) when testing with legitimate samples, but achieves a significant improvement in performance (0.1380) when testing adversarial samples. Especially in the latter case, DrLIM-DNN shows higher robustness when compared to adversarial training.

As previously introduced in Sect. 4, DrLIM is designed with the objective of preserving similarity between a pair of high dimensional samples when mapped to lower dimensional space. Figure 3(a) shows the 2D mapping result of legitimate examples. We notice some outliers and hence highlight them and their neighbours by showing their corresponding images.

Since the point of DrLIM is to preserve the similarity in a lower dimensional space, we further visualize the 2D mapping of adversarial samples in Fig. 3(b). The 2D mapping in this case is not as clear as that for legitimate samples, but the similarity between pairs of samples are still reasonably well-preserved. This result indicates that DrLIM-DNN will not suffer as much as a normal DNN would when confronted with highly confusing adversarial samples.

Table 3. Classification confidence obtained from normal DNN and DrLIM-DNN

Outlier no.	Classification confidence of testing adversarial samples	
	Normal DNN	DrLIM-DNN
1	0.9995	0.5196
2	0.9721	0.5290
3	0.9989	0.6220
4	0.9921	0.5646
5	0.9998	0.5903
6	0.9997	0.5402
7	0.9998	0.6596
8	0.9919	0.5638

Table 4. Classification performance of PCA-DNN and DLM-DNN testing with reconstructed adversarial samples by inverting PCA

Trained models		Classification error rates
Normal DNN		0.6596
Noise coefficient of 0.1	PCA(95%)	0.2846
	PCA(75%)	0.2011
	PCA(50%)	0.1447
	PCA(25%)	0.1131
	PCA(5%)	0.3691
Noise coefficient of 0.3	PCA(95%)	0.1864
	PCA(75%)	0.1729
	PCA(50%)	0.1449
	PCA(25%)	0.1884
	PCA(5%)	0.4766

In order to explore more of these outliers, in Table 3, we show the probabilities of making wrong classification decisions when testing a normal DNN and a DrLIM-DNN with these outliers. As shown in Table 3, these outliers cause a normal DNN to make wrong classification results with over 97% confidence. However, when processed with DrLIM-DNN, although these outliers are not mapped to ideal regions, the probabilities of being wrongly classified is significantly reduced to lower than 66%. This result indicates that a DrLIM-DNN is effective for responding to unfamiliar samples with lower confidence. Therefore, DrLIM-DNN will not suffer as much as a normal DNN would when confronted with highly confusing adversarial samples.

As our experimental results show, DrLIM-DNN provides the best performance when tested against adversarial samples.

5.3   Reconstruction Performance

As previously introduced in Sect. 4, both DLM-DNN and DrLIM-DNN are non-invertible for different reasons. More importantly, we have proven that recovering the original data from a low dimensional space induced by DrLIM is an NP-hard problem. In this subsection, we mainly focus on inverting the proposed dimensional reduction method DLM by approximating it with a linear transformation matrix. We obtain the linear transformation matrix by solving a linear regression problem. In case the original data is sparse, we further employ a linear regression with L_1 regularization. First, we demonstrate that when configuring DLM as pure PCA, the approach is not robust given that it may be effectively inverted and thus allow for reconstruction of adversarial samples. Next, we examine the reconstruction error obtained from inverting DLM, taking a percentage of PCA mappings less than 100%.

We evaluate the reconstruction performance when inverting one extreme case of DLM, where DLM uses only PCA mappings. We refer to this method as PCA-DNN for comparison. To examine this extreme case, we first configure DLM as pure PCA and map legitimate testing samples to a 100-dimensional space. Then we reconstruct these legitimate samples by inverting PCA, as explained in Sect. 4.

Now we assume that an adversary has acquired the lower dimensional mappings generated by PCA. Then this adversarial can easily generate their corresponding *lower dimensional adversarial mappings*. So the adversarial example can be easily reconstructed as mentioned in Sect. 4. We use the reconstructed adversarial samples to test a normal DNN model and a DLM-DNN under different settings. According to the testing results shown in Table 4, the reconstructed adversarial samples maintain their attack power against a normal DNN model. And these adversarial samples can be effectively defended by a DLM-DNN as shown in Table 2.

We finally investigate the reconstruction errors when inverting DLM-DNN. We present reconstruction errors when varying percentages of PCA mappings used and when varying sub-space dimensionality in Fig. 2. Our experiment shows that inverting a DLM-DNN leads to high reconstruction errors, regardless of how many PCA mappings are used what dimensionality is used. Recall the theoretical analysis of DrLIM-DLM in Sect. 4, we demonstrate that our proposed methods effectively build an adversary-resistant DNN.

6   Conclusion

We proposed a new framework for constructing deep neural network models that are robust to adversarial samples, based on an analysis of both the "blind-spot" of DNNs and the limitations of previous solutions. With our proposed framework, we developed two adversary-resistant DNN architectures that leverage non-invertible data transformation mechanisms. Then we empirically showed that crafting an adversarial sample for the first architecture will incur significant distortion and thus lead to easily detectable adversarial samples. In contrast, under the second architecture, we theoretically demonstrated that it is impossible for an adversary to craft an adversarial sample to attack it. This implies that our proposed framework no longer suffers from attacks that rely on generating model-specific adversarial samples.

Furthermore, we demonstrated that recently studied adversarial training methods are not sufficient defense mechanisms. Applying our new framework to the MNIST data set, we empirically demonstrate that our new framework significantly reduces the error rates in classifying adversarial samples. Furthermore, our new framework has the same classification performance for legitimate samples with negligible degradation.

References

1. Aman, S., Hongseok, N., John, D.: Certifiable distributional robustness with principled adversarial training. In: International Conference on Learning Representations (2018)
2. Bar, Y., Diamant, I., Wolf, L., Greenspan, H.: Deep learning with non-medical training used for chest pathology identification. In: SPIE Medical Imaging, International Society for Optics and Photonics, p. 94140V (2015)
3. Bhagoji, A.N., Cullina, D., Mittal, P.: Dimensionality reduction as a defense against evasion attacks on machine learning classifiers. arXiv preprint (2017)
4. Cisse, M., Bojanowski, P., Grave, E., Dauphin, Y., Usunier, N.: Parseval networks: improving robustness to adversarial examples. In: Proceedings of the 34th International Conference on Machine Learning (2017)
5. Dahl, G.E., Stokes, J.W., Deng, L., Yu, D.: Large-scale malware classification using random projections and neural networks. In: 2013 IEEE International Conference on Acoustics, Speech and Signal Processing, pp. 3422–3426. IEEE (2013)
6. Donoho, D.L.: Compressed sensing. IEEE Trans. Inf. Theory 52, 1289–1306 (2006)
7. Eckart, C., Young, G.: The approximation of one matrix by another of lower rank. Psychometrika 1, 211–218 (1936)
8. Fornasier, M., Rauhut, H.: Compressive sensing. In: Scherzer, O. (ed.) Handbook of Mathematical Methods in Imaging, pp. 187–228. Springer, New York (2011). https://doi.org/10.1007/978-0-387-92920-0_6
9. Gu, S., Rigazio, L.: Towards deep neural network architectures robust to adversarial examples. arXiv:1412.5068 [cs] (2014)
10. Hadsell, R., Chopra, S., LeCun, Y.: Dimensionality reduction by learning an invariant mapping. In: 2006 IEEE Computer Society Conference on Computer Vision and Pattern Recognition (2006)
11. Hadsell, R., et al.: Learning long-range vision for autonomous off-road driving. J. Field Robot. 26, 120–144 (2009)
12. Huang, R., Xu, B., Schuurmans, D., Szepesvári, C.: Learning with a strong adversary. CoRR, abs/1511.03034 (2015)
13. Jolliffe, I.: Principal Component Analysis. Wiley Online Library (2002)
14. Miyato, T., Maeda, S.-I., Koyama, M., Nakae, K., Ishii, S.: Distributional smoothing with virtual adversarial training, stat, 1050, p. 25 (2015)
15. Nguyen, A., Yosinski, J., Clune, J.: Deep neural networks are easily fooled: high confidence predictions for unrecognizable images. In: 2015 IEEE Conference on Computer Vision and Pattern Recognition (2015)
16. Ororbia II, A.G., Giles, C.L., Kifer, D.: Unifying adversarial training algorithms with flexible deep data gradient regularization. arXiv:1601.07213 [cs] (2016)
17. Papernot, N., McDaniel, P., Wu, X., Jha, S., Swami, A.: Distillation as a defense to adversarial perturbations against deep neural networks. arXiv preprint arXiv:1511.04508 (2015)
18. Pascanu, R., Stokes, J.W., Sanossian, H., Marinescu, M., Thomas, A.: Malware classification with recurrent networks. In: 2015 IEEE International Conference on Acoustics, Speech and Signal Processing (2015)
19. Raskutti, G., Wainwright, M.J., Yu, B.: Minimax rates of estimation for high-dimensional linear regression over-balls. IEEE Trans. Inf. Theory 57, 6976–6994 (2011)
20. Szegedy, C., et al.: Intriguing properties of neural networks. In: International Conference on Learning Representations (2014)

21. Vavasis, S.A.: Nonlinear Optimization: Complexity Issues. Oxford University Press Inc., New York (1991)
22. Wu, X., Jang, U., Chen, J., Chen, L., Jha, S.: Reinforcing adversarial robustness using model confidence induced by adversarial training. In: International Conference on Machine Learning (2018)
23. Yuan, Z., Lu, Y., Wang, Z., Xue, Y.: Droid-Sec: deep learning in android malware detection. ACM SIGCOMM Comput. Commun. Rev. **44**, 371 (2014)
24. Zeiler, M.D., Fergus, R.: Visualizing and understanding convolutional networks. In: Fleet, D., Pajdla, T., Schiele, B., Tuytelaars, T. (eds.) ECCV 2014. LNCS, vol. 8689, pp. 818–833. Springer, Cham (2014). https://doi.org/10.1007/978-3-319-10590-1_53

Extracting Implicit Friends
from Heterogeneous Information Network
for Social Recommendation

Zihao Ling[1], Yingyuan Xiao[1,2(✉)], Hongya Wang[3], Lei Xu[4],
and Ching-Hsien Hsu[5]

[1] Tianjin Key Laboratory of Intelligence Computing and Novel Software
Technology, Tianjin University of Technology, Tianjin 300384, China
yyxiao@tjut.edu.cn
[2] Key Laboratory of Computer Vision and System, Ministry of Education,
Tianjin University of Technology, Tianjin 300384, China
[3] College of Computer Science and Technology, Donghua University,
Shanghai 201620, China
[4] School of Management, Tianjin University of Technology,
Tianjin 300384, China
[5] Department of Computer Science and Information Engineering,
Asia University, Taichung City, Taiwan

Abstract. With the popularity of online social networks, social relation data is becoming increasingly important to alleviate the data sparsity and cold-start problem of the traditional recommender systems. Social relations, such as trust or friend relationships, are used as complement source to user feedback data (e.g. item rating). However, using explicitly issued social relations directly may generate sub-optional recommendation results because of the inherent drawbacks of explicit social relations. To address the inherent drawbacks of explicit social relation, we incorporate top-k implicit friends, who can be identified from a heterogeneous information network established by user feedback and user social relation data, into a matrix factorization method to make social recommendations. Experimental results on real-world datasets FilmTrust and Douban show that our method can improve the performance of rating prediction, compared to the social recommender systems using explicit social relation and non-social recommender system.

Keywords: Social recommendation · Heterogeneous information network · Network embedding

1 Introduction

Recommender systems have been widely adopted by many online websites, such as Netflix and Amazon, to provide personalized products to their users. Personalized recommendation technology also becomes an important and independent research area to alleviate the data overload problem caused by the rapid growth of information on the

© Springer Nature Switzerland AG 2019
A. C. Nayak and A. Sharma (Eds.): PRICAI 2019, LNAI 11672, pp. 607–620, 2019.
https://doi.org/10.1007/978-3-030-29894-4_49

Web. However, traditional recommender systems often suffer from the data sparsity and cold start problem because of lacking enough user feedbacks.

Recently, online social networks, such as Facebook and LinkedIn, have become popular. A user can not only make comments or give a rating to a product but also build relationships with other users (e.g., "Web of Trust" at Epinions.com). Inspired by the homophily theory [1], which assumes that people are more inclined to establish contact with persons who have the same characteristics as their own, social recommendation become an effective way to alleviate the data sparsity problem by utilizing the social relation [2–4]. However, incorporate social relations in a recommender system directly may only bring marginal gains in predictive accuracy for three reasons. First, just like rating data, social relation is often very sparse (e.g., the trust density in Epinions and Ciao is 0.029% and 0.23%, respectively) if it exists [5]. Second, there are various kinds of relationships online, such as trust, follow, and friendship. Treating them in the same way may generate suboptimal results. Last but not least, the trust or friend relationships may only exist in some specific aspects. For example, user A follows user B because of the same taste on books, but they may hold different opinions on foods.

To mitigate the issues mentioned above, we propose a novel IFHN (Implicit Friends Extraction from Heterogeneous Information Network) social recommendation method which extracts implicit and reliable friends from the heterogeneous information network (HIN) via carefully designed meta-paths. First, we combine the user-item bipartite network (e.g., item rating information) with user social network to build an HIN. Next, we carefully design some meaningful meta-paths and then explore the HIN by conducting biased random walks to generate a set of node sequences, which we called *behavior corpus*, under the guidance of meta-paths. Then, these node sequences are used to learn user representation through a heterogeneous network embedding approach proposed in [6]. Finally, the top-k implicit friends can be identified by computing the cosine similarity for each pair of two users w.r.t. their embeddings. Based on this, we incorporate the top-k implicit friends into an extended probabilistic matrix factorization method to make the prediction on ratings.

To summarize, our work makes the following contributions:

- We extract the top-k implicit friends of each user from the heterogeneous information network via meta-path based random walks and heterogeneous network embedding technique.
- We incorporate the implicit friends into an extended probabilistic matrix factorization model for rating prediction.
- We conduct extensive experiments to validate the effectiveness of IFHN. The experimental results on two real-world data sets show that our method achieves better performance than explicit social recommenders and non-social recommender.

The remainder of this paper is organized as follows. We first review the related work in Sect. 2. Section 3 defines the basic concepts and the problem studied in this work. In Sect. 4, we present the proposed method in details. Section 5 evaluates the proposed method through extensive experiments. Finally, Sect. 6 concludes the paper with a brief discussion on future work.

2   Related Work

Based on the intuition that a user's preference is similar to his or her socially connected friends, social relations have been widely used as a complementary resource to user feedback data to improve the performance of recommender systems. These kinds of recommender systems can be seen as social recommender system. Most existing social recommender systems are based on collaborative filtering (CF) techniques and can be classified into memory-based and model-based social recommender systems, according to the basic CF models adopted to build the systems [7]. Specifically, Ma et al. [8] proposed a factor analysis approach based on probabilistic matrix factorization (SoRec). The idea is to perform a co-factorization in the user-item matrix and the user-user social relation matrix by sharing the same user preference latent factor. Further, Ma et al. [4] proposed a social trust ensemble method RSTE which interpret the ratings in user-item matrix R as the representation mixed by both the user's own taste and his or her trusted friends tastes on the item. They fuse the users' own tastes and their trusted friends' tastes together by an ensemble parameter. Later on, Jamali et al. [3] proposed a regularization method, called SocialMF, which consider that a user's latent feature vector should be close to the average of her social relations. This closeness is enforced by the social regularization term in the objective function. In addition, Ma et al. [9] consider that trusted neighbors of a user may have diverse tastes. The authors design a pair-wise social regularization term, in which the preference closeness between a user and her social relations is determined by the similarity of their past rating pattern.

However, explicit social relation is not always available in recommender systems, and it, if exists, is always sparse and noisy [7]. Recent studies [10, 11] have shown the success of finding reliable implicit friends to make social recommendation. Ma et al. [10] propose to identify the top-k similar users of each user from the user-item rating matrix by calculating the Pearson Correlation Coefficient between them, when the explicit social relation is not available. Taheri et al. [11] build a novel recommendation model Hell-TrustSVD which uses Hellinger distance to extract implicit social relations in the user-item bipartite network.

Recently, motivated by the success of word embedding techniques [12], some random walk based network embedding algorithms have been proposed [13, 14]. The purpose of these algorithms is to learn dense node representations and preserve the structural information of nodes at the same time, so the learned embedding can be applied to further data mining task, such as recommender system. Zhang et al. [15] propose the CUNE method to identify implicit and reliable friends by embedding a collaborative user network, which is a homogeneous information network and transformed from a user-item bipartite network. And then, the authors extend MF and BPR methods using the top-k implicit friends for ratings prediction and items ranking, respectively. However, we argue that the only usage of rating information by CUNE can't fully catch the complicated relations between users. A recent study of heterogeneous information network embedding algorithm metapath2vec [6] makes it possible to build a heterogeneous information network utilizing both rating and trust information, and then learn user embedding through metapath2vec.

3 Preliminaries

In the section, we first define the concepts used in this paper, and then describe the problem studied in this work.

Definition 1. *Heterogeneous Information Network* (HIN): A h*eterogeneous informa-tion network* is defined as a directed graph $\mathbf{G} = (V, E, T)$ in which each entity v and each link e is tied with a mapping function $\phi(v) : V \rightarrow T_V$ and $\phi(e) : E \rightarrow T_E$, respectively. T_V and T_E denote the possible types of entity and link in the graph, respectively, with the restraint that $|T_V| > 1$ or $|T_E| > 1$.

For example, Fig. 1 illustrates an HIN established by item rating network and user relation network where three types of entity (i.e., user, item, and category) and three types of edge (i.e., rate, trust, and belong to) are involved.

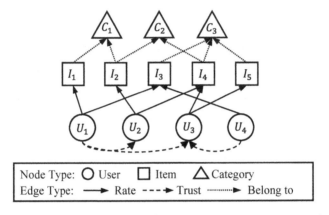

Fig. 1. An example of HIN

Definition 2. *Meta-path*: According to [16], a meta-path $\mathcal{P}$ is a path defined on the graph of network schema $T_G = (V, R)$, and is denoted in the form of $V_1 \xrightarrow{R_1} V_2 \xrightarrow{R_2} \cdots \xrightarrow{R_{n-1}} V_n$, which defines a composite relation $\mathbf{R} = R_1 \circ R_2 \circ \cdots \circ R_{n-1}$ between type V_1 and V_n, where $\circ$ denotes the composition operator on relations.

For example, $U \xrightarrow{rate} I \xleftarrow{rate} U$ is a meta-path which explores the implicit social rela-tionship between a user and another user who co-rated an item in a similar manner (i.e., positive or negative). In Fig. 1, $U_2 \rightarrow I_4 \leftarrow U_3$ is an instance of $U \xrightarrow{rate} I \xleftarrow{rate} U$, if U_2 and U_3 rated I_4 in a similar manner.

Definition 3. *Implicit Friends*: Implicit friends are defined as a pair of users who have similar preferences but do not directly connected in the social network. Correspond-ingly, explicit friends are defined as a pair of users who built relations in the social network with a single edge.

Finally, we define the social recommendation studied in this paper as follows: Given a heterogeneous information network $\mathbf{G}$ established by user-item rating information and user relation information, the task of social recommendation is to predict the missing values in the user-item matrix by means of **G**.

4   The Proposed Method

In this section, we will elaborate the IFHN method which consists of four consecutive steps: (1) designing meta-paths over HIN built by rating and social information; (2) collecting semantic behavior corpus via meta-path-based random walks; (3) learning users' latent representations through heterogeneous embedding; (4) identifying top-k implicit friends for each user and incorporating them into a matrix factorization model for rating prediction.

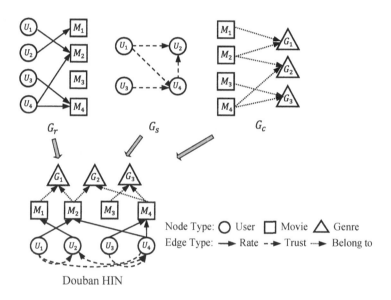

Fig. 2. Douban HIN merged by G_r, G_s, and G_c

4.1   Designing Meta-paths over HIN Built by Rating and Social Information

In this paper, we first build two HINs respectively using FilmTrust and Douban datasets. Figure 2 is an illustration of how to build the Douban HIN. In Fig. 2, rating information and user social relation in Douban dataset are represented in the form of user-movie rating bipartite network G_r and the user social network G_s, respectively. G_c denotes the movie-genre bipartite network using genre information from Douban dataset. Based on the assumption that these three networks share the same group of users and movies, we merge G_r, G_s and G_c into a Douban HIN shown in Fig. 2. In this way, we can discover the rich information shared by these three networks to identify implicit friends with similar preferences for each user.

Recent studies [16, 17] demonstrate the effectiveness of adopting meta-paths to perform data mining tasks in heterogeneous information network. Given a meta-path, say $\mathcal{P} = V_1 \xrightarrow{R_1} V_2 \xrightarrow{R_2} \cdots \xrightarrow{R_{n-1}} V_n$, the connection between a pair of objects $x \in V_1$ and $y \in V_n$ can be quantified by several similarity measures, such as Path count and PathSim [16]. In order to identify implicit friends with similar preferences for each user, we design a set of meta-paths with different semantic meaning. Specifically, we carefully design four meta-paths, demonstrated in Table 1, to model the complex relations between users. Next, we descript the meaning of these meta-paths one by one. P_1 connects a pair of users who rated a movie in a similar manner (i.e., positive or negative). Taking Douban HIN shown in Fig. 2 as an example, given U_1 as the root node, the path instance $U_1 \rightarrow M_2 \leftarrow U_4$ can reach U_4 after two steps under the guidance of P_1. P_2 further exploit the co-rating behavior and try to build a relation between two users who both like or dislike the same genre of movie. $U_1 \rightarrow M_2 \rightarrow G_2 \leftarrow M_4 \leftarrow U_3$ is a path instance of P_2, and it associates two socially unconnected user U_1 and U_3. It is worth noting that P_1 and P_2 are based on the idea of collaborative filtering. P_3 leverages the concept of trust propagation to discover the potential trust of friends without direct connections in the social network. $U_3 \rightarrow U_4 \rightarrow U_2$ is a path instance of P_3. P_4 associates a user with those who have similar preferences with someone he or she trusts. $o_3 \rightarrow U_4 \rightarrow M_2 \leftarrow U_1$ is a path instance of P_4. It is important to notice that we use all the four meta-paths on Douban dataset and use only P_1, P_3 and P_4 on FilmTrust dataset for the lack of genre information.

Table 1. Meta-paths designed for implicit friend extraction

	Path scheme	Semantic information
P_1	$U \xrightarrow{rate} M \xleftarrow{rate} U$	A pair of users who have both positive/negative feedback to the same movie can be similar
P_2	$U \xrightarrow{rate} M \xrightarrow{belong\ to} G \xleftarrow{belong\ to} M \xleftarrow{rate} U$	A pair of users who both positively/negatively rate the same genre of movies can be similar
P_3	$U \xrightarrow{trust} U \xrightarrow{trust} U$	A user may trust his/her friends' friends
P_4	$U \xrightarrow{trust} U \xrightarrow{rate} M \xleftarrow{rate} U$	A user may share similar taste with the one who have similar preference with his/her friends

4.2   Collecting Node Sequences via Meta-Path-Based Random Walks

To connect users who may share similar preferences, we conduct random walks over HIN and collect a set of node sequences called *behavior corpus*. However, different from the standard random walk which randomly selects a node from the neighbors of its predecessor, we select each successor node under the guidance of meta-path for a more reliable and meaningful node sequence. Here we elaborate the procedure of node sequences collection. Given a heterogeneous network $\mathbf{G} = (V, E, T)$ and a meta-path

$\mathcal{P} = V_1 \xrightarrow{R_1} V_2 \xrightarrow{R_2} \cdots V_t \xrightarrow{R_t} V_{t+1} \cdots \xrightarrow{R_{n-1}} V_n$, the transition probability at step k is defined as follows:

$$
p(v^{k+1}|v_t^k, \mathcal{P}) = \begin{cases} \dfrac{1}{|N_{t+1}(v_t^k)|} & (v^{k+1}, v_t^k) \in \left\{ \xrightarrow{rate}, \xleftarrow{rate}, \xrightarrow{belong\ to}, \xleftarrow{belong\ to} \right\}, \\[2ex] \dfrac{\psi(v^{k+1}, v_t^k)}{\sum\limits_{v' \in N_{t+1}(v_t^k)} \emptyset\left(v', v_t^k\right)} & (v^{k+1}, v_t^k) \in \left\{ \xrightarrow{trust}, \xleftarrow{trust} \right\}, \\[2ex] 0 & (v^{k+1}, v_t^k) \notin E. \end{cases} \tag{1}
$$

where $v_t^k \in V_t$, $N_{t+1}\left(v_t^k\right)$ denotes the V_{t+1} type of neighborhood of node v_t^k, $\psi\left(v^{k+1}, v_t^k\right) = \left|N_{t+1}\left(v^{k+1}\right) \bigcap N_{t+1}\left(v_t^k\right)\right|$. In other words, at each step of random walk, we select the successor node according to the pre-defined meta-paths. Specifically, given a specific meta-path, when the relation between the current node and its successor node should be *rate* or *belong to*, we uniformly select the next node. If *trust* relation connects two consecutive nodes under the guidance of meta-path, namely two users, we select the next node according to the number of overlapped neighbors with the current node. It means, the more mutual friends two users share, the more likely they choose each other as the next node. It is worth noting that the random walk is recursive, which means the length of each walk can be longer than meta-path scheme. When the pre-defined walk length exceeds a meta-path scheme, the meta-path scheme is repeated, namely $V_{n+1} = V_2$.

4.3   Learning User Embedding and Finding Top-k Implicit Friends

A number of recent works [12–14] demonstrate the effectiveness of network representation learning which can embed network vertices into a low-dimensional vector space and preserve network topology at the same time. With network representation learning, the similarity of vertices in a network can be quantified. However, these researches are mainly focused on representation learning for homogeneous network and cannot directly apply to HIN. Inspired by heterogeneous Skip-Gram [6], we feed the collected *behavior corpus* to it for learning user representations $\mathbf{Y} \in \mathbb{R}^{|V| \times d}$. The heterogeneous Skip-Gram maximizes the likelihood of nodes co-occurrence within a context. Formally, given a node sequence collected by meta-path-based random walk and the current node v^k, the objective function of heterogeneous Skip-Gram is defined as:

$$
\arg\max_{\mathbf{Y}} \sum_{v \in V} \sum_{v_t^m \in N(v^k)} \log p\left(v_t^m | v^k; \mathbf{Y}\right) \tag{2}
$$

where $N(v^k)$ is the context of v^k with the windows size w and $p(v_t^m|v^k; \mathbf{Y})$ is commonly defined as a softmax function, that is:

$$p(v_t^m|v^k; \mathbf{Y}) = \frac{e^{\mathcal{Y}_{v_t^m} \cdot \mathcal{Y}_{v^k}}}{\sum_{v \in V_t} e^{\mathcal{Y}_v \cdot \mathcal{Y}_{v^k}}} \tag{3}$$

where $\mathcal{Y}_v$ is the vth row of $\mathbf{Y}$, denoting the learned embedding vector of node v, and V_t is the node set with type t in G. When computing the normalization factor, heterogeneous Skip-Gram only considers nodes in the same type instead of all nodes, which makes it different from the common Skip-Gram model. In addition, to accelerate the learning, we adopt negative sampling [12] to avoid the complexity of computing $p(v_t^m|v^k; \mathbf{Y})$ in Eq. (2). Given a node type in $N(v^k)$ and the negative sample size S, we uniformly select S nodes with the same type from V for the softmax function. Next, we update Eq. (2) by maximizing the following objective function:

$$\mathcal{O}(\mathbf{Y}) = \log \sigma(\mathcal{Y}_{v_t^m} \cdot \mathcal{Y}_{v^k}) + \sum_{i=1}^{S} \mathbb{E}_{v_t^i \sim P_t(v_t)} \left[\log \sigma(-\mathcal{Y}_{v_t^i} \cdot \mathcal{Y}_{v^k}) \right] \tag{4}$$

where $\sigma(\mathcal{Y}) = \frac{1}{1+e^{-\mathcal{Y}}}$ and the sampling distribution $P_t(v_t)$ are determined by the node degree.

After the user embedding $\mathbf{Y}$ is learned, we compute the cosine similarity for each pair of users regarding their embeddings, and then we identify the top-k implicit friends for each user.

4.4   Incorporating Top-k Implicit Friends into MF

Given an $m \times n$ matrix R formed by the m users' ratings on n items, an matrix factorization (MF) model approximates R by a multiplication of l-rank user and item latent vectors, i.e., $R \approx U^T V$, where $U \in \mathbb{R}^{l \times m}$ and $V \in \mathbb{R}^{l \times n}$ with $l \ll \min(m, n)$. When user i's rating on item j is missing, MF can predict that rating by the inner product of the user latent vector u_i and item latent vector v_j, i.e., $\hat{r} = u_i^T v_j$. The assumption behind a MF model is that there are only a few factors influencing the preferences, and that a user's preferences vector is determined by how each factor applies to that user [18].

We incorporate the top-k implicit friends into MF as a social regularization term to constrain the objective function of MF, which is defined as follow:

$$\mathcal{L} = \frac{1}{2} \sum_{i=1}^{m} \sum_{j=1}^{n} I_{i,j}^R (r_{ij} - U_i^T V_j)^2 + \frac{\ddot{e}_U}{2} \sum_{i=1}^{m} U_i^T U_i + \frac{\lambda_V}{2} \sum_{j=1}^{n} V_j^T V_j$$
$$+ \frac{\lambda_S}{2} \sum_{i=1}^{m} \sum_{f \in \mathcal{F}_i^+} sim(i,f)(U_i - U_f)^T (U_i - U_f) \tag{5}$$

where $I_{i,j}^R$ is the indicator function which equals to 1 if user i rated item j and equals to 0 otherwise. In addition, λ_U and λ_V are the regularization parameter that controls model complexity to avoid over-fitting. We use the notation $\mathcal{F}_i^+$ denotes the top-k implicit friends of user i, and use the notation $\mathcal{F}_i^-$ denotes the set of users whose top-k implicit friends contains user i. The social regularization term in Eq. (5) is used to minimize the preference of user i and his/her implicit friends. λ_S controls the degree of the social constraint. Furthermore, in order to differentiate all top-k implicit friends, we add the term $sim(i,f)$, computed by the cosine similarity between the embedding of user f and user i, into the objective function.

A local minimum of the objective function given by Eq. (5) can be found by performing gradient descent on U_i and V_j for all users and all items,

$$
\frac{\partial \mathcal{L}}{\partial U_i} = \sum_{j=1}^{n} I_{i,j}^R \left(r_{ij} - U_i^T V_j\right) V_j + \lambda_U U_i + \lambda_S \sum_{f \in \mathcal{F}_i^+} \left(U_i - U_f\right) + \lambda_S \sum_{g \in \mathcal{F}_i^-} \left(U_i - U_g\right)
$$
$$
\frac{\partial \mathcal{L}}{\partial V_j} = \sum_{i=1}^{m} I_{i,j}^R \left(r_{ij} - U_i^T V_j\right) U_i + \lambda_V V_j \tag{6}
$$

5   Experimental Analysis

In this section, we first introduce the datasets we use and then report the experimental results of our method compared with several baseline methods. Then, we design an experiment to verify the effectiveness of our method to alleviate the cold start problem.

5.1   Experimental Settings

Datasets. We adopt two real-world datasets FilmTrust and Douban, both contain social relations and publicly available on the web, in our experiments. FilmTrust is a movie sharing and rating website where a user can rate movies and add other users as friends. The FilmTrust dataset consists of 1,508 users, 2,071 movies and 35,497 movie ratings issued by the users. In addition, there are 1,632 trust relationships explicitly declared by users. These trust relationships are direct, which means user A trusting user B does not necessarily imply B also trusting A. Douban is a Chinese Web 2.0 website providing user rating, review, and recommendation services for movies, books, and music. A Douban user can rate movies on a scale of 1 to 5 and build connections with other users. The Douban dataset consists of ratings from 2,965 users who rated a total of 39,694 movies. The number of social connections in the Douban dataset is 35,770. It's worth noting that the trust value in both datasets is binary. The main statistics of these two datasets are summarized in Table 2.

Table 2. Statistics of FilmTrust and Douban datasets

Datasets	Users count	Items count	Category count	Ratings count	Density	Social links
FilmTrust	1,508	2,071		35,497	1.136%	1,853
Douban	2,965	39,695	36	912,479	0.775%	35,770

Baseline Methods. In order to demonstrate the superiority of our method, we compare it with a set of existing methods for rating prediction.

- **PMF:** A widely used basic matrix factorization approach proposed in [19], which does not consider any social information.
- **SoRec:** A social recommendation method fuses the user-item rating matrix with the user's social network using probabilistic matrix factorization [8].
- **SocialMF:** A social recommender which makes the latent feature vector of each user close to the average feature vector of his direct friends in social network [3].

Evaluation Metrics. We use two popular metrics, the Mean Absolute Error (MAE) and the Root Mean Square Error (RMSE), to evaluate the prediction accuracy of our proposed method compared with other baseline methods.

$$MAE = \frac{\sum_{r_{ij} \in R_{test}} \left| r_{ij} - \hat{r}_{ij} \right|}{|R_{test}|}$$

$$RMSE = \sqrt{\frac{\sum_{r_{ij} \in R_{test}} \left(r_{ij} - \hat{r}_{ij} \right)^2}{|R_{test}|}}$$

where R_{test} denotes the test set, r_{ij} is the rating user i give to item j, and $\hat{r}_{ij}$ represents the prediction score made by a specific recommendation method. A smaller MAE or RMSE value means a better performance.

Configuration. For all the baseline methods, we adopt the parameters settings suggested in previous works or by experimental selection. Specifically, we set the regularization coefficient $\lambda_U = \lambda_V = 0.1$ and the dimension of latent features $K = 10$ for all models. For the methods using explicit social relations (SoRec and SocialMF), the social constraint coefficient is $\lambda_S = 0.2$. For the IFHN method using graph embedding, the number of walks is $n = 10$, the length of each walk $l = 7$, the window size is $w = 5$, the dimension of embedding is $E = 10$, and the number of implicit friends

$F = 10$ for FilmTrust, $F = 20$ for Douban. In addition, when collecting *behavior corpus*, all the designed meta-paths contribute evenly. We randomly select 80% of the dataset as the training set to train the model, and predict the remaining 20% of the dataset. The random selection was carried out 5 times independently, and we report the average results.

5.2 Performance Comparison

The experimental results are shown in Table 3, and the main findings can be summarized as follows.

- In all cases, our proposed method outperforms all the compared baseline methods. Specifically, the average RMSE scores of its predictions are around 0.87, 0.78 for FilmTrust and Douban datasets, respectively. The average MAE values of its results are around 0.65, 0.61 for FilmTrust and Douban datasets, respectively. The performance improvements, which are calculated by comparing our method with other methods, ranging from 1.69% to 6.28%.
- In most cases, the performance of the two social recommendation approaches is better than the traditional PMF approach. This finding shows that the social relation can be an effective complement to the rating information, regardless of explicit or implicit social information.
- Our implicit friend-based recommendation method outperforms the two explicit friend-based recommendation methods (SoRec and SocialMF). This result can be explained that the network embedding learning does a great job in modeling user's rating and social behavior. As a result, the identified top-k implicit friends can more precisely reflect the current user's preference than explicit friends.
- On Douban dataset, social recommendation method SoRec performs worse than traditional recommendation method PMF. It demonstrates that explicit social information is not always helpful to improve recommendation accuracy. The potential reason is that there are noises in explicit social relations which do harm to the recommendation performance.

Table 3. Performance comparison of our method and other baseline methods

Datasets	Metrics	PMF	SoRec	SocialMF	IFHN
FilmTrust	MAE	0.6853	0.6686	0.6732	**0.6573**
	Improve	4.08%	1.69%	2.36%	
	RMSE	0.9274	0.8917	0.9078	**0.8716**
	Improve	6.01%	2.25%	3.98%	
Douban	MAE	0.6343	0.6523	0.6324	**0.6113**
	Improve	3.61%	6.28%	3.34%	
	RMSE	0.8280	0.8342	0.8149	**0.7829**
	Improve	4.51%	6.14%	3.92%	

5.3   Performance on Cold-Start Users

In this subsection, we intend to confirm whether our method can alleviate the cold start problem. We consider users who rated less than 10 movies as cold-start users for both FilmTrust and Douban datasets. Following this definition, about 33% of FilmTrust users and 12% of Douban users are listed as cold-start users. Experimental results of RMSE and MAE values on cold-start users are shown in Fig. 3.

According to Fig. 3, we could clearly observe that the IFHN method outperforms other baseline methods in terms of the performance on cold-start users. In particular, the IFHN method gets considerable improvements (18.6% and 14.8%) over PMF and SoRec on FilmTrust dataset in terms of RMSE values, respectively. This improvement for cold start users is bigger than the improvement for all users which is shown in Table 3, which means that IFHN handles cold start users better than PMF and SoRec. This result shows that the identified implicit friends can provide valuable information for modeling the latent preference of the cold-start users.

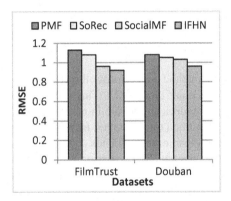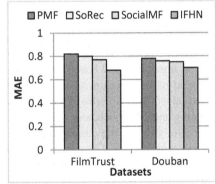

Fig. 3. Performance on cold-start users

5.4   Impact of Parameter λ_S

In our proposed method, the social regularization parameter λ_S plays an important role. It is used to control how much our method should incorporate the social relation information. On the one hand, a small value of λ_S can not fully take the advantages of implicit social relation, and result in a similar performance with non-social method. On the other hand, if we set a large λ_S, the implicit social relation information may have a bigger impact on user's latent representation than user's own rating information, which can degrade the performance of the recommender system. In this section, we analyze how different value of λ_S can affect the final recommendation accuracy. Specifically, we set λ_S value in the range between 0.01 and 2 to evaluate the performance of IFHN method on FilmTrust dataset.

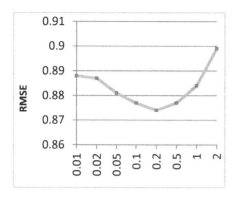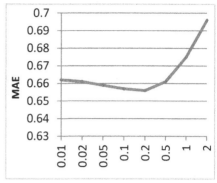

Fig. 4. Performance with different value of λ_S

As is shown in Fig. 4, the IFHN method achieves the best performance on both RMSE and MAE when $\lambda_S = 0.2$. The RMSE and MAE values decrease at first, but when λ_S goes above 0.2, the RMSE and MAE values increase with further increase of the value of λ_S. It seems that a small or big value of λ_S lead to a degradation in recommendation quality, which is consistent with our expectation.

6   Conclusions

In this paper, we investigate how to improve the performance of recommender systems by incorporating implicit social information. Inspired by the recent researches of network representation learning, we propose a novel implicit friend based social recommendation approach IFHN. Firstly, we build a heterogeneous information network using item-rating, social relation and item-category data. Then, we collect a set of node sequences over the HIN under the guidance of carefully designed meta-paths. After that, users are mapped into a common embedding space by network representation learning technique, which allows us to identify the top-k implicit friends for each user. Finally, we incorporate the top-k implicit friends into a matrix factorization approach for rating prediction. Experiments on two real-world datasets show that our method IFHN not only outperforms other baseline models in prediction accuracy, but also alleviates the cold-start problem.

Acknowledgment. This work is supported by the National Nature Science Foundation of China (91646117, 61702368) and Natural Science Foundation of Tianjin (17JCYBJC15200, 18JCQNJC00700).

References

1. McPherson, M., Smith-Lovin, L., Cook, J.M.: Birds of a feather: homophily in social networks. Annu. Rev. Sociol. **27**(1), 415–444 (2001)
2. Massa, P., Avesani, P.: Trust-aware recommender systems. In: Proceedings of the 2007 ACM Conference on Recommender Systems, pp. 17–24 (2007)

3. Jamali, M., Ester, M.: A matrix factorization technique with trust propagation for recommendation in social networks. In: Proceedings of the Fourth ACM Conference on Recommender Systems, pp. 135–142 (2010)
4. Ma, H., King, I., Lyu, M.R.: Learning to recommend with social trust ensemble. In: Proceedings of the 32nd International ACM SIGIR Conference on Research and Development in Information Retrieval, pp. 203–210 (2009)
5. Guo, G., Zhang, J., Yorke-Smith, N.: TrustSVD: collaborative filtering with both the explicit and implicit influence of user trust and of item ratings. In: AAAI, pp. 123–125 (2015)
6. Dong, Y., Chawla, N.V., Swami, A.: metapath2vec: scalable representation learning for heterogeneous networks. In: Proceedings of the 23rd ACM SIGKDD International Conference on Knowledge Discovery and Data Mining, pp. 135–144 (2017)
7. Tang, J., Hu, X., Liu, H.: Social recommendation: a review. Soc. Netw. Anal. Min. 3(4), 1113–1133 (2013)
8. Ma, H., Yang, H., Lyu, M.R., et al.: SoRec: social recommendation using probabilistic matrix factorization. In: Proceedings of the 17th ACM Conference on Information and Knowledge Management, pp. 931–940 (2008)
9. Ma, H., Zhou, D., Liu C, et al.: Recommender systems with social regularization. In: Proceedings of the Fourth ACM International Conference on Web Search and Data Mining, pp. 287–296 (2011)
10. Ma, H.: An experimental study on implicit social recommendation. In: Proceedings of the 36th International ACM SIGIR Conference on Research and Development in Information Retrieval, pp. 73–82 (2013)
11. Taheri, S.M., Mahyar, H., Firouzi, M., et al.: Extracting implicit social relation for social recommendation techniques in user rating prediction. In: Proceedings of the 26th International Conference on World Wide Web Companion, pp. 1343–1351 (2017)
12. Mikolov, T., Sutskever, I., Chen, K., et al.: Distributed representations of words and phrases and their compositionality. In: Advances in Neural Information Processing Systems, pp. 3111–3119 (2013)
13. Perozzi, B., Al-Rfou, R., Skiena, S.: DeepWalk: online learning of social representations. In: Proceedings of the 20th ACM SIGKDD International Conference on Knowledge Discovery and Data Mining, pp. 701–710 (2014)
14. Grover, A., Leskovec, J.: node2vec: scalable feature learning for networks. In: Proceedings of the 22nd ACM SIGKDD International Conference on Knowledge Discovery and Data Mining, pp. 855–864 (2016)
15. Zhang, C., Yu, L., Wang, Y., Shah, C., Zhang, X.: Collaborative user network embedding for social recommender systems. In: Proceedings of the 2017 SIAM International Conference on Data Mining, pp. 381–389 (2017)
16. Sun, Y., Han, J.: Mining heterogeneous information networks: principles and methodologies. Synth. Lect. Data Min. Knowl. Discov. 3(2), 1–159 (2012)
17. Shi, C., Zhang, Z., Luo, P., et al.: Semantic path based personalized recommendation on weighted heterogeneous information networks. In: Proceedings of the 24th ACM International on Conference on Information and Knowledge Management, pp. 453–462 (2015)
18. Candès, E.J., Recht, B.: Exact matrix completion via convex optimization. Found. Comput. Math. 9(6), 717 (2009)
19. Mnih, A., Salakhutdinov, R.: Probabilistic matrix factorization. In: Advances in Neural Information Processing Systems, pp. 1257–1264 (2008)

CD-ABM: Curriculum Design with Attention Branch Model for Person Re-identification

Junhong Chen, Jiuchao Qian$^{(\boxtimes)}$, Xiaoguang Zhu, Fei Wen, Yan Hong, and Peilin Liu

Shanghai Jiao Tong University, Shanghai, China
{lcchenjh,jcqian,zhuxiaoguang178,wenfei,
Hy2628982280,liupeilin}@sjtu.edu.cn

Abstract. Person re-identification (re-ID) is a challenging problem due to background clutter, illumination and pose variation, occlusion, and pedestrian misalignment. Current state-of-the-art methods commonly extract discriminative information by deep networks based on one-stage training. Though straightforward, using one-stage learning, the presence of pedestrian misalignment in practical applications may significantly degrade the performance of the learned model. To address this issue, we propose a novel model for person re-ID, called CD-ABM. It adopts a curriculum design to proceed training from easy to hard samples and generates an attention map in a supervised manner to further facilitate discriminative feature extraction. Compared with existing methods, CD-ABM has the following advantages: (1) The curriculum design can gradually improve the model capability through progressive learning. (2) The attention map enables the local branch to be associated with the global branch and better exploits both local and global information. Experiments on three benchmark datasets show that, CD-ABM can achieve competitive performance with the state-of-the-arts. Noteworthily, on the most challenging dataset MSMT17, it surpasses state-of-the-art methods by 15.9% in Rank-1 and 21.0% in mAP.

Keywords: Person re-identification · Attention · Curriculum learning · Training strategy

1 Introduction

Person re-identification (re-ID) aims to associate the images of a same person across non-overlapping surveillance cameras. More specifically, given a specified person, the goal of person re-ID is to find out all images of that person from a large gallery database. Due to its critical importance in video surveillance, person re-ID has attracted much research attention recently.

Generally, person re-ID in practical environment is challenging due to the presence of background clutter, illumination and pose variation and occlusion. Moreover, inaccurate bounding boxes from a pedestrian detector would result in

© Springer Nature Switzerland AG 2019
A. C. Nayak and A. Sharma (Eds.): PRICAI 2019, LNAI 11672, pp. 621–635, 2019.
https://doi.org/10.1007/978-3-030-29894-4_50

misalignment and, finally, significantly degrade the performance of person re-ID. An illustration of such situations is given in the Sub3 of Fig. 1. Consequently, how to extract discriminative features is the key to achieve robust person re-ID.

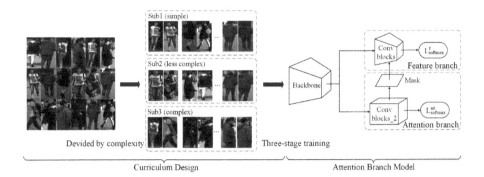

Fig. 1. Curriculum Design with Attention Branch Model architecture. Left is original samples with different challenges. Dataset is divided into three subsets by curriculum design (illumination variation, occlusion and pedestrian misalignment appear in Sub3). Then training proceeds with our training strategy. Attention branch model is used in the last stage.

Recently, deep learning based data-driven methods have achieved overwhelming advantage over traditional handcrafted ones [32]. A straightforward idea is to extract a global representation through deep networks [18,26]. Though simple, such methods cannot well capture informative details. Moreover, once obtaining misaligned images (e.g., images dominated by background), the features cannot be representative enough. To solve this problem, part-based methods have been proposed. Such methods can be generally classified into three categories: (1) Utilizing additional auxiliary knowledge such as person attributes [11,16], pose estimation [15,17,29], image segmentation [14,21], etc. This kind of methods aims to locate regions with structural information and extract better features for identities. These methods either require additional labels or need robust models from other domains, e.g., pose estimation. When there exists inconsistence between the datasets for pose estimation and person re-ID, it would lead to bad partition. (2) Dividing image (and also the corresponding feature map) by grids [1] or strips [5,19]. This helps pedestrian alignment to some extent and facilitates getting fine-grained details. However, such a fixed division destructs the interrelation among various parts. (3) Exploiting attention mechanism to allow the model to decide which regions to focus on [10,12]. These methods usually cannot separately supervise the generation of the attention map.

To address these limitations of existing methods, this work proposes a novel method, named curriculum design with attention branch model (CD-ABM), to more effectively extract discriminative representations for person re-ID. As shown in Fig. 1, our approach consists of two main pionts. Firstly, inspired by curriculum learning [4], we introduce a three-stage training strategy to train from easy to hard samples. Naturally, well-aligned images have strong similarities in one identity set, while the pedestrians with occlusion, inaccurate bounding boxes, or irregular shapes are different. As a result, the model is able to rank the training samples from easy to complex, since the complexity of images can be divided by their distribution density. Then, the divided samples are fed into the network by stage in our training procedure to gradually improve the presentation capability. The second is an attention branch model (ABM), which aims to generate the attention map in the last stage, supervised by an attention loss. Compared with [10,12], ABM can obtain more instructive attention map with supervision. On the one hand, ABM reinforces global features through the attention map. On the other hand, ABM can capture the correlation between global and local branches and exploit the interrelation among various parts in the local branch.

In summary, the main contributions of this paper are as follows:

- We adopt a curriculum design to divide training dataset by complexity, based on the distribution density data in a feature space. It helps to get representative descriptors by training from easy to difficult samples.
- An attention branch model is designed to further facilitate discriminative feature extraction, which reinforces global information by generating the attention map in a supervised manner and exploits the correlation between global and local branches.
- We present test results on three benchmark datasets to show that, the proposed method achieves consistent improvement, e.g., exceeds by 15.9% in Rank-1 and 21.0% in mAP on the MSMT17 dataset.

2 Related Work

Feature Extraction for Re-ID: Recent progress in person re-ID has benefited a lot from the adoption of deep learning. Typically, classic deep network models, such as ResNet-50 [9] and GoogleNet [20], pre-trained on ImageNet are used and fine-tuned for feature extraction in person re-ID. Generally, the considered feature representation can be classified into: (i) Global features, e.g., the output of a fully connected layer of a deep network [18,26], which cannot capture fine-grained details and cannot handle pedestrian misalignment. (ii) Part-based features, such as part convolution baseline (PCB) [19], which horizontally partition the feature map of a deep network and train multiple classifiers. Besides, another class considers the fusion of global and local information to get a better presentation. For example, Deep-person [3] integrates local features by LSTM and concatenates them with a global branch to form combined features. Instead of concatenating, our method bridge global and local branches through an attention map, which facilitates the exploitation of the interrelation between them.

Curriculum Learning: Curriculum learning (CL) [4] is inspired by human learning, which starts from easy conception and gradually learns more complicated contents. It has been shown that training a model from easy to hard is useful [24]. In person re-ID, PUL [6] iterates process between clustering and fine-tuning to progressively improve the initialization model trained on an irrelevant dataset. Moreover, the work [25] proposes a semi-supervised learning method based on progressive learning, which gradually exploits the unlabeled data for person re-ID. In these works, the main goal is to solve the label scarce problem. It has been shown in [2] that, gradually increasing the percentage of difficult samples can further improve the performance. Inspired by this concept and CurriculumNet [8], which adopts curriculum learning based on a divided dataset (in terms of label noise), our model estimates pedestrian complexity based on the distribution density of data in a feature space. Then, in the training procedure, difficult samples are gradually added to training procedure to improve network performance.

Attention Model: Attention model is useful to enforce a network to focus on salient regions. Recently, the attention model has been used in person re-ID to solve the misalignment problem. For instance, in DLPA [30], feature map is followed by a part-based net, which uses spatial attention to find aligned parts. Meanwhile, HydrapPlus-Net [12] trains multi-level and multi-scale attention features for fine-grained analysis. Moreover, HA-CNN [10] jointly learns soft pixel attention and hard regional attention to select attention for feature representations. Inspired by [7], our work uses a supervised attention branch to further extract features, which is able to enhance the global representation and better fuse global and local information.

3 The Proposed Method

In this section, we introduce how the proposed CD-ABM to extract discriminative features in detail. As is shown in Fig. 1, firstly, training samples $\mathcal{I} = \{\mathbf{I}_1, ..., \mathbf{I}_n\}$ are divided into three subsets $\mathcal{I}^s = \{\mathbf{I}_1^s, ..., \mathbf{I}_{n_s}^s\}$, $\mathcal{I}^m = \{\mathbf{I}_1^m, ..., \mathbf{I}_{n_m}^m\}$ and $\mathcal{I}^c = \{\mathbf{I}_1^c, ..., \mathbf{I}_{n_c}^c\}$, which is ordered by complexity. $\mathcal{I}^s$ represent simple training samples while complex samples are positioned into $\mathcal{I}^c$. Moreover, we introduce attention mechanism to our model to extract discriminative features in specific training stage. How such attention mechanism works in our model will be detailed in Sect. 3.2.

Specifically, we increase complexity into the training procedure progressively to improve the capability of the proposed model sequentially. Our model regards pre-trained ResNet-50 as backbone, which consists of shared layer $\boldsymbol{\theta}_S$, global branch $\boldsymbol{\theta}_G$, local branch $\boldsymbol{\theta}_P$, and attention branch $\boldsymbol{\theta}_A$. We train model with the global branch in the first two stages to extract the features of full identities in images roughly. At first, the model with the global branch is trained on the simple subset $\mathcal{I}^s$, which makes the model learn clean representations and basic features for identities. The optimization function in stage 1 is

$$L_G^s = -\frac{1}{n_s} \sum_{i=1}^{n_s} log \frac{e^{\boldsymbol{\theta}_G(I_i^s)}}{\sum_{k=1}^{C} e^{\boldsymbol{\theta}_G(I_i^s)}}, \tag{1}$$

where L_G^s is the optimization function in stage 1. After this model converges, the second stage starts, where less complex samples $\mathcal{I}^m$ are added to learn more diverse and meaningful information. It makes the model robust and improves its performance. The loss weights for simple and less complex subsets are set to 0.3 and 0.7, respectively. The optimization function in stage 2 is

$$L_G^m = -\left\{ \frac{0.3}{n_s} \sum_{i=1}^{n_s} log \frac{e^{\theta_G(I_i^s)}}{\sum_{k=1}^{C} e^{\theta_G(I_i^s)}} + \frac{0.7}{n_m} \sum_{i=1}^{n_m} log \frac{e^{\theta_G(I_i^m)}}{\sum_{k=1}^{C} e^{\theta_G(I_i^m)}} \right\}. \qquad (2)$$

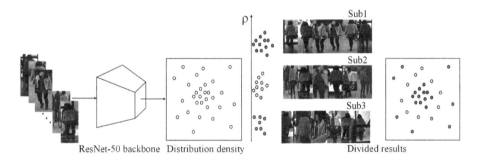

Fig. 2. Dataset division by the distribution density of data. The samples are mapped into the same feature space firstly, then the distance between each other is calculated for the value of density. The larger value of ρ represents similar images while complex samples have a sparse distribution with small value of ρ.

After model with global branch have a better learning capacity, we combine three subsets to train the whole ABM with three branches to further improve the generalization capability of the model. In this stage, the optimization function of ABM is formulated as:

$$L_{total} = L_G(\boldsymbol{y}, f(\boldsymbol{\theta}_S, \boldsymbol{\theta}_G)) + L_P(\boldsymbol{y}, f(\boldsymbol{\theta}_S, \boldsymbol{\theta}_P)) + L_A(\boldsymbol{y}, f(\boldsymbol{\theta}_S, \boldsymbol{\theta}_A)), \qquad (3)$$

where $\boldsymbol{y}$ is one-hot vector of ground truth and f represents the softmax cross-entropy loss. Similar to PCB [19], the feature of local branch is split into six part and each part is used to identify. Thus, the part classifier is defined as:

$$L_P = \sum_{i=1}^{6} L_{P_i}(\boldsymbol{y}, f(\boldsymbol{\theta}_S, \boldsymbol{\theta}_{P_i})), \qquad (4)$$

where L_{p_i} denotes the training loss of the i-th part in local branch. The attention branch is supervised by L_A, which is calculated as:

$$L_A = -\frac{1}{n} \sum_{i=1}^{n} log \frac{e^{\theta_A(I_i)}}{\sum_{k=1}^{C} e^{\theta_A(I_i)}}, \qquad (5)$$

where $\boldsymbol{I}$ stands for the whole training set and n is the number of it. Different baselines [18,19,29,30], we update model parameters stage by stage according to curriculum learning method, so that the learning capability of model achieve improvement aggressively. Moreover, we integrate attention branch into model to further capture discriminative information.

3.1 Curriculum Design

Compared with diverse complex samples, easy samples from one identity are more similar, which makes them closely clustered together in the same feature space. In comparison, complex samples are sparsely distributed. It is reasonable to measure the complexity of samples by their distribution density in a feature space, as shown in Fig. 2. In the beginning, we remove FC layer from the proposed ABM to obtain feature extactor f, and then use f to extract features of images $\mathcal{I}$. To measure the similarity between images, we use Euclidean distance to calculate the distance between image pairs:

$$D_{i,j} = \|f(\boldsymbol{I}_i) - f(\boldsymbol{I}_j)\|_2, \tag{6}$$

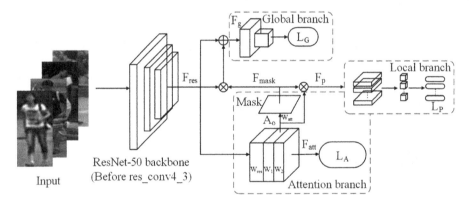

Fig. 3. The architecture of attention branch model, including global, local, and attention branches. An attention map generated from the attention branch to bridge global and local branches.

where $\boldsymbol{I}_i$, $\boldsymbol{I}_j$ are two images from the same category. The smaller the distance $d_{i,j}$, the more similar the two images are. A symmetric matrix $\boldsymbol{D} \in \mathbb{R}^{n \times n}$ contains the distances between each image pair, and n is the number of images in the current identity set. Then setting a threshold d_c, which is the median of the distance. A density ρ_i for the image i is computed as

$$\rho_i = \sum_j \Psi(\boldsymbol{D}_{i,j} - d_c), \tag{7}$$

where
$$\Psi(d) = \begin{cases} 1 & d < 0 \\ 0 & d \geq 0 \end{cases}.$$

It is considered that the closer similar images lead to a larger value of ρ. On the contrary, complexity would generate a smaller density for a relatively sparse distribution. With the distribution density, three clusters are generated by the k-means algorithm, then the corresponding clusters in each identity set are grouped together as a subset. Consequently, the dataset is divided in terms of complexity. The subset with a large density value is regarded as simple data, which represents more regular images. Inversely, the subset with a small density value has more complex samples, e.g., misalignment and occlusion. Accordingly, the dataset is split into three subsets as simple, less complex and complex ones as shown in Fig. 2, denoted by Sub1, Sub2, and Sub3, respectively.

3.2   Attention Branch Model

The attention branch model is used to generate an attention map in a supervised manner, which makes contributions to global branch and local branch as well. As is depicted in Fig. 3, ResNet-50 is used as backbone and we introduce another $conv\_5\_x$ block for attention branch. The $conv\_5\_x$ block removes the down-sampling operation to retain a proper receptive field, which gets more details of identities. Introduced attention branch generate feature map F_{mask} that can focus on salient regions and we leverage such region-interested feature to supervise local and global branches. In detail, the attention map generated in attention branch is computed as:

$$F_{mask} = \sigma(W_{mask} * f_{ReLU}(W_1 * W_{res} * F_{res})), \tag{8}$$

where σ is the sigmoid function, $*$ represents convolution with batch normalization, F_{res} is the output of $conv\_4\_x$ block, f_{ReLU} denotes the output from ReLU layer, and W_1 and W_{mask} represent the output of 1×1 convolution filters. The output dimension of W_1 is the number of identities and that of W_{mask} is 1. The attention branch separates after the $ReLU$ operation as

$$A_o = f_{ReLU}(W_1 * (W_{res} * F_{res})), \tag{9}$$

and the output F_{att} is calculated by:

$$F_{att} = f_{GAP}(W_2 * A_o), \tag{10}$$

where W_2 contains 1×1 convolution filters with the same output dimension as W_1. The attention branch guides attention generation in a supervised manner and ends directly by convolution, without a fully connected layer, which can reserve spatial information for salient regions.

We use PCB [19] as the local branch and insert the attention branch to exploit interrelation among various parts. The local branch with the attention branch operates as

$$F_p = A_o \odot F_{mask} \tag{11}$$

where $\odot$ denotes the element-wise product and $\boldsymbol{F}_{mask}$ is the attention map. Besides, a global branch is added to associate with the local branch by the attention map, which is operated by:

$$\boldsymbol{F}_g = \boldsymbol{F}_{res} \odot \boldsymbol{F}_{mask} + \boldsymbol{F}_{res}, \tag{12}$$

It shows that salient regions are aggregated according to the attention map. Then $\boldsymbol{F}_g$ is sent to the $conv\_5\_x$ block. The down-sampling rate of 2 in the $conv\_5\_x$ block is preserved, which obtains a large receptive field for integral images capture. Thus, we leverage attention map to supervise three branches and the whole optimization function of ABM is calculated in Eq. 3.

Table 1. The details of the three datasets, original and divided included. The blue font indicates the change in the number of identities.

Dataset	Train	Test	ID	Sub1	Sub2	Sub3	Total
Market-1501	12936/750	19732/751	725	5501	4700	2629	12830
DukeMTMC-reid	16522/702	17661/702	701	7963	5370	3183	16526
MSMT17	32621/1041	93820/3060	1040	13867	10357	6018	30242

4 Experiments

4.1 Datasets and Implementation Details

As listed in Table 1, experiments are presented on three benchmark datasets, including Market1501 [31], DukeMTMC-reid [33], and MSMT17 [22]. The pedestrian bounding boxes on the datasets are detected in different ways, e.g., Market-1501 by DPM, DukeMTMC-reid by hand-drawn, and MSMT by Faster R-CNN. MSMT17 is the most challenging dataset under the collection of various conditions. We adopt the official evaluation protocols in these datasets. All the experiments are under the single query setting and the performances are evaluated by the mean average precision (mAP) as well as the cumulated matching characteristics (CMC).

The CD-ABM model is implemented in Pytorch framework. During training, random horizontal flipping and random erasing are used for data augmentation. In the first-two stage, the inputs are resized to 256×128 while in the last stage are resized to 384×128. The batch size is set to 64 and the learning rate decays every 40 epochs by multiplying 0.1. Initially, the learning rate is 0.1 in the first and third stages and 0.001 for the second stage. For the pre-trained layers, the learning rate is delayed by $\times 0.1$. The stochastic gradient descent algorithm with a momentum 0.9 is used. In the first-two stage, the learning processes last for 60 epochs while in the last stage, it lasts 100 epochs. In the test phase, we concatenate all outputs except that from the attention branch to obtain final features.

Table 2. Comparison of our model with the state-of-the-arts on Market-1501. The compared methods are categorized into three classes: global, attentive, and part-based methods. We show our results in the global and attention branches (CD-ABM_G), and the whole model in the three branches (CD-ABM)

Methods	R-1	R-5	R-10	mAP
SVDNet [18]	80.5	91.7	94.7	55.9
PDC [15]	84.4	92.7	94.9	63.4
PAN [15]	84.4	92.7	94.9	63.4
HydraPlus [12]	76.9	91.3	94.5	-
DLPA [30]	81.0	92.0	94.7	63.4
AACN [27]	85.9	-	-	66.9
HA-CNN [10]	91.2	-	-	75.7
Spindle [29]	76.9	91.5	94.6	-
PSE [13]	87.7	94.5	96.8	69.0
GLAD [23]	89.9	-	-	73.9
Part-aligned [17]	91.7	96.9	98.1	79.6
Deep-person [3]	92.3	-	-	79.6
PCB [19]	92.3	97.2	98.2	77.4
PCB+RPP [19]	93.8	97.5	98.5	81.6
MAM [28]	93.5	-	-	81.8
CD-ABM_G(Ours)	91.6	97.1	98.5	79.3
CD-ABM(Ours)	**94.1**	**98.0**	**98.8**	**84.1**

4.2   Comparisons with State-of-the-Art Methods

Evaluation on Market-1501. CD-ABM is compared with 15 existing methods on Market-1501 in Table 2. These methods are categorized into three classes: global, attentive, and part-based methods. Our model uses the global and attention branches (CD-ABM_G) outperforms HA-CNN which also utilizes attention mechanism by 0.4% in Rank-1 and 3.6% in mAP, showing the effective of our attention mechanism in focusing on salient regions. Compared with MAM, which also takes global information and attention mechanism into account in part-based methods, our CD-ABM yields better results, reaching 94.1%(+0.6%) in Rank-1 and 84.1% (2.3%) in mAP.

Evaluation on DukeMTMC-ReID. Table 3 presents the comparison result on DukeMTMC-reID. With the help of curriculum design, our model achieves 84.8% in Rank-1 and 74.2% in mAP. It exceeds Part-aligned which utilizes extra pose information to align by 4.4% in mAP and 0.4% Rank-1, which means that CD-ABM is able to fully exploit discrimination information for the pedestrian misalignment.

Table 3. Comparison of our model with the state-of-the-arts on DukeMTMC-reID.

Methods	R-1	R-5	R-10	mAP
SVDNet [18]	67.7	80.5	85.7	45.8
PAN [15]	71.6	92.7	94.9	51.1
AACN [27]	76.8	-	-	59.3
PSE [13]	79.8	89.7	92.2	62.0
HA-CNN [10]	80.5	-	-	64.8
PCB [19]	81.8	-	-	66.1
PCB+RPP [19]	83.3	-	-	69.2
MAM [28]	83.5	-	-	69.8
Part-aligned [17]	84.4	92.2	93.8	69.3
CD-ABM(Ours)	**84.8**	**93.2**	**94.8**	**74.2**

Table 4. Comparison of our model with the state-of-the-arts on MSMT17.

Methods	R-1	R-5	R-10	mAP
GoogleNet [20]	47.6	65.0	71.8	23.0
PDC [15]	58.0	73.6	79.4	29.7
GLAD [23]	61.4	76.8	81.6	34.0
CD-ABM(Ours)	**77.3**	**87.5**	**90.8**	**55.0**

Evaluation on MSMT17. MSMT17 is the most challenging dataset with the largest number of identities in various conditions. From Table 4, we can find that our method achieves the most excellent results, which reach to 77.3% (+15.9%) in Rank-1 and 55.0% (+21%) in mAP, respectively. It means that the progressive learning and further feature extraction facilitation can improve the discriminative capability regardless of samples diversity.

4.3 Effectiveness of Attention Branch Model

As shown in Table 5, we evaluate the effectiveness of ABM in two aspects, without the local branch as global aspect (Baseline_G if without the attention branch) and with the local branch as the part-level aspect (Baselin_P if without the attention branch).

In the global aspect, ABM achieves better accuracy across all datasets. It indicates that, in a supervised manner, ABM focuses efficiently on salient regions, which alleviates the effect of pedestrians misalignment. Since bounding boxes annotated by humans (as mentioned above), the dataset DukeMTMC-reid is better aligned than Market-1501 and MSMT17 by algorithms, the improvement in DukeMTMC-reid is smaller than that in the other two.

In the part-level aspect, to highlight the effect of ABM in exploiting global and local information, we add a model only with local and global branches but without attention branch (+Global) as an additional set of comparison tests. ABM achieves an increase of 1.6%~4.5% in Rank-1 and 2.7%~5.4% in mAP, respectively. Meanwhile, the result shows that ABM can better fuse global and local representations.

Table 5. Comparison of ABM with global and local branches.

Dataset	Market-1501		DukeMTMT-reID		MSMT17	
	R-1	mAP	R-1	mAP	R-1	mAP
Baseline_G	88.7	72.8	77.5	61.1	38.9	24.9
ABM_G	90.9	77.2	78.0	63.2	44.1	31.1
Baseline_P	92.0	76.7	82.9	68.7	68.5	41.7
+Global	92.3	78.2	83.8	69.4	71.4	44.8
ABM_P	93.6	82.1	84.5	71.4	73.0	47.1

Fig. 4. The visualization of divided subsets in Market-1501, ranked by complexity from right to left. Sub1 stands for simple images set while sub3 represents complex one, with more diversity in it.

4.4 Effectiveness of Curriculum Design

We divide the datasets by their distribution densities as mentioned in Sect. 3.1. The detailed setting are given in Table 1. We have abandoned some badly divided identities, caused by the small number of samples or the lack of diversity.

Table 6. The performance of three-stage learning in the global and local branches (mainly different in the last stage).

Dataset	Market-1501		DukeMTMT-reID		MSMT17	
	R-1	mAP	R-1	mAP	R-1	mAP
Stage1	75.9	54.4	69.4	51.4	32.0	19.3
Stage2	84.9	66.1	75.0	56.7	36.2	22.3
Stage3_G	91.6	79.3	79.1	64.7	46.4	33.3
Stage3_P	94.1	84.1	84.8	74.2	77.3	55.0

In Market-1501, there are 750 origin identities training set, while only 725 after dividing. The other two datasets are reduced by one identity. Consequently, In our experiences, the two baselines (Baseline_G and Baseline_P) are trained with original training sets, while ABM and curriculum design are analyzed with divided ones. As shown in Table 5, the reduced identities do not degrade the performance of the model because of their complexity hard to adapt the model or their small quantity. Figure 4 shows different scenarios from Market-1501 divided by our curriculum design, where the complexity of scenario increases from left to right. Sub1 stands for simple images set while Sub3 represents complex one, with more diversity in it. Clearly, increasing complexity is caused by misalignment, occlusion, background clustering, and wrong labels.

The performance of three-stage learning is described in Table 6. We find that the capability of the model is gradually increased in all three subsets, which demonstrates the effectiveness of training sets division and training strategy from simpleness to complexity. Finally, ABM is added into the model in stage3. We train two models, with global and attention branches (stage3_G) and with three branches (the whole CD-ABM also as stage3_P). They all gain prominent results, especially stage3_P. The results show that CD-ABM, which stands for ABM with three-stage learning, can mine more valuable information from samples and learn a more robust representation.

5   Conclusions

We proposed a model called Curriculum Design with Attention Branch Model (CD-ABM) to excavate discriminative information for person re-ID. Based on the density distribution, a curriculum design with training strategy increasingly adds complexity into the training process, which significantly improves the capability of representation. Furthermore, we use an attention branch model (ABM) in the last stage to further promote representative feature extraction, with global information reinforcement and the exploitation of the correlation between global and local information. Experiments on three benchmark datasets showed that CD-ABM can achieve competitive performance to state-of-the-art methods, which reveals the effectiveness of our proposed framework.

References

1. Ahmed, E., Jones, M., Marks, T.K.: An improved deep learning architecture for person re-identification. In: Proceedings of the IEEE Conference on Computer Vision and Pattern Recognition, pp. 3908–3916 (2015)
2. Almazan, J., Gajic, B., Murray, N., Larlus, D.: Re-id done right: towards good practices for person re-identification. arXiv preprint arXiv:1801.05339 (2018)
3. Bai, X., Yang, M., Huang, T., Dou, Z., Yu, R., Xu, Y.: Deep-person: learning discriminative deep features for person re-identification. arXiv preprint arXiv:1711.10658 (2017)
4. Bengio, Y., Louradour, J., Collobert, R., Weston, J.: Curriculum learning. In: Proceedings of the 26th Annual International Conference on Machine Learning, pp. 41–48. ACM (2009)
5. Cheng, D., Gong, Y., Zhou, S., Wang, J., Zheng, N.: Person re-identification by multi-channel parts-based CNN with improved triplet loss function. In: Proceedings of the IEEE Conference on Computer Vision and Pattern Recognition, pp. 1335–1344 (2016)
6. Fan, H., Zheng, L., Yan, C., Yang, Y.: Unsupervised person re-identification: clustering and fine-tuning. ACM Trans. Multimed. Comput. Commun. Appl. (TOMM) **14**(4), 83 (2018)
7. Fukui, H., Hirakawa, T., Yamashita, T., Fujiyoshi, H.: Attention branch network: learning of attention mechanism for visual explanation. arXiv preprint arXiv:1812.10025 (2018)
8. Guo, S., et al.: CurriculumNet: weakly supervised learning from large-scale web images. In: Ferrari, V., Hebert, M., Sminchisescu, C., Weiss, Y. (eds.) ECCV 2018. LNCS, vol. 11214, pp. 139–154. Springer, Cham (2018). https://doi.org/10.1007/978-3-030-01249-6_9
9. He, K., Zhang, X., Ren, S., Sun, J.: Deep residual learning for image recognition. In: Proceedings of the IEEE Conference on Computer Vision and Pattern Recognition, pp. 770–778 (2016)
10. Li, W., Zhu, X., Gong, S.: Harmonious attention network for person re-identification. In: Proceedings of the IEEE Conference on Computer Vision and Pattern Recognition, pp. 2285–2294 (2018)
11. Lin, Y., Zheng, L., Zheng, Z., Wu, Y., Yang, Y.: Improving person re-identification by attribute and identity learning. arXiv preprint arXiv:1703.07220 (2017)
12. Liu, X., et al.: HydraPlus-Net: attentive deep features for pedestrian analysis. In: Proceedings of the IEEE International Conference on Computer Vision, pp. 350–359 (2017)
13. Saquib Sarfraz, M., Schumann, A., Eberle, A., Stiefelhagen, R.: A pose-sensitive embedding for person re-identification with expanded cross neighborhood re-ranking. In: Proceedings of the IEEE Conference on Computer Vision and Pattern Recognition, pp. 420–429 (2018)
14. Song, C., Huang, Y., Ouyang, W., Wang, L.: Mask-guided contrastive attention model for person re-identification. In: Proceedings of the IEEE Conference on Computer Vision and Pattern Recognition, pp. 1179–1188 (2018)
15. Su, C., Li, J., Zhang, S., Xing, J., Gao, W., Tian, Q.: Pose-driven deep convolutional model for person re-identification. In: Proceedings of the IEEE International Conference on Computer Vision, pp. 3960–3969 (2017)

16. Su, C., Yang, F., Zhang, S., Tian, Q., Davis, L.S., Gao, W.: Multi-task learning with low rank attribute embedding for multi-camera person re-identification. IEEE Trans. Pattern Anal. Mach. Intell. **40**(5), 1167–1181 (2018)

17. Suh, Y., Wang, J., Tang, S., Mei, T., Lee, K.M.: Part-aligned bilinear representations for person re-identification. In: Ferrari, V., Hebert, M., Sminchisescu, C., Weiss, Y. (eds.) Computer Vision – ECCV 2018. LNCS, vol. 11218, pp. 418–437. Springer, Cham (2018). https://doi.org/10.1007/978-3-030-01264-9_25

18. Sun, Y., Zheng, L., Deng, W., Wang, S.: SVDNet for pedestrian retrieval. In: Proceedings of the IEEE International Conference on Computer Vision, pp. 3800–3808 (2017)

19. Sun, Y., Zheng, L., Yang, Y., Tian, Q., Wang, S.: Beyond part models: person retrieval with refined part pooling (and a strong convolutional baseline). In: Ferrari, V., Hebert, M., Sminchisescu, C., Weiss, Y. (eds.) ECCV 2018. LNCS, vol. 11208, pp. 501–518. Springer, Cham (2018). https://doi.org/10.1007/978-3-030-01225-0_30

20. Szegedy, C., et al.: Going deeper with convolutions. In: Proceedings of the IEEE Conference on Computer Vision and Pattern Recognition, pp. 1–9 (2015)

21. Tian, M., et al.: Eliminating background-bias for robust person re-identification. In: Proceedings of the IEEE Conference on Computer Vision and Pattern Recognition, pp. 5794–5803 (2018)

22. Wei, L., Zhang, S., Gao, W., Tian, Q.: Person transfer GAN to bridge domain gap for person re-identification. In: Proceedings of the IEEE Conference on Computer Vision and Pattern Recognition, pp. 79–88 (2018)

23. Wei, L., Zhang, S., Yao, H., Gao, W., Tian, Q.: Glad: global-local-alignment descriptor for pedestrian retrieval. In: Proceedings of the 25th ACM International Conference on Multimedia, pp. 420–428. ACM (2017)

24. Wen, F., Chu, L., Liu, P., Qiu, R.C.: A survey on nonconvex regularization-based sparse and low-rank recovery in signal processing, statistics, and machine learning. IEEE Access **6**, 69883–69906 (2018)

25. Wu, Y., Lin, Y., Dong, X., Yan, Y., Bian, W., Yang, Y.: Progressive learning for person re-identification with one example. IEEE Trans. Image Process. **28**, 2872–2881 (2019)

26. Xiao, T., Li, H., Ouyang, W., Wang, X.: Learning deep feature representations with domain guided dropout for person re-identification. In: Proceedings of the IEEE Conference on Computer Vision and Pattern Recognition, pp. 1249–1258 (2016)

27. Xu, J., Zhao, R., Zhu, F., Wang, H., Ouyang, W.: Attention-aware compositional network for person re-identification. In: Proceedings of the IEEE Conference on Computer Vision and Pattern Recognition, pp. 2119–2128 (2018)

28. Yan, Y., Ni, B., Liu, J., Yang, X.: Multi-level attention model for person re-identification. Pattern Recognit. Lett. (2018, in press)

29. Zhao, H., et al.: Spindle net: person re-identification with human body region guided feature decomposition and fusion. In: Proceedings of the IEEE Conference on Computer Vision and Pattern Recognition, pp. 1077–1085 (2017)

30. Zhao, L., Li, X., Zhuang, Y., Wang, J.: Deeply-learned part-aligned representations for person re-identification. In: Proceedings of the IEEE International Conference on Computer Vision, pp. 3219–3228 (2017)
31. Zheng, L., Shen, L., Tian, L., Wang, S., Wang, J., Tian, Q.: Scalable person re-identification: a benchmark. In: Proceedings of the IEEE International Conference on Computer Vision, pp. 1116–1124 (2015)
32. Zheng, L., Yang, Y., Hauptmann, A.G.: Person re-identification: past, present and future. arXiv preprint arXiv:1610.02984 (2016)
33. Zheng, Z., Zheng, L., Yang, Y.: Unlabeled samples generated by GAN improve the person re-identification baseline in vitro. In: Proceedings of the IEEE International Conference on Computer Vision, pp. 3754–3762 (2017)

Non-stationary Multivariate Time Series Prediction with Selective Recurrent Neural Networks

Jiexi Liu and Songcan Chen[✉]

College of Computer Science and Technology, Nanjing University of Aeronautics and Astronautics, MIIT Key Laboratory of Pattern Analysis and Machine Intelligence, Nanjing, China
{liujiexi,s.chen}@nuaa.edu.cn

Abstract. Non-stationary multivariate time series (NSMTS) prediction is still a challenging issue nowadays. Methods based on deep learning, especially Long Short-Term Memory and Gated Recurrent Unit neural networks (LSTMs and GRUs) have achieved state-of-the-art results. However, the architecture of LSTM and GRU may contain some useless components that affect the training efficiency, thus it is possible that optional architecture exists. Recently, newly-introduced one gate Minimal Gated Unit neural networks (MGUs) have exhibited promising results in computer vision and some sequence analysis applications. In this paper, we first transplant the MGUs into NSMTS prediction and then evaluate the ability of LSTMs, GRUs and MGUs via experiments. During these trials, none of these neural networks can always dominate in performance over all the NSMTS. Therefore, we further propose a novel Selective Recurrent Neural Networks with Random Connectivity Gated Unit (SRCGUs) that train random connectivity LSTMs, GRUs and MGUs at a time. This model can not only reduce the number of parameters and save about 2/3 of time compared to the separate training but also adjust their importance weights dynamically to select a more appropriate neural network for prediction. Experimental results show that SRCGUs have better performance on the benchmarks used and flexibility. And to the best of our knowledge, this selective architecture has never been reported before.

Keywords: Non-stationary multivariate time series (NSMTS) ·
Selective Recurrent Neural Networks with Random Connectivity Gated Unit (SRCGUs) · Recurrent Neural Network (RNN) ·
Minimal Gated Unit (MGU) · Long Short-Term Memory (LSTM) ·
Gated Recurrent Unit (GRU)

This work is supported by the National Natural Science Foundation of China (NSFC) under the Grant No. 61672281 and the Key Program of NSFC under Grant No. 61732006.

A. C. Nayak and A. Sharma (Eds.): PRICAI 2019, LNAI 11672, pp. 636–649, 2019.
https://doi.org/10.1007/978-3-030-29894-4_51

1 Introduction

Time series prediction, which aims to forecast new trends or potential hazardous events, has a long history and literature as its applications are ubiquitous in our everyday life ranging from forecasting stock price [20], traffic jam situation [6], solar plant energy output [18] to weather condition [21]. Figure 1 shows that time-series databases (Time Series DBMS) have the fastest growing speed in types of databases for the last 12 months according to the DB-engines[1].

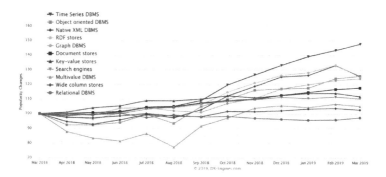

Fig. 1. The historical trend of the databases popularity for the last 12 months.

Typically, time series can be categorized into two types, one is stationary, the other is non-stationary. The definition of stationarity is that for two given sequences $x_{t_1}, \ldots, x_{t_k}$ and $x_{t_{1+\tau}}, \ldots, x_{t_{k+\tau}}$ in a time series, the joint statistical distributions of the above two sequences are identical for all τ. However, in practice it is difficult to meet the requirement of stationarity, instead, most real-world datasets are non-stationary. In addition, there are also many multivariate time series exist. Therefore, analyzing such non-stationary multivariate time series (NSMTS) has become a new hot spot in time series prediction domain [3,5].

Traditional approaches used to solve the time series prediction problems, like Exponentially Weighted Moving Average (EWMA) and Autoregressive Integrated Moving Average (ARIMA) [2,5] fail in forecasting NSMTS because there are some limitations in these methods: (1) they cannot deal with non-stationary time series or need special preprocess before training; (2) these approaches cannot solve the multivariate problems or capture and leverage the dynamic dependencies among multiple variables; (3) these kinds of statistical methods are inefficient and have some difficulties in dealing with big data. On the contrary, deep learning methods have achieved outstanding performance [1,14] in solving the

---

[1] DBMS popularity broken down by database model can be found at https://db-engines.com/en/ranking_categories.

prediction problems and they are also capable to overcome the above three disadvantages. Therefore, in this paper, we mainly focus on the more popular deep learning methods.

Deep learning methods, especially neural networks (NNs) based methods can indeed solve the prediction problems effectively, among which Forward Neural Networks (FNNs) [17], Fuzzy Neural Networks [17] and Recurrent Neural Networks (RNNs) [7] have been widely used. And with a chain-like structure and special gate mechanism, the recent advances in the variants of RNNs provide some useful and brand-new insights in tackling the NSMTS prediction problems.

However, there do not exist any researches on the choice of different variants of gated unit based neural networks. To alleviate this problem, in this paper, we evaluate the three gated units based neural networks (LSTMs, GRUs and MGUs) on five NSMTS datasets with traditional neural networks. Specifically, we first empirically compare the optimal performance of the three models concerning their separate well-selected parameter settings [4, 12] and conclude from the experimental results that it is hard to derive one suitable neural network for all data sets. This inspires us to propose a unified Selective Recurrent Neural Networks by selecting an appropriate neural network dynamically to achieve relatively higher prediction accuracy at the price of more parameters to tune during the training procedure. Considering that random topology formation of synapses can provide a sufficient foundation for specific functional connectivity to emerge in local neural microcircuits [9], we finally decide to adopt Random Connectivity gated units denoted as RCLSTM, RCGRU and RCMGU [11] to replace the traditional gated units in Selective Recurrent Neural Networks. Consequently, our newly designed SRCGUs are the combination of Selective Recurrent Neural Networks and Random Connectivity Gated Unit.

The contributions of this paper are multifold:

1. We apply the MGUs to the NSMTS predictions and compare the prediction efficiency of the MGUs with the LSTMs and the GRUs.
2. To the best of our knowledge, the proposal of the novel SRCGUs is the first work selecting a more appropriate gated unit based neural network for NSMTS datasets prediction by dynamically adjusting the importance weights of LSTMs, GRUs and MGUs at a time. And we also prove that there indeed exists the adjustment of the weights.
3. We demonstrate in experiments on various kinds of time series datasets (financial data, air quality data and Optical fiber data) that the proposed approach outperforms single neural network models, which saves time and further improves the accuracy in prediction.

In the second section, we will review the related work of time series prediction. Then the traditional model and our SRCGUs model will be introduced in the third section. Finally, we apply the above two models to the prediction problems and conclude by arranging the experimental results.

2   Related Work

Researchers have put forward a number of methods for time series prediction including traditional statistical methods and machine learning methods.

One statistical method used frequently in financial applications is called autoregressive integrated moving average (ARIMA) model. It is quite popular due to its statistical properties and the use of a well-known Box-Jenkins methodology [2] in the model selection procedure. However, with high computational cost, this model cannot deal with high dimensional multivariate time series forecasting problems efficiently [2]. In addition to ARIMA model, a simpler vector autoregression (VAR) [16] model and its variants have also become the most widely used models in multivariate time series analysis. Nevertheless, the model capacity of VAR grows quickly over the change of window size and the number of variables, so the inherited model will be very large and easy to overfit when dealing with long-range temporal patterns.

To assuage defects of these statistical methods, several machine learning approaches make some progress to some extent in dealing with time series problems. For example, standard linear regression models [16] with time-varying parameters have made some advances in handling multivariate forecasting problems [15] efficiently by using high-quality off-the-shelf solvers. Nevertheless, this kind of linear model has difficulty in capturing complex non-linear relationships between multivariate series. Another representative model is non-parametric Gaussian Process (GP) [19] that can capture dynamic phenomena by modeling distributions over a continuous domain of functions. However, the inverting of kernel matrix involved in the implementation of GP has cubic complexity over the number of observations.

3   Methodology

In this section, we first formulate the NSMTS prediction problem and briefly introduce two models for prediction, one is traditional neural network model, the other is novel SRCGUs proposed by us. Then, for completeness, we give a concise review of the RNN and the structures of three gated units (LSTM, GRU and MGU). Finally, we detail the structure of the SRCGUs and introduce the objective function and the optimization strategy.

3.1   Problem Formulation

In this paper, we primarily focus on NSMTS predictions by using simple rolling multi-step prediction method. Here, we use boldface letters to represent vectors. Specifically, given a series of known time series $Y = \{x_1, x_2, \ldots, x_T\}$, where $x_t \in \mathbb{R}^n$, n is the dimension of the time series and our goal is to predict x_{T+h}, in which h represents the desirable horizon ahead of the current time stamp. The horizon can be chosen according to the demands of the environmental settings in time series datasets ranging from a few seconds to a year and here we choose

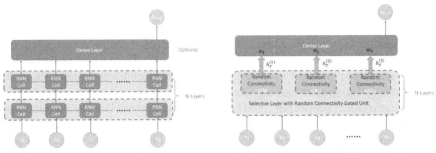

(a) The traditional model for simulations

(b) The designed SRCGUs model for simulations

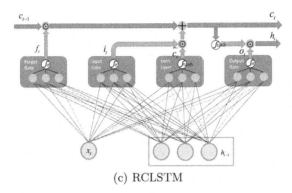

(c) RCLSTM

Fig. 2. The framework of two models and the structure of RCLSTM.

it manually for each dataset. Rolling prediction means that when we predict $\boldsymbol{x}_{T+h+1}$, the series $\{\boldsymbol{x}_1, \boldsymbol{x}_2, \ldots, \boldsymbol{x}_{T+1}\}$ is available. We then formulate the input matrix at time step T as $\boldsymbol{X}_T = \{\boldsymbol{x}_1, \boldsymbol{x}_2, \ldots, \boldsymbol{x}_T\} \in \mathbb{R}^{n \times T}$.

Figure 2(a) shows the structure of traditional neural network model for prediction, where the RNN unit can be replaced by LSTM, GRU and MGU. While the Fig. 2(b) gives an overview of the designed SRCGUs and this model will be detailed in Subsect. 3.3.

In this paper, we use index t to represent the t-th time point in the time series and assume a hidden state h_t to indicate the system status at time t. In addition to this, $\sigma(x)$ denotes the logistic sigmoid function $\sigma(x) = 1/(1 + \exp(-x))$, the symbol $\odot$ is the element-wise product between two vectors and tanh is an activation that applies to every element of the inputs.

3.2 RNN: LSTM, GRU and MGU

Recurrent Neural Networks (RNNs), the extension of Feedforward Neural Networks (FNNs), are neural networks with feedback loops, through which past information can be stored and exploited. Traditionally, the RNN unit updates its recurrent hidden state $\boldsymbol{h}_t$ by

$$h_t = f(h_{t-1}, x_t), \tag{1}$$

where f is a nonlinear mapping and one usual way to define f is to make it a linear transformation plus a nonlinear activation, like

$$h_t = \tanh(W[h_{t-1}, x_t] + b). \tag{2}$$

This kind of unidirectional RNNs are commonly denoted as SimpleRNNs.

Unfortunately, SimpleRNNs have difficulty in prediction problems not only because the gradients may vanish or explode during training, but also because the long-range dependencies are difficult to be captured. To alleviate this, several relatively sophisticated gated units are invented to capture long-range dependencies [4].

In this paper, we are more interested in the performance of these variants of RNN units (LSTM, GRU and MGU). For the completeness of further research, we first detail the typical gated units in the following.

Long Short-Term Memory: Apart from the short-range information, one important issue in time series prediction is that sometimes the long-range information can also impact the forecasting accuracy. When the gap between relevant information and the current time point is big enough, the SimpleRNNs cannot connect the information because their ability in capturing long-range dependencies is quite weak. However, the LSTMs do not suffer from this kind of problem due to the special gating mechanism and internal memory in LSTM controlling the flow of information [10]. Until now, the LSTMs still play a dominative role in real-world applications.

The gating mechanism in LSTM is easy to understand in intuition, it contains an internal memory c_t and three gates, i.e., a forget gate f_t, an input gate i_t and an output gate o_t. The hidden state of the recurrent units at time t is computed as,

$$\begin{aligned}
f_t &= \sigma(W_f[h_{t-1}, x_t] + b_f), \\
i_t &= \sigma(W_i[h_{t-1}, x_t] + b_i), \\
o_t &= \sigma(W_o[h_{t-1}, x_t] + b_o), \\
\tilde{c}_t &= \tanh(W_c[h_{t-1}, x_t] + b_c), \\
c_t &= f_t \odot c_{t-1} + i_t \odot \tilde{c}_t, \\
h_t &= o_t \odot \tanh(c_t).
\end{aligned} \tag{3}$$

Gated Recurrent Unit: As a commonly used variant of the LSTM, the GRU has a simpler architecture that it innovatively combines the forget gate f_t and input gates i_t into a single update gate z_t, it also proposes a reset gate r_t and removes the memory cell to merge it with the hidden state. The update rules of GRU are shown as below,

$$z_t = \sigma(W_z[h_{t-1}, x_t] + b_z),$$
$$r_t = \sigma(W_r[h_{t-1}, x_t] + b_r),$$
$$\widetilde{h}_t = \tanh(W_h[r_t \odot h_{t-1}, x_t] + b_h),$$
$$h_t = (1 - z_t) \odot h_{t-1} + z_t \odot \widetilde{h}_t. \tag{4}$$

Compared with traditional LSTMs, several experiments show that the GRUs slightly outperform the LSTMs when they have the same number of parameters [4] in several domains.

Minimal Gated Unit: In order to further simplify the architecture, a single gate unit should be taken into consideration. A newly-introduced gated unit called MGU is a minimal design among existed gated hidden units [22] and more importantly, MGUs can get comparable promising accuracy as LSTMs do in many existing experiments in computer vision and some sequence analysis applications.

When designing the MGU structure, the choice of the only gate is crucial. From the experimental aspect, it has been discovered that the forget gate is extremely significant by performing experiments to measure the importance of every component in LSTM [4,8,12]. Meanwhile, from the intuitive aspect, the forget gate can decide what information to store or forget that makes it crucial for capturing long-range dependencies.

So MGU is a simplified GRU and it further effectively shares the reset gate and update gate together by letting $r_t = f_t, \forall t$, and then use f_t to denote the forget gate. The update rules of MGU are computed as:

$$f_t = \sigma(W_f[h_{t-1}, x_t] + b_f),$$
$$\widetilde{h}_t = \tanh(W_h[f_t \odot h_{t-1}, x_t] + b_h),$$
$$h_t = (1 - f_t) \odot h_{t-1} + f_t \odot \widetilde{h}_t. \tag{5}$$

It is obvious that the structure of MGU is much simpler than that of LSTM or GRU. The number of parameter sets $\{W, b\}$ of MGU is only half of LSTM and two-thirds of GRU. Therefore, when the three gated units-based models achieve comparable prediction accuracy, MGU can be seen as an optimal choice for reducing training time.

3.3 Selective Recurrent Neural Networks with Random Connectivity Gated Unit (SRCGUs)

When dealing with NSMTS predictions with deep neural networks, the choice of the gated units based neural network is crucial because inappropriate model may affect the training efficiency and forecasting accuracy. However, traditional neural networks can only train one neural network each time which will result in the waste of hardware resources. Hence, we design a selective layer to train the LSTMs, the GRUs and the MGUs at a time to choose the most appropriate one.

Generally, the computing time for individual gated unit based neural network is proportional to the number of parameters, without customized hardware and software acceleration. If we use fully connected gated unit in our model, the number of parameters may raise the computation complexity. Thus, we replace them with randomly connected gated units [11] to reduce the number of involved parameters. The probability of unit connections is determined by certain randomness, which will be explained later.

Here we take the LSTM as an example. Since the trainable parameters in LSTM only exist between the input data $[x_t, h_{t-1}]$ of internal memory at time t and the functional part (i.e. the gate layers and the tanh layer). So the random connections exist between $[x_t, h_{t-1}]$ and the functional part. Figure 2(c) shows the architecture of RCLSTM as a representative structure of a random connection gated units in which the solid lines mean the pair of neurons is connected and the dashed lines indicate the disconnection. If all the connection lines are solid lines, this architecture can be seen as the typical fully connected LSTM.

The strategy for randomly selecting the connecting neurons is detailed below. The probability values that show the tendency of corresponding pair of neurons will be connected or not can obey arbitrary statistical distributions, and we choose uniform distribution in our simulations due to the high computational efficiency. We further assume all neurons are connected with the same probability and then use a threshold to determine whether the neurons are connected or prohibited. Therefore, the random connected gated units' structures can create some sparsity and considerably decrease the total number of involved parameters to be trained and reduce the computational load of the whole network [11].

Another component is the dense layer whose inputs contain three hidden states $h_t^{(i)}$ ($i = 1, 2, 3$) from each gated unit component at time step t and the output is the final prediction results that computed as,

$$\hat{\boldsymbol{Y}}_t = \sum_{i=1}^{3} w_i \boldsymbol{h}_t^{(i)} + b, \tag{6}$$

where $\sum_{i=1}^{3} w_i = 1$ and $w_i \in \{0, 1\}$.

3.4   Objective Function and Optimization Strategy

Since squared error is the default loss function for most of the prediction problems, so our objective function can be formulated as,

$$\begin{aligned}
&\underset{\Theta}{\text{minimize}} \sum_{t \in \Omega_{\text{Train}}} \|\boldsymbol{Y}_t - \hat{\boldsymbol{Y}}_{t-h}\|_F^2, \\
&\text{s.t.} \sum_{i=1}^{3} w_i = 1, \forall w_i \in \{0, 1\}
\end{aligned} \tag{7}$$

in which Θ represents the parameter set of our model, Ω_{Train} is the time series used for training and $\| \cdot \|_F$ is the Frobenius norm.

Our optimization strategy is the same as the widely used strategy in traditional time series prediction models. With an input time series $Y_t = \{x_1, x_2, \ldots, x_t\}$ at time step t, we then define a tunable window size k to reformulate the above series as $X_t = \{x_{t-k+1}, x_{t-k+1}, \ldots, x_t\}$. Subsequently, this issue becomes a regression task with a feature value pairs $\{X_t, Y_{t+h}\}$ and we adopt the Stochastic Gradient Decent (SGD) or its variants to solve it [13].

4 Experiments

In this paper, we first use the traditional neural network model to apply the MGUs to the NSMTS prediction problems and then compare the ability of MGUs in forecasting with LSTMs and GRUs by training them separately. We also perform experiments on the SRCGUs and compare the prediction accuracy and time costs for per epoch with the traditional neural network models above.

All models are implemented with the Keras library with TensorFlow[2] backend.

Table 1. Results and statistics of MGUs, GRUs and LSTMs on five datasets.

Dataset	#hidden units			#trainable parameter			Per epoch time		
				LSTMs	GRUs	MGUs	LSTMs	GRUs	MGUs
BAC	32			9,794	7,362	4,930	0.908	1.284	**0.865**
C	64			35,970	27,010	18,050	1.368	1.332	**1.155**
GS	48			20,834	15,650	10,466	0.917	1.203	**0.843**
Pollution	64			37,124	27,908	18,692	2.97	2.524	**2.169**
Optical	256			588,804	441,860	294,916	10.072	7.714	**7.537**
Dataset	RMSE			MAE			R^2		
	LSTMs	GRUs	MGUs	LSTMs	GRUs	MGUs	LSTMs	GRUs	MGUs
BAC	**0.167281**	0.179057	0.176892	0.136586	0.14298	**0.134421**	**0.997**	0.996	0.996
C	0.612668	**0.5632**	0.610662	0.496549	**0.456047**	0.462657	0.996	**0.998**	0.991
GS	1.305976	1.358861	**1.248959**	**0.99121**	1.121053	1.007991	0.997	0.996	**0.997**
Pollution	4.844758	5.449293	**4.467702**	3.124952	3.555733	**3.030868**	0.996	0.996	**0.996**
Optical	**13.92472**	14.59827	20.15546	**8.97219**	10.05284	12.97202	**0.995**	0.997	0.995

4.1 Datasets

We use 5 datasets to complete the experiments.

1. **Three stock price datasets**[3]: These three stock price datasets, denoted as "BAC", "C" and "GS", are collected from *Kaggle Datasets* and can be found on the Internet. All of them contain 5 features and the length of the sequence is 2517. We aim to predict the accurate "Close" price for each stock price dataset.

---

[2] https://keras.io/, https://www.tensorflow.org/.
[3] These three datasets are available at https://www.kaggle.com/rohan8594/stock-data.

2. **Air quality dataset**[4]: This dataset that denotes as "Pollution", contains 7 features and the length of the sequence is 43825. This dataset contains several missing value and we use mean to fill them. This task focuses on forecasting the pollution of the next hour.
3. **Optical fiber dataset:** The optical fiber dataset denoted as "Optical" is a real-world dataset that contains 30 columns and the sequence length is 259202. The dataset collects from several sensors in real production. However, it is a confidential dataset that cannot be downloaded from the Internet. Since the break of the optical fiber may cause catastrophic financial loss, it is crucial to predict when the optical fiber is going to break. In this experiment, we are going to predict the "fiber-tensor" and "line-speed".

Every dataset has been split into training set (60%), validation set (20%) and test set (20%) chronologically.

Table 2. Results and statistics of average results in the traditional neural network model and the SRCGUs.

Dataset	#hidden units	Best choice in traditional model	# average trainable parameter (100%)	Average per epoch time	Average RMSE	Average MAE	Average R^2
BAC	32	LSTMs	7,362	1.019	0.17441	0.137996	0.996
C	64	GRUs	27,010	1.285	**0.59551**	**0.471751**	**0.998**
GS	48	MGUs	15,650	0.987	1.304599	1.040085	0.996
Pollution	64	MGUs	27,908	2.554	4.920584	3.237184	0.996
Optical	256	LSTMs	441,860	8.441	16.22615	10.66568	0.995
Dataset	#hidden units	Best choice in SRCGUs model[a]	#trainable parameter (70%)	Per epoch time	RMSE	MAE	R^2
BAC	32	RCGRUs	7,660	1.032	**0.146752**	**0.108009**	**0.996**
C	64	RCGRUs	28,224	1.798	0.610032	0.462657	0.997
GS	48	RCMGUs	16,329	1.323	**1.267075**	**1.048628**	**0.997**
Pollution	64	RCMGUs	9,346	2.769	**3.775834**	**2.679569**	**0.997**
Optical	256	RCLSTMs	462,873	13.201	**15.33951**	**10.63967**	**0.996**

[a]The best choice in SRCGUs means the neural network whose importance weight becomes 1 during the training and the per epoch time is the per epoch training time for the whole SRCGUs model not for single neural network.

4.2   Metrics

We use three conventional evaluation metrics called Root Mean Square Error (RMSE), Mean Absolute Error (MAE), Coefficient of Determination (R^2) to evaluate the performance of models that defined as: $\text{RMSE} = \sqrt{\frac{1}{T}\sum_{t=1}^{T}(\hat{\boldsymbol{x}}_t - \boldsymbol{x}_t)^2}$,

---

[4] This dataset is available at https://raw.githubusercontent.com/jbrownlee/Datasets/master/pollution.csv.

MAE $= \frac{1}{T}\sum_{t=1}^{T}|x_t - \hat{x}_t|$ and $R^2 = 1 - \sum_{t=1}^{T}(x_t - \hat{x}_t)^2/\sum_{t=1}^{T}(x_t - \bar{x}_t)^2$, where x_t and $\hat{x}_t$ represents the actual and predicted values at step t for $0 < t \le T$ respectively, and $\bar{x}_t$ is denoted as $\bar{x}_t = \frac{1}{T}\sum_{t=1}^{T}x_t$.

4.3   Experimental Result

First, we use the traditional neural network model to conduct three experiments using LSTMs, GRUs and MGUs separately for each NSMTS dataset. We set the number of the hidden units ranging from 32 to 256, and choose the suitable hidden unit number for each dataset that shown in Table 1 to achieve the best prediction accuracy and the number of 'N' in 'N-layers' shown in Fig. 2(a) can be chosen ranging in the set of $\{1, 2, 3\}$. The dense layer in both model is optional, but when the dimension of the input matrix is not the same as the output matrix, the dense layer becomes necessary. Each network is trained for 100 iterations.

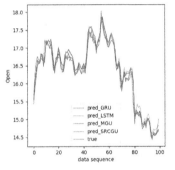

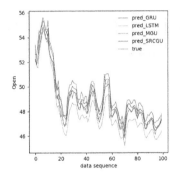

(a) Prediction curves of BAC dataset.

(b) Prediction curves of C dataset.

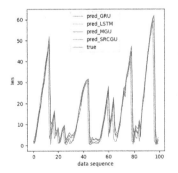

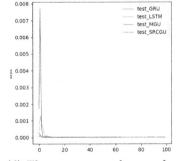

(c) Prediction curves of pollution dataset.

(d) The mean squared error of optical fiber dataset.

Fig. 3. The comparation of prediction results.

Since the MGUs have achieved good performance in computer vision and some sequence analysis problems, we intend to figure out whether this model can exhibit promising results in NSMTS prediction or not. As shown in Table 1, with a much simpler structure and fewer parameters, MGUs spend significant less training time but still achieve comparable accuracy with other two units that make it a good option for NSMTS with very small time interval.

However, from Table 1, there do not exist single gated unit base neural network that has prominent performance by comparing all five datasets. For example, GRUs achieve great performance in dataset "C" but fail in other datasets. In order to handle this problem, we further conduct a group of experiments by using SRCGUs to train the three neural networks at a time. This model setting is almost identical to the traditional neural networks with the same number of hidden units and depth of the neural networks for each specific dataset. As demonstrated by previous studies, 70% neural connectivity in the SRCGUs can achieve comparable RMSE with fully-connected models [11], so we choose this percentage of connection to do the simulation.

In Table 2, the SRCGUs can obtain more appropriate gated unit and achieve higher prediction accuracy with the average performance of traditional neural network models for most conditions. The best choices in SRCGUs model are shown in Table 2 and compared with the best choices in traditional models, the SRCGUs make the right decision for most of the time and this proves that there exists the adjustment in the importance weights. Since the traditional neural network model must be trained three times separately to find the gated unit that can achieve the highest prediction accuracy, the SRCGUs can finally save about 2/3 of the training time in total at the price of more parameters to train due to the combination of three neural networks.

The experimental results of evaluation among LSTMs, GRUs, MGUs and SRCGUs are shown in Fig. 3, in which (a,b,c) are the prediction results of two stock price datasets and the pollution dataset curves, while (d) is the test set mean squared error comparison for the optical fiber dataset.

5   Conclusion

In this paper, we newly transplant the MGUs into the NSMTS prediction problems and prove that it can achieve comparable prediction accuracy with LSTMs and GRUs. However, there do not exist a single gated unit based neural network that can show supreme performance over all the NSMTS. In order to relieve the problem, we use the SRCGUs to do the selection among three gated unit based neural networks. Since existing experiments show that our SRCGUs can achieve higher accuracy in time series prediction and this brings us a new perspective in NSMTS predictions. Hence, the SRCGUs can be seen as a suitable model for NSMTS prediction.

References

1. Althelaya, K.A., El-Alfy, E.S.M., Mohammed, S.: Stock market forecast using multivariate analysis with bidirectional and stacked (LSTM, GRU). In: 2018 21st Saudi Computer Society National Computer Conference (NCC), pp. 1–7. IEEE (2018)
2. Box, G.E., Jenkins, G.M., Reinsel, G.C., Ljung, G.M.: Time Series Analysis: Forecasting and Control. Wiley, New York (2015)
3. Chatfield, C.: The Analysis of Time Series: An Introduction. Chapman and Hall/CRC, London (2016)
4. Chung, J., Gulcehre, C., Cho, K., Bengio, Y.: Empirical evaluation of gated recurrent neural networks on sequence modeling. arXiv preprint arXiv:1412.3555 (2014)
5. Das, S.: Time Series Analysis. Princeton University Press, Princeton (1994)
6. Downs, O.B., Chapman, C.H., Barker, A.: Dynamic time series prediction of future traffic conditions, uS Patent 7,813,870, October 2010
7. Goodfellow, I., Bengio, Y., Courville, A., Bengio, Y.: Deep Learning, vol. 1. MIT Press, Cambridge (2016)
8. Greff, K., Srivastava, R.K., Koutník, J., Steunebrink, B.R., Schmidhuber, J.: LSTM: a search space odyssey. IEEE Trans. Neural Netw. Learn. Syst. **28**(10), 2222–2232 (2017)
9. Hill, S.L., Wang, Y., Riachi, I., Schürmann, F., Markram, H.: Statistical connectivity provides a sufficient foundation for specific functional connectivity in neocortical neural microcircuits. Proc. Natl. Acad. Sci. **109**(42), E2885–E2894 (2012)
10. Hochreiter, S., Schmidhuber, J.: Long short-term memory. Neural Comput. **9**(8), 1735–1780 (1997)
11. Hua, Y., Zhao, Z., Li, R., Chen, X., Liu, Z., Zhang, H.: Deep learning with long short-term memory for time series prediction. IEEE Commun. Magaz. **57**(6), 114–119 (2019)
12. Jozefowicz, R., Zaremba, W., Sutskever, I.: An empirical exploration of recurrent network architectures. In: International Conference on Machine Learning, pp. 2342–2350 (2015)
13. Kingma, D.P., Ba, J.: Adam: a method for stochastic optimization. arXiv preprint arXiv:1412.6980 (2014)
14. Lai, G., Chang, W.C., Yang, Y., Liu, H.: Modeling long-and short-term temporal patterns with deep neural networks. In: The 41st International ACM SIGIR Conference on Research & Development in Information Retrieval, pp. 95–104. ACM (2018)
15. Li, J., Chen, W.: Forecasting macroeconomic time series: lasso-based approaches and their forecast combinations with dynamic factor models. Int. J. Forecast. **30**(4), 996–1015 (2014)
16. Lütkepohl, H.: New Introduction to Multiple Time Series Analysis. Springer, Heidelberg (2005). https://doi.org/10.1007/978-3-540-27752-1
17. Maguire, L.P., Roche, B., McGinnity, T.M., McDaid, L.: Predicting a chaotic time series using a fuzzy neural network. Inf. Sci. **112**(1–4), 125–136 (1998)
18. Martín, L., Zarzalejo, L.F., Polo, J., Navarro, A., Marchante, R., Cony, M.: Prediction of global solar irradiance based on time series analysis: application to solar thermal power plants energy production planning. Solar Energy **84**(10), 1772–1781 (2010)
19. Roberts, S., Osborne, M., Ebden, M., Reece, S., Gibson, N., Aigrain, S.: Gaussian processes for time-series modelling. Phil. Trans. R. Soc. A **371**(1984), 20110550 (2013)

20. Schöneburg, E.: Stock price prediction using neural networks: a project report. Neurocomputing **2**(1), 17–27 (1990)
21. Xingjian, S., Chen, Z., Wang, H., Yeung, D.Y., Wong, W.K., Woo, W.C.: Convolutional LSTM network: a machine learning approach for precipitation now casting. In: Advances in Neural Information Processing Systems, pp. 802–810 (2015)
22. Zhou, G.B., Wu, J., Zhang, C.L., Zhou, Z.H.: Minimal gated unit for recurrent neural networks. Int. J. Autom. Comput. **13**(3), 226–234 (2016)

A Hybrid GA-PSO Method for Evolving Architecture and Short Connections of Deep Convolutional Neural Networks

Bin Wang[✉], Yanan Sun, Bing Xue, and Mengjie Zhang

School of Engineering and Computer Science, Victoria University of Wellington,
PO Box 600, Wellington 6140, New Zealand
{bin.wang,yanan.sun,bing.xue,mengjie.zhang}@ecs.vuw.ac.nz

Abstract. Image classification is a difficult machine learning task, where Convolutional Neural Networks (CNNs) have been applied for over 20 years in order to solve the problem. In recent years, instead of the traditional way of only connecting the current layer with its next layer, shortcut connections have been proposed to connect the current layer with its forward layers apart from its next layer, which has been proved to be able to facilitate the training process of deep CNNs. However, there are various ways to build the shortcut connections, it is hard to manually design the best shortcut connections when solving a particular problem, especially given the design of the network architecture is already very challenging. In this paper, a hybrid evolutionary computation (EC) method is proposed to *automatically* evolve both the architecture of deep CNNs and the shortcut connections. Three major contributions of this work are: Firstly, a new encoding strategy is proposed to encode a CNN, where the architecture and the shortcut connections are encoded separately; Secondly, a hybrid two-level EC method, which combines particle swarm optimisation and genetic algorithms, is developed to search for the optimal CNNs; Lastly, an adjustable learning rate is introduced for the fitness evaluations, which provides a better learning rate for the training process given a fixed number of epochs. The proposed algorithm is evaluated on three widely used benchmark datasets of image classification and compared with 12 peer Non-EC based competitors and one EC based competitor. The experimental results demonstrate that the proposed method outperforms all of the peer competitors in terms of classification accuracy.

Keywords: Evolutionary computation · Image classification ·
Convolutional Neural Networks · Shortcut connections

1 Introduction

Deep Convolutional Neural Networks (CNNs) have been the leading approach for solving image classifications tasks since it was introduced around 30 years ago [12].

© Springer Nature Switzerland AG 2019
A. C. Nayak and A. Sharma (Eds.): PRICAI 2019, LNAI 11672, pp. 650–663, 2019.
https://doi.org/10.1007/978-3-030-29894-4_52

Various CNN methods have been developed, e.g. VGGNet [16], Xception [2] and GoogLeNet [21]. Deep CNNs have achieved better and better accuracy on image classification tasks. However, the architectures of CNNs grow deeper and deeper (i.e. more and more layers), which makes the training of deep CNNs much harder due to the difficulty in the CNNs *architecture design* and *network training*.

Almost all of the state-of-the-art CNNs are with a manually designed architecture, which is very challenging to achieve without expertise both in CNNs and domain knowledge on the target problem. However, most real-world users often do not have such knowledge. In recent years, evolutionary computation (EC) has shown to be effective in *automatically* searching for the optimal architecture of CNNs [13,20,24].

Back-propagation with gradient descent optimisation is the most commonly used method for training CNNs, but the vanishing gradients problem often occurs when training a deep CNN [1,18]. Recently, *shortcut connections* have been introduced and shown to be effective in dealing with this problem [15]. Shortcut connections add extra connections between the current layer and the forward layers. Typical examples are ResNet [6] as shown in Fig. 1 and the densely-connected shortcuts in DenseNet [7] as illustrated in Fig. 2. As can be seen from Fig. 1, in ResNet, along with the direct forward connections between the current layer and the next layer, there are also jump connections, which connect the current layer to the layer after the next layer. DenseNet divides the CNN architecture into a number of blocks. Each layer can be connected to all of the forward layers of the same block, which is called densely-connected structure. Such shortcut connections have been heavily investigated in recent years with different variants [15,25]. However, such shortcut connections are manually designed and there still are a large number of open questions. For example, although the operations after shortcut connections are addition in ResNet and concatenation in DenseNet, it is unclear whether the shortcut connections in ResNet with the concatenation mechanism is better than DenseNet. Without rich expertise, it is still challenging to design the best shortcut connections to effectively and efficiently address a given problem. Therefore, it is needed to develop an approach to automatically searching for the shortcut connections.

Goals: we aim to develop a novel EC based approach that can automatically find the optimal CNN architecture and decide whether there should be shortcut connection(s) between one layer and its forward layer(s). A two-level encoding strategy is proposed, which is then used by a hybrid EC method of a genetic algorithm (GA) and particle swarm optimisation (PSO) to evolve both the network architecture and shortcut connections. Since both the architecture and the shortcut connections are dynamically decided during the evolutionary process without any human interference, the proposed method is named *DynamicNet*. The proposed method will be examined and compared with one EC based method and 12 state-of-the-art non-EC based methods on three of the widely-used datasets having different levels of difficulties. The specific objectives and contributions are:

– Design a new encoding strategy that includes both the CNN architecture and
the shortcut connections. Since the CNN architecture is decisive to the classification accuracy and the shortcut connections impact how well the CNN can
be trained, a two-level encoding is proposed with the first level representing
the CNN architecture and the second level representing the shortcut connections. These two levels are encoded as a vector with decimal values and a
vector of binary values, respectively;
– Develop a hybrid algorithm that can work with the two-level encoding. A
variable-length PSO algorithm is proposed to evolve the CNN architectures
due to PSO's promising performance on continuous optimisation while GA
is used to evolve the shortcut connections since it works well on optimisation
tasks with binary values;
– Propose a new fitness evaluation method to improve the effectiveness and
efficiency of the encoded CNN. Classification accuracy is used as the fitness
value of the proposed method. Each evaluation requires to train the encoded
CNN, which is an expensive process. Motivated by previous work [19], a small
number of training epochs is used to speed up the training. Furthermore, an
automation method is developed to search for the best learning rate among
a sequence of learning rates to improve the classification accuracy.

Fig. 1. ResNet architecture (image taken from [6])

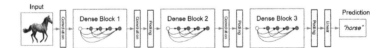

Fig. 2. DenseNet architecture (image taken from [7])

2   Background

2.1   ResNet

As shown in Fig. 1, the architecture is built on a plain CNN architecture called
VGG nets [17], which mostly contains convolutional layers with 3×3 filters;
while by inserting shortcut connections, the plain architecture is turned into the
recently proposed ResNet. The output is calculated based on Eq. (1), where x
is the input, $\mathcal{F}(x, W_i)$ represents the output of the convolutional layer with the

weights W_i, and W_s can be a constant of **1** if the dimension of the input is identical to that of the output of the convolutional layer; otherwise it will be a linear projection of the input in order to match the dimension of the output of the convolutional layer.

$$y = \mathcal{F}(x, W_i) + W_s x \tag{1}$$

2.2 DenseNet

DenseNet is a newly proposed CNN architecture in image classification tasks. As shown in Fig. 2, a DenseNet is composed of several dense blocks, and the convolutional layer and the pooling layer between the dense blocks which are referred to as the transition layer. To be more specific with the dense block, suppose a single image x_0 is passed to a dense block, which is composed of L layers. Each of the L layers implements a non-linear transformation $H_l(\cdot)$, and the output of the lth layer is denoted as x_l. As the output of the lth layer receives all of the feature maps of all preceding layers, the output x_l can be calculated according to Formula (2), where $[x_0, x_1, ..., x_{l-1}]$ refers to the concatenation of the feature maps obtained from layer 0, 1, ..., $l-1$, and H_l represents a composite function of three consecutive operations, which are batch normalization (BN) [8], a rectified linear unit (ReLU) [5] and 3×3 convolution (Conv).

$$x_l = H_l([x_0, x_1, ..., x_{l-1}]) \tag{2}$$

2.3 GAs and PSO

GAs. As an EC approach, GAs are inspired by the process of natural selection. The bio-inspired operators, such as mutation, crossover and selection, are utilised to evolve the population in order to obtain a high-quality solution [14]. The procedure of GA is composed of five parts: initialisation, selection, fitness evaluation, mutation, and crossover. At the stage of initialisation, a population of random vectors with a fixed dimension is generated; Next, the selection is performed by using a selection algorithm to select the individuals into a mating pool; After that, mutation is performed by selecting one individual from the mating pool and the value of each dimension is randomly chosen to be changed to evolve a new individual; Crossover is performed by selecting two individuals in the mating pool and combining a part of one individual's vector with that of the other. By iterating the fitness evaluation, selection, mutation, and crossover, the new population can be filled with new individuals with hopefully better solutions. The whole process terminates when the stopping criteria are met, and the best individual of all generations is reported as the evolved solution.

$$v_{id}(t+1) = w * v_{id}(t) + c_1 * r_1 * (P_{id} - x_{id}(t)) + c_2 * r_2 * (P_{gd} - x_{id}(t)) \tag{3}$$

$$x_{id}(t+1) = x_{id}(t) + v_{id}(t+1) \tag{4}$$

PSO. As one of the EC approaches, PSO is motivated by the social behaviour of fish schooling or bird flocking [4,9]. In PSO, there is a population consisting of a number of candidate solutions also called particles, and each particle has a position and a velocity. The representation of the position is $\mathbf{x_i} = (x_{i1}, x_{i2}, ...x_{id})$, where $\mathbf{x_i}$ is a vector of a fixed dimension representing the position of the ith particle in the population and x_{id} means the dth dimension of the ith particle's position. $\mathbf{v_i} = (v_{i1}, v_{i2}, ...v_{id})$ illustrates the velocity of a particle, where $\mathbf{v_i}$ is a fix-length vector expressing the velocity of the ith particle and v_{id} means the dth dimension of the ith particle's velocity. The way that PSO solves the optimisation problems is to keep moving the particle to a new position in the search space until the stopping criteria are met. The position of the particle is updated according to the update equation which incorporates two equations - the velocity update Eq. 3 and the position update Eq. (4). In Formula (3), $v_{id}(t + 1)$ indicates the updated dth dimension of the ith particle's velocity, r_1 and r_2 carry random numbers between 0 and 1, w, c_1 and c_2 are PSO parameters that are used to fine-tune the performance of PSO, and P_{id} and P_{gd} bear the dth dimension of the local best and the global best, respectively. After updating the velocity of the particle, the new position can be achieved by applying Formula (4).

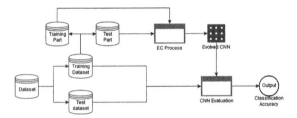

Fig. 3. The flowchart of the experimental process

3   The Proposed Method

3.1   Overall Structure of the System

Figure 3 shows the overall structure of the system (this structure is actually used by all of the experiments in this paper). The dataset is split into a training set and a test set, and the training set is further divided into a training part and a test part. The training part and the test part are passed to the EC process, which is the HGAPSO algorithm. During the fitness evaluations, the training part is used to train the neural network, and the test part is used to obtain the test accuracy of the trained neural network, which is used as the fitness value. EC produces the evolved CNN architecture, which is the best individual. Lastly, in the CNN evaluation procedure, the produced CNN architecture is trained on the whole training set, and the test accuracy of the trained CNN model is obtained, which is the final output of the system.

3.2 DynamicNet - The Evolved CNN Architecture

By comparing the figures of ResNet and DenseNet, it can be observed that in ResNet, each layer has at most two connections from previous layers. However, in DenseNet, the connections of each layer coming from previous layers are the number of previous layers due to the densely-connected structure. Therefore, the number of input feature maps is the sum of the numbers of feature maps of all previous layers, which results in the exploding growth of the number of feature maps, particularly for the layers near the output layer. The solution introduced in DenseNet is to divide the whole CNN into multiple blocks called Dense Block. Each block is followed by a transition layer, which comprises a convolutional layer and a pooling layer, to reduce the number of feature maps to half the number of input feature maps. The hyperparameters of the convolutional layer are fixed, which are 3 as the filter size, 1 as the stride size, and half the number of input feature maps as the number of feature maps; The pooling layer also has fixed hyperparameters, which are 2×2 as the kernel size and 2 as the stride size. As the proposed DynamicNet may be densely-connected, it might have the same exploding growth issue of the number of feature maps. Therefore, DynamicNet adopts the block mechanism of DenseNet.

Inside each block, there are a number of convolutional layers with a fixed filter size of 3×3 and a fixed stride size of 1. After each layer, the total number of input feature maps grows by the number of feature maps of the convolutional layer, which is called the *growth rate* of the block. In DenseNet, *the number of blocks*, *the number of convolutional layers* and *the* growth rate are manually designed, which requires good domain knowledge and a lot of manual trials to find a good architecture. In the proposed HGAPSO algorithm, these three hyperparameters will be also automatically designed.

3.3 HGAPSO Encoding Strategy

DynamicNet is comprised of a number of blocks which are connected by transition layers, and the shortcut connections are built between layers inside the block. Based on the construction pattern of the network, the hyperparameters of the architecture can be split into the architecture and the shortcut connections. Regarding the architecture of the network, there are various hyperparameters including the number of blocks, the number of convolutional layers in each block and the growth rate of the convolutional layer in the block, which need to be evolved. In addition to the densely-connected structure in DenseNet, different topologies of shortcut connections, i.e. the different combination of partial shortcut connections in each block, will be explored by the proposed HGAPSO method in order to keep the meaningful features and remove the unmeaningful features learned by previous layers.

Based on the analysis of the architecture and hyperparameters, the encoding process can be divided into two steps. The first step is to encode the hyperparameters of the CNN architecture. Each of the hyperparameters is a dimension of the architecture encoding, which is shown in Fig. 4a. The first dimension is the number of blocks, and the two hyperparameters of each block, the number of convolutional layers and the growth rate, as two dimensions are appended to the vector. The first step of the encoding is named the first-level encoding, which will be used by the first-level evolution. Based on the results of the first-level encoding, the shortcut connections can be encoded into a binary vector at the second-level encoding. An example of one block with 5 layers is illustrated in Fig. 4b. Each of the dimensions represents a shortcut connection between two layers that are not next to each other, and the two layers next to each other are always connected. Taking the first layer as an example, the three binary digits - [101] represents the shortcut connections between the first layer to the third, to the fourth, and to the fifth layer, respectively, where 1 means the connection exists and 0 means there is no connection. A number of similar binary vectors shown in Fig. 4b constitute the whole vector that represents the shortcut connections of the whole block.

3.4   HGAPSO Search

Overview. Based on the two-level encoding strategy, the algorithm is composed of two levels of evolution, which are described in Algorithm 1. The first-level evolution is designed to evolve the architecture of the CNNs encoded by the first-level encoding, and the second-level evolution is performed to search for the best combination of shortcut connections. There are a couple of reasons to separate the architecture evolution from the evolution of the shortcut-connection combination. First of all, since the architecture and the shortcut connections play different roles in the performance of CNNs, which are that the architecture including the depth and the width of the CNNs represents the capacity of network and the shortcut connections are to facilitate the training process of the network, the training process is only comparable when the architecture is fixed, which inspires the idea of splitting the evolution to two levels. Secondly, if the hyperparameters of both the architecture and the shortcut connections are combined into one encoded vector, it will bring some uncertainties to the search space, which, therefore, may deteriorate the complex search space by introducing more disturbance to the search space.

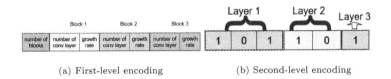

(a) First-level encoding   (b) Second-level encoding

Fig. 4. HGAPSO encoding

It is arguable that the computational cost of the two-level evolution may be high, but the two-level encoding strategy divides the complex search space into two smaller search spaces and reduces the disturbance in the search space, so

Algorithm 1. Framework of HGAPSO

$P \leftarrow$ Initialize the population with first-level encoding elaborated in Section 3.3;
$P_{best} \leftarrow$ Empty PSO Personal Best;
$G_{best} \leftarrow$ Empty PSO global best;
while first-level termination criterion is not satisfied **do**
    $P \leftarrow$ Update the population with first-level PSO evolution described in Section 3.4;
    for particle ind in population P **do**
        $P\_sub \leftarrow$ Initialize the population with second-level encoding based on the value of ind illustrated in Section 3.3;
        while second-level termination criterion is not satisfied **do**
            $P\_sub \leftarrow$ Update the population with second-level GA evolution described in Section 3.4;
            evaluate the fitness value of each individual;
            $P\_sub_{best} \leftarrow$ retrieve the best individual in P_sub;
        end while
        Update P_{best} if P_sub_{best} is better than P_{best};
    end for
    $G_{best} \leftarrow$ retrieve the best individual in P;
end while

the two-level evolution we believe will not perform worse than searching for the optima in a much more complex search space. Other than that, as the second-level evolution of searching for the best combination of shortcut connections only depends on the specific architecture evolved in the first-level evolution, the second-level evolution can be done in parallel for each of the individual of the first-level evolution, which can dramatically speed up the process if sufficient hardware is available.

HGAPSO First-Level PSO Evolution. Algorithm 2 shows the pseudo code of the PSO evolutionary process. Based on the encoded vector from the first-level encoding, the value of each dimension is a decimal value, and PSO has been proved to be effective and efficient in solving optimisation problems with decimal values, so PSO is chosen to perform the first-level search. However, the dimensionality of the encoded vector is not fixed, so an adapted variable-length PSO is proposed to solve this variable-length problem. Since the size of the input feature maps to each block is different and the specific block is trained and designed to learn meaningful features given the size of the input feature maps, when applying EC operators on two individuals, it is important to find the matched blocks which have the same size of input feature maps and apply the operators on the matched blocks. To be specific with the PSO evolution in HGAPSO, the length of the particle may be different from the length of the personal best and global best, so based on the blocks of the individual, the corresponding blocks in the personal best and the global best need to be matched by selecting the blocks with the same size of the output feature and the PSO algorithm is only applied on the matched blocks.

Algorithm 2. HGAPSO first-level PSO evolution

Input: The current particle ind, the personal best P_{best}, the global best G_{best}, the rate of changing the number of blocks r_{cb};

$rnd \leftarrow$ Generate a random number from a uniform distribution;

Find the matched blocks of the particle ind by comparing the feature map size;

Update the velocity and position of the matched blocks of the particle ind according to Equation 3 and 4;

if $rnd < r_{cb}$ **then**

    Update the velocity and position of the dimension of number of blocks of the particle ind according to Equation 3 and 4;

    Randomly cut or generate the blocks to the value of the number of blocks.

end if

The first dimension of the vector represents the number of blocks. When the number of blocks changes, the depth of the CNN architectures changes, which achieves the ability to evolve the depth of the CNN architecture and keeping the diversity of the PSO population. However, the change of the number of blocks incurs a dramatic change to the CNN architecture, and if it changes too often, each CNN architecture evolution might be too short to achieve good performance, so it is better to leave the evolution some time to optimise other hyperparameters given the specific number of blocks. In order to keep the diversity of the number of blocks and reduce the disturbance caused by frequently changing the number of blocks, the rate of changing the number of blocks in the vector is introduced, which is a real value between $[0, 1]$. Therefore, the preference for diversity or stability depending on specific tasks can be controlled by tweaking the rate of changing the number of blocks.

When the number of blocks is changed, some blocks need to be randomly cut or randomly generated in order to meet the requirement of the number of blocks in the first dimension. For example, suppose the number of blocks is increased from 3 to 4, the hyperparameters of the fourth block need to be randomly generated based on the first-level encoding strategy, which then are appended to the vector of 3 blocks; On the other way around, assuming the number of blocks is decreased from 4 to 3, the last block is removed. In the proposed HGAPSO method, whenever removing a block(s), it always starts from the last layer because it does not affect the feature map sizes of the other blocks.

HGAPSO Second-Level GA Evolution. According to the second-level encoding depicted in Sect. 3.3, once the CNN architecture is obtained from the first-level evolution, the dimensionality of the second-level encoding will be fixed, so the encoded vector can be represented by a fixed-length binary vector. Since GAs are good at optimising binary problems, a GA is chosen as the algorithm to perform the second-level evolution.

3.5   HGAPSO Fitness Evaluations

It can be observed from Algorithm 1 that fitness evaluation only takes place inside the second-level GA evolution, and the fitness of the best GA individual is used as the fitness of its corresponding particle of first-level PSO evolution. Backpropagation with Adam Optimiser [10] is used to train the network for a number of epochs on part of the training data. The accuracy of the trained CNN on the test part of the training data as the fitness value of the individual.

There are two hyperparameters for the fitness evaluations, which are the number of epochs and the initial learning rate of Adam Optimiser. In the experiment, 5 epochs are used by considering the hardware available and a fairly-short experimental time. After the number of epochs is chosen, DenseNet is used as a baseline to determine an initial learning rate for optimising a CNN with the given depth and width, i.e. after the architecture of the CNN determined, the network with fully-connected blocks are used to find a best initial learning rate among 0.9, 0.1 and 0.01.

In order to speed up the evolution process, a part of the training dataset is used for the second-level evolution because the second-level evolution consumes the most computation. While for the first-level evolution, as the computational cost is not that high, and in order to achieve a more stable performance given the architecture of a CNN, the full training dataset is used.

4   Experiment Design

4.1   Benchmark Datasets and State-of-the-Art Competitors

Due to our limited hardware resource, the DECNN method proposed in [23], which only requires a few days running of the experiment on a single GPU, is chosen as the peer EC competitor instead of the method proposed in [26], which takes 28 days on 500 GPUs to obtain the final result. The state-of-the-art machine learning algorithms used to compare with DECNN are also used as the peer Non-EC competitors. As DECNN did not perform well on CONVEX benchmark dataset [11], CONVEX dataset is selected as one of the benchmark datasets to see if the proposed HGAPSO algorithm able to achieve better performance. Apart from the CONVEX dataset, the MB and MDRBI datasets [11] are also used as benchmark datasets to evaluate the proposed algorithm across different complexities, as MB is the simplest dataset among the MB variants, and MDRBI is the most complicated variant of the MB datasets. On MB, the images represent the handwritten digits from 0 to 9, and there are 12,000 training images and 5,000 test images; MDRBI contains the same amount of training and test images, but some noises are added to the original MB dataset. The CONVEX dataset contains images with the shape of convex or non-convex, which are divided into the training dataset of 8,000 images and the test dataset of 5,000 images. Since EC methods are stochastic, the experiment will be run 30 times and statistical tests will be performed when comparing the proposed algorithm with its peer competitors.

As it would be more convincing to evaluate the proposed HGAPSO algorithm on larger datasets such as CIFAR-10, but the computational cost is too high, e.g. one run of HGAPSO on CIFAR-10 takes more than a week. Therefore, the experiment on CIFAR-10 will not be run for 30 times due to the very high

Table 1. Parameter settings

Parameter	Value	Parameter	Value
HGAPSO parameters		c_1, c_2	1.49618
the range of # of layers in each block	[4, 8]	w	0.7298
the range of growth rate in each block	[8, 32]	GA	
population size	20	mutation rate	0.01
generation	10	cross over rate	0.9
PSO		elitism rate	0.1

computational cost, our limited GPU resource and the time constraint. Instead, only one run of the experiment will be performed in order to obtain an initial result, which gives suggestions on whether it is worth continuing the experiments for 30 runs in the future when more GPU resources are ready.

4.2 Parameter Settings

All of the parameters are configured according to the conventions in the communities of PSO [22] and GAs [3] along with taking into account the computational cost and the complexity of the search space. The values of the parameters of the proposed algorithm are listed in Table 1.

5 Results and Discussions

5.1 HGAPSO vs. State-of-the-Art Methods

The experimental results and the comparison between HGAPSO and the state-of-the-art methods are shown in Table 2. In order to clearly show the comparison results, the terms (+) and (−) are provided to indicate the result of HGAPSO is significantly better or worse than the best result obtained by the corresponding peer competitor. The term (−) means there are no available results reported from the provider or cannot be counted.

It can be observed that the proposed HGAPSO method achieves a significant improvement in terms of the error rates shown in Table 2. HGAPSO significantly outperforms the other peer competitors across all the three benchmark datasets. To be specific, it further reduces the error rate over the best competitor by 5%, 1% and 10% on the CONVEX, MB and MDRBI datasets, respectively.

5.2 HGAPSO vs. DECNN

In Table 2, it can be observed that by comparing the results between HGAPSO and DECNN, both the mean error rate and the standard deviation of HGAPSO are smaller than that of DECNN, and from the statistical point of view, HGAPSO has a significant improvement in terms of the classification accuracy.

Table 2. Classification errors of HGAPSO and Competitors

Method	CONVEX		MB		MDRBI	
CAE-2		−	2.48	(+)	45.23	(+)
TIRBM		−		−	35.50	(+)
PGBM+DN-1		−		−	36.76	
ScatNet-2	6.50	(+)	1.27	(+)	50.48	(+)
RandNet-2	5.45	(+)	1.25	(+)	43.69	(+)
PCANet-2 (softmax)	4.19	(+)	1.40	(+)	35.86	(+)
LDANet-2	7.22	(+)	1.05	(+)	38.54	(+)
SVM+RBF	19.13	(+)	30.03	(+)	55.18	(+)
SVM+Poly	19.82	(+)	3.69	(+)	54.41	(+)
NNet	32.25	(+)	4.69	(+)	62.16	(+)
SAA-3	18.41	(+)	3.46	(+)	51.93	(+)
DBN-3	18.63	(+)	3.11	(+)	47.39	(+)
HGAPSO(best)	1.03		0.74		10.53	
HGAPSO(mean)	1.24		0.84		12.23	
HGAPSO(standard deviation)	0.10		0.07		0.86	
DECNN(mean)	11.19		1.46		37.55	
DECNN(standard deviation)	1.94		0.11		2.45	
P-value	0.0001		0.0001		0.0001	

5.3   Evolved CNN Architecture

After investigating the evolved CNN architectures, it is found that HGAPSO demonstrates its capability of evolving both the architecture of CNNs and the shortcut connections between layers. By looking into the evolved CNN architectures, it can be observed that not only the CNN architectures with various number of layers but also different topologies of shortcut connections are evolved. For example, one evolved CNN architecture has 3 blocks. In the first block, there are 4 convolutional layers, and [0, 0, 0, 0, 1], [0, 1, 0, 1], [0, 0, 1], [0, 0] and [1] represent the connections from the input, the first layer, the second layer, the third layer to the following layers, where 1 indicates the connection exists, and 0 means no connection; The second block is composed of 8 layers with the growth rate of 34, and the corresponding connections are [1, 0, 1, 0, 1, 0, 1, 0], [0, 1, 1, 1, 1, 0, 1], [1, 1, 1, 1, 1, 0], [1, 1, 1, 0, 1], [1, 0, 0, 0], [0, 0, 0], [1, 1] and [0]; In the third block, there are 5 layers with the corresponding connections of [0, 0, 1, 1, 0], [0, 0, 0, 0], [1, 0, 0], [0, 1] and [0], and the growth rate is 39.

5.4   One-Run Result on CIFAR-10 Dataset

As mentioned earlier, the computational cost of testing HGAPSO is extremely high. For one run of the experiment using one GPU card, it takes more than a week to evolve the CNN architecture, and it took almost 12 h to train the evolved CNN architecture. The classification accuracy of the specific run is 95.75%, which ranks the second among the state-of-the-art deep neural networks ranging from 75.86% to 96.53% that are collected by the rodrigob website[1]; However, all of the state-of-the-art deep neural networks require very highly specialised domain knowledge and tremendous experiments to manually fine-tune the performance, while HGAPSO has the ability of automatically evolving the CNN architecture without any human interference, which is considered as the biggest advantage.

---

[1] http://rodrigob.github.io/are_we_there_yet/build/classification_datasets_results.
html#43494641522d3130.

6   Conclusions

This paper developed an EC based method for automatically evolving both the architecture of CNNs and shortcut connections, without human intervention or domain knowledge in either CNNs or the target problem. The proposed method outperforms both the EC competitor and the Non-EC competitors on commonly used benchmark datasets. The first reason is that by evolving shortcut connections, the feature maps learned in previous layers can be reused in further layers, which amplifies the leverage of useful knowledge; Secondly, the shortcut connections make the training of very deep neural networks more effectively by passing the gradients through shortcut connections, which has been proven by DenseNet [7]. Furthermore, the classification accuracy of HGAPSO on CIFAR-10 is promising as it is very competitive with the state-of-the-art deep neural networks. In addition, the most advantage of HGAPSO is that it does not require any human efforts to design the architecture of CNNs, which is usually required for the peer state-of-the-art competitors.

In regard to the future work, firstly, due to the hardware limitation, the proposed algorithm has been tested on relatively small datasets. It would be more convincing if the algorithms could be tested on other larger datasets such as ImageNet dataset; secondly, as there are more and more new CNN architectures proposed with better performance, it would be helpful to investigate more recent CNN architectures, based on which EC methods can be applied to automatically evolve more advanced CNN architectures.

References

1. Bengio, Y., Simard, P., Frasconi, P.: Learning long-term dependencies with gradient descent is difficult. IEEE Trans. Neural Netw. 5(2), 157–166 (1994)
2. Chollet, F.: Xception: deep learning with depthwise separable convolutions. arXiv preprint 1610–02357 (2017)
3. Digalakis, J., Margaritis, K.: An experimental study of benchmarking functions for genetic algorithms. In: Proceedings of 2000 IEEE International Conference on Systems, Man and Cybernetics (2000). https://doi.org/10.1109/icsmc.2000.886604
4. Eberhart, Shi, Y.: Particle swarm optimization: developments, applications and resources. In: Proceedings of the 2001 Congress on Evolutionary Computation (IEEE Cat. No.01TH8546), vol. 1, pp. 81–86, May 2001. https://doi.org/10.1109/CEC.2001.934374
5. Glorot, X., Bordes, A., Bengio, Y.: Deep sparse rectifier neural networks. In: Proceedings of the Fourteenth International Conference on Artificial Intelligence and Statistics, pp. 315–323 (2011)
6. He, K., Zhang, X., Ren, S., Sun, J.: Deep residual learning for image recognition. CoRR abs/1512.03385 (2015). http://arxiv.org/abs/1512.03385
7. Huang, G., Liu, Z., Weinberger, K.Q.: Densely connected convolutional networks. CoRR abs/1608.06993 (2016). http://arxiv.org/abs/1608.06993
8. Ioffe, S., Szegedy, C.: Batch normalization: accelerating deep network training by reducing internal covariate shift. arXiv preprint arXiv:1502.03167 (2015)

9. Kennedy, J., Eberhart, R.: Particle swarm optimization. In: IEEE International Conference on Neural Networks, Proceedings, vol. 4, pp. 1942–1948, November 1995. https://doi.org/10.1109/ICNN.1995.488968
10. Kingma, D.P., Ba, J.: Adam: a method for stochastic optimization. arXiv preprint arXiv:1412.6980 (2014)
11. Larochelle, H., Erhan, D., Courville, A., Bergstra, J., Bengio, Y.: An empirical evaluation of deep architectures on problems with many factors of variation. In: Proceedings of the 24th International Conference on Machine learning, pp. 473–480. ACM (2007)
12. LeCun, Y., et al.: Backpropagation applied to handwritten zip code recognition. Neural Comput. **1**(4), 541–551 (1989)
13. Miller, J., Turner, A.: Cartesian genetic programming. In: Proceedings of the Companion Publication of the 2015 Annual Conference on Genetic and Evolutionary Computation, GECCO Companion 2015, pp. 179–198. ACM, New York (2015). https://doi.org/10.1145/2739482.2756571. http://doi.acm.org/10.1145/2739482.2756571
14. Mitchell, M.: An Introduction to Genetic Algorithms. MIT Press, Cambridge (1996)
15. Orhan, E., Pitkow, X.: Skip connections eliminate singularities. In: International Conference on Learning Representations (2018). https://openreview.net/forum?id=HkwBEMWCZ
16. Simonyan, K., Zisserman, A.: Very deep convolutional networks for large-scale image recognition, April 2015. https://arxiv.org/abs/1409.1556
17. Simonyan, K., Zisserman, A.: Very deep convolutional networks for large-scale image recognition. CoRR abs/1409.1556 (2014). https://arxiv.org/abs/1409.1556
18. Srivastava, R.K., Greff, K., Schmidhuber, J.: Training very deep networks. CoRR abs/1507.06228 (2015). http://arxiv.org/abs/1507.06228
19. Sun, Y., Xue, B., Zhang, M.: Evolving deep convolutional neural networks for image classification. CoRR abs/1710.10741 (2017). http://arxiv.org/abs/1710.10741
20. Sun, Y., Xue, B., Zhang, M., Yen, G.G.: Automatically designing CNN architectures using genetic algorithm for image classification. CoRR abs/1808.03818 (2018). http://arxiv.org/abs/1808.03818
21. Szegedy, C., et al.: Going deeper with convolutions. In: 2015 IEEE Conference on Computer Vision and Pattern Recognition (CVPR), pp. 1–9, June 2015
22. Vandenbergh, F., Engelbrecht, A.: A study of particle swarm optimization particle trajectories. Inf. Sci. **176**(8), 937–971 (2006). https://doi.org/10.1016/j.ins.2005.02.003
23. Wang, B., Sun, Y., Xue, B., Zhang, M.: A hybrid differential evolution approach to designing deep convolutional neural networks for image classification. In: Mitrovic, T., Xue, B., Li, X. (eds.) AI 2018. LNCS (LNAI), vol. 11320, pp. 237–250. Springer, Cham (2018). https://doi.org/10.1007/978-3-030-03991-2_24
24. Xie, L., Yuille, A.: Genetic CNN. In: 2017 IEEE International Conference on Computer Vision (ICCV), pp. 1388–1397, October 2017. https://doi.org/10.1109/ICCV.2017.154
25. Yamanaka, J., Kuwashima, S., Kurita, T.: Fast and accurate image super resolution by deep CNN with skip connection and network in network. In: Liu, D., Xie, S., Li, Y., Zhao, D., El-Alfy, E.S.M. (eds.) Neural Information Processing. LNCS, pp. 217–225. Springer, Cham (2017). https://doi.org/10.1007/978-3-319-70096-0_23
26. Zoph, B., Le, Q.V.: Neural architecture search with reinforcement learning. arXiv preprint arXiv:1611.01578 (2016)

Deep Feature Translation Network Guided by Combined Loss for Single Image Super-Resolution

Mingyang Guan[1], Dandan Song[1(✉)], and Linmi Tao[2,3]

[1] Beijing Engineering Research Center of High Volume Language Information Processing and Cloud Computing Applications, Beijing Lab of Intelligent Information Technology, School of Computer Science and Technology, Beijing Institute of Technology, Beijing 100081, China
sdd@bit.edu.cn
[2] Key Laboratory of Pervasive Computing, Ministry of Education, Beijing 100084, China
[3] Department of Computer Science and Technology, Tsinghua University, Beijing 100084, China

Abstract. Single image super-resolution (SISR) which aims to infer a high-resolution (HR) image from a single low-resolution (LR) image has wide applications such as surveillance and medical image processing. However, existing methods which aiming at minimizing the mean squared error (MSE) always get high objective quality, i.e., peak signal-to-noise ratios (PSNR), but their results are blurry which lacks high-frequency details thus are perceptually unsatisfying. Some recently proposed Generative Adversarial Networks enhance the perceptual quality greatly, but their objective quality is very low, which means their generated texture details are not faithful to the real image. In this paper, we adopt a multi-scale HR construction process to generate HR images gradually to achieve large upscaling factors. For each level, the generation of HR difference features from LR features is taken as a feature translation process, and deep image feature translation network (DFTN) is designed. To recover finer texture details, we combine three loss functions: content loss, a novel fine-grained texture loss and adversarial loss in our model optimization. We desire that the content loss ensures the LR results faithful to the original image, and the other two losses push our model to capture the manifold of natural images. Experiments confirm that our model can achieve the state-of-the-art results in different evaluating metrics, including both objective and perceptual quality evaluations. Therefore, our method can generate HR images with fine texture details and faithful to original images.

Keywords: Image super-resolution · Combined loss · Fine-grained texture loss · Feature translation network

© Springer Nature Switzerland AG 2019
A. C. Nayak and A. Sharma (Eds.): PRICAI 2019, LNAI 11672, pp. 664–677, 2019.
https://doi.org/10.1007/978-3-030-29894-4_53

1   Introduction

The reconstruction of high-resolution (HR) image from a low-resolution (LR) image is an important task, which is referred to as super-resolution (SR) or single image super-resolution (SISR). It has a wide range of applications, such as surveillance and medical image processing. Thus, it is a hot research area which attracted substantial attention from both academic and industrial communities. There are many classic methods for the SR problem, but this problem is still highly challenging because the reconstructed HR images always lack enough details and sharp edges.

In recent years, methods based on convolutional neural networks (CNN) [4, 9,13,16–18,24,25] are applied into the SR problem. They model the SR problem into the nonlinear low-resolution to high-resolution image mapping process, and the optimization target of these supervised SR algorithms is to minimize the pixel-wise difference such as mean squared error (MSE) between the HR image and ground truth. Therefore, their peak signal-to-noise ratio (PSNR) value exceeds traditional methods significantly in the objective quality. However, their resulted images are overly-smoothed and lack texture details, which are perceptually unsatisfying [19].

Generative adversarial networks (GANs) have shown strong ability on content generations, thus are also adopted in the SR problem. To generate more photo-realistic HR images, SRGAN [19] tries to apply perceptual loss and adversarial training on the SR problem. EnhanceNet [23] propose an application of automated texture synthesis with adding extra texture loss, besides the perceptual loss and adversarial loss. Their results show that these methods can generate images with high perceptual quality. However, their objective quality such as PSNR is very low, revealing that the results have enhanced textures but are not faithful to the original images.

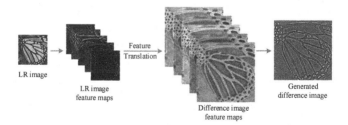

Fig. 1. Visualization of the feature translation process.

In this paper, we design a deep feature translation network (DFTN) to improve the super-resolution image quality. We adopt laplacian pyramid architecture which is a multi-scale reconstruction process that generates HR images with large upscaling factors gradually. In each level of the pyramid, for the generation of the difference image features from the LR image features, we model it as a feature translation process, and designed feature translation layers to deal with it. The intuitive visualization of the process is shown in Fig. 1. Inspired by the U-Net structure which has been successfully applied in biomedical image segmentation [22] and image-to-image translation [14], we apply a tailored U-net architecture for the DFTN structure, which consists of a contracting path to capture contexts and a expanding path to get precise localizations. Furthermore, to recover natural and realistic texture details, we combine three different losses for optimization, which contains the fundamental content loss, a novel fine-grained texture loss and the adversarial loss. We desire that the content loss ensures the SR results faithful to the original image, and the other two losses help to recover the realistic textures with high perceptual quality.

We conduct experiments on 6 benchmark datasets, and compare our model with other state-of-the-art methods using multiple evaluating metrics. Compared with methods whose optimization focus on pixel difference, our pre-trained model (DFTN-C) can obtain state-of-the-art PSNR, SSIM (Structure similarity) and IFC (Information Fidelity Criterion) scores, demonstrates the best objective quality of the results. Compared with adversarial methods, our method (DFTN-CTA) can achieve higher PSNR/SSIM/IFC scores while maintaining relatively lower FID values, which reflects better objective quality. And based on volunteers' judgment, our method achieves the highest MOS (Mean Opinion Score), satisfying to the human inception. Therefore, our method can generate natural and realistic HR images which are perceptually good and are faithful to the initial images.

2   Related Work

Prediction-based methods including bilinear interpolation, bicubic interpolation, Lanczos resampling [5] and so on have the advantage of fast speed, but their results were smoother and lack texture details. More powerful researches rely on the training data to establish a complex mapping between the LR and HR images. Example-based methods [6] always divide the entire image into small patches and create the example set to search enough examples for reconstruction. Compared to the example-based methods, dictionary-based methods [3] have higher computational efficiency since they don't need example images if they have learnt the prior knowledge.

In recent years, methods based on convolutional neural networks are applied in SR and significantly perform better than classical methods. SRCNN [4] uses a fully convolutional network to predict the nonlinear LR-HR mapping. Kim et al. propose two deep convolution network models: VDSR [16] and DRCN [17], where they show significant improvement by increasing the network depth to 20 convolutional layers. VDSR adopts global residual learning with inspiration of the success of ResNet [10]. DRCN introduces a network that contains multiple recursive layers with up to 16 recursions and adds skip connection to improve the performance. DRRN [25] combines the idea of the above two methods, using a deep recursive residual network containing 52 convolutional layers. LapSRN [18] introduce the laplacian pyramid structure to SR network, which takes coarse images and predicts high-frequency residuals. DSRN [9] proposes a dual-state recurrent network and exploits both LR and HR signals jointly. IDN [13] develops a deep but compact convolutional network to reconstruct the HR image, with fewer numbers of filters per layer and group convolution to achieve faster speed. However, the objective of above methods are aiming at minimizing the pixel-wise difference between HR image and real image, such as mean squared error (MSE). Therefore, their results have high objective quality, i.e., peak signal-to-noise ratios (PSNR). But they are always over-smoothed and lack detailed textures, thus have poor perceptual quality.

Since the generative adversarial networks (GANs) [8] came out, they have obtained great success in the field of content generation. Conditional GAN are applied to image-to-image translation problems, such as pix2pixGAN [14]. Inspired by their advancement of getting more perceptual results, some researchers have applied generative adversarial networks to the SR problems. SRGAN [19] adopt a deep residual network to recover photo-realistic textures from LR images. EnhanceNet [23] also use deep residual network trained by combined loss. These methods can achieve high perceptual quality, however, their objective quality is very low, which means their generated texture details are not faithful to the real image.

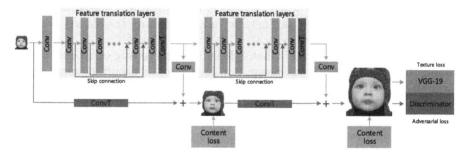

Fig. 2. Network architecture and training procedure for scale: ×4. Feature translation layers are responsible for translating the low-resolution features into the high-pass features, which has a series of skip connections and a transposed convolutional (ConvT) layer. Each level of network uses content loss and the output level has texture loss and adversarial loss. (Color figure online)

3   Proposed Method

3.1   Network Architecture

we design a deep feature translation network (DFTN) to improve the super-resolution image quality. It is a Laplacian Pyramid multi-scale structure, and feature translation layers are applied on each level.

Laplacian Pyramid. We design our multi-stage HR image reconstruction architecture to be a Laplacian Pyramid, because it can generate HR image gradually and we can apply supervised learning on each level. It can finally reach a high scale factor 2^N when the network has N levels. Figure 2 shows an example of a pyramid structure with two levels. In each level, the input image will pass 2 routes: difference image generation (green route in Fig. 2) and coarse image generation (blue route in Fig. 2).

(1) Difference image generation. The input image goes through a block of feature translation layers. These feature translation layers are responsible for translating the low-resolution features into the high-pass features, which stand for the edge structure. And the contained transposed convolutional layer upsamples the features to make its size doubled. Then the HR features pass a convolution layer and output the difference image.

(2) Coarse image generation. The $k * k$ input image goes through a transposed convolutional layer and is upsampled to be a $2k * 2k$ image. This upsampled image will be a coarse-version of the HR image.

The upsampled image is then added to the generated difference image to produce the output image (a HR image on its level). Note that these two routes are not simply fixed, but are jointly optimized in the training procedure.

Feature Translation Layers. For the generation of the difference image features from the LR image features, we model it as a feature translation process (as illustrated by Fig. 1). Accordingly, we add the feature translation layers to our super-resolution network.

Our another intuitive idea is that a defining characteristic of SR problems is to map a low resolution input image to a high resolution output image. However, the reality is that low resolution images contain less information while high resolution images need more information. Hence making full use of original information which LR image contains is very important.

Inspired of the success of image translation [14], we employ a tailored U-net structure which add the information of front layer to the back layer by using connection skips. Figure 3(a) shows our architecture of the feature translation layers. Specifically, it is a symmetrical structure and skip connections (red arrows) were placed between the i_{th} layer and the $(n-i)_{th}$ layer, where n is the total number of layers. Each skip connection concatenates all channels belonging to the i_{th} layer and the $(n-i)_{th}$ layer respectively.

Unlike previous U-net applications, this is a "feature" translation network to translate the LR image features into difference image features instead of the images. In addition, we modify the original U-net structure to adapt it for the SR task. The "barrel shape" is used in place of the "hourglass shape". More specifically, we reserve the width and height of feature maps to keep all the previous information, which is shown by Fig. 3(b).

3.2   Loss Functions

In order to get natural and realistic texture details, we use three different losses for optimization, which contains (i) content loss, (ii) fine-grained texture loss and (iii) adversarial loss. The total loss is described as follows:

$$Loss = L_{content} + \lambda_1 * L_{texture} + \lambda_2 * L_{adv} \tag{1}$$

Figure 2 shows an overview of our method for the scale of ×4. For the training phase, we downsample a training image to obtain its label images for each level. At each level, we compute the content loss between the output image and the target image. In addition, adversarial loss and fine-grained texture loss can be applied to the entire network. Note that each loss will compute the gradients from its position to the forefront LR input in the process of back propagation. We first train the DFTN using content loss only to obtain the pre-trained model and then add extra two losses.

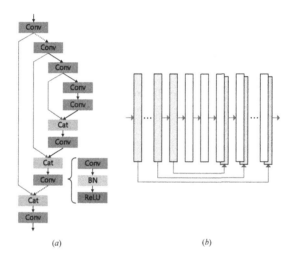

(a)   (b)

Fig. 3. Structures of our Feature Translation Layers. Here, "BN" refers to Batch Normalization, "Cat" refers to the concatenation operation. Red arrows express skip connections. Dashed arrows express the elliptical convolutional layers, which determine the depth of the total network. (Color figure online)

Content Loss. Let $\hat{y}_l$ ($l = 1, 2, 3, \ldots, L$) be the output image and the y_l be the corresponding ground truth image on the l_{th} level. The common ways are minimizing the mean square errors (MSE) between $\hat{y}_l$ and y_l. Instead of it, we adopt a differentiable variant of the L_1 norm: Charbonnier penalty function, and the total content loss is described as followed:

$$L_{content} = \sum_{l=1}^{L} \sqrt{(\hat{y}_l - y_l)^2 + \varepsilon^2} \tag{2}$$

where L is the number of levels in Laplacian pyramid. And ε is set to $1e - 6$.

Fine-Grained Texture Loss. One of the important differences between the output HR image and the target HR image is texture. In the training procedure, a patch of image would contain multiple textures because the patch size 128×128 is still large. Our intuition is that if we deal with texture in a smaller scale, the selected region would contain a same single texture. Hence, we propose a novel fine-grained texture feature extraction process, as Fig. 4 shows. We divide the whole image patch into several sub-patches and each sub-patch passes the convolutional layer to produce its own feature map. Then we join all the produced feature maps together into a tensor. Based on the tensor, the convolutional operator can conduct different weight parameters on different layers of feature maps, thus could deal with textures in a finer granularity.

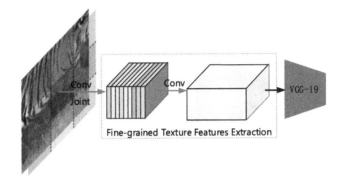

Fig. 4. An illustration of fine-grained texture features extraction.

For the detailed computation, we incorporate the method of [7,15] into our fine-grained texture loss computation. We extract fine-grained texture features of the target HR image and the generated image, and then computes the MSE differences between their Gram-matrix outputs of VGG-19:

$$L_{texture}(\hat{y}, y) = \frac{1}{BC} \|G(\phi(\hat{y})) - G(\phi(y))\|^2 \tag{3}$$

where B and C are the BatchSize and channel numbers, $\phi()$ is the output activations at ReLU5_4 of VGG-19, $\hat{y}$ and y represent the generated image and ground truth image of the last level of the Laplacian pyramid, respectively.

Conducted on an example image at $\times 4$ SR, Fig. 5 shows comparison of our model trained by content loss only, a combination of content and previous texture loss realization [7], and a combination of content and our proposed fine-grained texture loss. Obvious improvement can be noticed in the rightmost image, which demonstrates the effect of our proposed fine-grained texture loss. More visual results are available in the supplementary materials.

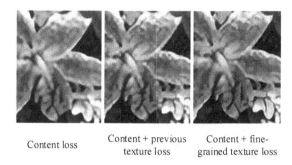

| Content loss | Content + previous texture loss | Content + fine-grained texture loss |

Fig. 5. A comparison of our model trained by content loss, "content + previous texture loss [7]" and "content + fine-grained texture loss" for an example image at ×4 SR.

Adversarial Loss. The training of Generative Adversarial Networks has obtained impressive results on many generation tasks including SR, so we also incorporate adversarial loss into our loss functions in order to get more realistic SR results. SRGAN [19] has been applied the generative adversarial network on the SR problem early and they adopt the original GAN [8]. However, the original GAN model suffers from training instability. Referring to WGAN [1] which obtains better convergence properties than the original GAN by replacing the Jensen-Shannon divergence with the Wasserstein distance, our target is designed as follows:

$$max \ \mathbb{E}_{\tilde{x} \sim \mathbb{P}_g}[D(\tilde{x})] - \mathbb{E}_{x \sim \mathbb{P}_r}[D(x)] \tag{4}$$

where $\mathbb{P}_g$ and $\mathbb{P}_r$ is the generator distribution and the real data distribution respectively.

4 Experiments and Results

4.1 Implementation Details

Similar to other SR researches, for the training set, we use 91 images from Yang et al. [28] and 200 images from the training set of Berkeley Segmentation Dataset [20], which contains 291 images totally. We evaluate our model with 6 widely used benchmark datasets: Set5 [2], Set14 [29], BSDS100 [20], Urban100 [12], Manga109 [21] and STL-10[1]. We apply data augmentation on the training set. Following [18], an image will go through three operations in turn, (1) Flipping; (2) Rotation; (3) Scaling. Then we crop HR image patches with the size of 128 × 128. We use bicubic downsampling operation to get the LR images. We implement two versions of our DFTN method with different loss functions: (1) DFTN-C: the pre-trained DFTN with content loss only; (2) DFTN-CTA: content + texture + adversarial loss.

For training strategy, we use Adam optimizer with default parameters to train our model (DFTN-C) with content loss in the pre-train procedure. As for

---

[1] http://cs.stanford.edu/~acoates/stl10.

our model DFTN (trained with combined loss), we use the RMSprop optimizer and its default setting in *Pytorch*. Note that parameters of DFTN-CTA are initialized by a pre-trained DFTN-C.

PSNR and SSIM are two classic metrics to evaluate pixel-wise and structure similarities between reconstructed and original HR images. And the IFC value which assesses the image quality based on natural scene statistics is thought to correlates well with human perceptions [27]. These three metrics are the most widely used objective quality evaluation metrics for SR task.

4.2   Evaluation on Pre-trained Model

Here we compare our pre-trained model DFTN-C with SR methods whose optimization goal is mainly using pixel-wise difference (i.e. MSE), which always achieve high objective qualities. Methods to be compared include two classic algorithms (Bicubic, A+ [26]) and six state-of-the-art CNN-based SR algorithms (SRCNN [4], DRCN [17], DRRN [25], lapSRN [18], DSRN [9] and IDN [13]).

Table 1. Quantitative evaluation of classic and convolutional neural network based SR algorithms on objective qualities: PSNR, SSIM and IFC. Red texts express the highest scores and underlined blue texts express the second highest scores.

Algorithm	Scale	Set5 PSNR/SSIM/IFC	Set14 PSNR/SSIM/IFC	BSDS100 PSNR/SSIM/IFC	Urban100 PSNR/SSIM/IFC	Manga109 PSNR/SSIM/IFC
Bicubic	×2	33.69/0.931/6.166	30.25/0.870/6.126	29.57/0.844/5.695	26.89/0.841/6.319	30.86/0.936/6.214
A+ [26]	×2	36.60/0.955/8.715	32.32/0.906/8.200	31.24/0.887/7.464	29.25/0.895/8.440	35.37/0.968/8.906
SRCNN [4]	×2	36.72/0.955/8.166	32.51/0.908/7.867	31.38/0.889/7.242	29.53/0.896/8.092	35.76/0.968/8.471
VDSR [16]	×2	37.53/0.959/8.190	33.05/0.913/7.878	31.90/0.896/7.169	30.77/0.914/8.270	37.22/0.975/9.120
DRCN [17]	×2	37.63/0.959/8.326	33.06/0.912/8.025	31.85/0.895/7.220	30.76/0.914/8.527	37.63/0.974/9.541
LapSRN [18]	×2	37.52/0.959/9.010	33.08/0.913/8.501	31.80/0.895/7.715	30.41/0.910/8.907	37.27/0.974/9.481
DRRN [25]	×2	37.74/0.959/8.671	33.23/0.914/8.320	32.05/0.897/7.613	31.23/0.919/8.917	37.92/0.976/9.268
DSRN [9]	×2	37.66/0.959/8.585	33.15/0.913/8.169	32.10/0.897/7.541	30.97/0.916/8.598	–
IDN [13]	×2	37.83/0.960/8.659	33.29/0.915/8.384	32.08/0.899/7.485	31.27/0.920/8.982	38.01/0.975/9.194
DFTN-C	×2	37.72/0.960/9.345	33.21/0.915/8.774	32.00/0.898/7.944	30.89/0.917/9.386	37.76/0.976/9.915
Bicubic	×4	28.43/0.811/2.337	26.01/0.704/2.246	25.97/0.670/1.993	23.15/0.660/2.386	24.93/0.790/2.289
A+ [26]	×4	30.32/0.860/3.260	27.34/0.751/2.961	26.83/0.711/2.565	24.34/0.721/3.218	27.03/0.851/3.177
SRCNN [4]	×4	30.50/0.863/2.997	27.52/0.753/2.766	26.91/0.712/2.412	24.53/0.725/2.992	27.66/0.859/3.045
VDSR [16]	×4	31.35/0.883/3.496	28.02/0.768/3.071	27.29/0.726/2.627	25.18/0.754/3.405	28.83/0.887/3.664
DRCN [17]	×4	31.54/0.884/3.502	28.03/0.768/3.066	27.24/0.725/2.587	25.14/0.752/3.412	28.98/0.887/3.674
LapSRN [18]	×4	31.54/0.885/3.559	28.19/0.772/3.147	27.32/0.727/2.677	25.21/0.756/3.530	29.09/0.890/3.729
DRRN [25]	×4	31.68/0.888/3.703	28.21/0.772/3.252	27.38/0.728/2.760	25.44/0.764/3.700	29.46/0.896/3.878
DSRN [9]	×4	31.40/0.883/3.500	28.07/0.770/3.147	27.25/0.724/2.599	25.08/0.747/3.297	–
IDN [13]	×4	31.82/0.889/3.744	28.25/0.774/3.282	27.41/0.731/2.757	25.41/0.764/3.685	29.42/0.895/3.881
DFTN-C	×4	31.75/0.889/3.772	28.24/0.774/3.285	27.37/0.730/2.767	25.31/0.761/3.714	29.26/0.894/3.933
Bicubic	×8	24.40/0.658/0.836	23.10/0.566/0.784	23.67/0.548/0.646	20.74/0.516/0.858	21.47/0.650/0.810
A+ [26]	×8	25.53/0.693/1.077	23.89/0.595/0.983	24.21/0.569/0.797	21.37/0.546/1.092	22.39/0.681/1.056
SRCNN [4]	×8	25.33/0.690/0.938	23.76/0.591/0.865	24.13/0.566/0.705	21.29/0.544/0.947	22.46/0.695/1.013
VDSR [16]	×8	25.93/0.724/1.199	24.26/0.614/1.067	24.49/0.583/0.859	21.70/0.571/1.199	23.16/0.725/1.263
DRCN [17]	×8	25.93/0.723/1.192	24.25/0.614/1.057	24.49/0.582/0.854	21.71/0.571/1.197	23.20/0.724/1.257
LapSRN [18]	×8	26.15/0.738/1.302	24.35/0.620/1.133	24.54/0.586/0.893	21.81/0.581/1.288	23.39/0.735/1.352
DRRN [25]	×8	26.18/0.738/1.307	24.42/0.622/1.127	24.59/0.587/0.891	21.88/0.583/1.299	23.60/0.742/1.406
DFTN-C	×8	26.22/0.745/1.389	24.46/0.624/1.184	24.58/0.588/0.924	21.93/0.589/1.388	23.66/0.749/1.480

We show our quantitative results on these objective quality metrics in Table 1. Our model has obtained competitive PSNR and SSIM results in most datasets and scales. Especially, we have improved a lot and achieved new state-of-the-art results in the Information Fidelity Criterion (IFC), which has been shown to reflect the human perception of SR results best [27]. Figure 6 show the visual comparisons of two examples from BSDS100 and Manga109 datasets. From this figure, we can easily draw a conclusion that our model has obtained more clear straight lines, more clear texts, and sharper edge, while other methods' results are more blurry.

Table 2. Comparison of PSNR, SSIM and IFC on state-of-the-art methods that focus on human perception for the scale ×4.

Algorithm	Set5 PSNR/SSIM/IFC	Set14 PSNR/SSIM/IFC	BSDS100 PSNR/SSIM/IFC	Manga109 PSNR/SSIM/IFC	Urban100 PSNR/SSIM/IFC
SRGAN	28.20/0.817/2.537	25.86/0.700/2.154	24.63/0.643/1.806	23.68/0.700/2.470	26.49/0.832/2.549
EnhanceNet	28.57/0.809/2.647	24.95/0.653/2.008	24.14/0.605/1.426	23.55/0.694/2.655	20.44/0.674/1.101
DFTN-CTA	**29.76/0.846/3.143**	**26.45/0.712/2.685**	**25.67/0.665/2.342**	**23.97/0.710/3.076**	**27.38/0.849/3.195**

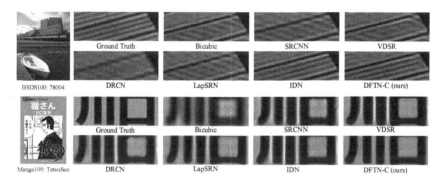

Fig. 6. Visual comparison on pre-trained model. **Top**: Results of "78004" from the BSDS100 with the scale ×2. **Bottom**: Results of "TetsuSan" from the Manga109 with the scale ×4.

4.3 Comparison with Adversarial Training Methods

Thanks to GAN's excellent performance in generating real data distribution, some GAN-based methods such as SRGAN [19] and EnhanceNet [23] have make progress in enhancing the perceptual quality of LR images. However, their reconstructed images have very low objective quality (with very low PSNR and SSIM values) and thus are not faithful to original images. As Table 2 shows, our model with combined loss functions (DFTN-CTA) performs better than SRGAN and EnhanceNet in the objective quality, with higher PSNR, SSIM and IFC. For example, DFTN-CTA improve PSNR with 1.04 dB and 1.53 dB over SRGAN and EnhanceNet in the BSDS100 dataset.

| SRGAN | EnhanceNet | DFTN-CAT | Ground truth |

Fig. 7. Visual comparison between our model and previous methods on two example images from Set5 and Set14 for the scale ×4.

Table 3. Comparison of FID on state-of-the-art adversarial training based methods in the STL-10 dataset for the scale ×4. Bold texts express the highest score and underlined texts express the second highest score.

Dataset	IDN	SRGAN	EnhanceNet	DFTN-C	DFTN-CTA
STL-10	107.872	**31.326**	35.411	97.671	<u>33.952</u>

Fréchet Inception Distance (FID) is a widely used quantitative evaluation metric to evaluate the perceptual quality of the generated images. Similar to the image generation task, super-resolution model get the LR image input and generate the HR images. Based on this similarity, we **first** introduce the Fréchet Inception Distance (FID) for quantitative SR results evaluation. According to [11], FID can measure the distance between two data distributions. The lower FID score indicates higher similarity between generated data distribution and real one. We desire it to be an overall indicator to reflect the similarity between the original HR images distribution and reconstructed one.

Table 4. MOS comparison results of state-of-the-art methods on the Set5 and Set14 for the scale ×4. Bold text express the highest score.

Algorithm	SRCNN	DRCN	LAPSRN	DRRN	IDN	SRGAN	EnhanceNet	DFTN-C	DFTN-CTA
Set5	2.28	2.97	3.02	3.15	3.26	3.38	<u>3.45</u>	3.28	**3.56**
Set14	2.43	2.91	2.91	2.98	3.21	3.30	<u>3.35</u>	3.22	**3.36**

More specifically, we use the dataset STL-10 as the benchmark dataset. We select 20000 images with the size of 96 × 96 from the unlabeled set and downsample them to get the LR images at the scale ×4. We apply SR algorithms to these LR images and compute FID between the set of original images and SR images.

As Table 3 shows, although the FID of our model is higher than SRGAN, our model DFTN-CTA get relatively low FID scores. Our pre-trained model DFTN-C also obtains lower FID than IDN [13], which has similar pixel-wise loss. Above results confirms the results of our method have better perceptual quality.

4.4   Mean Opinion Score Testing

Due to the disadvantages existing in current object and perceptual quality evaluation metrics, for a more reasonable and intuitive evaluation, following SRGAN [19], we use MOS testing to assess the comprehensive quality of images that are reconstructed by our model. Specifically, we invite 20 volunteers to rate on a five-point scale (1: bad quality, 5: excellent quality) on the SR results. Volunteers has rated different versions of images from dataset Set5, and Set14, which include SRCNN, DRCN, LAPSRN, DRRN, IDN, SRGAN, EnhanceNet and our four DFTN models. For each image of all datasets, we calibrate the raters by setting the bicubic (score: 1) and original HR (score: 5) versions for each image. We show the mean opinion score testing results by Table 4, our DFTN-CTA version has obtained the new state-of-the-art scores. The results confirm that our model can confirm to the human perception better.

We plot SR results from adversarial training based methods (SRGAN, EnhanceNet and DFTN-CTA) for the scale ×4, which are shown by Fig. 7. We can see that adversarial training based methods can produce clearer and sharper SR image, but some of their textures have many noisy points or artificial information which is different from the true HR images. Compared with SRGAN and EnhanceNet, our model DFTN-CTA reduces noise while looking into details, which not only improves the perceptual quality, but also reconstruct the images more faithful to the target HR images.

5   Conclusion

In this work, we propose a super-resolution deep feature translation network (DFTN) with Laplacian Pyramid architecture. At each level of pyramid, we translate the LR image feature into difference image feature. To enhance detail information, we combine three loss functions: content loss, fine-grained texture loss and adversarial loss in our model optimization. For different evaluation metrics including objective and perceptual quality metrics and MOS testing, the proposed DFTN achieve state-of-the-art results. Extensive experimental results confirm strongly that our model can improve perceptual quality and maintain object quality at the same time.

Acknowledgement. This work was supported by National Key Research and Development Program of China (Grant No. 2016YFB1000902) and the project of National Science Foundation of China (No.61672017).

References

1. Arjovsky, M., Chintala, S., Bottou, L.: Wasserstein GAN (2017)
2. Bevilacqua, M., Roumy, A., Guillemot, C., Morel, A.: Low-complexity single-image super-resolution based on nonnegative neighbor embedding. In: BMVC (2012)
3. Dai, D., Timofte, R., Van Gool, L.: Jointly optimized regressors for image super-resolution. Comput. Graph. Forum **34**(2), 95–104 (2015)
4. Dong, C., Chen, C.L., He, K., Tang, X.: Image super-resolution using deep convolutional networks. IEEE Trans. Pattern Anal. Mach. Intell. **38**(2), 295–307 (2016)
5. Duchon, C.E.: Lanczos filtering in one and two dimensions. J. Appl. Meteorol. **18**(8), 1016–1022 (1979)
6. Freeman, W.T., Jones, T.R., Pasztor, E.C.: Example-Based Super-Resolution. IEEE Computer Society Press, Washington, D.C. (2002)
7. Gatys, L.A., Ecker, A.S., Bethge, M.: Texture synthesis using convolutional neural networks. In: NIPS (2015)
8. Goodfellow, I.J., et al.: Generative adversarial networks. Adv. Neural Inf. Process. Syst. **3**, 2672–2680 (2014)
9. Han, W., Chang, S., Liu, D., Yu, M., Witbrock, M., Huang, T.S.: Image super-resolution via dual-state recurrent networks. In: Proceedings of the IEEE Conference on Computer Vision and Pattern Recognition (2018)
10. He, K., Zhang, X., Ren, S., Sun, J.: Deep residual learning for image recognition. In: IEEE Conference on Computer Vision and Pattern Recognition, pp. 770–778 (2016)
11. Heusel, M., Ramsauer, H., Unterthiner, T., Nessler, B., Hochreiter, S.: Gans trained by a two time-scale update rule converge to a local nash equilibrium. Adv. Neural Inf. Process. Syst. **30**, 6626–6637 (2017)
12. Huang, J.B., Singh, A., Ahuja, N.: Single image super-resolution from transformed self-exemplars. In: Computer Vision and Pattern Recognition, pp. 5197–5206 (2015)
13. Hui, Z., Wang, X., Gao, X.: Fast and accurate single image super-resolution via information distillation network. In: The IEEE Conference on Computer Vision and Pattern Recognition (CVPR), June 2018
14. Isola, P., Zhu, J., Zhou, T., Efros, A.A.: Image-to-image translation with conditional adversarial networks, pp. 5967–5976 (2016)
15. Johnson, J., Alahi, A., Fei-Fei, L.: Perceptual losses for real-time style transfer and super-resolution. In: Leibe, B., Matas, J., Sebe, N., Welling, M. (eds.) ECCV 2016. LNCS, vol. 9906, pp. 694–711. Springer, Cham (2016). https://doi.org/10.1007/978-3-319-46475-6_43
16. Kim, J., Lee, J.K., Lee, K.M.: Accurate image super-resolution using very deep convolutional networks. In: IEEE Conference on Computer Vision and Pattern Recognition, pp. 1646–1654 (2016)
17. Kim, J., Lee, J.K., Lee, K.M.: Deeply-recursive convolutional network for image super-resolution. In: IEEE Conference on Computer Vision and Pattern Recognition, pp. 1637–1645 (2016)
18. Lai, W.S., Huang, J.B., Ahuja, N., Yang, M.H.: Deep Laplacian pyramid networks for fast and accurate super-resolution. In: IEEE Conference on Computer Vision and Pattern Recognition, pp. 5835–5843 (2017)
19. Ledig, C., et al.: Photo-realistic single image super-resolution using a generative adversarial network. In: Computer Vision and Pattern Recognition, pp. 105–114 (2017)

20. Martin, D., Fowlkes, C., Tal, D., Malik, J.: A database of human segmented natural images and its application to evaluating segmentation algorithms and measuring ecological statistics. In: Proceedings Eighth IEEE International Conference on Computer Vision, ICCV 2001, vol. 2, pp. 416–423, July 2001. https://doi.org/10.1109/ICCV.2001.937655

21. Matsui, Y., et al.: Sketch-based Manga retrieval using Manga109 dataset. Multimed. Tools Appl. **76**(20), 21811–21838 (2017)

22. Ronneberger, O., Fischer, P., Brox, T.: U-Net: convolutional networks for biomedical image segmentation. In: Navab, N., Hornegger, J., Wells, W.M., Frangi, A.F. (eds.) MICCAI 2015. LNCS, vol. 9351, pp. 234–241. Springer, Cham (2015). https://doi.org/10.1007/978-3-319-24574-4_28

23. Sajjadi, M.S.M., Schölkopf, B., Hirsch, M.: Enhancenet: single image super-resolution through automated texture synthesis. In: IEEE International Conference on Computer Vision, pp. 4501–4510 (2017)

24. Shi, W., et al.: Real-time single image and video super-resolution using an efficient sub-pixel convolutional neural network. In: Computer Vision and Pattern Recognition, pp. 1874–1883 (2016)

25. Tai, Y., Yang, J., Liu, X.: Image super-resolution via deep recursive residual network. In: IEEE Conference on Computer Vision and Pattern Recognition, pp. 2790–2798 (2017)

26. Timofte, R., De Smet, V., Van Gool, L.: A+: adjusted anchored neighborhood regression for fast super-resolution. In: Cremers, D., Reid, I., Saito, H., Yang, M.-H. (eds.) ACCV 2014. LNCS, vol. 9006, pp. 111–126. Springer, Cham (2015). https://doi.org/10.1007/978-3-319-16817-3_8

27. Yang, C.-Y., Ma, C., Yang, M.-H.: Single-image super-resolution: a benchmark. In: Fleet, D., Pajdla, T., Schiele, B., Tuytelaars, T. (eds.) ECCV 2014. LNCS, vol. 8692, pp. 372–386. Springer, Cham (2014). https://doi.org/10.1007/978-3-319-10593-2_25

28. Yang, J., Wright, J., Huang, T.S., Ma, Y.: Image super-resolution via sparse representation. IEEE Trans. Image Process. **19**(11), 2861–2873 (2010)

29. Zeyde, R., Elad, M., Protter, M.: On single image scale-up using sparse-representations. In: Boissonnat, J.-D., et al. (eds.) Curves and Surfaces 2010. LNCS, vol. 6920, pp. 711–730. Springer, Heidelberg (2012). https://doi.org/10.1007/978-3-642-27413-8_47

Heterogeneity-Oriented Immunization Strategy on Multiplex Networks

Yingchu Xin[1], Chunyu Wang[1], Yali Cui[2], Chao Gao[1], and Xianghua Li[1(✉)]

[1] College of Computer and Information Science, Southwest University,
Chongqing 400715, China
li_xianghua@163.com
[2] Guangdong College of Business and Technology, Zhaoqing 526020,
Guangdong, China

Abstract. Many real-world complex systems can be treated as multiplex networks and there have constantly been unwanted diffusion (e.g., computer viruses, rumors, and epidemics) running on top of them. These type of network risks often lead to the global economic burden every year. Centrality-based immunization is an important approach to reduce the cost of preventing such unexpected massive outbreaks, for its effectiveness in cutting off the dissemination paths to delay the propagation. However, most of the current strategies on multiplex networks only focus on the topological structures when evaluating the influence of nodes, and the heterogeneity of individual behaviors has been less addressed. This paper proposes a heterogeneity-oriented (HO) immunization strategy for multiplex networks based on heterogeneous features of nodes. Specifically, the HO strategy treats nodes as independent agents, and the behaviors of them are defined and quantified in each layer. After coupling with the topological factor, this strategy is able to characterize the importance of nodes which can further be used for pre-immunization to delay the detrimental propagation. To testify the effectiveness, plenty of experiments are conducted based on a multi-agent email model. The results on large real-world and synthetic multiplex networks show that our strategy outperforms the existing representative strategies and effectively delay the propagation.

Keywords: Multiplex networks · Individual heterogeneity · Network immunization · Multi-agent systems

1 Introduction

Network theory is an important tool for analyzing complex systems [1,2]. From social to science fields, almost all the systems can be represented as the interconnected networks: "nodes" are defined as the individuals, and "edges" denote the ties between pairs of nodes. In the last years, more and more studies start to characterize the interactions between networks and other networks [3,4]. The system

© Springer Nature Switzerland AG 2019
A. C. Nayak and A. Sharma (Eds.): PRICAI 2019, LNAI 11672, pp. 678–690, 2019.
https://doi.org/10.1007/978-3-030-29894-4_54

composed of several layers of subnetworks is called multiplex network. In different layers, nodes still belong to the same sets [5], but the relationships and physical meanings of them differ extremely [6,7]. Through links within each subnetwork and external channels that connect all subnetworks, the dynamical processes could go all over the whole interconnected network. Hence, multiplex networks provide ideal inner structures for studying the real-world dynamics [8,9]. The problem of controlling different diffusion phenomena is also transformed into how to protect multiplex networks effectively.

Centrality-based immunization is an effective approach to achieve the goal. By immunizing (or removing) parts of the most important nodes to cut off the contagion paths, the propagation could be effectively delayed. In previous studies, a number of strategies have been proposed for the purpose of immunization [10,11]. For example, Betweenness [12] is a classical strategy which identifies centrality based on the shortest path within layers and between layers; PageRank [13] on the other hand, characterizes node centrality by considering the importance of its neighbors. Although these strategies have exploited the topological characteristics, the heterogeneous features of nodes have been less considered [8], especially when the complexity and diversity of real-world systems are emerging rapidly.

In the recent few years, more and more researches have revealed that heterogeneous peculiarities of nodes have a strong impact on the identification of node centrality [14,15]. In multiplex networks, the individual heterogeneity of nodes can be found in many fields. For instance, it can be denoted as the different tendencies towards innovation adoption [14]; or represents divergent awareness to the epidemic spreading process [15,16]. On the other hand, the heterogeneity provides a new view of nodes. Nodes are treated as the independent agents and they behave differently in the propagation process. Through this way, real situations could be simulated in a more general and comprehensive way, which is essential towards optimizing the immunization strategy. Hence, to measure the node centrality, both topology and heterogeneity factors should be taken into consideration.

In this paper, we define the *HO* strategy from three aspects: (1) structure centrality, (2) activity rank and (3) spread rank. Specifically, structure centrality measures the topological importance of nodes, activity rank and spread rank quantify the activity level and spread ability of the nodes, respectively. By tactfully combining the three elements and immunizing nodes based on the *HO* strategy, less cost and high efficiency could be achieved. For testing our strategy, plenty of experiments are conducted on large real-world and synthetic multiplex networks based on a multi-agent email model [17]. As shown in the results, our *HO* strategy outperforms the existing immunization strategies and can restrain the propagation process effectively [18]. Our main contributions can be summarized as follows:

(1) A unique heterogeneity-oriented immunization strategy is proposed. It could accurately measure the node centrality on multiplex networks, then through immunizing accordingly, the propagation could be delayed effectively.

(2) The effectiveness of our proposed strategy is testified on different types of multiplex networks, and the comparisons are made with the existing representative strategies.

The rest of the paper is organized as follows: Sect. 2 describes the model definition and algorithm. Section 3 provides the detailed descriptions and formulations of our proposed method. Section 4 represents some of the experiment results as well as analyses. Finally, Sect. 5 states conclusions.

2 Preliminary

This section provides the theoretical foundation of our work. Specifically, Sect. 2.1 introduces the dynamics of a multi-agent email model. Section 2.2 analyzes the model applicability on multiplex networks and presents the detailed propagation algorithm.

2.1 Model Descriptions

Email model [17] is an interactive multi-agent model which depends on two primary user behaviors: check email box and open email attachments. A node becomes activated when it is checking the email box, after this, it has a possibility to open the malicious attachments. Once the node gets infected, it would immediately send one malicious attachment to its neighbors. Assume a multiplex network with two layers, specifically, layer A and layer B own the same set of nodes but with the different edge pairs, and each layer represents one independent social and communication environment.

Consider the non-reinfection case, initially ρ_0 of nodes are selected as the first infected sources, in this paper $\rho_0 = 2/N$, namely two-origin infection. Let $D(x)$ denote the probability generating function of node degrees of each layer:

$$D(x) = \sum_{k=1}^{\infty} P_X(d = k)x^k \tag{1}$$

$P(d = k)$ is the probability that a node is of degree k in layer X. When all nodes have the same probability to open the malicious attachments, i.e., $P_i = p, (i = 1, 2, ...|V|)$, the lower bound of the $E[N_{\infty}^h]$ is derived which denotes the average number of uninfected nodes when the propagation is terminated:

$$E_A[N_{\infty}^h] \geq |V| \sum_{k=1}^{\infty} P_A(d = k)(1 - p)^k = |V|G(1 - p) \tag{2}$$

$$E_B[N_{\infty}^h] \geq |V| \sum_{k=1}^{\infty} P_B(d = k)(1 - p)^k = |V|G(1 - p) \tag{3}$$

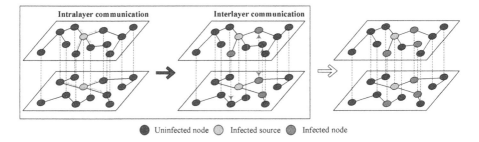

Uninfected node   ◯ Infected source   ◉ Infected node

Fig. 1. Illustration of a propagation on a double-layer multiplex network. There are two key points: (1) overlapped infection exists in the propagation; (2) a node is changed to infected state in all layers even if it gets infected in only one of them.

2.2 Propagation Algorithm

Different from the single-layer propagation, situations are more complicated in multiplex networks. First, the propagation proceeds simultaneously on all of the layers. This step is called **intralayer communication**. Then, during the propagation, the status of nodes would be updated to keep the consistency between layers. This step is called **interlayer communication**. The detailed mechanism can be seen in Fig. 1, and the process is specified in Algorithm 1.

Algorithm 1. Propagation on multiplex networks

Input: The edge and node information data of all X layers in a network G
Output: A matrix $R[k][t]$, which denotes the average proportion of infected nodes at each time step during k^{th} simulation

1. InitNetwork(filename);
2. /* **start propagation** */
3. **For** $k = 1$ to R **do** //An average value is obtained after running R times
4.   InitialInfection(ρ_0); //Initially infecting ρ_0 of nodes randomly
5.   **While** $t < T$ **do** //There are T time steps at each run
6.   **For** $i = 1$ to N in layer z ($z = 1,2,...,X$) **do** //Traverse every node in all
7. X layers
8.   **If** $v_z^i.timeInterval.get(t) == 0$ **then** //The node is activated now
9. $Prob$ = probGenerator(); //compute the probability of clicking a
10.   virus email based on β and $virusNum$
11.   **If** rand() $< prob$ **then**
12.   **If** $v_z^i.status ==$ danger **then**
13. $v_z^i.status =$ infected
14.   update v_z^i status ($z = 1,2,...,X$)
15. v_z^i spreading virus to its neighbors
16. $R[k][t] = I_t$;
17.   resetNode(); //reset the status of nodes

To estimate the performance of one propagation, the average proportion of infected nodes I at time step t is defined as follows:

$$I_t = \frac{\sum v_z^i | v_z^i.status = infected}{N_z} \quad z = \forall z \in (1, 2, ..., X) \tag{4}$$

X is the number of layers and N_z is the number of nodes in any of the layers. Notice that z is equal to any value in set $(1, 2, ..., X)$, this is because the status of nodes is updated among layers immediately.

3   Method

This section presents the detailed principals of our proposed method. The notions of activity rank are first defined in Sect. 3.1. Then, Sect. 3.2 gives the measurement of spread rank. Finally, Sect. 3.3 derives the final formulation of *HO centrality*.

3.1   Activity Rank

The activity rank measures the activity level of an entity [19], and the activities of entities are different in different situations. For example, in the email networks, agents may execute the email-box checking and clicking behaviors [17,18]; in the geographical networks [20], humans may have the migration behaviors; or in the movie networks [21], users may have the rating behaviors. In multiplex networks, one entity has different activity rank in a different layer of the network. Consider a Facebook-twitter double layer network, if an individual is a frequent Facebook user and an indifferent twitter user at the same time, the activity frequency it shows on these two different layers would vary in a great extent. In this paper, the expected values of activity time intervals are formulated to measure the level of such activities.

Given a multiplex network with X layers, for each layer z, the ith node is denoted as v_i, L_z^i is the corresponding activity time interval queue defined in Eq. (4). In this paper, the normal distribution $N(40, 20^2)$ is adopted to depict the attributes of L_z^i based on [17].

$$L_z^i = \{l_z^{i1}, l_z^{i2} \ldots l_z^{im}\} \tag{5}$$

The activity time interval queue implies the specific time point the node get activated and the length of one sleep time span. To measure the effect of activity time interval, the activity rank is defined as follows:

$$Q_z(i) = \frac{\sum_{h=1}^{m} l_i h}{m} \tag{6}$$

$$AR_z(i) = -\ln \frac{Q_z(i)}{\sum_{i=1}^{n} Q_z(i)} \tag{7}$$

By the definition of activity rank, the smaller $Q(i)$ is, the more active the node v_i becomes. After the transformation in Eq. (7), AR is able to describe the activity levels of nodes based on $Q(i)$.

3.2   Spread Rank

Besides the activity rank, the spread rank is the other heterogeneity feature of nodes, which quantifies the spread ability of a node. A parameter β is taken to measure such spreading capacity of nodes. The meanings of spread rank also differ as the definitions of the research fields vary. For instance, in the email networks, the spread ability represents the worm emails clicking probability [18]; or in the social networks, it means the information forwarding ability [22].

However, different from the activity rank, the spread rank of an individual is the same in any of the layers. In general, the spread ability is an inherent attribute of a node. Hence, for a specific node, such an intrinsic ability is stationary regardless of environments (i.e., layers). Besides, some studies have shown that the spread abilities of nodes in a network can be characterized by the normal distribution in a statistical way [17]. In other words, most of the nodes are normal spreaders, only a few nodes have extremely strong or weak spread abilities. In this paper, $N(0.5, 0.3^2)$ [17] is used to describe the distribution of β in each layer.

3.3   HO Centrality

Sections 3.1 and 3.2 have provided the definitions of two core heterogeneity factors, to derive the final formulation, one topology factor is added into our proposed *HO centrality*.

Our motivation is to formulate an immunization strategy which tactfully combines the topology and heterogeneity factors, and can finally be used to better characterize the importance of a node. Consequently, a balance is made between three factors, and the situations all of the layers are considered. In a multiplex network with X layers, the gross *HO centrality* of a node is defined as follows [11]:

$$HO\ centrality(i) = \frac{1}{X} \sum_{z=1}^{z=X} structure\ centrality_z(i) * AR_z(i) * \beta(i) \quad (8)$$

For node i, *structure centrality* and *AR* are different among layers while β stays the same. After averaging the effect of X layers, the final *HO centrality* could be derived. For the rationality, if a node takes an important topological position, but it is inactivated or it has no spread ability (i.e., $AR(i)_z = 0$ or $\beta(i) = 0$) in layer z, this node would be considered incapable of spreading in layer z. Vice Versa, a node cannot spread virus if it is isolated in layer z (i.e., *structure centraliy$_z$(i)* = 0). By such a fusion, extreme situations above could be simulated. The illustration of *HO* strategy is shown in Fig. 2.

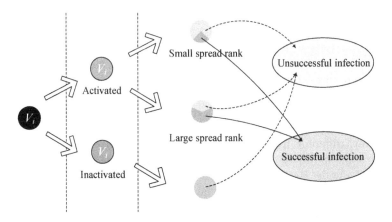

Fig. 2. Propagation details by initially immunizing nodes based on HO method. It can be seen that a successful infection only happens when the node is activated, and its possibility is higher when the spread rank is higher at the same time.

4   Experiments

The details of the experiments are stated in this section. Specifically, Sect. 4.1 describes the procedures of preprocessing data and datasets being used. Then in Sect. 4.2, the effectiveness of our proposed HO method is tested and its immunization efficiency is compared with structural strategies and AR methods [17].

4.1   Datasets and Preprocessing

In our experiments, two real-world and two synthetic multiplex networks with different layers are used as the import data. For real-world networks, G_1 is obtained from twitter [23], and three layers of relationships correspond to retweet, mentions, and replies observed between. G_2 is the biological network which contains three different types of genetic interactions [24] including (1) Direct interaction, (2) Physical association and (3) Association. Besides, for the two synthetic networks, G_3 is generated by BA algorithm [25] and G_4 is a random network. The detailed information is summarized in Table 1.

For preprocessing, there are three main steps in each simulation: (1) Sort the nodes in descending order based on their centralities calculated by different strategies; (2) Initially set $\rho_0 = 2/N$ of nodes as infected sources; (3) Start propagation based on Algorithm 1, and all results are averaged over 100 runs and the total simulation time is $T = 600$ in each run.

Table 1. Networks used in our experiments. The total number of nodes and edges of a network are denoted as $|N|$ and $|E|$, respectively. The number of layers is denoted by $|L|$. Type is the feature of edges and Range is main information of the network.

ID	Networks	$|N|$	E	$|L|$	Type	Range
G_1	NYClimateMarch2014	102439	102439	3	Undirected	Twitter
G_2	PLASMODIUM	1023	2521	3	Undirected	Biological
G_3	BA	10000	7182	2	Undirected	Synthetic
G_4	ER	1115	6932	2	Undirected	Synthetic

Based on the network data and procedures above, the node centrality could be extracted by applying different strategies. For the *HO centrality*, the calculation algorithm is specified in Algorithm 2.

Algorithm 2. Immunization on multiplex networks by *HO centrality*

Input: The edge and node information data of all X layers in network G
Output: Network G with $\rho_0 = 2/N$ immunized nodes
1. InitNetwork(filename);
2. **For** $i = 1$ to N **do**
3. $v_i.beta = $ betaGenerator(*average, variance*); //generate the spread rank
4.   based on the parameters of the normal distribution
5..   **For** $z = 1$ to X **do**
6. $v_z^i.timeInterval = $ timeGenerator(T); //generate the activity time interval
4.   queue based on simulation time
5. /* **Immunization by** *HO* **strategy** */
6. *sorted* = sort(); //sort all *centralities* in descending order
7. **For** $i = 1$ to $N * p\%$ of *sorted* in layer z ($z = 1, 2,...,X$) **do**
8. $v_z^i.status = $ immunized; //Selecting top $p\%$ ($p = 5\%, 10\%, 30\%$ in this paper)
9. $\cdot$ of nodes to be immunized

4.2 Evaluation of Performance

In this section, the efficiency of *HO* is evaluated by comparing with: (1) Degree [11]: Immunizing the nodes with the highest average number of neighbors between layers at once. (2) Betweenness [12]: Immunizing nodes based on shortest paths. (3) PageRank [13]: Immunizing the nodes which have the neighbors with the best qualities. (4) AR [19]: Immunizing the nodes by the fusion of activity rank with a topology-based strategy.

Figures 3, 4 and 5 illustrate the efficiency comparison results with immunization rate $p = 10\%$. Table 2 provides the statistical results between Degree and HO_{degree} in every 100 time steps as an example. It is conspicuous that:

(1) The speed of epidemic propagation is extremely high on multiplex networks, the infection rate is close to a steady state at $T = 400$. This is because, in every time step, the newly infected individuals have a significant diversity in different layers, and such an effect is cross-layer. In other words, because of the low-overlapping rate [14] of an infection, the virus could get disseminated more easily.

(2) Compared with the single topology-based immunization strategies, the heterogeneity-oriented methods (AR and HO) can improve the immunization efficiency remarkably under the same condition (i.e., the same immunization rate and network structures). At the same time, all the HO methods are more efficacious than the AR methods. Such results prove that the spread ability has a noteworthy impact on immunization efficiency and it could be applied on multiplex networks.

(3) Under the same condition, the HO methods combining with different structure centralities perform diversely due to the differences between networks. This is because when the heterogeneity factor is kept the same, the structure of a network is the main factor that makes the difference.

Table 2. Comparisons between average infected proportions of Degree and HO_{degree} in every 100 time steps. It's conspicuous that the propagation speed of HO_{degree} is much lower than Degree's.

Networks	TimeStep						
	Strategy	100	200	300	400	500	600
G_1	Degree	0.564	0.851	0.914	0.939	0.949	0.952
	HO_{degree}	0.305	0.751	0.862	0.906	0.915	0.919
G_2	Degree	0.019	0.428	0.900	0.973	0.892	0.899
	HO_{degree}	0.012	0.348	0.721	0.851	0.870	0.876
G_3	Degree	0.371	0.882	0.899	0.899	0.899	0.899
	HO_{degree}	0.151	0.734	0.868	0.886	0.886	0.886
G_4	Degree	0.182	0.582	0.799	0.867	0.875	0.875
	HO_{degree}	0.164	0.585	0.720	0.837	0.875	0.875

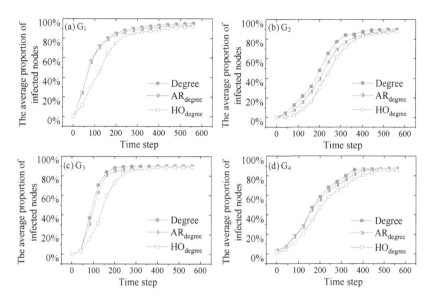

Fig. 3. Comparison results of the propagation in G_1–G_4 between Degree, AR_{degree} and HO_{degree}. It is obvious that the infection process is the slowest when immunizing nodes by HO_{degree}, which proves that the efficiency of HO method is better.

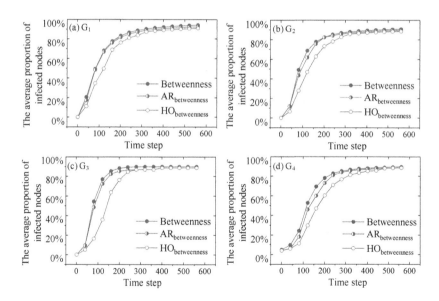

Fig. 4. Comparison results of the propagation in G_1–G_4 between Betweenness, $AR_{betweenness}$ and $HO_{betweenness}$. It is obvious that the infection process is the slowest when immunizing nodes by $HO_{betweenness}$, which proves that the efficiency of HO method is better.

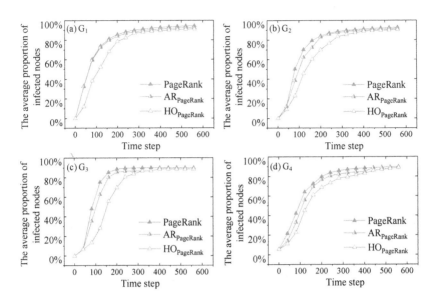

Fig. 5. Comparison results of the propagation in G_1–G_4 between PageRank, $AR_{PageRank}$ and $HO_{PageRank}$. It is obvious that the infection process is the slowest when immunizing nodes by $HO_{PageRank}$, which proves that the efficiency of HO method is better.

5   Conclusions

In this paper, a heterogeneity-oriented (HO) immunization strategy is proposed. To elucidate our strategy, two core elements (i.e., activity rank, spread rank) are first defined, then by tactfully combining with the structure centrality, the final formulation is derived. Besides, a multi-agent email model is presented as the simulation platform, and plenty of comparison experiments are conducted on large real-world and synthetic multiplex networks. The main findings can be concluded as: (1) HO strategy outperforms the single topology-based immunization strategies as well as the existing heterogeneity-oriented method (AR); (2) Due to the low-overlapping rate of the infection, the speed of the propagation on multiplex networks is typically high in different networks. However, HO strategy could still slow the spreading process to some extent.

Future works include (1) to find the effect of overlapping rate on the propagation and (2) to test the parameters of distribution on the efficiency of HO strategy.

Acknoledgement. This work is supported by National Natural Science Foundation of China (Nos. 61602391,61403315, 61402379), Natural Science Foundation of Chongqing (No. cstc2018jcyjAX0274), in part of Chongqing Training Programs of Innovation and Entrepreneurship for Undergraduates.

References

1. Pastor Satorras, R., Castellano, C., Van Mieghem, P., Vespignani, A.: Epidemic processes in complex networks. Rev. Mod. Phys. **87**(3), 925 (2015)
2. Goodarzinick, A., Niry, M.D., Valizadeh, A., Perc, M.: Robustness of functional networks at criticality against structural defects. Phys. Rev. E **98**(2), 022312 (2018)
3. Vespignani, A.: Modelling dynamical processes in complex socio-technical systems. Nat. Phys. **8**, 32–39 (2012)
4. Wang, Z., Wang, L., Szolnoki, A., Perc, M.: Evolutionary games on multilayer networks: a colloquium. Eur. Phys. J. B **88**(5), 124 (2015)
5. Alvarez Zuzek, L.G., Stanley, H.E., Braunstein, L.: Epidemic model with isolation in multilayer networks. Sci. Rep. **5**, 12151 (2015)
6. Zhao, D., Li, L., Peng, H., Luo, Q., Yang, Y.: Multiple routes transmitted epidemics on multiplex networks. Phys. Lett. A **378**(10), 770–776 (2014)
7. Massaro, E., Bagnoli, F.: Epidemic spreading and risk perception in multiplex networks: a self-organized percolation method. Phys. Rev. E **90**, 052817 (2014)
8. Zhao, D., Wang, L., Li, S., Wang, Z., Wang, L., Gao, B.: Immunization of epidemics in multiplex networks. PLoS ONE **9**(11), e112018 (2014)
9. Buono, C., Alvarez Zuzek, L.G., Macri, P.A., Braunstein, L.A.: Epidemics in partially overlapped multiplex networks. PLoS ONE **9**(7), e10473 (2014)
10. Battiston, F., Nicosia, V., Latora, V.: Structural measures for multiplex networks. Phys. Rev. E **89**, 032804 (2014)
11. Zhao, D., Li, L., Li, S., Huo, Y., Yang, Y.: Identifying influential spreaders in interconnected networks. Phys. Scr. **89**(1), 015203 (2014)
12. Chakraborty, T., Narayanam, R.: Cross-layer betweenness centrality in multiplex networks with applications. In: Proceedings of IEEE 32nd International Conference on Data Engineering, pp. 397–408. IEEE, Helsinki (2016)
13. Halu, A., Mondragón, R.J., Panzarasa, P., Bianconi, G.: Multiplex PageRank. PLoS ONE **8**, e78293 (2013)
14. Zhu, X., Tian, H., Chen, X., Wang, W., Cai, S.: Heterogeneous behavioral adoption in multiplex networks. New J. Phys. **21**, 019501 (2018)
15. Scatà, M., Di Stefano, A., Liò, P., La Corte, A.: The impact of heterogeneity and awareness in modeling epidemic spreading on multiplex networks. Sci. Rep. **6**, 37105 (2016)
16. Granell, C., Gómez, S., Arenas, A.: Competing spreading processes on multiplex networks: awareness and epidemics. Phys. Rev. E **90**, 012808 (2014)
17. Zou, C.C., Towsley, D., Gong, W.: Email worm modeling and defense. In: Proceedings of 13th International Conference on Computer Communications and Networks, pp. 409–414. IEEE, Chicago (2004)
18. Gao, C., Liu, J., Zhong, N.: Network immunization and virus propagation in email networks: experimental evaluation and analysis. Knowl. Inf. Syst. **27**(2), 253–279 (2010)
19. Li, X., Guo, J., Gao, C., Zhang, L., Zhang, Z.: A hybrid strategy for network immunization. Chaos, Solitons Fractals **106**, 214–219 (2018)
20. Gao, C., Liu, J.: Modeling and restraining mobile virus propagation. IEEE Trans. Mob. Comput. **12**(3), 529–541 (2012)
21. Chen, C., et al.: Node immunization on large graphs: theory and algorithms. IEEE Trans. Knowl. Data Eng. **28**(1), 113–126 (2016)
22. Yun, X., Li, S., Zhang, Y.: SMS worm propagation over contact social networks: modeling and validation. IEEE Trans. Inf. Forensics Secur. **10**(11), 2365–2380 (2015)

23. Omodei, E., De Domenico, M., Arenas, A.: Characterizing interactions in online social networks during exceptional events. Front. Phys. **3**, 59 (2015)
24. Stark, C., Breitkreutz, B.J., Reguly, T., Boucher, L., Breitkreutz, A., Tyers, M.: BioGRID: a general repository for interaction datasets. Nucleic Acids Res. **34**, D535–9 (2006)
25. Barabási, A.L., Albert, R.: Emergence of scaling in random networks. Science **286**(5439), 509–512 (1999)

Supervised Clinical Abbreviations Detection and Normalisation Approach

Xiaolong Huang[1,3]([✉]), Edmond Zhang[2,3], and Yun Sing Koh[1]

[1] Department of Computer Science, University of Auckland, Auckland, New Zealand
xhua342@aucklanduni.ac.nz, ykoh@cs.auckland.ac.nz
[2] Orion Health, Auckland, New Zealand
edmond.zhang@orionhealth.com
[3] Precision Driven Health Partnership, Auckland, New Zealand

Abstract. The ambiguous acronyms and abbreviations in clinical reports can be quite confusing for patients and doctors to understand, which will potentially lead to medical malpractice [15]. To solve this problem, we proposed a supervised approach to detect abbreviations in given clinical reports and normalise these abbreviations to medical concepts. In the step of detection, a seq2seq model with the attention mechanism was built and achieved the micro-average F1 score of 83.85% among 99 test reports. In the step of normalisation, we used both internal and external senses inventories to build one disambiguation classifier for each abbreviation. Finally, the proposed normalisation method achieved a micro-average accuracy of 74.7%, beating the first ranked team in the ShARe/CLEF eHealth 2013 competition, Task 2. This work provided a complete pipeline to handle ambiguous abbreviations in clinical documents, which is essential for healthcare providers and researchers to understand and subsequently leverage the clinical reports.

Keywords: Clinical abbreviations · Named Entity Recognition · Named Entity Normalisation · Word sense disambiguation

1 Introduction

Effective and adequate communication between different healthcare providers is essential for providing patients with high-quality medical care, and this communication is usually achieved through clinical reports [17]. As medical referrals become more convenient and frequent, more and more healthcare professionals are involved in the treatment of one patient. This tendency means that a patient's clinical reports will be read and referenced by many doctors with different backgrounds. However, this seemingly ordinary process faces enormous challenges due to the existence of ambiguous clinical abbreviations. A study in the UK showed that 90% of doctors from other profession were unclear about 6 of the 13 commonly used abbreviations in otolaryngology, which may potentially lead to medical misdiagnosis [5]. According to the "Institute of Safe Medicine

© Springer Nature Switzerland AG 2019
A. C. Nayak and A. Sharma (Eds.): PRICAI 2019, LNAI 11672, pp. 691–703, 2019.
https://doi.org/10.1007/978-3-030-29894-4_55

Practices" (ISMP), more than 7,000 people die from drug errors each year, and abuse of acronyms has made a significant contribution to this statistic [10].

Consequently, we urgently need to find an effective solution to detect abbreviations in clinical texts and normalise them into unified, clear and easy-to-understand forms. This task is challenging for the reason that (1) some tokens can refer to different concepts and (2) tokens referring to some concepts have different variations and these variations cannot exactly match terms in ontologies [11]. To solve this problem, this project aimed to develop:

- A clinical abbreviation detector, which can detect spans of medical abbreviations and their variations in given clinical reports.
- A clinical abbreviation normaliser, which can map the detected abbreviations to the concepts in the Unified Medical Language System (UMLS).

Our project contains two parts, "Named Entity Recognition" (NER) and "Named Entity Normalization" (NEN). In the part of abbreviation detection, we proposed a seq2seq neural network with the attention mechanism to predict the BIO labels of text segments sampled by the predefined sliding window; then we concatenated these labels to calculate the span indices of each abbreviation in the reports. Our method achieved the micro-average F1 score of 83.85% among 99 test reports; In the part of abbreviation normalisation, we developed one classifier for each abbreviation to predict possible meaning based on its context. The use of character-level word embedding and external acronym meta thesaurus [6] made our normaliser outperform the previous works on clinical abbreviation normalisation, by training SVM classifiers based on the average word embedding in the 20-word sampling window, our approach achieved a micro-average accuracy of 74.7%, beating the first ranked team in the ShARe/CLEF eHealth 2013 competition.

2 Related Work

In general, the main idea of machine learning-based abbreviation normalisation approach is that, building classifiers for each abbreviation by training massive clinical texts containing this abbreviation with its gold standard long-form labelled by professionals.

The first study on applying word embeddings to clinical text normalisation was proposed by Wu et al. [21], before that, researchers generally used some text-based features to train their models, such as part-of-speech (POS), N-grams text snippet, semantic types, position feature and stemmed words features [13, 19, 23]. They trained the word embeddings on 403871 unstructured clinical texts from the MIMIC II database using the framework proposed by Collobert et al. [4], and their method achieved a micro-average accuracy of 93.01% and 95.79% on the VUH and UMN dataset separately. Therefore, word embedding is proved as a dominant feature to improve the performance of word sense disambiguation in clinical texts.

In addition to improving the feature engineering, some scholars made some improvement in the model structure. In 2017, Yepes [22] proposed a "Long-Short

Term Memory" (LSTM) based recurrent neural networks (RNN) to do clinical abbreviations normalisation. They evaluated their model on the MSH WSD data set [8] and the NLM WSD data set [18], the results of their experiments showed that, when using same features, the proposed LSTM model outperformed the classical machine learning models including SVM, Naive Bayes and K-nearest neighbours (KNN) [22] largely. In 2018, Joopudi et al. [9] proposed an effective convolutional neural network (CNN) framework for abbreviation normalisation. Their framework took as input the concatenation of word embedding, positional embedding and POS embedding, and it avoided the feature engineering. They built CNN classifiers for each abbreviation and evaluated these classifiers on an auto-generated data set, and their proposed CNN classifiers improve 1 to 4% in the accuracy compared to SVM. Since this end-to-end framework did not involve feature engineering, the models kept promising performance on multiple data set. The above two examples show that deep learning models have great potential in clinical text normalisation, and these models are robust across different datasets.

3 Abbreviation Detection Methodology

The objective of detection is to locate all abbreviations in clinical reports so that we can subsequently track these abbreviations and normalise them. In this section, we will introduce how our detector extracted and transformed features and labels from the raw texts and made the final predictions.

3.1 Feature and Label Transformation

Word Embedding. In steps of clinical abbreviation detection and normalisation, all abbreviations and their surrounding contexts were represented using FastText word embedding, which overcame the limitations of word2vec models. Because the word2vec model regards each word as an atomic entity, it ignores the internal morphological features of words. For example, some words pairs, such as "apple" and "apples", "cook" and "cooker", have some common characters, and their semantical connections are tight. If using the word2vec model, internal morphological relations of such words will be lost because they are converted into different ids. To overcome this problem, FastText model uses character-level n-grams to represent a word, which regards n-characters as atomic entities rather than words. In FastText word embeddings, words with similar character combinations will be mapped to similar vectors. Such a mechanism is good at getting over variations of abbreviations. We leveraged Gensim package to train 200-dimensional word embeddings using all MIMIC III notes.

BIO Labeling. As for labels, BIO encoding is the most popular encoding in NER task, which tags each token as beginning-of-entity (B), inside-of-entity (I) or outside-of-entity (O). In this case, we can input a sequence of words to our model and get the same-length "B", "I", "O" sequences as results. However, the word numbers of different clinical reports may vary a lot. It would be quite challenging to map random-length sequences to random-length sequences with the fixed-size architectures. To solve this problem, we set a sliding window to sample the raw text. Therefore, we could get massive instances from reports, and each instance contained the same number of words. Figure 1 demonstrates what the training instances look like.

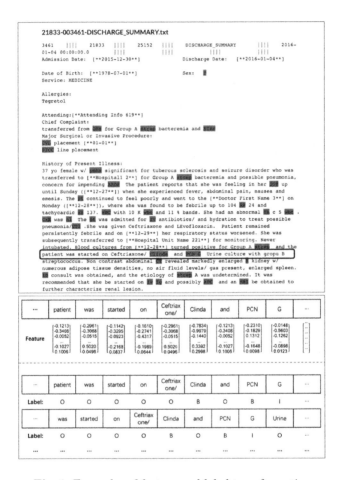

Fig. 1. Examples of feature and label transformation

3.2 Model Architecture

The seq2seq deep learning model used in this paper mainly leveraged the attention mechanism [2], which is a very influential and seminal improvement on the "Encoder-Decoder" model [3,16]. We adopted this model for the reason that the attention mechanism was good at finding detection-relevant source words for prediction according to the surrounding detection result. [2] defined the context variable $context^{<t>}$ as the weighted sum of hidden states of all timestamp for the timestamp t, by training these weights our model could easily find detection-relevant source words. The detailed structure is shown in Fig. 2, the diagram on the left shows the structure of our seq2seq model and the diagram on the right show only one "attention" step in this model to calculate the attention weights $a^{<t,t'>}$, which is used to calculate the context variable $context^{<t>}$ for each timestep in the output $(t = 1, \ldots, T)$, through the following formula:

$$context^{<t>} = \sum_{t'=1}^{T} a^{<t,t'>} a^{<t'>} \tag{1}$$

where the superscript $^{<i>}$ indicates the ith time step of variables. $a^{<t,t'>}$ indicates the weight of the influence of hidden state $a^{<t'>}$ on the context variable $context^{<t>}$, and $a^{<t,t'>}$ is based on the post-attention LSTM hidden state $s^{<t-1>}$ and the pre-attention Bi-LSTM hidden state $a^{<t>}$ (Fig. 2 right).

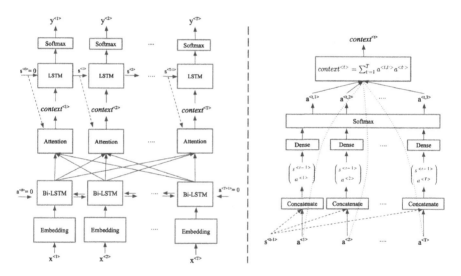

Fig. 2. The seq2seq deep learning model with the attention mechanism [1] to solve the task of clinical abbreviation detection

4 Abbreviation Normalization Methodology

After locating all abbreviations and their variations in clinical reports, we need to normalise them to UMLS concepts. In general, clinical abbreviations have multiple meanings and can refer to various concepts. Therefore, we converted this "word sense disambiguation" task into a concepts-classification task.

4.1   Overview and Strategy

We followed the strategy introduced in [19]; our abbreviation normalisation approach mainly consisted of two steps: (1) generating one senses inventory for each
abbreviation; (2) matching the most possible concepts (senses) to each abbreviation from their sense inventories.

In the first step, we generated two types of senses inventory. The first one
was the "internal senses inventory" generated from the training set by grouping
all concepts and their original text in reports. The other one was the "external
senses inventory". Grossman et al. [6] built one integrated senses inventory by
combining eight famous source inventories including UMLS LRABR, ADAM,
Berman, Vanderbilt, Discharge Summaries, Vanderbilt Clinical Notes, Stetson,
Columbia OBGYN and Wikipedia. We chose this integrated senses inventory as
our "external senses inventory", then for each abbreviation in this inventory, we
queried its long forms of all concepts in the MIMIC III database and collected the
corresponding source sentences. In this way, we generated our "complementary"
training corpus.

In the second step, we normalised each abbreviation to UMLS concept from
both the "internal senses inventory" and the "external senses inventory". When
predicting the concept of every target abbreviation, our normaliser first checked
whether this abbreviation was included in the "internal senses inventory", if not,
our normaliser then checked whether the "external senses inventory" covered
this abbreviation. For the abbreviations covered in "internal senses inventory"
or "external senses inventory", the mapping tasks had been transformed into
supervised classification problems. While for those "uncovered" abbreviations,
we directly called the UMLS Terminology Service API (UTS API) to find the
possible concepts. Figure 3 shows the working flow of the second step.

4.2   Model Architecture

The main idea of modelling was to capture the sentence-level meaning of words
surrounding the target abbreviation and used this meaning to predict the possible UMLS concept of this abbreviation. Because all possible concepts were
provided by the two senses inventories, for each abbreviation, we trained a classifier to pick the concept with the highest possibility.

We tried two methods to capture the sentence-level meaning. The first one
was "averaging method", and the other one was "long short-term memory
method", as shown in Fig. 4.

Averaging Method. Averaging method is our baseline method. For each target
abbreviation, we picked fixed-number of words before and after it, and used the
average value of these picked words' word embedding values to represent the
feature of this text fragment. The SVM model is good at dealing with high
dimensional data, so we trained one SVM classifier for each abbreviation from
"internal senses inventory" and "external senses inventory". We also compared
our averaging method with another two word embedding aggregating method

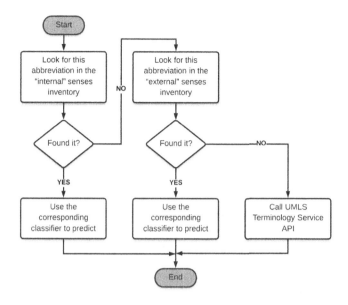

Fig. 3. Working flow of abbreviation sense disambiguation

defined in [21], namely "Left-Right Surrounding Based Embedding" (LR-SBE) and "MAX Surrounding Based Embedding" (MAX-SBE) with same classifier parameters.

Long Short-Term Memory Method. Although the above averaging method could train a large number of classifiers in a short time, its limitation was also obvious, that was, this method did not consider the order between words when acquiring sentence-level features. It was not difficult to understand that changing the order of words may change the meaning of a sentence. Therefore, using the LSTM model before averaging the vectors might be a better solution to solve this problem. This assumption was supported by [22], their work showed that adding one LSTM layer could improve the performance of word sense disambiguation of abbreviations. Therefore, we assumed that the LSTM model would still perform better than the averaging method in our task.

5   Dataset

The proposed approach was evaluated by the Shared Annotated Resources (ShARe) corpus, which was a subset of de-identified clinical reports from approximately thirty thousand ICU patients provided by MIMIC II database [14]. In ShARe/CLEF eHealth challenge task 2, 298 clinical reports were split into two parts, 199 clinical reports in the training set and 99 clinical reports in the test set. All the 298 reports had corresponding annotations of acronym/abbreviation

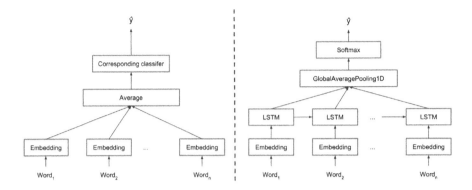

Fig. 4. Structures of our baseline classification model and LSTM-based model

spans and UMLS Concept Unique Identifiers (CUIs). In our project, we maintained this splitting method, used the annotated acronym/abbreviation spans to evaluate our detection model and used annotated UMLS CUIs to evaluate our normalisation model.

6   Evaluation and Results

We conducted two independent experiments to evaluate the performance of our multi-label classification model - abbreviation detector and our multi-class classification model - abbreviation normaliser. To compare our proposed approach with others' work, we did not re-split the data set, and all the performances were evaluated on the 99 clinical reports from ShARe corpus.

6.1   Task 1: Abbreviation Detection

In the first experiment, we used a sliding window to sample the pre-processed free texts in the training set. All the sampled text segments were fed into our seq2seq model; When predicting, we first split the pre-processed free texts into non-overlapping segments with the same length as training segments. Then, we made predictions for these segments separately. Finally, we concatenated these predicted sequences as our detection result on one pre-processed free text.

We used the hamming loss as the matrix to train our model. After we concatenated the predictions into one string, we could also evaluate our model by words as a single-label classifier. The size of the sliding window played an important role in the predictive accuracy of our model. If the window size was too small, some information that can be helpful to prediction might not be used; on the contrary, if the window size was too large, we might cover too much unnecessary information that did not contribute. Therefore, we tried different window sizes in the first experiment; every time the window size was changed, a new seq2seq model would be trained and evaluated.

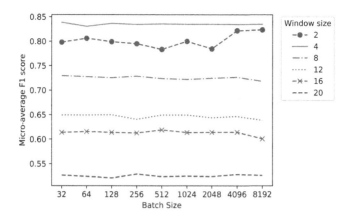

Fig. 5. Micro-average F1 score by batch size with different window sizes

We used 2, 4, 8, 12, 16, 20 as the size of our sampling window, trained and validated multiple seq2seq models respectively and calculated the micro-average F1 score on 99 test reports by different batch sizes. For each training, we set the maximum number of epochs as 50 and use early stopping with the patience parameter of 5. The result is shown in Fig. 5, choosing a window size of 4 got the highest micro-average F1 score on the validation set, and it achieved the micro-average F1 score of 83.85% on the test set.

6.2   Task 2: Abbreviation Normalisation

In the second experiment, our normalisation approach was evaluated independently. We normalised human-detected abbreviation spans in ShaRe CLEF corpus to compare the human-normalised results with ours. By using the strategy shown in Fig. 3, 3774 abbreviations in the test set were split into three parts: "internal" abbreviations, "external" abbreviations and "uncovered" abbreviations.

Because the training sets corresponding to the "internal" abbreviations were manually labelled by medical professionals, the data quality of which was relatively higher than our generated training data for external abbreviations. To avoid interference factors caused by poor data quality and to control a single variable, we validated our model only on these "internal" abbreviations and applied the same setting to "external" abbreviations when predicting. Similar to the practice in the first experiment, we first evaluated the effect of different window sizes on the classification accuracy of models, such as SVM, Random Forest and KNN.

As shown in Table 1, the random forest classifier was better than the other two models when the window size was relatively large; and when the window size became smaller, the SVM classifier gradually showed its advantage. When the window size was 20, the three models simultaneously reached their highest value and SVM classifiers achieve global optimal classification performance with the micro-average accuracy of 83.56%. With the same setting, we got the micro-average accuracy of 40.06% on the "external" abbreviations. Table 2 shows the overall performance of our normalisation baseline system.

Table 1. Micro-average accuracy of disambiguation for "internal" abbreviations with different window size. Best results for each model are shown in bold, best global results are shown underlined.

Window size	SVM	Random forest	KNN
10	83.02%	82.86%	81.74%
20	**83.56%**	**83.28%**	**81.83%**
50	82.77%	82.93%	80.99%
100	82.24%	82.55%	80.77%
200	81.14%	81.77%	80.45%
300	80.89%	81.80%	80.42%
400	80.89%	81.80%	79.76%

Table 2. Performance of our baseline on the test set

Type	#instances	#correct	Micro-average accuracy
Internal abbreviation	3187	2663	83.56%
External abbreviation	347	139	40.06%
Uncovered abbreviation	240	18	7.4%
In total	**3774**	**2820**	**74.72%**

We examined the two novel word embedding aggregation method proposed by Wu et al. [21] on our task. As shown in Table 3, the random forest model and KNN model had a slight improvement, but the overall highest micro-average accuracy did not exceed our baseline model.

We also trained one LSTM-based classifier for each abbreviation. Finally, we got 579 classifiers in total (382 classifiers for "internal" abbreviations and 197 classifiers for "external" abbreviations). It would be quite tricky and time-consuming to make parameter tuning for each LSTM based networks, so we did not do validation and use the default parameters for all 579 classifiers.

As shown in Table 2, our approach achieved the micro-average F1 score of 74.72%, which was higher than the first ranked teams' performance in the ShARe/CLEF eHealth 2013 competition. The information about other teams' performance is shown in Table 4.

Table 3. Micro-average accuracy of disambiguation for "internal" abbreviations with different aggregation method of word embeddings.

Features	SVM	Random forest	KNN
AVG20	**83.56%**	83.28%	81.83%
LR10	83.49%	82.90%	82.21%
AVG20+LR10	83.28%	83.09%	**82.33%**
MAX20	83.15%	82.77%	82.11%
AVG20+MAX20	83.21%	**83.31%**	82.30%

Table 4. Participating teams performances compared with our approach performance

Abbreviation normalization system	Accuracy
Our technique	**74.7%**
UTHealthCCB.B.1 [19]	71.9%
Majority Sense Approach [12]	69.6%
UTHealthCCB.B.2 [19]	68.3%
LIMSI.1 [23]	66.4%
THCIB.B.1 [20]	65.7%
TeamHealthLanguageLABS [13]	46.7%
WVU.1 [7]	42.6%

7   Conclusion

In this research, we proposed a complete solution for dealing with ambiguous abbreviations in clinical reports. This pipeline had two stages: abbreviation detection and abbreviation normalisation. In our work, a seq2seq neural network was built as the abbreviation detector, and 579 SVM classifiers were trained as parts of the abbreviation normaliser. Both of these approaches achieved a promising performance. There are two main contributions in our work. Firstly, we applied the attention-based model for language translation to the field of clinical abbreviations detection and achieved satisfactory results, which might provide new ideas for future researchers. Secondly, we provided an approach to automatically generate supplementary data sets when the human-labelled data is very limited. These external training set may play an important role when we extend our approach to other data set.

In future work, we will collect more abbreviation senses inventories and query in some larger medical or general corpus, such as PubMed and Wikipedia. We believe that, with more data set provided, our model will achieve much higher performance.

Acknowledgements. This research was supported and supervised by Precision Driven Health Partnership (www.precisiondrivenhealth.com). We thank the organizers of ShaRe/CLEF 2013 Task 2 for providing the data used in this work.

References

1. Andrew, N.: Deeplearning.ai: attention mechanism in sequence to sequence models. https://www.coursera.org/learn/nlp-sequence-models/lecture/lSwVa/attention-model
2. Bahdanau, D., Cho, K., Bengio, Y.: Neural machine translation by jointly learning to align and translate. arXiv preprint arXiv:1409.0473 (2014)
3. Cho, K., et al.: Learning phrase representations using RNN encoder-decoder for statistical machine translation. arXiv preprint arXiv:1406.1078 (2014)
4. Collobert, R., Weston, J., Bottou, L., Karlen, M., Kavukcuoglu, K., Kuksa, P.: Natural language processing (almost) from scratch. J. Mach. Learn. Res. **12**, 2493–2537 (2011)
5. Das-Purkayastha, P., McLeod, K., Canter, R.: Specialist medical abbreviations as a foreign language. J. R. Soc. Med. **97**(9), 456–456 (2004)
6. Grossman, L.V., Mitchell, E.G., Hripcsak, G., Weng, C., Vawdrey, D.K.: A method for harmonization of clinical abbreviation and acronym sense inventories. J. Biomed. Inform. **88**, 62–69 (2018)
7. Jagannathan, V., et al.: WVU NLP class participation in ShARe/CLEF challenge. In: CLEF (Working Notes) (2013)
8. Jimeno-Yepes, A.J., McInnes, B.T., Aronson, A.R.: Exploiting mesh indexing in medline to generate a data set for word sense disambiguation. BMC Bioinformatics **12**(1), 223 (2011)
9. Joopudi, V., Dandala, B., Devarakonda, M.: A convolutional route to abbreviation disambiguation in clinical text. J. Biomed. Inform. **86**, 71–78 (2018)
10. Kuhn, I.F.: Abbreviations and acronyms in healthcare: when shorter isn't sweeter. Pediatric nursing **33**(5), 392–398 (2007)
11. Li, H., et al.: CNN-based ranking for biomedical entity normalization. BMC Bioinformatics **18**(11), 385 (2017)
12. Mowery, D.L., et al.: Normalizing acronyms and abbreviations to aid patient understanding of clinical texts: ShARe/CLEF ehealth challenge 2013, task 2. J. Biomed. Seman. **7**(1), 43 (2016)
13. Patrick, J.D., Safari, L., Ou, Y.: ShARe/CLEF eHealth 2013 normalization of acronyms/abbreviations challenge. In: CLEF (Working Notes). Citeseer (2013)
14. Saeed, M., Lieu, C., Raber, G., Mark, R.G.: MIMIC II: a massive temporal ICU patient database to support research in intelligent patient monitoring. In: Computers in Cardiology, pp. 641–644. IEEE (2002)
15. Sheppard, J.E., Weidner, L.C., Zakai, S., Fountain-Polley, S., Williams, J.: Ambiguous abbreviations: an audit of abbreviations in paediatric note keeping. Arch. Dis. Child. **93**(3), 204–206 (2008)
16. Sutskever, I., Vinyals, O., Le, Q.V.: Sequence to sequence learning with neural networks. In: Advances in Neural Information Processing Systems, pp. 3104–3112 (2014)
17. Walsh, K.E., Gurwitz, J.H.: Medical abbreviations: writing little and communicating less. Arch. Dis. Child. **93**(10), 816–817 (2008)

18. Weeber, M., Mork, J.G., Aronson, A.R.: Developing a test collection for biomedical word sense disambiguation. In: Proceedings of the AMIA Symposium, p. 746. American Medical Informatics Association (2001)

19. Wu, Y., Tang, B., Jiang, M., Moon, S., Denny, J.C., Xu, H.: Clinical acronym/abbreviation normalization using a hybrid approach. In: CLEF (Working Notes) (2013)

20. Xia, Y., et al.: Normalization of abbreviations/acronyms: THCIB at CLEF eHealth 2013 task 2. In: CLEF (Working Notes) (2013)

21. Xu, J., Zhang, Y., Xu, H., et al.: Clinical abbreviation disambiguation using neural word embeddings. In: Proceedings of BioNLP, vol. 15, pp. 171–176 (2015)

22. Yepes, A.J.: Word embeddings and recurrent neural networks based on long-short term memory nodes in supervised biomedical word sense disambiguation. J. Biomed. Inform. **73**, 137–147 (2017)

23. Zweigenbaum, P., Deléger, L., Lavergne, T., Névéol, A., Bodnari, A.: A supervised abbreviation resolution system for medical text. In: CLEF (Working Notes) (2013)

Duo Attention with Deep Learning on Tomato Yield Prediction and Factor Interpretation

Sandya De Alwis[1,2]([✉]) [ID], Yishuo Zhang[1] [ID], Myung Na[3], and Gang Li[1] [ID]

[1] Deakin University, Geelong, VIC 3216, Australia
{sdealwi,chris.zhang,gang.li}@deakin.edu.au
[2] Guilin University of Electronic Technology, Guilin 541004, China
[3] Department of Statistics, Chonnam National University, Gwangju, Korea
nmh@chonnam.ac.kr

Abstract. Although many smart farming related approaches have been proposed to support farmers, crop modeling in smart farming and most effective factors for the yield remains an open problem. In this paper, we introduce Long Short Term Memory (LSTM) and Attention score mechanism, which gives the most effective factors to tomato yield using tomato growing under smart farm condition data set. Our finding shows that plant factors are more important as well as environmental factors. Next, we proposed DA-LSTM model for tomato yield prediction and best time frame for harvest based on a deep learning algorithm. This model shows high accuracy when compared with LSTM, XGBR and Support Vector Regression (SVR).

Keywords: Machine learning · Smart farming · Tomato

1 Introduction

Tomato *(Solanum lycopersicum)* is one of the most consumable foods in the whole world, not only as a fresh vegetable or fruit but also for other processed products such as sauce, paste, etc [1]. As health issues increase, people intend to eat more healthily, resulting in increased demand for healthy food like tomatoes. For this demand, it is essential that the market is continuously supplied even in extreme environmental conditions. The importance of smart-farming arises at this point. Smart farming developed as an application of Internet of Things (IoT) [15]. With this new technology, farmers are interested in growing tomatoes under the smart farming conditions to ensure the constant supply of the quality product and at the same time, targeting high yield as well as high profit.

All the environmental conditions can be monitored and changed in high tech plant houses. For example, if the temperature is too high in the plant house, it can be lowered using fans. Also, quality of the product could be enhanced with proper monitoring such as early detection of pest and disease [4]. Resource

© Springer Nature Switzerland AG 2019
A. C. Nayak and A. Sharma (Eds.): PRICAI 2019, LNAI 11672, pp. 704–715, 2019.
https://doi.org/10.1007/978-3-030-29894-4_56

management [14] and the minimum use of fertilizer and pesticides [11] are also an advantage of smart farming. A massive amount of data is extracted during the smart farming process. It is important to take full advantage of this data to gain high-quality product and maximum profit.

Smart farming data could be used for many applications. With the new technology, farmers monitor their farms in a range of dimensions such as temperature, water requirement and detection of pest and diseases [12]. Yield prediction, farm management, variety selection, and economic analysis are the other big data applications in smart farming. Yield prediction is beneficial for farmers together with policymakers, food marketing agencies, and governments for food security. Authorities can plan to either import or export according to yield prediction [7]. Therefore, accuracy in yield predicting is extremely important. Agriculture wants crop models for a huge variety of applications, including yield predicting, farm managing and policy analysis [5]. Various data mining methods are used in different approaches in yield prediction but accuracy is remaining a problem.

To fill this research gap, we attempted to discover knowledge from the tomato data sets obtained from a smart farm in South Korea. Two main research challenges are in this study. The first challenge is accurate yield prediction based on lots of features within the time series. Though existing works have used different techniques for the yield prediction models, input features are also important. Use of only climatic data such as temperature, rainfall, etc. are not enough to predict accurate yield. However, a large number of features could also make the prediction over-fitting. The second challenge is the difficulty of interpreting the results of many advanced methods, such as deep learning. But in the farming industry, environmental factors play the main role during the plant growth including the yield. Plant factors such as the number of leaves of the plant also determines the yield. In this paper, the duo attention mechanism has been implemented together with deep learning models. The attention mechanism not only could be solving the feature engineering challenge, but also give a great interpretation of the deep learning model.

Hence, in this paper, we attempt to address the following contributions towards the two challenges.

- We proposed the duo attention based deep learning model which is the best algorithm to predict yield
- We are using the two attention mechanisms to find out the factor/s or the particular weeks mostly influence the tomato yield with regards to individual farms and overall farm level.

We have investigated several methods to find out the best one for predicting the yield accurately using all the attributes in smart farming data. Our proposed method based on deep learning Long Short-Term Memory (LSTM)and attention mechanisms stand out of the comparison through the validation, which is more accurate when compared with XGBT-Regression and SVR. Specifically, by using the attention mechanism, our method gives factors and lags with the most impact on the yield.

2   Related Work

Jones [8] proposed source-sink relationship yield model for tomatoes in 1991. Effect of solar radiation and temperature before and after anthesis on tomato yield is another approach of tomato yield modeling [6].

Existing data mining techniques applied to yield prediction for other crops is as follows; Matsumura et al. 2015 [10] used both Artificial Neural Networks (ANN) and Multiple Linear Regression (MLR) techniques. The ANN model used in Matsumura et al.'s paper is the multi-layer perception, with one hidden layer to predict Maize yield against climate changes. Whereas, relationships between sunflower yields and soil, water and salinity is Dai et al. approach. ANN technics used to predict yield for wheat, sesame and sugar cane by [13], [3] respectively. On the other hand, Zheng et al. 2009 [17] predicted soybean yield using CART and Generalised Linear Models (GLM). According to their research, they have found that the most effective factor for the yield soil total potassium. Marko et al. [9] proposed a different method for yield perdition for soybean, weighted histograms regression(WHR). Furthermore, [2] proposed improved model using feature selection, feature engineering and model tuning. Recently, [16] have used remote sensing data for yield prediction based on Deep Gaussian Process.

However, the major limitation in those existing works is the accuracy of the prediction. The next problem is they have paid less attention to find out the most important time for harvesting and the features during the growth. Previous work hasn't recognized most affecting factors to the yield as they used few attributes for their yield prediction.

3   Materials and Methods

In this section, we will first introduce the notation we use in this paper to formalize the tomato harvest forecast problem. Then, we will present the proposed Duo Attention Long Short Term Memory (DA-LSTM) model with relevant deep learning technologies that has been used for this paper.

Problem Formation and Notations. The tomato harvest prediction is regarded as the multiple variate time series forecast problem. Hence, by given n variables on the series in the dataset $\mathbf{D}$, the input feature could be represented as $X = (\mathbf{x}^1, \mathbf{x}^2, \mathbf{x}^3 ..., \mathbf{x}^n)^\top$, and further by choosing the lag window of T, the input feature X on T lags is donated as $\mathbf{X} = (\mathbf{x}_1, \mathbf{x}_2, \mathbf{x}_3 ..., \mathbf{x}_T)^\top \in \mathbf{R}_{n \times T}$ where the $\mathbf{x}_t = (\mathbf{x}_t^1, \mathbf{x}_t^2 ..., \mathbf{x}_t^n)^\top \in \mathbf{R}^n$ is a vector with n exogenous features at time t. Same as the input $\mathbf{X}$, the target output $\mathbf{Y}$ is employed as $\mathbf{Y} = (y_1, y_2, y_3 ..., y_T)^\top \in \mathbf{R}$.

In our prediction problem, the essence of our forecast aims on using the lag window of T on input $\mathbf{X} = (\mathbf{x}_1, \mathbf{x}_2, \mathbf{x}_3 ..., \mathbf{x}_T)^\top$ with the corresponding target $\mathbf{Y} = (y_1, y_2, y_3 ..., y_T)^\top$ to predict on the next lag target value y_{T+1} by using the non-leaner mapping through the deep learning technology:

$$\hat{y}_{T+1} = F(y_1, y_2, y_3 ..., y_T, \mathbf{x}_1, \mathbf{x}_2, \mathbf{x}_3 ..., \mathbf{x}_T). \tag{1}$$

LSTM for Time Series Forecast. LSTM had been widely used in time series forecasting recently. The LSTM models are variants of the recurrent neural network which is designed to solve the gradient vanishing problems by adding multiple gates into each unit. These gates control how much information could be processed or forgot into next neural unit on each time step. The Fig. 1 is showing the LSTM unit structure. Each gates in Fig. 1 could be using below equation to express its functionality inside the LSTM unit on time step t:

$$f_t = \sigma(W_f \cdot [h_{t-1}, x_t] + b_f) \tag{2}$$

$$i_t = \sigma(W_i \cdot [h_{t-1}, x_t] + b_i) \tag{3}$$

$$\hat{C}_t = tanh(W_C \cdot [h_{t-1}, x_t] + b_C) \tag{4}$$

$$C_t = f_t * C_{t-1} + i_t * \hat{C}_t \tag{5}$$

$$o_t = \sigma(W_o \cdot [h_{t-1}, x_t] + b_o) \tag{6}$$

$$h_t = o_t * tanh(C_t) \tag{7}$$

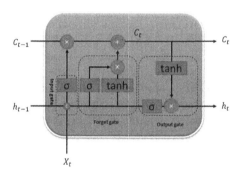

Fig. 1. LSTM unit structure

Attention on Deep Learning. Attention is a mechanism to help the deep learning model to better focus on the useful features on the final prediction. In our problems, our goal is to predict the y_{T+1} by using input of $(y_1, y_2, y_3..., y_T, \mathbf{x}_1, \mathbf{x}_2, \mathbf{x}_3..., \mathbf{x}_T)^{\top}$.

Given $n + 1$ dimensions feature with lags of T from the input $\hat{\mathbf{X}}$ on this problem, The attention mechanism is basically assigning a weight matrix of $\mathbf{W} \in \mathbf{R}_{(n+1) \times T}$ which will dot multiply on the input $\hat{\mathbf{X}}$. The weight matrix approach could be calculated by below equations:

$$W = softmax[(w_1, w_2, w_3..., w_t)] \tag{8}$$

where the $(w_1, w_2, w_3..., w_t)$ is from the model initialization and could be learned from the training until converge. The t is the length of the input vector.

Lag Attention. Particularly, by permuting the input vector, there are two kinds of attention which could be applied. When the initial input is $\hat{\mathbf{X}} \in \mathbf{R}_{(n+1) \times T}$, by applying the attention weights from Eq. 10, the weights length equals to the lag length of T.

Feature Attention. When the last dimension and second dimension of the input $\hat{\mathbf{X}} \in \mathbf{R}_{n+1 \times T}$ had been switched, then the new input could be expressed as $\hat{\mathbf{X}}^{\top} \in \mathbf{R}_{T \times (n+1)}$. So the attention will be applied on the features directly based on the Eq. 9.

$$Attention_f = softmax(tanh(W^f \cdot [\hat{\mathbf{X}}^{\top}] + e_f)) \cdot [\hat{\mathbf{X}}^{\top}] \qquad (9)$$

$$Attention_t = softmax(tanh(W^t \cdot [\hat{\mathbf{X}}] + e_t)) \cdot [\hat{\mathbf{X}}] \qquad (10)$$

In the equations, W^t and W^f are the weights which could be learned in the training in the attention layer, and the e_t and e_f are the bias. `tanh` and `softmax` is the activation function inside the attention layer.

Conceptual Model Structure. By applying the duo attention mechanism with LSTM, we proposed the DA-LSTM framework to predict the tomato harvest time series problem. The figure shows the structure of the proposed DA-LSTM framework.

The input of DA-LSTM is applied by two attention weights on top of it, and then the outcome of the two attention layers will be separately put into the two LSTM networks. After the computing of two LSTM networks, the hidden state of h_t will be concatenated together and pushed into the dense layers for getting the predicted target value of $\hat{y}$. Figure 2 shows the proposed framework structure.

3.1 Training Procedure

By minimizing the prediction error from the proposed model, we use the stochastic gradient descent (SGD) together with the Adam optimizer to train the model. The default loss function is the mean absolute percentage error:

$$\mathcal{L}(y_T, \hat{y}_T) = \frac{1}{N} \sum_{i=1}^{N} |\frac{y_T^i - \hat{y}_T^i}{y_T^i}| \qquad (11)$$

In the loss function, the N is the number of training samples from each epoch.

4   Experiment

The privet data set used in this approach collected from "Daphne" tomatoes grow under plant house with sensors (smart-farms with the area of $13,200\,\mathrm{m}^2$), five different locations in South Korea, from August, 2014 to July, 2015 (48

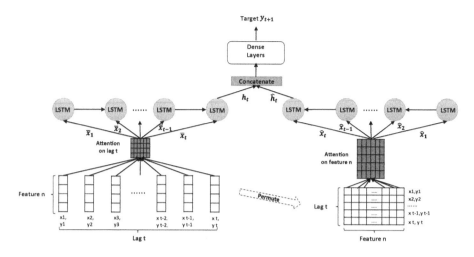

Fig. 2. Tomato Model for feature attention

weeks) with 46 features. Recordings of environmental and plants were taken throughout the period which represents one life cycle of the plant. In this data sets, the features could be split into three main part: the environment features, the plant measurement features and the fruit growth features. Environment features represent temperature, solar radiation, humidity, CO_2 level, water, electric conductivity and pH. Plant measurements were taken as follows; length and width of the leaflet, stem thickness (between third and fourth nodes), height of the flower, number of fruits, number of fruits per unit, flowering speed, and fruit set speed. Leaf Area Index (LAI) is a key factor in this data set, where LL is Leaf length, LW is Leaf width, NoL is Number of Leaves and PA is Penetration area.

$$LAI = \frac{(LL) * (LW) * (0.5) * (NoL) * (DENSITY)}{(10000) + (PA)} \tag{12}$$

For fruit growth in this data set, the attributes have a factor of fruit (FoF), which is considered as weight of tomato (WoT) per standard weight of tomato (SWoT). Here, standard weight considers as 175 g.

$$FoF = \frac{WoT}{SWoT} \tag{13}$$

The attribute Trans1 (T1) means amount of solar radiation received to the pant house. Here, Transmittance = 0.85

$$T1 = 24hr\,Radiationsum(J) * Transmittance \tag{14}$$

This value depends on the state of the greenhouse. Trans2 (T2) means amount of radiation received from the plant; where LA is Leaf area.

$$T2 = (LAI)^3 - (0.133 * LA(LAI)^2) + (0.606 * LA(LAI) + 0.003) \tag{15}$$

The last attribute of fruit grown in this data set is the average weight per unit.

4.1   Results

In this section, we are using the 5 different farms' data to evaluate the proposed model. In order to provide the best performances on the 5 farms with our proposed method, we use the walkthrough validation first to find out the best parameters. Then we will compare the proposed method with the proper parameters to compare with other models for showing its advantage on accuracy.

Validation and Parameter Settings. Several parameters in the proposed model are needed to be determined through the walk through validation. The walkthrough validation will need the training data on each week to be added by last weeks' validation data. On each week, when the model had been validated, the validation data will be added into the training data to form the next new training data for next week.

By using the walkthrough validation, the parameters such as the number of time steps in the lag window T, the size of the hidden unit in LSTM p, the dropout rate d, and the size of the dense layer q is determined. Practically the time window of $T \in \{3, 6, 9, 12\}$, the hidden unit size of $p \in \{128, 256, 512\}$, drop out rate of $d \in \{0.01, 0.3, 0.5\}$ and the dense layer $q \in \{32, 64, 128\}$ were evaluated in the validation. Finally the time window of $T = 3$, the hidden size on LSTM of $p = 256$, the drop out rate of $d = 0.3$ and the dense layer $q = 64$ had archived the best performance through the validation and they are used for the rest of the experiments.

Performance Evaluation. In order to compare effects on the performance of the proposed model, we have used three metrics to evaluate the model comparison, which are the root mean square error (RMSE), the mean absolute error (MAE) and the mean absolute percentage error (MAPE).

Particularly, when y_t is the target value and $\hat{y}_t$ is the prediction at time t, the RMSE is denoted as $\mathbf{RMSE} = \sqrt{\dfrac{1}{N} \sum_{i=1}^{N} (y_t^i - \hat{y}_t^i)^2}$, and the MAE is denoted as $\mathbf{MAE} = \dfrac{1}{N} \sum_{i=1}^{N} |y_t^i - \hat{y}_t^i|$. Because we are using 5 farms data to compare the proposed model with benchmark models. So MAPE is used at here which is defined as $\mathbf{MAPE} = \dfrac{1}{N} \sum_{i=1}^{N} |\dfrac{y_t^i - \hat{y}_t^i}{y_t^i}| \times 100\%$.

In model comparison, LSTM is the most commonly used method on time series prediction. ANN is the artificial neural network which is widely used in regression and time series prediction. XGBTR, the extreme gradient boosting tree regressor is a powerful tree model to solve the regression problems. The SVR is very broadly used in many multi-variate regression approaches. Each model will use the same validation method. For the XGBTR and SVR, they all use the past 3 month data as the input as the time window $T = 3$ from above parameter settings.

Form Tables 1, 2 and, 3, clearly we could observe that the DA-LSTM has the best performance over all three metrics over 48 weeks. LSTM has the second best performance as it has the closest structure with DA-LSTM excluding the two attention mechanisms. The XGBTR has the worst performances.

Table 1. MAPE Comparison on different Methods over 48 weeks

Farm	DA-LSTM	LSTM	ANN	XGBTR	SVR
A	2.46	4.78	4.80	13.60	6.93
B	2.02	2.21	5.36	8.46	8.01
C	2.80	3.5	4.31	11.46	6.22
D	3.60	3.7	6.24	8.46	7.16
E	0.93	1.12	3.34	7.46	5.11
Mean	**2.36**	3.06	4.81	9.89	6.69

Table 2. MAE Comparison on different Methods over 48 weeks

Farm	DA-LSTM	LSTM	ANN	XGBTR	SVR
A	0.054	0.112	0.121	0.452	0.302
B	0.061	0.072	0.151	0.293	0.322
C	0.131	0.191	0.221	0.671	0.412
D	0.109	0.182	0.347	0.511	0.381
E	0.011	0.021	0.108	0.361	0.237
Mean	**0.073**	0.116	0.190	0.458	0.331

Lag Importance. As attention had been implemented in the lags for each farm, so the interpretation of lag importance could be observed during the experiments. In the validation from performance evaluation, the time window of $T = 3$ had been selected for the best performance on the accuracy. Figure 3 shows the lag importance from the attention score.

From the Fig. 3, for farm A, C and D, the lag 2, which means the last-third week has the maximum contribution on the next week's yield.

Farm B and E, the lag 0 which means the last week gives the most important for the next week's prediction. Those patterns could give a great interpretation of how the model select the lag during the attention mechanism.

Table 3. RMSE Comparison on different Methods over 48 weeks

Farm	DA-LSTM	LSTM	ANN	XGBTR	SVR
A	0.162	0.353	0.372	1.021	0.716
B	0.168	0.178	0.392	0.780	0.701
C	0.176	0.210	0.315	0.926	0.691
D	0.213	0.235	0.577	0.782	0.637
E	0.092	0.104	0.202	0.651	0.652
Mean	**0.162**	0.223	0.372	0.676	0.680

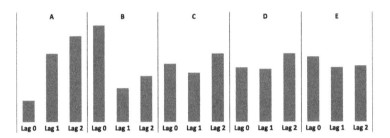

Fig. 3. Lag importance over 5 farms

Most Effective Features. The relationships between yield and other attributes and most effective factors to the yield with attention score were found out. First, we are presenting the top ten factors summarized for all the five farms as shown in Fig. 4.

The first three factors were plant factors which have top attention score on predicting yield. The flowering speed was the most significant factor in the data sets, showing significance difference from the second most important factor, set speed. The number of leaves is third. The CO_2 level is the most imperative environment factor according to our results followed by water usage, humidity and temperature. Leaf Area Index (LAI) and the average weight per unit are the next key features. Radiation sum during 24 hrs is the 10th factors with all summary.

To see the most effective factors to the yield at the different farm level, first, we normalized all the attention scores on all farms. Then summarized the related attributes and plotted the top twenty factors according to different farm levels as shown in Fig. 5.

This graph indicates which factors are most influenced by the yield. After comparing all the five farms, we can see that all the five farms have some similarities as well as some variations up to a certain range.

All the farms have shown that plant factors like flowering speed, set speed and leaf area index are most effective to the yield. Flowering speed and set speed are the most important factor in farm A and D. Farm B and D displayed different

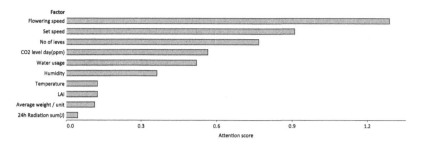

Fig. 4. Most effective features for the yield

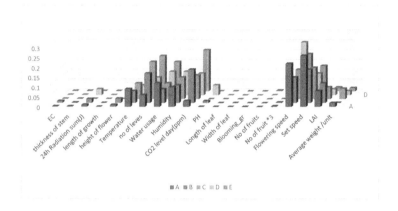

■A ■B ■C ▥D ▨E

Fig. 5. Most effective features for the yield in all farms

results from other farms, for example, the factor importance of PH and height of flower is significantly higher than other farms. The CO_2 level per day is the most important feature in farm E comparing to other farms. However, Farm A has the smallest effects by CO_2 level per day comparing to other farms.

For other factors, as seen in the graph, The LAI has a huge impact on farm A, B, and C, but quite a small impact on others. Humidity and temperature have a similar influence on all farms. The environment factors like humidity, temperature, CO_2 level per day water usage and the PH are all similar for farm B and C. Which means farm B and C has a similar growing environment for the tomato plant. Moreover, water usage has a more significant influence on farm A, D, and E, and solar radiation has more impact on farm B and D.

5   Conclusion

According to our results in proposed duo attention with LSTM and Attention score mechanism, we can conclude that plant factors such as flowering speed, set speed and number of leaves are most important for the tomato yield whereas carbon-dioxide level, water, humidity and temperature are the most effective environmental factors. The DA-LSTM model not only shows high accuracy against other existing applications but also could give a better interpretation on how the tomato features could affect the future yield growth. This paper used the common deep learning technologies with two attentions to successfully solve the time series prediction. The lag attention could let the model keep better. The lag importance to better predict the future and the feature attention could be working directly on each feature for enhancing the important features and fading the less important one.

Acknowledgment. We gratefully acknowledge support from Australian Government Research Training Program Scholarship. This work was supported by the International Cooperation Project of Institute of Information Engineering, Chinese Academy of Sciences under Grant No. Y7Z0511101, and Guangxi Key Laboratory of Trusted Software (No KX201528).

References

1. Amón, R., Maulhardt, M., Wong, T., Kazama, D., Simmons, C.W.: Waste heat and water recovery opportunities in California tomato paste processing. Appl. Therm. Eng. **78**, 525–532 (2015)
2. Bocca, F.F., Rodrigues, L.H.A.: The effect of tuning, feature engineering, and feature selection in data mining applied to rainfed sugarcane yield modelling. Comput. Electron. Agric. **128**, 67–76 (2016)
3. Emamgholizadeh, S., Parsaeian, M., Baradaran, M.: Seed yield prediction of sesame using artificial neural network. Eur. J. Agron. **68**, 89–96 (2015)
4. Freebairn, D., Ghahramani, A., Robinson, J., McClymont, D.: A tool for monitoring soil water using modelling, on-farm data, and mobile technology. Environ. Model. Softw. **104**, 55–63 (2018)
5. Gary, C., Jones, J.W., Tchamitchian, M.: Crop modelling in horticulture: state of the art. Sci. Hortic. **74**(1–2), 3–20 (1998)
6. Higashide, T.: Prediction of tomato yield on the basis of solar radiation before anthesis under warm greenhouse conditions. HortScience **44**(7), 1874–1878 (2009)
7. Johnson, M.D., Hsieh, W.W., Cannon, A.J., Davidson, A., Bédard, F.: Crop yield forecasting on the canadian prairies by remotely sensed vegetation indices and machine learning methods. Agric. For. Meteorol. **218**, 74–84 (2016)
8. Jones, J.W., Dayan, E., Allen, L., Van Keulen, H., Challa, H.: A dynamic tomato growth and yield model (tomgro). Trans. ASAE **34**(2), 663–0672 (1991)
9. Marko, O., Brdar, S., Panic, M., Lugonja, P., Crnojevic, V.: Soybean varieties portfolio optimisation based on yield prediction. Comput. Electron. Agric. **127**, 467–474 (2016)
10. Matsumura, K., Gaitan, C.F., Sugimoto, K., Cannon, A.J., Hsieh, W.W.: Maize yield forecasting by linear regression and artificial neural networks in Jilin, China. J. Agric. Sci. **153**(3), 399–410 (2015)
11. Moon, A., Kim, J., Zhang, J., Liu, H., Son, S.W.: Understanding the impact of lossy compressions on IoT smart farm analytics. In: 2017 IEEE International Conference on Big Data (Big Data), pp. 4602–4611. IEEE (2017)
12. O'Grady, M.J., O'Hare, G.M.: Modelling the smart farm. Inf. Process. Agric. **4**, 179–187 (2017)

13. Pantazi, X.E., Moshou, D., Alexandridis, T., Whetton, R., Mouazen, A.M.: Wheat yield prediction using machine learning and advanced sensing techniques. Comput. Electron. Agric. **121**, 57–65 (2016)
14. Suebsombut, P., Sekhari, A., Sureepong, P., Ueasangkomsate, P., Bouras, A.: The using of bibliometric analysis to classify trends and future directions on "smart farm". In: International Conference on Digital Arts, Media and Technology (ICDAMT), pp. 136–141. IEEE (2017)
15. Yoon, C., Huh, M., Kang, S.G., Park, J., Lee, C.: Implement smart farm with IoT technology. In: 2018 20th International Conference on Advanced Communication Technology (ICACT), pp. 749–752. IEEE (2018)
16. You, J., Li, X., Low, M., Lobell, D., Ermon, S.: Deep Gaussian process for crop yield prediction based on remote sensing data. In: AAAI, pp. 4559–4566 (2017)
17. Zheng, H., Chen, L., Han, X., Zhao, X., Ma, Y.: Classification and regression tree (cart) for analysis of soybean yield variability among fields in Northeast China: the importance of phosphorus application rates under drought conditions. Agric. Ecosyst. Environ. **132**(1–2), 98–105 (2009)

Fast Valuation of Large Portfolios of Variable Annuities via Transfer Learning

Xiaojuan Cheng[1,2] , Wei Luo[3]([✉]) , Guojun Gan[4] , and Gang Li[3]

[1] Xi'an Shiyou University, Shaanxi 710065, China
xiaojuan.cheng@tulip.org.au
[2] Guangxi Key Laboratory of Trusted Software,
Guilin University of Electronic Technology, Guilin, China
[3] Deakin University, Geelong, VIC 3216, Australia
{wei.luo,gang.li}@deakin.edu.au
[4] University of Connecticut, Storrs, CT, USA
guojun.gan@uconn.edu

Abstract. Variable annuities are important financial products that result in 100 billion sales in 2018. These products contain complex guarantees that are computationally expensive to value, and insurance companies are turning to machine learning for the valuation of large portfolios of variable annuity policies. Although earlier studies, exemplified by the regression modelling approach, have shown promising results, the valuation accuracy is unsatisfying. In this paper, we show that one main cause for the poor valuation accuracy is the inefficient selection of representative policies. To overcome this problem, we propose a novel transfer-learning based portfolio valuation framework. The framework first builds a backbone deep neural network using historical Monte Carlo simulation results. The backbone network provides a valuation-driven representation for selecting the policies that best represent a large portfolio. Furthermore, the transferred network provides a way to adaptively extrapolate from these representative policies to the remaining policies in the portfolio. By overcoming a major difficulty faced by the popular Kriging model, the need of matrix inversion, the transferred network can handle a large number of representative policies to sufficiently cover a diverse portfolio.

Keywords: Variable annuity · Deep representation · Transfer learning

1 Introduction

A variable annuity (VA) is a retirement insurance product. Guarantees embedded in variable annuities have complex risk profiles and many insurance companies manage the risk through dynamic hedging [11], which results in a large portfolio of individual policies. In order to simulate the performance of dynamic hedging and determine the stochastic reserve of VA products, insurance companies rely on nested Monte Carlo (MC) simulations [14]. However, the computation of MC simulations for a large VA portfolio is time-consuming because each VA policy

© Springer Nature Switzerland AG 2019
A. C. Nayak and A. Sharma (Eds.): PRICAI 2019, LNAI 11672, pp. 716–728, 2019.
https://doi.org/10.1007/978-3-030-29894-4_57

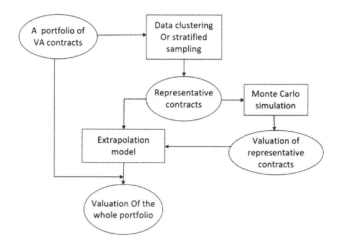

Fig. 1. Meta-modeling approach for VA portfolio valuation.

needs to be projected over many scenarios for a long time horizon. For example, [9] implemented the nested MC simulations in Java, and they calculated the partial dollar deltas along 1,000 real-world paths at annual steps. For a portfolio of 38,000 VA policies, the calculation would take about 2.97 years to complete. In practice, a portfolio needs to be reevaluated under multiple market assumptions. Repeating the MC simulation for each market assumption is simply infeasible.

Recently, meta-modeling approaches [16] have been proposed in the literature [5,10,20] to address the aforementioned computational problem. Figure 1 shows that the meta-modeling approach involves three main steps: First, we select a small number of representative VA policies by a clustering algorithm or a sampling method; Then, we run the MC simulation to generate the valuation of representative VA policies; Finally, we choose an appropriate meta-model (e.g., linear regression) to estimate the valuation of all policies in the large portfolio based on the valuation of representative policies. Meta-modeling approaches can significantly reduce the runtime because only a small number of representative policies are valuated by the high-accuracy MC simulation method, and the whole portfolio of policies are valuated by the meta-model. Although the meta-model may produce less accurate valuation for each policy, the aggregated valuation for the whole portfolio can achieve a low overall error due to the nature of dynamic hedging [5]. This attractive feature makes meta-modeling a popular VA valuation framework.

However, current VA meta-modeling approach relies on efficient selection of policies representing the whole portfolio. When a portfolio is large and with diverse policies, this task is challenging and usually results in poor valuation accuracy (See Sect. 3).

Our Contributions. We propose a new framework for accurate valuation of a large VA portfolio. It builds on the commonly adopted clustering-based

Table 1. Example predictor variables used for clustering VA policies.

Variable	Description
gender	Gender of the policyholder
age	Age of the policyholder
productType	Product type of the VA policy
gmwbBalance	Guaranteed minimum withdrawal benefit (GMWB) balance
gbAmt	Guaranteed benefit amount
FundValue$i$	Account value of the ith fund, for $i = 1,2,\ldots,$n
ttm	Time to maturity in years

approach. At the centre of our framework is the novel idea of clustering not at the predictors themselves, but at a deeper representation guided by the target performance of policies. This is done in a principled approach using deep neural network motivated by the *information bottleneck* [17] principle (see Sect. 4.2 for details).

The proposed method for selecting representative policies greatly improves the coverage of the diverse policies in a dynamically hedged portfolio. This contributes to superior performance in portfolio risk valuation. In addition to an abstract representation to improve clustering, the deep neural network provides a way to quickly re-estimate VA valuations under varying market assumptions. Extensive empirical evaluations have confirmed that our framework provides more accurate VA estimates, which also implies reduced dependency on the computational expensive Monte Carlo simulation. Finally, our framework addresses a major challenge faced by the state-of-the-art Kriging model, the need to compute matrix inversion which inhibits the use of a moderately bigger number of representative policies.

This paper is organized as follows. Section 2 reviews the related work, and Sect. 4 proposes the transfer-learning framework. The details of experiments and result analysis are presented in Sect. 5. Finally, in Sect. 6 we conclude the paper.

2   Related Work

During the past five years, a number of research papers on meta-modeling for VA valuation have been published [2,3,5–8,10,12,13,20]. In [2] and [6], the k-prototype algorithm was used to select representative VA policies and the Kriging model was used as the meta-model. To address the drawback that the k-prototype algorithm is not efficient for selecting a moderate number (e.g., 200) of representative VA policies, [3] proposed the Latin hypercube sampling (LHS) to select representative policies. In [5], a scalable clustering algorithm called the truncated fuzzy c-means (TFMC) algorithm was used to select representative policies. In [7], several methods for selecting representative VA policies were compared. The authors found that the clustering method and the LHS method produce similar results, and both are better than other methods such as random sampling.

In [12] and [20], neural networks were employed for the valuation of large VA portfolio. In [13], the valuation of large VA portfolios was formulated as a spatial interpolation problem. In [8], the authors studied the use of copula to model the dependency of partial dollar deltas and found that the use of copula does not improve the prediction accuracy of the meta-model. In [10], the authors used the GB2 (generalized beta of the second kind) distribution to model the fair market values. In [4], the author considered interactions between VA policy features in linear models and found that linear models with interaction terms can produce accurate predictions.

Among the meta-models considered in the aforementioned papers, the Kriging model is one of the top performers in terms of accuracy. Therefore in this paper, the Kriging model is used as the baseline for evaluating our proposed framework. To describe the ordinary Kriging model, let $\mathbf{z}_1$, $\mathbf{z}_2$, ..., $\mathbf{z}_s$ be the representative VA policies. For every $j = 1, 2, \ldots, k$, let v_j be the fair market value of $\mathbf{z}_j$ that is calculated by Monte Carlo simulation. Then the fair market value of the VA policy $\mathbf{x}_i$ in the portfolio is estimated as follows:

$$\hat{y}_i = \sum_{j=1}^{k} w_{ij} \cdot v_j, \tag{1}$$

where $w_{i1}, w_{i2}, \ldots, w_{ik}$ are the Kriging weights obtained by solving the following linear equation system [15]:

$$\begin{pmatrix} V_{11} & \cdots & V_{1k} & 1 \\ \vdots & \ddots & \vdots & \vdots \\ V_{k1} & \cdots & V_{kk} & 1 \\ 1 & \cdots & 1 & 0 \end{pmatrix} \cdot \begin{pmatrix} w_{i1} \\ \vdots \\ w_{ik} \\ \theta_i \end{pmatrix} = \begin{pmatrix} D_{i1} \\ \vdots \\ D_{ik} \\ 1 \end{pmatrix}. \tag{2}$$

In the above equation, θ_i is a control variable used to make sure the sum of the Kriging weights is equal to one,

$$V_{rs} = \alpha + \exp\left(-\frac{3}{\beta} D(\mathbf{z}_r, \mathbf{z}_s)\right), \quad r, s = 1, 2, \ldots, k, \tag{3}$$

and

$$D_{ij} = \alpha + \exp\left(-\frac{3}{\beta} D(\mathbf{x}_i, \mathbf{z}_j)\right), \quad j = 1, 2, \ldots, k, \tag{4}$$

where $D(\cdot, \cdot)$ denotes the Euclidean distance, and both $\alpha \geq 0$ and $\beta > 0$ are parameters.

One major drawback of the Kriging model is that the computational cost for large k can be inhibitive, due to the need for matrix inversion.

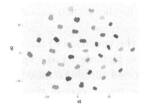  

(a) All variables including productType and Gender. Distinct clusters are formed for different product types.

(b) With productType removed and Gender kept. Two genders lead to two nearly identical clusters. But better mixture is achieved in each cluster.

(c) With both Gender and productType removed. The artefact due to Gender is also removed.

Fig. 2. t-SNE visualization of policies in a portfolio, forming clusters from which representative policies are selected.

3   Challenges in Representative Policy Selection

The success of meta-modeling relies on a set of well-balanced representative policies. However, finding such representative policies in a large portfolio remains some challenges. We will illustrate these challenges for clustering-based meta-modeling, which also apply to the sampling-based approach.

In the clustering-based approach, the representative policies are chosen from cluster centroids. The clustering of policies are based on a bag of variables assumed to be potentially predictive of the policy performance. These may include variables related to the policy holder and those related to the products themselves. Some example variables are shown in Table 1. Clearly until the simulation is completed, we do not actually know whether or how much these variables can predict the policy performance. Adding to this indiscriminating use of variables, the clustering also runs on bare categorical variables (e.g., gender and productType). Such categorical variables, especially those with a large number of levels, can create artificial clusters aligned mostly with their levels. Figure 2 demonstrates the inherent challenge of selecting 'representative' policies solely based on independent variables, which may or may not be predictive of target variable (policy valuation in this case). In other words, noisy or irrelevant policies-level features may impose undue influence on the clustering results, leading to unreliable 'representative' policies. Clearly the above difficulties of finding truly representative policies also apply to the sampling-based approach. The problem needs to be addressed for meta-modeling to achieve more reliable valuation.

4   Method

In this section, we present the transfer-learning (TL) based framework. Figure 3 shows the major steps in our framework, and the difference with Fig. 1

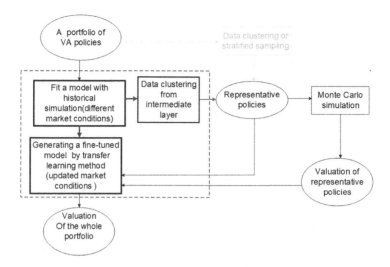

Fig. 3. The proposed model. The dashed line highlights the new components introduced. A deep neural network is trained using historical data or data from an approximate (simplified) simulation (Sect. 4.1). The trained network provides both a regulated space for robust policy clustering (Sect. 4.2) and a base model that can be transferred for extrapolation (Sect. 4.3).

(the traditional approach) has been highlighted with bold arrows in Fig. 3. In general, the proposed transfer-learning (TL) framework consists of the following five major steps.

1. Fit a multi-layered (deep) model based on a large number of historical simulations, under a potentially different market scenarios.
2. Obtain feature representations from an intermediate layer, which also forms a manifold of the portfolio, then use a data clustering algorithm to find a small number of representative policies.
3. With the configurations of the target market, run the Monte Carlo simulation for the valuation of representative policies.
4. Fine-tune the pre-trained model using simulation results of representative policies.
5. Use the transferred model to value all policies in the portfolio.

4.1   Build a Deep Neural Network Using Historical Data

This step builds a deep neural network that provides both a representation for clustering and a base model for transfer learning. Figure 4 shows the network architecture. To train such a network, we exploit available historical simulation data for similar VA products, potentially under a different set of market assumptions. When such historical simulation data is not available, we rely on the fact

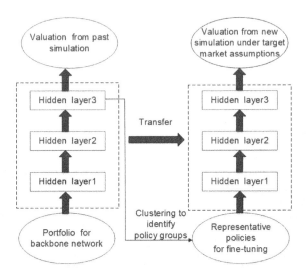

Fig. 4. The transfer learning architecture

that Monte Carlo simulation can be simplified with a much lower resolution to trade simulation accuracy for efficiency. A network trained on such a *proxy* target variable is often sufficient as a base model. With the proxy training labels, we train a dense network with three hidden layers.

4.2 Clustering on Hidden-Layer Representation

With the neural network trained, we perform the following steps to obtain the representative contracts from a portfolio.

1. Feed contacts to the network and obtain the hidden-layer representations.
2. Perform clustering on the obtained representations.
3. From the generated clusters, retrieve the cluster centers, which will become the representative policies.

Performing clustering on deep features can overcome the problem of inefficient clustering as shown in Fig. 2, because performing unsupervised learning on such features is a highly effective technique used by many deep learning practitioners. For example, deep representation was recently used to improve robustness in video anomaly detection [19]. Such representation can be extracted by deep neural network, which can transform input signals through multiple hidden layers to output layer. More specifically, when model training begins, the network receives an input X, and successively processes it through hidden layers, where the output of previous layer is the input of next layer. The closer the hidden layer is to the output layer, the more relevant features can be captured.

In our setup, the deep representation can be viewed as the result of regulating input features using the (proxy) target variable. Formally, it can be explained via the *information bottleneck* principle. The recent work by Tishby and Zaslavsky [18] provides a formal structure for understanding the latent representations in terms of information processing. The idea of *information bottleneck* principle is that a network rids noisy input data of extraneous details as if by squeezing the information through a bottleneck, preserving information in the data that is relevant to the outputs. As can be seen in Fig. 2, clustering on the original inputs cannot distinguish relevant information from irrelevant information.

More formally, assume an input random variable $X \in \mathcal{X}$, and an output random variable $Y \in \mathcal{Y}$, given a join distribution $p(X, Y)$, the *relevant information* is defined as the mutual information $I(X; Y)$, where we assume statistical dependence between X and Y. In this case, we can capture relevant features by a compressed mapping of input variable X that discards the information irrelevant to Y.

In a multi-layer network, the hidden layer representation H provides an information compression of X guided by Y. In terms of the mutual information, neural network training tries effectively to minimise $I(X; H)$ and maximise $I(H; Y)$.

4.3   Transfer Learning

The previous step produces a deep network that maps each policy to a proxy measurement of its valuation. It forms a base model that can recalibrate using the high-resolution Monte Carlo simulation results on representative policies under the target market condition.

Let (P) be the portfolio of policies as shown in Fig. 1. The pre-trained network can be viewed as a function $f(c; \theta^s)$ minimising $\sum_{c \in \mathcal{P}} L(f(c; \theta^s), y_c^s)$, where y_c^s is the valuation used for pre-training. With the set $\mathcal{R}$ of the representative policies, we fine-tune the network so that θ^s is replaced by θ^t that minimises $\sum_{c \in \mathcal{R}} L(f(c; \theta^t), y_c^t)$, where y_c^t is the valuation generated by high-resolution Monte Carlo simulation.

5   Experiment and Analysis

Due to the demanding computational requirement of Monte Carlo simulation, our experiment will be based on existing simulation results for a large VA portfolio under five different sets of market assumptions. We will treat the first set of simulation results as given and use it to train a deep neural network. From the remaining four sets of results, we will simulate the process of re-valuation of the representative policies under those market assumptions. They also provide the ground truth for evaluating the valuation accuracy of the transferred model.

5.1   Data Description

To evaluate the performance of our transfer-learning framework, we follow [5] and use a synthetic portfolio. The portfolio contains $38,000$ synthetic variable annuity policies, described by 34 features including 2 categorical features (See Table 1).

Five sets of deltas have been generated using Monte Carlo simulation as in [5] under different market assumptions. Figure 5 shows a histogram of the first set of deltas. We use this set of deltas to simulate the available historical data for training the backbone network. The remaining four sets of deltas will be used as the ground-truths for evaluating the transfer-learning model.

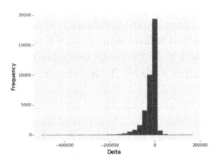

Fig. 5. A histogram of deltas in a portfolio under the first application market. The wide range of deltas reflects the diverse policies in a portfolio with dynamic hedging. It is crucial that the selected representative policies provide sufficient coverage of such a diverse portfolio.

5.2 Performance Metrics

To evaluate the accuracy of the proposed model, we follow the strategy in [5] and use the following two validation measures: the percentage error at the portfolio level and R^2. The percentage error and R^2 is respectively defined as

$$PE(\mathcal{P}) = \frac{\sum_{c_i \in \mathcal{P}}(\hat{y}_i - y_i)}{\sum_{c_i \in \mathcal{P}} y_i}, R^2 = 1 - \frac{\sum_{c_i \in \mathcal{P}}(\hat{y}_i - y_i)^2}{\sum_{c_i \in \mathcal{P}}(y_i - \mu)^2} \qquad (5)$$

where y_i describes the value of policy c_i in the portfolio $\mathcal{P}$ from the high-resolution Monte Carlo simulation. And $\hat{y}_i$ is the corresponding estimate from the neural network, $\mu = \frac{1}{n}\sum_{c_i \in \mathcal{P}} y_i$ is the average Delta value.

From the above equations we can see, PE and R^2 are complimentary measurements for the valuation accuracy. While R^2 measures the fitness at the policy level, PE directly measures the accuracy at the portfolio level. Therefore minimising PE is our primary objective.

5.3 Baseline Models

To verify the performance of proposed transfer-learning framework, two baseline models are set. One is the meta-model in [5]. In that model, the TFCM++

algorithm is used to obtain k cluster centres as representative policies. After obtaining the Monte Carlo simulated deltas for these k representative policies, Kriging is performed to extrapolate the delta values to other policies in the portfolio. Please see [5] for more details.

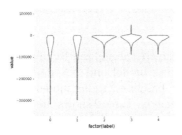 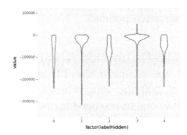

(a) clustering on the input space (policy-specific features).

(b) clustering on the hidden-layer representation.

Fig. 6. clustering on the input space (policy-specific features).

To demonstrate the value of transfer learning, we also use the neural network (NN) model trained directly on the representative policies as another baseline. For simplicity, we use the same representative policies selected by the backbone network, and corresponding deltas are acquired via the MC simulation. However, no fine-tuning is applied, the neural network starts with random parameter initialisation and is directly trained using the small number of representative policies under a target market assumption.

5.4   Implementation Details of the Proposed Model

The deep network. Using the first set of deltas, we train a three-layer densely connected network. From the third hidden layer, we obtain the representation of the policies and perform clustering using K-means to obtain the representative policies. The trained network is saved as the base network for transfer learning under a different set of market assumptions.

Transfer learning. For each of the remaining four sets of market assumptions, we obtain the deltas for representative policies. These additional deltas were used to fine-tune the saved basic network. Detailed illustrations are shown in Fig. 4.

5.5   Results

Quality of Representative Policy Selection. To verify that the hidden layer provides a better representation for selecting representative policies. We randomly sample 5,000 points on the input space and the representation space respectively, and then group them into 5 clusters. The corresponding delta value range and distribution are shown in Fig. 6. Some similar clusters are presented in Fig. 6a. For example, the leftmost two clusters have nearly identical distributions, and similarly for the remaining three clusters, which suggests that the clustering on the input features will result in redundant representative policies, and consequently inefficient use of the Monte Carlo simulation. In contrast, clusters in Fig. 6b have distinct distributions, and they will likely lead to more distinct representative policies.

Portfolio Estimation Accuracy. To demonstrate the superiority of proposed model, we compare the TL model with Kriging model and NN model when $k = 100$, 200 and 400. When k gets bigger, the baseline Kriging model becomes infeasible due to the need for inverting a large matrix. Table 2 shows the accuracy of three models. As we can see in this table, in each model, as the number of clusters increases, PE reduces but R^2 improves, which indicates that the larger the number of representative policies, the higher the prediction accuracy. On the other hand, in each setting, the accuracy of TL model is always the highest among these models. For example, when $k = 100$, PE of Kriging model is 0.115 whereas TL model's drops to 0.043. Similar trends can be observed in other clusters, too. Moreover, with the increase of k, the advantage of the TL model is more remarkable. The low R^2 for the Kriging model suggests a poor model fit. This is not surprising in views of the redundant clusters shown in Fig. 6a.

Overall, the transfer-learning framework outperforms the Kriging model and the vanilla deep neural network in terms of the valuation accuracy.

Computing Cost. Table 3 shows the runtime of major steps of Kriging model and TL model. The majority of the run time is still spent on generating Monte Carlo simulation for the representative policies. In general, transfer-learning framework does not take longer than the SoTA Kriging model, if a backbone network is available. The fine-tuning step is faster than Kriging, especially when the number of clusters k increases, because it avoids the need for matrix inversion. The training of the backbone network took 54.90 s, a constant that is independent of k.

Overall, the transfer-learning framework achieves improved accuracy (measured by PE) and shorter runtime (due to the avoidance of matrix inversion is more pronounced). The differences are more pronounced as the number of clusters k gets larger. For example, from Tables 2 and 3, when $k = 400$, PE of Kriging model is 0.035, while TL model's surprisedly drops to 0.001. This is achieved with a shorter run-time than Kriging model. Therefore, the proposed framework can have greater advantages in both estimation accuracy and computation time when a portfolio has a greater diversity and requires more representative policies for sufficient coverage.

Table 2. Accuracy comparison of three models. k denotes the number of representative policies.

$k = 100$			$k = 200$			$k = 400$		
	Kriging	NN	TL model	Kriging	NN	TL model	Kriging	NN	TL model
$\downarrow PE$	0.115	0.056	**0.043**	0.074	0.036	**0.024**	0.035	0.003	**0.001**
$\uparrow R^2$	0.324	0.437	**0.445**	0.392	0.452	**0.485**	0.446	0.577	**0.661**

Table 3. Runtime of the proposed TL framework and the baseline Kriging model.

	$k = 100$		$k = 200$		$k = 400$	
	Kriging	TL model	Kriging	TL model	Kriging	TL model
Clustering	1.63	**1.46**	3.35	**3.16**	8.10	**7.82**
Monte Carlo[a]	722.34	722.34	1,444.68	1,444.68	2,889.36	2,889.36
Kriging[b]/Fine-tuning	3.07	**2.65**	7.30	**2.86**	14.79	**3.88**
Total	727.04	**726.45**	1455.33	**1450.70**	2912.25	**2901.06**

[a,b] Estimations derived from the results reported in [5].

6   Conclusions

We have proposed a new framework to address two challenges that current meta-modeling approaches face in a large portfolio of VA policies: inefficient selection of representative policies and the need for matrix inversion in Kriging. Incorporating the principles of information bottleneck and transfer learning, the framework achieves empirically validated improvement on the representative policy selection and the policy re-valuation under varying marketing assumption. Furthermore, by avoiding matrix inversion in the popular Kriging model, the proposed framework is able to handle a large number of representative policies, which is critical for sufficient coverage of a diverse portfolio.

The current work can potentially be extended along several dimensions. In particular in [1], we show that the clustering can be performed in a space of reduced dimension, which can result in further improvement of the valuation accuracy.

Acknowledgement. This work was supported by the International Cooperation Project of Institute of Information Engineering, Chinese Academy of Sciences under Grant No. Y7Z0511101, and Guangxi Key Laboratory of Trusted Software (No KX201528).

References

1. Cheng, X., Luo, W., Gan, G., Li, G.: Deep neighbor embedding for evaluation of large portfolios of variable annuities. In: Douligeris, C., Karagiannis, D., Apostolou, D. (eds.) KSEM 2019. LNCS (LNAI), vol. 11775, pp. xx–yy. Springer, Cham (2019)

2. Gan, G.: Application of data clustering and machine learning in variable annuity valuation. Insur. Math. Econ. **53**(3), 795–801 (2013). https://doi.org/10.1016/j.insmatheco.2013.09.021

3. Gan, G.: Application of metamodeling to the valuation of large variable annuity portfolios. In: Proceedings of the Winter Simulation Conference, pp. 1103–1114 (2015)

4. Gan, G.: Valuation of large variable annuity portfolios using linear models with interactions. Risks **6**(3), 71 (2018). https://doi.org/10.3390/risks6030071

5. Gan, G., Huang, J.: A data mining framework for valuing large portfolios of variable annuities. In: Proceedings of the 23rd ACM SIGKDD International Conference on Knowledge Discovery and Data Mining, pp. 1467–1475 (2017). https://doi.org/10.1145/3097983.3098013

6. Gan, G., Lin, X.S.: Valuation of large variable annuity portfolios under nested simulation: a functional data approach. Insur. Math. Econ. **62**, 138–150 (2015)

7. Gan, G., Valdez, E.A.: An empirical comparison of some experimental designs for the valuation of large variable annuity portfolios. Depend. Model. **4**(1), 382–400 (2016). http://ssrn.com/abstract=2830879

8. Gan, G., Valdez, E.A.: Modeling partial greeks of variable annuities with dependence. Insur. Math. Econ. **76**, 118–134 (2017). http://ssrn.com/abstract=2844509

9. Gan, G., Valdez, E.A.: Nested stochastic valuation of large variable annuity portfolios: Monte Carlo simulation and synthetic datasets. Data **3**(3), 31 (2018). https://doi.org/10.3390/data303003110.3390/data3030031

10. Gan, G., Valdez, E.A.: Regression modeling for the valuation of large variable annuity portfolios. North Am. Actuarial J. **22**(1), 40–54 (2018). http://ssrn.com/abstract=2808088

11. Hardy, M.: Investment Guarantees: Modeling and Risk Management for Equity-linked Life Insurance, vol. 215. Wiley, Hoboken (2003)

12. Hejazi, S.A., Jackson, K.R.: A neural network approach to efficient valuation of large portfolios of variable annuities. Insur. Math. Econ. **70**, 169–181 (2016)

13. Hejazi, S.A., Jackson, K.R., Gan, G.: A spatial interpolation framework for efficient valuation of large portfolios of variable annuities. Quant. Finan. Econ. **1**(2), 125–144 (2017). https://doi.org/10.3934/QFE.2017.2.125

14. IAA: Stochastic Modeling: Theory and Reality from an Actuarial Perspective. International Actuarial Association, Ontario, Canada (2010). http://share.actuaries.org/Documentation/StochMod_2nd_Ed_print_quality.pdf

15. Isaaks, E., Srivastava, R.: An Introduction to Applied Geostatistics. Oxford University Press, Oxford (1990)

16. Kleijnen, J.P.C.: A comment on blanning's "metamodel for sensitivity analysis: the regression metamodel in simulation". Interfaces **5**(3), 21–23 (1975)

17. Tishby, N., Pereira, F.C., Bialek, W.: The information bottleneck method. Univ. Illinois **411**(29–30), 368–377 (2000)

18. Tishby, N., Zaslavsky, N.: Deep learning and the information bottleneck principle. In: 2015 IEEE Information Theory Workshop (ITW), pp. 1–5. IEEE (2015)

19. Vu, H., Nguyen, T.D., Le, T., Luo, W., Phung, D.: Robust anomaly detection in videos using multilevel representations. In: Proceedings of Thirty-third AAAI Conference on Artificial Intelligence (AAAI), Honolulu, USA (2019)

20. Xu, W., Chen, Y., Coleman, C., Coleman, T.F.: Moment matching machine learning methods for risk management of large variable annuity portfolios. J. Econ. Dyn. Control **87**, 1–20 (2018)

Forecasting of Currency Exchange Rate Using Artificial Neural Network: A Case Study of Solomon Island Dollar

James D. Kimata[1], M. G. M. Khan[1(✉)], Anuraganand Sharma[1],
Mahmood A. Rashid[2], and Tokaua Tekabu[1]

[1] The University of the South Pacific, Suva, Fiji
jamesdekimata@gmail.com,
{khan_mg, sharma_au, tekabu_t}@usp.ac.fj
[2] Victoria University Melbourne, Werribee, VIC 3030, Australia
mahmood.rashid@gmail.com

Abstract. The use of neural network models for currency exchange rate forecasting has received much attention in recent time. In this paper, we propose an exchange rate forecasting model based on artificial neural network. We tested our model on forecasting the exchange rate of Solomon Islands Dollar against some major trading currencies of the country such as, Australian Dollar, Great Britain Pound, Japanese yen, and Euro. We compared the performance of our model with that of the single exponential smoothing model; the double exponential smoothing with trend model; and Holt-Winter multiplicative and additive seasonal and multiple linear regression model. The performance of the models was measured using the error function, root mean square error (RMSE). The empirical result reveals that the proposed model is more efficient and accurate in forecasting currency exchange rate in comparison to the regression and time series models.

Keywords: Forecasting exchange rate · Neural network model · Multiple linear regression model · Time series models · Naive method

1 Introduction

Currency exchange rate plays an import role for a country in any international trading. Developing forecasting models for exchange rates is an on-going field of research because of its contribution to investors' confidence in the local currency, entrepreneurship development and also the performance of the stock market. Many time series models such as autoregressive integrated moving average (ARIMA), autoregressive (AR), Random Walk (RW), generalized autoregressive conditional heteroscedasticity (GARCH), and exponential smoothing models have been developed over the past decades to forecast exchange rates (Meese and Rogoff 1983; Zhang et al. 1998, 2003; Tambi 2005; Lee and Boon 2007; Maniatis 2012; Ahmed et al. 2013). However, these models are well known in the literature for their poor predictions, which are characteristically highly volatile, complex, noisy, nonstationary, nonlinear and chaotic (Meese and Rogoff 1983; Kuan and Liu 1995; Abhyanker et al. 1997;

© Springer Nature Switzerland AG 2019
A. C. Nayak and A. Sharma (Eds.): PRICAI 2019, LNAI 11672, pp. 729–733, 2019.
https://doi.org/10.1007/978-3-030-29894-4_58

Gencay 1999; Zhang 2003; Tambi 2005; Maniatis 2012). In 1970, Box and Jenkins popularized ARIMA and researchers use it to forecast economic time series for years as a benchmark model (Kadilar et al. 2009). ARIMA is a general univariate model and it is developed on the assumption that the time series being forecasted, is linear and stationary. But most of the time series are nonlinear and nonstationary which makes ARIMA not a good technique for forecasting (Kadilar et al. 2009; Ahmed et al. 2013). Recently, ANN has become a popular model for forecasting (Leung et al. 2000; Walczak 2001; Huang and Lai 2004; Kadilar et al. 2009; Pradhan and Kumar 2010; Egrioglu et al. 2012) and was found to be more effective than other econometric models with higher percentage of accuracy to predict (Walczak 2001).

In this paper, we develop an ANN-based forecasting model of exchange rates for SBD against its major trading currencies such as AUD, GBP, JPY and EUR. The proposed model forecasts the rate that minimizes the sum of squared errors and is based on three neurons in the input layer and four neurons in the hidden layer. As a learning algorithm, a generalized reduced gradient (GRG) is developed, which uses a tangent hyperbolic transfer function and is solved using Excel Solver.

The rest of the paper is summarized as follows. First two sections discuss the methodology of ANN and time series models with the measures of model evaluation and validation. The next section describes the Solomon's exchange rate data followed by the presentation of results and discussion of the forecasting time series and proposed ANN models. The paper ends with the discussion of results and conclusion with future directions.

2 Solomon Islands Exchange Rate Data

This paper used the daily exchange rate of AUD against SBD (AUD/SBD) and the three other major trading currencies, namely GBP, JPY and EUR from January 5, 1998 to June 30, 2014 collected from the Central Bank of Solomon Islands (CBSI 2005, 2014). The data contain 4150 observations, out of this, 3750 (90%) will be used for training and the remaining 400 (10%) will be used for forecasting, which excludes weekends and public holidays.

3 Methodology

The purpose of this paper is to develop an artificial neural network for forecasting the exchange rate of a country against its major trading currencies and to compare its performance with other time series models. We use the naive method as a benchmark method for the comparison of the proposed ANN model.

The main goal of a neural network is to make an accurate prediction in the dependent variable (output cell). The advantage of a neural network is that it uses less assumptions; it can fit a nonlinear model that can approximate any nonlinear function with higher accuracy; and has greater ability of prediction to be used in many different areas (Kamruzzaman and Sarker 2004; Wu and Yang 2007; Kadilar et al. 2009).

The ANN model designed in this paper is a multi-layered perception. The proposed model considers the most widely used neural network, known as the back propagation network. The network consists of one-hidden layer with different lags of exchange rate as neurons in the input layer. We used 2 to 6 (lag 2 to lag 6) nodes for the input layer, 3 to 5 nodes for the hidden layer and one output in the model topology. We experiment on different transformation or activation functions to map the inputs into the outputs and found that the tangent hyperbolic *tanh* function gives better performance so we use it in our model. The optimum weights and biases that yield the best forecasts are obtained by minimizing the sum of square error (SSE). Using the training data with the RMSE error measure for different number of nodes in the input and hidden layers we found ANN (3, 4, 1) to be the best so we take it as our final model.

We also constructed the multiple linear regression (MLR) and time series models for comparison purposes. For the selection of the number of time-lags that fits best a multiple linear regression model for forecasting AUD/SBD exchange rate, we consider the Akaike information criteria (AIC) and the Schwarz information criteria (SIC) and found that MLR (6), the multiple linear regression with 6 lags is the most preferred model because it is significant at the 1% level of confidence, and has the lowest values of AIC and SIC. We also generate the time series models using the exponential single and double smoothing models as well as the Holt–Winters (HW) additive and multi-plicative models for the training sample.

4   Forecasting Results and Discussion

We use the testing sample to forecast the Solomon Islands exchange rates against AUD, GBP, JPY and EUR using all the methods discussed above. For the comparison of various forecasting models and exchange rate series, we present the error measures in Table 1 for AUD, GBP, JPY and EUR. The results of the proposed ANN (3, 4, 1) model are presented in the last row of the table. It reveals that the proposed ANN (3, 4, 1) is the preferred model with lowest RMSE. We further benchmarked our proposed model with the naive method, which may appear to be the best forecasting method in many cases. Thus, the proposed ANN method should be compared to this simple method to ensure that the new method is better (Hyndman and Athanasopoulos 2014). The results for the naive method along with the proposed method are presented in Table 2. The table reveals that the proposed method outperformed the benchmarked method in all of the four exchange rate.

Table 1. RMSE measures for different models and exchange rate series using the testing sample.

Model	AUD ($\times 10^{-4}$)	GBP ($\times 10^{-4}$)	JPY ($\times 10^{-4}$)	EUR ($\times 10^{-4}$)
Single	10.49	12.33	12.74	7.26
Double	10.60	13.25	10.13	7.63
HW additive	9.31	12.33	8.53	7.20
HW multiplicative	9.31	12.33	8.53	7.20
MLR(6)	9.37	12.81	8.74	7.39
ANN (3, 4, 1)	**9.23**	**11.95**	**8.52**	**6.96**

Table 2. RMSE measures for benchmarking the proposed ANN model using the naive method for different currencies exchange rate.

Accuracy measure	AUD/SBD		GBP/SBD		Japanese Yen/SBD		EUR/SBD	
	Naive	ANN	Naive	ANN	Naive	ANN	Naive	ANN
RMSE ($\times 10^{-4}$)	164.91	**9.23**	37.61	**11.95**	246.66	**8.52**	36.95	**6.96**

5 Conclusion

In this paper, we propose an ANN model for forecasting Solomon exchange rates against four major trading currencies. The result of this study reports that the ANN (3, 4, 1) produces least values of RMSE. This proposed model is compared with regression and time series models and is found to be robust and superior. The proposed model also has the least value of RMSE over the benchmarked method for all the currencies. These empirical findings strongly indicate that ANN is an efficient tool for the forecasting the currency exchange rates more accurately. The immediate future direction is to use other exchange rate datasets with ANN or its variations such as recurrent neural network and cooperative coevolution neural network.

Acknowledgement. The authors would like to thank Mr. Ali Homelo from the Central Bank of Solomon Islands for providing the daily exchange rate data and the information on the basket of currencies.

References

Abhyanker, A., Copeland, L.S., Wong, W.: Uncovering nonlinear structure in real-time stock-market indexes: the S&P 500, The Dax, the Nikkei 225, and the FTSE-100. J. Bus. Econ. Stat. **15**, 1–14 (1997)

Ahmed, S., Khan, M.G.M., Prasad, B.: Forecasting Tala/USD and Tala/AUD of Samoa using AR (1), and AR(4): a comparative study. Math. Comput. Contemp. Sci., 178–186 (2013)

CBSI: CBSI quarterly review, vol. 17. Central Bank of Solomon Islands, Honiara, June 2005

CBSI: CBSI quarterly review, vol. 27. Central Bank of Solomon Islands, Honiara, June 2014

Egrioglu, E., Aladag, H.C., Yolcu, U.: Comparison of architect selection criteria in analysing long memory time series. Adv. Time Ser. Forecast. **3**, 18–25 (2012)

Gencay, R.: Linear, non-linear and essential Foreign exchange rate prediction with simple technical trading rules. J. Int. Econ. **47**, 91–107 (1999)

Huang, W., Lai, K.K.: Forecasting Foreign exchange rates with artificial neural networks: a review. Int. J. Inf. Technol. Decis. Mak. **3**, 145–165 (2004)

Hyndman, R.J., Athanasopoulos, G.: Forecasting: Principles and Practice. OTexts (2014)

Kadilar, C., Muammer, S., Aladag, H.C.: Forecasting the exchange rate series with ANN: the case of Turkey. Istanb. Univ. Econ. Stat. E-J. **9**, 17–29 (2009)

Kamruzzaman, J., Sarker, R.A.: ANN-based forecasting of Foreign currency exchange rates. Neural Inf. Process. Lett. Rev. **3**, 49–58 (2004)

Kuan, C.M., Liu, T.: Forecasting exchange rates using feedforward and recurrent neural networks. J. Appl. Econ. **10**, 347–364 (1995)

Lee, C.L., Boon, H.T.: Macroeconomic factors of exchange rate volatility evidence from four neighbouring ASEAN economies. Stud. Econ. Financ. **24**, 266–285 (2007)

Leung, M.T., Chen, A.S., Daouk, H.: Forecasting exchange rates using general regression neural networks. Comput. Oper. Res. **27**, 1093–1110 (2000)

Maniatis, P.: Forecasting the exchange rate between Euro and USD: probabilistic approach versus ARIMA and exponential smoothing techniques. J. Appl. Bus. Res. **28**, 171–192 (2012)

Meese, R.A., Rogoff, K.: Empirical exchange rate models of the seventies. Do they fit out of sample? J. Int. Econ. **14**, 3–24 (1983)

Pradhan, R.P., Kumar, R.: Forecasting exchange rate in India: an application of artificial neural network model. J. Math. Res. **2**, 111–117 (2010)

Tambi, M.K.: Forecasting exchange rate: a univariate out of sample approach. IUP J. Bank Manag. **0**(2), 60–74 (2005)

Walczak, S.: An empirical analysis of data requirements for financial forecasting with neural networks. J. Manag. Inf. Syst. **17**, 203–222 (2001)

Wu, W.P., Yang, H.L.: Forecasting New Taiwan/United States dollar exchange rate using neural network. Bus. Rev. **7**, 63–69 (2007)

Zhang, G., Patuwo, B.E., Hu, M.Y.: Forecasting with artificial neural networks: The state of the art. Int. J. Forecast. **14**, 35–62 (1998)

Zhang, G.P.: Time series forecasting using a hybrid ARIMA and neural network model. Neurocomputing **50**, 159–175 (2003)

CapDRL: A Deep Capsule Reinforcement Learning for Movie Recommendation

Chenfei Zhao$^{(\boxtimes)}$ and Lan Hu$^{(\boxtimes)}$

School of Mathematical Sciences, Peking University, Beijing 100871, China
{zhaochenfei,lh_math}@pku.edu.cn

Abstract. Recommender systems provide users with a personalized list based on individual interests. There are three main challenges in traditional movie recommendation models: (1) considering recommendation procedure as a static one; (2) not taking user's feedback into consideration; (3) it's hard to extract similar features of items rated by users effectively. To address these, we propose a Deep Reinforcement Learning method based on the Capsule Network for the movie recommendation, called CapDRL. Roughly speaking, to solve the first two problems, we formulate the task of sequential interactions between users and recommender systems as a Markov Decision Process and automatically learn the optimal strategies by deep reinforcement learning. For the third problem, we leverage Capsule Network to dynamically decide what and how much similar information need be transferred from each item, which can capture the user's preference. Experiments on real datasets indicate that CapDRL outperforms state-of-the-art methods, validating the effectiveness of our approach on the recommender system. In addition, we explore the effects of different features on the proposed model.

Keywords: Deep reinforcement learning · Capsule ·
Recommender system

1 Introduction

Recommender Systems (RS) tend to predict the probability that a specific user will like a specific resource. According to the past user behaviors, it will generate a personalized list of potentially relevant resources [3]. Compared to traditional recommendation methods [6,9], employing deep learning in RS draws wide attention [1,10] due to their capability of modeling complex user-item interactions. However, there are some defects in movie recommendation.

First, methods often consider recommendation procedure as a static one. User may have different interests as time goes by, and the properties of items cannot always keep the same. Besides, new items can be constantly incorporated into the system, which might influence users' interests. Methods based on recommender systems should model the dynamics of recommendation.

L. Hu—Equal contribution.

© Springer Nature Switzerland AG 2019
A. C. Nayak and A. Sharma (Eds.): PRICAI 2019, LNAI 11672, pp. 734–739, 2019.
https://doi.org/10.1007/978-3-030-29894-4_59

Second, most models do not take users' feedback into consideration for recommending the latest. The user either finds something interesting or gets bad experience then relinquishes this movie after trying for a while. Both the actions should be adopted as the feedback to improve the quality of recommendation.

Third, dealing with a wide variety of movies, it's hard to aggregate information about movies. Some common techniques such as concatenation and pooling are difficult to capture similar features of items and learn user's preference.

To handle these challenges in personalized movies recommendation, we propose a Deep Reinforcement Learning framework with the Capsule Network (CapsNet), called CapDRL. Our model derives the Deep Deterministic Policy Gradient (DDPG) [5] framework to capture users' dynamic properties with long-run planning and dynamic adaptation. CapsNet [2,8] is proposed and proven as a powerful alternative to CNNs and RNNs. We adopt CapsNet as an aggregation mechanism to cluster similar features together consciously. We take both a user's positive (rating score is 4 or 5) and negative (rating score is 1, 2, 3) rated movies' embeddings as the input of CapsNet. Adding negative behaviors will disturb the original data and alleviate the impact of over-personalization. Utilizing this clustering technique can guarantee the relevance and diversity of recommended items. CapsNet maps the user's behavior to a latent weight space, which represents the feature of user's preference.

Our contributions are three-fold. First, we propose a novel CapDRL model, and it's the first attempt to use DRL method based on the Capsule Network for movie recommendation to the best of our knowledge. Second, deep reinforcement learning method is utilized to model the sequential interactions between users and recommenders, while Capsule Network extracts movies' similar features as user's preference effectively. Third, we consider both content features and rating information. Besides, we crawl additional movie information as the priors. Experiments are conducted on MovieLens datasets to show that our method achieves significant and consistent improvement as compared to the other baselines.

2   CapDRL Model for Movie Recommendation

To solve the issues of static recommendation and ignoring user's feedback, we model the task of sequential interactions between users and recommender systems as Markov Decision Process (MDP). DDPG building upon the Actor-Critic architecture [4] is suitable for large action space and can also reduce the computation cost.

In this paper, we utilize the Actor Network to recommend a list of items for users. Critic Network is employed in evaluating whether the recommended items is suitable or not. Facing a variety of items in recommender systems, we should consider how to capture the similarity of items and describe user preferences more accurately. In contrast to both the pooling and concatenation aggregation, CapsNet proposed a novel aggregation mechanism to effectively capture the similarity property and alleviate information redundancy or information loss. The CapDRL architecture is depicted in Fig. 1.

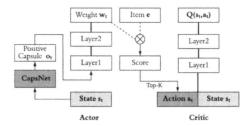

Fig. 1. The Architecture of CapDRL. Each state s_t is defined as previous N movies that user u rated before time t. Each action a_t is a recommendation list including Top-K movies generated by recommender agent (RA) based on s_t at time t. After RA takes action a_t on current state s_t, the user gives his/her positive $r = 1$ or negative $r = 0$ feedback based on the recommendation list.

Capsule Network. CapsNet provides a better understanding of users' demands, items' characteristics and their historical interactions. Compared with deep learning methods, CapsNet is more effective at extracting relationships between different features with the dynamic routing policy. This policy prefers to cluster similar features together consciously rather than use pooling to aggregate information. The vector-output capsule [2,8] can represent the specific properties, together with the existence of an entity. The predictions of higher-level capsules are determined by the lower-level capsules and a transformation matrix.

We call each positive or negative behaviors, or a group of neurons, as a capsule. Thus, the current state $\mathbf{s}_t$ denotes the input capsules for feature extraction, and $\mathbf{v}$ denotes the output capsules. The negative behaviors perturbed the feature detector, which can alleviate the impact of over-personalization. We describe the Capsule Network formally.

$$\mathbf{z}_j^{(l+1)} = \sum_i c_{ij}^{(l)} \hat{\mathbf{v}}_{j|i}^{(l)}, \quad \hat{\mathbf{v}}_{j|i}^{(l)} = \mathbf{W}_{ij}^{(l)} \mathbf{v}_i^{(l)}, \quad c_{ij} = \frac{\exp\left(b_{ij}\right)}{\sum_k \exp\left(b_{ik}\right)} \quad l = 1, \ldots, L \tag{1}$$

where $\mathbf{v}_i^{(l)}$ is the vector output of capsule i in layer l, $l = 1, \ldots, L$ and $\mathbf{v}^{(0)} = \mathbf{s}_t$. $\mathbf{z}_j$ is weighted sum over all outputs from the capsules in the layer below and $\hat{\mathbf{v}}_{j|i}$ is the "prediction vector". Coupling coefficient c_{ij} is the relevant between each lower-level capsule i and higher capsule j, it will determined by the iterative dynamic routing [8] process during the forward propagation, while other conv-parameters and $\mathbf{W}_{ij}$ in CapsNets need loss function to update. The b_{ij} are the prior values that capsule i should be coupled to capsule j, which can extract the relevant rather than the similarity from each capsule.

Then we squash $\mathbf{z}_j^{(l+1)}$ to confine $|\mathbf{z}_j^{(l+1)}| \in (0, 1)$ to a probability,

$$\mathbf{v}_j^{(l+1)} = \frac{\|\mathbf{z}_j^{(l+1)}\|^2}{1 + \|\mathbf{z}_j^{(l+1)}\|^2} \frac{\mathbf{z}_j^{(l+1)}}{\|\mathbf{z}_j^{(l+1)}\|}, \quad l = 1, \ldots, L \tag{2}$$

In this paper, there are two classes in the final layer, one for the user's positive feature and another for negative. Each class is represented by a low-dimension capsule, here we select the positive capsule as the output of Cap-sNet. The Positive capsule will be the feature of user's preference, representing the user's positively rated and user's like-minded feature. The output $\mathbf{o}_t$ is defined as follows.

$$\mathbf{o}_t = \mathbf{v}_{positive}^{(L)}. \tag{3}$$

The Actor Network. As introduced above, we use CapsNet mapping the user's current state $\mathbf{s}_t$ to feature embedding $\mathbf{o}_t$, which represents user's current preference. Then we assume the Actor Network to find Top-K recommendation list as follows:

$$f_{\theta^\pi} : \mathbf{o}_t \rightarrow \mathbf{w}_t, \tag{4}$$

$$score_i^{(t)} = \mathbf{w}_t \cdot \mathbf{e}_i, \tag{5}$$

where f_{θ^π} is a two-layer neural network with parameters θ^π that maps the feature representation to weight space, $\mathbf{w}_t$. $\mathbf{e}_i$ represents the embedding of movie i in movie embedding space. We select the Top-K movies as a_t with highest scores.

The Critic Network. The Critic Network is utilized for evaluating whether the action $\mathbf{a}_t$ generated by Actor Network suits for the user's current state $\mathbf{s}_t$. The goal of reinforcement learning is to learn the optimal action-value function $Q(\mathbf{s}_t, \mathbf{a}_t)$. At each time step, Actor in DDPG method outputs a deterministic action for Critic, which reduces the computational cost. The learning of the optimal function follows the Bellman equation as:

$$Q(\mathbf{s}_t, \mathbf{a}_t) = E_{\mathbf{s}_{t+1}}[r_t + \gamma Q(\mathbf{s}_{t+1}, \mathbf{a}_{t+1})|\mathbf{s}_t, \mathbf{a}_t]. \tag{6}$$

Many state-action pairs $(\mathbf{s}, \mathbf{a})$ may not be accessible. It's practical that the method of DDPG uses an approximate function to estimate the action-value function $Q(\mathbf{s}, \mathbf{a})$. DDPG creates the copy of the Actor and Critic networks as the target networks. Utilizing soft-update technique with parameter τ updates the parameters of target networks, which can improve the stability of learning. In this paper, we use a two-layer neural network with parameters θ^μ as Critic Network. The target networks adopt the same architecture parameterized by $\theta^{\pi'}$ and $\theta^{\mu'}$. The critic can be trained by minimizing a sequence of loss functions $L(\theta^\mu)$ as:

$$L(\theta^\mu) = E_{\mathbf{s}_t, \mathbf{a}_t, r, \mathbf{s}_{t+1}}[(y_t - Q_{\theta^\mu}(\mathbf{s}_t, \mathbf{a}_t))^2], \tag{7}$$

where

$$y_t = r + \gamma Q_{\theta^{\mu'}}(\mathbf{s_{t+1}}, \mathbf{a_{t+1}}). \tag{8}$$

3   Experiments

In order to evaluate the effectiveness of our model, we conduct experiments on the MovieLens-100k[1] and MovieLens-1M[2] datasets. In addition to rating information, gender, age and occupation are integrated to initialize user features and

---

[1]   https://grouplens.org/datasets/movielens/100k/.
[2]   https://grouplens.org/datasets/movielens/1m/.

movie description as movie features. For each movie, we use the mapping from the DBpedia ontology[3] to obtain the Wikipedia page from which are extracted the abstract of the entity as movie description. The purpose of our experiments is to recommend Top-K movies for users at each time step.

For CapDRL model, we use all movies rated by users before time t as current state s_t. At each time step, recommender agent recommends a list of $k = 5$ movies. The learning rate of Actor-Critic networks is set as 0.01 and 0.02. The rate for soft updates of target network $\tau = 0.01, \gamma = 0.9$. And the parameters in all models are set with the best performance. Due to the lack of an online platform, the experimental results in this paper are all from offline testing.

Table 1. Results on MovieLens Dataset $(\times 10^{-2})$

| | Using rating information | | | | Using rating-content information | | | |
| | MovieLens-100k | | MovieLens-1M | | MovieLens-100k | | MovieLens-1M | |
	nDCG@5	Precision@5	nDCG@5	Precision@5	nDCG@5	Precision@5	nDCG@5	Precision@5
PMF	0.1034	0.0212	0.1814	0.0532	-	-	-	-
RRN	0.1253	0.0247	0.1949	0.0473	-	-	-	-
DQN	0.1620	0.0343	0.2327	0.0633	0.1702	0.0412	0.2409	0.0586
DDPG	0.1632	0.0402	0.2419	0.0645	0.1762	0.0433	0.2477	0.0572
CapDRL	**0.1702**	**0.0445**	**0.2609**	**0.0659**	**0.1843**	**0.0556**	**0.2635**	**0.0632**

Evaluation Against Other Algorithms. PMF [6] uses a user-item rating matrix to product two lower-rank users matrix and items matrix for recommending new items to users without considering rating changes over time. In experiments, at each time step t, we apply user's history rating records before time t. As a variant of PMF, RRN [10] consider temporal aspects using Recurrent neural network to predict future behavioral trajectories, but their goals only focus on current reward, rather than the effect to the feedback. Deep Reinforcement Learning models outperform them in terms of the accurate recommendations in all experiments, which confirms the correctness of taking both the dynamic property and users' feedback into account. It benefits the recommendation accuracy significantly in the long run.

Evaluation on DRL. Comparisons of CapDRL, DQN [7] and DDPG [5] are conducted under the same settings with two layers for both Actor and Critic Networks. CapDRL based on MovieLens-1M dataset outperforms DDPG 7.28% on nDCG@5 and 2.17% on Precision@5, the results are depicted in Table 1. Note that, CapDRL, due to the CapsNet, is more stable, performs better and is more likely to capture similar features of movies that users rated. Only DRLs can use the rating-content information. The results using rating-content information only have a slight improvement on that using rating information. There are two possible reasons for this phenomenon. The first is that user's behavior is more

---

[3] http://dbpedia.org/ontology/.

realistic about user's interest in the movie domain, then the rating information is relatively sufficient to indicate the user's interest. Another is that we are limited in the amount of content information on MovieLens dataset we can extract.

4   Conclusions

In this paper, we have proposed a Deep Reinforcement Learning method based on the Capsule network (termed CapDRL model for short) for the movie recommendation. We modeled the sequential interactions between users and recommender agent as Markov Decision Process, and utilize DDPG method that can automatically learn the optimal recommendation strategies. We utilized an aggregation mechanism inspired by Capsule network to extract items' similar features as user's preference. We have validated our model compared with four baselines over MovieLens datasets. The experimental results show that CapDRL always performs best. In addition, we compared the result of CapDRL based on rating information with ones based on the rating-content information. There was no significant improvement. We will try to crawl more features in the future.

Acknowledgements. This work was partly supported by the National Natural Science Foundation of China under Grant No. 61572002, No. 61170300, No. 61690201, No. 61732001 and No. 61672049.

References

1. Guo, H., Tang, R., Ye, Y., Li, Z., He, X.: DeepFM: a factorization-machine based neural network for CTR prediction. In: IJCAI, pp. 1725–1731 (2017)
2. Hinton, G.E., Sabour, S., Frosst, N.: Matrix capsules with EM routing. In: International Conference on Learning Representations (2018)
3. Ricci, F., Rokach, L., Shapira, B.: Introduction to Recommender Systems Handbook. In: Ricci, F., Rokach, L., Shapira, B., Kantor, P.B. (eds.) Recommender Systems Handbook, pp. 1–35. Springer, Boston (2011). https://doi.org/10.1007/978-0-387-85820-3_1
4. Konda, V.R., Tsitsiklis, J.N.: Actor-critic algorithms. In: Advances in Neural Information Processing Systems, pp. 1008–1014 (2000)
5. Lillicrap, T.P., et al.: Continuous control with deep reinforcement learning. arXiv preprint arXiv:1509.02971 (2015)
6. Mnih, A., Salakhutdinov, R.R.: Probabilistic matrix factorization. In: Advances in neural information processing systems, pp. 1257–1264 (2008)
7. Mnih, V., et al.: Human-level control through deep reinforcement learning. Nature **518**(7540), 529 (2015)
8. Sabour, S., Frosst, N., Hinton, G.E.: Dynamic routing between capsules. In: Advances in Neural Information Processing Systems, pp. 3859–3869 (2017)
9. Schafer, J.B., Frankowski, D., Herlocker, J., Sen, S.: Collaborative filtering recommender systems. In: Brusilovsky, P., Kobsa, A., Nejdl, W. (eds.) The Adaptive Web. LNCS, vol. 4321, pp. 291–324. Springer, Heidelberg (2007). https://doi.org/10.1007/978-3-540-72079-9_9
10. Wu, C.Y., Ahmed, A., Beutel, A., Smola, A.J., Jing, H.: Recurrent recommender networks. In: Proceedings of the Tenth ACM International Conference on Web Search and Data Mining, pp. 495–503 (2017)

Portfolio Risk Optimisation and Diversification Using Swarm Intelligence

Kingshuk Mazumdar$^{(\boxtimes)}$, Dongmo Zhang, and Yi Guo

Western Sydney University, Penrith, Australia
{k.mazumdar,d.zhang,y.guo}@westernsydney.edu.au

Abstract. The ongoing global economic turmoil has got the asset management industry look into new ways of financial risk management. Portfolio optimisation and risk budgeting are at the heart of most computational finance studies by academics and practitioners. In this paper, we introduce and analyse a method to construct an equity portfolio based on decomposition of marginal asset risk contribution of each stock in a given universe and then formulate a diversification problem for unsystematic risk as an optimisation problem. We have illustrated the performance of our method by comparing with another diversification technique, known as the Risk Parity portfolio, and then benchmark our results against the global major indices.

Keywords: Portfolio optimisation · Particle Swarm Optimization · PSO · Portfolio diversification · Risk Parity · Risk budgeting · Swarm intelligence

1 Introduction

Portfolio optimization primarily concerns itself with choosing the best proportion of various assets that conforms to the investor needs. Markowitz [7] showed that investment is not just about picking stocks, but about choosing the right combination of stocks among which to distribute one's nest egg. The risk in a portfolio of diverse individual stocks will be less than the risk inherent in holding any one of the individual stocks. The fluctuations of the prices of the various assets are not independent, as they are exposed to common sources of risk, and thus become correlated. In the universe of stocks, the most common source of fluctuations is the price of the global equity factor, also called the market. Assets relatively insulated from the market are less risky, all things being equal, and thus yield less profit. Assets most exposed to the market deliver high profits for a higher level of risk. A portfolio is therefore typically exposed to two types of risks, namely systematic risk and unsystematic risk. In this paper, we propose a swarm intelligence based method to optimise unsystematic risk by diversifying our investments. Our method named, Maximum Diversification and Optimisation (MDO) strategy, constructs an equity portfolio based on decomposition of marginal asset risk contribution of each stock in a universe and then formulate

© Springer Nature Switzerland AG 2019
A. C. Nayak and A. Sharma (Eds.): PRICAI 2019, LNAI 11672, pp. 740–747, 2019.
https://doi.org/10.1007/978-3-030-29894-4_60

a diversification problem for unsystematic risk as an optimisation problem. We consider two popular portfolio construction techniques, namely Risk Budgeting [10] and Maximum Diversification Ratio [2] in this analysis. First, we derive the risk budget for all the equities in our universe based on equal weights and then filter out the maximum risk contributing assets to define a new universe of low risk contributing stocks. Secondly, we apply Particle Swarm Optimisation (PSO) [8], a swarm intelligence based meta-heuristic algorithm, to explore the weights of the selected securities that maximises the Maximum Diversification ratio of the portfolio. Finally, we illustrate the performance of our method by comparing with another diversification technique, known as the Risk Parity portfolio [6], and then benchmark our results against the major known indices.

2 Related Works and Our Contribution

Markowitz's portfolio theory [7] introduced that a portfolio is diversified if its variance could not be reduced any further at the same level of expected return. This definition implies that a portfolio's variance maybe used as a proxy for the fund's diversification level. Based on it, Maximum Diversification (MD) was proposed by Choueifaty et al. [2] along with the concept of a Diversification Ratio (DR). Choueifaty claimed that portfolios with maximal DRs were maximally diversified and that such portfolios provided an efficient alternative to market cap-weighted portfolios. In our proposed Maximum Diversification and Optimisation (MDO) strategy, we calculate the marginal risk contribution (MC_n) for each of the nth asset of a universe (U) of n risky assets, denoted as $U = (x_1, x_2, ..., x_n)$ and then select the least risk contributing assets to build a new portfolio P, denoted as $P = (w_1, w_2, \ldots, w_i)$, where w_i is weight for each asset in P. We then apply swarm based optimisation algorithm, PSO, to find the w_i for each of the ith asset. Within the stochastic programming framework, it is important to have an optimiser that can provide high-quality results, whilst maintaining a reasonable run time. For this purpose, we have considered a swarm intelligence optimiser, known as the Particle Swarm Optimisation (PSO), due to its potential for solving complex high-dimensional problems [5]. Empirical tests show the suitability of our method over different time horizon and compare results with another portfolio risk management strategy introduced by Maillard et al. [6], known as Risk Parity portfolio. We also provide benchmark comparison of our approach against leading global indices such as - S&P 500, S&P 100 and Dow Jones Industrial. The contribution of this paper is that our proposed Maximum Diversification and Optimisation (MDO) strategy, incorporates the interplay between marginal asset risk contribution and maximum diversification techniques, to construct an optimal portfolio allocation and diversification strategy using swarm intelligence. We also continuously evaluate market changes by recurrently applying PSO using unanchored walk forward analysis technique [3], to rebalance our portfolio over a configurable investment time horizon. It is, to the best of our knowledge, the first paper in the literature to combine the application of these factors together and dynamically optimise portfolio according to recent market performance over a multi-period investment horizon.

3   Preliminary

Particle Swarm Optimization. Particle Swarm Optimization (PSO) is a stochastic evolutionary algorithm based on swarm intelligence, which was first introduced by Kennedy and Eberhart in 1995 [5]. PSO uses a swarm of particles to simulate the behaviour of bird flocks in finding food. Each particle is a possible solution of the optimization problem and has a random initial position X and velocity V. The objective function targeted to be optimized is used to evaluate each particle position's fitness. Higher fitness means a better position. For each particle, PSO uses $pBest$ to record the best position this particle has arrived. For the whole swarm, $gBest$ is used to record the global best position achieved by all particles. At time t, PSO updates each particle's velocity using (1), where w is the inertia weight, c_1, c_2 are the acceleration coefficients and r_1, r_2 are two random numbers in the range between 0 and 1. After updating the velocity, each particle will move to a new position according to (2). This particle movement will repeat iteratively until all particles converge to the optimal position at last, like when birds find the food at the end of searching. The first term of (1) indicates an inertia for a particle wondering in the search space. The second term represents self-cognition of past experience of a particle, i.e., the particle tends to move towards its past best position. Similarly, the third term indicates that particles have social cognition to the whole swarm and are attracted by the global best position.

$$V_{t+1} = wV_t + c_1r_1(pBest - V_t) + c_2r_2(gBest - V_t) \tag{1}$$

$$X_{t+1} = X_t + V_{t+1} \tag{2}$$

Risk Parity Portfolio. The Risk Parity Portfolio was established in 1996 by Bridgewater Associates with the introduction of a risk parity fund, known as the All Weather fund [1]. In a Risk Parity portfolio the product of each security's portfolio weight, w_i, and its marginal contribution to the portfolio's volatility, σ_p, is the same for all (i, j) of the portfolio's securities [6], as given in Eq. (3) where $\delta\sigma_p$ is the marginal change in volatility of a portfolio and δw_i is the marginal change in its allocation weight.

$$w_i \frac{\delta\sigma_p}{\delta w_i} = w_j \frac{\delta\sigma_p}{\delta w_j} \tag{3}$$

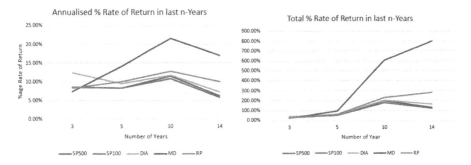

Fig. 1. Annualized rate of returns   **Fig. 2.** Compound rate of returns

4 Maximum Diversification and Optimisation (MDO) Method

Construction of long equity portfolios, based on optimal risk diversification of the stocks in the portfolio and their respective risk contribution, has been at the center of focus for investment managers in the last decade after the financial crisis in 2008. Studies conducted by practitioners on the root cause for sub-optimal performance during the period from 2007 to 2010, inspite of the belief that Markowitz's portfolio optimisation provides requisite diversification, helped realise a gap in existing investment techniques. Portfolio optimisation and risk budgeting are at the heart of most computational finance studies by academics and practitioners. This motivated us to study and propose a new technique to construct an equity portfolio based on decomposition of marginal asset risk contribution of each stock in the universe considered, and then formulate a swarm optimisation solution for a diversification problem in terms of unsystematic risk. In our method for portfolio construction, we use an ensemble of two techniques known as risk budgeting and Maximum Diversification portfolio. The MDO model has two phases - Learning Phase and Testing Phase. We have further divided the model's learning phase into 3 stages - Data Capture, Risk Budgeting and Optimised Risk Diversification. Data Capture module applies the walk forward analysis technique to rebalance our portfolio over a configurable investment time horizon. We then use an ensemble of marginal asset risk contribution and maximum diversification techniques, in Risk Budgeting and optimised Risk Diversification stages, to construct an optimal portfolio allocation and diversification strategy using swarm intelligence. **Learning Phase:Data capture** stage is responsible to collect input data for supervised learning. Prudent and effective choice of a finite set of equities that constitutes an individual portfolio can be a daunting task over period of time. Hence we utilise unanchored walk forward technique (WFA) [3] to constantly stay abreast with current market and make relevant changes to the portfolio. **Risk budgeting** is the analysis of a portfolio in terms of risk contributions rather than in terms of portfolio weights. Zhu et al. [10] has shown that risk contributions are not solely a mere mathematical decomposition of risk. They have financial significance as good predictors of the marginal contribution of each position to losses, especially for those of large magnitude. Let us consider our universe of n risky assets, as $U = (x_1, x_2, ..., x_n)$.

According to CreditMetrics^{TM} [4], the marginal risk contribution of the ith asset in U is defined in Eq. (4), where $Cov[R_i, Rj]$ is covariance of returns for i^{th}-asset compared to other assets, w_i is weight of the ith-asset in the universe U, $\sigma[R_p]$ is standard deviation of portfolio returns and MC_i is the marginal contribution to portfolio risk by i^{th}-asset. We calculate the marginal risk contribution for each of the ith-asset in our universe over the learning time horizon L_w and rank them so as to filter out the high risk assets, assuming that the portfolio is initialised to equally weighted assets. We pick the least risk contributors from the universe U and create a new set of assets, denoted as portfolio P. We pass the set P, to the next phase for finding the optimal combination of assets and their weights, that constructs a portfolio which maximises the asset diversification. **Optimised Risk Diversification**-The Diversification Ratio (DR), proposed and patented by Choueifaty [2], measures how much a given portfolio is diversified and as such, the ratio can be used to compare portfolios. The higher the DR, the more diversified the portfolio. It is important to emphasize that holding a large number of assets or investments does not necessarily increase a portfolio's DR. Rather, for a portfolio to be characterized by a high DR it must be exposed to a diversified number of sources of risk. A portfolio that maximizes the DR has the appealing characteristic of maximizing the effective number of independent sources of risk that it is exposed to. In that sense, a portfolio with a high DR is considered to be unbiased and built without using any views (i.e. market biases) regarding the future risk compensation of the constituent stocks. A truly diversified portfolio, in other words, does not reflect any speculative views from the marketplace. Let us consider a portfolio with n risky assets, represented as $P = (y_1, ..., y_n)$, where y_i denotes each asset allocated in P. Formally, the DR for portfolio P is denoted as given in Eq. (5), where σ_i is the volatility (standard deviation) of the returns of ith-asset, ω_i is the allocation weight of the ith-asset, σ_P is the volatility (standard deviation) of returns of the total portfolio P and DR_P is the Diversification Ratio of the portfolio P. At this stage, we apply particle swarm optimisation algorithm (PSO) to construct a portfolio that has maximum diversification so as to minimize the portfolio risk. We utilise the equation in (5) as our optimisation objective function. At the end of this phase, we start with the next period and apply Risk Parity Portfolio strategy to the set of assets in portfolio P, so as to find the optimal portfolio where each asset has the same equal risk contribution as explained in Eq. (3). **Testing Phase:** After each learning window, testing phase follows for period and the optimized portfolio weights $P = (w_1, w_2, \ldots, w_n)$ learnt during the learning phase are exploited to allocate stocks and construct a portfolio to achieve maximum diversification. We test our strategy and observe its performance over different time horizon and note the Sharpe Ratio and returns generated.

$$MC_i = w_i * \frac{\sum_{j=1}^{n} w_j * Cov[R_i, Rj]}{\sigma[R_p]} \tag{4}$$

$$DR_P = \frac{\sum\limits_{i=1}^{n} \sigma_i \cdot \omega_i}{\sigma_P} \tag{5}$$

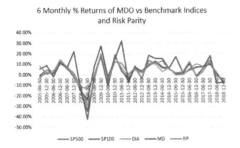

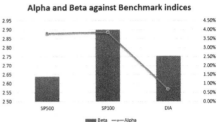

Fig. 3. Comparison of 6 monthly returns

Fig. 4. Risk measurement - alpha and beta

5   Experiments

In this section, we conduct extensive experiments to evaluate the effectiveness and efficiency of our proposed methods. We have kept our approach configurable and tried to avoid any kind of bias towards an upward or downward trend or any particular time period or industry, by including all 100 stocks from S&P 100 index in our universe over last 14 years period from 2005 till 2018. We have summarised the results of our experiments over multiple time period - 3 yrs, 5 yrs, 10 yrs and 14 yrs. Our benchmark reference for this evaluation is the Risk Parity portfolio construction method and the 3 well known global indices - Dow Jones Industrial (DIA), S&P 100 (OEM) and S&P 500 (SPY). **Observation 1:** Risk Budgeting and Stock Selection in each iteration. We evaluate results from the short-listed equities in our universe of stocks, for each 6 monthly iteration starting from Jan 2005 till Dec 2018. We observe that during the period Jul-Dec 2008, when the S&P 500 index dropped significantly by -42.31%, using MDO method, incurs much lower losses of -23.7%. We interpret that market downturn, like in year 2008 and 2018, can't mitigate systemic risk by risk budgeting and diversification. Though MDO strategy performed relatively better during second half of 2008 and 2018 periods, but might not help eliminate such systemic risks. **Observation 2:** Compound and Annualized Returns (Figs. 1 and 2). Annualised returns of MDO method over 4–14 years period outperformed all the benchmarks indices and the Risk Parity portfolio. Similarly, we find that the compound returns of MDO method over 3–14 years period outperformed all the benchmark indices and the Risk Parity portfolio. Based on our 60 observations, we conclude that the MDO method has significantly better performance when we compare results over 3 or more years horizon. **Observation 3:** Risk Measurement - Alpha,

Beta, Standard Deviation and Sharpe Ratio (Figs. 3, 4, 5 and 6). We find that
the Sharpe ratio [8] of our method is higher in comparison to the benchmark
indices and the Risk Parity portfolio, when we observe returns data for more
than three years. We also compare alpha ratio [9] against 3 different benchmark
indices and find that MDO has higher alpha by generating 4% excess returns.

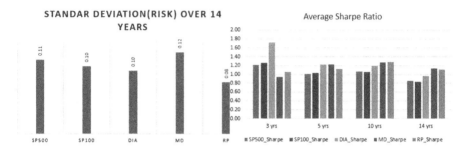

Fig. 5. Standard deviation of returns   **Fig. 6.** Sharpe ratio comparison

6   Conclusion

The MDO portfolio significantly outperformed the major US indices and the
Risk Parity portfolio, in terms of annualised and cumulative returns, when compared over an investment horizon of more than 3 years. But this also comes with
a high cost due to excess beta, which meant higher volatility. Again, the Sharpe
ratio of our portfolio outperforms the benchmark indices when the investor's
time horizon is above 3 years. In contrast, this method underperformed for
investors with a short term horizon of less than 3 years. To summarise, our
proposed method's performance was quite encouraging as a long term strategy
but also varied considerably in short term. Further analysis of the MDO strategy of portfolio allocation could be explored with a larger and wider universe of
stocks, which might allow for more scope in terms of diversification benefits as
well as the portrayal of better confidence on the technique presented.

References

1. Bridgewater: The all weather story (1996). https://www.bridgewater.com/reso-
   urces/all-weather-story.pdf
2. Choueifaty, Y., Coignard, Y.: Toward maximum diversification. J. Portfolio Manage. **35**(1), 40–51 (2008). https://doi.org/10.3905/JPM.2008.35.1.40. cited By 102
3. Davey, K.: Building Algorithmic Trading Systems a Trader's Journey from Data
   Mining to Monte Carlo Simulation to Live Trading (Wiley Trading). Wiley, Hoboken (2014)
4. Gupton, G., Finger, C., Bhatia, M.: CreditMetrics: Technical Document. J.P. Morgan Co., New York (1997)

5. Kennedy, J., Eberhart, R.: Particle Swarm Optimization, vol. 4, pp. 1942–1948. IEEE, Piscataway (1995). cited By 34585
6. Maillard, S., Roncalli, T., Teïletche, J.: The properties of equally weighted risk contribution portfolios. J. Portfolio Manage. **36**(4), 60–70 (2010). https://doi.org/10.3905/jpm.2010.36.4.060. cited By 145
7. Markowitz, H.: Portfolio selection*. J. Finance **7**(1), 77–91 (1952). https://doi.org/10.1111/j.1540-6261.1952.tb01525.x
8. Sharpe, W.: The sharpe ratio. J. Portfolio Manage. **21**(1) (1994). http://search.proquest.com/docview/195581284/
9. Wan, P.: Alpha and Risk Factors. Wiley (2015). https://doi.org/10.1002/9781119057871.ch11, cited By 0
10. Zhu, S.S., Li, D., Sun, X.: Portfolio selection with marginal risk control. J. Comput. Fin. **1** (2010). https://doi.org/10.21314/JCF.2010.213

Multi-peak Algorithmic Trading Strategies Using Grey Wolf Optimizer

Kingshuk Mazumdar[✉], Dongmo Zhang, and Yi Guo

Western Sydney University, Sydney, Australia
{k.mazumdar,d.zhang,y.guo}@westernsydney.edu.au

Abstract. In this paper, we propose a new method of algorithmic trading for short term investors in the financial markets, by applying swarm intelligence. We apply a well known meta-heuristic, known as Grey Wolf Optimizer (GWO), and find multi-peak optimisation solutions having different expected risk and return ratios, to propose 3 automated trading strategies. The novelty of our method is how we leverage three best swarm agents to construct multi-peak solutions that are best suited for the stochastic nature of financial markets. We utilise the variance between the positions of swarm agents in GWO to construct different algorithmic approaches to day trading, with an aim to diversify expected portfolio volatility. Our research showcases how the three best swarms of GWO are best suited to predict stochastic time series problems, as we typically find in the field of finance. Our experiments demonstrate the capability of our model compared to industry benchmark indices and evaluates the effectiveness of the proposed strategies.

Keywords: GWO · Algorithmic trading · Swarm intelligence · Risk · Volatility

1 Introduction

In the current global financial markets era, algorithmic trading is fundamental to investment strategies for achieving financial goals. With evolution of technology and new methods of algorithmic trading, financial markets have achieved more efficient execution of trade by lowering transaction costs, generating improved portfolio performance and by providing higher transparency [1]. Glantz [2] has shown a strong negative relationship between investment portfolio returns and volatility. High volatility leads to larger risks and high variability in returns compared to a portfolio with lower volatility. Our motivation for this paper, is drawn from this need for choice of optimum volatility by investors exposed to algorithmic trading. In this paper, we propose a swarm intelligence based method for day trading of stocks using multiform algorithmic trading strategies, where each strategy is recurrently evaluated and tuned for different levels of volatility. Our method is based on a meta-heuristic algorithm, known as Grey Wolf Optimizer (GWO), originally proposed by Mirjalili et al. [3]. We have proposed a variant of GWO algorithm, which utilises three best swarm agents (also known as the α, β and δ swarms) to formulate multi-peak optimisation solutions and derive them as short term trading strategies with different levels of volatility. We have defined these approaches as the α, β and δ trading strategies. Our method is an ensemble where, we first derive the relevant stock's technical indicators and their optimum threshold values

© Springer Nature Switzerland AG 2019
A. C. Nayak and A. Sharma (Eds.): PRICAI 2019, LNAI 11672, pp. 748–754, 2019.
https://doi.org/10.1007/978-3-030-29894-4_61

that best predicts the stock price movements to maximise returns at a minimum risk level, and then assign each of the indicators with weights that maps to their relevant entropy. Finally, we find the optimised threshold values that maximises the accuracy of prediction to buy, sell or hold trade decisions, thus achieving an overall objective to maximise the portfolio returns and minimise the risk level. We have illustrated the performance of our method by benchmarking our results against the major known indices - S&P 500, S&P 100 and Dow Jones Industrial.

2   Our Method and Related Works

Traditionally, portfolio managers have relied on technical and fundamental indicators to feel for the concentration of risk in their portfolios. But determining the relevance of these indicators at the asset allocation level, for a multi asset portfolio, has been a daunting task with so many indicators to pick from [1]. In our proposed solution, we create an ensemble of multi-threshold selection techniques, implemented as a two-step optimisation method. Let us consider, a universe of n risky assets in a portfolio, denoted as $P = (x_1, x_2, ..., x_n)$, and a universe of i technical indicators used by the trader, denoted as $F = (t_1, t_2, . . . , t_i)$. Firstly, we find the relevance of each t_i on every asset x_n in P, and optimise its threshold values to maximise the returns and minimise the risks. By capturing the effects of every technical indicator on each asset, and recognizing that not all indicators have the same impact across different assets and also that its impact changes with time, our method lays the foundation for the next step. Subsequently, we use the cumulative effect of the learnt threshold values for items in F, to calculate the final optimised threshold values for each asset (x_n). Our goal for each asset x_n, is to maximise the accuracy of prediction of asset price changes, so as to learn how to best classify the trades and make a decision to 'Buy', 'Sell' or 'Hold' trade over a given period. In a recent related work published by Sezer et al. [4], a multi-layer perceptron (MLP) artificial neural network (ANN) model is proposed by applying a single strategy for price prediction of 30 stocks from Dow Jones. In their method, asset risk was not considered as a parameter for optimisation. Applying our suggested model, we find that our method's annualized returns outperformed their results. Tawfik et al. [5] have applied Cuckoo search algorithm to optimize forex trading based on 3 technical indicators as predictors and depends on trend of 2 years historical data to maximize profit and sharpe ratio, but their method has proposed a single strategy to trade on limited currencies. Our method is different to both of them, as we propose a versatile method for constructing 3 distinct risk diversified strategies that can be opted by investors depending on their risk profiles or market perspective, which could be conservative or aggressive. We make two major contributions in this paper. Firstly, we propose a new variant of GWO for construction of multi-peak solutions, instead of a single best solution. Secondly it is, to the best of our knowledge, the first paper in the literature to combine the application of above explained factors together to propose multiple risk diversified day-trading strategies using single meta-heuristic.

3   Optimisation Method and Evaluation Strategy

Grey Wolf Optimizer. Grey Wolf Optimizer (GWO) is a population based meta-heuristic algorithm inspired by hunting behaviour of grey wolves (Canis lupus) [3]. The GWO algorithm mimics the leadership hierarchy and hunting mechanism of grey wolves in nature. In this paper, we introduce a variation of GWO, that retrofits the logic to update the position of the α, β and δ swarm wolves provided in the original GWO implementation [6]. Our motivation to retrofit the original logic, comes from the need to accurately map the multi-peak formation of the swarms as they depict the multiple strategies suggested by our method. In our proposed method, we have calibrated the logic to demote the current α agent to the position of the β swarm agent, when a new agent is found with a fitness better than the current α agent, as in Algorithm 1. In the original implementation, since typically we are only interested in the single best swarm, the position of α or β agents never got demoted.

Algorithm 1. Retrofitted GWO snippet - update position for maximisation problem

---

Input: $\alpha\_pos, \alpha\_score, \beta\_pos, \beta\_score, \delta\_pos, \delta\_score,$
$Positions, fitness, i$
Output: $\alpha\_pos, \alpha\_score, \beta\_pos, \beta\_score, \delta\_pos, \delta\_score$
Function: $Update\_Postition()$

1: **if** $fitness > \alpha\_score$ **then**
2:     Demote the current β position as the new δ position
3:     Demote current α position as the new β position
4: **if** $fitness < \alpha\_score$ and $fitness > \beta\_score$ **then**
5:     Demote the current β position as the new δ position
6: return $\alpha\_pos, \alpha\_score, \beta\_pos, \beta\_score, \delta\_pos, \delta\_score$

Objective Function. Our variant of the GWO algorithm, provides a trader with options to choose between different expected rate of returns and level of asset risks. We define the three solutions as the α, β and δ strategy, as they represent α, β and δ wolf packs of the GWO algorithm and have named our model as the $\alpha\beta\delta$ - **Trading Model**. The objective of the optimisation model is to maximize the portfolio returns and the Sharpe ratio [7]. Objective function for GWO is as given in Eq. (1), where i is the sequence of days of trading for the period 'n', R_i is the returns from trade on day 'i', R_f is the risk free rate of return for period 1 to n, and σ_r is the portfolio standard deviation depicting risk.

$$Maximize\_f(x) = \frac{\sum_{i=1}^{n} R_i * (\sum_{i=1}^{n} R_i - R_f)}{\sigma_r} \quad (1)$$

Research Evaluation Strategy. We evaluate the robustness of our proposed trading strategies on the basis of their capacity to perform effectively in a changing environment. Following hypothesis tests were evaluated across 60 cycles of independent tests, refer Table 1. **Hypothesis 1**-We expect that the portfolio returns from each of the α, β and δ strategies to be distinct from each other and to consistently generate different levels of returns, in accordance to their levels of risk. To prove this, we hypothesize that the δ trading strategy achieves higher returns compared to the α strategy, resulting in δ strategy as preferred stratagem for higher returns without considering risk associated with each of the strategies. **Hypothesis 2**-Our second research hypothesis evaluates the portfolio risks of the α, β and δ trading strategies. We hypothesize that due to the GWO's objective to minimise risk, the position of α swarm is closest to global optimum, and thus the δ strategy achieves higher returns at a cost of higher portfolio risk compared to the α strategy. **Hypothesis 3**-We further test and validate our method by comparing the sharpe ratio for each of the α, β and δ strategies and confirm that our method's calibration of portfolio returns and risk is correct. We hypothesize that sharpe ratio of the δ and β trading strategies are lower than the α strategy.

4   The $\alpha\beta\delta$ Trading Model

In this section, we provide details of how in our proposed method, we construct multiple strategies for algorithmic prediction of stocks from our universe of assets and trade on them. Our model has two phases - Learning and Testing Phase. We have further divided our model's learning phase into 3 stages - Data Capture, Feature Threshold Selection and Stock Threshold Selection. Let us consider, a universe of n risky assets in a portfolio, denoted as $P = (x_1, x_2, ..., x_n)$, and a universe of i technical indicators used by traders for stock price trend analysis, denoted as $F = (t_1, t_2, \ldots, t_i)$. **Learning Phase: Data capture** stage is responsible to collect input data for supervised learning. To start with, we fetch the historical stock market data for each stock (x_n) in our portfolio P for period L_w, defined as the learning time period. Subsequently, we calculate the technical indicators (t_i) for each stock and map to F, using the historical price movements of asset x_n. In **Feature Threshold Selection** phase, we begin supervised training with input feature vector, F, to predict stock price trends. Applying the GWO algorithm, we find the relevance of each indicator t_i in F on every asset x_n in P, over the period L_w. We then search for optimum threshold values for each t_i that maximises the returns and minimises the risks using the objective function, in Eq. (1). Subsequently, we rank the features in F on the basis of their information entropy to predict price trends accurately and create a new sorted list of features, as F_{opt}, with its relevant threshold values (to used for generating trade signals). In the last stage of **Stock Threshold Selection**, we aggregate the individual trade signals from the top 5 stock's price trend indicators in F_{opt}, to derive the cumulative effect of trade recommendation for each stock. Individual signal generated using threshold values of each technical indicator t_i in F_{opt} with length i, denoted as S_i, is aggregated based on the entropy rank r_i to derive S for each x_n, using Eq. (2). We then again apply GWO algorithm, to find the threshold values for each asset x_n, that maximises the prediction accuracy of asset price change and the precision to categorise trade decision into classifiers - 'Buy', 'Sell' or 'Hold', using S. For each stock x_n, we note the optimised positions of the α, β and δ wolves of GWO into vectors τ_α, τ_β and τ_δ and define them as the α, β and δ trading strategies for that individual stock. **Testing Phase:** During the testing period T_w, we trade on all assets in our portfolio $P = (x_1, x_2, ..., x_n)$ using the learnt optimized threshold values in τ_α, τ_β and τ_δ for each asset x_n. These threshold values facilitate the algorithmic trade decisions by classifying the daily trade calls into 'Buy', 'Sell' or 'Hold' positions, depending on recent stock price movements and aggregate signals from the preferred technical indicators of that asset x_n. We test and benchmark our strategies on the basis of the portfolio risk, portfolio returns and portfolio Sharpe Ratio over the duration T_w.

$$S = \sum_1^i S_i(1 - \frac{r_i}{i})$$ (2)

5 Experiments

We kept our approach configurable and have tried to avoid any kind of bias towards an upward or downward trend or any particular time period or industry, by including all stocks from Dow Jones Industrial index and run the tests on our model over 14 years, from 2005 till 2018. We have preselected 7 stock market technical indicators for our optimisation problem - Volatility index [8], Chaikin Volatility [9], Relative Strength Index [9], MACD [9], William %R [9] and Ultimate Oscillator [9]. For the experiments, the α, β and δ strategies close all trades over 'T+1' day.

Experiment Results and Benchmark Comparison. We evaluate the 3 hypothesis undertaken for our research and validate our model's performance based on the results. We observe in Figs. 1 and 2 that the annualised returns and profits of α, β and δ trading strategies proposed using our method, outperforms well known global benchmark indices in terms of profits and risk comparison. We gather further evidence by comparing the results with another meta-heuristic, known as Particle Swarm Optimisation (PSO) [10]. We observe in Table 1 that the δ trading strategy consistently achieves higher expected returns compared to the α strategy. We find that although absolute returns of the δ strategy is higher than the α strategy, but the risks involved are also high compared to the α strategy. As shown in Figs. 2, 4 and Table 1, δ strategy consistently takes higher risk compared to α strategy. We find in Fig. 3, the Sharpe ratio of δ strategy is less than α strategy and we can infer the same based on independent t-Test conducted, with a confidence level above 99.9%.

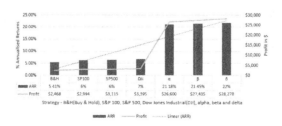

Fig. 1. Annualised returns and risk comparison

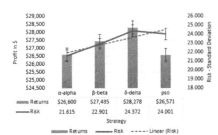

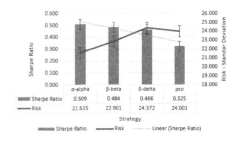

Fig. 2. Profit and risk comparison   **Fig. 3.** Sharpe ratio comparison

Table 1. t-Statistics for hypothesis testing of $\alpha\beta\delta$ trading model

Level of significance 0.01		D. freedom = 120		
		Decision	t-Statistic	Confidence
Hypothesis 1 - Portfolio Returns	$H_0 : \delta_{profit} - \alpha_{profit} \leq 0$	Rejected	14.13	99.9%
	$H_1 : \delta_{profit} - \alpha_{profit} > 0$	Accepted		
	$H_0 : \beta_{profit} - \alpha_{profit} \leq 0$	Rejected	5.22	99.9%
	$H_1 : \beta_{profit} - \alpha_{profit} > 0$	Accepted		
Hypothesis 2 - Portoflio Risks	$H_0 : \delta_{risk} - \alpha_{risk} \leq 0$	Rejected	13.51	99.9%
	$H_1 : \delta_{risk} - \alpha_{risk} > 0$	Accepted		
	$H_0 : \beta_{risk} - \alpha_{risk} \leq 0$	Rejected	5.55	99.9%
	$H_1 : \beta_{risk} - \alpha_{risk} > 0$	Accepted		
Hypothesis 3 - Sharpe Ratio	$H_0 : \alpha_{SR} - \delta_{SR} \leq 0$	Rejected	4.68	99.9%
	$H_1 : \alpha_{SR} - \delta_{SR} > 0$	Accepted		
	$H_0 : \alpha_{SR} - \beta_{SR} \leq 0$	Rejected	3.64	99.9%
	$H_1 : \alpha_{SR} - \beta_{SR} > 0$	Accepted		

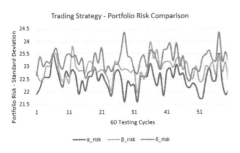

Fig. 4. Portfolio risk   **Fig. 5.** Portfolio returns

6 Conclusion

High market volatility, increased investor risk aversion, and additional interest in risk diversification in the equity market have prompted a surge of empirical research on alternate options of trading strategies. Empirical experiments suggest that the performance of our proposed α, β and δ trading solutions are efficient, consistent and reliable options to alternate methods of algorithmic trading. Our method offers investors with multiple trading alternatives instead of being complacent with a single strategy. We also find that for complex problems which are stochastic in nature like financial markets, GWO algorithm when used with an active learning technique, was able to provide a much more accurate prediction of future behaviour than PSO. Our findings add to the growing body of literature that explores studies on effectiveness of algorithmic trading strategies for global financial institutions, and offers insight into application of machine learning for researchers as well as investors in the area of computational finance (Fig. 5).

References

1. Kissell, R.: The Science of Algorithmic Trading and Portfolio Management. Elsevier Inc., Amsterdam (2013). Cited By 8
2. Glantz, M., Kissell, R.: Multi-Asset Risk Modeling: Techniques for a Global Economy in an Electronic and Algorithmic Trading Era. Elsevier Inc., Amstersdam (2013). Cited By 5
3. Mirjalili, S., Mirjalili, S., Lewis, A.: Grey wolf optimizer. Adv. Eng. Softw. **69**, 46–61 (2014). Cited By 1549
4. Sezer, O., Ozbayoglu, A., Dogdu, E.: An artificial neural network-based stock trading system using technical analysis and big data framework. In: ACMSE 2017, pp. 223–226 (2017). Cited By 7
5. Tawfik, A., Badr, A., Abdel-Rahman, I.: One rank cuckoo search algorithm with application to algorithmic trading systems optimization. Int. J. Comput. Appl. **64**(6), 30–37 (2013)
6. Mirjalili, S.: Grey wolf optimizer (2014). http://www.alimirjalili.com/gwo.html - implementation source code
7. Sharpe, W.: The sharpe ratio. J. Portfolio Mgmt. **21**(1), 49–58 (1994)
8. Bekaert, G., Hoerova, M.: The VIX, the variance premium and stock market volatility. J. Econ. **183**(2), 181–192 (2014). Cited By 114
9. Ciana, P.: New Frontiers in Technical Analysis: Effective Tools and Strategies for Trading and Investing. Wiley, Hoboken (2012). Cited By 1
10. Kennedy, J., Eberhart, R.: Particle Swarm Optimization, vol. 4, pp. 1942–1948. IEEE, Piscataway (1995). Cited By 34585

Author Index

Printed in the United States
By Bookmasters